Land of Promise
A HISTORY OF THE UNITED STATES

Cover: The oldest national flag bearing a regimental number—the "standard of the eagle" of the U.S. 1st Infantry Regiment, 1791. The American eagle rises serene in true Olympian majesty against a brilliant sunburst while 13 stars shine softly in the depths of a night-blue sky.

Land of Promise
A HISTORY OF THE UNITED STATES

Carol Berkin ☆ **Leonard Wood**

Contributing Authors
Sandra Deines
Dianne Ghertner

Scott, Foresman and Company
Editorial Offices: Glenview, Illinois
Regional Offices: Palo Alto, California · Tucker, Georgia · Glenview, Illinois · Oakland, New Jersey · Dallas, Texas

Authors

Dr. Carol Berkin is professor of history at Baruch College, The City University of New York. She has published several books, including *Jonathan Sewall: Odyssey of an American Loyalist* (1974), which won the Bancroft Prize, and *Women of America* (1979). Professor Berkin teaches American colonial and revolutionary history and women's history at Baruch, where she is chair of the Women's Studies Program Committee.

Dr. Leonard Wood is professor of history and director of cooperative education at Eastern Illinois University. He has also taught at Miami University in Ohio and at secondary schools in Pennsylvania. He has written many books on American and European history and book review articles in leading journals. He also has extensive experience in developing American history textbooks and other social science instructional materials for several major educational publishers.

Contributing Authors

Sandra Deines began teaching in 1971 at Ridgewood High School in Norridge, Illinois. Since then she has written a variety of classroom and teaching materials for high-school social studies.

Dianne Ghertner taught high-school social studies for 10 years in Illinois and Virginia and has written a variety of materials for high-school social studies. She is also on the executive board of the Historical Society of Oak Park and River Forest, Illinois.

Teacher Consultants

The authors and publisher would like to thank the following consultants for their reviews of *Land of Promise* during its developmental stage. They contributed valuable comments, chapter by chapter, on both the content and the level of difficulty. Their assistance has helped make *Land of Promise* a practical classroom text.

John E. Derby
Principal
Shonto Boarding School
Shonto, Arizona

Ernestine N. Madison
President, Mississippi Council of
   Social Studies
Social Studies Teacher
Vicksburg High School
Vicksburg, Mississippi

Herbert C. Martin
Secondary Staff Teacher, Social
   Science
Educational Services
Compton, California

Hilary L. Sullivan
American History Teacher
High School Division
Skyline Center
Dallas, Texas

Academic Consultants

Annotations for U.S. Constitution
David P. Currie
Professor of Law
University of Chicago

Visiting the Past Essays
Anthony C. Wood
Deputy Director
Municipal Art Society of New York
formerly staff, New York City
   Landmarks Preservation
   Commission

Contents

Junction of the Erie and Northern Canals, *by John W. Hill,
around 1830*

A Wisconsin couple displays the fruits of their harvest, 1895

UNIT EIGHT
PROSPERITY AND
DEPRESSION   573

Celebration of the nation's bicentennial in New York harbor, 1976

Swedish map, 1540

Maps

Atlas and Reference Section

A 15th-century geographer

The Geographic Setting

Presidential Gallery

Visiting the Past

"Rising sun" carving on the chair used by George Washington at the Constitutional Convention, 1787

Life in America

Portrait of Sarah Prince of Newburyport, Massachusetts, around 1801

From the Archives

To the Student

Land of Promise has been organized so that you will find it easy to use. The book is divided into 10 units and 35 chapters. Each chapter is divided into several sections. The **Table of Contents** and the **Index** will help you find what you need to know. Note that the Table of Contents includes a complete list of maps, charts, tables, diagrams, and special features. The Index gives birth and death dates for historic personages as well as hundreds of pronunciations. Also note that the end of the book includes an **Atlas and Reference Section** and a **Glossary.**

Chapter Organization
Each chapter includes an introduction, several sections, and a two-page chapter review. The section and sub-section headings show at a glance the main ideas of the chapter. **Key terms and names** are shown in boldfaced (heavy) print where they are first identified. At the end of each section are **Section Review Questions** that focus on these terms, names, and main ideas. By skimming a chapter and reading the headings, the boldfaced terms and names, and the Section Review Questions, you will get a good idea of what you will be studying.

Each chapter has two special content features. One, called **Life in America,** includes a variety of topics, such as family life, biographies, inventions, and popular culture. The other, labeled **From the Archives,** includes selections from major documents in American history and excerpts from songs, novels, and diaries. In addition, there is a capsule review of each President's term of office.

The two-page **Chapter Review** includes a review of the key terms and main ideas. A **Special History Skills** exercise is provided to sharpen your social studies skills, such as map reading, using the library, and recognizing bias and interpretation. There are also critical thinking questions, suggestions for projects, a brief bibliography, and a quiz. Use these pages to guide your study. If you can comfortably answer the questions, you know you are learning American history.

Unit Organization
Each unit begins with a page that features a photograph, the unit title, and a list of chapters in the unit. The end-of-unit test allows you to review the main ideas and facts from that unit.

The Geographic Setting
Scattered throughout the book are special essays that focus on the impact of geography on American history. These **Geographic Setting** essays look at the major regions of the United States and show how the natural features of the land—the climate, landforms, and vegetation—influenced human settlement.

Visiting the Past
Each **Visiting the Past** focuses on three historical sites that you can visit. These essays discuss the difference between original and reconstructed sites and show you the various ways that American history has been preserved.

Atlas and Reference Section
At the end of the book is a handy reference section that includes a wide variety of maps, historical statistics, facts about the states today, and other materials. This section also includes a **List of Presidents** and a **Glossary.**

Unit One

Colonial Origins

Chapters in This Unit

THE OLD WORLD FINDS THE NEW

The advisers to King Ferdinand and Queen Isabella of Spain were growing tired. Why could not this man Columbus see that his scheme to sail west to China was foolhardy? Furthermore, his geography was wrong! True, in theory China could be reached by sailing west across the Atlantic. But not in 3,000 miles! It was more like 12,000 miles, the advisers argued, and no ship of the day could sail so great a distance nonstop across the open sea.

The Queen appeared to give in to her advisers. The answer to Columbus would have to be "no." With heavy heart, he left the palace and prepared to leave Spain forever. Then something happened. We do not know why, but Queen Isabella changed her mind. A runner was sent to overtake Columbus. Back at court, he learned that he was to have the three small ships he had asked for after all.

Never mind that Columbus' geography was off by some 9,000 miles! The royal advisers were right on this. What matters was that out there—unknown to anyone in all of Europe—was a vast New World, located about where the captain expected to find China.

Thus a new chapter in world history opens with a story that is as fantastic as it is true. Thanks to a woman's decision and a sailor's stubborn faith in his mistaken geography, a whole new age was born.

Sections in This Chapter
1. The Age of Discovery
2. The First Americans
3. Spain and Portugal Claim the Americas

Opposite: Feather headdress presented by the Aztec prince Montezuma to Hernando Cortés, conqueror of Mexico

1. THE AGE OF DISCOVERY

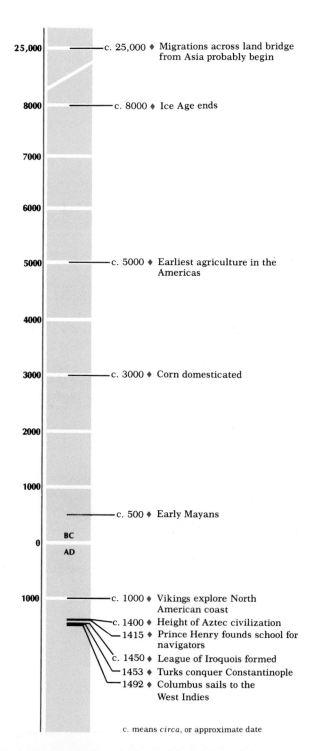

25,000 ——— c. 25,000 ♦ Migrations across land bridge from Asia probably begin

8000 ——— c. 8000 ♦ Ice Age ends

7000

6000

5000 ——— c. 5000 ♦ Earliest agriculture in the Americas

4000

3000 ——— c. 3000 ♦ Corn domesticated

2000

1000

500 ——— c. 500 ♦ Early Mayans

0 — BC / AD

1000 ——— c. 1000 ♦ Vikings explore North American coast
c. 1400 ♦ Height of Aztec civilization
1415 ♦ Prince Henry founds school for navigators
c. 1450 ♦ League of Iroquois formed
1453 ♦ Turks conquer Constantinople
1492 ♦ Columbus sails to the West Indies

c. means *circa*, or approximate date

Columbus was born in 1451 in Genoa, a seaport in northwestern Italy. At the time of his birth, Genoa was a thriving trade center. Look at the map on page 6 and you will see why. Notice that the Italian Peninsula is located in the Mediterranean Sea, midway between western Europe and trading centers to the east such as Constantinople and Damascus. All goods from Asia reached Europe by this route. Asia was the source of many valuable items of trade, such as gold, gems, spices, silks, sugar, glass, and steel. As a boy growing up in Genoa, Columbus must have seen ships unloading this rich cargo.

The Renaissance

Those years in the mid-1400s were an exciting time to be alive. For a hundred years or more the pace of life in much of Europe had been quickening. The peoples of the Italian Peninsula were at the center of much that was happening. Grown rich from trade, wealthy Italian families were interested in art and learning. They hired artists to decorate their palaces and churches. They sent scholars in search of old books and manuscripts that told of the wisdom of the ancient world. Much of this knowledge had been lost to the people of western Europe since the fall of Rome, a thousand years earlier. Now it was being brought to light again.

So much was happening, both in the discovery of new things and in the rediscovery of old, that this period is called the **Renaissance** [ren′ə säns], a word meaning "rebirth." Italy experienced the Renaissance first, but it soon spread along the routes of trade to Germany, the Netherlands, France, Spain, and Portugal. People seemed to have a new spirit, a new zest for life. The way they thought about politics, religion, and the world began to change.

With the Renaissance came a strong desire to experience new things and to learn about places outside of Europe. Of particular interest was Asia,

4

Merchant ships crowd a busy harbor in this Italian illuminated manuscript painted in the mid-1400s.

especially India, China, Japan, and the East Indies. Europeans of Columbus' day knew very little about these distant lands.

The Need for New Trade Routes

The eastern Mediterranean area was familiar to Europeans, but China and the East Indies were thousands of miles farther east. And the difficult journey took many months, sometimes years, to complete. Was there no easier route than the one by land and sea that stretched over trackless deserts and rugged mountains? A growing number of people asked this question.

It was not curiosity alone that aroused interest in a new and better route to eastern Asia. There were some down-to-earth practical reasons. For

one thing, not enough eastern goods were reaching western Europe. Consequently, prices were high, and the supply never kept up with the demand. Then, after 1453, when Constantinople fell to the Turks, trade with the East all but stopped. There was not enough gold and silver in western Europe to mint the coins needed to expand trade. In those days without refrigeration, spices were absolutely essential to preserve food and improve its taste. But pepper, ginger, cloves, cinnamon, nutmeg, and other spices were often hard to get.

Second, Europeans had plenty of woolen cloth, tin, and other items to trade for the things they wanted from the East. If a new source of gold and spices could be found or a shorter route to distant

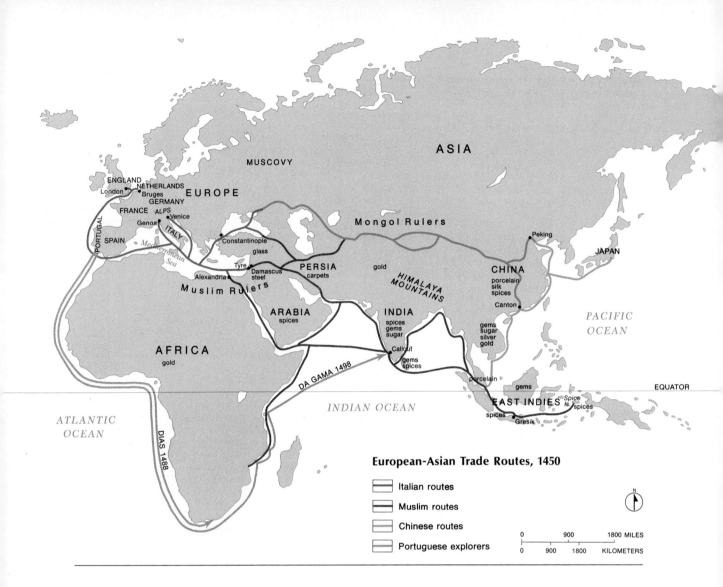

European-Asian Trade Routes, 1450

	Italian routes
	Muslim routes
	Chinese routes
	Portuguese explorers

Asia discovered, large profits could be made. Business could expand, and kings and queens could grow rich and powerful. The tight control over Asian trade that Genoa and Venice enjoyed could be smashed, and others could become wealthy in their turn.

A third powerful force was the desire to convert non-Christians to Christianity. **Queen Isabella** of Spain and other European rulers considered missionary work part of their Christian duty. The Church taught that a ruler who won souls for Christ would find favor with God and could hope to win a place in heaven.

Portugal Takes the Lead

In the search for new trade routes to the east, Portugal took the lead and made the first impor-

tant breakthrough. The curtain rises with a remarkable Portuguese prince on center stage. History knows him as **Prince Henry the Navigator.** Convinced that the Italian trade monopoly with Asia could be broken by finding an all-water route to the east, Prince Henry laid careful plans. In 1415, he set up a school for navigators and invited leading European sailors and scholars. There they studied and improved methods of sailing. They planned and built larger and more seaworthy ships. They became familiar with new and improved instruments of navigation, such as the compass and the astrolabe [as′trə lāb]. They developed maps and charts that took some of the mystery and uncertainty out of sailing out of sight of land. Building on this growing knowledge, Portuguese sea captains began searching for an all-water route to the Indies.

These explorers knew that the earth was round. But they also believed that it would be easier to reach East Asia by sailing around Africa. Thus, following Prince Henry's orders, Portuguese ship captains inched their way south along the African coast. It took great courage to undertake voyages of such length. Progress was slow. Years went by, but finally, in 1488, a Portuguese captain, Bartolomeu Dias, rounded the tip of Africa. Ten years later, in 1498, another captain, Vasco da Gama, followed the same route and sailed on to India. (See map, opposite page.)

The Portuguese captains did not find the coast of Africa to be very inviting. There were few ports or towns. In many places the interior appeared either completely barren or so choked with vegetation as to discourage exploration. But here and there they sent landing parties ashore to make contact with the Africans. In this way, the Portuguese began a limited trade with Africa, exchanging European goods for supplies and a few slaves. The slaves brought a good price back in Portugal and Spain, helping to pay for these costly voyages. Descendants of these slaves accompanied later Spanish explorers to America, becoming the first Africans to reach the New World. One is believed to have been a crew member on Columbus' first voyage.

The success of Portugal threatened to break the Italian trade monopoly with Asia and introduced the Age of Discovery. The rulers of other European countries were anxious to take part. Soon ship captains, many of them Italian by birth, enlisted in the service of Portugal's rivals. The rulers of Spain, England, and France listened eagerly to their plans. Among these captains was Christopher Columbus.

Columbus Finds New Lands

It is October 1492. Three small, storm-battered ships are lost at sea, sailing into an unknown ocean. A frightened crew has been threatening to throw their stubborn captain overboard, turn the ship around, and make for the safety of familiar shores.

Then a miracle: The sailors see some green branches floating on the water. Land birds fly overhead. From high in the ship's rigging the lookout cries, "Land, land ahead!" Fears turn to joy. Soon the grateful captain wades ashore and gives thanks to God.

FROM THE ARCHIVES

Columbus Announces His Discovery

Archives [är′kīvz] *are public records and other historical documents. The following is an excerpt from the first document in American colonial history: a letter from Columbus to the Queen's Keeper of the Privy Purse, written on the voyage homeward.*

Sir, forasmuch as I know that you will take pleasure in the great triumph with which Our Lord has crowned my voyage, I write this to you, from which you will learn how, in 20 days [actually 33 days]* I reached the Indies. . . . And there I found very many islands filled with people without number, and of them all have I taken possession for Their Highnesses, by proclamation and with the royal standard displayed, and nobody objected.

From Columbus' letter to Luís de Santangel, February 15, 1493.

If Columbus had not discovered the New World when he did, others soon would have. But he is the one who made the find. His discovery began a movement of people and ideas that in an amazingly short span of time was to bring great and powerful nations into being.

As is often pointed out, Columbus did not really "discover" America. When he arrived on this side of the Atlantic there were perhaps 20 or more million people already here, the product of migrations, possibly from Asia via the Bering Strait, many thousands of years earlier. These were the people Columbus called "Indians," thinking he was in the East Indies. The misnomer stuck, and although other terms such as "Native Americans" are sometimes used, the term "Indian" to describe these varied peoples is the more common.

*Quoted materials in this book show spelling and punctuation as they appeared in the sources from which they were taken. Words in brackets ([]) indicate changes from the original document or explanations added for clarity. Ellipses (. . .) indicate omissions from the original text.

Tapestry from a Viking queen's ship, around 800 A.D.

TIME GLOSSARY

Here is a "refresher course" on the terms that historians use to describe time periods. As you can see, some of the terms have precise meanings, while others are quite vague.

age a long or short span of time, often associated with a person or distinctive condition: *the Age of Discovery, the Age of Jackson, the Gilded Age, the space age.*

B.C. and A.D. Americans use the Christian calendar, which dates events from the birth of Jesus. B.C. means "before Christ," and A.D. means *anno domini,* which is Latin for "in the year of our Lord." Archaeologists often use B.P., which means "before present," to date their finds.

century a 100-year period. The 1900s are the 20th century. Columbus made his first voyage in 1492, which was near the end of the 15th century.

decade [dek′ād] a 10-year period. Recent periods are often characterized as decades, although events rarely fit into this neat pattern: *the Twenties, the Fifties, the Sixties.*

era a period in history; an age: *the Federalist Era, the era of the railroads.*

generation the average span of time from the birth of children to the birth of their children; about 25 years. People who share experiences are often considered members of a "generation": *the revolutionary generation, the postwar generation.*

millennium a 1,000-year period. The plural is "millennia."

period a long or short span of time; age; era: *the colonial period of American history, a period of economic growth.*

And of course there were the **Vikings!** These hardy Scandinavian sailors burst upon the world in the 10th and 11th centuries, plundering the coasts of Europe and landing on the North American continent in several places. (See map, page 22.) But except for a few scattered contacts with Indians, they made no impression on the land or people. They merely touched the shore briefly, and sailed away. Some think that a few may have traveled deep into the interior of the continent, but the evidence is very unclear. It is clear, however, that their deeds, except in song and legend, were quickly forgotten.

What had Columbus found? Not Asia, as he continued to believe, but two huge continents. Among the first to realize this was the Florentine explorer, **Amerigo Vespucci** [ve spü′chē], who went on several voyages to the new lands between 1497 and 1507. Some of the letters Vespucci wrote describing the beauty of the New World were widely read in Europe. Among the readers was a German mapmaker by the name of Martin Waldseemuller [vald sē myü′lèr]. Wanting to show the new lands on a map he was making, he decided to name them "America" after the writer of the letters. Other mapmakers began to do the same. Columbus died in 1506 unaware that the continents he had found would be known to history as America.

SECTION 1 REVIEW

Identify: Renaissance, Queen Isabella, Prince Henry the Navigator, Vikings, Amerigo Vespucci

Main Ideas

1. How did the Renaissance affect European attitudes toward the rest of the world?
2. List three reasons why European rulers wanted to find a water route to East Asia.
3. What was Prince Henry of Portugal's contribution to the Age of Discovery? What was Columbus' contribution?
4. What role did the Vikings play in the European exploration of America?
5. Why did Martin Waldseemuller name the newly discovered continents "America"?

THE GEOGRAPHIC SETTING

WINDS, CURRENTS, AND COLUMBUS

Geography is the study of the relationship between people and their environment—how people adapt to the earth's physical features, such as landforms, climate, bodies of water, vegetation, and soils. Let's look at the physical and human factors that combined to make Columbus' discovery possible.

Latitude and Longitude

First, look at the solid blue lines on the map at right. These represent the grid system, a system of imaginary lines invented to locate places on earth. There are two kinds of lines, latitude lines and longitude lines.

Latitude lines are also called parallels because they run parallel to the Equator. The Equator is an imaginary line that divides the earth into two equal parts, the Northern Hemisphere and the Southern Hemisphere. All points on the Equator are equally distant from the two poles. The Equator is numbered 0° (zero degrees). The other latitude lines are numbered in degrees north and south of the Equator. Thus, the Canary Islands (see map) are about 28 degrees north latitude, or 28°N.

The dashed blue lines are special parallels. The Tropic of Cancer (23.5°N) is the latitude which is the farthest north that the sun shines directly overhead. The

Tropic of Capricorn marks the farthest south that the sun shines directly overhead. The latitudes between these parallels are called the Tropics. Because the sun is directly or almost directly overhead, the Tropics are usually warm.

Columbus was able to determine latitude by using a small device called an astrolabe to measure the

angle of stars above the horizon. Even on the open sea, sailors in the 1400s had a pretty good idea how far north or south of the Equator they wcrc.

But Columbus and other seamen of his day were unable to determine their longitude. This part of the grid system was not established until the late 1700s, when the English and French

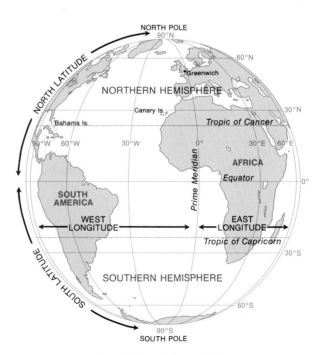

Latitude and Longitude

Astrolabe (top) and Venetian engraving of Columbus' departure

developed accurate clocks to help them calculate distances east and west on the open sea.

Longitude lines, also called meridians, run between the North Pole and the South Pole. Meridians are numbered 0° to 180° east and west of the Prime Meridian. The Prime Meridian—or 0°—runs through Greenwich, England, which is now part of London. The 180° meridian is exactly halfway around the earth from the Prime Meridian.

Find the Prime Meridian on the map on page 9. Now locate the Canary Islands. According to the grid system, these islands are about 15 degrees west of the Prime Meridian, or 15°W. By using the grid system you can describe the exact location of any place on earth.

Columbus' Voyage into the Unknown

Spain is located about 35°N to 40°N. Columbus knew that at these latitudes the winds usually blew from the west. He also knew that the winds off the Canary Islands usually blew *toward* the west. Furthermore, the Indies, he believed, lay due west about the same latitude.

Now trace the route Columbus took on his first voyage to the New World. (See map, opposite page.) He sailed from Palos, Spain, to the Canary Islands, then almost straight west across the Atlantic. After awhile his crew became worried, because the constant wind made sailing west so easy. Unable to determine longitude, they could not tell how far they had traveled. How would their sailing ships ever return to Spain?

Columbus and his crew did not know about the earth's great wind systems. Without these winds, Columbus would not have reached

Watling Island in the Bahamas in 33 days, or returned home to tell about it.

The Prevailing Winds

Most parts of the world, especially the oceans, experience prevailing winds. These are winds that usually blow from the same direction. All winds are caused by air moving from high-pressure areas to low-pressure areas. The direction of the prevailing winds is determined by several factors, including the rotation of the earth and the uneven heating of the atmosphere.

For example, look at the simplified diagram of the earth's wind systems on the opposite page. Note the low-pressure region at the Equator, created by warm air rising. High in the atmosphere, this warm air cools off and descends, creating a high-pressure belt at about 30°N and S. Some of this air will then flow toward the low-pressure zone at the Equator.

The global circulation of air would result in winds that blow directly north and south were it not for the Coriolis force, an effect of the earth's rotation. Because of this force, anything moving in the Northern Hemisphere tends to turn right, or clockwise. In the Southern Hemisphere, moving objects tend to veer left, or counterclockwise. Notice how water always swirls down your drain in a clockwise direction. In Argentina and Australia, water swirls down the drain in the opposite direction.

Now find the northeast tradewinds on the diagram. (Winds are named for the direction *from* which they come.) These are the winds that blew Columbus' ships to the New World.

In the higher latitudes, between 40° and 60°, winds called the prevailing westerlies blow toward the poles. As you can see from the map below, Columbus took advantage of the prevailing westerlies to sail home again to Spain.

As knowledge of the Atlantic increased, sailors learned to avoid the doldrum belt at the Equator and the horse latitudes at 30°N and S because in these calm waters sailing ships often became motionless. Columbus almost had a mutiny when his course took him briefly into the horse latitudes.

Ocean Currents

Columbus was also speeded on his journey to the New World by the Canary Current and the North Equatorial Current. Find them on the map below. Ocean currents are created by the wind, the Coriolis force, the mixing of cold and warm sea water, and the shape of the ocean bottom.

The Gulf Stream is a strong current of warm water that flows from Cuba up the North American coast to about 40°N. It then swings eastward and becomes the North Atlantic Drift, which warms the coast of Britain and Scandinavia.

It is documented in Columbus' journal that he steered southwest off his transatlantic course to follow a flock of birds toward what he thought would be land. If he hadn't done so, his ships would have entered the Gulf Stream and been carried northward. Perhaps Columbus would have discovered Georgia or South Carolina instead of the islands of the Caribbean!

Columbus was a gifted seaman who used the knowledge available to him. But he was also lucky. The prevailing winds and the ocean currents carried his ships to and from the New World on his voyage of discovery.

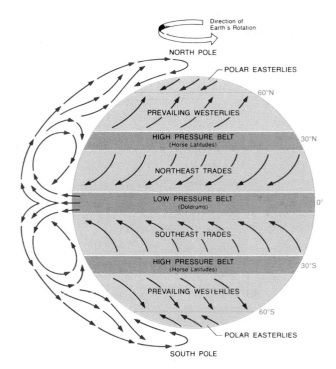

The Earth's Wind Systems

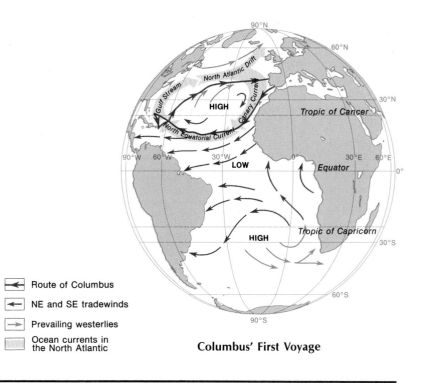

⬅ Route of Columbus

← NE and SE tradewinds

→ Prevailing westerlies

Ocean currents in the North Atlantic

Columbus' First Voyage

2. THE FIRST AMERICANS

Many archaeologists* believe that for tens of thousands of years before the arrival of Columbus, the people he called Indians had the Western Hemisphere all to themselves. It is generally believed that their ancestors came from Asia. If so, these varied peoples were the true discoverers of the American continent. The pre-Columbian phase of American history may have lasted about 27,000 years.

The Land Bridge to the Americas

Look at the map on page 14. Find the **Bering Strait,** the place where North America and Asia almost touch. The two continents are separated at this point by less than 60 miles of water. On a sunny day, a person standing on the Asian side can see land in North America.

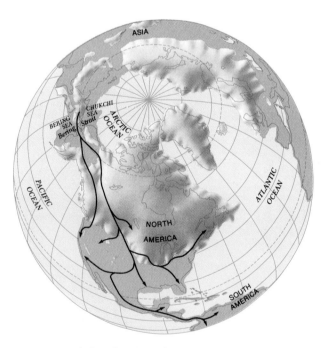

Routes of the First Americans

Places covered by glaciers during the Ice Age

Shape of ice-free parts of continents during Ice Age

Routes that were probably followed by migrating tribes

Travel from Asia to North America by way of the Bering Strait would have been quite easy during several periods in the last Ice Age, some 10,000 to 40,000 years ago. (See map, this page.) At times much of the water in the world was frozen in huge glaciers. The sea level was much lower, and it was possible to walk on dry land from Siberia to Alaska. It was during these icy periods that migrations of stone-age hunters from Asia to North America probably took place. In recent, warmer years, melting ice has created the Bering Strait, separating North America from Asia.

Great numbers of people might have crossed over into North America before the land bridge disappeared. They could have come over a long period of time, each group for reasons of its own. Most probably came in search of food, perhaps following herds of wild animals.

Although much of the land of North America was ice covered, a broad ice-free strip to the east of the Rocky Mountains stretched from Alaska southward. As the great herds of game animals moved southward, so did the hunters. The new land had other attractions too: fish, wild berries, fruit and nut trees, and edible plants. Over many thousands of years the first Americans could have spread out to occupy the lands that stretched from the Pacific to the Atlantic and from Alaska to the southernmost tip of South America.

Little is known about the history of these first Americans. There is evidence that by about 5000 B.C., some of them had begun to practice agriculture. Later—about 3000 B.C.—they domesticated corn, a plant that does not produce food in a wild state. The first Americans cultivated many other crops that were unknown in the Old World: potatoes, squash, pumpkins, beans, tomatoes, sweet potatoes, pineapple, cacao, tobacco, and peppers. Today corn, potatoes, and yams are major food crops, and the other plants add variety to the diets of people all around the world.

A Variety of Cultures

No one knows how many Indians lived in America in 1500 A.D. Estimates vary, ranging between

---

*archaeologist [ar/kē ol/ə jist] a person who studies the people, customs, and life of ancient times by examining material remains, such as tools, bones, seeds, pottery, buildings, and other evidence from the past.

Eskimo men and women catching fish in stone traps

20 and 40 million people. The vast majority lived in Mexico and Central and South America.

In the thousands of years before the first Europeans arrived in the New World the Indians of the Americas developed many different ways of living, or cultures. The word **culture** is used here to refer to all the things that describe how a group of people live. Included in culture are language, literature, art, religion, the way people organize their lives, how they govern themselves, and how they make a living. Many Indians lived in small tribes* with only a few hundred people. Others were members of federations, such as the Creek, Powhatan, and League of the Iroquois. Still others lived in huge, tightly run empires.

The large empires were all in Mexico and Central and South America. They may have developed in these areas because of favorable climate and abundant food supplies. Whatever the cause, by 1500 A.D. several large civilizations had developed south of what is now the United States. Among these were the Mayan of the Yucatán

*tribe an inexact term used to describe a group that differs from its neighbors in language or customs.

Peninsula, the Aztec in the Valley of Mexico, and the Inca of Peru. The Mayan civilization reached its peak from 1000 to 1200 A.D. The Aztec, a heavy borrower from older civilizations such as the Mayan, reached its highest point about 1400 A.D. but was still thriving when the Spanish arrived a century later. The Inca empire had been flourishing for hundreds of years when Pizarro found it in the lofty Andes Mountains. It extended all the way from southern Colombia to central Chile, some 2,600 miles, and may have included 16 million people.

Indians of the Present-day United States

The size of the pre-Columbian population in the lands north of Mexico is also unknown. Estimates range between 1 million and 12 million. The largest tribes had 10,000 or 20,000 members; the smallest were like large families. The map on page 14 shows the names of only a few of these peoples. Some were mainly hunters and seed gatherers. Others lived by fishing. Some combined agriculture with hunting and fishing. Most

ASIA

ARCTIC OCEAN

Bering Sea

Bering Strait

ALEUT

ESKIMO

KOYUKON

INGALIK

TANAINA

EYAK

TANANA

KUTCHIN

HARE

TUCHONE

KASKA

SLAVE

SEKANI

BEAVER

CHIPEWYAN

SARSI

ESKIMO

ESKIMO

ARCTIC

ESKIMO

ARCTIC CIRCLE

ESKIMO

Labrador Sea

Hudson Bay

ESKIMO

ESKIMO

SUB-ARCTIC

CREE

MONTAGNAISNASKAPI

BEOTHUK

TSIMSHIAN

NORTHWEST COAST

HAIDA

BELLA COOLA

NOOTKA

QUINAULT

CHEHALIS

TILLAMOOK

COOS

ROGUE RIVER

KLAMATH

ROCKY MTS

CARRIER

SHUSWAP

LILLOOET

KUTENAI

PLATEAU

SPOKANE

COEUR D'ALENE

FLATHEAD

NEZ PERCE

YAKIMA

UMATILLA

MODOC

PAIUTE

Bannock

BLACKFOOT

GROS VENTRE

ASSINIBOINE

CHIPPEWA (OJIBWA)

ALGONQUIN

ABANAKI

MICMAC

MALECITE

PENNACOOK

MOHEGAN

MASSACHUSETTS

Narragansett

Pequot

WAMPANOAG

DELAWARE

CROW

MANDAN

SANTEE

WISCONSIN

HURON

IROQUOIS

MOHAWK

ONEIDA

ONONDAGA

CAYUGA

SENECA

SUSQUEHANNA

MTS

CHEYENNE

TETON

SIOUX

YANKTONAI

YANKTON

SAUK

FOX

KICKAPOO

MENOMINEE

OTTAWA

WINNEBAGO

EASTERN

WOODLAND

ERIE

Mingo

PACIFIC OCEAN

COS

WINTU

MAIDU

POMO

COSTANOAN

MIWOK

YOKUTS

NORTHERN

SHOSHONE

Goshute

Uintah

GREAT BASIN

UTE

ROCKY MOUNTAINS

PONCA

ARAPAHO

OGLALA

OMAHA

IOWA

PAWNEE

MISSOURI

MIAMI POTAWATOMI

ILLINOIS

SHAWNEE

APPALACHIAN

TUTELO

CHEROKEE

CATAWBA

POWHATAN

TUSCARORA

ATLANTIC OCEAN

CHUMASH

CAHUILLA

SERRANO

SOUTHERN PAIUTE

MOJAVE

NAVAJO

HOPI

ZUNI

PUEBLO

JICARILLA

KIOWA

GREAT PLAINS

OSAGE

QUAPAW

CHICKASAW

CREEK

CALIFORNIA

TIPAI

YUMA

PAPAGO

PIMA

SAN CARLOS

CHIRICAHUA

MESCALERO

SOUTHWEST

APACHE

COMANCHE

WICHITA

CADDO

CHOCTAW

BILOXI

SOUTHEAST

ALABAMA

APALACHEE

TIMUCUA

COCHIMI

SERI

OPATA

CANITA

CONCHO

JUMANO

LIPAN

TONKAWA

ATAKAPA

KARANKAWA

COAHUILTEC

SEMINOLE

TOBOSO

GUAYCURA

NORTHERN MEXICO

TEPEHUAN

GUACHICHIL

TAMAULIPEC

Gulf of Mexico

TROPIC OF CANCER

CONCAZAPAN

GUAJIVE

CORA

TARASCA

AZTEC

MIXTEC

OTOMI

MIDDLE AMERICA

ZAPOTEC

MAYA

LENCA

Caribbean Sea

SOUTH AMERICA

MANGUE

OROTINO

**North American Tribes
and Culture Areas, 1500**

0   300   600 MILES

0   300   600
KILOMETERS

lived in communities with less than 100 people. In contrast to Europeans, individual Indians did not own land; instead it was owned in common by a tribe or village, and individuals had the right to use it.

There was so much variety among the Indians north of Mexico that we cannot speak of a "North American Indian culture" as though it meant the same thing everywhere. Furthermore, the Indians adapted quickly to the new conditions and new challenges that came with the European invaders. By the time the westward-moving pioneers reached the interior of the continent, the Indians who lived in the region had changed in many ways. We will meet many different Indian groups as we follow the history of European settlement in what is now the United States. First we must take a brief look at some representative North American Indians as they were when the first Europeans appeared.

Southwest Indians

The American Southwest is a dry and rocky land with stretches of desert where colorful canyons and bleak mesas meet the eye. Part of this region is home for the Hopi, Zuñi, and other Pueblo Indians. The history of these peoples is briefly discussed in Chapter 2. The name **pueblo** [pweb′lō] was given to them by the first Spanish to explore the area. The word means "village" in Spanish but refers to both the the Indians and to the homes of stone and adobe [ə dō′bē], or sun-dried clay, in which they lived.

Unlike most other North American Indians, the Pueblos lived almost entirely by farming. The dry sandy soil does not lend itself ideally to agriculture, but in this unpromising environment the Pueblo Indians successfully grew a variety of crops including corn, beans, squash, cotton, and tobacco. The Pueblos were excellent potters, weavers, and basket makers. Like many other Indians, Pueblo families belonged to clans (group of families who trace their descent through a common ancestor). In 1500, there were about 90 Pueblo villages. (Today there are about 30.) Customs and language varied from village to village, but the Pueblos usually traced descent through their mothers. Women owned the crops and houses, prepared food, and made baskets and pottery. Unlike other U.S. Indians, men did the farming and weaving.

Hopi sun symbol

Pueblo villages were usually built on cliffs with a good view of the surrounding country. From these heights, lookouts could spot approaching enemies, who were always near at hand. The houses were usually several stories high and built to serve as forts as well as homes. The ground floor had no doors or windows, and the only means of entry were ladders that could be pulled up to the second floor in case of attack.

More recent arrivals to the Southwest were the Apache tribes and their relatives the Navajos. At first the Apaches and Navajos were nomads who lived by hunting and gathering. But soon they took to farming, learning to grow corn, beans, and squash from their Pueblo neighbors. Although known as fierce fighters, the Apaches had another side. They were also basket makers, pottery makers, and part-time farmers.

California Indians

California of 500 years ago was the most densely populated region of the present-day United States. (Population density is a measure of the average number of people per square mile or kilometer.) California was home for 100,000 to 350,000 Indians. They belonged to over 200 different tribes and spoke many different languages. Among these peoples were the Yokuts, the Pomo, and the Wintun. The Californians appear to have come from all regions of North America to enjoy the sunshine, mild climate, and abundant food.

Finely worked Pomo feather and shell gift basket

Compared with other parts of the continent, life was easy in California. Little was required by way of clothing and shelter. The streams provided fish, the mountains contained a wealth of wild game, and the shoreline was teeming with shellfish. On the hillsides, seeds and berries were waiting to be gathered. The staple of the diet was bread made from acorns that had been shelled, ground, and soaked in several baths of water to remove the bitter taste.

As you might expect with so great a number of peoples, many different ways of living developed among the California Indians. But in every case, life was kept fairly simple, and the people were neither very rich nor very poor. They lived in small villages in stable, well-marked territories. Since most tribes were small, no elaborate kind of government or social organization developed. Religious ideas varied from tribe to tribe, and holy men and women were sometimes as important in the tribal organization as the chiefs.

In many tribes the women made exquisite baskets which were used for food storage, cooking, and even tightly woven water containers. The California Indians—especially the Pomo—were the most skilled basket makers in all of North America and perhaps the world. Special baskets made for gifts and ceremonies were elaborately decorated with tiny bright feathers and geometric designs, with stitches so fine that a magnifying glass is needed to count them.

Northwest Indians
The Pacific Northwest Coast, from Alaska south to northern California, was also a densely populated region. Here lived Indians who in some ways were even more favored by climate and geography than the California Indians to the south. (See map, page 14.) Despite the more northerly location, the climate was mild, warmed by the Japan Current along the coast. There was an abundance of fish, fruit, wood, and furs, especially in the lands of the Maida, Nootka, Tlingit, and other tribes in present-day Canada.

The chief source of food was the salmon that crowded the streams and coastal waters at certain times of year. Cod, herring, and halibut were also plentiful. Some tribes hunted whale, going out into the open sea in long dugout canoes.

Everything the Northwest Indians needed was near at hand. They built spacious houses from the wood in the great evergreen forests and made baskets, clothes, and bedding from the bark. The Northwest Indians are famous for their elaborate wood carvings, particularly the tall totem poles that decorated their homes and villages. These intricately carved and brilliantly painted totems were used to identify a family or clan or to tell a story.

Common among the Northwest Indians were great ceremonial feasts called **potlatches** (Nootka, for "giving") in which wealth was given away. The more wealth was given away, the greater the giver's prestige. Sometimes a wealthy Indian might give away everything he owned at a potlatch. He would in time receive as much or greater wealth when he attended the potlatches of his guests. A potlatch might be given for any one of a number of reasons, like a child's coming of age, a marriage, or a death in the family.

Unlike the California Indians, the tribal life of the Northwest Indians was highly organized. There were distinct classes and much concern about wealth and a person's rank in society—whether he or she was an aristocrat, a commoner, or a slave. Some Northwest Indians traced family descent through the mother but wealth was usually owned by the father. Among the U.S. tribes who shared these customs were the Chinook, the Quinault, and the Makah.

The Plains Indians
The Plains Indians lived on the vast stretch of land between the Rockies and the Mississippi River from southern Canada to Texas. (See map,

Mandan chief, painted by George Catlin around 1830

Eastern Woodland (Algonquin) portage across the Winnipeg River in present-day Canada. Painted around 1840.

page 14.) This almost treeless expanse of grassland was home to a number of tribes whose names appear and reappear in the history of the American West in the 1800s—Cheyenne, Mandan, Blackfoot, Comanche, Pawnee, Sioux (Dakota), and many others.

The river valleys and grasslands of the plains were well stocked with game, particularly the buffalo, or bison. When the first Spanish explorers came to the area, the Plains Indians hunted buffalo on foot with bows, arrows, and spears. Sometimes they would stampede a herd over a high cliff. So dependent were the Plains Indians on the buffalo that every part of the animal was used either as food or as raw material for making tools, shelter, or clothing.

Many of the eastern Plains Indians were farmers as well as buffalo hunters. Some, such as the Mandans, were town dwellers, living in earth-covered pole buildings grouped together in valleys or on the banks of streams. Using the shoulder blades of buffalo as hoes, they tended fields of corn, beans, and squash.

The life of the Plains Indians began to change radically about 100 years after the first Spanish explorers reached the area. The reason was the introduction of the horse and firearms. The horse had died out in North America in prehistoric times. But runaways from the Spanish expeditions in the 1500s multiplied rapidly. Soon there were sizable herds of wild horses roaming the grasslands. The Plains Indians were quick to take advantage. Mounted on horseback and armed with rifles, the Plains Indians became expert

LIFE IN AMERICA

THE CREEK CONFEDERACY

The Creeks lived in what are now the states of Georgia and Alabama, building their towns along the Coosa, Tallapoosa, Ocmulgee, and Chattahoochee rivers (thus the name "Creeks" given by Europeans to these Muskogean peoples). When Hernando de Soto first encountered the Creeks in 1540, they were one of the largest Indian groups north of the Aztec empire in Mexico.

The Creeks lived in villages that were loosely organized into an informal confederacy. Each town was like a small independent city-state, with its own chief, or *miko*. The confederacy grew to as many as 50 towns by including defeated tribes and later refugee groups from areas of English settlement. In the 1700s, the confederacy may have numbered about 10,000 people.

A Prosperous People

The Creeks were quite prosperous as farmers, hunters, and traders. Their villages centered around a public plaza or town square. On a mound facing the square were the meeting houses for the miko, his advisers, and the warriors. Here also was the hot house, or *chokofa*, a circular building sometimes 50 feet in diameter, which served as a meeting place for men during the colder winter months. The rest of the plaza was the *chungke* yard, where games, ceremonies, and dances took place. Beyond the square were streets lined with houses and gardens, and outside the town were the croplands.

Each family contributed part of its harvest to a public granary to use during war emergencies or bad harvests, to feed visitors, and to share with other towns. Towns in the north traded copper and flint for salt and dried fish from the Gulf Coast. Some scholars think that Creek traders traveled as far as Cuba in cypress dugout canoes.

White Towns and Red Towns

Creek towns and clans were divided into a "white" group and a "red" group. Mikos were selected from white clans, and the white clans and towns were in charge of peacetime administrations. Peace talks were always conducted in white towns, which were places of sanctuary where no one could be killed, even enemies or murderers.

The red clans and towns took charge during times of war, when both red and white towns and clans united against a common enemy.

Creek village. Note the circular hot house and granaries.

hunters and fighters. The art of hunting buffalo was revolutionized, and the people became much more mobile. Because food was plentiful, Indians from other regions also moved into the area and took up buffalo hunting as a way of life. Life became easier for the Plains Indians only to end in disaster when white settlers and hunters destroyed the buffalo herds in the 19th century.

Eastern Woodland and Southeast Indians

The entire area between the Atlantic Coast and the Mississippi River was once almost entirely covered by forests. Here lived an estimated 300,000 Indians. They are sometimes described in two regional groupings: Eastern Woodland and Southeast Indians.

The Eastern Woodland Indians belonged to two large groups—the Algonquin [al gong′kən] peoples and the Iroquois [ir′ə kwoi]. The Iroquois seem to have been latecomers to the East Coast, moving from the west into lands that the Algonquins had been living in for many centuries. Most of the Southeastern Indians spoke Muskogean [mus kō gē′ən] languages.

Although their ways of living varied depending on geography, climate, and soil, most of the Indians east of the Mississippi lived by combining shifting cultivation with hunting, fishing, and gathering. **Shifting cultivation** is a system found in many forested parts of the world. It is also called slash-and-burn agriculture because farmers clear a field within the forest by slashing the tree trunks. The trees die, the trunks are burned, and the wood ash is used to fertilize the soil. After a few years, the soil loses its fertility, and the farmers cultivate another area, allowing the trees to grow up in the former field.

The slash-and-burn method keeps the soil fertile, but the number of farmers that can be supported in a region is low. Early colonists often took over fields that had been cleared and farmed by Indians and then vacated temporarily. In most eastern tribes, the women were the farmers. They grew corn, beans, squash, pumpkins, sunflowers, and tobacco. The men hunted game or fished in streams and lakes for sturgeon, trout, and other fish. Those along the Atlantic shore reaped a rich harvest of shellfish.

Among the Algonquin peoples were many tribes that would interact with the English colonists, sometimes as friends, more often as enemies. In this group were the Narragansett, the Pequot, the Powhatan, the Delaware, and many others. Among the Iroquois peoples were the Huron and the Erie, as well as the five powerful tribes of the League of the Iroquois—the Mohawk, Oneida, Seneca, Cayuga, and Onondaga. Southeastern tribes included the Creek, the Chickasaw, and the Choctaw, and many smaller groups. Unlike the northerners, they often lived in towns of several

Iroquois longhouse. These houses were shared by 8 to 10 related families, usually sisters and their husbands and children. Beds and possessions were stored on shelves. Inside were several fireplaces, each one serving two families.

hundred people and had some customs similar to those of Mayans, Aztecs, and other Indians in Mexico.

Eastern Indians tended to organize into confederacies. The most powerful one was the **League of the Iroquois,** which may have formed around 1450 or 1500 A.D. Each autumn, 50 male councilors chosen by female clan leaders from each of the five tribes came together to discuss matters of concern to all. The League successfully ended the fighting within the five tribes and gave them unity in facing their enemies. The League became very powerful in the 1600s and 1700s and played an important role in early United States history.

The Iroquois controlled the area that is now New York State. This made them a key factor in the struggle between England and France for control of North America. Their decision to side with the English in the French and Indian War (1754–1763) helped drive the French from North America.

SECTION 2 REVIEW

Identify: Bering Strait, culture, pueblo, potlatch, shifting cultivation, League of the Iroquois

Main Ideas

1. How did the Ice Age probably affect migration to the Americas?
2. In 1500 where did most Indians live? Where were the larger empires located?
3. How did the Pueblos differ from other U.S. Indians?
4. Why were California and the Pacific Northwest Coast the most densely populated parts of the present-day U.S. and Canada? Compare the cultures of the Indians in these regions.
5. How did horses and firearms change the lives of the Plains Indians?
6. How did the Indians east of the Mississippi generally make their livings?
7. How did the League of the Iroquois affect early U.S. history?

3. SPAIN AND PORTUGAL CLAIM THE AMERICAS

When Columbus returned from his first voyage, claiming to have reached East Asia, the Portuguese were alarmed. They did not want Spain claiming lands they expected to reach in the very near future by sailing around Africa. The rulers of Spain and Portugal referred the dispute to the head of the Catholic Church, the Pope in Rome. The result was the **Treaty of Tordesillas** [tôr-də sē′yas], signed between Spain and Portugal in 1494.

The treaty set up a "line of demarcation" which ran from pole to pole, dividing the world in half. (See map, next page.) In the Atlantic Ocean any discoveries to the east of that line would belong to Portugal. Lands to the west would belong to Spain. In 1500, Pedro Alvares Cabral, a Portuguese captain, following Da Gama's route to India but swinging farther west, reached the coast of Brazil. Since Brazil was east of the papal line, Portugal claimed the new land. In later years, Catholic countries, with the exception of France, tended to honor the treaty. Protestant countries like England and Holland ignored it.

Discovery Leads to Exploration and Conquest

On his later voyages, Columbus explored along the coast of Central America and northern South America. His men were excited to learn from the coastal Indians that pearls and gold were common in the area. When this news reached Spain, it touched off a rush to explore the unknown lands in the hope of quick riches.

These expeditions proved to be of very great importance. The men who led them, known as **conquistadors** [kon kē′stə dôrz], were daring, ruthless captains who set out to win gold and glory. Before they were finished they had toppled the Aztec and Inca empires, killed or enslaved millions of Indians, and laid the basis for a new Spanish-Indian civilization.

The chart on page 23 lists some early Spanish explorations in the New World. The first Spaniard to set foot on land that is now part of the continen-

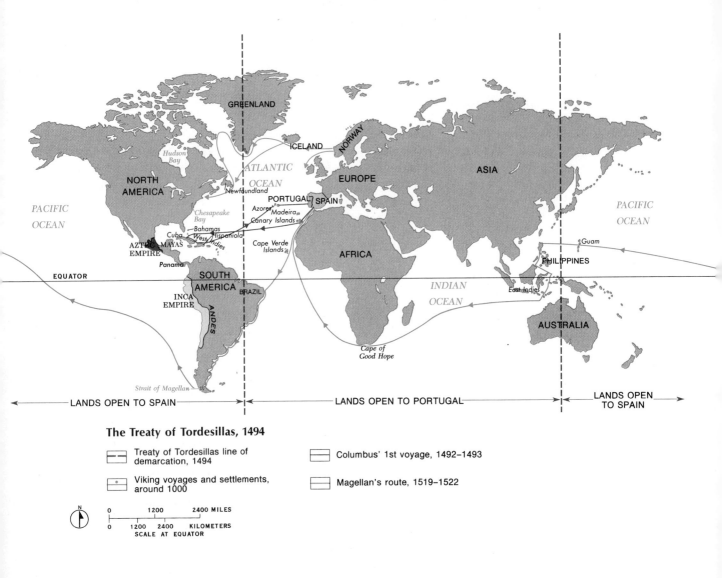

The Treaty of Tordesillas, 1494

Treaty of Tordesillas line of demarcation, 1494

Viking voyages and settlements, around 1000

Columbus' 1st voyage, 1492–1493

Magellan's route, 1519–1522

	1200	2400 MILES
0		
0	1200 2400	KILOMETERS

SCALE AT EQUATOR

tal United States was **Ponce de León.** Sailing north of Cuba in the spring of 1513, he discovered what he thought was a large island, which he named Pascua Florida, Spanish for "Easter." Here he hoped to find gold and also a fountain of eternal youth. By the time of his second visit in 1521, he realized that Florida was not an island. He planned to start a colony but was killed in a battle with Indians.

To the south, in Mexico, **Hernando Cortés** smashed the Aztec empire in 1521 and killed Montezuma, the Aztec ruler. On the ruins of the Aztec capital of Tenochtitlán, he built a new city—Mexico City—which became the capital of New Spain. Massive hordes of gold and silver

were gathered up and shipped to Spain.

A few years later, in 1532, another of the conquistadors, **Francisco Pizarro,** destroyed the empire of the Incas in South America. Again, stacks of gold and silver objects were collected, melted down, and shipped to Spain.

The Search for Gold Turns to the North

Reports of great riches to be seized by easy conquest inspired **Pánfilo de Narváez, Hernando de Soto,** and **Francisco Vásquez de Coronado** to strike out north of Mexico into land that is now part of the United States. (See map, page 30.) Without exception these three large expeditions were dis-

HIGHLIGHTS OF SPANISH EXPLORATION, 1492-1550

Date	Explorer	Goal	Accomplishment
1492-1504 (4 voyages)	Christopher Columbus	To reach eastern Asia by sailing west.	Discovered the West Indies and the Caribbean Sea.
1513, 1521	Juan Ponce de León	To find gold and a fountain of youth and to colonize Florida.	First European to explore land in present-day U.S. Failed to find gold or a fountain of youth or to conquer Florida.
1513	Vasco Nuñez de Balboa	To find gold and a sea reported to be west of America.	With the help of Indians, he crossed the Isthmus of Panama, becoming the first European to see the Pacific Ocean.
1519-1522	Ferdinand Magellan	To determine the size of the Pacific Ocean.	Killed in the Philippines, but the 18 survivors of this expedition were the first people in history to sail around the world. Proved that the Americas were not part of Asia.
1519-1521	Hernando Cortés	To find gold and conquer the Aztec empire.	Destroyed the Aztec empire in Mexico and seized vast amounts of gold.
1528-1536	Alvar Núñez Cabeza de Vaca and Estebanico	To find gold and conquer lands between Florida and Mexico.	Survivors of the ill-fated expedition led by Pánfilo de Narváez. First European and first African to explore the American Southwest, where they heard and spread reports of golden treasures in the "Seven Cities of Cibola."
1531-1533	Francisco Pizarro	To find gold and conquer the Inca empire.	Destroyed the Inca empire in South America and seized huge amounts of gold.
1539-1542	Hernando de Soto	To find gold and set up a colony in Florida.	Explored Florida and parts of what is now Georgia, Alabama, Mississippi, Arkansas, and Oklahoma, but failed to find gold or conquer Indians.
1540-1542	Francisco Vásquez de Coronado	To find gold and conquer the Seven Cities of Cibola.	Explored the American Southwest as far inland as Kansas but failed to find gold in the Seven Cities or elsewhere.

appointments. No gold was found. Thousands of Indians were slaughtered. The Spaniards who took part suffered incredible hardships. Both Narváez and De Soto lost their lives. The expeditions did, however, have important results: Much was learned about the interior of the North American continent.

By the mid-1500s, Spanish interest in North America had cooled. After the failure in 1542 of De Soto and Coronado to find gold or other treasure in the lands north of Mexico, Spain turned its attention to exploiting Central and South America and the islands of the Caribbean.

SECTION 3 REVIEW

Identify: Treaty of Tordesillas, conquistadors, Ponce de León, Hernando Cortés, Francisco Pizarro, Pánfilo de Narváez, Hernando de Soto, Francisco Vásquez de Coronado

Main Ideas
1. What happened to the Aztec and Inca empires when the Spanish learned of their golden treasures?
2. Why did the Spanish lose interest in the region north of Mexico in the mid-1500s?

CHAPTER 1 REVIEW

Key Terms
Explain the meaning of each of the following terms:

Renaissance
Vikings
Bering Strait
culture
pueblo

potlatch
shifting cultivation
League of the Iroquois
Treaty of Tordesillas
conquistadors

Reviewing the Main Ideas
Section 1
1. In what ways were the 1400s in Europe a time of great change?
2. Describe three reasons why Europeans wanted to find new trade routes.
3. How did Prince Henry help Portugal become a center for exploration?

Section 2
1. How did the Indians probably get to the Western Hemisphere?
2. Where and when did the largest Indian empires flourish?
3. Describe an outstanding cultural aspect of Indians in each of the following regions: Southwest, California, Northwest, Plains, Eastern Woodland, and Southeast.

Section 3
1. What was the purpose of the Treaty of Tordesillas?
2. What did the Spanish conquistadors accomplish in the 50 years after Columbus's first voyage?
3. Why did the Spanish consider their expeditions north of Mexico in the early 1500s unsuccessful?

Special History Skills:
Working with Charts
Charts can help you learn information quickly and communicate it clearly. For example, look at the chart on page 23. Note how it helps you answer the following questions: (1) What were the Spanish explorers' goals? (2) Which explorers accomplished their goals? (3) Which failed to do so?

Now make a chart that summarizes the information in this chapter about Indians north of Mexico around 1500. First decide what facts you want to show. List these as headings on a sheet of paper. See the examples below. Then fill in the chart. You may not be able to fill in every heading for every region or tribe mentioned in the text. Charts should always have titles, so make up a title for your chart. Suggested headings:

REGION   TRIBES   ORGANIZATION   ECONOMY   ARTS

Other Skill Activities
1. **The first European explorers**
   Find out more about the Vikings' early voyages to North America. Make a map and a written or oral report.
2. **Local tribes**
   Find out which Indian tribe lived in your area in 1500. Research the history and culture of that tribe. Try to use local resources, such as the public library and historical society.
3. **Navigation in 1492**
   Learn how a compass or astrolabe works. Demonstrate its use for your class.
4. **Time line**
   Make a time line of Spanish exploration starting with Columbus' first voyage and ending 50 years later. Use information from the chart on page 23 as your source.

Thinking Critically
1. It can be said that Columbus did not discover America. Give at least two reasons.
2. Why is it hard to describe a single "North American Indian culture"? Did the first Americans share any common aspects of culture that distinguished them from Europeans in 1500?
3. In what ways did the European invasion change the Indian ways of life? What influence did Indians have on Europeans? Use examples from the chapter.
4. Make lists of positive and negative accomplishments of the Spanish conquistadors. How would you summarize their place in history?

Further Reading

George Sanderlin. *Across the Ocean Sea: A Journal of Columbus's Voyage.* Harper & Row, 1966. Background information with excerpts from his journal and his son's biography.

Cyrus H. Gordon. *Before Columbus.* Crown Publishers, 1971. Excellent work on Indian history and traditions before Columbus.

Edwin Tunis. *Indians.* Thomas Y. Crowell, 1979. An illustrated description of American Indians before Columbus.

Meridel Le Sueur. *Conquistadores.* Franklin Watts, 1973. Easy reading; traces explorations of Columbus, Cortés, Pizarro, Cabeza de Vaca, and Coronado.

Morton J. Golding. *The Mystery of the Vikings in America.* J. B. Lippincott, 1973. Explores the evidence that the Vikings were the first Europeans to reach America.

Robin Lee Graham with Derek L. T. Gill. *The Boy Who Sailed Around the World Alone.* Golden Press, 1973. Ever thought of going on a voyage of discovery yourself? This 16-year-old did it.

TEST YOURSELF

WRITE YOUR ANSWERS ON A SEPARATE SHEET OF PAPER.

True or False

Read each statement below. Mark T if the statement is true, F if it is false. Change the italicized word in all false statements so that they are true.

1. Indians north of Mexico *did* share a common culture.
2. Europe in the 1400s was undergoing *great changes*.
3. People probably first traveled to America by way of the *Bering Strait*.
4. The largest Indian civilizations developed *north* of the area now the U.S.
5. North American Indians owned land as *tribes* or *villages*.
6. In 1500, *California* was the most densely populated region in the present-day U.S.
7. *Northwest* Indians were noted for their generosity.
8. Horses and firearms radically changed the life of the *Plains* Indians.

9. Some *California* Indians were organized into powerful confederacies.
10. Spanish explorations north of Mexico were considered *successful*.

Matching

Write the letter of the item that best matches the description below.

1. the New World was named after him
2. means rebirth or re-awakening
3. explorers who destroyed Aztec and Inca civilizations
4. first Spaniard to explore land that is now part of the continental United States
5. powerful Indian confederacy
6. set up a school for sailors and scholars
7. served as homes and forts for Southwest Indians
8. divided the world for Spanish and Portuguese exploration
9. financed Columbus' voyage of discovery
10. great ceremonial feasts among the Northwest Indians

    a. Renaissance
    b. conquistadors
    c. Treaty of Tordesillas
    d. League of the Iroquois
    e. Prince Henry the Navigator
    f. pueblos
    g. Amerigo Vespucci
    h. Queen Isabella
    i. potlatches
    j. Ponce de León

Time Line

Copy this time line and put the following items in the correct place on the line.

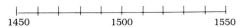

1450   1500   1550

1. Cortés conquers the Aztec empire
2. Columbus discovers America
3. De Soto explores Florida and the Southeast
4. Pizarro destroys the Inca empire
5. Ponce de León discovers Florida

Chapter 2

EUROPEAN EMPIRES IN AMERICA

The rulers of Spain were becoming enormously wealthy from their New World conquests. The king received a fixed share, the "royal fifth," of all the gold and silver seized by the conquistadors. Naturally, the rulers of other European countries became jealous of Spain. But because of serious problems at home, there was little they could do.

While Spain was gathering in its golden riches from Mexico and Peru and laying the foundation for a vast New World empire, England's king was worrying about staying on the throne. Not until the 1580s would English rulers be strong enough to challenge Spain.

France, also, was preoccupied for many years. A bitter struggle within France between Catholics and Protestants prevented the king from mounting an aggressive effort at New World discovery. Both England and France did, however, make feeble exploration efforts in the early 1500s that gave them claims to New World lands that would be important later. Building on these early voyages of discovery, England, France, and Holland began in the early 1600s to establish their own New World empires.

In Chapter 2 we will look first at the early attempts of England and France to explore North America and then at the Spanish, French, and Dutch empires in North America. The last section reviews the humble beginnings of the English colony of Virginia. Here was planted the first in a chain of 13 coastal English colonies that would later become the United States.

Sections in This Chapter
1. England and France Begin to Challenge Spain in Europe and America
2. Spain Builds Its New World Empire
3. France and Holland Start North American Colonies
4. England Plants the Jamestown Colony

Opposite: Mixtec gold from Monte Alban site, Oaxaca, Mexico

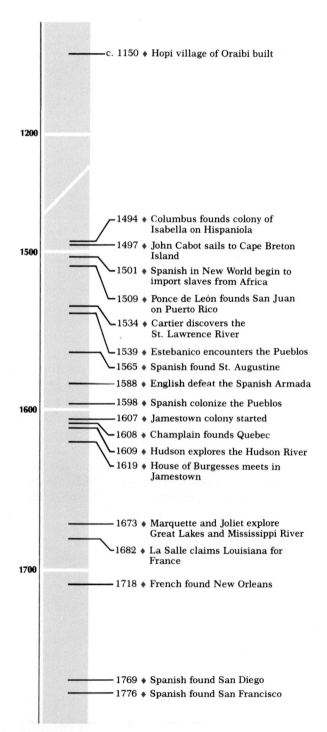

c. 1150 ♦ Hopi village of Oraibi built

1200

1494 ♦ Columbus founds colony of
Isabella on Hispaniola

1500

1497 ♦ John Cabot sails to Cape Breton
Island

1501 ♦ Spanish in New World begin to
import slaves from Africa

1509 ♦ Ponce de León founds San Juan
on Puerto Rico

1534 ♦ Cartier discovers the
St. Lawrence River

1539 ♦ Estebanico encounters the Pueblos

1565 ♦ Spanish found St. Augustine

1588 ♦ English defeat the Spanish Armada

1598 ♦ Spanish colonize the Pueblos

1600

1607 ♦ Jamestown colony started

1608 ♦ Champlain founds Quebec

1609 ♦ Hudson explores the Hudson River

1619 ♦ House of Burgesses meets in
Jamestown

1673 ♦ Marquette and Joliet explore
Great Lakes and Mississippi River

1682 ♦ La Salle claims Louisiana for
France

1700

1718 ♦ French found New Orleans

1769 ♦ Spanish found San Diego

1776 ♦ Spanish found San Francisco

1. ENGLAND AND FRANCE BEGIN TO CHALLENGE SPAIN IN EUROPE AND AMERICA

The earliest voyage to North America was made five years after Columbus' discovery. In 1497, **John Cabot**, by birth an Italian, sailed from Bristol, England, across the North Atlantic to what he hoped would be Japan. He had the permission of England's king, Henry VII, to sail to any part of the unknown world. With a crew of only 18 men, Cabot sailed his little ship *Matthew* west to what was probably Cape Breton Island in present-day Nova Scotia. (See map, page 30.) The following year he returned and explored the coastline as far south as New England. In 1509, his son, Sebastian Cabot, made a voyage to the same area.

Both father and son were looking for a water route that led to Japan and China. Finding none, the English lost interest. But the voyages of the Cabots gave England a claim to North America that would be important later when England was strong enough to challenge Spain and France for land in the New World.

France was the next European country to try to find a water passageway through the North American landmass. In 1524, **Giovanni da Verrazano** [və rä zä′nō], an Italian with French backing, hunted for this water route all along the North American coast from the Carolinas to Nova Scotia. Verrazano did not find any passage there, so the next French effort was made farther north.

In 1534 and again in 1535 and 1541, **Jacques Cartier** [zhäk kärt yā′] sailed in the service of the French king to what is now Canada. He discovered the St. Lawrence River (see map, page 30) and made an unsuccessful effort to start a settlement at Quebec. But not until the early 1600s would France be ready to follow up the discoveries of Verrazano and Cartier.

England Grows Strong

In the 1500s, during the reigns of Henry VIII and **Elizabeth I**, England grew in wealth, power, and influence. The increased production of wool and woolen cloth gave England a valuable commodity in great demand. Good management of the royal treasury put the country in sound shape financially. A growing navy gave the island kingdom security and a useful weapon against possible rivals. Above all, the brilliant and forceful leadership of England's great queen, Elizabeth I, gave the English people a feeling of national pride. This growing confidence soon led them to challenge Spain's leadership in Europe and America.

For many years, England had tried to keep on friendly terms with Spain. One reason John Cabot took the northern route across the Atlantic in 1497 was to avoid trespassing on Spanish claims to the south. But as England grew stronger, its desire to maintain Spanish friendship declined. Then, during the reign of Henry VIII, a real quarrel developed.

In the late 1520s, Henry VIII decided to end his marriage to Catherine of Aragon, a Spanish princess. Naturally, the Spanish were offended. In 1534, after the Pope refused to grant him a divorce, Henry VIII separated the English church from Rome and made himself its head. This action further angered the king of Spain, who was a strong supporter of the Roman Catholic Church. After Henry VIII's death, the English church (now called the Anglican Church) became more Protestant in its teachings, following the ideas of Martin Luther and other Protestant leaders.

After Elizabeth I came to the throne in 1558, hostility toward Spain increased. She completed the religious break with the Roman Catholic Church, and with the enthusiastic support of her people, she began to aid Spain's enemies.

English Pirates Attack Spanish Treasure Ships

Among Elizabeth's subjects were merchants and sailors who wanted to challenge Spain's power. The queen secretly gave them money and support. Known as **sea dogs,** * these men did not hesitate to steal Spanish treasure and sink Spanish ships even though England and Spain were officially at peace. To the English they were national heroes. To the Spanish, they were common pirates. Chief among the sea dogs whose deeds thrilled all of England were John Hawkins and Francis Drake.

*sea dog another name for dogfish, which are several species of small shark.

Queen Elizabeth I in coronation robes

Hawkins began his career in the 1560s as a slave trader, selling slaves seized in Africa to Spanish colonists in the New World. He was in trouble with Spain from the start because Spanish law forbade foreigners to trade with Spain's colonies. But the Spanish colonists wanted the slaves, and Hawkins simply ignored the law.

As he sailed in and out of Spain's colonial ports, Hawkins saw wagonloads of gold and silver ready for shipment to Spain. He organized raiding parties to seize these shipments. Among those who sailed with Hawkins was a young naval lieutenant who was to become the most famous of all the pirate-heroes, **Francis Drake**.

Drake was a dashing, fearless leader with winning ways. Elizabeth admired him and became a secret supporter of his piratical schemes. The boldest of these schemes began in December 1577, when he sailed from England with the goal of attacking the Spanish treasure ships in the Pacific Ocean, where they least expected it. Drake's plan was to sail through the Strait of Magellan and appear suddenly on the west coast

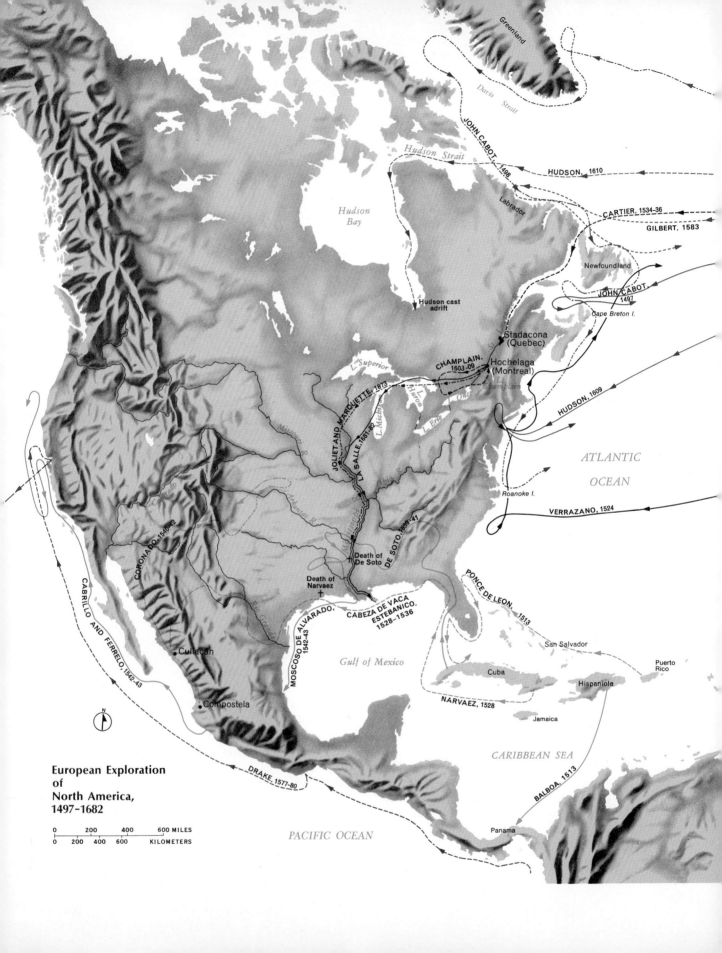

European Exploration
of
North America,
1497–1682

0   200   400   600 MILES
0 200 400 600 KILOMETERS

Greenland

Davis Strait

JOHN CABOT, 1498

HUDSON, 1610

Labrador

CARTIER, 1534–36

GILBERT, 1583

Hudson Strait

Hudson Bay

Hudson cast
adrift

Newfoundland

JOHN CABOT
1497

Cape Breton I.

Stadacona
(Quebec)

CHAMPLAIN,
1603–09

Hochelaga
(Montreal)

L. Superior

JOLIET AND MARQUETTE, 1673

L. Huron

L. Michigan

L. Erie

L. Champlain

LA SALLE, 1681–82

Missouri R.

Mississippi R.

Ohio R.

HUDSON, 1609

ATLANTIC

OCEAN

Roanoke I.

VERRAZANO, 1524

CORONADO, 1540–42

Colorado R.

Arkansas R.

Death of
De Soto

DE SOTO, 1539–41

Death of
Narvaez

PONCE DE LEON, 1513

MOSCOSO DE ALVARADO, 1542–43

CABEZA DE VACA
ESTEBANICO,
1528–1536

Rio Grande

CABRILLO AND FERRELO, 1542–43

Culiacán

Compostela

N

Gulf of Mexico

San Salvador

Cuba

Puerto
Rico

Hispaniola

NARVAEZ, 1528

Jamaica

CARIBBEAN SEA

DRAKE, 1577–80

BALBOA, 1513

Panama

PACIFIC OCEAN

of Central America. There he would attack the unarmed Spanish treasure ships that sailed north each year along the coast bound for Panama.

Drake's plan worked perfectly. His sudden attacks took the Spanish fleet by surprise. He swooped down on prize after prize. Then, his ships laden with an immense fortune in gold, silver, and jewels, Drake sailed north to what is now San Francisco Bay and on still farther north to the vicinity of Vancouver. From there he steered a westward course to the Philippines, the Malay Peninsula, and on home to England. Drake had sailed around the world! Gone three years, he had been given up for lost when his ship quietly sailed into an English harbor in September 1580.

Hearing of his safe return, Queen Elizabeth sent for Drake at once. Spain was threatening war if Drake was not executed for piracy. Many in England, wishing to keep the peace, expected the queen to sacrifice Drake. What would Queen Elizabeth do?

When the *Golden Hind* sailed up the Thames River to London, Elizabeth accepted an invitation from Drake to come aboard to a lavish banquet. There on the deck, with her ministers of state looking on, Elizabeth defied the Spanish king. Laughingly she said to Drake, "The king of Spain has demanded Drake's head of me, and here I have a gilded sword to strike it off." She then asked Drake to kneel before her. Touching him lightly on the shoulder with a golden sword, she declared, "I bid thee rise, *Sir* Francis Drake."

Early English Attempts at Settlement

While Drake was sailing his treasure-laden ship around the world, other Englishmen were busy with plans for colonizing North America. Eighty years had gone by, and no one had followed up the claims established for England by the voyages of John and Sebastian Cabot. Clearly, the best way to strengthen these claims was to establish permanent colonies.

Sir Humphrey Gilbert became the first to attempt colonization for England. In 1578 he received Queen Elizabeth's permission to start a settlement in Newfoundland. Gilbert made two voyages to explore the area, but could not talk his followers into becoming colonists on that bleak and foggy island.

After Gilbert's death at sea, his half brother, **Sir Walter Raleigh**, made another attempt to found a permanent colony. Queen Elizabeth granted him land north of Spanish Florida, which he named Virginia in her honor. In all, Raleigh made three attempts to colonize **Roanoke Island** in present-day North Carolina. None were successful.

The last of Raleigh's efforts was led by John White in 1587. All was going well with the little colony when White went back to England for more colonists and supplies. His return to Roanoke was delayed because of England's growing difficulties with Spain. When at last he got back in 1590, the settlers were gone. The word "Croatoan" carved on a post was the only clue to their fate. Possibly they had gone to live with the Croatoan Indians who lived nearby. But no trace of the settlers was ever found. Among the missing colonists was White's granddaughter, the infant Virginia Dare, the first English child born in America. Thus the 1500s ended for England as they began, without any successful settlements in the New World.

Explorers for England and the Netherlands	Explorers for Spain	Explorers for France
John Cabot, 1497, 1498	Juan Ponce de León, 1513	Giovanni da Verrazano, 1524
Humphrey Gilbert, 1583	Vasco Nuñez de Balboa, 1513	Jacques Cartier, 1534–1536
Francis Drake, 1577–1580	Pánfilo de Narváez (Cabeza de Vaca, Estebanico), 1528–1536	Samuel de Champlain, 1603–1609
Henry Hudson, 1609 for the Dutch, 1610 for the English	Hernando de Soto (Moscoso de Alvarado), 1539–1543	Louis Joliet and Jacques Marquette, 1673
	Francisco Vásquez de Coronado, 1540–1542	Robert de La Salle, 1681–1682
	Juan Rodriguez Cabrillo and Bartolomeo Ferrelo, 1542–1543	

Philip Sends the Armada Against Elizabeth

In the meantime, dramatic events in Europe were about to open the way for successful English colonization. King Philip II was furious with Queen Elizabeth for her support of the sea dogs and for the aid the English were giving the Dutch, who were in the midst of a bitter war against Spanish rule. The hero's welcome given Drake by the Queen quickly brought matters with Spain to a head.

In 1587, Spain began to amass a huge naval and military force to overcome the English fleet and invade England. Learning of the Spanish plans, Drake sprang again into action. In a lightning raid along the Spanish coast, he badly damaged some of the ships of the gathering armada. At length the damage was repaired. In the summer of 1588, the mighty **Spanish Armada*** set sail for England. It was the largest fleet that the world had ever seen, consisting of 130 ships carrying 30,000 troops and 2,400 pieces of artillery.

*armada [är mä′də] a large fleet of warships.

Drake and the English navy waited impatiently. When at last the Spanish sails were spotted on the horizon, the English sailed out to meet them. Taking full advantage of their smaller size and greater maneuverability, the English men-of-war* began to pick off the slow-moving Spanish galleons* one by one. Off and on for ten days the battle raged. When part of the armada took refuge in the French port of Calais, the English sent in fire ships to force them out. Thinking the burning ships were loaded with ammunition, the Spanish left the harbor in wild confusion. In hot pursuit, the English chased the remnants of the armada into the North Sea. The few galleons that were not wrecked in storms off the shores of Scotland made their way around the British Isles and back to Spain.

England's victory over the Spanish Armada was no accident. For many years the English had been slowly building their sea power, based on a growing merchant fleet, superior seamanship, and improved ship design.

*man-of-war a warship belonging to a navy.
*galleon a large, high ship with three or four decks.

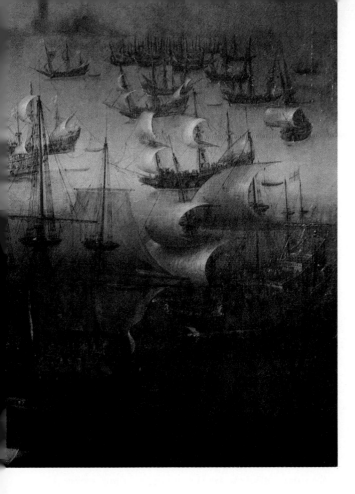

The defeat of the Spanish Armada in 1588 was a turning point in both English and American history. Up until then, England had made only feeble and unsuccessful efforts at New World colonization. Spain had been the dominant sea power, and the strongest European power in North America. After 1588, prospects for establishing English colonies in the New World were much improved.

SECTION 1 REVIEW

Identify: John Cabot, Giovanni da Verrazano, Jacques Cartier, Elizabeth I, sea dogs, Francis Drake, Walter Raleigh, Roanoke Island, Spanish Armada

Main Ideas

1. What parts of North America did the English and French explore? What were they looking for? How did these explorations become important later?

2. What events led to war between England and Spain in 1588? Why was the Spanish defeat a turning point in English and American history?

2. SPAIN BUILDS ITS NEW WORLD EMPIRE

The English victory over the Spanish Armada, although a serious setback for Spain, had little immediate effect on Spain's New World empire. As yet, neither England nor France had any settlements in the Western Hemisphere. Both had done little more than explore parts of the coast of North America. They had failed in their attempts to plant permanent colonies.

In comparison, by 1600 Spain had discovered, explored, and successfully colonized a vast empire which extended across two continents. (See map, next page.) The spectacular accomplishments of explorers like Columbus, Cortés, and Pizarro were matched by the successful colonizing efforts of thousands of other Spaniards who came to the New World as merchants, ranchers, miners, planters, soldiers, nuns, and priests.

A Far-Flung Empire

On his second voyage to America in 1494, Columbus had founded the colony of Isabella on the island of Hispaniola.* Twenty years later there were 17 Spanish towns on Hispaniola, of which Santo Domingo was the most important.

Meanwhile, in 1509 Ponce de León founded San Juan on Puerto Rico. Within a few years other successful Spanish settlements were made in Cuba, Jamaica, and along the coast of Central America. These centers became thriving communities in themselves and also served as military posts and staging centers for further exploration.

Within 50 years after Columbus' voyages, Spanish conquistadors had explored the major islands of the Caribbean, Central America, and much of North and South America. They had conquered the Aztecs and the Incas. They had also taken possession of Venezuela, Ecuador, Bolivia, and Chile, and founded Buenos Aires in Argentina.

The Spanish built cities and laid out farms and plantations. They constructed great cathedrals and dotted the countryside with missions. As early as 1551, they founded the great universities

---

*Hispaniola [his′pə nyō′lə] the second largest island in the West Indies. Today it is divided between Haiti and the Dominican Republic.

Spain's American Empire, 1600

| 0 | 1000 | 2000 MILES |
| 0 | 1000 | 2000 KILOMETERS |

San Juan 1598
Santa Fe 1609
Orista 1568
St. Augustine 1565
Culiacan 1532
San Antonio 1566
Havana 1515
Mexico 1521
VICEROYALTY OF NEW SPAIN
Santo Domingo 1496
San Juan 1509
Guatemala 1524
Panama 1519
Caracas 1567
Quito 1534
Lima 1535
BRAZIL (PORTUGUESE)
Santa Cruz 1548
VICEROYALTY OF PERU
Asuncion 1537
Santiago 1541
Buenos Aires 1536
ATLANTIC OCEAN
Caribbean Sea
PACIFIC OCEAN

had the power to make important decisions. When new lands were discovered, they belonged to the Spanish ruler.

To govern the Spanish lands in the New World, the king sent officials known as **viceroys**. The viceroy's job was to see that the king's laws and regulations were carried out. But the viceroys and other Spanish officials in the New World faced many difficult local problems. In many cases they found it difficult or impossible to enforce the royal laws. Often they had to act on their own authority and hope the king would uphold them later. Nowhere was the problem of carrying out the king's wishes more difficult than in governing the native American populations.

The Indians Under Spanish Rule

The Spanish viceroys were instructed to deal kindly with the Indians. The Indians were considered Spanish subjects, and one of the consistent aims of the king was to have them baptized as Christians and taught the Roman Catholic faith. Yet this view of the Indians conflicted with another important aim of the king: he expected his New World colonies to enrich Spain.

Spanish officials in the colonies soon learned that the wealth they were seeking required the labor of the Indians. Once the golden treasures of the Aztecs and Incas had been gathered up and shipped back to Spain, the remaining source of wealth was in the silver mines and the fertile fields that could grow sugar cane and other plantation crops.

To supply the labor needed in the fields and mines, the king began to give large tracts of land, called *encomiendas*, to important colonists from Spain. These gifts of land were feudal estates; that is, they also included the Indians who lived on them. The Indians were to continue living on the land in exchange for their labor, and the lords of the *encomiendas* were supposed to protect them and pay them wages. But the system led to many abuses. More often than not the Indians were treated as slaves. Millions—no one knows how many—died from harsh treatment or from European diseases for which they had no immunity.

The Catholic Church tried to protect the Indians from the evils of the labor system but with little success. The best known of the priests who protested the harsh treatment of the Indians was

of Mexico City and Lima. They opened libraries and set up printing presses. Long before the first successful English colonies were planted in North America, Spain had built a number of cities and towns in the Americas where life was as comfortable and luxurious as anywhere in the world.

From the earliest days of settlement Spanish ways of living began to change the way of life of the Indian peoples who lived in this vast area. A new Spanish-Indian way of living began to replace the original Indian cultures.

Spanish Colonial Government

When Spanish explorers discovered new lands, they always took possession of these lands in the name of the Spanish ruler. The rulers of Spain were **absolute monarchs**; that is, they controlled all the powers of government. They had many officials and advisers to help them, but they alone

Bartolomé de Las Casas. Las Casas enlisted the support of the king, who in 1542 ordered Spanish officials to end what amounted to slavery. But the evils continued.

The African Slave Trade Begins

As early as 1501, Spanish officials had begun to import black slaves from Africa. As the Indian population continued to decrease, particularly on the Caribbean islands, the African slave trade supplied more and more of the workers needed. By 1600, there were about 75,000 black slaves in the West Indies and northern South America. The arrival of many thousands of Africans to this area added a third important group to the population. In the Caribbean islands and northern South America a new way of life began to develop, which was a blend of Indian, Spanish, and African cultures.

Spanish Territories and Settlements in the Present-Day United States

Because the United States developed from a group of English colonies on the Atlantic Coast, we tend to think of our country as an offshoot of England. Furthermore, our language, government, and culture all had their origins in the colonial period under English rule. Yet vast portions of the present-day United States were Spanish, at least in name, until the 19th century—nearly 300 years.

These Spanish territories extended from Florida and South Carolina in the east to California in the west. In some places Spanish claims reached as far north as Canada. Half of what is now the United States was once part of the Spanish empire.

In much of this huge area Spain exercised little if any actual control. Refer to the map below. As late as 1776, only about 15,000 colonists had moved into these lands. Except for many place names, little remains to show that these areas were once part of New Spain. But in certain key areas Spanish colonists and missionaries planted thriving settlements. In these areas Spanish influences continue to be strong.

With so much thinly settled land under Spanish control to the south, why did Spain wish to control

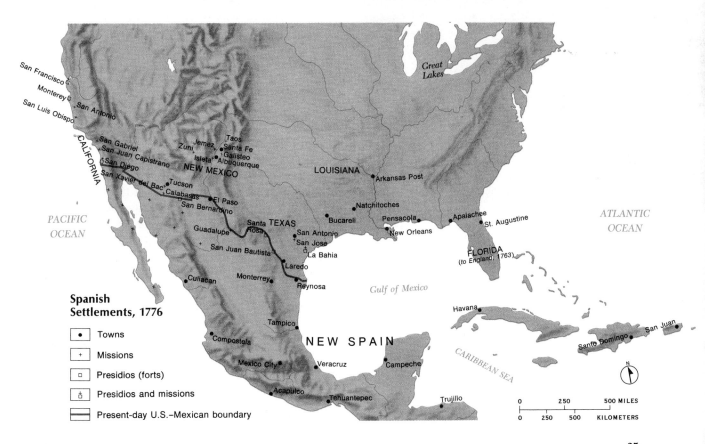

Spanish Settlements, 1776

- • Towns
- + Missions
- ◻ Presidios (forts)
- ⌓ Presidios and missions
- ▬ Present-day U.S.–Mexican boundary

Carvings in the Mexican church of Santa Maria Tonantzintla blend Spanish and Indian styles.

this distant northern territory? At first the area was believed to contain great wealth like that found in Mexico and Peru. Even when no gold or silver was found, the northern lands were still considered important for the defense of New Spain. So when these areas were threatened by other nations, Spain sent in colonists to protect them. It was mainly for this reason that the Spanish started settlements in Florida, New Mexico, Texas, and California.

Spain's Outpost in Florida

In 1565 the Spanish founded **St. Augustine** in Florida, the oldest European town in what is now the United States. (See map, page 34.) For years, English and French sea captains had been raiding the Spanish treasure fleet as it passed along the Florida coast bound for Spain. Thus a Spanish colony at St. Augustine could protect the treasure ships and aid Spanish vessels blown ashore by storms. Furthermore, the French established a base near what is now the city of Jacksonville that posed an even greater threat to Spanish control. Although little more than a defensive outpost, St. Augustine served its purpose well. The French were driven from Florida and the sea lanes protected from enemy raiders.

Early Settlements in New Mexico

Settlement of New Mexico began in 1598. In that year Juan de Oñate [hwän′ dā ō nyä′tä] established the first permanent settlement in New Mexico at San Juan pueblo (later called San Gabriel) on the banks of the Rio Grande. San Juan, the second oldest European town in the United States, was the capital of New Mexico until 1609, when Oñate's successor as governor founded Santa Fe. (See map, page 34.)

A major reason for this Spanish push north into New Mexico was to protect their mining settlements to the south. Also, after the defeat of the Armada, the Spanish feared that English explorers might find a water passageway through North America and threaten New Spain from the north.

The Spanish colonists in New Mexico settled in the narrow but well-watered Rio Grande Valley among the Pueblo Indians. Several times the Pueblo Indians rose against the Spanish but were always defeated. The governor at Santa Fe organized the surrounding territory and introduced the mission system to convert the Indians to Christianity and to teach Spanish ways. The Spanish settlements in New Mexico prospered, but the population remained largely Indian. By 1760, there were about 8,000 Spanish and Mexican settlers in the area.

Mission church of San Francisco de Asis, built around 1710 near Taos, New Mexico

Settlements in Texas

From time to time exploring parties from Santa Fe went east into what is now Texas. They made regular contact with some of the Indian groups in the area, and in 1659 Spanish priests started a mission at El Paso, which was then part of New Mexico. (See map, page 35.)

The first settlements in Spanish Texas date from 1690. By 1700, there were about 3,000 settlers in the region. After 1718, French settlement in New Orleans posed a threat to the Texas territory, and Spain made new colonizing efforts in Texas.

California

Just as in Florida and New Mexico, the Spanish began settlements in California to prevent other nations from muscling in on their claims. In the case of California, this threat came much later. Although Spanish explorers had sailed along the California coast in the 1500s and 1600s, they made no attempts at settlement. California was simply too far away from Spanish centers to the south and from Spain itself.

It was not until after Russia took over Alaska in the 1700s and threatened to expand southward along the Pacific coast that Spain took action. Spanish soldiers and missionaries occupied San Diego in 1769. The next year they raised the Spanish flag farther north at Monterey Bay. **Father Junípero Serra** [hü nē′per ō ser′rä] set about at once building a chain of missions between the two settlements. Another group of Spanish colonists came overland by way of northern Mexico to found San Francisco in 1776.

The Presidio and the Mission

Wherever Spain went in the New World, the Spanish soldier and the Catholic missionary

LIFE IN AMERICA

PUEBLO TOWNS: THE OLDEST IN THE UNITED STATES

Pueblo village of Taos, New Mexico

Most towns in the present-day United States were built within the last 200 years, but some Pueblo towns have been inhabited for over 800 years. The oldest known continuously inhabited town, the Hopi village of Oraibi in Arizona, was built around 1150 A.D.—400 years before St. Augustine.

Early History

The ancestors of the Pueblos were the Anasazi, a Navajo word meaning "ancient ones." They came to the Southwest perhaps as long as 4,000 years ago. For centuries they lived to the north of their present home, in the "Four Corners" area where the four states of Colorado, Utah, Arizona, and New Mexico come together. Here they built settlements such as the famous Cliff Palace at Mesa Verde, an eight-story dwelling that housed over 400 people. Another large structure was Pueblo Bonito, in the canyon of the Chaco River in northwestern New Mexico. Rising to five terraced stories, Pueblo Bonito had over 800 rooms and perhaps 1,000 inhabitants.

Tree Rings Reveal the Past

The Pueblos had no written history but preserved much of their long history through oral history. Archaeologists can identify some dates in the Pueblo past by using tree rings to determine the age of Pueblo ruins. They figured out construction dates for buildings by comparing the annual growth rings in the timbers of old buildings with the rings of very old trees felled in recent years. Once they found a match up or overlap of tree rings, they could work backward, dating older and older buildings.

Using this method, archaeologists were able to determine that Cliff Palace was built over a period of time from A.D. 300 to A.D. 1273. Other Pueblo ruins were traced back to the 1st century.

Pueblo settlements in the northern part of the Four Corners area were probably abandoned because of severe drought. Tree rings again tell the story. The rings show a 23-year rainless period after 1276. Raids from warlike tribes such as the Apache and Navajo may have been another reason for moving. In any event, it was at this time that the Pueblos moved south into Arizona and New Mexico.

The Spanish Come

In 1539, the Pueblos met their first foreigner from the Old World. He was Estebanico, a black slave from Morocco, who led an expedition of gold seekers into New Mexico. The next year Coronado's expedition marched through the region in search of the "Seven Cities of Cibola." They found instead the adobe villages of the Pueblos. Disappointed, the Spaniards withdrew.

Some 60 years later, in 1598, Oñate established the first Spanish colony of San Juan in the land of the Pueblos. The Spanish established *encomiendas* and tried to suppress the Pueblos' religion.

A Pueblo uprising temporarily ended Spanish rule in 1680. But after 12 years of freedom, the Pueblos were again conquered. They were still under Spanish rule when Mexico became independent in the 1820s. In the treaty ending the Mexican War in 1848, the Pueblo lands passed to the United States.

worked closely with Spanish colonists. This was particularly true in the borderland areas such as New Mexico, Florida, and California. Every Spanish outpost had its presidio and its mission. The *presidio* [pri sid′ē ō] was the military post or fortified area of the settlement. In case of enemy attack, everyone in the settlement took shelter within its walls. The **mission** was the settlement's religious center and also the place where much of the activity of the settlement took place. It was the headquarters of the priests or friars, usually Franciscan or Dominican monks, who devoted their lives to the task of converting the Indians to Christianity. They set up mission schools and taught the Indians various crafts such as spinning and weaving as well as Spanish ways of farming. In return the Indians introduced the Spanish to many things from their rich culture, such as irrigation methods for farming and crops that would grow in the hot, dry climate of the Southwest.

The Weaknesses of Spain's New World Empire

Spain's New World empire made it the leading nation of Europe in the 1500s. But during the 1600s and 1700s, England, France, and Holland forged ahead of Spain in Europe and began to challenge its power in both Europe and the Americas. Though the Spanish empire was fairly efficient, various weaknesses began to appear.

Size One weakness was the sheer size of this huge empire: it was hard to govern efficiently. In the 1500s and 1600s, means of communication were so slow that months might go by before a viceroy in America was able to reply to an order sent from Spain.

Lack of self-rule A second weakness was that colonists were allowed very little voice in their own affairs. This tended to stifle individual initiative. Most matters of importance were decided by the king or his officials. This was true of the economic life of the colonists as well as their political and religious life.

All colonial trade, for example, was strictly controlled. The colonies were not allowed to trade with each other or with foreign countries. All trade had to be with Spain itself so that Spanish merchants and the king's government could make a profit on the trade. This made the goods that the colonists needed more expensive than they would have been if bought directly from foreign merchants.

The restrictions in free trade led to much friction between Spain and its colonies. On many occasions they also led to wars with England, France, and Holland. These nations wanted to break the Spanish trade monopoly and, when possible, take over Spanish lands, particularly islands in the Caribbean that were easy to reach with naval power. In a series of wars that were fought in the 1600s and 1700s, Spain lost some of its Caribbean islands to England, France, and Holland.

Lack of resources A third weakness was that Spain simply did not have the resources to accomplish all it tried to do. In the 1500s and 1600s Spain over-extended itself fighting a war with the Turks and leading the Catholic nations in the wars between Catholics and Protestants then raging in Europe. Added to this was the enormous effort required to conquer, govern, and defend what was at the time the world's greatest empire.

Because of these weaknesses, Spain was unable to sustain the great lead over its European rivals that its early discoveries, explorations, and settlements had given it. As we shall see, by the early 1600s, England and France were ready to mount a successful challenge to Spain's colonial dominance.

SECTION 2 REVIEW

 Identify: absolute monarchs, viceroys, *encomiendas*, Bartolomé de Las Casas, St. Augustine, Junípero Serra, *presidio*, mission

Main Ideas

1. How was the Spanish system of government in the New World organized?
2. Why did Spanish officials import slaves from Africa?
3. Name the areas in the present-day United States that were colonized by the Spanish. Why did Spain found so few settlements north of Mexico?
4. Describe three weaknesses of the Spanish empire in the New World.

3. FRANCE AND HOLLAND START NORTH AMERICAN COLONIES

Colony of Biloxi on the Louisiana coast (present-day Mississippi), 1720

We have seen how France was first attracted to North America by the hope of finding a northwest passage through the continent to Japan, China, and the Spice Islands. Failing this, the French kings hoped to find another golden kingdom like Spain had found in Mexico and Peru. The early voyages of Verrazano and Cartier were disappointing on both counts. They did, however, give France a claim to parts of North America.

By the end of the 1400s, French fishermen had already learned, probably from the voyages of John Cabot, that the waters off Newfoundland were thick with cod and other fish. They began at once to make regular voyages to the Grand Banks of Newfoundland, an area which remains to this day one of the world's richest fishing grounds. (See map, page 98.)

When the French fishermen went ashore to repair their boats and dry their fish, they made contact with some of the coastal Indians and traded with them for furs. These early French visitors to North America were not interested in planting colonies in the wilderness. But they had hit upon two sources of wealth that would rival the gold of the Aztecs: fish and furs.

The Beginnings of New France

The first successful French settlements in the New World were the work of a remarkable soldier-statesman, **Samuel de Champlain**. In 1608 Champlain selected the Indian village of Stadacona, located on a mighty rock on the St. Lawrence River as the site of **Quebec**, the first successful French settlement in the New World. (See map, page 30.) The surrounding area, which the Indians called Canada, would soon become New France.

From Quebec, Champlain explored southward into present-day New York State, discovering the lovely lake which is now known as Lake Champlain. While in the area he made friends with the Huron Indians and helped them defeat their enemies, the Mohawks. This proved to be a costly mistake.

The Mohawks belonged to the powerful League of the Iroquois. From that day on, the Iroquois federation almost always sided with the enemies of the French, whether they were English, Dutch, or other Indians.

Champlain continued to explore into the Great Lakes region and along the North American coast. His aims were to gain control of the fur trade, convert the Indians to Christianity, and find the long-sought water route through the continent to the Far East. When he died after nearly 30 years of ceaseless labor, he had laid the foundations for New France.

The Work of Marquette, Joliet, and La Salle

The work of Champlain was taken up next by a remarkable team of French explorers, consisting of a Jesuit missionary and a daring fur trader. The missionary, **Father Jacques Marquette** [zhäk mar ket'], and his trader-companion, **Louis Joliet** [lü'ē jō'lē et], set out by canoe from western Lake Michigan in 1673, seeking a river that would lead west to the Pacific. Carrying their canoes overland they came to the Wisconsin River, which flows to the Mississippi.

Reaching the Mississippi, they floated down the mighty river for hundreds of miles, hoping it would turn west and bring them to the Pacific Ocean. When they reached the point where the Arkansas River joins the Mississippi (see map, page 30), they decided the river was taking them to the Gulf of Mexico. Not wishing to fall into Spanish hands, they turned around and returned to the Great Lakes.

A few years later, in 1681–1682, another French explorer, **Robert de La Salle**, led a party of explorers from the Great Lakes down the Mississippi River all the way to its mouth. (Refer again to the map on page 30.) He laid claim for France to "that river [the Mississippi], of all the rivers that enter into it, and all the country watered by them." In honor of the French king, Louis XIV, Robert de La Salle gave the name **Louisiana** to the whole vast area.

Thanks to the work of its great explorers, France now claimed all land extending from the mouth of the St. Lawrence River westward to the Rocky Mountains and south along the Mississippi to the Gulf of Mexico. To make good their claim to Louisiana, the French built a fort and settlement at New Orleans in 1718.

The Importance of the Fur Trade

French success in the New World rested mainly on the fur trade. The vast forested regions of New France were the natural habitat for beaver, otter, mink, fox, and other fur-bearing animals. Moose and deer were also plentiful. The trade in fur and hides grew rapidly and soon became well organized and highly profitable.

The fur trade required a close working relationship with the Indians who supplied the furs. With the exception of the Iroquois, the French got along well with the Indians. The Indians wanted to trade for French products, and since there were relatively few French settlers, the Indians did not see them as a threat to their tribal lands. French missionaries and fur traders lived with the Indians, converting them to Christianity and teaching them the French language and French ways of living. Since few Frenchwomen came to New France, many Frenchmen married Indian women and became members of their tribes.

Known as *coureurs de bois* [kü rər′ də bwa′], or runners of the woods, the French fur traders left Montreal on the St. Lawrence River each fall and headed for the interior. They paddled their canoes sometimes hundreds of miles to reach the lands of the Indians with whom they traded. The French stayed the winter with their Indian hosts and in the spring returned to Montreal, bringing with them fleets of Indian canoes piled high with furs collected during the winter.

For several weeks each year a carnival atmosphere prevailed along the banks of the St. Lawrence near Montreal. The Indians came to trade their pelts for knives, axes, hatchets, hoes, kettles, woolen blankets, colored calico*, gun powder, guns, and brandy. When all the trading was over, the Indians filled their canoes with supplies and returned upstream to their homes in the wilderness.

*calico a cotton cloth that usually has colored patterns printed on one side.

Weaknesses of New France

Lack of settlers For many years the prosperity of New France rested on profits from the fur trade. But New France remained weak because of the lack of settlers. By 1760, only about 80,000 settlers lived in all of French North America. (In contrast, in 1760 the population of the 13 English colonies was 1.5 million.) So, in the long run, the fur trade proved to be a weakness. Rather than building strong, self-supporting settlements along the St. Lawrence, young ambitious Frenchmen were drawn into the wilderness to make their fortune.

Furthermore, attempts of the French government to persuade farmers and craftworkers to settle in New France were never very successful. This was partly because the French ruler gave out the land to large landholders or nobles called *seigneurs* [sā nyėrz′] rather than to ordinary Frenchmen. The seigneurs then divided their estates into smaller parcels to be held by tenants, called *habitants* [äb ē täntz′].

In addition, only Roman Catholics were allowed to settle in New France. French Protestants who wanted to escape religious persecution at home were not welcome. Thus France lost many skilled workers who would have added strength to its New World empire.

Lack of self-government A second weakness was that the French government, like the Spanish government, exercised strict control over the settlers' lives. The colonists had no say in how they were governed. They were told what to do and how to do it. Since they were treated like children, they developed little initiative or self-reliance.

The Dutch in America

In 1609, a small Dutch ship, the *Half Moon,* commanded by **Henry Hudson,** crossed the Atlantic from Amsterdam. Hudson was sure he could find the Northwest Passage through North America that others had sought in vain. Searching every bay and inlet along the coast, he finally discovered what seemed to be a promising waterway leading north into the interior. What he discovered was not the passage he was hoping to find but the great river that today bears his name.

Hudson, an Englishman, was employed by the Dutch East India Company. This large trading company had grown wealthy from the Far Eastern trade once controlled by Portugal. If the company could find a water route through America to East Asia, making the trip shorter, it could lower costs and increase its profits enormously.

Settlements in the Hudson Valley

The Hudson River did not lead to the Spice Islands, but it did lead into the heart of the Iroquois country. On his trip up the river, Hudson dropped anchor where the city of Albany now stands. There he made some important friends among the powerful Mohawk Indians, one of the five Iroquois nations. They welcomed the opportunity to trade regularly with the Dutch, who in 1613 opened a permanent trading post at Albany, called Fort Orange. (See map, page 68.)

The Dutch soon set up a new trading company, the Dutch West India Company, to handle all of their growing interests in the New World. In 1626 the company bought Manhattan Island from the

French trapper, 1690

t' Fort nieúw Amsterdam op de Manhatans

The earliest known picture of New Amsterdam, dated 1651

local Indians. Here they established the colony of New Amsterdam to serve as the headquarters for their fur-trading operations. Although never large in population, New Amsterdam was a thriving trading center when it and all of New Netherland later fell to the English in 1664.

Next the company claimed control of the Hudson Valley between New Amsterdam and Albany and began dividing up the rich valley into large estates. Any member of the company who promised to bring 50 settlers from Holland was given one of these large tracts of land. These landowners, known as **patroons**, became powerful figures in New Netherland, the name given to all the Dutch holdings in the area.

Other Dutch Settlements and New Sweden

Later the Dutch extended their control over Long Island and northward into the Connecticut Valley as well as westward to the Delaware River. In 1655, they took over the small colony of New Sweden, which consisted of several fur trading posts and about 400 Swedish settlers. (See map, page 68.) Founded in 1638, this latter colony extended for about 35 miles along the Delaware River. Thus, by 1664 New Netherland extended in strips along the Hudson and Delaware rivers, its population numbering about 8,000 settlers of various nationalities.

SECTION 3 REVIEW

 Identify: Samuel de Champlain, Quebec, Marquette and Joliet, Robert de La Salle, Louisiana, *coureurs de bois*, *seigneurs*, *habitants*, Henry Hudson, patroons

Main Ideas

1. Why were relations between the Indians and the French generally good?
2. What two weaknesses did New France have in spite of the rich fur trade?
3. In what river valleys did the Dutch settle?

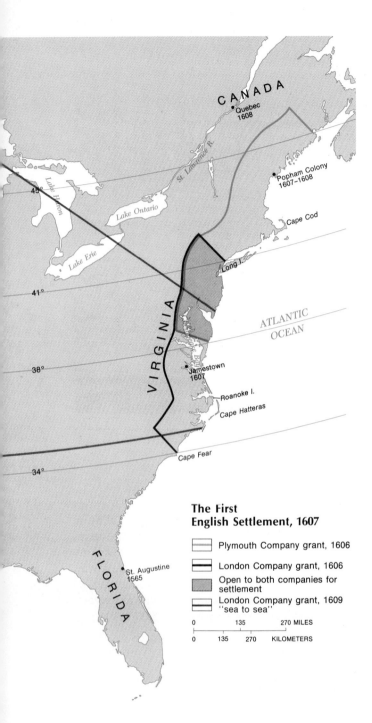

The First English Settlement, 1607

▭ Plymouth Company grant, 1606
▬ London Company grant, 1606
▨ Open to both companies for settlement
▭ London Company grant, 1609 "sea to sea"

0		135		270 MILES
0	135	270	KILOMETERS	

4. ENGLAND PLANTS THE JAMESTOWN COLONY

While France and Holland were starting New World colonies, the English had not been idle. Although Sir Walter Raleigh's Roanoke colony had failed, his idea of planting "a new English nation" in North America continued to fire the imagination of the English. They knew, however, that Raleigh had lost a fortune on his ventures. And a great deal of money would be needed to finance any new attempt at settlement. A way was needed to combine the resources of many people to share the financial risks.

Joint-Stock Companies Raise Money for Colonies

The answer was a new kind of business organization called the **joint-stock company** in which many individuals could invest small amounts of money. The joint-stock company—the ancestor of the modern corporation—was already proving highly successful in raising large amounts of capital for trading companies such as the British East India Company. Why not allow investors to buy shares in companies formed for the purpose of planting colonies in America?

With these ideas in mind, a group of London and Plymouth merchants went to King James in 1606. The king gave them a charter which allowed them to form two Virginia companies. The Virginia Company of Plymouth was given the right to colonize along the Atlantic coast of North America from Chesapeake Bay north to present-day Maine (see map, this page). The Virginia Company of London was granted the area south from Chesapeake Bay to Spanish Florida. The Plymouth Company made only one unsuccessful attempt at colonization: the Popham Colony on the coast of Maine. But the **London Company** began a movement of people across the seas which in time brought wealth and power to England—and resulted in the birth of the United States of America.

An Unpromising Beginning

On a gray December day in 1606 three small ships carrying 120 men left London and drifted down the Thames River bound for America. From the dock, friends and relatives waved hats and scarves in a gesture of farewell. Little did anyone realize the perils this small group of Virginia colonists faced in the days ahead.

Trouble began almost at once. Bad weather kept the ships along the English coast until mid-February. Rather than brave the North Atlantic in winter, the little ships took the southern route of Columbus, stopping at several places in the West Indies before steering north. It was not until early May that they sighted the Virginia coast. Some 16 of those who left London died during the voyage. Five months squeezed together in cramped quarters made everyone edgy. Fights broke out, and one of the men, John Smith, was placed in irons and held prisoner below deck for much of the trip.

The difficulties of the voyage soon faded when the colonists caught sight of Virginia and began sailing slowly up a broad river which they called the James in honor of their king. It was springtime. The dogwood was in bloom, filling the air with a sweet fragrance. Wild strawberries, far sweeter than those that grew in English gardens, were ripening on the hillsides. The banks of the river were a brilliant carpet of flowers. Everywhere there were marvels to greet the eye in this earthly paradise.

The settlers chose a spot 30 miles upstream from the coast to lay out their settlement. To further honor their king they decided to call it Jamestown. The location seemed at first to be ideal. It was on a narrow peninsula that had a commanding view of the river. Defense would be easy because the peninsula became an island at high tide. The men began at once building a fort to guard against Spanish attack. The colonists discovered too late that because of the low ground, the well water was brackish and polluted. Although they did not know it, the marshes and swamps nearby were a breeding ground for disease-carrying mosquitoes. Over the next few years scores of colonists died of malaria and typhoid.

Orders from Home

Before the colonists left England, the directors of the London Company gave them a sealed box that contained instructions to be opened on arrival. In addition to a list of seven men who were to be the

Southeastern Indians preparing for a feast. Engraving by Theodore DeBry, 1590.

leaders of the colony, the instructions listed three duties of the colonists:

(1) They were to search for gold and other valuable minerals. (2) They were to explore the surrounding area for the Northwest Passage to the Pacific Ocean, which was thought to be nearby. (3) They were to convert the Indians to Christianity.

The company also laid down a rule that the colonists were to hold all their goods in common. No one was to own anything, and all were to work for the common good. They were to receive only the food and supplies they needed.

Disaster Strikes

Much time and energy were wasted looking for gold and for the nonexistent passage to Asia. The time would have been better spent in laying in a supply of food and building snug homes that would be needed during the coming winter. None of these things were done, and the result was near disaster.

The company had not chosen well in picking the men who were to start the colony. Many of the settlers were English "gentlemen," which meant they had never done any manual labor. Men from this class had no idea what was needed to survive in the wilderness. They expected the company to feed them and take care of their needs while they looked for gold.

John Smith Takes Command

The man who saved Jamestown was the same **John Smith** who had arrived in disgrace. Once in America his luck quickly changed. When the company's box of instructions was opened, Smith learned that he was to be one of the seven leaders.

At first, the other six would not allow John Smith to serve, but soon his natural leadership talents won out. Smith was one of those rare men of action who can size up a situation and see what has to be done and then make sure that it gets done. A young man of 27, he had been chosen by the company because of his military background.

Although denied his council seat, Smith soon had the men working, cutting logs for the protective fort. He then began to explore the surrounding countryside with an eye to protecting the settlement against attack by the Indians or possibly the Spanish, who had settled at St. Augustine. He also, of course, looked for gold and for the Northwest Passage that was on everyone's mind.

On one of his scouting trips he fell into the hands of **Powhatan** [pou′ə tan′], chief of a confederation of 34 tribes. Smith was about to be clubbed to death when—according to legend—Powhatan's 12-year-old daughter, **Pocahontas,** came to his rescue and brought about his release.

John Smith's greatest service to Jamestown came during the first two years, when it seemed that disease and starvation would wipe out the little settlement. Only 38 of the original colonists survived the first winter.

During this crisis period, the members of the council were divided, unable to act. At this point, Smith took over complete control. He used his influence with the Indians to obtain corn to feed the starving. He sent men out under armed guard to fish and gather oysters. He introduced strict military discipline to end the bickering among the colonists. He marched the men out in the morning in small groups to clear fields, plant crops, and build additional fortifications.

John Smith (left) and a modern painting of Jamestown's marketplace in 1619

"The Starving Time"

In 1608 and 1609 about 500 new settlers joined the colony. But it was still in trouble when Smith was injured in a gunpowder explosion in 1609 and returned to England to recover. Before he left, he had shown the settlers that strict discipline and hard work were necessary to their survival.

Unfortunately, however, worse times were still ahead for Jamestown. The winter after John Smith left was so bad that those who survived always looked back on it as "the starving time." Only 60 of the 500 settlers lived through this terrible winter. When spring came, the survivors decided to give up the losing battle and return to England. But the timely arrival of a relief ship bringing more settlers and needed supplies changed their minds.

A new charter in 1609 reorganized the colony, giving it a more effective rule under a single governor. The new charter also added more territory to the original grant. (See map, page 44.)

Tobacco Saves the Colony

What Jamestown needed to survive as a colony and make a profit for the London Company investors was a marketable product. It found such a product in tobacco, which had been introduced into Europe by the Spanish and had become popular in England.

The Indians in the Virginia area grew tobacco for their own use, but it had a bitter taste and did not appeal to the English. One of the colonists, John Rolfe, introduced a milder tobacco plant from the West Indies. It grew well in Virginia and was easily sold in England for a good profit.

Soon tobacco was growing everywhere, even in the streets of Jamestown. Rolfe's discovery brought prosperity to Virginia. He later married Pocahontas, thereby softening for a time the bitterness of Powhatan against the colonists.

By 1619, Jamestown was prospering from the tobacco trade. Every ship from England brought

THE SMOKING AGE
OR
The Life and Death of Tobacco

Necotiana

Antismoking cartoon, 1640

Indentured Servants in Virginia

As the Virginia colony expanded, much of the labor needed to cultivate the fields of tobacco was provided by men and women who came to Virginia as **indentured servants**. An indentured servant was a person who had signed an agreement to work for a master for three to seven years in return for passage to America. Often the services of newly arrived indentured servants were sold to plantation owners at auction. When their period of indenture was up they were free.

Slavery was not part of the Virginia labor system in these early years. The first blacks to arrive in Virginia were brought in 1619 by a Dutch captain who had seized them from a Spanish slave ship. He sold them to Virginians, who treated them like other indentured servants, freeing them after a number of years. Other blacks who arrived in the early years of the colony were treated the same way. It was not until after 1650 that blacks were brought to Virginia for sale as slaves.

Self-Government Begins to Develop

When the London Company liberalized its policies in 1618, it decided to allow some of the settlers of Jamestown a voice in the government of the colony. The male colonists who owned land were allowed to elect representatives to an assembly. The assembly, later called the **House of Burgesses**, was to help the governor and his advisers make laws for Jamestown.

Thus it was that on a steaming hot day in July 1619, twenty-two newly elected members of the House of Burgesses crowded into the log church in Jamestown to meet with the governor and his council. They took part in the first meeting of a freely elected representative body in the colonies.

The London Company's new liberal policy was the work of investors who were prominent in English politics and who were eager to limit arbitrary government* whether it was the king in England or the governor in Virginia. They also took the occasion to assure the settlers that in the future they would be governed by English law and would have all the "rights of Englishmen."

This was good news in Jamestown. In the original charter of 1606, the London Company had

new settlers, many of them skilled craftworkers. New liberal policies introduced by the London Company in 1618 gave each male newcomer who paid his own passage a 50-acre grant of land. The earlier ban on owning property was lifted, and with this new incentive the economy began to boom.

Among the new arrivals in 1619 were some 60 unmarried women, sent over by the company to find husbands among the settlers. Until then there were very few women in the colony. Growing numbers of families soon added another element of stability in the Virginia colony. Despite a plague that took the lives of almost 4,000 settlers between 1619 and 1624 and a terrible Indian massacre in 1622 that killed 347 more, the colony survived and slowly expanded.

---

*__arbitrary government__ a government with unlimited power; the rulers can make any laws or regulations that they wish to make.

promised that settlers in Virginia would have all the rights they enjoyed in England. But during the difficult early years at Jamestown, this promise had not been kept.

The "Rights of Englishmen"

The "rights of Englishmen" was a phrase that had been around a long time. Ever since 1215, when the English barons forced King John to grant a charter of liberties called the **Magna Carta**, few English rulers had dared to govern as absolute rulers.

According to the Magna Carta, kings and queens had to obey the laws and customs of the land like anyone else. To see that the rulers lived up to this idea, the English developed a council called **Parliament.** While Parliament was not originally a democratic body, it continued to meet down through the centuries, frequently preventing kings and queens from overstepping their authority.

It was of very great importance that English colonists took with them to the New World these same guarantees against absolute rule. As we have seen, the colonists in New Spain and New France had no such rights. No council like Parliament existed in Spain or France. The absolutism of their rulers was extended to their New World colonies. With no say in their own affairs, Spanish and French colonists lacked the incentives that the English colonists enjoyed. For this reason more than any other, the English colonies soon outstripped all others in population and wealth.

Virginia Becomes a Royal Colony

The reforms introduced by the London Company brought lasting benefits to Virginia. But they did not solve the company's financial problems. A fortune in investors' money had been poured into Virginia to outfit supply ships and help the settlers survive the bad times. Just when the future looked brighter because of the success of the tobacco plantations, the company ran into serious political troubles at home.

The English ruler, King James I, believed in absolutism, even though he dared not practice it. Thus he did not like the new policies of the

*Parliament [pär′lə mənt] the national lawmaking body of Great Britain, consisting of the House of Lords and the House of Commons. The name is from the French word *parler*, "to speak."

England's House of Commons in the 1600s

company in Virginia. Some of the London merchants who were leaders in the company were the king's enemies in Parliament. Therefore, in 1624, the king decided to revoke the company's charter and make Virginia a royal colony under his direct control. He did not, however, disturb the assembly created in 1619. In the future, the governor was appointed by the king rather than by the London Company. But the elected House of Burgesses continued to meet and assist in making the laws for Virginia.

SECTION 4 REVIEW

Identify: joint-stock company, London Company, John Smith, Powhatan, Pocahontas, indentured servants, House of Burgesses, Magna Carta, Parliament

Main Ideas

1. How did the development of joint-stock companies help the colonization of Virginia?
2. What problems did the Jamestown colony face between 1607 and 1624?
3. How did John Smith and later tobacco help the colony survive?
4. How did the House of Burgesses help protect the "rights of Englishmen" in Virginia?

49

CHAPTER 2 REVIEW

Key Terms
Explain the meaning of each of the following terms:

sea dogs
Roanoke Island
Spanish Armada
absolute monarchs
viceroys
encomiendas
St. Augustine
presidio
mission
Quebec
Louisiana

coureurs de bois
seigneurs
habitants
patroons
joint-stock company
London Company
indentured servants
House of Burgesses
Magna Carta
Parliament

Reviewing the Main Ideas
Section 1
1. Describe briefly the explorations of the Cabots and Cartier. How would these become important in the 1600s?
2. What events led to war between England and Spain in 1588? How did the outcome affect the history of North America?

Section 2
1. How were Indians and Africans treated in Spain's New World colonies?
2. What were some weaknesses of the Spanish empire in the New World?
3. Why did Spain establish settlements north of Mexico? Why did it found so few of them?

Section 3
1. List the strengths and weaknesses of New France.
2. In what North American river valleys did the French, Swedish, and Dutch settle?

Section 4
1. What problems did the Jamestown settlers face between 1607 and 1624? What factors enabled the colony to survive?
2. Describe the significance of the House of Burgesses to English colonists.

Special History Skills:
Working with Maps
Which European country once sent explorers and settlers to claim the area in which you live? If you don't know the answer, make a conjecture, or guess. Check your conjecture—or prove your answer—by looking at a map of your state or local area. Identify place names that reflect the early Spanish, English, French, Swedish, Dutch, or Russian claims in your area. List these place names, grouping them into the following categories: (1) physical features, such as mountains, rivers, lakes, and bays, (2) towns and cities, (3) counties and states.

Other Skill Activities
1. **Awards for outstanding achievements**
   Review the chapter and choose three men or women who you think made an especially important contribution to European exploration and settlement of the New World. Write a brief explanation of why you chose the three.
2. **The Elizabethan Age**
   England's rise to power was an exciting historical period. Find out more about one of the following people in an encyclopedia or other source and report to your class: Queen Elizabeth I, Sir Walter Raleigh, Sir Francis Drake, John Smith.
3. **Goals of Spain**
   On a chart, match each of the following to a specific economic, religious, political, or military goal of the Spanish empire in the New World: *presidio*, *encomienda*, mission, viceroy.
4. **A Jamestown survivor**
   It is June 7, 1610. You are one of the 60 survivors of "the starving time" in the Jamestown colony. Write a letter to your cousin in London. (a) Describe your ordeal during the past winter. (b) Tell your plans for the future now that the relief ship has arrived. (c) Give your cousin advice about settling or not settling in Virginia.
5. **Making time lines**
   Using the chapter as your source, make four time lines, each from 1490 to 1720. Label them "European Exploration and Settlement in the New World." On each time line plot the events for one country: Spain, England, France, and Holland.

Thinking Critically

1. Why were so many explorers in the 1500s and 1600s eager to find a water passageway to Asia?
2. If you were an advisor to the king of Spain in 1600, would you have argued for greater efforts in settling the lands north of the Rio Grande? Explain.
3. The population of the United States is made up of many peoples. What evidence of this diversity can be traced to the earliest days of colonial settlement?

Further Reading

Tee Loftin Snell. *The Wild Shores: America's Beginnings.* National Geographic Society, 1974. Overview of the discovery and settlement of the New World. Beautiful photographs.

Peter Nabokov. *Native American Testimony.* Crowell, 1978. First-hand accounts by Indians of Indian-settler contacts.

W. J. Jacobs. *Robert Cavelier de La Salle.* Franklin Watts, 1975. Brief biography with authentic prints, documents, and maps. Easy reading.

TEST YOURSELF

WRITE YOUR ANSWERS ON A SEPARATE SHEET OF PAPER.

Matching

Select the letter of the answer that best matches each item below.

1. Samuel de Champlain
2. viceroys
3. John Smith
4. Francis Drake
5. patroons

a. carried out the king's orders in the Spanish empire
b. founded Quebec and other early French settlements
c. defeated the Spanish Armada and opened the seas to the English
d. Dutch landowners in the New York area
e. saved the Jamestown colony

Fill in the Blanks

(1) In the 1500s, _____ was the most powerful European country and the leader in New World exploration. (2) Explorers in the 1500s and 1600s searched for a Northwest Passage that would lead them to _____. (3–4) The _____ founded the oldest towns in the present-day United States; the oldest town settled by Europeans is _____. (5–6) Self-government in the English colonies began with the _____, started in the _____ colony in 1619. (7–8) The St. Lawrence and Mississippi rivers were explored by the _____ in the 1600s. (9–10) The Dutch started colonies along the _____ and _____ rivers.

Locations

Match the letters on the map with the place names listed below.

1. St. Augustine
2. Jamestown
3. Santa Fe
4. Quebec
5. Mississippi River

VISITING THE PAST

Mesa Verde, Colorado

Mesa Verde National Park in Colorado preserves more than natural wonders. The park protects one of the largest archaeological sites in the country. Ruins dating back before Columbus are nestled in among the ledges of the canyon walls. Because of its archaeological riches, Mesa Verde has been named by UNESCO as a "World Cultural Site" with international archaeological significance.

Mesa Verde, a Spanish name meaning "green tableland," has a rich history. Over 1,000 years ago, ancestors of the present-day Pueblo Indians began to live on this large plateau. In the soil of the mesa (plateau) they grew vegetables. They made baskets and pottery. Over time, their homes changed from pit-houses to row houses. Then the Indians moved off the plateau to the ledges of the steep mountain wall below.

The largest of the settlements built on these cliffs resembles a large pueblo tucked into the side of a mountain. Several hundred people could live there. The roof of one room would be the terrace of another. Ladders were used to move between the many levels. There were rooms for both storage and living. The most fascinating rooms were the kivas, large chambers that had a ceremonial function. On the roof of the kivas the Indians would dance in costumes representing their gods.

Mesa Verde is a place of wonder and mystery. There are no written records of its history. Archaeology provides us with most of our knowledge about it. But there still remain unanswered questions. Why did the Indians move off the plateau to the cliffs? Why did they later abandon their cliff dwellings? Several possible answers have been suggested. Someday, through archaeology, we may learn which are the right ones.

The ruins at Mesa Verde were so isolated that they remained undisturbed for hundreds of years. The largest ruins were discovered by accident in 1888. After the discovery, vandals were soon demolishing the ancient masonry walls of the apartmentlike dwellings. They were searching for Indian relics to sell. This destruction led to federal legislation to protect Mesa Verde and other important archaeological sites. The legislation was an important step toward the preservation of America's heritage.

St. Augustine, Florida

Even today, over 400 years after its founding, the main reason for the establishment of St. Augustine, Florida, is still obvious. Castillo de San Marcos, a star-shaped 17th-century Spanish fort with walls 30 feet high and 13 feet thick, points to the military purpose behind the settlement.

The Spanish settled St. Augustine in 1565 to stop French activity in Florida. Located on the route which Spanish galleons sailed to bring the riches of the colonies back to Spain, St. Augustine became a military outpost of great strategic significance. Sir Francis Drake, the daring Englishman, attacked and burned the settlement in one of his attempts to break Spain's link to these riches. This was only one of the many times that the settlement would be destroyed, only to be rebuilt.

The 235 years of Spanish rule have left their mark on St. Augustine. Today the town retains much of its Spanish flavor through the

Ruins of the "Cliff Palace," a pueblo that housed about 400 people. Mesa Verde, Colorado.

surviving architecture. The fort, the original street plan, the old city gates, and the surviving colonial buildings keep alive the town's special character.

Visitors to St. Augustine usually find the city's history interesting and exciting. "Old St. Augustine" gives the visitor a glimpse of life in Spanish colonial times. Costumed interpreters bring the past to life on a street lined with preserved and reconstructed colonial buildings.

Information from archaeological excavations has assisted in the accurate reconstruction of key colonial buildings. Such archaeological information has helped to fill in the gaps of written historical records by providing new information on the way St. Augustine's earliest settlers lived. Recent discoveries include what archaeologists believe to be the remains of buildings destroyed in Drake's raid during the summer of 1586.

Archaeology continues to increase our knowledge of how people lived and survived in the past. In St. Augustine, it is bringing us closer to the earliest days of this, the oldest permanent European settlement in the continental United States.

Traces of New Amsterdam

What city could be more modern than New York City? Skyscrapers soar high above the hustle and bustle of one of the world's most populated cities. Is it possible that this mighty metropolis still retains any of its humble colonial identity? Could any relics of those days have survived generations of unrelenting change?

Surprisingly, the answer is yes. On the southern tip of Manhattan, the narrow and random street patterns established in the early 17th century by the inhabitants of

Dutch New Amsterdam survive. These streets, as well as several added by the English in the early 18th century, still follow their original paths. This historic street pattern has played a dominant role in creating the present-day look of this distinctive part of lower Manhattan.

More amazing than the survival of the colonial street pattern is the discovery of colonial artifacts. Recently, archaeologists have unearthed the remains of 17th-century colonial New Amsterdam.

Excavating a site occupied only by buildings with shallow basements, archaeologists located the foundations of the first city hall: the 1640 Dutch Stady Huys. Next to it, they found the remains of an early famous tavern. In these buildings the political dramas of colonial New Amsterdam were conducted.

This dig is particularly exciting. The discovered artifacts had not been disturbed for hundreds of years. In the four tons of material salvaged from the site are pieces of such items as plates, wine bottles, and clay pipes. The success of this dig has made people realize that significant remains of colonial times might still survive even in a place that has undergone as much change as New York.

Just as the Dutch street pattern has left its mark on modern New York, so too will the recent dig. The foundation stones will be incorporated into the design for the plaza of the modern building that will rise on that site. More importantly, New York, like other urban centers, can now hope to learn more about its past through urban archaeology. Who knows what other archaeological treasures remain to be discovered under the sidewalks of New York?

UNIT 1 TEST

WRITE YOUR ANSWERS ON A SEPARATE SHEET OF PAPER.

Classifying (20 points)

Mark each of the following E if it is English, F if it is French, S if it is Spanish, or O if it represents some other nationality.

1. conquistadors
2. Elizabeth I
3. potlatch
4. Iroquois
5. patroons
6. John Smith
7. armada
8. Louisiana
9. sea dogs
10. *encomiendas*
11. Samuel de Champlain
12. Hernando Cortés
13. *coureurs de bois*
14. Jacques Cartier
15. Junípero Serra
16. Walter Raleigh
17. Francis Drake
18. Hernando de Soto
19. Prince Henry the Navigator
20. Robert de La Salle

Multiple Choice (20 points)

Write the letter of the answer that best completes each statement.

1. Which is the correct order in which these towns were settled?
   a. St. Augustine, Mesa Verde, Jamestown, New Amsterdam
   b. Mesa Verde, St. Augustine, Jamestown, New Amsterdam
   c. New Amsterdam, Mesa Verde, Jamestown, St. Augustine
   d. None are correct
2. The importation of African slaves into the New World
   a. was first introduced by the English.
   b. was designed to replace the Indians as workers.
   c. had no effect on the population and cultures of the Caribbean and South America.
   d. was known as *encomienda*.
3. Indians of the New World
   a. had not developed cultures when Europeans arrived.
   b. were misnamed by Columbus, who thought he had landed in the East Indies.
   c. prospered under European rule.
   d. lived in many tribes, all sharing similar cultures.
4. European nations financed voyages of discovery in order to
   a. find a water route to Asia.
   b. satisfy their curiosity about the world.
   c. convert non-Christians to Christianity.
   d. do all of the above.
5. How was the English colony at Jamestown different from Spanish or French colonies?
   a. The colonists searched for gold.
   b. Half the colonists were women.
   c. The colonists elected representatives to a governing assembly.
   d. Jamestown was not different from the Spanish or French colonies.

Time Line (20 points)

Match the letters on the time line with the events they stand for.

1. Jamestown colony started
2. Columbus sails to the West Indies
3. First African slaves imported into New World
4. Hopi village of Oraibi built
5. Ponce de León lands in Florida
6. Hudson explores the Hudson River
7. Spanish found St. Augustine
8. Vikings explore North American coast
9. League of Iroquois formed
10. De Soto and Coronado search for gold north of Mexico

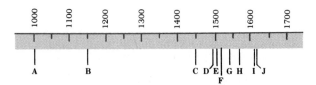

Essay Questions (40 points)

1. Describe at least three accomplishments and three weaknesses of Spain's New World empire.
2. Explain the "rights of Englishmen." How did these rights make England's colonies unique?

54

Unit Two

The Thirteen Colonies

Chapters in This Unit

Chapter 3

THE COLONIAL EXPERIMENTS IN THE NEW WORLD

1620–1732

It was 1600. On the streets of London, a young farm girl wandered, begging for food. A landlord had evicted her family from their farm only a week before. What lay in store for them now, she wondered. Was there some place they could go to escape this poverty?

In a quiet village a man sat by a midnight fire, going over his account books. He frowned. Prices in England kept rising, yet his income remained the same. Was there some place a hardworking shopkeeper could grow richer, not poorer?

At a small church in Plymouth, five men and women gathered to talk. One of their fellow Puritans had just been arrested. It was rumored that he had been roughly treated. Would his five friends share his fate? Was there some place they could go where they could worship in peace and safety?

In the elegant dining room of a London home, two prosperous merchants lingered over a glass of sherry. Before them lay a map. One man pointed to a vast area, marked off by bold black lines. Here they intended to start a colony that would make them richer. Their eyes sparkled. The New World was filled with business opportunities for adventurous Englishmen. Was there any place more exciting to go than America?

Why would Englishmen and women be willing to risk the perils of an ocean voyage and the dangers of an unknown world? What kind of societies did they hope to build on the other side of the Atlantic? You'll find some answers to these questions in this chapter.

Sections in This Chapter
1. The Background for Colonization
2. The New England Colonies
3. The Middle Colonies
4. The Southern Colonies

Opposite: "Plimoth Plantation": a reconstruction of the colony as it might have looked in the 1620s

1. THE BACKGROUND FOR COLONIZATION

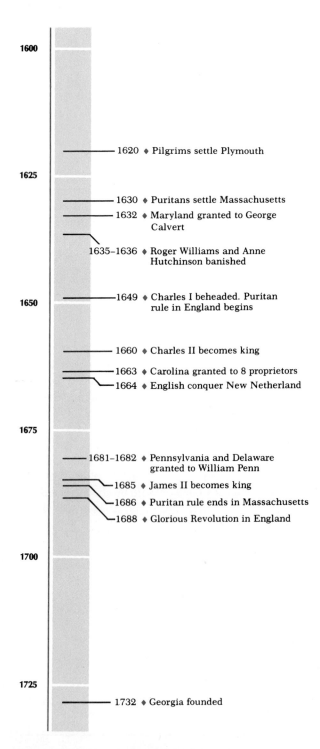

1620 ◆ Pilgrims settle Plymouth

1630 ◆ Puritans settle Massachusetts

1632 ◆ Maryland granted to George Calvert

1635–1636 ◆ Roger Williams and Anne Hutchinson banished

1649 ◆ Charles I beheaded. Puritan rule in England begins

1660 ◆ Charles II becomes king

1663 ◆ Carolina granted to 8 proprietors

1664 ◆ English conquer New Netherland

1681–1682 ◆ Pennsylvania and Delaware granted to William Penn

1685 ◆ James II becomes king

1686 ◆ Puritan rule ends in Massachusetts

1688 ◆ Glorious Revolution in England

1732 ◆ Georgia founded

During the 1600s, life in England was changing so rapidly and so drastically that men and women were suffering a form of "future shock." In the 1500s, when Spain was building its New World empire, England was a nation of carefully tended farms. Three out of every four Englishmen and women were tenant farmers* who rented their land from the wealthy gentry* or the nobility.* But by 1600, England had begun to shift to commerce and industry.

Commercial Agriculture and the Enclosure Movement

Textile, or cloth, production was at the heart of the new economy, and wool soon became the most valuable agricultural product in England. Throughout England landowners evicted their tenant farmers, converted the tilled fields into pasture for sheep, and fenced off, or enclosed, the pastureland that had formerly been used by the tenant farmers as common property. This shift from small tenant farming to commercial sheep raising was called the **enclosure movement**.

So it was that in the same year that Jamestown was founded, riots racked the English countryside. Farmers without farms marched together chanting, "Sheep eat men!" Their complaint against the new commercial agriculture was only one sign that England's growth as a world power was going to cause great hardships for England's people.

Slums and Poverty Everywhere

What became of the more than 2 million homeless and jobless people as a result of this enclosure movement? Many roamed the countryside, but most flocked to towns and cities, creating

*__tenant farmer__ farmer who raises crops and lives on land belonging to another, paying as rent a share of the crops.

*__gentry__ people of good social position belonging to the upper class of society below the nobility.

*__nobility__ people of noble rank, title, or birth, such as earls, countesses, knights, and ladies.

slums and massive overcrowding everywhere. Unable to find work, many of these farm people starved or turned to crime. The rioters who had cried out that "sheep eat men" were voicing their anger over an all too real poverty.

In 1610, the year of Jamestown's "starving time," probably 1.5 million of the 6 million English—a fourth of the population—lived below subsistence level, lacking adequate shelter, food, or medical care. An equal number eked out a bare existence, working at odd jobs for pitiful wages. The signs of poverty were everywhere. Malnutrition created a population deformed by rickets and scurvy. Smallpox spread through the slums, killing thousands and scarring the survivors for life. The young looked old—toothless and stooped with care.

Some among the small, prosperous upper classes were sympathetic to the plight of the poor. But most rich people believed that the problem lay in overpopulation. They believed that there were simply too many people on the small island of England. To those who believed this, an overseas empire was an attractive solution to the problem. Such an empire could provide a "dumping ground" for the poor. "We are a populous nation," said a character in a 17th-century play, "and increase so fast that if we are not sent abroad in colonies . . . we must starve or eat up one another."

The Middle Classes Become Poorer
Yet it was not the poorest people who made the journey to North America. Instead, the men and women who risked shipwreck, piracy, and starvation in the cold winters of America were members of the English middle classes: small landowners, shopkeepers, and artisans.* In an era of rising prices, many of them earned the same living in 1640 as their great-grandparents had earned in 1540. The promise of land in the colonies offered them an escape from poverty.

Religious Tensions in the 1600s
Ever since 1534, when King Henry VIII made England a Protestant nation, Englishmen and women had been quarreling over matters of church organization and forms of worship. After

*artisan [är'tə zən] a skilled worker in an industry or craft, such as carpenter, seamstress, weaver, blacksmith, goldsmith, potter, baker, or barrelmaker.

his break with the Catholic Church, Henry VIII seemed more interested in seizing Catholic Church property than in revising the Church of England's worship service to conform with Protestant beliefs.

Henry may not have been interested in issues of religious ritual and church organization, but many Englishmen and women cared deeply. Few English people were happy with the Anglican Church. Some wished to remain Catholic, while others felt that the Church of England was not yet Protestant enough. One large Protestant group, called **Puritans**, waged a century-long battle to reform, or "purify" the Anglican Church.

In the 1600s, the tensions between the many different Puritan sects and the Church of England were increasing. Persecution of the most active Puritan groups was common, and discrimination against both Puritans and Catholics kept the conflicts alive. By the mid-1600s, religious disagreement and intolerance would lead to civil war. But some men and women, driven by persecution or inspired by religious idealism, would seek a haven in the new American world.

Political Struggles in the 1600s
English politics were as unsettled as the economy and religious life in the 1600s. Henry VIII and Elizabeth I had centralized political power in England. The new, unified nation was able to support a navy and thus to protect the country's trade on the open seas. Without this centralization, the colonial empire would not have been possible. Yet the exact relationship between the monarchs who ruled and the people they governed had yet to be hammered out.

After Elizabeth's death in 1603, a struggle for power between the ruler and the Parliament took shape. Both ruler and Parliament demanded more control over taxation powers, over the right to make and interpret laws, and over the religious direction of the nation. These struggles led to several periods of violence.

Charles I dismisses Parliament, 1629 As you saw in Chapter 2, James I was an absolutist, believing in the "divine right of kings" to rule as they saw fit. During his reign from 1603–1625, James I controlled his impulses toward absolutism. But his son, **Charles I**, did not. In 1629, Charles I dis-

Charles II

BRITISH RULERS DURING THE COLONIAL PERIOD

Ruler	Period of Rule	Key Events in American History
Henry VII	1485–1509	John Cabot explores North American coast
Henry VIII	1509–1547	Founds Anglican Church; period of religious strife begins
Edward VI	1547–1553	
Mary I	1553–1558	
Elizabeth I	1558–1603	Defeats Spanish Armada, opening seas to English shipping
James I	1603–1625	Colony chartered in Virginia; Pilgrims settle Plymouth
Charles I	1625–1649	Colonies chartered in Massachusetts, Maryland, and Rhode Island
Oliver Cromwell and successors	1649–1658 1658–1660	
Charles II	1660–1685	Conquers New Netherland; colonies chartered in Connecticut, Carolina, New York, New Jersey, New Hampshire, and Pennsylvania (includes Delaware)
James II	1685–1688	
William III and Mary II	1689–1702 1689–1694	Parliament wins struggle with monarchy; New York gains representative government
Anne	1702–1714	
George I	1714–1727	
George II	1727–1760	Last mainland colony, Georgia, chartered
George III	1760–1820	The 13 colonies become independent

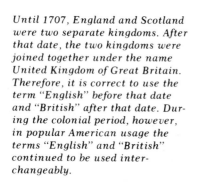

Until 1707, England and Scotland were two separate kingdoms. After that date, the two kingdoms were joined together under the name United Kingdom of Great Britain. Therefore, it is correct to use the term "English" before that date and "British" after that date. During the colonial period, however, in popular American usage the terms "English" and "British" continued to be used interchangeably.

missed Parliament and ruled for 11 years without any representative government.

The Puritan Revolt, 1642–1660 Thousands of people fled the country during Charles I's reign. His abuse of power, combined with an increase in religious persecution, prompted the Puritans to revolt. In 1642, these Puritans raised their own army, and civil war began. When Oliver Cromwell's Puritan "Roundheads"* defeated the king's "Royalists," Cromwell had Charles I beheaded. From 1649 to 1660, a Puritan Parliament ruled

*__Roundheads__ Puritans who supported Parliament during the English Civil War. The men wore their hair short in contrast to the long curls of the Royalists.

the country. But this government did not satisfy the English, and in 1660 the monarchy was restored.

The Restoration period, 1660–1685 In 1660, **Charles II** took the throne. The tone of his government was noticeably different from the somber mood of the Puritan regime. Charles II was a devoted follower of the good life, and he surrounded himself with an elegant, sophisticated, and pleasure-loving royal court. The Restoration monarchy, as his reign was called, was lively, and not a little scandalous.

The Glorious Revolution of 1688 The English people seemed willing to tolerate a little sin in high places during Charles II's reign, but they were not willing to tolerate a little Catholicism. James II, the next English king, was a Catholic. When he gained the throne in 1685, many believed that he would overthrow Protestantism and return the nation to the Catholic Church. Tensions mounted once again, and rumors spread of a second civil war. But James II was not willing to lose his head as his own father, Charles I, had done. In 1688, he fled the country when he learned that the Dutch Protestant prince, William of Orange, was coming to claim the English throne. Parliament chose James' daughter, Mary, and her husband, William of Orange, as co-rulers. Protestants called this bloodless change of power the "**Glorious Revolution.**" After this period, Parliament dominated the monarchy in English government.

English Rulers Affect American Colonies

As you'll see in the rest of this chapter, each of these changes in power affected American colonization. Yet, all who ruled England in the 17th century seemed to agree on the value of a colonial empire. From James I to Cromwell to William and Mary, these English rulers were empire builders. Supported by the new commercial class in England—the wealthy shippers, merchants, and factory owners—these rulers all supervised the growth of settlement in English America.

SECTION 1 REVIEW

 Identify: enclosure movement, Puritans, Charles I, Charles II, Glorious Revolution

Main Ideas

1. Why did the enclosure movement occur? How did it lead to massive poverty in England?
2. Why did some Englishmen and women decide to settle in America during the 1600s?
3. What issues divided the monarchy and the Parliament during the 17th century? How did the Glorious Revolution affect English government?

2. THE NEW ENGLAND COLONIES

In 1619, a group of Englishmen and women began to plan a new colony in America. Unlike the members of the Virginia Company who invested in the Jamestown colony, however, these people were neither rich nor concerned with profit. They were members of a small community of religious exiles living in Holland who called themselves the **Pilgrims.**

The Puritans had hoped to purify the Church of England. But the Pilgrims separated from it altogether and worshiped in their own congregations. As head of the Church of England as well as of the nation, James I viewed these separatists as political rebels, and drove them into exile.

In 1608, a modest postmaster from Scrooby Village named **William Bradford** led his fellow Pilgrims to Holland. Here they found the religious freedom and safety they were seeking. But as foreigners, the Pilgrims found it difficult to earn their living in the Dutch nation. And as parents, they worried that their children would forget the English language and abandon English traditions. When the London Company offered them a chance to emigrate to Virginia, about 35 Pilgrims seized the opportunity gladly.

The Pilgrims Establish the Plymouth Colony

The Pilgrims set out in the summer of 1620, stopping at Southampton, England, to pick up 80 additional passengers for the ocean crossing. In September, the three-masted *Mayflower* made for the open seas. But Captain Christopher Jones steered a northward course toward the rocky coastline of New England, rather than the southerly route for Virginia. After two months on rough seas, the Pilgrims and the other colonists traveling with them landed on the New England coast at Plymouth. (See map, page 66.)

The New England landing came as a rude surprise for the bedraggled and tired majority on board the *Mayflower*. The Pilgrims had decided to settle in this isolated region in order to be far from the watchful eye of the Anglican authorities.

Their traveling companions, however, had joined the expedition seeking economic opportunity in the Virginia tobacco plantations. Rumors of mutiny spread quickly.

The Mayflower Compact

To avoid rebellion, the Pilgrim leaders made a remarkable concession to the other colonists. They issued a call for every male on board, regardless of religion or economic status, to join in the creation of a "civil body politic," or government. Any man—master or servant, Pilgrim or not—who signed an agreement to abide by the new government's laws, would have a hand in selecting the government. This political agreement, or compact, was modeled on the church covenants that Puritans and Pilgrims alike made within their own church congregations. The Pilgrim leaders may have proposed this democratic government in order to restore calm and ensure the safety of their followers, but the **Mayflower Compact** stood as the colonies' first democratic government with full male participation.

With the political crisis passed, the colonists began their life at Plymouth Plantations.* They had chosen a good location for their first New England winter. Plymouth had a fresh and clean water supply, and nearby there were cleared fields abandoned by Indians. Despite these advantages, one-half the colony died before spring.

In the spring of 1621, the colonists were startled by a visit from an English-speaking Indian, Squanto. He had learned their language, he explained, from English fishermen who ventured into the New England waters each summer. Squanto taught the Pilgrims how to plant corn, squash, and pumpkins. Would the small band of settlers have survived without Squanto's help? We cannot say. But by the fall of 1621, colonists and Indians could sit down to several days of feast and thanksgiving to God (later celebrated as the first Thanksgiving), certain that the winter ahead would be a good one.

There would be 70 years ahead for this small community. Then, in 1691, Plymouth colony would be absorbed by the larger colony of Massachusetts that had grown up beside it on Massachusetts Bay.

The Puritan Experiment: The City upon a Hill

The Pilgrims had arrived in New England in an old and leaky vessel called the *Mayflower*. When their Massachusetts neighbors arrived in 1630, they came in 17 good ships, each loaded down with food, clothing, tools, and livestock to ease the difficulties ahead. Over 1,000 in number, these Puritans established their towns beside Boston Bay and along the Charles River.

These Puritan colonists were not poor exiles like the Pilgrims. Among them were college-educated ministers, prosperous landowners and merchants, and one of the few titled immigrants to America, Sir Richard Saltonstall. The rest were

---

*plantation another term in the 17th century for colony or settlement. Later, "plantation" meant only a commercial farm or estate in a warm climate on which the work was done by slaves or laborers.

yeoman farmers,* artisans, and independent shopkeepers.

Why did such people leave the comforts of home for New England? It was true that many of them were concerned about the rising prices and unstable economy in England. And as Puritans, they had all suffered persecution under James I and his church advisers. Yet these Puritans did not leave England as refugees from hardship or harassment. They came to Massachusetts Bay Colony with a positive sense of mission: to establish a perfect society.

The Puritans of Massachusetts Bay hoped to prove to the Anglican Church that a thoroughly reformed and purified society was both possible and practical. They had no opportunity to show

*yeoman farmers [yō/mən] farmers who owned their own small farms, as opposed to tenant farmers whose farms were owned by others.

A modern painting of Plymouth Colony based on data from a 1627 census and other information. Although the styles of individual houses are not known, it is clear that the buildings were wooden and that some houses had thatched roofs. The Pilgrims' meeting house was in the lower story of the fort.

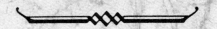
this at home, so they journeyed 3,000 miles to their "Wilderness Zion" to make their point. When the Massachusetts Bay Company leader, **John Winthrop**, spoke of his colony, he called it a "City upon a Hill." Like ancient Jerusalem, the Puritan colony was to be a model, shining and perfect, for English people everywhere to see.

The Puritans Combine Religion and Government

Life in the City upon a Hill was far different from life in Virginia or England. In Massachusetts, Biblical law was as strictly enforced as English law. Civil government and religion were joined together, and the daily life of every colonist was subject to the critical eye of the church and the Massachusetts Bay Colony leadership.

There was little left to personal choice in this colony. Everyone was required to attend the Puritan Congregational Church and to observe the

Sabbath. It was a crime as well as a sin in Massachusetts to drink, dance, or argue on Sunday. The church and the government regulated business practices, domestic quarrels, and even problems between parent and child.

Unlike the leadership in Virginia or Plymouth, the Massachusetts Bay Colony directors made no effort to establish a representative government. The small number of men who owned the colony only reluctantly allowed any participation in decision making by the colonists. When their fellow colonists forced the colony directors to allow such participation, they set up strict religious qualifications for both voting and officeholding. Only "**saints,**" that is, accepted members of the inner circle of the church, were citizens in this religious experiment called Massachusetts.

Religious Intolerance Breeds Dissent

In their eagerness to set a good example for England, the Puritan leadership created an atmosphere of intolerance in Massachusetts Bay. They had come to America for their own religious freedom, but they had no intention of granting that freedom to others. Nevertheless, religious dissent* was a problem from the earliest years of the colony. It came not from outsiders but from within the Puritan community itself. "Saints" rather than sinners challenged the Puritan experiment.

Roger Williams Calls for Reforms

In 1631, a young and brilliant minister named **Roger Williams** took the pulpit of the Salem church. Williams was a devout, brooding man, whose own standards of perfection were even more demanding than those of John Winthrop and his fellow company directors. Williams did not like what he saw in Massachusetts. He objected to the fact that the colony had not purchased its lands from the true owners, the Indians. He openly accused the colony of stealing. He also condemned the colony's combining of church and civil government. From his Salem pulpit, he preached that the church and state should never be united. Religious life, Williams said, was a

private matter, and the government should not interfere with it.

Williams infuriated the Puritan leadership with sermons like these. He was causing serious legal problems for them with his defense of Indian rights. He was also challenging the very basis of the Puritan experiment. In 1635, in the middle of winter, Roger Williams was banished from the colony forever.

Williams Founds Rhode Island

Williams took refuge with the Narragansett Indians to the south of Massachusetts. In the spring of 1636, he struck out on his own and built a crude cabin near Narragansett Bay. He called his new home Providence. (See map, page 66.) Williams did not remain in Providence alone, however, for he had not been forgotten by his friends and followers in Massachusetts. The members of his old congregation at Salem left their homes and joined Williams in his exile. Other men and women seeking religious freedom also found their way to Providence. Jews, Quakers, and dissatisfied Puritans flocked to Williams and his new settlement.

In 1644, Roger Williams secured a charter for this third New England colony, which he called Rhode Island. Rhode Island was true to its founder's most basic principles. Its charter established liberty of conscience for all citizens and a complete separation of church and state.

Anne Hutchinson Challenges the Ministers

The threat of Roger Williams had no sooner passed than a new challenge to the ministers arose. It came from **Anne Hutchinson**, a matronly housewife and the mother of a dozen children. She was no ordinary Puritan woman, however. Unlike most of her female friends, Anne Hutchinson could read, write, and interpret the Scriptures with a penetrating wit. Had she been born a man, friends said, she would surely have made a fine Puritan minister.

Soon after moving to the colony, Hutchinson began to hold Sunday afternoon discussion groups in her home. Here she criticized the sermons of the colony's leading ministers. No one was too famous or too popular to escape her criticism.

---

*dissent [di sent′] refusal to conform to the rules and beliefs of an established church.

LIFE IN AMERICA

A typical New England village of the 1600s

NEW ENGLAND VILLAGES

The New England towns tell us in a physical way what the Puritan sermons tell us in words: that living under the watchful eye of ministers and neighbors was the proper fate of a Puritan man or woman. The pattern of settlement in early New England reflected the nature of the Puritan experiment.

Close-Knit Villages

As you saw in Chapter 2, after 1618 the Virginians settled their colony as individuals, choosing to farm any plot of land that seemed promising. Puritans, however, settled in organized groups. Each new town was carefully laid out, the land often divided by lot among the adult males in the group.

The first task assigned to the colonists was the construction of the town church. No family was allowed to live beyond an easy walking distance from that church. Often all the people in a New England town already knew each other before they arrived. Entire church congregations in Old England had pulled up stakes and driven them down together in New England. But even strangers came to know each other well in these tightly knit communities.

Relics of the Middle Ages

As the map of Wethersfield shows, Puritan towns of the 1600s were compact villages surrounded by strip fields, a pattern of settlement that developed in England in medieval times. Towns were divided into village lots and field lots. Each village lot was large enough to include a house and several "outbuildings," such as a barn, dairy, and smokehouse. The field lots consisted of strips of cropland, meadowland, wood, and marsh so that each family had both good and bad land.

Within the village was a plot reserved for grazing, called the "common." After 1700, however, such commons were divided into private plots, and the strip fields were redistributed to make individual farms.

Houses and Blockhouses

New England houses resembled English houses, even to the overhanging second story, the casement windows that opened on hinges like doors, the steep-pitched shingle roof, and the central chimney for heating the entire house. Because of the harshness of the climate, overlapping boards called clapboards were added to the outside of the house.

An additional feature of such villages was the blockhouse, a fortress-like structure with an overhanging second story. Sometimes the meeting house (church) was used as the blockhouse. The compactness of the village kept the settlers close to the blockhouse where they could take refuge in case of attack.

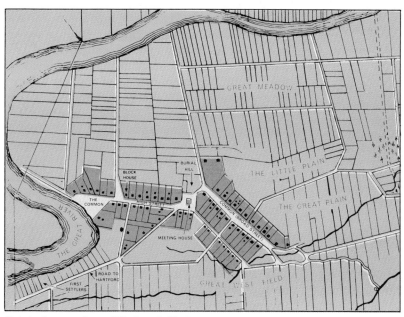
Original town plan of Wethersfield, Connecticut, 1641

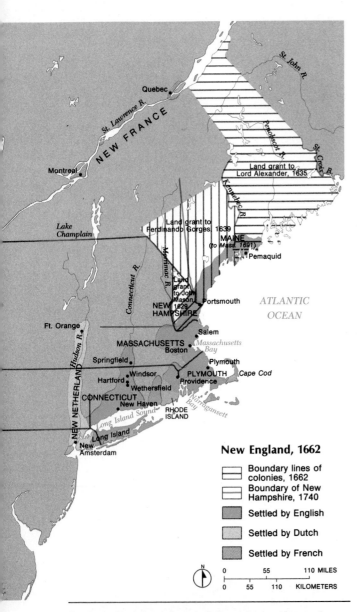

During the colonial period, boundaries changed many times. France, Spain, and England had conflicting claims, and so did individual colonies. See the map on page 84 for approximate boundaries around 1760. New Hampshire's western boundary was not fixed until 1764.

The conclusion that churches were unnecessary was too much for Puritan leaders to permit. When the Bay Colony government met in 1636, they held an elaborate and lengthy trial for Anne Hutchinson. They found her "unfit for our society" and banished her to the wilderness.

Anne Hutchinson found refuge at first with Roger Williams in Providence. Later she settled with her family in the Dutch colony of New Netherland. When Puritan leaders heard that she had been killed in New Netherland in 1643 during an Indian attack, they believed that justice had been done.

In many ways, the protests of Williams and Hutchinson were symptoms of a growing unhappiness among the Puritan colonists. During the 1630s the colony had grown too rapidly. In a "Great Migration" from England, 65,000 people had come to America, fleeing economic depression and religious persecution. Twenty thousand chose to make their homes in the Bay Colony. Few of these people, however, were committed to the difficult and demanding task of creating a "City upon a Hill." Instead, they wanted what colonists everywhere seemed to want: land and a chance to live a decent life.

The Origins of Connecticut

The desire for land led many Puritans to forsake the Bay Colony. In the spring of 1636, the Reverend Thomas Hooker and his congregation said their farewells to Massachusetts friends and set out into the forest southwest of the Bay Colony. Here, in the fertile Connecticut River Valley, they established the town of Hartford. Nearby other land-hungry Puritans established the towns of Wethersfield and Windsor. (See map, this page.)

When the men of these three towns met to form a mutual government, their Fundamental Orders of Connecticut (1639)—America's first written constitution—reflected the importance of economic opportunity over religious concerns. Property owning was the basis for citizenship here, not church membership.

In 1662, these three towns joined with neighboring New Haven and 11 other towns to form the independent colony of Connecticut. Thus the fourth New England colony was formally established.

She was critical of the role ministers played in the colony. She insisted that no minister's sermon could really assist a person in the search for salvation. She also felt that no church, even a Puritan church, could help to save a person's soul. In the end, Anne Hutchinson said, the true "saint" did not need a church at all.

New Hampshire and the Maine Settlements

During the 1630s Puritans also wandered northward from the Massachusetts Bay area and settled in what later became New Hampshire and Maine. Two Englishmen, Captain John Mason and Sir Ferdinando Gorges [gôr′jəs], already held charters to settle the region. But the land was largely empty, and Puritan pioneers simply made their homes upon it.

By the 1650s there were enough Puritan squatters* for Massachusetts to claim the regions by right of settlement. In 1679, New Hampshire broke free of Massachusetts and won a charter from King Charles II. Maine, however, remained a northern territory of Massachusetts until 1820, well after American independence.

Opposition to Puritan Rule Increases

When Cromwell's revolution began in England in the 1640s, emigration to Massachusetts ended abruptly. The eyes of the Puritan world were no longer upon the Bay Colony, but upon Oliver Cromwell and his army. The Cromwell victory was celebrated in Massachusetts, but not without some bitterness on the part of the leadership there. Cromwell had not once turned to these colonial leaders for guidance in establishing a proper Puritan society. To the new Puritan government, the "City upon a Hill" was only another colonial outpost.

During the next 20 years, Massachusetts colonists increased their pressures upon the Bay Colony government to end the rule of the saints. Wealthy Boston merchants and prosperous landowners were more preoccupied with the demands of their businesses than with church affairs. Because they were not "saints"—members of the inner church—these important men could neither hold office nor vote. Informally, however, many individual towns allowed all respectable male citizens to vote in local elections.

The End of Puritan Rule

When Charles II took the throne in England, he began to investigate the unusual rules and regulations of Massachusetts Bay Colony. Royal commissioners visited the colony during the 1660s and 1670s, and each recommended that the colo-

*squatter a person who settles on another's land without legal right.

ny's charter be revised or taken away. To the horror of the Puritan leaders, many of Massachusetts colony's most prosperous men supported the commissioners' recommendations.

In 1686, Massachusetts lost its standing as a separate colony and was linked with several other American colonies in a Dominion of New England. The governor of this Dominion was the hated **Edmund Andros**, a particularly haughty, high-handed, and greedy man with little patience for Puritan traditions.

Andros quickly revised Massachusetts laws and customs. To the shock of even the most lackadaisical Puritans, he established the Church of England in the Bay Colony. When the Glorious Revolution of 1688 sent King James II fleeing for his life, Massachusetts men wasted no time in imprisoning their enemy, Edmund Andros.

Massachusetts Becomes a Royal Colony

In 1691, Massachusetts was once again a separate colony, but it was now a royal colony. Its governor was appointed by the king, and its assembly was popularly elected. The Puritan experiment was over. The surest sign of the change that had taken place over 60 years was this: a man with 40 shillings worth of property could vote in Massachusetts, even if he was not a member of any church at all.

SECTION 2 REVIEW

Identify: Pilgrims, William Bradford, Mayflower Compact, John Winthrop, "City upon a Hill," "saints," Roger Williams, Anne Hutchinson, Edmund Andros

Main Ideas

1. Why did the Pilgrims decide to settle in America? What makes the Mayflower Compact a historic document?
2. What was the goal of the Puritans who settled in Massachusetts? Describe briefly the rules of this colony.
3. What reforms did Roger Williams and Anne Hutchinson call for?
4. Describe briefly the origins of (a) Rhode Island, (b) Connecticut, (c) New Hampshire, and (d) Maine.
5. When and why did Puritan rule in Massachusetts come to an end?

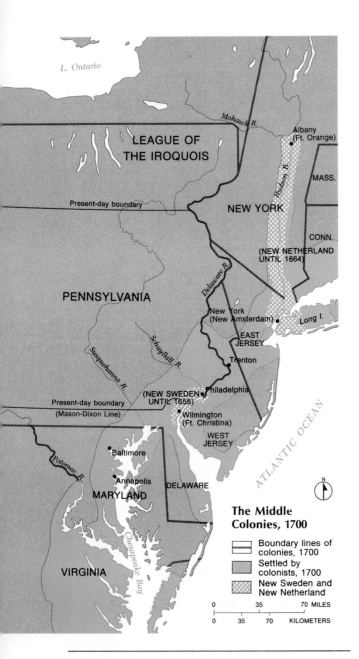

The Middle Colonies included New York, the Jerseys, Pennsylvania, and Delaware. In 1702, East and West Jersey united to form New Jersey. Delaware had its own legislature but was part of Pennsylvania until 1775.

This map shows the parts of Pennsylvania and New York that colonists settled by 1700. The League of the Iroquois controlled most of present-day New York. The boundaries of New York, Pennsylvania, and Maryland were in dispute throughout the colonial era.

3. THE MIDDLE COLONIES

For many years the Dutch had been a thorn in England's side. On the coast of Africa, Dutch vessels competed with English vessels. On the high seas, fast-moving Dutch ships seized English cargoes. And in America, Dutch ships smuggled goods to and from the English colonies. Between 1648 and 1673, the two rival nations would fight three wars, each hoping to destroy the commercial success of the other.

When **Charles II** came to the English throne in 1660, he decided to take drastic steps against the Dutch in North America. He had everything to gain by ridding his nation of the Dutch presence. First, New Netherland blocked English colonial growth. It divided the English territories neatly in half, cutting New England off from the southern colonies. (See map, this page.) Secondly, it occupied two fertile valleys, the Delaware River Valley and the Hudson Valley. Finally, the Dutch monopolized the profitable fur trade with the Iroquois in the Hudson Valley region.

The English Conquer New Netherland

In 1664, Charles II hatched a plot with his younger brother James, Duke of York (later to be James II). Charles offered James the entire Dutch holding in America if James could conquer it. The Duke wasted little time. As Lord High Admiral of England, he ordered a fleet of four frigates* to sail to New Netherland. In command of this naval force, James placed his trusted and loyal friend, Colonel Richard Nicolls.

On August 26, Nicolls' flagship, the *Guinea*, rounded Coney Island and anchored just below the Narrows, in full sight of the startled inhabitants of New Amsterdam. The excitable governor, **Peter Stuyvesant**, sent a messenger to Nicolls, asking exactly what the English wanted. "I do demand the town," Nicolls replied.

Stuyvesant stalled, spending several days in a desperate attempt to rouse the townspeople to their own defense. The New Amsterdam citizens only shrugged. It did not matter to them who

*frigate   a fast, three-masted sailing warship of medium size.

ruled, they told Stuyvesant, as they did not rule themselves. On September 8, 1664, Stuyvesant reluctantly signed the Articles of Capitulation. New Amsterdam became New York, and not a shot was fired.

Authoritarian Government in New York

When James took over New York he granted its Dutch inhabitants the right to keep their land, speak their language, practice their religion, and preserve their customs. It was a generous act, and a surprising one, for James. He was more in character when he laid heavy taxes on both Dutch and English inhabitants.

As proprietor (owner) of New York, James had vast powers, and he took advantage of them all. Through his hand-picked governors he controlled all political appointments in the colony. He also approved or drafted all laws, granted all trade monopolies, and set the customs duties (import taxes). There was no provision in his charter requiring a representative assembly for New York, and James made no effort to establish one. Except for one brief experiment with an assembly, New York was without representative government until after the Glorious Revolution of 1688.

James, Duke of York, copied the Dutch in formulating his land policy. He gave great tracts of land, called manors, to friends, followers, or admirers. His English "lords of the manor" had the same broad powers to govern their tenant farmers as the Dutch patroons enjoyed. English settlers, looking for land and a guarantee of their political rights, avoided New York in the years before 1688. Instead, Scots and French Huguenots* came to the Duke's colony, for the freedom of religion guaranteed to the Dutch was extended to them as well. By 1685, New York colony had 15,000 people, mostly from the non-English world.

Tensions in New York were common during the Duke's years as proprietor. There were intense rivalries between Dutch merchants and English merchants in New York City. Poorer settlers complained bitterly, but without success, about the heavy tax burden placed upon them. Up-and-

*Huguenots [hyōō′gə nots] French Protestants in the 1500s and 1600s. They were greatly persecuted by the French government, which was officially Catholic.

coming business people found their opportunities blocked by the special privileges and monopolies the Duke granted to his favorites in the colony. Finally, Albany citizens resented the growth of New York City as a commercial center.

The Dominion of New England and Leisler's Rebellion

All these tensions came to a head in 1686. That was the year James, now king of England, established the Dominion of New England in order to tighten royal control over colonial affairs. New York, New Jersey, Massachusetts, Plymouth, Rhode Island, Connecticut, and New Hampshire were all joined together under the centralized rule of Edmund Andros. New Yorkers had already experienced the heavy hand of Andros, for he had governed the colony in the 1670s.

When news came in the spring of 1689 that James was in flight for his life and that Andros was locked in a Boston jail, New Yorkers staged their own rebellion against the Dominion. The revolt was called **Leisler's Rebellion** after its leader, a German merchant named Jacob Leisler [lī′slèr]. The rebels seized the fort at New York City and established a representative government.

The new English king, William, did not accept this government, however. Instead, he sent his own appointed governor to the colony. When Leisler refused to surrender power, he was arrested, tried, and executed for treason. His execution was horrible: he was hanged, disemboweled, decapitated, and cut into pieces. This was the required punishment for treason in the English world. But Leisler's efforts to see a representative government established were honored, and after 1691, New Yorkers enjoyed the same rights as other English people.

The Beginnings of New Jersey

As Duke of York, James gave several generous gifts of land to friends and followers. The largest of these grants went to John, Lord Berkeley [berk′ lē] and Sir George Carteret [kär′tèr et], who, in 1664, received an area lying east and north of the Delaware River, which they called New Jersey.

In 1674, Berkeley sold his western share to a group of **Quaker** merchants. In 1680, Carteret sold his eastern section to another Quaker company. East Jersey (see map, page 68) filled slowly with Puritans, moving south from Massachusetts in search of land. West Jersey, however, became a Quaker settlement. For two decades, West Jersey's guarantee of liberty of conscience, due process of law,* jury trial, and a representative government stood in sharp contrast to James II's authoritarian rule in New York.

The Quakers who established West Jersey's liberal policy were members of a small Protestant sect that opposed the Anglican Church and were therefore persecuted. The purchase of New Jersey was their first attempt to establish a safe haven in the New World. Although they surrendered New Jersey to King William in 1702 (and the two divisions became one colony), the Quakers did not give up their hopes for life in America.

William Penn's Background

Among the Quakers who purchased West Jersey was a young gentleman named **William Penn**. Penn had been born into wealth and privilege; his father was Admiral Sir William Penn, conqueror of Jamaica. The younger Penn was a constant disappointment to his father. He was restless and appeared to be seeking something more in life than the material riches to which he was heir. He disgraced his father by being expelled from Oxford College for associating with religious radicals. Admiral Penn sent his son to Ireland, hoping that an enforced stay in the countryside would end young William's flirtation with radicalism. But in Ireland William Penn found the religious truths he had been seeking. He joined the most radical and persecuted of the dissenting Protestant sects, the Society of Friends, or Quakers. The name "Quakers" came from their founder's call for them to "tremble at the name of the Lord."

The Views of the Quakers

Because the Quakers believed that God spoke directly to individuals, they were outspoken critics of a professional ministry and of the Anglican bishops and church officialdom. The Friends had no ministers within their own churches. Their Sabbath service had no ceremony or ritual. They prayed silently in their meeting houses, speaking

aloud only to share a special thought with one another. Unlike the Puritans and Anglicans, who forbade women to speak in church, the Society of Friends welcomed any member's participation.

The Quakers' simple dress and simple religious services made them seem different. Their insistence that all people, of whatever race, class, or faith, were loved by God made them behave differently also. But the heavy persecution they suffered in England was probably due to their pacifism: opposed to all war, they refused to serve in the king's army or support his military budget. To the king, the Quaker commitment to pacifism was a form of treason.

The Founding of Pennsylvania

William Penn became a leading member of the Society of Friends. Four times in his life, Penn was jailed for publicly declaring his religious views. Having experienced religious persecution first-hand, Penn became active in the efforts to establish a colony for his fellow Quakers.

When his father died, Penn inherited a large estate. He discovered that the king owed the Penn family a sizable debt. In 1681, Penn asked Charles II to repay the debt by granting him land in America. Charles agreed at once. Penn was made the proprietor of a huge tract of land lying west of the Delaware River. (See map, page 68.) He called this colony Pennsylvania, or Penn's Woods, in memory of his father.

The Creation of Delaware

Pennsylvania was large, but it was landlocked. To remedy this, King Charles II gave Penn the additional region lying along the Delaware River where New Sweden had been. (See map, page 68.) This ensured Pennsylvania an outlet to the sea and allowed Penn to build his city of Philadelphia inland on the Delaware River. Except for this route to the sea, the Delaware area remained outside Penn's real interests. Throughout the colonial period, settlers in this section of Penn's properties governed themselves. In 1776, when American independence was declared, this region became the state of Delaware.

Penn's Holy Experiment

William Penn had been given extensive power as proprietor of his colony. Unlike James, the Duke of York, however, he was not anxious to rule

*due process of law lawful treatment. Anytime government threatens a person's life, freedom, or property, he or she is entitled to the protection of due process of law, with all the standard legal steps and no shortcuts.

Pennsylvania with an iron fist. Instead, Penn designed a **"Holy Experiment"** in keeping with Quaker principles of simplicity, truth, and peace. He drafted several plans for the governing of the colony until at last he was satisfied with Pennsylvania's political structure.

All Penn's Frames of Government guaranteed religious freedom and popular participation in politics. The colony had a unicameral or one-house legislature which allowed the elected representatives greater freedom than other assemblies enjoyed. The result in Pennsylvania was a very active and often quarrelsome political life. Occasionally, Penn would plead with his colonists: "For the love of God, me, and the poor country, be not so governmentish, so noisy, and open, in your dissatisfaction." Yet Penn never made any effort to deprive his colonists of their political privileges and powers.

Pennsylvania offered economic opportunity as well as political and religious freedoms. Every male settler was guaranteed 50 acres of land. In contrast to New York and other colonies held by proprietors, Penn's colony was consciously designed to avoid large land holdings by the few or the establishment of tenant farming. All land had to be purchased from the Indians of the region. As a Quaker, Penn also insisted that the people of his colony live at peace with these Indians.

Penn's Holy Experiment was certain to attract colonists. Yet he did not wait for settlers to learn of his colony. In 1681, Penn published a pamphlet which advertised to English, Welsh, Scots-Irish, and German farmers the advantages and opportunities awaiting them in the new colony. Thousands of men and women came to Pennsylvania. By 1685 there were 8,000 settlers, not only from England but from Ireland, France, Holland, Germany, Sweden, and Denmark.

When William Penn died in 1718 his colony was a remarkable success. Philadelphia hummed with the activity of Quaker merchants and shippers, and the western farmlands supported a prosperous population of non-Quakers. Yet there

Penn's Treaty with the Delaware Indians, 1683. Painted by Edward Hicks around 1830

were warning signs that the Quakers had not truly escaped their problems with England after all.

War Ends the Holy Experiment

The major problem following the Quakers to Pennsylvania was the warfare between England and its rivals in Europe. Several times after Penn's death, war broke out between France and England, and each time the colonies were drawn into the battle. On Pennsylvania's western frontier, Indians aligned with the French, and there was a danger of attack from these enemies. Settlers in this region demanded military protection by the government in Philadelphia, but the Quaker-dominated assembly refused to raise an army or send military supplies. Soon these Quaker pacifists and the non-Quaker groups on the frontier were at odds with each other.

In 1756 a major war—the Seven Years' War—began between France and England. (See Chapter 6.) The Pennsylvania Quakers realized that they could no longer keep their colony out of the struggle. Every Quaker in the colonial assembly resigned his office, and the government was turned over to non-Quakers. As members of the government, Quakers could no longer impose their pacifism on others. But as private citizens, they could remain true to their commitment to peace. Thus the "Holy Experiment" ended, but its democratic and tolerant spirit survived.

SECTION 3 REVIEW

Identify: Charles II, Peter Stuyvesant, Leisler's Rebellion, Quakers, William Penn, Holy Experiment

Main Ideas

1. List three reasons why Charles II decided to conquer the Dutch in North America. Why did the citizens of New Amsterdam surrender without a fight?
2. How did the rule of James, Duke of York, affect New Yorkers' (a) political rights, (b) religious freedom, (c) economic opportunities?
3. Describe briefly the settlement of East and West Jersey between 1664 and 1702. What is the origin of the state of Delaware?
4. What was William Penn's Holy Experiment? In what ways was the Pennsylvania experiment both a success and a failure?

4. THE SOUTHERN COLONIES

William Penn was not the first nor the only friend of a king to receive his own colony. In 1632, **Sir George Calvert**, Lord Baltimore, had won a similar favor from King Charles I. Calvert had recently converted to Catholicism. Fearing the persecution of his religious companions, he had decided to build a colony for them in the New World. Calvert named his Catholic haven Maryland, in honor of Charles' wife, Queen Henrietta Marie.

The Original Plan for Maryland

Sir George Calvert died before his colony could become a reality; his son, **Cecil Calvert**, was left to complete his father's dream. Unfortunately, Sir George's plan for Maryland was not a very realistic or promising one. An aristocrat, Calvert had designed an aristocratic colony. His plan called for Maryland to be divided into several large mini-kingdoms, or baronies, to be populated and farmed by peasant labor. You have seen the same idea in the Dutch patroon system and in the Duke of York's manorial system. Like the patroon system, the barony system failed. Few Englishmen or women wished to emigrate to Maryland to work on other people's land.

The Original Plan Is Changed

Cecil Calvert recognized that the opportunity to become a landowner was the most powerful motivation for colonial immigration. He scrapped his father's plan, and instead offered 100 acres to every husband and wife who settled in Maryland. For each servant the couple brought to the colony, they would receive an additional 100 acres. A teenage son or daughter was worth 50 more acres. And any man or woman who could bring five male colonists would receive a grant of 2,000 acres.

Those who decided to recruit five additional male colonists wisely decided not to make religious preference an issue. Thus, although Maryland was designed to be a refuge for Catholics, many of the settlers were Protestant. In fact, when the first 200 colonists arrived on the *Ark* and the *Dove* in 1634, the majority were Protestant artisans, laborers, and servants.

Events in England Affect Maryland

In the early years of Maryland's history, Protestant and Catholic settlers cooperated. But here, as in so many colonies, local affairs came under the influence of events in England. The Puritan revolution of the 1640s drove a wedge between the Marylanders and brought the colony close to civil war.

Cecil Calvert feared that the Protestant majority would outlaw Catholicism. To protect his people, Calvert issued a Toleration Act in 1649. But Cromwell's Puritan government repealed this guarantee of religious freedom the following year. Maryland was taken away from the Calvert family; and for ten years Catholics were in danger of persecution within their own colony.

When the monarchy was restored in 1660, the Calverts were again returned to power in Maryland. But in 1688 the Glorious Revolution in England spurred Protestants to do battle with their Catholic neighbors, and the colony was seized by its Protestant majority.

In 1691 the Protestant colonists petitioned for and received a royal charter for Maryland, and the proprietors were once again deprived of their colonial holdings. The Church of England was established as the official church of Maryland. For some time it appeared that the Calvert family would have to accept this loss of their American lands. But in 1713 Benedict Calvert converted to the Anglican faith just as his great grandfather, George, had converted to Catholicism over 60 years before. In 1715, King George I restored the colony of Maryland to Benedict's heir. Thus, Maryland was once again a proprietary colony, but its history as a Catholic one had ended.

Carolina: A Fanciful Plan

King Charles II was a man of elegant and expensive tastes. In his own way, he was also a very generous man. During his reign, he gave away millions of acres in America to his friends. In 1663, Charles II gave eight such friends an extremely generous gift. As the map above shows, its boundaries in 1665 ran from Virginia to northern Florida and extended westward all the way to the Pacific Ocean! The proprietors of this new colony called it Carolina in honor of their king.

No colony ever had more elaborate or more unrealistic plans drawn up for it than Carolina.

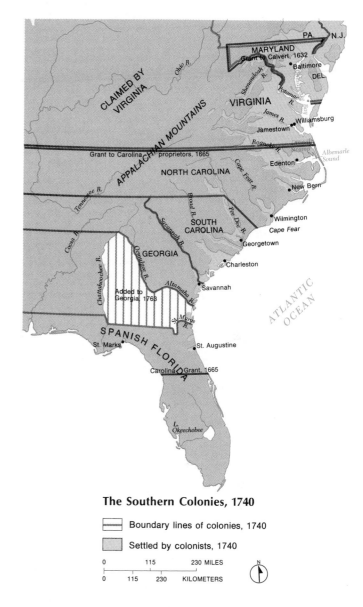

The Southern Colonies, 1740

⊟ Boundary lines of colonies, 1740

▨ Settled by colonists, 1740

0   115   230 MILES

0   115   230   KILOMETERS

Virginia once extended all the way from New York to South Carolina but English kings gave large land grants to various proprietors. Some English colonies claimed all the land from "sea to sea," but the French and Spanish also claimed the lands west of the Appalachians.

Together the aristocratic Sir Anthony Ashley Cooper and his secretary, the philosopher John Locke, drafted the colony's Fundamental Constitutions. The Fundamental Constitutions tried to bring to life a society long dead in the 17th century—a world of nobles and peasants which harkened back to the days before commerce became important in England.

This society was to be pyramid in shape, with a small number of rich and powerful nobles at its peak and a vast landless majority forming its base. At the very top, of course, were the eight proprietors, who each held 12,000 acres in every county of Carolina. Next came three fancifully named ranks of nobility: landgraves, caciques, and lords of the manor. They received thousands of acres of land. Far below these aristocrats came the ordinary freeholders, independent farmers who received only 50 acres. At the bottom of the Carolina pyramid were the leet-men, or peasants, who farmed the land owned by everyone else. African slaves were listed as property rather than people.

You may have already guessed that no such society ever actually existed in Carolina. Many men volunteered to be landgraves or caciques. But none wanted to serve as leet-men.

Two Colonies Develop in Carolina

The geography of the colony rather than the founders shaped its society. At the northern tip of Carolina, near the Albemarle Sound, a small settlement of Virginians was already established. (See map, page 73.) These families farmed tobacco, grew corn, and drew tar and rosin from the local pine trees. The great Dismal Swamp divided these colonists from Virginia proper, and swampland also isolated them from the Carolina settlements to the south. This Albemarle region developed as a colony within a colony. Undoubtedly Sir Anthony Ashley Cooper and John Locke would have been dismayed to see the rough-and-ready, poor but democratic society that developed here.

To the south, a very different colony evolved. Its center was Charles Towne, or Charleston as it was later called. Charleston's fine harbor and the fertile lands around it acted like a magnet to planters from the West Indian islands and to Scottish, French, and German settlers. To colonize this region, they risked Indian attack from the west and the threat of the Spanish from the south. The prize was worth the danger, however, for the rice plantations of the area made these settlers rich. By the 1690s the Carolina rice plantations had created an aristocracy not unlike the one dreamed of in the Fundamental Constitutions.

By 1719, Charleston planters had taken their region away from the original eight proprietors. Soon after, the Albemarle settlers did the same. Then, in 1729, the two regions separated, with South and North Carolina each becoming royal colonies.

Georgia and the Solution to Poverty

By 1715, Carolina colony had expanded west and south of the Savannah River into present-day Georgia. This expansion brought friction with the Yamassee Indians who lived in that region. With the help of the Spanish in Florida, the Yamassee began making raids into Carolina. The English defeated the Yamassee in early 1715, and sealed their victory by building forts and settlements in the conquered area. The Spanish were angered by this British expansion, and by 1727, Spanish troops had clashed with English soldiers on the Carolina frontier. What could be done to guarantee safety on the border?

The English government decided that border settlements were the best security against a Spanish invasion of South Carolina. These settlements would act as a buffer zone. Fortunately, just as England began to look for pioneers to settle this dangerous Georgia region, a group of wealthy Englishmen were meeting to plan a new colony.

In 1732, a group of troubled men sat down to consider the continuing problem of poverty in England. Two of these men, Viscount Percival and **General James Oglethorpe**, had served on a committee to investigate debtors' prisons. In these prisons lived men, women, and their children in hopelessness and squalor because they could not pay some small debt. Oglethorpe and his friends agreed that something must be done to help these debtors.

The result of this meeting in 1732 was the last mainland English colony, Georgia. In some ways Georgia was different from the other 12 colonies: First, the East Coast was no longer a wilderness when Georgia was founded. Second, unlike the other proprietary colonies (see chart, page 76),

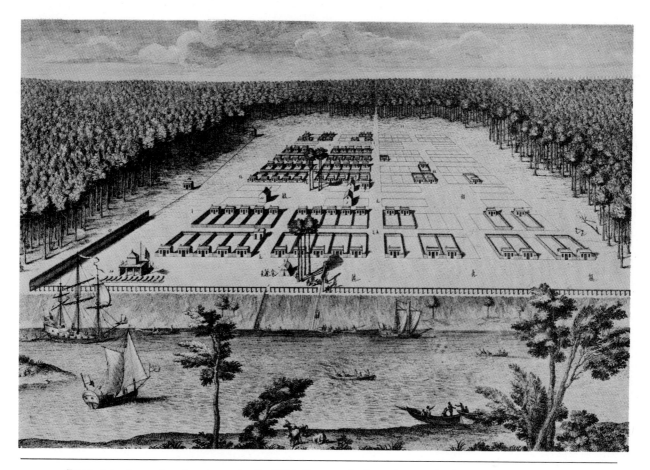

First steps toward ending poverty: In 1734, Savannah, Georgia, was little more than a clearing in the woods. Governor James Oglethorpe's tent is beneath the tall pines at center.

Georgia was not owned by its founders. Instead, Georgia's founders acted as its trustees or guardians and were not allowed to make any personal profit from the colony. Third, although poverty had long been a major problem in England, Georgia was the only colony purposely designed to help the poor.

Treated Like Children

The Georgia trustees were good men, but they knew little about the people they wished to help. They were rich men who looked upon poverty as a weakness of character. Thus they treated the colonists like children, planning every detail of their lives.

Because they were not required to pay taxes, the colonists had no representative government. Charity made them less than full English citizens. The trustees made rules about what crops the colonists could raise, how many acres of land they could own, and whom they could sell land to or buy it from. Colonists were even told what they could drink with their meals!

Oglethorpe and his fellow trustees imposed their rules on the Georgia colonists because they wished to reform them and make them hardworking, sober Christians. But most of the debtor colonists did not blame their imprisonment on laziness or drunkenness, but rather on the economic hardships of English life. They wished to take their own chances in the New World and to run their own risks of success or failure as free men and women.

The debtors resented the trustees' many laws regulating their daily lives. But the English government supported the trustees: Since the colo-

ORIGINS OF THE 13 COLONIES

COLONY AND SETTLEMENT DATE	FOUNDERS	REASONS	TYPE OF GOVERNMENT	IMPORTANT CHARACTERISTICS
New England Colonies				
Plymouth (1620)	William Bradford and other Pilgrims	To form separate religious community and keep English identity	Corporate (self-governing) until 1691*	Mayflower Compact. Became part of Massachusetts in 1691.
Massachusetts Bay (1630)	John Winthrop and other Puritans	To establish a perfect society based on Puritan ideals	Corporate, 1629–1686 Royal, 1691–1776	Dictatorship of "saints" until 1686.
Rhode Island (1636)	Roger Williams	Opposed Puritan rule; banished	Corporate, 1644–1776	Religious tolerance. Separation of church and state.
Connecticut (1636)	Thomas Hooker and other Puritans	Land	Corporate, 1662–1776	Fundamental Orders, 1639, was the first written constitution in the colonies.
New Hampshire (1623)	Puritans	Land, opposition to government in Massachusetts	Proprietary, 1622–1679 Royal, 1679–1776	Original proprietors were Mason and Gorges.
Middle Colonies				
New York (As New Netherland, 1626)	Dutch West India Company	Trade with Indians, land	Proprietary, 1664–1685 Royal, 1685–1776	Ruled without representative government until Glorious Revolution.
New Jersey (As New Netherland, 1626)	Dutch West India Company	Trade with Indians, land, Quaker ideals	Proprietary, 1664–1702 Royal, 1702–1776	Taken from Dutch and given to Berkeley and Carteret. Bought and developed by Quakers. Two separate colonies until 1702.
Pennsylvania (1682)	William Penn	Quaker ideals	Proprietary, 1681–1776	Holy Experiment tried pacifism and guaranteed religious and political liberty.
Delaware (As New Sweden, 1638)	Swedish colonists	Trade with Indians, land	Proprietary, 1664–1776	Part of Pennsylvania until 1776 but had own legislature.
Southern Colonies				
Virginia (1607)	London Company	Find gold and Northwest Passage, convert Indians to Christianity	Corporate, 1606–1624 Royal, 1624–1776	First successful English colony. Colonists guaranteed "rights of Englishmen." First elected legislature in colonies.
Maryland (1634)	George Calvert	Refuge for Catholics	Proprietary, 1632–1691 Royal, 1691–1715 Proprietary, 1715–1776	Toleration Act of 1649 guaranteed religious freedom to Catholics and Protestants.
North Carolina (1650)	8 proprietors	Land	Proprietary, 1663–1729 Royal, 1729–1776	Democratic society developed early in colony's history.
South Carolina (1670)	8 proprietors	Land	Proprietary, 1663–1729 Royal, 1729–1776	Rich rice-growing region. One of the wealthiest colonies.
Georgia (1733)	James Oglethorpe and other trustees	Protect South Carolina, help poor debtors	Proprietary, 1732–1752 Royal, 1752–1776	Did not develop until goal of helping debtors abandoned. Then settlers seeking land developed colony.

*Plymouth and 6 other colonies were briefly joined together in the Dominion of New England, 1686–1689. See Chapter 5 for a closer look at the three types of colonial government.

nists were also expected to serve as a military force in case of trouble with the Spanish in Florida, the English government wanted them sober and reliable. Over the years, the debtor colonists fought some rules and ignored others. When Georgia began to attract settlers who did not owe their freedom to the trustees, the new settlers refused to obey most of the rules at all. Despite the trustees' efforts, Georgia began to develop along the lines of South Carolina, with plantations and slave labor. By 1752, the Georgia charter had expired, and Oglethorpe and his friends gladly abandoned their experiment with poor people and turned the colony over to the king.

Georgia had failed as an experiment to end poverty. But it was successful as a buffer zone against Spanish Florida. The Georgia colonists defended their colonial borders twice during Oglethorpe's years, first, in 1739, during the English-Spanish War of Jenkin's Ear, and again in the 1740s, when King George's War broke out.

The Colonial Experiments Become Societies

None of the American colonies turned out as its founders had wished. No matter how carefully plans were laid, no matter how dedicatedly they were pursued, circumstances in America and at home in England worked to alter the character of each colony. In one sense, then, the colonial experiments were failures. Virginia did not make men and women instantly rich with gold and silver. Massachusetts did not become the most perfect and saintly society on earth. Maryland and Carolina did not create an American world of titled aristocrats and obedient peasants. Pennsylvania did not preserve a lasting peace between Indians and settlers. Georgia did not solve the problem of poverty in England.

Yet, as you have seen, the American colonies were successful in surprising and unexpected ways. Life changed for every man, woman, and child who reached the New World. Some, like the Africans, suffered a loss of freedom and family and heritage that they would not regain. But many white settlers found an opportunity for wealth, religious freedom, and political participation unimagined in their native lands. For most, the opportunity to own their own land, and to pursue their own destiny made their colonial worlds a success.

The trustees demanded that all families raise silkworms, even though the colonists soon realized that the worms would not survive on Georgia mulberry bushes.

Perhaps the most surprising fact of all was that the 13 colonies grew to resemble each other in their cultures, economies, and politics, and that an American sense of identity developed. It is the evolution of these similarities that you will study next.

SECTION 4 REVIEW

 Identify: George and Cecil Calvert, James Oglethorpe

Main Ideas

1. Why did Maryland become a haven for Catholics? How did religious strife in England affect Maryland between 1649 and 1715?
2. Why did two separate colonies develop in Carolina? How were they like or unlike the colony planned by the original proprietors?
3. Describe the goals and organization of the Georgia colony in its early years. Why did it later become more like South Carolina?
4. In what ways were the colonial experiments failures? How were they successes?

77

CHAPTER 3 REVIEW

Key Terms
Explain the meaning of each of the following terms:

enclosure movement   "City upon a Hill"
Puritans   "saints"
Glorious Revolution   Leisler's Rebellion
Pilgrims   Quakers
Mayflower Compact   Holy Experiment

Reviewing the Main Ideas
Section 1
1. What conditions led Englishmen and women to settle in America in the 1600s?
2. What issues divided the monarchy and Parliament in the 1600s?

Section 2
1. What were the aims of the founders of Massachusetts Bay Colony? What criticisms helped end the rule of the "saints"?
2. Explain the origins of Rhode Island, Connecticut, New Hampshire, and Maine.

Section 3
1. How did the rule of James, Duke of York, affect New York colony? How did New York get a representative government?
2. How did Quakers affect the development of New Jersey? What is the origin of Delaware?
3. Describe the strong and weak points of William Penn's Holy Experiment in Pennsylvania.

Section 4
1. What were the founders' original goals in Maryland, the Carolinas, and Georgia?
2. How did these colonies differ from their founders' goals?

Special History Skills:
Working with Maps
Draw a map of your town or neighborhood. If you live in a rural area, map the nearest community. Include places of worship, factories, stores, schools, residential areas (indicating apartments and houses), and major means of transportation.
1. By looking at your map, what could others tell about your neighborhood's or town's:
   religious beliefs
   economic activity
   educational services
   transportation
   where and how families live
   what people do for fun
   other
2. Compare your map with the map of Wethersfield on page 65. How are the two maps alike? How are they different?

Other Skill Activities
1. New foods and farms
Find out more about the farming techniques the Indians passed on to the European colonists. What new foods and technology did the Indians introduce to the world?

2. Do-it-yourself utopia
A utopia is a perfect society. Many groups besides the Puritans and Quakers have tried to create a utopia on American soil. You will read about some of these groups in later chapters.

Plan your own utopia in America. Describe where it will be located, what it will look like, what goals and rules it will have, who can live in it, and who can make and change rules.

Thinking Critically
1. In which colony would you have settled if your main goal were: religious freedom, the right to vote, farmland, a close religious community? Explain your choices.
2. Why was the Mayflower Compact a unique document for its time? Would you have signed it if you were a passenger on the *Mayflower*? Why or why not?
3. Defend or reject the following statement. Use at least six colonies as examples. "American colonies were failures because none of them turned out as their founders wished."
4. Have the reasons people want to settle in America changed, or have they stayed basically the same over the years? Explain your answer.

Further Reading

Deborah Crawford. *Four Women in a Violent Time*. Crown, 1970. Dramatized stories of Anne Hutchinson, Mary Dyer, and other women during the early years of New England and New York.

Howard S. Russell. *Indian New England Before the Mayflower*. University Press of New England, 1980. A scholar's account of the way of life of New England Indians before the colonists overwhelmed them.

John Anthony Scott. *Settlers on the Eastern Shore, 1607–1750*. Alfred A. Knopf, 1967. Description of English colonies and colonial issues. Many primary sources.

TEST YOURSELF

WRITE YOUR ANSWERS ON A SEPARATE SHEET OF PAPER.

True or False

Mark T if the statement is true, F if it is false. Change the italicized words in all false statements so that they are true.

1. *All* the English colonies turned out as their founders intended.
2. *Georgia* was founded as a buffer against the Spanish in Florida and to help the poor.
3. *Geography*, not the founders, shaped the societies of the Carolinas.
4. Although Maryland was designed as a refuge for *Protestants*, many settlers were *Catholics*.
5. Both *Pennsylvania and Massachusetts* were founded as religious experiments.
6. *Charles II* gave away millions of acres in America to his friends.
7. *Many* English settlers came to New York in the years before 1688.
8. The English conquered *New Netherland* without firing a shot.
9. *Anne Hutchinson and Roger Williams* were banished from Massachusetts because of their beliefs.
10. Three groups who came to America to establish religious communities were *the Pilgrims, the Puritans, and the Quakers*.

Matching

Select the letter of the answer that best matches each item below.

1. Pilgrims
2. Puritans
3. James Oglethorpe
4. George Calvert
5. William Penn
6. Quakers
7. James II
8. enclosure movement
9. Glorious Revolution
10. Peter Stuyvesant

a. Dutch governor who surrendered New Amsterdam
b. signed the Mayflower Compact
c. allowed religious freedom but no voting in New York
d. forced English farmers off their land
e. founded the "perfect society" in Massachusetts
f. wanted to help poor people
g. founded a colony as a refuge for Catholics
h. pacifists who resigned from government rather than raise an army
i. proprietor who founded a Holy Experiment in Pennsylvania
j. established Parliament over the monarchy in England

Charting the Main Ideas

Copy the chart below. Then fill in the missing information.

	COLONY	LOCATION	FOUNDER	IMPORTANT CHARACTERISTIC
1.			Quakers	part of Pennsylvania until 1776
2.	Georgia	southern colonies		
3.	Rhode Island			religious freedom
4.		New England		rule of the "saints"
5.		southern colonies	8 proprietors	Virginia settlers made this one of the most democratic colonies.

Chapter 4

THE COLONIAL ECONOMY

In 1760, 150 years had passed since the founding of Jamestown. English America was shaped like a new crescent moon, curving from Maine to Georgia. There were about 1.5 million colonists spread thinly along 3,000 miles of Atlantic coastline. In many areas great expanses of forest and wilderness separated farms and villages from each other. Bear and mountain lion could still loll in the sun of the Appalachian Mountains without fear of human presence. These mountains were a wall that separated the colonial world from a great unknown. The states, cities, and towns that most of you live in today were undreamed of by even the most farsighted colonist.

This colonial world of the mid-18th century might seem small and unimpressive to you. But it was large and breathtaking to the men and women who inhabited it. In 1760, it took a rider on horseback several weeks to go from Boston to Philadelphia. It took as long for a Carolina pioneer to walk to the nearest town. Mail and newspapers from England could take months to arrive. Mail from the colony next door probably took even longer. A farmer in Georgia was linked by the ocean to Europe more easily than by the land to Maine.

Yet, by 1760, the colonial economy linked the Georgian to the Virginian, and the Virginian to the farmer of Maine. These economic links are important to your understanding of the development of an "American" rather than a colonial history.

Sections in This Chapter
1. New England's Economy: Villages and Voyages
2. The Middle Colonies: Doorway to America
3. The Southern Colonies: Tobacco, Rice, Indigo, and Frontier
4. Free Workers, Indentured Servants, and Slaves
5. Social Mobility

Opposite: A golden harvest of grain flowed outward from the middle colonies.

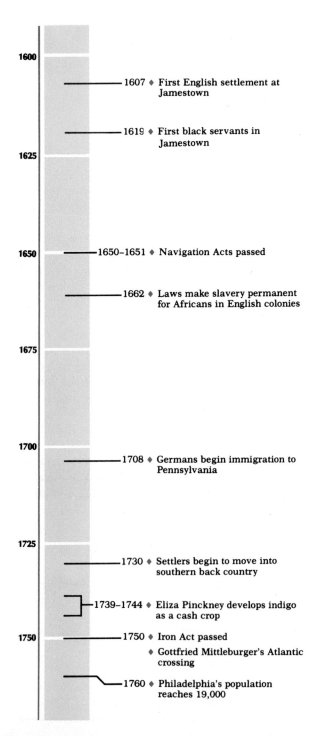

1600

1607 ◆ First English settlement at
Jamestown

1619 ◆ First black servants in
Jamestown

1625

1650 1650–1651 ◆ Navigation Acts passed

1662 ◆ Laws make slavery permanent
for Africans in English colonies

1675

1700

1708 ◆ Germans begin immigration to
Pennsylvania

1725

1730 ◆ Settlers begin to move into
southern back country

1739–1744 ◆ Eliza Pinckney develops indigo
as a cash crop

1750 1750 ◆ Iron Act passed

◆ Gottfried Mittleburger's Atlantic
crossing

1760 ◆ Philadelphia's population
reaches 19,000

1. NEW ENGLAND'S ECONOMY: VILLAGES AND VOYAGES

Like nine out of every ten colonists, the typical New Englander was a farmer. But, as an old and bitter joke went, the main crop of a New England farm was always the same: rocks. There was some truth to the jest. New England soil was rocky, and often infertile. Here was a frustrating contrast to the green fields of Old England and the rich lands of the middle and southern colonies. New England farming was difficult and not very productive.

A Subsistence Economy

New England farmers lived in a **subsistence economy**. That is, they used all that they produced for their families' daily existence. There was no surplus for sale and thus no profit in a subsistence economy.

Even if the New England soil and climate had been better, the topography, or shape of the land, would have made this a subsistence economy. For, unlike Virginia, New England had no system of navigable rivers that flowed to the ocean. This was important in the 1700s, for rivers were the highways of the colonial world. Without them, farmers could not get their crops to buyers quickly or cheaply.

However, by the 1840s technology would turn this disadvantage into an advantage: the streams and the waterfalls of New England would make excellent sources of waterpower for factories. But in the 1700s, Nature isolated most of New England from the marketplace.

The Connecticut Valley

The Connecticut River Valley region was the only exception to this New England rule. Here soil was rich, and a surplus was produced. Even tobacco grew in this valley. The Connecticut River flowed down to Long Island Sound (see map, page 66) and could be used as a route to the ocean. The wealthy farmers of this valley were called "River Gods," a clear sign that their prosperity was not typical.

A Comfortable Existence but Land Was Scarce

New England farmers were not poor, however. Most led comfortable lives. They ate well, for their gardens were full of vegetables and their orchards gave them quinces, pears, cherries, plums, and apples. Their poultry and livestock provided fresh eggs, roast chicken, milk, cream, slabs of bacon, and Sunday hams. The woods gave them all the materials they needed for homes, for furniture, and for the wooden tools they made.

These farmers also had the comfort of friends and family nearby. As you recall from Chapter 3, most New Englanders lived in compact towns. Side by side, these towns formed a chain of communication and interaction that was not possible in the southern or middle colonies. In fact, New England was the most urban region of America. And, because the land was distributed fairly evenly among the townsmen, most men had enough property to vote.

No world is a paradise, however. The happiness of New England depended upon the availability of farmland. By the 1760s, new land was scarce, and family farms had been divided and redivided among sons and daughters many times. Each farm grew smaller and smaller. Many New England farm boys found themselves packing their belongings and heading for the frontiers of other regions or for the cities of Boston, Newport, and New Haven.

Needlework farm scene

The World of New England Commerce

Happy farmers were not the only image that came to mind when people spoke of the "Yankees" of New England. (The nickname is Dutch, for "John Cheese.") Many people thought instead of the men and women of the seaport cities, who lived and worked in a commercial (profit-oriented) economy.

At first and even at second glance, New England seemed to have little that anyone would wish to buy. But the Yankees managed to create wealth out of some very ordinary resources.

There were tall oak and white pine trees in New Hampshire and Maine. Their tar and turpentine were valuable naval stores (ship supplies). Their timber was perfect material for shipbuilding. By 1631, Boston boasted a shipyard. Over the next century the shipbuilding industry of the region provided jobs for many workers. Shipwrights, coopers, and blacksmiths built every size vessel from the little fishing sloops to the grand three-masted square-riggers that Americans called "pinks."

New England also had waters crowded with fish. From Gloucester [glos′tər] and Marblehead, the fishing fleets sailed as far as the Grand Banks of Newfoundland to catch the Atlantic's halibut, herring, mackerel, and cod.

Even more adventurous than the fishermen of Gloucester were the whalers of Nantucket. Using only the harpoon, these men pursued and killed the great whales of the northern waters. Whales were an important source of materials. Colonists made fuel from the whale blubber. From the spermaceti [spėr′mə set′ē], a waxy substance,

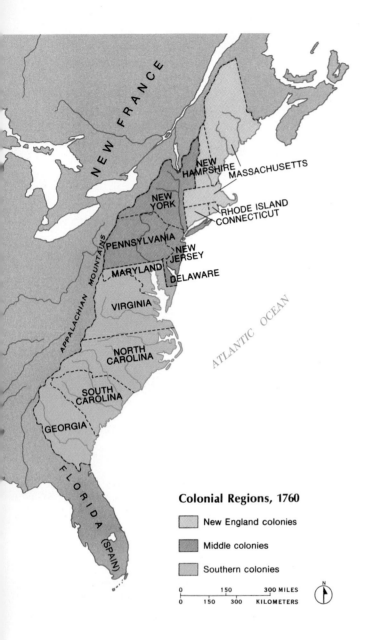

Colonial Regions, 1760

New England colonies

Middle colonies

Southern colonies

| 0 | | 150 | | 300 MILES |
| 0 | 150 | 300 | | KILOMETERS |

they made candles. From the ambergris [am′ bər grēs′], a secretion from the intestines, they made perfumes.

The Triangular Trades

New Englanders developed several markets for their native products. By a series of trading steps —each step exchanging one item for a more valuable one—they wound up with money in their pockets. These trade exchanges came to be known as the **Triangular Trades**. You can see how

this process got its name if you trace the lines of the trade routes. (See map, opposite page.)

One triangle went like this: New England ships carried lumber and salted or preserved fish to the sugar plantations of the West Indies. En route, they might also have stopped in New York or Philadelphia to pick up grain and meat. The fish (grain and meat) fed the thousands of slaves who labored in the sugar-cane fields there. West Indies planters paid for these supplies with sugar or molasses.* The New England ships then carried the sugar to England where they exchanged it for manufactured goods. The triangle was completed when the ships returned to the colonies, here to sell the goods for a tidy profit.

Another triangle began exactly as the first. (See map.) But this time the sugar was returned to New England to be made into rum. Rum distilleries became a special New England industry. Thus the descendants of the sober Puritans became world suppliers of liquor. The rum was carried to the West African coast and exchanged for African slaves. The third leg of the triangle was the Atlantic crossing to the southern colonies or to the West Indies, where slaves were paid for in silver, gold, or bills of credit.

New England traders worked many variations on this triangular system. But their purpose was always the same: to turn common and plentiful resources into cash through a series of sales and exchanges.

Mercantilism and the New World Colonies

England did not allow the colonists to make their profits entirely as they chose, however. Like most European countries, England operated under an economic system called **mercantilism**. This mercantilism reflected the principles of a merchant society, and therefore involved rules for buying, selling, trade, profit, and measuring one's wealth against one's rivals.

According to mercantilism, a nation, like a shopkeeper, must sell more than it bought. This "favorable balance of trade" brought gold into the country, and gold ensured power and prestige among all nations. To be a creditor rather than a debtor nation, a country must be as self-sufficient as possible. It must produce all the necessities of

*__molasses__ a sweet, brown syrup obtained in the process of making sugar from sugar cane or from raw sugar.

life for itself, and it must produce a surplus of goods that others want to buy.

The New World colonies became an important factor in the economy of all the mercantilist nations, which included Spain, Portugal, Holland, France, and England. These colonies could produce many of the raw materials that the European countries needed. And, they produced many new and desirable items, like tobacco, that could be sold for a profit. Furthermore, the people in the colonies were a steady market for all that their mother countries manufactured.

You can see that mercantilism put the English colonies in an inferior position to the Mother Country. England's colonies were valuable only because they served the needs of the English economy.

The Navigation Acts

England did not leave its prosperity to chance. All economic activities in the colonies were carefully regulated by trade laws called the Navigation Acts. Some of the earliest Navigation Acts were passed by Oliver Cromwell's government in 1650 and 1651. By 1691 England had a four-point trade policy for the colonies.

First, any ship carrying goods to and from America or England had to be English-built, and the majority of its crew had to be English citizens. (Americans were, of course, English citizens.) This Navigation Act was aimed at eliminating competing shippers, like the Dutch, from the colonial trade.

Second, the colonies were required to purchase all manufactured goods from England. The only

Each triangle represents the route of a typical New England sea captain around 1760.

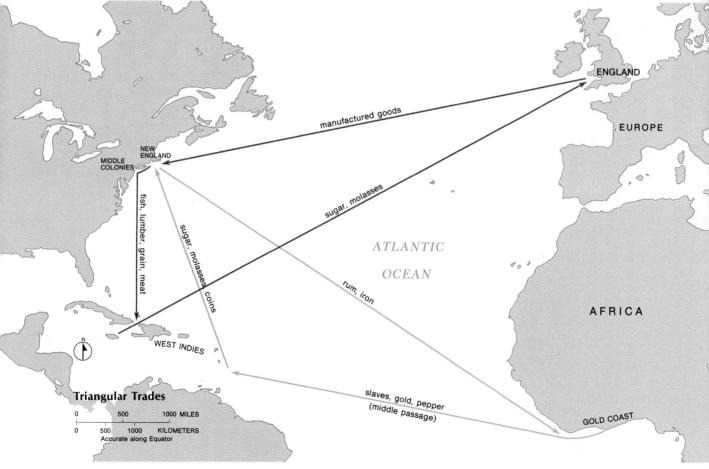

nies could not sell to the highest bidder. By 1750, almost everything produced on American farms was on this special enumerated, or named, list.

Finally, to prevent competition with English manufacturers, Americans were forbidden to produce any manufactured goods from their own raw materials. This meant that tobacco planters could not cure and process tobacco for smoking. As a result, colonial planters often made less from the growing of tobacco than English tobacco processors made from its sale.

The Navigation Acts defined the relationship of the colonies to the Mother Country. The colonies were like children, sent to America to help the family at home grow richer. They were nurtured and protected, but they were never allowed to compete with their English parents.

The Colonists Evade the Navigation Laws

New England merchants were not ashamed to break the Navigation Acts when they could. They traded with the French and Dutch West Indies as readily as they did with the English ones. They bought Dutch tea because it was cheaper than English tea. They imported foreign products without bringing them first to England. They did this because they believed that their economy depended on this smuggling. To a very great extent, they were correct.

SECTION 1 REVIEW

 Identify: subsistence economy, Triangular Trades, mercantilism, Navigation Acts

Main Ideas

1. Why was most New England farming subsistence farming? How did the prosperity of New England farmers gradually change in the 1700s?
2. Explain how the people of New England turned the following resources into wealth: lumber, fish, and whales.
3. What was the goal of the Navigation Acts? How did they affect the colonists?
4. Why did the American colonists try to evade the Navigation Acts?

Detail from Sea Captains Carousing in Surinam, *by John Greenwood, 1750*

exceptions were items that England did not produce, like the Spanish wine madeira [mə dir′ə]. Any non-English goods the colonists bought had to be shipped to England first and then resold to the Americans. An English duty, or tax, was placed on each of these goods. This meant that the colonists paid more for non-English products than people in England did.

Third, certain raw materials produced in the colonies could only be sold to England. The colo-

2. THE MIDDLE COLONIES: DOORWAY TO AMERICA

When the men and women on New England farms dreamed of fertile lands and sun-kissed climate, they were probably dreaming of the middle colonies: Pennsylvania, Delaware, New York, and New Jersey. In these four colonies there were long, navigable rivers like the Mohawk, the Hudson, and the Delaware. There were rich soils in the river valleys, rolling hills, and broad flatlands. The sun was bright, the temperature was moderate, the growing season was long. The middle colonies seemed tailor-made for agriculture.

Commercial Grain Farming

The typical farm in the middle colonies was larger than in New England. It was 200 acres, of which perhaps one-half were cleared and planted. The farmers grew vegetables and fruit, but their major crop was grain: wheat, barley, oats, rye, and corn. Even with the poor tools and the wasteful techniques of colonial agriculture, the Pennsylvania farmers could produce a surplus. Thus the middle-colony farmers were not just self-sufficient. They were **commercial farmers**. Their colonies were nicknamed the "bread colonies" because of all the grain they sold each year to the other English colonies and to Europe.

Huge Land Grants Hamper Settlement in New York and New Jersey

The abundant grain production is more impressive when you realize that the real potential of the region was not fully developed. The policy of land distribution in New York and New Jersey left thousands upon thousands of acres of good land untilled.

As you recall, in the 1660s James, Duke of York, set the pattern in both these colonies of making vast land grants to friends. New York land grants in the 1700s were also wastefully large, often 10,000 acres or more. But the landlords could not find tenants to work their acres. Although New England squatters improved some of the New York land, more than 80% of the rich soil of the colony was still uncultivated in 1760.

Pennsylvania Is the Land of Opportunity

It was Pennsylvania that best fulfilled the middle colonies' potential of commercial farming. William Penn's liberal land policy was still the rule in the 18th century. Farmers from Germany, Ireland, England, and France came to this colony to buy land cheaply from the Penn family.

But the Penn family did not guard its empty lands. Thus many immigrants did not bother to purchase the land; they simply took up their hoes and farmed it. By 1726, there were almost 100,000 of these squatters. Eventually many did pay for their farms. But news spread rapidly to new immigrants that Pennsylvania was a real "land of opportunity."

Most of the 18th century's eager immigrants entered America through the ports of Philadelphia or New York. In consequence, the middle colonies quickly took on the flavor of a "melting pot." Although you may associate this term with the 19th-century era of immigration, in fact, by 1760 Pennsylvania and New York were already filled with a variety of European peoples and cultures. The economy of the region thus influenced its human make-up.

The Pennsylvania Germans

In the early 18th century, the second largest group of immigrants to the colonies were the Germans from the Rhineland. Between 1708 and 1760, war, hunger, and persecution drove 100,000 of these men and women to America. Many settled in the middle colonies.

These people were poor, but they were excellent farmers. Unlike the English farmers, the Rhinelanders understood and honored many laws of conservation. They rotated crops, fertilized the soil, and did not abuse the land. At harvest time, the German farmers could be seen loading their crops and children into covered wagons and heading east to the market towns.

The Pennsylvania Germans maintained their own culture in the colonies, much as the Pilgrims tried to do in Holland a century before. They had their own Protestant churches, spoke their own language, and printed and read their own newspapers. Yet they could not remain entirely untouched by the English people around them. By the second generation, many Germans spoke a mixture of German and English which came to be

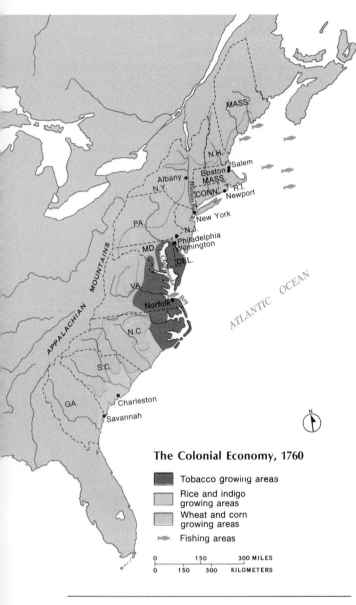

The Colonial Economy, 1760

- ■ Tobacco growing areas
- ▨ Rice and indigo growing areas
- ▧ Wheat and corn growing areas
- ➤ Fishing areas

0   150   300 MILES
0 150 300 KILOMETERS

All of the colonies also sold lumber and other wood products in England.

known as **"Pennsylvania Dutch"** (from *Deutsch*, meaning "German").

The Scots-Irish

The **Scots-Irish** were the largest immigrant group of the early 18th century. They were Scottish Presbyterians who had colonized northern Ireland in the 1500s. Because they were Presbyterians rather than Anglicans, they were persecuted by the English government. Between 1700 and 1763, almost 200,000 of these poverty-stricken people came to the English colonies. Many settled in the middle colonies, although others went farther south to the Carolinas.

Commercial Links to the Other Colonies and to Europe

Philadelphia and New York were like two doorways to the colonial world. In came the people and products of England and Europe. Out went the foodstuffs and raw materials of the colonies. In 1760, Philadelphia—the "City of Brotherly Love"—had 19,000 inhabitants. The largest town in the 13 colonies, it was a Quaker city of straight streets, neat brick houses, and window boxes of flowers. Its life was dominated by its port activities. The immigrant influence was everywhere. Even the street signs were printed in both English and German.

The commercial-farming economy of the middle colonies reached out to many parts of the world. It linked the grain farmers to men and women they had never met in Europe, the West Indies, the southern colonies, and New England. The wheat fed them all. It also helped sustain the major seaport cities of Philadelphia, New York, and Wilmington.

The Iron Act

Because of the wheat, flour milling was the main industry in Philadelphia, New York, and Wilmington. However, the iron industry was also important in the cities and countryside of the middle colonies. In New Jersey and Pennsylvania, "iron plantations" mined and processed ore, making bar or pig iron through a smelting process. Then urban iron mills were built to transform this bar iron into tools, nails, and other finished goods that were expensive to import from England. The English government, reacting to the competition, soon decided to regulate this expanding colonial industry.

In 1750, Parliament passed the **Iron Act**. This law encouraged the continued production of bar and pig iron, as long as it was sent to England in that form. But the English forbade any further production of tools and supplies. Colonial ironmasters sometimes defied the law, and their colo-

ENGLAND'S NEW WORLD COLONIES, AROUND 1760

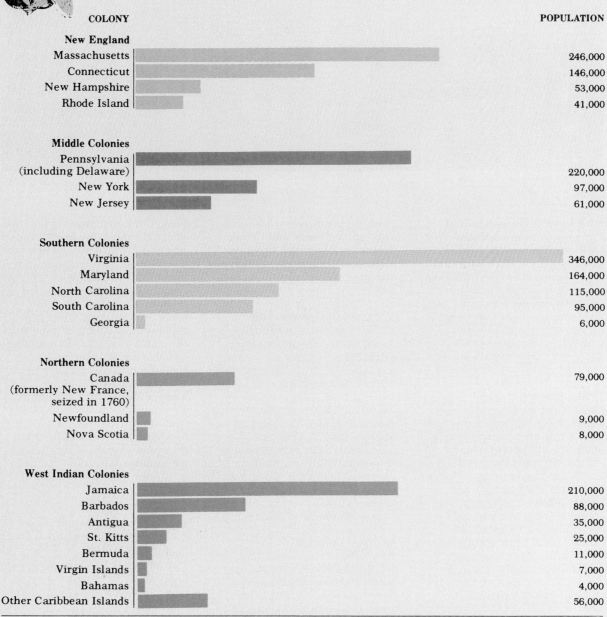

COLONY	POPULATION
New England	
Massachusetts	246,000
Connecticut	146,000
New Hampshire	53,000
Rhode Island	41,000
Middle Colonies	
Pennsylvania (including Delaware)	220,000
New York	97,000
New Jersey	61,000
Southern Colonies	
Virginia	346,000
Maryland	164,000
North Carolina	115,000
South Carolina	95,000
Georgia	6,000
Northern Colonies	
Canada (formerly New France, seized in 1760)	79,000
Newfoundland	9,000
Nova Scotia	8,000
West Indian Colonies	
Jamaica	210,000
Barbados	88,000
Antigua	35,000
St. Kitts	25,000
Bermuda	11,000
Virgin Islands	7,000
Bahamas	4,000
Other Caribbean Islands	56,000

Colonial officials did not count Indians in their censuses, probably because they were not considered members of the British empire. Note that many of the West Indian colonies were quite large, compared to the mainland colonies. Trade between the West Indian colonies and the 13 colonies was very important in this period.

LIFE IN AMERICA

NEW YORK CITY IN 1760

View of New York City from the Brooklyn shore, 1757

Even in 1760, life in New York City seemed more hectic and lively than anywhere else in America. The city was not large, extending only a mile north of the Battery at the southern tip of Manhattan Island. Walking north from the Battery, a visitor would soon be strolling through potato fields. But within the built-up area, everything was noise and congestion.

A Maze of Hazards
Unlike Philadelphia, New York City had not been carefully laid out as a Holy Experiment. Narrow winding streets crisscrossed each other. The city seemed to grow winding tentacles in every direction as the population grew. Rents were high, and housing was scarce. Streets were muddy and crowded. Carts, coaches, and riders on horseback created 18th-century traffic jams. Pedestrians had to keep an eye out for garbage falling from windows above, for pickpockets on the streets, and for reckless drivers racing by. The wooden houses and warehouses were fire hazards. In the winter, fuel bills soared as firewood and coal became precious commodities. The water was often unsafe to

drink, for it was polluted by ocean salts, animal waste, and garbage. Sanitation, like crime, was a constant topic of complaint. Smallpox and other plagues remained possibilities.

A Magnet of Opportunities
Yet, men and women flocked to New York and the other seaport cities. For the cities were the centers for trade, manufacturing, and the buying and selling of luxuries. It was home for the storekeeper, the sailor, the dressmaker, the peddler, and the theatrical performer. As early as 1703, more than 20 specialized trades were advertised in New York City, among them, merchant, goldsmith, baker, flour miller, carpenter, mariner, tailor, brickmaker—and seven men who were professional bell ringers.

A City of Contrasts
Over 2,000 of New York City's 14,000 inhabitants were slaves. Racial tensions and rumors of slave riots were common. There were ethnic conflicts as well. But there were taverns where men and women could learn the latest gossip about business or European politics; there were newspapers and

booksellers; there was theater; there were societies to improve the mind and to encourage wit and humor.

Flour the Foundation
New York's economy was based on the flour milling industry. For many decades the city had a monopoly on the milling of grain from the middle colonies. Although Philadelphia and Wilmington were competitors in this industry by 1750, colonial New York remained a city of flour millers and bakers. Flour was the focus of New York's flourishing trade with the West Indies, Europe, and England. It was the source of many of the mercantile fortunes of the city.

nial friends supported this lawbreaking. In Philadelphia, for example, a new iron mill opened right under the Pennsylvania governor's eye. Local citizens silently dared the government to close this valuable supply of building materials. It remained open until the Revolution.

The Commercial Network
Makes the Colonists "Americans"

The merchants, sailors, tradesmen and women, and the flour millers and ironmakers of the middle-colony cities were vital to the colonial economy. And they were also important in creating an American identity.

The merchants had friends and family members in other colonies with whom they did business. Sailors and merchants traveled the length and breadth of the colonial world, acting as news sources and personal links between the regions of the Atlantic coastline. Many of the commercial occupations gave men and women an overview of the growing strength of the colonial economy. Many merchants' account books would clearly reveal the interdependence of one colony with another.

These colonists were keenly aware of the burdens that the Navigation Acts and Iron Act placed on them and what these laws said about the relationship of the Mother Country to its colonies. It is not surprising that the movement for independence began in commercial centers like Boston, Philadelphia, and New York.

Above: Wedding scene from a 1756 sampler

SECTION 2 REVIEW

Identify: commercial farmers, Pennsylvania Dutch, Scots-Irish, Iron Act

Main Ideas

1. Why did the middle colonies become a region of commercial farming?
2. Why did Pennsylvania attract more immigrants than did New York and New Jersey in the colonial period?
3. Explain why Philadelphia, New York City, and Wilmington became important ports during this period.
4. How did trade to and from the middle-colony ports help create an "American" consciousness?

THE LARGEST CITIES IN THE 13 COLONIES, 1760	
City	**Population**
Philadelphia, Pennsylvania	19,000
Boston, Massachusetts	16,000
New York, New York	14,000
Charleston, South Carolina	8,000
Newport, Rhode Island	7,000
Marblehead, Massachusetts	5,000
Salem, Massachusetts	4,000

The cities in the 13 colonies were quite small. In 1760, Mexico City had more than 100,000 inhabitants, while London, the largest city in the world, had almost 700,000.

3. THE SOUTHERN COLONIES: TOBACCO, RICE, INDIGO, AND FRONTIER

Half of all the American colonists lived in the five southern colonies of Maryland, Virginia, North and South Carolina, and Georgia. These colonies were the apple of England's mercantile eye, for they produced the staple, or basic, crops that England wanted and needed. Only the sugar plantations of the British West Indies compared as model colonial children, helping the Mother Country compete with other European nations. Most of the southern colonists lived in the **Tidewater** region. This fertile low-lying coastal plain was so named because the networks of rivers that ran through it were reached by ocean tides.

The Importance of Tobacco
In Maryland, Virginia, and North Carolina, tobacco was the sole cash crop. In the Tidewater region around the Chesapeake Bay and along the

Detail from a map of Virginia for 1751

Potomac, Rappahannock, York, James, and Roanoke rivers, wealthy plantations and small family farms grew the same "sotweed" that John Rolfe had first planted a century ago.

The topography and climate were perfect for tobacco. There were long and hot summers, good soil, and a heavy rainfall. The extensive network of navigable rivers ran generally from west to east, ideal for shipping the crop to the ocean-going vessels waiting on the coast.

Tobacco Plantations and Family Farms
Half of all the tobacco was grown on large plantations that spread along the rivers. Each had its own small port facilities for shipping tobacco to and receiving goods from England. (See illustration, opposite page.) At the core of each plantation was a village, dominated by the elegant home of the plantation family. Nearby were the houses of the overseers, or field-work supervisors, and also of the skilled workers, such as blacksmiths, carpenters, brickmakers, and other artisans. Their workshops and sheds were also nearby. Other buildings housed the kitchen, laundry, smokehouse, and cider presses, whose work was supervised by the mistress of the plantation. A bit apart, and far more shabby, were the cabins of the slaves. Close to all these houses and workshops were the orchards, the gardens, and the pastures. Farther out lay the tobacco fields themselves.

These great farms resembled New England towns. However, most of the inhabitants were slaves. Because almost all the many men and women involved in the life of the plantation were Africans, the members of the white plantation family thought of themselves as isolated and alone, miles from their nearest neighbors. The slaves, however, had a tightly knit community life.

Half the colonial tobacco was produced on small, 100- to 200-acre family farms. These family farms varied greatly. Some were the modest enterprises of the poor "lubbers" or "buckskins." Others belonged to the younger sons of rich planters. These men had to start life on their own because in the tobacco colonies a father usually left his entire plantation to the oldest son. This custom, imported from England, was called **primogeniture**, meaning "first-born." Unlike New Englanders, who divided their lands among all

This typical Tidewater plantation was like a small town, with houses, mill, warehouses, and wharf.

the sons and daughters, the southern planters tried to avoid breaking the family holdings into smaller and smaller units. However, primogeniture often ensured riches for one son at the expense of the other children.

Soil Exhaustion and Land Speculation

Tobacco farming was very damaging to the soil, and after about seven years, the earth lost its fertility. Planters were always buying and readying new western lands for planting. This meant that a large part of the tobacco planter's income was tied up in land. It also meant that the steady movement westward from the coast was a necessity, not just a sign of an adventurous spirit.

The tobacco farmer operated in a one-crop world. But many of the wiser planters tried to expand their activities and thus to vary their source of income. Some, like Carter Braxton of Virginia, invested in slave ships and the importation of convict labor. Others became lawyers or merchants. Most were land speculators, purchasing western lands and then selling them to neighbors for a profit. George Washington was among the most active land speculators in the 18th century.

Rice and Indigo Regions

South Carolina and Georgia were rice and indigo-growing regions. Rice was a staple food, much in demand in Europe. The indigo plant yielded a blue dye that the cloth industry of England used for coloring.

Detail from a diagram explaining how indigo plants are processed into blue dye

At the very center of this hot, mosquito-ridden but prosperous area was the city of Charleston. Charleston was the jewel of the South, a showplace of elegant townhouses, grand ballrooms, and private clubs. Eight thousand people lived here, catering to the needs of the planter families who spent the hot summer months in the city.

The Currency Problem

Despite their wealth, the pockets of the southern planters were often empty because of debts and because of the currency problem in colonial America. England did not allow gold to leave the Mother Country for use in the colonies. No payment for crops or goods could be made in real currency. Instead, colonists received "bills of credit" which they could spend in English shops or warehouses to pay for manufactured goods. The real money always passed between the English shipper who bought the tobacco or rice and the English shopkeeper who sold the cloth, nails, or furniture.

What, then, could a colonist use when buying and selling at home? In the 1600s, colonists often used wampum, the Indian bead or shell money. Even in 1760, many farm people bartered, that is, exchanged goods and services without any money transactions. But large plantation owners and big shipping companies could hardly be expected to operate this way!

The colonists tried many ways to solve the currency problem. In the South, men and women used tobacco or rice "crop notes." These were the receipts from shippers showing how much tobacco or rice the planter had produced and sold. Crop notes were one proof of how much the planter was worth, and thus were accepted as a form of money. In Massachusetts, in the 1680s and 1690s, colonial leaders broke English law by minting coins of their own. But these "pine tree shillings" were quickly outlawed by the Mother Country.

Many colonial governments experimented with printing paper money that was backed by expected tax collections. But the value of this paper money was not steady, for no one could be certain if taxes would really cover the amount of money the government printed. Speculation* thus

The indigo plant originally came from Madagascar, a huge island off the eastern coast of Africa. Between 1739 and 1744, **Eliza Pinckney**, a South Carolina planter, perfected the process of growing indigo and producing the dye from the fresh-cut plants. Seeds from this crop were distributed, and indigo soon became one of the most valuable products in South Carolina until the Revolution ended the export trade.

The heart of the rice world was the **Carolina Low Country**, a region of swamps, rivers, sounds, and islands between Winyah Bay and the Savannah River. Here the plantations were far larger than in the tobacco colonies: the average planter owned at least 300–500 acres and a dozen or more slaves. South Carolina boasted the wealthiest group of colonists in America.

*speculation buying and selling when there is a large risk, with the hope of making a profit from future price changes.

caused the value of the paper money to go up and down too rapidly for it to be useful currency.

In the end, the only real solution was to acquire gold and silver coins from foreign countries. The English did not object to this, because they knew that eventually the coins would wind up in English shopkeepers' pockets.

Colonists were so eager to get foreign coins that they even welcomed pirates into the seaports of Charleston and Boston. Anyone from the notorious Blackbeard to the famous women pirates Mary Read and Anne Bonny were treated like guests in these cities. Their money was more important than their characters. (See pages 276–277 for more information about these and other pirates.)

The Currency Problem
Links the 13 Colonies

However, the most effective way of attracting foreign money was not by welcoming pirates. It was through trade. This is another reason why merchants engaged in the Triangular Trades felt the need to smuggle goods to and from the French and Dutch West Indies. Unlike English planters, these foreigners paid in coin. The currency problem was another economic link between southern planters, New York flour merchants, and New England shippers—colonists who might seem at first to have little in common.

The Southern Frontier

The southern frontier, or **back country**, was very different from the wealthy Tidewater regions. Here, subsistence farming was the rule. But these farms were not yet the comfortable farms of the New England towns. This inland region, stretching 600 miles along the Maryland and Virginia **Piedmont*** to the clay regions of Georgia, was the 18th-century's pioneer world. (See map, page 97.)

In 1730, Adam Miller led a band of fellow Germans through the forests to the Shenandoah Valley. They were the first of a steady stream of settlers to the back country of the South. Within 20 years this area was transformed from an Indian economy based on hunting and shifting culti-

*Piedmont [pēd/mont] foothills that extend between the Appalachian Mountains and the Atlantic Coastal Plain. They begin near the coast of New York and run southwest all the way to Alabama.

vation to a heavily populated colonial agricultural region.

On the eve of the American Revolution, there were 250,000 settlers here. Most of them were farmers, fur trappers, or village craftworkers. They were German and Scots-Irish, part of the waves of immigration that passed through the ports of Philadelphia and New York.

The settlers moved south along the "great wagon trail," a wandering dirt highway that was little more than an Indian footpath at many spots between Pennsylvania and Georgia. These pioneers were poor. They came south with two horses or a pair of oxen, a wagonload of family and household goods, and a few cows and chickens trailing behind.

Neither the Germans nor the Scots-Irish had any experience with pioneering or frontier survival. They learned by cruel experience how to build a log cabin and how to clear a forest to make a field. In the first year, a family was considered lucky if it had a roof overhead, a cabin with four full sides, and an acre or two of corn in the ground. Here, life was similar to colonial life along the Atlantic seacoast 150 years earlier. For still another 150 years, there would always be such a frontier region in America, with pioneer families re-creating the backbreaking struggles of the very first colonists who settled in the New World.

SECTION 3 REVIEW

Identify: Tidewater, primogeniture, Eliza Pinckney, Carolina Low Country, back country, Piedmont

Main Ideas

1. How did climate, geography, and economics help make tobacco the major cash crop in Maryland, Virginia, and North Carolina?
2. How was a large tobacco plantation similar to a New England town? How was it different?
3. How did soil exhaustion lead to land speculation and other occupations in the tobacco regions?
4. What English policies led to a lack of currency in the colonies? List measures the colonists took to deal with the problem.
5. What was it like to be a settler on the southern frontier?

THE GEOGRAPHIC SETTING

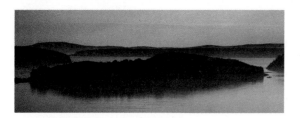

SETTLING THE EAST COAST

The settlers who eagerly viewed the eastern coast of North America saw a land remarkably similar to the one they had left in western Europe. No other ocean in the world, in fact, would leave so few surprises on the other side.

Although much of North America is farther south than Europe, the climate was similar. Thus, newcomers needed few changes in clothing or housing, and they could grow familiar foods.

The topography was also much the same. The bays and rivers, forests and low mountains were all familiar landforms to Europeans. Settlement along the rivers and into the interior was fairly easy.

Think how different North America's West Coast is! Look at the map of North America's physical features in the Atlas Section (Map 3). On the West Coast settlers would have found few bays to shelter their ships, and high mountains would have blocked their movement inland. The East Coast was much more friendly to European settlement.

The left map on the opposite page shows the parts of the East Coast that colonists settled by 1700 and by 1760. Looking carefully at this map, we can see several ways that the land influenced settlers. But first, look at the map of European claims in 1754. As you can see, France and Spain claimed huge sections of North America. The French and Spanish seem to hem in the British colonies along the coastline. It would be hard to

predict the importance and success of the English colonies from this map.

New France Fails to Develop

Now look at the settlement map. Note the area of French settlement in North America by 1700 (indicated by light green shading). Almost all the 15,000 French settlers lived along the St. Lawrence River. A small minority lived in fur-trading posts near the Great Lakes.

Later French settlement (marked in dark green) spread along Lakes Ontario and Erie and southward to the Ohio River. Thus New France controlled the East Coast's best natural route inland from the Atlantic Ocean. But New France never became heavily populated. By 1760, there were less than 80,000 European settlers in all the vast area called New France.

Spanish Claims: Colonies Without Colonists

Even more sparsely settled was the area of Spanish claim in Florida. The settlement map shows an early population around St. Augustine, established in 1565. This was to be the only area of permanent settlement in Florida, where the main goals were to convert the Indians to Christianity and to protect Spanish trade routes.

A few forts and missions were built along the coast and inland in northern Florida along a road, more like a path, called the Camino Real, or "royal road." Settlers along the northern coast of the Gulf of Mexico carried on trade

with the Creek Indian confederacy. But Spanish Florida never had more than about 6,000 settlers. It can truly be called a colony without colonists.

Likewise, Spanish territory west of the Mississippi did not attract colonists from Mexico or from Europe. In 1760, less than 15,000 settlers lived in the Spanish lands north of present-day Mexico.

The Bulk of the Population

In contrast, the English colonies on the East Coast were developing rapidly. Settlers occupied much more of the area of claim than did the French or Spanish. By 1760 about 1.5 million colonists lived in this region. This was probably more than all the other people—Indians and settlers combined—on the entire continent north of Mexico.

The Atlantic Coastal Plain

Now let's look briefly at some geographical aspects of English colonial settlement. In 1700, about 250,000 settlers lived on the East Coast. The area of settlement was mainly near the sea (light green shading). Two physical features were of prime importance to these early settlers: the Atlantic Coastal Plain and the river valleys.

The Atlantic Coastal Plain is a lowland area of sand, silt, and clay that extends all the way from Cape Cod in the north to the Yucatán Peninsula in Mexico. On land, this region gets wider as one proceeds south, and provided colonists with level land for farming. Beneath the sea the plain extends north to

Newfoundland, forming shallow places called "banks." These banks were of great importance to the colonists, for here the Yankee fishermen reaped the rich harvest of the sea: cod, herring, halibut, mackerel, and whale. (See map, next page.)

The River Valleys

The early settlers tended to settle along river valleys that led inland. In early Virginia, for example, settlement was in the Tidewater region along the James, the Rappahannock, and the Potomac. Early settlements in New Sweden and later Pennsylvania, Delaware, and New Jersey were along the Delaware. Note on the settlement map the Hudson River in New York and the Connecticut River in New England. They show the deepest penetration by Europeans in 1700.

A Dispute Between Colonies

Notice also the gray area in southern Delaware. Why was it unsettled as late as 1760? It seems that William Penn and the Calverts disputed this land for many years after it was taken from the Dutch. Not many settlers were interested in coming to this area until the 1760s, when two surveyors, Charles Mason and Jeremiah Dixon, tramped through swamps and forests to determine the exact boundaries between Maryland and Pennsylvania (which included Delaware). Their "Mason and Dixon Line" (1769) gained new significance at the time of the Civil War, when it became the symbol of the division between free and slave states.

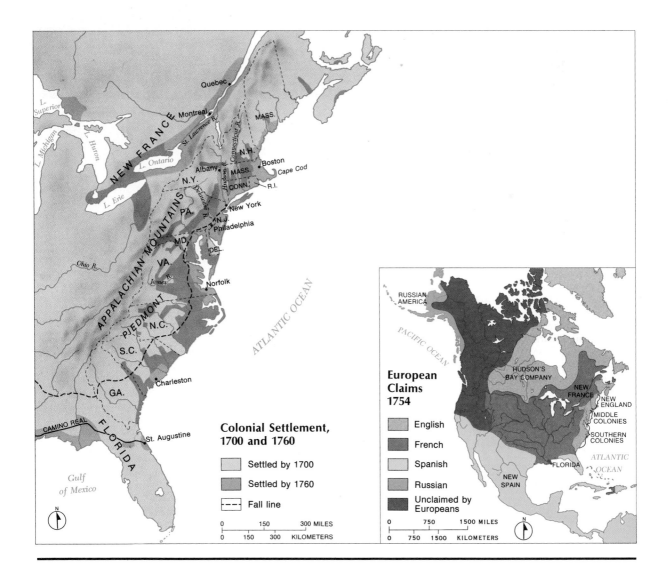

Colonial Settlement, 1700 and 1760

Settled by 1700
Settled by 1760
- - - Fall line

0   150   300 MILES
0   150   300   KILOMETERS

European Claims 1754

English
French
Spanish
Russian
Unclaimed by Europeans

0   750   1500 MILES
0   750   1500   KILOMETERS

THE GEOGRAPHIC SETTING

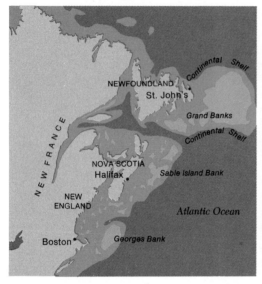

**Fishing Banks
off the Atlantic Coast**

0   200   400   600 MILES
0 200 400 600 KILOMETERS

Left: The light green areas show the shallow fishing banks. Here Yankee, English, and French sailors caught cod, herring, and other sea creatures. The medium green areas show the submerged coastal plain, also called the continental shelf. The dark green areas are the deeper parts of the ocean, while the gray areas are land.

Right: Many of the New England whalers were Pequot and other Indians. Catching whales was dangerous work, requiring two whale boats: one to kill the whale, the other to save the crew if the first boat were swamped.

The Piedmont

The next geographical area opened to European settlement was the region of low, rocky foothills that divided the coastal plain from the Appalachian Mountains. This area is called the Piedmont. The boundary between the flat coastal plain and the Piedmont is the "fall line," where waterfalls blocked transportation inland on the rivers.

Many cities eventually sprang up along this fall line—look for Trenton, New Jersey; Richmond, Virginia; Raleigh, North Carolina; Columbia, South Carolina; and Macon, Georgia, on Map 2 in the Atlas section. Water power was used to run factories in these cities when the Industrial Revolution came to America in the 1800s. In colonial times, however, the Pied-

mont was the frontier, or back country, settled by pioneers after 1730. By 1760, this region was beginning to appear more settled.

The Appalachian Mountains

Perhaps you've already noticed the dark gray shaded area on the settlement map. Here lie the Appalachians, which stretch from Newfoundland to present-day Alabama.

From Pennsylvania southward the mountains form parallel ridges and valleys that run in a northeast–southwest direction. Rivers flowing through these valleys drop to the Piedmont and then to the coastal plain. Some of the river valleys were the sites of frontier settlements in the mid-1700s. Notice on your map the tongues of

dark green in the westernmost settled parts of Pennsylvania, Maryland, and Virginia. They show how settlers followed the northeast–southwest direction of the river valleys in the Appalachians.

The Appalachians were only a temporary barrier to settlement in the English colonies. Population pressure and the desire for new and rich farmland made the area beyond the mountains attractive to many colonists. Soon guides like Daniel Boone would be leading groups of pioneers through gaps in the Appalachian ridges, despite the wishes of the British government. Desire for the land west of the mountains would become a major issue in the coming dispute between the colonies and the Mother Country.

4. FREE WORKERS, INDENTURED SERVANTS, AND SLAVES

In colonial society, work was always plentiful but labor was usually scarce. Prosperity depended almost totally on human labor (the Machine Age had not yet begun). One major aspect of the colonial economy, therefore, was the way in which free colonists solved their "labor problem." They developed three solutions to the problem: free labor, indentured labor, and slave labor.

Free Workers

Everyone from Judge Samuel Sewall in the 1680s to Abigail Adams in the 1780s complained about the high cost of labor. There were simply never enough skilled or unskilled workers to satisfy colonial wants and needs. Even the most highly skilled artisans shared with other colonists the belief that owning land was superior to providing a service. These values were a legacy from England, where land was scarce and labor was plentiful. But the workers' values did not change to meet colonial reality. Thus, even though wages were 50% higher in the colonies than in England in 1700, artisans and laborers usually wanted to be landowners.

How the Labor Shortage Helped the Free Workers

In the 1600s and early 1700s, colonial governments did what they could to maintain the class system that had grown up in England. There, workers were much poorer than their employers and never had much chance to improve their social position. So, colonial assemblies passed laws regulating hours and wages for paid labor. These laws tried to keep hours as long and wages as low as possible. Other laws, called "sumptuary laws," regulated the consumption by workers of various luxuries, like silk, lace, or gold buttons. In colonial America, it was feared, the rich and their servants would soon dress and live alike. In addition, ministers preached against artisans and laborers' demanding high wages because of the labor shortage. But the colonial laws could not be enforced, and the ministers' warnings had little effect. The labor shortage enabled workers to demand more money. For blacksmiths, dock workers, coopers, and other workers, America was clearly a land of opportunity.

Idleness Was a Crime

You will not be surprised to read that in this "labor poor" society, in most colonies it was illegal to be lazy. In Rhode Island for example, "rogues, vagabonds, sturdy beggars, and masterless men," that is, all idle able-bodied males, were classified together as notorious offenders of the law and of community values. An idle man could be whipped, fined, or assigned to forced labor on repairing roads, public buildings, and jails. Young people were expected to work hard, too. All boys and girls over 12 were kept busy working at home or a trade.

Apprentices and Indentured Servants

To deal with the problem of labor scarcity, the colonists transformed the old English practice of apprenticeship into a major colonial economic institution. **Apprenticeship** worked as follows: A worker, usually a young boy or girl about 10 years old, was "bound," or contracted, to work for a master or mistress. Girls served until they were 16 or 18. Boys' terms were longer. In exchange for the child's labor, the master or mistress pledged to provide room, board, clothing, and an opportunity for the servant to learn the "mystery" of a special craft.

Colonial America continued the practice of apprenticeship. Benjamin Franklin began his career as a printer's apprentice. Paul Revere, a first-class silversmith, took on several young men as apprentices. But bound labor also grew to be much more than a system of vocational training. From the early 1600s to the Revolution, thousands of poor men and women became bound laborers, or **indentured servants**, for three to seven years in exchange for passage to America.

A Record of Abuses

Fifty to 75 percent of all white colonists in the 1600s came to America as indentured servants. About one-third of these were women. The importation of indentured servants was a major business in the 18th century as well.

Many made the trip willingly. Others, however, were tricked into coming, lured by labor agents, called "newlanders," who misled them about the costs of the Atlantic crossing or the fate that awaited them in the colonies. Others came because they had no choice—among them, youths from English orphanages and convicted criminals from English jails. Finally, some were kidnapped, victims of the endless demand for labor in the colonies.

The Atlantic crossing was a nightmare. A few servants left journals of these voyages, which you may find as shocking as they did themselves. In 1750, for example, a boatload of German families made its way from Rotterdam to Philadelphia. Many of these 400 people had paid the ship captain a sum they believed would cover the cost of the journey. Quickly, however, they discovered that "hidden costs" would reduce them to indentured servants or "redemptioners," as the Germans were called. Here is a description of that voyage written by one passenger, Gottfried Mittelberger:

This journey lasts a whole six months. The people are packed into the big boats as closely as herring, so to speak. The bedstead of one person is hardly two feet across and six feet long.

During the journey the ship is full of pitiful signs of distress—smells, fumes, horrors, vomiting, many different kinds of sea sickness, fever, dysentery, headaches, heat, constipation, boils, scurvy, cancer, mouth-rot, and other afflictions. Add to all that very little food, hunger, thirst, frost, heat, damp air, fear, misery, anger, and sorrow as well as other troubles. Thus, for example, there are so many lice, mostly on the sick people, that they have to be scraped off the bodies. Along with everything else one must also suffer through two to three days and nights of storm, with everyone believing that the ship with all aboard is bound to sink. . . .

It is not surprising that many passengers fall ill, because warm food is served only three times a week, and at that is very bad, very small in quantity, and so dirty as to be hardly edible at all. And the water is often very black, thick with dirt, and full of worms. Even when very thirsty, one is almost unable to drink it without feeling disgust.

As the voyage dragged on, even rotten food became a luxury. Desperate passengers paid extra for any scraps of food or any help at all from the crew. When the ship docked at Philadelphia, most of the Germans aboard were facing several years of forced labor to pay for their survival. It was not unusual for a servant ship to dock with half its human cargo dead or dying.

Once a ship arrived in the colonies, the sale of the servants began. Buyers boarded the ships to inspect the merchandise, checking teeth, feeling muscles, looking for tell-tale signs of illness or for uncooperative personalities. Some bought only one or two servants. But in the 18th century, men called "soul drivers" bought wholesale. Rounding up dozens of servants, these buyers marched them inland, selling their contracts—and thus them—door to door. Sometimes children were separated from their parents, and husbands from their wives, never to see each other again.

Their Fate in the Colonies

Though roughly treated on their journey to America, indentured servants did have legal rights under the terms of their contracts. They could sue for their freedom if their masters or mistresses abused them. At the end of their terms, they were entitled to receive "freedom dues"—a small sum of money or some new clothing. In South Carolina, the freedom dues were 50 acres of land.

Some servants never waited for their terms of service to end. These runaways disappeared onto the frontier or into the crowded cities of the middle colonies. Of those who served out their terms, the 18th-century German redemptioners fared best. In the friendly environment of Pennsylvania and in the backwoods of the South, these men and women were usually able to establish themselves as independent farmers. But in the plantation economies of the South, where they were forced to compete with slave labor, the freed servants were often unable to keep their freedom. Eighty percent either re-indentured themselves or became dependent on public charity.

An Unsatisfactory Solution to the Labor Problem

Indentured servitude was one answer to the labor problem, and it worked well for many employers. But it had its price. Servants were expensive, for the purchase of their labor contract from a sea captain or a soul driver was a major investment for the average farmer. Also, indentured servants were only a temporary labor supply. When their contracts ended, their labor was gone.

Even the cheaper, long-term servant, the English convict, was a mixed blessing to a community. English laws of 1662 and 1717 authorized the "dumping" of criminals in the colonies. Most of the 50,000 convict servants sent to the colonies were dangerous criminals—robbers, cutthroats, and murderers. A planter might be willing to run the risk, but the neighbors often protested. Being murdered seemed too high a price to pay for solving the labor problem.

Slavery in America

The third and the most effective solution to the labor problem was slavery. It was also the most tragic. The English colonists did not create African slavery. As you'll recall from Chapters 1 and 2, the Portuguese began taking African slaves in the mid-1400s, and the Spanish used African slaves in their New World colonies as early as 1501—only nine years after Columbus' first voyage. But the English willingly took over the practice of slavery from the Portuguese and Spanish.

Until the 1680s, slaves were very expensive in the English colonies. Then England's Royal African Company moved to the forefront of the slave trade, making it possible for colonists to buy a seemingly endless supply of slaves at reasonable prices. By the eve of the American Revolution, 500,000 African captives had been brought to the 13 colonies. This was only 5% of the estimated 10 million men and women who were forced into slavery in the New World between 1500 and 1850. But it was enough to establish the world of master and slave in English America. By 1760, about 20% of the colonial population was held in slavery.

In the transatlantic slave trade, more than 20 million people were taken from Africa between 1500 and 1800. About 75% came from West Africa, 23% from Central Africa, and 2% from East Africa. Of those who survived the crossing, about 60% went to the West Indies, Central America, and northern South America; 35% went to Brazil; and 5% went to the U.S. The slave trade also continued between East Africa and the Middle East.

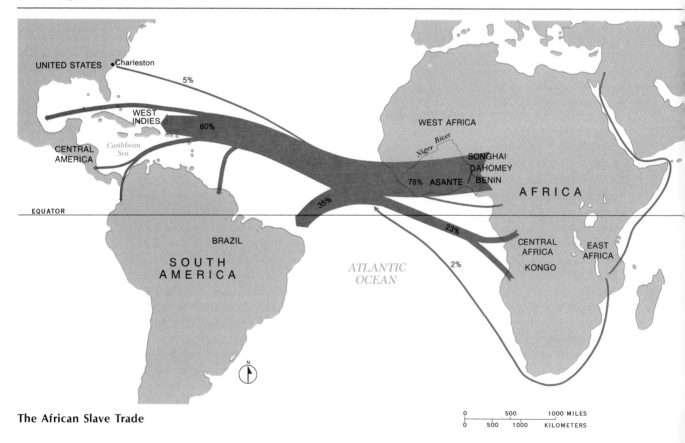

The African Slave Trade

The Beginnings of Slavery

The following court case shows how some black indentured servants were treated like slaves early in colonial history.

Whereas Hugh Gwyn hath . . . brought back from Maryland three servants formerly run away . . . the court doth therefore order that the said three servants shall receive the punishment of whipping and to have thirty stripes [lashes on the back] apiece.

One called Victor, a Dutchman, the other a Scotchman called James Gregory, shall first serve out their times with their master according to their indentures, and one whole year apiece after the time of their service is expired . . . and after that service . . . to serve the colony for three whole years apiece.

And the third being a Negro named John Punch shall serve his said master or his assigns for the time of his natural life here or elsewhere.

Adapted from a Virginia court decision, July 1640. Spelling and punctuation modernized.

In the 1600s and 1700s, racial prejudice against blacks eased the English colonists' minds over slavery. The English were not alone in this prejudice. They were part of a general western culture that feared and hated the "different."

Certainly the Africans looked different to the English. Blackness, the English concluded, was surely a curse from God for evil deeds or the sin of not being Christian. For the English "black" already brought to mind a host of sad, unlucky, and evil images: death, Satan, cruelty, murder, disaster. The English did not analyze their attitudes. Nor did they probably notice or care that Africans regarded the white race as just as strange, and just as likely to represent "evil" when first encountered.

Superior weapons, not logic, determined the question of "superiority" and "inferiority." By the time most English colonists encountered Africans, they were already in chains. The question was settled. And, for most colonists, matters of race and prejudice were far less important than the pressing fact that labor was needed.

The Development of Slave Codes

At first African captives were treated more or less like indentured servants. But, as the court case at left shows, they were not treated as well as white servants even in the early days. By 1662 the colonists had developed laws to ensure the permanent servitude of Africans in their midst. In that year, Maryland made slavery a hereditary, or inherited, condition. The Maryland law declared that a child born of a slave woman was a slave. Thus Marylanders made slavery a caste—a legally established and inherited position within society.

By the 1680s the colonial law books included complex **slave codes** that regulated all aspects of the institution of slavery. For example, they forbade any intermarriage between whites and blacks, and they required slaveholders to discipline their slaves properly. To prevent slave rebellions, most colonies forbade slaves to leave their plantations without passes, to congregate in groups, or to handle and carry weapons. Finally, the slave codes made clear that the slaves would suffer if they resisted their fate. Disobedience could bring whippings, brandings, maimings, and even death. The slaves had no rights at all. The slave codes completed the process of turning Africans into "chattels," or property.

The Horrors of the Middle Passage

Most of the slaves brought to America were West Africans who lived between the coast and about 100 miles inland. They were captured for the slave traders by coastal tribes, who were supplied guns and ammunition by the Europeans.

The Atlantic crossing for the slave was a "**middle passage**" between all that was familiar and all that was foreign. The horrors of this middle passage disturbed the consciences of few white men or women until the 1800s. On the slave ships, men, women, and children were chained together in twos, packed into spaces 5 feet by 16 inches, in holds crammed as full as possible. No one could stand, and even lying down fully extended was difficult. People had to curl up into "spoons," sleeping head to toe along the hard planks of their ocean prisons. Fresh air and exercise on the deck were allowed only at the two meals. When weather was bad, the slaves remained below in the stale air and dark dampness. Without decent sanitation, fresh food, or fresh air, many—sometimes half or more—became ill and died. Their bodies were tossed overboard, at times chained to a man or woman still alive. Beatings and attacks on the women were commonplace. All that could be said of the white servants' nightmare journeys was true here, and more. And, the Africans were headed for a lifetime of servitude.

Resistance to Slavery

Many slaves rebelled against their fate. They committed suicide on board ship. They ran away when they reached the shore. They mutinied.

The fear of rebellion haunted the white slaveholders. By 1750, 40% of the population of Virginia and 75% of the population of South Carolina were enslaved. Even in New York City, where 14% were slaves, the fear of rebellion was ceaseless.

There were enough riots and rebellions to keep those fears alive. In 1739, Cato's Conspiracy at the Stono, South Carolina, plantation left 44 blacks and 30 whites dead. In New York, the rumor of a black plot in 1741 led to the conviction of 101 blacks, of whom 18 were hung and 13 were burned alive.

There was, however, little chance of real freedom even for the most determined slave. Some fugitives found refuge in Indian villages. Most rebels, however, had nowhere to go once they were free of the plantation. Color was the badge of slavery, and few whites would protect a runaway slave. Few whites were even sympathetic to the slave's plight. In the 1720s, some Quakers began to feel that their belief in the equality of human souls must include Africans as well as whites. A Quaker, John Woolman, wrote the first antislavery pamphlet in 1762. But these voices were dim, and were rarely heard among the many satisfied slaveholders.

Free Blacks in Colonial Times

Even for the black man or woman who was freed by a slaveholder, life was difficult in the colonies. Free blacks were "segregated," that is, separated from white society as much as possible. They lived in black sections of New York, Boston, or Philadelphia. They worshiped separately or in "black pews" in the white-run churches. Black

Phillis Wheatley   *Benjamin Banneker*

men could not vote, even if they met the property qualifications. Nor could blacks testify in court against whites. Thus, the free community of blacks lived everywhere on the margins of the white-dominated society.

Despite all the barriers that free blacks faced, some made important contributions to the colonial culture and economy. **Benjamin Banneker**, a free black from Maryland, was a noted astronomer, a mathematician, and a surveyor—a man of practical sciences in a society that valued them greatly. **Phillis Wheatley**, formerly a Boston slave, became a distinguished poet in her new language. And **Paul Cuffe**, a Massachusetts sea captain who became a wealthy merchant, financed schools for free blacks and helped them gain positions in the otherwise unfriendly world around them.

SECTION 4 REVIEW

Identify: apprenticeship, indentured servant, slave codes, middle passage, Benjamin Banneker, Phillis Wheatley, Paul Cuffe

Main Ideas

1. How did the labor shortage benefit free workers?
2. What were some legal and illegal ways that workers became indentured? What rights did they have?
3. Why did African slavery become established in the colonies? What conditions made it almost impossible for blacks to escape from slavery?
4. Compare the indentured servants' and the slaves' voyages to America.

5. SOCIAL MOBILITY

A wealthy English visitor to America in 1760 might feel a sense of confusion about the colonies. Much about the colonial world looked familiar: its lively towns, its rich farmland, and the bustling seaports. Yet there was something peculiar about these colonies.

No Aristocracy

The first shock for our visitor might have been the absence of a genuine aristocracy. In England, an upper class of nobles was established by law. Family background, not wealth, entitled them to occupy the upper ranks of their society. Aristocracy, like slavery, was a caste.

There were no aristocrats in America because noblemen and women did not choose to emigrate to the colonies. And the colonists did not create a new aristocracy to fill their places. Here, wealth, not birth, determined a family's status.

A Chance for Wealth

A man or woman's success could erase his or her early beginnings as a servant, laborer, or even convict. This sense of opportunity made the laboring classes behave very differently in America than in England. American servants often seemed brash and even impolite, as if being a servant or a paid laborer were only a temporary situation.

Few Americans actually went from "rags to riches." Most went from poor to middle class. Famous success stories, like that of Andrew Lamb, are exceptions. Lamb was sentenced to be hanged in England but was "dumped" in the colonies instead. After seven years as an indentured servant in the tobacco fields of Virginia, he moved on to Philadelphia, where he made a good living as a craftsman. Next he moved to New York City, where no one knew of his criminal past. Here he married a wealthy woman, settled into a comfortable mercantile career, and saw his son become a leading local politician.

No Rich Idlers

The English visitor would also no doubt have been amazed to see what life at the top was like. In England, a "gentleman" would never do work. But on the magnificent Livingston Manor in New York colony, the "lord of the manor" rode from one tenant farm to another, checked the operation of the manor's gristmill, and advised the workers at the manor ironworks. In Virginia, the men and women of the Lee family, with servants and slaves to do their bidding, nevertheless put in a dawn-to-dusk day of supervision. Rich people did not pretend to be ignorant of how they got their wealth—in the colonies, they talked endlessly of prices, crops, and the art of buying and selling.

A New Kind of Society

What the visitor was observing was a society based on social mobility. **Social mobility** is the opportunity to move both upward and downward through the layers of a society's economy. This mobility did not result in economic or social equality. Like the English, Americans were divided into the rich, the "middling," and the "mean," or poor. Yet colonial society was unique in allowing men and women to accumulate wealth and improve their social position.

Why was there social mobility in the colonies? You may have gathered some clues already. First, few laws prohibited this mobility among free white men. Those that did proved unenforceable. Second, the lands and other resources of the 13 colonies were undeveloped. There was always a frontier, whose potential for profit lay waiting to be tapped. Third, the availability of land made it possible for a family of laborers to become landowners.

Social Barriers

Colonial society did limit sharply who was eligible to compete. You have seen that harsh laws trapped African slaves at the bottom rung of society. In every colony, free blacks and also Indians were kept on the margins of society. Furthermore, laws and discrimination made sex a barrier to equal competition.

Colonial wedding shoes

Although unmarried women or widows could operate businesses or work to support themselves, they were locked out of professions, and severely restricted by custom and unwritten "laws" of proper behavior for females. Most important, no matter how rich or successful, women were blocked from gaining any political power. Except for a few rare exceptions, only men had the vote.

In addition, economic conditions limited mobility for many white males, especially in the older, more settled parts of the colonies. In coastal Virginia, for example, newly freed indentured servants could not compete with the well-established tobacco planters. In New England, land grew scarce, and the price rose dramatically. In the seaport cities, competition was keen, and inherited wealth gave some merchants an edge over others. Here there was a growing population of poor people. In 1750, for example, 6% of Boston's population was on public charity. In Philadelphia, public almshouses (homes for very poor people) were an ordinary sight.

By 1760, the gap between rich and poor had widened in the colonies. But it was still small compared to England, where nobles lived in splendor while a third of the people starved.

Colonial society was thus a contradictory society. It slammed the door on huge groups within it. Yet, for its time and place in the larger western world, the American colonial society was unique in creating opportunities for many poor and landless people.

Americans Share Middle-Class Values

In 1760 the colonists would strike the English visitor as decidedly middle class. Except for slaves, most of the colonists were members of the "middling" ranks. But more importantly, the rich had risen out of the middle class and the poor looked forward to joining it. Thus colonists of all classes shared in common certain middle-class values, or attitudes: One was the distaste for idleness, even among the very rich. Another was the belief in reward for work and talent. A third was the belief that the law should never interfere with a white man's right to move up the colonial social ladder. As you'll see in the next chapter, colonists were willing to fight any group that tried to pass such laws.

Detail from a painting of the Pennsylvania farm of the Twining family as it looked in 1787

SECTION 5 REVIEW

 Identify: social mobility

Main Ideas
1. Why was there no aristocracy in the colonies?
2. What conditions made it possible for poor white immigrants to become richer in the colonies?
3. What social barriers prevented blacks, Indians, and women from competing on an equal basis with white male colonists?
4. Describe three "middle-class" values that united free Americans of all classes—rich, "middling," or poor.

CHAPTER 4 REVIEW

Key Terms
Explain the meaning of each of the following terms:

subsistence economy
Triangular Trades
mercantilism
Navigation Acts
commercial farmers
Pennsylvania Dutch
Scots-Irish
Iron Act
Tidewater

primogeniture
Carolina Low Country
back country
Piedmont
apprenticeship
indentured servant
slave codes
middle passage
social mobility

Reviewing the Main Ideas
Section 1
1. Explain how colonists in New England were able to create wealth from sparse resources.
2. How did the Navigation Acts affect New Englanders and other colonists?

Section 2
1. Why did the middle colonies become a region of commercial farming?
2. Why were immigrants attracted to Pennsylvania? Why did they avoid New York and New Jersey?
3. How did trade to and from cities like Philadelphia, New York, and Wilmington help create an "American" consciousness?

Section 3
1. What were the major cash crops in the southern colonies?
2. Describe briefly life along the coast and back country of the South.
3. What measures did the southern colonists and other colonists take to solve the currency problem?

Section 4
1. Why was there a labor shortage in the colonies? What three solutions to this problem did the colonists develop?

2. Which group(s) benefited from the labor shortage? Which suffered disadvantages? Explain your answers.
3. Describe the hardships that indentured servants and slaves encountered on their voyages to America.

Section 5
1. What conditions made social mobility possible for many poor white colonists?
2. What barriers made social mobility difficult for some groups?

Special History Skills:
Making Graphs
Graphs can show at a glance statistics and relationships. There are many different kinds of graphs.

A pie or circle graph can show how the parts of a whole are divided. A family budget, for example, could be illustrated on a circle graph.

A line graph can show changes over time, like changes in population or income between 1700 and 1760.

A bar graph makes comparisons easy. Populations of colonies or countries could be compared on a bar graph.

A line or bar graph is drawn on two perpendicular lines called axes. The horizontal axis usually shows time or items. The vertical axis usually shows value. To make a circle graph, divide a circle into wedge-shaped parts that correspond to the size of the portion.

Now graph the following information:
1. In the 1600s, 50% of all white colonists came to America as indentured servants.
2. In 1760, about 20% of the colonial population were slaves.
3. In 1760, Philadelphia's population was 19,000; Boston's was 16,000; New York City's was 14,000; and Charleston's was 8,000.

Other Skill Activities
1. Famous black colonists
   Find out more about the lives of one of the following colonists: Benjamin Banneker, Phillis Wheatley, Paul Cuffe.
2. A letter to friends
   You are a New England villager visiting a cousin on a large rice plantation in South Caro-

lina. Write a letter to your family at home describing similarities and differences in climate, topography, settlement, crops, and lifestyle.

3. A frontier map

Trace the left-hand map on page 97. Shade the 1760 frontier area. Label important mountain ranges and rivers. Provide an arrow pointing north. In which direction will the frontier move in the next century?

Thinking Critically

1. The Navigation Acts, the Iron Act, and the currency shortage were all products of mercantilist policies. Explain why opposition to them would help link the colonies together.
2. Why do you think there was so little opposition among white colonists to the growth of slavery in the colonies?
3. America had a frontier for 300 years of its history. How do you think this shaped our society and attitudes?
4. Do you think that most Americans still believe in the three middle-class values of hard work, just rewards, and no government interference in a person's attempt to get rich? Explain.
5. A basic concept in the study of economics is the idea of "scarcity"—no one can have everything that he or she wants. The colonial economy illustrates the idea of scarcity. What was scarce in the colonies? What was plentiful? How did colonists shape their economy in response to scarce and plentiful resources? Are the same resources scarce and plentiful in America today?

Further Reading

Lillie Patterson. *Benjamin Banneker: Genius of Early America.* Abingdon, 1978. Biography of 18th-century astronomer, mathematician, biologist, surveyor, author, and musician.

William S. Sachs and Ari Hoogenboom. *The Enterprising Colonials: Society on the Eve of the Revolution.* Argonaut, 1965. Examines colonial society from the vantage point of the colonial businessman.

Edwin Tunis. *Colonial Living.* World Publishers, 1957. Accompanied by numerous drawings, this book explains the everyday life and objects of colonial America.

TEST YOURSELF

WRITE YOUR ANSWERS ON A SEPARATE SHEET OF PAPER.

Matching

Write the letter of the term that best matches each description below.

1. system that uses up all it produces
2. laws regulating all aspects of slavery in the colonies
3. frontier area; also called the Piedmont
4. form of vocational training in skilled colonial trades
5. voyage of slaves from Africa to America
6. practice of leaving land to eldest son
7. people who worked without wages to pay off cost of voyage to America
8. economic theory based on the view that a country should sell more than it buys
9. largest city in the 13 colonies in 1760
10. elegant southern colonial port

a. middle passage
b. Iron Act
c. primogeniture
d. apprenticeship
e. social mobility
f. slave codes
g. mercantilism
h. subsistence economy
i. Charleston
j. New York City
k. indentured servants
l. Philadelphia
m. currency problem
n. Triangular Trades
o. back country

Locations

Match the letters on the map with the places listed below.

1. Chesapeake Bay
2. Massachusetts Bay
3. James River
4. Connecticut River
5. Delaware River

Chapter 5

A MATURING SOCIETY

I n the early years of settlement, the colonists thought of themselves in Old World terms, as Britons, Dutch, or Germans transplanted to a new environment. Later, their sons and daughters identified themselves by their colony— as Rhode Islanders, Virginians, or New Yorkers. Few, if any, of these men and women would have described themselves as "Americans." Yet during the 18th century, the colonists were becoming just that: Americans. Puritans and southern planters, Scots-Irish pioneers and Quaker merchants were slowly forging an American character and an American culture.

In Chapter 4, you saw how the economy of the colonies linked men and women all along the eastern seacoast, creating a growing interdependence among farmers, merchants, and planters. In this chapter you will see how trends in religion, education, and government helped form this new American identity. Even certain problems— religious and political tensions, for example— would help create an American way of looking at life and dealing with its difficulties.

Sections in This Chapter
1. Religious Toleration Develops
2. A Talented Colonial Leadership
3. The Rise of the Colonial Assemblies
4. 150 Years of Warfare

Opposite: The first Hebrew grammar book published in America (1735). Colonial college students studied ancient history in the original Hebrew, Greek, and Latin. Soon they would apply these lessons about struggles for freedom and justice and the nature of governments to their own lives.

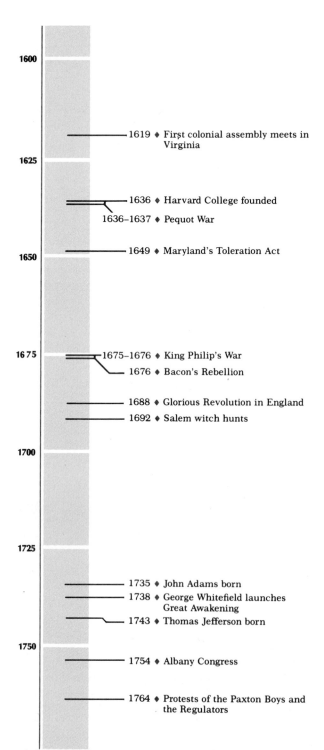

1600

1619 ◆ First colonial assembly meets in Virginia

1625

1636 ◆ Harvard College founded
1636–1637 ◆ Pequot War

1650

1649 ◆ Maryland's Toleration Act

1675

1675–1676 ◆ King Philip's War
1676 ◆ Bacon's Rebellion

1688 ◆ Glorious Revolution in England
1692 ◆ Salem witch hunts

1700

1725

1735 ◆ John Adams born
1738 ◆ George Whitefield launches Great Awakening
1743 ◆ Thomas Jefferson born

1750

1754 ◆ Albany Congress

1764 ◆ Protests of the Paxton Boys and the Regulators

1. RELIGIOUS TOLERATION DEVELOPS

In the summer of 1692, in the small community of Salem Village, Massachusetts, 9-year-old Betty Parrish and her 11-year-old cousin Abigail Williams began to suffer terrifying nightmares. Soon, they wore a dazed and worried look as they did their household chores. Their troubles seemed to be contagious, for several of their friends began to suffer the same troubled sleep. The girls, seven in all, grew steadily worse. They ate little, slept little, and in their waking hours they cried out that "spirits" were taunting and attacking them. Their strange behavior led the local minister to conclude that the Devil himself had come to Massachusetts.

The girls blamed their condition on the Parrish family slave, Tituba. Tituba, they said, had the power to bewitch them. When the West Indian woman was questioned, she shocked the authorities by freely admitting to the practice of voodoo and black magic. But, Tituba added, she was hardly the only witch in town. With fear and fury, New England's most important judges and ministers began the **Salem witch hunts.**

Within six months, over 100 Puritans all over Massachusetts Bay Colony had been condemned as devil worshipers and witches. Twenty were executed, among them a kind and gentle woman named Rebecca Nurse and a minister, George Burroughs. One elderly man had died denying the charge, but a 5-year-old child, Dorcas Good, had confessed to witchcraft. The witch-hunters soon went too far, however, when they accused the most highly respected people in the community of witchcraft, including Lady Phips, the wife of the governor. People were appalled and began to doubt the accusations. In December 1692, Governor Phips, who had been in England, returned to Massachusetts and forbade any further witch hunts.

Only a generation later, Massachusetts Puritans would find it unbelievable that such an event as the witch hunt had taken place within their church. They no longer believed in themselves as a special people with a religious mission. And they certainly no longer believed in demons, witches, and black magic.

Religion had changed in Massachusetts. In fact, it had changed throughout the English-speaking world. The Salem witch hunt, with its religious intensity and its vision of an earthly battle between good and evil, was part of a tradition that English people everywhere were beginning to reject. Almost two centuries of religious warfare and persecution were ending in Europe and in England. And as the struggle to impose one religion on all the people ceased, the belief in "witches, devils, and demons" also seemed to die.

The Causes of Religious Toleration

As early as the 1660s, English rulers like King Charles II began to worry less about how people worshiped and more about the peace and prosperity that religious toleration could bring. Charles was a Catholic, but he welcomed Protestants and Jews into his kingdom if they were hard-working and loyal to England.

After the Glorious Revolution of 1688, England's new Protestant rulers, William and Mary, made toleration legal. The **Toleration Act of 1689** marked the beginning of a new era: English men and women could worship as they pleased.

In America, however, belief in freedom of religion was *already* a tradition. In 1634, **Roger Williams** had declared that "forced worship" was false worship. The laws of Rhode Island reflected this opinion, and there was complete freedom of religion in that colony.

Quakers also generally believed in religious freedom, and the Quaker colonies of West Jersey and Delaware did not impose religious laws on their colonists. However, in Pennsylvania and East Jersey, Jews and other non-Christians could not vote or hold office.

Jews had first begun to settle in the colonies in 1654, when 23 Jewish colonists arrived in New Amsterdam. By the time of the Revolution, there were about 2,500 Jews in the 13 colonies, mainly in Newport, New York, Philadelphia, Charleston, and Savannah.

From the very beginnings of settlement, few colonies could afford to turn settlers away because of their religious beliefs. Recall the serious labor shortage described in Chapter 4. Massachusetts was the only exception to this rule because a steady flow of English Puritans kept the Massachusetts population growing for several decades. Thus, in 1660, Mary Dyer, a Quaker, could still be

Touro Synagogue in Newport, Rhode Island, dedicated in 1763, is the oldest in America.

hanged in Boston for entering the colony to protest the persecution of other Quakers.

But Maryland was more typical of the colonial world. Here the Roman Catholic proprietor, **Cecil Calvert,** fearing that the Protestant majority in the colony would ban Roman Catholic practices, supported the passage of a **Maryland Toleration Act** in 1649. The act provided that all who believed in the Trinity, both Catholics and Protestants alike, could practice their religion in the colony. However, the goal of the act was to maintain peace in the colony, not to promote toleration. Thus the law imposed harsh penalties upon those who did not support the established view of God and religion.

Though Maryland and the other colonies remained overwhelmingly Protestant, on the eve of the Revolution about 25,000 Roman Catholics lived in English America. Throughout the 1700s, the 13 colonies boasted an almost dazzling variety of religions. There were Anglicans, of course, and in New England, Puritan Congregationalists. But there were also Quakers, Dutch and German Reformed, Baptists, Roman Catholics, Jews, Lutherans, Presbyterians, Mennonites, Schwenkfeldians, Dunkers, and Anabaptists. No group was ever large enough to dominate the others. Therefore, toleration was a practical fact.

Quaker meeting house

The Decline of Established Churches

Religious toleration was not, however, the same thing as the "separation of church and state." In colonial times, the "separation of church and state" meant that no established church was given legal status. An **established church** is an official religion. In 9 of the 13 colonies, every citizen had to pay taxes for the upkeep of the established church and the wages of its ministers. In Virginia, Georgia, Maryland, the Carolinas, and New York, the established church was the Church of England. In Massachusetts, Connecticut, and New Hampshire, the Puritan Congregational Church was the official church.

By the 1750s, however, protests against paying taxes to support any single church were already strong. In almost every colony with an established church, the other religious groups had already won or were in the process of winning their battle to be treated equally under the law.

A Falling Away from Religion

Religious freedom was also winning support in America because of religious apathy (lack of interest). In 1720, most colonists were not members of any church at all. Even in New England, only about one in seven colonists was a member of a church. In the middle colonies, the figure was one in fifteen. In the South, fewer than one in fifteen supported a church.

Why did religion seem so much less important to these colonists than it did to previous genera-

tions? Some of the decline in membership was the result of frontier circumstances. Many new immigrant groups, for example, lived in the back country of the southern colonies without a minister to help them organize a church. But it was also true that many of the older, more settled groups in the colonies concentrated on economic interests rather than on religious ones. Economic opportunity and economic prosperity appeared to be creating a secular (nonreligious) society.

Some Americans Become Deists

In addition, the mid-1700s saw a growth of rational thought. In France, men such as Rousseau and Voltaire developed an outlook on life that became known as **deism.** Strictly speaking, deism was not a religion, since it had no organized church. It was a philosophy toward God, humans, and the organization of society.

Deists believed that God was like a Clockmaker: He made the Universe, then He either abandoned it or simply watched it. In either case, He did not interfere with it. Thus deists did not believe in miracles, did not pray for divine intervention, and did not believe that God influenced what humans did. Humans alone were responsible for their condition.

Deism reflected a growing interest in rational thought and, as such, may also have influenced the decline in church membership. Toward the end of the 1700s, deism was very popular among many of the new nation's leaders, such as George Washington, Thomas Jefferson, and Benjamin Franklin.

The Great Awakening

Changes in the churches themselves may have helped to explain their declining membership. Church services were more formal, less emotional, more intellectual and ceremonial than they had been in the 1600s. The original Calvinist notion of salvation by God's grace had been softened even in the Puritan and Presbyterian churches. Now, good works, or moral behavior, were stressed.

This emphasis on moral behavior rather than on the emotional search for God's grace suited the well-educated and the prosperous. But many of the poorer and less educated people felt that the church did not offer them the emotional fulfillment that Protestantism had once offered. All this would change suddenly in the 1730s and 1740s. For a brief moment, religious intensity would be reborn, and a **Great Awakening** of religious feelings would sweep across the colonies.

The roots of this Great Awakening were planted as early as 1720. In that year, a young German minister came to the middle colonies. Theodore Frelinghuysen was a powerful and emotional preacher, quite unlike the colonial ministers of the day. While most ministers reasoned calmly with their congregation, Frelinghuysen startled and aroused his audience with the importance of saving their souls. Soon, Frelinghuysen had a following of like-minded ministers. Men such as William Tennent and his fiery son, Gilbert, brought emotional intensity back to their Presbyterian services. Their appeal to faith, not good works or reason, was called an "evangelical approach."

Even among the graduates of Yale, there were some who began to doubt if the "head" was the only gateway to the soul. The brilliant young Puritan minister **Jonathan Edwards** was one such man. He shocked his fellow ministers in 1731 by criticizing their preaching methods. In 1734–1735 Edwards led a revival among the people of Northampton, Massachusetts. He drew hundreds of people back to the church with terrifying sermons reminding them that they were "sinners in the hands of an angry God," apt to be struck down at any moment, perhaps to spend their immortal days in a fiery hell.

In 1738, the Methodist evangelical minister, **George Whitefield,** came to preach in the colonies. The Great Awakening had begun in earnest. Whitefield was a naturally gifted orator. He was such a persuasive preacher that even the deist Benjamin Franklin once rose to his feet with excitement as Whitefield spoke. George Whitefield preached the traditional Calvinist notion that men and women were saved by God's grace alone rather than by their own good behavior. But

Christening a baby. From a book of sketches by Lewis Miller, a German immigrant.

where once the Puritans had said that only a few people were chosen to be saved, Whitefield assured the thousands who heard him that God would "open the Gates of Heaven" to them all.

The men who continued Whitefield's work when he left were a new breed of ministers. They were often men of humble backgrounds, without much education. They could speak to the poorer colonists in their own language and on their own terms. There was a democratic undercurrent, therefore, to the Great Awakening.

By the 1760s the intensity of the Great Awakening had faded, but the revival of religious interest was seen in the growth of church membership in the colonies. Between 1740 and 1780, membership rose 470% among Baptists, 310% among Presbyterians, and 290% in the Dutch and German Reformed Churches.

In some cases, the results of the Great Awakening were divisions within churches, especially in New England, where theological disputes became quite bitter, dividing the religious community into people who called themselves "New Lights" and those who called themselves "Old Lights." Later, the more liberal-minded "Old Lights" would develop into Unitarians.

The Great Awakening also was the thrust behind the founding of several colleges, including Princeton, Rutgers, and Dartmouth. And, because the Great Awakening spread throughout the colonies, it helped unify the colonists in opposition to things English, including the Anglican Church and those who supported it.

SECTION 1 REVIEW

Identify: Salem witch hunts, Toleration Act of 1689, Roger Williams, Cecil Calvert, Maryland Toleration Act (1649), established church, deism, Great Awakening, Jonathan Edwards, George Whitefield.

Main Ideas
1. Give two reasons why religious toleration quickly became an American tradition.
2. Why did many colonists call for an end to the established churches?
3. Why did colonists tend to be less religious in the 1700s than in the 1600s?
4. How did the Great Awakening affect colonial society?

2. A TALENTED COLONIAL LEADERSHIP

As individual personalities, John Adams and Thomas Jefferson were worlds apart. Adams was short, stocky, bursting with nervous energy. Jefferson was tall, lanky, slow-moving, and deliberate. Adams had a fierce desire for fame. Jefferson seemed modest and retiring. Adams made few friends and many enemies. Jefferson was liked by almost everyone who knew him. Adams was a man of action. Jefferson was an intellectual.

Despite these differences, the two men were alike in very important ways. They became members of an outstanding American political leadership that Jefferson himself called an "aristocracy of talent."

Education in the Colonies
Jefferson and Adams were both products of an American education. As a New Englander, Adams came from an educational system almost as old as Massachusetts itself. Harvard College was founded in 1636. Soon after, a system of public schools was begun, because Puritans considered education a defense against evil. In 1647, Massachusetts passed a law requiring every town with 50 households to provide a teacher of reading and writing. Every town with 100 households had to set up a Latin grammar school for boys going on to college.

In the 1700s, New England education put far less stress on religion. But if John Adams read fewer sermons in his school books, he was not spared the long and tiring regimen of education. In the winter months, a New England boy was expected to be at his desk by 6 A.M. and to sit at a grammar lesson or a Latin translation until 11 o'clock. He was back at his desk by 1 P.M. and worked on until 6 o'clock. In the summer, he labored at his studies from dawn to dusk, with only a two-week vacation. A New England boy seemed, in fact, to be in one perpetual state of study.

Jefferson had not trudged to school at daybreak. In the plantation world of the South, young people from wealthy families received an education in their homes. Prosperous families like the Jeffersons hired private tutors. These tutors were often indentured servants imported from England to teach the sons and daughters of the planters how to read, write, do geometry, speak French, play the harpsichord, and dance. In the middle colonies, church-run schools operated by Quakers, Anglicans, Jews, the Dutch Reformed Church, and other sects were the rule.

In none of the middle or southern colonies was there public education. Poorer children learned their reading, arithmetic, and writing in private **dame schools** (combination day-care and elementary schools), as apprentices, in night schools for working people in the seaport cities, or from their mothers and fathers. The literacy rate is not known, but the majority of free Americans probably did learn to read.

Just when John Adams and Thomas Jefferson were about to go to college, the girls of their families found their education at an end. Not all 18th-century men believed, as the old Puritan leader John Winthrop had, that too much reading could cause a woman to go insane. But most colonial fathers did think that the female brain was different—weaker and unsuited to serious study.

Occasionally a girl's desire to study was indulged. In Massachusetts, John Adams' friend, Mercy Otis, read beside her brother as he studied. Even when James Otis went to college, he sent home his reading assignments and his class notes to his sister. Mercy Otis Warren later became a famous poet and novelist, as well as the new American nation's first historian. In New York, Governor Cadwallader Colden allowed his daughter, Jane, to become a "bookish" woman. Jane Colden grew up to be a leading colonial botanist. But these two educated women were exceptions to the rule.

College Life in the 1700s

Only the sons of the well-to-do went on to college. Few parents could afford to pay the £150 that five years at Harvard, Yale, or King's College (later Columbia) would cost. College was a dividing line, therefore, between the elite and the ordinary colonist. The boys usually entered college at 15 or 16, several years earlier than most college students today.

Girl with hornbook, 1661. A hornbook is a thin sheet of animal horn attached to a wooden paddle. It was used to teach children the alphabet.

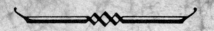

FROM THE ARCHIVES

A Tutor on a Virginia Plantation

The following is from a letter by Philip Fithian, tutor to the Carter family at Nomini Hall in 1773–1774. Mr. Carter was a councilor in the Virginia legislature.

[Mr Carter] has two sons, and one Nephew; the oldest Son is turned of seventeen, and is reading Salust [a Roman poet] and the greek grammar; the others are about fourteen, and in english grammar and Arithmetic. He has besides five daughters which I am to teach english, the eldest is turned of fifteen, and is reading the spectator [an English periodical]; she is employed two days in every week in learning to play the Forte-Piana, and Harpsicord —The others are smaller, and learning to read and spell.

[Mr] and Mrs Carter have a manner of instructing and dealing with children far superior, I may say it with confidence, to any I have ever seen. . . . The children are more kind and complaisant to the servants who constantly attend them than we are to our superiors in age and condition. Mr Carter has an overgrown library of Books of which he allows me the free use. It consists of a general collection of law books, all the Latin and Greek Classicks, vast numbers of Books on Divinity chiefly by writers who are of the established Religion; he has the works of almost all the late famous writers, as Locke, Addison, Young, Pope, Swift, Dryden, &c., in Short, Sir, to speak moderately, he has more than eight times your number—His eldest Son, who seems to be a Boy of genius and application is to be sent to Cambridge University, but I believe will go through a course either in Philadelphia or Princeton College first.

From Philip Fithian's letter to Reverend Enoch Green, December 1, 1773.

At college, the young colonist learned rhetoric, geometry, astronomy, and natural science. He studied logic, ethics, and metaphysics. Finally, he pored over ancient history for its lessons, reading it in the original Hebrew, Greek, or Latin.

Despite the full day of classes and the long nights of study, some New England college boys found time for riots, rowdiness, and general misbehavior. Though John Adams was not interested in joining in the campus food riots, some of his Harvard classmates engaged in all-night gambling and drinking bouts. Life at William and Mary, Jefferson's alma mater, was less rowdy. But at King's College, the young Alexander Hamilton joined his classmates in chasing the school president through the streets of New York City.

The embattled college professors did manage to educate these young men, however. Colonial orators such as James Otis came out of Harvard's rhetoric classes. Fine political theorists such as William Smith, Jr., and Thomas Jefferson were college products. Each year young men graduated with a knowledge of Jewish history, with its examples of covenants, legal justice, and struggles for freedom, and of Greek and Roman history, with their examples of tyrants and republics.

An Elite Linked by Friendship and Marriage

By the eve of the American Revolution there were eight American colleges: Harvard, William and Mary, Yale, the University of Pennsylvania, the College of New Jersey (Princeton), Brown, King's College (Columbia), and Dartmouth. These schools created an elite group of literate and sophisticated colonial leaders. And they also helped create a colonial network of friendships, bringing together the sons of North Carolina planters, Massachusetts merchants, and New Jersey shippers. Their five years together were not easily forgotten.

Friendship was not the only personal link among the colonial leaders. There was also the connection of marriage. During the 18th century, family ties began to crisscross the colonial world. News about births, deaths, and other family events flew from the pens of daughters of Virginia and Maryland, now wives and mothers living in Rhode Island and Connecticut. In a world of large families and strong family loyalties, these connections were important links joining the leaders of all the colonies.

An Elite with Legal Training

Thomas Jefferson and John Adams were both members of a new and important profession: the legal profession. Becoming a lawyer was actually a new career choice in the mid-1700s. For almost 100 years, colonists had felt no need for full-time lawyers. Colonial law was simple and much more flexible than the formal legal system of England. There were few trained judges, and citizens brought their own lawsuits and acted in their own defense. It was an age of amateur lawyers.

But by the mid-1700s, the American economy had outgrown the simple frontier approach to the law. Business transactions had become too complex for amateurs. More and more colonists were coming face to face with the complicated English trade laws and navigational acts. Merchants and sea captains in seaport cities needed skilled lawyers to defend them when the English Board of Trade accused them of smuggling or breaking some new trade regulation.

Therefore, the professional lawyer made his appearance. Colonists traveled to England to study law at the London Inns of Court, then returned to teach others the "mysteries of the craft." Young law students like John Adams and Thomas Jefferson might have been momentarily overwhelmed by English law, with its "codes, pandects, digests, institutes, reports, entries, commentaries, actions, and pleas." But they were also impressed by the beauty of English legal theory, by the procedures for fair trial and the protection of property, and by the tradition of rights and liberties upon which the English formal law was based.

By the 1760s law and the intellectual approach to problems it encouraged were another link between the leaders of the colonial world. In almost every wealthy family, one son was a member of the legal profession. For example, William Livingston, the New York City lawyer, was related to the Livingston manor lords, to Livingston merchants, and to Livingston government officials. In the plantation society, men who were mainly tobacco or rice planters found the study of the law a handy skill to keep in the family. Not surprisingly, most colonial leaders found a legal education a great help in politics. It was no accident that debates in the colonial governments on the eve of the Revolution were like carefully reasoned courtroom arguments.

The Habit of Command

Colonial leaders also shared in common what they called **"the habit of command."** These men were experienced in the management of large plantations, businesses, and trading firms. They were skilled problem-solvers, excellent organizers, and self-confident managers. They were accustomed to being listened to, and they took their responsibilities seriously.

Equally important, they were familiar with the demands of political office and the local problems

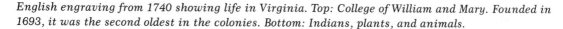

English engraving from 1740 showing life in Virginia. Top: College of William and Mary. Founded in 1693, it was the second oldest in the colonies. Bottom: Indians, plants, and animals.

LIFE IN AMERICA

THE DAILY LIVES OF ORDINARY COLONISTS

While members of the colonial elite were practicing law or running their businesses and plantations, ordinary colonists were going about their daily tasks.

Life on the Family Farm

Most colonial Americans made their living on the farm. Here, husband and wife, daughters and sons, were all important members of the family work force. Men and boys worked in the fields, sowing, planting, and harvesting the crops. Women and girls worked in the home and the dairy, in the orchard and the garden.

Housekeeping was a constant round of vital activities: feeding the poultry, milking the cows, tending the vegetable garden, making butter and cheese, slaughtering pigs and making sausage, preserving meat for the winter, dipping candles, making soap, tending beehives for sweet fresh honey, cooking, baking, laundering, and sewing. The most tiring but necessary of women's chores was cloth making. Teenage daughters bemoaned their fate, for they were assigned the tasks of combing, carding, spinning, and weaving for the family.

The Importance of the Fireplace

The typical colonial home had one room, and the focus of that room was the fireplace. Not just a cozy attraction on a wintry evening, the hearth had to be fired 24 hours a day, 365 days a year. It provided heat for cooking; dryness for preserving food; warmth for sleeping; heat for candlemaking; and light for reading, sewing, and embroidering.

How the Colonists Cooked

Most fireplaces were bigger than the ornamental ones we know today. In the average home the hearth was about 3 feet high, 3 feet deep, and often 10 feet wide. The bake oven was an opening in the brick wall, either at the back of the hearth or to the side. It was covered with an iron door. After hot embers from the fireplace had heated the bricks of the oven, a woman would usually test the readiness of the oven by sticking her bare arm in it. If she could stand to keep her arm in the oven for 30 seconds, but no longer, the oven was ready for the bread, beans, or pies. But first the ashes had to be shoveled out of the oven and stored in the ash pit, an opening beneath the oven. Then the cook would hoist into place the oven's iron door. As if that were not hazardous enough, one must remember that all this shifting of hot ashes and embers was done by women wearing floor-length skirts.

Cooking in the fireplace was no easy task either. Meat for roasting was first skewered on a spit then placed on andirons (metal racks). Young children and sometimes dogs were given the task of turning the meat so that it would be evenly cooked. Although this may sound like a Girl Scout cookout, it was not. To preserve meat, the colonists often covered it with a few inches of lard, then wrapped it in greased paper. Sparks and, indeed, flames would often fly.

Cozy but Deadly

If the chimney was not cleaned twice a year, the constant accumulation of greasy soot could catch fire. So, too, could the mortar of the oven bricks. And naturally, if the fire were not properly damped at night, sparks could ignite the herbs hung to dry on the ceiling beams or the apples strung to dry over the fireplace. If someone's cornhusk-stuffed mattress was close by, it too could burst into flame. Thus life in a colonial home could be quite hazardous.

A woman's normal routine included hog butchering.

of government long before they took their seats in the colonial council or assembly. This was because many of the same families had held office in each colony for many generations. Officeholding was often passed from fathers to sons. Therefore the younger men had the opportunity to ask advice from their parent and to gain much knowledge that only experience could provide. There was continuity in American politics because there was a continuity in the leadership.

Informed and Active Citizens
The political leaders in each colony shared another common bond: They governed an informed and politically active people. Although their education was less formal, the free white colonists of the middle and lower classes were interested in politics and learning. In cities like Philadelphia and Boston, artisans and shopkeepers met to discuss history, morality, poetry, and science, as well as politics. By 1750, there were public libraries in Charleston, Newport, New York and other cities. These libraries allowed men and women to borrow books that they could not afford to buy.

The tendency of the average colonist to read improved the general level of conversation, Benjamin Franklin said. It also made America's "common people as intelligent as most foreign gentlemen." More important, Franklin added, reading made the colonists better informed and thus more outspoken in demanding their rights as English citizens.

The presence of an informed public influenced the decisions of colonial leaders everywhere. The leaders in the colonies were trained to believe that they were guardians of the public interest. And the people were quick to remind them of this fact, if the leaders ever forgot their duty.

SECTION 2 REVIEW

Identify: dame schools, "the habit of command"

Main Ideas
1. What was education like for most Americans during the colonial period?
2. Why were college friendships important to communication among the colonies?
3. What were four common characteristics of colonial leaders?
4. How did the citizens influence the leaders?

3. THE RISE OF THE COLONIAL ASSEMBLIES

The English government in 1760 was a remarkable one for its time and place in history. France and Spain were governed by absolute monarchs who ruled by whim rather than by law. Few countries anywhere guaranteed their citizens basic rights. Yet in the 13 English colonies, the colonists lived under the protection of the English constitution and participated in representative government.

As you saw in Chapter 2, the early settlers in Virginia were granted the "rights of Englishmen." The nature of these rights, however, was not well established until after the Glorious Revolution of 1688.

The struggles between Parliament and the monarchy during the 1600s hammered out a basic understanding between the English people and their rulers. After the Puritan Revolt of the 1640s, kings and queens could not rule as absolute monarchs. Lawmaking was reserved to Parliament, which had two houses. The upper house, or House of Lords, represented the English aristocracy. The House of Commons represented the rest of the English people—the middle class and even the ordinary citizens—although the common people had not yet won the right to vote for members of the House of Commons. Thus the English government balanced the interests of royalty, nobility, and the rest of the people.

By the early 1700s, the House of Commons had won for itself two important powers needed to protect the people's interests: Only the House of Commons could pass taxation bills, and it alone controlled the military forces of the nation.

The Puritan Revolt and the Glorious Revolution also provided a new theory of government, the idea of the **social contract** between the rulers and the people. According to this theory, the "contract" required the ruler to protect the property and the lives of the people. In return, the citizens were obliged to be loyal, to pay taxes, and to obey the laws. If the government broke the terms of the social contract, it no longer had the right to govern. In such a case, the people had a right, even a duty, to rebel against that government.

The most influential spokesman for the idea of the social contract was **John Locke,** the philosopher of the Glorious Revolution. According to Locke's *Treatise on Civil Government* (1690), the people also had certain **inalienable rights**, that is, basic rights that could never be taken away. By the early 1700s, the English believed these basic rights included (1) the right to have their representative assembly determine the taxes they must pay; (2) the representative assembly must control the military; (3) every citizen enjoyed the right to a trial by a jury of his or her equals. Taken together, England's government of "balanced powers," the theory of the social contract, and the concept of inalienable rights made the English system the most democratic of its day.

The English System in America

The 3,000-mile journey across the Atlantic may have separated the colonists from English daily life. But the colonists did not for a moment expect to be separated from their English rights and liberties. Thus, each colony developed a system of representative government—a miniature version, in fact, of the English government. But American society was different from England's in some very basic ways, and so, therefore, were these colonial governments.

By 1700, every colony except Pennsylvania had a governor and a bicameral, or two-house, legislature. The upper house was called the council, and the lower house was called the assembly. Pennsylvania had a unicameral, or one-house, legislature.

The colonial governor In the eight royal colonies, the governor was appointed by the king or queen. The governor was responsible for carrying out the monarch's interests and for insuring that colonists obeyed the laws of England. To aid the governor, there was an attorney general and several officials who helped enforce England's navigation laws.

The governor could veto any colonial laws that he believed did not follow English policy. He also had the right to appoint colonial judges and to dismiss the colonial legislature if he felt it had acted improperly.

In Maryland, Pennsylvania, and Delaware, the proprietors appointed the colonial governor. Only in the two self-governing (corporate) colonies of Connecticut and Rhode Island were the governors chosen by the colonial assemblies—and therefore indirectly by the colonists themselves.

The colonial council The colonial councils were similar to the English House of Lords. In most colonies the governors appointed the council members.

The council provided support and advice to the governor. It was expected to protect the interests of England rather than the colony. And, like the English House of Lords, the council was supposed to check the popular will as expressed by the assembly if it became too strong. The council therefore had the power to veto (reject) certain bills the assembly might pass.

Ordinarily, men from the very richest and most prestigious families were chosen for these councils. But unlike the members of the House of Lords, the colonial councilors were not aristocrats; they did not represent a special class that separated them from the assembly members. The councilors were colonists with colonists' concerns.

The colonial assembly Like the English House of Commons, this was the "people's" branch of the government. The men who served in office were not ordinary or "common" men themselves, but they did pledge themselves to represent the ordinary man or woman's best interests.

The first assembly was Virginia's House of Burgesses, which met in 1619. By 1700, all the existing colonies had popularly elected assemblies. In the 1600s, many colonies had religious restrictions on who could vote. As you have seen, this was no longer the case in the 1700s. By then, for white males, property holding was the key to voting rights.

During the 150 years of colonial history, the power of the **colonial assemblies** increased dramatically. These assemblies often began as mere conveniences. They were a practical means of settling local problems, because the proprietors or colony directors were too far away to make quick decisions. The assemblies were convenient, too,

COLONIAL GOVERNMENTS

Royal Colonies

After 1753, Massachusetts, New Hampshire, New York, New Jersey, Virginia, North Carolina, South Carolina, and Georgia were all royal colonies.

A **royal colony** was the property of the **Crown** (the king or queen), who ruled with Parliament according to the laws and needs of England. The Crown's representative in the colony was the royal governor.

The **royal governor**'s job was to enforce English laws. He could veto any laws passed by the local government that ran contrary to English policy. It was his duty to enforce English trade laws and foreign policy.

The Crown appointed the governor and also the colony's attorney general, judges, and customs officials, often on the advice of the royal governor.

The governor appointed the **council**, or upper house of the colonial legislature, except in Massachusetts where the lower house elected the council. This was a tradition left over from Massachusetts' days as a corporate colony. The council was an advisory group of wealthy and prominent local citizens. They advised the governor on local matters since the governor was usually a stranger to the colony. The council could veto certain bills passed by the assembly.

The **assembly**, or lower house, had broad powers to govern local affairs. It raised and distributed tax money, paid the salaries of the royal officials, and governed religious affairs.

The assembly in a royal colony was elected by the **eligible voters**. As a general rule, all free white adult males who were Christians and respectable property owners could vote for the assembly.

English law called for a man to hold 40 shillings worth of property in order to vote. In England, where land was scarce and belonged to the aristocracy, this requirement left most tenant farmers unable to vote. In the colonies, however, there was a great deal of land and few people. Thus landowning was widespread, and voting was too.

In several colonies, some men who did not own land were allowed to vote in town or county elections. But indentured servants, Jews, slaves, free blacks, and women of all classes were barred from political participation.

Proprietary Colonies

Nine colonies began as proprietary colonies, but by the Revolution there were only three: Maryland, Pennsylvania, and Delaware.

A **proprietary colony** was the property of an individual or group of individuals who had been granted American lands by the Crown. The proprietor had the same rights in his colony as the king had in a royal colony. The proprietor was, of course, expected to obey English laws and to follow English policies in trade and foreign affairs.

Like the king, the proprietor usually appointed a **governor** to represent his interests.

The **council** was like the royal colony council. The governor or the proprietor appointed council members.

The **assembly** was like the royal colony assembly. Members were elected by the **eligible voters** of the colony.

Corporate Colonies

Rhode Island and Connecticut were **corporate**, or self-governing, **colonies**. These colonies were created when the Crown approved a charter submitted by the settlers. Thus, the peopling of these colonies came before the colony was official. Virginia and Massachusetts were also once corporate colonies.

In the corporate colonies, the **eligible voters** elected the **governor**, the **council**, and the **assembly**. As in the other two types of English colonies, colonial laws were expected to conform to English laws and policies.

French and Spanish Colonies

The tradition in these countries was a highly centralized bureaucracy of both State and Church. Thus, the political and religious affairs of their colonies were also tightly controlled.

Both Crown and Church sent out officials from the Mother Country, and these officials governed. The colonists had no representative government.

House of Burgesses in Williamsburg, the capital of Virginia

because they won the cooperation of the settlers. The English rulers supported them because they raised local taxes to pay the costs of the colony's royal government. Without assemblies, the ruler would have had to foot the bill for the governor's salary, the judges' salaries, and the general upkeep of colonial administration. Nevertheless, even in the mid-1700s, the kings still regarded the assemblies as temporary conveniences, rather than as legitimate branches of government.

The colonists did not share the kings' views, however. To them, their colonial assembly was like the House of Commons itself—a sacred and vital part of the social contract. During all the 1700s, the assemblies performed many of the same duties as the House of Commons. They raised taxes. They authorized the organization of the militia, or citizen-soldiers, for local defense. This power was like the House of Commons' power over England's armed forces.

How the Colonial Assemblies Won More Power

The assemblies also won other powers through patient and clever manipulation of the colonial governors' weaknesses. Even excellent governors found their jobs difficult. Their detailed instructions seldom met the real needs of the colonies. The king and his advisers could not predict the kinds of problems that might arise in the colony. Thus the colonial governor usually could not outmaneuver the assembly, which could change its political strategy as quickly as the situation demanded. Also, because the governor's salary was paid by the assembly out of local taxes, the colonial leaders could, and very often did, refuse to pay his salary until he surrendered on an issue.

Secondly, the typical governor was not very good or talented or even honest. Few able and experienced men wanted to be stationed in the colonies. For them, this was like being exiled to the hinterlands. The governor, therefore, was probably one of three types. First, he might be a young man without experience but eager to perform well and move on to a post in England. He wanted his term of office in America to be short, peaceful, and easy. He would often allow the assemblymen anything they wanted if they would not argue or cause trouble for him. If they wished to take over the appointment of sheriffs from him,

for example, he did not object. Once such a power had been won, however, the assembly never gave it up.

The second type were men like Lord Culpeper, governor of Virginia, or William Cosby of New York. These men were greedy and came to the colonies to make quick fortunes. They abused their privileges, granting themselves huge tracts of colonial land or special business advantages. Such men could be difficult and heavy-handed, but just as often they could be bribed. Colonial assemblies did not hesitate to award such governors salary "bonuses" if they cooperated with assembly demands.

Finally, a third type of governor was neither ambitious nor corrupt, but only incompetent. Many of these men were appointed as favors to their influential relatives in England. This kind of **patronage**, the granting of offices as a favor, was a common practice in that era. Sometimes the nephew or brother-in-law given the job turned out to be a good administrator. Usually, he did not. But patronage was the oil that greased the bureaucratic machinery of the English government. Such a governor was no match for politically experienced men of the colonial assembly. Few governors of any type were.

The assemblymen lived in the colony and cared deeply about its government's activities. They were, as you have seen, a talented and educated group of men who knew each other and who had worked closely together for many years. Like a well-coached team, they outmaneuvered and outplayed their opponents in the governor's chair. By 1760, the assembly was the most powerful branch of government in every colony.

SECTION 3 REVIEW

 Identify: social contract, John Locke, inalienable rights, colonial assemblies, patronage

Main Ideas
1. How did the political struggles in England in the 1600s benefit the American colonists?
2. What did the English believe were inalienable rights in regard to (a) taxes, (b) the military, and (c) juries?
3. List the reasons why the colonial assembly became the most powerful branch of government in every colony.

4. 150 YEARS OF WARFARE

The colonies were plagued by wars, both Indian wars and wars for empire. They also suffered conflicts between seaboard communities and communities on the frontier. Few colonies escaped bloody and brutal warfare between Indians and settlers. The pattern in each colony was roughly the same. In the beginning, Indians treated the colonists as neighbors and allies in the struggle for power among tribes. Often they helped struggling whites to survive. But tensions mounted as the white population expanded, taking more and more land that the Indians used for farming and hunting.

Indians and settlers had sharply contrasting attitudes toward land ownership. Indians regarded the land in the same way we regard the sea: a tribe or country with the strength to hold a territory has the right to use it, but the area is not usually divided into clearly marked individual plots. The settlers believed in individual land ownership and took over tribal territories permanently. Furthermore, they were land-hungry. Thousands made the Atlantic crossing just to get land, for land was the measure of a European's wealth.

It is difficult to say if any compromise between settlers and Indians would have been possible. Certainly prejudice and misunderstanding stood in the way. Most whites measured the Indians by European standards and values and judged them, like the Africans, to be inferior people.

In the wars that inevitably followed, many colonists lost their lives. But the Indians suffered greater defeats. Not only did warriors fall in battle, but men, women, and children also died from exposure to Old World diseases. The most terrible of these infections—smallpox—swept through Indian villages, killing most it touched. Thus in Virginia alone, the Indian population shrank from an estimated 30,000 in 1600 to a mere 2,000 by 1760. In New England, warfare and disease destroyed entire tribes. In the 1630s, Puritans wiped out almost all the Pequots [pē′kwots] in a vicious war that had about it an air of a religious crusade.

King Philip's War

Although **King Philip's War** was especially fierce, its causes and outcome were typical. By 1675, the white population of New England had grown to more than 50,000. The colonists forced the Indians to obey them and were putting great pressure on the Indians for land.

In the summer of 1675, **Metacomet** [met ə-kom′ət], or King Philip, leader of the Wampanoags, led an attack on Plymouth colony. The threat of white settlers had united Metacomet's people with several other Algonquin tribes. In this bloody conflict some 600 colonists and possibly 3,000 Indians lost their lives, and more than 20 colonial settlements were burned to the ground. But in the end the Indians were defeated. Metacomet was betrayed and shot, and his wife and 9-year-old son were sold into slavery in the West Indies. Sporadic fighting continued for three years, but the power of the Indians in southern New England was broken. Some survivors fled to Canada where they joined with the French.

This struggle between cultures had united some of the Algonquin tribes. It had also temporarily united several New England colonies for defense. King Philip was defeated by the army of the New England Confederation, a defense league formed in 1643 by Massachusetts, Connecticut, Plymouth, and New Haven. The Confederation was the first attempt by American colonies to form a federation. By King Philip's War, however, the Confederation was in decline. It lasted until 1684, when Charles II reorganized some of the colonial governments.

Colonial Rebellions

Indian attacks did not always unite the colonies. In Pennsylvania, as you remember, a disagreement over Indian policy between Quakers and the non-Quakers on the frontier forced the Quaker government to resign. In Virginia, Indian raids

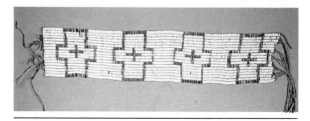

Wampum belt marking Penn's 1683 purchase of SE Pennsylvania from the Delaware Indians

on the frontier led to a major rebellion.

In 1676, farmers on the Virginia frontier called on Governor William Berkeley to defend them from Indian attack. Berkeley refused, for he made a tidy sum each year from the fur trade with the Indians. The farmers then took matters into their own hands. Their leader was a young newcomer to Virginia named Nathaniel Bacon. He was bold, brave, and an instant hero to frontier families in Virginia. When Bacon led a raid against the Indians, Berkeley was furious and declared Bacon a traitor. Tempers soon cooled, and Berkeley dropped these charges. Bacon was, after all, the governor's own nephew. Later, Berkeley would regret his generosity to his relative, for he had not heard the last of Nathaniel Bacon.

Bacon's followers were unhappy about more than Indian matters. They disliked the high taxes they paid and the poor services they received for their money. Demands for roads, new courthouses, and new land offices were not met as quickly as men like Bacon thought they should be. Nor were these "back counties," as they were called, given their fair share of representatives in the colonial government. The population of the back counties grew, but their voice in government did not. Bacon's followers thought that the colonial government, made up of those from the seacoast areas, ignored their demands purposely. In Virginia and in other colonies, these suspicions were often correct.

Bacon's men decided to make war on their own government. They marched on Jamestown and took control of the House of Burgesses. The amazed Governor Berkeley fled town. The rebels promptly voted in a reform program suited to their needs. In the midst of their triumph, however, Nathaniel Bacon caught malaria and died.

The governor's troops soon recaptured the colony, and Berkeley hanged 23 of Bacon's rebels, without allowing them a trial by jury. When King Charles II heard of Berkeley's high-handed action, he dismissed him. "That old fool has hanged more men," Charles was heard to say, "than I have done for the murder of my father."

Bacon's Rebellion was short-lived. But the problems of the colonial back country produced other rebellions. Wherever colonists felt that they were being unfairly treated, they rose up in protest. In 1764, for example, a band of western Pennsylvanians, calling themselves the **Paxton Boys** marched

toward Philadelphia to protest Indian attacks and underrepresentation in the assembly. Benjamin Franklin was sent to calm them down. His assurances that the assembly would agree to many of their demands prevented a rebellion.

The governments of North and South Carolina were less agreeable. In these colonies a movement called the **Regulator Movement** developed in 1764, about the same time as the Paxton Boys. In North Carolina the Regulators were protesting the corrupt and expensive legal machinery in their counties. Legal fees were too high, they said, and there were too many of them. Every time a colonist signed a deed, sold some cattle, or had land surveyed, a host of justices of the peace, lawyers, and court officials demanded money. The government turned a deaf ear to these complaints, and even jailed some of the Regulators.

After angry Regulators committed several acts of violence, Governor Tryon raised an army of 1,200 militiamen in 1771 and attacked the Regulators at the Alamance River. The 2,000 poorly armed backwoods farmers were defeated in two hours, and six of their leaders were then executed. The bitterness in North Carolina ran deep for many years after the Battle of the Alamance. When the American Revolution came, many former Regulators fought with the British against their old enemies from the seaboard counties.

In South Carolina, the Regulators were protesting the lack of local government. They wanted the colonial assembly to pay for courts, sheriffs, and other machinery for law and order in their counties. Like the Paxton Boys, these Regulators believed their troubles stemmed from unequal representation in the assembly. The cry of "no taxation without representation" was not always the complaint of colonists against the Mother Country. It was also the complaint of colonists against colonists in a growing country.

Imperial Wars and the Colonies
Even if there had been no Indian wars and no colonial rebellions, life would not have been peaceful in America. The colonies were pieces in a great game of empire-building, a game that pitted France and Spain against England for over 100 years.

England and France fought four separate wars between 1689 and 1763. Although three of these wars began in Europe, they inevitably reached

American shores. The first war, King William's War, began in 1689 and ended in 1697. Americans participated by waging attacks on Nova Scotia and Florida. In 1702, Queen Anne's War began, and again, New Englanders joined up to fight the French in Canada. The peace treaty ending Queen Anne's War in 1713 increased England's holdings in America, giving it Hudson Bay, Newfoundland, and Acadia (Nova Scotia).

In 1744, war broke out for the third time. King George's War produced a great victory by New England troops, who took the French stronghold of Louisbourg on Cape Breton Island. Colonists were proud and elated, and even the fact that the peace treaty in 1748 made them return the island did not diminish their sense of glory.

These imperial wars meant more to colonial life, however, than uniforms, military honors, and the thrill of conquest. For one thing, they meant that no 18th-century colonist could look back on a lifetime of peace. Every New Englander had a relative or friend who had battled the French. Most Georgians and Carolinians were related to a veteran of attacks by or on the Spanish (allies of the French) in Florida.

The frequent wars also meant a disruption of colonial trade, unemployment, and inflation. Taxes were usually increased to pay for American activity in the wars. Many colonists, therefore, sincerely hoped for peace. But, in the 1750s, the colonial world braced itself for a fourth imperial war (see Chapter 6).

A Call for Union

Both France and England were clearly preparing for a final showdown. This threat of a full-scale French attack on the colonies prompted an intercolonial meeting to discuss defense. This was the first intercolonial congress since the decline of the New England Confederation. In June 1754, delegates from 7 of the 13 colonies attended the **Albany Congress**. Among the delegates were some of the most distinguished colonial leaders of the day. Delegate Benjamin Franklin led the group in calling for a permanent union of the colonies.

Franklin had already begun a campaign to win popular support for the idea of a union. In his *Pennsylvania Gazette* he published a cartoon of a snake cut into several pieces. The snake represented the separate and thus vulnerable colonies. Under the snake was the motto: JOIN OR DIE.

Franklin's cartoon was probably based on the myth of the "snapping snake," which broke into pieces to protect itself, but had to rejoin quickly, or die.

Franklin's plan of union was adopted by the Albany Congress. But not a single colony approved the plan. Why was it so roundly defeated?

Each colonial assembly was jealous of its right to raise taxes, of its powers over western land and Indian affairs, and of its special local interests. Even though the French army was gathering at their borders, the colonial leaders were not yet ready to give over the powers their own assemblies had so painstakingly won.

Only 20 years later, however, the colonies would unite against a common enemy. But it would not be France. And, JOIN OR DIE would be the motto of the American Revolution.

SECTION 4 REVIEW

 Identify: King Philip's War, Metacomet, Bacon's Rebellion, Paxton Boys, Regulator Movement, Albany Congress

Main Ideas

1. What happened to the eastern Indians during the colonial period?
2. Describe briefly the tensions between the frontier farmers and the people of the seaboard counties in (**a**) Virginia, (**b**) Pennsylvania, (**c**) North Carolina, and (**d**) South Carolina.
3. How did the struggle between England and France affect the American colonists?
4. Why did the colonies reject the Albany Plan?

CHAPTER 5 REVIEW

Key Terms

Explain the meaning of each of the following terms:

Salem witch hunts
Toleration Act of 1689
Maryland Toleration Act (1649)
established church
deism
Great Awakening
dame schools
"the habit of command"
social contract
inalienable rights
colonial assemblies
patronage
King Philip's War
Bacon's Rebellion
Paxton Boys
Regulator Movement
Albany Congress

Reviewing the Main Ideas

Section 1

1. Why did religious toleration take hold quickly in the 13 colonies?
2. Why did many colonists call for an end to the established churches? Why did they want to achieve a separation between church and state?
3. How did religious apathy and deism affect religion in the colonies in the 1700s?
4. How did the Great Awakening affect colonial society?

Section 2

1. What was education like for most Americans during the colonial period?
2. How did college life and legal training link colonial leaders?
3. How were ordinary citizens involved in colonial politics?

Section 3

1. How did the political struggles in England during the 1600s benefit the American colonists?
2. Describe the role of the colonial governors, councils, and assemblies.
3. Why did the colonial assemblies become the most powerful branch of government in every American colony?

Section 4

1. What happened to the Indians on the East Coast during the colonial period?
2. Why were the people in the back counties discontented with the colonial governments?
3. How did the wars between England and France affect the American colonists?
4. What was the goal and outcome of the Albany Congress?

Special History Skills:

Comparing Sources of Information

Today we have many more sources of information about political affairs than the colonists had.

(1) Make a list of all such sources of information you can think of that are available to us today.

(2) Divide them into two groups—those which were also available to the colonists, and those which were not.

(3) Star those sources that you think are the most important for an informed citizenry today. Discuss your choices with your class.

Other Skill Activities

1. **Write a letter**

   Write a letter to a colonial student and compare your school day and routine to his or hers.

2. **Attitudes toward land**

   Colonial and Indian attitudes, especially toward land, were very different. Can you think of any other ways besides warfare to resolve this difference of opinion? Write your views in a short essay.

3. **Religious minorities**

   Find out more about one of the religious groups mentioned in this chapter—the Quakers, Catholics, Jews, Lutherans, Mennonites, etc.—during the colonial period.

Thinking Critically

1. In what ways could religious toleration help colonial unity?
2. Monarchs based their right to govern partly on tradition. On what ideas did the colonial elite probably base their leadership?
3. How did the education of leaders and common citizens contribute to colonial unity?
4. How could John Locke's theory of the social contract be used to justify revolution? What are the weaknesses of his theory?
5. Why can the political struggles in England during the 1600s be considered part of "American" history?

Further Reading

Ravina Gelfaund. *Freedom of Religion in America*. Lerner Publications, 1969. Discusses religious freedom—from intolerance in early America to questions surrounding the First Amendment today.

Sally Sheppard. *Indians of the Eastern Woodlands*. Franklin Watts, 1975. A brief look at the customs and history of Algonquin and Iroquois tribes of northeastern America. Includes illustrations and many quotations.

Shirley Glubok. *Home and Child Life in Colonial Days*. Macmillan, 1969. Discusses housekeeping, education, recreation, needlecraft, dress, religion, and travel in the American colonies. Many illustrations.

Edwin Tunis. *Colonial Living*. World Publishers, 1957. Accompanied by numerous drawings, this book explains everyday life and objects of colonial America.

John Loeper. *Going to School in 1776*. Atheneum, 1973. First-hand accounts of teachers, textbooks, and games. Easy reading.

TEST YOURSELF

WRITE YOUR ANSWERS ON A SEPARATE SHEET OF PAPER.

Matching
Write the letter of the definition that best matches each term below.

1. religious toleration
2. established church
3. habit of command
4. social contract
5. Maryland Toleration Act of 1649

a. freedom to worship as one chooses
b. protected freedom of religion for Catholics and Protestants
c. an official religion
d. ability to govern or lead
e. a view of government's responsibilities and citizens' rights
f. law that called for free public education

Fill in the Blanks
Four connections that linked colonial leaders from all the 13 colonies were (1) _____, (2) _____, (3) _____, and (4) _____. The (5) _____ in the colonies were like the English House of Commons, while the (6) _____ were like the English House of Lords. Defender of the Glorious Revolution of 1688, (7) _____ wrote about the theory of (8) _____, an idea which became popular in the colonies. By 1750, the (9) _____ was the most powerful branch of government in every one of the 13 colonies. At the Albany Congress of 1754, (10) _____ devised a plan for the colonies to unite, but not one colony supported his plan.

Classifying
Mark U for factors that tended to unify the 13 colonies. Mark D for factors that caused disunity.

1. jealousy of colonial assemblies
2. religious toleration
3. college-educated elite
4. belief in the rights of English citizens
5. threat of French attack

VISITING THE PAST

Williamsburg, Virginia

Colonial Williamsburg is one of the best known historic sites in America. The capital of colonial Virginia, Williamsburg is known not only because of the historic events that happened there, but also (and mainly) because of the way the town has treated its past.

In 1926, Williamsburg, Virginia, looked very different from how it does today. Its colonial buildings were covered with new additions. Gas stations and modern buildings hid the special character of the town. Then, something special happened. With the financial backing of John D. Rockefeller, the reconstruction of Williamsburg as the capital city of colonial Virginia began. Modern buildings were removed. Colonial structures were restored. Lost buildings were rebuilt.

Colonial Williamsburg miraculously began to re-emerge. In this process of turning back the hands of time, special skills and knowledge about restoring the past were developed. Old crafts that were needed to restore and rebuild the past were revived. Williamsburg was undertaking an ambitious and unique project. Instead of restoring one or two isolated buildings, it re-created a historic feeling, an experience.

This reconstructed 18th-century town of Williamsburg has caught the imagination of many of its visitors. The town is shaped by its colonial plan. Streets are lined with small frame and brick homes and shops. Backyards have gardens, and trees line the streets. Some crafts, such as the making of silver items and musical instruments, are demonstrated in shops. The colonial taverns use the food and songs of the past to entertain the visitors who flock there from all over the world.

The Colonial Williamsburg that you see today is much nicer than the one that really existed. A bus takes visitors on a tour through the almost spotless streets. The buildings are all in tiptop condition. Although here the past has been glamorized a bit, one can learn much about colonial architecture, crafts, and life. Williamsburg has taught us the value and attraction of preserving a complete historic setting.

Plimoth Plantation, Massachusetts

Colonists hoe the corn, work at crafts, and prepare dinner. It is another typical day in the year 1629 at Plimoth Plantation on the coast of New England. The only thing in the settlement not in keeping with the early 17th century is you, the visitor.

Walking from the parking lot to the settlement, you feel as though you were traveling through time. The muddy path to the palisade takes you by the scrawny corn trying to grow. No tour buses or modern objects detract from the authenticity of the site. Here is a living world of colonial crafts, cooking, farming, dancing, military drills, and people.

Plimoth Plantation in Massachusetts is an unusual, exciting, and special type of historical site. The goal of its planners was to reconstruct a moment in time. At this living museum, historical tools are seen in use, not on display. Crafts and cooking are done using techniques of the 1600s. Dressed in costumes of the period, the museum interpreters actually live the

Governor's Palace in colonial Williamsburg

lives of the settlement's inhabitants. You can hear colonists speaking the dialect of the time. The hard work, the dirt, and the occasional joys of this young settlement occur around you.

You can easily spend a day walking around and around the palisaded community, learning amazing things about how the people lived. Their beds consisted of a thin mattress slung across ropes supported on a frame. The beds were small, the rooms were small. There was little light, for the windows were small, also. There were no closets. The few clothes the people owned were hung on hooks.

The museum is not on the actual site of early Plymouth, but the life and look of the settlement in 1629, including mud, pigs, and flies, have been simulated as accurately as historical research can determine. All of the "old" buildings are actually new. They can be changed if research tells us something new about how Plimoth Plantation looked.

The museum re-creates a complete historic environment. The visitor learns while enjoying the sights and sounds of history—history brought to life and filled with action.

Colonial Charleston

Charleston, South Carolina, may bring to mind the bombardment of Fort Sumter and the Civil War. However, the golden age of this city was the 18th century, before the fort was built. At that time Charleston was the major cultural center of the South. Reminders of this period are plentiful.

In 1670, Charleston was settled by the English. Within a decade its citizens relocated it across the Ash-ley River on a peninsula. As Charleston grew, the lines on the city plan were filled with real streets. The port city prospered on the wealth of the rice and indigo plantations that surrounded it. Plantation owners spent summers in Charleston, away from the dangers of malaria.

The flavor of 18th-century Charleston survives. In 1931 the city made preservation history by establishing the first of many historic districts in the country.

The creation of a historic district does not turn part of a city into a museum, as in Williamsburg, or stop the clock in a particular year, as does Plimoth Plantation. The creation of a historic district protects the history and architecture of a place by regulating change. Modern life continues in and around the historic buildings and streets.

In Charleston, hundreds of buildings from before 1840 still exist. These structures give the city its flavor. Charleston's architectural heritage is not limited to one style or period. Yet much of its distinctiveness results from the way colonial architecture adapted to the climate.

The narrow sides of many old houses face the street, with main entrances facing private enclosed gardens. The long two-story porches of the houses overlook the gardens. The houses are situated to catch the summer breeze and the winter sun. First floors were elevated to protect from flooding as well as to raise the parlor to catch the breeze.

Charleston's past is an important part of its present. The past gives Charleston the special sense of place that makes it famous.

129

UNIT 2 TEST

WRITE YOUR ANSWERS ON A SEPARATE SHEET OF PAPER.

Matching (20 points)
Match each person with a description from the list below.
1. Anne Hutchinson
2. Benjamin Franklin
3. Benjamin Banneker
4. Metacomet
5. John Locke
6. Phillis Wheatley
7. Roger Williams
8. James Oglethorpe
9. Eliza Pinckney
10. Peter Stuyvesant

a. founder of Georgia
b. Dutch governor who surrendered New Amsterdam to the English
c. perfected the growing and processing of indigo
d. banished from Massachusetts because of her religious beliefs
e. noted astronomer and mathematician
f. established religious freedom in Rhode Island
g. poet
h. proposed the Albany plan of union
i. philosopher of the social contract
j. leader of the Wampanoags
k. founder of Maryland

Multiple Choice (20 points)
Write the letter of the answer that best completes each statement.
1. Speculation is
   a. unjust treatment by a government.
   b. buying and selling when there is a high risk.
   c. using all that is produced, with no surplus for sale.
2. Someone who raises crops and lives on land belonging to another, paying rent as a share of the crops, is
   a. a commercial farmer.
   b. an artisan.
   c. a tenant farmer.
3. *Due process of law* refers to
   a. dissent.
   b. protection provided by the standard legal steps.
   c. arbitrary government.
4. The theory that requires a ruler to provide protection in return for a citizen's loyalty is called
   a. "the habit of command."
   b. social mobility.
   c. the social contract.
5. The foothills that extend between the Appalachian Mountains and the Atlantic Coastal Plain are called the
   a. Piedmont.
   b. Carolina Low Country.
   c. Tidewater.

Time Line (20 points)
Match the letters on the time line with the events they stand for.
1. Albany Congress
2. Settlers begin to move to the southern back country
3. Glorious Revolution in England
4. Navigation Acts passed
5. Maryland Toleration Act
6. Jamestown founded
7. Protests of Paxton Boys and the Regulators
8. Pilgrims settle Plymouth
9. Pennsylvania granted to William Penn
10. Salem witch hunts

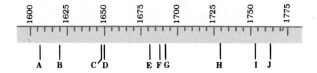

Essay Questions (40 points)
1. Why did religious toleration develop in the colonies while intolerance flourished in Europe?
2. Describe three economic, social, or political factors that led to growing independence in the colonies before 1760.

130

Unit Three

The Revolutionary Era

Chapter 6   1754–1776

THE COMING OF THE AMERICAN REVOLUTION

On a summer day in 1774, John Adams and Jonathan Sewall argued as they walked among the hills overlooking Maine's Casco Bay. These friends were leaders of opposing sides in the rift between the American colonies and Great Britain. Adams and Sewall would soon go their separate ways.

Adams would serve in a Continental Congress that would surely denounce England's rule over the colonies. Sewall was to serve the king in a new Massachusetts government. By their acts they were declaring themselves—Adams a Patriot and Sewall a Loyalist.

Sewall reminded his quick-tempered friend that Great Britain was powerful—that only tragedy could come of defying the mother country. But Adams, committed to liberty, would, in his words, "swim or sink, live or die, survive or perish with my country."

The men said farewell and embraced. They would not meet again until 1784, when Adams was minister to England from the United States, and Sewall was a poor and broken exile, living in a London rooming house.

What led the American colonies to revolution and a war for independence? The answer to that question lies, in part, in the natural development of the colonial economy and the evolution of colonial institutions, which you read about in earlier chapters. But it was the escalating tensions between 1763 and 1776 that forced Americans to choose between colonial dependence and nationhood.

Sections in This Chapter
1. The French and Indian War and Its Aftermath
2. The End to "Salutary Neglect"
3. More Taxes, More Protest
4. The Path Toward Independence

Opposite: Flag of the "United Company of the Train of Artillery," a Rhode Island regiment formed in 1775

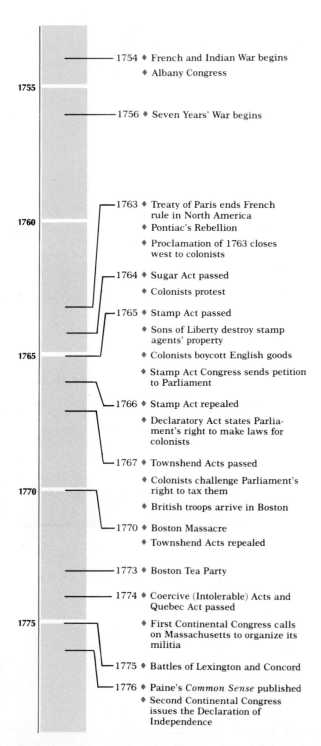

1754 ◆ French and Indian War begins
     ◆ Albany Congress

1755

1756 ◆ Seven Years' War begins

1760

1763 ◆ Treaty of Paris ends French
       rule in North America
     ◆ Pontiac's Rebellion
     ◆ Proclamation of 1763 closes
       west to colonists

1764 ◆ Sugar Act passed
     ◆ Colonists protest

1765 ◆ Stamp Act passed
     ◆ Sons of Liberty destroy stamp
       agents' property
1765 ◆ Colonists boycott English goods
     ◆ Stamp Act Congress sends petition
       to Parliament

1766 ◆ Stamp Act repealed
     ◆ Declaratory Act states Parlia-
       ment's right to make laws for
       colonists

1767 ◆ Townshend Acts passed
     ◆ Colonists challenge Parliament's
       right to tax them

1770 ◆ British troops arrive in Boston

1770 ◆ Boston Massacre
     ◆ Townshend Acts repealed

1773 ◆ Boston Tea Party

1774 ◆ Coercive (Intolerable) Acts and
       Quebec Act passed

1775 ◆ First Continental Congress calls
       on Massachusetts to organize its
       militia

1775 ◆ Battles of Lexington and Concord

1776 ◆ Paine's *Common Sense* published
     ◆ Second Continental Congress
       issues the Declaration of
       Independence

1. THE FRENCH AND INDIAN WAR AND ITS AFTERMATH

In 1754, independence was far from the minds of the American colonists. They knew that to their north and to their west, French and Indian troops were preparing for a final contest for control of North America. Only the British army and navy stood between the colonists and the death and disaster a fourth war could bring.

The French and Indian War Begins

You'll recall from Chapter 5 that the French and English had long been rivals and enemies. Since 1689, they had fought three major wars for a world empire. In North America, both powers claimed the territory between the Great Lakes and the Mississippi River. The British and the colonists had their eyes on this area for colonial settlement. They viewed this land as part of Virginia under the charter of 1609. Also at stake was the rich fur trade with the Indians.

In 1747, a group of Virginia planters formed the Ohio Company to develop the fur trade and to sell land in the Ohio Valley. Hoping to keep the British colonists hemmed east of the Appalachians, the French soon built a string of forts from Lake Erie to the Ohio River.

In 1754, the governor of Virginia sent a 22-year-old officer named George Washington to build a fort at the point where two rivers join to form the Ohio River (the site of modern Pittsburgh). The purpose of Washington's mission was to assert the Virginia claim. But the French had already built a fort there called Fort Duquesne [dü kān′]. They and their Indian allies drove away Washington's forces in a battle on July 4, 1754. This was the first engagement in a world war that would reach across the globe.

Less than a month later, delegates from seven colonies met at Albany to try to win the support of the Iroquois and other Indians, and to develop colonial plans for their common defense. As you saw in Chapter 5, the Albany Plan for union which the delegates proposed failed to gain support among the colonies. Thus, during the war the colonies fought separately and inefficiently.

In the colonies, the war lasted nine years, from 1754 to 1763. Here it was called the **French and Indian War**. By 1756, all the major powers of Europe were at war. England, Portugal, and Prussia were aligned against France, Austria, Russia, Sweden, various German states, and later Spain. In Europe it is known as the **Seven Years' War**. Battles raged across the world, from the West Indies and Germany to India and the Philippines. But the major action was in North America —in the Ohio Valley, along the southwestern frontier, in New England, and in Canada.

For the first few years, the French and their allies seemed to be winning, but after 1758, when William Pitt became Britain's secretary of state, the tide turned in favor of the British. In 1758, the British took Fort Duquesne and the French stronghold of Louisbourg on Cape Breton Island. (See map, page 140.) In 1759, the British took Quebec, and in 1760, they conquered Montreal. The war dragged on for another three years, but North America was in British hands.

The war was the bloodiest of the many contests between France and England. It was also the costliest. To support the far-flung army and navy, the English people were taxed heavily and steadily. The government also borrowed money from private financiers, and the British national debt soared.

Celebrating England's Victory

In the end, England was victorious and became the ruler of the largest empire since Roman times. When news of the peace treaty in 1763 reached the colonists, they celebrated England's victory with bonfires and parades. In the churches, ministers preached the virtues of English valor. Men and women, separated from their mother country by 3,000 miles of ocean, drank toasts to Parliament, to William Pitt, to the generals and the admirals, and to King George III. "Nothing," the governor of Massachusetts declared as he watched the joyous celebrations, "can eradicate from the colonists' hearts their natural . . . affection to Great Britain."

At that moment, the governor was correct. The men and women of the 13 English colonies had, after all, every reason to rejoice in 1763. They and their forebears had lived for a century or more hemmed in on all sides by the French and the Spanish. Now the fear of invasion was over.

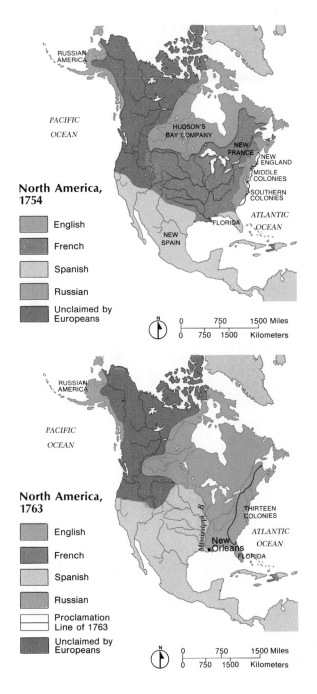

North America, 1754

- English
- French
- Spanish
- Russian
- Unclaimed by Europeans

North America, 1763

- English
- French
- Spanish
- Russian
- Proclamation Line of 1763
- Unclaimed by Europeans

The colonies were secure. Canada, Florida, and the land between the Appalachians and the Mississippi River were in British hands. When the bonfires died down and the parades were over, American colonists went home to dream of new lands, of a new fur trade, and of a world without threat of enemy attack.

The Problems Victory Brought

In London, however, the sweetness of victory faded fast. For the king and his ministers, there were definite benefits to this victory, but there were thorny problems as well.

First among the problems was the size of the new empire. With the signing of the **Treaty of Paris of 1763** England's North American possessions had nearly doubled in size. (See maps, page 135.) Under the terms of the treaty, France gave Britain all the lands east of the Mississippi, except New Orleans. Spain ceded Florida to Britain. Britain also gained control of India. In return for Spain's aid in the war, France gave Spain New Orleans and all French holdings west of the Mississippi. All that remained of a once impressive French empire in North America were some tiny fishing villages on Miquelon and St. Pierre, two little islands off the Newfoundland coast. (See Map 2 in the Atlas section.)

In Britain, a bigger empire meant more natural resources and more power, but it also meant more physical area to defend. The cost was staggering. Before the war, the North American colonies had cost the government £70,000 a year. Now the king's advisers estimated a budget five times that amount.

Second, these new territories were not empty lands, but conquered provinces. In North America, the British flag flew over settlements peopled by defeated French citizens and Indian nations. These new English subjects—formerly bitter enemies—would have to be watched carefully as well as governed diplomatically. Somehow, their loyalties would have to be won. Such tasks required patience, skill, and money.

Finally, England's old enemy, France, could not be ignored. France had lost the war, but remained a mighty nation. Were England to show the slightest signs of weakness, France might make war again. England would need a strong army and the best of navies to keep what it had won. And military strength was expensive to maintain.

The central issue of the next decade, therefore, was money. How and from whom would the money needed to support the empire be raised? The government needed a sensible overall policy for governing the empire, a policy that would divide the costs of maintaining it between colonies and mother country. No such policy had ever existed.

The Character of the English Government

The English government was poorly equipped to deal with the great challenges of the 1760s. A small group of wealthy, ambitious, and self-centered people ruled the nation. Their struggles over prestige and quarrels over patronage had disappointed, and finally disgusted, the English public. English men and women of the middle classes viewed Parliament and its leaders as "debased and rotten."

The English leaders knew almost nothing about the colonies they governed. They lived in London or on country estates, and had no desire to visit

King George III in his coronation robes, 1760

the outposts of their empire. To them, Maryland or Virginia or New York was still no more than a wilderness settlement, peopled by convicts, low-class refugees, religious dissenters, and foreigners of all sorts.

The development of an educated elite and a prosperous, well-informed population in the colonies was unknown to the English who were to govern the empire. To them, the colonists were country bumpkins—necessary parts of the empire, but certainly not equal members in it.

The king himself did little to provide an atmosphere in which genuine statesmen could work. **George III** was a tense and excitable man who suffered long bouts of mental illness as he grew older. In 1763 he was a young king, unhappy, sensitive, and lonely. His greatest wish was to follow his mother's advice to "be king"—to be a powerful and active leader of his government. To achieve this he wooed members of Parliament to his side with offers of riches and rewards. This helped create an atmosphere of competition and conflict among political leaders just when cooperation was most needed.

The government of the 1760s was filled with factions, or political parties, that formed around George III or around his enemies. Each faction criticized the others, and political suggestions were judged by whether they were put forth by the right or the wrong political party. In this setting, it was difficult to produce wise solutions to the problems that came as an aftermath to the French and Indian War.

SECTION 1 REVIEW

 Identify: French and Indian War, Seven Years' War, Treaty of Paris of 1763, George III

Main Ideas
1. Describe the causes and results of the French and Indian War.
2. Why did the English government need money after the war? What policies did the government need to take in regard to its French and Indian subjects?
3. Describe the weaknesses of the English government in the 1760s.

2. THE END TO "SALUTARY NEGLECT"

Almost immediately after the war ended, the government had to decide what to do about a major Indian rebellion west of the Allegheny Mountains. In the spring of 1763, Pontiac, an Ottawa leader, formed an alliance with members of other nations, including Delaware, Miami, Shawnee, Potawatomi, and Chippewa. They wanted to keep the colonial settlers from taking more land. In lightning raids, the Indians under Pontiac seized and destroyed 8 of the 11 forts along the northwestern frontier, killing hundreds of settlers. In return, a mob of angry colonists—the Paxton Boys—had massacred 20 Conestoga, a peaceful tribe in western Pennsylvania. Two thousand soldiers and settlers and uncounted Indians died before the English finally negotiated an end to **Pontiac's Rebellion.**

The Proclamation Line of 1763

The bloodshed was tragic and costly. To keep Indians and colonists at arm's length from each other, in 1763 the English government issued a proclamation limiting westward movement. The Ohio Valley and all lands west of a demarcation line were temporarily off-limits to settlers and land speculators. (See map, page 140.)

Solitary adventurers like Daniel Boone simply ignored the **Proclamation Line of 1763.** But to families beginning to establish themselves in areas like Kentucky, this policy was a severe blow. It was equally hard on Virginia and Pennsylvania investors with money tied up in land companies laying claims in the Ohio Valley.

The Proclamation Line of 1763 angered many colonists. They felt the English government was cheating them out of the fruits of victory, maybe permanently. The suspicion that the English government would keep Americans crowded on the seacoast added to colonial resentment at English interference in people's lives. The English government did not notice this warning sign of colonial discontent. Its attention was elsewhere.

The English government was worrying about finances. What the English saw in the colonies was a prosperous population of farmers, artisans, merchants, and planters who, they felt, had not paid a penny for the running of the empire.

LIFE IN AMERICA

FRANKLIN AND JEFFERSON: DISCIPLES OF THE ENLIGHTENMENT

Benjamin Franklin and Thomas Jefferson are famous for their contributions to the founding of our government. Both men were leaders in the revolution and the period following the establishment of the new nation. Both were also members of an influential group of colonial intellectuals whose talents covered a variety of fields.

Printer and Public Servant

Benjamin Franklin (1706–1790) has been called America's first "self-made man," a pioneer in breaking down class barriers. He was born to a poor family of candlemakers and at age 12 was apprenticed to his half-brother, a printer. An avid reader, Franklin studied the classics on his own and became an accomplished writer. At age 24, he acquired his own business and through hard work became a prosperous printer and the publisher of the popular *Poor Richard's Almanack*.

In colonial times, almost every family owned an almanac that contained information about tides, weather, and medical remedies. *Poor Richard's Almanack* also gave its readers bits of Franklin's philos-

Benjamin Franklin

ophy tucked in odd spaces on the pages, such as "Never leave that till tomorrow which you can do today" and "The sleeping fox catches no poultry."

Franklin took his own advice. At age 17 he wrote a list of admirable qualities he intended to pursue, including temperance, sincerity, efficiency, and avoidance of idleness and extravagance. He devoted one week to each virtue. No one knows how long this regimen lasted, but Franklin was able to retire in 1751 at the age of 42 from his publishing and printing business and devote his time to public service and to science.

As a public servant, Franklin was efficient and ingenious. He helped establish the first public library in the 13 colonies. He served as postmaster, militia organizer, colonial representative in England, and diplomat in France, to name only a few of his positions.

Franklin's Studies of Electricity

But it was his career as a scientist that made him known internationally as "Dr. Franklin." He first began experimenting with electricity in 1747. By 1752 he reasoned that lightning and static electricity had similar characteristics. To test his theory, he devised his famous kite experiment, an experiment astounding in its simplicity and importance. Franklin's theory of electricity, later called the electron theory, became the basis on which further advances in the study of electricity were made. He had created a new way of thinking about electricity and a new vocabulary as well. Electrical terms such as "armature," "battery," "conductor," and "positive and negative charges" were all coined by Franklin.

Sketch for bifocals

Franklin's "Pennsylvania fireplace"

Poor Richard's Almanack

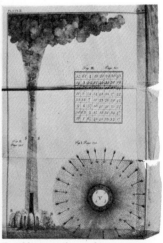

Franklin's analysis of waterspouts

Jefferson as Scholar and Scientist

Thomas Jefferson (1743–1826) represented the best that social advantage could offer in the colonies. At the College of William and Mary he studied law, the classics, literature, history, mathematics (his favorite subject), science, and music. He also began buying books while a student, and in 1812 he sold his personal library of 10,000 volumes to the government, to form the nucleus of the Library of Congress. A political leader and scientist, he was also one of the finest architects of his time.

Jefferson's career as public servant was impressive: among other things, he wrote the Declaration of Independence and served two terms as President.

As a scientist, he was a careful observer of natural phenomena and keeper of records. He regularly noted such details as temperature readings in his notebooks and carried a thermometer on his many journeys to Williamsburg and Philadelphia. Thanks to Jefferson, we know that it was 68°F in Philadelphia on the morning of July 4, 1776.

Jefferson used his observations and the reports of others to compile his *Notes on the State of Virginia* (1784). It described topography, minerals, birds and animals, trees and vegetables, military forces, In-

Thomas Jefferson

dians, counties and towns, legal and educational institutions, religion and manners, manufacturing and commerce, and the frontier. It was the most accurate and sweeping scientific catalogue of America in its day and was popular reading on both sides of the Atlantic.

The Enlightenment in America

In 1780 Thomas Jefferson was elected a member of the American Philosophical Society, an organization founded in 1743 by Benjamin Franklin "for the promoting of Useful Knowledge." Its honorary membership also included George Washington and James Madison. These men represented a circle of talented American intellectuals whose ideals were those of the Enlightenment.

The Enlightenment was a philosophical movement in Europe in the 1700s that emphasized rational thought and scientific discovery. Intellectuals of the Enlightenment believed that theoretical knowledge was useful in practical ways. Thus, Franklin, who developed a theory of electricity, also invented bifocals, the lightning rod, and the Franklin stove. Jefferson, the classical scholar and accomplished violinist, experimented with crop rotation, invented a plow, and designed the buildings of the University of Virginia and the state capitol at Richmond.

But above all, these disciples of the Enlightenment believed in the power and freedom of the mind. Typically, a quote from Jefferson says it best, "I have sworn upon the altar of God eternal hostility against every form of tyranny over the mind of man."

Jefferson's code machine and music stand

Jefferson designed the University of Virginia, an architectural masterpiece

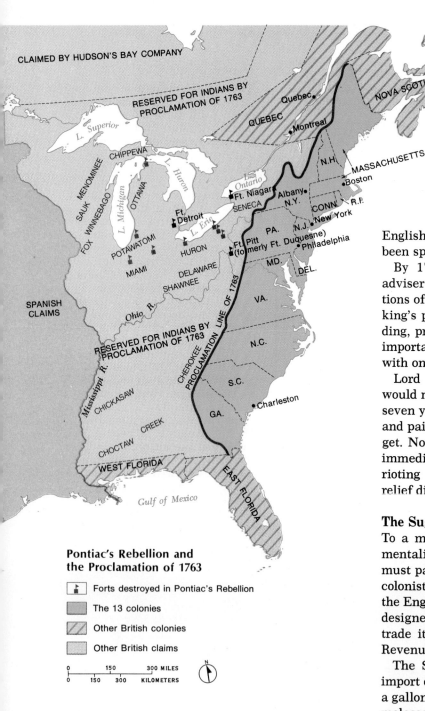

Pontiac's Rebellion and the Proclamation of 1763

- ⚐ Forts destroyed in Pontiac's Rebellion
- The 13 colonies
- Other British colonies
- Other British claims

| 0 | 150 | 300 MILES |
| 0 | 150 | 300 KILOMETERS |

Who Should Pay?

The English said their recent war had been fought for the sake of the colonies, and the colonies should have paid for it. The truth is, the war had been fought to protect England's economic and military interests in North America, not to protect the colonists. Yet it is easy to see how the English public could believe their money had been spent to aid the Americans.

By 1764, the anxious king and his harried advisers decided to revise the financial obligations of the colonies to their mother country. The king's prime minister, George Grenville, a plodding, practical man, probably did not realize the importance of this decision. He was concerned with one thing: raising money for the Treasury.

Lord Grenville knew that the English people would not, and probably could not, pay more. For seven years the English had tightened their belts and paid extra taxes to support the military budget. Now that the war was over, they demanded immediate tax reductions. Grenville knew that rioting was possible in the streets of London if relief did not come soon.

The Sugar Act

To a man with George Grenville's bookkeeping mentality, the problem was simple. Someone must pay for the years of war, and the American colonists must be that someone. Thus, in 1764, the English government passed the first trade act designed to raise money rather than to regulate trade itself. This act was called the American Revenue Act, or Sugar Act.

The Sugar Act actually lowered the existing import duty on molasses or sugar from 6 pennies a gallon to 3 pennies a gallon. This tax on foreign molasses might seem lower, but in reality it was not. For until 1764, no one had ever paid the tax on foreign molasses at all. French West Indian molasses was one of the main items in the respectable smuggling trade of New England.

What England had once winked at was now to be prevented. The law would be enforced. Suddenly in 1764, each colonial port had customs collectors with nosy assistants who checked the cargo decks of ships and searched for hidden barrels of molasses in the dark corners of the ship's hold. Customs inspectors even raided the warehouses of American shippers, looking for illegal cargoes unloaded in the dead of night.

New England businessmen resented these meddling inspectors and collectors even more than they resented the 3 pennies import tax. Rich and prominent citizens like Boston's John Hancock did not like being told how to run their businesses by "snoops and spies."

The Traditional Policy of Salutary Neglect

Technically, of course, the English government had every legal right to enforce trade regulations, based upon the doctrine of mercantilism. But, for over half a century England had been lax in governing the colonies. This was as much a conscious policy as a sign of real neglect.

Leaving the colonies to their own devices had been economical and profitable, as long as the Americans were steady providers of raw materials and steady customers for manufactured products. This silent agreement not to over-regulate the colonies was called **salutary neglect**, which means "healthy" neglect. You have seen one of its side effects in the high degree of self-government that developed in the colonies.

Until 1764, the policy of salutary neglect had generally satisfied both the mother country and the colonies. Now, without considering long-range consequences, George Grenville swept aside this traditional agreement. In 1764 colonial merchants found that their habit of bending the trade laws was now labeled smuggling. What they had become used to considering their rights now became their crimes.

Colonists did not think it was their duty to foot the bill for keeping troops in America. As they understood it, protecting their homes from attack was England's obligation. Here after all was the basic trade-off of mercantilism: the mother country was responsible for keeping the colonies safe, as long as the colonies helped make the mother country rich.

The Stamp Act

Americans hardly had time to recover from the surprise of the Sugar Act when Lord Grenville

shocked them again. In 1765 Parliament passed a Stamp Act to raise tax money directly from the colonists.

Collecting taxes by the use of stamps was not new to the taxpayers. Colonial governments had collected revenue this way because the method was fast and efficient. All the government had to do was print up special stamps and insist that they be attached to certain goods sold in the colony. Merchants and shopkeepers bought these stamps from the government's agent and glued them to the product. Then they passed the cost of the stamp along to the customers.

Stamp taxes were familiar, but a stamp tax *by Parliament* definitely was not. The American colonists had never paid direct taxes like this to England. Now Parliament had decided to raise money from the colonists by requiring stamps on legal documents, newspapers, dice, playing cards, and even marriage licenses. Almost every colonist was touched in some way by the Stamp Act of 1765. Sailors shooting dice, country gentlemen playing a hand of cards, merchants thumbing through the advertisements in a local paper, young brides- and grooms-to-be, even an angry colonist suing a neighbor—all would have to pay the tax.

Colonists Oppose the Stamp Act

Protest went up all over the colonies. Petitions were sent to Parliament demanding that the Stamp Act be repealed. Colonial assemblies passed resolutions insisting that Parliament was in error.

The fiery young lawyer Patrick Henry spoke in Virginia's House of Burgesses of a conspiracy against the rights of colonial Englishmen. In a speech that came dangerously close to treason, Henry warned George III to remember the fates of tyrants like Caesar of Rome and Charles I of England. Henry's warning carried added power because of the recent **Quartering Act**. This act required colonists to supply room and board to British troops; it seemed to suggest a tyrant's plan for military occupation.

Newspaper editors joined political leaders in their protest and urged the people to resist the infringement of their civil rights. Men and women demonstrated in the streets against the Stamp Act. Scarecrows dressed to look like George Grenville were carried through Boston and New York and burned on nearby hills. Violence soon erupted.

Men calling themselves the **Sons of Liberty** destroyed the home of Andrew Oliver in Massachusetts when they learned he had been appointed stamp agent for their colony. A crowd also sacked the home of Lt. Governor Thomas Hutchinson because they had heard that he supported the Stamp Act.

Two Points of View

Grenville and the king could hardly believe their eyes when they read of all the commotion in the colonies. They wondered what had gotten into those people in America. What had? Most colonists feared that their most important rights had been challenged. As you saw in Chapter 5, colonists believed that they, like all English citizens, had a right to select and elect the people in government who taxed them. That meant there should be no taxation without representation.

Stamp agent hanged and stoned in effigy

The London government and the colonists disagreed completely over what this phrase meant. For the colonists it was clear: no Americans voted in Parliament; so, although Parliament could govern the empire, it could not tax the people of the colonies. As Grenville and the other English leaders saw it, the phrase "no taxation without representation" meant that the House of Commons was the only branch of English government that could tax. Neither the king nor the House of Lords could tax, for this was a right won by the branch of Parliament that represented the "commoners" or the people.

In the English view, since the House of Commons was pledged to represent fairly *all* common Englishmen and women, it did not matter where these citizens lived or even if they had the right to vote. This interpretation of "no taxation without representation" was called **virtual representation**.

The Stamp Act Congress

By the summer of 1765, many colonists openly defied English law and signed pledges not to use the government stamps. Merchants in seaports pledged not to buy or sell any English products until the hated Stamp Act was repealed. These "nonimportation agreements" (or boycotts, a term not used until the late 1800s) were major steps toward cooperation among the sometimes quarrelsome colonies.

Political leaders joined forces, also. In October 1765, the month before the Stamp Act was to go into effect, leaders from nine colonies met in a **Stamp Act Congress** in New York City. Each delegate believed that he was acting as a true and loyal English patriot should, exercising the right and duty to preserve the liberties of the people.

After much debate, the delegates to the Stamp Act Congress agreed upon a declaration to be sent to the king and to the Parliament. This "Declaration of Rights and Grievances" pledged continuing colonial loyalty, but called for an end to any taxation except by local colonial assemblies.

The colonists won their battle with the mother country. Their boycott of English goods hurt British merchants badly, and these merchants urged Parliament to repeal the Stamp Act. The riots and the political protest helped persuade Parliament as well.

In truth, England could not enforce the tax, since American citizens were not willing to distribute the stamps, and few would buy them. Not a single penny was ever raised by this first attempt on the part of the English government to tax the American colonists directly.

Results of the Stamp Act Crisis

The Stamp Act was repealed in March 1766. Peaceful times returned, but things were not as they had been before 1763. Americans had learned three lessons from the Stamp Act crisis.

First, they learned that England needed them as much as they needed England, and perhaps more. Without American business, English merchants could not continue to make their great profits. Second, Americans learned the power of cooperation among the colonies. Finally, and most significantly, colonists learned to distrust the English government.

The repeal of the Stamp Act did not mean that Parliament was persuaded by the political arguments of the colonists. In fact, immediately after voting for repeal, Parliament passed the Declaratory Act of 1766. This act asserted Parliament's absolute right to make laws for English citizens everywhere "in all cases whatsoever."

The English government considered repeal of the Stamp Act a gesture of good will, not an admission that the Americans were right. If colonists read the Declaratory Act, they chose to ignore it. But England still expected to make the colonies pay more of the cost of maintaining the safety of the empire. There would be no return to the era of salutary neglect.

SECTION 2 REVIEW

 Identify: Pontiac's Rebellion, Proclamation Line of 1763, salutary neglect, Quartering Act, Sons of Liberty, virtual representation, Stamp Act Congress

Main Ideas

1. Why did the British pass the Proclamation of 1763, the Sugar Act, and the Stamp Act?
2. Why did the colonists oppose these measures so strongly?
3. What were the results of the Stamp Act Congress?
4. What three things did the colonists learn from the Stamp Act crisis?
5. How did Parliament respond to this crisis?

3. MORE TAXES, MORE PROTEST

The year 1767 began gloomily for King George III and Parliament. The government needed income, and the king's key adviser, George Grenville, had not found a satisfactory way to raise the money. The king decided to replace Grenville. Instead of choosing an experienced and talented statesman for the job, George III picked a handsome, dashing young nobleman for the post, Charles Townshend [toun′zend]. His nickname was "Champagne Charlie," a tribute to the extravagant lifestyle that would leave him dead at age 41.

Townshend, like his predecessor, believed the solution to England's financial problems lay in tapping the pocketbooks of the Americans. Reviewing the disaster of the Stamp Act, Townshend decided that direct taxation upset the colonists more than fund-raising through enforcement of trade regulations. Therefore, in 1767, he proposed import duties on paper, tea, paint, lead, and many other everyday items the colonists needed. Import taxes under the Townshend Acts were not just on smuggled or foreign goods, but on manufactured goods from England as well.

Colonists Challenge Parliament's Right to Tax Them

Rumors spread. Royal governors in the colonies, who knew the mood of the people, warned their superiors in England that trouble would follow any attempt to tax the Americans, either directly or indirectly. In the colonial assemblies, the Townshend Acts were debated and condemned. Most American leaders challenged Parliament's right to raise revenue by imposing *any* taxes, direct or indirect, on the colonists.

Slowly but surely such debates were leading to the larger questions of England's right to govern the colonies at all. Some who saw this began to fear for the future. What would happen if these struggles between Parliament and the colonists continued? When did protest become open treason? Some colonists recalled with a shudder that many Stamp Act protests in 1765 had turned into violent attacks on the property of wealthy local citizens. These colonists feared the power of mobs as much as they feared Parliament. What was in store, they wondered, if the people learned to protest everything they did not like?

Other colonists, including Boston radical **Samuel Adams**, looked eagerly toward the future. Adams believed that England had grown too corrupt to govern the empire well, and that Parliament's members lacked respect for the liberties and rights guaranteed under the British Constitution. Adams did not think that "Champagne Charlie" and his luxury-loving companions should govern the sober, hard-working men and women of the colonies.

Samuel Adams had no fear of the "mob." He worked closely with these artisans, dock workers, and laborers. He had confidence in their judgment and in the judgment of all working and farm people, and he knew how to influence them. As early as 1767, Adams was ready to see Americans free of Parliament's rule entirely.

Few American political leaders or their followers shared Samuel Adams' view in 1767. Most were troubled and angry, but they were sincere in seeking a compromise between mother country and colonies. Perhaps **John Dickinson**, a lawyer from Pennsylvania, spoke for the majority in his *Letters from a Farmer in Pennsylvania* (1768).

In these newspaper articles, Dickinson pleaded for a repeal of the Townshend Acts, and for an end forever to Parliament's interference in American daily affairs. Let Parliament continue to regulate the empire's trade, he wrote, as it had always done. But let the colonists see to their own taxation through their own elected assemblies.

Boycotts and Violence

Colonists were ready to fight for their right to local control of taxation. Popular protest against the Townshend Acts came quickly. Once again petitions flooded Parliament. Once again colonial merchants signed nonimportation agreements, and citizens everywhere boycotted British goods. Ladies' Associations devoted to banning tea-drinking sprang up in New York, in Philadelphia, and in small towns like Edenton, North Carolina. Women in New York City formed spinning clubs to produce quantities of yarn so that their families could wear homespun clothing rather than imported woolens from England.

This time the boycott was not entirely voluntary. The Sons of Liberty enforced nonimportation, smearing merchants' shop windows with paint or threatening them if they did not comply.

The most active protest seemed to be in Boston. Mobs chased customs collectors through the city streets in 1767 and 1768 and beat them with clubs. Anyone suspected of importing or selling English goods risked being coated with hot tar and then covered with feathers.

British Troops Arrive

The Massachusetts governor, customs officers, and their staffs grew so frightened that they fled the city of Boston. There was no police force in the 18th-century colonies. If the governor wanted to restore order he had to call on the army. By the end of 1767 several regiments of British soldiers had landed in Boston.

The arrival of troops was supposed to return Boston to its former peace and quiet. But their presence made matters worse. The soldiers themselves were often young and inexperienced. While they drilled in the city's common, or town square, dressed in their bright red coats and shiny black boots, the local people taunted them. "Lobsterback!" the Bostonians shouted, and often they threw snowballs or stones at the soldiers.

Samuel Adams alerted colonists to the dangers of an army in their midst by publishing inflammatory articles in the *Boston Gazette* that detailed incidents of violence committed by the soldiers against private citizens. Such incidents may have been fanciful rather than factual. It is hard to say who was more frightened, soldier or citizen, during the Boston military occupation.

The Boston Massacre

On the evening of March 5, 1770, violence broke out. Some dock workers and soldiers had a fist fight. Later that night, a gang of local youths began to taunt a young sentry on guard duty at the Customs House. The sentry struck one boy on the head with his musket.

A growing crowd began to pelt the sentry with ice, shouting "Kill him, kill him." The troop commander sent reinforcements to see the soldier safely to his barracks. But the reinforcements, led by Captain Thomas Preston, were quickly surrounded by the crowd and cut off from their headquarters. The crowd continued to shout insults and throw rocks and snowballs. The soldiers could hardly hear their orders over the noise and were frankly nervous.

View of the Boston Massacre by Paul Revere, artist and silversmith, who later made a famous midnight ride

Someone in the crowd threw a club that knocked a soldier to the ground. What happened next is hard to know. A shot rang out. Did the soldier's musket go off as he fell? Then a shout of "Fire!" was heard. Muskets went off. When the confusion was over, five colonists lay dead in the snow. The next day the dead were carried through the streets in a solemn funeral procession. One victim was a black man, possibly a seaman, named Crispus Attucks. The other four were white Boston workingmen.

Who had given the order to fire on the crowd? Captain Preston swore he had not. A jury found the soldiers innocent of intentional murder. But the **Boston Massacre**, as this event was labeled, was not forgotten by the colonists. American newspapers now warned their readers that England would kill in order to enforce laws.

Repeal and a Momentary Calm

A little more than a month later, on April 12, 1770, the Townshend Acts were repealed. The political protests, the violence in Boston, and especially the economic boycott of English goods had combined to force Parliament once again to give up its program of taxation. Townshend himself did not live to see the failure of his program.

The new chief minister, Frederick North, tried to salvage what he could of English pride in this political defeat. Lord North made it clear that England still maintained Parliamentary supremacy over the colonies. To prove that England still had the right to tax the colonies, the government kept on the law books the tax on tea.

After the repeal of the Townshend Acts a calm seemed to settle over the colonies. Most men and women devoted their energies once more to the private matters of family, farm, or shop. Royal government officials breathed a sigh of relief. In Boston, the governor, Thomas Bernard, moved back into the city. But keen observers noted that the quiet felt like the calm before a violent storm.

Several incidents did occur. In June of 1772, for example, a rich Rhode Island merchant named John Brown took revenge on the customs officers who had hounded him for the last few years. When the customs patrol boat, the *Gaspee*, ran aground off the coast of Providence, Brown and his brothers led a band of men on board the boat. The colonists killed the commanding officer, then evacuated the *Gaspee*'s crew and burned the boat to ashes. Many Rhode Islanders witnessed the burning of the *Gaspee* and knew the men who did it. The accused were to be sent to England for trial. When English officials looked for witnesses to testify against the Browns, no one spoke up.

Attitudes Harden on Both Sides

The English resented this defiance among the colonists. Their mistrust of the Americans in-

145

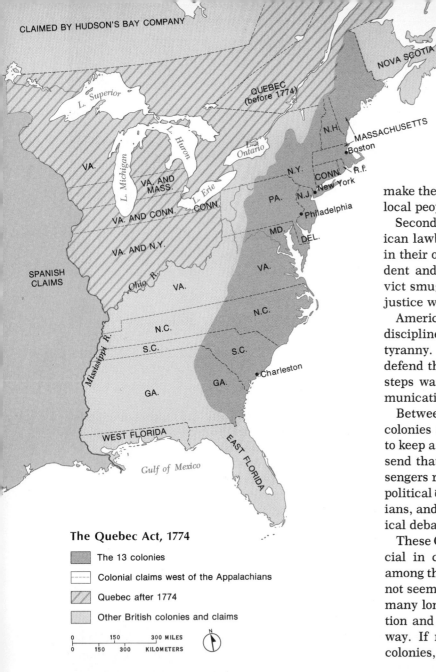

CLAIMED BY HUDSON'S BAY COMPANY

NOVA SCOTIA

QUEBEC (before 1774)

L. Superior

L. Huron

L. Michigan

L. Ontario

L. Erie

VA.

VA. AND MASS.

VA. AND CONN.

CONN.

VA. AND N.Y.

N.H.

MASSACHUSETTS

Boston

N.Y.

CONN.

R.I.

New York

PA.

N.J.

Philadelphia

MD.

DEL.

SPANISH CLAIMS

Ohio R.

VA.

VA.

Mississippi R.

N.C.

N.C.

S.C.

S.C.

GA.

GA.

Charleston

WEST FLORIDA

EAST FLORIDA

Gulf of Mexico

The Quebec Act, 1774

The 13 colonies

Colonial claims west of the Appalachians

Quebec after 1774

Other British colonies and claims

0   150   300 MILES

0   150   300 KILOMETERS

N

make these officials independent of the will of the local people.

Second, the government decided to bring American lawbreakers to trial in England rather than in their own colony. Because of the *Gaspee* incident and several unsuccessful attempts to convict smugglers, the English were convinced that justice would not be done by American juries.

American leaders saw the English efforts to discipline them as another dark sign of a growing tyranny. They felt compelled to take steps to defend themselves. The most important of these steps was the development of an effective communications network among the colonies.

Between 1772 and 1774, leaders in the various colonies appointed **Committees of Correspondence** to keep a record of events in their own colony and send that record to all their sister colonies. Messengers rode night and day, carrying the news of political decisions in Massachusetts to the Virginians, and returning with reports on Virginia political debates.

These Committees of Correspondence were crucial in creating a sense of unity and purpose among the colonists. The English government did not seem to realize that people spread out over so many lonely miles could unite themselves in action and in ideas. But the colonists had found a way. If new trouble arose anywhere in the 13 colonies, Americans were ready to work together.

The Boston Tea Party

New trouble did arise in 1773. That May, Lord North and his government made a special agreement with the East India Tea Company. The company had been hard hit by the colonial boycott during the Townshend Acts protest, and at that moment, had 17 million pounds of tea in its warehouses. Unless the company could unload this tea, it was in danger of bankruptcy.

Lord North's government made a special ruling called the **Tea Act** that allowed the East India Tea Company to sell its tea directly to the American colonies. The ruling eliminated the cost of retail-

creased just as the American suspicions of them grew. More and more, the English government began to think in terms of a "get-tough" policy toward the colonies. Money, though still important, was no longer the only issue. The English wanted to discipline the colonies and to teach the people in America to respect Parliament, the King, and English supremacy.

Signs of this decision to discipline the colonies appeared between 1770 and 1773. First, the English government decided to pay the salaries of the judges and the governor of Massachusetts, instead of having the colonists pay them, in order to

ers and the expense of shipping the tea first to England and then to the colonies. Thus the price of the company's tea would be considerably lower than its competitors'.

This should have been good news to the colonists, North thought, since tea was the favorite drink of the 18th century, and the colonists were always on the lookout for a bargain. But, when Americans heard of the arrangement with the East India Tea Company, something struck them as suspicious.

Many Americans thought they saw a plot. Was the English government trying to create a tea monopoly? This year the East India tea might be a bargain, but the company might charge sky-high prices in 1774, once it had driven all its competitors out of business. And perhaps this monopoly was only the first of many that the government intended to create.

It is hard to say whether or not the Americans were correct in their suspicions. However, one thing is clear: the English government did want to help the East India Tea Company, especially since many members of Parliament owned stock in the company. And the government was willing to bend colonial laws to do it.

No one will ever know if the price of tea would have risen in 1774. For, on the evening of December 16, 1773, Samuel Adams led a band of colonists disguised as Mohawk Indians on board the tea ships in the Boston harbor. These colonists dumped the company's tea into the water. Thousands of dollars worth of merchandise floated for a moment on the water's surface, and then sank.

Lord North and his advisers were outraged at this destruction of property in the "**Boston Tea Party**," as the incident was called. It was time, they decided, to teach the colonists a lesson they would not forget. In 1774, the English government issued the **Coercive Acts**, a series of orders that Americans called the "Intolerable Acts."

First, the port of Boston was closed to all shipping. The Royal Navy was stationed in the harbor to see that not a single ship entered or left. No supplies of any kind would be allowed to reach the city until Boston paid for the tea that had been destroyed in the Boston Tea Party.

Second, Parliament made major changes in the Massachusetts government structure. It revoked the charter of 1691, cut back the powers of the colonial assembly, and forbade town meetings without the governor's permission. The Massachusetts council, always elected before, was now to be appointed by the governor.

Third, a new Quartering Act provided that British troops could be lodged among the people as well as in barracks.

Fourth, British officials charged with murder committed while enforcing British laws would have their trials in England, not the colonies. This measure led to the fear that British soldiers would be more likely to fire on the populace.

Parliament also passed the **Quebec Act** in 1774. This law had nothing to do with punishing the colonists but was aimed at establishing good relations with the French colonists in Canada. The Quebec Act granted political and religious freedom to Catholics, recognized aspects of French law (including trial without jury), and enlarged the boundaries of Quebec to include a huge territory in the west claimed by Virginia, New York, Massachusetts, and Connecticut. (See map.) The Quebec Act outraged colonists from New Hampshire to Georgia, who viewed it as a continuation of the policy limiting westward movement. They also saw it as a plot to spread Catholicism.

Lord North was determined to make an example of Massachusetts. He felt certain he could isolate and inflict special burdens on the colony without protest from the remaining colonies. But the years of the Stamp Act Congress and the Committees of Correspondence had united the colonists. "The cause of Boston," said Virginian George Washington, "now is and ever will be the cause of America."

SECTION 3 REVIEW

 Identify: Samuel Adams, John Dickinson, Boston Massacre, Committees of Correspondence, Tea Act, Boston Tea Party, Coercive Acts, Quebec Act

Main Ideas
1. Why did Townshend believe that import duties would be acceptable to the colonists even though the Stamp Act was not?
2. What was the nature of England's "get-tough" policy? How did the colonists respond?
3. What was the cause of the Boston Tea Party and who "threw" the party?
4. How did the Coercive Acts and the Quebec Act affect colonial unity?

LEADERS OF THE AMERICAN REVOLUTION

John Hancock   Patrick Henry

John Adams (born in Massachusetts, 1735; died in Massachusetts on July 4, 1826, exactly 50 years after the adoption of the Declaration of Independence—the same day that Thomas Jefferson also died) lawyer, farm owner, newspaper propagandist against Britain, defense attorney in the trial of British soldiers for the Boston Massacre, member of the Massachusetts Assembly (1770–1771), member of the Massachusetts Revolutionary Provincial Congress (1774–1775), delegate to the 1st and 2nd Continental Congresses, helped draft the Olive Branch Petition, advised Jefferson on the writing of the Declaration of Independence and was a signer of it, served as Chairman of the Board of War and Ordnance during the early years of the war, member of the U.S. team—along with Benjamin Franklin and John Jay—to negotiate peace with Britain, 1st Vice-President and 2nd President of the United States.

Samuel Adams (born in Massachusetts, 1722; died in Massachusetts, 1803) failed businessman (bankrupt brewery), tax collector for Boston (1756–1764), member of the Caucus Club—a radical organization in Boston, propagandist for the revolution, chief tactician of the Massachusetts protest against the Stamp Act, helped organize the Sons of Liberty in 1765, organizer of the Nonimportation Association in 1768, member of the Massachusetts Assembly (1766–1774), initiated the Massachusetts Committee of Correspondence in 1772, leader of the Boston Tea Party (1773), delegate to the Continental Congress (1774–1781), signer of the Declaration of Independence.

John Dickinson (born in Maryland, 1732; died in Delaware, 1808)

lawyer in Philadelphia, member of the Delaware Assembly (1760–1762), member of the Pennsylvania Assembly (1762–1765, 1770–1776), pamphleteer during the revolutionary era, member of the 1st Continental Congress for Pennsylvania and the 2nd Continental Congress for Delaware, worked on the Olive Branch Petition, coauthored with Thomas Jefferson the "Declaration of the Causes and Necessity of Taking Up Arms" (1775), opposed but did not vote against the Declaration of Independence, head of the committee to draft the Articles of Confederation (1776).

Benjamin Franklin (born in Boston, 1706; died in Philadelphia, 1790) printer, author, philanthropist, scientist, member of the Pennsylvania Assembly (1751–1764), postmaster of the colonies (1753–1774), delegate to the Albany Congress in 1754, agent in England for Pennsylvania, Georgia, and Massachusetts in the 1760s, member of the 2nd Continental Congress, helped draft and was a signer of the Declaration of Independence, member of the U.S. delegation to negotiate peace with Britain.

Alexander Hamilton (born in Nevis in the British West Indies, 1755; died in New York City, 1804) lawyer, pamphleteer for the revolution, aide-de-camp for General Washington, a key supporter and propagandist for the Constitution, 1st Secretary of the Treasury of the United States.

John Hancock (born in Massachusetts, 1737; died in Massachusetts, 1793) merchant, took part in the Stamp Act protest (1765), member of the Massachusetts Assembly (1769), head of the Boston town committee (1770), elected president of the Massachusetts Provincial Congress (1774); he and Samuel Adams were the only two men denied amnesty in General Thomas Gage's Proclamation of June 12, 1775; delegate to the 2nd Continental Congress (1775), president of the 2nd Continental Congress (1775–1777), 1st signer of the Declaration of Independence.

Patrick Henry (born in Virginia, 1736; died in Virginia, 1799) lawyer, orator, planter, member of Virginia's House of Burgesses after

Thomas Paine   Mercy Otis Warren

writs of assistance (1761), member of the Massachusetts Assembly in the 1760s, patriot pamphleteer, Stamp Act Congress delegate (1765), by 1770s suffered from mental illness which incapacitated him. He died when struck by lightning on May 23, 1783.

Thomas Paine (born in Norfolk, England, 1737; died in New York City, 1809) jack-of-many-manual-trades, came to the colonies in 1774, wrote two of the most important pamphlets of the revolution: *Common Sense* (1776) and the series, *Crisis* (1776-1783). *Common Sense* is believed to have converted thousands to the cause of revolution and independence. The opening passage of the first *Crisis* paper was read to Patriot troops in army camps. It read: "These are the times that try men's souls. The summer soldier and the sunshine patriot will, in this crisis, shrink from the service of their country; but he that stands it *now*, deserves the love and thanks of man and woman." These words inspired many troops to stay and fight despite harsh conditions.

Mercy Otis Warren (born in Massachusetts, 1728; died in Massachusetts, 1814) leading propagandist for the revolution in Massachusetts, author of patriotic poems, plays, and satiric verse between 1772 and 1776, influential in the creation of the first Committee of Correspondence (1772), one of the first historians of the American Revolution. Her 1805 book, *History of the Rise, Progress and Termination of the American Revolution*, was begun in the late 1770s.

George Washington (born in Virginia, 1732; died in Virginia, 1799) planter, surveyor, military officer, member of the Virginia House of Burgesses from 1759, delegate to the 1st and 2nd Continental Congresses, commander-in-chief of the Continental Army as of June 1775, and 1st President of the United States.

1765, leader against the Stamp Act in Virginia, leading force in reassembling the House of Burgesses when the royal governor dissolved it in 1774, made a famous speech on March 23, 1775, calling for resistance to England in which he cried, "Give me liberty, or give me death!", member of the 1st Continental Congress, helped draft the Virginia Constitution of 1776, governor of Virginia (1776-1779), opposed the ratification of the U.S. Constitution, and a key figure in the winning of the Bill of Rights.

John Jay (born in New York City, 1745; died in New York, 1829) lawyer, member of the 1st and 2nd Continental Congresses (1774-1776) and of the New York Provincial Congress (1776-1777), member of the U.S. delegation to negotiate peace with Britain, 1st Chief Justice of the Supreme Court of the United States.

Thomas Jefferson (born in Virginia, 1743; died in Virginia, 1826) lawyer, author, planter, scientist, architect, member of the Virginia House of Burgesses (1769-1775), delegate to

the 1st and 2nd Continental Congresses, wrote and signed the Declaration of Independence, member of the Virginia legislature (1776-1779), governor of Virginia (1779-1781), member of the Confederation Congress and later 1st U.S. Secretary of State, 3rd U.S. President.

James Madison (born in Virginia, 1751; died in Virginia, 1836) chairman of the Committee of Public Safety for Orange County, Virginia (1775), helped draft Virginia's Constitution in the Virginia Convention (1776), served in the Continental Congress (1780-1783), and helped form the compromise plan that led to the acceptance of the Articles of Confederation. Later he was a major figure in the adoption of the Constitution, author of the Bill of Rights, Secretary of State under Jefferson, and 4th President of the United States.

James Otis (born in Massachusetts, 1725; died in Massachusetts, 1783) brother of Mercy Otis Warren, lawyer, resigned his office as king's advocate general of the vice-admiralty court to argue against general search warrants called

4. THE PATH TOWARD INDEPENDENCE

Americans took speedy action against the Coercive Acts and against the English government. In September 1774, the **First Continental Congress** met in Philadelphia to plan a response to the crisis. All the colonies except Georgia sent delegates.

Most leaders who attended the meeting now came much closer to agreeing with Samuel Adams than they had back in 1767. The group took bold steps almost immediately. The Congress called on the people of Massachusetts to arm themselves and to organize their militia, or citizens' army.

This warlike order, known as the "Suffolk Resolves," troubled many moderate-minded delegates. Joseph Galloway of Pennsylvania tried to persuade the Congress to seek peaceful compromise with England. He proposed a plan for uniting the colonies, giving Parliament the right to make laws for the colonies but not to tax them. By a close vote his plan was rejected. In the fall of 1774 his fellow delegates no longer believed that Parliament had *any* right to govern the colonies. In their minds, the 13 colonial assemblies and the English Parliament were equal governments, linked—as John Adams put it—only by their loyalty to the king of England.

The view that the colonial governments were equal to Parliament was a radical vision of the empire. Yet the members of the First Continental Congress stopped short of declaring their independence from England. "We want no revolution," said a delegate from North Carolina. Instead, the Congress appealed to King George III to end the punishment of Boston and to take an active part in restoring peace.

In England, however, an angry king had already declared the New England colonies to be in a state of rebellion. "Blows must decide," wrote George III.

Fighting Begins

Blows did decide. In Massachusetts two armies were preparing for confrontation. Colonists in small towns and villages practiced marching and musket loading on their village greens. English troops paraded on Boston streets.

Rumors of surprise attacks by the Redcoats spread through the colony. At Salem, Massachusetts, Redcoats and militia had almost clashed when they met accidentally at the Salem bridge. Then, on April 18, 1775, news came that the English troops were planning to march on Concord, where an ammunition depot [dep/ō] was located. (See map, opposite page.)

The English were under orders to seize these supplies. They were also planning to arrest the two most important leaders of the resistance in the colony, Samuel Adams and the merchant John Hancock.

Quickly, colonial spies sent a signal to warn their country neighbors. In the bell tower of Boston's North Church a lantern flashed, once, then once again. The signal had been given: the English were crossing the Charles River to march toward Concord. It was late at night. Paul Revere and William Dawes of Boston mounted their horses and, taking separate routes, rode out to warn Hancock and Adams to flee.

Revere reached Lexington around midnight. He warned the people that the Redcoats were coming and then rode on with Dawes and Samuel Prescott toward Concord. A British patrol captured Revere and forced Dawes to turn back, but Prescott reached Concord and warned the militia to hide the weapons and supplies.

At Lexington, the defenders waited on the village green. When dawn came, the road from the coast was still empty. Perhaps the English were not coming after all. Suddenly, a man came galloping toward them, shouting "They are coming!" Lexington militia captain John Parker hurriedly mustered his 70 men and boys together on the green.

The Lexington militia did not block the path to Concord. The pathway and bridge to that neighboring town were clear. Parker's militia meant only to make a show of solidarity with their fellow colonists. But the approaching British soldiers, tired from the all-night march, were nervous and hostile.

The English troops were thousands of miles from home, thrust among people who jeered at them and hated them. A British major rode onto the Lexington green and shouted at the colonists to disperse.

Before the militia broke ranks, British soldiers poured onto the green, cheering. Some militiamen scattered; others held their ground. Shots rang out. Eight Americans died, and ten fell wounded. As suddenly as it began, the **Battle of Lexington** was over. But "the shot heard 'round the world" had entered history.

The English troops marched on to Concord. Here they were met by streams of militiamen, pouring in from neighboring farms and nearby towns. At Concord's North Bridge, shots were fired for the second time that day. As the Redcoats tried to make their way back to Boston, the Americans continued the assault. Farmers-turned-soldiers fired at the retreating lines of British infantrymen from behind their barns and from the cover of fences and bushes. A war that was not yet really a war had begun in earnest.

Last Efforts at Reconciliation

Even as the battle was fought on Lexington Green, delegates from the colonies were on their way once again to Philadelphia for the **Second Continental Congress**. Sobering images of battle and death hung over this group of distinguished colonial leaders. The delegates knew that they must make speedy preparations for war, even as they continued to hope for peace.

The Congress took several important military steps. They invited patriot ship captains to create a colonial navy by arming their vessels and sailing as privateers (privately owned warships). They appropriated funds to recruit a continental army, and appointed generals to lead American forces should peace efforts fail. **George Washington** of Virginia was named commander-in-chief.

To justify these military activities, the delegates composed a legal argument in their defense. Like the good lawyers that most of these men were, they reviewed the events of the last decade and explained the colonists' position. The result was a "Declaration of the Causes and Necessity of Taking Up Arms," adopted on July 6, 1775. Yet this statement was no formal declaration of war. In truth, the delegates were even busier pursuing peace.

At the same time, Congress also sent an Olive Branch Petition to George III, proposing an end to all violence and a lifting of the Coercive Acts. The delegates knew that many Americans were ready to fight to protect their liberties—and would do so throughout 1775 and early 1776. But how many Americans, the troubled delegates wondered, were ready to break the binding ties to the Mother Country entirely, and forever?

Hopes for peace were still alive in England too. In Parliament, Edmund Burke addressed his fellow members of the House of Commons with a brilliant plea for conciliation between mother country and colonies. He reminded Parliament

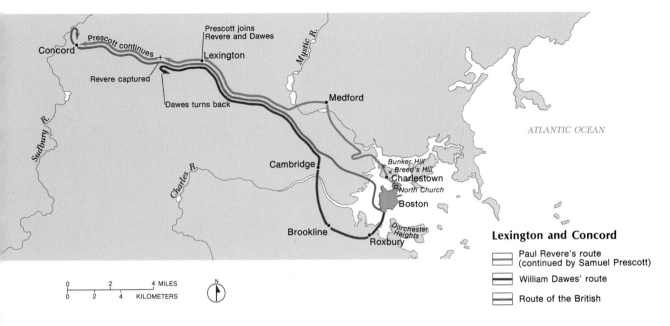

Lexington and Concord

- Paul Revere's route (continued by Samuel Prescott)
- William Dawes' route
- Route of the British

Year	British Law	Colonial Reaction
1763	**Proclamation of 1763** forbids colonial settlement west of the Appalachians.	Colonists protest; some ignore the law.
1764	**Sugar Act** cuts in half the import duty on foreign molasses but enforces law strictly.	Colonists raise cry of "no taxation without representation" and boycott British products.
1765	**Quartering Act** requires colonists to furnish food and lodging for British troops. **Stamp Act** levies a tax on newspapers, marriage licenses, and other documents.	Colonial assemblies pass resolutions. Colonists boycott British products. Sons of Liberty attack stamp agents. Stamp Act Congress sends Declaration of Rights and Grievances to Parliament.
1766	**Repeal of Stamp Act.** Parliament passes Declaratory Act stating its right to tax the colonists.	New York refuses to enforce Quartering Act. Colonists ignore Declaratory Act.
1767	**Townshend Acts** impose duties on paper, tea, paint, lead, and other items. **Suspension of New York Assembly** for its refusal to enforce Quartering Act.	Colonial assemblies pass resolutions challenging Parliament's right to tax them. Colonists boycott British products. Sons of Liberty enforce boycotts. Colonists rally to the support of New York. Numerous protests held.
1770	**Repeal of the Townshend Acts** except the tax on tea.	Colonial boycotts ended and calm restored.
1773	**Tea Act** gives the East India Company a monopoly on the colonial tea trade.	In the Boston Tea Party incident, colonists dump the company's tea into the Boston harbor. In other colonies the company's ships are not allowed to unload, or the tea is confiscated.
1774	**Coercive (Intolerable) Acts** punish Boston for the Tea Party. (1) Boston's port is closed. (2) Britain takes tighter control of Massachusetts' government. (3) The Quartering Act directs colonists to find housing and certain supplies for British troops. (4) British soldiers will be tried in England for certain crimes. **Quebec Act** sets up a civil government and recognizes certain French laws in Quebec. It grants religious and political freedom to Catholics in Quebec. It also extends the boundaries of Quebec southwestward to the Ohio and Mississippi rivers.	Colonists interpret the Quebec Act as evidence that Britain wants to close the west to settlers from the 13 colonies. Protestants are alarmed over religious provisions of the act. Because of the Quebec Act and the Coercive Acts, all the colonies except Georgia send delegates to the Continental Congress. Congress calls for defense measures against British attack, authorizes another boycott against British goods, and appeals to King George III to restore the peace.
1775	**First battle of Revolutionary War** results when British troops encounter colonial militia at Lexington while en route to Concord to seize military supplies.	

that the colonies were worth far more as a market for English manufactured goods than any tax bill would ever profit the government.

To lose the colonies because they resisted taxation would be a foolish, self-defeating act, Burke argued. But Parliament turned a deaf ear, and the king was determined to crush colonial resistance. In late autumn, 1775, Parliament issued an American Prohibitory Act. This act ordered the Royal Navy to seize American ships "as if the same were the ships and effects of open enemies." Here, in fact, was a declaration of war.

A Crisis of Loyalties

By the end of 1775 the crisis of loyalties was at hand for every American. Each would have to decide: must I be loyal to the king or loyal to my fellow Americans?

Revolution and rebellion were not easy ideas for colonists to contemplate. They had been raised to respect the king and to honor the British Constitution. One radical, **Thomas Paine**, did much to help the colonists throw off their old affections for the mother country. In January 1776, Paine published a pamphlet he called *Common Sense*.

In *Common Sense*, Paine argued that the separation between the parent, England, and the children, the colonies, was a natural part of growth and change. Independence meant adulthood, and its time had come. Paine openly criticized the king, something few colonists had ever done. Americans had criticized Parliament and the king's advisers, but never the king himself.

Paine shocked Americans, but he also convinced many of them. By the spring of 1776, the decision to break with England had separated **Patriots** (rebels) from **Loyalists**. Loyalists, like John Adams' friend Jonathan Sewall, opposed the call for revolution. These men and women were no different from their Patriot neighbors: they were rich, poor, white, black, farmers, housewives, merchants, ministers, slaves. But they did not favor fighting for independence.

Some Loyalists feared revolution and the confusion it could bring to human life. Some feared that the poor would kill the rich, once war began. Some feared that the slaves would learn rebellion from their masters. Many feared that God would punish people who rose up against their lawful king. Most white Loyalists believed, above all, that England would crush the rebellion and that thousands would die needlessly. They loved their colonies, and they did not wish to see rebellion destroy them. Only black Loyalists viewed the war with optimism. These slaves of Patriots hoped that loyalty to and military service for the king would win them freedom.

Almost all of the white colonists had moments of doubt. Even Thomas Jefferson, John Adams, and Benjamin Franklin came only reluctantly to believe that revolution was the only way to defend the liberties Americans cherished. Yet about one-third of the colonists chose to support the struggle against the king and Parliament.

FROM THE ARCHIVES

Thomas Paine's *Common Sense*

I have heard it asserted by some, that as America hath flourished under her former connection with Great Britain, that the same connection is necessary toward her future happiness, and will always have the same effect. Nothing can be more fallacious than this kind of argument. We may as well assert that because a child has thriven upon milk, that it is never to have meat, or that the first twenty years of our lives is to become a precedent for the next twenty. . . . I answer roundly, that America would have flourished as much, and probably much more, had no European power had anything to do with her. The commerce by which she hath enriched herself, are the necessaries of life, and will always have a market while eating is the custom of Europe.

On July 2, 1776, the 56 delegates to the Second Continental Congress approved a **Declaration of Independence**, written by **Thomas Jefferson** with the help of John Adams, Benjamin Franklin, Robert Livingston, and Roger Sherman. On July 4th, the colonists learned that they were now struggling not just to defend their homes, but to be a nation.

SECTION 4 REVIEW

Identify: First Continental Congress, Battle of Lexington, Second Continental Congress, George Washington, Thomas Paine, *Common Sense*, Patriots, Loyalists, Declaration of Independence, Thomas Jefferson

Main Ideas

1. What request did the First Continental Congress send to King George III? What was his response?
2. What events led to the battles of Lexington and Concord?
3. What steps did the Second Continental Congress take to prepare for war? To achieve reconciliation?
4. Why did the Second Continental Congress declare independence?

The Declaration of Independence

IN CONGRESS, JULY 4, 1776. THE UNANIMOUS DEC-LARATION OF THE THIRTEEN UNITED STATES OF AMERICA—When in the Course of human events, it becomes necessary for one people to dissolve the political bands which have connected them with another, and to assume among the powers of the earth, the separate and equal station to which the Laws of Nature and of Nature's God entitle them, a decent respect to the opinions of mankind requires that they should declare the causes which impel them to the separation.

We hold these truths to be self-evident, that all men are created equal, that they are endowed by their Creator with certain unalienable Rights, that among these are Life, Liberty and the pursuit of Happiness.

That to secure these rights, Governments are instituted among Men, deriving their just powers from the consent of the governed,

That whenever any Form of Government becomes destructive of these ends, it is the Right of the People to alter or to abolish it, and to institute new Government, laying its foundation on such principles and organizing its powers in such form, as to them shall seem most likely to effect their Safety and Happiness. Prudence, indeed, will dictate that Governments long established should not be changed for light and transient causes; and accordingly all experience hath shown, that mankind are more disposed to suffer, while evils are sufferable, than to right themselves by abolishing the forms to which they are accustomed. But when a long train of abuses and usurpations, pursuing invariably the same Object evinces a design to reduce them under absolute Despotism, it is their right, it is their duty, to throw off such Government, and to provide new Guards for their future security.

Such has been the patient sufferance of these Colonies; and such is now the necessity which constrains them to alter their former Systems of Government.

The history of the present King of Great Britain is a history of repeated injuries and usurpations, all having in direct object the establishment of an absolute Tyranny over these States. To prove this, let Facts be submitted to a candid world.

He has refused his Assent to Laws, the most wholesome and necessary for the public good.

He has forbidden his Governors to pass Laws of immediate and pressing importance, unless suspended in their operation till his Assent should be obtained; and when so suspended, he has utterly neglected to attend to them.

He has refused to pass other Laws for the accommodation of large districts of people, unless those people would relinquish the right of Representation in the Legislature, a right inestimable to them and formidable to tyrants only.

He has called together legislative bodies at places unusual, uncomfortable, and distant from the depository of their public Records, for the sole purpose of fatiguing them into compliance with his measures.

He has dissolved Representative Houses repeatedly, for opposing with manly firmness his invasions on the rights of the people.

He has refused for a long time, after such dissolutions, to cause others to be elected; whereby the Legislative powers, incapable of Annihilation, have returned to the People at large for their exercise; the State remaining in the mean time exposed to all the dangers of invasion from without, and convulsions within.

He has endeavoured to prevent the population of these States; for that purpose obstructing the Laws for Naturalization of Foreigners; refusing to pass others to encourage their migration hither, and raising the conditions of new Appropriations of Lands.

He has obstructed the Administration of Justice, by refusing his Assent to Laws for establishing Judiciary powers.

He has made Judges dependent on his Will alone, for the tenure of their offices, and the amount and payment of their salaries.

He has erected a multitude of New Offices, and sent hither swarms of Officers to harass our people, and eat out their substance.

He has kept among us, in times of peace, Standing Armies, without the Consent of our legislatures.

He has affected to render the Military independent of and superior to the Civil power.

He has combined with others to subject us to a jurisdiction foreign to our constitution, and unacknowledged by our laws; giving his Assent to their Acts of pretended Legislation:

For quartering large bodies of armed troops among us:

For protecting them, by a mock Trial, from punishment for any Murders which they should commit on the Inhabitants of these States:

For cutting off our Trade with all parts of the world:

For imposing Taxes on us without our Consent:

For depriving us in many cases, of the benefits of Trial by Jury:

For transporting us beyond Seas to be tried for pretended offences:

For abolishing the free System of English Laws in a neighbouring Province, establishing therein an Arbitrary government, and enlarging its Boundaries so as to render it at once an example and fit instrument for introducing the same absolute rule into these Colonies:

For taking away our Charters, abolishing our most valuable Laws, and altering fundamentally the Forms of our Governments:

For suspending our own Legislatures, and declaring themselves invested with power to legislate for us in all cases whatsoever.

He has abdicated Government here, by declaring us out of his Protection and waging War against us.

He has plundered our seas, ravaged our Coasts, burnt our towns, and destroyed the lives of our people.

He is at this time transporting large Armies of foreign Mercenaries to compleat the works of death, desolation and tyranny, already begun with circumstances of Cruelty & perfidy scarcely paralleled in the most barbarous ages, and totally unworthy the Head of a civilized nation.

He has constrained our fellow Citizens taken Captive on the high Seas to bear Arms against their Country, to become the executioners of their friends and Brethren, or to fall themselves by their Hands.

He has excited domestic insurrections amongst us, and has endeavoured to bring on the inhabitants of our frontiers, the merciless Indian Savages, whose known rule of warfare, is an undistinguished destruction of all ages, sexes and conditions.

In every stage of these Oppressions We have Petitioned for Redress in the most humble terms: Our repeated Petitions have been answered only by repeated injury. A Prince, whose character is thus marked by every act which may define a Tyrant, is unfit to be the ruler of a free people.

Nor have We been wanting in attention to our Brittish brethren. We have warned them from time to time of attempts by their legislature to extend an unwarrantable jurisdiction over us. We have reminded them of the circumstances of our emigration and settlement here. We have appealed to their native justice and magnanimity, and we have conjured them by the ties of our common kindred to disavow these usurpations, which, would inevitably interrupt our connections and correspondence. They too have been deaf to the voice of justice and of consanguinity. We must, therefore, acquiesce in the necessity, which denounces our Separation, and hold them, as we hold the rest of mankind, Enemies in War, in Peace Friends.

WE, THEREFORE, the REPRESENTATIVES of the UNITED STATES OF AMERICA, in General Congress, Assembled, appealing to the Supreme Judge of the world for the rectitude of our intentions, do, in the Name, and by Authority of the good People of these Colonies, solemnly publish and declare, That these United Colonies are, and of Right ought to be FREE AND INDEPENDENT STATES; that they are Absolved from all Allegiance to the British Crown, and that all political connection between them and the State of Great Britain, is and ought to be totally dissolved; and that as Free and Independent States, they have full Power to levy War, conclude Peace, contract Alliances, establish Commerce, and to do all other Acts and Things which Independent States may of right do. And for the support of this Declaration, with a firm reliance on the protection of Divine Providence, we mutually pledge to each other our Lives, our Fortunes and our sacred Honor.

John Hancock

Button Gwinnett
Lyman Hall
George Walton
William Hooper
Joseph Hewes
John Penn
Edward Rutledge
Thomas Heyward, Junior
Thomas Lynch, Junior
Arthur Middleton
Samuel Chase
William Paca
Thomas Stone
Charles Carroll of
  Carrollton
George Wythe
Richard Henry Lee
Thomas Jefferson
Benjamin Harrison
Thomas Nelson, Junior
Francis Lightfoot Lee
Carter Braxton
Robert Morris
Benjamin Rush
Benjamin Franklin
John Morton
George Clymer
James Smith

George Taylor
James Wilson
George Ross
Caesar Rodney
George Read
Thomas McKean
William Floyd
Philip Livingston
Francis Lewis
Lewis Morris
Richard Stockton
John Witherspoon
Francis Hopkinson
John Hart
Abraham Clark
Josiah Bartlett
William Whipple
Samuel Adams
John Adams
Robert Treat Paine
Elbridge Gerry
Stephen Hopkins
William Ellery
Roger Sherman
Samuel Huntington
William Williams
Oliver Wolcott
Matthew Thornton

CHAPTER 6 REVIEW

Key Terms
Explain the meaning of each of the following terms:

French and Indian War
Seven Years' War
Treaty of Paris of 1763
Pontiac's Rebellion
Proclamation Line
  of 1763
salutary neglect
Quartering Act
Sons of Liberty
virtual representation
Stamp Act Congress
Boston Massacre
Committees of
  Correspondence

Tea Act
Boston Tea Party
Coercive Acts
Quebec Act
First Continental
  Congress
Battle of Lexington
Second Continental
  Congress
Common Sense
Patriots
Loyalists
Declaration of
  Independence

Reviewing the Main Ideas
Section 1
1. What problems did Britain face after winning the Seven Years' War?
2. Why was the British government poorly equipped to handle these problems?

Section 2
1. Why did the colonists oppose the Proclamation of 1763, the Sugar Act, and the Stamp Act?
2. What was the British view of these laws?
3. What important things did the colonists learn from the Stamp Act crisis?

Section 3
1. How did the Townshend Acts, Coercive Acts, and Quebec Act anger and unify the colonists?
2. Why did the British government feel that it must discipline the colonies?

Section 4
1. How did King George III respond to the First Continental Congress' call for reconciliation?
2. What events led to the battles of Lexington and Concord?
3. Why did the Second Continental Congress declare independence?

Special History Skills:
Making Time Lines
A time line is a list of events. It can help you tell when important events occurred and how close in time they were to other events. For example, a brief time line of your life might look like this:

Birth 1st step 1st day of school   Now

You can tell from the time line that your first step was closer to your birth than to your first day of school.

Now draw a time line showing major events between 1763 and 1776 that led to the American Revolution. List at least ten events. Do events get closer in time or further apart during the years 1763–1776? How might this affect attitudes in the colonies and in England?

Other Skills Activities
1. Loyalist or rebel?
If you had been a colonist, would you have been a Loyalist like Jonathan Sewall or a rebel like John Adams? Write a letter to a fellow colonist convincing him or her to remain loyal. Or, write a letter telling a friend why you decided to rebel. Give your letter a specific date and discuss actual events.

2. Revolutionary puzzle
Make a crossword puzzle using the names of the actions of Parliament and the actions of the colonies. Be sure your puzzle clues include the year in which the various acts occurred.

3. Revolutionary leaders
Write short biographies of two American revolutionaries. In what ways are their backgrounds and ideas similar and different?

4. Protest songs
Compose a protest song or poem which expresses the feelings of an American in 1767. Write a second song or poem, but date it 1776. What is the difference between your two works?

Thinking Critically
1. Should England or the colonies have paid for the Seven Years' War? Give at least two reasons why each side should pay and two reasons why each should not pay.

2. What methods did the colonists use to fight against the Sugar Act, Stamp Act, and Intolerable Acts? Imagine that you were a colonist. How would you have felt about these actions? Would you have considered any of them immoral and/or treasonous?
3. At what point do you think the Revolution was inevitable? When the first colonists arrived in 1607? In 1766, after the Stamp Act crisis? When England changed to a "tough" policy in 1770–1773? After the Battle of Lexington? Other? Defend your decision with facts.
4. Which was more "revolutionary," the British attempt to enforce trade laws and tax the colonists, or the colonists' attempt to rule themselves?

Further Reading

Bruce Bliven. *A Mirror for Greatness: Six Americans.* McGraw-Hill, 1975. Biographies of Franklin, Adams, and Jefferson are included.

Theodore Taylor. *Rebellion Town, Williamsburg, 1776.* Crowell, 1973. Brings to life clashes with the king's government, debates between Loyalists and rebels, and the drafting of Virginia's Declaration of Rights and Constitution. Emphasizes the setting of Williamsburg.

Jean Poindexter Colby. *Lexington and Concord, 1775: What Really Happened.* Hastings House, 1975. Examines events before, during, and after the first battles of the American Revolution. Many photos and descriptions of sites still standing are included.

Esther Forbes. *Johnny Tremain.* Houghton Mifflin, 1945. A classic novel of growing up and adventure for a boy apprentice in revolutionary Boston.

TEST YOURSELF

WRITE YOUR ANSWERS ON A SEPARATE SHEET OF PAPER.

True or False

Mark T if the statement is true, F if it is false.
1. The Proclamation Line of 1763 temporarily closed the door to colonial settlement west of the Appalachian Mountains.
2. Colonists opposed the Stamp Act because it was the first attempt of Parliament to tax them directly.
3. The Townshend Acts closed the port of Boston to all shipping.
4. Thomas Paine's *Common Sense* inspired many colonists to break colonial ties with England.
5. The Coercive Acts and Quebec Act did much to forge colonial unity.

Matching

Select the letter of the answer that best matches each item below.
1. Committees of Correspondence
2. Lexington Green
3. Second Continental Congress
4. Samuel Adams
5. Declaratory Act
6. Thomas Jefferson
7. Stamp Act
8. Coercive Acts
9. Pontiac's Rebellion
10. salutary neglect

a. wrote the Declaration of Independence
b. tax collected on documents and newspapers
c. led to the Proclamation of 1763
d. policy of not regulating the colonies closely
e. stated Parliament's right to tax the colonists
f. revolutionary leader in Massachusetts; one of the first to call for independence
g. effective line of communication between the 13 colonies
h. revoked the Massachusetts charter of 1691 and changed its government
i. first battle between the British and Americans
j. issued the Declaration of Independence

Classifying

Classify each of the following British laws. Mark M if it was designed to raise money, P if it was meant to punish the colonists, and A if it had another purpose.
1. Sugar Act
2. Coercive Acts
3. Townshend Acts
4. Quebec Act
5. Stamp Act

THE WAR FOR INDEPENDENCE

Between 1763 and 1775 the Americans had often amazed and annoyed the British. For the next eight years, they would continue to do so. The Redcoats were professional soldiers, with officers from the aristocracy and fighting men from the poor, the desperate, and the hopeless. They faced an undisciplined force of American citizen-soldiers, who did not fight according to the established rules.

The Redcoats were accustomed to the formal, patterned warfare of Europe. There, battles were fought on open fields in good weather in daylight. Opposing armies faced each other, with artillery, cavalry, and infantry carefully separated for their different tasks. When the muskets were empty, the cannons silent, the sabers in their sheaths, then the side with the most survivors would claim victory.

In the wars of Europe there were no midnight raids nor attacks from behind barns, trees, and bushes. But in the American Revolution, there were all these guerrilla tactics, and more. American armies—outnumbered and untrained—did not stand and fight. For two years, George Washington's men ducked and darted, raided and ran, keeping the revolution alive by avoiding capture.

England's army was the strongest in the world and the most professional. Its navy was mistress of the seas. Yet there was hope for the Americans. England had to wage a war 3,000 miles from home. The Americans were on their own soil, and they were willing to fight for their independence.

Sections in This Chapter
1. The War in the North, 1775–1776
2. The War in the South and the Middle Colonies, 1776–1777
3. Women in the Revolutionary War
4. From Saratoga to Yorktown, 1777–1781
5. The Peacemakers and Their Treaty

Opposite: A silent snowfall covers the quiet cannons of Fort Ticonderoga in upstate New York.

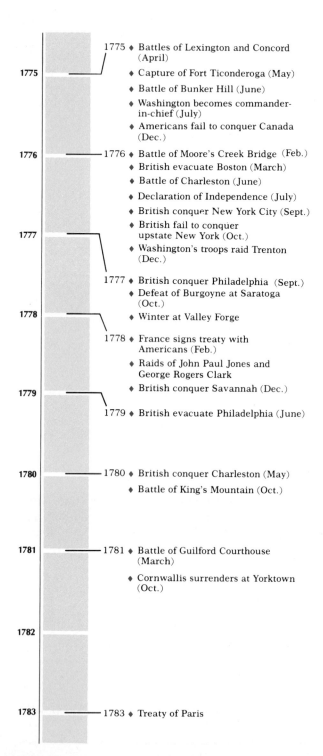

1775 ◆ Battles of Lexington and Concord (April)

◆ Capture of Fort Ticonderoga (May)

◆ Battle of Bunker Hill (June)

◆ Washington becomes commander-in-chief (July)

◆ Americans fail to conquer Canada (Dec.)

1776 ◆ Battle of Moore's Creek Bridge (Feb.)

◆ British evacuate Boston (March)

◆ Battle of Charleston (June)

◆ Declaration of Independence (July)

◆ British conquer New York City (Sept.)

◆ British fail to conquer upstate New York (Oct.)

◆ Washington's troops raid Trenton (Dec.)

1777 ◆ British conquer Philadelphia (Sept.)

◆ Defeat of Burgoyne at Saratoga (Oct.)

◆ Winter at Valley Forge

1778 ◆ France signs treaty with Americans (Feb.)

◆ Raids of John Paul Jones and George Rogers Clark

◆ British conquer Savannah (Dec.)

1779 ◆ British evacuate Philadelphia (June)

1780 ◆ British conquer Charleston (May)

◆ Battle of King's Mountain (Oct.)

1781 ◆ Battle of Guilford Courthouse (March)

◆ Cornwallis surrenders at Yorktown (Oct.)

1783 ◆ Treaty of Paris

1. THE WAR IN THE NORTH, 1775–1776

When the war began at the Battle of Lexington, America had no professional army. General Washington did forge a small army for Congress out of the Continental recruits, but in large part the war was fought by citizen-soldiers, or **militia**. The militia was a home guard of able-bodied men, aged 16 to 60, in every community. These troops were raw, inexperienced, and undisciplined. Yet, fired by patriotism, they were often moved to remarkable bravery. A militia was a motley crew, but it was always there—in New England, in New York, in Pennsylvania, in the South—when the Continental army needed help. The Revolution was a people's war, not just a battle between armies. Women, children, old men, and young all aided their chosen cause.

The Beginning of the War

Throughout 1775 and early 1776, the center of hostilities was Boston. The British army, under General Thomas Gage, occupied the city. The American forces were scattered in the neighboring countryside. The army that awaited George Washington in Massachusetts in July 1775 was a ragtag collection of 10,000 militiamen and a small band of Continental soldiers. Since the battles at Lexington and Concord, it had been largely the militia's job to hold the Redcoats at bay in Boston. Surveying his troops, Washington must have despaired. His officers were inexperienced. Henry Knox, the tactical genius of the American army at Boston, was a bookseller who had learned everything he knew about military matters from the books in his shop! The enlisted men looked no more promising. Many were too young or too old. They were poorly equipped and undisciplined. There were rivalries between troops from different colonies, and the army was dangerously short of ammunition.

The British army in Boston, on the other hand, boasted well-armed reinforcements and a trio of newly arrived gentlemen generals. The tall, handsome General William Howe, a man devoted to beautiful women and fine wines as much as to combat, had joined General Thomas Gage in Boston. The ambitious but much too cautious General Henry Clinton and the young, witty "Gentleman Johnny" Burgoyne were also at Gage's headquarters.

The Battle of Bunker Hill

Despite the military presence in Massachusetts, the only major battle there after Lexington and Concord between Patriot and Redcoat forces occurred in June 1775, a month before Washington's arrival. On June 12, General Gage issued a proclamation declaring all armed Americans to be traitors. However, the proclamation offered amnesty [am′nəs tē], or pardon, to any colonist who laid down his arms and returned home. Only John Hancock and Samuel Adams were denied pardons. The Americans greeted Gage's offer with stony silence.

Gage's army then fortified nearby Dorchester Heights. (See map, page 151.) On June 16, the Americans responded by fortifying Breed's Hill and occupying Bunker Hill. Gage read this action as a challenge and decided to attack.

On June 17, General Howe led 2,400 men against the American fortification at Breed's Hill. The Redcoats, each carrying a 100-pound knapsack on his back, approached the American position in march formation. This frontal attack was a mistake that cost the lives of 40% of these British soldiers.

Only 1,200 Americans were on Breed's Hill, but by staggering their loading and firing, they kept up a steady barrage against the oncoming soldiers. But they ran out of ammunition midway through the battle, and confusion behind the battle lines delayed the arrival of reinforcements and supplies. In the end the British took Breed's and Bunker hills.

Though most of the action took place on Breed's Hill, the battle is usually called the **Battle of Bunker Hill.** It was the first direct confrontation between American and British troops. In terms of human life it was the costliest in the entire war.

The Capture of Fort Ticonderoga

It was clear to the Americans that no attack on enemy-held Boston was possible without artillery (cannons and other heavy firearms). But the Americans had no cannons. Even before Washington arrived in Boston, therefore, a plan had been hatched to capture artillery from the enemy. Back in May 1775, the young military wizard **Benedict Arnold** took a detachment of 400 Patriots westward toward the British-held **Fort Ticonderoga.** (See map, next page.)

This fort on Lake Champlain in New York colony had just the heavy cannon and supply of shot the Patriots needed. However, Benedict Arnold was not the only man with his eye on Ticonderoga. Almost simultaneously, Vermont leader **Ethan Allen** gathered up his private army of **Green Mountain Boys** and headed toward the fort.

Both Arnold and Allen had strong wills and stubborn pride, and both craved the limelight. Each demanded that the other abandon his plan of attack. After much argument, the two men finally agreed to join forces and fight the British rather than each other.

On May 10, 1775, Arnold, Allen, and 83 hand-picked Green Mountain Boys surprised the garrison at Fort Ticonderoga. The commander, asleep when the attack began, surrendered the fort before he even had his breeches on. After this victory, the two American leaders parted company. Allen and his men went on to take the fort at Crown Point, north of Ticonderoga, and Benedict Arnold's troops seized Fort St. John across the border in Canada. The first genuine victories of the war had been won by Americans.

With the capture of Ticonderoga, the American army now had artillery. But how could Washington use it in Boston while it sat 300 miles away? The young bookseller, Henry Knox, figured out the answer. He had the Patriots construct sledges to be pulled by teams of oxen. In December the cannons were loaded on the sledges and pulled across the winter snows to Boston. By January 25, 1776, General Washington had his artillery.

Victory in Massachusetts

The British had done nothing to destroy the American army since the previous June at Bunker Hill. Gage, and his successor in command, William Howe, seemed content to sit tight in Boston, waiting, perhaps, for warmer weather. Their inactivity proved their undoing.

On March 4, 1776, Washington's soldiers seized the abandoned fortifications at Dorchester Heights. From this elevated spot, the Americans could easily bombard the city. General Howe

Overview of the
Revolutionary War

▨ The 13 colonies

▨ Other British colonies and claims

☒ Battles

looked up the next day to see cannon pointing down on an unprotected Boston.

Howe recognized defeat when he saw it. On March 17, the British army evacuated Boston, loading troops, horses, supplies, weapons, and over 1,000 refugee Loyalists into the transport ships in Boston Harbor. Howe moved to conquer New York City as the new British base of operations. Washington hurried to defend the Revolution there. Henry Clinton took his troops to South Carolina. With that, the English turned Massachusetts over to its rebel inhabitants forever.

The Americans Fail to Conquer Canada

While Washington faced the British at Boston, a second American army was on its way to conquer Canada. Unfortunately, these Americans would not let military inexperience stand in the way of their dreams of glory.

At first, the Continental Congress forbade the invasion of Canada, hoping that the Canadians would join the rebellion. Ambassadors had even been sent north to test the political mood of the French inhabitants.

However, in the fall of 1775, intelligence reports came to Congress that Sir Guy Carleton, the Governor General of Canada, was planning a full-scale invasion of New York. This news—or rumor—altered the situation. Congress now approved the move against Canada as a security measure.

The first American successes in Canada were deceptive. On October 13, 1775, Montreal fell to the Patriot troops. (See map.) On November 13, Benedict Arnold stood with his Patriots on the banks of the St. Lawrence River, staring up at the sheer cliffs that must be scaled to reach Quebec.

In the 18th century, European armies did not fight in winter. But the Americans broke the pattern. This time, American willingness to improvise proved foolish. On December 3, a second force of 300 Americans, led by Richard Montgomery, joined Arnold outside Quebec. Their situation was not promising. Winter had begun in earnest, and it was bitterly cold. Supplies were short, and the soldiers' enlistments were almost up. The men were uncomfortable and restless.

But Arnold would not abandon his scheme. The combined forces of Arnold and Montgomery stormed the gates of Quebec on December 31, in the midst of a raging blizzard. Almost immediately, Montgomery was killed by cannon fire, and Arnold was wounded. Half the American troops were captured or killed. The British soldiers were shocked at the folly of their enemy.

Despite this defeat, Arnold lingered near Quebec. All winter long his soldiers lay siege to the city. But 500 Americans in the ice and snow were no real threat to a walled city of 5,000, reinforced by 1,500 Redcoats and equipped with 148 cannons. When the spring thaw came, and the British fleet could again reach Quebec, Arnold retreated to Crown Point.

The British Fail to Conquer New York

Now the pursuers became the pursued. The Canadians under Sir Guy Carleton set out after Arnold, to take New York. The Governor General led 13,000 troops south toward Albany. General William Howe's army, which, as you will see, had taken New York City, was to sail up the Hudson River and join the Canadian army at Albany.

Benedict Arnold now realized the danger to the American cause that his Canadian campaign had provoked. If the two British armies met at Albany, upstate New York would be lost, and New

This 1775 German engraving shows barefooted Continental soldiers wearing homemade buckskin uniforms.

England would be cut off from the rest of the colonies. Arnold now put his bravery and daring to the task of delaying Carleton's progress southward.

Arnold had his men build ships on Lake Champlain. Then they sailed north to challenge the approaching British fleet. On October 11, 1776, Arnold's makeshift navy met Carleton at Valcour Island. The flimsy American ships were destroyed, but Carleton lost precious time in his naval battle with Arnold. Winter came, and Carleton's hopes for a campaign against New York had to be given up. Arnold's quick thinking and bold move had preserved the unity of the 13 colonies.

SECTION 1 REVIEW

 Identify: militia, Battle of Bunker Hill, Benedict Arnold, Fort Ticonderoga, Ethan Allen, Green Mountain Boys

Main Ideas
1. What events enabled Washington to win Massachusetts? What mistakes did the British make?
2. Explain why the Americans failed to conquer Canada.
3. How did Benedict Arnold save upstate New York from a British takeover?

2. THE WAR IN THE SOUTH AND THE MIDDLE COLONIES, 1776–1777

Throughout the war, the English military efforts suffered because English leaders did not understand conditions in the colonies. Policymakers in England were convinced that sentiment for the revolution was not widespread or very deep.

This view was based in large part on reports by wealthy New England Loyalists who flocked to London to wait out the war. These New Englanders, like former Governor Thomas Hutchinson and Jonathan Sewall of Massachusetts, believed the revolution was strictly a New England event. The Loyalists insisted that the ordinary people were deluded by ambitious men and political fanatics who held people under a political spell.

The head of the British war office, Lord George Germain, accepted this notion of the revolution as a New England conspiracy. Therefore, Germain's military strategy in 1776 was based on the assumption that the southern colonies would welcome the return of the king's peace.

There were, of course, many Loyalists in all the colonies. In the Carolinas, in particular, the bitter memory of the Regulator struggles made many back-country people ready to fight for the Crown. But the English never found the solid support they expected. Not until they lost the war did they accept the fact that the desire for independence was strong throughout the 13 colonies.

The Battle of Moore's Creek Bridge
A British army moved south in January 1776. From the beginning, the campaign went badly for the English. Two forces, one under General Henry Clinton and a second under Charles, Lord Cornwallis, were to meet with Loyalist forces in North Carolina. Admiral Sir Peter Parker was to give these armies naval support. But the commanders did not keep to their schedule. The Loyalist troops, alone and outnumbered by Patriot forces in North Carolina, were badly beaten at the **Battle of Moore's Creek Bridge** on February 27, 1776. (See map, page 162.) Instead of restoring the king's peace, British incompetence lost North Carolina entirely. This failure of the British high command

to cooperate well and to keep to their rendezvous schedules would be an important factor in other campaigns.

The Battle of Charleston
In June 1776, General Clinton shifted his attack plan to South Carolina. His target was Charleston. But there the Americans were saved by good luck combined with bungling by British scouts.

The city's main defenses were constructed on Sullivan's Island in the Charleston harbor. Here the Patriots had slapped together a fort made of logs from the local palm tree, the palmetto. What looked like the flimsiest of fortifications proved to be the perfect defense.

The palmetto wood was porous. Instead of splintering when it was hit, it absorbed the cannon balls fired by the British fleet. This accident of nature left the surprised, and relieved, Patriots inside the fort free to return fire on Admiral Parker's ships.

Nature turned against the British in other ways. Several of Parker's ships, caught in the shallows, lay helpless. The ground troops fared no better. Clinton and his army landed on a neighboring island recommended by scouts who assured the general that, at low tide, the army could walk to Sullivan's Island. Low tide proved to be 7 feet of water. Clinton was stranded.

The **Battle of Charleston** was a humiliating defeat Clinton would not forget. With the army marooned and the navy disabled, the British gave up hope of capturing Charleston. In fact, Clinton returned to New York City, abandoning his plans to conquer the southern colonies. Not for almost three years would the British attempt a second southern campaign.

The British Move Against New York City
As you saw, when **General William Howe** left Boston in March 1776, his army headed for New York City. The move made good military sense. Control of New York would allow the British to isolate New England. And the city was an excellent jumping-off point for other military expeditions.

General George Washington rushed to challenge General Howe. But he held out little hope of defending New York City against the British. New York City was on an island (Manhattan), and naval power was the key to its control.

On July 2, 1776—the very day that the Declaration of Independence was approved—Howe and 10,000 troops landed on nearby Staten Island. On July 12, the General's brother, Admiral Richard Howe, sailed into the harbor with a fleet of battleships and 150 transport vessels. By mid-August, Admiral Parker, with Clinton and Cornwallis and their soldiers in tow, arrived from the South. In all, it was an impressive display of English power and military strength.

The Howes had every advantage against Washington's army, with 32,000 professional soldiers pitted against 23,000 Americans, mostly militiamen. Throughout most of the New York campaign, General Washington was in retreat and General Howe in pursuit. Follow the American army's movements on the map on page 166.

Washington Retreats into New Jersey

First, General William Howe drove the Americans off the position they had established at Brooklyn Heights. He might have won the war right then, by pursuing the Americans immediately. But in the midst of victory, William Howe showed a strange hesitation that he would reveal

again and again. Instead of following Washington's men in flight, Howe kept his army at Brooklyn Heights for a full day.

The desperate but grateful Washington took full advantage of Howe's peculiar military behavior. In the dead of night, on August 29–30, the American army escaped across the East River, with Colonel John Glover's Marblehead fishermen rowing the tired troops silently to safety on Manhattan Island.

On September 14, Howe roused himself at last. He crossed the river to the north of Washington's troops, in a good position to trap the American army on southern Manhattan. Sensing that they were caught between one Howe on land and another Howe at sea, many of Washington's militiamen panicked and ran.

Again, William Howe had George Washington and the entire American army at his mercy. Again, he delayed. For two mysterious hours, Howe did not make a move. The Americans rushed, helter-skelter, to safety. Washington was disheartened by his men's performance, but thankful to see them on the way to safety. At

Americans won the Battle of Charleston after their palmetto fort withstood a furious barrage of cannonballs.

Harlem Heights, the American troops stood their ground against a force of Redcoats. This pleased Washington, since he believed his surrender was likely.

Then, as Washington put it, "Providence or some good honest fellow" came to his rescue. On September 20, flames ripped through Manhattan, destroying much of the city. Howe gave up his pursuit of Washington to fight the fire. Although a division of Redcoats engaged the exhausted American troops once more at White Plains, New York, the battle did not halt Washington's retreat. By November 1776, the commander-in-chief and his army had slipped out of reach of the Howe brothers. The Revolution remained alive!

Washington's Raids on Trenton and Princeton

The battle for New York taught George Washington that he could not yet meet the experienced British head-on in battle. He had neither the supplies nor the trained troops he needed. Nor could Washington expect to keep control of sea-coast cities against the combined naval and mili-

Washington's Retreat and the Trenton/Princeton Victories

- - - - American retreat
━━━ American advance
× Battles

```
0        25        50 MILES
0    25    50    KILOMETERS
```

tary strength of the British. Five months of harrowing retreat had taught him this.

What could Washington do? He could harass the enemy and then slip away into the familiar and friendly countryside. It was this kind of guerrilla warfare that General Washington decided upon in the winter of 1776.

December found Washington in the Pennsylvania countryside with a small band of less than 500 men. The bulk of his army was in White Plains and Peekskill, New York. The troops with the General were restless and full of complaints. Their enlistment terms were running out. To raise sagging American morale and to lower British self-confidence, Washington masterminded a Christmas attack on the British garrison at **Trenton**, New Jersey. Loading his troops on boats, Washington crossed the Delaware River and returned to the Jersey shore.

Colonel Johann Gottlieb Rall was commander for the British at Trenton. Rall, like most of the men of his garrison, was a German mercenary, one of 30,000 soldiers hired by George III to fight in the British army. Most of these mercenaries came from the principalities of Hesse-Kassel or Hesse-Hanau and thus were known as **Hessians**. The Hessians were good soldiers, but they had no real stake in the outcome of the war. Many of them, in fact, would later desert to the American side after seeing the rich farmlands of Pennsylvania and New Jersey.

But Colonel Rall's Hessian soldiers were not thinking of desertion on Christmas, 1776. Like their commander, they were celebrating the holiday season with rum, song, and recollections of home. Rall was quite drunk when, suddenly, at 8 A.M. the next morning, a band of Patriots swept in and took the garrison. It was over in an hour. Nine hundred Hessians were captured. Only four Americans were injured in this daring raid, one a young lieutenant from Virginia named James Monroe—the future President.

While Rall was surrendering at Trenton, William Howe was settling in for a peaceful winter at New York City. The news of Washington's raid shattered Howe's calm. On January 1, he sent troops from New York to New Jersey, but Washington eluded them.

By making a night march to **Princeton**, New Jersey, Washington and his soldiers surprised the British garrison there just as they had done at

Washington Crossing the Delaware, *by Emanuel Leutze, 1851. Though important details are inaccurate (the flag, the ice floes, the boats, Washington's stance), the drama of the painting has made it famous.*

Trenton. The Princeton victory was important, for the garrison provided Washington's troops with many of the supplies they needed for the winter ahead. Triumphant, Washington again crossed the Delaware and returned to the safety of Pennsylvania's woods.

Washington's men called their New Jersey campaign "the Nine Days' Wonder." When it was over, the British were almost eliminated from New Jersey, and American spirits were revived.

The American Victory at Saratoga

In February 1777, the British returned to their strategy of isolating New England from the other colonies. Again they planned to take the Hudson Valley by moving south from Canada and north from New York City. Like Carleton's plan in 1775, this campaign depended upon the perfect timing of troop movements in both directions.

General John Burgoyne drew up a three-pronged attack. He would move south from Canada; Howe would sail up the Hudson; and a third force under Colonel Barry St. Leger would cut east across the Mohawk Valley from Fort Oswego on Lake Ontario. The three forces would meet at Albany.

George III enthusiastically approved the plan himself. But communications must have failed between the king and his war minister, Lord Germain. For at the very same time, Germain had approved a campaign by Howe to capture Philadelphia. Howe could not be in two places at once.

The campaign began well for the optimistic "Gentleman Johnny" Burgoyne as he proceeded southward from Canada in June 1777. (See map, next page.) On July 5, he recaptured Fort Ticonderoga and, chasing the New York Patriots southward, pressed on to meet St. Leger and Howe.

But Burgoyne began to make some costly errors. For example, he was unfamiliar with the terrain of New York and lost time and supplies by marching his army through a marshland near Lake George. Burgoyne's troops took 24 days to go 23 miles.

Soon after, Burgoyne received word that one of his Indian allies, a Wyandot, had killed a young Loyalist named Jane McCrea. The residents of the Mohawk Valley were shocked and outraged, but the General could not punish the man involved. To do so might have infuriated his Indian allies, who included the powerful Iroquois, and

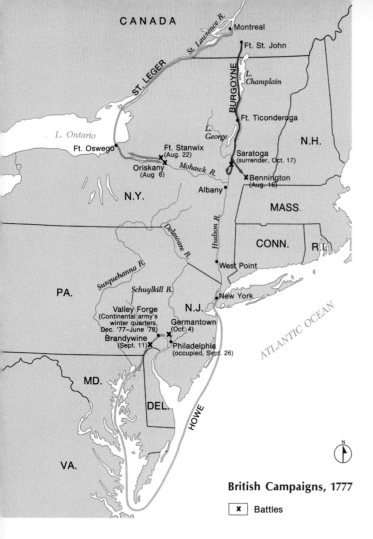

British Campaigns, 1777

☒ Battles

1777, the British general made a last, desperate attempt to break past the American lines and retreat northward. But **General Horatio Gates** and his Patriot troops held firm. On October 17, General John Burgoyne surrendered.

General Gates and his army had won a stunning victory that October day, and a politically important one. European nations that had hesitated to support the American cause came forward. As a result of the **victory at Saratoga,** France signed a treaty with the Americans in 1778.

Although both France and Spain had secretly provided money and supplies like gunpowder since 1776, this open statement of alliance and support was a genuine triumph. For England now faced an international war, not just a colonial rebellion. The Saratoga victory might be seen as the true birth of our nation, for it brought recognition of American independence as well as money and supplies from France and other nations.

The Winter at Valley Forge, 1777–1778

Saratoga was also important for its effect on American military morale. In September 1777, Howe had crushed Washington's troops at Brandywine Creek and captured Philadelphia. Washington's army had suffered another serious defeat in October while trying to attack Howe's army at Germantown. In December Washington's army set up winter quarters at Valley Forge, Pennsylvania, 20 miles northwest of Philadelphia.

News of Burgoyne's surrender did much to make the **winter at Valley Forge** bearable for Washington and his troops. They were wintering at

Soldiers try to keep warm at a Valley Forge campfire.

destroyed what shaky control over them he had. The murder of Jane McCrea and Burgoyne's refusal to punish the Wyandot probably converted more New Yorkers to the Patriot cause than even Thomas Paine's *Common Sense* had done.

Burgoyne's luck finally ran out on August 16 when part of his force was destroyed by Green Mountain Boys at Bennington, where his troops were trying to gain needed supplies. Then, on August 22 at Fort Stanwix, Benedict Arnold's troops forced St. Leger to retreat to Oswego.

When Burgoyne finally reached Saratoga on September 12, 1777, he was a changed man. By now he realized that Howe was not going to come north as promised. He also realized that his troops were far from their supply base and in hostile territory. In their first battle with Americans at Saratoga, Burgoyne's troops suffered heavy losses. They were trapped, and could do nothing without reinforcements from New York City.

No help came for Burgoyne. On October 7,

Mount Joy, a heavily wooded hill that did not live up to its name. The troops were housed in huts and tents that provided poor protection against the cold and snows. Few of Washington's soldiers had blankets, many had no shirts, and some were entirely naked except for rags.

Food was scarce, and soldiers filled their stomachs with "fire cake," a lump of dough baked over the campfire. General Anthony Wayne said that he would rather fight the British once a week than see his troops suffering as they were.

Yet, under Washington's fatherly care, the men endured. There was no talk of mutiny, no word of surrender. Despite the cold, the men roused themselves and assembled each morning on the drilling field. Here the Prussian drillmaster, Baron Friedrich von Steuben, barked orders in French, Prussian, and English. Von Steuben transformed Washington's men into a disciplined army. Like the young Marquis de Lafayette of France, the German Baron de Kalb, and Polish Count Casimir Pulaski, von Steuben had volunteered his services in the cause of liberty.

Hundreds of American soldiers died of hunger, fever, and dysentery at Valley Forge while General Howe and his officers danced and dined in elegant comfort 20 miles away in Philadelphia. "These are the times that try men's souls," Tom Paine had written in 1776. The 11,000 soldiers who remained with Washington knew exactly what Paine meant. Only the memory of the Saratoga victory and the news of the French alliance brought any warmth to Washington's army in the terrible winter of 1777–1778.

SECTION 2 REVIEW

Identify: Battle of Moore's Creek Bridge, Battle of Charleston, William Howe, Hessians, raids on Trenton and Princeton, John Burgoyne, Horatio Gates, victory at Saratoga, winter at Valley Forge

Main Ideas

1. Why did the British tend to be overconfident throughout the war?
2. Why did the British abandon their southern campaign in 1776?
3. What foolish mistakes did General Howe make during his conquest of New York City?
4. What made the American victory at Saratoga so important?

3. WOMEN IN THE REVOLUTIONARY WAR

The times that tried men's souls troubled women's souls as well. Because the American Revolution was fought on American farmlands and in American cities, the war touched the women's lives as it did the men's.

Organizing Supplies

Almost immediately after the battle on Lexington Green, women mobilized to support the troops, collecting money and supplies for the newly formed Continental army. They organized scrap drives to gather household items that could be transformed into ammunition. In a metal-scarce society, pewter plates, candlesticks, and even window weights were all melted down to make cannonballs and shot. Spinning clubs and sewing circles became an unofficial **quartermaster corps*** which produced clothing for the Patriot army. No one appreciated the importance of these unofficial troops more than General Washington. He took the time to write personal notes of thanks to these women throughout the war.

Women were inventive in their battles against shortages of food and supplies. After 1776, the English cut off normal channels of trade to the Americans, and families soon found themselves in need of salt, pins and needles, sugar, and medicines.

The lack of salt was especially serious, because salt was used to preserve meat for the winter months. Women found a substitute preserving agent in walnut ash. Although it tasted bad, it preserved winter meats throughout the war. Women also created herbal medicines, herbal teas, and a corn liquor for the Patriot army to replace the usual rum rations.

For women whose husbands and sons were away at war, life was extremely difficult. Many faced the task of managing farms, shops, or businesses, as well as large families, by themselves.

***quartermaster corps** section of an army that provides food, clothing, shelter, and transportation for troops. In the Revolutionary War, this part of the American army scarcely functioned.

Lack of money was a constant worry, for a soldier's pay was low and did not come regularly.

At the Front

Many women packed up their children and belongings and joined their husbands. The young Jane McCrea, who was killed by Burgoyne's Indians, was riding to join her fiance's military unit. The presence of hundreds of wives, children, and sweethearts in military camps was common in all 18th-century wars. The armies were actually mobile communities, and the camps were temporary towns.

Thus, winter quarters at Valley Forge were more like a bustling city than a military installation. The women cooked, sewed and mended, and served as nurses in the military hospitals. General Washington's own wife, Martha, joined him in the terrible winter at Valley Forge. The presence of high-ranking officers' wives serving as cooks and nurses helped enlisted men to see the willingness of rich as well as poor to endure hardships for the patriotic cause.

The women who followed the army often saw combat during the Revolution. In forts and garrisons, women loaded guns, tended wounds, and carried water to the thirsting men. If a husband fell in battle, the wife sometimes took his place. Mary Ludwig, one of the many women nicknamed "**Molly Pitcher**" because of their water-carrying chores, was 24 years old and pregnant when she took the gun from her wounded husband and fired on the British. Washington promptly commissioned her a sergeant so that she could receive a pension. Some of the many "Molly Pitchers" were recognized by Congress after the war for their military heroism. Margaret Corbin, for example, was granted a military pension after she was wounded, captured, and disabled for life.

Some women took up arms against the enemy on their own. A number of American regiments discovered that women, disguised as men, had enlisted and served their terms. The most famous of these women soldiers was a farm girl named **Deborah Sampson** who served with General Washington as Private Robert Shirtliffe. When Private Shirtliffe was stricken in an epidemic, her real sex was discovered. Washington had Deborah Sampson discharged from the army, but in 1804 Congress granted her a military pension.

Women As Spies

Women made excellent spies, as they could often cross military lines without rousing suspicion. Fifteen-year-old Betheland Moore canoed upstream on the Little River to carry vital information to American troops in South Carolina. Deborah Champion of Massachusetts was captured and interrogated as she carried a message for General Washington, but she outwitted the Redcoats and rode free. Patriot women spied on British planning sessions as they served the officers their food and drink. It was said that General William Howe's fatal two-hour delay in pursuit of Washington's army in 1776 was the work of Mary Murray, who invited the British general to her home for cake and tea and spiked his cup with liquor.

Hundreds of women—Patriots and Loyalists alike—sacrificed their safety and their homes to support their chosen cause. They harbored hunted men in their basements, delayed troop movements by creating diversions, or burned their fields or buildings to destroy supplies that would aid the enemy. Martha Bratton, a South Carolina Patriot, for example, blew up her barn to keep supplies from falling into Loyalist hands. Organized spy rings also served both the Loyalist and the Patriot causes. For example, on Long Island Anna Strong, a Patriot, directed the **Culper Ring** during the British occupation of New York City. In 1779 a woman in Mrs. Strong's group was captured by the British and died while confined in one of the dreaded prison ships in New York harbor.

SECTION 3 REVIEW

Identify: quartermaster corps, Molly Pitchers, Deborah Sampson, Culper Ring

Main Ideas

1. How did women help supply the materials needed in the American army?
2. What conditions made it possible for many women to serve as "Molly Pitchers"?
3. Why did Congress grant some women military pensions after the war?
4. Why were women particularly effective as spies during the Revolutionary War?

4. FROM SARATOGA TO YORKTOWN, 1777–1781

The American victory at Saratoga prompted the English government to rethink its policy toward its colonies. Saratoga had drawn France into the war, and neither the king nor Lord North wanted to fight on both a European and an American front. The English leaders considered the French threat far more serious than the American rebellion. Thus, in February 1778, Lord North sent a peace commission to America. The English terms were similar to Joseph Galloway's plan of union that Congress had rejected in 1775. The offer came too late. In 1778, the firm goal of the American government was independence.

How the French Helped the Americans

The Americans had high hopes that the French alliance would make an immediate difference in the war. Diplomatically it did, for it prompted the peace offer. Militarily, the entrance of the French navy into the war also had some effect. General Howe had conquered Philadelphia in September 1777 while Burgoyne was en route to defeat at Saratoga. However, in June 1778, General Clinton evacuated Philadelphia when he realized that French ships in the Delaware River could isolate him from his supply base in New York.

But the first efforts at actual cooperation between the French navy and the American land troops were failures. The Americans did better in 1779 with their own privateers than with the mighty French fleet.

John Paul Jones and George Rogers Clark

American privateers challenged the British navy throughout 1779. For example, the British man-of-war *Serapis* was attacked by the American privateer *Bonhomme Richard*. The *Bonhomme Richard*, named in honor of Benjamin Franklin's almanac character, Poor Richard, was a French merchant ship converted for battle by the Scotsman **John Paul Jones**. In a remarkable moonlight battle, Jones outmaneuvered the 44-gun *Serapis* and forced its captain to surrender. Jones also conducted raids with his privateer on the English and Scottish coasts.

Although privateers like Jones could harass the British navy, the Americans sorely needed the support of a well-armed fleet to carry troops and supplies and to challenge British control of coastal areas. America's 100 ships were no match for the British navy.

Individual heroic acts like those by Jones were common in the American Revolution. For example, in 1778 a reckless but brave Kentucky surveyor named **George Rogers Clark** sailed 900 miles down the Ohio River with a small force of 175 Kentucky and Virginia volunteers. Their goal was the nearly impossible task of driving the British out of the Ohio Valley.

Clark and his men seized Kaskaskia, Vincennes, and other distant frontier outposts (see map, page 162). For a brief and glorious moment in 1779, the frontier belonged to the Americans. But British military superiority soon reasserted itself, and by 1780, Clark and his men were in retreat. At the close of the war, they still held onto Kentucky and much of the region north of the Ohio River. Their efforts helped win these western lands for the new American nation.

The Second Southern Campaign

In the last two years of the fighting, all the major battles took place in the South. Late in 1778 the British once again began a southern campaign.

The Bonhomme Richard *battles the* Serapis, *1779.*

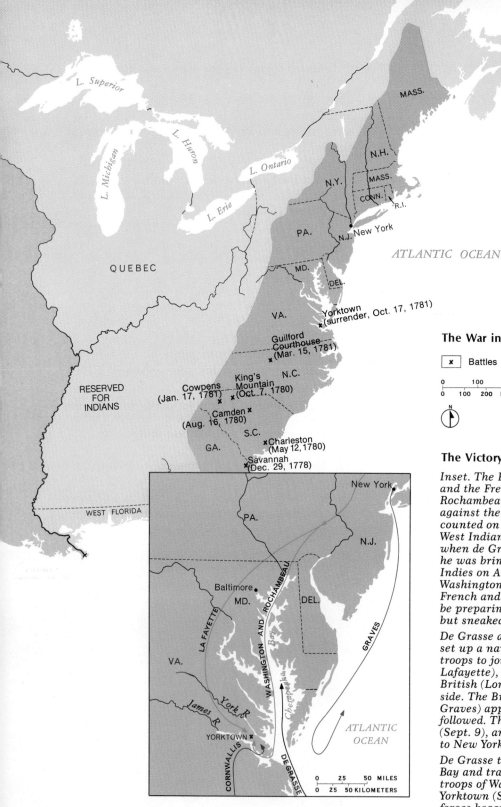

The War in the South, 1778–1781

| x | Battles |

```
0        100      200 MILES
0    100   200  KILOMETERS
```

The Victory at Yorktown

Inset. The Patriots (led by Washington) and the French (led by Comte de Rochambeau) planned a joint attack against the British in New York. They counted on the support of the French West Indian fleet (Comte de Grasse). But when de Grasse notified Washington that he was bringing the fleet from the West Indies on August 13 to Chesapeake Bay, Washington decided to head south. The French and Patriot troops pretended to be preparing an attack on Staten Island but sneaked through New Jersey.

De Grasse arrived off Yorktown (Aug. 13), set up a naval blockade, and landed his troops to join the French (Marquis de Lafayette), who were blockading the British (Lord Cornwallis) from the land side. The British fleet (Admiral Thomas Graves) appeared, and a sharp action followed. The French fleet was reinforced (Sept. 9), and the British fleet withdrew to New York for repairs (Sept. 10).

De Grasse then sent ships up Chesapeake Bay and transported the bulk of the troops of Washington and Rochambeau to Yorktown (Sept. 14–24). The combined forces began the siege of Yorktown. Cornwallis was forced to surrender (Oct. 17).

LIFE IN AMERICA

BENEDICT ARNOLD'S TREACHERY

One of the most respected heroes of the war was Benedict Arnold. But in 1779, Arnold shocked Patriots throughout the colonies when it was revealed that he had turned to treason.

In part, success proved the major general's undoing. He was a favorite of General Washington, and his rise was rapid. After a brilliant military performance at Saratoga, Arnold was rewarded with the prestige of commanding American forces in Philadelphia in 1779.

Success Breeds Discontent

In Philadelphia, Benedict Arnold, like the British general William Howe before him, was wined and dined by the city's social elite. Arnold found the life of a gentleman full of charm, and he fell in love with a beautiful heiress named Peggy Shippen, whom he married.

Living beyond his means, Arnold was soon pursued by creditors. His financial difficulties may have created discontent in the young officer, for he began to complain that Congress did not really appreciate him.

Peggy Shippen, who was both ambitious and a Loyalist sympathizer, fed the fires of Arnold's discontent. By May 1779, Benedict Arnold had offered the British his services as a double agent for a high price. For 13 months Arnold was both a Patriot officer and an informer. In May 1780 he devised a scheme to prove his worth to the British.

Arnold's plan was to get himself transferred to command the garrison at West Point, and then to turn the garrison over to the British. West Point was a crucial fortification on the Hudson River; the army that held it controlled New York. (See map, page 168.) If Arnold's scheme worked, England could at long last divide New England from the rest of the American states.

The Plot Revealed

Arnold had no trouble winning his transfer to West Point. But his plot failed. His British go-between, Major John André, was captured by American soldiers as he slipped out of a secret meeting with Arnold at West Point. Papers found on André exposed the plot. Major André was hanged. But Arnold's luck held out, and he escaped to safety behind British lines, where he fought for the British in Virginia and Connecticut.

Benedict Arnold's treason saddened American political and military leaders, but the failure of the West Point plot insured the security of the nation. After the war, Arnold went to London, where he spent his life scorned and impoverished.

An effigy of Benedict Arnold is paraded at Philadelphia in 1780.

They believed that if they controlled the ports, the Loyalists would rise up and throw out the Patriot forces in the interior. Moving swiftly, British forces took Savannah on December 29, 1778, and overran most of Georgia soon after. The leader of the English troops in Georgia could proudly write: "I have ripped one star from the rebel flag of America."

In May 1780, the British finally took Charleston. Soon after, all of South Carolina was in British hands. Feeling confident, General Clinton departed for New York City, leaving General Cornwallis to finish the conquest of the South.

For a time, the British seemed unstoppable.

Even General Horatio Gates, the hero of Saratoga, could not stop Cornwallis' march toward North Carolina. Gates was beaten badly at Camden, South Carolina, in August. (See map, opposite.)

The Battle of King's Mountain

At last, on October 7, 1780, the Americans struck their first effective blow at the British invaders. At **King's Mountain**, South Carolina, the Patriot forces isolated the Loyalist battalions marching with Cornwallis, and engaged them in battle. The fierce fighting of American against American at King's Mountain reminds us that the Revolution was not only a war for independence but a civil war as well. Loyalist Captain Patrick Ferguson's cause was hopeless, yet he refused to surrender. He rode among his troops, hacking down with his saber any white flags they raised.

The Patriots, for their part, were eager for bloodletting. They bitterly remembered that the previous May, a Loyalist force under the brutal command of Banastre Tarleton had massacred surrendering and wounded Patriot troops at Waxhaw, South Carolina. As the Patriots fell upon the Loyalists at King's Mountain, they were ready to butcher the Loyalists. Fortunately, the cooler heads among them prevailed, and no massacre occurred.

The King's Mountain battle saved North Carolina from British invasion. Cornwallis decided to return to South Carolina to regroup. The new American commander in the South, General Nathanael Greene, decided that guerrilla warfare was the best strategy for a while. Using his best officers, like Daniel Morgan, Greene harassed Cornwallis' army, slowly eliminating the Loyalist support troops. The Patriots won another important victory at Cowpens in January 1781. By March, Greene felt ready to do battle directly with Cornwallis.

Greene had the advantage when he met Cornwallis at Guilford Courthouse, North Carolina, on March 15, 1781. (See map, page 172.) The Patriot troops under Greene had fresh reinforcements, while the British had lost their Loyalist allies. Although Greene's troops did not win the battle, they made the British victory costly. Cornwallis lost a fourth of his army.

The Siege* of Yorktown Ends the War

Abandoning North Carolina, Cornwallis pushed on to Virginia in the spring of 1781. He was tired,

*siege [sēj] the surrounding of a fortified place by enemy forces trying to capture it.

he wrote his superiors, of "marching about the country in search of adventure." He asked Clinton to send him massive reinforcements for a final and decisive campaign.

But Clinton, ever cautious, did not wish to concentrate all his strength in one place. As commander-in-chief in America, Clinton had his way. He ordered Cornwallis to find a good location in Virginia, to settle in, and to stay put. This is how Cornwallis came to be at Yorktown, Virginia, on the York River, in the fall of 1781.

George Washington had not intended to attack Cornwallis at Yorktown. In fact, Washington was busy making plans for a French and American campaign against New York. As usual, however, coordination between the French fleet commanders and the Americans did not proceed smoothly.

The commander of the French fleet, Admiral de Grasse, did not head for New York City, as Washington hoped. Instead he sailed into the Chesapeake Bay that summer. Washington speedily revised his plans and headed his own army south toward Virginia. Henry Clinton was all too slow in realizing what had happened. He sent the British fleet to Chesapeake Bay to rescue Cornwallis, but de Grasse's navy repulsed them.

By September 25, 1781, Washington's army had united with a southern Patriot force under the Frenchman **Marquis de Lafayette**, and was in position near Yorktown. The Americans outnumbered the British two to one, with 15,000 French and American troops against only 7,500 Redcoats. Cornwallis and his army were trapped between the American army and the French fleet.

The **siege of Yorktown** began in October 1781. Under a constant cannon barrage, Cornwallis was helpless. His only hope, and it was a slim one, was a midnight retreat across the York River. But Nature intervened. A storm blew up, and the evacuation of Yorktown was impossible. On October 17, Cornwallis surrendered.

At the surrender ceremony on October 19, Cornwallis could not face his duties. He sent a second-in-command to deliver up his sword. Thus General George Washington was cheated of the full taste of victory. He had to send his second-in-command to receive the British sword. As the representatives of the most powerful nation in the world surrendered to representatives of the newest, the military band played a tune called "The World Turned Upside Down."

FROM THE ARCHIVES

The World Turned Upside Down

The song the British military band played at the surrender at Yorktown is from an old nursery rhyme.

If buttercups buzzed after the bee,
If boats were on land, churches on sea,
If ponies rode men, and if grass ate the corn,
And cats should be chased into holes by the mouse,
If the mammas sold their babies to gypsies for half
    a crown,
If summer were spring, and the other way 'round,
Then all the world would be upside down.

When Lord North, who had directed English policy through the 1770s, heard of the Yorktown surrender, he exclaimed, "Oh God! It is all over." And so it was.

SECTION 4 REVIEW

Identify: John Paul Jones, George Rogers Clark, Battle of King's Mountain, Marquis de Lafayette, siege of Yorktown

Main Ideas
1. How did the French help Americans during the Revolutionary War?
2. What was the long-range significance of George Rogers Clark's capture of the frontier outposts?
3. In what way was the Battle of Guilford Courthouse a turning point in the war?
4. Explain how Washington was able to force Cornwallis to surrender at Yorktown.

Eyewitness view of the surrender at Yorktown. Note the British troops laying down their arms.

5. THE PEACEMAKERS AND THEIR TREATY

The American Congress sent four peacemakers to Europe. The first was **John Jay**, the New York lawyer, a thin, somewhat sour-faced man who lacked great charm but was respected by those who knew him. Jay had spent the last years of the war in Madrid, trying without success to convince Spain to recognize the American government. Spain had declared war on England in 1779 as an ally of France, not of the United States.

John Adams of Massachusetts was the second American negotiator. As always, Adams was full of nervous energy, eager to begin the talks, both worried and confident at the same time. His past efforts to win support abroad for the United States had gone well. He had convinced the Dutch to recognize American sovereignty [sov′ran tē], or independence, and to lend the American cause some much-needed money. Adams was delighted with the Dutch, and with himself.

Heading the delegation was the most celebrated American of his day, **Benjamin Franklin.** Franklin had been in France throughout the war, representing his country in the delicate secret negotiations that had finally resulted in the American-French alliance. He was the toast of France. A portly man in his 70s, whose wit delighted the French, Franklin was widely admired for his charm, his scientific knowledge, and his diplomatic abilities. To the French, Franklin was the grand old man of America.

A fourth commissioner, Henry Laurens, was captured by the British as he sailed to Europe. He could not join his colleagues in Paris in 1782, because he was imprisoned in the Tower of London. By the time he won release, the peace treaty was almost complete.

In the hands of three men, therefore, rested the American future. How well would Jay, Adams, and Franklin do against the experienced empire builders of England and France? Compared to the French Comte Vergennes or the English Lord Shelburne, the Americans were mere innocents at diplomacy.

All fears proved groundless. The Americans stood rock firm on the demand that the English negotiators recognize American independence before any further discussion could take place. Lord Shelburne, England's new postwar prime minister, stalled. He wanted an end to war, but not an end to England's American empire. At last, however, he gave way, and his commissioners at the peace table negotiated with "the Commissioners of the United States of America."

The Terms of the Treaty

In the **Treaty of Paris of 1783** the Americans won a resounding victory, gaining far more than they had to concede. First, they won recognition as a sovereign nation. Second, they gained most of the lands between the Great Lakes, the Appalachian Mountains, and the Mississippi River—the region that had been closed to them in 1763. (The French had hoped to regain this region, but the Americans conducted secret negotiations with the British, who preferred to give it to the United States.) Finally, the United States won the right to continue fishing off the coast of Canada.

The Americans made two concessions to British demands. They agreed to recommend to the individual states that all debts owed to British merchants from before the war be honored. They also agreed to urge that all land confiscated from the Loyalists be returned or paid for.

The Fate of the Indians and the Loyalists

Two groups of Americans suffered by the peace of 1783. The first group of victims were the Indians of the frontier. Most of the tribes had fought as loyal allies to the British because they believed that England would honor their claims to the land.

When the English went to the peace table, however, they did not defend the rights of their Indian allies. Much of the land that England ceded (gave) to the Americans belonged by treaty to the Indian nations. In upper New York, the Iroquois rose up in fury after the peace and refused to honor an agreement that stole their lands from them.

The second group of victims were the Loyalists.

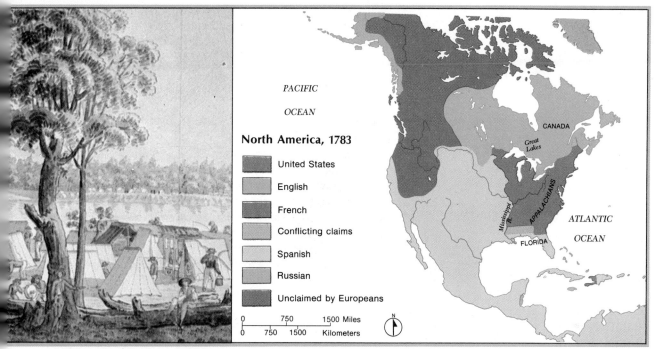

PACIFIC

OCEAN

North America, 1783

- United States
- English
- French
- Conflicting claims
- Spanish
- Russian
- Unclaimed by Europeans

CANADA

Great Lakes

Mississippi R.

APPALACHIANS

ATLANTIC

OCEAN

FLORIDA

0   750   1500 Miles
0   750   1500   Kilometers

Loyalist refugee camp on the St. Lawrence River in Canada

For almost 200 years after the Revolution, historians ignored the story of these thousands of men and women who remained faithful to the king and their mother country.

Recently, we have come to appreciate how difficult the decision for or against rebellion was for the American colonists, and how much like a civil war the Revolution was. Families were divided by the crisis of loyalties in 1775–1776, and often brothers opposed brothers, and wives renounced their husbands.

Over 100,000 Americans left the country after the war was over. These exiles went to Canada, to the West Indies, to England, and to Africa. Many of them were freed slaves who had won their liberty by fighting with the British. Some fared well in their new lives. But for many, the war was a turning point from prosperity to misery. Wealthy men who had held responsible offices in the colonial government found themselves living on the charity of the English government with no profession to pursue and no job to fill their days.

The letters and diaries of the Loyalists reveal how homesick for American life they were. No matter where they settled, New England Loyalists remained New Englanders at heart. New York and Pennsylvania families longed for their farms in America.

About 40,000 of these Loyalists went to Canada. They became the founders of a strong English-speaking society in Canada that would eventually outnumber the French. Descendants of the Loyalists would become the political leaders of the Canadian world. Yet, the loss of these thousands of American men and women, with their skills and talents and their genuine love of their American homes, was a serious blow to the new nation.

SECTION 5 REVIEW

Identify: John Jay, John Adams, Benjamin Franklin, Treaty of Paris of 1783

Main Ideas

1. What did the United States gain in the Treaty of Paris of 1783?
2. How did the treaty affect Indians on the frontier?
3. What happened to the Loyalists after the war? Why can the Revolutionary War be considered a civil war?

177

CHAPTER 7 REVIEW

Key Terms
Explain the meaning of each of the following terms:

militia
Battle of Bunker Hill
Fort Ticonderoga
Green Mountain Boys
Battle of Moore's Creek Bridge
Battle of Charleston
Hessians
raids on Trenton and Princeton
victory at Saratoga
winter at Valley Forge
quartermaster corps
Molly Pitchers
Culper Ring
Battle of King's Mountain
siege of Yorktown
Treaty of Paris of 1783

Reviewing the Main Ideas
Section 1
1. Why were the Americans able to win control of Massachusetts early in the war?
2. Why did the American army fail to conquer Canada? How did Benedict Arnold save upstate New York from a British takeover?

Section 2
1. What misinformation led the British to launch their southern campaign in 1776?
2. Why was Washington able to save his army despite the superior forces of General Howe?
3. Why was the American victory at Saratoga so important?

Section 3
1. In what ways did women participate in the Revolutionary War?
2. What were some problems women faced on the home front during the war?

Section 4
1. Why was the French involvement in the American Revolution so important?
2. What British mistakes led to the surrender at Yorktown?

Section 5
1. What did the Americans gain as a result of the Treaty of Paris of 1783?
2. How did the Treaty of Paris affect the Indians on the frontier?
3. What happened to many Loyalists after the war?

Special History Skills:
Working with Military Maps
Maps of military campaigns can help explain why important historical events turn out as they do. Look at the map on page 168, showing British campaigns in 1777. The objective of the British in 1777 was to capture the Hudson Valley and cut New England off from the colonies to the south. The original British strategy for doing this centered on Albany, New York.

1. Using the map and your text as sources, draw a diagram of the original British military plan. Label the diagram with the names of the British generals, key places involved, and directions the British troops were to move.
2. Use your diagram and the map on page 168 to explain what went wrong with the original plan. (Note: General Burgoyne left Fort St. John on June 17, 1777, and General Howe left New York City on July 23, 1777.)
3. Check the map on page 168. How far is it from Fort St. John to Bennington? How long did it take General Burgoyne to cover this distance? (Remember, he left Fort St. John on June 17.) Working with the map and the text, explain why it took him that long.
4. Refer to the map on page 168 and the text to explain why the map could also have been named "An American Victory at Saratoga."
5. Using the map and the text, describe the campaign between General Howe's troops and the Continental army in the fall of 1777.

Other Skill Activities
1. **A good peace?**
   Franklin thought the peace of 1783 was a good one. Would you agree if you are (**a**) an American rebel, (**b**) an American Loyalist, (**c**) an American Indian? Write a paragraph response for each individual.
2. **Colonial women**
   Find out more about the activities of colonial women at home or in the war. Topics might

include home remedies for diseases, clothing and food production, political activities, famous spies, or a biography of one of the women mentioned in the text.

3. **Chart the war**

   Make a chart with two columns. In the first column list points at which the English could have ended the war. Be sure to include battles and peace commissions. In the second column explain why the war did not end.

Thinking Critically

1. Some historians believe that without the victory at Saratoga the Americans would have lost the war. Explain why you agree or disagree.
2. Did the Americans win the war, or did the British lose it? Explain your answer, using specific examples from the text.
3. "The American Revolution was a civil war." Defend or dispute this statement.
4. Why do you think the British allowed the United States to take over the land between the Appalachians and the Mississippi, even though the Americans did not really succeed in occupying it militarily?

Further Reading

Michael Pearson. *Those Yankee Rebels*. G. P. Putnam's Sons, 1974. An account of the Revolution from the British viewpoint.

Scott O'Dell. *Sarah Bishop*. Houghton Mifflin, 1980. A young girl loses her family and home when the British invade New York.

Sally Smith Booth. *The Women of '76*. Hastings House, 1973. A chronicle of women's opposition and support of the Revolution.

John and Patricia Beatty. *Who Comes to King's Mountain?* Morrow, 1975. A well-documented tale of conflicting loyalties.

Edwin Tunis. *The Tavern at the Ferry*. Crowell, 1973. Suspense and intrigue lead to Washington's Delaware crossing.

David G. Chandler. *Atlas of Military Strategy*. The Free Press, 1980. Pages 6–17 cover the Revolutionary War.

Michael Calvert and Peter Young. *A Dictionary of Battles, 1715–1815*. Mayflower Books, 1979. Useful reference book.

TEST YOURSELF

WRITE YOUR ANSWERS ON A SEPARATE SHEET OF PAPER.

Time Line
List the following events in the order in which they occurred.
1. Battle of Bunker Hill
2. Victory at Saratoga
3. France enters the war
4. Winter at Valley Forge
5. British defeat at Trenton
6. Victory at Yorktown
7. Treaty of Paris signed
8. Capture of Fort Ticonderoga
9. Battles of Lexington and Concord
10. Iroquois refuse to accept the Treaty of Paris

Multiple Choice
Write the letter of the phrase that best completes each statement. There may be more than one correct answer.
1. Benedict Arnold was
   a. a Green Mountain Boy.
   b. a traitor to the Revolution.
   c. a hero of the Revolution.
2. The French entered the war after
   a. the siege of Yorktown.
   b. the Treaty of Paris.
   c. the Battle of Saratoga.
3. George Washington's troops
   a. surprised the Hessians at the Battle of Trenton.
   b. captured New York City after a battle at Harlem Heights.
   c. were well supplied and well paid.
4. Women aided in the war effort in a variety of ways, such as
   a. helping supply American troops with ammunition, food, and clothing.
   b. joining their husbands in fighting the British.
   c. spying and carrying messages.
5. The Treaty of Paris
   a. gave the United States most of the land between the Great Lakes, the Appalachians, and the Mississippi River.
   b. did not honor Indian land rights.
   c. gave the United States the right to fish off the coast of Canada.

Chapter 8

FROM CONFEDERATION TO CONSTITUTION

The American colonists of the 1600s and 1700s were highly self-sufficient. Most of the colonists grew their own food, spun and wove their own clothing, and built their own homes. In government, as in other activities, they figured out the things that needed to be done, and they did them themselves. The colonial governments had little direct influence on their lives, and the colonists liked their freedom from government control.

Between 1775 and 1787, an independent nation was created in America. People gathered together to establish local and national governments. Despite their revolution against England, these American political leaders were proud of their English political heritage. They drew upon that heritage as they shaped their governments. They preserved what they believed was good from their colonial past: representative government, due process of law, the tradition of a constitution, and the doctrine of a separation of powers.

The earliest efforts at creating governments —the state constitutions and the Articles of Confederation—focused on the past. The political leaders who worked on these documents tried to correct the errors and injustices of colonial politics. The later effort—the Constitution—focused on the present problems and the future needs of the new republic.

Sections in This Chapter

1. The State Constitutions and the Articles of Confederation
2. The Critical Period
3. The Constitutional Convention
4. The Struggle over Ratification of the Constitution

Opposite: Interior of the State House of Pennsylvania, now called Independence Hall. In this austere but elegant room the Declaration of Independence was adopted and the U.S. Constitution written.

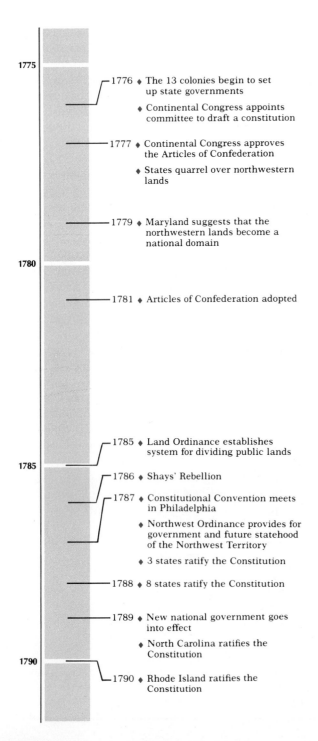

1775

1776 ◆ The 13 colonies begin to set up state governments

◆ Continental Congress appoints committee to draft a constitution

1777 ◆ Continental Congress approves the Articles of Confederation

◆ States quarrel over northwestern lands

1779 ◆ Maryland suggests that the northwestern lands become a national domain

1780

1781 ◆ Articles of Confederation adopted

1785 ◆ Land Ordinance establishes system for dividing public lands

1785

1786 ◆ Shays' Rebellion

1787 ◆ Constitutional Convention meets in Philadelphia

◆ Northwest Ordinance provides for government and future statehood of the Northwest Territory

◆ 3 states ratify the Constitution

1788 ◆ 8 states ratify the Constitution

1789 ◆ New national government goes into effect

◆ North Carolina ratifies the Constitution

1790

1790 ◆ Rhode Island ratifies the Constitution

1. THE STATE CONSTITUTIONS AND THE ARTICLES OF CONFEDERATION

Even before the Declaration of Independence was issued, most Americans found themselves free of English rule. During 1775 and 1776, royal government in the colonies simply faded away. News of the battle at Lexington Green sent many governors hurrying home to England. Loyalists who were serving in the colonial councils and on the governors' staffs also fled for safety. Customs officers deserted their posts. With surprising ease and speed, political independence soon became a reality.

While most Americans rejoiced at the end of English rule, few wished to live without any formal government. When the Continental Congress advised each colony to establish a new government in May of 1776, political leaders and followers everywhere were eager to comply. By the end of 1776, ten colonies had completed the transition to statehood. By 1780, all 13 states had adopted written constitutions.

The New State Governments

These new state governments are worth examining, even though many were reorganized later. These governments reflect the revolutionaries' commitment to local self-government and their fear of a strong central power.

Four features stand out in these new governments. First, all the states had written constitutions. American leaders were determined that their society would be ruled by laws and not by the whims of individuals. In this concern, they revealed their English heritage.

Second, every state constitution established the people as the sovereign rulers. This meant that government existed solely because it served the people's needs, and they alone had the power to establish or dissolve a government.

Third, all states had restricted powers. No state was allowed a permanent army. Government officials could not search a person's home or business without a specific warrant. The memory of customs officers raiding warehouses and shops was strong among Americans. Nor could the states interfere with the basic freedom that Americans, like their English ancestors, believed men and women naturally enjoyed.

The government, for example, could not deny its citizens free speech, free press, or the right to petition when a grievance was felt. To protect people against government abuses such as secret trials and unrestricted punishments, all citizens, rich or poor, were entitled to a trial by jury, and to "due process of law," that is, uniform procedures of arrest, charge, trial, and punishment. Most states followed Virginia's decision to list these liberties in a special Bill of Rights.

Fourth, all the new governments increased the powers of the legislature and weakened the powers of the executive branch. For example, nine states denied the governor a veto power over laws passed in the legislature. Nine states limited the governor's term to a single year. Eight states put the selection of the governor in the hands of the legislators. Pennsylvania constitution makers eliminated the office of the governor entirely and divided that job among legislative committees.

It is not hard to understand why American constitution makers went so far in shifting power from the executive to the legislative branches. All their troubles with England seemed to stem from a distant, centralized power represented by the royal governor. Yet, farsighted men like John Adams recognized that the state constitution makers had gone too far. The governor no longer represented the king, but served the people.

Adams urged that the executive be effectively used rather than feared. He pointed out that even the legislature could become dangerous if its powers were too great and were unchecked. In correcting one evil, the planners risked another. When Massachusetts created its government in 1780, that state heeded Adams' warning. And, over the next decades, most states restored the balance between the two branches of government.

The First National Government

Forming a national government was harder than forming state governments. While few revolutionaries denied that a central government ought to exist, most were afraid to create a strong one. In the decade after the Declaration of Independence, few political leaders would heed Alexander Hamilton's call to "think continentally." Instead, they wished to guard the rights of the new states they represented.

A committee to draft a constitution was appointed by the Continental Congress on June 12, 1776. But the first American constitution, the **Articles of Confederation**, was not adopted until March 1781, almost five years after independence was declared. **John Dickinson** of Pennsylvania, who drafted the Articles, was careful to respect the mood of the day. The Confederation government was a loose alliance that preserved the independence of each state.

This central government had very limited and very specific powers. It could make war and peace, maintain an army and a navy, and negotiate treaties and alliances with foreign nations. These powers, as you can see, were the same ones that the Continental Congress already enjoyed. The new government was also authorized to borrow money and to create a national post office.

There were five important powers denied to the new government. First, the Confederation government could not raise taxes. Revolutionary leaders, fresh from their struggles with the English Parliament over taxation, wished to keep the "power of the purse" in the hands of the local governments. The Confederation treasury could only *request* funds from the states. As long as the national government depended on the states for its budget, it could not challenge state freedom and independence.

Second, the Confederation could not regulate trade for the new nation, either between the states or with other nations. After a century and a half of England's Navigation Acts, no state was ready to let decisions on commerce out of its hands.

Third, the Confederation could not forbid a state to issue its own money. Like most limitations on a new government, this one had its roots in a colonial problem. In Chapter 4, you saw how severely crippled the colonies were by English currency laws that forbade the colonies to print paper money or to mint coins. The new states were determined that they, not the central government, would control their currency.

Fourth, the Confederation had no executive branch. The legislature was to handle all executive functions, as the state legislature in Pennsylvania did. By eliminating the executive office,

LIFE IN AMERICA

VISITORS TO THE NEW NATION

Even before the peace treaty ending the Revolutionary War was signed, Europeans began visiting the new nation and reporting home their observations. Travel books about the new country became so popular in France that enterprising authors even began inventing accounts. One travelogue went through eight editions before it was discovered that the author had never stepped foot in America!

Bizarre Stories

Many visitors found the American landscape fascinating. They thought it more vast, more beautiful, and yet more harsh than anything they had experienced. One French scientist theorized that the American continent was newly formed and had not yet dried; thus it produced inferior plants and animals. This made Thomas Jefferson, in Paris at the time, so annoyed that he sent home for a moose skeleton. Others wrote about wondrous plants that grew two different kinds of fruit, and the potato, which grew everywhere as free food.

An Unusual People

The entire country is a vast forest, noted one traveler. An Englishman described the Americans' aversion to trees: wherever there were people on the frontier, he found tree stumps left to rot. Farmers planted crops right up to their front doors—with no flowers to decorate nor trees to shade their houses.

Europeans were also amazed at the readiness of these pioneers to move onto new land. In Europe, families lived for generations in the same neighborhood or on the same farm.

Europeans were constantly surprised by the condition of equality among citizens. Important men took public stagecoaches and bought their own food in the market. Retired generals became innkeepers and apothecaries (druggists). Common laborers and servants were well paid and well fed, and not too shy to ask foreigners a lot of questions.

The visitors also noted the involvement of the people in the politics of the day. One Frenchman was probably exaggerating when he wrote, "From the landlord to the housemaid, they all read two newspapers a day."

If Americans were not as sophisticated as their French observers, no one denied that they were a different breed in their equality, simplicity, and eagerness to make changes. Americans seemed unique: They had brought about the Revolution and were ready to create a new nation for themselves unlike any other in the world.

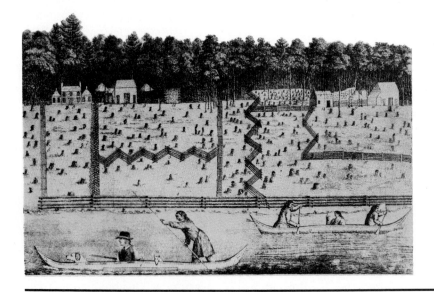

Tree stumps cover a newly cleared farm, 1793.

political leaders hoped to avoid any possibility of an American tyrant arising.

Finally, the Confederation had no judiciary (court system). The national government depended entirely upon the states and their courts to enforce its laws. In practical terms, this meant that a state could annul (make void) any federal law it disliked simply by refusing to enforce it.

The Confederation government was carefully designed to protect the independence of the states as they acted within it. Each state had one vote in the Confederation legislature. No important decision could be made unless nine states favored it. No additional powers could be granted and no amendments could be made to the Confederation constitution unless all 13 states agreed.

The Problem of the Northwest Territory

The Continental Congress approved the Articles of Confederation on November 17, 1777. Why, then, did it take over three more years for the Confederation government to begin? The long delay was caused by one state's refusal to ratify the constitution until a major controversy was resolved. This time, the problem was not a fear of the central government, but jealousy among the states.

The controversial issue was ownership of the northwestern territory. Several states claimed this vast land which lay between the Great Lakes and the Ohio River. (See map at right.) Each insisted that its colonial charter entitled it to the region. Virginia, Maryland, Pennsylvania, and Connecticut were all determined to add the Northwest to their states as soon as peace returned.

Leaders in Maryland, however, began to doubt that they would be able to assert their state's claims against larger and more powerful states like Virginia. Maryland refused, therefore, to ratify the Articles of Confederation unless the issue of the Northwest Territory were settled. Maryland suggested that the states give up their claims to the region and that the central government make it a national domain. Here was one instance in which a state wished to strengthen the central government rather than weaken it.

The Maryland suggestion was made in 1779. For almost a year, Virginia refused to agree. But in 1780, with Cornwallis and his army at the border, Virginia surrendered all claim to the Northwest. In March 1781, the Confederation was, at last, established.

The Achievements of the Confederation Government

Between 1781 and 1787 the Confederation government could boast of several important achievements. It finished a successful war and won a favorable peace. Its most significant domestic accomplishment was the handling of the Northwest Territory. (See map, next page.) Through the Land Ordinance of 1785 and the Northwest Ordinance of 1787, the Confederation established the rules for settling and governing the first national domain.

The **Land Ordinance of 1785** drew upon the colonial New England pattern of settlement. It established a system of townships in the Northwest,

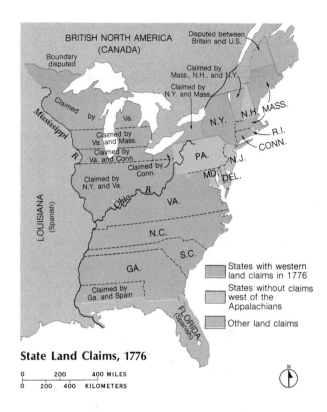

State Land Claims, 1776

States with western land claims in 1776

States without claims west of the Appalachians

Other land claims

```
0        200        400 MILES
0    200    400   KILOMETERS
```

each six miles square. Each township was divided into 36 sections, and each section measured 640 acres. (See diagrams, page 188.) When the township had been surveyed, the government auctioned off the 36 sections at $1 an acre. The proceeds from one section were carefully set aside for the creation and support of public schools.

The Land Ordinance ensured an orderly settlement of the northwest frontier. The sale of lands also brought the Confederation government a small income it badly needed.

The **Northwest Ordinance of 1787** provided for the governing of the Northwest Territory. First, Congress appointed a territorial governor. As soon as a region had 5,000 adult white males, however, these men could elect their own legislature and send a nonvoting delegate to the national Congress. When 60,000 people lived in the region, the citizens could draft their own state constitution. That constitution, when approved by Congress, would establish a new state on an equal basis with the original states. Not more than five nor less than three states were to be carved out of the Northwest Territory. None would be permitted to have slavery.

185

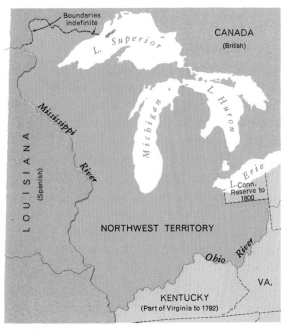

The Northwest Territory, 1787

0   100   200 MILES
0   100   200 KILOMETERS

N

In 1784, Thomas Jefferson, a Virginia congressman, suggested that the region be divided into 9 states, including Assenisipia, Polypotamia, Saratoga, Metropotamia, and Cherronesus.

Because of the Northwest Ordinance, the new American government did not create colonies of its own. Instead, the Confederation government ensured that the United States would grow as a nation, not as an empire.

SECTION 1 REVIEW

Identify: Articles of Confederation, John Dickinson, Land Ordinance of 1785, Northwest Ordinance of 1787

Main Ideas

1. How did the new state governments distribute power among the branches of government?
2. Why was it more difficult to form a national government than state governments?
3. Make a list of powers granted to the central government under the Articles of Confederation. Make a list of powers denied to the central government.
4. What were the achievements of the Confederation government?

---

2. THE CRITICAL PERIOD

Despite its successes, the Confederation government had many critics. As time passed, political leaders began to feel that they had limited their central government too severely. Their fears of tyranny faded, and their fears that the nation was endangered by a weak central government grew. These leaders, like Alexander Hamilton, "thought continentally." Among them were respected figures like George Washington, John Adams, and James Madison. These "nationalists" shared General Washington's opinion that "if the powers of Congress are not enlarged, the blood that has been spilt . . . and the distresses we have undergone will avail us nothing."

Why did the nationalists feel that the nation was in crisis? A number of conditions existed that led people to call the years of the Confederation a **"critical period"** in America's history.

Independence Brings Economic Problems

First, the nation was suffering from an economic depression during the 1780s. This was due in part to the ups and downs that usually follow when a country shifts from a war economy to a peacetime economy. In part, independence itself had created the depression.

For 150 years the American economy had been geared to the British mercantile system. American crops had their markets in England. American ships made their profits carrying goods to and fro between the mother country and the colonies. New Englanders thrived from their trade with the West Indies. Now the British navigation laws were gone, but so too were the advantages of being part of the empire.

Americans needed time to establish new markets and to develop their own manufacturing. The new government needed time to find out how to protect American trade at sea. It was also crucial that the new nation win a firm treaty with England so that the two countries could reestablish many of the trade patterns that had aided them both.

America was making progress toward many of these economic goals during the Confederation years. Ships flying the new Stars and Stripes were making their way to Africa and China. Many states had already begun programs to encourage and to support local manufacturing efforts. These states passed their own protective tariffs, or Navigation Acts, that taxed imported products in order to encourage or protect their own local industries. The major stumbling block remained the British government's refusal to negotiate a workable commercial treaty.

State Rivalries Hurt the Economy

Economic rivalry between the states was also harming the economy. The Confederation government could not regulate trade between states. Therefore, each state was free to tax the others. New York charged New Jersey for shipping or receiving goods through the port of New York. New Jersey retaliated, charging New York for the construction of a harbor lighthouse on the New Jersey side of the Hudson River. Virginia taxed Pennsylvania farmers who shipped their wheat to the Carolinas along Virginia highways and roads.

To further complicate matters, each state issued its own money. Some states were responsible financial agents, taking care that any paper bills they printed were backed by gold or silver. This meant that a citizen could exchange the paper money for gold or silver coins. Other states issued paper bills without gold or silver backing, but with a guarantee that citizens could use these bills to pay state taxes. This meant the paper money did not become worthless. But some states printed a bulk of worthless paper money. Rhode Island, for example, printed so much worthless paper money that it became known as "Rogue's Island" currency.

All the different kinds of money circulating throughout the states confused consumers and merchants alike. Was a Virginia dollar worth the same as a North Carolina dollar? How many paper bills equaled one silver coin? Even the most ordinary shopping expedition could confuse an American consumer.

To many thoughtful Americans, the economy seemed like a horse without a rider, galloping first one way and then another. Unless some agency was given authority to regulate trade, to issue a single currency, and to end the competition between the states, the nation could not develop its resources and live up to its economic potential.

The Government's Prestige at Home and Abroad

Besides depression and state economic rivalries, a third problem that nationalists pointed to was the Confederation government's low prestige, both at home and abroad. Some delegates to the Congress never bothered to attend. There were many sessions when so few delegates were present that no business could legally be done. Some of the most respected political figures resigned from the Confederation government and returned to state politics or to private life.

American prestige abroad was embarrassingly low. The highly centralized governments of Europe had no respect for the Confederation, and did not trust its ability to keep its promises. English diplomats sarcastically suggested that 13 separate treaties were needed on any issue, because the 13 states held all real power.

Of course, the American nation was young, and it probably would not have commanded much respect under any governmental system. Yet, nationalists felt that the Confederation would never be strong enough to win the United States a place among the powers of the world. As long as the government lacked the "power of the purse," nationalists said, no nation and no citizens of this nation, would respect the country's government.

The Confederation could not even pay its bills. The government owed $40 million to foreign and domestic creditors who had lent funds for the war. The paper notes issued by the Continental Congress to cover these debts were now worthless. "Not worth a Continental" had become the popular phrase to describe anything that was without value.

Shays' Rebellion and the Survival of the Nation

Finally, the nationalists feared that the nation might break apart. Rivalries between the states often erupted into violence. Pennsylvania and Virginia went to war over the possession of the Pittsburgh region. Connecticut settlers battled with Pennsylvanians for the right to farm the Wyoming Valley in what is now northeastern Pennsylvania. Squabbling threatened to tear apart the "league of friendship" among the states.

European nations, allies and enemies alike, seemed to hover nearby, ready to carve up the

THE GEOGRAPHIC SETTING

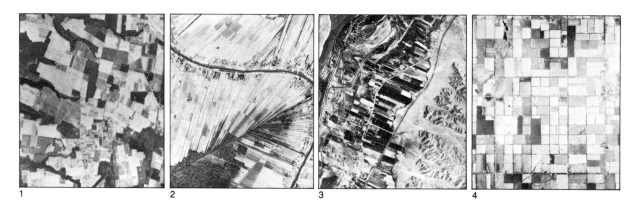

1   2   3   4

THE LAND ORDINANCE OF 1785

Different groups of people divide land in different ways. If you compared the United States with other countries, you would quickly see some striking differences. Land division reflects a people's history. Recall, for example, the New England villages described in Chapter 3. Here Puritans settled in compact villages whose center was the church.

The Indian System

The first Americans were the Indians. Although their customs varied from tribe to tribe, in general, Indians claimed whole territories as tribal property but did not divide the land into plots owned by individuals. In the traditional Indian view, land is a public natural resource, like air or water. "My reason teaches me that land cannot be

sold," declared Black Hawk, a 19th-century Sauk chief. Some Indian tribes still own large tracts of land in common. The largest undivided Indian lands are marked in dark brown on the Land Division map.

The English System

In the colonial period, settlers in the English colonies divided the land into irregular fields that followed the land's natural shape. This system had been used in England. The parts of the United States divided according to the "traditional English system" are marked in medium brown. An aerial view of this irregular pattern of land division is shown above in photograph 1. The photograph shows farmlands on Virginia's Eastern Shore.

The French System

The French settled small areas along the rivers and lakes of New France and Louisiana. They developed a special pattern of long, narrow plots of land which gave everyone access to water transportation. See photograph 2 above of Bayou Lafourche, Louisiana. The areas marked in red on the map show where the "long-lot system" was once used in the present-day United States.

The Spanish System

Spanish settlers divided land in a

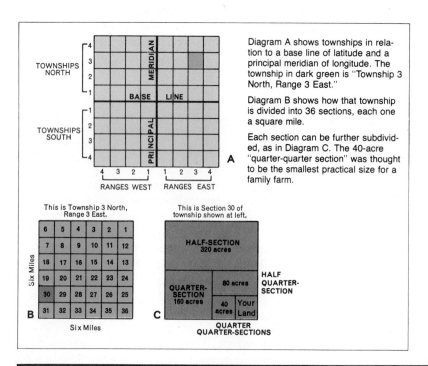

Diagram A shows townships in relation to a base line of latitude and a principal meridian of longitude. The township in dark green is "Township 3 North, Range 3 East."

Diagram B shows how that township is divided into 36 sections, each one a square mile.

Each section can be further subdivided, as in Diagram C. The 40-acre "quarter-quarter section" was thought to be the smallest practical size for a family farm.

TOWNSHIPS NORTH

TOWNSHIPS SOUTH

MERIDIAN

BASE LINE

PRINCIPAL

RANGES WEST   RANGES EAST

A

This is Township 3 North, Range 3 East.

6	5	4	3	2	1
7	8	9	10	11	12
18	17	16	15	14	13
19	20	21	22	23	24
30	29	28	27	26	25
31	32	33	34	35	36

Six Miles

B   Six Miles

This is Section 30 of township shown at left.

HALF-SECTION
320 acres

QUARTER-SECTION
160 acres

80 acres

HALF QUARTER-SECTION

40 acres   Your Land

C   QUARTER QUARTER-SECTIONS

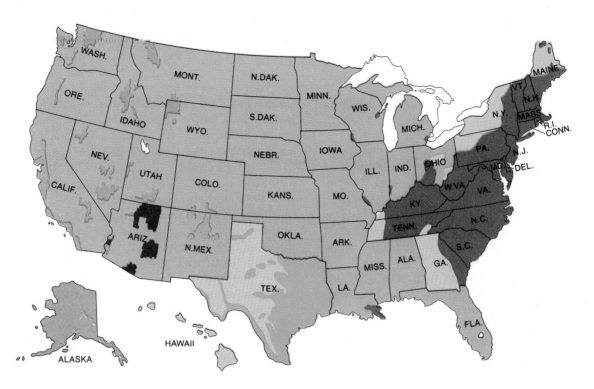

Land Division in the U.S. Today

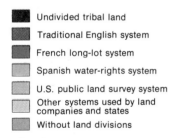

- ■ Undivided tribal land
- ■ Traditional English system
- ■ French long-lot system
- ■ Spanish water-rights system
- ■ U.S. public land survey system
- ■ Other systems used by land companies and states
- ■ Without land divisions

variety of ways. In dry lands where irrigation was necessary, lots were arranged along a river or irrigation channel similar to the French system. Note photograph 3 of Bernalillo, New Mexico. Find on the map the regions where the Spanish "water-rights system" was used.

The Township-and-Range System

By far the most widely used U.S. land-division system is the "township-and-range system," devised by a committee headed by Thomas Jefferson and made law by the Land Ordinance of 1785.

Jefferson believed that all Americans should own land. This would ensure a democratic society. The township-and-range system offered a way to sell land so that ordinary people could afford to buy it. About three-fourths of all U.S. land was divided according to this system.

The township-and-range system made use of latitude and longitude lines to establish a grid of townships, each one 6 miles long and 6 miles wide (supposedly the ideal size for a farming community). The three diagrams show how land is divided according to this system.

The Impact of the System on American Society

As you can imagine, this rigidly geometric system of land division had a huge impact on settlement. Photograph 4, taken in southern Michigan, shows the obvious effect of this system: The land is divided into hundreds of little rectangles!

The township-and-range system has affected road patterns. These, in turn, have determined where towns, schools, businesses, and local government districts are located. Even the streets within cities have been influenced by this system.

Undivided Lands

Vast tracts of land in the United States have not been divided. The gray areas on the map mark some of these regions. Road maps of the states where these areas are located will show you that they are mainly national parks and military sites.

Note also that most of Alaska is still undivided. This huge state is almost entirely public land. Some people think that it should be kept that way as a national treasure. Others believe that the land should be divided and sold to private developers, as was done with the bulk of public land in the other states.

new nation if the opportunity arose. The future looked dark; Washington and other leaders thought collapse might be nearer than most Americans realized.

The "critical period" reached its climax in the minds of these leaders in the summer of 1786. In late August of that year, civil war broke out in Massachusetts. The trouble began when the state legislature refused to help central and western Massachusetts farmers who were deeply in debt.

The farmers had been hard hit by the postwar depression. Most had mortgages on their property and could no longer meet the payments. People who had been Patriots in the Revolution saw their tools, their livestock, and finally their farms turned over to their creditors by the courts. Farmers were jailed for debt or were sold into indentured servitude.

The plight of these farmers was made worse by the policies of the state legislature, which was controlled by Boston businessmen. The legislators used their power unjustly to shift the tax burden to land rather than commerce. Thus, just when the farmers could least afford to pay, their taxes rose sharply.

When the Massachusetts legislature ignored their requests for relief, the farmers armed themselves and marched on the courthouses in Worcester [wůs′tər] and Northampton counties. They forced the courts to close, so that no more actions could be taken against them for debt. The leader of the revolt, Daniel Shays, then led his men to Springfield where he intended to seize the ammunition in the state arsenal.

The governor, hearing of the rebellion, raised a well-armed state militia. The militia easily defeated the farmers' army, and Daniel Shays fled the state. The danger of rebellion was over. As it turned out, many citizens in the state sympathized with the farmers and criticized the governor for his actions. The rebels were all pardoned, the governor was not re-elected, and the legislature voted changes in the law to help the farmers.

News of **Shays' Rebellion** spread quickly throughout the nation. Rich property owners and people who were creditors firmly opposed any rebellion against legitimate debts. Visions of debtors rising up everywhere against their creditors filled many a head. Yet even among those who sympathized with the embattled farmers, there was a concern that law and order were giving way to vigilante* action. Suddenly, society seemed very fragile under the Confederation.

Shays' Rebellion provoked fears of mob violence.

SECTION 2 REVIEW

 Identify: "critical period," Shays' Rebellion

Main Ideas

1. Why did nationalists like Washington and Hamilton feel that the nation's economy was in crisis? How did independence and state rivalries bring economic problems?
2. How did the weakness of the Confederation government affect foreign affairs?
3. What events led nationalists to fear for the survival of the nation?
4. Why did wealthy people fear the spread of actions like Shays' Rebellion?

*vigilante [vij′ə lan′tē] member of a self-appointed and unauthorized group of citizens organized to punish lawbreakers or unpopular citizens.

3. THE CONSTITUTIONAL CONVENTION

In September 1786 a small group of leaders from five states gathered in Annapolis to discuss the problems of interstate commerce. The conversation moved quickly to other issues, however, and soon to the state of the nation itself. Before disbanding, they decided to ask for a convention to revise the Articles of Confederation. The Confederation Congress hesitated, but in the end agreed to arrange such a convention. Members of Congress hoped the delegates would strengthen the Confederation's authority and give the government the right to raise revenue through taxation.

The Delegates Gather

The convention met in Philadelphia in May 1787. The 55 delegates who journeyed to the City of Brotherly Love had all played active roles in the Revolution, in forming state governments, or in the Confederation itself.

Six delegates had signed the Declaration of Independence. Three had been officers in the Continental Army. Many had represented their states in the Continental Congress or in the Confederation Congress. Two delegates would later become President of the United States. Two would serve as Chief Justice of the Supreme Court. Over a dozen would be governors of their states. The delegates had education, wealth, and political and diplomatic experience.

Thomas Jefferson, who was watching events from his diplomatic post in France, felt the convention was a gathering of "demigods." More accurately, the delegates were part of that "natural aristocracy of talent" to which Jefferson also belonged. The delegates were young. Five were in their 20s, and five in their 30s. Most were in their early 40s, making the 55-year-old General Washington a senior member of the group. Benjamin Franklin, a sprightly 81, was surely a grandfather figure to the delegates around him.

Not surprisingly, Alexander Hamilton, James Madison, and George Washington were in Philadelphia. But three of the most noted patriots, John Adams, Thomas Paine, and Thomas Jefferson, were absent because their duties or their interests had carried them to Europe.

Two of the most radical revolutionaries were also missing. Patrick Henry had refused to attend, for he opposed any effort to increase the powers of the central government. Samuel Adams, whose support of the poor and the working people of Boston had continued after the Revolution ended, was not chosen to attend by his own state's legislature. Thus, the most democratic strains in American politics were not represented at the convention, although the delegates who were there did represent fairly democratic thought.

Secret Proceedings

The air was humid and the temperature was rising when the delegates began their deliberations on May 25. Despite the heat, no windows were open to catch the breeze and the doors were all bolted tight. The delegates had decided to conduct their meetings in strictest secrecy.

Why were the proceedings to be secret? There were three main reasons. First, many of the delegates to the Philadelphia Convention intended to go beyond their instructions to amend the Articles of Confederation. They meant to press for a completely new constitution. This intention bordered on treason, and thus these delegates wished to proceed with caution and with a sense of security. If their views were reported and reacted to from day to day, opponents might not allow them to complete their work.

Second, the delegates all realized that they were about to debate controversial issues. They preferred to discuss these issues in privacy so that each delegate could speak freely and frankly. Third, the delegates worked in secrecy to avoid airing American disagreements before the other nations of the world.

Whether the delegates were justified in holding their meetings in secret is still debated today. Most of the men gathered in Philadelphia believed that the nation was in crisis and that extreme measures were necessary. Yet many of their contemporaries did not agree. Modern-day Americans often find themselves caught up in a similar debate over the people's right to know and the right of those in government to conduct important and sensitive negotiations in secrecy.

Since the convention was secret, how do we

know what happened in it? **James Madison** of Virginia kept careful and detailed notes of each day's debate. A convention secretary also took notes, and these were made public in 1818. Together, these records tell us how the present-day Constitution of the United States came into being.

The Convention Begins

The first order of business was the selection of a chairman. George Washington was the unanimous choice. Next, the rules of procedure were set for the convention. Each state had a single vote on all the issues, just as it did in the Confederation Congress. But here, a simple majority would decide all issues.

Over the course of the next four months, there would be many heated arguments. Yet, on some of the most fundamental issues the delegates were already in full agreement. They all approved of a written constitution. They all assumed that the states would continue to exist. They all agreed that the American government should continue to be republican in form, with laws passed by elected representatives. All assumed that there would be a separation of powers between the branches of the government and between the state and national levels of government. So basic were these assumptions that the delegates probably were not aware of them as issues.

A Background for Compromise

Because the delegates shared the same English and colonial political heritage, they were able to compromise at every crucial point. As you will see, the Constitution would emerge as a "bundle of compromises."

Debates began in earnest on the third day of the convention when **Edmund Randolph** rose to present a "Virginia Plan" to the delegates. James Madison, who had drafted the Virginia Plan, meant for the convention to move directly to the main issue: Were the delegates there to draft a new government or only to amend an old one? The mood of the group was clear; the delegates wanted to create a *new* government whose authority would be the "supreme law of the land." The few delegates who opposed this decision to draft a new government left the convention long before its work was done.

The Virginia Plan

The **Virginia Plan** called for a new, strong central government, with powers to levy taxes, to regulate foreign and domestic trade, and to enforce its laws through a national court system. These were the main powers denied to the Confederation government.

The Virginia Plan called for a government with three branches: an executive, a judiciary, and a legislature with two houses. The lower house, or Assembly, was to be popularly elected. The upper house, or Senate, was to be chosen by the Assembly from a list of candidates submitted by the state legislatures. The number of seats that a state held in either house would be determined by the state's population.

Delegates from the small states of New Jersey, Delaware, and Connecticut protested. If seats in Congress were distributed according to state populations, the larger states would dominate the legislature. The small states were willing to give the Confederation government the right to raise taxes and regulate commerce. But they wanted to preserve the principle of government as a "league of friendship" among states that were equals, regardless of population. On June 14, **William Paterson** of New Jersey made a counter-proposal.

The New Jersey Plan

Paterson's **New Jersey Plan** called for a single-house legislature, with seats distributed equally among the states regardless of population. Paterson's proposal also called for a return to an executive committee chosen by the Congress rather than an independent executive branch. As you can see, the New Jersey Plan was a return to the structure of the Confederation government.

For three days the delegates sat arguing the pros and cons of the New Jersey Plan. James Madison pleaded for a truly national government, not a mere confederation, while representatives of the small states clung to the principle of equal representation for all states in the Congress.

At last a vote was taken on whether or not the convention should continue to consider the Virginia Plan as the basis for discussion. The delegates answered yes, voting seven states to three, with one state delegation divided. Thus, the convention rejected the New Jersey Plan and confirmed its intention to draft a new constitution for a new government.

Connecticut Offers a Compromise

The issue of representation had not been solved. For two weeks a deadlock continued. Then, a delegate from Connecticut named **Roger Sherman** put a suggestion before the convention: Let there be two houses in Congress. Let representation in the lower house be based on a state's population, but let each state have an equal number of representatives in the upper house, or Senate.

Sherman's **Connecticut Compromise** wove together all points of view. The plan respected the sovereignty (independence) of the states by making the Senate their forum. It offered protection to the small states by ensuring equal representation in that Senate. It also preserved the principle Madison so devotedly endorsed, that the legislature represent the people of the nation, not just the states themselves. Representation in the lower house based on population upheld that principle.

Of course, no one was entirely happy with the Connecticut Compromise, or the **Great Compromise**, as it was later called. Nevertheless, the delegates realized that it was the best solution to their problem. On July 2, the South Carolina delegation moved that the convention turn the question of representation over to a committee for discussion and recommendations. The convention agreed. The committee was to be composed of one member from each state, selected by his colleagues.

The mood of the convention was clearly revealed in the choice of the committee members, for no stubborn supporter of either the Virginia Plan or the New Jersey Plan was selected. On July 5, the committee reported in favor of the Connecticut Compromise.

The Three-fifths Compromise

The convention breathed a collective sigh of relief. The greatest hurdle, Madison said, was over. But the issue was not really settled yet. A new problem immediately arose regarding representation. If the seats in the lower house were to be apportioned (distributed) according to population, how was population to be determined?

Behind this question was the question of slavery. Were slaves to be counted as *people* for the sake of determining congressional representation? The northern states said no. Slaves were legally *property*, not people. But the southern delegates stood firm on counting slave men and women in their census. Unless slaves were included, southern states would have far smaller representation in the government than populous states like Pennsylvania. Half the inhabitants of South Carolina, for example, were slaves.

Again, a compromise was hammered out. The northern states agreed—in part—to count slaves as population when assigning congressional seats. The South agreed—in part—to have them counted when tax assessments were levied by the new federal government. Thus, for purposes of both representation and taxation, five slaves were to be considered as three people. This three-fifths formula was an old one, used by the Confederation Congress when it set state requisitions for funds in 1783.

The delegates to the Constitutional Convention knew that it made no moral or logical sense for a slave to be counted as three-fifths of a person. But the **Three-fifths Compromise** did make political sense, and thus it was approved.

At last, the full Connecticut Compromise, with all its amendments, was ready to be decided upon. This Great Compromise was passed by a vote of 5 to 4, with one state's delegation divided.

More Compromises

With the Virginia Plan's basic design for the government agreed upon, and with the Connecticut Compromise established regarding representation, the most difficult times were over for the delegates. Other issues were resolved more quickly, either by compromise or by sending the matter to a committee for resolution.

Electing a President For example, the Virginia Plan called for a single executive or President, but it did not spell out how that person would be elected, by whom, or for how long. Alexander Hamilton, whose views were sometimes out of touch with those of his colleagues, suggested a President for life. Not even the most conservative delegates took Hamilton's proposal seriously. James Wilson, a nationalist like Madison, wanted to see the President elected directly by the people. Many delegates balked at this suggestion. They were not defenders of state governments, but on the other hand, they did feel that the leaders in those governments had better judgment than ordinary citizens. You must remember that the delegates to the Constitutional Convention were members of an educated elite and believed that many major decisions were best left to responsible members of their group.

George Mason of Virginia spoke for this elite when he suggested the indirect election of the President, through a system of presidential electors chosen by each state. The convention sent the matter to a committee, which reported the following compromise: An **electoral college** would select the President, but the members of the college could be chosen in any manner a state saw fit. If no candidate won a majority in the college balloting, then the choice of the President fell to the lower house of the Congress. Here, each state would have one vote.

A COMPARISON OF THE ARTICLES OF CONFEDERATION AND THE CONSTITUTION	Weaknesses of the Articles of Confederation	How Remedied by the Constitution
	There was no separate executive branch to carry out the laws of Congress.	A separate executive department was created, headed by the President. Its job was to enforce the Constitution and laws enacted under it and to conduct foreign relations.
	There was no national judiciary to handle offenses against the central government's laws and to settle disputes between states.	A judicial department was created, headed by a Supreme Court, to handle offenses against federal laws, disputes between states, and cases involving foreign diplomats.
	Congress did not have the power to levy taxes. It could only requisition, or request, contributions from the states.	Congress was given the power to levy and collect taxes, thus freeing it from dependence upon financial contributions by the states.
	Congress could not regulate interstate and foreign commerce.	Congress was given the power to regulate commerce between the states and with foreign nations, thus enabling it to make enforceable trade treaties with foreign nations.
	The states, as well as Congress, had the power to coin money.	Only Congress was given the right to coin money and regulate its value, in order to provide a single national monetary standard.
	Congress was in no position to support an army and navy, since it could not collect taxes. It had to depend on the support of state militias.	Congress, with power to tax, could afford to create a national army and navy, thereby freeing the central government from dependence upon state militias. In addition, state militias were put under the control of Congress.
	It was difficult to pass laws under the Articles, since at least nine states had to approve each proposal.	Under the Constitution the process of lawmaking was made easier. Bills needed only a simple majority vote of Congress to become laws.
	The requirement of unanimous consent of all the states made amendment of the Articles almost impossible.	The Constitution provided for amendment by two-thirds of Congress and three-fourths of the states. This made change more possible, although still difficult.

There was little argument over the committee report. Most delegates were not deeply concerned with the issue, since they were certain that George Washington would be the first President, no matter what election system was used. The convention quickly settled on a four-year term for a President, with no limit on the number of terms the President might serve.

The tariff and the slave trade The summer days dragged on. The heat grew worse, yet the delegates managed to keep their tempers cool. It was late July when, suddenly, a new logjam arose. The convention was working on the new government's authority to regulate trade. Northern and middle states wanted a national **protective tariff** (tax on imports) for American manufacturing, much like the ones the states had recently passed. Such a tax would be levied specifically to raise prices on foreign products in order to drive them from the market. This would protect the sales of American items.

The southern delegates objected. Their citizens were consumers rather than manufacturers of finished goods. They would be paying higher prices on their purchases, if imports were taxed.

To balance this sacrifice by southern planters, the convention offered to extend the slave trade for 20 years and to forbid any government tax on farm exports like wheat or tobacco. The compromise was accepted. But, as you will see in the chapters ahead, later generations of southern leaders would sorely regret this compromise.

The Delegates Vote for the New Constitution

On July 26, the delegates turned their rough draft of the Constitution over to a Committee on Detail. The committee's complete draft was debated, point by point, throughout August and the early

The signing of the Constitution. Washington stands at right. In the foreground are Madison and Franklin.

days of September. Then, on September 10, the convention voted to approve the Constitution. The document next went to a Committee on Style, where **Gouverneur Morris,** a noted writer of elegant prose, produced the final version of the Constitution. On September 16, 1787, the Constitutional Convention approved this document, and on the following day a tired and thankful George Washington adjourned the convention.

Not everyone shared the evident satisfaction and optimism of Benjamin Franklin when their task was done. Two New York delegates had left the convention in anger in July. Luther Martin of Maryland had departed on September 4. And Edmund Randolph, who had begun it all with the introduction of the Virginia Plan, refused to put his name to the Constitution he helped produce. Even those who believed in the document they had drafted reserved their celebration and their enthusiasm. They knew that a long struggle loomed ahead before the Constitution would be accepted by the nation.

SECTION 3 REVIEW

Identify: James Madison, Edmund Randolph, Virginia Plan, William Paterson, New Jersey Plan, Roger Sherman, Connecticut Compromise (or Great Compromise), Three-fifths Compromise, electoral college, protective tariff, Gouverneur Morris

Main Ideas

1. Briefly describe the delegates who gathered at Philadelphia.
2. Why did the convention's delegates decide to meet in secret?
3. On what basic issues did all the delegates agree?
4. What were the main differences between the Virginia and the New Jersey plans?
5. What major problem was settled by the Three-fifths Compromise?
6. How did northern delegates get southern delegates to agree to a protective tariff?

4. THE STRUGGLE OVER RATIFICATION OF THE CONSTITUTION

Supporters of the Constitution, or "**Federalists,**" immediately began to map out a strategy for ratification (adoption) of the new government. They realized that the Confederation Congress would not support the Constitution, for it was designed to replace the old government entirely. They also knew that the state legislatures would oppose the proposal for a new government because the Constitution weakened the powers of the states.

Thus, these Federalists decided to bypass both the Confederation Congress and the state legislatures, and take the Constitution directly to the voters. They issued a call for special conventions to meet in each state to discuss the Constitution and to decide its fate. As soon as nine of these ratifying conventions approved the Constitution, the new government would go into effect for those states.

The Strengths of the Federalists

Even with the system of ratifying conventions, the Federalists feared that they might lose their battle for the Constitution. Most Americans, they knew, remained hostile to the idea of a strong central government. Most Americans still had a strong attachment to their state and local governments.

The conviction that any strong central government, no matter how it was designed, would eventually become an oppressive government was deeply rooted in the minds of this revolutionary generation. The Federalists would have to persuade the voters that the Constitution could protect their liberties.

The Federalists faced many difficulties, but they had several advantages as well. These men had political skills and wealth and the know-how to organize an effective campaign. They managed to get many of their own candidates elected to the ratifying conventions. Even where a majority of the citizens were opposed to the Constitution, the delegates chosen for the ratifying conventions were often Federalists.

In the ranks of the Federalists were some of the most persuasive political writers of the day. Men like John Adams of Massachusetts, John Jay and Alexander Hamilton of New York, and James Madison of Virginia took up their pens to argue the virtues of the Constitution in the newspapers. In New York, where opposition was quite strong, Hamilton, Jay, and Madison published a series of 85 brilliant newspaper essays, later known as the *Federalist* papers. These essays carefully answered every criticism of the new government, and gave powerful arguments for adopting the Constitution.

The influence of the essays was great, as was the influence of Federalist writers in all the states. It was an added advantage to have national heroes like George Washington endorse the Constitution. More than any other American, Washington was known and loved by the nation. Many voters, and many delegates to the conventions, were swayed by Washington's statements in favor of the new government.

The Federalists also had the advantage of a concrete proposal to put before the voters. Their opponents had no alternative proposal to offer. These opponents were placed in the unenviable position of being nay-sayers, or negative voices, in the convention debates. The Federalists dubbed their opponents **Antifederalists**, thus emphasizing the negative position they took.

The Federalists sometimes used their wealth to gain an unfair advantage. They controlled most of the newspapers in the new nation, and frequently refused to print letters or essays by the Antifederalists. Their papers carried only Federalist editorials, Federalist accounts of the debates in other state conventions, and essays urging ratification by the voters. The Federalists sometimes tried to frighten readers into supporting the Constitution by insisting that the nation was on the verge of chaos, invasion by foreign countries, or economic collapse. Thus the "critical period" grew into a doomsday in the hands of some overzealous supporters of the Constitution.

Some Questionable Tactics

The Federalists' strategy was to press for quick ratification wherever possible. They wisely reasoned that if they could get a few states to ratify quickly, then the momentum would be on their side. Occasionally Federalists resorted to questionable tactics. In Pennsylvania, for example, the Antifederalists refused to call a ratifying con-

vention. These opponents argued that no one in the state had had time to read the Constitution or evaluate it. Therefore, the convention should be delayed. To make sure that no action was taken, these Antifederalists stayed away from the state legislature. Without them, there was no quorum* and thus no votes could be taken on any issue.

The Pennsylvania Federalists responded to this delaying tactic with physical force. They broke into the Antifederalists' rooms and dragged them through the streets to the legislature. Antifederalists were kept locked in the State House, where the legislature met. Their forced attendance assured a quorum, and the motion to call a ratifying convention was passed. Antifederalists, of course, were not above similar questionable behavior during the course of the ratification struggle. There were those on both sides who felt that the ends justified the means.

The Antifederalists and Their Arguments

Who were the Antifederalists? Many of these opponents of the Constitution came from the same background as the Federalist leaders. They were political figures of education and wealth. Some opposed the new government because they were leaders in state governments and state politics, just as some Loyalists had opposed the Revolution because they held offices by appointment from the Crown.

*****quorum** number of members of an assembly required on hand to carry on legal business.

But many Americans opposed the Constitution for intellectual and ethical reasons. They believed that strong local governments were more democratic than strong central governments. They believed that local self-rule was the true goal of the Revolution. Their criticism of the Constitution focused on these points.

What dangers did the Antifederalists see in the Constitution? First, they believed that a national Congress could not be truly representative of the many different interests of a growing nation. There were too few representatives in the lower house, and too many voices to be heard.

Second, they believed the Constitution gave the executive branch too much power.

Third, they wished to see greater rotation in office in all branches of government. In the Confederation Congress, no member could run for re-election. The Antifederalists believed that rotation in office prevented any individual or group from growing too powerful.

Finally, the Antifederalists pointed to the absence of a Bill of Rights in the Constitution. Why, they asked, had the Constitutional Convention failed to ensure individual liberties?

Perhaps the Antifederalists were too pessimistic about people's motives once they had power. Perhaps they failed to appreciate the needs of the new nation for an active federal government. Yet, many of their concerns about a distant, unresponsive, and overly powerful central government have remained concerns of Americans throughout our history.

The Battles in the States

The Federalist strategy appeared to be working well in the early stages of the ratification struggle. Delaware, New Jersey, Georgia, and Connecticut all endorsed the Constitution without long debate. As you can see, the Connecticut Compromise was proving a wise one, for these four states were all small states.

The first major battle was in Pennsylvania. Here, those involved in commerce and business lined up against the farmers on the question of ratification. The business people staked their hopes on a federal government that could bring order to American commerce. The Federalists won the day, defeating the opponents of the Constitution by a vote of 46 to 23.

Parade to celebrate the Federalist victory in New York, where the Constitution was ratified by only 3 votes

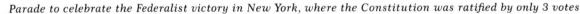

In Massachusetts, the convention heard long and impassioned arguments on both sides. Massachusetts Antifederalists voiced the fear of many ordinary men and women that the rich would control the federal government and thus control the nation. The lawyers, the college educated, and the men with leisure time to devote to politics would swallow up the "little folks" said one Antifederalist, "just as the whale swallowed up Jonah."

Fears such as these arose in part from the absence of a Bill of Rights in the Constitution. Although the Federalists won their battle for ratification in Massachusetts by a narrow margin, their opponents managed to have the convention formally recommend that a Bill of Rights be added to the Constitution immediately.

By May of 1788, only a year after the Constitutional Convention had first been called to order, it appeared that the Constitution was well on its way to adoption. However, even if nine states did ratify, the Union would not be secure without two key states: Virginia and New York. These large and prosperous states actually held the fate of the Union in their hands.

Many of the most respected Federalist leaders were Virginians. But many of the most influential figures in state politics were staunch Antifederalists. Patrick Henry, for example, fought the new government with every skill he had. Federalists everywhere held their breaths, as first one side and then the other seemed to gain ground in the Virginia ratifying convention. Yet, on June 25, when the vote was at last taken, the Federalists triumphed, 89–79. Virginians, like the Massachusetts convention, demanded that a Bill of Rights be added to the Constitution.

The Federalist victory in Virginia turned the tide in New York. Here the most powerful figure in the state, Governor George Clinton, led the anti-Constitution forces. Why, Clinton asked, should a prosperous state like New York give over so many of its powers to a central government? Most of the delegates to the ratifying convention agreed. Yet, after six weeks of debate, the convention finally ratified the Constitution by three votes. It was futile to resist, now that Virginia and nine other states were in the Union.

New York was the 11th state to ratify the Constitution. The Confederation Congress held its last meeting in October 1788, and in January 1789 national elections were held to choose the new government. Eleven months later, in November 1789, North Carolina came straggling into the Union. Rhode Islanders, who had ignored the call to the Constitutional Convention in 1787, tried to ignore the Constitution itself as long as possible. It was May 1790 before this small but independent-minded state ratified the new government.

Two columns needed to complete the "Federal Edifice"

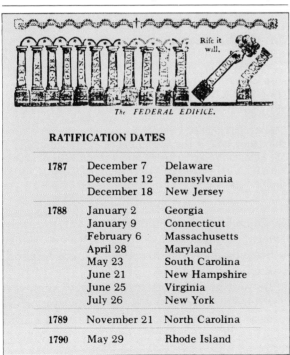

The *FEDERAL EDIFICE*.

RATIFICATION DATES

1787	December 7	Delaware
	December 12	Pennsylvania
	December 18	New Jersey
1788	January 2	Georgia
	January 9	Connecticut
	February 6	Massachusetts
	April 28	Maryland
	May 23	South Carolina
	June 21	New Hampshire
	June 25	Virginia
	July 26	New York
1789	November 21	North Carolina
1790	May 29	Rhode Island

SECTION 4 REVIEW

 Identify: Federalists, *Federalist* papers, Antifederalists

Main Ideas

1. Why did the supporters of the Constitution call for special state ratifying conventions?
2. What advantages did the Federalists have over the Antifederalists?
3. Who were the Antifederalists? What were their arguments against the Constitution?
4. Why was ratification by Virginia and New York so important? What problems did the Federalists face in these states?

199

CHAPTER 8 REVIEW

Key Terms
Explain the meaning of each of the following terms:

> Articles of Confederation
> Land Ordinance of 1785
> Northwest Ordinance of 1787
> "critical period"
> Shays' Rebellion
> Virginia Plan
> New Jersey Plan
> Connecticut Compromise
>   (or Great Compromise)
> Three-fifths Compromise
> electoral college
> protective tariff
> Federalists
> *Federalist* papers
> Antifederalists

Reviewing the Main Ideas
Section 1
1. What were the outstanding features of the new state governments?
2. What powers were given to the national government under the Articles of Confederation? What important powers were denied to this government?
3. What were the provisions of the Land Ordinance of 1785 and the Northwest Ordinance of 1787? Why were these important achievements of the Confederation government?

Section 2
1. What economic problems did the new nation face? How did the weakness of the Confederation government make these problems worse?
2. How did the weakness of the Confederation government affect foreign affairs?
3. Why did nationalists fear that the nation might break apart?

Section 3
1. What were the major differences between the Virginia Plan and the New Jersey Plan?
2. How did the Connecticut Compromise (Great Compromise) resolve this controversy?

3. What was the Three-fifths Compromise, and why was it made?
4. Why did the delegates decide to create the electoral college for presidential elections?

Section 4
1. What advantages did the Federalist leaders have over the Antifederalists?
2. What criticisms of the Constitution did the Antifederalists raise?

Special History Skills:
Recognizing Historians' Interpretations
Historians often view the same facts quite differently. When you read history, always keep in mind that the historian is giving you his or her interpretation of the facts, not just the facts themselves. Some people think that historians should "stick to the facts," but this is impossible. They can never give you *all* the facts (and, of course, they can never know all the facts), so they must pick and choose the ones that they think are the most important. At the same time, they will make a judgment about the meaning and significance of the facts that they have selected. This is their interpretation.

Some historians support the view of nationalists like George Washington and James Madison that the Confederation years were a "critical period" in American history. Other historians disagree. Read the following quotations and then answer the questions.

"Congress had steadily declined in power and in respectability . . . and there was reason to fear that . . . the scarcely formed Union would break into pieces . . . setting up thirteen little republics."   John Fiske

"Merchants owned more ships at the end of the 1780s than they had at the beginning of the Revolution. . . . Freedom from the British Empire resulted in a surge of activity in all phases of American life. Of course not all problems of the new nation were solved by 1789."
          Merrill Jensen

1. Which historian would be most likely to use the term "critical period" to describe the United States under the Articles of Confederation? Explain your choice.
2. Do you think the historian, Carol Berkin, who wrote Chapter 8 viewed the Confederation era as a "critical period," or did she use the term as a way of explaining the views of the nationalists of that era? Give reasons for your answer.

Other Skill Activities

1. Land division

What kind of land-division system was used in your local area? How does the land-division system affect real estate in your area? If you're not sure, call a real estate office.

2. The Constitution makers

The following people were major figures in the writing and adoption of the Constitution: James Madison, Edmund Randolph, William Paterson, Roger Sherman, Gouverneur Morris, Alexander Hamilton, and George Washington.

(**a**) Review Chapter 8 to see what role each one played at the convention or in the ratification process. Jot down your findings.

(**b**) Use an encyclopedia or biographical dictionary to find out more about the views and role of each one. Write a short paragraph about each one, summarizing your findings.

(**c**) Why is James Madison sometimes called the "Father of the Constitution"?

3. Voting on the Constitution

You are a delegate at a state ratifying convention. Would you vote for or against the Constitution (**a**) if you were a farmer, (**b**) if you were a successful merchant? Explain your answers in writing or prepare an oral argument to present to your class.

4. State constitutions

Refer to a copy of your state constitution. Find two ways that it is similar to and two ways that it is different from the federal Constitution.

Thinking Critically

1. In the introduction to Chapter 8, the author says that the state constitutions and the Articles of Confederation focused on the past, and the Constitution focused on the present and future. Find examples in the chapter to support or refute this idea.

2. What would North America be like today if the fears of the nationalists had come true, and the Union had broken apart by the early 1800s? How might your own life be different?

3. What might the United States be like today if the Articles of Confederation had remained in operation? List as many ideas as you can.

4. How would the United States be different today if only the original 13 colonies were permitted to be states and all its other lands were administered as territories?

5. Which, if any, criticisms of the Constitution by the Antifederalists are valid in your opinion?

Further Reading

Marion Starkey. *Lace Cuffs and Leather Aprons: Popular Struggles in the Federalist Era, 1783–1800.* Knopf, 1972. Primary sources on the "critical period," the Constitutional Convention, and foreign visitors. Easy reading.

Catherine Drinker Bowen. *Miracle at Philadelphia.* Little, Brown & Co., 1966. The story of the Constitutional Convention, May to September 1787.

TEST YOURSELF

WRITE YOUR ANSWERS ON A SEPARATE SHEET OF PAPER.

Matching

Write the letter of the item that best matches each description below.

1. first constitution of the United States
2. insured the orderly settlement of the Northwest Territory
3. gave new states equality with the original 13 states
4. caused men and women of property to fear that law and order were breaking down
5. group that supported the new Constitution
6. determined how slaves would be counted for taxation and representation
7. provided for the indirect election of the President
8. one of the authors of the *Federalist* papers
9. group that opposed the new Constitution
10. last state to ratify the Constitution

a. Alexander Hamilton
b. Patrick Henry
c. New Jersey Plan
d. Virginia Plan
e. Three-fifths Compromise
f. Great Compromise
g. Articles of Confederation
h. electoral college
i. Shays' Rebellion
j. Land Ordinance of 1785
k. Northwest Ordinance of 1787
l. Rhode Island
m. New York
n. Federalists
o. Antifederalists

Suits at Common
according to the
the Common Law.
shall not
or to
Test

Chapter 9

EXAMINING THE CONSTITUTION

he Americans who wrote the Constitution faced four major challenges. First, they needed to create a workable relationship between the states and the national government. Second, they wanted to protect the people's liberties. Third, they had to find a way to distribute power to the various branches of government. Finally, they tried to design a constitution that would be flexible enough to meet the changing needs of the nation.

When the Constitution was written, Americans were not (as 18th-century men and women would have said) "in a state of nature." That is, Americans already had governments, laws, political loyalties, and other bonds of community. Thus the delegates to the Constitutional Convention could not ignore existing realities. They had to design a government that the American people would accept.

The success of the delegates in meeting their challenges did not mean that there was no work left to be done by future generations of Americans. The task of creating a free and equal people remained, said the patriot Dr. Benjamin Rush, part of an "unfinished revolution."

Sections in This Chapter
1. Federalism
2. Protection of Civil Liberties
3. The Three Branches of Government
4. A Design That Permits Change
5. The Unfinished Revolution

NOTE: The complete Constitution is printed at the end of this chapter, along with a section-by-section paraphrase.

Opposite: The seal of the state of New York on the document ratifying the Constitution

1. FEDERALISM

As you saw in Chapter 8, the state governments were part of the reality that the delegates always had to keep in mind. There were some delegates, like James Madison of Virginia, who would have preferred to eliminate the states entirely and establish a single national government. But most of the delegates at the Philadelphia convention wished to preserve the states. Also, they knew they had no choice. No constitution would be accepted by Americans which did not honor the right of the states to exist. Thus, the Constitution began as a compromise between a national and a local system of government. The compromise is called **federalism**.

Federalism means that all Americans live under two systems of law and two governmental structures. Each American is a citizen of a state and of a nation. Although federalism respects the existence of the states and their laws, the Constitution and the nation's laws and treaties are "the supreme law of the land."

No state may annul* a federal* law, and no state may refuse to allow the federal government to enforce its laws equally upon all U.S. citizens. Through the federal court system, the national government reaches into every state to govern the people directly.

The federal system is complicated. The Constitution actually creates five categories of governmental powers. There are (1) powers delegated to the federal government, (2) powers denied to the federal government, (3) powers retained by the states, (4) powers denied to the states, and (5) **concurrent powers** held in common by the state and federal governments.

Powers Delegated to the National Government

You are already familiar with most of the important powers delegated to the national government. They include the power to tax, to borrow and coin money, to regulate interstate and foreign trade, and to maintain an army and a navy.

*annul [ə nul′] destroy the force of; make void; nullify; cancel.

*federal When used to refer to U.S. law, the government, the court system, taxes, etc., the word "federal" refers to the *national* government.

Detail, The Tontine Coffee House, Wall Street, Home of the New York Stock Exchange, *by Francis Guy, 1797*

Powers Denied to the National Government

The federal government is denied such power as the right to tax articles exported by the states. Also, the national government cannot make rules or levy taxes which favor the ports of some states and not others.

Powers Retained by the States

It was understood, in making the Constitution, that the states kept any power not specifically granted to the federal government. This understanding was restated in the Tenth Amendment, also known as the "reserved power amendment."

Powers Denied to the States

The states are denied the power to negotiate or sign separate treaties with other nations. They are not allowed to coin money. They cannot impair the obligation of contracts (declare contracts void). They cannot tax imports and exports unless Congress agrees. The states cannot maintain their own troops, or keep warships in times of peace without the consent of Congress.

Concurrent Powers

Despite the emphasis on a division of powers, there are actually many powers that the states and the federal government hold concurrently (share). These are the basic powers that every government needs. The most important are the right to raise taxes and borrow money, the right to establish a court system, and the right to create a law enforcement agency.

Federalism is a complex, and often cumbersome, system of government. But it has proved to be a safeguard against the tyranny of a too powerful government.

FROM THE ARCHIVES

The Tenth Amendment

The powers not delegated to the United States by the Constitution, nor prohibited by it to the states, are reserved to the states respectively, or to the people.

SECTION 1 REVIEW

 Identify: federalism, concurrent powers

Main Ideas

1. Were the delegates to the Constitutional Convention free to create any form of government they wanted to? Why or why not?
2. Explain how federalism can be described as a compromise between a national and a local system of government.
3. Give an example of each of the five categories of governmental powers created by the Constitution.

GOVERNMENT POWERS IN THE FEDERAL SYSTEM

Powers Delegated to the National Government
- Coin money
- Regulate interstate and foreign trade
- Conduct relations with foreign countries
- Establish post offices
- Govern territories and admit new states
- Grant patents and copyrights
- Maintain the armed forces
- Declare war and make peace
- Establish immigration and naturalization laws
- Fix standards of weights and measures
- Make all laws necessary and proper for carrying out the delegated powers

Powers Denied to the National Government
- Tax articles exported by the states
- Give preference to the trade of one state over another

Powers Reserved to the State Governments
- Provide for local governments
- Conduct elections
- Make laws about contracts, wills, and domestic relations
- Proivde for and supervise schools
- Regulate commerce within the states
- Ratify constitutional amendments
- Assume power not granted to the United States nor prohibited to the states

Powers Denied to the State Governments
- Negotiate or sign separate treaties with other nations
- Coin money
- Impair the obligation of contracts
- Tax imports or exports without the consent of Congress
- Maintain troops or warships without the consent of Congress

Concurrent Powers
- Tax
- Borrow money
- Charter banks
- Pass bankruptcy laws
- Establish courts
- Build roads
- Promote agriculture, industry, and science
- Protect the health, safety, and morals of the people
- Take property for public purposes
- Pay debts

2. PROTECTION OF CIVIL LIBERTIES

The concern for **civil liberties*** has a long history in America. It runs like a thread throughout the colonial period and the Revolution. The writers of the state constitutions devoted much thought to protecting various freedoms. The delegates at the Philadelphia convention wove several safeguards against tyranny into the fabric of the Constitution.

Section 9 of Article 1 gives the following right:. The government cannot arrest and imprison people without stating the charges against them. If a citizen is arrested but not formally charged with a crime, the person can demand a **writ of habeas corpus** [ha′bē əs kôr′pəs]. The writ demands the prisoner be immediately released unless the government can produce concrete evidence against him or her of a specific crime.

If there were no right to a writ of *habeas corpus,* any citizen who angered or criticized government authorities might be jailed indefinitely. The President can suspend the right of *habeas corpus* only in the most extreme cases of rebellion or invasion, when the safety of the society is threatened.

Section 9 also forbids Congress from passing bills of attainder and *ex post facto* laws. A **bill of attainder** is a law passed by a legislature to convict a person of a crime. ***Ex post facto*** **laws** penalize people for actions that were legal when committed, but declared illegal later.

In Article 3, the Constitution writers took special care to define treason, for they knew that governments often used this charge to punish dissenters and critics.

According to the Constitution, **treason** against the United States shall "consist only in levying war against them, or in adhering to their enemies, giving them aid and comfort." No one can be convicted of treason unless two witnesses can testify to having seen the deed committed, or unless the accused confesses in open court. Without these protections and the narrow definition set for treason, a citizen's freedom of press, speech, or petition would be meaningless.

*****civil liberties** the freedom of a person to enjoy the rights guaranteed by the laws or constitution of a state or country without any undue restraint by the government.

The Bill of Rights

The original Constitution did not contain a **Bill of Rights.** It is likely that the delegates did not think that a list of guaranteed freedoms was necessary because most state constitutions already included one. However, the federal government honored the requests of the ratifying conventions to adopt a special list of rights. These are described in the first ten amendments to the Constitution.

Reading over these ten amendments, you will recognize many rights that the state constitutions took care to guarantee. You will also recall their historical roots in the Magna Carta of 1215 and in the principles established as the "rights of Englishmen" during the 1600s.

For example, the First Amendment grants to Americans freedom of religion, speech, the press, peaceable assembly, and petition. The Second Amendment guarantees the right of the people to "keep and bear arms." People of the revolutionary generation did not want to see the citizens disarmed, especially when the government had been given the right to create a permanent army. The Fourth Amendment forbids, as the state constitutions did, "unreasonable searches and seizures" of a citizen's home or person.

The Bill of Rights devotes much of its attention to the **"due process of law."** As you know, this includes the right to know what crime you are charged with and the right to answer those charges before a jury. The Eighth Amendment, for example, insures reasonable bail and protection from cruel and unusual punishments, such as the torture and dismemberment suffered by Jacob Leisler in colonial New York.

Limits on Civil Liberties

The writers of the Constitution realized that individual rights must be balanced against the rights of others and against the legitimate needs of the society. Thus, the Constitution does not protect the right to slander* as part of the right of freedom of speech. And, as you have seen, certain rights like *habeas corpus* can be suspended temporarily in a national crisis. However, the suspension of rights has always been controversial in the United States. Even in wartime many citizens oppose the suspension of *habeas corpus*.

---

*slander   spread false statements in order to harm a person's reputation. If written or published, such false statements are called "libel."

THE BILL OF RIGHTS

First Amendment
Freedom of religion, speech, the press, peaceable assembly, and petition

Second Amendment
The right to keep and bear arms

Third Amendment
Rules about stationing troops in citizens' homes

Fourth Amendment
Protection against unreasonable searches and seizures

Fifth Amendment
Rules about trials for serious crimes. Rules against the taking of life, liberty, or property without due process of law

Sixth Amendment
The rights of the accused. These include a speedy and public trial, a defense lawyer, the right to hear the charges, call witnesses, and be present when witnesses speak in court.

Seventh Amendment
The right to a trial by jury

Eighth Amendment
Protection against excessive bail and cruel and unusual punishments

Ninth Amendment
Mention of certain rights in the Constitution does not mean that these are your only rights nor that the unnamed rights are less important.

Tenth Amendment
Powers not delegated to the U.S. nor prohibited to the states are reserved to the states or to the people.

Determining when a limit on civil liberties is proper is usually the job of the courts. The courts are also called upon when Americans wish to expand the scope of their rights.

SECTION 2 REVIEW

Identify: civil liberties, writ of *habeas corpus*, bill of attainder, *ex post facto* law, treason, Bill of Rights, due process of law

Main Ideas

1. Why was it so important for treason to be narrowly defined in the Constitution?
2. What were some of the historical roots of the Constitution's Bill of Rights?
3. Which branch of government usually decides when to limit or expand civil liberties?

3. THE THREE BRANCHES OF GOVERNMENT

The writers of the Constitution thought that a national government had to perform three major functions: pass laws, carry out laws, and interpret those laws through some form of court system.

The Constitution makers decided to divide these jobs among three branches of government: Congress passes the laws. The President, or chief executive, carries out those laws. The judiciary, or court system, interprets the laws.

This, they believed, would offer protection against tyranny because power would be divided rather than concentrated. This principle of the **separation of powers** is the heart of the Constitution.

To insure that no single branch of the government could acquire tyrannical powers over the others, the Constitution makers created an elaborate system of "checks" on each branch by the other branches. These checks guarantee a **balance of powers** in addition to the separation of powers within the government.

Checks on Congress

Article 1 of the Constitution gives Congress the power to make the laws of the nation. What are some of the checks on this authority?

First, the President can veto [vē′tō], or reject, any bill passed by Congress. Although Congress can then vote to override the veto, it is hard for Congress to muster the necessary two-thirds vote to defy the President's wishes.

Second, Congress is checked by the President's prestige and ability to influence public opinion. The President can put pressure on Congress to pass a certain bill by appealing to the voters. The President can call a press conference, deliver a message to the nation supporting the bill, and ask the citizens to make their views known to their representatives in Congress. The President can also call a special session of Congress if it has not acted on the bills the Executive supports. Furthermore, the President can influence how strongly a law passed by Congress is enforced.

Another check on the power of Congress comes from the judiciary. The Supreme Court can check the law-making powers of Congress by ruling on the constitutionality of a law. This power—called the power of judicial review—was not written into the Constitution. It developed early in the 1800s, as you'll see in Chapter 11.

Furthermore, because the Congress has two houses, each with separate functions, there is an internal checking system in the legislative branch. A bill must be approved in both the House and the Senate before it is ready to go to the President's desk to be signed into law.

Checks on the President

Article 2 of the Constitution gives the President the power to carry out the laws. What are some of the checks on this authority?

First, Congress can remove the President if the Executive is found guilty of misusing power. In such a case, the House of Representatives draws a bill of impeachment* which charges the President. Then the Senate tries the case. President Andrew Johnson was impeached in 1868, and an impeachment hearing was held in 1974 during the administration of Richard Nixon. No President has ever been convicted and removed from office.

A second check on the power of the President is in the area of approving appointments. The President appoints various government officers. However, no appointment becomes final until it is confirmed by a majority vote of the Senate.

Third, the President's power to make treaties with foreign nations can be checked. Before a treaty becomes official, it must have the approval of two-thirds of the Senate.

Fourth, the President's power to veto a bill passed by Congress, which is a check on the legislative branch, can itself be checked. The Congress can override a veto by a two-thirds vote.

Fifth, the President can create programs, but Congress can check them through its "power of the purse." Because Congress controls taxation and government spending, it can greatly influence the Executive's program.

---

*bill of impeachment formal accusation that commits an accused public official for trial. A simple majority of the House is sufficient to impeach.

Checks on the Judiciary

Article 3 of the Constitution gives the judiciary the power to interpret the laws of the nation. What are the checks on this authority?

First, Congress has the same power to impeach and remove a federal judge as it has to impeach and remove a President. This power has been used many times.

Second, the Senate has the power to approve or reject the appointment of judges.

Third, to overturn Supreme Court decisions, Congress can propose constitutional amendments and submit them to the states for approval.

Fourth, because Congress establishes the number of justices on the Supreme Court, it can influence the Court's opinions. Today, there are nine members of the Court, but in the past there have been as many as ten and as few as five.

Fifth, the President has the power to appoint federal judges, with the approval of the Senate. This power of appointment gives the President great influence over how the law is interpreted. By selecting men or women who share a President's own legal and political viewpoint, the Executive can influence decisions. Note that this appointment power checks more than the judiciary: It also operates as a check on Congress because the Court can rule unfavorably on congressional legislation.

Sixth, the President has the power to check

CHECKS AND BALANCES IN THE FEDERAL GOVERNMENT

Executive Branch
Enforces laws

- can veto laws
- influences public opinion
- calls special sessions of Congress
- controls how vigorously laws are enforced

- appoints judges
- controls how vigorously court orders are enforced
- can pardon people convicted of federal crimes

- House can impeach President and other high officials
- Senate approves presidential appointments
- Senate approves treaties
- Congress can overturn President's vetoes
- Congress controls President's programs through "power of the purse"

- once appointed, judges are free from President's control
- can declare President's actions unconstitutional

Legislative Branch
Passes laws

- House can impeach judges
- Senate approves appointment of judges
- Congress establishes number of Justices on Supreme Court
- Congress can propose amendments to overturn Supreme Court decisions

Judicial Branch
Interprets laws

- decides on the meaning of laws
- can rule that laws are unconstitutional

Supreme Court interpretation by determining how vigorously the law will be enforced.

Finally, the President can also decide to pardon men or women convicted and sentenced to prison by federal judges, thus checking judicial power.

Checks and Balances in Federalism

An additional example of checks and balances at work is one that the delegates to the convention did not purposely create. That example is federalism. Because of federalism, two systems of government cooperate, but they also compete. When the goals of the state government and the goals of the national government differ, the tensions between the two can serve as a check on each.

Protecting Diversity

The separation of powers, with its built-in system of checks and balances, was created to protect Americans against governmental tyranny. The people who drafted the Constitution also had another goal. They wanted to make the nation's government a safe forum for competing interests and viewpoints. They believed that it was the nature of human beings to differ. As James Madison pointed out in the *Federalist* essay number 10, there are rich and poor, debtors and creditors, people in commerce and in agriculture, citizens with one religious creed and with another. Government had to handle this human diversity.

Government might see diversity as a threat, Madison said, and try to force all people to have "the same opinion, the same passions, and the same interests." This would require a government to turn its back on a commitment to civil liberties. Such a government, Madison warned, would create a tyranny of uniformity.

A second way to handle the natural tendency of people to differ might be to allow these differences, but forbid them to compete. This, too, would require a severe restriction on civil liberties.

The delegates to the Constitutional Convention rejected both of these solutions. Instead, they designed a government that allowed the differing interests to compete—according to the rules of law. In this way violence might be prevented. The problem in designing a government was to find a way to ensure that no person or single interest group could seize control of the government and dominate it for selfish ends.

Preventing tyranny by a minority The separation of powers seemed to ensure against such a tyranny. In order to control the United States government, a minority interest group would have to win a majority in Congress, win election to the presidency, and gain the majority of seats on the Supreme Court. Such a combination is not easy to achieve. Also, the staggered terms for senators, representatives, and the President would make it hard for any group to capture all these offices at once.

Preventing tyranny by the majority However, Madison and his fellow delegates felt that the greatest threat to liberty might come from a determined majority. The "tyranny of the majority" would surely infringe on the liberties of others as it asserted itself. In the *Federalist* papers, Madison wrote eloquently of the rights of a minority. When he wrote this, Madison was thinking specifically of the rights of the wealthy to enjoy their property. Shays' Rebellion was on Madison's mind. But the principle of minority rights logically extends to other minorities in matters of race, sex, religion, and political views.

The separation of powers and the elaborate system of checks and balances can slow the process of government. But those who created this system believed that efficiency was less important than safeguarding liberty.

SECTION 3 REVIEW

 Identify: separation of powers, balance of powers

Main Ideas
1. What are the three major functions of government?
2. Explain how the separation of powers and the balance of powers help protect against tyranny.
3. Name four ways that congressional power is "checked" by the other government branches.
4. Name four ways that presidential and judicial power are checked.
5. How does federalism serve as another check against tyranny?
6. How did the framers of the Constitution ensure that no single group could dominate the government?

4. A DESIGN THAT PERMITS CHANGE

The delegates at the Philadelphia convention were well read in history. They looked to examples of republics in the past to aid them in designing their own American republic. But although they could read the past, they could not predict the future.

Because the delegates were intelligent enough to realize this, they took care not to burden future generations with a totally completed Constitution. Instead, they labored to create a solid framework upon which others could build. This is why as times change, our government has also been able to change.

Changes Through Legislation

The Constitution has several procedures for change. The most obvious one is Congress' power to pass new laws. Thus, under the right to regulate commerce, we have many 20th-century laws governing the modern airplane. Even Benjamin Franklin, a man of scientific vision, could not have anticipated this means of transportation!

The Constitution also has a provision known as the **elastic clause.** In Section 8 of Article 1, Congress is empowered:

To make all laws which shall be necessary and proper for carrying into execution the foregoing powers, and all other powers vested by this Constitution in the government of the United States, or in any department or officer thereof.

Over the years, Congress has employed this elastic clause widely. In the 20th century, for example, laws governing the working conditions of employees have been judged "necessary and proper" to the regulation of interstate trade. There are few challenges to the wisdom of having the elastic clause. But there has been much controversy over who ought to determine if a law is "necessary and proper." The Constitution is silent on the matter.

John Marshall, the forceful and brilliant Chief Justice of the Supreme Court between 1801 and 1833, insisted that the court have the right to rule on the application of the elastic clause. Marshall's assertion has come to be accepted by the government.

On the whole, use of the elastic clause requires the cooperation of all three branches of the government. The President has usually proposed an expansion of government activity through the elastic clause. The Congress has then responded with new laws. And finally, the Supreme Court has ruled on their constitutionality.

Changes Through Amendments

The Constitution established a formal amendment procedure. Because an amendment can change the basic framework of government, this procedure was made slow and difficult.

An amendment can be proposed either by Congress or by a special national convention called at the request of two-thirds of the states. All the amendments except one (the 21st: repeal of Prohibition) have originated in Congress. An amendment must be ratified by three-fourths of the state legislatures or by special ratifying conventions.

Supporters of reforms have had a hard time carrying their proposals through the amendment process. Many have criticized the Constitution for setting such a difficult procedure. Other citizens, however, want important changes to be carefully considered before becoming part of the Constitution.

Only one amendment has ever been passed and later repealed. This was the 18th Amendment,

Modern view of the U.S. House of Representatives

which prohibited the manufacture or sale of intoxicating liquors. Only 16 amendments have been adopted since the Bill of Rights.

Some amendments, such as women's suffrage, would have surprised the delegates to the Philadelphia convention. Others, like the amendment abolishing slavery, would have produced either satisfaction or dismay. Yet all the amendments were made possible by the willingness of these delegates to permit the government to adapt to change.

The Supreme Court's Power to Interpret Laws

The Supreme Court has also played an active part in making the Constitution flexible. The justices who sit on the Court change over the years, and a new Court often rethinks old questions.

The most famous example of a new interpretation is in the area of civil rights. In the 1896 case *Plessy* v. *Ferguson*, the Supreme Court ruled that separate public facilities* for black Americans were legal so long as the facilities were equal to those provided for white citizens. In 1954, a different Supreme Court reversed this decision. In *Brown* v. *Board of Education of Topeka*, the Supreme Court found the separate-but-equal doctrine unconstitutional. Court cases have traditionally been a way of redefining civil liberties.

*public facilities These include both private and public services, such as railroads, restaurants, schools, parks, theaters, etc., that are open to the general public.

Entrance to the U.S. Supreme Court

The "Unwritten Constitution"

Because the Constitution was designed to be flexible, both tradition and practical experimentation can play their roles in remolding the government as the times require. You might be surprised to realize how many important aspects of modern political life the Constitution does not mention at all.

For example, the Constitution makes no provisions for political parties. In fact, many people in the revolutionary generation opposed all political parties or "factions." The belief that political parties are useful, and can help our government run smoothly, grew slowly over the 19th century. And as that notion grew, parties found their place in the government.

Various solutions to everyday problems have also become established customs. For example, the Congress has an elaborate system of standing committees to handle matters like foreign affairs or the budget. The Constitution does not provide for such a committee system.

A third example of a custom establishing itself within the government is seniority. The seniority of a member of Congress is measured by years in office. That seniority determines the member's rank on congressional committees. Thus, a congressman or woman with seniority can exercise great influence on government policy while chairing an important committee.

Changes shaped by tradition or by practical considerations have been called part of the "**unwritten constitution**" of the nation. Your own generation will certainly make additions to that unwritten constitution.

SECTION 4 REVIEW

Identify: elastic clause, "unwritten constitution"

Main Ideas
1. In what three ways can the Constitution be changed?
2. Are amendments always proposed and passed by the same governing bodies? Explain.
3. What role has the Supreme Court played in making changes in the Constitution?
4. What are some examples of the "unwritten constitution" operating in our political life today?

5. THE UNFINISHED REVOLUTION

The revolutionary generation who drafted the new nation's first political documents—from the Declaration of Independence to the state constitutions to the federal Constitution of 1787—knew that contradictions to the principles of freedom and equality existed within their society.

Slavery and Free Blacks

The most glaring contradiction was slavery. While Patriots cried out against a king who threatened to reduce them to slavery, many Americans were slaveholders themselves. At the time of the Revolution, about 20% of the colonial population were slaves. The subject of slavery was often discussed in letters, in newspaper essays, in the private diaries of planters, and at public gatherings.

Uneasy consciences Men and women of conscience, like Henry Laurens of Virginia—who had once been a slave trader—admitted that slavery haunted them. Yet, it was hard to give up the economic advantages that slavery provided to the southern planter. Patrick Henry, a champion of liberty, confessed that he would not free his slaves because of the "general inconvenience of living . . . without them."

Simple self-interest was not the only reason that slaveholders hesitated to end slavery. Thomas Jefferson, for instance, agreed that slavery was morally wrong. Yet, he could not imagine any alternative to it in the new nation.

What role, Jefferson asked, would the tens of thousands of blacks play in the United States if they were free? Surely, he wrote, black people could never be American citizens.

In saying this, Jefferson revealed himself as a man of his times. Like most white men of his generation, Thomas Jefferson saw physical differences like skin color and sex as signs of inferiority. As long as such a belief prevailed, slavery would remain a "necessary evil."

Freedom for some Despite the self-interest of some people and the pessimism of others, many slaves were given their freedom after the Revolution. As early as July 1774, the democratic-minded state of Rhode Island declared that any black person entering the colony was to be considered free. In the next decade, Pennsylvania, Massachusetts, New Hampshire, Connecticut, Delaware, Maryland, Virginia, North Carolina, and South Carolina all passed laws that either abolished slavery or slowed down its growth. In these states, the importation of slaves was discouraged or forbidden.

In Maryland, the number of free blacks rose 350% between 1755 and 1790. By the time the Constitution was a decade old, almost a quarter of Maryland's 110,000 black people were free.

When, in 1782, Virginia made it legal for private citizens to manumit (free) their slaves, many planters did so. By 1790, there were 12,000 free black people in that state, about 4% of the state's black population. George Washington was among the many revolutionary leaders who manumitted their slaves in their wills. Between 1770 and 1810, the number of free blacks in the United States rose to 200,000.

One route to freedom was through military service. Thousands of black slaves enlisted in the cause of the British during the Revolution. Black Loyalist troops fought against their former masters, wearing sashes across their uniforms that read "Liberty to slaves." When the war ended, these black Loyalist veterans left the country, making new homes in Canada, England, the West Indies, and even in colonies in Africa.

Freedom was also gained by enlisting in the American army. In several cases, southern state legislatures stepped in to guarantee that the promise of freedom was kept for black soldiers. After the war many black Patriots returned to their states as free men. Most took new names, moved away from the scene of their slave years, raised families, and built their own schools and churches. Some, like the successful North Caroli-

na barber John C. Stanly, devoted their lives to freeing other slaves. By 1810, Stanly had purchased the freedom of more than two dozen black people.

Nevertheless, free black Patriots were not made equal citizens with white Patriots. Wherever a free black went, he or she met with economic discrimination and social segregation. Political rights were denied.

The Constitution did not challenge the institution of slavery. In fact, by the Three-fifths Compromise, and by the extension of the slave trade to 1808, the Constitution indirectly confirmed the legality of slavery. Like many controversial issues, the problem of slavery was left to the states.

Some states, like Rhode Island, Pennsylvania, and Massachusetts, soon abolished slavery. But most did not do so immediately. A movement began during the 1770s and 1780s to see slavery ended by the national government. In 1775, Philadelphia Quakers formed the first antislavery society. As you will read, the movement to abolish slavery grew strong in the 19th century.

Limited Suffrage for White Men
The Revolution did not bring universal participation in politics for white men. Neither the right to hold office nor to vote was open to all white male citizens. Political leaders of the revolutionary generation, like their colonial fathers, assumed that only men with property—men with a "stake in society"—should be heard in the new governments of the Republic.

Property qualifications for office holding, although not for voting, actually rose sharply as some colonies made the transition to statehood. In Maryland and New Jersey, for example, a member of the upper house of the state legislature was expected to own land worth £1,000. (This was an enormous sum. In Maryland, for example, an estimated 90% of the farmers had farms worth less than £500.) Other states required even more property for office holding. Thus although white men of modest means could vote, they could not generally hold office themselves.

The American Constitution did not specify property qualifications for voting or office holding. It left this matter to the states. Since most state legislators had to meet a property qualification, it was assumed that they would select only prosperous candidates for the U.S. Senate.

This indirect check prevented citizens of average income from serving in the U.S. Senate. The 17th Amendment, passed in 1913, finally removed this restriction by establishing the direct election of U.S. senators.

The Rights of Women
The political and legal rights of women were a third part of the unfinished revolution. Although women like Abigail Adams urged their Patriot husbands to "remember the ladies" and give women more legal rights, the revolutionary leaders probably did less thinking about sexual inequality than about any other social problem. Tradition prevailed, and tradition dictated that women were the dependents of their fathers or husbands, rather than independent adults. Men were expected to take fatherly responsibility for all women within the family circle.

The laws of colonial society had reflected this view of women as a dependent sex. For example, when a woman married, all that she owned became her husband's property. If she worked, her wages were his. Even her personal clothing was his.

A married woman was assumed to have no need to enter the courts of law in her own interest. Thus, she could not sue or be sued. She could not make contracts with others or sign deeds. She could not be held responsible for her own debts. She was not the guardian of her family, and in cases of separation or the rare instances of divorce, her husband acquired custody of the children.

Unmarried women, either spinsters or widows, were less restricted by colonial laws than married women. Referred to legally as a *feme sole* (from the French, for "woman alone"), the unmarried woman's need for certain rights was recognized by the courts and the legislatures.

A single woman could run a business, pay or collect wages, sign deeds, and enter into legal contracts. The *feme sole* was always considered exceptional, however. Except in rare cases, regardless of a woman's personal wealth, or her business success, or her education, she was not entitled to vote or hold office.

Because men of the times—Thomas Jefferson, Alexander Hamilton, or even the worldly Benjamin Franklin—believed that American men protected and represented women, they saw no need

LIFE IN AMERICA

COLONIAL BUSINESSWOMEN

Colonial society felt that women belonged within the "domestic circle." But, poor women, unmarried women, and widows often worked outside the home.

In colonial cities, needy women earned wages as domestic servants or by sewing for others. Some enterprising women became shopkeepers. Others were skilled craftswomen, who generally worked at traditionally female trades, like hat making, dressmaking, and embroidering. Such artisans often took on young girls as apprentices.

Women also sold the products of their kitchens or home laboratories: special pastries and preserves, cosmetics, and medicines. Some turned domestic arts into paying arts by opening taverns, boardinghouses, or inns.

Widows often took over their husbands' businesses if there were no adult sons to carry the burden.

Furrier's shop, 18th century

Thus, in colonial newspapers we find advertisements by women printers, blacksmiths, pewter makers, shipwrights, glassmakers, and brewers.

Most women did not run their own businesses after they were married, but there were some notable exceptions. In New York, for example, a number of women were active in the fur trade, and several New Yorkers became wealthy merchants, such as Margaret Philipse, who also owned two sailing ships.

---

for women to have a separate voice in the new governments. Neither the state constitutions nor the national Constitution reformed the colonial laws governing women's lives. Women continued to be represented in the society only by and through the males of the household. Single women were not represented politically at all.

This arrangement for American women was similar to the English notion of **virtual representation.** As you recall from Chapter 6, the English argued that colonial Americans were represented in the House of Commons even though there were no actual colonists in the House. The members of the Commons could be relied upon, English politicians explained, to act in the best interests of all commoners, no matter who they were or where they lived.

American Patriots did not accept this idea of virtual representation. They did not wish to depend on others. They wanted the power to vote on the issues that affected their lives.

In 1920—almost 150 years after the Revolution—the 19th Amendment granted women the same right to self-rule that men had won in the War for Independence.

SECTION 5 REVIEW

 Identify: *feme sole,* virtual representation

Main Ideas

1. Why didn't the revolutionary generation end slavery? How could slaves become free?
2. Why was it assumed that only men with property should hold office in the new state governments? How did this affect the new national government?
3. Through what political and legal means were women required to be dependents of men? How was the *feme sole* treated differently from other adult women? What right was denied to most women until 1920?

CHAPTER 9 REVIEW

Key Terms
Explain the meaning of each of the following terms:

federalism
concurrent powers
civil liberties
writ of *habeas corpus*
bill of attainder
ex post facto law
treason
Bill of Rights

due process of law
separation of powers
balance of powers
elastic clause
"unwritten constitution"
feme sole
virtual representation

Reviewing the Main Ideas
Section 1
1. Explain how federalism is a compromise between local and national government.
2. Name some powers delegated to the national government and some powers retained by the state governments.

Section 2
1. What parts of the Constitution were designed to protect civil liberties? Which freedoms seemed most important?
2. How did the Constitution balance individual rights with the needs of an orderly society?

Section 3
1. What are the duties of each branch of the government?
2. List some powers of each branch. Then list "checks" that the other branches have on those powers.

Section 4
1. Describe three ways that the Constitution can be changed.
2. What common aspects of political life today are not provided for in the Constitution?

Section 5
1. What were three contradictions to the principles of equality and freedom held by the revolutionary generation? Why didn't the Constitution clear up these contradictions?

Special History Skills: Reading Newspapers
You have learned in this chapter that the Constitution has undergone many changes and reinterpretations over the years. This ongoing process is apparent in the news of the day—court cases, new laws, proposed amendments, etc.

News articles usually follow a basic plan. Knowing it, the skilled reader can gain much information in a short time. First, look at the headline. This gives you a clue about the main parts of the news story. The first paragraph of the news article usually gives the most information. Paragraphs at the end contain the least important information. A typical news article will answer the questions: *who? what? where?* and *when?*

Another kind of newspaper article is the feature. Feature stories are more loosely constructed essays about people, issues, and ideas. They do not follow the basic rules that apply to news stories. The headline may plant a question in your mind rather than give you information. Important points may appear in a conclusion at the end of the article.

Look at this week's newspapers. Photocopy or clip (if the paper is your own) a news article or feature story about one of the following topics that relate to the Constitution: (1) new laws passed by Congress, (2) women's rights, (3) minority rights, (4) changes in the "unwritten constitution," (5) use of the elastic clause, (6) proposed amendments.

As you read, underline what you think are the article's most important points. Then determine whether it is a news article or a feature story. Finally, write a paragraph summarizing the article and another paragraph expressing your opinion on the subject.

Other Skill Activities
1. **The Supreme Court**
   What cases is the Supreme Court hearing this year? Consult magazines and newspapers and discuss one case in depth with your class. How might this case reinterpret the Constitution?
2. **The unwritten constitution at work**
   Find out what committees your congressman or woman is on. What seniority do they have on these committees? Call their local offices or write to them in Washington.

Thinking Critically

1. A criticism of the Constitution was that it took too much power away from local government and made government more impersonal. Do you agree or disagree that government is too impersonal to help the average person? Explain your answer.
2. What might be the advantages and disadvantages to the United States if the legislative, executive, or judicial branch of government became more powerful?
3. Why is it important that the framers of the Constitution did not burden future generations with a totally completed Constitution?
4. Do you agree with colonial leaders that only people with property should be able to hold government office? Why or why not?

Further Reading

1. Joyce L. Stevos. *The Constitution.* Scott, Foresman, 1978. A short, illustrated explanation of the Constitution. Included are a brief history, the full text, and a section-by-section paraphrase at an easy reading level.
2. Mary H. Manoni. *Our Bill of Rights.* Scott, Foresman, 1970. Tells why the first ten amendments were added to the Constitution and explains each amendment through case studies.

TEST YOURSELF

WRITE YOUR ANSWERS ON A SEPARATE SHEET OF PAPER.

Matching

Write the letter of the definition that best matches each term below.

1. federalism
2. writ of *habeas corpus*
3. *ex post facto* law
4. treason
5. due process of law
6. separation of powers
7. balance of powers
8. elastic clause
9. "unwritten constitution"
10. virtual representation

a. the three branches of government
b. penalizes a person for an action that was legal when it was committed
c. permits new laws for new circumstances
d. political arrangement for women before the 19th Amendment
e. a combination of local and national systems of government
f. making war against the United States or giving its enemies aid and comfort
g. requirement that concrete evidence be presented that an individual committed a crime
h. includes the right to a jury trial, reasonable bail, and protection from cruel and unusual punishment
i. created by checks on each government branch by the others
j. common political customs and structures not created by the Constitution

Scrambled Outline

Use the items below to create an outline called "The Separation of Powers." Some items are headings. Others belong under those headings as examples.

THE SEPARATION OF POWERS

I.
A.
B.
C.
D.

II.
A.
B.
C.
D.
E.

III.
A.
B.

carries out laws
draws bill of impeachment against President or federal judge
executive branch
approves treaties
makes treaties
legislative branch
rules on constitutionality of legislation
appoints government officials
judicial branch
confirms presidential appointments
vetoes legislation
interprets the laws
makes the laws

VISITING THE PAST

MOUNT VERNON, VIRGINIA

While there are many historic sites in our country that are thought to be national shrines, only a few can live up to such a claim. One of the few that can is Mount Vernon, Virginia. Mount Vernon is not a town, but a house—an impressive house with outbuildings and lovely gardens. However, it is not the architecture or age of the house that makes this a landmark. It is the man who lived there, George Washington, who makes it special. Mount Vernon is also special because of its place in the history of how we have preserved pieces of our past.

In the 1850s the country was on the verge of civil war. At times of national crisis, Americans often look toward their history for inspiration. Washington had already become a giant in the national consciousness. With the Union threatened, it was not surprising that the popularity of a figure so closely associated with the birth of the nation would increase further. At this time Washington's heirs were considering selling Mount Vernon. There were even rumors that Mount Vernon might be developed as a resort.

The idea that Washington's home would be something less than a shrine to his memory shocked many Americans. One, Ann Pamela Cunningham, was spurred into action. She launched a crusade to preserve the landmark by forming the Mount Vernon Ladies Association of the Union. Cunningham became head of the organization, with the title of Regent. Vice-regents were appointed in 30 states.

The campaign to save Mount Vernon became the first successful nationwide preservation campaign. The effort to save Wash-

ington's home involved people from all across the country. Edward Everett, a famous speaker and senator from Massachusetts, toured the nation speaking about Washington and promoting the effort to save Mount Vernon. Cunningham's group and its campaign set an example for future preservation efforts. Today, as you walk through Mount Vernon's restored rooms or explore its glorious gardens, you can see how successful this effort was.

The preservation of sites associated with famous Americans was the beginning of our country's efforts to maintain physical pieces of its past. Though the success at Mount Vernon would not easily be repeated elsewhere, it did signal the country's growing interest in preserving its history.

Fort Ticonderoga, New York

America's history is full of great adventures and daring deeds. One

favorite episode is that of "America's first victory," the capture of Fort Ticonderoga.

It was less than a month after the "shot heard round the world" had been fired at Concord. The colonies were engaged in a struggle with one of the most powerful nations in the world—England. Was there any hope that they could win? Benedict Arnold and Ethan Allen would soon give the emerging nation a reason to believe that it could!

On May 10, 1775, Patriot troops led by Arnold and Allen captured Fort Ticonderoga in New York colony from its sleeping British occupants. The fort was strategically important, for its cannon controlled the mighty inland water route connecting New York and Canada.

Its location had earned Fort Ticonderoga the nickname "key to a continent." Originally the fort had been a French earthen-wall construction. As the French and Eng-

lish battled for the area, the fort was developed into a stone fortress. The cannon and ammunition from the fort were dragged to Boston in the dead of winter and used by General Washington to break the English grip on that city.

After the Revolutionary War, Fort Ticonderoga was abandoned and fell into ruins. These ruins captured the imagination of a family. Over the course of several generations they bought, protected, and ultimately restored the fort. The work of the Pell family greatly interested the public, and the fort became a museum and historic site.

A visit to Fort Ticonderoga puts one in touch with our history. Standing on the south wall, overlooking Lake Champlain, you can imagine Ethan Allen and his men coming across the lake, ready to fight for their freedom. Walking the walls, touring the barracks, and seeing the massive cannon, you may feel the words in the history books come to life.

Fort Ticonderoga, like many historic sites, keeps alive the memory of an important event in the Revolution. But even more important, it is a symbol of the courage and spirit of self-sacrifice that helped create our nation.

Boston's Quincy Market

There is the hum of excitement in the air. The old building is crowded with people. Its small shops are full of the latest fashions and goods. Its restaurants are varied and full. This setting has the vitality of the latest, most fashionable urban shopping place. It also happens to be a historic place—Quincy Market, Boston.

Washington did not live here. No famous battles were fought here. Yet, with its distinguished architecture and long role as a city market, Quincy Market is an important piece of Boston's history.

Quincy Market is a three-story Greek Revival building with a cop-

per dome. On either side of the market are brick and stone five-story buildings. Architect Alexander Paris designed the building for Josiah Quincy, Boston's mayor. On August 26, 1826, the market opened.

One hundred and fifty years later, on August 26, 1976, the market reopened as one of the most dynamic and successful urban retail centers in the nation. In the 150-year period between the two openings, the market prospered, declined, and ultimately fell victim to partial abandonment, fires, and vandalism. By the 1960s things had reached the point where demolition was being contemplated.

Still sturdy and beautiful, the old buildings caught the imagination of people with vision. These people believed that the market could once again play an important role in the life of the city. It could be reborn as a new urban market, and with its rebirth would come the revival of its neighborhood. After a struggle, the supporters of this plan found financing. With the cooperation of the city, they moved forward with their ambitious project.

The success of the project is history. Over 150 stores in the market complex attract over 150 million visitors a year. Boston's success has inspired other cities. Urban retail centers are appearing in recycled buildings across the country. A crucial element in their success is the special atmosphere and distinct image of the historic structures that house them.

Quincy Market has demonstrated that a preserved past can play an active role in the economic and social life of contemporary urban America.

UNIT 3 TEST

WRITE YOUR ANSWERS ON A SEPARATE SHEET OF PAPER.

Multiple Choice (40 points)
Write the letter of the answer that best completes each statement.

1. Which British act closed the port of Boston?
   a. one of the Coercive Acts
   b. Sugar Act
   c. Stamp Act
2. What was the first battle of the American Revolution?
   a. Trenton
   b. Bunker Hill
   c. Lexington
3. Who wrote the Declaration of Independence?
   a. Thomas Jefferson
   b. George Washington
   c. Samuel Adams
4. After which battle did the French enter the American Revolution?
   a. Yorktown
   b. Trenton
   c. Saratoga
5. The Treaty of Paris
   a. gave the United States most of the land between the Great Lakes, the Appalachian Mountains, and the Mississippi River.
   b. honored Indian land rights.
   c. gave the United States the right to fish off the coast of Florida.
6. The Articles of Confederation were weak because
   a. its writers feared the power of a central government.
   b. British Loyalists wanted it to fail.
   c. there was no need for a strong central government.
7. Under the Articles of Confederation all the states had a
   a. permanent army.
   b. powerful executive.
   c. written constitution.
8. The Northwest Ordinance of 1787

   a. was soon made ineffective by the adoption of the Constitution.
   b. provided for the governing and eventual statehood of the land in the Northwest.
   c. established a system for dividing the land in the Northwest.
9. The Constitutional Convention was conducted in secret because
   a. delegates were unsure of their positions.
   b. delegates wanted to debate freely.
   c. most delegates wanted to maintain the Articles of Confederation.
10. The U.S. Constitution
   a. allows the President to veto bills passed by Congress.
   b. denies the states the power to levy taxes.
   c. does not guarantee civil liberties.

Time Line (20 points)
Match the letters on the time line with the events they stand for.

1. Proclamation of 1763
2. Shays' Rebellion
3. U.S. government under the Constitution goes into effect
4. Boston Tea Party
5. French and Indian War begins
6. Continental Congress approves the Articles of Confederation
7. Declaration of Independence
8. Stamp Act
9. Pontiac's Rebellion
10. Battle of Bunker Hill

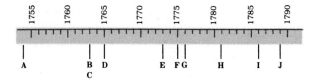

Essay Questions (40 points)
1. List and discuss the weaknesses of the Articles of Confederation and how they were remedied in the Constitution.
2. Defend or reject: The colonists won the Revolutionary War partly through skill and tenacity and partly because of British error.

In the pages that follow, the Constitution is printed in black. Parts that are no longer in force have been crossed out. The spelling and punctuation have been modernized. An explanation of the Constitution is printed in color. The explanation and the headings are not a part of the Constitution.

The Constitution of the United States

Preamble

We the people of the United States, in order to form a more perfect Union, establish justice, ensure domestic tranquillity, provide for the common defense, promote the general welfare, and secure the blessings of liberty to ourselves and our posterity, do ordain and establish this Constitution for the United States of America.

The writers of the Constitution had six goals: (1) to have a stronger central government than they had under the Articles of Confederation, (2) to improve the court system, (3) to have peace in all the states, (4) to protect the country from enemies, (5) to have good living conditions, and (6) to have freedom for themselves and for future Americans. Most importantly, the Preamble says that "we the people" are the authority for the Constitution.

Article 1 Legislative Branch

The Constitution created a government for the whole United States, which we call the federal government. It is divided into the legislative, executive, and judicial branches. Article 1 explains what the federal legislature is and what it can or cannot do. It also puts some limits on the state governments.

SECTION 1
CONGRESS
Who has the power to make laws?

All legislative powers herein granted shall be vested in a Congress of the United States, which shall consist of a Senate and House of Representatives.

Legislative power is the power to make laws. All of the federal government's power to make laws is given to a group of people called *Congress*. Congress is divided into two parts, called *houses*. One house is called the Senate; the other, the House of Representatives.

SECTION 2
HOUSE OF REPRESENTATIVES
Who chooses representatives, and how long is a representative's term?

Sec. 2, clause 1. The House of Representatives shall be composed of members chosen every second year by the people of the several states, and the electors in each state shall have the qualifications requisite for electors of the most numerous branch of the state legislature.

Representatives are chosen every two years by the voters of each state. People who are allowed to vote for state legislators are also qualified to vote for their representative in the national legislature. This clause gives each state the power to decide who is qualified to vote for members of Congress. Several amendments have put limitations on the voting laws states can make. Today, nearly every adult citizen is qualified to be a voter.

Who can be a representative?

Sec. 2, clause 2. No person shall be a representative who shall not have attained to the age of twenty-five years, and been seven years a citizen of the United States, and who shall not, when elected, be an inhabitant of that state in which he shall be chosen.

A representative must be at least twenty-five years old, must have been a United States citizen for at least seven years, and must live in the state from which he or she is chosen.

How many representatives are there?

Sec. 2, clause 3. Representatives and direct taxes shall be apportioned among the several states which may be included within this Union, according to their respective numbers, ~~which shall be determined by adding to the whole number of free persons, including those bound to service for a term of years, and excluding Indians not taxed, three fifths of all other persons.~~

221

The actual enumeration shall be made within three years after the first meeting of the Congress of the United States, and within every subsequent term of ten years, in such manner as they shall by law direct.

The number of representatives shall not exceed one for every thirty thousand, but each state shall have at least one representative; and until such enumeration shall be made, the state of New Hampshire shall be entitled to choose three, Massachusetts eight, Rhode Island and Providence Plantations one, Connecticut five, New York six, New Jersey four, Pennsylvania eight, Delaware one, Maryland six, Virginia ten, North Carolina five, South Carolina five, and Georgia three.

The number of representatives a state has is based on the number of people in the state. A *census*, or count of the people, must be taken every ten years. Congress decides how the count shall be made and uses the census results to decide how many representatives each state shall have. Because of Amendments 13 and 14, the three-fifths clause is no longer in force. Since 1910, Congress has limited the number of representatives to 435. Since 1940, Indians have been included in the census.

How are vacancies filled?

Sec. 2, clause 4. When vacancies happen in the representation from any state, the executive authority thereof shall issue writs of election to fill such vacancies.

If a representative dies or leaves office, the governor (the *executive authority*) of the state calls an election to fill the vacancy.

Who organizes the House, and who has the power to impeach?

Sec. 2, clause 5. The House of Representatives shall choose their speaker and other officers; and shall have the sole power of impeachment.

Every two years, a new Congress meets. At that time, the House elects its presiding officer, or *speaker*, as well as other officers.

Only the House of Representatives has the power to *impeach*. This is the power to decide whether or not high executive or judicial officers should go to trial for serious misbehavior in office.

SECTION 3
SENATE
What is the Senate?

Sec. 3, clause 1. The Senate of the United States shall be composed of two senators from each state, chosen by the legislature thereof, for six years; and each senator shall have one vote.

The Senate is made up of two senators from each state. Each senator is elected for a six-year term and has one vote. Until 1913, senators were chosen by the state legislatures, but Amendment 17 changed this.

When do senators serve?

Sec. 3, clause 2. Immediately after they shall be assembled in consequence of the first election, they shall be divided as equally as may be into three classes. The seats of the senators of the first class shall be vacated at the expiration of the second year, of the second class at the expiration of the fourth year, and of the third class at the expiration of the sixth year, so that one third may be chosen every second year; and if vacancies happen by resignation, or otherwise, during the recess of the legislature of any state, the executive thereof may make temporary appointments until the next meeting of the legislature, which shall then fill such vacancies.

Only one-third of the senators are elected in any one election year. Unlike the House, which can change greatly after one election, the Senate changes slowly.

Who can be a senator?

Sec. 3, clause 3. No person shall be a senator who shall not have attained to the age of thirty years, and been nine years a citizen of the United States, and who shall not, when elected, be an inhabitant of that state for which he shall be chosen.

A senator must be at least thirty years old, a U.S. citizen for at least nine years, and must live in the state that he or she represents.

How is the Senate organized?

Sec. 3, clause 4. The Vice-President of the United States shall be president of the Senate, but shall have no vote, unless they be equally divided.

Sec. 3, clause 5. The Senate shall choose their other officers, and also a president pro tempore, in the absence of the Vice-President, or when he shall exercise the office of President of the United States.

The Vice-President presides at Senate meetings, but votes only if there is a tie.

The Senate chooses its other officers, including a person to preside at Senate meetings when the Vice-President is absent. This person is called the president pro tempore, or pro tem for short.

How does the Senate try impeachments?

Sec. 3, clause 6. The Senate shall have the sole power to try all impeachments. When sitting for that purpose, they shall be on oath or affirmation. When the President of the United States is tried, the Chief Justice shall preside; and no person shall be convicted without the concurrence of two-thirds of the members present.

Only the Senate has the power to try officials impeached by the House of Representatives. The Senate sits as a jury, and the senators must take an oath to try the case fairly. (The writers of the Constitution knew that some religions do not allow people to take oaths. So they provided that a senator could swear or affirm. *Affirm* means "to declare positively that something is true.") If the President is on trial, the Chief Justice of the United States presides over the trial. In other cases the Vice-President presides. To convict, two-thirds of the senators present must vote guilty.

Impeachment gives Congress a check on both the President and the judicial branch. However, this check is rarely used. In all, the House has impeached only twelve individuals, including one President, Andrew Johnson. Only four, all judges, were found guilty by the Senate.

How are convicted officials punished?

Sec. 3, clause 7. Judgment in cases of impeachment shall not extend further than to removal from office and disqualification to hold and enjoy any office of honor, trust, or profit under the United States; but the party convicted shall nevertheless be liable and subject to indictment, trial, judgment, and punishment, according to law.

The Senate's power to punish a convicted official is limited. All it can do is remove the official from office and keep him or her from ever holding another office in the United States government. However, the official may also be punished by the regular courts.

SECTION 4
ELECTIONS AND MEETINGS
When is Congress elected?

Sec. 4, clause 1. The times, places, and manner of holding elections for senators and representatives shall be prescribed in each state by the legislature thereof; but the Congress may at any time by law make or alter such regulations, except as to the places of choosing senators.

Each state may decide when, where, and how elections for its senators and representatives are held, unless Congress disagrees.

When does Congress meet?

Sec. 4, clause 2. The Congress shall assemble at least once in every year, and such meeting shall be on the first Monday in December, unless they shall by law appoint a different day.

Congress must meet at least once a year. Amendment 20 set January 3 as the regular meeting date.

SECTION 5
RULES OF PROCEDURE
Who judges the qualifications of members, and how many members make a quorum?

Sec. 5, clause 1. Each house shall be the judge of the elections, returns, and qualifications of its own members, and a majority of each shall constitute a quorum to do business; but a smaller number may adjourn from day to day, and may be authorized to compel the attendance of absent members, in such manner, and under such penalties as each house may provide.

The House of Representatives decides if members are entitled to be in the House. The Senate decides if senators are entitled to be in the Senate. This power is mainly used when an election is so close that the winner changes each time the ballots are recounted.

Neither the House nor the Senate can hold meetings for business unless it has a *quorum*. That is, more than half the members must be present. The Senate and the House of Representatives can each make rules and set penalties for not attending meetings.

Who makes the rules for Congress?

Sec. 5, clause 2. Each house may determine the rules of its proceedings, punish its members for disorderly behavior, and, with the concurrence of two-thirds, expel a member.

The House and the Senate may each make rules for conducting business and punish their members for not following these rules. In either the House or the Senate, two-thirds of the members must agree if they wish to expel a member.

How shall records be kept?

Sec. 5, clause 3. Each house shall keep a journal of its proceedings, and from time to time publish the same, excepting such parts as may in their judgment require secrecy; and the yeas and nays of the members of either house on any questions shall, at the desire of one-fifth of those present, be entered on the journal.

The House of Representatives and the Senate must each keep a record of what is done at its meetings. Most of what is said (and much that is not said) is printed in the *Congressional Record*. When the members decide to keep some matters secret, those things are not printed in the record. If one-fifth of the members present favor it, the record must show how each member voted on any question.

How can Congress recess?

Sec. 5, clause 4. Neither house, during the session of Congress, shall, without the consent of the other, adjourn for more than three days, nor to any other place than that in which the two houses shall be sitting.

During the period when Congress is in session, neither the House nor the Senate shall let three days pass without holding a meeting, unless both houses agree to a longer recess. Both houses must meet in the same city.

Along with other parts of this section, this clause gives Congress power to decide when and where it should meet. This power is important in keeping Congress independent.

SECTION 6
PRIVILEGES AND RESTRICTIONS
What privileges do members of Congress have?

Sec. 6, clause 1. The senators and representatives shall receive a compensation for their services, to be ascertained by law, and paid out of the treasury of the United States.

They shall in all cases, except treason, felony, and breach of the peace, be privileged from arrest during their attendance at the session of their respective houses, and in going to and returning from the same; and for any speech or debate in either house, they shall not be questioned in any other place.

Senators and representatives are paid out of the United States Treasury according to the law that sets their salaries.

When members of Congress are attending meetings of Congress, or are going to and from meetings, they cannot be arrested except for treason, serious crime, or breaking the peace. They cannot be sued for anything they say or do in their legislative business, and no one can punish them for it, even if it is criminal, except the house to which they belong.

This clause also protects the independence of Congress. Representatives and senators are protected from interference in doing their duty.

What restrictions do members face?

Sec. 6, clause 2. No senator or representative shall, during the time for which he was elected, be appointed to any civil office under the authority of the United States which shall have been created, or the emoluments whereof shall have been increased during such time; and no person holding any office under the United States shall be a member of either house during his continuance in office.

Senators and representatives cannot hold other U.S. government offices while they are members of Congress. During the term for which they have been elected, they cannot take a government position that was created during that term nor any position for which the salary was increased during that term. *Emoluments* means "salary" or "pay."

SECTION 7
HOW BILLS BECOME LAWS
Who proposes money bills?

Sec. 7, clause 1. All bills for raising revenue shall originate in the House of Representatives; but the Senate may propose or concur with amendments as on other bills.

All bills for raising money must begin in the House of Representatives, which originally was the only body in the U.S. government that was directly elected by the people. The Senate may amend these bills and usually does. In fact, it often substitutes an entirely different bill.

What happens if the President vetoes a bill, and how does a President affect bills by not acting?

Sec. 7, clause 2. Every bill which shall have passed the House of Representatives and the Senate, shall, before it becomes a law, be presented to the President of the United States. If he approves, he shall sign it, but if not he shall return it, with his objections, to that house in which it shall have originated, who shall enter the objections at large on their journal, and proceed to reconsider it. If after such reconsideration two-thirds of that house shall agree to pass the bill, it shall be sent, together with the objections, to the other house, by which it shall likewise be reconsidered, and if approved by two-thirds of that house, it shall become a law. But in all such cases the votes of both houses shall be determined by yeas and nays, and the names of the persons voting for and against the bill shall be entered on the journal of each house respectively.

If any bill shall not be returned by the President within ten days (Sundays excepted) after it shall have been presented to him, the same shall be a law, in like manner as if he had signed it, unless the Congress by their adjournment prevents its return, in which case it shall not be a law.

For a bill to become a law, it must first pass both houses of Congress. It then becomes a law in one of three ways: (1) the President signs it within ten days (not counting Sundays) of its having been presented, or (2) the President does not sign it, but also does not veto it within the ten-day period, or (3) the President vetoes the bill, but a two-thirds majority of both houses overrides the veto.

Bills passed in the last ten days that Congress is in session must be signed by the President or they do not become law. The President's refusal to sign one of these bills is called a *pocket veto*.

This clause includes checks on both the President and Congress. Congress must pass a bill before the President can sign it or veto it. Thus, Congress checks the President. The President's veto is a check on Congress. However, Congress has another check on the President. It can override the veto.

When is the President's consent needed?

Sec. 7, clause 3. Every order, resolution, or vote to which the concurrence of the Senate and House of Representatives may be necessary (except on a question of adjournment) shall be presented to the President of the United States; and before the same shall take effect, shall be approved by him, or being disapproved by him, shall be repassed by two-thirds of the Senate and House of Representatives, according to the rules and limitations prescribed in the case of a bill.

The President's approval is needed for matters other than laws. If an order, resolution, or vote must be approved by both houses of Congress, it must be approved by the President. As with bills, the President can veto any of these actions, and Congress can override the veto. However, Congress does not need the President's approval to end its meetings for the year.

SECTION 8
POWERS OF CONGRESS

Section 8 of Article 1 describes the powers of Congress. It is, therefore, one of the most important parts of the Constitution, for the list of congressional powers is also a list of the major powers of the United States government.

What taxing power does Congress have?

Sec. 8, clause 1. The Congress shall have power to lay and collect taxes, duties, imposts, and excises, to pay the debts and provide for the common defense and general welfare of the United States; but all duties, imposts, and excises shall be uniform throughout the United States.

Congress has the power to raise money by taxing. Taxes can be used (1) to pay the debts of the national government, (2) to defend the country, and (3) to provide services for the good of all the people. Most federal taxes must be the same in all parts of the country.

How else can Congress raise money?

Sec. 8, clause 2. To borrow money on the credit of the United States;

Congress has the power to borrow money for the government to use. The Constitution sets no limit on the amount of money the government can borrow.

What controls does Congress have over commerce?

Sec. 8, clause 3. To regulate commerce with foreign nations, and among the several states, and with the Indian tribes;

Congress can pass laws to control trade with other countries, among the states, and with groups of Indians. The power to regulate commerce has been interpreted broadly. Among other things, it has been used to set up national banks and to regulate radio and television broadcasting.

What powers concerning naturalization and bankruptcy does Congress have?

Sec. 8, clause 4. To establish a uniform rule of naturalization, and uniform laws on the subject of bankruptcies throughout the United States;

Congress can pass laws that say how people born in other countries can become U.S. citizens. This is the process of *naturalization.* Congress can also pass a bankruptcy law that is the same in all the states. Bankruptcy laws set up rules for paying off debts when a person goes broke.

How are money and measurement systems provided?

Sec. 8, clause 5. To coin money, regulate the value thereof, and of foreign coin, and fix the standard of weights and measures;

Congress has power to coin money and to say how much it is worth. It also has the power to say how much foreign money is worth in American money. Congress has the power to define weights and measures so that they will be the same throughout the nation.

What control over counterfeiters does Congress have?

Sec. 8, clause 6. To provide for the punishment of counterfeiting the securities and current coin of the United States;

Congress has power to punish persons who make fake government bonds or money.

Who controls the postal services?

Sec. 8, clause 7. To establish post offices and post roads;

Congress can provide a postal service and roads to be used in delivering the mail.

Who issues copyrights and patents?

Sec. 8, clause 8. To promote the progress of science and useful arts, by securing for limited times to authors and inventors the exclusive rights to their respective writings and discoveries;

Congress can encourage science, industry, and the arts by passing patent and copyright laws. Such laws prevent others from profiting from the work of inventors and writers for a specified period.

Who sets up the court system?

Sec. 8, clause 9. To constitute tribunals inferior to the Supreme Court;

Congress has the power to set up courts that are lower in authority than the Supreme Court.

What powers does Congress have concerning piracy and international law?

Sec. 8, clause 10. To define and punish piracies

and felonies committed on the high seas, and offenses against the law of nations;

Congress has power to make laws about crimes committed on the seas or oceans. Congress also has power to make laws to punish those who violate treaties or international customs (international law).

Who has power to declare war?

Sec. 8, clause 11. To declare war, grant letters of marque and reprisal, and make rules concerning captures on land and water;

Congress has the power to declare war. Congress was originally allowed to give persons permission to capture or destroy ships and goods of enemy nations without being guilty of piracy. This practice was given up in 1856 when Congress agreed to follow a rule of international law. Congress makes rules about seizing enemy property on land or sea.

What control over the military forces does Congress have?

Sec. 8, clause 12. To raise and support armies, but no appropriation of money to that use shall be for a longer term than two years;

Sec. 8, clause 13. To provide and maintain a navy;

Sec. 8, clause 14. To make rules for the government and regulation of the land and naval forces;

Congress has the power to raise an army and a navy and to give them supplies. But Congress may not provide money for the army for more than two years at a time. No time limit was put on appropriations for the navy. Congress also has the power to make rules for the organization and regulation of the armed services.

When can Congress use the state militias?

Sec. 8, clause 15. To provide for calling forth the militia to execute the laws of the Union, suppress insurrections and repel invasions;

The volunteer armed forces of the different states used to be called the *militia*. Since the National Defense Act of 1916, the militia have been called the National Guard. This clause gives Congress the power to call out the Guard (1) to enforce the national laws, (2) to put down rebellion, and (3) to drive out invading armies.

What control over the state militia does Congress have?

Sec. 8, clause 16. To provide for organizing, arming, and disciplining the militia, and for governing such part of them as may be employed in the service of the United States, reserving to the states respectively the appointment of the officers and the authority of training the militia according to the discipline prescribed by Congress;

Congress has the power to organize, arm, and discipline the National Guard. Each state has the power to appoint the officers of its Guard and to see that the soldiers are trained according to rules made by Congress.

What provisions are there for a national capital?

Sec. 8, clause 17. To exercise exclusive legislation in all cases whatsoever, over such district (not exceeding ten miles square) as may, by cession of particular states, and the acceptance of Congress, become the seat of the government of the United States, and to exercise like authority over all places purchased by the consent of the legislature of the state in which the same shall be, for the erection of forts, magazines, arsenals, dock-yards, and other needful buildings;

This clause gives Congress the power to govern the District of Columbia, the national capital. In 1974, Congress gave the District a charter allowing a mayor and a 13-member city council. Still, Congress can overrule city council actions. Congress also governs all places bought from the states for forts, ammunition storage, navy yards, and other uses.

What other powers does Congress have?

Sec. 8, clause 18. And to make all laws which shall be necessary and proper for carrying into execution the foregoing powers, and all other powers vested by this Constitution in the government of the United States, or in any department or officer thereof.

Congress has the power to make all laws needed to carry out the power granted in clauses 1–17. Congress also has the power to make all laws needed to carry out powers that other clauses of the Constitution grant to Congress or to other federal officials. Clause 18 is called the "elastic clause" because it stretches Congress's powers. It does *not* give Congress power to do whatever it wants. However, this clause has been interpreted generously so that the federal government has a good deal more power than you might think from reading the first 17 clauses.

SECTION 9
POWERS DENIED TO THE FEDERAL GOVERNMENT

Section 9 of Article 1 lists some of the things that Congress or other branches of the United States government may not do.

What can Congress do about the slave trade?

Sec. 9, clause 1. The migration or importation of such persons as any of the states now existing shall think proper to admit, shall not be prohibited by the Congress prior to the year one thousand eight hundred and eight, but a tax or duty may be imposed on such importation, not exceeding ten dollars for each person.

This clause was part of the compromise over commerce. It said that Congress could make no law before 1808 to forbid the international sale of slaves. By agreeing that the foreign slave trade might possibly be ended 20 years later, those who favored slavery gained a more favorable wording of the commerce and treaty clauses. However, Congress was allowed to place a tax as high as $10 on each slave brought into the country. The writers did not use the word *slave* anywhere in the original Constitution. Even the expression "such persons" was part of a compromise.

When is habeas corpus guaranteed?

Sec. 9, clause 2. The privilege of the writ of habeas corpus shall not be suspended, unless when in cases of rebellion or invasion the public safety may require it.

The government cannot arrest and imprison people without reason to believe that they have broken the law. When a person is arrested, the friends or family can go into court and ask for a *writ of habeas corpus* [hā′bē əs kôr′pəs]. This order directs the jailer to bring the prisoner immediately into court. The arresting officials must then show that they have the right to hold the prisoner, or else he or she will be released. Clause 2 says that only when the country is in danger of rebellion or invasion can Congress remove this important guarantee of personal liberty.

What are some laws that Congress is forbidden to pass?

Sec. 9, clause 3. No bill of attainder or ex post facto law shall be passed.

Congress cannot pass a *bill of attainder*—a law convicting or punishing a particular person. Congress cannot pass an *ex post facto* law—a law that makes unlawful something that was not illegal at the time it was done.

What restrictions are there for direct taxes?

Sec. 9, clause 4. No capitation, or other direct, tax shall be laid, unless in proportion to the census or enumeration herein before directed to be taken.

If Congress is to levy "head" taxes or land taxes, they must be based upon population; the wealth or physical size of states cannot be considered. An income tax is a direct tax, but because of Amendment 16, it does not have to be based on population.

What taxes are forbidden?

Sec. 9, clause 5. No tax or duty shall be laid on articles exported from any state.

Congress cannot tax goods or products being sent out of any state.

What treatment is guaranteed to state ports?

Sec. 9, clause 6. No preference shall be given by any regulation of commerce or revenue to the ports of one state over those of another; nor shall vessels bound to, or from, one state, be obliged to enter, clear, or pay duties in another.

Congress cannot make laws that favor one state's harbors over another's. Ships from any state may enter the ports of other states without paying duties.

What rules affect spending?

Sec. 9, clause 7. No money shall be drawn from the treasury, but in consequence of appropriations made by law; and a regular statement and account of the receipts and expenditures of all public money shall be published from time to time.

Government money can be spent only if Congress passes a law for that purpose. An account of how much money is collected and how it is spent must be made public.

What rules cover titles of nobility and gifts?

Sec. 9, clause 8. No title of nobility shall be granted by the United States; and no person holding any office of profit or trust under them, shall, without the consent of the Congress, accept of any present, emolument, office, or title, of any kind whatever, from any king, prince, or foreign state.

The U.S. government cannot give a title of nobility (such as count, duchess, earl) to anyone. No one in the service of the United States can accept a title, a present, or a position from another country without permission of Congress. This clause was intended to prevent foreign governments from corrupting U.S. officials.

SECTION 10
POWERS DENIED TO THE STATES
What are some actions that the states are forbidden to take?

Sec. 10, clause 1. No state shall enter into any treaty, alliance, or confederation; grant letters of marque and reprisal; coin money; emit bills of credit; make anything but gold and silver coin a tender in payment of debts; pass any bill of attainder, ex post facto law, or law impairing the obligation of contracts, or grant any title of nobility.

This clause lists eight things states cannot do. (1) States cannot make treaties with other countries. Nor can they become a part of some other country. (2) States cannot give private citizens permission to fight other countries. (3) States cannot coin their own money or issue paper money. (4) States cannot pass laws that allow anything other than gold and silver to be used as money. (5) States cannot pass laws declaring a particular person guilty of an offense and describing the punishment. (6) States cannot pass laws that would punish a person for something that was not against the law when it was done. (7) States cannot pass laws that excuse people from carrying out lawful agreements. (8) States cannot give titles of nobility.

What actions by the states require congressional approval?

Sec. 10, clause 2. No state shall, without the consent of the Congress, lay any imposts or duties on imports or exports, except what may be absolutely necessary for executing its inspection laws; and the net produce of all duties and imposts, laid by any state on imports or exports, shall be for the use of the treasury of the United States; and all such laws shall be subject to the revision and control of the Congress.

Sec. 10, clause 3. No state shall, without the consent of Congress, lay any duty of tonnage, keep troops or ships of war in time of peace, enter into any agreement or compact with another state, or with a foreign power, or engage in war, unless actually invaded, or in such imminent danger as will not admit of delay.

These two clauses list actions that states may take only with the approval of Congress. States cannot tax goods coming from or going to other countries unless Congress agrees. However, states may charge an inspection fee if necessary. Any profit from state import or export taxes approved by Congress must go into the United States Treasury, and these state tax laws may be changed by Congress. Unless Congress provides otherwise, states may not tax ships, or keep troops (except the National Guard) or warships in time of peace. States cannot make agreements with other states or with foreign countries unless Congress agrees. For example, if three states want to form a compact to deal with a river that flows through their land, they must get the permission of Congress. States cannot go to war unless they have been invaded or are in such great danger that delay would be disastrous.

Article 2 Executive Branch

Article 2 outlines the powers of the President, says who can be President, and describes how the President is chosen.

SECTION 1
PRESIDENT AND VICE-PRESIDENT
Who has executive power and for how long?

Sec. 1, clause 1. The executive power shall be vested in a President of the United States of America. He shall hold his office during the term of four years, and, together with the Vice-President, chosen for the same term, be elected as follows:

Executive power is the power to carry out the laws. This power is given to the President, who is the chief executive of the United States government. The President serves a four-year term of office. The Vice-President is elected at the same time as the President and serves the same term.

Who elects the President?

Sec. 1, clause 2. Each state shall appoint, in such manner as the legislature thereof may direct, a number of electors, equal to the whole number of senators and representatives to which the state may be entitled in the Congress; but no senator or representative, or person holding an office of trust or profit under the United States, shall be appointed an elector.

The people do not elect the President directly, although they do have a great deal to say about who will be elected President. A group of electors known as the *electoral college* votes the President into office. Each state legislature decides on the way its electors are chosen. The number of electors from each state is equal to the total number of senators and representatives the state has in Congress. No senators or representatives and no one holding a position in the national government may be an elector.

How was the President formerly elected?

Sec. 1, clause 3. The electors shall meet in their respective states, and vote by ballot for two persons, of whom one at least shall not be an inhabitant of the same state with themselves. And they shall make a list of all the persons voted for, and of the number of votes for each; which list they shall sign and certify, and transmit sealed to the seat of the government of the United States, directed to the president of the Senate. The president of the Senate shall, in the presence of the Senate and House of Representatives, open all the certificates, and the votes shall then be counted. The person having the greatest number of votes shall be the President, if such number be a majority of the whole number of electors appointed; and if there be more than one who have such majority, and have an equal number of votes, then the House of Representatives shall immediately choose by ballot one of them for President; and if no person have a majority, then from the five highest on the list the said House shall in like manner choose the President. But in choosing the President, the votes shall be taken by states, the representation from each state having one vote; a quorum for this purpose shall consist of a member or members from two-thirds of the states, and a majority of all the states shall be necessary to a choice. In every case, after the choice of the President, the person having the greatest number of votes of the electors shall be the Vice-President. But if there should remain two or more who have equal votes, the Senate shall choose from them by ballot the Vice-President.

This clause describes the original way of electing the President and Vice President. It was changed by Amendment 12.

When are electors chosen?

Sec. 1, clause 4. The Congress may determine the time of choosing the electors, and the day on which they shall give their votes; which day shall be the same throughout the United States.

Congress chooses the date that electors are chosen and the date they vote. That day must be the same throughout the United States. Congress has set the Tuesday after the first Monday in November in every fourth year as the date for choosing electors. The electors cast their votes on the Monday after the second Wednesday in December.

Who can be President?

Sec. 1, clause 5. No person except a natural-born citizen, or a citizen of the United States at the time of the adoption of this Constitution, shall be eligible to the office of President; neither shall any person be eligible to that office who shall not have attained to the age of thirty-five years, and been fourteen years a resident within the United States.

To be President, a person must have been born a citizen. The person must be at least thirty-five years old and must have lived in the United States for fourteen years. The only persons eligible to be President who were not born citizens were those who were citizens when the Constitution was adopted.

What happens if the President leaves office?

Sec. 1, clause 6. In case of the removal of the President from office, or of his death, resignation, or inability to discharge the powers and duties of the said office, the same shall devolve on the Vice-President, and the Congress may by law provide for the case of removal, death, resignation or inability, both of the President and Vice-President, declaring what officer shall then act as President, and such officer shall act accordingly, until the disability be removed, or a President shall be elected.

This clause describes the original method for the Vice-President to become President. It has been changed by Amendment 25. Congress still has power to say who becomes President if both President and Vice-President are unable to serve. Under today's law the Speaker of the House is next in line.

What rules affect the President's salary?

Sec. 1, clause 7. The President shall, at stated times, receive for his services, a compensation, which shall neither be increased nor diminished during the period for which he shall have been elected, and he shall not receive within that period any other emolument from the United States, or any of them.

The President's salary cannot be lowered or raised during his or her term of office. While in office the President cannot receive any other salary from the U.S. government or from any of the state governments.

What is the President's oath of office?

Sec. 1, clause 8. Before he enter on the execution of his office, he shall take the following oath or affirmation:—"I do solemnly swear (or affirm) that I will faithfully execute the office of President of the United States, and will to the best of my ability, preserve, protect and defend the Constitution of the United States."

Before taking office, the President must take an oath of office, promising to carry out the duties of the job and make sure the Constitution is obeyed.

SECTION 2
POWERS OF THE PRESIDENT
What military and civil powers does the President have?

Sec. 2, clause 1. The President shall be commander in chief of the army and navy of the United States, and of the militia of the several states, when called into the actual service of the United States; he may require the opinion, in writing, of the principal officer in each of the executive departments, upon any subject relating to the duties of their respective offices, and he shall have power to grant reprieves and pardons for offenses against the United States, except in cases of impeachment.

The President commands all of the armed forces in the United States, including the National Guard when it is called into national service. The writers of the Constitution made the President commander in chief because they wanted civilian control of the military forces.

The President is the boss of all the department heads in the executive branch. The President may call on heads of executive departments, like the Attorney General, for advice.

The President can postpone the sentences of those convicted of federal crimes, or pardon them altogether. However, the President cannot interfere with impeachment cases.

What treaty and appointment powers does the President have?

Sec. 2, clause 2. He shall have power, by and with the advice and consent of the Senate, to make treaties, provided two-thirds of the senators present concur; and he shall nominate, and by and with the advice and consent of the Senate, shall appoint ambassadors, other public ministers and consuls, judges of the Supreme Court, and all other officers of the United States, whose appointments are not herein otherwise provided for, and which shall be established by law; but the Congress may by law vest the appointment of such inferior officers, as they think proper, in the President alone, in the courts of law, or in the heads of departments.

The President has power to make treaties with foreign countries. But at a meeting of the Senate, two-thirds of the senators present must approve any treaty.

The President appoints ambassadors, justices of the Supreme Court, and many other government officials. Many of these appointments must be approved by a majority vote of the Senate. The requirement that the Senate must approve treaties and appointments is a check on the President. The leaders of the executive departments—the *Cabinet*—are among the officials who must be approved by the Senate. However, the President alone has the power to fire them.

Congress may pass laws allowing the President, the courts, or heads of government departments to appoint less important officials.

What temporary appointments may the President make?

Sec. 2, clause 3. The President shall have power to fill up all vacancies that may happen during the recess of the Senate, by granting commissions which shall expire at the end of their next session.

The President may temporarily appoint people to federal offices that become vacant while Congress is not in session. These appointments last until the end of the next meeting of the Senate.

SECTION 3
DUTIES OF THE PRESIDENT
He shall from time to time give to the Congress information of the state of the Union, and recommend to their consideration such measures as he shall judge necessary and expedient; he may, on extraordinary occasions, convene both houses, or either of them, and in case of disagreement between them, with respect to the time of adjournment, he may adjourn them to such time as he shall think proper; he shall receive ambassadors and other public ministers; he shall take care that the laws be faithfully executed, and shall commission all the officers of the United States.

This section is an important source of the President's role in the legislative process. It calls for the President to speak regularly to Congress about the nation's problems. This is the State of the Union message the President gives at the beginning of each session of Congress. Only Congress can make laws, but the President has power to suggest laws that Congress should pass. This power gives the President enormous influence.

In emergencies, the President may call a meeting of either or both houses of Congress. If the houses of Congress disagree about when to end their meeting, the President may decide when to end it.

The President is the official who meets with representatives of other countries. This power makes the President chief foreign-policy maker because the power to receive ambassadors is the power to recognize foreign governments.

It is the duty of the President to see that the laws of the country are followed. The President must sign the papers that give officers the right to hold their positions.

SECTION 4
IMPEACHMENT
The President, Vice-President and all civil officers of the United States, shall be removed from office on impeachment for, and conviction of, treason, bribery, or other high crimes and misdemeanors.

The President, Vice-President, and other officers of the United States government (except congressmen and military officers) will lose their position in government if they are impeached and convicted of certain crimes. *Treason* is giving help to the nation's enemies. Nobody is sure exactly what *high crimes* and *misdemeanors* are, but the basic idea is that an officer can be removed if he or she has seriously abused his or her power.

Article 3 Judicial Branch

The writers of the Constitution gave Congress the job of creating most of the courts to be run by the United States government. They also listed the kinds of cases that might be heard in the federal courts.

SECTION 1
FEDERAL COURTS
What courts are there, and how independent are the judges?

The judicial power of the United States shall be vested in one Supreme Court, and in such inferior courts as the Congress may from time to time ordain and establish. The judges, both of the supreme and inferior courts, shall hold their offices during good behavior, and shall, at stated times, receive for their services, a compensation, which shall not be diminished during their continuance in office.

Judicial power is the power to decide cases in a court of law. This power is given to the Supreme Court and to lower courts set up by Congress. Once appointed, judges hold office for life or until they have been impeached and found guilty of wrongful acts. The salary paid to a judge cannot be lowered so long as he or she holds office. The writers of the Constitution wanted judges to be free of political pressures. The provisions about judges' salaries and terms check both Congress and the President.

SECTION 2
EXTENT OF JUDICIAL POWERS
What power do federal courts have?

Sec. 2, clause 1. The judicial power shall extend to all cases, in law and equity, arising under this Constitution, the laws of the United States, and treaties made, or which shall be made, under their authority;—to all cases affecting ambassadors, other public ministers and consuls;—to all cases of admiralty and maritime jurisdiction;—to controversies to which the United States shall be a party;—to controversies between two or more states; between a state and citizens of another state;—between citizens of different states;—between citizens of the same state claiming lands under grants of different states; and between a state, or the citizens thereof, and foreign states, citizens or subjects.

Federal courts hear cases that have to do with the Constitution, with laws of the United States, with treaties, and with ships and shipping. They hear any case in which the United States government is one of the two opposing sides. They settle disputes between two or more states. They originally heard cases involving a state and people from another state or from a foreign country. Amendment 11 took away this power except when the state is the one that takes the case to court. They settle disputes between citizens of different states; disputes about certain claims to grants of land; disputes between a state and a foreign country or its people; and disputes between an American and a foreign country or its people.

One power that the courts have that is not described in the Constitution is *judicial review.* It is the power to say that a law or executive action is unconstitutional. To be constitutional, a law must not violate or go beyond the powers given to the government by the Constitution.

What cases does the Supreme Court hear?

Sec. 2, clause 2. In all cases affecting ambassadors, other public ministers and consuls, and those in which a state shall be party, the Supreme Court shall have original jurisdiction. In all the other cases before mentioned, the Supreme Court shall have appellate jurisdiction, both as to law and fact, with such exceptions, and under such regulations as the Congress shall make.

Jurisdiction [jŭr′ is dik′ shən] is the right of a court to hear a particular kind of case. The Supreme Court has *original jurisdiction* in all cases involving a representative from a foreign country or involving a state. This means that it hears the facts of the case and decides which side wins the case. All other cases must be tried in the lower courts first. The decision of the lower courts can then be appealed to the Supreme Court, which has *appellate jurisdiction.* Congress decides which kinds of cases can be appealed.

What rules govern trials?

Sec. 2, clause 3. The trial of all crimes, except in cases of impeachment, shall be by jury; and such trial shall be held in the state where the said crimes shall have been committed; but when not committed within any state, the trial shall be at such place or places as the Congress may by law have directed.

Any person accused of committing a crime against the United States has the right to a trial by jury. The trial is held in a federal court in the state where the crime was committed. Congress describes by law where trials are held in places that are not states (in territories, for example). The only exceptions to these rules are impeachment trials, which are tried as described in Article 1.

SECTION 3
TREASON
What is treason?

Sec. 3, clause 1. Treason against the United States shall consist only in levying war against them, or in adhering to their enemies, giving them aid and comfort. No person shall be convicted of treason unless on the testimony of two witnesses to the same overt act, or on confession in open court.

Treason is defined as carrying on war against the United States or helping enemies of the United States. Convicting a person of treason is difficult. At least two witnesses must testify in court that the accused person committed the same act of treason. Any confession by the accused must be made in court. Confessions made elsewhere are not accepted as evidence.

How is treason punished?

Sec. 3, clause 2. The Congress shall have power to declare the punishment of treason, but no attainder of treason shall work corruption of blood or forfeiture except during the life of the person attainted.

Congress has the power to decide the punishment for treason. It can only punish the guilty person. No punishment can be set for heirs or family of the guilty person. *Corruption of blood* is punishment of the family of a wrongdoer. It involves taking away a wrongdoer's right to pass an estate or title on to the family. *Forfeiture* involves taking away the goods and honors of the wrongdoer during his or her lifetime.

Article 4 The States

Article 4 describes how the states are to deal with one another. It also sets out a procedure for the addition of territories and states.

SECTION 1
RECOGNITION OF EACH OTHER'S ACTS
How shall one state treat the laws of other states?

Full faith and credit shall be given in each state to the public acts, records, and judicial proceedings of every other state. And the Congress may by general laws prescribe the manner in which such acts, records, and proceedings shall be proved, and the effect thereof.

All states must accept the laws, records, and court decisions of other states as legal and binding. Congress has the power to make laws that force the states to respect each other's laws, records, and court decisions.

SECTION 2
CITIZENS' RIGHTS IN OTHER STATES
How will each state treat citizens from other states?

Sec. 2, clause 1. The citizens of each state shall be entitled to all privileges and immunities of citizens in the several states.

A citizen from another state has basically the same rights as the citizens of the state where he or she happens to be. He or she is not to be treated as a foreigner.

What happens to accused criminals who escape to one state from another?

Sec. 2, clause 2. A person charged in any state with treason, felony, or other crime, who shall flee from justice, and be found in another state, shall on demand of the executive authority of the state from which he fled, be delivered up, to be removed to the state having jurisdiction of the crime.

People cannot escape justice by running out of state. Anyone accused of a crime in one state who flees to another state must be returned if the governor of the state where the crime was committed requests it. This process is called *extradition*.

What happened to escaping slaves?

Sec. 2, clause 3. No person held to service or labor in one state, under the laws thereof, escaping into another, shall, in consequence of any law or regulation therein, be discharged from such service or labor, but shall be delivered up on claim of the party to whom such service or labor may be due.

Persons held to service or labor were slaves, indentured servants, or apprentices. They could not become free by escaping to another state. They had to be sent back to their owners.

SECTION 3
NEW STATES AND TERRITORIES
How shall new states enter the Union?

Sec. 3, clause 1. New states may be admitted by the Congress into this Union; but no new state shall be formed or erected within the jurisdiction of any other state; nor any state be formed by the junction of two or more states, or parts of states, without the consent of the legislatures of the states concerned as well as of the Congress.

Congress has power to add new states to the United States. (No way is provided for a state to leave the Union.) No state may be divided to make another state without the consent of the original state and Congress. The consent of Congress and the states involved is also needed for a new state to be made by putting parts of two or more states together.

How shall territories be treated?

Sec. 3, clause 2. The Congress shall have power to dispose of and make all needful rules and regulations respecting the territory or other property belonging to the United States; and nothing in this Constitution shall be so construed as to prejudice any claims of the United States, or of any particular state.

Congress can sell or give away government lands and property. It has power to make laws governing lands and property. This clause is the source of power for Congress to decide how territories are governed before they become states. Nothing in the Constitution is intended to favor one state over another, or over the United States, in disputes over land claims.

SECTION 4
GUARANTEES TO THE STATES
The United States shall guarantee to every state in this union a republican form of government, and shall protect each of them against invasion; and on application of the legislature, or of the executive (when the legislature cannot be convened) against domestic violence.

The federal government promises that every state in the Union shall have a government in which representatives are elected by the people. It promises to protect each state from invasion. It also promises to send help in putting down riots. The help must be requested by the state legislature or, if the state legislature cannot meet soon enough, by the governor.

Article 5 Amending the Constitution

The writers of the Constitution realized that if their work was to last, they would have to provide ways to adapt the Constitution to changes in society. Article 5 provides several ways.

What is the amendment procedure, and what amendments are forbidden?

The Congress, whenever two-thirds of both houses shall deem it necessary, shall propose amendments to this Constitution, or, on the application of the legislatures of two-thirds of the several states, shall call a convention for proposing amendments, which, in either case, shall be valid to all intents and purposes, as part of this Constitution, and when ratified by the legislatures of three-fourths of the several states, or by conventions in three-fourths thereof, as the one or the other mode of ratification may be proposed by the Congress; provided that no amendment which may be made prior to the year one thousand eight hundred and eight shall in any manner affect the first and fourth clauses in the ninth Section of the first Article; and that no state, without its consent, shall be deprived of its equal suffrage in the Senate.

There are two ways of proposing amendments to the Constitution. One way is for two-thirds of both the Senate and the House of Representatives to vote for a specific amendment. The other way is for the legislatures of two-thirds of the states to ask Congress to call a special convention to propose amendments. All proposed amendments must be ratified by the states. An amendment can be ratified in one of two ways. The legislatures of three-fourths of the states can approve the amendment, or conventions in three-fourths of the states can approve the amendment. Congress chooses the method of ratification at the time an amendment is proposed.

No amendment proposed before 1808 could stop the international slave trade or allow a different method of figuring direct taxes. No amendment can decrease the number of senators a state has unless the affected state agrees to the change.

Article 6 National Supremacy

What happened to existing debts?

All debts contracted and engagements entered into, before the adoption of this Constitution, shall be as valid against the United States under this Constitution, as under the Confederation.

All debts and treaties that Congress made under the Articles of Confederation are binding on the United States under the Constitution.

Which laws are supreme?

This Constitution, and the laws of the United States which shall be made in pursuance thereof; and all treaties made, or which shall be made, under the authority of the United States, shall be the supreme law of the land; and the judges in every state shall be bound thereby, anything in the constitution or laws of any state to the contrary notwithstanding.

This Constitution and federal laws or treaties constitutionally made are the highest law of the land. State judges must follow this law, even if state laws or constitutions contradict it.

What do officials promise?

The senators and representatives before mentioned, and the members of the several state legislatures, and all executive and judicial officers, both of the United States and of the several states, shall be bound by oath or affirmation, to support this Constitution; but no religious test shall ever be required as a qualification to any office or public trust under the United States.

All federal and state officials must promise to support this Constitution. However, no officials or public employees can ever be required to take any kind of religious test in order to hold office.

Article 7 Ratification

Article 7 describes how the Constitution could be approved by the states.

How can the Constitution be ratified?

The ratification of the conventions of nine states shall be sufficient for the establishment of this Constitution between the states so ratifying the same. Done in convention by the unanimous consent of the states present the seventeenth day of September in the year of our Lord one thousand seven hundred and eighty seven and of the independence of the United States of America the twelfth. In witness whereof we have hereunto subscribed our names.

Government under this Constitution could begin after nine states approved it at special conventions. (Nine states ratified the Constitution by June 21, 1788.) This Constitution was signed on September 17, 1787, in the twelfth year of the country's independence. These were the signers:

George Washington—
President and deputy
from Virginia

New Hampshire
John Langdon
Nicholas Gilman

Massachusetts
Nathaniel Gorham
Rufus King

Connecticut
William Samuel Johnson
Roger Sherman

New York
Alexander Hamilton

New Jersey
William Livingston
David Brearley
William Paterson
Jonathan Dayton

Pennsylvania
Benjamin Franklin
Thomas Mifflin
Robert Morris
George Clymer
Thomas FitzSimons
Jared Ingersoll
James Wilson
Gouverneur Morris

Delaware
George Read
Gunning Bedford, Junior
John Dickinson
Richard Bassett
Jacob Broom

Maryland
James McHenry
Daniel of St. Thomas
  Jenifer
Daniel Carroll

Virginia
John Blair
James Madison, Junior

North Carolina
William Blount
Richard Dobbs Spaight
Hugh Williamson

South Carolina
John Rutledge
Charles Cotesworth
  Pinckney
Charles Pinckney
Pierce Butler

Georgia
William Few
Abraham Baldwin

Amendments to the Constitution

The date given in parentheses is the date that ratification of the amendment was completed. Most of the amendments were added to meet specific needs as the country grew and changed. The first ten amendments make up the Bill of Rights. They were written by the First Congress at the request of the states. They limit the powers of the national government and protect the rights of individuals. All three branches of government are limited by the Bill of Rights.

AMENDMENT 1 (1791)
RELIGIOUS AND POLITICAL FREEDOM
Congress shall make no law respecting an establishment of religion, or prohibiting the free exercise thereof; or abridging the freedom of speech, or of the press; or the right of the people peaceably to assemble, and to petition the government for a redress of grievances.

Congress cannot set up an official religion for the country or pass laws to stop people from following their own religion.

Congress cannot make laws that stop people from speaking and writing what they wish. (However, sedition and slander are not always included. *Sedition* is speech or writing to cause rebellion against the government. *Slander* is the spreading of false statements against a person's character.)

Congress cannot make laws that stop people from holding peaceful meetings or from asking the government to correct a wrong.

AMENDMENT 2 (1791)
RIGHT TO BEAR ARMS
A well regulated militia being necessary to the security of a free state, the right of the people to keep and bear arms shall not be infringed.

The people have the right to protect themselves by serving as armed citizens (militia), and Congress cannot stop them. However, Congress has restricted the possession of particular weapons. For example, private ownership of sawed-off shotguns, concealed weapons, and machine guns is prohibited by federal law.

AMENDMENT 3 (1791)
QUARTERING OF SOLDIERS
No soldier shall, in time of peace be quartered in any house, without the consent of the owner, nor in time of war, but in a manner to be prescribed by law.

In peacetime, citizens cannot be forced to give soldiers a place to sleep or meals in their homes. In wartime, this may be done only in the way Congress describes in a law.

AMENDMENT 4 (1791)
SEARCH AND SEIZURE
The right of the people to be secure in their persons, houses, papers, and effects, against unreasonable searches and seizures, shall not be violated, and no warrants shall issue, but upon probable cause, supported by oath or affirmation, and particularly describing the place to be searched, and the persons or things to be seized.

A person cannot be arrested, and his or her house cannot be searched and property or papers taken, except in ways that follow the law. Courts can issue search warrants and arrest warrants, but whoever asks for a warrant must explain why, exactly where the search is to be made, and who or what is to be taken. A *search warrant* authorizes a police officer or sheriff to seize evidence that could prove who committed a crime. The purpose is to prevent the evidence from being destroyed.

AMENDMENT 5 (1791)
LIFE, LIBERTY, AND PROPERTY
No person shall be held to answer for a capital, or otherwise infamous crime, unless on a presentment or indictment of a grand jury, except in cases arising in the land or naval forces, or in the militia, when in actual service in time of war or public danger; nor shall any person be subject for the same offense to be twice put in jeopardy of life or limb; nor shall be compelled in any criminal case to be a witness against himself, nor be deprived of life, liberty, or property, without due process of law; nor shall private property be taken for public use, without just compensation.

Before anyone can be tried in a federal court for a serious crime, a grand jury must formally accuse that person in an indictment [in dīt′ ment]. This rule does not cover members of the armed forces in times of war or public danger.

Once found not guilty of committing a particular crime, a person cannot be tried again for that crime by the federal government. However, if the offense is also a crime under state law, the person can be tried as well in a state court. If the offense hurts someone, the accused person can be made to pay for damages.

No one can be forced to say anything that would help convict himself or herself of a federal crime. This provision prevents the use of torture in getting a confession.

The federal government cannot take a person's life, freedom, or property except in the exact ways written in law, and the law must give him or her a fair trial. Amendment 14 applies this rule to the states too.

The government cannot take a person's property without paying a fair price for it. This power is called *eminent domain*. When the government takes a person's property, it must be used for the benefit of all the people.

AMENDMENT 6 (1791)
RIGHTS OF THE ACCUSED
In all criminal prosecutions, the accused shall enjoy the right to a speedy and public trial, by an impartial jury of the state and district wherein the crime shall have been committed, which district shall have been previously ascertained by law, and to be informed of the nature and cause of the accusation; to be confronted with the witnesses against him; to have compulsory process for obtaining witnesses in his favor, and to have the assistance of counsel for his defense.

An accused person has the right to a prompt, public trial by jury. The jury must be chosen from the state and district where the crime was committed, and the district must be one that has already been described in law. The accused must be told of the charges and must be present when witnesses speak in court. The accused has the right to a lawyer and has the power to make witnesses come and speak in court.

AMENDMENT 7 (1791)
RIGHT TO JURY TRIAL
In suits at common law, where the value in controversy shall exceed twenty dollars, the right of trial by jury shall be preserved, and no fact tried by a jury shall be otherwise re-examined in any court of the United States than according to the rules of the common law.

In many disputes that involve more than twenty dollars, either side in the dispute can insist on having a jury trial. Or both can agree not to have a jury. The second clause of this amendment limits the power of judges to interfere with a jury's decision.

AMENDMENT 8 (1791)
BAIL AND PUNISHMENT
Excessive bail shall not be required, nor excessive fines imposed, nor cruel and unusual punishments inflicted.

Bails, fines, and punishments must not be excessive or cruel and unusual. *Bail* is the money or property an accused person gives to a court as a guarantee he or she will show up for the trial.

AMENDMENT 9 (1791)
ALL OTHER RIGHTS
The enumeration in the Constitution of certain rights shall not be construed to deny or disparage others retained by the people.

The mention of certain rights in the Constitution does not mean that these are the only rights that people have and does not make other rights less important.

AMENDMENT 10 (1791)
RIGHTS OF STATES AND THE PEOPLE
The powers not delegated to the United States by the Constitution, nor prohibited by it to the states, are reserved to the states respectively, or to the people.

This is the "reserved power amendment." The states or the people have all powers that have not been assigned to the federal government or prohibited to the states.

AMENDMENT 11 (1798)
SUITS AGAINST A STATE
The judicial power of the United States shall not be construed to extend to any suit in law or equity, commenced or prosecuted against one of the United States by citizens of another state, or by citizens or subjects of any foreign state.

Citizens of other states or foreign countries cannot sue a state in the federal courts without its consent.

AMENDMENT 12 (1804)
ELECTION OF PRESIDENT
The writers of the Constitution wanted the President and the Vice-President to be the two best qualified persons. For that reason, the original election method provided for the Vice-President to be the person who came in second in the election. This plan worked during the first three presidential elections. In 1800, however, the vote was tied between the Republican candidates for President and Vice-President. The election had to be decided in the House of Representatives.

In the House, the tie was not broken until the 36th ballot. Soon after the election, this amendment was

235

proposed and ratified. It says that the Vice-President is specifically elected to that office.

The electors shall meet in their respective states and vote by ballot for President and Vice-President, one of whom, at least, shall not be an inhabitant of the same state with themselves; they shall name in their ballots the person voted for as President, and in distinct ballots the person voted for as Vice-President, and they shall make distinct lists of all persons voted for as President, and all persons voted for as Vice-President, and of the number of votes for each, which lists they shall sign and certify, and transmit sealed to the seat of the government of the United States, directed to the president of the Senate;

The president of the Senate shall, in the presence of the Senate and House of Representatives, open all the certificates and the votes shall then be counted;

The person having the greatest number of votes for President, shall be the President, if such number be a majority of the whole number of electors appointed; and if no person have such majority, then from the persons having the highest numbers not exceeding three on the list of those voted for as President, the House of Representatives shall choose immediately, by ballot, the President. But in choosing the President, the votes shall be taken by states, the representation from each state having one vote; a quorum for this purpose shall consist of a member or members from two-thirds of the states, and a majority of all the states shall be necessary to a choice.

~~And if the House of Representatives shall not choose a President whenever the right of choice shall devolve upon them, before the fourth day of March next following, then the Vice-President shall act as President, as in the case of the death or other constitutional disability of the President.~~

The person having the greatest number of votes as Vice-President, shall be the Vice-President, if such number be a majority of the whole number of electors appointed, and if no person have a majority, then from the two highest numbers on the list, the Senate shall choose the Vice-President; a quorum for the purpose shall consist of two-thirds of the whole number of senators, and a majority of the whole number shall be necessary to a choice.

But no person constitutionally ineligible to the office of President shall be eligible to that of Vice-President of the United States.

The electors meet in their own states, where they cast separate ballots for President and Vice-President. At least one of the candidates they vote for must live in another state. After the vote, the electors make a list of the persons voted for as President and another list of persons voted for as Vice-President. On each list they write the total votes cast for each person. Then they sign their names, seal the lists, and send them to the president of the Senate in Washington, D.C.

In a meeting attended by both houses of Congress, the president of the Senate opens the lists from all the states, and the votes are counted.

The person having the most votes for President is President. However, the number of votes received must be more than half of the total number of all electors (now 270 or more). If no person has this many votes, the House of Representatives selects the President from the three candidates who have the largest number of electoral votes. Each state has one vote, no matter how many representatives it has. Two-thirds of the states must be represented when this vote is cast. The candidate who receives a majority of the votes of the states is President.

If the House of Representatives does not elect a President before the date set for the new President to take office, the Vice-President acts as President. (The date for this was changed by Amendment 20.)

The person who receives the most electoral votes for Vice-President becomes Vice-President. However, he or she must get more than half the electoral votes. If no person has more than half, the Senate chooses a Vice-President from the two candidates with the most votes. Two-thirds of all the senators must be present when the vote is taken. To be elected Vice-President, the candidate must receive the votes of more than half (now 51 or more) of all the senators.

A person who does not have the qualifications for President of the United States cannot be Vice-President.

AMENDMENT 13 (1865)
ABOLITION OF SLAVERY

Sec. 1. Neither slavery nor involuntary servitude, except as a punishment for crime whereof the party shall have been duly convicted, shall exist within the United States, or any place subject to their jurisdiction.

Slavery is not allowed in the United States or in any lands under its control. No one may be forced to work unless a court has set that as punishment for committing a crime.

Sec. 2. Congress shall have power to enforce this article by appropriate legislation.

Congress has the power to make laws that will put this amendment into effect.

AMENDMENT 14 (1868)
CIVIL RIGHTS IN THE STATES

Amendment 14 did several things. It gave citizenship to former slaves and their decendants, gave them equal rights, canceled the clause counting three-fifths of the slaves in deciding how many representatives a state would have, punished Confederate officers, and canceled Confederate debts.

Sec. 1. All persons born or naturalized in the United States, and subject to the jurisdiction thereof, are citizens of the United States and of the state wherein they reside. No state shall make or enforce any law which shall abridge the privileges or immunities of citizens of the United States; nor shall any state deprive any person of life, liberty, or property, without due process of law; nor deny to any person within its jurisdiction the equal protection of the laws.

Everyone who was born or naturalized in the United States and is subject to the country's laws is a citizen of the United States and also of the state in which he or she lives. States cannot make or enforce laws that prevent any citizen from enjoying rights given by federal law. This amendment also makes the due-process clause of the Fifth Amendment apply to the states as well as to the federal government. The Supreme Court has said that it makes other parts of the Bill of Rights, such as freedom of speech, apply to the states too. The "equal protection" clause is very important. One thing it does is to make it illegal for states to discriminate on unreasonable grounds, like the color of a person's skin. By defining state citizenship, the amendment made it impossible for states to have their own citizenship requirements that keep blacks from being state citizens.

Sec. 2. Representatives shall be apportioned among the several states according to their respective numbers, counting the whole number of persons in each state, excluding Indians not taxed. But when the right to vote at any election for the choice of electors for President and Vice-President of the United States, representatives in Congress, the executive and judicial officers of a state, or the members of the legislature thereof, is denied to any of the male inhabitants of such state, being twenty-one years of age, and citizens of the United States, or in any way abridged, except for participation in rebellion, or other crime, the basis of representation therein shall be reduced in the proportion which the number of such male citizens shall bear to the whole number of male citizens twenty-one years of age in such state.

All people, except untaxed Indians, are counted in order to determine how many representatives in Congress each state is to have. This section amended Article 1, Section 2, clause 3, in which slaves were counted as three-fifths of a free person. A state will lose representatives in proportion to the male citizens over twenty-one who have not committed crimes that it prevents from voting. This provision, intended to force states to allow black men to vote, has never been enforced. However, Amendment 15 has been used to enforce black voting rights.

Sec. 3. No person shall be a senator or representative in Congress, or elector of President and Vice-President, or hold any office, civil or military, under the United States, or under any state, who, having previously taken an oath, as a member of Congress, or as an officer of the United States, or as a member of any state legislature, or as an executive or judicial officer of any state, to support the Constitution of the United States, shall have engaged in insurrection or rebellion against the same, or given aid or comfort to the enemies thereof. But Congress may by a vote of two-thirds of each house, remove such disability.

Congress worded Section 3 so that Confederate leaders who had previously held national or state office were no longer able to vote or hold office. On June 6, 1898, Congress removed this barrier.

Sec. 4. The validity of the public debt of the United States, authorized by law, including debts incurred for payment of pensions and bounties for services in suppressing insurrection or rebellion, shall not be questioned. But neither the United States nor any state shall assume or pay any debt or obligation incurred in aid of insurrection or rebellion against the United States, or any claim for the loss or emancipation of any slave; but all such debts, obligations, and claims shall be held illegal and void.

The states or the federal government cannot pay any part of the Confederate debt. The payment of the Union debt cannot be questioned. No payment can be made for slaves who have been emancipated.

Sec. 5. The Congress shall have power to enforce, by appropriate legislation the provisions of this article.

Congress has power to make laws that will put this amendment into effect.

AMENDMENT 15 (1870)
BLACK SUFFRAGE

Sec. 1. The right of citizens of the United States to vote shall not be denied or abridged by the United States or by any state on account of race, color, or previous condition of servitude.

Sec. 2. The Congress shall have power to enforce this article by appropriate legislation.

Neither the United States nor any state has the right to keep citizens from voting because of their race or color or because they were once slaves.

Congress has the power to make laws that will put this amendment into effect.

AMENDMENT 16 (1913)
INCOME TAX

The Congress shall have power to lay and collect taxes on incomes, from whatever source derived, without apportionment among the several states, and without regard to any census or enumeration.

This amendment changes Article 1, (Section 2, clause 3, and Section 9, clause 4 by saying that Congress has the power to put a tax on income *without* dividing the amount due among the states according to population.

AMENDMENT 17 (1913)
DIRECT ELECTION OF SENATORS

Sec. 1. The Senate of the United States shall be composed of two senators from each state, elected by the people thereof, for six years; and each senator shall have one vote. The electors in each state shall have the qualifications requisite for electors of the most numerous branch of the state legislatures.

Sec. 2. When vacancies happen in the representation of any state in the Senate, the executive authority of such state shall issue writs of election to fill such vacancies: *Provided,* That the legislature of any state may empower the executive thereof to make temporary appointments until the people fill the vacancies by election as the legislature may direct.

Sec. 3. This amendment shall not be so construed as to affect the election or term of any senator chosen before it becomes valid as part of the Constitution.

This amendment changed the method of selecting senators described in Article 1, Section 3, clause 2 to say that senators would be elected by the people of each state, not by the state legislatures.

AMENDMENT 18 (1919)
NATIONAL PROHIBITION

Sec. 1. After one year from the ratification of this article the manufacture, sale, or transportation of intoxicating liquors within, the importation thereof into, or the exportation thereof from the United States and all territory subject to the jurisdiction thereof for beverage purposes is hereby prohibited.

One year after this amendment was ratified it became illegal in the United States and its territories to make, sell, or carry intoxicating liquors for drinking purposes. It became illegal to send such liquors out of the country and its territories or to bring such liquors into them.

Sec. 2. The Congress and the several states shall have concurrent power to enforce this article by appropriate legislation.

The states and the federal government shared enforcement duties.

Sec. 3. This article shall be inoperative unless it shall have been ratified as an amendment to the Constitution by the legislatures of the several states, as provided in the Constitution, within seven years from the date of the submission hereof to the states by the Congress.

This amendment would not have become a part of the Constitution if it had not been ratified by the legislatures of the states within seven years. The need for ratification within seven years was written into several amendments.

AMENDMENT 19 (1920)
WOMEN'S SUFFRAGE

The right of citizens of the United States to vote shall not be denied or abridged by the United States or by any state on account of sex.

Congress shall have power to enforce this article by appropriate legislation.

Neither the United States nor any state can keep a citizen from voting because she is a woman. Congress has the power to make laws that will make this amendment effective.

AMENDMENT 20 (1933)
"LAME-DUCK" AMENDMENT

Sec. 1. The terms of the President and Vice-President shall end at noon on the twentieth day of January, and the terms of senators and representatives at noon on the third day of January, of the years in which such terms would have ended if this article had not been ratified; and the terms of their successors shall then begin.

Sec. 2. The Congress shall assemble at least once in every year, and such meeting shall begin at noon on the third day of January, unless they shall by law appoint a different day.

Sec. 3. If, at the time fixed for the beginning of the term of the President, the President-elect shall have died, the Vice-President-elect shall become President. If a President shall not have been chosen before the time fixed for the beginning of his term, or if the President-elect shall have failed to qualify, then the Vice-President-elect shall act as President until a President shall have qualified; and the Congress may by law provide for the case wherein neither a President-elect nor a Vice-President-elect shall have qualified, declaring who shall then act as President, or the manner in which one who is to act shall be selected, and such person shall act accordingly until a President or Vice-President shall have qualified.

Sec. 4. The Congress may by law provide for the case of the death of any of the persons from whom the House of Representatives may choose a President whenever the right of choice shall have devolved upon them, and for the case of the death of any of the persons from whom the Senate may choose a Vice-President whenever the right of choice shall have devolved upon them.

Sec. 5. Sections 1 and 2 shall take effect on the fifteenth day of October following the ratification of this article.

Sec. 6. This article shall be inoperative unless it shall have been ratified as an amendment to the

Constitution by the legislatures of three-fourths of the several states within seven years from the date of its submission.

A person who holds office after his or her replacement has been chosen does not have much influence, and so is known as a "lame duck." This amendment shortens the "lame duck" period. Formerly a President and Vice-President elected in November did not take office until March 4. Now they are sworn in in January. Formerly, new members of Congress waited 13 months to take their seats. Now they wait only about two. Sections 3 and 4 give procedures for the selection of President and Vice-President in situations not covered by Amendment 12. This amendment had to be approved within seven years of its being sent to the states.

AMENDMENT 21 (1933)
REPEAL OF PROHIBITION

Sec. 1. The eighteenth article of amendment to the Constitution of the United States is hereby repealed.

This amendment repeals Amendment 18. Prohibition is no longer a national law.

Sec. 2. The transportation or importation into any state, territory, or possession of the United States for delivery or use therein of intoxicating liquors, in violation of the laws thereof, is hereby prohibited.

A state can forbid liquor for drinking purposes. Carrying liquor across state boundaries for use in a "dry" state is a crime against the United States as well as against the state.

Sec. 3. This article shall be inoperative unless it shall have been ratified as an amendment to the Constitution by conventions in the several states, as provided in the Constitution, within seven years from the date of the submission hereof to the states by the Congress.

Amendment 21 had to be ratified by state conventions chosen specifically for their views on the issue. The conventions had to approve the amendment within seven years.

AMENDMENT 22 (1951)
PRESIDENTIAL TERM OF OFFICE

Sec. 1. No person shall be elected to the office of the President more than twice, and no person who has held the office of President, or acted as President, for more than two years of a term to which some other person was elected President shall be elected to the office of the President more than once. But this article shall not apply to any person holding the office of President when this article was proposed by the Congress, and shall not prevent any person who may be holding the office of President, or acting as President, during the term within which this article becomes operative from holding the office of President or acting as President during the remainder of such term.

No person can have more than two terms as President. Holding the office of President or acting as President for more than two years will be considered as one full term. This amendment did not apply to Harry Truman, who was President at the time this amendment was both proposed by Congress and ratified by the states.

Sec. 2. This article shall be inoperative unless it shall have been ratified as an amendment to the Constitution by the legislatures of three-fourths of the several states within seven years from the date of its submission to the states by the Congress.

This amendment had to be ratified within seven years in order to take effect.

AMENDMENT 23 (1961)
VOTING IN THE DISTRICT OF COLUMBIA

Sec. 1. The district constituting the seat of government of the United States shall appoint in such manner as the Congress may direct:

A number of electors of President and Vice-President equal to the whole number of senators and representatives in Congress to which the District would be entitled if it were a state, but in no event more than the least populous state; they shall be in addition to those appointed by the states, but they shall be considered, for the purposes of the election of President and Vice-President, to be electors appointed by a state; and they shall meet in the district and perform such duties as provided by the twelfth article of amendment.

Sec. 2. The Congress shall have power to enforce this article by appropriate legislation.

This amendment gives people living in Washington, D.C., a voice in choosing the President and Vice-President. It says the District of Columbia may choose electors in the election of the President and Vice-President of the United States. The number of electors is limited to the number of electors from the state with the smallest population. The electors follow the rules for elections described in Amendment 12. Congress can pass laws to put this amendment into effect.

AMENDMENT 24 (1964)
ABOLITION OF POLL TAXES

Sec. 1. The right of citizens of the United States to vote in any primary or other election for President or Vice-President, for electors for President or Vice-President, or for senator or representative in Congress, shall not be denied or abridged by the United States or any state by reason of failure to pay any poll tax or other tax.

Sec. 2. The Congress shall have power to enforce this article by appropriate legislation.

Neither the United States nor any state can make the payment of a poll tax or any other tax a requirement for voting in any election for national officers. This rule applies to the election of the President, Vice-President, electors of these, senators, and representatives in Congress. The amendment does not make poll taxes illegal in elections of state officials. However, it makes them unlikely and impractical because to require a poll tax in state elections but not in federal elections, a state would have to keep two different lists of voters and print two different kinds of ballots. Congress can make laws to enforce this amendment.

AMENDMENT 25 (1967)
PRESIDENTIAL DISABILITY AND SUCCESSION

Sec. 1. In case of the removal of the President from office or of his death or resignation, the Vice-President shall become President.

If the President dies or resigns, or is removed from office, the Vice-President becomes President.

Sec. 2. Whenever there is a vacancy in the office of the Vice-President, the President shall nominate a Vice-President who shall take office upon confirmation by a majority vote of both houses of Congress.

The President appoints a Vice-President if no one is serving in that office. The appointment must be approved by a majority vote in both houses of Congress.

Sec. 3. Whenever the President transmits to the president pro tempore of the Senate and the speaker of the House of Representatives his written declaration that he is unable to discharge the powers and duties of his office, and until he transmits to them a written declaration to the contrary, such powers and duties shall be discharged by the Vice-President as Acting President.

If the President notifies Congress in writing that he or she is unable to perform official duties, the Vice-President takes over as Acting President until the President notifies Congress in writing that he or she is again able to serve.

Sec. 4. Whenever the Vice-President and a majority of either the principal officers of the executive departments or of such other body as Congress may by law provide, transmit to the president pro tempore of the Senate and the speaker of the House of Representatives their written declaration that the President is unable to discharge the powers and duties of his office, the Vice-President shall immediately assume the powers and duties of the office as Acting President.

Thereafter, when the President transmits to the president pro tempore of the Senate and the speaker of the House of Representatives his written declaration that no inability exists, he shall resume the powers and duties of his office unless the Vice-President and a majority of either the principal officers of the executive departments or of such other body as Congress may by law provide, transmit within four days to the president pro tempore of the Senate and the speaker of the House of Representatives their written declaration that the President is unable to discharge the powers and duties of his office. Thereupon Congress shall decide the issue, assembling within forty-eight hours for that purpose if not in session. If the Congress, within twenty-one days after receipt of the latter written declaration, or, if Congress is not in session, within twenty-one days after Congress is required to assemble, determines by two-thirds vote of both houses that the President is unable to discharge the powers and duties of his office, the Vice-President shall continue to discharge the same as Acting President; otherwise, the President shall resume the powers and duties of his office.

If a disabled President is unable or unwilling to notify Congress of his or her disability, the Vice-President may. In such a case, a majority of the Cabinet, or some other group named by Congress in law, must agree. Then the Vice-President becomes Acting President.

The President may notify Congress of a recovery and resume the powers and duties of office. However, if the Vice-President and a majority of the designated group do not agree that the President has recovered, they must notify Congress before four days have passed. Congress must meet within forty-eight hours. They have twenty-one days to discuss the issue. If two-thirds or more of each house votes against the President, the Vice-President continues to serve as Acting President. Otherwise, the President resumes office.

AMENDMENT 26 (1971)
EIGHTEEN-YEAR-OLD VOTE

Sec. 1. The right of citizens of the United States, who are eighteen years of age or older, to vote shall not be denied or abridged by the United States or by any state on account of age.

Sec. 2. The Congress shall have the power to enforce this article by appropriate legislation.

The United States and the state governments cannot say that eighteen-year-olds are too young to vote. Congress can pass laws to enforce this amendment.

Unit Four

The Young Republic

Chapter 10

1789–1800

THE FEDERALIST ERA

On April 14, 1789, the news that everyone had been waiting for reached Mount Vernon: George Washington had been elected the first President of the United States! For the General, it was sobering news, but not surprising. As he packed his trunk for the journey to New York City, the temporary capital, friends told him about the election. He had been the unanimous choice of the 69 electors. Even his old political foe, Patrick Henry, had voted for him. John Adams was the new Vice-President, and Congress was filled with staunch Federalists.

On April 16, Washington set out for New York City. The journey took a full week, for all along the way his progress was slowed by the crowds that greeted him. The cheers were as much for the miracle of American independence as for the President himself.

On April 30, Washington took his oath of office. Then he stepped onto the balcony of Federal Hall to greet the people. Standing on the balcony, he perfectly symbolized the new nation. His clothing was an odd blend of the republican future and the colonial past, for his suit was made of American homespun cloth, but his stockings were imported from England. The magnificent dress sword, gleaming against his drab brown suit, was a reminder of America's victory in the Revolution. The silver buckles shining on his shoes marked him as a member of the elite class that governed America even though it was a republic.

Sections in This Chapter
1. The Start of a Government
2. Washington's First Term and Hamilton's Economic Program
3. Washington's Second Term and the Foreign Policy Crisis
4. John Adams, Political Parties, and the Quasi-War
5. The Alien and Sedition Acts and the Defeat of the Federalists

Even at the nation's beginning Americans turned toward space. Opposite: Model of the solar system built around 1770 by David Rittenhouse, a noted astronomer and the first director of the U.S. Mint.

Timeline

1788

1789 ◆ George Washington elected first President

◆ Congress passes the Judiciary Act, drafts the Bill of Rights, passes a small tariff, and establishes the President's cabinet

◆ French Revolution begins

1790

1790 ◆ Congress accepts most of Hamilton's economic proposals

1792

1793 ◆ French king and queen beheaded

◆ England and France at war

◆ Washington issues Proclamation of Neutrality

1794 — 1794 ◆ Whiskey Rebellion crushed in western Pennsylvania

1795 ◆ U.S. and England sign Jay's Treaty

◆ U.S. and Spain sign Pinckney's Treaty

1796 — 1796 ◆ Washington submits Farewell Address

◆ John Adams elected President

1797 ◆ XYZ Affair encourages war against France

1798 — 1798 ◆ Quasi-War against France

◆ Alien and Sedition Acts curtail civil liberties

1800 — 1800 ◆ Adams makes peace with France

◆ Thomas Jefferson elected President

1801 ◆ Outgoing President Adams appoints Chief Justice John Marshall and the "midnight judges"

1802

1. THE START OF A GOVERNMENT

The new President did not underestimate the tasks that lay ahead for this first administration. "Ten thousand embarrassments, perplexities, and troubles" awaited him. His administration was the first under the new Constitution, and everything he or his government did would serve as a model for the future. There was no tradition to draw upon. His government must create that tradition.

Congress shared Washington's concern for setting the right tone for the new national government. Were elaborate ceremonies and a touch of splendor proper for the republic? Should the President keep his distance from the people as European royalty would do? At the heart of such questions lay the problem of winning respect for a new and untried government. Even the plain-dressed and straightforward John Adams was willing to approve some aristocratic touches in the first administration. He urged that Washington be addressed as "Your Highness" or "Your Excellency." A wit responded that the chubby Vice-President Adams could then be called "Your Rotundity." In the end, the Congress decided to uphold republican principles, and call the President simply "Mr. President."

Washington was quite satisfied to be Mr. President. Nevertheless, he did work hard to introduce touches of formality and elegance into his office. He held formal receptions each week and kept an impressive staff of servants. He rode in a canary-yellow coach, drawn by six cream-colored horses. When on horseback, the President sat upon a leopard-skin saddle. These gestures were probably less important than the natural dignity Washington brought to his office. He was tall, erect in his bearing, immaculate in his dress, and a reserved man even with his closest friends. President Washington looked and acted the part of a national leader.

Organizing the Government
The business of organizing the government got underway in May. A host of "perplexities and troubles" faced the administration. The Constitution had set down the framework for the govern-

Cheering crowds greet George Washington, America's first national hero.

ment, but the Congress and the President would have to create the actual machinery. There were no courts. No taxes had yet been raised. Debts had to be paid, but there was no treasury. The Chief Executive had no staff at all.

By the **Judiciary Act of 1789,** Congress created a federal court system. A Chief Justice and five associate justices were to make up the Supreme Court. In addition, thirteen district courts and three circuit courts were established. Washington was the only President to have the opportunity to appoint an entire Supreme Court. The men he chose were Federalists. Their leader was to be Chief Justice John Jay of New York. Congress also added a clause to the Judiciary Act which confirmed the power of the Supreme Court, rather than a state court, to rule on the constitutionality of all laws and treaties.

Congress next drafted the Bill of Rights, and readied these amendments for ratification by the states. Then, to raise money, Congress passed a small tariff (tax on imports). This 5% duty was the first use of the right to regulate foreign trade.

Finally, Congress created a **cabinet** for the President. Three departments were set up: a Department of State to direct foreign affairs, a Department of Treasury to handle finances, and a De-

George Washington (1732–1799)

IN OFFICE: 1789–1797

From Virginia. Washington's administration set many precedents for the new government. He established a foreign policy of strict neutrality, followed Hamilton's fiscal policies, and demonstrated the power of the federal government by suppressing the Whiskey Rebellion. Though Washington felt himself to be above party politics, he generally followed Federalist policies.

partment of War to administer military matters. Washington selected these department heads with care. He appointed fellow Virginian **Thomas Jefferson** as Secretary of State, New York lawyer **Alexander Hamilton** as Secretary of the Treasury, and the Boston bookseller and military genius Henry Knox as head of the War Department.

The Constitution had not considered the duties of a cabinet, but Washington knew that these executive officers would supply advice and counsel on their special concerns. Not all cabinet heads would have the same influence on Washington, however. The President always believed that he was the best judge of foreign affairs. Therefore Jefferson's power within his department was quite limited. On the other hand, Washington always took the young Hamilton's advice on matters of finance.

Hamilton's power exceeded that of all other advisers. This was partly because of Washington's confidence in him, and partly because of Congress' distrust of the Department of Treasury itself. Congress was eager to keep control over government finances. Therefore, it required the Treasury secretary to make regular reports to the legislature on his activities. This restriction turned out to increase Hamilton's influence, for it ensured him direct access to the Congress. He could lay his programs before them for immediate action.

In addition to the three departments, two other executive agencies were created. The office of the Attorney General was filled by Edmund Randolph, former governor of Virginia, and the first Postmaster General was Samuel Osgood. These positions were not of cabinet rank until later.

Rivalry Between Hamilton and Jefferson

Washington sought talented and forceful men for his first cabinet, and he found them. But they did not all share the same vision for the new nation. Now that the government was ready to act, there

---

THE PRESIDENT'S CABINET TODAY

Since President Washington's day, the number of cabinet departments has grown. The dates show when these departments were established.

Agriculture
1889. Helps farmers grow high quality crops; inspects and grades crops, meat, eggs, and dairy products; helps with pest and flood control; administers price supports.

Commerce
1913. Fosters domestic and foreign trade, manages Bureau of the Census, registers trademarks, provides weather forecasts.

Defense
1949. Provides military defense. Coordinates activities of the three major divisions of the armed forces—the Army, the Navy, and the Air Force.

Education
1979. Runs various educational programs, such as schools for children of members of the armed forces stationed overseas, programs for handicapped students, and bilingual education.

Energy
1977. Operates the nuclear weapons program, regulates the price and use of certain energy supplies, conducts energy research.

Health and Human Services
1953 (as Department of Health, Education, and Welfare). Runs Social Security Administration, Food and Drug Administration, and other programs to protect health and prevent disease, drug abuse, and malnutrition.

Housing and Urban Development
1965. Provides loans and grants for housing and community development.

Interior
1849. Administers federal lands; develops and conserves natural resources; runs national parks, U.S. Geological Survey, Bureau of Indian Affairs, Bureau of Mines, and other agencies.

Justice
1870. Helps enforce federal laws; represents U.S. in legal matters; runs Immigration and Naturalization Service, Federal Bureau of Investigation, Bureau of Prisons, and other law enforcement agencies.

Labor
1913. Promotes the welfare of wage earners and enforces certain laws regulating wages and working conditions.

State
1789. Helps develop foreign policy, negotiates treaties and agreements with foreign nations, supervises U.S. representatives abroad.

Transportation
1966. Runs Coast Guard, Federal Aviation Administration, National Highway Traffic Administration, and other transportation agencies.

Treasury
1789. Collects taxes and customs duties, manufactures coins and paper money, manages national finances.

was little agreement among Washington's advisers on what policies and programs should be pursued. Tensions between Alexander Hamilton and Thomas Jefferson were often personal, yet they did reflect the contrast between Hamilton's vision of a powerful, commercial nation and Jefferson's vision of a quiet, agricultural society.

Hamilton envisioned a federal government that took an active role in the economic growth of the nation. He wanted the government to encourage new American industries and manufacturing. To protect new enterprises, Hamilton proposed that a high protective tariff be placed on all competing European and English goods in order to drive foreign products from the market. Hamilton wanted economic self-sufficiency for Americans.

Hamilton also wanted the national government to fund education, encourage technological development, and promote immigration. If such a vigorous program were followed, Hamilton believed, the nation would become an urban, commercial society. This new society would employ free labor rather than slaves, and in the end, Hamilton believed, all would profit from the change.

Thomas Jefferson spoke for a small, non-meddling government and for the preservation of a quiet agricultural world. Like many agrarian (farm) leaders, Jefferson distrusted cities, and feared that people who worked for wages would be the political slaves of their employers when they voted. A republic, Jefferson believed, rested on widespread landownership.

Jefferson spoke for small farmers, but he also spoke for the interests of the slaveholding planters. The society Hamilton proposed would decrease the power and the importance of the planters because it would reduce agriculture to the role of a servant to commerce.

SECTION 1 REVIEW

 Identify: Judiciary Act of 1789, cabinet, Thomas Jefferson, Alexander Hamilton

Main Ideas
1. What special problems did Washington's administration face as the very first American presidency?
2. List four accomplishments of the first Congress.
3. Compare and contrast Hamilton's and Jefferson's vision for the new nation.

2. WASHINGTON'S FIRST TERM AND HAMILTON'S ECONOMIC PROGRAM

In 1790, Hamilton presented his first report to Congress. This *Report on the Public Credit* was a plan to restore the nation's credit reputation by repaying all outstanding debts. Americans owed $12 million to France, Spain, and Holland. Continental Congresses and the Confederation had borrowed the money during the Revolutionary War. The government also owed $44 million to U.S. citizens.

The revolutionary governments had raised this money from Americans in two ways. They issued paper money, and they sold bonds, or certificates that promised repayment with interest. As you learned in Chapter 8, these paper "Continentals" were not backed by gold or silver and had quickly grown worthless. The certificates also had declined sharply in value.

Most bond holders had lost faith that they would ever be repaid. Farmers and shopkeepers eagerly sold the certificates to wealthy speculators, who bought them at far less than the original holders had paid. The certificates had changed hands many times during the 1780s, each time sinking in value as the nation's credit reputation sank.

Payment of the National Debt at Face Value

In his *Report on the Public Credit,* Hamilton proposed that the federal government raise taxes and set aside a portion of all tax money to pay the national debt. All certificates would be honored at par, or face value. Even if a speculator had paid only $1 for a $50 certificate, the government would repay the full $50.

Congressman James Madison objected. He felt it was immoral to allow speculators to profit in this way. He proposed that only the original holders receive face value, while speculators would receive a reduced sum.

Madison's concern was not entirely a moral one. Most speculators were from New England. If the certificates were honored at par, a great profit would be handed to northern commercial interests. Furthermore, the money to pay those speculators would be raised by taxing all Americans.

Taxes from southern pockets would end up in New England pockets.

Hamilton argued that speculators had shown faith in the nation during the critical years and ought now to profit. But more important, the government bonds would help serve as a sound currency. There was a shortage of gold and silver coin in the country, and other forms of currency were needed. Simply printing paper money would only cause inflation. But government bonds could circulate like money if people had faith in them— if people knew that the bonds could be redeemed in gold at face value. Hamilton was determined to launch the new government with a sound money system. After much debate, Congress finally passed his plan.

Federal Payment of the State Debts

Hamilton's *Report on the Public Credit* also proposed that the federal government assume (take over) the $25 million in state debts from the revolutionary period. Hamilton's proposal was not prompted by generosity. He knew that only a portion of the tax money collected each year would go to the payment of the debts. The federal treasury could use the rest to promote economic growth.

Again, Madison and the southern congressmen objected. First, northern speculators also held most state bonds. Second, state debts were not equally shared. Georgia and North Carolina, for example, had repaid much of their debt, and Virginia had no debt at all. Most of the states heavily in debt were north of Virginia. Madison saw no reason for southern taxpayers to pay the debts of these northern states.

Sentiment ran against Hamilton on this issue. Realizing this, Hamilton appealed to Jefferson for his support. The two men made a deal. Jefferson agreed to support the national assumption of state debts, and Hamilton agreed to support the location of the nation's permanent capital in the south. Thus, "Federal City," later called Washington, D.C., came to be built on land donated by Virginia and Maryland.

The Wealthy Support the Government

With the passage of the Assumption Bill in 1791, the first phase of Hamilton's program was complete. He had succeeded in restoring the national credit. He had given the government a legitimate reason to raise taxes. Equally important, Hamilton had linked the fate of the new government with the fortunes of many wealthy Americans.

Speculators could reap their profit on the certificates only if the federal government continued to function successfully. Thus, the government's creditors must be its active supporters. Most of Hamilton's programs were designed to reward the wealthy for their continued loyalty to the government. To ensure the loyalty of average citizens, as you shall see, he was willing to use force.

The Bank of the United States

In December 1790, Hamilton proposed a government-chartered Bank of the United States, with one large central bank and several branch banks in major cities. The Bank would be owned and directed by both private investors and the government. The government would receive one-fifth of the Bank's shares in exchange for depositing all tax revenues in the Bank. The remaining 25,000 shares would be sold at $400 each. These shares and the government deposits would provide the Bank's working capital.

The Bank was an example of Hamilton's financial genius. It was actually a device for collecting in one large pool the financial resources of the young nation. Tax monies and private investments would be joined together so that the Bank could make large loans to the government and to enterprising businessmen. With a $10 million pool, the Bank could help build factories, roads, or other major projects.

Hamilton stressed the services such a Bank could provide, particularly its ability to further his plan for a "sound uniform currency" for the nation. The bank notes (paper money) that the Bank issued would be sound, for each note would be backed by government tax deposits. The notes would also be uniform, because they would have the same value in every state.

Hamilton's bank was modeled on the Bank of England, which was almost 100 years old in 1790. Yet a banking system was a radical idea to most Americans. Only three state banks existed in 1790, and most states did not have any bank at all.

Jefferson condemned the Bank as an institution that only served the rich. At $400 a share, he noted, few Americans could afford to invest in the

Bank. The government's money would be used by the Bank to make loans, and any interest earned on these loans would go to the shareholders. Thus, taxpayers' money would make the rich richer.

After long debate, the Congress approved the Bank bill. Washington, however, hesitated to sign it into law. He was concerned about the constitutionality of the Bank. He asked both Jefferson and Hamilton to state their opinions on the constitutionality of the Bank.

Jefferson argued that the Constitution makes no provision for creating such an institution. He was offering a narrow interpretation, or **strict construction,** of the powers granted to the government by the Constitution.

Hamilton argued that certain powers were implied by the specific powers granted to the government in the Constitution. The right to collect taxes, for example, implied the right to build a bank to house the money in. Hamilton's was a **loose construction,** or broad interpretation, of the Constitution.

Hamilton also cited the "elastic clause," declaring that a bank was "necessary and proper" to fulfill the government's taxing power. Jefferson argued that "necessary" meant "essential or indispensable." Hamilton said it simply meant "useful."

Washington signed the bill. Over the years, this loose construction has been favored, since it adds flexibility to the Constitution. As President, Jefferson would use the loose-construction argument to defend his purchase of Louisiana in 1803.

Despite Hamilton's success on public credit and the Bank, he was not able to persuade Congress to play an active role in the growth of American manufacturing. The government rejected his proposal for high protective tariffs made in his 1791 *Report on Manufactures.*

The Whiskey Tax and the Whiskey Rebellion

Hamilton's fourth, and last, major proposal to Congress was an excise tax* on distilled liquor. Distilling was an important home industry along the frontier. The farmers here lived too far away

Alexander Hamilton

from market towns to transport their surplus rye and corn. Rather than waste their grains, frontier farmers turned them into "Monongahela Whiskey." The liquor could be carted along country trails to Pittsburgh or other cities for sale.

Hamilton's tax was high: 25% on all sale and production of liquor. It was not designed, however, for revenue. The excise tax was purposely intended to pressure the frontier distillers into disobeying a federal law. Hamilton was deliberately trying to provoke resistance so that he could prove the government's ability to enforce its laws.

By the summer of 1794, western Pennsylvania farmers were in open rebellion against the tax on whiskey. The **Whiskey Rebellion** was very much like the Stamp Act riots of 1765. The "Whiskey boys" terrorized the tax collectors, closed the county courts, and demanded repeal of the hated tax. But the federal government was more than ready to crush the resistance. In late summer of 1794, George Washington rode toward the frontier with an army of 13,000 militia. When he reached Philadelphia, Washington turned over the command, but Hamilton continued on with the

---

*__excise__ [ek′sīz] __tax__   a tax on the manufacture, sale, or use of certain articles made, sold, or used within a country.

troops, eager to prove that his new government could restore order anywhere it was necessary.

The Whiskey boys were rebels, but they were not fools. Faced with an army larger than the one Washington had commanded during the Revolution, the rebels vanished into the hills. The federal troops rounded up only 20 prisoners. Of the 20, only 2 were convicted of treason. Washington pardoned them both, explaining that one was a "simpleton" and the other was "insane."

It is difficult to judge if Hamilton's show of force had the effect he desired. Jefferson felt that the government looked more like a bully than a defender of law and order. Nevertheless, because Shays' Rebellion of 1786 still lingered in people's minds, Hamilton thought that the defeat of the Whiskey rebels had built confidence in the new government.

Hamilton's Place in History

In 1795, Alexander Hamilton resigned from public office and returned to his legal practice in New York. His work was completed. Hamilton was undisturbed by critics who accused him of sacrificing the interests of the average citizen in order to aid the wealthiest Americans. He believed the entire nation would benefit in the long run from his assistance to the rich. He did not care to be remembered as a democrat or a man of the people. He wished only to be remembered as the architect of a great and powerful nation.

SECTION 2 REVIEW

Identify: strict construction, loose construction, Whiskey Rebellion

Main Ideas

1. Why were government bonds and American money almost worthless in 1789?
2. What were the main points of Hamilton's 1790 *Report on the Public Credit*? What were Madison's main objections?
3. What was the purpose of Hamilton's proposed Bank of the United States? What were Jefferson's criticisms?
4. How did Jefferson and Hamilton interpret the Constitution with regard to the Bank of the United States?
5. What was Hamilton's motive for proposing an excise tax on whiskey? Did it have the effect Hamilton desired?

3. WASHINGTON'S SECOND TERM AND THE FOREIGN POLICY CRISIS

In 1789, the same year that the new Constitutional government began in America, a revolution began in France. Americans watched with enthusiasm as French men and women rose up against the king and aristocracy. The French revolutionaries called for "liberty, equality, and fraternity," and this appeal struck a sympathetic note with the Americans. Patriots like Thomas Paine journeyed to France to sit in the revolutionary councils. **Democratic Societies,** dedicated to the principles of the French Revolution, sprang up in American towns and cities. Men and women wore the French tricolor in their hats to show their enthusiasm for this new battle for liberty.

The governments of Russia and England did not wish to see the democratic spirit spread to their own peoples. Their opposition to the revolution hardened. Soon the politics of the new French government also grew more extreme. In 1793, the French king and queen were beheaded, and a Reign of Terror replaced the early promises of democracy.

England and France Insult American Sovereignty

By February 1793, the two old rivals, England and France, were once again at war. Both nations immediately pressured the United States for support. The French navy seized American ships carrying goods to and from England. England seized American ships carrying supplies to the French.

In addition, England claimed that many of the sailors on the captured American vessels were actually deserters from the Royal Navy. The British therefore impressed (forced) some of these seamen into duty aboard their ships. Some sailors undoubtedly were deserters from the cruel life of the English navy, but most of these impressed seamen were American citizens. The American public viewed **impressment** as an insult to their country's independence.

France, too, insulted American sovereignty. In April 1793, the French minister to the United

States, **Citizen Edmond Genêt,** arrived in Charleston, South Carolina. Without presenting his credentials to the President, he began recruiting for France. He traveled from town to town, calling on American citizens to fight for France, and he signed up four privateers to attack English ships off the American coast.

The United States Tries to Remain Neutral

President Washington had just begun his second term of office when the Anglo-French War began. His government, he knew, must declare its position on that war. Washington asked Hamilton and Jefferson to submit written opinions on this matter of foreign policy.

Secretary of State Jefferson urged the United States to support the French revolutionary government. Jefferson hated the English and argued that the United States must honor its 1778 treaty of alliance with France. Hamilton, on the other hand, feared that a war with England would cut off commerce with that nation and create a new economic depression in the United States. He argued that the 1778 treaty was no longer valid since it had been signed by a Continental Congress with a Royalist French government, neither of which now existed.

Washington accepted Hamilton's reasoning. Washington's own opposition to the French Terror may have influenced his decision, but it is clear that Washington wanted, above all, to avoid going to war. In April 1793, Washington issued a **Proclamation of Neutrality.** Popular opinion ran against the President, but Congress supported him by passing a Neutrality Act.

It was one thing to proclaim neutrality, but it was another to enforce it. Washington's proclamation was really a request. Would the two warring nations honor America's desire for neutrality?

The French response was promising. France did not make an issue of the Treaty of 1778. It reasoned that the United States was more valuable as a neutral supplying food and goods than as a military ally. America had, after all, no professional army or navy. Soon after Washington's proclamation, France opened up a once-forbidden trade between its French West Indies and the United States.

England immediately objected. In November 1793, the English government ordered that American vessels trading with the French colonies be seized. England insisted that trade routes closed to a neutral country during peacetime could not be opened during war. English seizures of American ships swung popular sentiment against the British.

On the frontier, in particular, anti-British feeling ran high. England had not yet evacuated its forts in the Northwest Territory, and frontiersmen and women believed the English provoked Indian attacks against their settlements.

Washington resisted popular pressure once again. In the spring of 1794 he sent Supreme Court Justice John Jay to England as a special minister, where he negotiated a treaty.

Jay's Treaty

Jay had little bargaining power. He could not realistically threaten military action against Britain. **Jay's Treaty** was not, therefore, a diplomatic victory for America. Jay won a few concessions,

John Jay hanged in effigy to protest his 1795 treaty

most importantly, the promise that British troops would be gone from the Northwest by 1796, leaving Americans in full control of that region. But most concessions went to England.

England was permitted to trade in all U.S. ports and to continue its prosperous fur trade in the Northwest Territory. The United States also agreed to settle the debts Americans, especially southern planters, still owed to British creditors from pre-revolutionary years. England owed southern planters compensation for the slaves the British army carried away after the war, but this was dropped. On the issue that most insulted American pride, impressment, the treaty was silent.

Jay and Washington knew that the treaty would be unpopular. The President kept the terms secret for four months, hoping that anti-British feelings would soften during the winter of 1794. But by March 1795, Americans learned of their diplomatic defeat.

FROM THE ARCHIVES

Washington's Farewell Address

The great rule of conduct for us, in regard to foreign Nations, is, in extending our commercial relations, to have with them as little *Political* connection as possible. So far as we have already formed engagements, let them be fulfilled with perfect good faith. Here let us stop.

Europe has a set of primary interests, which to us have none, or a very remote relation. Hence she must be engaged in frequent controversies, the causes of which are essentially foreign to our concerns. . . .

Our detached and distant situation invites and enables us to pursue a different course. If we remain one People, under an efficient government, the period is not far off, when we may defy material injury from external annoyance. . . .

'T is our true policy to steer clear of permanent alliances, with any portion of the foreign world. . . .

Taking care always to keep ourselves, by suitable establishments, on a respectably defensive posture, we may safely trust to temporary alliances for extraordinary emergencies.

Abridged from George Washington, *Farewell Address*, September 17, 1796.

The reaction was as hostile as Washington had feared. John Jay was publicly ridiculed. Jefferson, who had resigned in anger from the cabinet in December 1793, led the congressional attack on ratification of the Jay Treaty from his home at Monticello. Hamilton rushed to defend the treaty with a series of newspaper essays.

The fight over ratification was long and bitter. In the end, however, the Senate bowed to the President's wishes. In June 1795, Jay's Treaty was approved. The Senate vote revealed how divided the national leadership was. The southern politicians had opposed the treaty, while the New Englanders had forced its approval.

Pinckney's Treaty

Jay's Treaty did have one positive result. News of the reconciliation between Britain and the United States worried Spain, which was just about to join France. Spain wanted to protect its Florida and Louisiana territories against American attack. Sensing an opportunity, Washington dispatched Thomas Pinckney to Madrid. By October 1795 Pinckney had completed the Treaty of San Lorenzo, or **Pinckney's Treaty.**

Pinckney's Treaty was a boost to American morale. The United States won three important concessions from Spain. First, Spain recognized U.S. boundary claims between Georgia and Florida. (See map, page 177.) Second, the Spanish government agreed to stop provoking Indian attacks on Georgia frontier settlements.

Third, Spain granted Americans the right to navigate the Mississippi River to its mouth and to export goods from the port of New Orleans without customs charges. After 1796, western farmers could float their crops down the Mississippi on barges to ships waiting at New Orleans. This river trade was important to the American economy for decades to come.

Washington's Farewell Address

In 1796, George Washington announced his retirement from public life. Despite Hamilton's pleas, the President would not consent to a third term. Washington was satisfied that he had steered the nation through its first difficult years. He was proud that the country was making a sound economic recovery and that it remained at peace despite both European and American popular pressures. But Washington was ill, tired, and eager to be free of political responsibilities. Before returning to his Mount Vernon home, Washington decided to address the nation and to offer Americans his advice for the future.

Throughout the summer of 1796, Washington worked on his **Farewell Address.** Madison had helped him draft such a speech as early as 1792. Now Hamilton labored with the President to revise and expand those thoughts. Washington drew upon the suggestions of both men, but the final draft of the Farewell Address was his own.

The Farewell Address was never read publicly by the President. Washington submitted it to his cabinet on September 15, 1796, and it was printed in a Philadelphia newspaper four days later. In his address, Washington stressed three dangers facing the nation. The first was the rise of political factions, or parties, which Washington believed would divide Americans and destroy the cooperation needed in national government. The second was sectionalism, or political divisions based on geographic loyalties. The third was involvement in the European rivalries that repeatedly drove those nations to war. The retiring President urged Americans to continue to steer a neutral course in foreign affairs.

In 1801, President Thomas Jefferson repeated Washington's sentiments, warning the United States to avoid "entangling alliances" with other nations. We have come to think of the phrase "entangling alliances" as Washington's words because Washington expressed the thought in his Farewell Address.

SECTION 3 REVIEW

Identify: Democratic Societies, impressment, Citizen Edmond Genêt, Proclamation of Neutrality, Jay's Treaty, Pinckney's Treaty, Farewell Address

Main Ideas

1. What actions did England and France take in 1793 that created foreign policy problems for the United States?
2. What solutions did Jefferson and Hamilton propose? Which foreign policy did Washington adopt, and why?
3. How did England and France react to America's neutrality?
4. Against what three dangers did Washington warn in his Farewell Address?

4. JOHN ADAMS, POLITICAL PARTIES, AND THE QUASI-WAR

In 1789, George Washington had been the unanimous choice for President. In 1796, however, no one candidate enjoyed such esteem. The contest between Thomas Jefferson and Aaron Burr, representing one faction, and John Adams and Thomas Pinckney, representing another, reveals how rapidly political parties developed in the United States.

The Rise of Political Parties

The first government had begun as a united Federalist government. But, as you have seen, Hamilton's economic program divided the political leadership and the voters. Clustered around Jefferson and Madison were the southern planters and the small farmers of the nation. Supporting Hamilton were the commercial interests.

Washington thought of himself as above party preferences, but most political leaders saw him as a firm member of the Hamiltonian Federalist faction. The followers of Washington and Hamilton retained the name Federalists for their party. The Jefferson-Madison group became known as Jeffersonians, or Democratic-Republicans, or simply **Republicans.** By 1792, attacks and accusations flew between the two factions. Jefferson's resignation in 1793 marked the end of a nonpartisan administration. Washington's new cabinet was made up entirely of Federalists.

Foreign affairs heightened the differences between the two parties. When the Democratic Societies began to appear in American towns in the 1790s, Washington correctly accused them of being political clubs with two purposes. The first was to express support for France. The second was to organize voters for the Republicans. At the same time, the official government policy seemed to lead to greater friendship with England than with France.

The Federalists controlled the national government. They made little effort to win popular support and did not believe in taking their case to the people. They were leaders of the nation, not followers of the popular will. The Republicans, perhaps for the very reason that they were not in control of the government, turned to organizing popular support for their party.

Jefferson had a genius for organizing on a local level and for creating a loyal political machine to win elections. Thus, throughout Washington's second term, the Jeffersonian strategy was to admit defeat in the federal government and to devote all energies to winning local or state offices. The Republicans took care to discuss local issues with the voters, while the Federalists concentrated on national affairs and diplomacy. The Jeffersonians already strong in the South, allied themselves with the old Antifederalist groups in New York, headed by the governor of the state, George Clinton. Thus, two powerful states, Virginia and New York, were joined together.

Neither the Federalists nor the Republicans liked to think of themselves as party men. Instead, each accused the other of the sins of "factionalism." The attacks were far from restrained, for although the politicians were gentlemen, politics in that era was not gentlemanly. Every effort was made to embarrass the opposition, and attacks on a man's character, his morals, and even his person were common. Duels were fought between Republicans and Federalists. Scuffles with canes, spitting—even nose-pulling contests in the Senate were not unheard of.

The principle of impartial journalism was unknown in the 18th century, and newspapers were used to insult, expose, and ridicule the opposition. Both parties financed their own newspapers, which aimed furious barbs at their opponents. On several occasions, the Republicans tried to convict Hamilton of using his office for personal financial gain, despite the fact that Hamilton was known to have perfect integrity in such matters.

The politics of the day were vicious, yet the political leaders of the 1790s were generally responsible men. There were no attempts to overthrow the Washington government despite the strong opposition to it. In 1796, the major test of constitutional government—the peaceful transfer of power from one administration to another—was achieved without any violent incident.

The Election of 1796

The 1796 election was not a smooth one. Both the Federalist and the Republican candidates were selected by a caucus, or small meeting, of leading congressmen. The states then chose the presidential electors. The Constitution did not require an elector to cast both votes for the candidates of a single party, since the Constitution did not provide for political parties. In 1796, the candidate who received the most votes was President; the candidate with the next highest tally was Vice-President. But complications arose.

Alexander Hamilton was busy in the background, trying to influence the election. Hamilton did not like John Adams, largely because he could not control Adams as well as he could many other people. Hamilton urged the South Carolina electors to withhold their two votes from Adams, cast their votes for Thomas Pinckney, and thus make their own state's nominee the second President of the United States.

Hamilton's plan backfired. When New Englanders learned of the scheme, several responded by withholding their electoral votes from Pinckney. When the balloting was over, John Adams had squeaked by with 71 votes, but Thomas Jefferson, the Republican leader, had polled 68 votes, beating Pinckney. The new administration was neither Federalist nor Republican, but an uncomfortable mixture of the two.

The Quasi-War with France

When John Adams took the oath of office on March 4, 1797, he immediately faced a new crisis in foreign affairs. This time it was the French government that threatened America's delicate neutrality. A new French government began to seize American ships carrying goods to England. France's change in policy prompted Adams to send a three-man commission to Paris.

When Charles Cotesworth Pinckney of South Carolina, John Marshall of Virginia, and Elbridge Gerry of Massachusetts arrived in the French capital, they were rudely refused an audience with the French Minister of Foreign Affairs, **Talleyrand.** In May of 1797, however, the greedy Talleyrand sent three French gentlemen to make a private call on the Americans. These men, known later only as X, Y, and Z, told the commissioners that no negotiations could begin until three conditions were met.

First, the American government must publicly apologize for statements the President had made that France considered to be anti-French in tone. Second, the United States must approve a loan to the French government. Finally, Messieurs X, Y, and Z said that a "gift" of $250,000 could buy the Americans their meeting with Talleyrand.

Such bribery was common in French politics at the time. European diplomats had been forced to line the pockets of Minister Talleyrand before he signed a treaty or shared military information. In this way, the Frenchman had restored his personal fortune, lost during the French Revolution. The American commissioners were both shocked and offended by Talleyrand's demands. They rejected the terms set by the mysterious visitors and returned home to make their report.

John Adams allowed the report on the **"XYZ Affair"** to be made public. The response was outrage. Republicans as well as Federalists protested the French insult to their nation. "Millions for defense, but not one cent for tribute," was the slogan of the day.

The truth is that Americans were already paying millions of dollars in tributes to Mediterranean pirates on the Barbary Coast of North Africa. For a number of years the American government had been bribing pirates from Algiers, Tripoli, Tunis, and Morocco to prevent raids on American vessels. But Adams was determined not to bow to such pressures from the French.

Popular demand for war with France grew louder throughout the winter. The Adams administration took steps to increase the army and raised taxes to pay for military preparation. A Navy Department was established. American harbors were fortified and ships built and equipped with cannon. George Washington was called upon to serve as commander-in-chief once again. No one was more delighted with this turn of events than Alexander Hamilton, who spent hours plotting an American invasion of Florida and Louisiana.

Although war was not formally declared, American warships had captured 80 French vessels by the end of 1798. This **Quasi-War with France,** as the conflict is called, brought the Federalists a popularity that they had never enjoyed before. The Republicans were discredited in the public eye. John Adams became a hero. "Adams and Liberty" was the general cheer, and wherever he went a band struck up "The President's March."

Neutrality Maintained

Adams enjoyed his popularity. But he decided to rise above politics and practice statesmanship. The President realized that a long and expensive

John Adams (1735–1826)

IN OFFICE: 1797–1801

Federalist from Massachusetts. During John Adams' administration the most pressing problem was the increased hostility with France. When war with France threatened, the Federalists passed the Alien and Sedition Acts (1798) in order to ensure unanimity of opinion. These repressive measures resulted in Adams' loss of popularity and helped cause the downfall of the Federalist party.

war was no better for the young Republic in 1799 than it would have been in 1793. Washington's policy of neutrality remained the wisest course.

By 1799, there was a new government in France. Its leader, Napoleon Bonaparte, gave Adams reason to believe that a second American commission to Paris would be properly and cordially greeted. When Adams informed his cabinet that he was sending a peace commission to France, his fellow Federalists were stunned. The three American commissioners were promptly dispatched to Paris, and in 1800 an agreement was reached.

Popular resentment against France still ran strong, and John Adams was not applauded for ending the Quasi-War. The newspapers that had so recently sung his praises now condemned him. He did not recover his reputation in his own lifetime. His statesmanlike behavior, however, has been admired by Americans of later generations.

SECTION 4 REVIEW

 Identify: Republicans, Talleyrand, XYZ Affair, Quasi-War with France

Main Ideas
1. Identify the leaders and policies of the two rival political parties in the 1790s.
2. How did the Quasi-War with France help the Federalists and hurt the Republicans?
3. What difficult decision did President Adams make? What did this do to his political future?

5. THE ALIEN AND SEDITION ACTS AND THE DEFEAT OF THE FEDERALISTS

The Federalists' domestic policies contributed to the party's decline after 1799. During the two years of the Quasi-War, the Federalist-dominated Congress passed four laws known as the Alien and Sedition Acts. Although supporters claimed that these laws were security measures for the nation, the target of the Alien and Sedition Acts was really the Republican party.

Unlike Americans today, the 18th-century politicians did not accept the principle of a "loyal opposition." In politics, a loyal opposition means that the party out of power is free to criticize the administration and its policies without being accused of treason. In the late 1790s, both Federalists and Republicans saw their own party as the only true American one, and viewed their opponents as enemies of the Constitution.

The Laws Against Aliens

During the Adams administration, many Federalists behaved as if the nation were suffering through a new "critical period." Visions of France as a "devouring monster," ready to destroy the United States, ran through the speeches and the newspaper essays of leading Federalists. The Republicans were accused of being agents of the French monster, rather than patriotic citizens. It was not enough for some Federalists that fathers warned their daughters that it was "better to be married to a Felon or a Hangman" than to a Republican. These determined Federalists wanted the Republican party totally destroyed.

In June 1798, Federalists introduced the first of their four measures, the **Naturalization Act.** It required immigrants to reside in the country 14 years before becoming citizens. The original requirement was only 5 years.

The real motive behind the Naturalization Act was political. Most immigrants to the United States, whether French or Irish or English, joined Jefferson's party, for it appealed to the average and the poorer citizen. By extending the residency requirement to 14 years, Federalists hoped to choke off new recruits to the opposition party.

The Naturalization Act did little to help the Federalists. Because each state established its own residency laws, the Federalists did not eliminate the new voters. Many states allowed new arrivals to vote in local elections with even less than 5 years residency.

Congress also passed an **Alien Act** authorizing the President to expel any foreigner he judged to be "dangerous to the peace and safety of the United States." Citizen Edmond Genêt was clearly in the minds of the Federalists when they drafted this law. Next, Congress passed the **Alien Enemies Act**, permitting the President to imprison or banish a foreigner he considered dangerous during wartime or time of invasion. With these two acts, the President could silence opposition by declaring criticism "dangerous." The powers of the acts were not used, but their existence served to threaten many critics of the Federalists.

The Sedition Act

Finally, Congress passed the **Sedition Act,** a law directed at American citizens. It gave the government authority to fine and imprison any American who wrote, uttered, or printed "false, scandalous, and malicious" comments that might damage the reputation of the government, the Congress, or the President. Thus, criticizing officeholders was labeled sedition, an attempt to stir up rebellion.

Given the vicious and slanderous nature of journalism in the 1790s, it was not hard to find Republican newspapermen to prosecute under the Sedition Act. Ten newspaper editors were arrested, and fined or imprisoned. The most famous of these was the grandson of Benjamin Franklin, Benjamin "Lightning Rod, Jr." Bache, whose nickname came from his grandfather's experiments with electricity. Bache's newspaper, the *Aurora,* sent out its own kind of sparks, attacking every Federalist from Adams to Hamilton to the idolized George Washington himself. The fiery newspaperman died in prison before his trial began.

Not all of the victims of the Sedition Act were political leaders or influential newsmen. A New Jersey man named Luther Baldwin got drunk one afternoon and expressed a desire to see John Adams shot in the backside by the cannons that were saluting the President nearby. For this remark, Baldwin was imprisoned.

Alexander Hamilton was the lone voice in the Federalist party against the Alien and Sedition Acts. George Washington had supported these four measures, but Hamilton considered them foolish and provocative. He warned that the acts carried a threat of civil war. "Let us not establish a tyranny," Hamilton wrote, warning that tyranny promotes rebellion.

The Alien and Sedition Acts confirmed the Republican belief that the Federalists did not respect the freedoms guaranteed in the Bill of Rights. Thus, the Republicans also saw the Quasi-War years as a "critical period," with the Federalists undermining the Constitution and American liberties.

The Virginia and Kentucky Resolutions

In response to the Alien and Sedition Acts, Jefferson drafted the first of the **Kentucky Resolutions,** and Madison drafted a similar set of **Virginia Resolutions.** These resolutions introduced a serious challenge to the concept of an indivisible Union. They asserted the right of each state to nullify (make void, not binding) any federal law the state opposed. The basis for this claim was a states' rights, or compact, theory of the Constitution.

The compact theory held, first, that the states had created the federal government and had authorized it to act as their agent in specific matters. As you can see, this theory incorporates Jefferson's strict construction of the Constitution.

Second, the compact theory held that the states had every right to criticize federal government activities or laws, and if necessary, the states could nullify those laws. In other words, Jefferson was saying that the states, not the Supreme Court, were the final judges on the constitutionality of congressional laws.

The Virginia and Kentucky Resolutions were not supported by other states. Most state legislatures were controlled by Federalist majorities. But even a Republican legislature might have hesitated to support a theory that led, logically, to the right of a state to secede from (leave) the Union.

The Election of 1800

Federalist popularity declined rapidly in 1799, as popular concern over civil liberties grew. Also, internal problems plagued the Federalists as Al-

exander Hamilton and John Adams fought to control the party. When the Federalist caucus met in 1800, Adams just managed to win the nomination for a second term. Charles Cotesworth Pinckney was selected as vice-presidential candidate. The Republicans chose Thomas Jefferson for the presidency and New York politician Aaron Burr as Jefferson's running mate.

The campaign was waged in the free-wheeling style of the era. Federalists attacked Jefferson for being a deist* rather than a member of a Protestant church. "God—and a Religious President," their slogan read, "or Jefferson—and no God!" The issue did not seem to stir the people. The Republicans continued to accuse the Federalists of endangering civil liberties. But it was the organizing skills of the Republicans that brought them victory. At rallies and meetings in each state, the Republicans were careful to discuss local issues as well as national ones.

In 1800, as in 1796, the balloting by electors produced confusion. There was a tie between the two Republicans, Jefferson and Burr. The Constitution did not specify one candidate for the presidency and another for the vice-presidency. The decision had to be made in the House of Representatives.

The Federalists, who had a majority in the House, saw power for themselves in the situation. They were able to prevent Jefferson from winning

*deism a form of Christianity popular among intellectuals in the late 18th century. See Chapter 5.

THE ALIEN AND SEDITION ACTS, 1798

Naturalization Act
Required an immigrant to live in the United States for 14 years before becoming a citizen.

Alien Act
Allowed the President to expel foreigners from the United States if he thought they were dangerous to the peace and safety of the nation.

Alien Enemies Act
Allowed the President to imprison or expel foreigners considered dangerous in time of war or invasion.

Sedition Act
Barred American citizens and others from saying, writing, or publishing any false, scandalous, or malicious statements against the U.S. government, Congress, or the President. Persons convicted of doing so could be fined $2,000 and imprisoned for 2 years.

LIFE IN AMERICA

THE DUEL BETWEEN HAMILTON AND BURR

On the morning of July 10, 1804, two enemies met on a small ledge beneath the heights of Weehawken, just across the Hudson River from New York City. The challenger was Aaron Burr, the Vice-President of the United States. He arrived first. A few minutes before seven o'clock, Alexander Hamilton, Federalist leader, former cabinet officer, and unceasing critic of Burr's character, climbed to the ledge with his "second," Mr. Pendleton, while the doctor waited with the boatman.

The "seconds" paced off ten steps, checked the pistols and loaded them. On the word "Present!" by Mr. Pendleton, Burr raised his gun, aimed, and hit Hamilton on his right side, the bullet lodging in his spine. Hamilton's gun fired into the air as he pitched forward. Burr was hurried away by his friends while the doctor tended to Hamilton's wound. Hamilton died the afternoon of the next day.

The Origin of Dueling

This was perhaps the most famous duel in American history, but it was not the first one nor the last. America had early inherited the European custom of dueling. The first recorded American duel took place in 1621 at Plymouth, Massachusetts. The origin of the custom can be traced back to 501 A.D. when a French king legally established the trial by combat, or judicial duel, as a better alternative to trials by oath (which encouraged lying) or ordeal (which were gruesome, even for medieval tastes).

The judge or king established the time, place, and weapons, and God, it was believed, determined the winner. The challenger threw down a gauntlet, or glove. The opponent accepted when he picked up the gauntlet.

This type of trial was open to all free men. Clergy, women, the sick, and those under 20 or over 60 were exempt, although sometimes pro-

fessional fighters or "champions" were hired to fight for them. Not until Henry II of England (1154–1189) instituted a new alternative, trial by jury, did the popularity of judicial duels decline, but they were not outlawed in England until 1819.

The Duel of Honor

The "duel of honor," a private fight between two opponents according to strict rules, developed among European gentlemen during the 1500s. Duels might be fought over property, charges of cowardice or deceit, or insults to the honor of a lady or to one of the participants. The favorite weapon was the sword, but as 18th- and 19th-century technology improved the accuracy and dependability of firearms, matched sets of dueling pistols became the most popular weapons.

Dueling "codes" were published to help gentlemen conduct their affairs with decorum. The challenge was very formal and most often de-

---

a majority. Thirty-five ballots were taken, and thirty-five times, no majority was won. With Inauguration Day only a few weeks away, the deadlock was serious.

Once again, Alexander Hamilton entered the scene. Hamilton thought Burr was dishonest and without principles. Burr returned the hatred. Within four years, these two men would face each other in a pistol duel, and Hamilton would fall mortally wounded on the cliffs of Weehawken, New Jersey.

Hamilton persuaded the Federalist members of the House to support Jefferson. Hamilton was confident that Jefferson would not dismantle the Bank or the economic programs of the Federalist government. His judgment proved correct.

On February 17, 1801, on the 36th ballot, Thomas Jefferson was chosen the third President

of the United States. In 1804, the 12th Amendment to the Constitution provided for separate ballots for the President and Vice-President. Thus, the Constitution was adjusted to meet the realities of a party system in American politics.

Midnight Judges and a Chief Justice

In the elections of 1800, besides losing the presidency, the Federalists also lost their majorities in the Congress. They were determined, however, to secure the judicial branch for their party. Before the Republicans took over, the Federalist Congress passed a new Judiciary Act of 1801, which increased the number of judges in the circuit and lower courts. Then, John Adams signed the commissions for these Federalist judges, working all day and well into the evening of his last day in office, March 3. Many of these **"midnight judges"**

livered as a letter, not in the heat of argument. In America and England the choice of weapons was up to the man challenged. Each participant or "principal" was accompanied by one or more trusted friends, called "seconds," who conducted the duel according to agreed-upon rules and sometimes took over for their fallen friends. Since most states had laws against dueling, the event had to take place in a secluded spot. Doctors were commonly in attendance.

Americans Take Up Dueling

Dueling became popular in America after the Revolution, which produced a new group of army and navy officers, lawyers, and politicians interested in defending their "honor." Many noted citizens, including Henry Clay and Andrew Jackson, fought duels during the period between the Revolution and the Civil War.

The American duel began to take on a few unique characteristics. Whereas in Europe a little blood usually satisfied the duelists, Americans had the nasty habit of killing their opponents. Sometimes unusual weapons were chosen, such as rifles, double-barreled shotguns, bowie knives, and even harpoons. Another American custom was "posting." The challenger would publish a notice in a newspaper of some public place declaring that "so-and-so is a villain and a coward." Some scholars say that the classic gunfight of the Old West was another American contribution to the art of dueling.

More people would have died in duels had it not been for the fact that most people weren't very good marksmen, and even those who were had to fight with smooth-bore pistols that didn't shoot straight. The stance taken by most duelists also cut down on casualties. The custom was to stand sideways with

head bent in toward the shoulder and arm bent in at the elbow, protecting the side of the body.

Public Outrage

But there were many deaths caused by duels, and public opinion turned strongly against the practice. The shocked public outcry at the death of Alexander Hamilton immediately produced opposition to dueling in the northern states, although it continued until the Civil War in the South. As for Aaron Burr, the "winner" was disenfranchised by the laws of New York for having fought a duel and was charged with murder in New Jersey. Amazingly, he finished his vice-presidential term, but he never regained his reputation and died in poverty in 1836.

Today a plaque and small park mark the area above the ledge in Weehawken where these two men fought.

were later removed when Jefferson took office.

In his last weeks in office, Adams also appointed the extraordinary **John Marshall** of Virginia as Chief Justice of the Supreme Court. For 34 years, John Marshall would play a major role in shaping our understanding of the Constitution. Marshall would ensure that the Federalist perspective on economics and politics would dominate long after the Federalist party itself had faded. His opinions from the bench firmly asserted the supremacy of the national government over the states. Marshall established the principle that the Supreme Court could reverse a decision of a state court. He also ruled that the Court could set aside any state law that was contrary to the Constitution.

As you will see in the coming chapters, the conflict between states' rights and national supremacy would continue for over half a century.

SECTION 5 REVIEW

Identify: Naturalization Act, Alien Act, Alien Enemies Act, Sedition Act, Virginia and Kentucky Resolutions, midnight judges, John Marshall

Main Ideas
1. Why did the Federalists pass the Alien and Sedition Acts?
2. What were the main points of the states' rights, or compact, theory of the Constitution developed by Jefferson and Madison?
3. Why did the Federalist party decline by 1800? How did the Federalists lose the election of 1800, yet choose the President?
4. What would some of John Marshall's accomplishments as Chief Justice be in his 34 years on the bench?

CHAPTER 10 REVIEW

Key Terms
Explain the meaning of each of the following terms:

Judiciary Act of 1789
cabinet
strict construction
loose construction
Whiskey Rebellion
Democratic Societies
impressment
Proclamation of Neutrality
Jay's Treaty
Pinckney's Treaty
Farewell Address
Republicans
XYZ Affair
Quasi-War with France
Alien and Sedition Acts
Virginia and Kentucky Resolutions
midnight judges

Reviewing the Main Ideas

Section 1
1. What were the main problems facing the first American presidential administration?
2. What laws did the first Congress pass?
3. How did Hamilton and Jefferson differ in their ideas about government and the kind of nation the United States should be?

Section 2
1. What was Hamilton's plan to repay America's foreign and domestic debts? Why did he want the federal government to assume state debts?
2. What services did Hamilton's Bank of America provide? Why did Jefferson oppose it?
3. How did the whiskey tax serve to strengthen or weaken people's confidence in the new government?

Section 3
1. How did the French Revolution create problems for the United States? What policy did Washington adopt in order to deal with these problems?
2. Why was Jay's Treaty considered a failure and Pinckney's Treaty considered a success?
3. In his Farewell Address Washington warned against three dangers. What were they?

Section 4
1. What were the strategies and beliefs of the Federalists and Republicans? Who were their leaders?
2. The Quasi-War with France helped the Federalists. Why? Why didn't Adams declare war on France?

Section 5
1. What laws attacking the Republicans caused instead the decline of the Federalists?
2. Explain the states' rights or compact theory of the Constitution. Which branch loses power under this theory?
3. Why did Hamilton help Jefferson win the presidential election of 1800?

Special History Skills:
Using Specialized Reference Books
Special American history reference books can be found in most high-school and public libraries. These include specialized encyclopedias, dictionaries, and historical atlases. Almanacs can also be useful reference tools.

These references will help you find information about people, places, events, laws, and ideas. They are an important first step when doing research. They won't tell you everything, but they'll get you started with a core of facts. The next step in your research would be to find books, magazines, and perhaps newspaper articles.

Make a list of 5 to 10 specialized American history reference books in your school or public library. Then use one to locate more information about one of the following topics:

George Washington, Alexander Hamilton, John Adams, Thomas Jefferson, John Jay, Thomas Pinckney, John Marshall, the French Revolution, impressment, early plans for Washington, D.C., the Sedition Act, the duel between Aaron Burr and Alexander Hamilton, another topic of your choice

Other Skill Activities
1. **Visions for a young nation**
Hamilton and Jefferson had differing visions of the best future for America. What is your vision of what is best for America in the future? Write your ideas as if you were going to give a speech.
2. **You be the judge**
Treason is very narrowly defined in the Constitution to prevent the government from prose-

cuting its critics. If you were on the Supreme Court in 1798, how would you rule on the constitutionality of the Alien and Sedition Acts? Consult the Constitution for the basis of your ruling.

3. **Your cabinet**

If you could start a new cabinet, like President Washington did, what departments would you create? Explain your choices.

4. **States' rights**

States' rights is still an important issue in American politics. Find three newspaper or magazine articles dealing with states' rights issues. Underline the main points of the articles. Write one paragraph summarizing each article and one paragraph explaining your opinion of each issue.

Thinking Critically

1. Compare the government's action during the Whiskey Rebellion with the role the Confederation played in Shays' Rebellion. What does this show about the new federal government?
2. Washington kept Jay's Treaty a secret for four months. Could a President withhold the terms of a treaty for four months today? Explain.
3. Washington warned against political parties. Yet he was called a "party man" by many contemporaries. Do you think this is a valid observation? Why or why not?
4. Both Federalists and Republicans saw the Adams administration as a "critical period." What were each group's reasons?
5. What, if any, were the enduring contributions of the Federalist party to policies of the American government?

Further Reading

Donald Barr Chidsey. *Mr. Hamilton and Mr. Jefferson.* Thomas Nelson Co., 1975. An easy-to-read book describing the politics of the Federalist era.

Thomas P. Abernathy. *The South in the New Nation, 1789–1819.* Louisiana State University Press, 1961. Includes a scholarly account of the Whiskey Rebellion and Alien and Sedition Acts.

Richard B. Morris. *The First Book of the Founding of the Republic.* Franklin Watts, Inc. 1968. A simply written book which shows the peaceful transition of power from the Federalists to the Republicans.

TEST YOURSELF

Fill in the Blanks

Choose the correct word from the pair that follows each statement.

1. Opponents of Hamilton's Bank of the United States objected on the basis of a _____ interpretation of the Constitution. (strict–loose)
2. The federal government sent a strong military force to put down _____ Rebellion. (Shays'–the Whiskey)
3. _____ Treaty was considered a diplomatic victory for the new nation. (Jay's–Pinckney's)
4. _____ gained political power by concentrating on local issues and building strong organizations. (Republicans–Federalists)
5. Peace with European nations was urged by the _____. (Proclamation of Neutrality–XYZ Affair)
6. The _____ tried to dampen criticism against the Adams administration. (Sedition Act–Virginia and Kentucky Resolutions)
7. _____ established the power of the Supreme Court over state laws and state courts. (John Adams–John Marshall)
8. _____ advocated the right of states to nullify federal laws. (Jefferson–Hamilton)
9. Politics ended _____ presidency after one term. (Adams'–Washington's)
10. _____ began impressing American sailors in the 1790s despite government protests. (France–England)

Classifying

Write F if the item characterized the Federalists, R if it characterized the Republicans.

1. represented farmers
2. favored France
3. Alexander Hamilton
4. South
5. New England
6. James Madison
7. George Washington
8. won election of 1800
9. loose interpretation of Constitution
10. favored a powerful central government

Chapter 11   1801–1824

ISSUES OF AMERICAN NATIONALISM

On March 4, 1801, Thomas Jefferson left his boarding house and walked along the dirty streets of the nation's new capital, Washington, D.C. He kept his eyes on the road, stepping carefully around the mud puddles and avoiding the tree stumps that cropped up on the path to the Capitol. But Jefferson's mind was not on the dismal conditions of the city. Today, he would take the oath of office as the third President of the United States.

What did the new century hold in store for the United States? The President was a thoughtful and intelligent man, but he surely could not predict the many surprising events of the next 25 years. Before Jefferson even left office in 1809, the nation would more than double in physical size. This remarkable growth would create new economic opportunities. But it would also cause tensions between slaveholders and the free farmers of the North and Northwest, as these groups battled for control of the new western lands.

Tensions with other nations would also grow. By 1812, America and England would once more be at war. This war would test American unity and American patriotism. In the years that followed, political leaders would work to strengthen the national government so that it could perform the necessary tasks for our expanding and often troubled country. In this chapter, you will see—as Jefferson himself saw—the growth of a young nation.

Sections in This Chapter
1. Jefferson Reforms the Government and Re-shapes the National Boundaries
2. The Eagle Is Challenged by the Tiger and the Shark
3. The War of 1812
4. An Era of Good Feelings—and Some Bad Ones

Opposite: Quilting is a distinctly American art. This intricate "Bird of Paradise" quilt is typical of "album" or friendship quilts made around Baltimore.

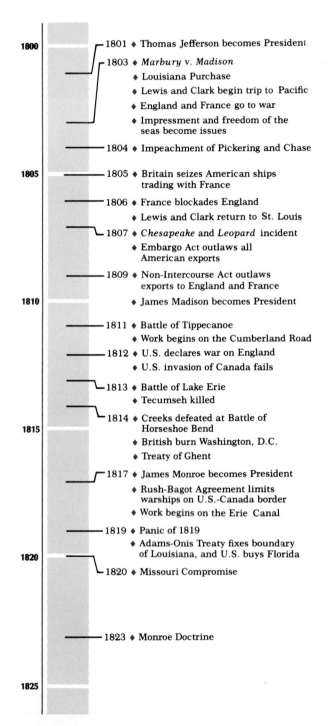

1800

1801 ♦ Thomas Jefferson becomes President

1803 ♦ *Marbury* v. *Madison*
♦ Louisiana Purchase
♦ Lewis and Clark begin trip to Pacific
♦ England and France go to war
♦ Impressment and freedom of the seas become issues

1804 ♦ Impeachment of Pickering and Chase

1805

1805 ♦ Britain seizes American ships trading with France

1806 ♦ France blockades England
♦ Lewis and Clark return to St. Louis

1807 ♦ *Chesapeake* and *Leopard* incident
♦ Embargo Act outlaws all American exports

1809 ♦ Non-Intercourse Act outlaws exports to England and France
♦ James Madison becomes President

1810

1811 ♦ Battle of Tippecanoe
♦ Work begins on the Cumberland Road

1812 ♦ U.S. declares war on England
♦ U.S. invasion of Canada fails

1813 ♦ Battle of Lake Erie
♦ Tecumseh killed

1814 ♦ Creeks defeated at Battle of Horseshoe Bend
♦ British burn Washington, D.C.
♦ Treaty of Ghent

1815

1817 ♦ James Monroe becomes President
♦ Rush-Bagot Agreement limits warships on U.S.-Canada border
♦ Work begins on the Erie Canal

1819 ♦ Panic of 1819
♦ Adams-Onís Treaty fixes boundary of Louisiana, and U.S. buys Florida

1820

1820 ♦ Missouri Compromise

1823 ♦ Monroe Doctrine

1825

When Thomas Jefferson read his inaugural address that March morning in 1801, almost no one in the crowded room could hear a word of it. The President's voice never rose above a whisper. Yet his message rang out loud and clear. He intended to create a revolution in government, to sweep out old Federalist programs and old Federalists, and to establish a republican government.

Jefferson's plan to reform the government took up most of his first term. The Jeffersonians repealed the whiskey tax and let the hated Alien and Sedition Acts expire. They cut back federal spending and took steps toward balancing the federal budget. Jefferson even reformed the lifestyle in the new capital. Washington and Adams had been formal men. Jefferson was casual. Visitors found it hard to stand on ceremony with a President who greeted them in a torn dressing gown and carpet slippers!

Some of Jefferson's reforms were a matter of politics, not principles. Like most Presidents after him, Jefferson believed that his own loyal supporters ought to be rewarded with offices. In his speeches, Jefferson claimed, "We are all Republicans; we are all Federalists." But 180 Federalists lost their jobs during Jefferson's first term. The Republicans who replaced them, however, were honest and capable men.

Jefferson Battles the Judiciary

Jefferson was especially eager to reform the judiciary. This branch of government was a Federalist stronghold. The President was determined to break the Federalist power on the bench. He asked Congress to impeach and remove from office several Federalist judges.

Congress did remove the district judge of New Hampshire, John Pickering. Pickering had not committed any crime in office, but he was emotionally unstable and drank too much.

Jefferson's next target, however, was a more powerful figure. Supreme Court Justice Samuel Chase was the man who had presided over many of the Sedition Act trials. He was ornery and unpopular, but like Pickering, Chase was innocent of any genuine criminal act. It was clear to everyone that Jefferson wanted Chase impeached because of the judge's Federalist politics.

Congress did not bow to Jefferson's wishes. Many senators believed that the Constitution intended impeachment only as a punishment for criminal acts, not for unruly personal behavior. Chase was acquitted, and Jefferson gave up his plan to remove other Federalist judges. No President since Jefferson has ever tried to impeach a judge for political loyalties.

The Importance of *Marbury* v. *Madison*

Jefferson's trouble with the judiciary was not over. In the case of *Marbury* v. *Madison* in 1803, the President did battle with the Chief Justice, John Marshall—and lost. William Marbury was one of the many "midnight judges" appointed by John Adams in 1801. Marbury never received his commission, however, for when President Jefferson took office he ordered his Secretary of State, James Madison, to withhold that commission.

Marbury protested. His appointment was legal. He appealed to the Supreme Court, asking Chief Justice Marshall to order Madison to do his duty. By challenging the President, an ordinary man named William Marbury became a famous figure in American constitutional history.

Chief Justice Marshall was in a difficult situation, and he knew it. If he ruled in favor of Marbury, Secretary Madison would simply ignore the court order. This would expose the judiciary's basic weakness: it could not enforce its rulings without the cooperation of the executive branch.

On the other hand, if Marshall ruled against Marbury, the Court would appear to approve Jefferson's actions. Marshall seemed trapped. But he was a brilliant politician as well as a fine judge. He ruled that Marbury deserved his commission according to the Judiciary Act of 1789. But he also declared that part of the act unconstitutional.

Marshall thus avoided a confrontation with the President. At the same time, he established the Court's power of **judicial review**—the right of the Court to strike down a law passed by Congress. The decision gave the Court an important "check" in the system of "checks and balances." Many people had assumed that the Court had the

power of judicial review, but it was not actually spelled out in the Constitution. *Marbury* v. *Madison* was the first case in which the Court actually overturned a federal law. The Court would not use the power again for more than 50 years (in the 1857 Dred Scott decision).

In the end, Jefferson's "revolution" was not so drastic as Federalists feared it might be. New faces filled old offices, but important old programs and policies remained. The federal government continued to bear the mark of Alexander Hamilton. Jefferson himself acknowledged this. "We can pay off his debt," the President sighed, "but we cannot get rid of his financial system."

The Louisiana Purchase

Thomas Jefferson had been to Paris, but he had never traveled more than 50 miles west of his Virginia plantation, Monticello. The President knew, however, that America's future lay in the vast, uncharted areas west of the Mississippi River. Although these lands belonged to Spain, Jefferson did dream that someday they would be part of an "American Empire for Liberty."

In 1800, Spain secretly turned over much of its lands west of the Mississippi to France. News of this exchange reached the President six months later. Jefferson was alarmed. Did France's powerful new ruler, **Napoleon Bonaparte**, intend to build a French empire in the West? Such a French plan

Thomas Jefferson (1743–1826)

IN OFFICE: 1801–1809

Republican from Virginia. Although Jefferson believed in the theory of a limited central government, his actions often expanded the role of the federal government. During his administration, the Louisiana Territory was purchased (1803), war was fought with the Barbary pirates (1801–1805), and the Embargo Act (1807) was passed in an effort to protect neutral rights.

would put an end to Jefferson's own dream of American farms and towns there.

With congressional approval, in 1803 Jefferson wrote to the U.S. minister in France, Robert R. Livingston. He instructed Livingston to offer $2 million for the port of New Orleans and West Florida. (See map, below.) By purchasing these southern lands, the United States could at least safeguard the use of the Mississippi River.

Jefferson sent his friend, James Monroe, to Paris to help Livingston arrange the purchase. The two Americans expected difficulty in persuading Napoleon to agree to the sale. Imagine their surprise when the emperor offered to sell them not only New Orleans but the entire Louisiana territory!

Bonaparte was not a rash man. Why did he suddenly decide to give up a territory as large as France itself? The truth is, Napoleon Bonaparte's plan for an American empire had already failed. To colonize Louisiana, France needed a secure naval base in the Caribbean. But a slave revolt on the island of Santo Domingo in the 1790s had made such a naval base impossible.

Despite all Napoleon's efforts, his troops could not reconquer the island. In 1802, the former slaves, led by **General Toussaint L'Ouverture** [tü san′ lü ver tür′] soundly defeated the French troops. Their victory had a great impact on the development of the American West: Napoleon now turned his attention to a new and grander scheme—the conquest of all Europe.

To conquer Europe, the emperor needed ready cash. Thus he offered France's American lands to Livingston and Monroe for only $15 million. The two American diplomats had no orders to cover such a sudden windfall. Taking the chance that Jefferson would approve, they accepted Napoleon's proposal.

Jefferson did indeed approve of this action. However, in buying all of Louisiana in 1803, he acted independently of Congress, even though he knew that the Constitution did not give him the specific right to do so. Federalists, borrowing the

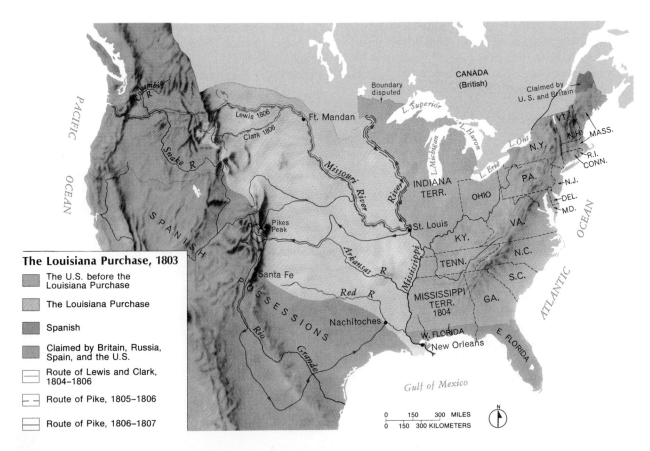

The Louisiana Purchase, 1803

- The U.S. before the Louisiana Purchase
- The Louisiana Purchase
- Spanish
- Claimed by Britain, Russia, Spain, and the U.S.
- Route of Lewis and Clark, 1804–1806
- Route of Pike, 1805–1806
- Route of Pike, 1806–1807

strict constructionist view usually taken by Republicans, insisted that the Constitution did not allow Jefferson to make the **Louisiana Purchase**. But Jefferson argued that the constitutional power to govern territories *implied* the right to buy them (the loose constructionist view). In the end, the enthusiasm of American farmers and settlers in favor of the Louisiana Purchase proved more important than the constitutional and political debate.

The Lewis and Clark Expedition

In early 1803—months before the Louisiana Purchase—Jefferson had persuaded Congress to grant secretly a small sum to finance a western expedition. Motivated by scientific curiosity and military interests, he also wanted to find new sources for the fur trade and to discover, if possible, the long-sought-for water route to the Pacific Ocean. Jefferson invited his young secretary, Meriwether Lewis, to head the expedition, and Lewis recruited a veteran of Indian wars, William Clark, to join him. In the winter of 1803–1804, **Lewis and Clark** met with a few dozen soldiers and adventurers near St. Louis. (See map, opposite.) Thus began their exciting journey to the Far West.

In the spring of 1804, the expedition traveled up the Missouri by keel boat. By late fall, they had reached present-day North Dakota, land of the Mandan Indians. Here they camped for the winter. By April 1805, the snows had melted, and Lewis and Clark started west.

Before them lay the most difficult part of their adventure—the trek across the Rocky Mountains. Fortunately, the travelers found an excellent interpreter in the Mandan village. **Sacajawea** [sak′ə jə wē′ə] was a Shoshone, whose own people lived west of the Rockies. With her young baby strapped securely to her back, Sacajawea led the Americans across the Continental Divide. By November 1805, Lewis and Clark stood gazing at "this great Pacific Ocean, which we have been so long anxious to see."

On their return, the expedition split in two for a while, with Lewis and Clark exploring different areas. It was almost a year later that the tired band of adventurers reappeared in St. Louis with the trophies of their trip: maps and samples of plant, animal, and insect life from the Far West. At the same time, other explorers were adding to their country's store of knowledge of the conti-

Sioux village. Painted by George Catlin around 1830

nent. In 1805, **Zebulon Pike** led an expedition north from St. Louis in search of the source of the mighty Mississippi River. Pike failed to find the river's beginnings, but he did learn much about the lands of the upper Mississippi. In 1806, Pike set out again, this time heading west toward the Rockies. On this trip, he discovered the craggy Colorado mountain now called Pikes Peak.

SECTION 1 REVIEW

Identify: *Marbury* v. *Madison*, judicial review, Napoleon Bonaparte, Toussaint L'Ouverture, Louisiana Purchase, Lewis and Clark, Sacajawea, Zebulon Pike

Main Ideas

1. What changes did Thomas Jefferson bring to government during his first term as President?
2. Explain why Jefferson wanted to impeach important federal judges. Why did Congress refuse to convict Justice Chase?
3. How did Chief Justice John Marshall help strengthen the power of the Supreme Court in the case of *Marbury* v. *Madison*?
4. Why did Napoleon want to sell Louisiana? Why was the United States happy to buy it? What constitutional issues were raised?

267

2. THE EAGLE IS CHALLENGED BY THE TIGER AND THE SHARK

When Jefferson looked back on his first administration, he undoubtedly felt proud. The American voters shared his satisfaction and re-elected him by a landslide. Yet, when Jefferson retired from office only four years later, he was a troubled, tired, and ailing man. Rheumatism had robbed him of his spry step, and piercing headaches plagued him. More than the physical illnesses, however, the burdens and disappointments of office had aged the President. His troubles began—as newspapers of the day described the problem—when the French "tiger" and the English "shark" started challenging the American "eagle."

War Begins in Europe

As you saw in Section 1, Napoleon Bonaparte was determined to conquer Europe. England was determined to stop him, and by 1803, the two rival nations were once more at war. The French strength lay in its army, which prowled the European continent like a hungry tiger. England's might was on the seas, where, like a shark, the Royal Navy tried to devour the commerce of its enemy. England's strategy was to cut off France's imports and vital supplies. Napoleon, on the other hand, meant to destroy the English economy by cutting off British markets in the rest of Europe.

The two nations were thus evenly, if oddly, matched. Neutral powers like the United States were important, for their support could tip the scales of victory. Thus, neither England nor France would allow the Americans to remain neutral. Sometimes the two nations tried to woo American friendship. But just as often, they were willing to bully the young Republic.

Impressment Angers Americans

England's navy was always short of able seamen. Many sailors deserted ship, and in wartime, desertion was particularly serious. In 1803, therefore, England once again began the hated practice of **impressment**.

As you saw in Chapter 10, the English practice of boarding American vessels and seizing sailors was a serious blow to American pride in the 1790s. Now, the English were even more insulting, for their impressment gangs boarded U.S. ships lying within American territorial waters. Between 1803 and 1812, about 5,000 sailors were snatched from ships flying American colors.

The most shocking example of English contempt for American sovereignty occurred in June 1807. That month the British frigate *Leopard* hailed down the U.S. frigate *Chesapeake* in United States coastal waters. The British commander demanded the right to board and search for deserters. The *Chesapeake* captain refused. The *Leopard* let loose a volley at the American naval vessel. Three men were killed, 18 were wounded, and 4 were pressed into British service.

Although the British government disowned this action, the *Chesapeake* and *Leopard* incident outraged Americans. There was a great outcry for revenge against this attack on the nation's honor and independence.

The Freedom of the Seas

Impressment was not the only crisis Jefferson faced. There was also the broader question of the **"freedom of the seas."** Americans argued that neutrals had the right to trade with anyone they wished, at any time. Neither France nor England accepted this view. Both needed American aid, and both demanded exclusive rights to American trade.

Napoleon relied heavily on American shippers to ensure his nation's lifeline with the rest of the world. Supplies from French colonies in the Caribbean were important, but the small French navy could not be spared to protect this trade. To solve his problem, Napoleon opened up this trade to the Americans.

New England shippers were delighted to oblige the emperor. England, however, frowned on the arrangement. According to England's "Rule of '56" a neutral nation could not establish *new* trade routes in wartime. The Royal Navy stood ready to seize any American vessel found breaking the "Rule of '56."

There was, however, a loophole in the "Rule of '56." If the American vessel carried the French product to a U.S. port first, the cargo could be reshipped to France as an American product.

New England sea captains quickly arranged "broken voyages," anchoring briefly in an American port and then sailing on to France. Soon the "broken voyage" trade was booming.

The British then closed the "broken voyage" loophole. In 1805, British courts upheld the right of their navy to seize *any* American ship involved in the Caribbean trade with France. Over 500 American ships were captured.

New England shippers, however, had no intention of giving up the French trade. Even if one in every three ships were captured by the Royal Navy, the profits from the safe arrival of the other two made the risk worthwhile. Jefferson realized that American profit-seeking was threatening American neutrality.

Blockades and Yet More Blockades

Jefferson's worst fears were soon realized. In the 1806 Berlin Decree, Napoleon declared a blockade of England. In the Orders-in-Council of 1807, England forbade neutral nations from trading in any port that banned English ships, unless the neutral ship stopped first at a British port. Because Napoleon controlled most of Europe, this limited most American trade to British ports. Napoleon countered with the Milan Decree of 1807; he ruled that any neutral ship submitting to British inspection would be seized by the French.

Thus, the tiger and the shark created an impossible situation for the United States. The young Republic's demand for "freedom of the seas" fell on deaf ears. The United States was being driven to choose sides in the Old World's struggle for empire.

The Embargo on Foreign Trade

Jefferson wanted to avoid war. He was willing to take drastic measures to preserve the peace. In December 1807, he issued an unusual order, calling for the embargo (ban) of foreign trade. Congress quickly passed the **Embargo Act**, which forbade any American exports to foreign nations. Why did the President do this? First, he hoped that by removing American ships from the seas he could end the seizures and impressment. Second, he hoped to use the only weapon his nation had against England and France. If American trade were so important to these countries, perhaps by denying it to them, he could force recognition of American rights.

Jefferson's search for a peaceful solution did not mean that he was a pacifist (opposed to all warfare). He had, after all, drafted the Declaration of Independence, calling for revolution. And in 1801, when the ruler of Tripoli (in present-day Libya) raised the price he charged to "protect" American ships from his own Barbary Coast pirates, Jefferson was quick to send the navy to the trouble spot. (Americans won a favorable peace treaty with Tripoli in 1805, but continued to pay tribute to other Barbary Coast pirates until 1816.)

Even as the President drafted the Embargo Act, he was also making military preparations. Gunboats were built, garrisons constructed, and state militias put on alert. But the President sincerely hoped his countrymen and women would prefer economic sacrifice to war.

Americans Protest the Embargo

Many Americans did not agree with Jefferson's policies. Merchants and shippers were his strongest critics. Smuggling began immediately. Just as colonial New Englanders had once ignored English trade laws, now American shippers ignored the Embargo Act. The President responded harshly. He used the new gunboats and the state militias to arrest smugglers and enforce his unpopular law. But the smuggling went on.

The results of the embargo were disastrous. Economic depression swept the nation. Even with

The Embargo Act was nicknamed the Oh! Grab Me Act. Spell embargo backwards to see why.

smuggling, exports dropped 80% in 1808. Government revenues also dried up, for Jefferson's administration depended on customs duties for its income. Unemployment and discontent rose. Idle sailors filled the streets of Boston. Prices skyrocketed, and merchants went bankrupt.

By the summer of 1808 many Americans feared that Jefferson had led them to the brink of civil war. Most New Englanders showed their anger that fall at the polls. Federalist candidates were elected to Congress in 1808. Other New Englanders actually spoke of disunion.

The President tried to ease the price of peace to the nation. In 1809, he signed a partial repeal of the embargo. The **Non-Intercourse Act** allowed shippers to export to all nations except England and France. This act was a poor one, for it breathed instant life into smuggling. Ship captains lied about their destinations and headed directly for the forbidden ports. Jefferson's hopes for peaceful persuasion in foreign affairs had failed badly.

Madison Declares War

Despite the opposition to Jefferson's policy, the nation's voters still had faith in the Republican party. In 1808, James Madison, the third of the Virginia planter Presidents, defeated the Federalist candidate, Charles Cotesworth Pinckney of South Carolina.

James Madison (1751–1836)

IN OFFICE: 1809–1817

Republican from Virginia. Madison's presidency was dominated by the issues of neutral rights and impressment, which led to the War of 1812. Mismanagement of the war, as well as economic hardship, led to the threat of secession by a group of Federalists in New England. In 1816, the second Bank of the United States was chartered and a high tariff was passed, marking a return to Hamiltonian ideas.

Madison was not overconfident. The nation was severely divided. Sectionalism had reared its head in New England, where talk of a separate Northern Confederacy in 1804 was now remembered. Smuggling had undermined the law of the land. American ships were once again being captured on the open seas. Troubled days lay ahead for "Jemmy" Madison.

Madison's policy on international trade was like Jefferson's, but milder. In May 1810, Congress declared that trade with the English and French could begin anew. If, however, either country publicly acknowledged the American right to "freedom of the seas," then trade with the other nation would stop. War with the more stubborn nation was sure to follow.

On August 5, 1810, Emperor Napoleon declared his recognition of American neutral rights. Madison heard the news in November (communications were very slow in those days) and, all too trustingly, he moved to honor the American pledge to cease trade with England. Unfortunately, Napoleon was lying. Secretly, he gave the order to his navy: sell all American ships being held in the ports of France!

England was slower to act than France. But on June 16, 1812, England, too, recognized American "freedom of the seas." However, there was never time to test Britain's sincerity. For on the very next day, long before the slow traveling news could reach Washington, the United States declared war on England.

SECTION 2 REVIEW

Identify: impressment, "freedom of the seas," Embargo Act, Non-Intercourse Act

Main Ideas
1. Why were England and France at war by 1803? What strengths and weaknesses did each have in this war?
2. Explain the American demand for "freedom of the seas." Why did England and France refuse to grant these neutral rights?
3. How did Jefferson think the Embargo Act would help the United States? Why did it fail? Why did the Non-Intercourse Act lead to increased smuggling?
4. Why did relations with England become worse than those with France after 1810?

3. THE WAR OF 1812

It would be wrong to think that the Americans went to war with England only because of Napoleon's trickery. Nations, like people, usually have many motives for their actions. What, then, were the other causes for the War of 1812?

National Honor

The British seizure of American ships and the impressment of American sailors challenged American honor. As early as 1810, young **"War Hawks"** like Henry Clay of Kentucky demanded war with England. "Harry of the West," as Clay was called, was not personally involved in the shipping industry. But he, like Representatives Felix Grundy of Tennessee and John C. Calhoun of South Carolina, wished to see the American flag respected—even if it cost lives. For congressional leaders like the War Hawks, national honor was the reason for the war.

Troubles on the Frontier

Problems on the western frontier were a second motive for war. On November 7, 1811, a bloody battle occurred between Shawnee, Delaware, and other Indians of the Northwest and American troops at Tippecanoe in the Indiana Territory. Many Americans believed that the British in Canada had inflamed the Indians and provided them with weapons.

The Indian uprisings were led by a Shawnee chief named **Tecumseh** [tə kum′sə]. A statesman as well as a warrior, Tecumseh dreamed of creating a separate and independent Indian nation in the Ohio Valley. Tecumseh set about to unify the many tribes of the Northwest, much as John Adams and other Patriots had once set about to unify the colonies. Tecumseh's brother, Tenskwatawa, who was a religious leader known as the Prophet, helped weld the Shawnee, Delaware, Ottawa, Chippewa, and other tribes into an Indian confederacy.

In early November 1811, the governor of the Indiana Territory, **William Henry Harrison,** led about 1,000 troops north from Vincennes toward the Prophet's town on the Wabash and Tippecanoe rivers. (See map, page 274.) The Prophet's town was destroyed in the battle that followed.

Harrison's victory was glorified in the newspapers. He later became known as "Old Tippecanoe," and his reputation as an Indian fighter carried him all the way to the White House 30 years later. The Indian wars were not over after the Battle of Tippecanoe, however. The battles went on for years. People like Grundy and Harrison blamed the British for the Indian trouble. It probably never occurred to Harrison that the people he called "wretched savages" might be able, and willing, to fight for their own survival, without British direction.

Land Hunger and Agricultural Depression

Many Americans believed that the prairie lands of the Midwest were useless to farmers. A war with England could mean a chance to conquer Canada and to settle its farmlands. In the South, the Florida territory held by England's ally, Spain, looked desirable. This land hunger was another reason for war in 1812.

An agricultural depression in the southern and western states and territories also led some farmers to be hawks in favor of war rather than doves, or peace supporters, on the war issue. Prices for wheat, tobacco, and other crops were falling during the early 1800s. These hard times were probably the result of local problems like poor transportation routes. But unhappy farmers were willing to believe that Britain's control of the seas was to blame. They insisted that freedom of the seas would reduce their costs and restore prosperity.

New England Opposes the War

Where, you must wonder, were the War Hawks of New England? After all, it was New England ships and sailors who bore the brunt of the "shark's" attacks. New England had no War Hawks. The people of this region opposed what they called "Mr. Madison's War."

Like the late Alexander Hamilton, New England shippers understood the importance of their economic ties with Britain. Sudden profit might be made from Napoleon's blockade, but the French emperor could not create the lasting commercial ties that linked English and American consumers and producers. New Englanders tended to take the cynical view that the War Hawks wanted Canadian lands more than they wanted freedom of the seas.

By June 1812, however, the debate over the war was ended. The nation had declared a war that some called madness and other hailed as the "Second War for American Independence."

The U.S. Tries to Conquer Canada

Patriotism alone does not win wars. In fact, the nation was badly prepared for the War of 1812. The army was small. Recruitment went slowly. Only 4,000 men answered the call to arms in 1812. The generals were old and had little military experience. The navy's officers were young and talented, but even naval genius could not make up for a lack of ships, guns, and skilled sailors. Morale was a major problem. Despite the rousing speeches of the War Hawks, enthusiasm for the war quickly faded. Westerners were not as ready to march to war as Felix Grundy had thought. America's best fighting forces, the New England militias, had no intention of joining "Mr. Madison's War."

Despite the problems, military leaders laid their plans for a major invasion of Canada. On paper, the chances looked good. Canada's population was small (about 400,000), and its militia tiny by comparison with that of the United States. There were 5,000 crack British troops defending Canada, but they could not count on reinforcements as long as England's main armies were busy with Napoleon.

The invasion was a disaster! American generals divided their army into three parts. One was to head north through Detroit into Canada. A second was to follow the Niagara River into Canada. The third was to go by way of Lake Champlain to Montreal. (See map, page 274.)

Delays left the Detroit-bound army open to Indian attack. Fearing an Indian massacre, the commander surrendered Detroit to the British on August 16, 1812, without a fight. In addition, the day before, Indians massacred Americans at Fort Dearborn (now Chicago). Thus, the Northwest was lost, and by the end of 1812, the British flag flew over all the territory north and west of Ohio.

Things went no better for the remaining two armies. In October the Niagara expedition, outnumbered, turned back when New York state militia members refused to leave their state to reinforce the American army in Canada. The campaign against Montreal in November dissolved at the Canadian border when, again, state militia units refused to cross the borders of their states. The call to avenge national honor had clearly not created national unity.

Naval Victories Spark Excitement

The only welcome news in 1812 came from the navy. Three dramatic ocean battles were won by American captains. In August, the American frigate *Constitution* destroyed the proud British warship, *Guerriere*, off the Nova Scotia coast. In October, Stephen Decatur's *United States* captured the British *Macedonian*. In December, in the warm waters off Brazil, the *Constitution* defeated the British frigate *Java*. These victories had little real effect on the outcome of the war, but they did boost Americans' flagging morale.

The American public cheered its navy, but it remained uneasy about the war. Dissatisfaction sparked a new interest in the Federalist party. But in the 1812 election, Madison won re-election.

Victory on Lake Erie

1813 came, and the Americans tried to recover their losses. In a pattern of attack and counterattack, British and American troops exchanged advantages along the northern borders. Not until spring did the Americans score a solid victory. Once again, it was the navy that deserved the credit.

At Presque Isle on the shore of Lake Erie, Captain **Oliver Hazard Perry** supervised shipbuilding activities. The British, jealously guarding Lake Erie and Lake Ontario, hurried a fleet into place to blockade Perry. Perry then moved his ships to a better position off the island of Put-in-Bay. (See map, page 274.) On September 10, 1813, the British fleet challenged Perry.

The three-hour Battle of Lake Erie was a bloody one. The crew of Perry's own flagship was hit hard. The dead and the dying were strewn across the deck. But the Americans gave blow for blow to the enemy, and more. Perry sent the news of victory to William Henry Harrison: "We have met the enemy, and they are ours." Perry's victory put Lake Erie under American control.

Indian Dreams of Independence Die

The American navy's success seemed to inspire the army to its own victories. With Lake Erie lost,

This kerchief titled "Huzzah for the Navy" depicts exciting battles from the War of 1812.

the British decided to abandon Detroit and pull back to the north. Harrison gathered an army of over 4,000, and pursued the British troops. In early October 1813, the two armies met at Moravian Town, in Canada north of Lake Erie. (See map, page 274.)

Harrison's troops carried the day. Many people died at Moravian Town, but the most important casualty was the great chieftain, Tecumseh. With Tecumseh's death, Indian dreams of a separate nation died too. Indian resistance was broken. In July 1814, the Treaty of Greenville formally

marked the defeat and surrender of the northwest Indians. A heritage of bitterness remained.

The War of 1812 was also a turning point in the struggle between the southern Indians and the American government. At the Battle of Horseshoe Bend (March 27, 1814) in what is now Alabama, troops under **Andrew Jackson** of Tennessee decisively defeated the Creek Indians. In August, the Treaty of Fort Jackson forced the Creeks to surrender claims to two-thirds of their huge territory. These lands, which included southern Georgia and most of present-day Alabama, would soon become the heart of a rich new "Cotton Kingdom."

The British Invasion from Canada Fails

At the beginning of the war, Britain needed its warships for its fight against Napoleon. In the spring of 1813, it was able to spare more ships to blockade the United States. By 1814, a floating chain of British warships stretched from Maryland to the Canadian border. Americans were once again prisoners on their own shores.

Now chilling news came to the Americans. Napoleon had been defeated, and the European war was over. Suddenly, thousands of British

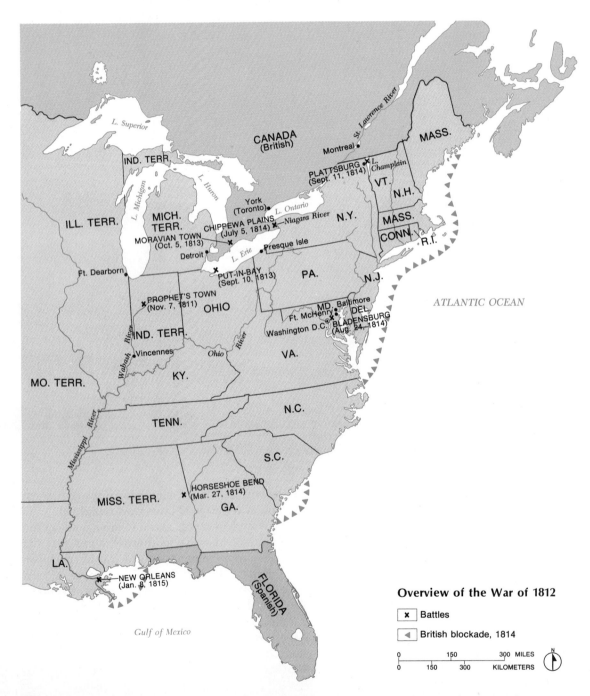

Overview of the War of 1812

| ✗ | Battles |

| ◀ | British blockade, 1814 |

troops were free to fight in America. British commanders promptly organized an invasion from Canada.

Fortune, however, smiled on the Americans. In July 1814, Winfield Scott led American troops against the British at Chippewa Plains, on the Canadian side of the Niagara River. (See map, opposite page.) Scott's soldiers drove the invading English back. In September, after fierce fighting on Lake Champlain, the American navy turned back another British invasion force near Plattsburg, New York.

The Capital in Flames

In August the British had hoped to divert American fighting forces from the Canadian borders by launching an attack on the Chesapeake region. One of the targets was Washington, D.C.

After defeating American militia at Bladensburg, Maryland, on August 24, the invaders headed for Washington. That evening, the President was just sitting down to dinner when word came to flee. Madison hurried away to safety in a boat across the Potomac. The British soldiers ate his dinner, then burned down the Executive Mansion, the Capitol, and other government buildings in retaliation for the American burning of York (Toronto) in April 1813. It would take two years to rebuild the Capitol. The Executive Mansion, stained by smoke, was given a fresh coat of white paint. Thus it came to be known as the White House.

The Tide of Battle Turns

The burning of Washington seemed to exhaust the energies of the British. In a battle near Baltimore on September 12, 1814, the American militia stood its ground. The British navy moved up the Chesapeake to assist its army. But Americans at Fort Covington and Fort McHenry held off the ships. The British commander realized that he must destroy the two harbor forts in order to take the city. A furious barrage began. Bombs, caseshot rockets, and incendiary rockets rained upon the two forts. The attack, dazzling to the eye but deadly, raged throughout the night of September 13–14.

By dawn, 2,000 missiles had been fired at the forts, yet the Americans did not surrender. The amazed British departed. Francis Scott Key, a prisoner of the British who had watched the

FROM THE ARCHIVES

The Star-Spangled Banner

Originally called "Defense of Fort McHenry," Key's poem was distributed as a handbill to Baltimore citizens the day after the bombardment. The tune was a popular English drinking song, "To Anacreon in Heaven." The song did not become the official national anthem until 1931.

Oh, say! can you see by the dawn's early light,
What so proudly we hailed at the twilight's last
    gleaming,
Whose broad stripes and bright stars, thru the perilous fight,
O'er the ramparts we watched were so gallantly
    streaming?
And the rocket's red glare, the bombs bursting in
    air,
Gave proof thru the night that our flag was still
    there.
Oh, say, does that Star-Spangled Banner yet wave
O'er the land of the free and the home of the
    brave?

incendiary rockets' red glare through the long night, preserved the American victory in his "Star-Spangled Banner."

Peace—At Last

The third year of war was almost at an end. But, who was winning? To most thoughtful observers, it appeared that no victor would emerge. A negotiated peace was the only sensible answer. In fact, peace efforts had begun almost simultaneously with the declarations of war. In July 1814, these negotiations began in earnest in the Belgian town of Ghent.

Few points of disagreement existed. Impressment had stopped as soon as the war in Europe ended. At first the British tried to create an independent country for the northwest Indians. When the Americans protested, the British backed down, abandoning their Indian allies to their fate. Both sides agreed to return the Canadian-American borders to their shape before the war. On Christmas Eve, 1814, the Treaty of Ghent was signed. The War of 1812 officially passed into history.

LIFE IN AMERICA

PIRATES

Jean Lafitte's help in the Battle of New Orleans was not a result of patriotism or love of liberty. For a number of years he had plundered ships in the Gulf of Mexico near the mouth of the Mississippi. Because of political connections in New Orleans he worked with a free hand. Many merchants in that wide-open city were only too happy to provide a market for stolen goods.

When the War of 1812 broke out, Lafitte had no feelings for either side. So both the British and Americans tried to gain his help. The British offered £30,000 and a captaincy in the Royal Navy. Jackson offered a pardon for his acts of piracy. Lafitte took the pardon, and the rest is history.

The Age of Piracy

Actually, Lafitte is a minor figure in the annals of piracy, which had its Golden Age much earlier, 1630 to 1725. Piracy provided an easy way to get rich in those years. Huge amounts of goods and gold were traveling the Atlantic sea lanes, and many merchant ships were unarmed or heavily outgunned by pirate men-of-war. Furthermore, the conditions and pay in the navy were dismal, and many sea captains were cruel or incompetent. Thus, few sailors were willing to lay down their lives to protect a ship's cargo from hijackers on the high seas.

Physical conditions aboard pirate vessels were also rough. Rats, roaches, and poor rations were facts of life on board any ship. But some crude forms of democracy made it worthwhile. Generally each pirate had a vote in the operations of the ship and equal rights to the ship's provisions. Even pirates who had lost a limb were guaranteed a place in the crew, sometimes for life.

Pirates sailing for Bartholomew Roberts divided the loot as follows: "The captain and quartermaster shall each receive 2 shares of a prize, the master gunner and boatswain 1½ shares, all other officers 1¼ and private gentlemen of fortune 1 share each." Often each crew member would earn £1,000, a princely sum for the time.

Some Famous Pirates in American History

No one knows the real worth of the plundered riches or can separate truth from myth regarding pirate captains. The famous Captain Kidd, for instance, was probably the greatest of all non-pirate pirates. William Kidd was actually a privateer. This means that he was authorized by the king or governor to attack enemy ships.

In 1695 Kidd entered into a privateering contract with Earl of Bellomont, governor of New York

The Battle of New Orleans

History, however, was not yet done with this war: its most spectacular battle was yet to be fought. In December 1814, a combination of British naval and land forces began a campaign to capture New Orleans and take control of the Mississippi River. News traveled too slowly in this era for either the British or the Americans to know of the peace negotiations coming to a close at Ghent.

On December 23—one day before the signing of the peace—the two armies faced each other for a showdown. Eight thousand seasoned British regulars faced Andrew Jackson's hastily assembled army of 5,000 troops—mainly militiamen, sailors, local citizens, and a company of Jean Lafitte's pirates.

After days of indecisive fighting, the tide turned on January 8, 1815, when the British made a frontal attack on Jackson's main position—and were slaughtered. The British suffered 2,000 casualties, the Americans 21. The Battle of New Orleans was an unquestioned American triumph —and a totally unnecessary one. But it made Andrew Jackson into a national hero. Jackson's fame, like Harrison's, would take him all the way to the White House.

and New England. The governor, however, was in the deal for his personal gain, and when Kidd was brought to trial as a pirate, his backers deserted him. This left Kidd out on a limb—a gallows limb. His execution is a classic example of the fine line between privateer and pirate.

Edward Teach, better known as Blackbeard, was a real pirate. A privateer turned pirate, he operated off the Virginia coast and the West Indies in 1717. In North Carolina he found a haven under an Act of Grace from Governor Charles Eden. The colony was hungry for trade—even pirate loot. From there Blackbeard ravaged South Carolina.

Teach had a powerful build, which he used to cultivate the pirate image. Other than a knack for leadership, his greatest asset was his beard, which he let grow to great dimensions and tied up with ribbons.

Constantly drunk, in battle Blackbeard would put long, smoldering matches under his hat, rattle cutlasses, brandish guns, and in general appear to be the Devil incarnate. Indeed, even his death took on heroic proportions as he was shot five times and his throat was slit.

Although women pirates were rare, two became famous. Mary Read's mother had dressed her as a boy in order to pass as her dead brother and collect an inheritance. As she grew, Read continued to disguise her sex and joined the Royal Navy. After she spent a brief spell as a happily married woman, her husband died and she again put to sea.

When her ship was taken by the pirate Calico Jack Rackham she was pressed into piracy along with the other crew members. As boisterous and bloody as the rest, no one suspected Mary Read's identity until she attracted the attentions of a crewmate—Anne Bonny, also in disguise! Rackham discovered this but was persuaded to keep them on because of their fierce nature and because he loved Anne Bonny.

Although they were outlaws, they were welcomed in the American colonies because they brought needed coin to merchants in the port cities. (Recall the currency shortage described in Chapter 4.) But Mary Read and Calico Jack Rackham came to a bad end: Read died in prison, and Rackham was hanged. Anne Bonny was sentenced to die on the gallows but was reprieved, and then disappeared from history.

News of peace and the smashing victory at New Orleans brought wild celebrations everywhere except among the New England Federalists. In December 1814, 26 Federalists had gathered in secrecy in Hartford, Connecticut, to organize a protest against the war and to demand the right of individual states to reject those national policies and laws they found hateful. Suddenly, the war was over and the Federalists at the **Hartford Convention** looked both foolish and unpatriotic. Republicans hinted that the Federalists were guilty of treason. The war had revived Federalism in 1812, but the peace killed it in 1815.

SECTION 3 REVIEW

Identify: War Hawks, Tecumseh, William Henry Harrison, Oliver Hazard Perry, Andrew Jackson, Hartford Convention

Main Ideas

1. Give four reasons (besides impressment and "freedom of the seas") why the U.S. went to war in 1812.
2. Why did New England oppose the War Hawks?
3. Was America ready for war in 1812? Name some problems and some victories.
4. How did the War of 1812 affect Indians?

4. AN ERA OF GOOD FEELINGS—AND SOME BAD ONES

"Americans! Rejoice!" boomed the headlines of the *Daily National Intelligencer* on February 16, 1815. News of the peace treaty had arrived. The postwar period began on that note: rejoice. In the next decade the Republicans had every reason to be happy. Their party's third President was inaugurated in 1817. Tall, awkward, solemn, **James Monroe** seemed to float on the waves of postwar pride and patriotism. As one Boston newspaper put it, this was an "era of good feeling."

The Postwar Boom

Overseas trade had quickly revived, and sailors, shippers, and sea captains were busy once more. Seaport cities continued to grow, with New York reaching almost 125,000 people by 1820. Philadelphia had over 100,000, and the port of Baltimore, 60,000. The newest American port city, New Orleans, already had 27,000 residents.

The national population climbed steadily—from 7 million in 1810 to 9.5 million in 1820 to 13 million in 1830. Many of these Americans were Irish, German, and British immigrants, who poured into the country after the War of 1812.

James Monroe (1758–1831)

IN OFFICE: 1817–1825

Republican from Virginia. The period of Monroe's presidency, known as the "era of good feelings," was characterized by a lack of strong party rivalry. During his term of office, the Great Lakes were demilitarized (1817), part of the northwest boundary between Canada and the United States was fixed (1818), Florida was purchased from Spain (1819), the Missouri Compromise was made (1820), and the Monroe Doctrine was announced (1823).

New states continued to be carved out of the west and the south. Mississippi, Alabama, Indiana, Illinois, Maine, and Missouri were all added to the Union between 1816 and 1821. The growth of the South was due largely to the widespread use of the cotton gin, invented by Eli Whitney back in 1793. This device, which separated the hundreds of seeds from the boll of cotton, made the production of cotton a profitable enterprise. The new southern states were part of a growing Cotton Kingdom.

American pride in the nation's growth and economic prospects showed itself in popular national symbols. The design of the Stars and Stripes was established in 1818. The number of stripes was fixed at 13, while the tradition of adding a new star for each state was continued.

Americans were proud, too, of their political unity. The peace of 1814 brought a spirit of cooperation that the war had failed to bring. The United States now had a one-party government, and for once political leaders did seem to fit the old motto: "We are all Republicans; we are all Federalists." Certainly, the Republicans had learned the value of a strong national government during the war years. They were now "outfederalizing the Federalists" in their policies.

Far-ranging roadbuilding and other programs on a national scale were proposed in this era of good feelings by political leaders who had once insisted that "the government that governs least governs best." "Harry of the West" **Henry Clay** was the chief supporter for an **American System**, his name for a development program that combined protective tariffs with federal funds for internal improvements, such as highways and canals. Representative **John C. Calhoun,** who would later be the leading defender of states' rights, was also a nationalist in 1817. He too called for a federal program of internal improvements. "Let us, then," Calhoun urged, "bind the Republic together with a perfect system of roads and canals. Let us conquer space." (See The Geographic Setting, pages 283–285.)

Both northern and southern Republicans supported the reestablishment of the Bank of the United States. The Bank's charter had been allowed to expire in 1812, causing severe financial problems during the war. A new charter for the Bank was issued in 1816, after the confusions of wartime had taught the Republicans the value of a sound and uniform currency. Alexander Hamilton would have been amazed and delighted to see the Republicans praise his financial system.

Even on the issue of protective tariffs—import duties on foreign goods—unity reigned. As you saw in the debates in the Constitutional Convention, New Englanders wanted such tariffs to protect their budding industries. Southerners, however, wanted to buy their manufactured goods at the best price, no matter where they were produced. From the beginning, then, the tariff was a sectional issue. Yet after the war, congressmen of both regions united to pass the Tariff of 1816. This tariff placed high enough duties on imported goods to prevent English manufacturers from selling low-cost goods in the United States. Had England been allowed to "flood the market," American industry might have been killed before it was firmly established.

Court Decisions Reflect the New Nationalism

The new concern to strengthen the national government is best seen in the three landmark Supreme Court cases of the era. In *McCulloch* v. *Maryland* (1819), Chief Justice Marshall ruled that neither Maryland nor any other state could tax the nationally chartered Bank of the United States. "The power to tax," Marshall observed, "involves the power to destroy." No state could thus threaten a national institution by taxing it.

In 1819, the Court also ruled on the *Trustees of Dartmouth College* v. *Woodward*. This decision also chipped away at the power of the states. The Chief Justice said that the state of New Hampshire could not alter the original colonial charter of the college. A charter is a contract, Marshall noted, and the federal Constitution guarantees that all contracts must be honored. The Chief Justice asserted once again that the Supreme Court could set aside any state law it judged unconstitutional.

The third important postwar case, *Gibbons* v. *Ogden* (1824), removed a state's attempt to restrict interstate transportation. New York had tried to grant a monopoly on steamboat traffic on the Hudson River to Robert Fulton, who had built the first commercial steamboat in 1807. Marshall ruled that New York could not grant such a

Russian artist Pavel Svinin painted this view of oyster sellers in Philadelphia around 1811.

monopoly. The Hudson River carried traffic between two states, New York and New Jersey, and thus was subject to federal regulation. Marshall went on to say that the federal power to regulate interstate and foreign commerce does not stop at a state boundary.

Speculation and the Panic of 1819

"Brother Jonathan" or "Uncle Sam," as the nation had nicknamed itself, appeared content and vigorous. But tensions rippled below the calm surface. First, the nation's rapid economic growth infected Americans with a get-rich-quick fever. Farmers and planters borrowed heavily to expand their farms and plantations. New England merchants, encouraged by the protective tariff, borrowed to build new factories. Citizens everywhere speculated in land and stocks. The recklessness spread to bankers, who issued bank notes (paper money) backed by optimism rather than by sound currency or deposits.

In 1819 the bubble temporarily but dramatically burst. The Bank of the United States, acting as a watchdog over American financial affairs, challenged the local state banks to prove the soundness of their bank notes. The Bank called in all its loans to these banks. In turn, local bankers demanded that mortgages and loans be paid by private citizens. Panic struck. Families lost their farms and businesses because they could not meet their debts. Banks closed their doors. Life savings disappeared. Many Americans blamed the Bank of the United States for the **Panic of 1819**. But American overconfidence was surely a culprit too.

The Balance of Power Between Regions

There were also serious political problems that no "era of good feelings" could hide or solve. These problems were reawakened by the very westward expansion and growth of the Cotton Kingdom in which Americans took such pride. In part, the problems centered around who should control the federal government and set its policies.

In the postwar period, with the federal government growing stronger each day, the struggle for control between the commercial-industrial North and the plantation South increased. This rivalry was known by the political shorthand: "slave states versus free states."

Until 1819, the political power in the federal government was roughly equal for the slave and free states. As the table below shows, there were 11 free states and 11 states in which slavery was both legal and widespread. The free states controlled the House of Representatives, for their populations were greater than those of the southern states. But the South could block any legislation it opposed in the Senate.

The "Fire Bell in the Night"

Trouble arose during the debates over the admission of Missouri into the Union. In 1819 Representative James Tallmadge of New York proposed an amendment to outlaw further slavery in Missouri and to free all children born of slaves in that state when they reached the age of 25. The **Tallmadge Amendment** shocked many and angered even more. For the New Yorker spoke as a moral opponent of slavery, not just as a politician. "It is the cause of the freedom of man," Tallmadge thundered. And, in chilling tones he added, "If a dissolution of the Union must take place, let it be so!" The morality of the institution of slavery, an issue long kept out of national politics, had been raised on the floor of Congress itself.

Tallmadge's amendment was defeated in the Senate. But the wound to national unity was deep and raw. Thomas Jefferson saw immediately that attacks on slavery as a southern way of life would surely destroy the Union. The Missouri dispute, he wrote, "like a fire bell in the night, awakened and filled me with terror." Thus, Jefferson's Louisiana Purchase had come home to haunt him. Instead of the "Empire for Liberty" he had dreamed of, the lands west of the Mississippi had become a battleground for opposing societies.

The Missouri Compromise

On March 2, 1819, Congress organized the Arkansas Territory, with a northern boundary at latitude 36°30'N. Slaveholders had settled Arkansas,

STATES IN THE UNION, 1819

	Free states	Slave states
Original 13 states	Massachusetts New Hampshire Rhode Island Connecticut New York Pennsylvania New Jersey	Delaware Maryland Virginia North Carolina South Carolina Georgia
Admitted 1791–1819	Vermont (1791) Ohio (1803) Indiana (1816) Illinois (1818)	Kentucky (1792) Tennessee (1796) Louisiana (1812) Mississippi (1817) Alabama (1819)

and slavery was to be legal in the territory and in the future state. But a second New York congressman, John W. Taylor, rose to demand that slavery be barred in Arkansas. A shudder spread through the Congress. The morality of slavery had been raised again. Taylor's wishes were not heeded, but on December 19, 1819, the House showed its antislavery bias by passing the Tallmadge Amendment for a second time.

The Senate again defeated the Tallmadge Amendment. Thus a stalemate had occurred. Something must be done, as the nation's leaders well knew. Settlers in the western territories had to be guaranteed the right to statehood. How could this be assured if the balance of power between slave and free states also had to be maintained?

Developments in New England resolved the crisis temporarily. In 1820, the people of Maine applied for statehood. A compromise was now possible between free-state politicians and slave-state supporters. On February 18, 1820, it was agreed that Missouri would enter the Union as a slave state and Maine as a free one. Slavery was banned north of latitude 36°30'N except for Missouri. (See map, below.) The **Missouri Compromise** preserved the balance of powers in the national government. But could this balance last?

Three Important Treaties

The United States had not won the War of 1812, but the willingness of its government to fight for American rights impressed the nations of the world. Important diplomatic successes followed the Treaty of Ghent. Between 1815 and 1824, the young nation played a bolder and firmer role in world affairs.

In 1817, English and American representatives negotiated the question of military defenses on the Canadian border, preventing a threatened naval-armaments race on the Great Lakes. The Rush-Bagot Agreement revealed that the two nations were genuinely at peace with each other. Each nation was allowed to keep only one warship on Lake Champlain, one on Lake Ontario, and two on each of the other Great Lakes. (By 1871, the entire U.S.–Canadian border would be completely demilitarized.)

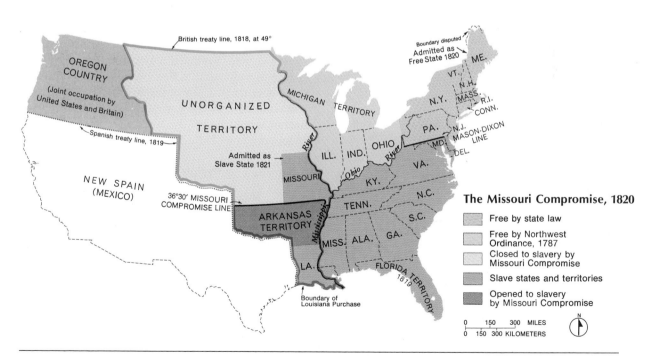

The Missouri Compromise kept the balance of power in the Senate by admitting Missouri as a slave state and Maine as a free state. It temporarily settled the argument over slavery in the territories: slavery was banned north of 36°30' except for Missouri.

In another important agreement, known as the Convention of 1818, the British and Americans drew the northern boundary of the Louisiana Purchase at the 49th parallel. (See map, page 281.)

Americans also settled border issues with Spain. In 1819, Secretary of State John Quincy Adams and the Spanish diplomat Luis de Onís established the western boundaries of the Louisiana Purchase territory. (See map, page 281.) The United States renounced its claims to Texas, and Spain renounced its claims to the Oregon Country. The Adams-Onís Treaty also gave the United States legal title to all of Florida.

The Monroe Doctrine

Nothing revealed America's new confidence in international affairs as much as the **Monroe Doctrine** of 1823. For the first time, the United States was ready to set policy rather than respond to the policy set by European powers.

In the early 19th century, Europeans still controlled much of the Americas. Russia claimed the Alaskan peninsula. Britain held Canada, British Honduras, British Guiana, and the British West Indies. France and Holland clung to their West Indian and South American possessions. Spain's American empire, once so mighty, had shrunk to Cuba, Puerto Rico, and Mexico.

The desire for independence had reshaped Mexico and Central and South America, however. When Napoleon took control of Spain in 1808, many Latin American colonies staged successful revolutions. But in 1822, four European nations united in an effort to try to restore the Spanish king to his throne and to recover his American empire for him. Austria, France, Prussia, and Russia, known as the Quadruple Alliance, laid plans to send a powerful army to reconquer Latin America. The United States government was suspicious. What would prevent such an army from attempting new conquests in the Americas?

Secretary of State John Quincy Adams urged President Monroe to stand firm against the European powers. Monroe agreed. Adams also advised the President to stand alone, even though Britain had invited the United States to issue a joint statement on the matter. In his message to Congress in December 1823, President Monroe announced: "The American continents . . . are henceforth not to be considered as subjects for future colonization by any European powers." The President also made clear that his nation recognized the revolutionary governments of Latin America.

The United States did not actually have the power to enforce the **Monroe Doctrine**. However, the Doctrine was a promise of things to come. As you shall see, by the end of the 19th century, the nation would be ready, and able, to enforce the independence of the New World from the Old.

FROM THE ARCHIVES

The Monroe Doctrine

The American continents, by the free and independent condition which they have assumed and maintain, are henceforth not to be considered as subjects for future colonization by any European powers. . . .

[We] consider any attempt on their [the Quadruple Alliance's] part to extend their system to any portion of this hemisphere as dangerous to our peace and safety. With the existing colonies or dependencies of any European power we have not interfered and shall not interfere. . . .

Our policy in regard to Europe, which was adopted at an early stage of the wars which have so long agitated that quarter of the globe, nevertheless remains the same, which is, not to interfere in the internal concerns of any of its powers.

From President James Monroe's 7th Annual Message to Congress, December 2, 1823

SECTION 4 REVIEW

 Identify: James Monroe, Henry Clay, John C. Calhoun, American System, Panic of 1819, Tallmadge Amendment, Missouri Compromise, Monroe Doctrine

Main Ideas

1. On what issues was the nation unified during the 1815–1824 "era of good feelings"?
2. How did the three famous court cases of the era reflect the strong nationalism of Americans?
3. Explain the crisis over Missouri statehood.
4. What prompted the creation of the Monroe Doctrine? What policy for the future did the Doctrine establish?

THE GEOGRAPHIC SETTING

TRANSPORTATION ROUTES WEST OF THE APPALACHIANS

Americans interested in settling in the West in the early 1800s had two major geographic problems. The first was getting themselves, their children, and their belongings over the Appalachian Mountains. Except for the Cumberland Gap on the border of Virginia, Tennessee, and Kentucky, and the Mohawk Valley in New York, there were few natural routes over this mountain barrier.

Once the settlers got across the mountains and settled in their new homes, they faced a second problem—how could they ship their farm products back to the markets in the East? Eastern farmers had always shipped their products on waterways. Beyond the Appalachians, however, the rivers flowed generally westward toward the Mississippi River. The price paid

for farm produce in Spanish-held New Orleans was not enough to make the trip profitable. And shipping loads 25 miles over bad country roads cost western farmers more than their produce was worth.

Clearly something had to be done to make the transportation of people and goods across the Appalachian barrier easier. Thus, some political leaders like Henry Clay and John C. Calhoun became champions of "internal improvements," namely roads and canals, to solve these two problems.

The Cumberland Road Is Built

Until the building of the Cumberland Road (see map), "roads" on

the frontier were pack trails called "traces," or private turnpikes. Turnpikes were roads financed by tolls collected at barriers or "pikes" which turned or lifted after payment. In 1802 the Congress, aware that good public roads were desperately needed on the frontier, passed an act providing for roads built with the profits from land sales in Ohio. Finally, in 1811 construction of the Cumberland Road began.

Only 100 miles long at first, the road not only crossed the Appalachians, but linked two major rivers: As you can see on the map, the Cumberland Road connected Cumberland, Maryland, on the Potomac River with Wheeling, Ohio, on the Ohio River.

The Cumberland Road was 30 feet wide, made of crushed stone

The Cumberland Road

Built by the federal government, 1811–1818

Built by the federal government, 1825–1838

Built by Illinois and Missouri after 1840

0   50   100   150 Miles
0   50 100 150 Kilometers

Two major internal improvements of the era of good feelings were the Cumberland Road and the Erie Canal. The Cumberland Road was the first national road built in the United States. It greatly helped the settlement of the states through which it passed.

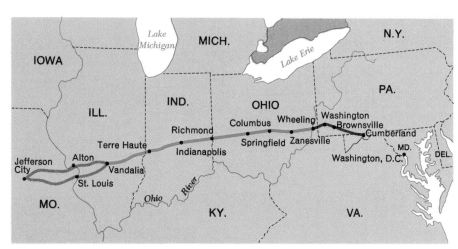

THE GEOGRAPHIC SETTING

Pioneer wagons jam the Frederick Road in Maryland on their way across the Appalachians to the West.

layered on a foundation of larger rocks. Drainage ditches and bridges were also built. The total cost was $1.75 million.

Later the Cumberland Road, often called the National Road, was extended to Vandalia, then the capital of Illinois. This section was not as well-built; often it was just a dirt road because stone for construction was scarce in these areas. By 1840 federal funds had run out, so Illinois and Missouri built the last sections of the road.

Thousands of tons of freight and hundreds of stagecoaches rumbled over the Cumberland Road every year. In fact, it was used so heavily that it began to wear out as soon as it was built. Heavy Conestoga wagons made ruts and ripped up the shoulders. Local farmers fenced in sections of roadside and carted off stone. Freight and coach costs remained too high for poor emigrants and farmers. A cheaper means of transportation was therefore needed.

The Erie Canal

Canals were to meet that need. If a convenient stream to the West did not exist, reasoned "internal improvement" supporters, why not build one? Nothing was cheaper than water transport, and Europe had many canals. The United States would have them too!

Governor DeWitt Clinton of New York thought the Mohawk Valley was the perfect location for a canal connecting the Hudson River with Lake Erie. The Mohawk Valley was a natural gap in the Appalachians. Although existing rivers were too swift, too slow, or flowed in the wrong direction, an artificial waterway could provide cheap, dependable transportation on barges pulled by horses.

Clinton provided the driving force to get the project approved in

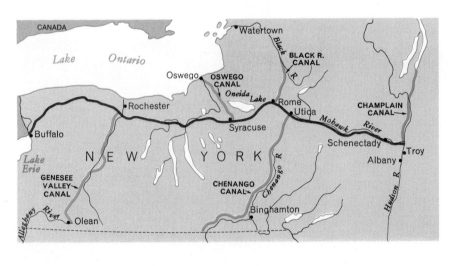

The Erie Canal

▬ Erie Canal, built 1817–1825
▭ Other canals in New York, built by 1840

In 1817, the "Canal Age" began when work was started on the Erie Canal. It was completed in 1825 and ran for 363 miles, connecting the Hudson River to Lake Erie. Its huge success made New York City a commercial giant and sparked a canal-building mania in many states. (See map, opposite page.) Though few other canals were as profitable, they lowered the cost of transport and helped develop the country's interior.

1817 and completed in 1825. At ceremonies marking the Erie Canal's completion, he poured a keg of Lake Erie water into New York harbor, symbolizing the union of the Great Lakes and the Atlantic Ocean. (See map, opposite page.)

The Erie Canal was an engineering marvel of its time. It was 363 miles long. A series of locks were used to raise and lower canal boats along the route. These boats were raised 425 feet between Utica, New York, and the Hudson River. Aqueducts carried the canal across existing rivers. Later, several connecting canals were built in New York (see map).

Freight rates dropped from $32 a ton for 100 miles by wagon to $1 a ton by canal boat. Furthermore, the trip from New York City to Buffalo took only half the time it did in pre-canal days. Trade along the canal was brisk, making New York the "Empire State" and New York City the busiest port in the United States.

Canal Fever in the Northwest

The success of the Erie Canal touched off a "canal fever" that soon swept surrounding states. On the map at right find the canals that crossed Ohio, Indiana, and Illinois linking Lake Erie with the Ohio River and Lake Michigan with the Mississippi River. Pennsylvania's Grand Canal was the most ambitious, with an inclined plane to transport canal boats over the Appalachian Mountains.

By 1840 there were 3,300 miles of canals in the United States. In combination with roads and navigable rivers, a complex transportation network had been created in the states north of the Ohio River. The southern states still lacked transportation routes over the mountains, but as you can see on the map at right, navigable rivers served for moving cotton to coastal ports. Several southern roads, such

as the Fall Line Road, permitted access to new lands suitable for cotton growing.

None of the later canals was as successful as the Erie Canal, and Indiana's canal bankrupted the state. But the Illinois & Michigan Canal helped make Chicago the most important port on the Great Lakes, and the Ohio canals helped boost the state's population to third in the country. The canals opened the northern regions of Ohio, Indiana, and Illinois to settlement and led to statehood for Michigan in 1837 and Wisconsin in 1848.

Lasting Effects of the Canals

Today only small sections of the once-great canal system remain.

By 1850 canal fever had been cured by a new mechanized means of transportation—the railroad. Yet, though the Canal Age was brief, in the space of 25 years canals had made possible the movement of people and goods unprecedented in our history. They helped create population and commercial centers that are still important today. Early roads and canals of the frontier helped Americans push that frontier farther west.

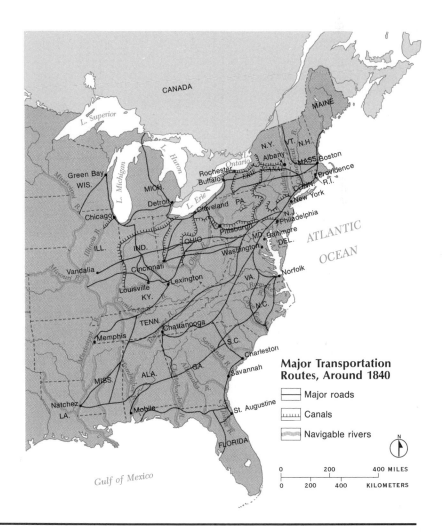

Major Transportation Routes, Around 1840

⎯⎯ Major roads

⊥⊥⊥⊥ Canals

≈≈≈ Navigable rivers

CHAPTER 11 REVIEW

Key Terms
Explain the meaning of each of the following terms:

> *Marbury* v. *Madison*
> judicial review
> Louisiana Purchase
> impressment
> freedom of the seas
> Embargo Act
> Non-Intercourse Act
> War Hawks
> Hartford Convention
> American System
> Panic of 1819
> Tallmadge Amendment
> Missouri Compromise
> Monroe Doctrine

Reviewing the Main Ideas

Section 1
1. What issues occupied Jefferson during his first term? In which areas did he succeed? In which did he fail to achieve his goals?
2. How did John Marshall strengthen the Supreme Court's powers in *Marbury* v. *Madison*?
3. How did the United States happen to acquire Louisiana? What constitutional questions were raised?

Section 2
1. Why did England and France both attack American ships after 1803? Why did the English impress sailors on American ships?
2. What was the purpose of the 1807 Embargo Act, and why did it fail? Why did the Non-Intercourse Act of 1809 also fail?
3. Why did relations with England deteriorate after 1810?

Section 3
1. What other causes besides impressment and freedom of the seas led to war with England?
2. Why did New England oppose the war?
3. Why did the U.S. fail to conquer Canada? Why can the war be considered a stalemate?

4. What happened to the northwestern and southern Indians as a result of the War of 1812? How did the Treaty of Ghent affect them?

Section 4
1. What issues united Americans during the "era of good feelings"?
2. What problem was highlighted by the fight over Missouri's entry into the Union? How was this issue settled temporarily?
3. Explain how the Rush-Bagot Agreement (1817) and the Adams-Onís Treaty (1819) benefited the United States.
4. Why did James Monroe proclaim the Monroe Doctrine? Why did it have little significance in 1823?

Special History Skills:
Working with Maps
A map can give you many kinds of information through the use of colors, symbols, and labels. Look at the map on page 281, which presents information about the Missouri Compromise and several boundary treaties. Use the map to answer these questions:

The Missouri Compromise
1. In what year did the Missouri Compromise take effect?
2. What state besides Missouri was involved in the compromise?
3. What was the name of the area opened to slavery by the Missouri Compromise?
4. Is this area east or west of the Mississippi River?
5. About how large is this area from east to west at its widest point?
6. Was the unorganized territory west of the Mississippi open to slavery?

Boundary Treaties
1. What two European nations made boundary treaties with the United States in 1818–1819?
2. Which nations claimed the Oregon Country in 1820?
3. What areas on this map are part of the Louisiana Purchase of 1803? (Refer also to the map on page 266.)
4. After its revolt from Spain in 1821, which country controlled the land that later became the state of Texas?

Other Skill Activities

1. Lewis and Clark

Find out more about the Lewis and Clark expedition. What items did they bring back? Why did these things cause such interest?

2. Crossword puzzle

Make a crossword puzzle using the names of people, events, and terms described in this chapter.

3. Military heroes who became President

William Henry Harrison and Andrew Jackson were war heroes who became President. Find out which other Presidents were once famous for their battlefield exploits.

Thinking Critically

1. How would the United States be different if Jefferson had decided not to buy Louisiana?
2. Some people think that the United States won the War of 1812. Others think that the United States lost it. Some think that the only real losers were the Indians. What is your opinion?
3. Jefferson tried to keep the United States out of war by getting Americans to accept a severe economic depression in place of war. What is your opinion of his policy? Could such a policy work today?
4. If you were an adviser to Jefferson, what would you have suggested that he do in response to the challenges of the "tiger" and the "shark"?
5. In 1819, Jefferson heard that "fire bell in the night." Forty-one years later, his worst fears would come true when the Union did break up after bitter disputes over the issue of slavery in the territories. Could anything have been done in 1820 to solve the problem before it grew more serious?

Further Reading

Walter Lord. *The Dawn's Early Light.* W. W. Norton and Co., 1972. Excellent history of the War of 1812.

Richard B. Morris. *The First Book of the War of 1812.* Franklin Watts, 1961. Easy reading that details land and naval battles in this conflict.

David C. Cooke. *Tecumseh: Destiny's Warrior.* Julian Messner Co., 1959. Shows Tecumseh as a military strategist, statesman, and humanitarian who was devoted to the cause of Indian unity and independence.

TEST YOURSELF

WRITE YOUR ANSWERS ON A SEPARATE SHEET OF PAPER.

Matching

Select the letter of the name that best matches each description below.

1. Chief Justice who defied Jefferson
2. Jefferson's secretary and explorer
3. Shoshone interpreter and explorer
4. President at time of the Missouri Compromise
5. tried to create an independent Indian nation
6. victor in the Battle of Tippecanoe
7. victor in the Battle of Lake Erie
8. wrote the "Star-Spangled Banner"
9. hero of the Battle of New Orleans
10. President during the War of 1812

a. Meriwether Lewis
b. William Henry Harrison
c. Oliver Hazard Perry
d. James Monroe
e. Francis Scott Key
f. Henry Clay
g. Sacajawea
h. Tecumseh
i. James Madison
j. Thomas Jefferson
k. Andrew Jackson
l. John Marshall

Fill in the Blanks

Events in Europe had much to do with shaping American history between 1801 and 1824. France's leader, (1) _____, needed money to fight a war against (2) _____ so he sold (3) _____ to the United States.

The United States carried on trade with both France and England. (4) _____ used its mighty navy to kidnap sailors from American ships and force them to serve in its navy. This practice was called (5) _____. Even though this angered Americans, Jefferson wanted to avoid war, so the (6) _____ was passed, which forbade all sea trade. This resulted in a depression which hurt the (7) _____ section of the country. The people of this region did not support the war, however, because of their commercial ties with England.

War finally broke out because the War Hawks wanted to defend the national (8) _____. They also claimed the British were helping (9) _____ on the frontier. In addition, they wanted to conquer (10) _____.

Chapter 12

THE AGE OF JACKSON

A new image of manhood developed in the 1820s and 1830s. Few flesh-and-blood men actually fit that ideal, yet it had a great influence on the way white males interpreted their daily lives and their political institutions.

What was this new American man like? Let us draw a sketch of him. He is white, Protestant, and native-born. His parents were hard-working, patriotic people of humble or "common" origins. Thus, he has no aristocratic background, no advantages of education, breeding, or what the revolutionary generation called "the habit of command."

He does, however, have self-confidence, ambition, and good common sense. He is practical, resourceful, without a head cluttered by "bookish notions." He is always keen to better his situation and ready to move on when opportunity calls. He has his eye on the future, not the past. He is a man of action and quick decision. Neither Nature nor any man can bend his will or defeat him. He is what his friends call a "self-made man." Like them, he reserves his respect for men who have made their fortunes by their own hands. He has contempt for lazy men, for elite men, and for racial groups he believes are inferior. Above all, he resents any law that ensures privileges to a few at the expense of "common men" like himself.

In this chapter we will look at the origins of this new image of the ideal American male. We will also see how the image affected politics.

Sections in This Chapter
1. The New American Man
2. A New Style and a New Party
3. The Jackson Presidency
4. The New Politics and Its Critics

Part of a "Protect Home Industries" metal banner from the 1840 Harrison-Tyler campaign. The tools represent various trades, such as shoemaking, carpentry, and tanning.

1. THE NEW AMERICAN MAN

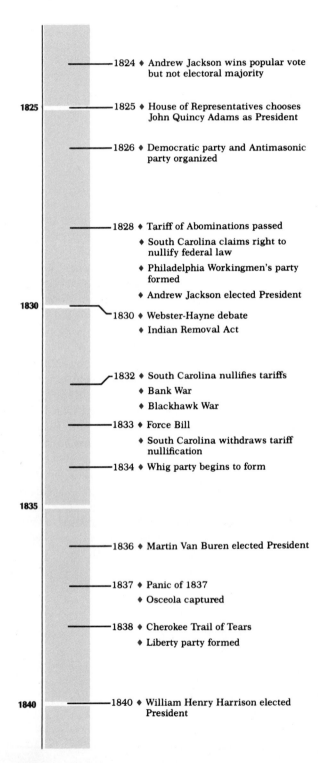

1824 ♦ Andrew Jackson wins popular vote but not electoral majority

1825

1825 ♦ House of Representatives chooses John Quincy Adams as President

1826 ♦ Democratic party and Antimasonic party organized

1828 ♦ Tariff of Abominations passed
   ♦ South Carolina claims right to nullify federal law
   ♦ Philadelphia Workingmen's party formed
   ♦ Andrew Jackson elected President

1830

1830 ♦ Webster-Hayne debate
   ♦ Indian Removal Act

1832 ♦ South Carolina nullifies tariffs
   ♦ Bank War
   ♦ Blackhawk War

1833 ♦ Force Bill
   ♦ South Carolina withdraws tariff nullification

1834 ♦ Whig party begins to form

1835

1836 ♦ Martin Van Buren elected President

1837 ♦ Panic of 1837
   ♦ Osceola captured

1838 ♦ Cherokee Trail of Tears
   ♦ Liberty party formed

1840

1840 ♦ William Henry Harrison elected President

The new ideal of the "**self-made man**" reflected several important changes in American life in the early 1800s. First, the era was one of great economic growth: the factory system arose, manufacturing increased, and profits from farming wheat, corn, and cotton soared. The average American expected to share in the new wealth of the nation and dreamed of going from rags to riches.

Second, America's rapid westward expansion weakened the power of the gentlemanly class over American life. The elite families of the eastern seaboard did not journey west toward the Mississippi, just as the aristocracy of England had not migrated to America in colonial times. Thus, new leaders arose in western communities, and new political power came to settlers in Indiana, Mississippi, and other new states. It is doubtful that many of these new leaders fit the rags-to-riches myth. However, few of them had family ties to the old aristocracy of the Northeast or the tobacco and rice regions of the South.

Third, and most important, were the changes in the American political system. These reforms encouraged ordinary men to believe that power and prestige could come to the talented among them. What were these remarkable reforms in American politics?

More White Men Could Vote

After the Revolution, a more democratic political system gradually developed. By the 1820s the vote had become the right of every free white male citizen. The newer western states led this reform by dropping restrictions on suffrage (voting) for white males. Soon, the older seaboard states followed suit. By 1818, Connecticut had opened up politics to all white men; Massachusetts and New York did the same a few years later. Although political leaders called this change "universal suffrage," it was not. Women, most free blacks, slaves, and Indians were excluded. Thus the majority of Americans still could not vote or hold office.

The new suffrage laws did mean many thousands of new voters at the polls each year. The "common man" was indeed a new force in politics. As political leaders learned, this new voter often wanted to elect "self-made men" to office.

The Voter's Power Increased

The actual power of the voter also increased in the 1820s. Most of the new and amended state constitutions called for popular election of officers who had traditionally been appointed. Nearly all state and county administrators now had to run for election. In some states, even judges were elected to the bench. The choice of presidential electors was placed directly in the hands of the voters in every state but Delaware and South Carolina.

New techniques for nominating candidates were developed in the 1820s. Instead of relying on senators, congressmen, and other party leaders to **caucus** (select candidates in private), voters supported **nominating conventions**. These conventions, like our party conventions today, included more people in the decision-making process.

The Reality of the Rags-to-Riches Dream

It is important to remember that the successful, self-reliant, self-made man was an ideal, not an everyday reality. He was a product of wishes and dreams. In fact, there was not much actual social mobility. The gap between the rich and the poor was greater in this "era of the common man" than it had ever been before.

Wealth was concentrated in the hands of a small number of industrialists, planters, and businessmen. Economic growth was very uneven and unpredictable. Panics and depressions became regular events in a cycle of boom-and-bust. This business cycle continued through the century. As you saw in Chapter 11, the Panic of 1819 wiped out many people's savings. In this chapter, you will see that the Panic of 1837 did the same.

Though families moved frequently, selling their farms for new opportunities farther west, few actually moved up the ladder of success. The likelihood of going from rags to riches was even slimmer in the cities of the older states. Here working people, especially unskilled immigrants, had little hope of rising out of poverty. Even their children rarely managed to improve the family's economic status. These urban poor could not escape to the frontier. Transportation west, farm

Election Day in Philadelphia, 1816

tools, and even the low-priced public lands were beyond their financial means. Though historian Frederick Jackson Turner and others would later speak of the frontier as a "safety valve" for the problems of poverty, it did not really serve as one.

SECTION 1 REVIEW

 Identify: self-made man, caucus, nominating convention

Main Ideas

1. How did (**a**) economic growth, (**b**) westward expansion, and (**c**) changes in the political system encourage the ideal of the self-made man?
2. To whom was the right to vote extended in the early 1800s? How did the voter's power increase?
3. How realistic was the rags-to-riches dream for farmers and city dwellers? Why?

2. A NEW STYLE AND A NEW PARTY

If you were a young Kentucky boy or girl in 1824, you would certainly have heard of Andrew Jackson. Your older brother, already sporting his own Kentucky rifle, would be singing or humming the most popular song of the day, "The Hunters of Kentucky." The countless verses of this song told of Jackson's heroic victories in the Battle of New Orleans.

Your father would be about to cast his vote for Andy Jackson as President of the United States. For your father, and for hundreds of western farmers like him, "Old Hickory" was the symbol of a new era dawning. He was the perfect example of the "self-made man." That is why both his contemporaries and historians today call the period from 1824 to 1840 "The Age of Jackson."

The Death of the Rebublican Party

In 1824, American politics was in a state of confusion. For 24 years the Republican party had dominated the government. Unity and solidarity had seemed to reign. An almost stately procession of Virginia gentlemen-planters filled the presidency, with Jefferson selecting his Secretary of State, James Madison, to succeed him, and Madison picking his Secretary of State, James Monroe, to follow him. But this **Virginia Dynasty**, as these administrations were called, came to an end when Monroe retired from office in early 1825. Monroe's Secretary of State, the brilliant but crotchety John Quincy Adams, was a faithful son of Massachusetts.

When Monroe stepped down from the presidency, more ended than the Virginia Dynasty. The Republican party collapsed. Torn apart by competition in its leadership, it was no longer one party, but many parties.

The division in the party began during Monroe's second term. It became clear when party leaders went to select a presidential nominee. Five men put themselves forward to the party caucus.

Down With "King Caucus"!

The Republican party caucus selected William Crawford of Georgia to carry the party's standard. The four disappointed candidates did not accept this choice. Three of them vowed to defy the party's tradition of one candidate and declared they would stay in the race. They publicly attacked the caucus method of choosing candidates as "undemocratic." Each candidate then held carefully staged nominating conventions in various states. Thus they entered the race for the presidency as popular candidates rather than as the choice of "King Caucus."

When the election returns were counted, the Tennessee lawyer and judge, Andrew Jackson, had carried the popular vote. This western slaveholder and military hero received 154,000 votes to John Quincy Adams' 109,000. "Harry of the West," Henry Clay, won 47,000 votes. Crawford, who had been paralyzed by a stroke in September 1823, polled only a few hundred less than Clay.

Over 350,000 men had gone to the polls to pick their President. They had clearly chosen the newcomer, Jackson. But he did not win! In the electoral college he did not gain the necessary majority. Jackson won 99 votes to Adams' 84; the remaining 78 votes were divided between William Crawford and Henry Clay.

The House Elects the President

The election went to the House of Representatives. Immediately, a new round of electioneering began. Adams had a slight edge in the House, with nine states favoring him. Clay realized that his cause was hopeless and threw his support to Adams. Clay's four states gave Adams 13 votes, and thus a majority. The sixth President of the United States was **John Quincy Adams**.

Down with Corrupt Bargains!

The Jackson forces were still smarting from their defeat when Adams made public his appointment of Clay as Secretary of State. The choice was a logical one, because the two shared similar views on government planning and assistance to promote economic growth. Jackson backers, however, screamed "corrupt bargain," insisting that Clay had sold the presidency to Adams in exchange for this cabinet post. Thus, even before Adams began his term in office, Jackson was campaigning for the presidency in 1828. "The Puritan and the Blackleg,"* as Jackson men nicknamed Adams and Clay, were in for a difficult four years.

*blackleg a popular term meaning "pirate."

"A Lighthouse in the Sky"

Even without Jackson's fierce opposition, John Quincy Adams would not have been likely to succeed in office. Like his father, John Adams, he was a man of learning and vision. Like his father, he was stubborn and self-defeating. The bold program of government planning that Adams proposed required a more diplomatic and politically cunning man to steer it through Congress and to convince the voters of its value.

In his inaugural address, Adams called for broad federal development programs, including laws to promote agriculture and industry and aid to the arts and sciences. He proposed a national university and an astronomical observatory to study the heavens. Few congressmen were willing to vote funds for this "lighthouse in the sky." They might have approved some of Adams' proposals if he had actively campaigned for them. But Adams would not wheel or deal. He refused to use his great powers of patronage to win congressional votes. He even refused to replace with friends known political enemies in federal offices. In four years he removed only 12 people from office.

By 1827, Congress was controlled by Jackson forces, who harassed President Adams and embarrassed him politically at every opportunity. Stubbornly, and to the great delight of the Jacksonians, the proud New Englander committed political suicide.

The Election of 1828

Jackson's supporters were more than ready for the 1828 campaign. Over the last three years they had worked to form a coalition (alliance of interests) between the West and the South. John C. Calhoun's support ensured their success. Jacksonians had also won support in key northern states such as New York and Pennsylvania. By 1828, New England—and Adams—were politically isolated.

The mastermind of this new coalition was not Jackson. It was **Martin Van Buren**, a short, redheaded son of Dutch tavernkeepers from Kinderhook, New York. "Van" was the most striking example of the new American politician and the self-made man. He had risen from humble origins by his wits and talent. Like many of the new political figures, he loved the excitement of mass politics, with its nominating conventions, lavish campaigns, and techniques of wooing the voter.

He was openly a party man. He believed that getting elected to office and staying in power were the party man's main goals. The people, he was fond of saying, would turn out of office anyone they did not like. This was, after all, the essence of democracy. Van Buren's confidence that party politics and open office-seeking were good for America is the most striking difference between the revolutionary generation and the new generation of American leaders.

Van Buren was a brilliant political organizer. His own New York party machine, the "Albany Regency," was a tightly run, successful organization for office-getting and office-holding. It was built on patronage, party loyalty, and discipline. Van Buren created a similar machine for Andrew Jackson.

When 1828 came, this new **Democratic party** was ready. The campaign was a spectacle of rallies, speeches, songs, and slogans. Jacksonians spent over a million dollars to get their candidate elected. The Democrats labeled Adams an aristocrat and a friend of privilege. In the newly written verses to the "Hunters of Kentucky," Jackson the Democrat was compared to Adams the Elitist:

> We are a hardy free-born race
> Who always fight for glory
> And never give our votes to place
> As President, a Tory.

John Quincy Adams (1767–1848)

IN OFFICE: 1825–1829

From Massachusetts. Adams was elected by the House of Representatives because the election of 1824 failed to give any one candidate a majority of electoral votes. Adams favored a program of extensive internal improvements, but Congress did not cooperate with him. The Tariff of Abominations (1828), passed during his term, hurt his chances for re-election.

Adams' supporters were less well organized, but they could sling mud also. They attacked Jackson as a gambler, a drunkard, and a murderer of innocent Indian women and children. Raking up an event of about 35 years before, they called Jackson an adulterer, for his beloved wife Rachel's divorce from her first husband may not have been totally legal. Jackson never forgot this last accusation. When Rachel Jackson died shortly after her husband became President, Jackson blamed the campaign slurs for her death.

Few real issues were raised amidst all the hoopla. Everyone knew what Adams stood for, and most voters thought they knew what Andy Jackson represented. He appeared to the average American as the ultimate self-made man—a man who managed to be exceptional and common at the same time.

Over a million voters felt the choice between Adams and Jackson was important. Jackson won 647,000 votes to Adams' 508,000. However, the electoral college vote told the real story of the Jackson party victory. Jackson received 178 electoral votes to Adams' 83. The campaign tactics of winning over key states had carried Jackson to the White House. Thus, in 1828 both a new party and a new style of politics were born.

SECTION 2 REVIEW

 Identify: Virginia Dynasty, John Quincy Adams, Martin Van Buren, Democratic party

Main Ideas
1. Describe the 1824 election. In what ways was it unusual?
2. Was Henry Clay's support for Adams "corrupt"? Why did Jackson supporters claim that it was?
3. Why did John Quincy Adams fail to win support for his broad federal programs? Why wasn't he re-elected President?
4. What was the winning strategy of the Democratic party in 1828?
5. What was the long-range significance of the election of 1828?

3. THE JACKSON PRESIDENCY

The nation almost lost its new President on Inauguration Day. Mobs of people crashed the President's reception at the White House. They knocked over tables of ice cream, cake, and punch in a mad press to meet their hero. Jackson was nearly trampled to death! The President was as shocked as anyone by the events of the day. His opponents, however, thought that the wild scene was just what Jackson deserved. After all, they said, Old Hickory's election was a victory for "King Mob."

Jackson Settles into Office
Jackson did not let "King Mob" rule. He did, however, bring many new faces to the capital. Unlike John Quincy Adams, the new President dismissed old officeholders, and appointed loyal party members in their places. As Democratic politician William Marcy, senator from New York, put it in 1831: "To the victor belongs the spoils." And government jobs were the choicest spoils of the day.

Jackson saw nothing wrong with this use of **patronage** (which opponents called the "spoils system"). He believed that any ordinary American could satisfy the job requirements of a government position. He reasoned that if each President's own loyal supporters were appointed to the jobs that needed doing, the result would be a rotation in office. This rotation in office, Jackson said, was democratic. This combination of practical politics and democratic principles was typical of the seventh President.

Jackson proved to be a strong and forceful national leader. He appointed to his cabinet men he could dominate and ran his cabinet meetings the way a general runs a military staff meeting. He used the presidential veto 12 times to kill laws he did not like. All the Presidents before him had used the veto very sparingly, and only to prevent laws they felt were unconstitutional.

The Tariff of Abominations
Jackson's first serious crisis in office came almost immediately. It was, in part, the result of his own efforts to gain the presidency.

In 1828, Jackson supporters in Congress had introduced a new, and shockingly high, protective tariff that would price certain imported raw materials like iron off the market. The Jacksonians thought this gesture would win them support in the industrial areas of Pennsylvania and New York. But they also felt confident that President Adams would veto the tariff. Thus none of the consumer states of the South or West would actually suffer. Adams did not veto the tariff, however. Southern leaders immediately denounced the new legislation as a "**Tariff of Abominations.**"

When Andrew Jackson took office in 1829, he faced angry southern congressmen who felt that their section of the country was being treated unfairly. **John C. Calhoun**, Jackson's own Vice-President, was the strongest voice in the southern protest. The 1828 Tariff of Abominations had led Calhoun to give up his nationalist views and to champion southern rights.

At the request of the South Carolina legislature, Calhoun drafted a position paper on the new tariff. This *South Carolina Exposition and Protest* (1828) raised once again the troubling question: which government held the ultimate power in the United States—an individual state or the federal government? Like Jefferson in his Kentucky Resolves and the Federalists at the Hartford Convention, Calhoun argued that a state had the right to nullify (cancel; make void) any federal law that threatened its welfare.

The Nullification Issue Heats Up
In January 1830, the nullification issue reached the floor of the Senate. A debate arose between a Connecticut and a Tennessee senator over the government's policy on the sale of western lands. Suddenly, Robert Y. Hayne of South Carolina took the floor, eager to show the western senators that the South was their true and natural ally in politics. This struggle to win the support of the West was an important contest between the northern and southern interests. In this case, Hayne's efforts proved disastrous. Hayne quickly moved from a discussion of western lands to a discussion of the nature of the federal union itself. Soon he was in the midst of an impassioned lecture on states' rights.

Senator Daniel Webster of Massachusetts, a big, burly man, who some said could out-talk the Devil himself, rose to answer Hayne. Thus began the dramatic **Webster-Hayne debate**, which lasted more than a week. Webster defended the supremacy of the national government under the Constitution. Hayne defended the sovereignty of the states. Webster closed his oration with the words that became the rallying cry of Union forces: "Liberty *and* Union, now and forever, one and inseparable!"

The President soon entered the unfolding drama. Jackson's politics were often vague and contradictory, but on one issue he was clear: the Union could not be dissolved. At a Jefferson Day dinner in April, Jackson and Vice-President Calhoun exchanged verbal fire. During a long round of toasts, the President rose and lifted his glass: "Our Union—it must be preserved." Calhoun, eyes blazing, rose to respond: "The Union—next to our liberty, most dear!"

Civil War Threatens
In 1832, efforts were made to lower the protective tariff rates and calm southern anger. But later that year, a special South Carolina state convention met and nullified both the original tariff of 1828 and the new 1832 tariff. The state also declared that no federal customs would be collected in South Carolina after January 31, 1833. The regular state legislature then voted funds for a military force.

Senator Hayne resigned from the Senate and returned to his home state to be governor and

Andrew Jackson (1767–1845)

IN OFFICE: 1829–1837

Democrat from Tennessee. Jackson's administration promoted the "spoils system," checked the program of federal internal improvements, and vetoed the recharter of the second Bank of the United States (1832). He asserted the authority of the federal government in the issue of nullification, and greatly expanded presidential power. During his term the eastern Indians were forced to move to lands west of the Mississippi.

commander-in-chief of South Carolina's army. Andrew Jackson, outraged by these events, issued a proclamation in December 1832 condemning nullification. He called South Carolina's military provisions "positive treason." The **nullification crisis** had begun in earnest.

In January 1833, Congress voted a Force Bill, approving the use of federal troops to collect customs duties in South Carolina. As the year began, bloodshed seemed likely. But cooler heads now began to prevail. Henry Clay produced a compromise tariff. In South Carolina, moderates also took the stage. They reminded firebrands like Hayne that South Carolina stood alone and unaided in this struggle.

The nullification crisis ended when South Carolina withdrew its nullification of the two tariffs. The principle of nullification and states' rights was not given up, however. The state legislature voted to nullify the federal Force Bill. It was only a gesture, for troops were no longer needed. But it was a sign of trouble to come. States' rights—once a concern of New Englanders as well as southerners—was now a purely sectional issue.

The Role of the Bank

In 1832, Andy Jackson went to battle once again, this time against the Bank of the United States.

Cartoon poking fun at Jackson's "Bank War"

Jackson declared the Bank a "Monster" and determined to kill it before it killed American democracy.

What was there about the Second Bank of the United States, you might wonder, that roused the passions of the President? The Bank, chartered for 20 years in 1816, was one of the country's few national institutions. Like the first Bank, its stock was held by the government and by private investors, both American and foreign. Nicholas Biddle had been president of the Bank since 1823, and distinguished politicians like Daniel Webster served on the Bank's board of directors.

The Bank seemed to be doing its job well, keeping the nation's currency stable and regulating inflation. It did this in two ways. First, it checked up on local banks, watching the amount of paper money, or bank notes, these banks issued. By requiring these banks to redeem their notes in specie (metal money; coin), the Bank of the United States made sure that gold and silver actually backed the paper money. This policing action helped prevent inflation. However, it also kept the specie holdings of local banks small, and thus loans to local business owners were costly.

The Opponents of the Bank

As you can imagine, ambitious local bankers and ambitious local business people resented the Bank's power. Other groups opposed the Bank too. New York financiers and politicians did not like the fact that all the customs duties collected in New York were sent to Philadelphia, where the Bank's main branch was located. Democratic party leaders held a grudge against Biddle and his Bank because they suspected it had supported John Quincy Adams in the 1828 election.

Finally, some fiercely nationalistic Americans were suspicious of the Bank because foreign investors held stock in it. We now know that this patriotism was misguided, because foreign capital was needed to develop American factories, roads, and canals in that era. But at the time this viewpoint seemed reasonable; many Americans feared that foreigners would use the Bank to control the nation's affairs.

The greatest enemy of the Bank was Old Hickory himself. Jackson was convinced that the "Monster" stood for privilege and special treatment, which were out of place in a democracy. To some extent, this was true. The richest businessmen did benefit from large loans from the Bank. But it was not necessarily true that the death of the Bank would benefit ordinary Americans.

Jackson Slays the Monster

The Bank's charter was not up for renewal until 1836, but Henry Clay convinced Bank president Biddle to reapply in 1832. When Congress approved the rechartering of the Bank, Jackson promptly vetoed the bill. In a rousing veto message, Jackson announced that democracy had triumphed over special privilege. The Monster was dead. Thus did Jackson win his **Bank War**.

Pet Banks, Inflation, and Panic

Did ordinary Americans benefit from the victory? Unfortunately, Jackson had no effective alternative to a central bank. Where would government tax monies be kept? How would paper money be regulated? Who would prevent fly-by-night banks from rising up and cheating the public? Jackson's only action was to remove the government's deposits from Biddle's bank and put them in various state banks. Jackson's opponents observed that these "**pet banks**" were now the privileged banking institutions.

The pet banks could do little to regulate their competitors. Soon paper money of little or no value began to flood the nation. The destruction of the Bank was a major cause of the **Panic of 1837**. In that year, banks collapsed, inflation spread, and many small business owners and farmers were ruined. As Jackson left office in 1837, a major depression was on its way.

The Removal of the Indians

The American concern for equal opportunity and greater democracy had big blind spots. For example, Andrew Jackson, and many Americans like him, did not consider the Indian nations worthy of concern or protection. As you saw in Chapter 11, the War of 1812 spelled the defeat of Indians in the South and Northwest in their struggle against westward expansion. During Jackson's administration, almost all these Indian peoples were dispossessed—driven out of their homes and off their lands. They were forced to move west beyond the Mississippi River to "Indian Country." This was a vaguely defined region on the Great Plains which was then thought to be a desert and therefore useless for white settlement.

About 53,000 Creeks, Cherokees, Choctaws, and Chickasaws still lived in the South when Jackson took office. But white farmers, gold-seekers, and land speculators pressured state governments to force the Indians to sell their lands. These whites argued that all Indians were "savages" who did not cultivate the land and who blocked the progress of civilized people.

This image of the Indian as a hunter-savage was so convenient that people refused to give it up even in the face of reality. For example, the Cherokees of Georgia had been farmers for many decades. They were a rich and literate community, with books in their native language and a weekly newspaper, the *Cherokee Phoenix*. Many

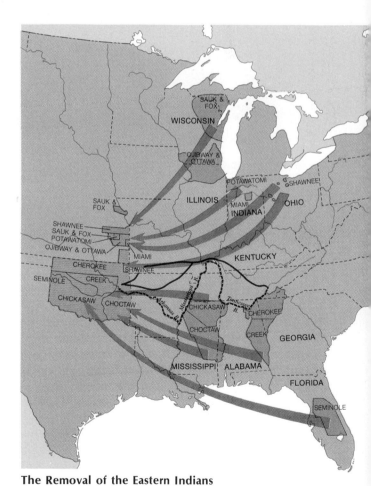

The Removal of the Eastern Indians

━━━ Cherokee Trail of Tears land route

----- Cherokee Trail of Tears water route

◀━━ Other Indian removals

0   150   300 MILES
0   150   300   KILOMETERS

Modern painting of the Trail of Tears by Jerome Tiger, a Creek-Seminole

were wealthy slaveholders. By the standards of the times, the Cherokees were "model" Americans. But they were not white Americans.

In 1828, the Georgia legislature denied the Cherokee nation's right to their farmland. It ordered them off the land and out of the state. In 1830, Jackson's administration passed an **Indian Removal Act** which allowed the federal government to seize most Indian lands so long as some compensation was paid for the property.

The Cherokees took their case to the Supreme Court. In 1832, Chief Justice John Marshall ruled that the Georgia action was unconstitutional. But Marshall could not hold back the tide of Indian removals. It was up to the executive branch of government to enforce the law. The President himself ignored the Supreme Court's ruling and gave his wholehearted support to the massive relocation of the Cherokee Indians.

In 1838, the American army **uprooted** the Cherokees of Georgia and placed **them** in detention camps. Then 15,000 men, women, and children were forced to march westward, mostly on foot, to what is now Oklahoma. (See map, page 297.) About 4,000 of these victims of land-hunger and racism died on the brutal journey known to history as the **Trail of Tears**.

The other Indians of the South and the Northwest suffered similar fates. In Illinois, the Sauk and Fox nations were driven west in 1831 after squatters took over their lands. The Sauk and Fox encountered enemy Indian nations to the west and, led by Chief Black Hawk, some of them fled back to Illinois for protection. In 1832, they could be seen, hungry and weary, on their old lands. But these Indians were not welcomed. In the

Tiger '66

FROM THE ARCHIVES

The Trail of Tears

The following excerpts are from two eyewitness descriptions of the Trail of Tears.

The sick and feeble were carried in waggons . . . a great many ride on horseback and multitudes go on foot—even aged females, apparently ready to drop into the grave, were traveling with heavy burdens attached to the back—on the sometimes frozen ground, and sometimes muddy streets, with no covering for their feet except what nature had given them. . . . We learned from the inhabitants on the road where the Indians passed, they buried fourteen or fifteen at every stopping place.

She could only carry her dying child in her arms a few miles farther, and then she must stop in a stranger-land and consign her much loved babe to the cold ground, and that too without pomp or ceremony, and pass on with the multitude. . . . I turned from the sight with feelings which language cannot express and wept like childhood then.

Quoted in *Indian Removal* by Grant Foreman. Norman, Oklahoma, Press, 1953, pp. 306, 307.

Black Hawk War of 1832 an Illinois militia unit attacked and massacred about 1,000 of these starving refugees.

Beginning in 1835, the Seminoles of Florida resisted United States efforts to deport them beyond the Mississippi. Chief **Osceola**, with the help of black fugitives from slavery, led his people's fight until 1837, when he was treacherously captured by an American general who had invited him to talk peace under a flag of truce.

The **Seminole War** continued until 1842, and it cost the United States 2,000 soldiers' lives and millions of dollars to defeat the Seminole nation. In fact, it was, up to that time, one of the bloodiest and costliest wars that American troops had ever fought. But the victory was complete, for the Seminole Indians were almost all killed by the military.

SECTION 3 REVIEW

Identify: patronage, Tariff of Abominations, John C. Calhoun, Webster-Hayne debate, nullification crisis, Bank War, pet banks, Panic of 1837, Indian Removal Act, Trail of Tears, Black Hawk War, Osceola, Seminole War

Main Ideas

1. How did Andrew Jackson explain his policy of removing enemies in office and replacing them with friends?
2. What led to the South Carolina nullification crisis? How was the crisis resolved?
3. List the arguments for and against the rechartering of the Bank of the United States.
4. How did the "death" of the Bank affect the economy?
5. What led white people to ignore the legal and moral rights of the Indians? What tribes were relocated during this period?

4. THE NEW POLITICS AND ITS CRITICS

Like much of American life, American politics was transformed during the 1820s and 1830s. More men voted, and a new kind of man got elected. Officeholding was no longer the obligation and right of only the wealthy and well-educated. Instead, the men who sought office were often professional politicians, whose careers revolved around getting and keeping public office.

The new politicians tended to avoid controversial issues in their campaigns. They concentrated on what we might call their "image" and presented themselves as common men and champions of the people. They relied on party organizations to get elected. They waged lavish campaigns, and, at least every four years, treated the voter as if he were a king.

The Rise of the Whigs

By 1834, two national parties had emerged: the Democratic party of Andrew Jackson and the Whig party of his enemies. These parties were mainly vast vote-getting machines that challenged each other in local, congressional, and presidential elections. Yet, because they were *national* parties, they helped preserve the Union. As you will see in the coming chapters, party loyalty held the nation together during several sectional crises. But the price for party loyalty was often the avoidance of important political and economic issues.

Who became a Democrat? Who became a Whig? The Democratic party was led by wealthy southern planters and ambitious, rising businessmen. It usually won the voting support of ordinary farmers, small town businessmen, and the new urban immigrants. For these voters, Jackson and his new party represented equal economic opportunity and concern for the common people.

The **Whig party** was led by the wealthiest city people. Most of New York City's 1,000 richest citizens were Whigs. But many southern planters were also active Whigs. At the polls, the more successful commercial farmers, small businessmen in prosperous areas, and non-immigrant workers were likely to vote the Whig ticket.

Were the two parties different in their approach to the voter? Not really. In 1836, when Old Hickory was about to retire from office, the Whig party was young and still divided. It ran three candidates for the presidency that year, William Henry Harrison of Ohio, Daniel Webster of Massachusetts, and Hugh White of Tennessee. **Martin Van Buren**, the Democratic nominee, won the election easily.

By 1840, the Whigs had learned to manage a presidential campaign as well as their opponents.

Martin Van Buren (1782–1862)

IN OFFICE: 1837–1841

Democrat from New York. Van Buren's popularity declined as a result of the Panic of 1837 and a severe economic depression which began several months after his inauguration. His plan to replace the second Bank of the United States with an independent treasury system was put into effect in 1840. He was the presidential nominee of the Free-Soil party in 1848.

William Henry Harrison (1773–1841)

IN OFFICE: 1841

Whig from Ohio. Harrison's campaign, based on the popular appeal of parades, songs, and mass meetings, set a new pattern for presidential campaigns and won him the presidency. He called a special session of Congress to enact his party's program, but his death from pneumonia, one month after his inauguration, prevented him from carrying out his legislative plan.

That year they nominated **William Henry Harrison**, the hero of the Battle of Tippecanoe. They took care to present Harrison as a rough-cut, honest, simple man of the frontier. Along the campaign trail, Harrison traveled with a miniature log cabin, a symbol of his alleged humble origins. In parades and at rallies, the Whigs sang:

> Farewell dear Van
> You're not our man.
> To guide the ship
> We'll try old Tip.

The Whigs portrayed Van Buren as an elitist, a snob, and a man who had failed to bring the nation out of the depression that followed the Bank War. As you remember, Jacksonians had used similar tactics against Adams in 1828.

Over 2.4 million voters went to the polls in 1840. William Henry Harrison and his running mate, John Tyler of Virginia, carried the day. The Age of Jackson was over; it was the era of "Tippecanoe and Tyler too."

LIFE IN AMERICA

CAMPAIGN MEMORABILIA

As the number of people who could vote grew, so did the amount of campaign memorabilia—election junk. Buttons, banners, and bumper stickers have been with us almost from the start of the Union. A clothing button proclaiming, "Long Live the President" and the initials "G.W." was distributed in 1789 after Washington's election. Even before that, however, a potter had printed "J. Hanson and Trade Forever" on a pitcher. (John Hanson was our first U.S. President under the Articles of Confederation.)

At first, various political items were used to commemorate a person's election, but soon they became part of the election campaign itself. Over the years, politicians have had their names on everything from cast-iron frogs to ballpoint pens. The trend has been away from usable items (the frog could be used as a doorstop) to throwaways like ribbons and pins.

In 1828, Jackson appealed to the electorate by advertising himself as the hero of the Battle of New Orleans. His supporters made much of the fact that Jackson had won the popular vote in 1824 by a large majority. A crock from the 1828 election, for example, shows a ship, an American flag, and the inscription, "25,000 majority Gnl. Jackson."

Two souvenirs of Jackson's 1824 campaign: a cast-iron frog and a sewing box

Since not everyone could read, candidates soon began to advertise themselves using symbols. The most popular symbol was the log cabin, which suggested a candidate's humble origins. The first candidate to use this symbol may have been William Henry Harrison, who spent most of his adult life as an officer and governor on the Indiana frontier. But his origins were not at all humble. He was from a distinguished and wealthy family of Virginia planters.

The Rise of Third Parties

There were men and women who felt that a choice between Whigs and Democrats was no choice at all. During the 1820s and 1830s several smaller political parties arose to speak out on controversial issues or to speak up for certain minority groups. The most important of these parties were the workingmen's parties, the Antimasonic party, and the Liberty party.

The Workingmen's Parties

In 1828, bricklayers, painters, glassmakers, carpenters, and a host of other craftsmen joined to form the Philadelphia Workingmen's Party. This independent party planned to nominate candidates who supported "the interests and the en-

Spinning cotton in an early 19th-century factory. Note the small child working behind the threads.

lightenment of the working classes." Similar **workingmen's parties** quickly rose up across the nation. The largest ones were in Philadelphia and New York, but many were formed in rural areas by farmers who considered themselves "workingmen" too.

These workingmen's parties called attention to real and pressing needs of ordinary citizens. They demanded shorter work hours, better working conditions, free tax-supported schools, inexpensive legal services, an end to debtor's prisons, clean streets and better sanitation, and reforms in land laws. The "10-hour day" was a rallying call for factory workers in the Northeast.

The workingmen's parties did not object to nominating wealthy candidates for office, so long as they were committed to reform platforms. Thus the candidates were often men of a different class from the voters. The party leadership remained workingmen, however.

The workingmen's parties rarely survived more than five years, for their leaders were inexperienced, the newspapers were usually hostile, and the major parties opposed them. Yet they were influential: the reform demands of these workingmen were often adopted by the major parties.

The Antimasonic Party

To some, secret societies like the Masons were elitist threats to American democracy. The Masons had once been a political and religious organization in Europe, but in America Masonic lodges were largely social clubs. Many of the wealthiest and most influential American leaders were members of this secret fraternity, among them Andrew Jackson and Daniel Webster.

The Masons often helped lodge brothers find jobs, supported each others' businesses, and provided what we would call "an old boys' network" throughout the country. But charges that Masons planned to take over the country were what led many voters to fear the society.

The **Antimasonic party** rose to public attention in 1826, when William Morgan, a critic of the Masons, mysteriously disappeared. Morgan had been in a New York state jail on what his supporters called trumped-up charges. On his release, a man came to pick up Morgan, who was never heard from again. Antimasons claimed that lodge brothers had kidnapped Morgan in order to silence him.

The Morgan disappearance prompted many rural New Englanders and New Yorkers to join the Antimasonic crusade. These people were fresh from a religious revival that had swept across the northern states (see Chapter 13), and they brought an air of a moral crusade to the Antimasonic movement. The leaders of the new party, however, were professional politicians much like the leaders of the Democratic and Whig parties. In 1831, William Wirt, who had once been a Mason himself, converted suddenly to Antimasonism—just in time to be the party's first candidate for the presidency.

For almost a decade, the Antimasonic party was strong in Vermont, Rhode Island, Pennsylvania, and New York. It forced many Masonic lodges to disband. In the 1830s the party also began to support reform issues like temperance* and abolition. But as the Whig party also began to take up these issues, the Antimasonic voters gradually began to vote as Whigs.

The Liberty Party

Congress and the major parties made every effort to keep silent about slavery. When petitions for the abolition of slavery in Washington, D.C., flooded the Congress in 1836, the Senate passed a **gag rule** to forbid discussion of the issue. The following year a stronger gag rule was passed. Even the House of Representatives, which was controlled by the free states, tried to ignore the demands for abolition in the nation's capital.

Most members of Congress believed that a debate on slavery in the District of Columbia would lead to a much-feared confrontation between the North and the South. Only John Quincy Adams, who had become a representative from Massachusetts, spoke out against the gag rules. His defense of the freedom of petition earned him the title "Old Man Eloquent."

Outside the Congress, voices were being raised on slavery. As you will see in the next chapter, antislavery societies multiplied during this era. In 1838, a small group of abolitionists met to form the **Liberty party**. Its first candidate for the presidency was James Birney, a former slaveholder from Kentucky.

In the election of 1840, Birney received only 1/10 of 1% of the vote. This did not reflect the strength of the antislavery movement, however. Many abolitionists preferred to use moral persuasion rather than politics in their struggle against slavery. Others felt it was unwise to create a third party. They wanted to win a major party to their cause.

The Liberty party did greatly influence American politics, however. In 1844, for example, its strong showing in New York State cost Henry Clay the presidency. Like many third parties in American history, the Liberty party could not win an election, but it could make the difference between victory and defeat for a major party candidate.

The workingmen's parties, the Antimasons, and the Liberty party all tell us something about the nature of politics in the "era of the common man." They arose to fill a vacuum created by the major parties' avoidance of troublesome issues and concentration on personalities. These third parties took seriously the major ideals of the day: an end to privilege, greater opportunity for the ordinary citizen, and freedom for all Americans. In the next chapter, you will see how vigorously other Americans worked to make these ideals a reality.

SECTION 4 REVIEW

Identify: Whig party, Martin Van Buren, William Henry Harrison, workingmen's parties, Antimasonic party, gag rule, Liberty party

Main Ideas
1. What was the "new politics," and who were the new politicians?
2. Who led the Democratic party? The Whig party? What were the main differences between the Democrats and the Whigs?
3. Describe some important aspects of the 1840 presidential campaign.
4. Why did third parties arise in the 1820s and 1830s? Discuss one of these parties and explain its importance.

---

*temperance movement against the excessive use of alcoholic beverages.

CHAPTER 12 REVIEW

Key Terms
Explain the meaning of each of the following terms:

self-made man	nullification crisis
caucus	Bank War
nominating	pet banks
convention	Panic of 1837
Virginia	Indian Removal Act
Dynasty	Trail of Tears
Democratic	Black Hawk War
party	Seminole War
patronage	Whig party
Tariff of	workingmen's parties
Abominations	Antimasonic party
Webster-Hayne	gag rule
debate	Liberty party

Reviewing the Main Ideas

Section 1
1. Why did the "self-made man" become the ideal American at this time? How realistic was this image?
2. What political changes made the voter more important?

Section 2
1. Why was the election of 1824 unusual?
2. What political problems did John Quincy Adams face during his presidency?
3. What was the significance of the 1828 election?

Section 3
1. How did Jackson justify his use of patronage to reward political supporters?
2. How did sectional disagreement over a tariff almost lead to civil war? How was the crisis resolved?
3. Why did many people criticize the Bank of the United States? What happened when it lost its charter?
4. What happened to Indians of the South and the Northwest during Jackson's administration? How were these acts justified?

Section 4
1. How did political campaigns change during the 1820s and 1830s?
2. Who were Whigs? Who were Democrats? What campaign tactics made these two major parties similar?
3. What third parties arose in the 1820s and 1830s? Why were they important?

Special History Skills:
Develop Your Economics Vocabulary
Several important economics terms are used in this chapter that will be used again in the text. You will also see them used in discussions of current economic issues.

Look up the definition of each of the following words in the glossary of this text and in a dictionary. Write a definition for each; then use each word in a sentence or two to show that you understand its meaning.

investor	capital
inflation	panic
specie	depression
financier	

Other Skill Activities
1. **Growing voter participation**
   Using the information given in the text, make a chart that shows the number of voters casting ballots in the 1824, 1828, and 1840 presidential elections. Then make a line graph with the same information.
2. **Defend or reject**
   Prepare to defend or reject the following statement in class: "Professional politicians are masters at manipulating the voters and later disregarding their wishes."
3. **The Trail of Tears**
   Find out more about conditions on the Cherokee Trail of Tears. Why was this journey so dreadful?
4. **The new home**
   Find out more about one of the other tribes forced to relocate west of the Mississippi. Where did they settle? What happened to the tribe after relocation?

Thinking Critically
1. Is the ideal American man of the 1820s–1830s still the ideal today? If so, give examples. If not, describe the ideal that has replaced it.

2. The Virginia Dynasty and the other "gentlemen" in politics were replaced by professional politicians during the Age of Jackson. What kind of public servant is most common today? Which is best for the country, in your opinion?
3. What do you think a fair policy toward Indians would have been?
4. How have third parties and third-party candidates influenced recent elections, both national and in your local area?
5. Jackson has often been blamed for inventing the "spoils system." Use this book as your source to find earlier examples of patronage in American politics.
6. One advantage of the use of patronage is "rotation in office." What are some disadvantages?

Further Reading

Burke Davis. *Old Hickory: The Life of Andrew Jackson.* Dial Press, 1977. Describes his colorful life, his ideas, and his place in American history. Length makes it for the advanced or interested student.

Alex W. Bealer. *Only the Names Remain: The Cherokees and the Trail of Tears.* Little, Brown & Co., 1972. Recounts the history of the Cherokees, their contact with whites, and their removal to the west.

Kenneth M. Jones. *War with the Seminoles: 1835–1842.* Franklin Watts, 1975. An easy-to-read account of the Seminoles' fight to keep their Florida homeland.

Manfred G. Reidel. *A Kid's Guide to the Economy.* Prentice-Hall, Inc., 1976. Basic economic ideas and terms are explained. Shows how they relate to everyday life.

TEST YOURSELF

WRITE YOUR ANSWERS ON A SEPARATE SHEET OF PAPER.

Matching

Write the letter of the item that best matches each description below.
1. demanded better working conditions and shorter hours
2. denied the federal government had power over the individual states
3. economic problems caused by the destruction of the Bank of the United States

4. relocation of the Cherokees west of the Mississippi River
5. justified the removal of political enemies from government jobs

a. Trail of Tears
b. Panic of 1837
c. nullification crisis
d. Virginia Dynasty
e. gag rule
f. patronage
g. workingmen's parties

Labeling

Copy the list of politicians below. Next, mark each with the letter or letters that apply to them.
1. Henry Clay
2. John Quincy Adams
3. Andrew Jackson
4. Martin Van Buren
5. John C. Calhoun

President of the United States - mark P
Advocate of compromise - mark A
Advocate of states' rights - mark R
Forced eastern Indians to move west of the Mississippi River - mark I
Mastermind of winning elections - mark M
Member of Adams' cabinet - mark C
Left political enemies in office - mark O

Classifying

Mark with a W any statement that applies to the Whig party in the 1830s. Mark with a D any statement that applies to the Democratic party. Mark B if a statement applies to both parties.
1. leaders were mainly wealthy southern planters and ambitious businessmen
2. usually supported by small farmers and immigrants
3. built by Andrew Jackson
4. built by Andrew Jackson's opponents
5. had a rich, northern city leadership but also attracted many southern planters
6. avoided serious issues of the day
7. huge vote-getting machine in local, state, and national elections
8. its candidate, Harrison, won in 1840
9. its national support helped preserve the Union during several sectional crises
10. its candidate, Van Buren, won in 1836.

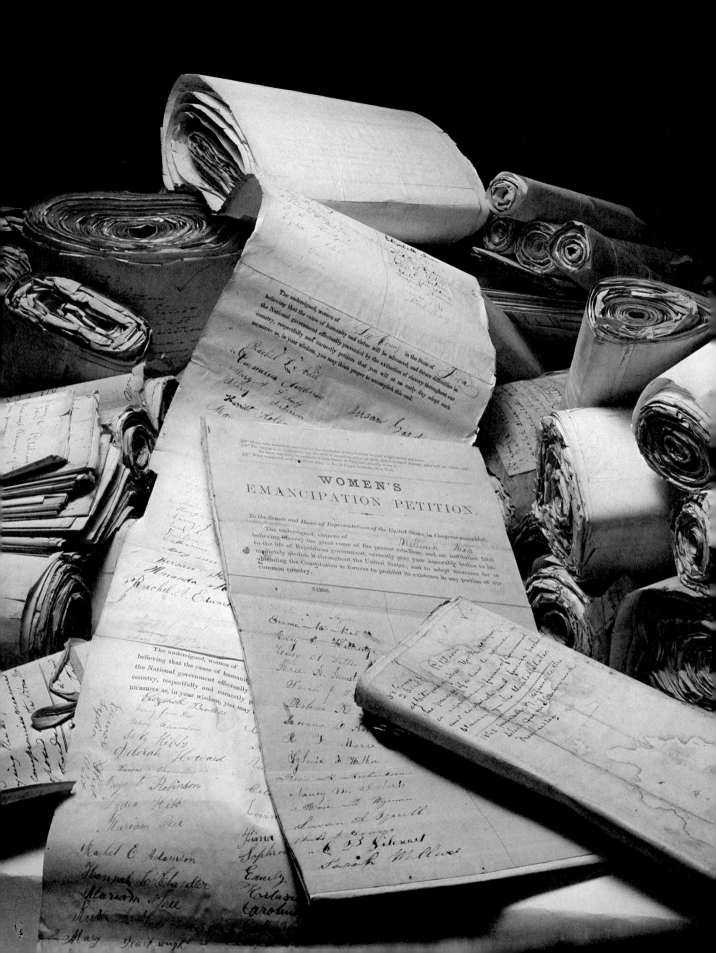

Chapter 13

1820–1850

THE AGE OF REFORM

I n the 1830s the buzz and hum of textile factories could be heard in New England. The whir and whish of the steamboat engine could be heard along the Hudson River and the Mississippi. The grind and gnash of the cotton gin could be heard throughout the deep South. These were the sounds of a growing and changing America.

But sounds of a different kind of activity could also be heard across the land. These were the voices of men and women trying to change the way Americans thought, what Americans felt, and how Americans lived. Their rallying cries were "Reform!" and "Improve!" These energetic men and women founded new religions and brought life back into old ones. They pioneered new treatments for and attitudes toward the insane, the deaf, and the blind. They designed a new educational system. They promoted pride in American literature and art. They called on slaveholders to end slavery and on men to grant equal citizenship to women.

Joseph Smith, Sojourner Truth, Henry David Thoreau, Margaret Fuller, Herman Melville, Sarah and Angelina Grimké, Frederick Douglass, and Horace Mann—these are the names of just a few of the remarkable Americans who created some of the social sounds of the period. The American Temperance Union, the *Appeal*, the New England Anti-Slavery Society, and the Seneca Falls Convention—these are just a few of the organizations they formed. In this chapter you will read about the sounds of social change in the Age of Reform.

Sections in This Chapter
1. Religion in the Age of Reform
2. The People's Choice: Popular Culture and Works of Genius
3. The Reformers and Their Crusades
4. The Rise of the Abolitionists
5. The First Women's Movement for Equality

Opposite: Some of the many antislavery petitions that flooded Congress before the Civil War

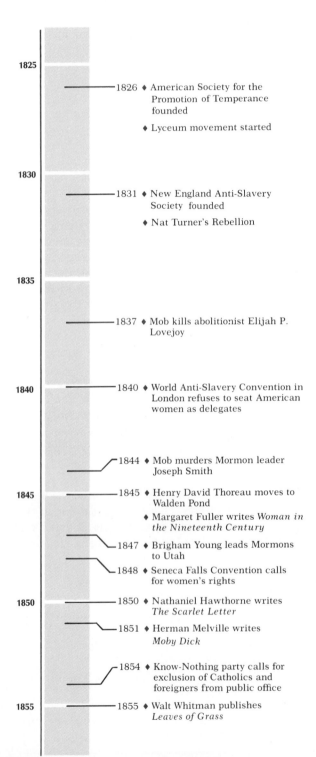

1825	
	1826 ♦ American Society for the Promotion of Temperance founded
	♦ Lyceum movement started
1830	
	1831 ♦ New England Anti-Slavery Society founded
	♦ Nat Turner's Rebellion
1835	
	1837 ♦ Mob kills abolitionist Elijah P. Lovejoy
1840	1840 ♦ World Anti-Slavery Convention in London refuses to seat American women as delegates
	1844 ♦ Mob murders Mormon leader Joseph Smith
1845	1845 ♦ Henry David Thoreau moves to Walden Pond
	♦ Margaret Fuller writes *Woman in the Nineteenth Century*
	1847 ♦ Brigham Young leads Mormons to Utah
	1848 ♦ Seneca Falls Convention calls for women's rights
1850	1850 ♦ Nathaniel Hawthorne writes *The Scarlet Letter*
	1851 ♦ Herman Melville writes *Moby Dick*
	1854 ♦ Know-Nothing party calls for exclusion of Catholics and foreigners from public office
1855	1855 ♦ Walt Whitman publishes *Leaves of Grass*

1. RELIGION IN THE AGE OF REFORM

In 1823, a tall, handsome young man named **Charles G. Finney** gave up his law practice to enter the ministry. Like many other Americans of that decade, Finney had been swept up by a religious revival. This **"Second Great Awakening"** spread from upstate New York to the frontier across the Mississippi. Finney became an important preacher of the new gospel, which optimistically promised salvation for all who sought it. In language that appealed to the ordinary citizen, Finney called on his audiences to trade their "old hearts" for new ones. Hundreds, if not thousands, of Americans heeded the call. New churches sprang up around the country. By 1860, there were over 38,000 church buildings in America.

Reform Based on Optimism

The religious revival encouraged an optimism about reform in American society. Ministers urged their congregations to overcome all their bad habits and to reshape their characters. On the western frontier, especially, Methodist ministers spoke out against gambling, drinking, and violence. In cities, Finney and his fellow clergy preached against greed and corruption. Finney's followers, called the "Holy Band," worked to reform the moral atmosphere in Philadelphia, New York, Boston, and the towns of upstate New York.

Enthusiasm generated by the religious revival spilled over into public life. New voluntary associations arose to spread the gospel of moral improvement. In 1826, for example, the Reverend **Lyman Beecher** created the American Society for the Promotion of Temperance. Like many Americans, Beecher believed that alcohol prevented men and women from leading successful and prosperous lives. In 1836, the American Tract Society was created to place literature on the Bible in every home. With organizations such as the American Bible Society and the American Sunday School Union, these voluntary groups formed what 19th-century Americans called the **"Benevolent Empire."**

Although the Benevolent Empire led many Americans into the two great social reform movements of the day—abolition and women's rights—there was a darker side to the religious revival of the era. It produced a strong anti-Catholic movement, too.

Anti-Immigrant and Anti-Catholic

Catholics were a small minority in America in the 1600s and 1700s. Even in 1810, only one out of every 100 Americans was a Roman Catholic. By 1860, however, one out of every ten Americans was a Catholic. This increase was largely the result of Irish immigration. In the 1840s a terrible famine drove one-fifth of Ireland's people to the American shores.

These Irish immigrants were rarely welcomed by their new neighbors. Pamphlets claiming to expose terrible secret practices of the Church poured out of some Protestant presses. Anti-Catholic mobs burned a convent in Massachusetts, and in Tennessee and Kentucky, Catholic churches were set afire. A riot in Philadelphia in 1844 left immigrants wounded and their homes in ashes. Even that otherwise admirable man, Lyman Beecher, joined the frantic campaign against Catholics between 1830 and 1860. Reverend Beecher called on "native" Americans to repel the spread of the "foreign religion," Catholicism. By 1854, anti-Catholic and anti-immigrant sentiments were given political shape under the banner of the **"Know-Nothing" party.** Officially named the American party, the "Know-Nothing" party* called for the exclusion of Catholics and foreigners from public office. It also called for immigrants to reside in America for 21 years before they could become citizens. Religious leaders such as Lyman Beecher confused a perfect American society with a society in which all citizens thought and worshiped alike.

The Formation of Utopian Societies

In the midst of the religious revival, many new religious sects grew and flourished. Some were **utopian societies,** led by men and women with new ideas about organizing American life. A utopian society was one which set up laws and living conditions that were thought to insure a perfect life for everyone, a life free from want or discrimination. Many of these utopian communities were

---

*Know-Nothing party Members of the party were sworn not to reveal its mysteries. When asked about the party, they answered "I know nothing about it," hence the nickname.

Know-Nothing cartoon depicting Irish and German immigrants stealing a ballot box

also socialist, based on the principle that all profits from manufacture or farming should be shared among the members of the group equally. During the 1840s and 1850s, hundreds of such utopian societies were formed, from New England to Texas, and everywhere between. These communal (owned jointly by all) experiments were not always successful, but two, the Oneida [ō nī′də] and the Amana societies, prospered.

The Oneida Society was founded in Oneida, New York, in 1848. Its members owned all property in common and practiced common care of the children. The members manufactured silverware, which is made in Oneida to this day. Likewise, the Amana Society, formed in 1855 in Iowa, was organized communally. The Amana Society still exists today.

The Mormons

One new religion that made an important mark on American history was the **Mormon Church,** or the Church of Jesus Christ of Latter-day Saints. This religion, founded in upstate New York by the son of a poor Vermont family, suffered a stormy beginning and provoked great controversy in the American Midwest.

In the 1820s, the Mormon founder, **Joseph Smith,** was a young man living with his family in western New York State. Smith acquired an enthusiastic and devoted following when he announced that he had found and translated a buried holy script that he called the *Book of Mormon.* This text, Smith explained, had been written by the last survivor of a lost tribe of Israel. The *Book of Mormon* told of the wanderings and warfare between the two "lost" tribes of Israel who had found their way to North America thousands of years before the first European settlers. Based on the revelations and the moral teachings of the *Book of Mormon*, Joseph Smith established a new —and entirely American—religion. Devoted followers of Smith joined and helped build the Church of Jesus Christ of Latter-day Saints.

During the 1830s the Mormon Church grew rapidly. It attracted many poor but hardworking families. But opposition to it and distrust of it grew, too. Mormons were not welcome in many states, and Smith's followers felt forced to move from New York to Ohio to Missouri and finally, in 1839, to an Illinois town called Nauvoo.

By 1844, Nauvoo was the largest city in Illinois, with 15,000 hardworking and dedicated Mormon residents. The dislike that "mainstream" Americans felt for the Mormon Church, however, continued to grow. In 1844, it turned to hostility and mob violence. The violence was precipitated by two events. The first of these was the announcement by Smith of a new Church policy: certain male members of the inner circle of the Church were permitted to practice polygamy (multiple marriage).

Most Americans were shocked by the notion of a man wed to several women. Tensions were increased by a second event: Smith created what he called the Nauvoo Legion, a military organization designed to defend his followers from their angry neighbors. Soon rumors spread that Smith intended the Legion as an attack force to seize control of the entire Ohio Valley. Smith was arrested, and a frenzied mob stormed the jail and murdered him.

Smith's murder stunned the Mormon community. Once again they decided to move west. In 1847, their new leader, Brigham Young, led 5,000 Mormons to the barren salt flats of Utah. Here, they built a thriving city, Salt Lake City, that is still the base for their church organization.

Transcendentalism: a Philosophy of Self-Reliance

Transcendentalism, like Mormonism, was another uniquely American movement born in the Age of Reform. It is difficult to define **Transcendentalism,** however. It was a religious movement, but it had no church. It captured the spirit of optimism, but it did not call for any particular reforms. In fact, it was more of a philosophy, or attitude toward life, than a movement or organization.

Transcendentalism celebrated feelings over rationality. Its leaders urged Americans to rise above Reason, which sometimes told a person that an ambition was foolish, a goal was too high, or a dream could not come true. Faith in oneself, said the Transcendentalists, could make the impossible possible. Americans should develop self-reliance, they argued, and confidence, and, above all, individuality. The Transcendentalists also urged Americans to stop admiring European culture and to take pride in things American.

Transcendentalism never attracted a large following. A small circle of New Englanders created it and kept its spirit alive in their essays, lectures, and books. These men and women were such exceptional individuals, however, that they influenced an entire age. In fact, the period of Transcendentalism coincided with "the flowering of New England," which was a bursting forth of great American literature.

The most famous of this lively, intellectual, and individualistic circle were Ralph Waldo Emerson, Henry David Thoreau, and Margaret Fuller. **Ralph Waldo Emerson** was a tall, quiet man, whose eloquent sermons in the 1820s and early 1830s thrilled and shocked his audiences. In 1832, Emerson quit the ministry and retired to Concord, Massachusetts, to think, to write, and later to travel the country lecturing and urging Americans to "hitch their wagons to a star."

In 1837, Emerson gave a speech to the graduating class at Harvard. His speech, "The American Scholar," called for Americans to trust themselves: "We have listened too long to the courtly muses of Europe. The spirit of the American freeman is already suspected to be timid, imitative, tame. Public and private avarice make the air we breathe thick and fat." The answer, said Emerson, was to "work with our own hands" and "speak with our own minds."

Henry David Thoreau, who graduated from Harvard in 1837 and heard Emerson's famous speech, worked in his father's pencil shop and taught school. He constantly read the writings of Emerson. In 1845, he left the comforts of his middle-class life and went to live in the woods beside Walden Pond. Thoreau built his own cabin and furniture and grew his own food. He meant to prove that a person could live simply and self-sufficiently. His record of this experience, *Walden,* was an attack on American conformity and a tribute to the abilities of the individual.

Margaret Fuller was the third of the leading Transcendentalists. She was a child prodigy, reading Latin, Greek, and the classical philosophers before she was ten years old. In a world that frowned on intellectual and independent women, Fuller was a controversial figure. She wrote the first American feminist book, *Woman in the Nineteenth Century* (1845), in which she said that women can be anything they want to be, including the captains of ships. Such ideas were shocking to most Americans. She edited *The Dial,* a magazine dedicated to Transcendentalist thought. She also organized "conversations," or seminars for women who wished to discuss ideas, world events, and the role of women in society. Fuller lived the Transcendentalist promise by defying the limits placed on women of her era.

The religious revival, the rise of native religions, and Transcendentalist thought were all products of America's new cultural independence from Europe. For two centuries, America had been part of the English and European world of ideas, although American circumstances had reshaped those ideas. Now Americans began to generate a uniquely American culture. In the next section, you will read about a new generation of American artists, novelists, and poets.

SECTION 1 REVIEW

Identify: Charles G. Finney, Second Great Awakening, Lyman Beecher, Benevolent Empire, Know-Nothing party, utopian societies, Mormon Church, Joseph Smith, Transcendentalism, Ralph Waldo Emerson, Henry David Thoreau, Margaret Fuller

Main Ideas

1. What were some positive and negative results of the religious revival of the Age of Reform?
2. Describe the origin of the Church of Jesus Christ of Latter-day Saints and the difficulties the early Mormons faced.
3. What was the Transcendentalist philosophy? Who were some well-known Transcendentalists, and what did they do?

2. THE PEOPLE'S CHOICE: POPULAR CULTURE AND WORKS OF GENIUS

A pride in America was one of the positive results of the War of 1812. By the 1820s and 1830s, this pride showed itself as a pride in America's history, the character of its people, and the natural wonders of its landscape.

American Themes in Literature and Art

Poets and novelists looked to American themes for inspiration. In New England, **Henry Wadsworth Longfellow** wrote of the vanishing world of the American Indians in his epic poem, *Hiawatha.* Longfellow became the nation's poet-historian, telling the story of the Revolution in *Paul Revere's Ride.* In *Evangeline* he told the story of the French and Indian War, in which the British expelled French Canadians (Acadians) from Nova Scotia in 1755. *Evangeline* tells how some of the Acadians journeyed to Louisiana, where their descendants live today.

In the South, William Gilmore Simms of South Carolina published two dozen novels and several books of poetry that drew upon his region's history. His most popular novel, *The Partisan* (1835), was set on the southern frontier during the Revolution. Writers such as Simms, William Cullen Bryant, and James Fenimore Cooper helped Americans think of their own past as a legitimate theme for the arts.

American artists took up their brushes to paint the natural wonders of the country. The most famous group of landscape painters was called the **"Hudson River School."** Men such as Asher Brown Durand and Thomas Cole were leaders of this school of painting. On their canvases, these painters captured the untamed beauties of the Adirondack Mountains and the mighty Hudson River of New York. Other artists showed Americans at work and play, engaging in ordinary activities on farms or in town and cities. George Catlin's portraits of American Indians sold as well as portraits of English kings and nobles had sold a century before.

The appeal to a wider, popular audience was

Lake George, *painted in 1869 by John Frederick Kensett, a member of the "Hudson River School"*

another development in the American arts. Instead of culture for the few, Americans demanded culture for the masses. Often, however, the popular eye was less critical than it should have been. Many of the best-selling books of the early 19th century were overly sentimental and badly written, with unbelievable plots and characters. Much of the art that hung in private homes has not stood the test of time.

Critics protested that quality, not sales figures, ought to be the measure of talent. They pointed to "hack" writers who sold millions of copies of silly books while genuine artists went unread. In particular, critics attacked the "women scribblers" of the day, whose romantic stories resemble our modern soap operas. Nevertheless, American writers such as Susan Warner, Maria Cummins, and Mary Jane Holmes were entertaining millions.

Four Literary Geniuses
Popular novelists did sell books, but so did four serious writers of the era. Edgar Allan Poe, Nathaniel Hawthorne, Herman Melville, and Walt Whitman produced the first great works of American literature.

Edgar Allan Poe was born in 1809, the son of two theater people. He was orphaned at the age of three and raised by a wealthy Virginian, John Allan. Poe's personal life was as dark and tragic as his writings. He was both an alcoholic and a drug addict, leading a wild, undisciplined existence and dying at 40. Yet Poe's poems and stories were the products of a skilled craftsman who showed discipline and a drive for perfection.

Poe was a master of the short story, and he is given credit for originating the detective story in the Western Hemisphere. Poe's themes were often bizarre or supernatural, as in the horror tale, "The Pit and the Pendulum." The tremendous popularity of Poe's poem, "The Raven," showed that Americans did support good literature as well as the works of "scribblers."

Like Poe, **Nathaniel Hawthorne** had an unhappy childhood. His father died when Nathaniel was small, and his grieving mother shut herself off from the world. Hawthorne grew up lonely, with only books and his imagination as companions. Hawthorne, turning to America's historic past for his subjects, wrote imaginative tales with strong moral lessons. *The Scarlet Letter* (1850), for example, was set in colonial Massachusetts and was about a woman who committed adultery. *The House of the Seven Gables* (1851), began in America's past and ended in its present.

Although he wrote of the past, Hawthorne was active in the issues of the day. He was a Democrat and wrote a campaign biography of his friend, President Franklin Pierce. Hawthorne's wife's family, the Peabodys, were active in the abolition and women's rights movements. Hawthorne's novels, especially the two mentioned, were seriously concerned with issues of individual and community morality. His books were heavily philosophical, yet thousands of American readers bought, read, and cherished them.

Herman Melville was born in New York in 1819. He, too, lost his father as a young boy. But unlike the lonely Hawthorne or the wild Poe, Melville was a man of action and adventure. He went to sea at 18, working on a whaling vessel. In 1842, the daring Melville jumped ship at a South Seas island and lived for over a year with cannibals. When he returned to America in 1844, he wrote about his adventures.

In 1846, Melville's *Typee* was published. It was an instant success. Adventure, bravery, and the exploration of new worlds were themes that Americans warmed to. *Omoo,* published in 1847, was equally popular. Melville could have continued to write high seas tales, but he did not. Instead, he began to read widely, to educate himself, and to ponder the same questions of good and evil, human weakness, and morality with which his new friend Nathaniel Hawthorne grappled. Then, in 1851, Melville published the powerful masterpiece, *Moby Dick.* The public did not like this changed, heavily philosophical Melville, and *Moby Dick* sold badly. Melville never recovered his audience, but *Moby Dick* is today recognized as one of the greatest American novels.

Poe, Hawthorne, and Melville shared a pessimism about human character that set them apart from their generation. Neither Transcendentalist optimism nor the era's belief in progress could persuade these three men that the darker side of the human heart could be defeated.

Walt Whitman was not a pessimist. He was an optimist who shouted his optimism to the world. Or, as he put it in his most famous poem, "I sound my barbaric yawp over the roofs of the world." Whitman's poetry abounds with a love for everything around him. Not even the carnage of the Civil War could defeat Whitman's optimism.

Like Melville, Whitman was born in New York in 1819. He quit school at 13 to wander, taking odd jobs and learning several trades. Whitman's fame came when he published at his own expense *Leaves of Grass* (1855), a book of 12 poems celebrating himself, his nation, and life itself. All the poems' subjects are American; all their references are to the American past, present, and future. With its free verse and undisciplined enthusiasm, *Leaves of Grass* seemed to capture the intense optimism of the Age of Reform.

The Lyceum Movement: Participation in Ideas

Americans, it seemed, could not get enough culture, could not get enough ideas. After 1826, they flocked to lyceums, or lecture halls, to hear new ideas and exchange opinions with speakers on science, religion, politics, and morality.

The **lyceum movement** was founded by Josiah Holbrook, who earned his living lecturing from town to town. The first lyceum was held in 1826 under the open skies of Millbury, Massachusetts. By 1831, over 1,000 lyceums were in operation. Scholars, artists, and reformers, as well as charlatans, quacks, and schemers traveled the lyceum circuit. The desire for self-improvement motivated men and women to attend lyceum programs on every subject from Transcendentalism to Graham flour diets to mesmerism (hypnotism) to hydrotherapy (the belief that baths can help cure ills) to phrenology (the "science" of reading a person's character by studying the bumps on his or her head).

SECTION 2 REVIEW

Identify: Henry Wadsworth Longfellow, Hudson River School, Edgar Allan Poe, Nathaniel Hawthorne, Herman Melville, Walt Whitman, lyceum movement

Main Ideas

1. What was new about culture and the arts during the age of reform?
2. What were Poe, Hawthorne, and Melville's views of human nature? How did their views differ from those of most Americans at the time?
3. What was Whitman's view of human nature?
4. Why was the lyceum movement popular?

3. THE REFORMERS AND THEIR CRUSADES

The belief that individuals could be reformed and their characters perfected prompted many Americans to tackle serious social problems in the Age of Reform. Between 1820 and 1850, campaigns for educational reform, prison reform, and new and humane treatment of the handicapped and insane were launched.

The Reform of Education

It was not difficult to see that the American system of formal education for the young was in sore need of reform. Schools across the country were in poor condition, with leaking roofs, crumbling steps, and broken windows. Teachers, most of them male, were untrained, and students were bunched together in a single classroom regardless of age or skills. In the newly thriving cities, truancy was fast becoming a social problem. Gangs of delinquent boys were disturbing the peace, and children were begging in the streets. Many of the poorer families took their children out of school so that they could work and bring home needed money.

What kind of citizens would these poorly taught or wholly untaught children become? This was the question that troubled reformers such as Reverend Lyman Beecher and educators such as Boston's Horace Mann. Both these men saw that economic growth and geographical expansion were not enough to insure American democracy. "We must educate! We must educate!" Beecher exclaimed, "or we must perish by our own prosperity." For educational reformers, the classroom offered an opportunity to shape the moral character of the next generation. They were beginning to see the school, not the family setting, as the major arena for promoting good citizenship.

The most famous educator of the era was **Horace Mann,** head of Boston's Board of Education from 1837 to 1848. Mann was the champion of free public schooling for all children. He transformed the Massachusetts educational system, creating a model other states would follow. Mann's system established tax-supported schools.

Mann and others called tax-supported public schools a debt that the rich owed to their country. These schools were free of any specific denomination's religious instruction. This rule was designed to calm Catholic fears that their children would come under Protestant influence.

In his educational reform work, Mann was especially critical of the undereducated, unskilled, and temporary teaching staffs in public schools. He urged a trained, professional staff of women teachers. To supply such a teaching staff, states established normal schools, or teacher-training academies, for women. Out of this educational reform, a new career for women was born.

Mann also changed the organization of classrooms. Students were separated into grades based on age and abilities. A student progressed from grade to grade by promotions based on achievements. The same graded textbooks were used in each Massachusetts school. Each school was directed by a principal, although a Board of Education oversaw the entire school system. You should recognize many of Mann's reforms in your own educational experience today. By 1850, the educational reformers had succeeded in creating tax-supported public school systems in the free, northern states that gave generations of American-born and immigrant children intellectual tools that they otherwise would have lacked.

Temperance: From Moderation to Total Abstinence

In colonial America drunkenness was a crime in Puritan colonies, and ministers everywhere preached against the evils of "demon rum." But no organized crusade for **temperance,** or moderation in drinking, was organized until the 1820s.

In 1826, Lyman Beecher formed the American Society for the Promotion of Temperance to stamp out the abuses of alcohol. Members pointed to broken homes, ruined lives, and criminal acts that resulted from drinking. To some extent, their campaign against drunkenness masked their dislike of the new immigrant cultures in America. These reformers often spoke as if drinking was a "foreign" custom, introduced to American society by the newest arrivals in Eastern cities. As you will see, this mixture of anti-immigrant feeling and genuine concern for the ills caused by alcoholism remained characteristic of the movement for over 100 years.

The American temperance movement began as an effort to cut back drinking by persuading Americans of the dangers involved. By 1830, 1 million Americans had joined the campaign. In 1836, many temperance organizations united to create the American Temperance Union. In 1840, a group of reformed alcoholics created their own organization, the Washingtonians. Members of the Washingtonians traveled the country to testify against alcoholism and to tell of their own climb up from drunken despair to new lives of sobriety. They ended their talks with appeals to the audience to "sign the pledge" and give up drink.

By the 1850s, temperance people had shifted from moral persuasion to legal action to fight against the drinking of alcohol. They now sought enforced abstinence (doing without) from alcohol. The temperance people demanded a prohibition of the sale and manufacture of any alcoholic beverages. In 1851, Neal Dow, the mayor of Portland, Maine, convinced his state to pass the first prohibition law. The Maine law forbade the sale or manufacture of any alcoholic drink. By 1856, eight other states had some form of prohibition. As you will see in Chapter 25, Americans experimented with prohibition on a national level in the 20th century.

Prison Reforms

While people such as Horace Mann concentrated on shaping the characters of children, other reformers felt it was never too late to remold adults. Many reformers were confident that even criminals could be rehabilitated—if the proper environment for repentance, reflection, and self-reform were provided.

In the 1830s two plans emerged for redesigning the American prison environment. The first, called the **Philadelphia system,** isolated each prisoner in a plain but sanitary cell. This strict solitary confinement was expected to help prisoners concentrate on the error of their ways. After months, or perhaps years of solitary reflection, said the reformers, the prisoner was sure to mend his or her ways. In reality, however, the Philadelphia system often drove the lonely prisoners to madness.

The second, or **Auburn system,** allowed prisoners limited contact with each other during work periods. Total silence was required, however. Talking was punished by flogging. The Auburn

"Father Come Home." Illustration from T. S. Arthur's 1854 temperance novel Ten Nights in a Bar-Room

system was expected to reform the criminal by giving him or her merely a taste of the social contact decent members of society enjoyed.

Both the Philadelphia and the Auburn systems seem cruel and harsh to us. Yet humane reformers sincerely believed these plans would cure all but the most depraved prisoners of their criminal tendencies.

Help for the Mentally Disturbed and the Handicapped

The great champion of the mentally disturbed was **Dorothea Dix,** who devoted 30 years of her life to improving the conditions in asylums and mental hospitals across the country. Hers was a disappointing and lonely crusade. Dix traveled from state to state, inspecting mental institutions and publicizing their abuses. She exposed, for example, the horrors of the Massachusetts asylums, where inmates were locked in closets and in cages, chained and often naked.

In theory, the men who ran these asylums and the public officials who created them intended to cure their patients. They upheld the concept of an environment of order, calm, quiet, and freedom from the pressures of the outside world for the asylum and hospital inmates. Yet funds were always lacking, staff was unavailable, and no one knew how to deal with violent and suicidal inmates. The work of Dorothea Dix, however, did help better the conditions for the mentally ill.

Efforts to help the handicapped were more successful than prison or asylum reforms. Here, scientific methods and improved environments did work small miracles. For the deaf, Americans adopted the teaching methods of Thomas Hopkins Gallaudet. By 1851, 14 states had special schools for teaching Gallaudet's technique. For the blind, **Dr. Samuel Gridley Howe** designed books printed with raised letters that could be "read" with the hands rather than the eyes. Dr. Howe helped educate Laura Bridgman, the first blind, deaf, and mute person to be educated in America. This success helped spur the growth of education for the handicapped.

Not all of the reformers' ideas were sound, and not all of their solutions worked. Some, such as the temperance people, seemed to meddle in the private choices of other citizens. Others, such as the educators, seemed too certain of the superiority of their way of life over the customs of the poor and the immigrants. Yet all shared a humane impulse to help perfect the people of their nation during the Age of Reform.

SECTION 3 REVIEW

Identify: Horace Mann, temperance, Philadelphia system, Auburn system, Dorothea Dix, Samuel Gridley Howe

Main Ideas

1. What was the educational system like before the age of reform? How did Horace Mann help change the educational system? Which of his reforms are in effect today?
2. Describe the history of the temperance movement. What were its first beliefs, and how did they change?
3. Discuss this statement: the motives of the reformers were a mixture of genuine concern and a feeling of superiority.
4. How were the mentally disturbed treated before the age of reform? How did Dorothea Dix fight against this treatment?
5. What changes did reformers make in the treatment of the handicapped?

4. THE RISE OF THE ABOLITIONISTS

By 1830, there were 2 million slaves, but until the 1830s, there was little organized protest against slavery. The largest organization, the **American Colonization Society,** formed in 1819, did not call for the abolition of slavery and citizenship for freed blacks. Instead, it urged that the "race problem" be solved by sending all blacks, slave and free, to Africa. Thus in 1822 the society founded the colony of Liberia on the west coast of Africa.

The society worked to encourage slaveholders to free their slaves and send them to Liberia. But few slaveholders heeded the society's call to voluntarily give up their labor force. And few free blacks chose to leave their native land for a colony in Africa. Still, by 1860 over 15,000 American blacks had become colonists in Liberia.

Liberia became independent in 1847, its government modeled on that of the United States. The American blacks who went there in the 19th century became the nation's ruling class. Their descendants, the "Americo-Liberians," now form about 2.5% of the country's population. They controlled the country until a military coup in 1980 overthrew their political leaders.

Despite the efforts of the American Colonization Society, the problem of slavery remained. Beginning in 1829, a series of events dramatized the pressing need for white Americans to rethink their positions on slavery. The majority of citizens continued to ignore the moral and economic dilemma. But a small group of reformers did answer the challenge.

In 1829, a free black of Boston, **David Walker,** published a radical volume called *Appeal*. *Appeal* urged slaves in America to revolt against their masters immediately. It warned white Americans to do justice by the black population—or face the tragic consequences.

The Fear of Slave Revolts

There had never been a mass uprising of slaves across the southern states. But a few attempts at revolt in the past had revealed the tensions of the slave system. As you learned in Chapter 4, in colonial times Cato's Conspiracy of 1739 had cost the lives of 74 blacks and whites. In 1741 the rumor of a slave plot in New York City had led to the execution of 31 slaves.

Two incidents also occurred in the young nation. In August 1800, James Monroe, who was then governor of Virginia, sent in the militia to quell a large, well-organized revolt. The slaves' leader, **Gabriel,** commanded over 1,000 determined rebels. Their plan to kill their masters and then ride to Richmond to torch the city was exposed at the last minute. Governor Monroe had Gabriel put to death. In 1822, in the crowded, elegant city of Charleston, South Carolina, **Denmark Vesey** planned an uprising among the trusted household slaves of the wealthy residents. The plot was discovered, and 35 blacks were hung.

In both the Gabriel and the Vesey revolts, it was the slaves who suffered the violence of punishment. But white southerners lived with the fear that someday such a revolt would succeed. Rules governing the movement of slaves, their right to congregate, and their chance to learn to read and write were designed to prevent revolts. Despite all precautions, however, rumors of a plantation house in flames, a poison plot, or a revolt nipped in the bud grew throughout the 19th century.

Walker's *Appeal* seemed to be an omen of things to come, for in 1831 a slave named Nat Turner led 70 comrades in a hopeless but bloody uprising in Southampton County, Virginia. **Nat Turner's Rebellion** struck terror into the white southern population. Thereafter, until the Civil War, southern whites felt constantly threatened by rumors of slave revolts, and southern state legislatures enacted harsher slave laws.

The same year as Nat Turner's Rebellion, the Jamaican slave revolt also began. Then, in 1833, England emancipated all slaves held in British territories. Americans could no longer comfort themselves that slavery was the universal way that white nations solved the "race problem."

The Abolitionists Organize

The fear of future violence and the encouragement of the British abolitionist movement helped convince American reformers that it was time to act. Perhaps the most important factor in the rise of the American abolitionist movement, however, was the religious revival of the 1820s and 1830s. Many leaders of the abolitionist campaign were ministers or followers of the religious revival.

From Finney's "Holy Band," from the seminaries and church organizations of the "Benevolent Empire" came the men and women who openly opposed slavery as a moral sin.

While men in government tried desperately to avoid the issue of slavery, abolitionists did their best to publicize and dramatize it. In 1831, **William Lloyd Garrison** struck the determined note of abolition in the first issue of his newspaper, the *Liberator.* "I will be as harsh as truth, and as uncompromising as justice . . . I will not retreat a single inch—AND I WILL BE HEARD."

Few Americans wished to hear Garrison's call for an immediate end to slavery. Yet the *Liberator,* with its small circulation, did trouble men in power. The Georgia legislature, for example, offered a reward for Garrison's kidnapping and delivery into their hands for trial.

William Lloyd Garrison was opposed to the work of the American Colonization Society. He did not believe that colonization was the answer. In 1831, he helped found the New England Anti-Slavery Society. Garrison was an effective writer and speaker and a dramatic personality. He called for the North to secede from the Union because the Constitution permitted slavery. He called the Constitution "a convenant with death and an agreement with Hell." At one abolitionist meeting in New England, Garrison publicly burned a copy of the Constitution.

Around Garrison and his New England Anti-Slavery Society gathered a small but tireless band of activists. **Theodore Weld,** a minister converted by Charles Finney, created a similar organization called the New York Anti-Slavery Society. By 1833 the two groups had merged as the **American Anti-Slavery Society.** The people who represented this society often sounded impractical or unrealistic to the average citizen. They had no concrete plan for ending slavery, or for the well-being of the blacks afterwards.

Weld, for example, wished to stamp out slavery but recognized the economic and social confusion that abolition would produce. He called therefore for "immediate" emancipation—"gradually achieved." Garrison was untroubled by the movement's lack of a solution to the problems of emancipation. The job of abolitionists, he said, was to stir American feelings of horror, shame, and sympathy for the slave, and to force the nation to action. It was for others—political and economic

LIFE IN AMERICA

FREDERICK DOUGLASS AND THE AMERICAN DREAM

Perhaps no figure in American history represents the ideal of the American dream better than Frederick Douglass. Born a slave, Douglass, through determination and daring, gained his freedom and lived to become a renowned reformer, best-selling author, ambassador, and honored spokesman of American blacks.

Frederick Douglass was born Frederick Augustus Washington Bailey on the Eastern Shore of Maryland, possibly in 1817. No one recorded the slave-child's birth, so the year is only an estimate. The young Frederick Bailey was separated from his mother and spent his childhood in Baltimore shipyards. There the energetic and inquisitive youth convinced several co-workers to teach him to read. But with the death of his master, he had to return to the plantation.

Two Escape Attempts—and Freedom!

At the plantation the young slave proved to be uncooperative and was hired out to a "slave-breaker." Only by taking an incredible risk and fighting back did he stop the beatings he received. This experience convinced him that he must be free. He planned a getaway with five other slaves, only to end up jailed and in chains when the plot was discovered.

Sent back to the Baltimore shipyards, Frederick Bailey learned ship-caulking and planned another escape. With "protection" papers borrowed from a free black seaman, he boldly boarded a north-bound train in 1838. He arrived in New York City safely. There he took the name of Douglass, which he used ever after, and was joined by his free black wife-to-be.

The new couple soon settled in

Frederick Douglass

New Bedford, Massachusetts, where Douglass hoped to work in the shipyards. He found, however, that a black caulker was not welcome. Freedom was not without its problems in 1838.

Douglass Speaks Out

August 1841 marked another turning point in Frederick Douglass' life. He attended an abolitionist meeting and was asked to speak of his slavery experience. Douglass' speech was so moving that the famed orator, William Lloyd Garrison, who was in the audience, immediately hired Douglass to speak for abolition. From that day on, he spoke out against slavery and discrimination in towns and cities throughout the North. People came to see Douglass as well as hear him. His distinguished appearance and his well-chosen words showed clearly that this former slave was a man, not a "thing" to be owned by another.

In 1845 his *Narrative of the Life of Frederick Douglass* became the first of his best-sellers in America and Britain. A speaking tour of the British Isles brought more fame and, unexpectedly, his technical freedom. It was bought from his master by an English abolitionist group.

"Agitate! Agitate! Agitate!"

In 1848 Frederick Douglass began publishing his own newspaper, *The North Star,* in Rochester, New York. In the paper, he spoke out in favor of many reform causes. He once wrote: "I am for any movement whenever and wherever there is a good cause to promote, a right to assert, a chain to be broken, a burden to be removed, or a wrong to be redressed." Abolition, temperance, desegregation, and the women's rights movement all received his support. His advice to other reformers was "Agitate! Agitate! Agitate!" In 1848, Douglass was the only man to play a prominent role at the Seneca Falls Convention, where he urged women to demand the right to vote.

Later in his life, Douglass was an honored guest at President Lincoln's White House, recruited black troops, and served as Ambassador to Haiti. He continued to speak out whenever and wherever he saw injustice. On the very day of his death in 1895 he had addressed a meeting of the National Council of Women.

Frederick Douglass' life showed what could be possible in America. His words were and still are a reminder of what should be. He stood for basic human rights and the equality of all persons. To later generations of Americans, his life has become an enduring symbol of protest against all forms of injustice. Frederick Douglass fought for the American dream for all.

leaders—to solve the practical issues.

The abolition movement slowly spread. At Lane Theological Seminary in Ohio, Theodore Weld gave speeches against slavery and converted 70 of his students to abolition. This "band of 70" helped organize abolitionist societies in the West. When Weld was fired for his views, the wealthy abolitionist Arthur Tappan established Oberlin College in Ohio. Here, at Oberlin, abolitionists were welcome to study and teach.

The abolitionists used the mass techniques of the Age of Jackson. Like Jacksonian politicians organizing a political campaign, Weld and others mapped out their moral campaign. Millions of antislavery leaflets and flyers were distributed. Rallies were held. Petitions were drawn up and sent to local governments and to Congress. Testimonials against slavery were offered.

The most moving of these testimonials were by former slaves themselves. The stately **Frederick Douglass** was the most famous of those who had experienced slavery and escaped to tell of it. His *Narrative of the Life of Frederick Douglass* became a major antislavery document. Sojourner Truth, also a former slave, spoke against the "peculiar institution." By 1836, the mass campaign bore its fruits: over 500 antislavery societies existed. By 1837, there were perhaps a thousand.

Soon, however, the opposition to the abolitionist movement also took shape. Men of wealth and property whose textile factories needed southern cotton and whose ships traded in southern ports were firmly against the abolitionists. Antiabolitionist riots, organized by respectable gentlemen, broke out in northern cities. Abolitionists were insulted at public rallies and injured by rocks, clubs, and fists. Women abolitionists, such as the South Carolina sisters Angelina and Sarah Grimké, were particular targets of angry crowds, who considered it indecent for women to address a mixed audience of men and women, no matter how urgent the cause. In 1838, Pennsylvania Hall in Philadelphia was burned by a mob that opposed the gathering of white women abolitionists, blacks, and white men in one place.

In 1837, a New England abolitionist named **Elijah P. Lovejoy** journeyed to Alton, Illinois, just across the Missouri River from slaveholding St. Louis. In Alton, Lovejoy set up an antislavery printing press and began organizing an antislavery society. Slaveholders from St. Louis were incensed. A group crossed into Alton by cover of night and attacked and destroyed two of Lovejoy's presses. The Illinois police looked the other way.

When a mob tried to destroy Lovejoy's third and last press at his warehouse, the abolitionist and his followers fought back. In the confrontation, Lovejoy's people shot a local boy. The mob then set fire to the warehouse, and when Lovejoy fled the flames the mob killed him. Lovejoy's death brought a wave of sympathy from northerners.

The abolitionist ranks soon divided over troubling questions of tactics and strategy. Some, like Garrison, insisted on remaining aloof from political parties. They wished to continue their campaign of moral education and prodding. Others, however, became convinced that political action was needed to reach the majority of Americans. As you saw in Chapter 12, these abolitionists formed a third party, the Liberty party, in 1840.

Abolitionists were not the only people against slavery in the age of reform, but they were the only ones who believed that slavery was such a terrible wrong that it had to be ended immediately. There were Americans who were against slavery but believed it should be tolerated until the South decided to give it up. And there were Americans who were against the *spread* of slavery but not against slavery itself. Of all these groups, however, the abolitionists were the most vocal.

No one can measure the impact abolitionists had on the nation and on the events that led to the Civil War. But these men and women put into words the long unspoken guilt of a nation that tolerated the "peculiar institution."

SECTION 4 REVIEW

Identify: American Colonization Society, David Walker, Gabriel, Denmark Vesey, Nat Turner's Rebellion, William Lloyd Garrison, Theodore Weld, American Anti-Slavery Society, Frederick Douglass, Elijah P. Lovejoy

Main Ideas
1. What events and factors, both national and international, helped create an American abolitionist movement? What two distinct approaches did the movement take?
2. What techniques did abolitionists use in their campaigns? How did opponents react? Why?

5. THE FIRST WOMEN'S MOVEMENT FOR EQUALITY

As you saw in Chapter 12, the Jacksonian era produced a new image of the ideal man. A new image of the American woman also developed, and it would lead to a century of struggle for women's rights.

Republican Motherhood: A Public Role for Women

A new feminine ideal was actually born in the years of the young Republic. In that era, the Founding Fathers called upon women to serve their country as the teachers and moral instructors of the next generation of Americans. As mothers, said John Adams, women were best suited to instill the values of and teach the virtues necessary for a democracy. **"Republican Motherhood,"** as this new role for women was called, did not take women beyond the household sphere or give them full citizenship. Yet it did give them a civic, or public, role for the first time in American history.

Loom operators in Lowell, Massachusetts, 1833

By the 1820s, women had expanded the duties of Republican Motherhood. They became active outside the home as teachers, as philanthropists (public benefactors), and as crusaders for public morality. Women became leaders and followers in many of the major reform movements of the era.

Women Develop a Different Self-Image

As reformers, women had experiences that drastically changed their concepts of themselves. Those who worked in public education had gone to school themselves and now found independent careers in teaching. Those who battled for prison reform, temperance, or abolition acquired many skills at organizing, fund raising, and public speaking that gave them confidence in their abilities. Those who argued for the dignity of the handicapped or the slave began to recognize their own inequality in society. Abolitionism in particular seemed to lead to the belief that women should have equal rights. "We have good cause to be grateful to the slave," wrote abolitionist and feminist Abbey Kelley. "In striving to strike his irons off, we found most surely that we were manacled ourselves."

Abolitionists such as **Sarah Grimké** and **Lucretia Mott** shared Kelley's views. Grimké, for example, noted with sadness that most male abolitionists were unwilling to extend the same legal and political rights to women as they wished to secure for black men. In her *Letters on the Condition of Women and the Equality of the Sexes* (1838), Grimké argued that women, too, must be citizens in a democracy. Thus, by the end of the Age of Reform, a small but determined group of women were calling for another reform: full citizenship for women.

The Seneca Falls Convention, 1848

It was an insult which eventually led to the now-famous Seneca Falls Convention of 1848. In 1840, the World Anti-Slavery Convention met in London, England. The American delegation included female abolitionists such as **Elizabeth Cady Stanton** and Quaker minister and orator Lucretia Mott. The World Anti-Slavery Association refused to seat these women delegates, arguing that decent women would not wish to participate in a political gathering. The American delegation protested, but could win only a humili-

LEADERS OF THE WOMEN'S MOVEMENT, 1840–1920

Elizabeth Cady Stanton

Sojourner Truth

Susan B. Anthony

★

Angelina Grimké (1805–1879) and **Sarah Grimké** (1792–1873). The Grimké sisters were born to an aristocratic slaveholding family of Charleston, South Carolina. During a visit to Philadelphia in the 1830s, Sarah, the older of the two, was converted to the Quaker faith. Sarah in turn converted Angelina, and the two sisters moved to the North, where they began to speak out against slavery and against inequality of women under the law. In 1835, Angelina wrote *An Appeal to the Christian Women of the South*, urging them to oppose the institution of slavery. In 1838 Sarah wrote *Letters on the Equality of the Sexes and the Condition of Women*. In 1838 Angelina married Theodore Weld, the minister who converted his students to abolitionism and who was probably the single most important figure in the abolitionist movement.

★

Lucretia Coffin Mott (1793–1880) was born in Massachusetts and lived in Philadelphia. A Quaker,

Mott taught school, lectured for temperance, against slavery, and for women's rights. She was, in addition, a Quaker minister. In 1833 Mott formed the Philadelphia Female Anti-Slavery Society. She was also a member of the American Anti-Slavery Society and, with Elizabeth Cady Stanton and others, attended the World Anti-Slavery Convention in London in 1840, where she and other female delegates were refused seats by the men who ran the convention.

★

Elizabeth Cady Stanton (1815–1902). Along with Lucretia Mott, she helped call the Seneca Falls Convention of 1848. After the Civil War, when black men were granted the vote but women were not, Stanton, along with Susan B. Anthony, helped found and edit *Revolution*, a newspaper that called for equal rights for women in all spheres of life. In 1869, she helped organize the National Woman Suffrage Association. Stanton wrote an autobiography in 1898: *Eighty Years and More*. Despite the lifetime she had

put in struggling for women's rights, neither Stanton nor her friend Anthony lived to see women vote.

★

Susan B. Anthony (1820–1906) was born in Massachusetts. A Quaker, she, too, like many women of her times, became a teacher. Anthony quickly abandoned teaching, however, to fight for other causes. Called the "Napoleon of the Women's Rights Movement," Anthony was a tireless organizer and uncompromising in her beliefs. When an organization known as the Sons of Temperance would not let women join, Anthony promptly founded the Daughters of Temperance. Anthony fought against slavery, for equal pay for women, for decent wages for all workers, and for the right of women to vote. When the 15th Amendment granted the right to vote only to black males, and not to black and white women, Anthony refused to support the bill. For her uncompromising stand, she lost much support in the women's rights movement. With Elizabeth Cady Stanton, Anthony helped found the newspaper, *Revolution*, advocate of women's rights. Anthony was president of the National Woman Suffrage Association and a member of the Working Woman's Association. In 1872 she caused a sensation by attempting to register to vote in Rochester, New York. She was arrested, tried, and sentenced to a fine, which she refused to pay. Susan B. Anthony was a key figure in the women's rights movement for more than 60 years, until her death in 1906.

★

Lucy Stone (1818-1893) was born in Massachusetts and graduated from the strongly abolitionist Oberlin College, Ohio, in 1847. Immediately upon graduation, Stone began to speak for the American Anti-Slavery Society as a regular lecturer. But she also spoke out for women's rights. When abolitionists urged her to be silent about women's issues, she responded: "I was a woman before I was an abolitionist.
I must speak for the women." In 1855 Stone married a fellow abolitionist, Henry Browne Blackwell,

but stunned American society by continuing to use her own name. Thus was coined a phrase, "Lucy Stoner," which meant a married woman who used her own name. It was one of Stone's lectures which converted Susan B. Anthony to the women's rights cause. In 1869, Stone helped found the American Woman Suffrage Association and edited *Women's Journal*, the organization's newspaper.

★

Sojourner Truth (c. 1797-1883) was a black woman who was born a slave but was freed. In 1843 she was convinced that "voices" told her to change her name and become a preacher. She changed her name to Sojourner Truth, which is how she was known from that day on. Until 1850, Truth spent most of her time in evangelical religious work and abolition. An intense, powerful speaker, Truth was tall, gaunt, and muscular. When she spoke out against slavery she was often accused of not being a woman. If these accusations upset Sojourner Truth, she did not let it show. Her battle

was for women's rights, not for any standards of femininity.

★

Charlotte Perkins Gilman (1860-1935) was born in Connecticut and was the great-granddaughter of Lyman Beecher, the famous minister. Gilman wrote many articles on the question of women's rights, as well as the famous book *Women and Economics* (1898). Starting in the 19th century, she criticized the exclusion of women from the work force, discussed the problems of careers and marriage, attacked the sexual stereotypes of men and women, debated the issue of "anatomy is destiny" for women, discussed the nature of housework, and analyzed the nuclear family—all basic questions in our society today. In 1915 Gilman also wrote a utopian novel, *Herland*, which was serialized in a magazine and published in book form in 1979.

★

Carrie Chapman Catt (1859-1947) was born in Wisconsin and raised in Iowa. In 1900, Catt took over the reins of the women's suffrage movement from the aging Stanton and Anthony. The winning of the 19th Amendment was Catt's greatest achievement, and it is to her and Susan B. Anthony that American women owe their right to vote. It was Catt who formulated the "Winning Plan" which led to the passage of the 19th Amendment. Catt's "Winning Plan" consisted of winning the right to vote in individual states while, at the same time, fighting for passage of women's suffrage on a national level. Catt served as president of the National American Woman Suffrage Association, helped form the Woman's Peace Party (1915), and helped organize the League of Women Voters in 1919.

Protest meeting against low wages held in New York's City Hall in 1845

ating compromise from the convention: the women could sit, silently, behind a curtain in the balcony!

While the men debated slavery, Mott and Stanton strolled through London, debating the woman reformer's dilemma. Stanton concluded that, while they must continue to help others, they must also help themselves.

On a summer day in July 1848, Stanton met once again with Lucretia Mott. It had been eight years since the London convention, but Stanton had not forgotten their discussions. With three other women, Mott and Stanton planned a convention for women to debate their rights. The next day, July 14, the *Seneca County Courier* carried this modest announcement: "Women's Rights Convention—a convention to discuss the social, civil, and religious rights of women will be held . . . on Wednesday and Thursday, the 19th and 20th of July." This meeting became known as the **Seneca Falls Convention.**

For the convention, Stanton prepared a "Declaration of Sentiments." She modeled this appeal for women's rights on the Declaration of Independence. "We hold these truths to be self-evident," Stanton wrote, "that all men and women are created equal. . . ."

The day of the convention dawned sunny and warm. Mott and Stanton had no idea whether any one in this upstate New York farming region would attend. In fact, 300 people came from a 50-mile radius, traveling by foot, horseback, and wagon. Together they debated the issues Stanton raised in her Declaration, among them the rights of married women to own and sell their own property, the rights of women for custody of their children, the rights of women to higher education and to enter professional schools, and, finally, the right to vote.

Most of the resolutions passed unanimously, but number nine, the question of suffrage, raised heated debate. Lucretia Mott herself felt it was too radical a demand. "Thou will make us ridiculous," she told Stanton. "We must go slowly." But the former slave Frederick Douglass stood up for Mrs. Stanton and warmly supported women's suffrage. In the end, resolution number nine carried, and the first formal request for the vote had been made.

Few of the goals set at Seneca Falls were achieved before the Civil War ended the Age of

FROM THE ARCHIVES

Resolutions from the Seneca Falls Convention

Resolved, That all laws which prevent woman from occupying such a station in society as her conscience shall dictate, or which place her in a position inferior to that of man, are contrary to the great precept of nature, and therefore of no force or authority.

Resolved, That woman is man's equal—was intended to be so by the Creator, and the highest good of the race demands that she should be recognized as such.

Resolved, That the same amount of virtue, delicacy, and refinement of behavior that is required of woman in the social state, should also be required of man, and the same transgressions should be visited with equal severity on both man and woman.

Resolved, That it is the duty of the women of this country to secure to themselves their sacred right to the elective franchise.

Resolved, That the speedy success of our cause depends upon the zealous and untiring efforts of both men and women, for the overthrow of the monopoly of the pulpit, and for the securing to women an equal participation with men in the various trades, professions, and commerce.

From the Seneca Falls Declaration of Sentiments, 1848.

Reform. Many would be won during the last quarter of the 19th century. Yet only one woman who attended the Seneca Falls Convention in 1848, 19-year-old Charlotte Woodward, lived to vote for the President of the United States. It would be another 72 years before women's suffrage was won.

SECTION 5 REVIEW

 Identify: "Republican Motherhood," Sarah Grimké, Lucretia Mott, Elizabeth Cady Stanton, Seneca Falls Convention

Main Ideas

1. What factors contributed to the rise of a women's rights movement during the Age of Reform?
2. What issues were discussed at the Seneca Falls Convention in 1848?

CHAPTER 13 REVIEW

Key Terms
Explain the meaning of each of the following terms:

Second Great Awakening
Benevolent Empire
Know-Nothing party
utopian societies
Mormon Church
Transcendentalism
Hudson River School
lyceum movement
temperance
Philadelphia system
Auburn system
American Colonization Society
Nat Turner's Rebellion
American Anti-Slavery Society
"Republican Motherhood"
Seneca Falls Convention

Reviewing the Main Ideas
Section 1
1. Describe the rise of religious fervor in the 1820s. What were its positive and negative sides?
2. Describe the origin of the Mormons and the problems they faced.
3. How did Transcendentalism reflect new attitudes about America and Americans? Who were some of the leading Transcendentalists?

Section 2
1. How did new attitudes about America affect culture and the arts?
2. How did Poe, Hawthorne, and Melville differ from other writers of the time in their beliefs about human nature?
3. How was the lyceum movement an expression of popular culture?

Section 3
1. List the reform movements of the 1820s and 1830s, their leaders, and their goals.
2. How did the attitudes of many reformers reflect both genuine concern and feelings of superiority? Give examples.

Section 4
1. What events led to the creation of abolitionist societies?
2. How did the abolitionist movement gain new members? What problems did it face?

Section 5
1. Why did a women's rights movement arise during the Age of Reform?
2. What issues were discussed at the 1848 Seneca Falls Convention?

Special History Skills:
Using the Card Catalog
The key to any library is the card catalog. By knowing how to use it, you can unlock the wealth of information the library has to offer. The card catalog is arranged alphabetically. It contains at least three cards for each book in the library—an author card, a title card, and a subject card. Each card contains similar information—title, author, publisher, and date of publication. The contents of each book are usually briefly described.

Each card in the card catalog has a number which indicates where in the library the book (or pamphlet, tape cassette, or film) can be found. Most libraries use either the Dewey decimal system or the Library of Congress system of arranging their nonfiction books according to subject. Fiction is usually arranged alphabetically by author's last name.

When you know the specific book you need, look for the title or author card in the catalog. If you have a topic but no specific title, look up the subject. If you don't find the subject, think of another way of stating it ("cars" might be under "automobiles," for example), or ask the librarian.

1. What type of card—author, title, or subject— would you look for in the card catalog to find each of the following?
   (a) a book on women's rights in the 1800s
   (b) a biography of Elizabeth Cady Stanton
   (c) *Paintbox on the Frontier*
   (d) a novel by Nathaniel Hawthorne
2. Use the card catalog in your library to find a book on each of the following topics. Copy the information you find on the card.
   (a) the Mormon Church
   (b) art in the 1820s–1850s
   (c) famous American feminists of the 1800s
   (d) a biography of Frederick Douglass

Other Skill Activities

1. A letter to Horace Mann

Write a letter to Horace Mann describing the strengths and weaknesses of American education today. Mention his reforms in your letter.

2. Start a reform movement

Suppose that you were to start a reform movement today. Give a five-minute speech explaining what you would try to reform, why, and why people should join your organization.

3. The popular versus the lasting

Choose a current painting, song, or novel that you think has lasting value. Have another student choose a current painting, song, or novel that he or she thinks is merely popular and has no lasting value. Give presentations to the class on your beliefs.

4. Crossword puzzle

Make a crossword puzzle using the names of reformers and movements during the Age of Reform.

Thinking Critically

1. Explain the following statement made in your textbook: "Religious leaders such as Lyman Beecher confused a perfect American society with a society in which all citizens thought and worshiped alike." Do you agree or disagree with this statement? Why?

2. You have learned about an era of religious revival and reform. Compare this to the era in which you live. How are the two periods the same? How are they different?

3. How did the Nat Turner Rebellion and the rise of abolitionism strengthen proslavery and antislavery attitudes in the period 1830–1850? How would this probably affect relations between the North and the South?

Further Reading

Abby Slater. *In Search of Margaret Fuller.* Delacorte, 1978. Easy reading with excerpts from the writings of an early feminist.

Mary Sayer Haverstock. *Indian Gallery: The Story of George Catlin.* Four Winds Press, 1973. A beautiful volume of his paintings.

Miriam Gurko. *The Ladies of Seneca Falls.* Macmillan, 1974. Discusses the birth of the women's rights movement and its leaders.

Nathaniel Hawthorne. *The House of the Seven Gables.*

TEST YOURSELF

WRITE YOUR ANSWERS ON A SEPARATE SHEET OF PAPER.

Identify

Write the letter of the description that best matches each name listed below.

1. Margaret Fuller
2. Joseph Smith
3. Henry David Thoreau
4. Horace Mann
5. Frederick Douglass
6. Edgar Allan Poe
7. Dorothea Dix
8. Theodore Weld
9. Elizabeth Cady Stanton
10. Henry Wadsworth Longfellow

a. founder of the Mormon Church
b. went to Walden Pond to live self-sufficiently
c. former slave who became a leading abolitionist
d. master of the short story
e. Transcendentalist editor and feminist
f. the new nation's poet-historian
g. early feminist leader at Seneca Falls
h. worked for better care for the insane
i. minister who organized abolitionist societies
j. reformed public education

True or False

Mark T if the statement is true, F if it is false.

1. Abolitionists had a carefully planned program for the end of slavery.
2. Most Americans supported the efforts of abolitionists and feminists.
3. Reformers eagerly accepted the ways of new immigrants as part of American society.
4. By the 1850s temperance reformers were working for legal prohibition of liquor.
5. Many women abolitionists became feminists in order to free their own sex.
6. The Philadelphia and Auburn systems were designed to reform criminals.
7. By 1850, education reformers had created a tax-supported public school system in many states.
8. Poe, Hawthorne, and Melville shared the reformers' optimism about human character.
9. Though the Mormon Church grew slowly, it was welcome in every state it entered.
10. The 1820s and 1830s were a time of pride in the new American culture, art, and literature.

VISITING THE PAST

Washington, D.C.

Clues to the origins of most cities can be found in their geography. One city, however, owes its existence and location entirely to politics. Washington, D.C., was created especially to serve as the home of the United States government.

It was 1790. Congress decided to build its permanent home in a new city "worthy of the nation." A political compromise led to the decision to build the capital on the Potomac River. After years of moving, the federal government would spend the next decade in Philadelphia, and then, in 1800, move for one last time.

George Washington selected Major Pierre L'Enfant to be the architect of the new city. L'Enfant went to the site in the spring of 1791 and began making his plans. He placed the most important building, the Capitol, in the most prominent spot on the landscape. The President's house, the other key government building, was situated on another prime spot. The two were to be connected by a grand avenue. Out from the Capitol, like the spokes of a wheel, radiated the major avenues of the city. Spreading forth from the Capitol was a mall. The city plan included parks, monuments, and other elements needed to give the city the dignity of a national capital.

It would take years for the city to achieve that dignity. In 1800, when the government moved in, neither of the two major buildings was finished. The grand avenues were lines on maps, nothing else.

The city grew in size and grandeur, however, and as it flourished it deviated from L'Enfant's plan. Its special character as a city designed to be a capital was threat-

ened. In the early 1900s action was taken. An updated plan was formulated. Height limitations for new buildings preserved the horizontal flavor of the city and emphasized the prominence of the government buildings.

Today, Washington, D.C., more closely resembles L'Enfant's vision than it did a century ago. His plan still helps shape the city.

A new plaza at the White House end of Pennsylvania Avenue, features a replica of L'Enfant's plan etched in marble paving. As you look at it, and the city it shaped, you can see the power of a vision.

Washington, D.C., is a city full of landmarks. Many visitors are unaware that the design of the city itself is also a major landmark.

Madison, Indiana

Before the highway and the airplane, Americans moved on one of nature's own transportation systems: the rivers. As pioneers moved west, towns sprang up along the rivers. One such town is Madison, Indiana, located on the Ohio River.

Madison was first settled between 1806 and 1809. At one time it was Indiana's largest city, and its future was thought to include becoming the state capital. The 1830s through 1850s were Madison's Golden Age, its prosperity based on pork packing, boat building, milling, and iron foundries.

By 1847 railroads had become the new national transportation network. Madison's geography made it difficult for the railroad to get to town. Eventually, the railroad bypassed Madison completely. With the railroad went prosperity.

This part of Madison's story is not unique. Just as the railroad replaced the river, the airplane and the highway would undermine

towns that depended on the railroad for their prosperity. Even today, a highway re-routing can turn a busy town into a quiet village. But Madison's story is special. Madison still retains, virtually intact, 130 blocks of buildings dating from its Golden Age. As you walk through this rich architectural inheritance, with its decorative ironwork, its restored Federal and Greek Revival brick homes, and its tree-lined streets, you see how these historic blocks give Madison its special sense of place.

By 1960 the value of Madison's architectural inheritance was recognized. A group called Historic Madison, Inc., was formed to help preserve this heritage.

When the railroad left Madison behind, the town's future was in doubt. Today, there is no doubt that Madison's future lies in the beauty and extent of its early 19th-century buildings.

New Orleans' Vieux Carré

New Orleans is famous for its historic French Quarter, also called the Vieux Carré ("old square"). Founded in 1718 by the French, New Orleans has a rich history. Though it became part of the United States in 1803, the flavor of the old city is still European. Its years as a French and then Spanish city are reflected in its architecture. Much of this architecture has survived fires and floods. Each rebuilding added new elements to the traditional ones. The result is a charming Old World city with narrow streets, brick walls, attractive street lamps, balconies framed with decorative ironwork, small shops, intimate gardens, and lovely homes.

As the special physical character of the district evolved over time, so too did its distinctive population. With the introduction of industry to the area, many of the old Creole (person of French or Spanish heritage) families moved out and were replaced by a variety of immigrant groups. As a deteriorating, low-rent area, the once elegant French Quarter attracted writers, artists, musicians, and show people. Eventually the charm of the area was rediscovered by others. Today the French Quarter is again a fashionable area.

The Vieux Carré is well known for its antique stores, book shops, and specialty stores. Its restaurants and bars are world renowned. The diversity of its population, its distinctive environment, and the richness of its commercial activity have created its identity. It was this *tout ensemble* ("all taken together")—the general effect— that the City Council hoped to preserve when it designated the French Quarter a historic district in 1937.

Much has happened since 1937. The district's immense popularity has led to change. Today the population has become less diverse as rents have soared. The variety of shops still exists, but often the small specialty shop is replaced by the more prosperous tourist gift store. The Old World feeling of the environment dominates, though the streets are often crowded with tour buses and visitors.

The *tout ensemble* has eroded but still survives. The French Quarter is now recognized as an essential part of the city's economic health. Its success has led to the rediscovery of other old and elegant neighborhoods. Will the Vieux Carré be able to keep alive its *tout ensemble* in the face of the pressures that success has created? That is the challenge facing New Orleans today.

UNIT 4 TEST

WRITE YOUR ANSWERS ON A SEPARATE SHEET OF PAPER.

Matching (20 points)
Match each person with a description from the list below.

1. Horace Mann
2. Tecumseh
3. Dorothea Dix
4. Nat Turner
5. Daniel Webster
6. Margaret Fuller
7. John C. Calhoun
8. Elizabeth Cady Stanton
9. John Marshall
10. Frederick Douglass

a. helped organize the Seneca Falls Convention
b. Quaker minister and orator
c. defeated during the War of 1812
d. led a slave uprising
e. Transcendentalist author and editor
f. Chief Justice of the Supreme Court
g. worked to improve treatment of the mentally ill
h. states' rights advocate
i. abolitionist orator
j. senator who defended the supremacy of the federal government
k. reformed public education

Multiple Choice (20 points)
Write the letter of the answer that best completes each statement. There may be more than one correct answer.

1. The Erie Canal
   a. touched off a canal-building craze in Ohio, Indiana, and Pennsylvania.
   b. was an engineering marvel of its time.
   c. solved the problem of cheap transportation from the western frontier to the eastern markets.
   d. All of the above are correct.
2. Strict construction of the Constitution
   a. was advocated by Alexander Hamilton.
   b. is justified by the "elastic clause."
   c. was used by Thomas Jefferson to defend his purchase of Louisiana in 1803.
   d. None of the above are correct.
3. Select the answer that correctly matches the

Presidents with their political party.
   a. Jefferson–Republican, Jackson–Democrat, Harrison–Whig
   b. John Adams–Republican, Monroe–Federalist, Van Buren–Democrat
   c. Washington–Federalist, Madison–Republican, Jackson–Republican
   d. None of the above are correct.
4. America went to war in 1812
   a. to uphold the national honor.
   b. to destroy Indian power on the frontier.
   c. to satisfy the New England War Hawks.
   d. to conquer Canada.
5. Politics in the Age of Jackson
   a. was characterized by low voter turnout.
   b. appealed to the elite groups in America.
   c. continued the style established by the Virginia Dynasty.
   d. featured campaigns focused on images, not on issues.

True or False (20 points)
Read each statement below. Mark T if the statement is true, F if it is false. Rewrite the italicized words in all false statements to make them true.

1. *Pinckney's Treaty* granted Americans valuable rights to the mouth of the Mississippi River.
2. The Supreme Court's decision in *Marbury* v. *Madison* established the Court's power of judicial review.
3. The Battle of New Orleans made *William Henry Harrison* a national hero.
4. "Universal suffrage" in 1820 meant that for the first time *the majority of Americans* could vote and hold office.
5. Transcendentalism was an optimistic philosophy that called upon Americans *to develop self-reliance, confidence, and individuality.*

Essay Questions (40 points)
1. In his Farewell Address, George Washington warned the new nation against political parties, sectionalism, and involvement in European rivalries. Discuss how well his advice was taken in each of these three areas between 1796 and 1850.
2. What trends and events provided a foundation for the abolitionist and women's rights movements in the Age of Reform?

Unit Five

Expansion, Civil War, and Reconstruction

Chapters in This Unit

Chapter 14   1840–1850

MANIFEST DESTINY SWEEPS THE NATION WESTWARD

Texas and Oregon! The words ring magically in the ears. In the 1840s the dream of adding these lands to the United States seems about to come true. Some Americans even dream of adding California, though few think it is possible—yet. But the belief is widespread that one day the Stars and Stripes will wave over all these lands, and others as well. Perhaps Canada will be added. And why not Mexico, too?

So many Americans in the 1840s believed in the dream of an expanding nation that a new phrase was born—"Manifest Destiny." First used by a New York editor, the phrase caught on. "Manifest Destiny" had no exact definition, but somehow everyone seemed to know exactly what it meant. It carried the idea that nothing could stop the young, vigorous nation from becoming a transcontinental power. Nothing could prevent Americans from spreading their democratic institutions throughout the Western Hemisphere and putting their stamp of freedom on the whole New World. This was to be the American destiny. It was written in the stars!

This kind of thinking swept the nation in the 1840s. It provided a welcome if only temporary relief from the growing disagreements over slavery and the tariff. Here at least was an issue on which many southern planters, western farmers, and New England merchants could agree enthusiastically.

Sections in This Chapter
1. The United States Adds Vast New Lands in Oregon
2. Texas Wins Independence from Mexico
3. The United States Wins a War with Mexico
4. The California Gold Rush
5. The Compromise of 1850

Opposite: part of a Mountain Man's gear—an iron-mounted flintlock rifle, a hunting pouch, and a painted buffalo robe

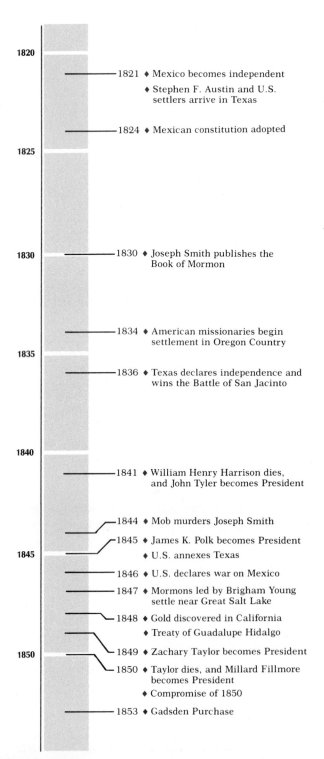

1820

1821 ◆ Mexico becomes independent
◆ Stephen F. Austin and U.S. settlers arrive in Texas

1824 ◆ Mexican constitution adopted

1825

1830 ◆ Joseph Smith publishes the Book of Mormon

1830

1834 ◆ American missionaries begin settlement in Oregon Country

1835

1836 ◆ Texas declares independence and wins the Battle of San Jacinto

1840

1841 ◆ William Henry Harrison dies, and John Tyler becomes President

1844 ◆ Mob murders Joseph Smith

1845 ◆ James K. Polk becomes President
◆ U.S. annexes Texas

1845

1846 ◆ U.S. declares war on Mexico

1847 ◆ Mormons led by Brigham Young settle near Great Salt Lake

1848 ◆ Gold discovered in California
◆ Treaty of Guadalupe Hidalgo

1849 ◆ Zachary Taylor becomes President

1850

1850 ◆ Taylor dies, and Millard Fillmore becomes President
◆ Compromise of 1850

1853 ◆ Gadsden Purchase

1. THE UNITED STATES ADDS VAST NEW LANDS IN OREGON

By the early 1840s Americans from New England to the Mississippi Valley had come down with a bad case of what was called "Oregon fever." Around many a dinner table, discussion turned to the merits of pulling up stakes and joining one of the wagon trains leaving Missouri every spring for the Pacific Northwest. Newspapers and pamphlets urged their readers to stake out claims to the rich farmland beyond the Rocky Mountains. A magnet seemed to be drawing an ever growing number of Americans to the **Oregon Country.** (See map, page 334.)

In the early years of European exploration and colonization, several nations claimed the Oregon Country. None of them paid the least attention to the fact that the land was already occupied—that the Northwest Indians (see Chapter 1) had lived and thrived in the Pacific Northwest for countless centuries. Of the various claimants to Oregon—Spain, France, Russia, Britain, and later the United States, all but two had dropped out of the competition by 1825. The two remaining, Britain and the United States, both based their claims on discovery and exploration. As you may recall, in 1579 Francis Drake sailed along the Pacific coast on his famous voyage around the world, thereby giving Britain an early claim. Later, British sea captains, including Captain James Cook in the 1770s, visited the area, adding weight to the British claim. Still later, when the North American fur trade began to shift to the Far West, a British concern, the Hudson's Bay Company, developed a near monopoly on the fur trade of the area.

The United States claim was more recent but also soundly based. In the late 1780s, Captain Robert Gray stopped along the Oregon coast on a voyage westward from Boston to China. He traded with the Indians, exchanging goods for sea otter furs, which he then sold in China. On a later voyage in 1792 he discovered the Columbia River. Soon thereafter, many New England ship captains stopped regularly along the Oregon coast en route to China.

Shortly after Gray's visits, Lewis and Clark made their celebrated trip from St. Louis to the

Trappers and traders met every summer at a fur marketing fair, or "rendezvous," for several days of trading and entertainment. Above: the 1837 rendezvous in the Wind River Mountains of present-day Wyoming.

mouth of the Columbia River. Their reports stimulated enough interest in Oregon for the United States to openly challenge the British claim. Since neither nation was in a position to exercise firm control, in 1818 they agreed to occupy Oregon jointly. Clearly, when the day came to decide the future of Oregon, the nation that had done the most to occupy the land would have a distinct advantage.

Mountain Men and Missionaries

In the early 1800s, American fur traders operating from the Rocky Mountain area, began to challenge the British monopoly of the fur trade in the Oregon Country. They were not very successful in opposing the British in Oregon, and after a time they withdrew eastward. But these **Mountain Men**, as they were called, mapped out the best routes over the mountains from the Missouri River to both Oregon and California. These routes became famous in the settlement of the Far West.

From time to time, missionaries interested in Christianizing the Indians joined parties of fur

traders on their journeys into Oregon Country. In 1834, a Methodist minister, Jason Lee, founded a mission in the fertile Willamette [wi lam'it] Valley, near modern Salem. The following year, a group led by two Presbyterian ministers, Samuel Parker and **Marcus Whitman**, began to work among the Nez Percé Indians of Oregon.

Whitman's enthusiasm for the new country caused him to return East to lead another group of settlers in 1836. This time he and other male settlers were accompanied by their wives, who worked with them in converting Indians and in starting a new settlement. In letters to friends in the East, Whitman did much to stir interest in the Oregon Country. His vivid description of the beauty of the land, its rich soil, mild climate, and abundant rainfall helped bring on the "Oregon fever" that swept over much of the East and Midwest.

The Oregon Trail

The early 1840s marked the turning point in deciding whether Britain or the United States

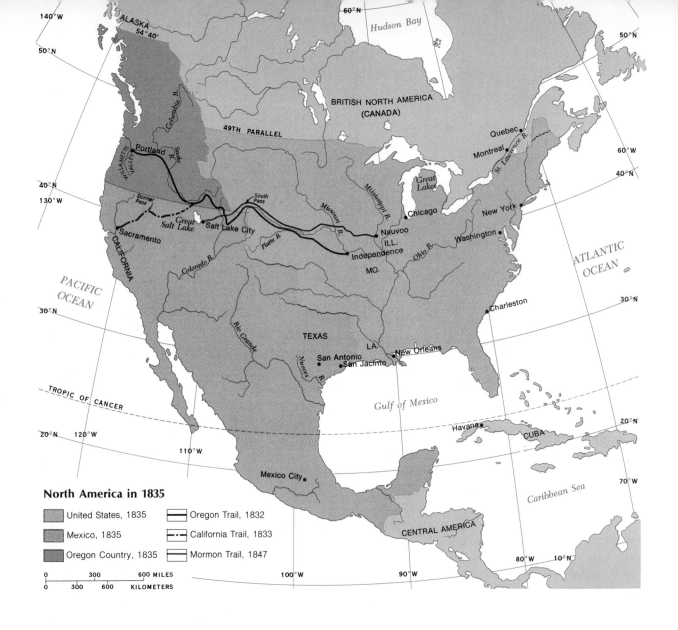

North America in 1835

▨ United States, 1835	▬ Oregon Trail, 1832
▨ Mexico, 1835	▬·▬ California Trail, 1833
▨ Oregon Country, 1835	▭ Mormon Trail, 1847

0 300 600 MILES
0 300 600 KILOMETERS

would win the contest for Oregon. As late as 1839, there were less than 100 Americans in all of Oregon. By 1846, there were 10,000. Most went to Oregon via the **Oregon Trail**, using routes mapped earlier by the Mountain Men. The Oregon Trail began at Independence, Missouri, and followed the winding Missouri and Platte rivers for 1,000 miles across the Great Plains to the Rocky Mountains. (See map above.) The trail cut through the mountains by way of South Pass, the only route wide enough for the covered wagons. Once through the Rockies, the trail stretched on for another thousand miles, proceeding along the Snake River Valley into Idaho, through the rugged Blue Mountains, and down to Fort Vancouver,

headquarters of the Hudson's Bay Company. In 1845, Portland was founded near this fort.

With the ease with which we fly today from St. Louis to Seattle, it is almost impossible to imagine the hardships endured on the Oregon Trail in the 1840s. The journey took six months. As the wagon train crept along at two miles per hour, Indian arrows, disease, starvation, and sheer exhaustion brought death to many. "The cowards never started, and the weak died along the way," became a common saying in the West.

The Settlers Organize a Government

With the great influx of Americans into the Oregon Country, the question of how they would be governed quickly arose. The Americans did not want to be ruled by the Hudson's Bay Company, which until then governed the area.

With the same kind of foresight that led the Pilgrims to meet in the cabin of the *Mayflower* and draw up the Mayflower Compact, a group of American immigrants met in an abandoned warehouse in Oregon and drew up a provisional constitution, which was ratified by settlers at a meeting on July 5, 1843. The constitution set down rules the settlers would live by until the United States took over Oregon.

There was already a growing chorus of support back East for the annexation of Oregon. The issue came up dramatically in the election of 1844 when the Democratic party called for the annexation of all of Oregon to 54°40' north latitude, that is, to the southern border of Alaska. This took in a vast area north of the Columbia River where there were almost no American settlers.

Polk Becomes President

In the presidential campaign of 1844, Democratic candidate **James K. Polk** ran against the Whig party's Henry Clay. The Democrats campaigned vigorously, using the phrase "Fifty-four Forty or Fight!" as their rallying cry. Polk won by a comfortable electoral majority, and when he entered office, he set about resolving the Oregon question. Polk never seriously intended to insist on all of Oregon to 54°40'N. Several earlier Presidents had tried to persuade the British to draw the boundary line at 49°N. Much of the U.S.–Canadian boundary had already been established on this parallel. Polk did not object to a compromise.

A New Territory

President Polk was eager for a quick settlement, particularly since war with Mexico threatened over the troubling issue of Texas. When the British suddenly suggested dividing the Oregon Country at the 49th parallel, Polk readily agreed. With the Americans rapidly winning the race to settle the southern part of the disputed area, the British also saw the wisdom of compromise.

With the signing of the treaty of 1846, the United States and Britain gained an undisputed border all the way from the Atlantic to the Pacific. After a bitter debate over the future of slavery in Oregon, Congress voted in 1848 to organize it as a territory with a free-soil government.

John Tyler (1790–1862)

IN OFFICE: 1841–1845

From Virginia. Although originally a Democrat, Tyler was elected Vice-President on the Whig ticket. Upon Harrison's death one month after his inauguration, Tyler succeeded to the presidency. His veto of the bills for a new national bank alienated him from the Whigs, and he again aligned himself with the Democrats. This alliance foreshadowed the gradual absorption of conservative Southern Whigs by the Democrats.

James K. Polk (1795–1849)

IN OFFICE: 1845–1849

Democrat from Tennessee. Polk achieved all the major objectives of his campaign platform. Texas was admitted to the Union (1845); the Oregon boundary dispute with Britain was settled (1846); the territories of California and New Mexico were acquired as a result of the Mexican War (1846–1848); the tariff was lowered (1846); and the independent treasury system was reestablished (1846).

SECTION 1 REVIEW

 Identify: Oregon Country, Mountain Men, Marcus Whitman, Oregon Trail, James K. Polk

Main Ideas

1. On what did the United States base its claim to the Oregon Country?
2. What attraction did Oregon hold for settlers?
3. How did Oregon settlers gain a government?
4. How was the issue of a U.S.–Canadian border resolved?

THE GEOGRAPHIC SETTING

THE SEA OF GRASS: THE GREAT PLAINS

Those who caught "Oregon fever" in the 1840s did not appreciate the grasslands that they had to cross to get to the Far West. These pioneers had never before encountered such flat, dry, and treeless plains. In fact, much of what we call the Great Plains today was then considered to be a desert.

The Desert That Wasn't

Zebulon Pike recommended in 1810 that American settlement end at the Mississippi and Missouri rivers. Stephen H. Long, an Army engineer and explorer, wrote in 1820 that "The whole of this region seems peculiarly adapted as a range for buffalos. . . . It is . . . of course, uninhabitable by a people depending on agriculture." Long labeled a map of the area between the Missouri River and the Rocky Mountains the "Great American Desert."

This desert soon became a standard feature on maps of the United States. Americans were so convinced that white farmers would never settle on the Great Plains that they decided to reserve the seemingly useless region for the Indians. Thus, in the 1830s, they deported the eastern Indians to the edges of this treeless, forbidding land. (See Chapter 12.)

Americans believed the plains were useless because the region did not look like the forestlands that they were used to. The plains

appeared to be an endless ocean, where waves of grass and flowers rippled in the wind. The lack of trees seemed to indicate that the soil was infertile. The average annual rainfall was less than appeared necessary for agriculture. Furthermore, centuries of decaying vegetation had formed a thick crust of sod on top of the soil. This could not be cultivated by the plows of the day.

The Plains Begin to Attract Ranchers and Farmers

Systematic scientific study of the Great Plains began to change people's minds. Between 1838 and 1863 the Army Corps of Topographical Engineers explored, surveyed, and mapped the West. Plans for a transcontinental railroad led to other government exploration of possible routes across the plains.

Explorers and surveyors were followed by prospectors and cattlemen. By 1870 the "Great American Desert" had miraculously disappeared, as farmers moved in with steel "sod buster" plows to cut through the thick sod.

Some tried to justify the earlier mistaken notions by suggesting that cultivation had improved the climate and increased rainfall. "Rain follows the plow" was a popular saying in the mid-1800s. Better-than-average rainfall between 1875 and 1880 brought many farmers to the plains, but recurring cycles of drought proved that the plow theory was wrong. The plains receive more rain in some years than in others.

An Enormous Area

The Great Plains extend all the way from the Arctic Ocean in Canada to the coastal plain of Texas. This, then, is a physical feature of immense size, extending from north to south for 3,000 miles! (See Map 3 in the Atlas Section.) From west to east the plains stretch about 400 miles. In the present-day United States, the Great Plains include parts of North and South Dakota, Nebraska, Kansas, Oklahoma, Texas, Montana, Wyoming, Colorado, and New Mexico.

The overwhelming aspect of this region is its flatness. The Llano Estacado, or "Staked Plains," of northwestern Texas are typical of extensive areas in early days. The natural landscape was so flat and featureless that early travelers often lost their way on this "sea of grass," and stakes or buffalo bones were set out to mark the routes of travel.

The plains are not entirely flat, however. The Black Hills of South Dakota and various stone outcroppings like Chimney Rock in Nebraska interrupt the plains in several places. The plains gently slope downward from the Rocky Mountains. At the edge of the Rockies, the plains are over a mile high, while they are only about 1,500 feet high at their eastern edges. This gradual slope was caused by the erosion of the mountains, the material of which is carried by rivers flowing eastward to the Mississippi.

On your map note the major cities along the Missouri River, where steamboats and keelboats carried people and goods in the 1800s. The Platte River was too shallow for navigation, but its valley made an excellent roadbed and the trees that grew along its banks were sources of fuel.

The 100th Meridian Is the Boundary Line

The Great Plains, sometimes called the high plains, end at about the 100° west meridian. This dry region, where 60 or so million buffalo grazed in the mid-19th century, is now famous for cattle ranching and wheat production, often with the use of irrigation and dry farming methods.

East of the Great Plains is another broad, flat plains region, called the Central Lowlands. This region receives more rainfall and has become one of the most productive farming regions of the world. Moist air from the Gulf of Mexico travels northward, dropping 20–40 inches of rain per year on the Central Lowlands. In contrast, the Great Plains receive only 10–20 inches of rain per year from drier winds crossing the Rockies.

A Land of Golden Harvests

Life has never been easy on the Great Plains. The climate is severe and unpredictable. In winter temperatures can change 50 degrees Fahrenheit in the course of a day. Weeks of summer drought are often followed by sudden hail and fierce, drenching thunderstorms.

But the Great Plains are no longer a wasteland reserved for conquered Indian tribes or a vast highway to somewhere else. Americans, once ill-suited for life on the prairie, altered their equipment, techniques, even their way of life. Sod houses, barbed wire fences, windmills, and irrigation typify their adaptation. The Great Plains were opened to agriculture in the 1860s and 1870s, about the same time as the railroads made cheap transportation to eastern markets available. This lucky coincidence provided America with an unrivaled food supply. In just 50 years the "Great American Desert" had become part of America's breadbasket.

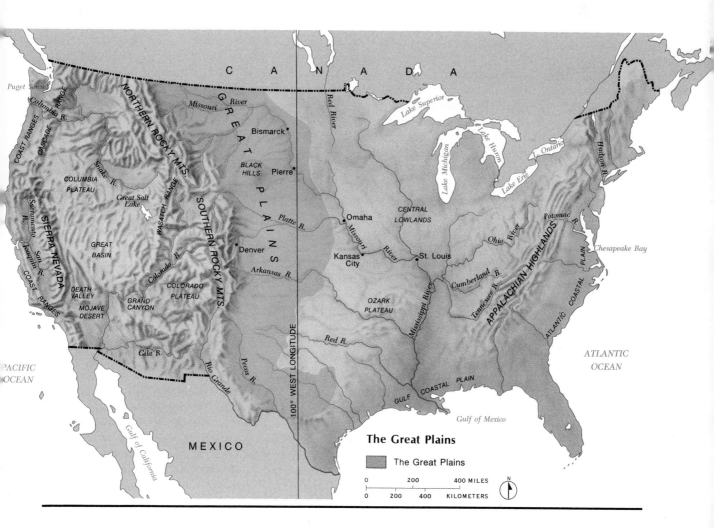

The Great Plains

The Great Plains

0   200   400 MILES
0   200   400   KILOMETERS

2. TEXAS WINS INDEPENDENCE FROM MEXICO

In the early 1820s, when the Mountain Men were blazing trails through the Rocky Mountains to Oregon and California, other Americans were setting out for Texas. Moses Austin, a Connecticut-born resident of Missouri, obtained a grant of land from the Spanish authorities in 1821. He got permission to bring 300 families to Texas, then part of New Spain and ruled from Mexico City. After Moses Austin's death later the same year, his son **Stephen F. Austin** obtained the right to take over his father's grant.

In December 1821, the first Americans arrived in Texas. They arrived only to learn that Mexico had declared itself independent of Spain. But fortunately for the settlers, the new Mexican government gave its approval to Austin's plan. Both the Spanish and later the Mexican governments made it clear that the American immigrants were to become citizens of their adopted country, obey its laws, and become Roman Catholics. The colonists brought by Austin had no quarrel with these conditions. They received generous land grants and set about building a prosperous community along the Brazos River. (See map, opposite page.)

Texas Under Spain

As you saw in Chapter 2, Texas was part of the Spanish borderlands that stretched from the Gulf of Mexico to the Pacific. This vast area was considered important for the defense of New Spain. Although only thinly populated, Texas had been the home of settlers from Spain and Mexico for over 200 years before American immigration began. When Austin's first colonists arrived, the colonial population of Texas was roughly 5,000, centered mainly at San Antonio, La Bahía (Goliad), and Nacogdoches. The people were varied, consisting of Spaniards, creoles (American-born of Spanish descent), mestizos (mixed Spanish and Indian), blacks, Indians, and various mixtures. In addition, some 25,000 Comanches, Kiowas, Apaches, and other tribes still hunted throughout the enormous region.

Spanish civilization in Texas was based on the missions, the *presidios* [pri sid'ē ōz], or forts, and the towns that grew up around them. Usually run by Franciscans, the missions worked to Christianize the Indians and to teach them farming, spinning, and weaving. Once this was accomplished, the Indians became *peons* (laborers) on the large estates. The presidios protected the missions and the towns.

The towns carried on a wide variety of farming and other activities. Most of the settlers raised farm animals, particularly sheep for their wool and cattle for meat and hides. The cattle industry was particularly important. Introduced from Spain by the earliest settlers, the cattle increased rapidly and by the early 1800s roamed wild in the bush country. Over time, they developed into the famous Texas longhorns.

The Spanish cowboys, or *vaqueros* [va ker'ōz] as they were called, invented or developed the arts of cattle herding later famous in the American West—tending cattle from horseback, roping, branding, the roundup, and the overland trail to market.

Before Spanish rule ended in 1821, the Spanish had explored most of Texas, Christianized some of the Indians, named most of the streams and inlets, built a number of thriving missions and settlements, and laid the basis for the cattle industry. The region remained sparsely populated, however. Spain had failed to attract enough settlers to cultivate the fertile farmland and develop the economy. It was mainly because of this lack of settlers that the Spanish and Mexican governments looked favorably on the plans of Moses and Stephen Austin.

The American Settlements

As with any new settlement, the Americans in Texas faced many problems and frustrations. But the select group of settlers who made up the "Old Three Hundred," as the pioneers of the Anglo-American Texans came to be called, were unusually industrious and ambitious. They astonished the Hispanic Texans by their rash of activity, but aroused no real resentment or cultural conflict.

The newcomers were especially pleased with the part of the new Mexican constitution of 1824 that established a framework for a large measure of local self-government. New colonization laws and liberal land grants soon attracted more American colonists. So pleased were the settlers that they wrote back to hometown newspapers urging friends and relatives to join them.

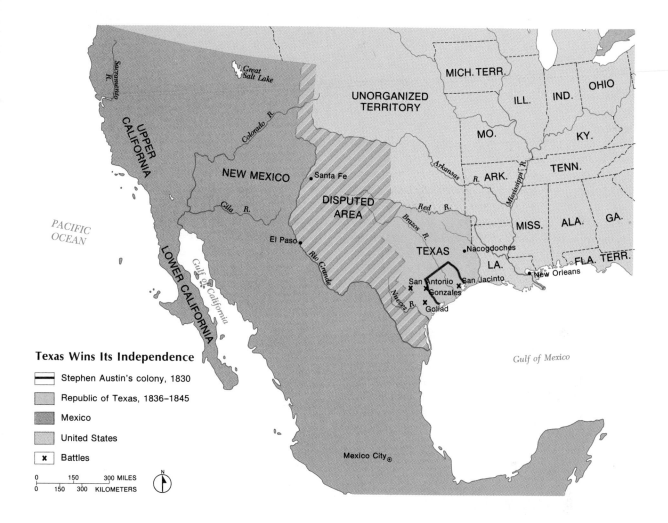

Texas Wins Its Independence

— Stephen Austin's colony, 1830

▨ Republic of Texas, 1836–1845

▨ Mexico

☐ United States

✗ Battles

0   150   300 MILES
0   150   300 KILOMETERS

All newcomers were required to become Mexican citizens, join the Catholic Church, and give evidence of good character. Most of the ex-Americans were Protestants, but the requirement that they convert to Catholicism was only laxly enforced and caused little trouble. Many of the settlers were from the cotton states of the South and brought their slaves with them. Although Mexican law prohibited slavery, it was not strictly enforced. Slaveholders evaded the law by calling the slaves "servants with lifetime contracts."

Mexico Gets a Dictator

Pleased though the Mexican authorities were with their new citizens in 1824, five years later they had grown alarmed. By 1830, the newcomers numbered 20,000. An official report complained that Texas was becoming Americanized.

The result was a series of new laws, including a ban on further immigration into Mexico and cancellation of land grants not already taken up.

The new laws were brought on by political upheavals in Mexico. In the early 1830s, the Mexican government was taken over by leaders who did not believe in the liberal democratic constitution of 1824. Some of the new laws took away rights guaranteed in the constitution, and placed the government in the hands of a dictator.

The Texans were not the only Mexicans to complain. As the Mexican government grew more dictatorial, rebellion broke out in a number of Mexican states. These rebellions were efforts to force the government to restore the constitution of 1824 which the dictator, **General Antonio López de Santa Anna** [san′tə an′ə], formally canceled in 1835.

Texans Resist

The first resistance in Texas took place in Gonzales. Mexican authorities at San Antonio demanded the return of a cannon given to the citizens of Gonzales for defense against Indians. The citizens refused. In an unsuccessful attempt to seize the cannon, a Mexican dragoon* was killed. Word of this episode, sometimes called the "Lexington of Texas," spread like a prairie fire. Volunteers streamed to the defense of Gonzales.

Meanwhile, Texas leaders hastily formed a provisional government. Significantly, they did not declare independence. Instead, they adopted a declaration in support of the federal constitution of 1824, which they wanted restored. Austin was sent to the United States to appeal for aid. The Texans drove a large Mexican force from San Antonio in fierce house-to-house fighting. To avenge this humiliation, General Santa Anna set out for San Antonio with a large army, bent on subduing the rebels.

On the day Santa Anna arrived in San Antonio at the head of a large army, the small rebel force of Texans under the command of William Travis withdrew behind the walls of an abandoned mission known as **the Alamo**. On the following day,

*__dragoon__ [drə gün'] mounted soldier trained to fight on foot or on horseback.

The Alamo today, San Antonio, Texas

February 24, 1836, one of history's immortal sieges began.

Outnumbered by more than 30 to 1, the defenders of the Alamo could not have hoped to win. They could easily have escaped. They chose to stand and die. This choice, freely made, was of enormous symbolic importance. For 13 days the siege went on until Santa Anna's veterans scaled the walls and wiped out the tiny force within.

The guns fell silent, but the deed lived on as a symbol of sacrifice and martyrdom to the Texas cause. Shortly after the fall of the Alamo, another small band of Texans was overpowered at Goliad. The decision of the Mexican authorities to have the survivors of Goliad shot as traitors further aroused the wrath of Texans, who termed the incident a massacre.

Texas Declares Independence

While the assault on the Alamo was still in progress, Texans met in a convention to decide the future. This time they decided to declare their independence from Mexico. At the same convention, they drew up a constitution and appointed **Sam Houston**, an old friend of Andrew Jackson, commander-in-chief of the Texas forces.

The following month, April 1836, Houston lured Santa Anna to **San Jacinto** and there turned the tables on the Mexican dictator. Caught off guard, the Mexicans were badly defeated by the smaller Texan army that marched into battle with shouts of "Remember the Alamo" and "Remember Goliad." Santa Anna himself was captured. After agreeing to accept the independence of Texas, an agreement he had no intention of keeping, Santa Anna was released. Texas was free—at least for the moment. However, a hostile Mexico on the border made the future anything but certain.

SECTION 2 REVIEW

 Identify: Stephen F. Austin, Antonio López de Santa Anna, the Alamo, Sam Houston, Battle of San Jacinto

Main Ideas

1. Why did Spain and Mexico encourage American settlement of Texas?
2. What did the Spanish accomplish in Texas before the American immigration began?
3. What happened when Texas resisted the dictatorship of Santa Anna?

3. THE UNITED STATES WINS A WAR WITH MEXICO

When the Texans won their independence from Mexico, they hoped and expected to become part of the United States. But because of the slavery issue, annexation was delayed for almost ten years. During that period, from 1836 to 1845, Texas maintained itself as an independent nation—the **Lone Star Republic**.

Mexico continued to view Texas as a Mexican territory in rebellion. Thus Texas needed United States protection. What were the Texans to do when it was denied them? As an independent nation, Texas was free to make whatever arrangements it could with other powers. As it happened, both Britain and France were interested in Texas. These European nations wanted an independent Texas as a source of cotton and as a low-tariff market for their manufactured goods. Britain was particularly friendly, offering the Texans a treaty guaranteeing their boundary and their independence.

The United States Annexes Texas

Britain's offer to Texas put the United States on the spot. Fearing that Texas might become an ally of a powerful European nation, the United States made renewed efforts at annexation. An attempt to get an annexation treaty through the Senate in 1844 failed when the required two-thirds vote could not be mustered.

But early the next year, a joint resolution, requiring only a simple majority, passed both houses of Congress, admitting Texas as a state. Texas accepted and joined the Union in December 1845.

The decision of Congress to annex Texas came early in 1845, in the closing days of the Tyler administration. In the election of 1844, held the previous November, Manifest Destiny was a leading issue. The winner and President-elect, James K. Polk, came out strongly during the campaign for the annexation of both Oregon and Texas. Polk was among those expansionists who hoped that once Oregon and Texas were added, the United States could obtain the rest of northwestern Mexico—by purchase if possible or by conquest if Mexico refused to sell.

Mexico Refuses Polk's Offer

When word reached Mexico City that the United States had finally annexed Texas, the Mexicans did what they had threatened to do. They broke off diplomatic relations with the U.S. and prepared for war. This occurred just as Polk was taking office. One of his first acts as President was to send an army under **General Zachary Taylor** to protect Texas in the event of a Mexican invasion.

Polk also went ahead with his plans to try to persuade Mexico to sell California and New Mexico to the United States, and to settle other issues. For example, the Mexican government owed money to a number of U.S. citizens. Attempts to collect these debts in the past had failed. Another problem was the American citizens in Mexican jails. The American government maintained that many prisoners were unjustly held and badly treated. Finally, there was the problem of the Texas boundary.

In annexing Texas, the United States took on the responsibility of settling the boundary dispute between Texas and Mexico. As an independent nation, Texas claimed the Rio Grande as its boundary with Mexico, although as a Mexican state its boundary had been the Nueces River (see map, page 339). Mexico considered the Nueces to be the Texas boundary. Polk intended to support the Texas claim.

In the hope of solving all these issues, Polk sent John Slidell to Mexico City in 1845 to negotiate a treaty. Polk instructed Slidell to offer Mexico $25 million for California and $5 million for New Mexico* as part of an overall settlement.

When Slidell arrived in Mexico, feeling against the U.S. was running high because of the annexation of Texas. The Mexicans continued to regard Texas as Mexican territory, and they were insulted by Polk's offer to buy a huge additional part of their country. The result was that the Mexican government refused even to talk to Slidell.

Taylor Advances to the Rio Grande

When word reached Washington early in 1846 that Mexico had refused to receive Slidell, Polk concluded that force would probably be needed to achieve his goals. Thus he ordered General Zachary Taylor, whose troops were stationed at Corpus

---

*New Mexico In the 1840s, this name referred to the area generally making up the present-day states of Arizona, New Mexico, Nevada, Utah, and Colorado.

Christi along the Nueces, to advance to the north bank of the Rio Grande near its mouth.

With the troops of the two countries facing each other across the river, an incident leading to a clash of arms was highly likely. The clash came on April 25 when a force of Mexican troops which had crossed the Rio Grande captured an American scouting party, killing or wounding 16 American soldiers.

Hearing of this incident, Polk at once asked for and received from Congress a declaration of war against Mexico. Polk claimed that the U.S. had been attacked and that American blood had been shed on American soil. Mexico considered the claim absurd because the clash occurred in the area between the Nueces and the Rio Grande.

Americans and Mexicans Support War

Now that war had been declared, Polk was determined to win by force of arms what he had failed to obtain by negotiations. In his war message to Congress he stated that the American aim was to "acquire California, New Mexico, and other further territory" as compensation for American expenses and losses. Most Americans supported the war with enthusiasm. New England was the exception, largely because of fear that territory won from Mexico would become slave territory. A young Whig congressman from Illinois by the name of Abraham Lincoln was among the few to question the American action on moral grounds. When Polk claimed that Mexico had shed American blood on American soil, Lincoln introduced a resolution questioning whether the spot where the clash occurred was American or Mexican.

Most Mexicans also welcomed the war, seeing in it an opportunity to regain Texas. Although smaller in population and economically weaker than the United States, Mexico had a larger standing army and the advantage of fighting a defensive war. Mexican spirits were high. They believed that U.S. forces, which had failed to win Canada in the War of 1812, would be equally unable to take territory from Mexico. They also believed that Britain might join them in a war against the upstart Americans. Events would soon show that Mexico had badly miscalculated.

Polk's War Strategy

The American campaign to win the war was carried forward in three areas—New Mexico, Cal-

ifornia, and in Mexico itself. In New Mexico and California, victories were won with relative ease and with very little bloodshed. In fact, a movement was already underway before war was declared to wrest California from Mexico.

In the spring of 1845 an exploring party of 62 sharpshooters, authorized by Polk and led by **John C. Frémont**, set out for California. Rumors were circulating that Britain was planning to seize California. Polk was aware of this danger, and Frémont's expedition was part of a two-part plan to win California for the United States: (1) Americans living in California were encouraged to rebel against Mexican rule. (2) American naval units had instructions to take possession of California in the event of war with Mexico.

At first, Frémont avoided a direct challenge to the Mexican authorities. Later, in July of 1846, he lent support to a party of armed frontiersmen led by William N. Ide who had taken over Sonoma in northern California and formed the **Bear Flag Republic.** Their hastily made flag showed a grizzly bear and a red star on a white background.

At almost the same time, U.S. naval forces commanded by Commodore John D. Sloat took control of Monterey on the California coast without opposition. (See map, opposite.) After absorbing the Bear Flag frontiersmen, Frémont's army moved south and, with the help of Commodore Robert F. Stockton, captured Los Angeles. There they were later joined by the troops of Brigadier General Stephen W. Kearny. Kearny's soldiers had arrived in California after gaining control of New Mexico on a grueling overland march from Fort Leavenworth by way of Santa Fe.

On to Mexico City

Militarily, the conquest of New Mexico and California was a sideshow to the major conflict. It was clear from the beginning of the war, that Mexico would not agree to the loss of Texas, to say nothing of New Mexico and California, unless forced to do so by defeat. This meant invading Mexico and overcoming the Mexican army.

Two colorful American generals, General Zachary Taylor and General Winfield Scott, led the troops who accomplished the task. "Old Rough and Ready," as General Taylor was affectionately called by his soldiers, led off with victories in northern Mexico along the Rio Grande. In a hard fought battle at Buena Vista (see map), Taylor's

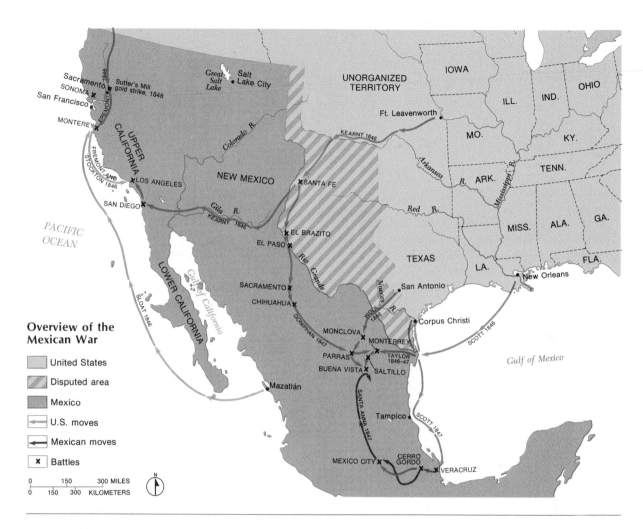

Overview of the
Mexican War

■ United States

▨ Disputed area

▓ Mexico

← U.S. moves

← Mexican moves

✗ Battles

| 0 | 150 | 300 MILES |
| 0 | 150 | 300 KILOMETERS |

THE MEXICAN WAR, 1846–1848

California and New Mexico

(July 1846–January 1847)
The U.S. fleet commanded by John D. Sloat sailed from Mazatlán, Mexico, and took Monterey, California (July 7, 1846). Meanwhile, troops led by Stephen W. Kearny left Fort Leavenworth and headed for California. They occupied Santa Fe (Aug. 18), set up a temporary government there, and moved on. They occupied San Diego on Dec. 12. The fighting ended after the combined forces of the army (Kearny and Captain John C. Frémont) and navy (Commodore Robert F. Stockton, who had replaced Sloat) took Los Angeles (Jan. 10, 1847).

Northern Mexico

(September 1846–March 1847)
After some early skirmishing, U.S. troops led by General Zachary Taylor attacked and captured Monterrey (Sept. 24). From Monterrey, the U.S. forces went to Saltillo, which they occupied (Nov. 13). Meanwhile, troops from San Antonio (General John Wool) had been sent to take Chihuahua. They won a battle at Monclova (Oct. 29) and then occupied Parras (Dec. 5). They joined Taylor's troops at Saltillo (Dec. 21). The combined forces captured Buena Vista (Feb. 27). Other U.S. troops (Colonel Alexander Doniphan) defeated the Mexicans at El Brazito (Dec. 25), El Paso (Dec. 27), and Sacramento (Feb. 28). Doniphan occupied Chihuahua (Mar. 1).

Central Mexico

(March–September 1847)
The deciding campaign of the war began with the landing of U.S. troops under General Winfield Scott at Veracruz (Mar. 9) and the capitulation of that city (Mar. 27). U.S. forces routed the Mexicans at Cerro Gordo (Apr. 18) and at nearby Contreras (Aug. 19–20). The U.S. suffered heavy casualties at Churubusco (Aug. 20), but the Mexicans were forced to withdraw to Mexico City. After a heavy bombardment and an assault, the Mexican defenders were finally overcome (Sept. 14). U.S. forces entered Mexico City and occupied it. After several more days of fighting, the shooting war was finally over. The Treaty of Guadalupe Hidalgo (Feb. 2, 1848) formally ended the war.

army won an important victory over a larger Mexican force commanded by Santa Anna, the old enemy of Texas independence.

Thereafter the war shifted farther south to central Mexico, where General Winfield Scott landed a large force at Vera Cruz. Known as "Old Fuss and Feathers" because of his fondness for strict discipline and dazzling uniforms, Scott battled his way inland from Vera Cruz over rugged terrain and against stiff Mexican resistance to capture Mexico City. With its capital occupied, Mexico at last agreed to sign a treaty of peace.

By the terms of the **Treaty of Guadalupe Hidalgo** (1848), Mexico acknowledged the American title to Texas, New Mexico, and California. These lands included those three present-day states as well as Nevada, Utah, and parts of Arizona, Oklahoma, Kansas, Colorado, and Wyoming. In return, the United States agreed to pay Mexico $15 million and to take over Mexican debts owed to American citizens amounting to $3.4 million.

Five years later, in 1853, the United States paid Mexico an additional $10 million for another piece of Mexican land south of the Gila River. Known as the **Gadsden Purchase**, the land was acquired for a transcontinental railroad. With the Gadsden Purchase, the United States rounded out its present southern boundary. (See map below.)

Mexican Americans

The territory won from Mexico by the Treaty of Guadalupe Hidalgo was not unoccupied country. Approximately 200,000 Indians and 75,000 Mexicans lived in New Mexico and California. The Mexican culture was a blend of Spanish and Indian. With the Treaty of Guadalupe Hidalgo, the Mexicans of the area became American citizens. The United States assumed the responsibility of giving them fair and equal treatment with other citizens and of honoring their land titles received from Mexico or Spain.

The Mexican Americans traced their ancestry

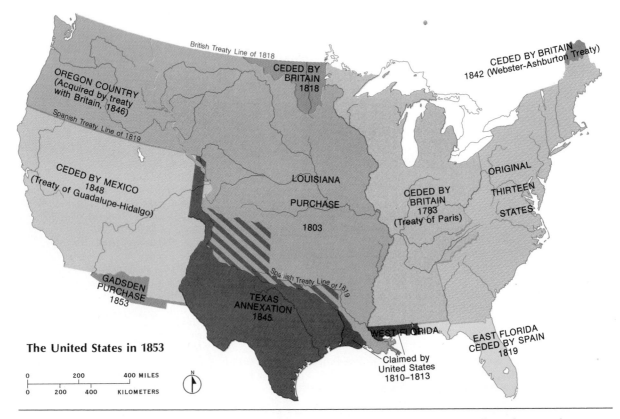

The United States in 1853

By 1853, the United States stretched from the Atlantic to the Pacific, controlling the area that eventually made up the first 48 states. In only 70 years since the Treaty of Paris of 1783, the country had tripled in size.

344

back to the age of colonization under New Spain. They were part of the south-to-north frontier movement that led to the settlement of Santa Fe and parts of Texas and California in the 1600s and 1700s. In language and culture, the Mexican Americans looked mostly to Spain and southern Europe, just as the majority of the colonists along the Atlantic coast of North America looked to England and northern Europe. Now, in the mid-1800s, with the westward push of the young United States, the two frontiers met in what had been the northern borderlands of New Spain—Texas, New Mexico, and California.

Many difficulties and much suffering awaited the Mexican Americans after the American victory in 1848. Despite treaty promises, the United States did not uniformly honor the Mexican land titles. The great influx of Americans into New Mexico and California put a great strain on patterns of living that were long established and which had changed little for many generations.

Many Mexicans had joined the American forces in the Texas rebellion of the 1830s. Others had welcomed the American takeover in California and New Mexico in the 1840s. But they were soon outnumbered by their new Anglo American neighbors, and they often became the victims of the prejudice toward Spaniards many Americans carried over from the days of English-Spanish rivalry in the period of colonization. The Mexican War rekindled these old prejudices and began a new period full of difficulty for Mexican Americans.

SECTION 3 REVIEW

Identify: Lone Star Republic, Zachary Taylor, John C. Frémont, Bear Flag Republic, Treaty of Guadalupe Hidalgo, Gadsden Purchase

Main Ideas

1. Why was Texas annexation delayed? What factors finally led to its admission as a state?
2. What differences did Polk's administration and the Mexican government have? What incident sparked the outbreak of war?
3. Many Americans and Mexicans welcomed the war. Why? Who opposed it? Why?
4. Briefly describe President Polk's war strategy.
5. Who were the Mexican Americans? What problems did they face after 1848?

4. THE CALIFORNIA GOLD RUSH

In their haste to add California to the nation, not even the most optimistic believers in Manifest Destiny dreamed of the riches about to be discovered. The ink was hardly dry on the Treaty of Guadalupe Hidalgo when the electrifying words "Gold strike!" resounded from the California hills. The ripple effect of those spine-tingling words was felt throughout the United States and in many foreign countries.

Hordes of gold seekers descended on the sleepy foothills of the Sierra Nevadas. Boom towns sprang up like mushrooms. The tiny seaport village of San Francisco was transformed into a bustling international harbor. Fortunes were made and lost in the twinkling of an eye.

With the bonanza of growth and wealth came problems that demanded early solution. California was soon urgently in need of a civil government. This raised the issue of statehood, and with it, of slavery in the territories won from Mexico. Congress would soon have to decide: "Was the West to be slave or free?"

Routes to California

Gold was first discovered in California in January 1848 at **Sutter's Mill** near present-day Sacramento. (See map, page 343.) During the year and a half after the discovery, 80,000 gold hunters made their way to California. The gold seekers from the East had a choice of three routes to California, all of them long and full of danger.

Some gold seekers went entirely by land. Traveling in covered wagons, they followed the Oregon Trail across the plains and deserts and through the Rockies by way of South Pass. (See map, page 334.) After passing north of the Great Salt Lake, they veered southwestward to scale the high Sierras at Donner Pass and then to descend into California's Central Valley. Starting out in the spring from settlements in the Mississippi Valley, with luck they reached the gold fields five months later. Many were lost along the way, victims of disease, starvation, Indian attack, or sheer exhaustion.

The shortest route in time and distance was by ship to Central America, by land through the disease-infested jungles of Panama, and by ship

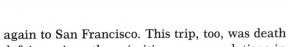
again to San Francisco. This trip, too, was death defying, given the primitive accommodations in Panama and overcrowding aboard ship. The easiest, longest, and most expensive route to California was by fast clipper ship around South America.

California Requests Statehood

On reaching California, the "**Forty-Niners,**" as the gold seekers were called, began the mad scramble. Equipped with picks, shovels, and wash basins, they roamed the hills and valleys, sifting through tons of soil and gravel. Only a few found much gold, and even fewer struck it rich. But stories of how newly arrived prospectors picked up huge nuggets of pure gold kept spirits high.

Bustling little communities such as San Francisco struggled to provide the food, supplies, and housing demanded by the hordes that arrived each week. Enterprising individuals soon discov-

ered that get-rich-quick schemes were not confined to the gold fields. Many Forty-Niners drifted into other kinds of work, and some found the fortune in business that they had failed to find in the diggings.

When the gold rush began, California was under the U.S. military government that took over when Mexican rule ended. Most of the people who came flooding in were U.S. citizens. They wanted a civil government organized as soon as possible. The non-Indian population of California skyrocketed from 6,000 at the beginning of 1848 to more than 85,000 in a little over a year.

In September 1849, the call went out for a convention to meet at Monterey to write a state constitution. The delegates drew up a document and forwarded it to Washington. But California's request to enter the Union as a free state sparked intense opposition in Washington from the slave-holding states of the South. California would have to wait while political leaders tried desperately to find an acceptable compromise.

The Mormons Settle Utah

On the overland route to California, many Forty-Niners passed through the newly settled Mormon communities in what is now Utah. You'll recall from Chapter 13 that an angry mob killed Mormon leader Joseph Smith in 1844. Led by Brigham Young, 15,000 Mormons withdrew beyond the edge of civilization and settled in the Great Salt Basin. Here they hoped to escape persecution and to build an ideal community, undisturbed. Arriving in 1847 when the area around the Great Salt Lake was still under Mexican rule, they found the isolation they desired.

Mexico had never tried to colonize the remote northern stretch of dry and barren land near the Great Salt Lake. And earlier pioneers had hurried across the uninviting country on their way to the more promising land of Oregon and California. Accustomed to hardships and challenge, the Mormons set to work to make the desert bloom. They constructed irrigation ditches to bring life-giving waters from the mountains to their fields of grain and vegetables. Their experiment was a success, and their settlements thrived. But as it turned out, the land they had selected was directly in the path of Manifest Destiny.

The Mormons were able to provide much-needed assistance to the weary California-bound

LIFE IN AMERICA

SAN FRANCISCO IN THE GOLD RUSH

A boom town is a town that grows up almost overnight, usually for an economic reason. San Francisco was such a city, and gold was the reason. When Commander John B. Montgomery raised the American flag on July 9, 1846, there were about 500 people in the little Spanish settlement, then called Yerba Buena.

On January 24, 1848, gold was discovered at Sutter's Mill on the American River, about 100 miles to the northeast. Within a few days, the word spread to San Francisco, where pandemonium broke out. Overnight the place became a ghost town (with seven inhabitants remaining) as sailors deserted their ships and merchants abandoned their shops in a mad dash for the gold fields.

This was only the beginning of what quickly became a stampede. News of the discovery soon reached the East, where President Polk announced in his message to Congress in December 1849 that gold was plentiful in the western mountains. Droves of easterners boarded ships, sailed around Cape Horn, and landed at San Francisco. In January of 1849 the population of the town was 2,000. By December it was a bustling seaport with 25,000 people, its harbor packed with ships delivering the goods and people to build a boom town and supply the mobs heading for the gold fields.

San Francisco was built, burnt, and rebuilt six times between 1849 and 1851. The fires were a result of the wooden shanties and tents that comprised the mushrooming city. But each fire merely cleared the way for the next building boom. Legend has it that the contracts to rebuild were signed in the glow of the fires.

The cost of real estate soared. Values increased sevenfold in six months of 1848. Land was at such a premium that parts of the harbor were filled in to create more of it. Some ships became more valuable as stores or hotels when landfill surrounded them.

Rents skyrocketed, and the cost of labor leaped from $1 to $30 per day. Goods of all kinds brought unheard-of prices because demand outstripped supply. At one point eggs sold for $6 a dozen, tooth-brushes and suspenders went for ten times their original cost; even carpet tacks cost $16 a box. Because of rats in the seaport, one sea captain was able to sell a shipload of stray cats for $10 each.

Between sailors looking for a good time and miners bent on spending their gold (it was considered bad luck to return to the mines without spending everything) the boom must have seemed like an explosion. On the "Barbary Coast," vice and crime ran rampant. Gambling flourished in the 46 gaming houses, and hundreds of saloons served the thirsty sailors and prospectors. The authorities could not keep the criminal element under control. As a result, citizens organized vigilante squads to catch, try, convict, and hang suspected criminals.

After the 1850s the gold ran out, and the boom slowed down. Unlike other boom towns, however, San Francisco continued to grow, its commercial success favored by its excellent harbor and location as a doorway to East Asia. No longer is it a slapdash, wooden shantytown. After the gold rush it became one of our most elegant and most charming cities.

pioneers, and they profited greatly by selling food and supplies to the Forty-Niners. But their isolation was destroyed. Other difficulties resulted when their area became part of the United States with the Treaty of Guadalupe Hidalgo.

Until then, the Mormons had governed themselves, mainly through their church organization. When their lands became part of the United States, their leaders hoped to form a territorial government and then enter the Union.

The question of providing a territorial government for the Mormon settlements arose in 1850, at the same time that California was applying for admission as a free state. But because of prolonged disagreements between the United States authorities and Mormon leaders over polygamy and other issues, Utah did not become a state until 1896.

SECTION 4 REVIEW

 Identify: Sutter's Mill, Forty-Niners

Main Ideas

1. Why did settlers flock into California after 1848? What routes did they follow?
2. Why did California's admission as a state spark opposition?
3. Why did the Mormons settle in the barren country around the Great Salt Lake? How did they help the Forty-Niners?
4. Why was Utah's admission as a state delayed until 1896?

Two flags that once flew over independent republics: the Lone Star Flag of Texas and the Bear Flag of California

5. THE COMPROMISE OF 1850

In 1846, when the Mexican War was just getting under way, a Pennsylvania congressman, David Wilmot, proposed an amendment to an appropriations bill on the sensitive issue of slavery. His bill, known thereafter as the **Wilmot Proviso**, would have outlawed slavery in any territory acquired from Mexico in the war. Bitterly opposed by southerners, the bill passed several times in the House of Representatives but was always defeated in the Senate. The debate over slavery touched off by the Wilmot Proviso died down during the war but was revived with a new intensity with the coming of peace.

The Election of 1848

In the election of 1848 both the Democrats and the Whigs avoided taking a stand on the Wilmot Proviso. The Whigs nominated the Mexican War hero, General Zachary Taylor. Although Taylor was a southerner and a slaveholder, he was believed to have moderate views. Since President Polk had decided not to seek re-election, the Democrats had to turn to another candidate. They finally settled on General Lewis Cass, a colorless, aging veteran of the War of 1812.

Cass personally believed in what was called **"popular sovereignty,"** a doctrine which meant letting the people who lived in a territory decide by popular vote whether or not slavery would be allowed there. This idea later gained many supporters, but Cass avoided any mention of slavery in his campaign. Clearly, neither of the major party candidates wanted to risk offending voters, North or South, by taking a stand on the most explosive and most talked about issue of the day, the Wilmot Proviso.

But in the North a new party, the **Free-Soil party**, broke the silence and came out four square against the extension of slavery in the territories. The Free-Soil candidate, ex-President Martin Van Buren, took enough votes from Cass in New York State to throw the election to Taylor.

Furthermore, the Free-Soilers elected 12 members of Congress, enough to hold the balance in the House of Representatives, which was about equally divided between Whigs and Democrats.

The submerged issue of the campaign, the future of slavery in the territories, was certain to come out in the open when Congress convened and began to debate the question of statehood for California.

The Debate over California

When the new President, Zachary Taylor, took the oath of office in March 1849, California and New Mexico were still under military rule. Something would have to be done soon. The military government could not keep law and order in the mining camps and boom towns with their drifting populations.

The normal procedure would have been for Congress to give California a civil government by organizing it as a territory. But to do this would be to raise at once the issue of whether or not slavery was to be permitted in the territory. Congress would then have to decide, thus bringing up again the bitter issue raised by the Wilmot Proviso.

With the problem growing daily more urgent, President Taylor decided to act. He hinted to leaders in California that they might skip the territorial stage. Instead, they might call a constitutional convention, elect officials, and apply for admission as a state. The issue of slavery in the territories would be avoided, and no one questioned the right of a state to decide for itself whether it was to be slave or free. As we have seen, Californians took the hint. In a constitutional convention that met at Monterey, they went through the necessary steps and applied for admission to the Union as a free state.

But President Taylor had badly miscalculated in thinking he had solved the problem. Instead of solving it, he precipitated the very crisis he had tried to avoid. Southerners accused him of trickery, of trying to steal California for the North. If California entered the Union as a free state, the existing balance of 15 free and 15 slave states would be destroyed. Ever since the Missouri Compromise of 1820, a balance had been fairly well maintained. Whenever a free state had been admitted, it was balanced by a new slave state. As southerners looked to the future, they feared they would become a permanent minority in the national government. There was no new slave state to balance California. Nor was there much likelihood that slavery would take root in the other lands won from Mexico.

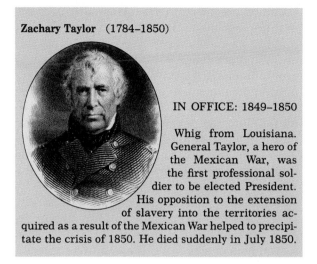

Zachary Taylor (1784–1850)

IN OFFICE: 1849–1850

Whig from Louisiana. General Taylor, a hero of the Mexican War, was the first professional soldier to be elected President. His opposition to the extension of slavery into the territories acquired as a result of the Mexican War helped to precipitate the crisis of 1850. He died suddenly in July 1850.

Other Issues Divide North and South

Thus it was that the application of California for statehood, followed a few months later by a similar request from New Mexico, triggered an angry North-South debate. Three other slavery-related issues also quickly surfaced.

One was a boundary dispute between Texas and New Mexico. If Texas, a slave state, were to lose territory to New Mexico, this would mean a setback for the South. Another issue was the slave trade in the District of Columbia, an area governed directly by Congress. Equally explosive was the growing demand in the South for a stronger fugitive slave law. In the absence of such a law, the South was losing as many as a thousand runaway slaves a year.

Taken together, these issues were dynamite. The fuse was lit by Taylor's support of California's application for statehood. When Congress assembled in December 1849, no less an issue than the survival of the Union was at stake.

A Burst of Oratory

As the session opened, three towering figures of the American political scene—John C. Calhoun, Henry Clay, and Daniel Webster—were on hand to lead the debates. Calhoun, staunch defender of slavery, was there to argue forcefully, and for the last time, for his beloved South. He argued that the Constitution protected slavery, and hence the institution could not legally be excluded from the territory won from Mexico.

Calhoun went one step further and declared that the North was an aggressor in pushing for restrictions on slavery. He stated that if this continued the South would have no choice but to secede from the Union. He demanded a constitutional amendment to restore and preserve the North-South balance. So ill that he had to be carried into the Senate chambers, Calhoun sat hollow-eyed while his speech was read for him by a colleague. His death a few weeks later removed from the political scene the ablest foe of compromise.

Clay and Webster, although opposed to slavery, were willing to compromise to save the Union. Both men had grown up with the nation, had served many years in Congress, and were determined now in their old age to preserve the Union they loved.

At the age of 73, Henry Clay was back in the Senate, leader of the forces favoring compromise. One of the most popular men in the nation, Clay had narrowly missed election as President in 1844 and now had no further political ambitions. His leading role in the passage of the Missouri Compromise 30 years earlier had won for him the title of "the great compromiser." Would he be able to put together a new agreement in the charged atmosphere of 1850?

Clay introduced an Omnibus Bill, so-called because it included all the issues under consideration. In the bill, Clay carefully balanced North-South issues in an attempt to counter Calhoun's uncompromising stand. Clay's proposals received the support of Daniel Webster of Massachusetts, probably the greatest orator of the day. In a powerful speech, Webster called on his listeners to accept the compromise and save the Union. In taking this stand, Webster turned his back on abolitionist supporters in New England who were dead set against a strong fugitive slave law and other concessions to the South. Equally, Webster condemned all talk of secession.

A Difficult Solution

All through the summer of 1850, the debate dragged on. The situation seemed hopeless because President Taylor took a strong stand against Clay's compromise proposals. Much to the dismay of the southern Whigs, Taylor had come under the influence of William Seward, a strong antislavery senator from New York. The

Millard Fillmore (1800–1874)

IN OFFICE: 1850–1853

Whig from New York. Fillmore, who became President when Taylor died, signed the bills that made up the Compromise of 1850. His enforcement of the Fugitive Slave Law cost him support in the North. He ran unsuccessfully on the American (Know-Nothing) party ticket in 1856.

President favored a pro-northern settlement that would probably have caused the South to secede.

But fate intervened. Taylor's unexpected death from typhus in July 1850 brought Vice-President **Millard Fillmore** to the White House. President Fillmore favored compromise, and with his support a solution was found. A young senator from Illinois, **Stephen A. Douglas**, played a vital role. Douglas saw that while there were not enough votes to pass Clay's Omnibus Bill as a whole, there was enough support to pass its parts separately. By using different combinations of support, the skillful Douglas found the votes necessary to enact the **Compromise of 1850.** As finally passed, the Compromise of 1850 balanced sectional interests, along the lines of Clay's original proposal, in five major provisions:

1. California was admitted to the Union as a free state, a concession to the North.
2. The rest of the land won from Mexico was divided into the territories of New Mexico and Utah, with no restriction on slavery. This was a concession to the South.
3. In the Texas boundary dispute, Texas was paid $10 million for the loss of territory to New Mexico. Here the interests of North and South were balanced.
4. The slave trade (but not slavery) was abolished in the District of Columbia, a concession to the North.
5. A strong Fugitive Slave Law, as favored by the South, was passed.

An Uneasy Truce

At best, the Compromise of 1850 brought an uneasy truce. Many southerners believed that the South received the worst of the bargain. California was lost to slavery, upsetting the balance between slave and free states in favor of the North. Few people, North or South, believed that slavery would win out in New Mexico and Utah. The safeguards for the South demanded by Calhoun were not part of the compromise.

The new **Fugitive Slave Law of 1850** was the one positive gain for the South. But this soon proved to be of questionable value. The Fugitive Slave Law required federal, state, and local officials to help retrieve runaway slaves; established severe penalties for citizens who helped runaway slaves; and deprived blacks accused of being fugitives of the right to testify in their own defense and to a jury trial. The measure was so unpopular in the North that attempts to enforce it broke down immediately. In fact, the new Fugitive Slave Law was largely responsible for a new wave of antislavery and antisouthern feeling that swept the North.

The Compromise of 1850 had the support of the business interests, North and South, and probably that of most voters. The nation was entering an unparalleled period of growth. For a time, sectional bitterness over slavery died down. Many leaders, North and South, worked hard to maintain the compromise, believing that the growing prosperity would heal the sectional wounds opened during the angry debates in Congress.

Clay and Webster went to their graves in 1852, believing that their efforts to preserve the Union had succeeded. The tried-and-true formula of compromise had once again triumphed. There remained, however, one haunting question. Would the nation be as fortunate when the next inevitable crisis over slavery arose?

SECTION 5 REVIEW

 Identify: Wilmot Proviso, popular sovereignty, Free-Soil party, Millard Fillmore, Stephen A. Douglas, Compromise of 1850, Fugitive Slave Law of 1850

Main Ideas

1. What issue delayed organizing California as a territory? How effective was President Taylor's solution to the problem?
2. What issues divided the North and South in 1849?
3. What positions did Calhoun, Clay, and Webster take in this crisis?
4. What were the provisions of the Compromise of 1850? Which section benefited by each?

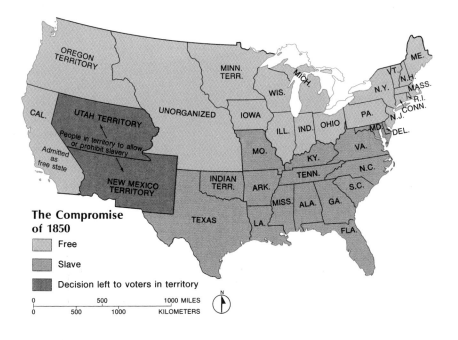

The Compromise of 1850

- Free
- Slave
- Decision left to voters in territory

0   500   1000 MILES
0 500 1000 KILOMETERS

The Compromise of 1850 temporarily settled the question of slavery in the lands won from Mexico. California was admitted as a free state. New Mexico and Utah were organized as territories, and the question of slavery was left open to the voters. In addition, Texas was paid $10 million for the loss of land to New Mexico; the slave trade was abolished in Washington, D.C.; and a harsher fugitive slave law was passed.

CHAPTER 14 REVIEW

Key Terms
Explain the meaning of each of the following terms:

Oregon Country
Mountain Men
Oregon Trail
the Alamo
Battle of San Jacinto
Lone Star Republic
Bear Flag Republic
Treaty of Guadalupe
 Hidalgo

Gadsden Purchase
Sutter's Mill
Forty-Niners
Wilmot Proviso
popular sovereignty
Free-Soil party
Compromise of 1850
Fugitive Slave Law
 of 1850

Reviewing the Main Ideas
Section 1
1. Describe the location and attraction to settlers of the Oregon Country.
2. How was the U.S.–Canadian border dispute finally resolved?

Section 2
1. Why did Spain and Mexico encourage American immigration in Texas?
2. What did the Spanish accomplish in Texas before the American immigration began?
3. Why did Texans rebel against the Mexican government?

Section 3
1. Why was Texas annexation delayed? Why was it finally admitted to the Union?
2. What issues led to the war between the U.S. and Mexico? Why did the war begin?
3. What areas of the present-day United States were won from Mexico? What special problems faced the residents of these areas after the peace treaty?

Section 4
1. Why did settlers flock into California after 1848? What routes did they take to get there?
2. Why did the Mormons settle in Utah? How did they help the Forty-Niners?
3. Why did the proposed entry of California and Utah into the Union spark opposition?

Section 5
1. What issues divided the North and South in 1849? How did they affect California? Why was the survival of the Union at stake?
2. What were the provisions of the Compromise of 1850? Why was it a compromise?

Special History Skills:
Working with Maps
Maps can show historical developments over a period of time. Look at the map on page 339 which helps explain historical relations between Mexico, Texas, and the United States. What is the earliest date shown on the map? The latest date? Refer to the map and the text to answer the following questions about that period.

Stephen F. Austin's Colony
1. About how large was Austin's colony in land area from east to west?
2. Find Texas on Map 2 in the Atlas section and compare the size of Austin's colony with present-day Texas. How many miles is Texas today at its widest point?

The Republic of Texas
1. Four battle sites are shown on the map. Which battle was called the "Lexington of Texas"? Where did the siege of the Alamo occur? Where were some Texans shot as traitors? In which battle were the Mexicans decisively defeated?
2. When did Texas win its independence from Mexico?
3. How long did Texas remain independent?

Boundary Disputes
1. Which two nations claimed land in the "disputed area"?
2. According to Mexico, which rivers formed the northern and southern boundaries of Texas?
3. Which rivers did the Texans claim as forming the northern and southern boundaries of Texas?
4. What river forms the southern boundary of Texas today?

Other Skill Activities
1. **From sea to shining sea**
 (a) Make a time line for the years 1607–1853 and mark the following events: Texas annexation; acquisition of Florida; Louisiana Pur-

chase; first English settlement at Jamestown; Mexican cession; Proclamation Line of 1763; territory won in the War for Independence; northern boundaries of Maine, Louisiana Purchase territory, and Oregon Country established; and Gadsden Purchase. (b) Illustrate your time line with a map like the one on page 344. (c) Write a caption that compares the first half of American history with the second half from the point of view of territorial acquisition.

2. **Goin' West**
Write ten journal entries describing your family's move from Pennsylvania to California in the 1850s. Include details you learned in the chapter.

3. **Spanish influence**
Look at a map of the western United States. Make a list of names of cities, states, and physical features that show a Spanish influence in this area.

Thinking Critically

1. "Texas and California were unique in the way in which they entered the Union." Find examples in the chapter to support this statement.
2. How would you feel about the addition of Mexican land to the United States in 1849 if you were (a) a Mexican citizen of California, (b) an American who had emigrated to Texas in the 1820s, (c) a northern abolitionist, (d) a southern planter?
3. Was the United States the aggressor in the Mexican War, or did Mexico provoke the fight? Was there right on both sides? Use information from the chapter to back up your opinion.
4. What would the United States be like today if it had not annexed Texas or fought and won the war with Mexico?

Further Reading

Irving Werstein. *The War with Mexico*. W. W. Norton and Co., 1965. Explains Manifest Destiny and describes Texas' fight for independence and Mexican War battles. Many illustrations.

Suzanne Hilton. *Getting There: Frontier Travel Without Power*. The Westminster Press, 1980. Describes travel by horseback, stagecoach, canal boat, covered wagon, and sailing ship.

TEST YOURSELF

WRITE YOUR ANSWERS ON A SEPARATE SHEET OF PAPER.

Matching

Write the letter of the item that best matches each description below.

1. went to California to search for gold
2. settled Americans in Texas
3. fur traders and explorers in the Rocky Mountains and the Oregon Country
4. settled on land near the Great Salt Lake
5. expansionist President
6. ceded Texas, California, and New Mexico to the United States
7. belief that the United States should stretch from coast to coast and even beyond
8. touched off a debate on slavery in the territories gained from Mexico
9. belief that territories should vote on whether to allow slavery
10. a symbol of resistance in the fight for Texas independence

a. Manifest Destiny	**g.** James K. Polk
b. Mountain Men	**h.** Forty-Niners
c. Mormon Church	**i.** Stephen F. Austin
d. Treaty of Guadalupe Hidalgo	**j.** the Alamo
e. popular sovereignty	**k.** John C. Frémont
f. Oregon Trail	**l.** Wilmot Proviso
	m. Lone Star Republic

Locating

On the map below find the letter that represents each of the following items.

1. purchased from Mexico
2. site of the 1849 gold rush
3. settled by the Mormons
4. the Lone Star Republic
5. boundary of this area settled by compromise

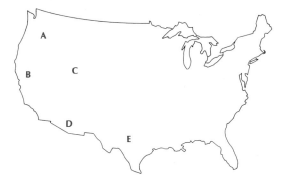

Chapter 15

SECTIONAL DIFFERENCES LEAD TO SECESSION

1850–1860

In the spring of 1852, when the Compromise of 1850 still held promise of quieting sectional strife, a young landscape architect by the name of Frederick Law Olmsted set out from his home in New York to visit the South. Olmsted shared the views of many moderates, North and South, toward the Compromise. He hoped that the great sectional differences in the country had been laid to rest and that the Compromise of 1850 would be permanent. Olmsted did not believe in slavery, but he was not an abolitionist. He believed the South should give up slavery voluntarily, rather than being forced by law to do so.

Olmsted was personally familiar with the free labor system of the North. He thought he knew what its strengths and weaknesses were. Since he had no direct experience with the economic system of slavery, he wanted to tour the South and learn about the system first hand. An extended visit to the "Cotton Kingdom" seemed the best way to fill in the gaps in his knowledge.

Over a 14-month period, Olmsted took three separate trips to the South, visiting every state and living, traveling, and talking with southerners from every walk of life. The *New York Times* and other newspapers published his reports and comments from the South. At the time, Olmsted's reports were much praised by both North and South. Both sections considered his reporting fair and factual. Later historians, also, have generally praised Olmsted's impartiality. Thus for us Olmsted is an important eyewitness to what the South was like in the decade that led to secession.

Sections in This Chapter
1. The South in the 1850s
2. The North in the 1850s
3. A New Sectional Crisis Erupts over Slavery
4. The Sectional Crisis Deepens
5. A Final Crisis Brings Secession

Opposite: Farm equipment like this antique hay rake helped lighten the load of the American farmer in the mid-19th century.

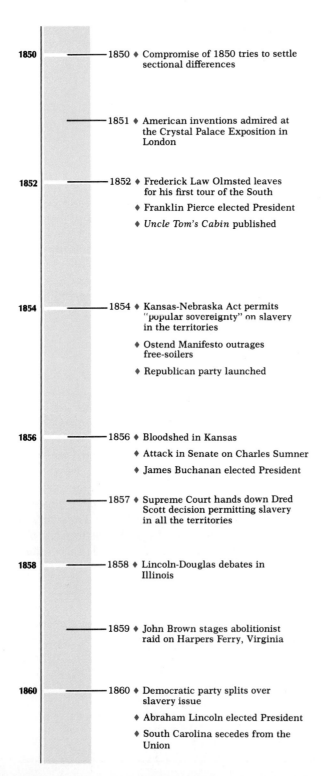

1850 ◆ Compromise of 1850 tries to settle
sectional differences

1851 ◆ American inventions admired at
the Crystal Palace Exposition in
London

1852 ◆ Frederick Law Olmsted leaves
for his first tour of the South

◆ Franklin Pierce elected President

◆ *Uncle Tom's Cabin* published

1854 ◆ Kansas-Nebraska Act permits
"popular sovereignty" on slavery
in the territories

◆ Ostend Manifesto outrages
free-soilers

◆ Republican party launched

1856 ◆ Bloodshed in Kansas

◆ Attack in Senate on Charles Sumner

◆ James Buchanan elected President

1857 ◆ Supreme Court hands down Dred
Scott decision permitting slavery
in all the territories

1858 ◆ Lincoln-Douglas debates in
Illinois

1859 ◆ John Brown stages abolitionist
raid on Harpers Ferry, Virginia

1860 ◆ Democratic party splits over
slavery issue

◆ Abraham Lincoln elected President

◆ South Carolina secedes from the
Union

1. THE SOUTH IN THE 1850s

What did **Frederick Law Olmsted**, the young landscape architect, learn on his travels? What conclusions did he reach about slavery when he compared it to the free labor system in the North? What did he find to be the key differences between life in the North and the South? Olmsted did not single out facts that might show the southern way of life in a bad light. Nor did he glamorize it as the land of "moonlight and magnolias," the way some novelists and film makers have done. Olmsted succeeded admirably in his goal of reporting accurately what he saw and experienced.

The Land of Cotton

The prosperity of the South, Olmsted was quick to see, depended more on its agricultural products than on anything else. (See map, page 358.) Of the various southern cash crops, cotton was king, easily outdistancing the others. Virginia and other parts of the upper South grew tobacco. South Carolina and Georgia grew rice. Louisiana produced sugar cane. Virginia, Kentucky, and Tennessee grew wheat and corn. Although all of these crops were important, none could begin to equal the importance of cotton to the region. Cotton, the principal cash crop, was grown throughout the **Cotton Kingdom**—a broad band extending from the Carolinas south and west into Texas.

In his travels, Olmsted noted that there were two contrasting types of southern agriculture. There were the small subsistence farms, growing mainly wheat, corn, and livestock, and there were the great plantations, growing broad acres of tobacco, rice, sugar cane, and above all, cotton. The subsistence farms of the South were much like those of the North and West. They provided a decent living for their owners, but they were not a source of great wealth. The owners of the large plantations, however, were often wealthy. By 1850 the cotton crop alone was worth more than $100 million annually. Most of it was sold abroad or to northern factories. The cotton crop made up more than half of the total foreign trade of the United States. The percentage increased annually as the demand for cotton continued to grow.

Planters and Subsistence Farmers

The social, political, and economic life of the South was dominated by the people of the wealthy **planter class**. They controlled politics, education, religion, and society. Although they were a small minority of the total population of the South, they were the leaders and their views were usually taken as representative of the region. This led to many widely believed myths about the South. One of these was the belief that the great white-columned mansion at the end of an avenue of great oaks, where the wealthy planters gave balls and barbecues, was typical of the South. This was a myth. Such places did, of course, exist, but in reality 75% of all white southerners lived on small subsistence farms and owned no slaves, while others owned only a few slaves.

The Demands of King Cotton

The particular demands of cotton agriculture help explain the existence of the plantation system and its dependence on slave labor. (See map, page 359, for a view of the areas where slave labor was used.) The climate of much of the South—ample rainfall and long, hot summers—was ideal for growing cotton. Cotton grew best on rich soil, which it quickly depleted. But there were vast expanses of land farther west that could be opened up as older fields gave out. To plant, cultivate, and harvest huge fields of cotton required a large work force. The South did not have a large pool of workers who would hire themselves out to plant, tend, and harvest cotton. But it did have slaves, who could be forced to do the work. With cotton bringing a good price on world markets, enterprising planters bought more and more land. The new lands partially offset the losses from declining soil fertility, but bringing new acres under cultivation required more and more slaves and larger investments of capital.

Was the slave system economically sound? Olmsted and other observers had doubts. They pointed out that the price of slaves—as much as $1,500 for a strong field hand—added greatly to a planter's capital investment. The dependence of the South on agriculture, to the near exclusion of industry, they said, meant that money earned from the sale of cotton found its way into the pockets of northern bankers and merchants. Furthermore, they argued, the depletion of the soil and the rising cost of land and slaves kept many planters in debt, notwithstanding their grand and elegant lifestyle.

Some modern historians disagree with these

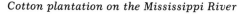

Cotton plantation on the Mississippi River

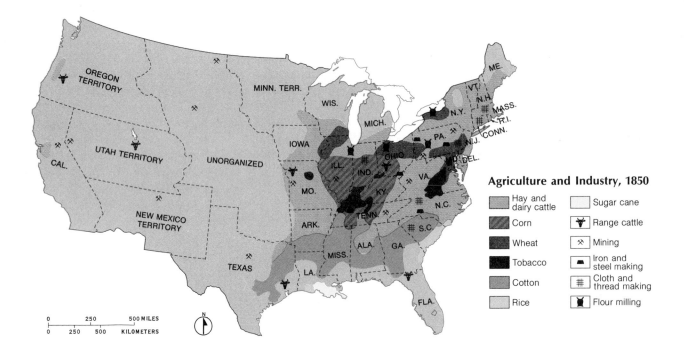

Agriculture and Industry, 1850

- Hay and dairy cattle
- Corn
- Wheat
- Tobacco
- Cotton
- Rice
- Sugar cane
- Range cattle
- Mining
- Iron and steel making
- Cloth and thread making
- Flour milling

doubts, however, and insist that the South was flourishing. Slave labor was more productive than free labor, these historians say, and slavery was profitable for the slaveholders.

The Lives of the Slaves

What was it like to be a slave in the American South? We have a great variety of answers. Some come from visitors like Olmsted. Others come from slaveholders, writing in account books, letters, and diaries about plantation management. Still others come from abolitionists who tended to paint a stark picture of brutality. We also have accounts of slaves who escaped to freedom, telling how the system worked and how it affected them and their families. Lastly, there are census records and other government statistics. From all these varied sources, we can put together a general picture of what it was like to be a slave.

Southerners who defended slavery referred to it as their "peculiar institution." By this they meant it was distinct and well suited to the special needs of the South. Although, as we have seen, the vast majority of southerners did not own slaves, they nonetheless saw the institution as useful and necessary to their way of life.

Slaveholders used their slaves to perform a wide variety of tasks. The most common use of slave labor was on the plantations where cotton,

tobacco, rice, and sugar cane were grown as cash crops. But southerners also used many slaves as house servants and as skilled workers or artisans. The slave's standard of living and comforts depended to a large extent on how his or her labor was used as well as on the character of the owner.

Beyond any doubt many owners treated their slaves well. But there is evidence of some masters punishing their slaves with beatings and overwork. During the growing season, field hands worked from dawn to dark planting, cultivating, and harvesting the crop. Unwilling slaves were sometimes beaten by overseers or slave drivers, although abolitionist writers tended to exaggerate the frequency of this kind of treatment. Slaves were too valuable to their owners to be so mistreated as to be unable to perform their tasks.

House servants usually lived better than field hands. Often they lived in the master's house and developed bonds of real affection for members of the master's family. Many slaves learned trades, becoming skilled artisans such as bricklayers, coopers, carpenters, and blacksmiths. When not needed by their owners, these skilled workers were often hired out for wages. Some earned enough money to buy their freedom.

Whether field hands, house servants, or artisans, slaves could never forget that they belonged to someone else. Slaves had no legal rights. Although often ignored, there were laws throughout the South against teaching slaves to read and write. Most slaves were not allowed to leave the property of their owners and were forbidden to gather in large groups with other slaves. Slaves might and often did attempt to escape, but punishment usually awaited them if caught. Slaveholders tended to keep families together. However, some slaves were sold by slaveholders who needed to raise cash or settle an estate. For the slave, this meant the anguish of parting from a wife, husband, child, or other family members.

The Issue of Slavery

Olmsted's observations seemed to confirm the growing conviction that the dependence of southern cotton planters on slavery was the number one problem of the United States. Geography and history had combined to plague the nation with a problem that no political compromise seemed

able to solve. Who was to blame? Slavery by 1850 was so woven into the economic and social fabric of the South that reform seemed hopeless. Southerners had inherited from the past a labor system more and more out of step with 19th-century thought and practice. But how to end it? Even if there had been the will, there seemed to be no acceptable solutions.

The attempts of some southern leaders earlier in the century to abolish slavery and transport blacks to a new life in Africa were no longer acceptable to anyone, black or white. Many thought that freeing the slaves without making provisions for their welfare would have created even greater problems. It would also have meant economic ruin for the former owners. Consequently, freeing the slaves and adopting an alternative system of free labor was not considered an option by most southerners.

Furthermore, although the vast majority of

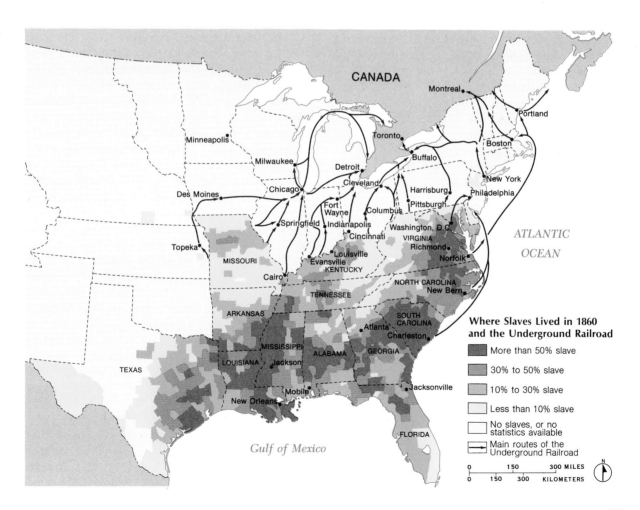

Where Slaves Lived in 1860 and the Underground Railroad

- More than 50% slave
- 30% to 50% slave
- 10% to 30% slave
- Less than 10% slave
- No slaves, or no statistics available
- Main routes of the Underground Railroad

0   150   300 MILES
0 150 300 KILOMETERS

southerners owned no slaves, they thought they had an important stake in the future of the institution. Whites, whether they owned slaves or not, feared for the supremacy of their race if blacks were to become free. Thus slavery was supported by all classes in the South. From once apologizing for the system as a necessary evil, southern leaders had moved to the position of defending it as a positive good. In making his observations on slavery, Olmsted might have added that the belief in white supremacy was by no means confined to the South. The many legal and social restrictions imposed on free blacks in the North show that it was a national attitude.

It did not help matters that the abolitionists of the North, in their zeal to bring slavery to an end, ignored many practical realities that stood in the way of achieving their goal. Abolitionists gave little consideration to the fact that immediate emancipation, even if possible, would create turmoil for blacks as well as whites, North as well as South. In a calmer atmosphere, moderate leaders, identified neither with the abolitionists nor with the southern extremists, might have found a way out. But with the South reacting defensively and belligerently to those who wanted to end slavery, hope of a peaceful resolution seemed to fade as each new crisis arose. The danger was growing that voices of reason and moderation, from whichever section they came, would be heard less and less. This was Olmsted's fear on the completion of his southern journey.

SECTION 1 REVIEW

Identify: Frederick Law Olmsted, Cotton Kingdom, planter class

Main Ideas

1. What were the two types of southern agriculture in the 1850s? Which was more economically important? Why?
2. What role did the planter class play in southern life?
3. What was life like for the southern slaves? In your answer, consider (**a**) living conditions, (**b**) types of work, (**c**) education, (**d**) legal rights, and (**e**) family life. What sources of information tell us about life under slavery?
4. What "realities" did abolitionists tend to ignore when they called for immediate emancipation?

2. THE NORTH IN THE 1850s

While Frederick Law Olmsted was touring the land of cotton, well-to-do southern families followed their annual habit of escaping the summer heat by vacationing at northern resorts such as Newport, Rhode Island, and Saratoga, New York. This practice, begun early in the century, continued to be popular. Southern leaders maintained many business and social ties with the North. Many upper-class southerners had gone to school in the North and had sons at West Point, Harvard, Yale, or Princeton. As long as relations between the sections remained reasonably friendly, these ties remained strong.

A Changing North

By 1852 these visits to the North took southern vacationers through large cities, thriving towns, and rich farmlands. The sights they saw both amazed and alarmed them. The North was changing rapidly—much more rapidly than the South. Although much that was happening disturbed the travelers, they were also impressed with the signs of prosperity. They could see that while the South continued to be almost entirely agricultural, the North was emerging as an industrial giant. They could see, too, that with the opening of more lands in the West and the completion of hundreds of miles of canals and railroads, more and more of the nation's commerce was following East-West routes rather than North-South ones. While the plantation system was keeping the South relatively static, free labor, immigration, and industrial growth were transforming the North.

The remarkable transformation that by midcentury was creating a great industrial society in the North was the result of many interrelated factors. Among these were the great number of new inventions and the growing abundance of raw materials.

New Inventions and Raw Materials

By the 1850s the United States was attracting world attention with the number of inventions and gadgets it was producing. At the London Crystal Palace Exposition of 1851, the United

States exhibits so impressed the British government that it sent special agents here to study American techniques.

Among the hundreds of new inventions there were a few key ones that quickly transformed the way goods were produced in American factories. In the early 1800s, the use of interchangeable parts, pioneered by **Eli Whitney**, revolutionized the making of rifles, watches, clocks, and tools. Whitney's work laid the basis for the modern assembly line and mass production. **Elias Howe's** invention of the sewing machine in 1846 created the ready-to-wear garment industry and made possible the large-scale manufacture of shoes. The invention of vulcanized rubber by **Charles Goodyear** in 1839 gave another boost to the shoe industry. The completion of the first telegraph lines by **Samuel F. B. Morse** in 1844 opened up a whole new system of instant communications.

New inventions for the farm were no less spectacular. New steel plowshares, the invention of **John Deere** in 1837, turned the tough prairie sod of the Middle West, opening vast new areas for growing wheat and corn. In 1831 **Cyrus McCormick** demonstrated the mechanical reaper, which solved the problem of how to harvest an expanding wheat crop. Other new farm machines— mechanical drills for planting, horse-drawn rakes for harvesting hay, and threshing machines for separating grain from its husks—gave a great boost to agricultural production.

The great expansion of agriculture, made possible by new inventions and the opening of new farmlands to the west, provided American industry with most of its raw materials. By midcentury, cotton from the South kept New England textile mills humming. One-fourth of the annual cotton crop went to northern textile mills. Wheat and corn crops kept the flour and grain mills busy producing flour and meal for both domestic consumption and export. (See map, page 358.) Cattle and sheep farmers provided the raw materials that kept the shoe factories and woolen mills of the North operating to capacity. The forests, North and South, supplied lumber for industry, railroad construction, and home building.

New and Expanding Industries

The first American factories were located along the banks of streams and used waterpower. Textile factories, both in New England and in the South, were usually located near the fall line, the boundary between the Piedmont and the coastal plain where there were many waterfalls. (See map, page 97.) These waterfalls could provide needed power. But with the development of steam engines, factories could be built near sources of labor, raw materials, and transportation routes. Improved steam engines with more power could increase production. They could also operate in all seasons of the year. Many of the older mills switched over to steam, and new industries depended on it exclusively.

Much of the industrial expansion experienced by the North in these years grew indirectly from new inventions. Each new industry created a kind of ripple effect. The vigorous cotton textile industry, for example, created a demand for cotton and provided cloth for the ready-to-wear clothing industry. The same industry also created a demand for new looms and other machines. This demand, in turn, stimulated the growth of the machine-tool industry, metal working shops, iron foundries, and iron and coal mining. Once a strong machine-tool industry was created, it greatly promoted the building of locomotives and other equipment for railroads and factories.

Transportation: New Methods and New Directions

Southern leaders were both surprised and disappointed by the way the North was beginning to influence the nation's transportation system. For many years the Mississippi River had been the great North-South artery. From the earliest days of settlement, produce from western farms found its way to market by being shipped down the mighty river to New Orleans. With their market in New Orleans, westerners had more in common with the South than with the East.

This situation began to change, however, with the opening of the **Erie Canal** in 1825. (See maps and text, pages 284–285.) The canal connected the Great Lakes to the Hudson River. The farmers in the West could ship their produce East more directly. Although New Orleans continued to be an important port, it had to share more and more of the western commerce with Buffalo, the western terminus of the Erie Canal. Soon more canals were built that linked the West with the East.

The East-West commercial ties created by the canals were later made even stronger and more

LIFE IN AMERICA

ELI WHITNEY'S INVENTIONS

In 1792 Eli Whitney, a young man from Massachusetts, went to Georgia to be a tutor. Whitney, who had tinkered with machines and tools all his life, was in Georgia only a few days before he invented the cotton gin (short for engine). This invention, which brought wealth to many (but not to Whitney), made it possible for southern slaveholders to expand westward into new lands, taking their slaves with them.

How the Cotton Gin Worked

When Whitney went south in 1792, he learned that there were two types of cotton: long staple and short staple. Long staple cotton grew only along the coasts. The seeds of this type were easily separated from the fiber by running the fiber through a roller. Short staple cotton, which could practically grow anywhere in the South, had short fibers which clung tenaciously to small green seeds. There was no easy way to deseed short staple cotton.

Eli Whitney put sawtooth disks on the rollers used in deseeding long staple cotton. This simple invention made it possible to deseed short staple cotton. As the crank

was turned, the cotton was snared by the teeth; the seeds, which were too large to pass through a comb-like screen, fell to the bottom of the gin while a brush, rotating in the opposite direction, caught the fibers. By using the cotton gin, a worker could clean up to 50 pounds

Cotton gin in operation

of short staple cotton a day. The cotton gin made the growing of short staple cotton profitable, thereby helping to extend slavery throughout the South.

Whitney wanted to set up "ginning" stations across the South. He patented his machine, but since it was so simple that any good blacksmith could—and did—make it, there were soon hundreds of cotton gins in production. Whitney took legal actions to stop these patent violations, but the legal battle put Whitney in debt and did nothing to stop the production of cotton gins.

The Concept of Interchangeable Parts

In May 1798 Whitney, who had moved to Connecticut, won a government contract which he hoped would end his debt. He promised to produce 10,000 muskets in 28 months—an unheard-of speed. In those days each gun was usually produced individually by hand by a skilled craftsman.

Whitney's idea was to produce machines to make thousands of identical parts, then to assemble the parts into muskets. In this fashion a broken part could be replaced instead of being newly crafted. All the guns would be the same.

It took Whitney ten years, not 28 months, to deliver the last of the rifles, but his concept of interchangeable parts laid the groundwork for America's industrial predominance in years to come.

---

permanent with the coming of the railroads. Introduced in the United States in the 1830s, the railroads had to overcome many problems before they could compete with the canals. Railroads were expensive to build and for many years were neither safe nor reliable. They required heavy iron rails, solid roadbeds, special bridges, and efficient brakes, all of which took time to develop. Most of the locomotives in the early days of railroading were not powerful enough to pull cars over steep grades and around sharp curves.

Gradually, however, these difficulties were overcome. After the Mexican War, railroad expansion was rapid. Smaller systems consolidated, and new standard gauge tracks were built (56½ inches between rails). By 1851, Lake Erie was linked by rail with the Hudson Valley. In 1852, the first train pulled into Chicago from New York.

The growth of the railroads provided a great stimulus to northern industry. The demand for rails, cars, and locomotives kept the iron industry busy. The towns and cities through which the railroads passed (and particularly terminus cities such as New York, Baltimore, and Chicago) benefited greatly. In addition, railroads ended the isolation of the western farmers. Iron rails linked them with eastern markets and made them an integral part of the industrial North.

Clipper Ships: A Brief Rule

The North was also taking the lead from the South in overseas commerce. From the early days of the Republic, trade tended to center in certain port cities—New York, Boston, Philadelphia, Baltimore, and New Orleans. By the 1850s, northern ports, especially New York, were far in the lead. The amount of trade handled by these ports increased dramatically between 1830 and 1850.

The attention of the world in the 1840s and 1850s was drawn to spectacular, perfected sailing vessels, called **clipper ships**. The most famous of these vessels were designed by Donald McKay of Boston. Sporting towering masts and displaying clouds of canvas, McKay's ships outdistanced all other vessels of the day. One of his ships covered 465 nautical miles in 24 hours, a record for sailing vessels that has never been surpassed.

The speed of these graceful monarchs of the sea made them favorites for the New England trade with China and for the long trip around South America to the gold fields of California. The desire for quick passage to distant ports was but one of several factors that promoted America's merchant marine in the 1850s. Another was the opening of Britain as a market for grain. Wherever speed of ocean transport was needed, the clipper ships ruled. But their days of glory were brief. The clipper ships were invented after the development of steam power. Slowly but surely, the larger steamships began to take over ocean transportation. By 1880, the swift, elegant clipper ships were ships of the past.

Immigrants Help Build the Industrial North

During the 1850s, some 2.5 million immigrants entered the U.S. from Europe. Joining the millions already here, they provided a pool of cheap labor without which the phenomenal industrial expansion of the North could not have taken place.

The vast majority of mid-century immigrants were from Ireland, Germany, and Scandinavia. A potato blight in Ireland between 1845 and 1849 and crop failures in Germany drove well over 2 million Irish and Germans to seek a better life in America. The failure of liberal revolutions in Europe in 1848–1849 produced many political refugees. Once they arrived here, many of the German and Scandinavian immigrants who had the means to do so pushed on to settle in the lush farmlands of the Middle West—in Ohio, Indiana, Illinois, and Wisconsin. The Irish, too poor to move west, usually settled in large eastern port cities, where they took whatever jobs they could find. Most of them were desperately poor and soon found themselves despised by other workers, whose jobs they frequently took. Free blacks in particular often lost out in the labor market to the newly arrived Irish.

Southerners familiar with living and working conditions in northern industrial cities claimed that slaves in the South were much better off than these wretched, half-starved "wage slaves" in northern factories. This criticism was largely true. The difference, of course, was that the Irish immigrants, impoverished and exploited though they were, remained free. Their families could not be broken up and sold by a slaveholder, and their children were born free with at least a chance to better their conditions.

The Andrew Jackson, *a sleek, fast, medium-size clipper built in 1855*

The great influx of immigrants into the northern states gave the North a diverse population, lacking in the South. The industry and skill of millions of hard-working immigrants gave the North other advantages as well. Businesses and industries could draw on a cheap, mobile labor supply. Many immigrants were from the professional ranks of society—doctors, lawyers, engineers—and many were skilled workers. Together, they added enormously to the cultural and material development of the North.

STATES IN THE UNION, 1860

	Free states	Slave states
Original 13 states	Massachusetts New Hampshire Rhode Island Connecticut New York Pennsylvania New Jersey	Delaware Maryland Virginia North Carolina South Carolina Georgia
Admitted 1791–1819	Vermont (1791) Ohio (1803) Indiana (1816) Illinois (1818)	Kentucky (1792) Tennessee (1796) Louisiana (1812) Mississippi (1817) Alabama (1819)
Admitted 1820–1865	Maine (1820) Michigan (1837) Iowa (1846) Wisconsin (1848) California (1850) Minnesota (1858) Oregon (1859)	Missouri (1821) Arkansas (1836) Florida (1845) Texas (1845)

SECTION 2 REVIEW

Identify: Eli Whitney, Elias Howe, Charles Goodyear, Samuel F. B. Morse, John Deere, Cyrus McCormick, Erie Canal, clipper ships

Main Ideas

1. What factors helped the North become an industrial society?
2. How did changes in transportation stimulate industrial growth in the North?
3. What events led millions of immigrants to come to America in the 1840s and 1850s?
4. What led southerners to say that slaves were better off than immigrant laborers of the North? How did immigration help the North?

3. A NEW SECTIONAL CRISIS ERUPTS OVER SLAVERY

The congressional leaders who put together the Compromise of 1850 believed that they had won an important victory in their fight to save the Union. What they had won, it turned out, was a fragile truce. The great majority of Americans probably supported the Compromise and saw no reason to disturb the peace and prosperity that followed the victory over Mexico. But a determined, vocal minority kept the old issues alive. For them, the issue of slavery was too fundamental for compromise. Thus the four years immediately following the Compromise of 1850 became a kind of contest between those who sought to keep slavery out of national politics and those who tried to use the government either to extend the institution or to abolish it.

The Election of Franklin Pierce

The first victory in the developing contest went to those who wanted to calm the waters. The test came in the presidential election of 1852. Because both Whigs and Democrats came out in support of the Compromise, the election campaign was a relatively calm one. The Democrats chose **Franklin Pierce**, a northerner whose southern leanings made him acceptable to slaveholders. The divided Whigs, hoping to win again with a military hero, nominated General Winfield Scott. The victory went to Pierce, whose moderate views fit the national mood. In his inaugural address, Pierce expressed the hope that sectional quarrels would not again threaten the nation and its prosperity.

The new President's good intentions were soon put to the test. Unfortunately, he proved to be a weak leader, unable to control the forces that used each opportunity to advance their particular views of the slavery issue.

Conflict over the Fugitive Slave Law

There was no way that President Pierce or anyone else could control the way many northerners felt about the **Fugitive Slave Law** that was a key part of the Compromise of 1850. This act allowed any slaveholder to reclaim a runaway slave simply by swearing that the fugitive was his or her slave. The black person claimed as a slave was not allowed to testify and was not entitled to a jury trial. The law, as part of the Compromise, was enforced by federal marshals, who received $10 when a slave was returned to a slaveholder, and $5 when he or she wasn't. No doubt a number of free blacks were forced back into slavery under the Fugitive Slave Law. Opposition to the act was immediate and violent in the North. Mobs swarmed in the streets of Boston, New York, and Syracuse, in some cases rescuing blacks from jail.

Newspaper stories reporting attempts to enforce the Fugitive Slave Law inflamed opinion both North and South. Southerners who were waiting to see if the North would live up to the Compromise of 1850 viewed these developments as proof of bad faith on the part of the North. And northerners who otherwise were willing to let slavery alone were enraged when they saw the law in action.

Many northerners continued to aid escaped slaves by hiding them. Eventually, many of these blacks made their way to Canada by way of the **"Underground Railroad."** The Underground Railroad was the term used to describe the many escape routes from the slave states to Canada. (See map, page 359.) The "railroad" was run by people who hid the escaped slaves by day and moved them by night from one "station" to the next.

Uncle Tom's Cabin

Out of northern opposition to the Fugitive Slave Law came the controversial novel, *Uncle Tom's Cabin*, one of the most influential books ever written. The author, **Harriet Beecher Stowe**, was against slavery but was not an abolitionist (one who wanted to end slavery immediately and unconditionally). Stowe's goal was to convince readers that slavery harmed everyone who had anything to do with it, North or South. The book was an instant success. The first printing of 10,000 copies in 1852 was sold in a week. Some 300,000 copies sold within a year.

Stowe had only limited firsthand knowledge of slavery, and her book contained inaccuracies. In general, however, she tried not to overstate her case. She portrayed southern slaveholders as kind and sensitive people and characterized the cruel slave driver, Simon Legree, as a transplanted northerner. The novel contained long descriptions of how human beings, black and white, suffered when slave families were broken up and sold. Powerful as a book, *Uncle Tom's Cabin* became even more effective when staged as a play. Audiences in the North wept openly when the young slave Liza, bloodhounds at her heels, crossed the frozen Ohio River to freedom, and when Little Eva and Uncle Tom died and went to Heaven. Southerners denounced Stowe's account of slavery as false and evil, which only made more readers for the book in the North.

The Ostend Manifesto:
A Southern Expansionist Plan Fails

Violent agitation in the North over the Fugitive Slave Law convinced southerners that they had been short-changed in the Compromise of 1850. To restore the balance, they sought some countermeasure that would be a gain for slavery and their section. Some southerners demanded a reopening of the African slave trade. Others looked southward to slaveholding in Cuba. Earlier, President Polk had tried to buy Cuba from Spain for $100 million. If it were annexed to the United States, Cuba could have been divided into several slave states. This would have gone far toward restoring the political balance lost to the South in the Compromise of 1850.

In 1854 the Pierce administration became involved with a southern plan to gain Cuba. The

Franklin Pierce (1804–1869)

IN OFFICE: 1853–1857

Democrat from New Hampshire. Pierce extended the southern border of the United States (Gadsden Purchase, 1853). After signing the Kansas-Nebraska Act (1854), he supported the proslavery faction in Kansas. This lost him the support of Northern Democrats, and he was not renominated.

plan was to make another purchase offer to Spain which, if refused, would be followed by a United States takeover of the island. To further the plan, the United States ministers in London, Paris, and Madrid met at Ostend, Belgium, to consider what the reaction in Europe would be. In a confidential dispatch to Washington, the ministers endorsed the plan and went on to say that if Spain refused to sell, the United States would be justified in taking Cuba by force.

Pierce's enemies in the House of Representatives demanded and obtained publication of the dispatch, known as the **Ostend Manifesto**. A howl of protest from free-soilers caused the plan to be scrapped. But the incident added fuel to the abolitionists' charges that there was a great "**slave-power conspiracy**" to spread slavery to the territories, to other lands, and ultimately to the free states themselves.

The Kansas-Nebraska Act, 1854

Even before the plan to acquire Cuba fell apart, the stage was set for a new crisis over slavery, one far greater than any thus far experienced. The crisis came early in 1854 when Senator Stephen A. Douglas of Illinois began to guide through Congress a measure known as the **Kansas-Nebraska Act**. The bill called for division of the Nebraska territory into two territories, Kansas and Nebraska. As part of the Louisiana Purchase north of the Missouri Compromise Line, this area had not been open to slavery. (See maps, opposite page.) Douglas, seeking southern votes, proposed to remove the restriction on slavery and substitute the principle of "**popular sovereignty**." The principle of "popular sovereignty" gave the voters of a new territory the right to decide whether that territory would be slave or free.

Douglas was at once denounced in the North for violating a sacred pledge. At the time of the annexation of Texas in 1845, Douglas had strongly defended the Missouri Compromise as a law that "no ruthless hand would ever be reckless enough to disturb." Why, then, had he changed his mind? Why would a man who had worked with Henry Clay to enact the Compromise of 1850 propose, four years later, a law that opened all the old wounds that the Compromise was intended to heal?

Douglas, a leading Democrat and one of the most astute politicians of the day, hoped to be-come his party's candidate for President. Without southern support, he had little chance of winning the nomination. Douglas knew that the opening of Kansas and Nebraska to popular sovereignty would please the South. There was at least a chance that Kansas, to the west of slaveholding Missouri, would vote for slavery. Personally, Douglas believed that slavery would not win out in either Kansas or Nebraska. But by allowing the voters to decide, Douglas could have it both ways. The South would be pleased by the removal of the prohibition of slavery during the territorial stage, but the North would ultimately win the area for free soil.

Douglas was also interested in promoting a transcontinental railroad that would run from Chicago to California, passing through the Kansas territory. As soon as the area was organized, plans for the railroad could get underway. All of these considerations may have been in the Senator's mind when he took the fateful step of introducing the Kansas-Nebraska Act into Congress in January 1854.

Whatever his motives, Douglas badly miscalculated. He was hardly prepared for the violent reaction that now set in. After months of bitter debate, the bill finally passed in May. Many in the North cried out that they had been betrayed. Never would they allow soil made free by the Missouri Compromise to be opened to slavery. All of the passions aroused by the Fugitive Slave Law were rekindled and fanned to a white heat. Antislavery groups in New England began making plans to send settlers to Kansas, where they might outnumber proslavery families expected to cross the border from slaveholding Missouri. An ugly fight was shaping up on the plains of Kansas. It would pit North against South and again place the Union in danger.

The Birth of the Republican Party

One of the chief casualties in the congressional struggle over the Kansas-Nebraska Act was the Whig party. No northern Whig would support the measure. Many southern Whigs, alienated by all the furor over the Fugitive Slave Law, went over to the Democrats. Even before the Kansas-Nebraska bill became law, a group of northern Whigs joined with antislavery Democrats and Free-Soilers in the call for a new party that would oppose the extension of slavery. Formally launched at Jackson, Michigan, on July 6, 1854, the new party adopted the name **Republican party**. Opposition to the expansion of slavery did not mean that the new party had any real concern for the welfare of blacks. It was "free soil" for white Americans, not freedom for slaves, that concerned the new party.

Blood on the Plains of Kansas

For two years following the passage of the Kansas-Nebraska Act, intermittent violence flared on the Kansas plains. Free-soil immigrants from New England, supplied by the Boston-based Emigrant Aid Society, founded Topeka, Lawrence, and other towns in Kansas. Proslavery groups from Missouri started settlements at Atchison, Leavenworth, and Lecompton. Then came a crucial test—the framing of a constitution and organization of Kansas as a territory. Would the territorial constitution permit slavery?

Swelled by proslavery voters who crossed the Missouri border to vote on election day in Kansas, the proslavery party won. Not to be outdone by those tactics, the free-soilers called another convention and drafted an antislavery constitution. Both groups sought recognition from Washington as the territorial government of Kansas. President Pierce recognized the proslavery government, but that did not settle the issue.

In the spring of 1856, a proslavery group marched on the town of Lawrence, setting fire to homes and looting stores. One person was killed. A few days later, **John Brown**, an abolitionist, accompanied by four of his sons, led a group of armed men against a proslavery town on Pottawatomie Creek. In an act of pure revenge, they killed five proslavery men in cold blood, in an incident known as the "Pottawatomie Massacre." Bands of armed men roamed the Kansas countryside, raiding farms and villages. In all, some 200 persons were killed before federal troops arrived to try to restore order to "**Bleeding Kansas**."

Acts of violence on the Kansas plains had their counterpart in the nation's capital. Shortly after the attack on Lawrence, **Senator Charles Sumner** of Massachusetts delivered a blistering speech in the Senate on the "Crime Against Kansas." Sumner denounced the southern leaders who were supporting the proslavery forces in Kansas, singling out Senator Andrew P. Butler of South Carolina for special abuse. Two days later, Repre-

Slave and Free Territory, 1820–1854

☐ Free or gradual abolition

☐ Slave

☐ Decision left to voters in territory

The Missouri Compromise, 1820
As part of the Missouri Compromise, Maine was admitted to the Union as a free state, and Missouri was admitted as a slave state. But slavery was prohibited in all other parts of the Louisiana Purchase north of 36°30'.

The Compromise of 1850
California was admitted as a free state, but the Compromise of 1850 kept alive the possibility that there would be more slave states. It allowed the voters in the Utah and New Mexico territories to decide if they wanted slavery.

The Kansas-Nebraska Act, 1854
The Kansas-Nebraska Act allowed the voters in the Kansas and Nebraska territories to decide about slavery. This law canceled part of the Missouri Compromise.

sentative Preston Brooks, Senator Butler's nephew, approached Sumner as he sat at his desk in the Senate and beat him senseless with a cane. Seriously injured, Sumner did not return to the Senate for many months. The atmosphere was so charged with hate that members regularly went about the halls of Congress armed for protection against their colleagues.

The Election of James Buchanan

With violence still flaring in the West, the nation prepared to hold the presidential election of 1856. The events in Kansas were enough to destroy President Pierce's chances for renomination. The Democrats, anxious for a candidate who might hold the northern and southern wings of their party together, fastened on **James Buchanan** of Pennsylvania, a northerner who was acceptable to the South. Douglas, who had sought the nomination, was thought to be too controversial because of his part in the furor over Kansas.

The new Republican party, gaining strength as the strife in Kansas continued, nominated John C. Frémont, who had won fame in California during the Mexican War. Although the Republicans made a strong showing, victory again went to the Democrats.

SECTION 3 REVIEW

Identify: Franklin Pierce, Fugitive Slave Law, Underground Railroad, *Uncle Tom's Cabin*, Harriet Beecher Stowe, Ostend Manifesto, slave-power conspiracy, Kansas-Nebraska Act, popular sovereignty, Republican party, John Brown, Bleeding Kansas, Charles Sumner, James Buchanan

Main Ideas

1. How did the Fugitive Slave Law increase hostility between the North and the South? How did *Uncle Tom's Cabin* increase hostility?
2. What were Senator Douglas' motives in proposing the Kansas-Nebraska Act of 1854?
3. What was the reaction in the North and South to the Kansas-Nebraska Act? What happened in Kansas as a result?
4. What groups joined to create the Republican party? What did the Republican party stand for?

4. THE SECTIONAL CRISIS DEEPENS

The year 1857 brought a new President to the White House and new woes to the nation. "Old Buck," as James Buchanan was affectionately known, had been in office only two days when the Supreme Court handed down a decision that rocked the nation.

The Dred Scott Decision

For some months the Supreme Court had been reviewing the case of Dred Scott, a slave who was suing for his freedom on the grounds that he had lived with his master for five years in free territory. On the surface the case of *Dred Scott* v. *Sandford* was simple enough. The Court could rule one way or another on whether residence on free soil entitled Dred Scott to his freedom. But instead of treating it as a simple legal matter, the Court turned it into a political issue.

To begin with, the Supreme Court ruled that Dred Scott was a slave, that slaves were not United States citizens, and hence had no right to sue in the federal courts. The Court could have stopped there and thrown the case out on a technicality. Instead, under the leadership of Chief Justice Roger B. Taney [tô′nē] from the slave state of Maryland, the Court went on to dispose of a broad range of issues relating to slavery in the territories. It was clear that the pro-southern majority on the Court intended to end the national debate on this issue in a manner favorable to the South.

Stated in simple terms, what the Court did was to rule that slaveholders could take their slaves into a territory without restrictions. To deprive slaveholders of this right would be to deprive them of their property "without due process," a violation of the Fifth Amendment to the U.S. Constitution. The Supreme Court was saying that Congress had no constitutional right to exclude slavery from the territories. The Court was saying that Congress had a constitutional duty to protect property, including slave property, in the territories. According to the **Dred Scott decision**, the Missouri Compromise had *always* been unconstitutional.

As President-elect and a good friend of Chief Justice Taney, Buchanan had had advance notice of how the Court would rule. He was pleased with the Dred Scott decision, believing it would finally settle the thorny issue of slavery in the territories. He told the country in his inaugural address that he would support the decision, "whatever it turned out to be," and that he expected all good citizens to do likewise. If Buchanan really believed this possible, he was out of touch with the strong feelings developing against the expansion of slavery. The Dred Scott decision did not smooth over sectional differences—instead it deepened the growing divisions over slavery.

Not surprisingly, southerners hailed the Dred Scott decision as sound doctrine. But in the North and West it was viewed as a political decision handed down by a Supreme Court that had a proslavery majority. It was further evidence of the "slave-power conspiracy." Moderates who opposed the expansion of slavery, but not slavery itself, were thoroughly alarmed. Did the Dred Scott decision mean that slavery would be free to spread throughout the entire country? In the days ahead, candidates for public office would be expected to tell the voters where they stood on this question.

The Panic of 1857

Deeply troubled by the Dred Scott decision and apprehensive over bloodshed in Kansas, the country reeled under still another blow when it suffered a business depression late in 1857. The North in particular was hard hit by bank failures, business collapses, and widespread unemployment. The agricultural South was little affected by this "**Panic of 1857**" and took its good fortune as proof that the southern economy was immune to the ups and downs of business and that Cotton was indeed King.

Northern business interests, already jittery over the nation's future in view of the slavery controversy, tended to blame the times on the policies of the pro-southern Presidents, Pierce and Buchanan. Sectional differences over slavery had so poisoned the air that the bad times were interpreted in partisan sectional terms.

Stephen A. Douglas

In 1858 Stephen A. Douglas returned to Illinois to run for re-election to the U.S. Senate. Douglas was optimistic about his chances. It was true that he had suffered some severe reverses during his

James Buchanan (1791–1868)

IN OFFICE: 1857–1861

Democrat from Pennsylvania. Although he believed that slavery was morally wrong, Buchanan supported the Supreme Court decision in the Dred Scott case. In 1860, as the southern states began to secede, he denied their right to do so, but refused to use force to keep them in the Union.

second term. The Kansas-Nebraska Act had turned out badly. He had failed to capture his party's nomination for President in 1856. Things were going badly in Kansas. He had come to an open break with President Buchanan, who was supporting proslavery politicians in Kansas. And, finally, there was the Dred Scott decision, which seemed to many people to run directly counter to Douglas' doctrine of popular sovereignty.

But these difficulties aside, Douglas could point to some real advantages. He was a nationally known figure, perhaps the best known politician in America. He was still a comparatively young man, only 45 on his last birthday. He was still popular in the South even if some of his friends there seemed not always to trust him. His chances of becoming his party's candidate in 1860 and being elected President were highly promising.

Douglas believed that the Illinois race presented no problems. If his fellow citizens would challenge him on the doctrine of popular sovereignty, Douglas would explain that his support of the doctrine was in no way an endorsement of slavery expansion. It was simply that he believed in grass-roots democracy. He had always said that if the people of a territory were allowed to decide between free soil and slavery, they would choose the former. Douglas believed that he would need only to go among the home folks with his brilliant blend of jovial informality and old-fashioned oratory to put their minds at rest.

Douglas' opponent on the Republican side was to be **Abraham Lincoln**, a well-known local lawyer with a reputation for wit and wisdom, a one-term congressman, but not really in Douglas' class. Lincoln looked like what he was: a small-town lawyer with no polish or style. Douglas sported the latest fashions and caused a flurry of excitement wherever he went. So Lincoln was not a problem. Douglas had known "Old Abe" for 20 years, and they were friends. The debates they agreed to hold in the seven congressional districts of the state would be a pleasant relief from the angry scenes in the Senate. But Douglas would need to choose his words carefully in the debates —Lincoln was a sharp lawyer and would probably try to catch him in some inconsistency.

The Lincoln-Douglas Debates

What followed were the **Lincoln-Douglas debates**, perhaps the most famous senatorial contest in American history. With the public mind—North, West, and South—highly agitated over slavery, the contest at once took on national significance. Large crowds followed the candidates, and the national press printed full accounts of the debates.

As expected, Lincoln put sharp, lawyerlike questions to Douglas. At Freeport, Illinois, scene

Lincoln and Douglas. Photographs by Mathew Brady.

of the first debate, Lincoln, with the Dred Scott decision in mind, asked Douglas to explain how a territory could forbid slavery if Congress could not. A territory was created by Congress. Did it have more power than the Congress that created it? Either way the Senator answered, he stood to lose votes. The Dred Scott decision was strongly supported in the South. The Kansas-Nebraska Act, which permitted a territory to vote for or against slavery, was popular in Illinois, where there was strong support for a transcontinental railroad. Southern votes were not at stake in 1858, but they would be in 1860 when Douglas again planned to run for the presidency.

In what became known as the "**Freeport Doctrine**," Douglas tried to sidestep the issue by answering that it did not matter what the Supreme Court said about congressional authority over slavery. As a practical matter, slavery could not exist "for a day or an hour" in a territory unless it was supported by local police regulations. Without them, no slaveholder would risk bringing valuable slave property into the territory.

It was during the Lincoln-Douglas debates that Abraham Lincoln was supposed to have said, "You can fool all of the people some of the time, and some of the people all of the time, but you cannot fool all of the people all of the time." These words, however, did not keep Douglas, the "Little Giant," from winning re-election. Although Lincoln won the popular vote, Douglas won the vote in the state legislature and was thus elected to another term. But he had badly damaged his standing in the South by admitting that the people in a territory might keep slavery out. In the South, the Freeport Doctrine was called the "Freeport Heresy." Lincoln lost the election, but the debates made him a national figure and put him forward as a potential Republican nominee for the presidency in 1860.

John Brown at Harpers Ferry

While politicians argued the slavery issue in the halls of Congress and on the campaign trail, others prepared to take matters into their own hands. John Brown, the man who had gone unpunished for the murder of five proslavery men in Kansas, moved East with a plan for a more direct blow against slavery. Believing himself commanded by God to free the slaves, Brown came up with a scheme to seize a federal arsenal in the

Virginia mountains. With secret aid from a group of abolitionists, Brown set out for **Harpers Ferry** on the Potomac River. His plan was to seize the arsenal, use it as a base, and from there send out armed bands to free the slaves. The freed slaves would be provided with arms from the arsenal. They would collect in the hills, organize into a black republic, and from there go on to liberate all the slaves in the South.

Brown and his men captured the arsenal but were quickly overpowered by a detachment of marines under the command of Colonel Robert E. Lee. Brown was captured, tried for treason against the state of Virginia, and hanged. At his trial, Brown maintained that his only desire was to end slavery.

The news from Harpers Ferry sent shock waves throughout the nation. Abolitionists in the North hailed Brown as a Christian martyr. Comparing Brown's death with that of Jesus, the poet Ralph Waldo Emerson wrote that Brown had "made the gallows glorious like the cross." In the South, Brown was denounced as a tool of Satan. The fear of a slave revolt, aided and abetted by northern abolitionists, arose once more to haunt the public mind. The hero's acclaim accorded Brown in the northern press seemed proof to the South that there were powerful groups in that section of the country bent on destroying slavery and with it all that the South held dear.

SECTION 4 REVIEW

Identify: Dred Scott decision, Panic of 1857, Abraham Lincoln, Lincoln-Douglas debates, Freeport Doctrine, Harpers Ferry

Main Ideas
1. What did the Supreme Court rule in the Dred Scott decision? What did this mean for the Missouri Compromise, the Compromise of 1850, and popular sovereignty?
2. Why did the Dred Scott decision make moderates fear that slavery would spread?
3. Why were the Lincoln-Douglas debates important? How did they affect the careers of the two men?
4. What was the result of John Brown's raid on Harpers Ferry? How did people in the North and South react?

5. A FINAL CRISIS BRINGS SECESSION

John Brown, martyr or murderer, went to the gallows in December 1859. The passions he had aroused across the land continued at a fever pitch. The spring of 1860 was not a good time to choose candidates for public office, but American presidential elections are determined by the calendar, not the national mood. The stately old city of Charleston, especially beautiful in springtime, prepared to welcome the chieftains of a badly divided Democratic party.

The Democratic Party Fails to Name a Candidate

The Democratic party that assembled in April 1860 was the only remaining national political organization of importance. The other parties were either old and dying, like the Whigs, or purely sectional, like the Republicans. Thus when the gavel came down opening the convention, more than party unity was at stake. The last cords that bound the North and South together were strained. If they should snap, the Union itself might fall apart.

The prospects for a harmonious result were not good. The leading contender, Stephen A. Douglas, was no longer acceptable to the South because of his "Freeport Doctrine"—his admission that a territory could in effect vote to exclude slavery. Added to this was the anger of southern Democrats arising from the raid on Harpers Ferry.

The Charleston convention quickly disintegrated into angry name calling. The South would not support Douglas; the North and West would support no one else. The unruly delegates, hopelessly deadlocked, finally adjourned without naming a candidate. Many of the southern delegates had already withdrawn in anger. With little hope of reconciling differences, the leaders nevertheless agreed to try again in June in Baltimore.

The Republicans Choose Lincoln

Meanwhile, a throng of high-spirited Republican delegates descended on Chicago, the rough boom city on the shores of Lake Michigan. Jubilant over the troubles of the Democrats in Charleston, and smelling victory in the air, the delegates began assembling in a hastily constructed convention hall called the "Wigwam." By this time the Republican party had adopted a number of important issues in addition to its opposition to the spread of slavery. Among these were a call for free homesteads for western settlers, protective tariffs for northern industry, internal improvements, and a railroad to the Pacific. All these measures, favored by the North and West, had been blocked in Congress by the desire to compromise with the South.

The leading contender for the Republican nomination was William Seward, a senator from New York and a well-known spokesman for free soil. Just about everyone's second choice was Abraham Lincoln of Illinois. Since the Lincoln-Douglas debates, Lincoln had traveled widely in the East and delivered many speeches. Although Lincoln was not given much chance of capturing the nomination, the holding of the convention in Chicago played into the hands of his supporters. Amid wildly cheering throngs who hailed him as "Abe the Rail Splitter" and "Honest Abe," Abraham Lincoln won nomination on the third ballot.

The Republican party's candidate gives a striking example of the opportunities a democratic system offers to persons of talent no matter how humble their origins. Lincoln was born in a log cabin in the backwoods of Kentucky, with none of the educational and social advantages available to many. To the young Lincoln, obstacles along the way became challenges to overcome. Reading a borrowed book late at night by the glow of a flickering candle had put him on the road to what was largely a self-education. The struggles of the Lincoln family as they moved from Kentucky, to Indiana, and finally to Illinois were part of a larger story—the westward movement of count-less frontier families little different from the Lincolns. Lincoln, however, had extraordinary leadership abilities—qualities that had always been present, but had never been put to the test.

The Fateful Election of 1860

When the Democrats reconvened in Baltimore, matters had gone from bad to worse. Many of the southern delegates were more interested in secession than in healing the split in party ranks. The spirit was defeatist on the part of northern Democrats and defiant on the part of southern Democrats. Again, many southern delegates bolted the convention. Those remaining chose Douglas, who became in effect the candidate of the northern wing. The southern wing, meeting in a separate convention in another part of the city, nominated John C. Breckenridge of Kentucky.

Meanwhile in May another group, consisting mainly of former Whigs and thoroughly alarmed over the prospect of disunion, met in their own hastily called convention, also in Baltimore. Fearful lest they offend free-soilers on the one hand or slave-state voters on the other, the delegates adopted the name of Constitutional Union party and refused to say anything specific about the slavery issue. They stressed their loyalty to the Union and their determination to uphold the Constitution—principles which they hoped a majority would agree with without asking for details. The Constitutional Unionists chose John Bell of Tennessee as their candidate.

Of the four candidates in the election of 1860, only Stephen A. Douglas waged a national campaign. He made a special point of touring the South, urging the voters to stay in the Union no matter what the results of the election. Lincoln stayed in Springfield, Illinois, and made no

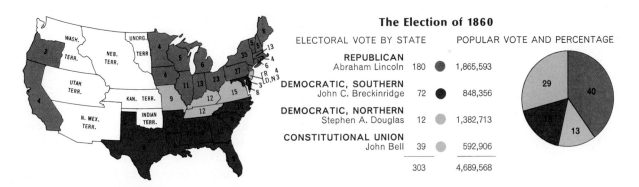

The Election of 1860

ELECTORAL VOTE BY STATE		POPULAR VOTE AND PERCENTAGE
REPUBLICAN Abraham Lincoln	180	1,865,593
DEMOCRATIC, SOUTHERN John C. Breckinridge	72	848,356
DEMOCRATIC, NORTHERN Stephen A. Douglas	12	1,382,713
CONSTITUTIONAL UNION John Bell	39	592,906
	303	4,689,568

speeches. His views against the spread of slavery were well known, he said, and so also was his promise not to disturb slavery where it existed. He believed that any further statement on the subject would be taken as a sign of weakness. By election day, Lincoln's election seemed certain. The only uncertainty was over what would follow.

When the results were in, it was clear that Abraham Lincoln had won, receiving 40% of the popular vote. Douglas was second with 29%, Breckenridge third with 18%, and Bell fourth with 13%. Lincoln carried all the states of the North and West, for a total of 180 electoral votes. (See map.) His three opponents, with a combined total of 60% of the popular votes, won only 123 electoral votes. Douglas carried only Missouri and part of New Jersey, while Breckenridge swept the South and split the border states with Bell.

In choosing Lincoln, the nation had elected a sectional President. In ten southern states he was not on the ballot and had not received a single vote. Repeatedly, the South had vowed to secede from the Union if Lincoln should win.

Seven States Secede from the Union!

With newspapers across the nation carrying banner headlines proclaiming the election of Lincoln, southern leaders prepared to make headlines of their own. They believed that they could no longer trust the government in Washington. The new President-elect was opposed to the expansion of slave territory. Thus there seemed to be no hope that the South could regain its lost influence in the political life of the nation. What choices did the South have? As many southerners saw it, secession was the only way out.

The election of Lincoln had provided the spark, and the long-dreaded, long-threatened secession of South Carolina was at hand. It came on December 20, 1860, and was swiftly followed by similar action on the part of the states of the lower South—Mississippi, Florida, Alabama, Georgia, Louisiana, and Texas. Delegates from the seceding states met in February at Montgomery, Alabama, and set up the Confederate States of America, or the **Confederacy**.

The Montgomery delegates drew up a constitution that in all but a few respects was a copy of the federal Constitution. It did, however, declare that no law ending or impairing the right to hold slaves could be passed, and it stressed the

FROM THE ARCHIVES

South Carolina's Ordinance of Secession

Right after Lincoln's election, the South Carolina legislature called a convention to consider secession. Chosen by popular vote, the delegates met in Charleston on December 17, and on the 20th they voted unanimously for secession.

An Ordinance to Dissolve the Union between the State of South Carolina and the other States united with her under the compact entitled the Constitution of the United States of America:
We, the people of the State of South Carolina, in Convention assembled, do declare and ordain, and it is hereby declared and ordained, that the ordinance adopted by us in Convention, on the 23rd day of May, in the year of our Lord 1788, whereby the Constitution of the United States of America was ratified, and also all Acts and parts of Acts of the General Assembly of this State ratifying the amendments of the said Constitution, are hereby repealed, and that the union now subsisting between South Carolina and other States under the name of the United States of America is hereby dissolved.

"sovereign and independent character" of each state. The President would have a 6-year term of office but would not be eligible for re-election.

The delegates then chose **Jefferson Davis** of Mississippi as provisional President and **Alexander Stephens** of Georgia as provisional Vice-President. The decades of impossible compromises were over: the deep South had seceded from a Union that no further compromise could hold together.

SECTION 5 REVIEW

Identify: Confederacy, Jefferson Davis, Alexander Stephens

Main Ideas
1. Why was unity among Democrats so important to the Union? What happened at the Democratic conventions in Charleston and Baltimore?
2. Explain why the Republican party was a sectional party, not a national one.
3. Why did Lincoln's election cause seven states to secede from the Union?

CHAPTER 15 REVIEW

Key Terms
Explain the meaning of each of the following terms:

Cotton Kingdom
planter class
Erie Canal
clipper ships
Fugitive Slave Law
Underground Railroad
Uncle Tom's Cabin
Ostend Manifesto
slave-power conspiracy
Kansas-Nebraska Act

popular sovereignty
Republican party
Bleeding Kansas
Dred Scott decision
Panic of 1857
Lincoln-Douglas debates
Freeport Doctrine
Harpers Ferry
Confederacy

Reviewing the Main Ideas
Section 1
1. What role did cotton and cotton planters play in the South in the 1850s?
2. What sources tell us about the lives of the southern slaves? Give a brief description of life under slavery, including living and working conditions, education, legal rights, and family life.
3. What issues did the abolitionists ignore when they called for "immediate emancipation"?

Section 2
1. Explain four factors that combined to help northern industry grow rapidly in the 1850s.
2. Why did many immigrants come to the United States in the 1840s and 1850s?
3. How did immigration help industrial growth in the North?

Section 3
1. How did the Fugitive Slave Law, *Uncle Tom's Cabin*, and the Kansas-Nebraska Act increase hostility between North and South?
2. What groups formed the Republican party? What were the new party's goals with regard to slavery?

Section 4
1. How did the Dred Scott decision change the issue of slavery in the territories? What was the reaction in the North? In the South?
2. What effect did the Lincoln-Douglas debates of 1858 have on the election of 1860?
3. Why did John Brown's actions at Harpers Ferry shock both North and South?

Section 5
1. What happened to the unity of the only national party in 1860? Explain.
2. On what platform did Abraham Lincoln run for President? Was he a "national" President? Explain.
3. What was the result of Lincoln's election?

Special History Skills:
Considering the Causes of Events
What caused the Civil War? This short question has no universally agreed-upon answer. Among the many conclusions of historians and other people are the following:
1. states' rights
2. slavery
3. the expansion of slavery
4. the abolitionists
5. *Uncle Tom's Cabin*
6. John Brown's raid
7. sectional rivalry and political ambition
8. patriotism
9. economic differences, such as the fight over the tariff
10. fanaticism on both sides
11. an inability of the democratic process to deal with a major moral issue (slavery) or with a conflict over the fundamental structure of society (states' rights vs. majority rule)
12. the Dred Scott decision
13. the election of Lincoln
14. the firing on Fort Sumter (see Chapter 16)

As you can see, some of the possible causes are specific events, while others are general trends and conditions. Which events, trends, or conditions *most* contributed to the breakup of the Union? Use the information given in this chapter and other sources, if you so desire, to help you pick out one or more *major* causes of the Civil War. Back your views with specific examples.

Other Skill Activities
1. Inventions aid industry
Research one of the inventions mentioned in the chapter. What led to this invention? How

did the invention affect industry? Write a report that includes a sketch of the invention and a short biography of the inventor.

2. **Railroad routes map and poster**

In an atlas or encyclopedia, find a map of the major railroad routes in the U.S. today. Do most rail lines still run east and west? Is there a network of lines that connects all parts of the country? Draw a map of the railroad lines on a poster.

Thinking Critically

1. Historians disagree about what the experience of the slaves was like. Some think that slavery was a very harsh system, while others think that on the whole the slaves were fairly well treated. Why might it be difficult for historians —and other Americans, as well—to come to an agreement on this subject?

2. On page 360 the text says: "In a calmer atmosphere, moderate leaders identified neither with the abolitionists nor with the southern extremists might have found a way [to end slavery]." Do you agree or disagree? Can you think of any peaceful solutions that might have been worked out to end slavery? Or could it have been ended only by war?

3. When Abraham Lincoln met Harriet Beecher Stowe, he is supposed to have said, "So this is the little lady who started the big war." He was referring to the emotions aroused by her book, *Uncle Tom's Cabin*. What effect do you think literature has on popular feelings? What other books have influenced history?

4. Did popular sovereignty work in Kansas? Why did Douglas propose it, and why did it backfire?

Further Reading

Leonard F. James. *Following the Frontier*. Harcourt, Brace, & World, 1968. Discusses the Erie Canal, early railroads, steamboats, and the Pony Express.

Elizabeth F. Chittenden. *Profiles in Black and White*. Charles Scribner's Sons, 1973. Ten biographies of men and women who fought against slavery. Includes stories of the Underground Railroad and Fugitive Slave Law.

Frank L. Dennis. *The Lincoln-Douglas Debates*. Mason/Charter, 1974. Includes quotations from the debates and discussion of the issues and the importance of the debates.

TEST YOURSELF

WRITE YOUR ANSWERS ON A SEPARATE SHEET OF PAPER.

Matching

Write the letter of the term that best matches each description below.

1. his election brought secession
2. author of *Uncle Tom's Cabin*
3. fanatic who planned a slave revolt
4. upheld slaveholders' rights to their property anywhere in the United States
5. gave residents the chance to vote on the issue of slavery in a territory
6. inventor of the steel plow
7. important in the careers of two 1860 presidential candidates
8. helped escaping slaves to reach freedom
9. his "Freeport Doctrine" lost him votes
10. created by groups opposed to the spread of slavery

a. Stephen A. Douglas
b. Dred Scott decision
c. Kansas-Nebraska Act
d. John Deere
e. Eli Whitney
f. Harriet Beecher Stowe
g. Lincoln-Douglas debates
h. Republican party
i. Underground Railroad
j. Erie Canal
k. Abraham Lincoln
l. John Brown

Classifying

For each item listed, mark N if it describes the North in the 1850s. Mark S if the item describes the South. Mark B if the item describes both. Mark O if the item describes neither.

1. most whites believed in white supremacy
2. economy based almost entirely on agriculture
3. supported the Dred Scott decision
4. many European immigrants settled here
5. leaders were a small group of wealthy planters
6. inventions and new means of transportation
7. voted for Abraham Lincoln
8. willing to compromise in 1860
9. economy increasingly based on industry
10. *Uncle Tom's Cabin* brought a strong reaction

Chronological Order

Place the following events in chronological order.
Compromise of 1850——Harpers Ferry raid—— Dred Scott decision——Lincoln elected—— Kansas-Nebraska Act

Chapter 16

THE CIVIL WAR

1861–1865

South Carolina seceded from the Union on December 20, 1860. By February 1, 1861, six other states—Mississippi, Florida, Alabama, Georgia, Louisiana, and Texas—had also seceded. Though many people in these states had opposed secession, on the whole the withdrawal of the seven states of the lower South had been accomplished quickly and with much public rejoicing.

Far different was the scene in the North. President-elect Lincoln was still in Springfield, Illinois, when Jefferson Davis was inaugurated President of the Confederacy. An air of uncertainty hung over Washington, D.C. The eight slave states that remained in the Union warned the federal government that they, too, might secede if force were used against the seceding seven. The populations of these states were deeply divided in their loyalties. In the free states, most Americans had greeted the secession crisis with a mixture of surprise and anger. As yet, there were few firm views on how to meet the situation. Only a few—mainly abolitionists—were glad to see the slave states leave the Union. Most wanted the Union restored. But how? Indecision reigned.

President James Buchanan, who would remain in office until March 4, 1861, presided over a government that was rapidly falling apart. Southerners were leaving federal service in droves. Men who had been close friends and colleagues for years were parting. With heavy hearts they said their farewells, not knowing if ever they would meet again. If they did it would probably be as enemies on some battlefield.

Sections in This Chapter
1. Compromise Gives Way to Conflict
2. A Slow Start to a Long Struggle, 1861–1862
3. The War Leads to the End of Slavery
4. Four Years of Fighting Bring a Northern Victory
5. Behind the Lines, North and South
6. Wartime Politics, Politicians, and Programs

Opposite: Haunting relics of long and cruel war

1. COMPROMISE GIVES WAY TO CONFLICT

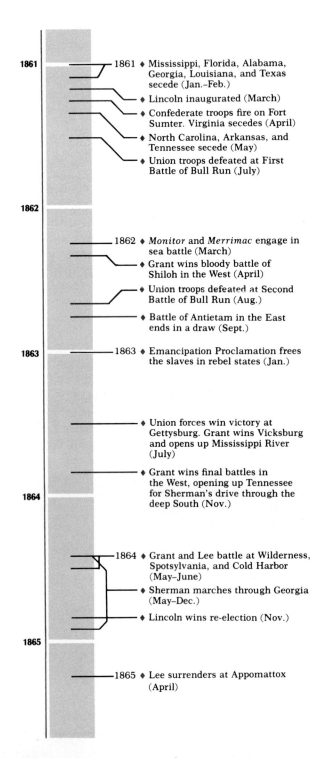

1861 ◆ Mississippi, Florida, Alabama, Georgia, Louisiana, and Texas secede (Jan.–Feb.)

◆ Lincoln inaugurated (March)

◆ Confederate troops fire on Fort Sumter. Virginia secedes (April)

◆ North Carolina, Arkansas, and Tennessee secede (May)

◆ Union troops defeated at First Battle of Bull Run (July)

1862 ◆ *Monitor* and *Merrimac* engage in sea battle (March)

◆ Grant wins bloody battle of Shiloh in the West (April)

◆ Union troops defeated at Second Battle of Bull Run (Aug.)

◆ Battle of Antietam in the East ends in a draw (Sept.)

1863 ◆ Emancipation Proclamation frees the slaves in rebel states (Jan.)

◆ Union forces win victory at Gettysburg. Grant wins Vicksburg and opens up Mississippi River (July)

◆ Grant wins final battles in the West, opening up Tennessee for Sherman's drive through the deep South (Nov.)

1864 ◆ Grant and Lee battle at Wilderness, Spotsylvania, and Cold Harbor (May–June)

◆ Sherman marches through Georgia (May–Dec.)

◆ Lincoln wins re-election (Nov.)

1865 ◆ Lee surrenders at Appomattox (April)

In the final days of Buchanan's administration hope was fast fading that last-minute compromise efforts, undertaken by moderates in Congress, would succeed. Chief among those searching frantically for a compromise solution was John Crittenden, senator from the border state of Kentucky. On December 18, he had introduced a peace resolution known as the **Crittenden Compromise**, which called for a series of constitutional amendments. One would have restored the Missouri Compromise line: slavery would be banned north of latitude 36°30′N, but it would be permitted south of that line in all present and future territories. Other constitutional amendments would guarantee the permanence of slavery and strengthen the power of slaveholders to recover fugitive slaves.

For border state leaders such as Crittenden, a compromise solution of some kind was the only way out of an impossible situation. Sentiment for the Union was strong in the border states, as shown by their support of Bell and Douglas in the 1860 election. But support for states' rights and the right of secession was also strong. If the North used force against the states that had left, the upper South would reluctantly leave the Union.

It was obvious that no compromise could succeed without the support of the President-elect. But Abraham Lincoln would not support the Crittenden proposal. He had built his political career on opposition to the expansion of slavery in the territories. He had just won election largely on that issue. When Lincoln's opposition became known, all hope for the Crittenden Compromise faded. A similar effort made by Virginia in February 1861 failed for the same reason.

Lincoln's view was that the issue of slavery in the territories would only have to be faced again. It was also time, he thought, to be firm on the question of secession. If the losers in a national election could get what they wanted by threatening to secede, effective democratic government would be at an end. At this point, Lincoln did not view the secession crisis as an issue of peace or war. It was only after he arrived in Washington that he saw how critical the situation had become.

Meanwhile, Buchanan remained President and did almost nothing to meet the crisis of secession. He said he was opposed to secession, but when seven states left the Union, he did nothing. Buchanan knew that if he used force, war would result. Thus he took no action when the Confederacy moved quickly to take over federal arsenals, forts, and other government property within its borders.

When Buchanan attempted to send supplies to **Fort Sumter** in South Carolina (one of two southern forts still in federal hands), the relief ship was fired upon and turned back. Sumter remained under federal control but would not be able to hold out for very long unless supplied. This was the situation when Abraham Lincoln was inaugurated 16th President of the United States.

The New President Takes Over
On March 4, 1861, the task of charting a course of action for a divided nation fell to Abraham Lincoln. Seven states had left the Union. Others were threatening to leave. What would Lincoln's attitude be? Would he accept the loss of federal property in the seceding states? Would he surrender Fort Sumter to the Confederacy without a fight? Would he use force against the Confederacy?

In a general way, Lincoln dealt with all of these questions in his inaugural address. He spoke frankly and compassionately concerning the national peril. To the South he addressed words that showed understanding rather than ill will. But he was firm. He made it clear that, unlike Buchanan, he would do whatever was necessary to defend and preserve the government. His speech was a moving 11th-hour appeal to the South, combined with a statement of what he intended to do:

In your hands, my dissatisfied fellow countrymen, and not in mine, is the momentous issue of civil war. The government will not assail you. You can have no conflict without yourselves being the aggressor. You can have no oath registered in heaven to destroy the government, while I shall have the most solemn one to preserve, protect and defend it.

And then Lincoln closed his inaugural address with one of those expressive passages for which history will always remember him:

Abraham Lincoln (1809–1865)

IN OFFICE: 1861–1865

Republican from Illinois. Lincoln was the first President belonging to the modern Republican party. The news of his election prompted the secession of seven southern states before his inauguration (March 1861). Lincoln's policies as President were based on a belief in the supremacy of the Union. He proclaimed the Emancipation Proclamation (1863) and guided the Union forces to victory. His plan for quickly restoring the South to the Union was thwarted by his assassination a few days after the end of the war (April 1865).

We are not enemies but friends. We must not be enemies. Though passion may have strained, it must not break our bonds of affection. The mystic chords of memory stretching from every battlefield and patriot grave, to every living heart and hearthstone, all over this broad land, will yet swell the chorus of the Union, when again touched, as surely they will be, by the better angels of our nature.

Confederate Forces Shell Fort Sumter
On the problem of what to do about Fort Sumter, Lincoln moved cautiously. Informed the day after inauguration that Fort Sumter would have to be surrendered if supplies and reinforcements were not sent at once, Lincoln decided to send supplies only. He informed the governor of South Carolina of what he planned to do. The next move was up to the Confederacy. One of Lincoln's chief considerations was to avoid any act of open aggression that would give the states of the upper South and the border states reason to join the Confederacy.

Confederate leaders, on the other hand, were unwilling to leave Fort Sumter, strategically located at the entrance to Charleston harbor, in federal hands. When the troops at Fort Sumter rejected the demand for immediate surrender on April 11, **General P. G. T. Beauregard** [bō′rə gärd], Confederate commander in Charleston, trained the shore batteries on Sumter on April 12 and gave the order to begin shelling the stronghold. For 35 hours bursting shells lit up the skies over

The Union and the Confederacy

Free states and territories
Slave states loyal to Union
Confederate States of America
Territory supporting Confederacy
Indian territory

The Indian Territory did not have a unified government. Some tribes supported the Confederacy while others backed the Union. The Arizona Territory declared its independence in 1861 and later became a Confederate territory. In 1862, it was captured by the Union. The next year it became a Union territory with entirely different boundaries. West Virginia seceded from Virginia in 1861 and was admitted to the Union in 1863.

the harbor. Unable to hold out longer, its walls in shambles, the fort surrendered on April 13. The small defending garrison was allowed to sail away in the supply ships that waited off shore.

The fall of Fort Sumter electrified the North. The long months of uneasy waiting were over. A great wave of patriotic feeling greeted the news that the flag had been fired upon and that the nation was at war. When Lincoln called immediately for 75,000 volunteers to serve for 90 days to crush the rebellion, the call was quickly oversubscribed.

In the South the reaction was equally swift. Lincoln's call for an army to crush the South was viewed as an act of naked aggression. It led at once to the secession of Virginia, Arkansas, Tennessee, and North Carolina. (See map above.) The western counties of Virginia, however, were opposed to secession, and in 1863 they entered the Union as the new state of West Virginia.

The Confederacy, now composed of 11 states, shifted its capital from Montgomery, Alabama, to Richmond, Virginia. The war had begun. However, both sides expected the war to be over quickly.

The Strengths and Weaknesses of Each Side

The fighting that began with the bombardment of Fort Sumter went on for four years. The long and bitter war became known in history by a number of names—the Brothers' War, the War for Southern Independence, the Revolution, the War Between the States, the War Between the North and the South, the War of the Great Rebellion, the War of Northern Aggression, and the Civil War.

On the surface it appeared to be an uneven struggle. As the map and charts on the facing page show, the North had far greater resources than the South. The population of the North in 1860 was 22 million to the South's 9 million, of whom 3.5 million were slaves. Almost all of the nation's manufacturing was located in the North. The North controlled far greater resources of food, raw materials, and transportation than did

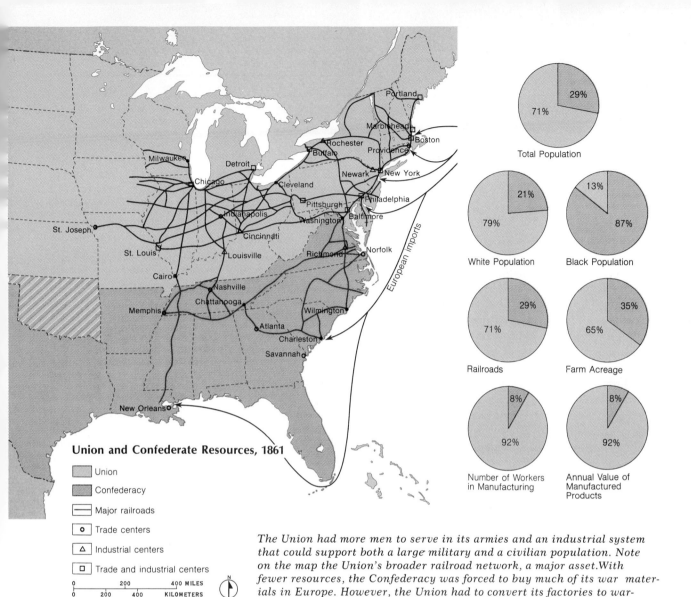

Union and Confederate Resources, 1861

Legend:
- Union
- Confederacy
- Major railroads
- ○ Trade centers
- △ Industrial centers
- □ Trade and industrial centers

0   200   400 MILES
0   200   400 KILOMETERS

Pie charts:
- Total Population: 71% / 29%
- White Population: 79% / 21%
- Black Population: 87% / 13%
- Railroads: 71% / 29%
- Farm Acreage: 65% / 35%
- Number of Workers in Manufacturing: 92% / 8%
- Annual Value of Manufactured Products: 92% / 8%

The Union had more men to serve in its armies and an industrial system that could support both a large military and a civilian population. Note on the map the Union's broader railroad network, a major asset. With fewer resources, the Confederacy was forced to buy much of its war materials in Europe. However, the Union had to convert its factories to wartime production, and it took time for the economic advantages to be felt.

the South. In any lengthy struggle, the vastly superior manpower and manufacturing might of the North would probably be decisive. In addition, the North owned most of the nation's shipping and enjoyed control of the seas. Its navy would play a leading part in preventing supplies from reaching the South.

But surface appearances were misleading. The South could count on several important factors that seemed to weigh heavily in its favor. First among these were strategic considerations. Geographically, the South was a compact unit. For the Confederacy, it would be a defensive war. Southerners would be fighting to defend their homes and fields against invasion. They had only to beat back northern armies to win their independence, whereas the North would have to invade and conquer the South and hold it against its will. The South would not need to use any of its forces to hold subjugated (defeated) territory. Hence northern superiority in numbers would be offset.

Second, the South had a strong military tradition. White male southerners of all classes knew how to manage horses and had been schooled since youth in the use of firearms. The U.S. Army, before secession, was dominated by southerners, so much so that many promising northern officers had left the service. Most of these southern officers, including some of the best in the nation's history, resigned their commissions and became the bright hope of the Confederacy. The greatest of the southern officers, **General Robert E. Lee**, had been offered command of the Union armies. But when his native state joined the Confederacy, Lee felt honor-bound to fight for Virginia. The loss of Lee and other talented officers was a severe blow to the Lincoln government, which spent most of the war developing generals with equal ability.

A third factor that seemed to give the South an advantage was the place of cotton in the world economy. Cotton could be exchanged in western Europe for the weapons, ammunition, and manufactured goods needed to win the war.

Finally, to the people of many foreign countries, the South appeared to have a superior cause. Ending slavery was not yet a northern war aim. With Maryland, Delaware, Kentucky, and Missouri supporting the Union cause, there were slave states on *both* sides of the conflict. Furthermore, Lincoln stated repeatedly that his only objective was to preserve the Union. It is not surprising then that the war was viewed by many in Europe and elsewhere as a war for freedom on the part of an emerging nation. It seemed very much like the 19th-century wars of independence in Europe waged by the Greeks and Italians. The North was fighting a war to hold the South against its will, very much as England in 1776 had tried to hold the American colonies against their desire to become an independent nation.

SECTION 1 REVIEW

 Identify: Crittenden Compromise, Fort Sumter, P. G. T. Beauregard, Robert E. Lee

Main Ideas
1. Give two reasons why Lincoln did not support the Crittenden Compromise allowing slavery south of the Missouri Compromise line.
2. Name three problems facing Lincoln as he took office.
3. List four advantages the North had at the beginning of the war.
4. List four advantages the South had at the beginning of the war.

2. A SLOW START TO A LONG STRUGGLE, 1861–1862

As the spring and summer of 1861 wore on, the northern belief in a quick end to the war slowly vanished. After the fall of Fort Sumter, the 75,000 volunteers called by Lincoln began arriving in Washington. The aging General Winfield Scott of Mexican War fame, now commander of all the federal forces, advised Lincoln that raw recruits could not invade the South. Months of training would be needed before an effective army could take the field. Slowly an army was formed, but it was far from battle-ready when impatient northern newspapers began to chant "On to Richmond!"

There was similar impatience in the South, where a growing number of leaders were convinced that the North would give up the struggle as soon as it suffered a defeat in battle. The main southern army, under General P. G. T. Beauregard, had taken up position at Manassas Junction, Virginia, a major rail center near Washington, D.C. Union General McDowell, leading 30,000 troops, was given the task of moving against Beauregard.

The resulting battle, fought on July 21 at a stream called Bull Run, became the **First Battle of Bull Run**. (See the upper map, page 386.) It was a northern disaster, with the federal forces falling back on Washington in wild disarray. Fortunately for the North, the victorious Confederate army was in no condition to pursue the routed federal forces. Had the Confederates been able to do so, the war might have ended then and there, with the South winning its independence. Instead, both sides settled back and prepared for a long, grim struggle.

After the Bull Run fiasco, the North adopted a three-part strategy for defeating the Confederacy. First, the North would mount a naval blockade that would halt cotton shipments and prevent supplies from abroad reaching southern ports. Second, the North would gain control of the Mississippi River and open the way for an attack on Georgia and South Carolina from the west. Third, the North would put together a new, well-trained army that could protect Washington, D.C., and undertake a new offensive against Richmond.

The Blockade of the South

Shortly after the fall of Fort Sumter, Lincoln ordered a blockade of the Confederacy. Months passed, however, before the blockade inflicted real hardship on the South. When the war began, the federal navy was not prepared to patrol 3,500 miles of Confederate coastline and stop all vessels coming to and from southern ports. The North did, however, have a certain advantage. What there was of a navy was in Union hands. Furthermore, the Northeast, with its seafaring tradition, was home of the U.S. merchant marine. Under the superb direction of Gideon Welles, the North's energetic Secretary of the Navy, an effective blockading force gradually came into being. Within a year and a half, almost all major Confederate ports had fallen into Union hands, and the blockade was causing shortages in the South. The blockade runners that slipped through the net could bring in only a fraction of the ammunition and supplies needed by the Confederacy.

The First Ironclads Battle on the Sea

There were moments, however, when the Confederacy took hope that the blockade could be smashed. One of these moments came on March 8, 1862, when the *Virginia*, a rebuilt steam frigate formerly named the **Merrimac**, steamed out of Hampton Roads, Virginia, flying the Confederate flag. Covered with 4-inch iron plate and equipped with an iron ram, the *Merrimac* (or *Virginia*) made quick work of several wooden blockading vessels at Hampton Roads. Their shells bounced off the *Merrimac*'s iron sides and fell harmlessly into the sea. If the *Merrimac* could destroy the blockade, supplies could reach Richmond. This was not to be, for on March 9 an equally strange northern ironclad, the **Monitor**, steamed into Hampton Roads. After a four-hour battle, during which neither ship was able to inflict serious damage on the other, the *Merrimac* returned to port. Both sides began to produce other ironclad ships for their rapidly expanding navies.

Union sailors aboard the U.S.S. Mendota, *1864*

The South Hopes for Foreign Intervention

The only other real hope of lifting the blockade rested on the possibility of foreign intervention. Many in the South believed that England and France, deprived of southern cotton, would use their modern navies to smash the wooden ships of the northern blockading fleet.

An incident early in the war almost led to a British intervention. The North stopped a British mail steamer, the *Trent*, on the high seas. The *Trent* was carrying southern diplomatic agents bound for England and France. If the North had refused to yield to the British demand to release the diplomats, war might have resulted. Lincoln wisely released the men, and England did not go beyond reinforcing British forces in Canada.

The South was, however, able to buy a number of commerce raiders in England. These raiders preyed on northern merchant shipping. The most famous of these ships, the *Alabama*, lit up the skies around the world with the burning hulks of northern merchant ships. In all, Confederate raiders destroyed 257 northern merchant ships. This kind of destruction, while highly damaging to the North's merchant marine, did nothing to ease the northern blockade of southern ports.

Grant Leads the War in the West

After the First Battle of Bull Run, the war shifted for a time to the West. Notice on the upper map on page 386 how the Appalachian Mountains separate the Ohio and Mississippi valleys from the coastal plain of Virginia, North and South Carolina, and Georgia. The mountains divided military operations into two quite distinct theaters of war, the "East" and the "West."

Attention in the West centered first on Missouri and Kentucky. In Missouri a struggle developed between the pro-southern governor and Union sympathizers. By March of 1862 the Union forces enjoyed uneasy control. In Kentucky there was strong southern support, but the pro-Union spirit of Henry Clay was also strong. The Confederacy hoped to win Kentucky, which would enable them to block any northern invasion attempt from the west. Northern strategy to win control of the Mississippi River and thereby isolate Texas, Louisiana, and Arkansas from the rest of the South also depended on holding Kentucky and capturing Tennessee.

By the end of 1861, Kentucky was safely in Union hands. But in Tennessee the Confederates still held Fort Henry on the Tennessee River and Fort Donelson on the Cumberland. In early 1862 both forts fell to **General Ulysses S. Grant**.

The next important action in the West came on April 6 and 7, when Grant at first lost and then narrowly won the bloody battle of Shiloh in southwestern Tennessee. More than 24,000 Americans were killed or wounded at Shiloh—13,000 Union troops and 11,000 Confederate troops. In June, a Union army seized Memphis, Tennessee, and continued on down the Mississippi.

These important victories in the West, combined with the capture by Admiral David G. Farragut later in 1862 of New Orleans and Baton Rouge in the south, nearly split the Confederacy. Except for a small stretch between Vicksburg, Mississippi, and Port Hudson, Louisiana, the mighty river was in northern hands. The hero of the war in the West was General U. S. Grant. He won the admiration of the North by his dogged determination. His demand at Fort Donelson for "unconditional surrender" caught the popular imagination and won for him the nickname "Unconditional Surrender" Grant. If he could capture Vicksburg, the war in the West would be all but over.

Stalemate in the East

After the First Battle of Bull Run, Lincoln gave overall command of the Union forces to **General George McClellan**. An able, methodical commander, McClellan began building a first-rate army, transforming northern volunteers into the superb Army of the Potomac.

Excessively cautious, however, McClellan was not ready to do battle in the East until April 1862. His plan was to approach Richmond by way of the peninsula formed by the York and James rivers. (Thus the fighting that followed is called the Peninsular Campaign.) But McClellan's unwillingness to take chances gave the initiative to the southern commanders, General Robert E. Lee and **General Thomas J. "Stonewall" Jackson**.

In a bitter series of battles near Richmond, known as the Seven Days' Battle, McClellan failed to take the Confederate capital. Always overestimating enemy strength, McClellan repeatedly requested reinforcements from the army guarding Washington under the command of Gen-

This photograph of the Battle of Antietam is one of the earliest combat photos ever made.

eral McDowell. Lincoln refused the requests because of the fear aroused by Lee's fast-moving field commander, "Stonewall" Jackson. Jackson's lightning raids around Washington had the capital in a panic. With the failure of the Seven Days' Battle, Lincoln ordered McClellan back to Washington and removed him as commander.

The new commander, General Henry W. Halleck, now placed the army protecting Washington under the command of General John Pope. A greater disaster than McClellan's Peninsular Campaign quickly followed. In August 1862, Pope was forced to make a stand near Manassas, in the same general area as the First Battle of Bull Run. In this engagement, the Second Battle of Bull Run, Pope was completely outclassed and his troops routed with heavy losses.

For want of a better solution, Lincoln turned again to McClellan to rebuild the shattered northern armies. Despair swept the North. Now was the time for Lee to press his advantage.

Bloody Antietam: A Military Draw

Lee's plan was to take the war to the North. If southern arms could win an important battle on northern soil, England and France might be persuaded to extend diplomatic recognition to the Confederacy. A move north might also win Maryland, where pro-southern sentiment was strong.

Lee's forces swept into Maryland, capturing the arsenal at Harpers Ferry on the way. At nearby Antietam [an tē′təm] Creek, on Maryland soil, Lee met McClellan, in command of the Army of the Potomac. There, on September 17, 1862, occurred the bloody **Battle of Antietam**. About 5,000 were killed and 19,000 wounded on that terrible day. The result of the awful slaughter was a military draw. After the battle, Lee withdrew across the Potomac and fell back toward Richmond. McClellan, much to Lincoln's disgust, did not follow in pursuit.

SECTION 2 REVIEW

 Identify: First Battle of Bull Run, *Merrimac* and *Monitor*, Ulysses S. Grant, George McClellan, "Stonewall" Jackson, Battle of Antietam

Main Ideas
1. Describe the North's three-part plan to defeat the South.
2. Why was it important for the South to lift the blockade, and how did they hope to do so?
3. Describe the Union victories in the West. What did these victories accomplish?
4. Give two reasons why Lee was anxious for a victory on northern soil.

385

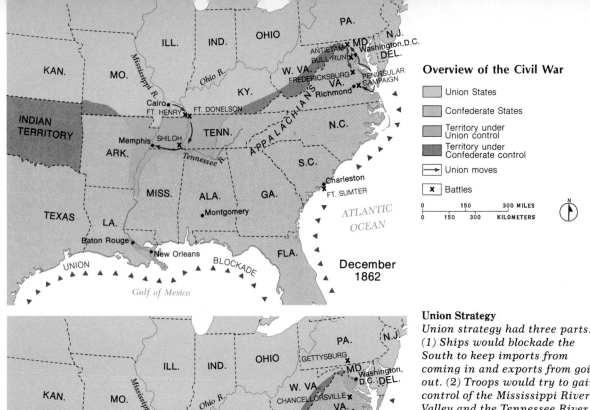

Overview of the Civil War

Union States

Confederate States

Territory under Union control

Territory under Confederate control

Union moves

Battles

| 0 | 150 | 300 MILES |

| 0 | 150 | 300 | KILOMETERS |

December 1862

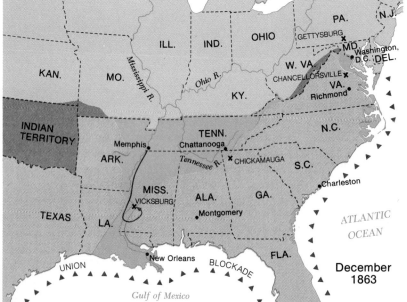

December 1863

March 1865

Union Strategy

Union strategy had three parts: (1) Ships would blockade the South to keep imports from coming in and exports from going out. (2) Troops would try to gain control of the Mississippi River Valley and the Tennessee River Valley, thus splitting the South in two. (3) Union forces would try to capture Richmond, the Confederate capital.

Confederate Strategy

Confederate strategy also had three parts: (1) Troops would defend the South from attack. (2) Confederate ships would try to break the blockade. In addition, England and France might be persuaded to recognize the Confederacy and help break the blockade. (3) Confederate troops would try to gain control of Washington, D.C., Maryland, and central Pennsylvania, thus cutting off the Northeast from the Midwest.

The Location of the War

As the three maps show, most of the fighting took place in the South. Note on the upper map how the Appalachian Mountains separated the two theaters of war: the East, where both capitals were located, and the West. Note also the vast extent of the Union blockade. It stretched more than 3,500 miles and became increasingly effective as the war dragged on, bringing extreme hardship to the South.

General William T. Sherman
President Abraham Lincoln

General Robert E. Lee

General Ulysses S. Grant
General "Stonewall" Jackson

July 1861 to December 1862

The upper map shows the early stages of the war. The Confederates won important victories in the East at Bull Run (July, Aug. 1861), in the Peninsular Campaign (May–July 1862), and at Fredericksburg (Dec. 1862). But "Bloody Antietam" (Sept. 1862) was a draw. As a result, Lincoln announced the Emancipation Proclamation, and the Confederacy failed to win foreign recognition.

Meanwhile, the Union gained control of Missouri and Kentucky and won major battles at Forts Henry and Donelson (Feb. 1862) and Shiloh (Apr. 1862), thus winning the upper Mississippi Valley. Admiral Farragut's capture of New Orleans and Baton Rouge (Apr. and May 1862) opened up the lower Mississippi Valley to the Union forces.

January 1863 to December 1863

The middle map shows the war in 1863. In May the Union forces suffered a crushing defeat at Chancellorsville. With the North demoralized, this was the high noon of the Confederacy. But in July the Union won two major victories: The capture of Vicksburg split the Confederacy in two. The victory at Gettysburg halted the Confederate invasion of the North and dashed Confederate hopes for foreign recognition and aid.

The Confederates won the Battle of Chickamauga (Sept. 1863), but Union forces gained control of Chattanooga (Nov.). Thus, by the end of 1863, Union troops were in position to march through Georgia to the sea.

January 1864 to April 1865

The bottom map shows the final stages of this long, bloody conflict. Sherman's march through Georgia (May–Dec. 1864) left a 60-mile-wide path of destruction through the state. His troops then moved north through the Carolinas (Jan.–Mar. 1865).

Meanwhile, from the Battle of the Wilderness (May 1864) to the end of the war, Union forces under Grant hammered at the Confederates in the attempt to take Richmond. Tens of thousands of young men died. With Lee's forces finally diminished to less than 30,000 troops, the surrender came in April 1865 at Appomattox Court House.

3. THE WAR LEADS TO THE END OF SLAVERY

It is often said that slavery was the chief cause of the Civil War and that the abolition of slavery was the main result. Is this correct? Broadly speaking, yes. But to people living in the 1860s the situation was much more complicated. They recognized, of course, that slavery was at the heart of North-South differences. But when Lincoln called for 75,000 volunteers to put down the rebellion, it was to save the Union, not to free the slaves. Time and again he told the South that its domestic institutions were safe in his hands. If abolition was not a northern war aim, why was slavery abolished?

Lincoln Considers Slavery Legal

Abraham Lincoln's views on slavery were well known by the time he was elected President of the United States. Lincoln disliked slavery. He thought it was wrong. But he was not an abolitionist. Time and again he expressed the hope that the slave states would some day end slavery voluntarily and that all men and women would be free. Yet he saw many obstacles in the path to such freedom.

As a lawyer, Lincoln understood very well the legal basis given slavery by the U.S. Constitution. The Constitution made it clear that the federal government did not have the power to interfere with the "domestic" institutions of the states. Slavery was a domestic institution—states were free to adopt it or to reject it.

In all the prewar arguments over slavery, no political leader of stature made the abolition of slavery a party measure. Only the abolitionists did that, and the steps they demanded to end slavery were considered unconstitutional by most Americans. The South considered the Republican party a threat in 1860 not because it called for an immediate end to slavery, but because it opposed expansion of slavery in the territories. This was the issue. It was Lincoln's refusal to back away from the Republican position on the expansion of slavery that caused the 11th-hour efforts at compromise to fail in 1861. Repeatedly, Lincoln assured the South that his purpose was to preserve the Union, not to abolish slavery.

Even had Lincoln thought it legal to abolish slavery, there were highly important practical reasons why he could not make abolition a war aim. The border states of Kentucky, Missouri, Maryland, and Delaware were vital to the Union cause. All were slave states, and all remained loyal to the Union. Thus there were slave states fighting on *both* sides in the war. Had Lincoln called for an end to slavery, these border states probably would have left the Union, thereby greatly strengthening the Confederacy.

Lincoln personally believed the best solution to the slavery problem was gradual emancipation undertaken by the states. He favored colonization of freed slaves in Africa or Central America. Lincoln also believed that the federal government should pay slaveholders for the loss of their property. He urged such a solution on the border states early in the war, but they rejected it.

The War Changes Lincoln's Attitude

As the war progressed, Lincoln's views changed with changing conditions. The strongest supporters of the war in Congress were the **Radical Republicans**, who believed that slavery should be abolished and that the South should be treated harshly. The Radicals were close to the abolitionists in their views on slavery. Early in the war they began to urge the President to abolish slavery. By the summer of 1862, the war was not going well for the North. McClellan had withdrawn after the Seven Days' Battle, and Pope had been routed at the Second Battle of Bull Run. England and France seemed about to extend diplomatic recognition to the Confederacy. There was a growing danger that these nations might intervene in the war in support of the South. At the same time, antislavery sentiment in these countries was strong. A statement from Lincoln that he planned to abolish slavery as a war measure might forestall foreign recognition of the Confederacy. It would also please the Radicals, who were becoming more and more critical of the conduct of the war.

Still another argument for emancipation was supplied by the blacks themselves. As Union armies invaded the South, thousands of blacks fled to safety behind Union lines. Many attempted to join in the fighting on the Union side but were turned away. Mobilizing the former slaves could strengthen the Union militarily.

LIFE IN AMERICA

HARRIET TUBMAN: CONDUCTOR ON THE UNDERGROUND RAILROAD

Her name was Harriet Tubman, but she was called "Moses." The biblical Moses led his people out of bondage in Egypt to freedom in the Promised Land. During the 1850s, Harriet Tubman made 19 journeys into the border states where she led small groups of slaves to freedom. She is believed to have aided as many as 300 fugitives and never lost a "passenger" on this Underground Railroad. Among those she brought to freedom were a sister with two children, a brother, and her elderly parents.

Heroism and a Brush with Death at 13

Tubman was born around 1821 on Maryland's Eastern Shore. As a child, she worked as a domestic servant and a field hand. Later she also helped her father, who was hired out as a woodcutter.

When she was about 13 years old, she was working in the fields when an overseer came by, chasing a slave. Tubman would later say that she gave no thought to what she did next: she placed herself between the overseer and the slave. The overseer beat her on the head with a club, fracturing her

skull. She lay near death for three months while her owner tried, unsuccessfully, to sell her. For the rest of her life she would suffer periodic blackouts. But her injury never stopped her determination.

In 1849, Tubman heard rumors that she and other slaves would be sold out of state. She decided to make her break for freedom. Her husband, a free black, decided to remain in Maryland, but she went to the home of friendly whites, where she was hidden in a wagon and covered with vegetables headed for market in Pennsylvania.

She reached Philadelphia and found employment in a hotel, but she chose to risk her freedom again and again on her trips into the slave states. Ingenious in her methods, she always managed to evade her pursuers.

Spy and Nurse in the Civil War

Harriet Tubman soon became famous among abolitionists, and occasionally spoke at their meetings. Around 1858, she moved to a farm near Auburn, New York, which

was sold to her by Senator William H. Seward. When the war broke out, she served as a spy in South Carolina, visiting slaves to gain military intelligence and encouraging them to join the Union forces. During the war she also worked as a nurse and continued this work briefly at a freedmen's hospital after the war.

Returning to her New York farm, she gave shelter to orphans and elderly people. This was the beginning of the Harriet Tubman Home for Indigent Aged Negroes.

Although she had friends in high places, such as Seward (now Secretary of State), she fought unsuccessfully for many years to receive compensation for her wartime service. As one biographer observed, "Red tape proved too strong even for [Seward], and her case was rejected, because it did not come under any recognized law." Finally, in 1896 Congress enacted a special law which gave her a small monthly pension. She continued to run her home for the aged and died in 1913 when she was in her 90s.

Harriet Tubman (left) with some slaves that she helped to free. Late 1800s

Looking at all of these factors, Lincoln decided to act. He told his cabinet in the summer of 1862 that he was thinking of issuing a proclamation freeing the slaves in the states that were in rebellion. They persuaded him to wait for a Union victory before making the announcement.

Lincoln waited until the Battle of Antietam. In that battle a Union army turned back a Confederate invasion of the North. Lincoln considered it enough of a victory; he issued a preliminary proclamation which set January 1, 1863, as the date for the **Emancipation Proclamation** to take effect.

The Importance of the Emancipation Proclamation

Lincoln, of course, had no way of enforcing the Emancipation Proclamation. It applied only to the states in rebellion, and he had no control over them. It did not apply to the loyal states or to southern areas occupied by Union armies. Even though the Emancipation Proclamation freed no slaves, it was a document of very great significance, ranking in importance with the Declaration of Independence and the Constitution.

The Emancipation Proclamation set a course toward freedom that would not be reversed. In 1860, 13% of all Americans were enslaved. In the Confederate states, 37% of the total population were slaves. Slavery was as old as America itself. It had begun to develop only a few years after the founding of Jamestown. But now, after 250 years in bondage, black Americans would be free people. The Emancipation Proclamation was the first in a series of steps leading to the 13th Amendment, adopted in 1865, that ended slavery throughout the United States. The claim that America was the "land of the free" would no longer have a hollow ring.

Blacks Fight for Their Freedom

As soon as they were permitted to do so, many blacks enlisted in the Union army. By the end of the war, over 180,000 had enlisted, more than half of them from the Confederate states. Of those who served, 40,000 lost their lives.

In their efforts to save the Union and obtain freedom, black soldiers faced many difficulties not faced by white soldiers. Usually black recruits were formed into all-black units that were called **"United States Colored Troops."** Most of these units were commanded by white officers. For the most part, white Union soldiers did not want to treat blacks as equals. Until near the end of the war, black units were used mainly for guard duty, in building fortifications, and for everyday chores around the camps. Usually black troops were paid less, and less attention was paid to their well-being. Before the war was over, however, black troops were making organized raiding parties be-

Gun crew, 2nd U.S. Colored Light Artillery, 1864

hind Confederate lines. They were excellent spies and scouts and saw action in every theater of war.

Confederate leaders complained that, by enlisting blacks in the army, the North was promoting a slave insurrection, urging slaves to rise and murder their masters. When black soldiers were captured, they were frequently treated as rebellious slaves rather than as prisoners of war. They were sometimes sold into slavery or shot. For example, when Fort Pillow, Tennessee, fell to the Confederate forces in 1864, Confederate General Nathan Forrest would not allow blacks to surrender. Instead, they were shot or burned to death.

In the wartime South, Confederate officials faced new problems in controlling the slaves. Many slaves remained loyal to their masters, but slave loyalty could not be taken for granted. The problem of runaways became acute as the war continued. Wherever Union forces appeared in the South, many slaves simply walked away from the plantations. The Union army provided them with food and clothing. To avoid large-scale desertion, Confederate officials began to move the slave population away from war zones.

Throughout the war, the Confederacy was heavily dependent on slave labor. Slaves produced much of the labor on farms and in factories, including the great ironworks in Richmond. Slaves also worked in the iron and salt mines and did much of the hard labor required by the army in building fortifications and roads.

Until the end, the South refused to use blacks as soldiers. Finally the Confederate government changed its mind, and blacks were recruited and promised freedom after the war. But by this time, the Confederacy was all but defeated.

SECTION 3 REVIEW

Identify: Radical Republicans, Emancipation Proclamation, United States Colored Troops

Main Ideas

1. Why was Lincoln cautious about ending slavery in the early years of the war?
2. Give three reasons why Lincoln decided to issue the Emancipation Proclamation. What were its short-term and long-term effects?
3. What kinds of prejudice did black troops face? Why was it especially dangerous for them to be captured?

4. FOUR YEARS OF FIGHTING BRING A NORTHERN VICTORY

The bloody battle of Antietam in September 1862 ended in a draw. After the battle, McClellan's exhausted troops allowed Lee to cross the Potomac to the safety of the Shenandoah Valley. In Washington, Lincoln was disgusted that McClellan had not gone in pursuit. Why was it, Lincoln wanted to know, that able though he was, McClellan always lacked the extra drive needed to win a clear-cut victory? One such victory would have opened the road to Richmond and ended the war. Clearly, McClellan must go. So, for the second time, Lincoln replaced him. But as before, Lincoln chose as a replacement a general less able than McClellan. His choice this time was General Ambrose Burnside.

Fredericksburg and Chancellorsville Demoralize the North

The new commander of the Army of the Potomac was no match for General Lee, who had entrenched his army on high ground above the town of Fredericksburg, Virginia, halfway between Washington and Richmond. On December 13, 1862, General Burnside, aware that his orders were to attack, tried a disastrous frontal assault. The result was a crushing defeat and the loss of 12,000 men. Thereafter, the two armies dug in for a dreary winter. When spring came, Burnside had been replaced by "Fighting" Joe Hooker. Lincoln was still searching for a winning general.

Hooker's plan was to outflank Lee and force him either to retreat or be caught in a trap. But once again a Union general was outfoxed by Lee and his dashing field commander, "Stonewall" Jackson. At the Battle of Chancellorsville in May 1863, Lee boldly divided his smaller army, sending Jackson to attack Hooker's exposed flank. Jackson's swift maneuver caught Hooker by surprise. Lee now moved in for the kill. Together, Lee and Jackson defeated an army of 130,000 men with a force half that size.

Hooker managed to save his army, but losses were heavy. The victory was also costly for Lee. Among the casualties was "Stonewall" Jackson, shot in the darkness by one of his own men, who

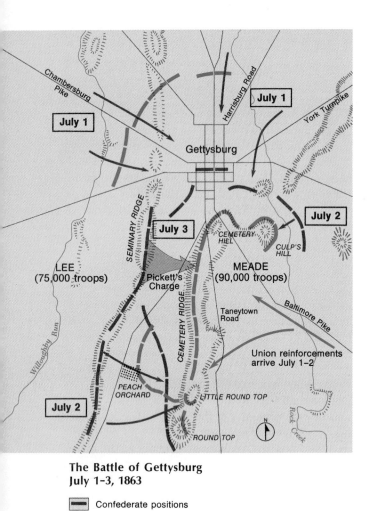

**The Battle of Gettysburg
July 1–3, 1863**

▬	Confederate positions
→	Confederate movements
▬	Union positions
→	Union movements

0 _____ 1 MILE
0 _____ 1 KILOMETER

The Battle of Gettysburg

The Battle of Gettysburg ended the Confederate attempt to invade the North. It also ended Confederate hopes for support from European nations which were considering recognition of the independence of the South. The battle at Gettysburg lasted three days (July 1–3, 1863) and cost more than 51,000 lives.

July 1
Confederate troops led by General Lee met Union forces north and west of the town of Gettysburg. Union troops were driven back through Gettysburg and took positions south of the town on Cemetery Ridge, Cemetery Hill, and Culp's Hill. The Confederates set up facing positions. Union reinforcements under General Meade arrived during the night of July 1, and the Union defense was arranged in a "fishhook" pattern on the high ground.

July 2
The Confederates attacked at Cemetery Ridge and Culp's Hill. They broke through a Union line at the Peach Orchard and advanced to Little Round Top, but Union forces held that hill. Union troops also held the line on Cemetery Ridge and Culp's Hill. At the end of the day, all Union main positions had held.

July 3
The Confederates, led by Major General Pickett, made a direct attack on Cemetery Ridge. The forces in this attack included 15,000 Confederate troops; the moving front was a mile long. Union forces, well-entrenched on Cemetery Ridge, drove back the Confederates after heavy fighting, with great loss of life on both sides. The next day, July 4, the Confederate army under General Lee began a retreat to the South.

mistook him for the enemy. The combination of Lee and Jackson had been unbeatable. The loss would be severely felt.

The victories at Fredericksburg and Chancellorsville were the highwater mark of the Confederacy. The North was thoroughly demoralized. Lee saw in the situation an opportunity to carry the war again to the North. If he could strike a telling blow on northern soil, the shaken government in Washington would be forced to make peace. To carry out his bold plan, Lee asked that he be given every possible Confederate soldier. But Jefferson Davis, mindful that the war in the West was reaching a critical stage at Vicksburg,

would allow Lee only what he already had. Not wishing to let the opportunity pass, Lee pushed ahead without reinforcements and without his indispensable "right arm," "Stonewall" Jackson.

Gettysburg Turns the Tide
Northward along the now familiar route of the Shenandoah Valley went Lee in command of the Army of Northern Virginia. His objective was Harrisburg, Pennsylvania, with the key railroad bridge over the Susquehanna River—the vital transportation link between the Northeast and the Northwest. Following a roughly parallel route, keeping always between Lee and the capi-

tal at Washington, went Hooker, in command of the Army of the Potomac. Here and there along the northward march the two armies made contact. One of these encounters, at Brandy Station, Virginia, resulted in the largest cavalry battle in American history. Before the main armies met, however, Hooker had been replaced by General George Meade.

Lee advanced toward Harrisburg so rapidly that his communications were disrupted, and he did not know where Meade's Union army was. Meade was equally in the dark as to Lee's whereabouts. With each force looking for the other, it was by chance that advance units of the two armies met near the small market town of Gettysburg in southern Pennsylvania. (See middle map, page 386.) Unit by unit and corps by corps the forces of Lee and Meade arrived and took up positions on the rolling hills around Gettysburg. It was the first of July, and the fields were yellow with ripening grain. The beauty of the land was in marked contrast to the grim tragedy about to unfold.

The Union forces quickly claimed the high ground south of Gettysburg, digging in along the slope of Cemetery Ridge. (See map opposite.) To the west, separated from Cemetery Ridge by a broad valley, lay Seminary Ridge. Here Lee's troops took positions. The greatest battle ever fought in the Western Hemisphere was about to begin.

The **Battle of Gettysburg** lasted three days. The first day belonged to the Confederates, the bulk of Meade's army having not yet arrived. The second day's fighting left neither side with any important gains. The third day saw the failure of a Confederate attempt to break around Meade's entrenched positions.

With his efforts at encirclement repulsed, would Lee try a direct assault across the valley and up the slope of Cemetery Ridge? The answer came at one o'clock when the Confederate forces began the heaviest artillery barrage of the war. This effort to weaken the Union position had little effect. Through the smoke, Meade's men could see the Confederate forces massing for a frontal assault. Across the fields they came, wave upon wave. Mowed down by deadly Union fire, they closed ranks and kept on coming. Pickett's Charge, as the valiant suicidal assault is known, failed, and the Union forces carried the day. A badly battered Lee, having lost a third of his force,

FROM THE ARCHIVES

The Gettysburg Address

On November 19, 1863, Lincoln gave this brief and moving speech at the dedication of the national cemetery at Gettysburg.

Four score and seven years ago our fathers brought forth on this continent, a new nation, conceived in Liberty, and dedicated to the proposition that all men are created equal.

Now we are engaged in a great civil war, testing whether that nation or any nation so conceived and so dedicated, can long endure. We are met on a great battle-field of that war. We have come to dedicate a portion of that field, as a final resting place for those who here gave their lives that that nation might live. It is altogether fitting and proper that we should do this.

But, in a larger sense, we can not dedicate—we can not consecrate—we can not hallow—this ground. The brave men, living and dead, who struggled here, have consecrated it, far above our poor power to add or detract. The world will little note, nor long remember what we say here, but it can never forget what they did here. It is for us the living, rather, to be dedicated here to the unfinished work which they who fought here have thus far so nobly advanced. It is rather for us to be here dedicated to the great task remaining before us—that from these honored dead we take increased devotion to that cause for which they gave the last full measure of devotion—that we here highly resolve that these dead shall not have died in vain—that this nation, under God, shall have a new birth of freedom—and that government of the people, by the people, for the people, shall not perish from the earth.

crossed the Potomac and once more fell back to northern Virginia. The Union had won a decisive victory. Never again would the Confederacy be able to mount a major offensive against northern armies. To win the war, it would have to exhaust the Union's will to fight.

Grant Captures Vicksburg

Far away to the west, on the same July 3rd, another critical battle was fought. The struggle for the Mississippi River, open to Union forces except for a stretch between Vicksburg and Port

Hudson, had continued through the winter of 1862–1863. Confederate control of the river bluffs near Vicksburg let herds of cattle and supplies from Arkansas, Louisiana, and Texas reach the Confederate forces in the East. The fall of Vicksburg would be a serious blow to the South.

The attacking Union forces had great obstacles to overcome. Chief of these was strongly fortified Vicksburg itself, with its wealth of natural protection on all sides. The city could be taken only by siege. The **siege of Vicksburg** began on May 22, 1863, and ended with Grant victorious, on the same day that Meade won at Gettysburg. Shortly thereafter, Port Hudson in Louisiana fell to a Union army. When informed of the great victory in the West, Lincoln penned his famous line, "The Father of Waters again goes unvexed to the sea."

The Battles for Chattanooga

After the fall of Vicksburg, the Union goal in the West was the capture of Chattanooga, on the Tennessee River near the Georgia border. (See middle map, page 386.) This would open the way for an invasion of Georgia and the lower South. In September 1863, Union General William Rosecrans battled Confederate General Braxton Bragg for control of Chattanooga. Bragg won at Chickamauga Creek, but Rosecrans, with the timely aid of troops under General George H. Thomas, saved his army to fight another day.

In October, Grant arrived on the scene, having just been made supreme commander in the West by Lincoln. Reinforced with fresh troops, Grant and his able subordinate generals, Thomas, Hooker, and Sherman, won two difficult battles— Lookout Mountain and Missionary Ridge (November 23–25). These stunning victories won Chattanooga and cleared the way for Sherman's advance into Georgia the following spring.

The grand Union strategy was working at last. The blockade and Emancipation Proclamation had just about ended the southern hope of significant material aid from Europe. The Mississippi River was in Union hands, with a federal army poised for a march into Georgia. The Confederate capital at Richmond was defended by an army that had suffered a serious reverse at Gettysburg. Lincoln now sought to hasten the end by bringing Grant, the hero of so many western battles, to the East and placing him in overall command.

Sherman's Destructive March Through Georgia and the Carolinas

Left in the West with 100,000 troops to begin the invasion of Georgia was **General William Sherman**. The main Confederate army in Georgia, under the command of General Joseph E. Johnston, retreated before the advance of Sherman's far superior numbers. Johnston's troops tried to delay the enemy advance by blowing up roads and bridges, but in early September of 1864 Sherman was in Atlanta. From there he set out in November on a 300-mile **march to the sea** through Georgia to Savannah near the coast. In an effort to crush the South's will to resist, Sherman's troops laid waste to a 60-mile corridor as they went. From Savannah Sherman turned northward and began an even more destructive march through the Carolinas.

Sherman believed in practicing "total" war—

anything that might help the enemy resist should be seized or destroyed. In his march through Georgia and the Carolinas, his troops were cut off from their supply base. They were totally dependent on the countryside for provisions. But much of what was taken was simply destroyed. "War is cruel," said General Sherman, "and you cannot refine it."

The Last Battles: The Wilderness to Appomattox

Meanwhile Grant, now commander-in-chief of the Union armies, turned his attention to the Virginia campaign. He set out at once in pursuit of Lee, the man who had denied every Union general sent against him the honor of a clear-cut victory over the Army of Northern Virginia.

In May of 1864, Grant marched his men into the Wilderness north of Richmond, where earlier Union armies had tasted defeat. This time the Union forces were led by a general who would call, if need be, upon the numerical superiority of the northern forces and fight on to victory no matter what the cost. Even Grant may not have imagined how ghastly the price would be. Thus began the most desperately fought campaign of the entire war. The grim news from the front shocked even a northern public grown accustomed to the tragedy of lengthening casualty lists.

Lee, brilliant and under most conditions unbeatable, was gradually worn down by the superiority of numbers. This was Grant's winning card, and he proceeded to play it to a triumphant and bloody end. Through the long months of 1864 and into the spring of 1865 reports from the front told the grim story. In the Battle of the Wilderness, fought in early May 1864, Grant lost 18,000 men. In the five-day Battle of Spotsylvania, Grant lost 12,000 more. In the Battle of Cold Harbor, the costliest assault of the war, 9,000 men were killed in a few hours. Grant's soldiers went into battle with their names and addresses written on pieces of paper pinned to their backs so that the dead could be identified. In a month's time, Grant lost 60,000 men (equal to Lee's entire army), and he was no nearer to Richmond than McClellan had been two years before!

Next Grant tried a flanking movement in an effort to take Richmond by way of Petersburg. Again, Lee blocked the way. Eight thousand more men died as Grant settled down for a nine-month siege of Petersburg. But now Lee's lines were growing ever thinner. Sherman had broken through to take Atlanta, was marching through the Carolinas, and would soon be closing in on Virginia. General Philip Sheridan with another Union army had devastated the Shenandoah Valley and was closing in on Richmond from the north.

At last Lee pulled his forces from the trenches defending Petersburg and slipped away toward the west in the direction of Lynchburg, hoping to join forces with General Johnston. Grant entered Richmond and went in pursuit of Lee. Finding his way blocked to the west, his exhausted army without rations, Lee sent out a horseman bearing

Pennsylvania artillery in the siege of Petersburg, June 1864

a white flag. There remained only a moving sur-render scene at **Appomattox Court House** where the two commanders met and arranged terms. The war was all but over. The Army of Northern Virginia passed into history, leaving behind a tradition of undying valor that has become the heritage of a reunited nation of North and South.

DEATHS IN AMERICA'S MAJOR WARS

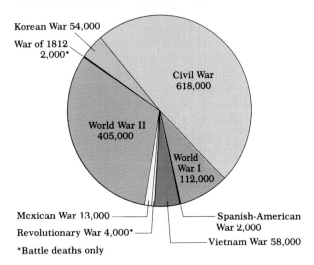

Korean War 54,000

War of 1812 2,000*

Civil War 618,000

World War II 405,000

World War I 112,000

Mexican War 13,000

Revolutionary War 4,000*

Spanish-American War 2,000

Vietnam War 58,000

*Battle deaths only

Because of inadequate field hospital facilities the survival rate for Civil War wounded—North and South alike—was shockingly low. There were far too few doctors, surgeons, and nurses in either army to cope humanely with the large number of wounded. The suffering of dying men, for whom no pain-killing drugs were available, was a common sight after every major Civil War battle.

SECTION 4 REVIEW

Identify: Battle of Gettysburg, siege of Vicksburg, Sherman's march to the sea, Appomattox Court House

Main Ideas

1. Why did Lee feel that the South had a good chance of winning the war after its victories at Fredericksburg and Chancellorsville? What was his plan for winning the war?

2. What was the importance of the Battle of Gettysburg, the capture of Vicksburg, and the battles of Lookout Mountain and Missionary Ridge?

3. What was the purpose of Sherman's march through Georgia and the Carolinas?

4. What was Grant's biggest advantage in the Northern Virginia Campaign of 1864–1865?

5. BEHIND THE LINES, NORTH AND SOUTH

In all wars, attention centers on military campaigns. Armies in the field must win battles or the cause for which they are fighting will ultimately be lost. But to achieve victory in modern warfare, a nation must have many things in addition to an effective fighting force. Much will depend, particularly in a long war, on the ability to mobilize human, industrial, financial, and agricultural resources.

The Civil War is called the first "modern" war because it was the first conflict in which industrialization was a key factor. Railroads, the telegraph, and steamships all played an important part. On the home front, factories turning out weapons and war materials were as important to victory as winning on the field. The Civil War involved the total economy—North and South—as no previous war had done.

As we have seen, the North had many advantages over the South in size, population, and resources. But these alone did not add up to certain victory. Shortly after the conflict began, both governments began to face up to the enormous problems of fighting a full-scale war.

The Southern War Effort

In raising and equipping an army to beat back the expected northern invasion, the South faced tremendous difficulties. At first, volunteers for the army were plentiful. President Davis' call in April 1861 for 100,000 volunteers to serve for 12 months was quickly oversubscribed. The problem was how to equip and supply this army. A year later, with a long war in prospect, the Confederacy had to resort to a draft. The draft law made all men between 18 and 35 liable for military service for three years. It allowed many exemptions, mainly favoring the rich. This led to much grumbling that it was "a rich man's war and a poor man's fight." In all, about 1 million men wore the gray uniform of the Confederacy, about half the number that served the Union.

Far more serious for the South than the disadvantage of smaller numbers was its smaller industrial base. Southern troops often lacked blankets, shoes, uniforms, food, and supplies. Trailing the North by more than 5 to 1 in manufacturing capacity, there was no way the South could make up the difference. The hope of exchanging cotton for needed products abroad did not materialize. Shortages of manufactured goods developed early in the war and soon became critical. In addition, lack of adequate railroads hindered the distribution of food supplies. People in a war zone might be near starvation while barns less than 100 miles away were bulging with grain.

The strong southern belief in states' rights also hurt the Confederacy. The Richmond government often had difficulty enforcing its laws. The problems it faced were quite similar to those faced by the American colonists under the Articles of Confederation. Some of the Confederate states, for example, refused to enforce the draft. There were widespread objections to other wartime measures curtailing the people's liberties. When Jefferson Davis suspended *habeas corpus* and ordered persons under suspicion held in jail without trial, there was a loud outcry. On more than one occasion, South Carolina threatened to secede from the Confederacy just as it had from the Union.

With so much of its wealth in land and slaves, the South had trouble financing the war. The hope of collecting custom duties at southern ports was soon dashed with the increasing effectiveness of the northern blockade. Another serious problem was the absence of good banking facilities. The people of the South gave generously to the Confederate cause, but their cash reserves were soon exhausted. Efforts to obtain loans in Europe were not successful. After a time, the only answer was to print paper money to pay bills. Before the end of the war, the Confederacy had issued more than $1.5 billion in paper money. The result was runaway inflation and financial ruin. By 1865, the Confederate dollar was worth less than one cent in gold.

The Northern War Effort

When Lincoln called for 75,000 volunteers to serve for 90 days, young men of the North responded enthusiastically. After the Union disaster at the First Battle of Bull Run, Congress issued a new call for 500,000 volunteers to serve for three years. By 1863 it was clear that the volunteer system by itself was not enough. Congress now passed a conscription act instituting a draft, as the South had done a year earlier. The 1863 draft law made all men between 20 and 45 liable for service, although blacks were not enrolled until 1864. In all, some 2 million men served in the Union forces, most of them volunteers.

The results of the draft were disappointing. The law provided that a drafted man could supply a substitute, or he could pay $300 and be exempted entirely. The draft supplied an insufficient number of recruits, but it did give a boost to the volunteer system. Young men about to turn 20 preferred to volunteer and avoid the stigma of conscription. Volunteers could collect special state and local bounties and could choose the regiment they wanted to join. A volunteer could collect as much as $1,000 in bounty money. This led to the dishonest practice of "**bounty jumping**." The same individual would enlist, collect his bounty, and then desert, only to re-enlist somewhere else, collect a second bounty, and so on. There were cases of bounty jumpers repeating the process as many as 25 times.

The draft was extremely unpopular and led to serious riots, particularly in northern cities where the war was unpopular among Irish immigrants. Already at the bottom of the wage scale, the Irish feared competition from blacks, a fear that increased with the Emancipation Proclamation. In New York City, blacks were hired to replace striking workers, touching off ugly race and antidraft riots. The situation became so bad in New York City that the army was brought in to restore order. The rioting ended only when the soldiers swept the streets with artillery fire. The riots in the North came in the summer of 1863. Had Lee won at Gettysburg, his victory in combination with the antidraft sentiment might have doomed the Union cause.

When it came to supplying the men at the front, the North had every advantage over the South. The war proved to be a great stimulus to business and industry, and much expansion took place. Many new companies were formed to compete for profitable government contracts. But there was also much graft and corruption and many examples of companies delivering shoddy merchandise to the armed services, or even smuggling goods into the South.

With no shortages to speak of, with industry and manufacturing already well established, the

Confederate spy Rose O'Neal Greenhow and her daughter

Southern women turned out war goods despite the blockade.

North experienced boom times. Wages were high, profits large, and the market for the produce of farm and factory constantly on the rise. Unlike the men in gray, the men in blue were almost always well fed and well clothed.

Financing the Northern War Effort

The methods used by the North to finance the war were much more effective than those used by the South. The huge cost of the Union war effort could not possibly be met by taxes, although taxes were increased and new ones added. For the first time in American history, an income tax was collected. Individuals earning from $600 to $5,000 paid 5% of their income. Those earning over $5,000 paid 10%.

By far the largest part of the war costs was met by bond sales to the public. This form of borrowing was popular. People saw it as a good investment and a way of showing their patriotism.

Another measure that helped war financing was the National Banking Act, passed by Congress in 1863. The act gave the United States its first national banking system since the death of the Second Bank in the 1830s. Through member banks, the new system provided a means of sell-ing government bonds. The system also added to the nation's money supply, as member banks were permitted to issue national bank notes based on their assets.

Finally, the government printed paper money called **greenbacks**. The government issued some $400,000 in greenbacks. Without a gold reserve backing them, the greenbacks quickly dropped in value. At one time they were worth only 39 cents on the dollar. By the end of the war, however, when the Confederate dollar was worth almost nothing, the federal greenbacks had risen in value to 60 cents.

Women in the War

Women in both the North and the South served as replacements for men on farms, in factories, and as nurses in military hospitals. Like the women of the Revolution, women in the Civil War were deeply involved in the war effort.

In the South, women of the planter class be-came plantation managers and overseers. Running a plantation under wartime conditions was far more taxing than in peacetime. Yet many southern women kept the fields producing in the face of many obstacles—deserting slaves, occupy-

The U.S. Sanitary Commision aided wounded troops.

ing armies, and broken-down machinery. Many women worked the fields, sometimes by hand, as horses and mules were taken by the army.

Frontier women in the Middle West had the added burden of fending off Indian attacks once protective garrisons were called to serve in the East and border states. Accustomed to rough conditions and grinding labor, some frontier women took on the additional responsibilities of homesteading. They took advantage of the new **Homestead Act** passed during the war. Under the terms of this 1862 law, an individual could obtain a farm free by working it and building a home there.

The work of women nurses at military hospitals was vital to the armies of both sides. Traditionally, the army used only male nurses in field hospitals. This barrier soon disappeared with the mounting casualty lists. Under the leadership of women such as **Clara Barton**, **Elizabeth Blackwell**, Dorothea Dix, and Mary Ann Bickerdyke, women nurses quickly proved their worth. Dr. Blackwell, the nation's first woman medical school graduate, organized a training program for Union army nurses.

Women also played a leading part in organizations such as the United States Sanitary Commis-

sion and the American Freedman's Aid Commission. The United States Sanitary Commission supervised a number of volunteer groups that provided medical supplies, nurses, and food to the armed forces in the North. Under the auspices of the American Freedman's Aid Commission, hundreds of northern women went south as schoolteachers to help blacks uprooted by the war.

SECTION 5 REVIEW

Identify: bounty jumping, greenbacks, Homestead Act, Clara Barton, Elizabeth Blackwell

Main Ideas

1. What was the biggest disadvantage the South faced in its war efforts?
2. Describe two difficulties the South faced in financing the war.
3. In what ways did northerners react to the draft?
4. Why did the North experience boom times during the war? What methods did it use to finance the war?
5. How did women participate in the war effort?

399

6. WARTIME POLITICS, POLITICIANS, AND PROGRAMS

The American Civil War tested democracy's ability to survive in an emergency. The Union and Confederate governments, fighting for their existence, were constantly tempted to overextend their constitutional powers. Under the plea of "wartime emergency," they exercised powers that in peacetime would not have been tolerated long by the public. Men anxious to remain in office used emergency powers in an effort to silence critics. In the name of patriotism and national defense, officials North and South overstepped the powers of their offices.

Congressional leaders, too, saw in the special wartime conditions opportunities to push for laws favorable to their interests. The result, particularly in the North, was a flurry of new legislation, much of it favorable to special interests.

Wartime Leaders: Davis and Lincoln

Both the Union and the Confederacy had reasonably able leadership at the top. Jefferson Davis came to the presidency of the Confederacy from years of public service. A somewhat cold and stiff man, Davis was able, hard-working, and thoroughly dedicated to the Confederate cause. Although skilled as an administrator, he was not at his best in the day-to-day rough-and-tumble of the political world. He frequently quarreled with subordinates and with the Confederate Congress. He fancied himself a military strategist and would have preferred a military command. He kept the general overall direction of the war in his own hands when it would better have been left to his able generals. Preoccupied with military affairs, he did not have enough time to devote to other pressing concerns.

Lincoln came to the presidency with little experience in elective office, but with leadership qualities of the highest order. These qualities were largely unknown and untested at the time of his election. Once on the job, he quickly showed that he was a superb leader with clear purpose, steadfast resolve, and infinite patience. As commander-in-chief, he proved more effective than Davis. Lincoln proved to be an ideal man for a crisis, seeming to grow in stature when difficulties increased. That the nation survived was largely due to his leadership. He was bold, flexible, and not given to panic. He had the wisdom to select strong men for cabinet positions and as commanders in the field, but he always remained their master.

Both Presidents were much criticized at the time and later for dictatorial acts. Lincoln made far-reaching decisions without consulting Congress and even spent money before it was appropriated. More seriously, he ignored constitutional rights of citizens, suspending *habeas corpus*, and ordering civilians suspected of disloyalty held without trial. President Davis acted in much the same way, claiming as Lincoln did that the war emergency justified his actions.

Politics During the War

The Confederate constitution provided for a six-year presidential term. Since the Confederacy did not last six years, the only presidential election came at the beginning when Jefferson Davis was chosen without opposition. There were, however, three congressional elections during the life of the Confederacy, and in these contests the campaigns were spirited.

Much of the attention centered on President Davis' policies and on the many changes he made in his cabinet. There was constant dissension over the rights of the states and the wisdom of government policy. At no time was there real harmony and effective cooperation between the

Confederate battle flag, the "Stars and Bars;" Jefferson Davis

Confederate Congress and President Davis. Dissension at the top had a paralyzing effect on government action and seriously weakened the Confederate war effort.

Meanwhile, in the North, Lincoln's troubles seemed at times greater than those of Davis. Particularly in the beginning months of the war, when the North was unable to win on the battlefield, criticism of Lincoln reached alarming proportions. Many in the President's own party found him too conservative for their tastes. They wanted him to pursue the war with vigor and blamed him for a lack of determination when defeat after defeat befell the northern armies. Early in the war the Radical wing of the Republican party set up a Joint Committee on the Conduct of the War. The Committee was frequently outspoken in criticizing war strategy and gave Lincoln little peace.

The Republican Program Is Implemented

The Republican party saw in the election of 1860 a national mandate to pass laws proposed in the party platform. Among the measures that now became law were proposals advanced for years by Whigs and northern Democrats. The departure of southerners from Congress opened the way for the following important laws:

(1) The Morrill Tariff of 1861 raised import duties to 47%, giving protection and encouragement to growing northern industries.

(2) The National Banking Act of 1863 gave northern business and financial interests a centralized banking system which they could dominate and which could provide the financial resources needed for business and industrial expansion.

(3) The Homestead Act of 1862 was a great spur to immigration and to the continuing westward movement, now almost exclusively a northern interest.

(4) The Morrill Land Grant Act of 1862 benefited farmers by giving support, through generous grants of public land, to colleges where agricultural and mechanical courses were emphasized.

(5) Also in 1862, Congress approved a measure to build a railroad to California using the central route, another measure blocked earlier by southern votes.

The Election of 1864

Unlike the Confederacy, the Union went through a presidential election in the midst of war. In a sense, this was the supreme test of democracy. With an enemy at the gates of the national capital, the election was held on schedule and the results accepted quietly. Lincoln was renominated by the Republicans who, in a bid for unity, chose **Andrew Johnson**, a "war Democrat" (a supporter of the Union cause) from Tennessee, for Vice-President. Many Democrats joined the Republicans in support of the Lincoln-Johnson ticket. To make the ticket more attractive to the voters, the name Republican was dropped and the name National Union party adopted.

The Democrats nominated General George McClellan, the popular commander who had not lost a major battle, but who had not won decisively, either. The campaign came at a time when morale in the North was exceedingly low. The war had gone on and on, and as late as the summer of 1864 there was still no end in sight. Many in the North supported some form of negotiated peace with the South. The inability of the North to win after three years of fighting gave new hope to a large northern group which had opposed the war from the beginning. This group, labeled "**Copperheads**" after the deadly snake of that name, openly opposed the northern war effort. Perhaps the most outstanding Copperhead was Clement L. Vallandigham, a congressman from Ohio. His activities were adjudged treasonable, and he was arrested and convicted.

In the early stages of the campaign, Lincoln was convinced he would lose. But by election day, the war news was encouraging. With Sherman's capture of Atlanta, Lincoln's prospects brightened. The vote on election day showed Lincoln the victor with 55% of the popular vote.

SECTION 6 REVIEW

Identify: Andrew Johnson, Copperheads

Main Ideas

1. What problems did Davis face as President of the Confederacy?
2. List two of Lincoln's leadership qualities. What criticism did he face?
3. In what way was democracy tested during the war in both the Confederacy and the Union?
4. Describe five Republican-sponsored bills passed by the Union during the war.

CHAPTER 16 REVIEW

Key Terms
Explain the meaning of each of the following terms:

      Crittenden Compromise
      Fort Sumter
      First Battle of Bull Run
      Merrimac and *Monitor*
      Battle of Antietam
      Radical Republicans
      Emancipation Proclamation
      United States Colored Troops
      Battle of Gettysburg
      siege of Vicksburg
      Sherman's march to the sea
      Appomattox Court House
      bounty jumping
      greenbacks
      Homestead Act
      Copperheads

Reviewing the Main Ideas

Section 1
1. What problems faced Lincoln as he took office?
2. Name four advantages that the North had at the beginning of the war.
3. What advantages did the South have at the beginning of the war?

Section 2
1. What was the North's three-part plan to win the war? How did the blockade hurt the South?
2. How did Grant's victories in the West in 1862 help the Union cause?
3. Why did Lee want a victory on northern soil?

Section 3
1. Why was Lincoln cautious about ending slavery before 1863?
2. What were the short-range and long-range effects of the Emancipation Proclamation?

Section 4
1. Give two reasons why the Battle of Gettysburg was important.
2. What was the significance of the following military actions: the siege of Vicksburg, the battles of Lookout Mountain and Missionary Ridge, and Sherman's march through Georgia and the Carolinas?
3. How did Grant defeat the Army of Northern Virginia in 1864–1865?

Section 5
1. What was the Confederacy's most serious disadvantage in its war efforts?
2. How did the North and South finance the war?

Section 6
1. Discuss Lincoln's and Davis' leadership qualities.
2. What political problems did Davis and Lincoln face during the war?
3. Name five long-debated proposals which became law during the war.

Special History Skills:
Working with Military Maps
As explained in the text, the Battle of Gettysburg was a turning point in the Civil War for both Confederate and Union forces. It was also the most costly battle in terms of casualties—killed, wounded, and missing. The 51,000 deaths in this one battle almost equal the total number of deaths (58,000) during the entire Vietnam War.

The map on page 392 shows the main troop movements of the battle and gives some indication of why losses were so high. Study the map and caption to answer the following questions.

1. Where did the first confrontation between Confederate and Union troops occur?
2. What was the outcome of this opening fight?
3. What was the land like in the area south of Gettysburg?
4. What was the troop strength on both sides by the second day of battle?
5. The Union positions have been described as a "fishhook." What hills marked the "hook" of these positions?
6. What was the approximate length of the Union "fishhook" position?
7. Which army, Confederate or Union, did most of the attacking on the second and third days of the battle?
8. What was the objective of the Confederate attack led by Pickett?
9. Why were Confederate casualties during this last attack so heavy?

10. *Using hindsight*: What options were available to the commanders of both sides by the beginning of the third day of battle? Refer to the map and then discuss reasons why these options might or might not have succeeded.

Other Skill Activities

1. Union or Confederate?
Was your state involved in the Civil War? With your friends or family visit a nearby battlefield or monument and report to the class on its importance. If your state was not in the war, what was its history during 1861–1865?

2. The General and the President
Research the lives of Robert E. Lee and Jefferson Davis after the war. How did they spend the rest of their lives?

3. The start of nursing
If you are considering nursing as a career, you might be interested to know that Clara Barton began the profession during the Civil War. Give a report on medicine and battlefield surgery during the Civil War.

4. The bloodiest war
The Civil War took more American lives than any other war in our history. Using the information given in the chart on page 396, make a bar graph comparing military deaths in America's wars.

Thinking Critically

1. Do you think that Lincoln should have reached a compromise with the South which allowed slavery but avoided a Civil War?
2. Do you think the Civil War was inevitable? Explain.
3. What might the United States be like today if the Crittenden Compromise had been accepted, the seceding states had rejoined the Union, and slavery had not been ended by a civil war? List as many possibilities as you can.
4. Discuss states' rights versus the Union. Should states be allowed to secede if they want to? Do they have the authority to secede if they wish?

Further Reading

Jerome Beatty. *Blockade*. Doubleday & Co., 1971. The true story of a young man stationed on a Union gunboat in rebel territory. Easy reading.

Bell Irvin Wiley. *Confederate Women*. Greenwood Press, 1975. This account of southern women is taken from their letters and diaries.

Irene Hunt. *Across Five Aprils*. Grosset & Dunlap, 1978. A beautifully written novel about a family during the war.

Robert Hunt Jones. *The Civil War in the Northwest: Nebraska, Wisconsin, Iowa, Minnesota, and the Dakotas*. University of Oklahoma Press, 1960. An account of an arena seldom covered in Civil War books.

TEST YOURSELF

WRITE YOUR ANSWERS ON A SEPARATE SHEET OF PAPER.

True or False
Mark T if the statement is true, F if it is false.
1. Lincoln was an abolitionist.
2. The Emancipation Proclamation freed all slaves.
3. Lincoln opposed slavery in new territories.
4. Black and white troops were treated equally in the Union army.
5. The war created many new businesses in the North.
6. The northern blockade kept the South from exporting much of its cotton.
7. The North went to war to preserve the Union.
8. Southern railroads kept supplies evenly distributed.
9. Northerners happily accepted the draft.
10. General Lee's northern victories won international aid for the Confederacy.

Matching
Below are listed advantages which were enjoyed by the North, the South, or both. For each item listed, write N for northern advantage, S for southern advantage, or B for both.
1. had a large navy
2. had a complete railroad system
3. had good banking facilities
4. had a strong military tradition
5. had a larger population
6. had a larger industrial base
7. was a geographically compact unit
8. had the cause of independence
9. had an important world commodity
10. had an established monetary system

1865

MY ♥ IS GLAD MY Country is Free

Chapter 17   1865–1877

REUNION AND RECONSTRUC- TION

Lincoln's re-election in 1864 was a vote of confidence in his wartime leadership. The war, which the North at last was winning, would soon be over. The President could then turn his and the nation's attention to the problems of peace. In Lincoln's mind, the most important problem of peace centered around this question: How could the southern states best be restored to their old position in the Union?

Differences of opinion on how best to restore the rebel states to the Union were already developing. Some, such as Lincoln, advocated forgiveness and leniency. Others, such as the Radical Republicans, favored harsh measures against the defeated rebel states. These differences quickly led to an intense struggle between the President and Congress. The one thing that Lincoln hoped to avoid was a period of bitterness and strife. Yet the result of the differences between the President and Congress was just that—a period of intense bitterness and strife.

This troubled period in American history, called Reconstruction, began before the Civil War was officially over and lasted until 1877, when the last federal troops were withdrawn from the South. The ill will that this period left behind and the problems it left unsolved lingered on far into the 20th century.

Sections in This Chapter
1. Conflicting Plans for Restoring the Union
2. The Failure of Presidential Reconstruction
3. The Impeachment of President Johnson
4. Radical Reconstruction—a Mixed Record
5. The Triumph of White Supremacy

Opposite: Banner made by a former slave, 1865

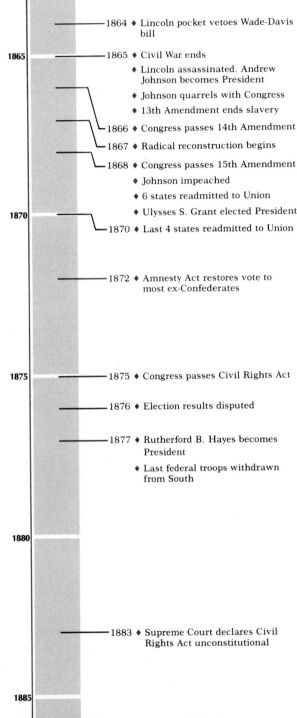

1864 ♦ Lincoln pocket vetoes Wade-Davis bill

1865

1865 ♦ Civil War ends

♦ Lincoln assassinated. Andrew Johnson becomes President

♦ Johnson quarrels with Congress

♦ 13th Amendment ends slavery

1866 ♦ Congress passes 14th Amendment

1867 ♦ Radical reconstruction begins

1868 ♦ Congress passes 15th Amendment

♦ Johnson impeached

♦ 6 states readmitted to Union

♦ Ulysses S. Grant elected President

1870

1870 ♦ Last 4 states readmitted to Union

1872 ♦ Amnesty Act restores vote to most ex-Confederates

1875

1875 ♦ Congress passes Civil Rights Act

1876 ♦ Election results disputed

1877 ♦ Rutherford B. Hayes becomes President

♦ Last federal troops withdrawn from South

1880

1883 ♦ Supreme Court declares Civil Rights Act unconstitutional

1885

1. CONFLICTING PLANS FOR RESTORING THE UNION

Early in the war Lincoln had shown that when it came to making peace he intended to be forgiving. Perhaps he believed that defeat was in itself sufficient punishment for the people of the South. He went further in the direction of conciliation when he said that the North should be willing to shoulder part of the blame for the war. It was a measure of Lincoln's greatness as a man and as President that he could give voice to sentiments of forgiveness in the midst of a bitter civil war. He never allowed a spirit of vengeance to guide his actions. As a result, the American Civil War—one of the costliest civil wars in history in terms of lives lost in battle—brought at its end no mass executions of defeated leaders, no firing squads, and no massacre of rank and file citizens.

Lincoln Faced Many Peacetime Problems

President Lincoln was of course aware that many problems other than bringing the seceded states back into the Union would have to be faced. One of these problems was the issue of abolition raised by the Emancipation Proclamation. Lincoln thought that a constitutional amendment would probably be needed to guarantee freedom for blacks. There was the related issue of race relations once blacks would be free. Were the races to have equal rights? If so, how could this be brought about when the ex-slaves had no property or economic position, and, in most cases, little or no education?

There was also the question of rebuilding the South, which had suffered great material damage. Southerners had expended much of their wealth in an unsuccessful bid for independence. All of the capital invested in slaves was lost. How could the shattered southern economy be rebuilt?

Until victory was achieved, however, all of these problems would remain secondary to the actual winning of the war. How they would be solved depended on the spirit in which reconstruction was carried out. And here Lincoln's policy of forgiveness would face stiff opposition from many in the North. In his second inaugural address, given in March of 1865, Lincoln repeated sentiments he had voiced so often during the war. His thoughts continued to be on "binding up the nation's wounds." If the President had his way, reconstruction would be carried out "with malice toward none and charity for all."

Lincoln's Reconstruction Plan

As the war progressed and northern armies pushed their way into the South, Lincoln appointed military governors for the conquered areas. The governors' authority to act came from the President and was backed by Union soldiers. These measures were seen as temporary arrangements by Lincoln. By 1863 Lincoln had outlined general procedures for establishing loyal governments in the defeated South. He had always maintained that a state could not legally secede. It followed logically from this that the states of the South had never really left the Union. According to this view, what had happened was that some of the inhabitants of these states had been in rebellion against the United States.

Included in **Lincoln's reconstruction plan** was an offer to pardon, with a few exceptions, Confederates who would agree to take an oath to support the U.S. Constitution. When in any state 10% of those who had voted in 1860 agreed to take an oath of loyalty and set up a state government which abolished slavery, Lincoln would recognize that government as legal. The state would again be a full member of the Union with all of its rights restored. Citizens of the state could elect senators and representatives whom Congress must then approve.

Lincoln added that reconstruction should be based on the principle of civil and political equality for blacks and that there should be a broad pardon for those who fought against the Union. On still another occasion he expressed the belief that blacks who had fought for the Union and those who had some education should be allowed to vote. And, finally, in the early months of 1865, Lincoln worked hard for the passage of the 13th Amendment to abolish slavery.

Radical Republicans Object to Lincoln's Plan

Lincoln's reconstruction policies had the support of many Republican moderates in Congress. There was, however, a small group of **Radical Republicans** who thought the policies of the President were far too lenient. Foremost among them were **Thaddeus Stevens** of Pennsylvania and **Charles Sumner** of Massachusetts.

Although the Radicals did not agree among themselves on everything, they all agreed that the South should be punished. They also believed there should be "ironclad" guarantees of loyalty before there could be any talk of letting the rebel states back into the Union. The Radicals wanted to make sure that those who had led the secession movement would never again gain power. Otherwise, they believed, the sacrifices of the North would have been in vain. Furthermore, the Radicals believed, if the old leaders of the South came back to power, they might join with northern Democrats and end Republican control of Congress. If this should happen, the new protective tariff, the national banking system, the transcontinental railroad, and other laws passed during the Civil War might be lost.

Among the chief concerns of some of the leading Radicals was the future of the former slaves. How were the blacks to fit into a reconstructed South? Unlike Lincoln, the Radicals did not want to leave the solution of the great moral and social problem of the blacks' future to former slaveholders. The Radicals also saw that giving the vote to ex-slaves would strengthen the Republican party against the Democrats. Thus the Radicals were motivated by both unselfish and selfish considerations.

In general, the Radicals supported Lincoln while the fighting continued, but began to criticize his plans for restoring the nation once southern armies surrendered. Mild at first, Radical criticism became sharper and sharper.

The Wade-Davis Bill

The Radicals' answer to Lincoln's reconstruction plan was the **Wade-Davis bill**, passed in Congress in July of 1864. The Wade-Davis bill proclaimed the right of Congress, not the President, to decide how the seceded states might rejoin the Union. The process outlined in the bill was much more severe than the Lincoln plan. First, the defeated states were to be placed under military rule. Then, instead of the 10% called for in the Lincoln plan, a majority of those voting in 1860 would have to take an oath of loyalty before forming a new government. Furthermore, anyone who had

LIFE IN AMERICA

THE AFTERMATH OF THE WAR IN THE SOUTH

Both the defeated Confederate army and the victorious Union army dispersed quickly in 1865. But soldiers in gray and blue returned home to very different situations. The northerner found his hometown undamaged, its economy expanding, and the people confident in the future. The southerner returned to a homeland devastated by war—in economic and physical ruin, and in the midst of social upheaval.

The Human Losses

The Civil War was the most costly in American history, both in human and material losses. The North counted 360,000 dead, the South 258,000. But while the North lost 1.5% of its population, the South lost 4% of its. This would be as if America lost 6 million troops in World War II instead of 400,000!

The loss of men and leadership created a great hardship for the South. It is estimated that 25% of the men between the ages of 18 and 40, potential leaders of their communities, were killed or maimed. One-fifth of Mississippi's state revenue for 1866 was spent on artificial limbs for Confederate veterans.

Burned Cities and Ruined Farms

The total cost of the Civil War, including war expenses, loss of slaves, pensions, and destruction of property, has been estimated at $20 billion. The South suffered by far the greatest material loss. The cities of Jackson, Charleston, Mobile, Richmond, Atlanta, and Savannah were burned. Most major campaigns had been fought on southern soil, with both invading and defending armies living off the land.

Southern transportation and communication lines were war casualties. Roads were a mass of ruts; telegraph lines were in tangles. Two-thirds of the railroad lines in the South were too badly damaged to operate trains.

Even where armies had not marched and foraged, roads, farms, and equipment stood neglected and in disrepair. Not until the 1890s were food production and livestock in the South back to prewar levels.

Economic Chaos

Perhaps the biggest blow to the southern economy was the collapse of its monetary and credit system. Confederate currency and bonds were worthless. Life and fire insurance companies went bankrupt. The freeing of 3.5 million slaves meant a capital investment loss to former slaveholders of several billion dollars. Without capital, the South could not put its land and labor back to work. Thousands of refugees, black and white, roamed the land in search of a new life.

supported the Confederacy would be excluded from the process. The new state governments formed under the plan were to prohibit slavery and refuse to honor the Confederate war debt.

The Wade-Davis bill put Lincoln on the spot. He did not agree with it because of its severity. But he was too shrewd a politician to break openly with Republican leaders, especially right before the presidential election of 1864. Thus he sidestepped the issue, allowing the bill to die by a pocket veto.* He tried to avoid Radical criticism of his action by referring to the Wade-Davis bill as "a proper plan for any state that wished to follow it." Of course no state would prefer it to the easier presidential plan. And the Radicals were furious with the President because of his veto.

Lincoln Is Assassinated

Lincoln's plan for reconstruction was still in the developmental stage when the nation suffered a tragic blow. The President, elated by the news of Lee's surrender at Appomattox, celebrated by attending a Washington theater with Mrs. Lincoln on the night of April 14. As Lincoln sat watching the play, a half-crazed actor, John Wilkes Booth, gained entrance to the presidential box and shot him in the head. Lincoln never regained consciousness and, to the great sorrow of the nation, died the next morning.

To Vice-President **Andrew Johnson** fell the task of completing Lincoln's plan for reconstruction and resolving the growing differences with Congress over the issue. Johnson was a former Democrat and a southerner who had been elected to the Senate from Tennessee in 1857. Although he had owned a few slaves, Johnson did not belong to the planter class. When Tennessee seceded, Johnson refused to go along, remaining in the Senate. Lincoln later appointed him military governor of Tennessee. In 1864 Johnson was chosen to run with Lincoln on the National Union party ticket.

Andrew Johnson was born in a log cabin in grinding poverty. His early life paralleled that of the murdered Lincoln. Like Lincoln, Johnson was handicapped in early life by the lack of educational and cultural opportunities. Starting out as a tailor's apprentice, Andrew Johnson ran away from home while still in his teens and set up a

*pocket veto   method of vetoing a bill presented within 10 days of the end of a session of Congress. If the President does not sign the bill before Congress adjourns, it does not become a law.

business on his own. He never attended a day of school in his life, but his wife taught him how to read and write. His self-education, his industry, and his absolute integrity commended him to his neighbors, and he rose rapidly in the democratic society of his native Tennessee.

Elevated suddenly to the presidency on Lincoln's death, Johnson lacked the degree of popular support that Lincoln had come to enjoy. Johnson also lacked Lincoln's ability to get along with political opponents and critics. He was given to bursts of rage and intemperate language and sometimes lapsed from official dignity. His enemies exaggerated his lack of decorum, accused him of drunkenness, and declared him unfit for high office. Johnson was absolutely honest in all his dealings, but he was stubborn and unyielding. He could not make the day-to-day compromises that are the daily bread of the successful politician. With passions at fever heat in postwar Washington, it is not surprising that Johnson quickly ran into serious problems as President.

FROM THE ARCHIVES

A Diary from Dixie

Here are excerpts from Mary Boykin Chesnut's account of the end of the war in South Carolina.

April 19th.—[The Yankees] pay us a compliment we would never pay them. We fought to get rid of Yankees and Yankee rule. How different is their estimate of us! To keep the despised and iniquitous [sinful] South as a part of their country, they are willing to enlist millions of men at home and abroad and to spend billions, and to have killed three for our one. We hear they have all grown rich. Genuine Yankees can make a fortune trading jack knives!

April 22nd.—Colonel Cadwallader Jones came with a dispatch, sealed and secret. It was for General Chesnut. I opened it. Lincoln, Old Abe Lincoln, killed, murdered! Seward wounded! Why? By whom? It is simply maddening. I sent off messenger after messenger for General Chesnut. I have not the faintest idea where he is, but I know this foul murder will bring down worse miseries on us.

From *A Diary from Dixie* by Mary Boykin Chesnut.

Johnson's Reconstruction Policies

After Lincoln's assassination, sentiment in the North favored a harsher peace. The new President was expected to fall in with the Radicals on reconstruction policy. But much to the disgust of Thaddeus Stevens and other Radicals, Johnson continued with Lincoln's lenient policy. The new President soon found himself in trouble not only with the Radicals in the Republican party but with the moderates as well.

Congress was not in session in April 1865, and did not reconvene until December. This gave Johnson the chance to continue the work of reconstruction without congressional interference. His aim was to complete the work by December. In May, he issued a proclamation of general amnesty, pardoning all but a few of those who had been in rebellion against the United States. He then appointed military governors for the seceded states and ordered state conventions held. These conventions repealed the ordinances of secession and drew up new constitutions. The voters then elected state officials and state legislatures. These bodies repudiated state war debts and ratified the 13th Amendment outlawing slavery (which became law in December 1865). The reconstructed states chose senators and representatives and sent them off to Washington. When Congress reconvened in December, every Confederate state except Texas had elected senators and representatives who were on hand ready to take their seats.

SECTION 1 REVIEW

Identify: Lincoln's reconstruction plan, Radical Republicans, Thaddeus Stevens, Charles Sumner, Wade-Davis bill, Andrew Johnson

Main Ideas

1. What peacetime problems faced President Lincoln at the end of the Civil War?
2. Why did the Radical Republicans think that Lincoln's reconstruction plan was too lenient? Why did they fear the political power of the former leaders of the South?
3. How and why did Lincoln prevent the Wade-Davis bill from becoming law?
4. How did Andrew Johnson continue Lincoln's policies after the assassination?

2. THE FAILURE OF PRESIDENTIAL RECONSTRUCTION

The reconstruction policies of Lincoln and Johnson had the merit of allowing the states that had seceded to return promptly to the Union. Their policies did not, however, take into account the fact that four years of bitter war had created a deep distrust in the North of the southern way of life.

Was it wise to allow the states of the Confederacy to assume their former place in the Union without requiring some basic changes in southern society? The Radical answer to this question was an emphatic "No." Thus, Stevens, Sumner, and other Radicals watched the progress of presidential reconstruction with growing suspicion. And they did not like what they saw. They felt Congress must act quickly or the opportunity to set things right would be lost. The Radicals were especially disturbed that laws regulating the lives of ex-slaves were being enacted by the newly assembled southern legislatures.

The Black Codes

The white people of the South were trying to adjust to the reality of defeat. This meant learning to cope with the losses from the destruction of lives and property. It also meant adjusting to a new relationship with blacks. Southern whites accepted the fact that blacks were now free. The war, the Emancipation Proclamation, and the 13th Amendment had decided that issue. But it was not yet clear what this meant in practical terms for the two races. Although free, the blacks were a landless, even homeless people. All that the vast majority of ex-slaves had to offer was their labor. The white landowning class needed their labor. Thus some new arrangement would have to be made that allowed the freedmen and women to work for wages.

But this was only a small part of the problem. The 13th Amendment did not make blacks citizens or give them the vote. Beyond setting them free, the 13th Amendment did nothing to protect their rights or guard their interests. Nothing had been said on these important questions by the government in Washington. The Lincoln-Johnson policies left these matters to the states.

Thus it was that during presidential reconstruction southern legislatures turned their attention to the whole problem of race relations. The measures they passed to govern the conduct of the ex-slaves were called the **black codes**. Although the codes varied from state to state, they were highly restrictive everywhere. The codes denied blacks the right to vote and to serve on juries. Blacks were to be segregated socially and not allowed to intermarry with whites. Their labor was closely regulated. They were, in fact, required to work. The court could arrest unemployed blacks and sell their labor to employers.

The codes did recognize that the blacks now had certain limited civil rights. They could own property, enter into legal marriages, and sue and be sued in court. But their status was to be that of dependent farm workers—a class apart. In many respects the codes were like the slave codes of prewar days.

The South Defends the Black Codes

Many northerners saw the black codes as evidence of the South's unwillingness to accept defeat. To the Radicals, many of whom sincerely believed in racial equality, the codes were intolerable. They demanded that the codes be abandoned and that the whole course of reconstruction be radically altered.

To southerners, the codes were passed not to defy the North but to deal with an urgent problem created by the war—a problem not faced in the North. Although now free, the vast majority of blacks remained in the South. Many were confused, not knowing what to do. Many, understandably, were waiting for something to happen. They did not know what. Great numbers had left the plantations and were wandering over the countryside. Some had gone to the cities where they were without jobs or other means of support.

White southerners accepted the fact that the labor of the ex-slaves would be on a wage basis. But they feared that unless some regulations were adopted to guide the process, the disruptions caused by the war and emancipation would continue. Crops would not be planted. Both the white and the black population would starve. The unemployed would turn to violence and crime. Economic recovery would not be possible. To most white southerners, then, the black codes seemed to be a social and economic necessity.

Congress Creates the Joint Committee of 15

Returning to Washington in December 1865, the Radicals began to undo the reconstruction work of Lincoln and Johnson. Their first step was to refuse to seat southern representatives elected by the reconstructed governments. Radicals were horrified to find among those waiting to take their seats former Confederate leaders, including Alexander Stephens, Vice-President of the Confederacy. To the Radicals and other Republicans, these men were traitors, unfit to hold office.

To moderate as well as Radical Republicans in Congress, the answer to presidential reconstruction and the black codes was to create the **Joint Committee of 15**. This committee, composed of six senators and nine representatives, began to assert the congressional viewpoint on all aspects of reconstruction.

The Freedmen's Bureau and Johnson's Veto

The Joint Committee of 15 sponsored measures giving economic aid to ex-slaves and providing federal protection of their rights. The first of these measures continued the life of the **Freedmen's Bureau**. This agency, under the War Department, had been in operation since March of 1865. It was engaged in the important work of feeding and caring for war refugees, black and white. The main task of the Freedmen's Bureau was to assist ex-slaves in finding jobs and to protect them

Andrew Johnson (1808–1875)

IN OFFICE: 1865–1869

From Tennessee. Johnson was the only southern senator to remain loyal to the Union during the Civil War. Although a Democrat, he was elected Vice-President on the National Union ticket in 1864 and became President upon Lincoln's assassination. His conflicts with Congress over reconstruction policies led to an attempt to remove him from office; that attempt failed by only one vote (1868). During his term of office, Alaska was purchased from Russia (1867).

against discrimination. The bill to extend its life had the support of moderates as well as Radicals.

President Johnson would have been wise to sign the Freedmen's Bureau bill and thereby establish a working relationship with Congress. Instead, he vetoed the bill on the ground that it would mean continuing a wartime measure in peacetime. He also said that it was an invasion of the judicial and legislative power of the states. Now that state governments were functioning again in the South, this meant that blacks would have to look to white southerners for assistance and protection, rather than to the federal government.

Johnson Vetoes the Civil Rights Act

Congress was unwilling to let matters stand as they were. It next passed a **Civil Rights Act**. This measure guaranteed citizenship to blacks and gave the federal government the right to intervene in the affairs of the states to protect the civil rights of blacks. The bill had nearly unanimous support from the Republicans in Congress. But it, too, was vetoed by President Johnson, who said it was unconstitutional. His actions disturbed many of his supporters. The President and Congress were on a collision course over the whole broad issue of reconstruction.

In the rapidly developing confrontation between the President and Congress, the personality of the President was a key factor. A stubborn

Mrs. Green's school for freedmen in Vicksburg, Mississippi, 1866

man, Johnson seemed completely unable to compromise. His inflexibility contrasted with Lincoln's willingness to consider opposing views and change his policies to gain support. Instead of bending, Johnson hardened his position and began to attack the Radicals with hot-tempered and ill-considered statements. His verbal abuse of the Radicals in speeches around the country cost him the support of many moderates who would have preferred to work with him. With the added support of the moderates, the Radicals were able to win the two-thirds vote needed in both houses of Congress to override the veto of the Civil Rights Act and of a new Freedmen's Bureau bill. These actions showed that the Radicals now had the votes to undo the reconstruction work already completed.

The 14th Amendment

In passing the Civil Rights Act the Radicals had won a major victory. The federal government now had the authority to interfere in the states where the civil rights of blacks were violated.

But what if a later Congress were to repeal the Civil Rights Act? What if the Supreme Court were to declare it unconstitutional? To guard against these possibilities, the Radicals now drew up a 14th Amendment to the United States Constitution. This important proposal became a key element in the congressional plan for reconstruction that was beginning to take the place of the discredited Lincoln-Johnson plan.

The proposed **14th Amendment** provided for the following: (1) It proposed to make ex-slaves citizens of the United States. (2) It stated that no state could deny its citizens equal protection of the law or take away anyone's life, liberty, or property without due process of law. (3) It provided that any state that denied the vote to any of its male citizens would lose some of its seats in the House of Representatives. (4) It disqualified former Confederate officials from federal and state office unless Congress, by a two-thirds vote, removed this disqualification.

With the Radicals in control, Congress demanded that the southern states accept the new amendment as a condition for regaining their seats in Congress. Had it not been for the hostility that now existed between President Johnson and the Radicals, the southern states might have accepted this condition. But Johnson denounced the amendment. In the congressional elections of 1866 he worked openly to defeat Republican candidates who supported it. On a speaking tour that he called a "swing around the circle," he lashed out at his enemies. In off-the-cuff stump speeches he made wild accusations and answered hecklers with abusive language. The President's highly undignified behavior lost him much of his support. His tactics backfired, and the Radicals won a solid victory. Johnson's enemies won enough seats in Congress to give them more than the two-thirds majority they needed to pass reconstruction measures over the President's veto.

Johnson Urges the Southern States to Reject the 14th Amendment

Johnson was angered over the election results. He personally urged the southern states to reject the 14th Amendment. Ten of the eleven states followed his advice, enough to defeat the measure. Tennessee was the only former Confederate state to ratify. Sentiment elsewhere in the South was divided on the amendment. Many southern leaders believed it wise to accept the measure and avoid further trouble with Congress on the issues it raised. They pointed out that the 14th Amendment did not *require* them to give the vote to blacks, although they would lose some of their representation in Congress if they failed to do so. By following Johnson's advice and rejecting the 14th Amendment, the South invited the hostility of a united Republican Congress. The way was open for harsher measures that would completely undo the reconstruction work of Lincoln and Johnson.

SECTION 2 REVIEW

 Identify: black codes, Joint Committee of 15, Freedmen's Bureau, Civil Rights Act, 14th Admendment

Main Ideas

1. Why did the southern legislatures enact black codes? What was the northern reaction?
2. What legislation did Congress pass to aid the ex-slaves?
3. How did President Johnson increase hostility between the North and the South? How did he increase hostility between himself and Congress?

3. THE IMPEACHMENT OF PRESIDENT JOHNSON

Radicals in Congress responded to the defeat of the 14th Amendment swiftly and drastically. They believed that they had offered the President a reasonable compromise. But the stubborn Johnson had rejected it. In March 1867, therefore, the angry Congress passed a package of new reconstruction laws. Thus, two years after the war ended, reconstruction was started all over again.

Radical Reconstruction Begins

In March of 1867, over President Johnson's veto, Congress enacted the following Radical reconstruction measures:

(1) The governments of the ten states that had refused to ratify the proposed 14th Amendment were declared illegal. These states reverted to the status of territories, over which Congress had complete and sole authority.

(2) The ten states were divided into five military districts with a major general in command of each. (See map, page 420.) The commanding general was made responsible for protecting life and property in his district, with power to use for that purpose either the ordinary civil courts or special military tribunals.

(3) A former state could regain its representation in Congress only by following a series of prescribed steps. *First*, it must call a constitutional convention, with members elected by blacks as well as whites. Former Confederate officials were excluded from voting or becoming delegates. *Second*, the constitutional convention was to draft a constitution that contained the same restrictions on voting and officeholding. *Third*, the constitution was to be ratified by the same voters and then approved by Congress. *Finally*, the legislatures elected under the new constitution must ratify the proposed 14th Amendment. Once this had been done, and the 14th Amendment had become part of the U.S. Constitution, the state would be readmitted to the Union and its representatives and senators allowed to take their seats in Congress.

The Radicals Restrict the President

To keep control of reconstruction in congressional hands, in March 1867 the Radicals also passed two laws to restrict the powers of the President. The **Tenure of Office Act** forbade the President to remove officeholders, including members of his cabinet, without the consent of the Senate. The Command of the Army Act forbade the President to issue orders to the army except through the General of the Army, General Grant. This, the Radicals believed, would prevent the President from using his authority as commander-in-chief to interfere in military reconstruction.

President Johnson was furious. He decided to test the constitutionality of the Tenure of Office Act. The act had been passed to prevent Johnson from dismissing his Secretary of War, Edwin Stanton, the lone Radical in the cabinet. When Johnson decided to remove Stanton, he walked into the trap the Radicals had prepared for him.

The President was the only remaining obstacle to complete Radical control of the government. The Radicals had bullied the Supreme Court into overlooking the unconstitutional actions of Congress in setting aside civil courts in the South in a time of peace and replacing them with military tribunals. Now if the Radicals could catch the President in a violation of the law, they might be able to remove him from office through the **impeachment** process as provided for in the Constitution. To "impeach" an elected official means to bring him or her to trial before the proper body for violation of laws. With both the Supreme Court and the President silenced, Congress would have complete control of the federal machinery.

The House Impeaches Johnson

A few days after Johnson removed Stanton from office, the House of Representatives voted to impeach the President. This meant that the President would be tried before the Senate, with the Chief Justice of the Supreme Court presiding. If found guilty, he would be removed from office.

The Radicals were confident of success since the Republicans controlled the necessary two-thirds vote in the Senate. A House committee drew up a list of charges against Johnson, most of which related to alleged violations of the Tenure of Office Act. Other charges were that Johnson had delivered "inflammatory and scandalous" speeches designed "to bring into disgrace, ridi-

cule, contempt, and reproach the Congress of the United States."

The impeachment trial of President Johnson created a sensation. The Constitution provides that a President may be removed from office only if found guilty of "high crimes and misdemeanors." Whatever his indiscretions, Johnson had committed no crime. Clearly, the Radicals wanted Johnson removed from the White House because he opposed their reconstruction policies.

Johnson Remains in Office

The impeachment trial of President Johnson lasted two months and was the talk of Washington. Each day large crowds swarmed to Capitol Hill. Those lucky enough to get seats packed into the galleries of the Senate chamber. There they heard the Radical prosecutors heap abuse on the President.

The Radicals expected all the Republicans in the Senate to vote for conviction. This would give them six more votes than the two-thirds majority needed to convict. But the Radicals overplayed their hand. In the final vote, seven Republicans voted with twelve Democrats against conviction. President Johnson stayed in office by the margin of one vote!

Had it not been for the courage of these seven Republicans in rising above the pressures of partisan politics, a dangerous precedent would have been set. Future Presidents would have been at the mercy of strong congressional majorities. Instead of a system of checks and balances in which Congress, the President, and the Supreme Court share authority, Congress would have become the most powerful branch of government, able to dictate to the other two.

Anti-Johnson cartoon. Note the tailor's scissors.

The Election of 1868

President Johnson was saved from dismissal, but he no longer had influence. For the election of 1868, the Republicans turned to **General Ulysses S. Grant**, the war hero. Grant had no previous political experience. He had served both Lincoln and Johnson but had fallen out with Johnson. The Republican platform called for a continuation of Radical reconstruction and payment of the federal government's war debt in gold.

The Democrats nominated Horatio Seymour of New York, a wealthy former governor. Their party was seriously handicapped, however, because of its past association with secession. The Democratic platform denounced Radical recon-

struction as unconstitutional. It also supported a plan to pay off the government debt in greenbacks, a plan that appealed to debtors.

The campaign was nasty. The Radicals reminded the voters of the battle losses in the Civil War, which they blamed on the Democrats. This campaign tactic, known as **"waving the bloody shirt,"** became a regular feature of Republican campaigns for many years. The Republicans hoped to win by convincing voters that the Democrats were disloyal.

With strong support in the South, where blacks had the vote and former Confederate leaders did not, Grant won the election. It was a close call for the Republicans, however. Their control of the national government in the future seemed to depend on black suffrage in the South.

SECTION 3 REVIEW

Identify: Tenure of Office Act, impeachment, Ulysses S. Grant, "waving the bloody shirt"

Main Ideas

1. Describe the three parts of the Radicals' reconstruction plan.
2. How did the Radicals try to remove President Johnson from office? Why did they fail?
3. What factors led to the Republican presidential election victory in 1868?

Ulysses S. Grant (1822–1885)

IN OFFICE: 1869–1877

Republican from Illinois. Grant, a hero of the Civil War, had no political experience prior to his terms as President. During his administration, the 15th Amendment, guaranteeing black suffrage, was added to the Constitution (1870); the Treaty of Washington was signed with Britain (1871); and civil service reform was begun. The reputation of his administration was severely damaged by the disclosure of corruption in the cabinet.

415

4. RADICAL RECONSTRUCTION— A MIXED RECORD

As we have seen, in March of 1867 Congress set aside presidential reconstruction and returned the South to military rule. Under military supervision, the southern states were required to call new conventions and write new constitutions along the lines laid down by Congress. They then elected new legislatures which ratified the 14th Amendment as required. All but four completed the process and were readmitted to the Union in time for the presidential election of 1868. The remaining four—Georgia, Mississippi, Texas, and Virginia—were not readmitted until 1870. By that time, a new condition had been added. To gain readmission, the four states had to ratify the 15th Amendment, which guaranteed the vote to black males.

New Groups in Power in the South

The new constitutions had a number of good features and were in general a considerable improvement over those they replaced. They provided for public school systems for the first time and for agencies to aid the homeless, the handicapped, and the unemployed. They set up a new tax system that was much fairer than the old. And they gave state governments the power to assist economic recovery by supporting programs to rebuild roads, bridges, and railroads.

But the governments established under the new constitutions were strongly disliked by many white southerners. They resented the new groups to whom Radical reconstruction gave control: blacks, **"carpetbaggers,"** and **"scalawags."**

Most white southerners of all classes looked down on the first group, the blacks, as an inferior people. Allowing former slaves to vote and hold office on an equal basis with whites was a shocking idea to most southerners at the time. The fact that most northern states had denied the vote to blacks living in the North suggested that black suffrage was being forced on the South as punishment. White southerners who were denied the vote because of past support to the Confederacy were especially angered.

The second group were northerners who for one reason or another had migrated south. Whatever their purpose, all northerners were resented and lumped together in the minds of southerners as "carpetbaggers," so called because some came carrying a type of luggage popular at the time made of carpeting material. Some were former soldiers who had fought in the Union army and stayed on or returned to the South after the war. Others were northern businessmen who had gone south to take advantage of economic opportunities opened up by the war. With money to invest, they bought plantations and mines (often for no more money than the tax owed upon them), built railroads, and started factories. Still others were northern volunteers who had gone south as teachers and ministers or as members of organizations that wanted to aid the ex-slaves. Finally, there were numerous agents of the federal government such as tax collectors, customs officers, and Treasury agents.

The former Confederates who had served in the war and were now without the vote saved their greatest hatred for the third group, the white southerners who cooperated with the new governments. They labeled all such persons "scalawags," a word that originally meant a small, runty cow or horse but now was used to mean scoundrel or traitor to the South.

The Record of the Reconstruction Legislatures

Because of the postwar bitterness, the record made by the Radical state legislatures has been much distorted. These governments were denounced as corrupt, inefficient, and incapable. The majority of white southerners detested them and became more determined than ever to restore white supremacy at the earliest opportunity. This view of Radical reconstruction is far from accurate. These governments had their faults, but they were not dominated by ignorant blacks and lazy, no-good whites, as was charged. Nor were they any more corrupt and dishonest than postwar governments elsewhere in the nation. As you will see in Chapter 19, the postwar years were a period of low public morality. The fraud practiced by the Tweed Ring in New York City (see page 453) far outdid anything that took place in the Radical legislatures in the South.

The reconstruction legislatures sponsored

worthwhile programs, many of them much needed and long overdue. The fact that these programs cost money, requiring tax increases and heavy borrowing, added to the charge of waste and corruption. Providing free public education for the first time was a great step forward. But it cost a great deal of money. And if taxes were increased to help pay the bill, they were at least more evenly distributed than in the past. Other reforms included changes in the legal system to protect the rights of blacks, women, and persons unable to pay their debts.

When it is remembered that many of the legislators had little if any previous experience in government, their record of accomplishment is the more remarkable. A number of the blacks elected to the reconstruction legislatures were educated and capable leaders, but without experience. It is important to note that the blacks did not use their votes against their former white masters. Although they hoped to obtain land for themselves, the blacks did not advocate taking it from white landowners. In fact, they supported efforts to give back the vote to the white leaders who had lost it.

Resistance to Radical Reconstruction

The former leaders of the South were in no mood to look upon the positive side of Radical reconstruction. They were embittered by defeat, economic hardships, and the loss of their civil rights. They blamed the victorious North for all their misfortunes and for what they claimed was "black rule." Although blacks won a number of offices and briefly enjoyed a majority in the legislature of South Carolina, they were never really in control in any state. But Radical reconstruction gave black men political equality with white men. And it was black votes that kept the reconstruction governments in office. To white southerners, this was the key fact of Radical reconstruction.

Almost all classes of the native white population opposed any idea of racial equality. They had always regarded blacks as an inferior race whose correct place in society was that of dependent laborers. Blacks might now be free, but nothing else had changed except that outside radicals had come in, given blacks the vote, and tried to upset the natural order of society based on white supremacy. Race prejudice was not something that could be readily changed even had the reconstruction governments been popular.

Portraits of the Radical Republican members of the South Carolina legislature, 1868

The Loyal League and the Ku Klux Klan

The Radical Republicans reached the blacks through an organization called the **Loyal League**. The League taught black voters Republican party principles and saw to it that blacks voted on election day. In some cases the League used threats to win the votes of blacks. For a time the League was highly successful in lining up solid black support. Given those circumstances, it is not surprising that southern whites tried hard to prevent blacks from voting in order to weaken Republican control.

Some of the efforts used to defeat the Republicans depended on violence and terror. Secret societies sprang up whose main purpose was to frighten or terrorize blacks and keep them from exercising their rights as voters. Societies such as the **Ku Klux Klan**, the Knights of the White Camelia, the White Brotherhood, the White League, and many others spread terror throughout the black community. Blacks were threatened, and if the threats did not keep them from voting and attending political meetings, violence followed. Soon there were reports throughout the South of beatings, torture, and killings carried out by the secret societies. Although many moderate southerners denounced the violence, secret societies represented a serious threat. They were a threat to the civil rights of southern blacks as well as a direct challenge to Radical reconstruction itself.

The 15th Amendment: Congress Strikes Back

The Republicans in Congress watched these developments in the South with growing alarm. If blacks were prevented from voting by the secret societies, the reconstruction governments would collapse. Grant's narrow popular vote majority in the 1868 presidential election would not have been possible without heavy black majorities in the South. To preserve the voting rights of blacks in face of these challenges, Congress hurriedly passed and submitted to the states the **15th Amendment**. The new amendment banned the denial of male suffrage "on account of race, color, or previous condition of servitude."

But other measures were needed to counter the terrorist societies. Thus three enforcement acts were passed. The first gave the President the power to use the army to enforce the 14th and 15th amendments. The second provided for federal supervision of registration and voting in national elections. The third, sometimes called the Ku Klux Klan Act, outlawed terrorist societies and gave the President the right to suspend the writ of *habeas corpus* if necessary to enforce the act.

SECTION 4 REVIEW

Identify: carpetbaggers, scalawags, Loyal League, Ku Klux Klan, 15th Amendment

Main Ideas
1. How did the new southern state constitutions differ from previous ones?
2. Describe the groups that had political power in the South during Radical reconstruction.
3. In what ways was the record of the reconstruction governments a "mixed" one?
4. What was the reaction of most southern whites to Radical reconstruction? Why?
5. How did Congress try to protect black voters?

5. THE TRIUMPH OF WHITE SUPREMACY

As the years went by, it became increasingly clear that Radical reconstruction was failing to achieve its goals of integrating blacks into American society. One of the reasons for failure was the inability or unwillingness of Congress to do anything meaningful to end **racial segregation**. This practice of "separating the races" usually meant barring blacks from public facilities.

Segregation Laws Passed in the South

The practice of segregation was so widespread, both North and South, that it was difficult to change. One man who tried to change it was Charles Sumner, senator from Massachusetts. Time and again Sumner introduced bills in Congress to outlaw segregation in schools, railroad cars, inns, theaters, and other places of amusement. But his efforts failed. Although a Civil Rights Act was passed in 1875, it did not promote school integration. In 1883, the Supreme Court declared the act unconstitutional.

This action by the Court and the general failure of society to counter the practice of segregation led to the passage in the 1880s and 1890s of what were called **Jim Crow laws**. More thorough than the black codes of 1865, the Jim Crow laws segregated blacks almost everywhere in the South—in streetcars, parks, restaurants, schools, hotels, railroad stations, restrooms, cemeteries, and barbershops. The Jim Crow laws made second-class citizens of the black population.

A Landless Class

"Our reconstruction measures were radically defective," wrote Frederick Douglass in 1880, because they failed to give the ex-slaves any land.

They left the former slave completely in the power of the old master, the loyal citizen in the hands of the disloyal rebel against the government. . . . When the serfs of Russia were emancipated, they were given three acres of ground upon which they could live and make a living. But not so when our slaves were emancipated. They were sent away empty-handed, without money, without friends, and without a foot of land to stand upon. Old and young, sick and well, were turned loose to the open sky, naked to their enemies.

For some years there was talk of giving each freedman "forty acres and a mule." But government leaders did not want to confiscate (seize) the land of the defeated rebels. Lincoln had considered such a policy during the war, and some land had actually been taken over and given to ex-slaves. But after the war, even these lands were returned to their former owners.

In 1866 Congress passed a Southern Homestead Act, but few blacks were in a position to take advantage of it before it was repealed in 1876. Failure to provide land for the freedmen was a serious shortcoming of Radical reconstruction. Without land or other economic assets, the ex-slaves soon lost what little influence they had.

The Sharecropping System

Having no land, and having only their labor to offer, many blacks became sharecroppers. The **sharecropping system** developed in the South after the war out of necessity. Many large plantations were broken up. The slaves were free, and there was no money to hire day labor. The freedmen wanted land but had no money to buy it. To a degree, the sharecropping system solved all these problems. Under this system, which became common among landless whites as well as blacks, a farm family made a contract with a landlord. They became tenants, agreeing to pay for the use of the land with a share of the crop. The landlord supplied the tools and seeds and provided the tenant farmers with the land, a mule, and a house or shack to live in.

Since the sharecroppers had no money, they obtained food and other necessities through credit. This meant that the crops they would sell at harvest time were mortgaged. Frequently, the sharecroppers found that the value of the crop was less than the bill, plus interest, that they had run up at the local store. Before long most of the sharecroppers in the South found themselves deeply in debt.

To make matters worse, laws were passed forbidding sharecroppers to leave the state until their debts were paid. Over the years a sharecropper's debts tended to increase. Thus there was no escape from the system. A family of sharecroppers was as tied to the soil as the slaves had been before emancipation.

A Shift in the National Mood

After a time the people of the North lost interest in the whole broad issue of reconstruction. Many of the Radical leaders were passing from the scene. Thaddeus Stevens died in 1868 and Charles Sumner in 1875. Memories of the war were fading. Other issues were demanding attention. The nation suffered a business panic in 1873 and the Grant administration was racked with scandals that were beginning to come to light.

Many northerners began to think that the South should be allowed to solve its problems without interference from Washington. Reports of fraud and stolen elections put the carpetbag and Republican governments in a bad light. The federal government had freed the blacks, made them citizens by the 14th Amendment, and given them the vote by the 15th. Many in the North believed that this was all that could or should be done. Racism had not disappeared. Now that war memories were fading, northerners began to agree with the view of white southerners on "the Negro question." The Supreme Court decided in 1883 that blacks were no longer entitled "to be the special favorite of the laws." And without the protection of the laws, equality and civil rights were largely a fiction.

Most sharecroppers were desperately poor.

419

The End of Reconstruction

Without the protection of Congress and the President, Republican regimes in the South collapsed one by one. In 1872 Congress passed the Amnesty Act, which restored the right to hold office to all but a few ex-Confederates. By this time various ways had been found to discourage blacks from voting or else to convince them to vote against Republican candidates. A favorite and successful method involved outright intimidation and violence. In contrast to the undercover activities of secret societies, the new efforts were highly visible. In Mississippi, white rifle companies drilled in public. Blacks were openly threatened, and some were publicly whipped. In cases where the blacks resisted, race riots occurred, with many black casualties. These activities demoralized white Republican party workers as well as black voters. County after county came under the control of native white rule.

With indifferent support from Congress, carpetbaggers and scalawags made their peace with southern conservatives. The victory of anti-reconstruction whites could no longer be delayed. They had always outnumbered the Radical reconstruction combination of blacks, carpetbaggers, and scalawags. They owned most of the land and other economic assets of the South. Without interference from the outside, they were certain sooner or later to dominate the political life of the region. All over the South, carpetbag governments collapsed and "home rule" was restored.

As we have seen, Grant would not have won the presidency in 1868 without heavy black majorities in the southern states. In the presidential election of 1872, Grant's re-election again benefited from the electoral vote of the South. But by 1876 the picture had changed. Most of the southern states had been "reconstructed," and federal troops—which had been used to protect black voters and certain carpetbag governments—had been withdrawn, except from South Carolina and Louisiana. The Republican candidate, **Rutherford B. Hayes**, received fewer popular votes than his Democratic opponent, Samuel Tilden. But there was a dispute over the electoral vote. The dispute was settled by a compromise: Hayes received the presidency, and as part of the bargain, he agreed to remove the last of the federal troops from the South.

The bitter decade of Reconstruction was over. White Americans turned away in relief from the problems of the South. The bright prospects of deliverance that the northern victory in 1865

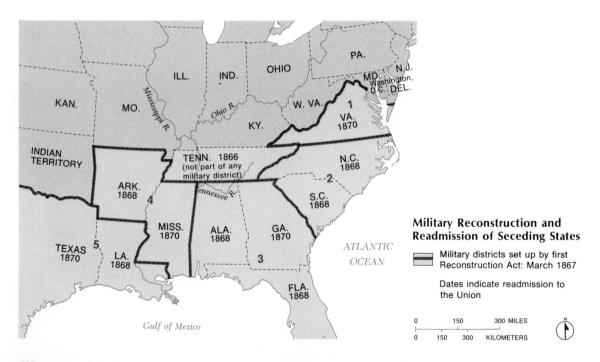

Military Reconstruction and Readmission of Seceding States

▬ Military districts set up by first Reconstruction Act: March 1867

Dates indicate readmission to the Union

seemed to open up for the black people of America were dashed. Blacks would wait until the mid-1950s—90 years later—before the nation was again ready to honor the original meaning of the 14th and 15th amendments.

In the South, the association of blacks with the Republican party during Reconstruction convinced white southerners that the Democratic party was the party of white supremacy. Thus was born the one-party system that delivered the **"Solid South"** to Democratic candidates for many decades to come.

SECTION 5 REVIEW

 Identify: racial segregation, Jim Crow laws, sharecropping system, Rutherford B. Hayes, Solid South

Main Ideas

1. Why did Radical reconstruction fail to provide blacks with equal status in society?
2. How were southern blacks discouraged from voting?
3. How did the sharecropping system answer the needs of both the landowners and the laborers? How did it tie the laborers to the land?
4. Why did white southerners vote Democratic for many decades following Reconstruction?

HIGHLIGHTS OF RECONSTRUCTION, 1865–1877

Between 1865 and 1877, control of the southern state governments went through three phases.

Phase 1: 1865 and 1866
The legislatures were dominated by white ex-Confederates. Black codes were passed restricting the rights of blacks to own property and move freely.

Phase 2: 1866 to early 1870s
See map, opposite page. Republican legislators, white and black, formed the majorities in the state governments. After one to three years of military rule, these governments completed the actions required by Radical reconstruction laws: Eligible voters ratified new state constitutions and elected new state legislatures. These legislatures ratified the 14th and, some, the 15th Amendment. The states were then readmitted to the Union. Dates of readmittance were:

1868	Alabama, Arkansas, Florida, Louisiana, North Carolina, South Carolina
1870	Georgia, Mississippi, Texas, Virginia

Phase 3: Early 1870s to 1877
See map below. Although military rule had ended, the new state governments sometimes called upon federal troops to protect Republican voters. Despite these efforts, black and white Radical Republicans lost power. White Democrats regained control of the southern legislatures in the following years:

1869	Virginia (before state was readmitted)
1870	North Carolina
1871	Georgia
1873	Texas
1874	Alabama, Arkansas
1875	Mississippi
1877	South Carolina, Louisiana, Florida

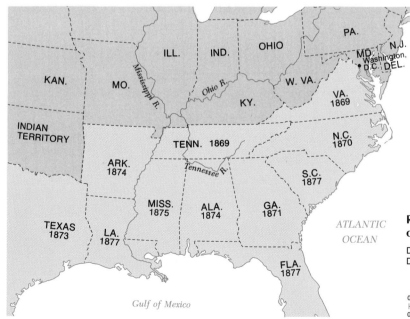

Return to Government of White Democrats

Dates indicate when white Democrats regained control

CHAPTER 17 REVIEW

Key Terms
Explain the meaning of each of the following terms:

Lincoln's reconstruction plan
Radical Republicans
Wade-Davis bill
black codes
Joint Committee of 15
Freedmen's Bureau
Civil Rights Act (1866)
14th Amendment
Tenure of Office Act
impeachment
"waving the bloody shirt"
carpetbaggers
scalawags
Loyal League
Ku Klux Klan
15th Amendment
racial segregation
Jim Crow laws
sharecropping system
Solid South

Reviewing the Main Ideas

Section 1
1. What peacetime problems faced Lincoln in 1865?
2. Describe Lincoln's reconstruction plan. What did Johnson do to continue this plan?
3. What did the Radical Republicans propose as a reconstruction plan?

Section 2
1. Why did the southern states pass black codes after the war?
2. What legislation did Congress pass to aid the former slaves? Why did Johnson veto these bills?

Section 3
1. Describe the three parts of the Radical Republicans' reconstruction plan.
2. What were the grounds for President Johnson's impeachment? What was the result of the impeachment?

Section 4
1. What group or groups had political power in the South during Radical reconstruction? What did they accomplish?
2. What was the reaction of southern whites to Radical reconstruction? Why?
3. What was the 15th Amendment designed to accomplish?

Section 5
1. Radical reconstruction failed to provide equality to ex-slaves. Why?
2. How was the sharecropping system an outgrowth of the conditions that prevailed in the South after the Civil War?

Special History Skills:
Speculation
Science fiction writers love to speculate. That is, they love to use their knowledge and imagination to try answering the question, "What if?" For example, "What if life was discovered on other planets?" "What if a new, abundant liquid fuel was discovered?" Write down a few of the consequences you can think of for these questions.

Now try speculating about these historical "What If's?" Write down all the consequences that would result from these events. Use your knowledge and imagination.
1. What if the South had won the Civil War?
2. What if Lincoln had not been assassinated?
3. What if Johnson had been removed from office?
4. What if women had been included in the 15th Amendment?
5. What if Radical reconstruction had provided land for former slaves?

Other Skill Activities
1. **How would you vote?**
   How would you have voted in the impeachment trial of President Johnson? Explain your answer in the form of a two-minute speech.
2. **Differing viewpoints**
   Make a two-column chart which compares presidential plans for reconstruction with congressional reconstruction.
3. **Write a play**
   Write a dialog between a sharecropper and a landowner at the end of a growing season. Imagine that the sharecropper has come to give the landowner his or her share of the crop.

4. Was Radical reconstruction harsh?

After World War II, the United States occupied Japan. Americans have usually viewed this occupation as a model of fairness and justice. Read about this occupation in an encyclopedia or other source and then compare it to the measures taken during Radical reconstruction. You might consider comparing (a) treatment of former officials, (b) treatment of the defeated population, (c) changes in laws, (d) goals of occupation.

5. Black codes and other special laws

During Reconstruction, the South enacted black codes. Choose one other country in history that has or had codes regulating the behavior of some of its citizens. Discuss the codes. Do you think codes regulating part of a population are legal? Moral? Explain why or why not.

Thinking Critically

1. The balance of powers created by the Constitution came close to breaking down in 1868. Explain what this statement means.
2. Did the terms for readmission to the Union remain consistent, or did they change during Reconstruction? How do you think this affected the South?
3. Radical Republicans were concerned with more than rights for ex-slaves when they pushed for passage of the 15th Amendment. Explain what this statement means.
4. Many democratic governments—Britain and Norway, for example—have a government in which the chief executive is obliged to follow the wishes of the assembly. If Johnson had been convicted, perhaps such a system would have developed in the United States. In your opinion, would such an outcome be desirable or undesirable?

Further Reading

Jim Bishop. *The Day Lincoln Was Shot.* Harper & Row, 1955. A record of events that took place April 14, 1865.

Allen W. Trelease. *Reconstruction.* Harper & Row, 1971. An analysis for good readers.

Margaret Mitchell. *Gone with the Wind.* Macmillan, 1936. A novel of historical drama and romance depicting life during the Civil War and Reconstruction.

William H. Armstrong. *Sounder.* Harper & Row, 1969. Award-winning story of a sharecropper.

TEST YOURSELF

WRITE YOUR ANSWERS ON A SEPARATE SHEET OF PAPER.

Matching

Write the letter of the item that best matches each description below.

1. designed to trap President Johnson
2. Lincoln's assassin
3. Republican campaign tactic
4. tied ex-slaves to the land
5. Radical Republican leader
6. outlawed segregation in public places, but was declared unconstitutional
7. established segregation in the 1880s and 1890s
8. group formed to prevent blacks from voting
9. post-Reconstruction pattern of voting for Democrats
10. group to register and organize black Republicans

   a. "waving the bloody shirt"
   b. Loyal League
   c. Ku Klux Klan
   d. Jim Crow Laws
   e. sharecropping system
   f. John Wilkes Booth
   g. black codes
   h. Charles Sumner
   i. Freedmen's Bureau
   j. Civil Rights Act (1875)
   k. Solid South
   l. Tenure of Office Act

Classifying

Mark an item P if it applies to presidential reconstruction. Mark an item C if it applies to congressional (Radical) reconstruction.

1. ended in 1867
2. required southern states to ratify the 14th and 15th amendments
3. stressed leniency
4. was designed to punish the South
5. was based on the idea that no state had left the Union
6. gave former slaves citizenship and voting rights

UNIT 5 TEST

WRITE YOUR ANSWERS ON A SEPARATE SHEET OF PAPER.

Matching (20 points)
Match each person with a description from the list below.

1. Stephen F. Austin
2. Stephen A. Douglas
3. Eli Whitney
4. John Deere
5. John Brown
6. Harriet Beecher Stowe
7. Jefferson Davis
8. Robert E. Lee
9. Elizabeth Blackwell
10. Charles Sumner

a. supported Radical reconstruction
b. brought American settlers to Texas
c. wrote *Uncle Tom's Cabin*
d. tried to start a slave uprising
e. invented the mechanical reaper
f. helped popularize the Oregon Country
g. leader of the Army of Northern Virginia
h. invented the cotton gin
i. Confederate President
j. organized a training program for nurses during the Civil War
k. invented the steel plow
l. opposed Lincoln in a Senate campaign

Multiple Choice (20 points)
Write the letter of the answer that best completes each statement. There may be more than one correct answer.

1. The Mexican War
   a. was fought to win Texas independence from Mexico.
   b. was welcomed by most Americans and Mexicans.
   c. was fought to gain California.
   d. started with a skirmish on land claimed by both the United States and Mexico.
2. The Compromise of 1850
   a. was opposed by Henry Clay, Daniel Webster, and Stephen A. Douglas.
   b. appeased the North with a weak Fugitive Slave Law.
   c. permitted voters in New Mexico and Utah to allow or to ban slavery.
   d. banned the slave trade in Washington, D.C.
3. Stephen A. Douglas tried to win southern support for his candidacy by means of
   a. the Kansas-Nebraska Act.
   b. the Dred Scott decision.
   c. *Uncle Tom's Cabin.*
   d. the establishment of the Republican party.
4. Reconstruction of the South
   a. was opposed by secret societies such as the Ku Klux Klan.
   b. was planned jointly by President Lincoln and Congress before the end of the war.
   c. accomplished some reforms.
   d. was followed by segregation laws.

Time Line (20 points)
Match the letters on the time line with the events they stand for. Then write the name of the President in office at the time from the following list: Franklin Pierce, Andrew Johnson, Abraham Lincoln, Rutherford B. Hayes, John Tyler, Ulysses S. Grant, James Buchanan, Millard Fillmore, Zachary Taylor.

1. annexation of Texas
2. Radical reconstruction begins
3. Dred Scott decision
4. Mexican War
5. the President narrowly escapes removal from office
6. Kansas-Nebraska Act
7. California admitted as a free state
8. Civil War
9. remaining federal troops leave the South
10. Gadsden Purchase

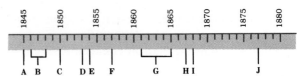

Essay Questions (40 points)
1. The Civil War has been called an "irrepressible conflict." Explain why you agree or disagree, and back your viewpoint with examples.
2. List some of the changes accomplished during the era of Reconstruction. Which were permanent, and which were temporary?

424

Unit Six

Industrial Transformation

Chapter 18

THE ERA OF THE RAILROADS

I n a famous story, Rip Van Winkle fell asleep one day and woke up 20 years later to find that he had missed the Revolutionary War. Suppose Rip had begun his nap in 1870. In 1870 the United States was still mainly a nation of farmers who tilled their own land, of independent craftsmen and women making goods in workshops, and of small entrepreneurs running their own businesses. It was a country made up of thousands of little economic islands—communities isolated from each other by great distances and differing interests. But in 20 years, life in America was transformed.

By 1890, the independent craft worker was gone, replaced by the unskilled immigrant factory worker. The small workshop was also gone, replaced by the massive and crowded industrial plant. Thousands of independent entrepreneurs had been displaced by a tiny group of powerful industrialists.

In the short space of 20 years, the country had become an industrial nation. Its vast expanses were bridged by fast-moving railroad trains and instantaneous messages over telegraph wires. The economic islands were isolated no longer, but tied together into a complex national economy. Rip might scratch his head and consider the results of all this change. Much in American life in 1890 would strike him as new and better. But he might also see that a whole way of life had disappeared, and with it something had been lost.

Sections in This Chapter
1. The Railroad Creates a National Economy
2. The Conquest of the Western Indians
3. The New Tycoons and the Corporation
4. Mass Production and Immigration
5. Social Darwinism and Its Critics

Opposite: The building of the railroads transformed the economy and bound Americans together with ribbons of steel track.

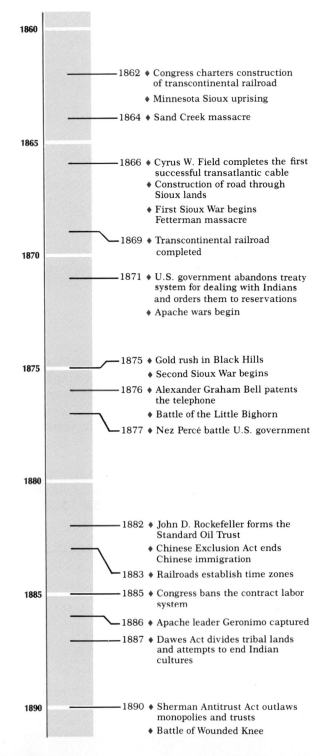

1860

1862 ◆ Congress charters construction of transcontinental railroad

◆ Minnesota Sioux uprising

1864 ◆ Sand Creek massacre

1865

1866 ◆ Cyrus W. Field completes the first successful transatlantic cable

◆ Construction of road through Sioux lands

◆ First Sioux War begins Fetterman massacre

1869 ◆ Transcontinental railroad completed

1870

1871 ◆ U.S. government abandons treaty system for dealing with Indians and orders them to reservations

◆ Apache wars begin

1875 ◆ Gold rush in Black Hills

◆ Second Sioux War begins

1876 ◆ Alexander Graham Bell patents the telephone

◆ Battle of the Little Bighorn

1877 ◆ Nez Percé battle U.S. government

1880

1882 ◆ John D. Rockefeller forms the Standard Oil Trust

◆ Chinese Exclusion Act ends Chinese immigration

1883 ◆ Railroads establish time zones

1885 ◆ Congress bans the contract labor system

1886 ◆ Apache leader Geronimo captured

1887 ◆ Dawes Act divides tribal lands and attempts to end Indian cultures

1890 ◆ Sherman Antitrust Act outlaws monopolies and trusts

◆ Battle of Wounded Knee

1. THE RAILROAD CREATES A NATIONAL ECONOMY

By the beginning of the Civil War, the major eastern cities of the United States were connected by railroad lines. The ride might be rocky and uncomfortable, but you could plan a trip by train from New York to Philadelphia, or from Boston to Washington, D.C. However, a train trip to the Pacific Coast was not possible. If you had consulted a railroad map in the 1860s, you would have seen an intricate pattern of railroad tracks covering the eastern portion of the United States. (See the upper map, page 430.) From Chicago westward, however, the map would have been almost blank. The Pacific Coast was physically isolated from the rest of the country. To get to California, or to send goods or messages, took months of rugged travel over mountains and across deserts or a voyage around Cape Horn.

The Government Backs the Railroads

During the Civil War the federal government saw the need for a fast route to the west. The railroad was the quickest way to move troops, ammunition, and medical supplies. In 1862, Congress decided to unify the nation by building a railway to the Pacific Coast. It therefore passed the Pacific Railway Act, which chartered two transcontinental railroad lines. The first, the Union Pacific, would build a rail system extending from Omaha, Nebraska, westward. The second, the Central Pacific, would build its half of the line eastward from Sacramento, California.

Such a massive undertaking took vast amounts of money. Thus the federal government assisted the companies by giving **subsidies** (grants of money) to their projects in the form of loans and land grants. Each railroad company was given loans of $16,000 for every mile of track laid on flat land, and $48,000 for each mile over mountainous terrain. Public land on both sides of the rail route was divided up in checkerboard fashion, and the government reserved alternate tracts, each 20 miles square, for the railroad companies' use. In return for this aid, the railroads agreed to transport federal troops and federal mail at reduced rates.

The Union Pacific builds a bridge over the Green River, near Citadel Rock, Wyoming, 1868.

Building the Tracks

Building the transcontinental lines was a difficult task performed by thousands of Union and Confederate veterans, former slaves, and immigrant workers, mainly Irish, German, Japanese, Chinese, and Mexican. Their work was difficult, slow, and dangerous. Most of it was heavy physical labor, done with only picks and shovels, in the terrible heat of the desert or in the freezing cold of mountain passes. These workers were hired by private construction firms, but the railroads often made extra profits by secretly controlling those companies.

On May 10, 1869, the tracks of the two lines met at Promontory Point, Utah. The Union Pacific had laid 1,086 miles of track; the Central Pacific, 689 miles. At the celebration a final golden spike was driven into the ground by a silver sledgehammer. The country was at last physically united! The trip across America would take one week. Nowadays, when you can cross the country by plane in a matter of hours, a journey that takes a week seems long. But in 1869, men and women marveled at this fast and direct route from coast to coast.

The Railroads Bring Settlers Westward

The success of the transcontinental rail line inspired other rail companies to undertake similar grand projects. By the 1890s there were four more lines extending from the Midwest to the Pacific Coast: the Southern Pacific; the Northern Pacific; the Great Northern; and the Atchison, Topeka & Santa Fe. These major routes, or **trunk lines**, were not the only railroads built in the period. Hundreds of **feeder lines**, connecting local towns and cities to the trunk lines, were also constructed.

Land grants from state and federal governments helped in the building of all these lines except the Great Northern. The railroads didn't use these land grants just to build track and stations. Instead, they sold the land to settlers and businesses. In this way, the railroads helped to populate the West. They made their land especially attractive to customers, often by offering low fares to people interested in purchasing western property. Some rail companies sent salesmen as far as Europe, equipped with elaborately illustrated brochures to convince people to emigrate to the American West. In one case, the Atchison,

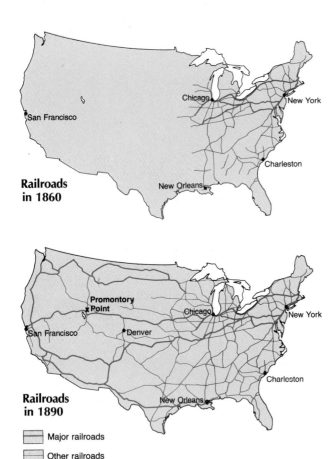

Railroads in 1860

Railroads in 1890

Major railroads

Other railroads

Abilene, Kansas. Here, in Abilene, the cattle were boarded on railroad cars of the Kansas Pacific Line and delivered to the East Coast. Between 1867 and 1872 almost 1.5 million steers arrived in Abilene.

The long drives to Abilene, and soon to other cattle towns along the railroad lines, were handled by a new type of worker: the **cowboy**. Many of the cowboys were blacks or Mexican Americans. The cowboys guided their herds of a few thousand steers the many miles over rough trails. Their dangerous jobs, and their wild celebrations once the herd was safely delivered, became legendary around the world.

Faster, Farther, and More Comfortable

That railroad map you might have consulted in the 1860s would have to have been repeatedly revised as the century progressed. From less than 35,000 miles of track laid in 1865, the amount increased to 52,000 miles in 1870, and 74,000 in 1875. But this increase was small compared to construction in the 1880s and 1890s when almost 5,000 miles of track were laid every year. By 1890 your map would have resembled a spider's web of 167,000 miles of track. (See the bottom map at left.)

The quality of railroad travel was improving as well. Once an unreliable, cramped, and halting means of travel, the railroad became safer, faster, and more comfortable by 1890. Technological innovations caused this improvement. For example, double sets of tracks were laid so that train traffic could go in two directions at once. Also, a uniform gauge was set so that cars could be transferred between railroad lines. Coal replaced wood as fuel, making for more powerful locomotives. George Westinghouse's invention of the air brake soon permitted all the cars of a train to be stopped together in an emergency.

There were other innovations which made railroad travel more efficient. One that you may take for granted today was the **standardization of time** in 1883. In that year, the United States (except Alaska) was divided into four time zones, differing from one another by one hour. Until these zones were established, railroad schedules had been confusing and contradictory, for each locality had made noon whatever time the sun was highest in the local sky. Passenger comfort im-

Topeka & Santa Fe Company persuaded 1,900 Mennonites to travel from Russia to settle in Kansas.

The Railroads Create the Cowboy

Roaming herds of wild longhorn cattle were a common sight on the ranges of the southwestern United States. These cattle were just the source of protein needed by the growing populations of the eastern cities. But, until the railroad, there was no way to transport the longhorns to the waiting markets of the East.

By the 1860s, an enterprising group of cattle dealers recognized the new opportunities that the railroad provided for profits. These men rounded up longhorn herds in southern Texas and drove them to the nearest large railroad depot for transportation east. The first of these experiments in cattle driving were failures. But by 1867, herds were successfully moving over the wild grasslands of Texas along the **Chisholm Trail**, which stretched all the way from San Antonio, Texas, to

proved further when George Pullman created a train with separate sleeping cars, dining car, and parlor cars. Despite all these improvements, there was still danger on the tracks, and terrible accidents were commonplace.

The Battle for Business

In their flurry of growth and improvement, the railroad companies seemed not to notice that there were not enough passengers or freight to go around. Companies often found themselves losing money and falling into debt. In areas where several companies competed for customers, **rate wars** developed. In a rate war the competing firms lowered prices, granted secret rebates (discounts) to businesses, bribed officials, and took other desperate actions to get passengers and freight. This kind of "cut-throat competition" was so bad that by 1879, 65 railroad lines had gone bankrupt. On the other hand, rates skyrocketed where there was no competition. The strange result was that sometimes it cost more to travel or ship goods a short distance in one area than to travel long distances in another.

The Communications Revolution

While the railroad was shrinking distances between people, innovations in communication were also bringing Americans closer together. During the Jacksonian era, the American inventor **Samuel F. B. Morse** and the English scientist Charles Wheatstone had created a system of communications along an electric wire called the telegraph. As the railroads expanded, the telegraph system expanded too, for rail companies quickly saw the advantage to them of speedy communication. The major telegraph company, Western Union, agreed to exchange telegraph service for free railroad shipment of telegraph equipment. Soon messages could be sent from New York to San Francisco in a matter of seconds. At the same time as telegraph wires began to cross the continent, communication between America and Europe also improved. In 1866, **Cyrus W. Field** laid the first successful transatlantic cable, a bundle of wires that carried messages across the Atlantic Ocean.

These communication developments were followed by another invention that would touch the lives of Americans everywhere. In 1876, **Alexander Graham Bell** patented his telephone, which he had invented while trying to design a machine to help deaf-mute people speak. At the spectacular 1876 Philadelphia Centennial Exposition, Bell exhibited his telephoning device as part of a competition among the technical wonders of the age. Bell won the gold medal. Four years later, 85 localities possessed telephone networks that linked their residents and businesses with each other. By 1900, telephone wires crisscrossed the nation, part of a communications revolution dominated by the American Telephone and Telegraph Company, which had been founded in 1885.

Even older forms of communication were improved during this era. After 1863, most city dwellers received their mail at home, instead of having to pick it up at a central post office. By the end of the 19th century, rural Americans were also getting home delivery in the countryside.

The growth and change in communications after the Civil War narrowed the distance between Americans: now they could visit each other, talk to each other, or write to each other more easily and cheaply than their parents could have ever imagined.

The Railroad's Impact on American Industry

The growth of the national network of railroads depended, of course, on the production of iron and steel. Without these metals, there could be no locomotives to pull the cars, or rails to carry the trains, or bridges to span the rivers and valleys. The tremendous construction needs of the railroads spurred iron and steel production and prompted the discovery of more efficient ways to make them.

The strength and durability of steel as a building material made it superior to the iron from which it was made. The girders supporting our modern buildings and bridges testify to steel's unique qualities. But in the early 19th century, steel was very expensive and was used only to make small objects. Two inventions made steel cheaper and better. Thus a steel era began.

First, in the 1850s, the English inventor Henry Bessemer, and William Kelly, an American, created a new technique that enabled steel workers to produce large quantities of steel at a fraction of the former cost. The **Bessemer converter** shot a stream of air into the molten iron and burned off

LIFE IN AMERICA

THE TRAIN BRINGS THE CIRCUS

Life in postwar, small-town America was busy, but often dull. There were no radios, stereos, televisions, or movie houses to help people pass the time. Then—right in the middle of the long, sleepy summer —it would happen! The advance wagon of the circus would come to town. The wagon displayed only a few of the many delights to be seen in this very town only two days hence. But the children would be

the impurities, leaving steel. A second technique, called the **open-hearth process**, was imported from Europe. The open-hearth process was slower than the Bessemer technique, but it improved the quality of the steel by allowing constant testing of the purity of the molten metal. Steel production quickly mushroomed, growing from 77,000 tons in 1870 to 1.39 million tons in 1880, to 4.79 million tons in 1890!

The railroads depended on the steel industry, and the steel industry depended upon the railroads. Both depended upon coal, the major source of energy for industry in the late 19th century. Railroad and steel companies quickly took over control of many of the country's coal mines in Pennsylvania, West Virginia, and the Midwest.

A National Economy

The transportation, communication, and technological revolutions bound the nation together. As the railroad map on page 430 shows, by 1890 Americans had become united by a complicated network of steel tracks and humming wires. What the map cannot show you however is the growing awareness Americans had of their unity and interdependence. The distances that separated markets from suppliers in different parts of the United States were bridged by the railroads. The

filled with eager anticipation of the exotic, unimaginably lavish and heroic splendors that awaited them. "Don't delay," the barker on the advance wagon would shout, "Hurry, Hurry, Hurry!"

The circus can trace its roots all the way back to the Circus Maximus of ancient Rome. But circuses as we know them go back to London in the 1770s when Philip Astley began a horseback-riding show with stunts and acrobatics.

Soon after the "golden spike" united the continent, Dan Castello's circus began its first transcontinental trip. Soon bigtoppers realized that railroads afforded them many advantages. Bigness became the measure of the shows, and railroads enabled them to grow to gigantic proportions.

At first, owners rented flat cars from railroad lines, but by the heyday of railroad circuses in the 1880s they had acquired their own. They modified the cars to suit their special needs (elephants, for example), lengthening the flat cars from the standard 40 feet to 72 feet.

A typical circus train had 25% stock cars, 50% flat cars, and 25% coach cars. Some trains carried 100 cars of wild beasts, dancing horses, red-uniformed bands, zany clowns, and death-defying trapeze artists—100 cars filled with thrills and chills for children of all ages. "Step right up and see the greatest show on Earth!"

great resources of the nation became available to all citizens for the first time. So successful was this shift from isolated economic communities to a national economy that today we take our interdependence for granted.

Try this simple test. Look around your home and consider where some everyday items come from. Your bicycle tires were made in Ohio. The oranges in the bowl on the dining-room table came from Florida. The paper you do your homework on is from Oregon. The ease with which goods and services flow from one part of the country to another separates our modern world from the world before the coming of the railroad.

SECTION 1 REVIEW

 Identify: subsidies, trunk lines, feeder lines, Chisholm Trail, cowboy, standardization of time, rate wars, Samuel F. B. Morse, Cyrus W. Field, Alexander Graham Bell, Bessemer converter, open-hearth process

Main Ideas

1. How was the construction of the transcontinental railroads financed?
2. How did the railroads help populate the West? How did they "create" the cowboy?
3. Describe how the growth of railroads helped the national economy.

THE GEOGRAPHIC SETTING

Slicing through the Colorado Plateau is the Grand Canyon, the world's largest canyon. This natural wonder is 280 miles long, 4 to 18 miles wide, and in places more than a mile deep.

THE INTERMONTANE REGION

The ceremonies marking the completion of the transcontinental railroad were held on a sagebrush desert just north of Great Salt Lake, on the edge of the Great Basin. Look at the map on the facing page. Locate the Great Basin between the Rocky Mountains and the Sierra Nevadas. To the northwest lies the Columbia Plateau; to the southeast is the Colorado Plateau. The Great Basin and the Columbia and Colorado plateaus form a unique and fascinating geographic area: the Intermontane Region. (Intermontane means "between the mountains.") Many Americans are unaware this region exists; yet it is more than 600 miles wide and 1,300 miles long.

Sparsely populated, the Intermontane Region is generally high in elevation; even the valleys of the Great Basin are 2,000 feet above sea level. Rainfall rarely exceeds 10 inches per year, and much of the region is desert.

The Great Basin

The Great Basin was named in 1843 by the explorer John C. Frémont, who discovered that the area, unlike any other in the United States, has no outlet to the sea. All rivers flow into lakes within the basin or evaporate because of the hot, dry climate. The Humboldt River, which many California goldseekers followed, flows west across Nevada, only to vanish at Humboldt Sink.

The Great Basin is like a bowl whose sides are rimmed by the Sierras and the Rockies. But the bottom of this huge bowl is not level. As you can see on the map, there are many low mountain ranges within the basin running north and south like a herd of caterpillars.

Although glaciers did not cover the Great Basin, the Ice Age was important in its geological history. Meltwater unable to reach the sea formed huge lakes in the basin. Great Salt Lake in Utah is a small remnant of ancient Lake Bonneville, whose shoreline is still visible, 1,000 feet high on the neighboring Wasatch Mountains.

The Great Basin is considered a "cool mountain and bolson (basin) desert." Though summers are hot, the high elevation causes cold winters. Annual rainfall is usually less than 10 inches and occurs on the western slopes of mountains. Heavy downpours on the steep slopes result in flooded streams, which carry eroded sand and gravel down to the basin floor. There rivers form shallow, temporary lakes called playas. Rapid evaporation soon leaves nothing but a layer of salt on the dry lake bed.

The Ute, Paiute, and Shoshone have lived in the Great Basin for thousands of years. The Mormons were the first and most successful of the recent settlers. They built Salt Lake City and Ogden and raised abundant crops using runoff from the Wasatch Mountains for irrigation. With the railroad came transportation for cash crops— cattle feed, sugar beets, and potatoes—and contact with outsiders who had to change from Union Pacific to Central Pacific trains at Ogden. Gold and silver mines at the western rim of the basin attracted others, who built Reno and Carson City. More recently, Las Vegas in the south has become a desert playground.

The Colorado Plateau

The Colorado Plateau forms much of Utah, Arizona, Colorado, and New Mexico (see Atlas Map 2). It was once a broad flat plain which was raised 10,000 feet high when the Rockies and other western ranges were formed about 70 million years ago. Since then, the Colorado River and its tributaries have been working at cutting down the plateau.

Rainfall averages only 10 inches a year, but the runoff cuts deep into the soft rock of the plateau, which is a desert and thus unprotected by plants. This erosion has created spectacular buttes, bridges, mesas, and canyons, including the Grand Canyon.

The layers of rock in the Grand Canyon reveal 3 billion years of geological history. Scientists have learned to read the exposed rock strata like a history book of the region. The Colorado River, which formed the Grand Canyon, flows 1,400 miles from the Rockies into the Gulf of California.

Vegetation and wildlife are sparse on the Colorado Plateau, and few people besides the Hopi, Navaho, Apache, and other Southwest Indians have made permanent homes here.

The Columbia Plateau

The Columbia Plateau includes parts of Idaho, Oregon, and Washington (see Atlas Map 2). It was formed by huge flows of lava gushing from cracks in the earth's surface. Part of the plateau, the Snake River Plain, is strewn with relatively fresh (2,000 years old) volcanic rubble. This stark, forbidding country has been used by astronauts training for moon landings. On the Idaho-Oregon border the Snake River has cut through the plateau to form Hells Canyon, which is deeper even than the Grand Canyon.

The wheatfields of eastern Washington end abruptly at the northern edge of the Columbia Plateau, where the rocky "scablands" are gouged by canyons and deep ripple marks. Here occurred a major geological catastrophe—the Spokane Floods. This event, which probably happened 18,000 to 20,000 years ago, was caused by meltwater from an Ice Age glacier. The meltwater formed Lake Missoula in western Montana, which was a large lake about half the size of present-day Lake Michigan. Scientists believe that the ice dam holding back the waters of Lake Missoula broke, sending ice, house-sized boulders, and a huge flood of water down onto the Columbia Plateau, grinding and washing away soil as it rushed to the Pacific! The Nez Percé and other Indians of the Columbia Plateau have legends of vast floods that may describe this deluge.

Today, the plateau is a sparsely settled agricultural and wilderness area. Most settlers going to Oregon bypassed this region on their way to the rich valleys near the Pacific. Hardy farmers and ranchers, some with ancestors from Europe's mountainous regions (such as Spain's Basque region), make a living on the plateau.

SPANISH WORDS FOR LANDFORMS

The Spanish explorers who first entered the Intermontane Region used familiar words to describe the landforms they saw. Here are five of them:

bolson pocket
canyon an old Spanish word for street
colorado red or reddish
mesa table
playa shoreline or beach

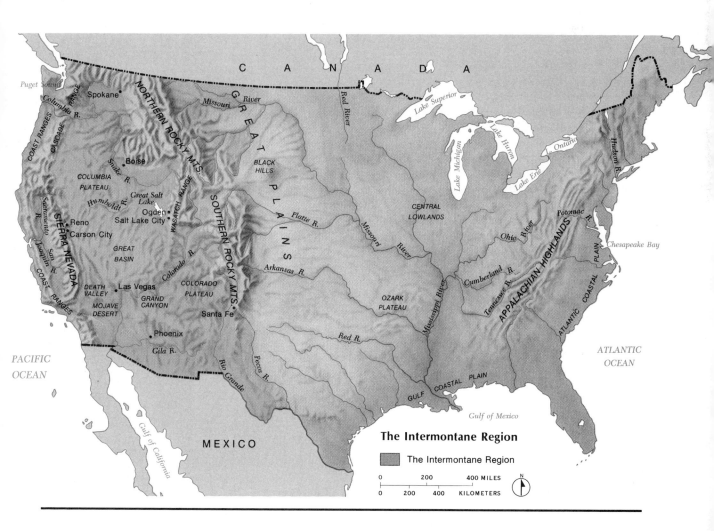

The Intermontane Region

■ The Intermontane Region

0 — 200 — 400 MILES
0 — 200 — 400 KILOMETERS

2. THE CONQUEST OF THE WESTERN INDIANS

There was one important obstacle to the expansion of the railroad and the migration of settlers that came with it: People already lived on the land that was being settled. At the beginning of the Civil War, some American Indians still roved nomadically over the western part of the United States. Unlike the eastern tribes, most of these Indians were not farmers, but hunters. It may be hard to imagine now, but about 225,000 Indians belonging to many different tribes peopled an area making up almost half of the continental United States. This vast and varied land, ranging from high mountains and plateaus to deserts and sweeping plains, was also the home of the buffalo. Millions of these great, lumbering beasts wandered about the plains. The buffalo was the source of food, clothing, and shelter for most of these Indians.

After the Civil War, these Indians were conquered. Their hunting grounds were transformed into territories and then states. The buffalo paths were crisscrossed by railroad tracks. New settlements of white families crowded out Indian and buffalo alike.

The Invasion of the Indians' America

The Indians were actually caught between two great migrations of people, one coming from the West Coast, the other from the settled lands to the east. From the Pacific Coast, miners moved eastward into the Rocky Mountains in search of gold and other precious metals. From the east, farmers came in search of new land to cultivate.

By law, the Indian lands were protected from these invaders, for the federal government had signed treaties with the western tribes. The government declared the Indian tribes to be independent nations within the borders of the United States. Thus, the treaties were like treaties made with foreign countries, honoring the tribes' territorial borders. But settlers pressed into these lands, ignoring government treaties and Indian rights. The American government could not, and would not, protect the Indians and their land.

The Indians of the plains and mountains knew well what the invasion of white settlers meant to their own race. They remembered what happened to the tribes of California when gold was discovered in that region in 1849. In that year and the years to follow, thousands of miners poured into California and destroyed whole Indian villages. In the ten years between 1850 and 1860, killings, disease, and other evils reduced the Indian population of California from 100,000 to 35,000!

The federal government did try to ease the problem between the Indian and the white people by confining the Indians on **reservations** scattered around the West. A reservation was a tract of land under the jurisdiction of the U.S. government. Indians on these reservations were wards (dependents) of the government, who received food and shelter as long as they remained confined. The lands chosen for the reservations were not good farmlands, and so were not expected to attract the envy of white farm families. As one Indian commissioner put it: "That these reservations will cause any considerable annoyance to the whites, we don't believe. They consist, for the most part, of ground unfitted for cultivation."

Many western Indians resisted both the reservation movement and the invasion of their hunting lands. The result was a quarter century of almost constant war. Presidents like Hayes sent the U.S. army to do battle with the tribes, yet Hayes did admit the justice of the Indian cause. "Many, if not most, of our Indian wars," Hayes said in 1877, "have had their origin in broken promises and acts of injustice on our part."

Indian Resistance in the 1860s

The first great resistance to white settlement in the West came from the Plains Indians, especially the Sioux of Minnesota and the Dakotas. As settlers poured into their hunting areas during the Civil War years, the Plains Indians complained to the federal government, but without success. In 1862, Minnesota Sioux led by Little Crow went to war, attacking frontier settlements and killing and capturing about 1,000 civilians. The war ended in 1863 when Little Crow was killed. The Sioux lands in Minnesota were confiscated and the tribe relocated.

In 1865, the U.S. government began construction of a wagon road to aid miners and travelers along the Bozeman Trail between Fort Laramie, Wyoming, and Virginia City, Montana. That road ran through the best hunting grounds of the Sioux.

As the government's road progressed, the buffalo fled. The Sioux, threatened by hunger, grew desperate. In 1866 they began a war, attacking wagon trains and ambushing an army force led by Captain W. J. Fetterman, killing all 82 troops.

The Americans could be equally brutal in their warfare against the Indian tribes. In 1864, a peaceful settlement of Cheyenne Indians was massacred at **Sand Creek**, Colorado, by Colorado militia. Here, Colonel J. M. Chivington, who had once been a Protestant minister, ordered the deaths of 300 Indian men, women, and children. "Kill and scalp all, big and little," Chivington ordered. "Nits make lice."

The Government Changes
Its Indian Policy

In 1867, to end the wars with the Plains Indians, the federal government decided to change its tactics. Battling the Sioux, Cheyenne, and other tribes was too costly in human life and in dollars. Instead the government began to negotiate with individual chiefs of the various Plains tribes. They tried to convince these chiefs that a move out of the path of the railroad was the best guarantee of peace and safety. Two reservation areas were marked off: one in the Black Hills region of Dakota Territory, the other, in what would become Oklahoma. All tribes who agreed to the relocation would have to give up the hunting life and become farmers. Making them farmers, it was believed, was the best way to turn them into good Americans.

Many chiefs agreed to the relocation. But many refused to be confined. The government had little patience with those who said no. In 1871, Congress announced that it would no longer deal with the tribes as independent nations. No treaties would be made again. Instead, the U.S. government asserted the right to order all Indians to reservations.

The Department of the Interior was responsible for Indian policy and for managing the reservations. Their officials were shockingly incompetent and corrupt. This made the difficult task of adjusting to reservation life even harder for the Indians. In addition, railroad construction crews and gold seekers continued to enter Indian lands. Soon, several tribes decided to fight rather than be governed by the United States. A new series of Indian wars began.

The Indian Wars of the 1870s and 1880s

Once again, the Sioux led the way in battling for independence. In 1874, gold was found in the Black Hills, and despite treaty guarantees, gold-hungry whites poured into Sioux territory. Sioux chiefs **Sitting Bull** and **Crazy Horse** declared war. The Indians' most stunning victory came in 1876, at the Little Bighorn River in Montana. Here, on June 25, 1876, the fiery and overconfident young lieutenant colonel, **George A. Custer**, led his 264 U.S. troops into battle against 2,500 Sioux and Cheyenne. Custer and his entire force were killed. Despite the victory at the **Battle of the Little Bighorn**, the Sioux surrendered to the United States in 1877, thus ending the second Sioux war.

Also in 1877, the once-peaceful Nez Percé [nez′ pérs′] Indians of Oregon and Idaho went to war when ordered to give up their land and settle on a reservation. Sensing that his cause was lost, their brilliant chief, **Chief Joseph**, made one last desperate attempt to save his people from a reservation. He took his remaining followers on a harrowing 1,700-mile trek to Canada. (See map below.) Only 30 miles from the border, the Nez Percé were captured and sent south again to Oklahoma. An exhausted and defeated Chief Joseph declared: "Hear me, my chiefs, I am tired;

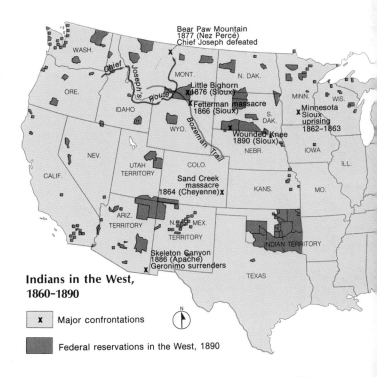

Indians in the West, 1860–1890

x Major confrontations

Federal reservations in the West, 1890

The Battle of the Little Bighorn, *by Amos Badheart Buffalo, a Sioux eyewitness*

my heart is sick and sad. From where the sun now stands, I will fight no more forever."

Perhaps the cleverest and the most determined of the mountain tribes were the Apaches of Arizona and New Mexico. These Apaches were led by **Geronimo**. For over ten years Geronimo's warriors evaded capture, although the U.S. army followed them doggedly. The Apaches did surrender, however, when the U.S. troops captured the women of the tribe. Geronimo remained free until 1886, when, at last, the army seized and imprisoned him. Some of the Apaches were moved to Oklahoma, but most remained on reservations in Arizona and New Mexico.

The Destruction of a Way of Life

The Indians were eventually defeated by the superior forces of the U.S. army. But, it was really the railroad that led to the Indians' downfall. The railroad transported the military troops as well as the farmers, ranchers, and other settlers who entered tribal lands. More importantly, the railroad brought the sportsmen and hunters who systematically destroyed the buffalo. By 1885, only 1,000 buffalo remained!

The death of the buffalo made the Plains Indian way of life impossible. The U.S. government

made it illegal. In 1887, Congress passed the **Dawes Act** to deal with the Indians now confined to reservations. The Dawes Act was designed to bring an end to tribal life and to convert Indians to white peoples' ways. The tribes themselves were dissolved, and tribal ownership of lands ended. Individual land ownership, a European-American concept, was enforced. Each married Indian male was allotted 160 acres to farm, while each adult single man or woman received 80 acres. The Dawes Act also made it possible for non-Indians to settle on land that was not allotted to individual Indians.

The efforts to turn the Plains Indians into farmers were often doomed to failure because the land granted them was poor and infertile. Most Plains Indians knew little about agriculture and farming techniques anyway. Too often, these hunters-turned-farmers were cheated out of their land by greedy whites.

Many of the Sioux found themselves facing a bleak future. The despair that some of them felt led to a tragic incident in 1890. Some of the Teton Sioux had turned to a messianic religion that seemed to offer hope. They awaited an Indian Messiah who would make the whites disappear and restore the land to the Indians. Part of the religion included dancing until the dancer fell into a trance; thus the religion became known as the Ghost Dance Religion. Many people in the Dakota area, both Indians and whites, feared that the Ghost Dance Religion might incite some of its followers to violence. Troops were sent to disarm a group of Indians who seemed to pose a threat. The Indians and troops were camped at a place called **Wounded Knee**. According to some accounts, one Indian shot at some soldiers, and a melee began. When it ended, 170 Sioux and 29 soldiers had been killed, and many others wounded.

The period around 1900 marks the low point of Indian life in the United States. The great loss of Indian land can be seen in the following figures: In 1873, at the beginning of the reservation policy, the Indian reservations contained about 150 million acres. In 1887, when the Dawes Act was passed, the amount had dropped to 138 million acres. By 1934, when the Dawes Act was repealed, the Indians had only 52 million acres.

The Indian population, which may have numbered in the millions at the time of Columbus, had declined to a low of 237,000. In 1900, it was believed that Indians were "vanishing Americans" and that the tribes would soon disappear as separate groups. But the Indians did not vanish. Their cultures remained alive, and their population rose dramatically in the 20th century, reaching 1.4 million by 1980.

SECTION 2 REVIEW

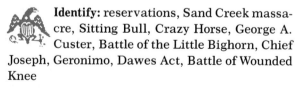

Identify: reservations, Sand Creek massacre, Sitting Bull, Crazy Horse, George A. Custer, Battle of the Little Bighorn, Chief Joseph, Geronimo, Dawes Act, Battle of Wounded Knee

Main Ideas
1. Why did the federal government establish reservations?
2. How did the government's Indian policy change in 1871?
3. Describe the efforts of the Sioux, the Nez Percé, and the Apaches to maintain their independence in the 1870s and 1880s.
4. How did the railroad, the destruction of the buffalo, and the Dawes Act affect the Plains Indians?

3. THE NEW TYCOONS AND THE CORPORATION

As you have seen, the building of a railroad network that stretched across the nation spurred the manufacture of other products, especially steel, iron, and coal. Thus the railroads produced a boom in the construction of new factories and the development of new manufacturing techniques. At the beginning of the Civil War, Britain, France, and Germany were the major manufacturing countries of the world. But, by the turn of the century, the United States had overtaken them all, producing nearly as many products in 1900 as those three countries combined. As you may imagine, this rapid rise of industry had a tremendous impact on American life.

Social and Physical Change

In order to see how business changed in the late 19th century, let's first go back in time to the pre–Civil War period. Imagine that it is 1860 and you own a business—a shoe company, perhaps. You probably live in a small town, and know most of the other residents there. You own a small workshop or factory near your home. You may have a partner, or it may be a family business. Either way, no more than a few people own the factory. Every morning you go to the workshop to supervise the people who work for you. There are not many shoemakers in the shop, and you probably know each of them by name and the names of their wives or husbands, sons, and daughters as well. You know how to make shoes yourself, so you can handle any problems in the shop personally. You might have disputes with your workers, of course, or conflicts with your neighbors, but everyone wants to work things out because you all live in the same town and care about the quality of life in that town.

The roar of the locomotive completely changed this way of life after the Civil War. The total number of workshops and factories greatly declined, yet their size and the amount they could produce grew rapidly. The steel industry, which you read about earlier, was typical of this change. The number of small forges producing steel declined as new, more efficient methods were adopted. These required larger factories, expensive equipment, and many additional workers. By the 1890s, only a few large companies now existed, where many small forges had been before.

Where an American worked, whom he or she worked with, and the relationship between the worker and the boss all changed as large factories replaced the small shops of the older era. Huge plants, located in large cities, employed hundreds or sometimes thousands of workers who did not know each other. The employer, too, was a stranger, often living in a different part of the country and rarely visiting the factory. The personal tie between employer and employee was thus broken, replaced by a system of hired supervisors who watched and directed the workers but who did not own the company.

The Rise of the Corporation

The huge new industries required great sums of money, or capital. There were factories to build, expensive and complicated equipment to buy and operate, large amounts of material and resources to obtain, and thousands of workers to pay. The individual proprietors (single owners) or the partners of the pre–Civil War period could not raise that kind of capital. Even the joint-stock companies, in use since the 17th century, could not satisfy the new demands of industrial growth. The joint-stock company allowed several investors to buy stock in a venture, but the company could not sell stock later on in order to raise additional badly needed capital. In its place a new form of business appeared: the **corporation**.

A corporation is created when three or more people apply for a charter, or license, from a state government. Such a charter permits these people to form a corporation and to sell shares of **stock** (certificates of partial ownership) in order to raise the capital needed for their business. In return for their money, the stockholders receive dividends, a portion of the company's profits. A corporation can raise much more capital by selling shares than an individual owner of a business could hope to save or borrow. As you recall, the railroads needed great sums of money for construction and equipment. Thus they became one of the first American businesses to form corporations and sell their stock on the open market.

The corporation is much different than the individually owned business. The law recognizes the corporation as an entity, or "person," apart from the people who own it. Therefore, a corporation can make its own contracts, buy and sell property, or take legal action in court. A corporation is a much safer way than a proprietorship or partnership for people to invest their money: If the business formed through a corporation fails, the stockholders can only lose what they originally invested. They are not responsible for the corporation's debts. This freedom from responsibility for a corporation's debts is called **limited liability**. Only the joint-stock company shared this advantage of limited liability.

Because of its ability to raise large sums of money and because of its limited liability, the corporation became the most common form of business organization for large companies after 1860. The table below shows how important corporations are in our economy today. Note that most businesses are sole proprietorships, but corporations earn most of the nation's money.

The Rise of the Trusts

The trend toward "bigness" in the size of factories was matched by the growth in the size of the companies that owned them. In the 1870s and 1880s, corporations in the same industries consolidated (merged), uniting to create larger, more powerful businesses. These mergers took over most of America's major industries of the period, including steel, oil, sugar refining, tobacco, leather, meat packing, and even the manufacturing of matches, nails, and bicycles. These consolidations usually had the same results: they limited or completely destroyed competition within their industry.

Consolidation took many forms. The railroads introduced one of the earliest, called the **pool**. Companies in a pool agreed to behave as if they were one large business. They divided up the market, agreed on rates and charges, and shared

U.S. BUSINESSES TODAY

	Number of businesses, 1980	Money received for goods and services, 1980
Sole proprietorships	11.4 million (78%)	$375 billion (9%)
Partnerships	1.1 million (8%)	$160 billion (4%)
Corporations	2.1 million (14%)	$3,606 billion (87%)

their profits. There were problems with the pool as a form of merger, however. Member companies often violated their pool agreements. Because the courts considered pools to be against the public interest, there was no way the agreements could be legally enforced. Furthermore, in 1887 the government took steps against the pools. In that year, the Interstate Commerce Act declared that pools were illegal. Soon after, the pool as a form of merger disappeared.

The **trust** became the most common type of business consolidation in the 1880s and early 1890s. In a trust, the stockholders of several companies turned over their shares to "trustees" in return for certificates entitling them to dividend payments. The trustees then held a majority of the member companies' stocks, and so controlled the member companies. The trustees could thus run several large firms as if they were one giant company. Operations could be coordinated, with individual plants making only one part of the industry's product instead of competing with each other in the production of the same items. The owners could save money because the trusts could make deals more easily than individual companies with suppliers of raw materials, with railroads that transported the products, and with banks for loans. Finally, through the creation of trusts, corporations in the same industry replaced cut-throat competition with cooperation.

What was to the advantage of the trusts, however, was not necessarily in the best interest of the ordinary American. Through consolidation, a trust could destroy smaller businesses. It could raise or lower prices as it needed to, while the smaller company could not. The results of trusts was **monopoly**: complete control of a whole industry. A monopoly is able to raise its prices as high as people will pay, because it has no competitors who might try to sell more goods by offering lower prices. As long as the monopoly doesn't raise its prices so high that people find substitutes for its product, it can charge as much as it wants to and make enormous profits. Small businesses, consumers, and workers were often hurt by the ability of trusts to control industries.

As you can imagine, many Americans called for laws to control the trusts. In 1890, Congress passed the **Sherman Antitrust Act** which outlawed all monopolies and banned "every contract, combination in the form of trust or otherwise, or conspiracy in restraint of trade." This law was not enforced until the early 1900s, when trusts were banned. However, other forms of merger continued, and the word "trust" continued to be applied to businesses that gained a giant share of their markets.

The New Tycoons: The Industrial Capitalists

With the rise of the corporation and the trust, a new type of business leader emerged—the **industrial capitalist**. Often called "captains of industry" or "new tycoons," these self-made men possessed wealth and power unheard of before their time. These tycoons came to control the major industries of the nation, and much of American life as well. They won their power by using their talents to bring new technology and organizing methods to industry. But they were also condemned for their ruthlessness and their exploitation of workers and business rivals. Two of the most famous of these industrialists were John D. Rockefeller and Andrew Carnegie.

John D. Rockefeller was born on a New York farm in 1839. He made his early fortune before the Civil War, selling produce to the government. During the war, Rockefeller began to invest in the new oil-refining industry. By the end of the war, he was actively involved in the oil business.

Rockefeller was a bold and adventurous oilman, always ready to try new production techniques. By 1870, his Standard Oil Company of Cleveland was a major firm, and Rockefeller himself controlled about 40% of the oil industry. He let little stand in his way: he cut prices to eliminate competitors, made secret deals with railroads, bribed officials and politicians, and won numerous rate wars. Even fellow tycoon Andrew Carnegie was struck by Rockefeller's behavior, calling him "Rockafellow."

By 1879, John D. Rockefeller had taken over most of his competitors and controlled a full 90% of the industry. Soon, oil prices soared. In 1882 Rockefeller capped his success by forming the Standard Oil Trust, a combination of 39 major oil companies that together controlled the production, refining, and marketing of oil in the United States. It was Standard Oil that led people to associate "trust" with "monopoly." By 1890, this brash farm boy from New York State was worth $80 million, an astonishing sum at that time.

Andrew Carnegie came to the United States in 1848, a boy of 12. The young Scot began his career working in a cotton mill for $1.20 a week. By the age of 20, however, Carnegie was earning $50,000 a year. Careful saving and wise investments had made him a prosperous young man. Carnegie entered the iron and steel industry just as it was expanding, and by 1880 he had become a leading producer.

Like Rockefeller, Carnegie was able to organize production and to take advantage of the newest technology. He also took care to surround himself with the most talented assistants he could recruit. Carnegie was as ruthless as "Rockafellow," but he also had a disarming wit. By 1890, he had won a series of rate wars and dominated the steel industry.

At the turn of the century Carnegie decided to retire from business and devote the rest of his life to philanthropy (using his money for public benefit). J. P. Morgan, the financier, bought the Carnegie Steel Company and soon organized a massive trust called United States Steel. United States Steel included all Carnegie's vast holdings plus ten of its largest competitors.

The New Tycoons: The Financial Capitalists

American industries continued to expand in the late 19th century, and as they grew, even more capital was needed to finance their needs. **Financial capitalists**, investment bankers like **J. P. Morgan**, became influential in the running of many corporations because of the capital they provided. By the 1890s, many of the great businesses were actually controlled by these bankers.

Morgan and other bankers devised new means of business consolidation. One technique was the **holding company**. In a holding company a new corporation is chartered, and stocks are issued. With the money collected from the sale of these stocks, the directors of the new company buy up controlling shares in a company actually engaged in producing goods or services.

Another method developed by the financial capitalists was the **interlocking directorate**, in which the same group of directors took control of several companies. The companies remained legally separate but operated as one large business, able to favor some suppliers and customers, and to freeze out competing businesses.

Cycles of Boom and Bust

American business and industry did not grow steadily in the late 19th century. As you saw in the case of the railroads, sometimes production outdistanced public demand. This overproduction often led to lost revenues and even bankruptcy. Also, in the hope of making big profits quickly, businesses gambled on risky deals over stocks, contracts, or equipment. Sometimes they made fortunes when the deals worked out, but just as often they ruined their companies. The post–Civil War period was, therefore, a time of boom and bust, with years of business expansion followed by years of depression. The early 1870s were a period of growth, followed by a depression beginning in 1873. The late 1870s and early 1880s were again years of business expansion, but depression hit in 1884. The economy boomed again in the early 1890s, only to end in 1893 in the most serious depression of the century.

This late-19th-century roller-coaster ride showed how much American life had changed since the Civil War. Businesses rose and fell, affecting investors who had put money into the firms, consumers who relied on their goods and services, and workers whose wages depended on their operation. A person could easily feel the impact of decisions made in distant parts of the nation. What Morgan did in New York, or Carnegie in Pittsburgh, or Rockefeller in Cleveland, affected the entire nation and its economy.

SECTION 3 REVIEW

Identify: corporation, stock, limited liability, pool, trust, monopoly, Sherman Antitrust Act, industrial capitalist, John D. Rockefeller, Andrew Carnegie, financial capitalist, J. P. Morgan, holding company, interlocking directorate

Main Ideas
1. Describe pre–Civil War business and how it changed with the rise of the corporation.
2. List two advantages and two disadvantages of trusts and monopolies.
3. Why did the U.S. economy experience marked periods of boom and bust during the late 19th century? How did these business cycles affect Americans?

4. MASS PRODUCTION AND IMMIGRATION

In 1892 there were 4,000 millionaires living in the United States. Almost all of them were "new tycoons" who had made their fortunes in the business world of the late 19th century. At the same time, the number of nonfarm workers had grown to about 14 million, of whom about 6 million people—men, women, and children—were employed in manufacturing and construction. By 1900, 18 million people made up America's nonagricultural work force. What was the impact of the rise of the corporation and the trust, of boom and bust, on these millions of workers? Who were these people who produced the nation's goods and services?

Manufacturing Before the Civil War

Let us go back to our pre–Civil War shoe factory, but this time to see things from a different point of view. Imagine that you are a shoemaker, or "cordwainer," as the trade was called then. Most likely you live in that small town we described earlier and work in a workshop with several other cordwainers. In the shop, too, are one or two young apprentices who are learning the trade by working under your direction. As a skilled shoemaker, you know every aspect of making a shoe, for you, too, once studied the craft as an apprentice. Each person in the shop creates his or her own product from start to finish, beginning with cutting out the leather pattern and ending with sewing on the soles. In the course of the day, you might stop for a moment to take in the view from the window by your workbench, or pause to sip a drink for refreshment. The time it takes you to make a pair of shoes and the way you work depends on your skill. You have a day-to-day relationship with your employer, and when problems or grievances come up, you and your employer settle them directly.

The New World of Mass Production

That kind of work style was no longer characteristic of American life after the rise of the railroads. Now—in 1880—instead of a shop, you go to a newly built factory filled with noise and crowded with hundreds of workers. You no longer make a pair of shoes from start to finish. In this new world, you perform one small task over and over and over. You receive a partially completed shoe from one worker, add your part to its construction, and pass it on to the next worker. This **division of labor** often requires you to tend a machine. You no longer determine the time it will take for you to do your job, for the machine forces you to do your job at a specific speed. Usually, your monotonous and limited tasks must be performed at a furious pace.

This drastic change in the pattern of work, called **mass production**, was the basis for the mushrooming of manufacture during the late 19th century. This pattern could first be seen in the textile mills of New England before the Civil War. It was unique to them in 1850; by the 1880s, it was common to all industry. In every industry, production processes became standardized, and every part became identical and interchangeable with other parts. The worker was not permitted to use his or her own judgment or to make decisions because each function was planned ahead of time. The way a person worked depended on the parts used and the speed of the machine. Factory supervisors now made decisions that the individual artisan had once made. The supervisors were themselves only a part of the process and had to answer to the owners regularly.

Work in the new factory was often tiring, and the hours were long. Men, women, and even very young children frequently started work before the sun rose and finished well after it had set. A work day could last 10 to 15 hours, even longer. A work week did not mean the five days we think of today, but six and sometimes seven days. Working conditions were often dangerous, for there were no safeguards on the machines and no compensation for accidents or deaths on the job. Wages averaged about $1.50 a day. Luckily, the cost of living during the period dropped so that workers found they could buy more with their limited wages as time went by. However, a person could not count on a steady income. The boom-and-bust nature of the economy often threw millions of people out of work. The depressions of 1873 and 1893 hit working people especially hard. Many spent years looking for work, or only found temporary jobs.

Shoemakers and other skilled workers lost their respected positions in society as their crafts were replaced by machines. Craftsmen and women could no longer deal with their employers on an equal basis because their skills were no longer in demand. At the same time, a new generation of unskilled workers entered the work force. Eventually, as you will see, both skilled and unskilled workers banded together to demand better working conditions and wages.

The New Immigration

Mass production demanded unskilled workers, and the need for them increased as business expanded. Most native-born Americans still lived on farms, however. American industry solved its labor problem by recruiting a new work force of landless immigrants.

Between 1877 and 1890, more than 6.3 million people came to the United States. From 1878, when 138,000 immigrants arrived, the flow increased steadily. By 1892, 789,000 men, women, and children reached our shores each year. The cramped steamships the immigrants traveled in usually arrived in New York harbor, just as the ships carrying indentured servants to colonial

Italian immigrants on shipboard. Photograph by Lewis Hine, early 1900s

America had earlier done. For those who arrived after 1886, the newly erected Statue of Liberty seemed to wave a welcome to America.

Who were these new Americans, and where did they come from? The vast majority were poor and unskilled young men, ranging from 15 to 40 years old. All were anxious to find work in their new country. Most settled in the cities of New England and the Middle Atlantic states, for this was the heart of America's industrial economy, and here jobs were to be found. By the turn of the century, over half the people in this part of the country were either immigrants or the children of immigrants.

Before the Civil War, immigrants had come mainly from northern and western Europe—from England, Ireland, Scotland, Germany, and Scandinavia. These "**old immigrants**," as they were later called, came to a nation of farmers. Thus, many of these immigrants followed the movement westward, migrating to the Midwest and the Great Plains, where they settled on the land. Others, particularly the Irish who had fled from the terrible potato famine of the 1840s, became our country's first unskilled industrial workers. They made up a large part of the early work force in the new textile industry of New England.

In contrast, most of the immigrants of the post–Civil War era found a United States rapidly transforming itself into an industrial nation. As late as 1883, 85% of all immigrants still came from northern and western Europe, but, for a variety of economic and political reasons, an ever increasing number now started their journey in eastern and southern Europe or in Asia. By 1896, more than half of all immigrants were coming from these areas. They were called the "**new immigrants**."

The cities of the Northeast soon had growing populations of people speaking languages many Americans had never heard before: Italian, Yiddish, Hungarian, Polish, and Czech. There were new languages to be heard on the West Coast as well, for here Japanese and Chinese immigrants landed, seeking work. Many immigrants endured the hard trip across the Atlantic or Pacific oceans in order to settle permanently in the United States. Others only wanted to earn enough money to buy a farm in their homeland. Thus thousands of immigrants returned to Europe and Asia after several years of work in America.

Unfortunately, the new immigrants were not always as welcome as the beaming Statue of Liberty seemed to suggest. Like the Irish immigrants before them, the Italians, Poles, Jews, and Hungarians often received angry and hostile responses from native-born Americans. Part of this attitude, called **nativism**, was simply the kind of response that people everywhere have toward anything new. Thus the varied languages, religions, and customs of the immigrants, which appeared both strange and exotic to the established Americans, provoked nativist sentiment. But much of the hostility had an economic basis. There was harsh competition for jobs, particularly during the periods of depression. Many immigrant workers were impoverished and willing to accept lower wages than the native-born American workers were accustomed to receiving. Employers frequently took advantage of this willingness to work cheaply. By pitting the new workers against the old, they were able to pay everyone less.

Some Immigration Restriction Laws Are Passed

To try to protect their jobs and wages, American workers urged the federal government to stop or cut down the number of people entering the country. The employers, however, pressed for the opposite, urging the government to allow even more immigrants into the United States. In the end, three limited immigration restriction laws were passed in the 1880s. These laws did little to lessen the flow of potentially cheap labor into the country.

The immigration laws reflected some of the confusion Americans felt about the waves of immigrants entering the United States in the late 19th century. For example, an 1885 law put an end to one of the most exploitative forms of immigration, the **contract labor** system. Contract laborers were brought to the United States under a prearranged work contract with an employer, often a railroad construction firm. These immigrants, usually Chinese or Italian, found themselves working under the very worst conditions and for the lowest of wages. If they complained, their employers could have them sent back to their own countries. They were not free to look for other jobs, no matter how bad conditions might get. One 1882 law prevented insane people, crim-

FROM THE ARCHIVES

The Statue of Liberty

The mammoth copper statue in New York harbor is officially named "Liberty Enlightening the World." Erected in 1886, it was a gift from the French people to honor a century of American independence. In 1902, Emma Lazarus' poem, "The New Colossus" was inscribed in bronze on its base.

Not like the brazen giant of Greek fame,
With conquering limbs astride from land to land
Here at our sea-washed sunset gates shall stand
A mighty woman with a torch, whose flame
Is the imprisoned lightning, and her name
Mother of Exiles. From her beacon-hand
Glows world-wide welcome; her mild eyes command
The air-bridged harbour that twin cities frame.
"Keep, ancient lands, your storied pomp!"
  cries she
With silent lips. "Give me your tired, your poor,
Your huddled masses yearning to breathe free,
The wretched refuse of your teeming shore.
Send these, the homeless, the tempest-tost to me,
I lift my lamp beside the golden door!"

inals, paupers, and people suffering from certain diseases from immigrating. But the most serious law passed reflected the lengths to which nativism and racism could go. In 1882, the **Chinese Exclusion Act** banned the immigration of Chinese workers into the United States.

SECTION 4 REVIEW

 Identify: division of labor, mass production, old immigrants, new immigrants, nativism, contract labor, Chinese Exclusion Act

Main Ideas

1. List three ways the world of work changed from the pre–Civil War to the post–Civil War period.
2. Why did employers encourage immigration after the Civil War? How did the flow of immigration change between 1870 and 1890?
3. Explain some of the reasons for the rise of nativism. List the three immigration restriction laws passed in the 1880s.

CHAPTER 18 REVIEW

Key Terms

Explain the meaning of each of the following terms:

subsidies	corporation
trunk lines	stock
feeder lines	limited liability
Chisholm Trail	pool
cowboy	trust
standardization of time	monopoly
	Sherman Antitrust Act
rate wars	industrial capitalist
Bessemer converter	financial capitalist
open-hearth process	holding company
reservations	interlocking directorate
Sand Creek massacre	division of labor
	mass production
Battle of the Little Bighorn	old immigrants
	new immigrants
Dawes Act	nativism
Battle of Wounded Knee	contract labor
	Chinese Exclusion Act

Reviewing the Main Ideas

Section 1

1. Describe the effects of the railroad on the development of the West.
2. How did the growth of the railroads influence the steel and communications industries?
3. List specific improvements in transportation, communication, and other technology in the postwar period.

Section 2

1. Why did the U.S. government establish reservations in the West after the Civil War?
2. Why did the Plains Indians battle the U.S. government in the postwar era? Describe the efforts of the Sioux, Nez Percé, and Apache to keep their independence.
3. How did the railroad and the policies of the U.S. government combine to destroy the Plains Indians' way of life?

Section 3

1. List three differences between pre– and post–Civil War business.
2. Why did large businesses tend to be corporations?
3. Why did Americans fear trusts and monopolies?
4. Why did the economy experience marked periods of boom and bust in the late 19th century?

Section 4

1. How did the world of work change after the Civil War?
2. Why did employers encourage immigration in the period 1870–1890? How did the sources of immigration change in that period?
3. What were the causes of nativism? How did the immigration laws of the 1880s reflect mixed feelings toward immigrants?

Special History Skills:

Making Graphs

Make a graph that illustrates the growth in miles of railroad track in the United States between 1865 and 1890. Then make a graph that shows the increase in U.S. steel production between 1870 and 1890. All the information you will need is in this chapter. Next, use the figures on this chart to make a graph:

PIG IRON PRODUCTION, 1870–1900

Year	Tons
1870	1,481,850
1880	3,413,150
1890	8,190,670
1900	12,272,210

Other Skill Activities

1. **Write a story**

   Write the Rip Van Winkle story of someone who fell asleep in 1870 and woke in 1890. What changes would Rip see? What would surprise him the most, least, and not at all?

2. **You can't take it with you**

   Both Carnegie and Rockefeller were philanthropists. Find out what good causes received their wealth.

3. **Recent immigrants**

   In the 1970s and 1980s, many Southeast Asians, Cubans, and Haitians immigrated here. Find out how they were received. Were they greeted by nativism? Discuss.

Thinking Critically

1. Is it a good idea for the government to help industries financially as it did in the case of the railroads? Why or why not?
2. Were the U.S. policies toward the Plains Indians in the postwar era fair? Why or why not?
3. Could the U.S. government have conquered the Indians without trying to make them abandon their traditional ways of life? Discuss.
4. Defend or reject: "The jobs and industries created by men like Carnegie and Rockefeller justify their ruthless business practices."
5. Should the United States permit anyone to immigrate? Why or why not?

Further Reading

Horatio Alger. *Brave and Bold, Luck and Pluck,* and *Risen from the Ranks* are only three of Alger's more than 120 novels on the theme of how to go from rags to riches—a favorite topic in the post–Civil War era. Millions were sold; your family or local library may still have a few of these best-sellers from the 1870s and 1880s. Some of his stories have been reprinted in paperback.

Paul Hastings. *Railroads: An International History.* Praeger Publishers, 1972. A short history of railroads around the world and the people who built, financed, and were affected by them.

Robert M. Utley. *Frontier Regulars: The United States Army and the Indian, 1866–1891.* Macmillan, 1973. An excellent history for advanced students.

S. L. A. Marshall. *Crimsoned Prairie.* Charles Scribner's Sons, 1972. A well-written military history, also for advanced students.

John S. Garraty. *The New Commonwealth, 1877–1890.* Harper & Row, 1968. A history that seeks to explain the disappearance of individualism and the rise of the corporation in all phases of American life.

Joseph J. Thorndike, Jr. *The Very Rich.* American Heritage Co., 1976. A fascinating review of rich families.

TEST YOURSELF

WRITE YOUR ANSWERS ON A SEPARATE SHEET OF PAPER.

True or False

Read each statement below. Mark T if the statement is true, F if it is false. Rewrite the italicized words in all false statements to make them true.

1. The country would not have grown as rapidly as it did without *railroads*.
2. The Bessemer converter led to the *invention of the telegraph*.
3. The law treats a corporation as *an individual*.
4. *Limited liability* means that a person can only lose the amount of money he or she invests in a company.
5. Andrew Carnegie and John D. Rockefeller were *financial capitalists*.
6. The first concern of industrial capitalists was *the welfare of their employees*.
7. Immigrants from all over the world were *warmly welcomed* to the United States between 1870 and 1890.
8. Nativism means that *a person is a native of the United States*.
9. The development of *railroads* led to the development of large-scale circuses.
10. Investment bankers like *J. P. Morgan* ran many corporations because of the capital they provided.

Listing

1. List five items which contributed to the growth of the railroads.
2. List two new industries that developed because of the railroads.
3. List three new or improved forms of communication in the period 1860–1890.

Interpreting a Photograph

Look closely at the photograph on page 444. Try to imagine the immigrant family's situation. Write a paragraph which describes or explains the life that they will probably lead in the United States. Use the terms: opportunity, nativism, division of labor, mass production, and new immigrants.

Chapter 19   1870–1890

POLITICS IN THE GILDED AGE

Politics was the great American pastime in the late 19th century. Americans flocked to mass rallies, cheering and chanting for their favorite candidates. On election day voters went to the polls in droves. Their feelings about politics resembled what you might feel at a football or baseball game today when your home team makes a touchdown or hits a home run, and the crowd around you goes wild. A century ago, Americans got that same kind of excitement from politics.

Like the ball game, however, politics in that era was basically a spectator sport. The campaign was exciting, yet it didn't seem to make much difference who won. In the post–Civil War years, just as in the age of Andrew Jackson, politicians avoided the serious issues and pressing concerns of most Americans. In the title of their 1873 novel, *The Gilded Age*, humorists Mark Twain and Charles Dudley Warner gave a name to the last decades of the 19th century. The Gilded Age was just as they portrayed it in their book: a time of extravagance, irresponsibility, and outrageous political behavior.

In this chapter you will see the workings of Gilded Age politics and the motives of its politicians. You will see how battles over government hiring policies led to civil service laws, one of the limited reforms the era produced. When you have read the chapter, you will also see why third parties arose to challenge the major parties on important social and economic issues.

Sections in This Chapter
1. Corruption in Postwar Politics
2. From the Spoils System to the Civil Service
3. To Reform or Not to Reform

Opposite: Exhibit in the Smithsonian Institution in Washington, D.C., displays the elegant fixtures of Stohlman's Confectionary Shop (1865–1957), where Gilded Age Americans ate cake and ice cream.

1. CORRUPTION IN POSTWAR POLITICS

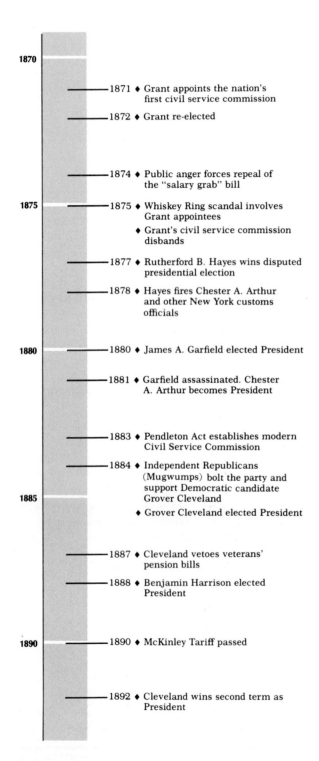

1870

1871 ♦ Grant appoints the nation's first civil service commission

1872 ♦ Grant re-elected

1874 ♦ Public anger forces repeal of the "salary grab" bill

1875

1875 ♦ Whiskey Ring scandal involves Grant appointees
♦ Grant's civil service commission disbands

1877 ♦ Rutherford B. Hayes wins disputed presidential election

1878 ♦ Hayes fires Chester A. Arthur and other New York customs officials

1880

1880 ♦ James A. Garfield elected President

1881 ♦ Garfield assassinated. Chester A. Arthur becomes President

1883 ♦ Pendleton Act establishes modern Civil Service Commission

1884 ♦ Independent Republicans (Mugwumps) bolt the party and support Democratic candidate Grover Cleveland
♦ Grover Cleveland elected President

1885

1887 ♦ Cleveland vetoes veterans' pension bills

1888 ♦ Benjamin Harrison elected President

1890

1890 ♦ McKinley Tariff passed

1892 ♦ Cleveland wins second term as President

As you learned in the last chapter, the new industrial age was changing American life, creating problems as well as benefits for millions of Americans. Never before, and never again, would such a high percentage of voters participate in the electoral process as during the Gilded Age. Yet no serious issues were resolved at the polls.

One major reason for the emptiness of American politics was the close balance between the Democratic and Republican parties. These parties almost evenly divided the nation's votes between them. Thus elections were always very close, and a few extra votes made the difference between victory and defeat. Neither party wanted to lose voters by taking stands on controversial issues. So they stressed the candidate's personality, praising their own nominee and slinging mud at their opponents. For example, in the 1884 presidential contest between Republican James G. Blaine and Democrat Grover Cleveland, the Democrats publicized letters showing Blaine's role in corrupt deals while he was Speaker of the House. Blaine's men, in turn, pointed out that Cleveland had fathered a child out of wedlock. They encouraged a popular chant that went:

> Ma! Ma! where's my pa?
> Gone to the White House,
> Ha! Ha! Ha!

Supporters of the Republican Party

Although both major parties avoided major issues, each party drew its supporters from particular geographical, social, and political groupings.

Four main groups supported the Republicans: (1) the farmers of the North and West, where antislavery sentiment had been strong before the Civil War, (2) veterans of the Union Army, (3) the freed black males of the South, and (4) the wealthy industrial capitalists of the Northeast. As you can imagine, nearly any social or political decision that pleased one of these groups would anger another. So the Republican party took great care to stress the one element that united them all: their loyalty to the Union during the Civil War. At every election, Republican candidates "waved the bloody shirt," reminding the voters that the Democratic party represented their old enemy, the South, in the Civil War. Almost every Republican presidential candidate during this era had been an officer in the Union Army. Voters were urged to "Vote the way you shot."

Supporters of the Democratic Party

Democrats had a firm base in the rural "Solid South" after 1877. They also attracted many of the bankers and merchants of the northern states. Perhaps the most important keys to the Democrats' ability to win national office, however, were the powerful Democratic **machines** in large northern cities. A machine is an organized group which controls the activities of a political party.

Like Tammany Hall and the "Albany Regency" of Andrew Jackson's era (see Chapter 12), these political machines could make or break a politician or a political platform. In the Gilded Age, the machines in northern cities won the support of urban immigrants in exchange for helping them survive in a rough new environment.

The Bosses of the "Millionaires Club"

The unity of both major parties was threatened by the existence of competing factions (competing alliances within the party). You might think that these factions reflected the conflicting interests of farmers, businessmen, southerners, and urban immigrants. But they did not. Party factions were based on the personal rivalries between political leaders, or **bosses**. These bosses were usually senators, for the Senate attracted the richest and most powerful politicians in the Gilded Age. It was nicknamed the "Millionaires Club." To the bosses, politics was a game played with money, influence, and the hopes of voters. The bosses played the game for a single end: to further their personal ambitions.

The Republican party was divided into two powerful factions, the Stalwarts and the Half-Breeds. The **Stalwarts** were controlled by **Senator Roscoe Conkling**, an elegant, wealthy gentleman from New York. Conkling was once described as "a great fighter, inspired more by his hates than his loves." The man Conkling hated most was not a Democrat, but a fellow Republican, **Senator James G. Blaine** of Maine. Blaine, who led the **Half-Breeds**, was one of the most popular political figures of his generation. Although the Half-Breeds claimed to support political reform, the real difference between the two factions was not the party platform. It was the struggle between Blaine and Conkling for leadership of the party. A third faction, the **Independent Republicans**, rejected both of these political bosses, but they had little influence in the party.

Senators like Blaine and Conkling dominated Gilded Age politics. Because of their intense rivalry, however, they had difficulty winning majorities for their favorites at party conventions. Even when a boss himself managed to get the presidential nomination, the rival faction would often fail to support him in the general election, giving victory to the Democratic candidate. As a result, a "compromise candidate" was often nominated. This nominee was usually a man the voters had never heard of or knew little about. For example, Rutherford B. Hayes was called the "Great Unknown" when he ran for office in 1876. Other such compromise candidates were James A. Garfield and Benjamin Harrison. Once in office these compromise candidates were usually honest but weak Presidents. They could not break the power of the "Millionaires Club."

Corruption Becomes a Way of Life in Government

Why did people enter politics in the Gilded Age? One of the major reasons was to become wealthy. Politics became a type of "business." Political office could mean a giant step up the social ladder, bringing money, power, and the flattering attention of social and business leaders. Businesses, corporations, and individuals offered handsome rewards to officeholders who voted their way. As one senator is reported to have explained the formula to a group of businessmen:

You send us to Congress. We pass laws under the operation of which you make money; . . . and out of your profits you further contribute to our campaign fund, to send us back again, to pass more laws to enable you to make more money.

This kind of bribery was commonplace, and both parties profited from it. Between 1866 and 1872, for instance, the Union Pacific Railroad spent about $400,000 on bribes to politicians in *both* parties. That was only a modest sum compared to the Central Pacific's payoffs of $500,000 doled out each year between 1875 and 1885.

On election day, each party pointed an accusing finger at the other, screaming "Corruption!" Henry Adams, grandson of President John Quincy Adams, and a great political commentator of the Gilded Age, wrote this judgment on the era:

One might search the whole list of Congress, Judiciary, and Executive during the twenty-five years 1870 to 1895 and find little but damaged reputations. The period was poor in purpose and barren in results.

If you compare cases of government corruption today with the Gilded Age shenanigans, you will see a striking difference. Today, when a newspaper uncovers a political scandal, it is presented as shocking news and as something illegal, performed behind closed doors. But Gilded Age corruption was often very public, reflecting the attitude that "everybody's doing it." Washington newspapers ran advertisements by office seekers who boldly sought government positions—at competitive prices! One such ad read:

"A Group of Vultures Waiting for the Storm to Blow Over. Let Us Prey." T. Nast view of Tweed Ring, 1871.

Scandals in the Grant Administration

The widespread corruption of President Grant's administration set the tone for the Gilded Age. When Grant became President in 1869, he entered office as a highly respected public figure. He was deeply honored as the man who had helped save the Union. But Grant was inexperienced and unsophisticated in the complicated world of politics. Although he was personally honest, he appointed dishonest men to important posts. These men easily deceived him and used their political offices to amass great fortunes.

In the **Crédit Mobilier scandal** of 1872, for example, a New York newspaper discovered that Vice-President Schuyler Colfax, James A. Garfield, and other highly placed Republicans had received shares in the Crédit Mobilier [kred′it mō bil yā′] construction company in return for helping the company avoid investigation of large stock swindles and fraudulent government contracts.

The remaining years of Grant's term brought a seemingly endless series of scandals. Grant's third Secretary of the Treasury uncovered more corruption. He found a widespread conspiracy among whiskey distillers and politicians to evade payment of liquor taxes. One of the key participants in this **"Whiskey Ring"** was the President's private secretary! Before Grant's years in office ended, his Secretary of War, of the Navy, and of the Interior had all been caught in bribery and corruption scandals.

When Ulysses S. Grant left office, his reputation was shattered. A sympathetic Henry Adams could only shake his head and write: "The progress of evolution from President Washington to President Grant, was alone evidence to upset Darwin." Politics, in short, was growing far worse, rather than better, in the United States.

Corruption also ran through the halls of Congress. Every election contained some element of bribery, ballot-box stuffing, or conspiracy. On the last day of the 1872 congressional session, both houses of Congress voted themselves a 50% pay raise. The public, however, rebelled against this "salary grab." Popular reaction was so strong that Congress was forced to withdraw the salary bill at the beginning of the next session.

The Tweed Ring of New York City

The "business of politics" descended down the ladder of government to state and city politics. The most famous case involved the **"Tweed Ring"** of New York City. Under the leadership of William Marcy Tweed, the city's Democratic machine stole between 50 and 200 million dollars in the 1860s and 1870s. The "Ring" took money from people seeking city jobs. They collected bribes from companies bidding on contracts to perform profitable city services. They also juggled the city's accounts to steal millions of dollars.

Political favors did not always take the form of money. Today, city and state governments often provide aid to poor or needy citizens through social services like welfare, unemployment insurance, and public housing. But in the Gilded Age, men like Boss Tweed gained much of their power by providing immigrants with jobs, housing, and financial aid at a time when public services did not exist.

Tweed arranged for new immigrants to become citizens, and thus voters, very quickly. On election day, he was confident that they would cast their ballots for the Democratic party. City workers helped the machine win elections because they knew that their jobs depended on the machine's election victories.

The Tweed Ring had its counterparts in other cities, such as those led by "King" James McManes in Philadelphia, Ed Butler in St. Louis, and Abraham Ruef in San Francisco. These party machines, like the Tweed Ring, gained widespread public support because they provided needed services to the voters and provided jobs for city workers. Urban corruption was thus a complicated matter. Although machine politics meant personal wealth for many individual politicians, it also provided vital assistance to impoverished city residents.

The search for personal gain in politics echoed the practices of the "new tycoons" you studied in the last chapter. The behavior of industrial and financial leaders served as a model for politicians. Like the tycoons, the bosses combined genuine organizational talents with cold-blooded and often illegal tactics. One standard for success in the Gilded Age was the accumulation of wealth and power. When personal gain was the only goal, the result was often corruption and scandal.

FROM THE ARCHIVES

The Gilded Age

The following is an excerpt from The Gilded Age, *by Mark Twain and Charles Dudley Warner. The postwar era takes its name from this 1873 novel.*

Mr. O'Riley furnished shingle nails to the new Court House at three thousand dollars a keg, and eighteen gross of 60-cent thermometers at fifteen hundred dollars a dozen. . . . When they were paid, Mr. O'Riley's admirers gave him a solitaire diamond pin of the size of a filbert [nut], in imitation of the liberality of Mr. Weed's friends, and then Mr. O'Riley retired from active service and amused himself with buying real estate at enormous figures and holding it in other people's names.

By and by the newspapers came out with exposures and called Weed and O'Riley "thieves,"— whereupon the people rose as one man (voting repeatedly) and elected the two gentlemen to their proper theater of action, the New York legislature.

The newspapers clamored, and the courts proceeded to try the new legislators for their small irregularities. Our admirable jury system enabled the persecuted ex-officials to secure a jury of nine gentlemen from a neighboring asylum and three graduates from Sing-Sing [a prison], and presently they walked forth with characters vindicated. The legislature was called upon to spew them forth—a thing which the legislature declined to do. It was like asking children to repudiate their own father.

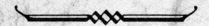

SECTION 1 REVIEW

Identify: machines, bosses, Stalwarts, Roscoe Conkling, James G. Blaine, Half-Breeds, Independent Republicans, Crédit Mobilier scandal, Whiskey Ring, Tweed Ring

Main Ideas

1. Why did the two major parties avoid serious issues during election campaigns in the Gilded Age?
2. Describe the main groups that supported the Republican and Democratic parties.
3. Name the two major factions splitting the Republican party. Who were their leaders?
4. What was one of the main reasons people entered politics in the Gilded Age? Give one example each of corruption in the executive branch, the Congress, and in city government.

2. FROM THE SPOILS SYSTEM TO THE CIVIL SERVICE

"To the victor belong the spoils," said William Marcy in the 1820s. But even Marcy would have been amazed at the spoils system of the Gilded Age. The spoils system, or **patronage system,** allowed politicians to offer voters and campaign workers government jobs in return for their help in winning the election. You can get some idea of the power of patronage during this era if you consider the massive growth in federal government jobs. At the end of the Civil War, 53,000 people worked for the federal government. By 1884, there were 131,000. Seven years later the number had grown to 166,000. The spoils system helped create a large and inefficient federal government. And, of course, every time an administration changed in Washington, most of the federal employees changed too!

The spoils system appealed to many people, despite the harm it did to good government. You, too, might have been a spoils seeker in the 1870s. If you had contributed money, or time and energy, to the campaign of a successful candidate, you would expect your rewards. One of the richest centers for political rewards was the Customs House in New York City. There were so many federal jobs under the roof of that one building, that the Collector of the Customs House often controlled New York State politics.

If you were lucky enough to be a New York spoils seeker, you would journey to the Customs House with hundreds of other hopefuls. You would stand in a long line that wound through the building's corridors. Everyone in that line was waiting to meet the Collector himself. When your turn came, you would boast to the Collector of all you had done to ensure his election and his party's continuing success. With a little luck, and some good personal connections, you might win a post. So spoils seeking was, in its way, a long, difficult, and exhausting process for both the office seeker and the man in power. In 1881, the new President James A. Garfield summed it up. Overwhelmed by spoils seekers, he cried out in exasperation: "My God! What is there in this place that a man should ever want to get into it!"

Grant and Hayes Try to Reform the Spoils System

Reformers looked at the waste and corruption of the spoils system and demanded that patronage be replaced by a merit system. A **merit system** would judge applicants for government jobs on their merits, or abilities, rather than on their political loyalties.

Even the scandal-torn Grant administration had attempted some reform in the civil service. The **civil service** is the branch of government service responsible for the routine maintenance and running of the government. It does not make government policy, but does handle a wide range of necessary operations, such as tax collection, surveying, and public health. In 1871, President Grant created a civil service commission to administer competitive tests for federal jobs. Four years later the commission head resigned, saying he could do nothing in the corrupt atmosphere that surrounded him. The commission was allowed to go out of business.

In 1872, a group of reform-minded independent Republicans organized the Liberal-Republican party to oppose Grant's re-election. The Democratic party joined them in a coalition that ran the reformer Horace Greeley for President. Greeley supporters chanted the slogan: "Turn the rascals out!" But Grant won an easy re-election.

As you may recall from Chapter 17, President Rutherford B. Hayes took office in 1877 after a disputed election that a special commission decided along party lines. Despite this somewhat clouded start, Hayes also made efforts to reform the spoils system. He appointed political independents to major cabinet posts. One of these men was a highly respected reformer named **Carl Schurz.** Schurz reorganized his Department of the Interior along the lines of a merit system. President Hayes also issued an executive order barring federal employees from participating actively in party politics. Unfortunately, this order was ignored.

Next, Hayes shocked politicians everywhere by ordering an investigation into the practices of the New York Customs House. The collector in 1876 was **Chester A. Arthur**, a man notorious for demanding campaign contributions from his employees. Arthur was also a man who loved luxury at other people's expense. He once redecorated the interior of the Customs House in red, white, and blue, with stars and stripes. To pay for this patriotic design, Arthur deducted 10% from every employee's salary.

The President's special investigating commission found many cases of corruption and inefficiency in Arthur's mini-kingdom. Yet when Hayes dismissed Chester Arthur and other officials, he angered the powerful Stalwart faction boss, Senator Roscoe Conkling, who took the move as a personal challenge to his power over New York politics. In a fury, Conkling took his revenge. He persuaded the Senate to reject every replacement Hayes recommended to the vacant posts. The President was forced to be patient, to name man after man, until the Senate grew tired and approved new officeholders. The battle cost him the support of a united party, however, and a weary Hayes refused to run for re-election in 1880.

The Election of 1880

With Hayes out of the presidential picture, the Republicans had to find a new candidate in 1880. Who would satisfy both Stalwarts and Half-Breeds? The answer was former Civil War general **James A. Garfield**. Garfield was an independent, but won the nomination with support from Blaine's Half-Breeds. To keep Conkling's Stalwarts happy, one of their people had to win the vice-presidential slot. Who should the choice be but Chester A. Arthur! The Democrats ran another former Union general, Winfield Scott Hancock. The campaign that followed was typical of the Gilded Age, with a heavy focus on the personalities of the candidates. James A. Garfield carried the day by a narrow margin of 10,000 votes out of 9 million cast.

Assassination—and Reform

Like Grant, Garfield was an honest man with a good record in the military and in Congress. But he was an insecure and indecisive President who bowed easily to pressure from supporters of the spoils system. His appointments favored the Half-Breeds, and Blaine became Secretary of State. These appointments enraged Conkling and his many supporters.

The fury and frustration of Conkling's Stalwarts climaxed on July 2, 1881. On that day, Charles J. Guiteau, a jobless and mentally disturbed Stalwart, stepped up to Garfield and shot the President twice in the back. As Garfield fell,

Rutherford B. Hayes (1822–1893)

IN OFFICE: 1877–1881

Republican from Ohio. The dispute over the election of 1876 was settled by a special commission appointed by Congress. Hayes was declared the President in return for the Republican promise to withdraw federal troops from the South and to provide money for southern internal improvements. Hayes was an advocate of government reform; he was opposed to political patronage and established the merit system in several departments.

James A. Garfield (1831–1881)

IN OFFICE: 1881

Republican from Ohio. Garfield, who had served in both the House and Senate, was a moderate Republican who wished to promote government reforms. He was fatally shot by a disappointed office seeker shortly after his inauguration. His death did much to convince people of the necessity of making a positive effort toward major civil service reform.

Guiteau exclaimed: "I am a Stalwart, and Arthur is President now!" Garfield survived for 80 days, but died on September 19, 1881.

The assassination shocked the nation. That one act of violence seemed to expose all the evils of the spoils system. A stunned public realized how far the political system had sunk when a President was faced with the ultimatum, "An office— or your life." Public pressure mounted for civil service reform. Senator George H. Pendleton, an Ohio Democrat, introduced a bill to create a merit system.

The Pendleton bill became the focus of intense and bitter debate. Many senators fought the merit system because it would end the spoils system as the source of their political power. Others opposed the new system because they feared it would create a permanent elite class of officeholders. The uneducated and poor would be driven from their jobs. Like the Jacksonians of the 1820s, these senators insisted that the common sense of the "common man" was as good a basis for office as a formal education.

Despite this coalition of selfish and unselfish opposition, the Pendleton bill passed in 1883. To the surprise of everyone who knew him from his Customs House days, President Arthur came out strongly in favor of the bill. The shock of Garfield's assassination seemed to have changed the old spoilsman's outlook, much to the sorrow of the Republican bosses.

How did the new system work? Under the **Pendleton Act**, the civil service law, the President appointed a Civil Service Commission of three people from both parties. The commission made a list of **"classified jobs"** that would be filled on the basis of competitive examinations. The number of classified jobs was small at first, only about 14,000 out of some 117,000 appointive positions. But the law allowed Presidents to add to the classified list. Each President took advantage of this provision by extending "classified" status to jobs held by his own appointees. In this way he prevented his successors from replacing them with their own favorites. So the number of government jobs under the merit system tended to increase with each new administration. By 1900 almost 100,000 positions were classified. The Pendleton Act also forbade the collection of campaign contributions from federal employees.

Despite the civil service law, politicians found ways to keep the spoils system alive. The Civil Service Commission usually accepted several candidates for each classified position and then left the final appointment to department heads. This allowed them to choose candidates from their own faction or party. Also, most high-paying jobs remained under the spoils system for several decades. In spite of its early weaknesses, however, the Pendleton Act became the foundation on which American Presidents were able to build the modern civil service system.

There was one unexpected consequence of the Pendelton Act of 1883. Under the old spoils system, office seekers and government employees had financed the campaigns of their political patrons. The rise of the merit system meant a sharp decline in these campaign funds. Politicians, seeking money for re-election or election, were forced to tap other sources. They came to rely even more than before on business leaders and industrialists, whose contributions depended on getting political favors in return. Business influence on legislation thus increased dramatically after 1883.

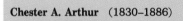
Chester A. Arthur   (1830–1886)

IN OFFICE: 1881–1885

Republican from New York. Although a powerful supporter of the spoils system before becoming President, Arthur reversed his position after Garfield's assassination. During his administration, Congress passed the first civil service act, the Pendleton Act (1883), which set up a merit system for the employment of federal workers.

SECTION 2 REVIEW

 Identify: patronage system, merit system, civil service, Carl Schurz, Chester A. Arthur, James A. Garfield, Pendleton Act, classified jobs

Main Ideas

1. How did Grant try to reform the civil service? What were the results of his efforts?
2. List one accomplishment and one failure of Rutherford B. Hayes' attempt to reform the civil service.
3. What effect did the Garfield assassination have on civil service reform?
4. Why did some political leaders oppose the Pendleton Act? Describe its effects on officeholding and elections.

LIFE IN AMERICA

NINETEENTH-CENTURY MEDICINE

On the morning of July 2, 1881, as he walked through the Washington, D.C., train station, President Garfield was shot in the back. Eighty days later he died as a result of receiving the best medical treatment the country had to offer.

The Practice of Bleeding

Medical standards in the last half of the 19th century had not progressed much in the previous hundred years. In 1799 George Washington caught a cold which turned to pneumonia. Following the practice of the day, his doctor "bled" him, that is, drew out some of his blood.

For centuries doctors had seen that persons short of breath could be helped by being bled. Such treatment was sometimes useful to someone with heart problems because it would lower the blood pressure. But the practice of bleeding also deprived patients of oxygen and probably harmed more people than it helped.

Lack of Anesthesia

Anesthesia was unavailable before 1846, and little surgery was done. Broken bones were set with only a liberal dose of alcohol to kill the pain. Often these crude methods failed, and amputation became necessary.

Ignorant Doctors and Dangerous Drugs

Throughout most of the 19th century, a person's best hope for recovery was his or her own body's defenses and not a doctor's help. "Heroic practice" was the term used to describe the treatment of the day—and heroic it was. For example, doctors routinely prescribed strong and dangerous drugs. Garfield was given morphine to help him sleep and quinine to prevent malaria. Opium was widely pre-scribed for common sprains and other simple ailments with hardly a thought about the dangers of addiction. In the 50 years between 1840 and 1890, opium prescribed by doctors increased more than 20 times to 500,000 pounds a year.

Alcohol, too, was used as an all-purpose cure-all. Even babies were given ½ to 2 teaspoons every three hours. Doctors commonly prescribed mercury, strychnine, and arsenic (deadly poisons!) to treat various symptoms. They did not know the causes of most of the ills they treated.

The Cause of Garfield's Death

In the 1850s, Louis Pasteur, a French scientist, discovered that microorganisms cause disease. In 1867 Joseph Lister, an Englishman, introduced the revolutionary idea of antiseptic surgery. Until then, doctors with unclean hands or instruments often caused their patients' wounds to become infected. This, and not the gunshot wound, was the real cause of President Garfield's death. Dr. D. W. Bliss infected the President as he probed for the bullet. He then compounded his mistake by sending Garfield to bed.

The infection and the lack of activity proved fatal. The lack of activity caused Garfield to lose 80 pounds in 11 weeks and reduced his body's ability to fight the infection. His lungs grew weak, and small parts even collapsed. Eventually this led to pneumonia. Medical historians today believe that the President may finally have died from a blood clot or a heart attack precipitated by his lack of activity.

Garfield's assassin portrayed as an armed robber

3. TO REFORM OR NOT TO REFORM

Who were the reformers who backed the reform of the civil service? They tended to be educated and wealthy Republicans, members of the old American elite before the rise of the "new tycoons." Twice during the Gilded Age the members of this Independent faction had bolted the Republican party: in 1872, in opposition to Grant's re-election, and again in 1884, when the party chose Half-Breed boss James G. Blaine for the presidency. Blaine represented everything these reformers hated, for he had risen to power on the back of the spoils system.

In 1884, therefore, the reformers marched out of the Republican convention hall. They announced that they would support any decent candidate that the Democrats might nominate. Newspapers labeled these Republican reformers **"Mugwumps,"*** but the Republican party called them traitors. The leaders of the Mugwumps were distinguished men like Carl Schurz, the former Secretary of the Interior, E. L. Godkin, the editor of the *Nation* magazine, and Charles Francis Adams, son of John Quincy Adams and father of the Henry Adams quoted earlier.

The Democrats, seeing their chance to capture the White House for the first time since Buchanan won in 1856, nominated a reform governor of New York, **Grover Cleveland**. True to their pledge, the Mugwumps threw their support behind the Democratic nominee. Cleveland had a reputation as a strong and honest administrator who had shown the courage to defy Tammany Hall by insisting on reform during his term as governor.

The Election of 1884
The 1884 campaign became particularly bitter and loud. Each candidate's past was raked over for fraud, flaws, and major or minor mistakes. Cleveland's illegitimate child was a campaign issue. But Democrats countered with charges of corruption on Blaine's part. They exposed secret deals that Blaine had made during his term as

*****Mugwumps** From an Algonquin word meaning "chief." The term was used in the 19th century to mock people who acted in a self-important manner.

Speaker of the House. "Blaine, Blaine, James G. Blaine, the continental liar from the state of Maine," chanted the marchers in Democratic parades. The only positive aspect of this campaign was the end of the "bloody shirt" as an effective strategy. Neither candidate had served in the military during the Civil War.

Grover Cleveland won the election by a nose, capturing the key state of New York by only 1,149 votes. Most political odds-makers had expected Blaine to carry New York, since he was popular with the Irish Catholic voters. But, at the last moment of the campaign, a Protestant minister visiting Blaine in New York denounced the Democratic party as the party of "Rum, Romanism, and Rebellion." This slur managed to imply in only four words that immigrants drank too much, that the Catholic Church was evil, and that the Civil War was the fault of the Democrats! Blaine should have immediately condemned the statement, but he did not. The Democrats lost no time in spreading the news. On election day, Irish Catholic voters deserted Blaine in large numbers and helped Grover Cleveland become the first Democratic President in 28 years.

The Mugwump Reformers
The Independent Republicans wanted social reform, but like the "new tycoons," they believed that government should stay out of economic matters. The Mugwumps were often **Social Darwinists,** who thought that in the "struggle for existence," only the "fittest" survived and that government should not help the "unfit." This was an interpretation of the English scientist Charles Darwin's theory of evolution, published in 1859.

Reform to a Mugwump meant the creation of a disinterested (impartial) government, run by an educated elite. That educated elite meant, of course, people like themselves. Corruption disturbed the Mugwump because it was immoral. But even worse, it created a government acting in the interests of one particular social group. The reformers saw such favoritism through corruption as a form of government intervention in society.

You may be surprised by the limited view of reform held by the Mugwumps, since today we have large-scale government programs like Social Security and Medicare, and many agencies

Gilded Age elections as sport: Below is the 1884 "baseball game." Above right: Cleveland and Harrison on a seesaw. Above left: Cleveland wins his "fish."

that regulate business and economic activities. But the Republican reformers were not champions of social and economic reform; their target was corruption.

Mugwumps believed in the importance of states' rights and limited government. They believed that life in America would run smoothly and justly as long as the government did not intervene. But other people disagreed about the value of such a **laissez faire*** approach. They saw the problems that the industrial revolution had brought to Americans. Many farmers, workers, small businessmen and women, black Americans, women, and immigrants felt victimized by the Gilded Age social and economic structure. Many of these people wanted laws that would improve their lives and would restrict unfair business practices. Men and women from these ranks called for reform in currency, banking, and credit. They demanded changes in business organizations, improvements in the work environment, action on public health and safety, and guarantees of their civil rights.

In Chapters 20 and 21 you will read more about these demands and the movements that arose to fight for them. The Mugwumps' opposition to active government involvement separated them from the great mass of American voters. The Mugwump struggle for impartial and honest government was a noble ideal, but it did not feed or clothe people. In the Gilded Age, the poor wanted practical help. This was one of the reasons why corrupt political machines received popular support despite their outrageous behavior. For these and other reasons, Gilded Age laissez-faire reformers usually lost elections.

The Laissez-Faire President
The President who best symbolized laissez-faire government was the reformers' hero, Grover Cleveland. Cleveland was perhaps the most courageous President of the era. He faced down the attempts of various groups to use the government for selfish purposes. He set a new record for presidential vetoes in his war against special-interest legislation. For example, he vetoed over 200 special pension bills for Civil War veterans because they were designed to fill the pockets of

***laissez faire** [les′ā fer′] the belief that government should not interfere with business activity. From a French phrase, meaning "to let one do."

many people who did not qualify under the existing laws. All in all, Cleveland vetoed almost two-thirds of the bills that crossed his desk.

Grover Cleveland believed above all in limiting government intervention. He opposed bills to assist the poor as well as the powerful. He took back over 80 million acres of public land that railroads, timber companies, and rich ranchers had held illegally for years. He also vetoed a bill that would have supplied money to needy Texas farmers to purchase grain seed after a severe drought.

Cleveland's attack on the tariff reflected his attitude about government involvement in the economy. During the Civil War, as after the War of 1812, Congress had passed high tariffs to protect American industry. Industrialists wished these protective tariff rates to continue in peacetime. Many farmers and workers also supported this **protectionist** stance. Other Americans, however, complained that high tariffs kept the price of manufactured products artificially high. As consumers, they opposed the tariff. Mugwumps opposed the tariff because they believed that it was special-interest legislation and did not conform to their laissez-faire views.

The argument over the tariff continued for many years. Protectionists set up a powerful lobby headquarters in Washington and paid large sums of money to senators and congressmen who supported their views. By the time Cleveland

Grover Cleveland (1837–1908)

IN OFFICE: 1885–1889, 1893–1897

Democrat from New York. Cleveland was the first Democrat to be elected President after the Civil War and the only President to serve nonconsecutive terms in office. During his first term, the Interstate Commerce Act was passed (1887). During his second term, the nation was faced with a severe economic depression (1893–1897), which Cleveland was unable to combat successfully.

entered the White House, the high tariff was earning the government about $100 million more than it spent each year.

Cleveland approached the tariff problem as he did all economic and social welfare legislation. He felt the tariff was a major reason behind greedy legislation like the pension "grabs" he had vetoed. The excess money in the treasury, he said, encouraged waste and corruption. It was the tariff, he said, that gave the trusts their great power over American life. His call for a lower tariff became the major issue of the 1888 presidential campaign. Cleveland supporters warned him that his outspoken position might cost him the election. The President replied: "What is the use of being elected or re-elected unless you stand for something?"

Harrison Replaces Cleveland

Grover Cleveland paid dearly for his wish to "stand for something." He lost the election to Republican **Benjamin Harrison**, grandson of "Old Tippecanoe." Harrison's protectionist stand brought huge amounts of corporation money into his campaign. When the votes were counted, Cleveland had carried the popular vote by over 95,000. But Harrison's victory in New York gave him the electoral-college majority.

Harrison proved to be another honest but ineffective President, unable to control the sharks in

Harrison tries to keep out greedy supporters. Cleveland says: "Aha! Now you know how it is yourself, Ben!"

his own party. He allowed many of Grover Cleveland's reforms to be undone by Congress. Civil War pensions mushroomed, and in 1890 the **McKinley Tariff** was passed, raising duties on imported goods even higher. Cleveland's political career did not end in 1888, however. Only four years later he turned the tables on Harrison and returned to the White House as President. Such were the unpredictable fates of politicians and of political issues in the Gilded Age.

Benjamin Harrison (1833–1901)

IN OFFICE: 1889–1893

Republican from Indiana. President Harrison exercised little personal leadership and allowed the party leaders to control the administration and its policies. Pensions to war veterans were increased, the tariff was raised (1890), and the Sherman Silver Purchase Act was passed (1890). The Sherman Antitrust Act was also passed (1890), but not enforced. Six new states were added to the Union: North and South Dakota, Montana, Washington, Idaho, and Wyoming. Benjamin Harrison was the grandson of President William Henry Harrison.

SECTION 3 REVIEW

Identify: Mugwumps, Grover Cleveland, Social Darwinists, laissez faire, protectionists, Benjamin Harrison, McKinley Tariff

Main Ideas

1. What were the Mugwumps' views on reform and laissez-faire government? Why did they fail to win many voters to their views?
2. Why did the Democrats win the election of 1884? Why did this election mark the end of the "bloody shirt" as a campaign issue?
3. What actions did Cleveland take in support of his views on laissez-faire government?
4. Which groups supported a high tariff, and which groups opposed it?
5. How did the actions of President Benjamin Harrison differ from those of Cleveland?

461

CHAPTER 19 REVIEW

Key Terms
Explain the meaning of each of the following terms:

machines
bosses
Stalwarts
Half-Breeds
Independent Republicans
Crédit Mobilier scandal
Whiskey Ring
Tweed Ring
patronage system

merit system
civil service
Pendleton Act
classified jobs
Mugwumps
Social Darwinists
laissez faire
protectionists
McKinley Tariff

Reviewing the Main Ideas
Section 1
1. Why did politics during the Gilded Age center on personalities and not issues?
2. Which groups supported the Republicans, and which groups supported the Democrats?
3. What were the two major Republican factions? How did they differ, and who were their leaders?
4. Why did machines become powerful in northern cities during the Gilded Age?

Section 2
1. Why was reform of the civil service slow during the Grant and Hayes administrations?
2. What event brought public pressure for civil service reform?
3. Why did some senators oppose the Pendleton Act? What effects did the Pendleton Act have on the civil service and on elections?

Section 3
1. What were the views of the Mugwumps on reform and laissez-faire government? Why did they fail to win many supporters to their views?
2. What actions did Grover Cleveland take in defense of his views on laissez-faire government?
3. Why did some Americans support a high tariff? Why did others oppose it?
4. How did Benjamin Harrison's administration differ from that of Grover Cleveland?

Special History Skills:
Interpreting Political Cartoons
Thomas Nast was one of America's most famous political cartoonists. His cartoons in *Harper's Weekly* against Boss Tweed, such as the one below and on page 452, attracted widespread attention and led to Tweed's downfall—and also to Tweed's identification after he escaped prison!

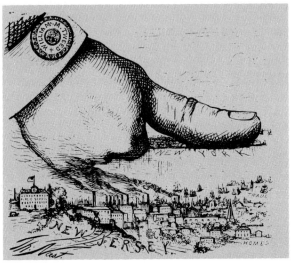

"Under the Thumb," by Thomas Nast, 1871

1. Look at the cartoon and then answer the following questions:
   (a) Whose thumb is in the cartoon? (b) Why is the thumb so big? (c) What is under the thumb? (d) What does "under the thumb" mean?
2. Write a paragraph summarizing the ideas that Nast meant to convey with this cartoon.

Other Skill Activities
1. **Working with graphs**
   Make a graph which shows the number of federal jobs between 1865 and 1891. Use the information given in this chapter.
2. **Civil service melodrama**
   Write the dialogue of a debate between supporters and opponents of the Pendleton bill.
3. **Crime detecting**
   The text says that political corruption during the Gilded Age was accepted and commonplace, while today it is a matter of news and outrage. Find a newspaper or magazine article about suspected political corruption today. Underline the parts of the article which suggest a crime has been committed.

4. Protect protectionism

Stage a debate between protectionists and non-protectionists. Use a present-day industry such as automobiles for your debate.

Thinking Critically

1. Put yourself in the place of the following New York City residents: new immigrant, industrial tycoon, unskilled laborer, small shopkeeper. In each situation, tell why you would or would not support the Tweed Ring.
2. Why did the spoils system flourish after the Civil War? Suggest as many reasons as you can. Why did the Garfield assassination affect people's views on the spoils system?
3. If you were a small farmer, what arguments might convince you to support a protective tariff? What arguments might persuade you to oppose it?

Further Reading

Beatrice and Calvin Criner. *Jobs in Public Service.* Lothrop, Lee and Shepard Co., 1974. Examines careers in government and civil service.

Nathan Miller. *The Founding Finaglers.* David McKay Co., Inc., 1976. This book reminds us that bribery and graft have been with us since the first settlers. The vocabulary is descriptive and sometimes difficult, but the topic and treatment are fascinating.

Leo Hershkowitz. *Tweed's New York: Another Look.* Anchor Press/Doubleday, 1977. The author examines Boss Tweed not as a corrupt politician but as a key figure in the development of New York as a big city with parks, social services, and cultural attractions.

TEST YOURSELF

WRITE YOUR ANSWERS ON A SEPARATE SHEET OF PAPER.

Matching

Write the letter of the item that best matches each description below.

1. view that the government should not interfere with economic activity
2. wanted honest, impartial, laissez-faire government run by an educated elite
3. New York boss
4. laissez-faire President
5. using the Civil War as a campaign issue
6. created the Civil Service system
7. Half-Breed boss
8. Stalwart boss
9. jobs should be given on the basis of political support
10. jobs should be given on the basis of ability

a. merit system
b. Pendleton Act
c. laissez faire
d. Mugwump
e. spoils system
f. Roscoe Conkling
g. "waving the bloody shirt"
h. Grover Cleveland
i. William Marcy Tweed
j. James G. Blaine

Getting the Presidents Straight

Match the date of the administration with the name of each Gilded Age President listed below.

1. Benjamin Harrison
2. James A. Garfield
3. Ulysses S. Grant
4. Chester A. Arthur
5. Grover Cleveland
6. Rutherford B. Hayes

a. 1869–1877
b. 1877–1881
c. 1881
d. 1881–1885
e. 1885–1889, 1893–1897
f. 1889–1893

Multiple Choice

Write the letter of the answer that best completes each statement.

1. Rutherford B. Hayes
   a. was responsible for the blossoming of the spoils system after the Civil War.
   b. tried to end corruption in the New York Customs House.
   c. was the chief figure in the Whiskey Ring.
2. Half-Breeds and Stalwarts were divided mainly
   a. by their views on the issues.
   b. by their personal loyalty to bosses.
   c. by their Civil War military records.
3. President Garfield was assassinated by
   a. a member of the Tweed Ring.
   b. a mentally disturbed Stalwart.
   c. a reform-minded Mugwump.
4. Chester A. Arthur
   a. was fired for corruption as New York collector of customs.
   b. was elected President on the Liberal-Republican ticket.
   c. fought against the Pendleton bill.

Chapter 20

1870–1900

A NEW SPIRIT OF REFORM

Gilded Age politicians may have ignored the social problems around them, but many ordinary Americans did not. A new spirit was rising in the towns and cities of the nation: the spirit of reform. The people it reached came from many walks of life, from the coal mines of Pennsylvania, the elegant parlors of Boston, the dormitories of American colleges, and the slums of New York.

The reformers looked at the danger, the long hours, and the low wages of the workplace and said "something must be done." They looked at the laws that prevented women from voting or holding office, and they said "something must be done." They looked at the crowding, disease, and dirt of city housing, and said "something must be done."

Many of the reformers believed that the doctrine of laissez faire stood in the way of needed improvements and changes. Thus they challenged that doctrine. They called on the government to recognize the right of workers to organize unions that could bargain for higher wages and better working conditions. They called on the government to grant political and legal equality for women. And they called on the government to improve urban housing, transportation, and recreation.

In this chapter you will meet some of the people who led these reform movements. You will see how each movement tried to bring basic changes to American society. And, you will find out where the Gilded Age reformers succeeded and failed.

Sections in This Chapter
1. Labor Struggles for Reform
2. Women Fight for Equality
3. The Problems of the Cities

Opposite: The inventions of the Gilded Age make that era seem close to our own times. Here are turn-of-the-century examples of the typewriter, the light bulb, the telephone, and the time clock.

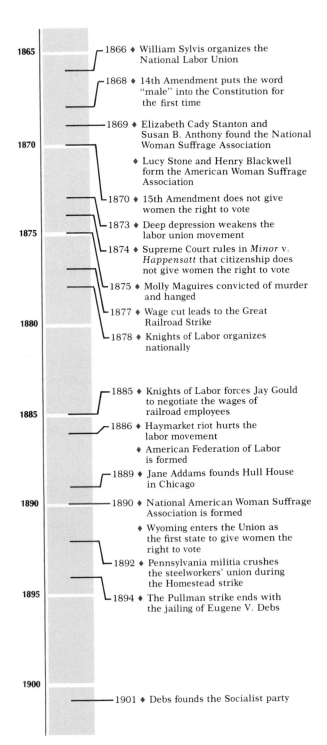

1865

1866 ♦ William Sylvis organizes the National Labor Union

1868 ♦ 14th Amendment puts the word "male" into the Constitution for the first time

1869 ♦ Elizabeth Cady Stanton and Susan B. Anthony found the National Woman Suffrage Association

1870

♦ Lucy Stone and Henry Blackwell form the American Woman Suffrage Association

1870 ♦ 15th Amendment does not give women the right to vote

1873 ♦ Deep depression weakens the labor union movement

1875

1874 ♦ Supreme Court rules in *Minor* v. *Happensatt* that citizenship does not give women the right to vote

1875 ♦ Molly Maguires convicted of murder and hanged

1877 ♦ Wage cut leads to the Great Railroad Strike

1880

1878 ♦ Knights of Labor organizes nationally

1885 ♦ Knights of Labor forces Jay Gould to negotiate the wages of railroad employees

1885

1886 ♦ Haymarket riot hurts the labor movement

♦ American Federation of Labor is formed

1889 ♦ Jane Addams founds Hull House in Chicago

1890

1890 ♦ National American Woman Suffrage Association is formed

♦ Wyoming enters the Union as the first state to give women the right to vote

1892 ♦ Pennsylvania militia crushes the steelworkers' union during the Homestead strike

1895

1894 ♦ The Pullman strike ends with the jailing of Eugene V. Debs

1900

1901 ♦ Debs founds the Socialist party

1. LABOR STRUGGLES FOR REFORM

Imagine that you were a coal miner in Schuylkill County, Pennsylvania. Poverty probably forced you to quit school as a boy and join your father in the deep pits of the anthracite mines nearby. Here you lived your life in darkness, for you rose before the sun each morning and spent your day in the blackness beneath the earth. You earned little for your labor, because there was no minimum wage and no recognized voice to represent the interests of the miners. Although you lived with the threat of gas explosions, cave-ins, and death, your employers took no responsibility for working conditions in mines. In the Gilded Age, labor unions struggled to improve your life and the lives of other miners.

The Growth of Unions

As the nature of the workplace changed, workers' organizations, or unions, changed too. A union was formed by workers to protect them when employers lowered wages or increased working hours. The idea behind the union was that one worker alone was weak, but many workers together were strong enough to stand up against an employer. Before the Civil War, unions were largely local organizations, made up of skilled workers in the same trade who lived in the same city or neighborhood. The shoemaker you met in Chapter 18, for example, might have belonged to the Society of Journeymen Cordwainers in his home town. But by 1870 these small local unions found that they could not hope to bargain with the huge national corporations that employed an increasing percentage of American workers. Union leaders realized that workers, too, would have to organize on a national level.

As early as 1866, the first attempt to form a national federation of unions arose. In that year several trade unions in Baltimore joined together to create the **National Labor Union (NLU)**. Its leader was William Sylvis, head of the iron molders' union. The NLU was small, but its program was bold. Sylvis and his supporters called for sweeping reforms in working conditions, starting with the 8-hour work day.

The work day would remain a major issue well into the next century. As late as 1900, three-fourths of all industrial workers put in 10 hours or more, six or seven days a week. Some industries, like steel, worked their employees 12 hours a day, seven days a week.

Political leaders turned a deaf ear to the NLU platform. In frustration, the NLU entered the world of politics. In 1872 the organization formed a new third party, the Labor Reform party, and nominated candidates for President and other national offices. The party's candidates for U.S. President and Vice-President withdrew, however. Soon both the party and the NLU dissolved.

The following year a major depression hit the United States and continued for five years. Unemployed workers searched desperately for jobs, and accepted whatever wages and conditions employers offered. Of 30 national unions, 21 had disappeared by 1877. The depression destroyed these early national efforts by labor, but it did not interrupt anti-labor activity. Business owners were hostile to the idea of their employees uniting to make demands. They decided to strike a blow against the weakened unions.

The most powerful weapon in the hands of employers was the "**blacklist.**" Once a worker was fired and placed on this list of "troublemakers," it was impossible for him or her to find a new job. To protect their members, unions became secret organizations. But factory and mine owners found ways of uncovering troublemakers. They hired private police to pose as workers and spy on the employees, and report any union activity. Sometimes they attended union meetings and acted as *agents provocateurs* [ä zhän′ prô vô kà tèr′], who incited workers to violence so that employers could prove that the unions aimed to take power by criminal means.

Railroad companies waged the most vigorous anti-union campaigns. They hired agents from the Pinkerton National Detective Agency, a well-known and feared organization. It was inevitable that trouble would break out between these private police and workers.

The Molly Maguires

The most famous, and the most tragic, confrontation took place in Schuylkill County, Pennsylvania. Here, in coal mines owned by the Reading Railroad, Irish miners formed a secret organiza-

Young boys who worked as coal sorters, around 1900

tion called the **Molly Maguires.*** The Mollies were bitter about the company's anti-union activities. They decided to fight violence with violence, and they committed acts of sabotage and murder. In 1875 a Pinkerton agent, James McParlan, infiltrated their ranks, and his testimony led to the arrest of 24 miners. Ten of these men were convicted of murder and hanged. The rest were sentenced to jail for two to seven years. The Mollies were thus defeated.

***Molly Maguire** the name given an unknown leader of an Irish rebel society in the early 1800s.

Although the Molly Maguires were not successful in forcing the mine owners to recognize a miners' union, their goals of better working conditions remained alive among miners. As you will see, miners would soon organize openly with the help of the Knights of Labor.

The Great Railroad Strike of 1877

More trouble began in July 1877. In the midst of the economic depression, the Baltimore & Ohio Railroad Company announced a 10% wage cut. Angry workers in Martinsburg, West Virginia, responded by going out on strike. Like wildfire, the strike spread to other railway lines. Union and non-union workers lay down their tools and quit their work. Within days, the strike covered all the railroad lines in the East and Midwest. It brought about two-thirds of the country's trains to a halt. To show their support, workers in other industries also went on strike. What began as a revolt against a pay cut had grown into a general strike!

With tempers high and tensions higher, violence soon exploded. Crowds of workers and their supporters battled with police in Martinsburg, Chicago, Pittsburgh, Baltimore, San Francisco, and other major cities. In Pittsburgh alone, the

Tracks in Pittsburgh torn up in the 1877 strike

violence left more than 30 dead. All the city's railroad cars, including 160 locomotives, were destroyed, and crowds leveled all the railroads' buildings and tore up miles of track. The state governors could not guarantee anyone's safety, and called for federal action. President Hayes sent federal troops to Martinsburg and Pittsburgh, and the strike collapsed.

The "**Great Railroad Strike of 1877**" shocked many Americans. The rise of the railroad and the corporation had certainly concerned and divided Americans. But it was not until the 1877 strikes that the desperation of workers and the power of the railroads became apparent. Many Americans feared violence more than the power of the railroad owners. They were convinced that the violence had been brought about by foreign "agitators." In this atmosphere of fear and distrust, anti-union activity increased.

The Knights of Labor

The failure of the Great Railroad Strike did not end the efforts to organize unions. The return of prosperity in the 1880s led to a return of interest in national labor organizations. The most important of these was the "Noble and Holy Order of the Knights of Labor," which had kept its organization and membership secret since 1869.

The **Knights of Labor** organized nationally in 1878. It aimed to be more than simply a coalition of skilled labor unions. It opened its membership to all workers—skilled and unskilled, male and female, black and white, immigrant and native-born. It looked for leadership from any member with talent, regardless of race or sex. Thus, Chicago's 80,000 Knights were led by Mrs. George Rodgers, a housewife and mother of 12 children. In the South, one-third to one-half of the Knights were black.

A Knight need not be a worker, for the Knights welcomed any member of the "producing classes," which, they said, excluded liquor dealers, professional gamblers, bankers, and lawyers. Their motto, "An injury to one is the concern of all," attracted a wide variety of Americans unhappy with the quality of life in the new industrial society. Farmers, housewives, storekeepers, doctors, and journalists joined, and by the 1880s the Knights had given up their secrecy and become a public organization. The broad platform of the Knights reflected their concerns. They demanded an end to child and convict labor, equal pay for women, safety codes at the workplace, the 8-hour day, and the nationalization (public ownership) of railroads and telegraph lines.

The Knights believed in self-help as well. They established libraries for worker education and organized cooperative stores and factories. They also participated in electoral politics, endorsing candidates who opposed monopolies and favored reform.

One of the genuine assets of the Knights was their "Grand Master Workman," **Terence V. Powderly**. With his elegant mustaches and his Irish brogue, the Pennsylvania machinist cut an impressive figure in a meeting hall or at a rally. Yet Powderly's organization owed much of its popularity to its support of successful strikes. For example, many Americans were impressed when the Knights took on Jay Gould's Wabash Railroad and won higher wages. The victory over Gould was especially sweet, for he had always shown contempt for his workers. "I can hire one half of the working class to kill the other half," Gould once bragged. After the Wabash victory in 1885, membership in the Knights of Labor reached 700,000.

The future seemed less bright by the end of 1886, however. The year was filled with strikes. By December, more than half a million people had participated in some effort for union recognition or for the 8-hour day. Strike after strike ended in failure, the result of poor planning and disunity between skilled and unskilled workers. With each labor defeat, membership in the Knights dropped. The fatal blow came on May 4, 1886, the date of the Haymarket riot.

The Haymarket Riot

The Haymarket incident seemed like a sad echo of the Boston Massacre a hundred years before. It began at the McCormick Harvester Works in Chicago, where a fight between strikers and police had erupted. On the night of May 4th, a crowd gathered in Chicago's Haymarket Square to protest police violence. As the rally broke up, someone threw a bomb into a group of policemen who had been watching the heretofore peaceful demonstration. The explosion killed one policeman, and the others began to fire into the crowd. Four civilians and six more officers died in the melee. Many more were injured in the **Haymarket riot**.

The events in Chicago shocked the nation. Quickly, eight German immigrants were arrested and tried for the crime. These eight men were **anarchists**, who opposed all forms of government. Their radical views and the fact that many American labor union members were becoming attracted to this "foreign doctrine" made them guilty in the eyes of many Americans even before the trial. Judge Joseph Gary convicted the anarchists on the basis that they had "incited"* the bomb-throwing, and so were as guilty as the actual bomb throwers. No substantial evidence was brought against them. Four were hanged, and one committed suicide in jail. Six years later, Illinois Governor **John Peter Altgeld** pardoned the remaining three. Newspapers across the country bitterly accused him of supporting anarchism.

The Knights of Labor had played no part in the terrorism of the Haymarket riot, but they were blamed for creating an atmosphere of violence. After Haymarket, anti-labor activities again increased, and factory owners and corporations took the offensive against union organizing. Membership in the Knights dwindled to about 100,000 in 1889. Skilled workers, in particular, retreated to their separate local unions. The Noble Order faded away.

The Homestead and Pullman Strikes

The decline of the Knights of Labor did not mean an end to labor-management violence. In fact, two of the biggest and bloodiest strikes took place in the 1890s. The first was the **Homestead strike**, which occurred in 1892 at Andrew Carnegie's Homestead steelworks near Pittsburgh. The chairman of the steel company, Henry Clay Frick, cut wages that year. He also demanded that workers at Homestead disband their union, the Amalgamated Association of Iron and Steelworkers. The workers refused. Frick responded by locking the men out of the Homestead plant. He then sent for 300 hired police to guard the plant while he hunted up strikebreakers to run the machines.

Traveling on barges pulled up the Monongahela River, the 300 Pinkerton police reached Home-

---

*August Spies, editor of the *Arbeiter-Zeitung*, a radical newspaper, had advocated violence in retaliation for the troubles at the McCormick plant. He was one of the speakers at the rally at Haymarket Square.

Socialist workers' parade in New York City, early 1900s

Another deep depression, which began in 1893, led to a second major defeat for strikers in the 1890s. This episode—the **Pullman strike**—took place in 1894 at Pullman, Illinois. Pullman was a company town owned by the Pullman Palace Car Company, the leading manufacturer of sleeping and parlor cars for railroads. The Pullman Company tried to run a "model town," offering its workers pleasant housing, parks, lakes, gardens, and libraries. When the depression came, however, life in the town changed. The company cut wages several times in 1893 and 1894, but did not lower the rents on the workers' houses. Soon the workers who made the rail cars faced a desperate situation. Their rent ate up their salaries, leaving them no money for food or clothing.

In 1894 the workers struck, and called on the new American Railway Union for help. Like the 1877 strike against the Baltimore Railroad, this strike soon spread from Chicago to California. Illinois Governor Altgeld thought he could handle the crisis, but President Grover Cleveland insisted upon stepping in. After naming a railroad lawyer to direct federal action, Cleveland rushed federal troops to Pullman to break the strike. The President claimed that the strikers were breaking federal laws by interfering with the U.S. mail.

Altgeld wrote the President a long letter, arguing the states' rights view that the President had no right to send troops into a state without the consent of the state government. He said:

The jurists have told us that this is a government of law, and not a government by the caprice of an individual. . . . Yet the autocrat of Russia could certainly not possess . . . greater power than is possessed by the executive of the United States, if your assumption is correct.

Governor Altgeld's protest against the federal intervention went unheeded.

Soon the courts dealt another blow to the Pullman strikers' hopes. A federal judge issued an **injunction** (court order) requiring the leader of the American Railway Union to end the strike. The union leader, **Eugene V. Debs**, refused. Debs and several other unionists were sent to prison for defying the injunction. Like the Homestead strike, the Pullman strike was defeated by government intervention on the side of employers.

Twice in the 1890s—at Homestead and at Pullman—the federal government had ignored its own laissez-faire policy and aided employers

stead early in the morning. They were met by about 3,000 angry strikers, and a pitched battle began. Three Pinkerton men and ten strikers were killed, and many others were wounded.

The strikers won the battle, but the state government stepped in five days later to crush the workers' victory. The steelworkers held out against the Pennsylvania state militia for months and won widespread popular support. During the course of this strike, an anarchist, Alexander Berkman, attempted to assassinate Frick in his own office. This act swung public opinion against the union and made the hated Henry Frick something of a hero. In the end, the alliance between Carnegie and the state government prevailed. The steelworkers surrendered, and their union was destroyed. Not until the 1930s did another strong union develop in the steel industry.

against workers. For 20 years more, labor injunctions would be used as a powerful weapon against the union movement.

The American Federation of Labor

The Knights of Labor had tried to combine into one organization skilled and unskilled workers, labor issues and other social issues. But, by the late 1880s, many union leaders had begun to feel that this approach was unrealistic. In the anti-labor and anti-union atmosphere of the Gilded Age, these union leaders argued for practicality rather than idealism. Unions, they said, should focus their energies on labor issues only. And, they should recruit skilled workers rather than all workers. Experience seemed to prove that the weakest link in a union strike was the unskilled laborer. These men and women could be easily replaced in the factory or shop, and the strike could be broken. This emphasis on unions for skilled workers lay at the heart of a new organization, the **American Federation of Labor (AFL)**.

The AFL was formed in 1886 from about 25 labor organizations. Its founder was the short, crusty labor organizer, **Samuel Gompers**, who led the AFL for the next 40 years. Gompers was an English-born cigarmaker, who made the AFL's goal "pure and simple" unionism. By this he meant that it was only concerned with workplace issues like wages, hours, and safety on the job. Unlike the Knights of Labor, the AFL ignored broad social issues. Nevertheless, the AFL did work to improve the circumstances in which millions of Americans toiled. It called for the 8-hour day, the 6-day week, better wages, laws to protect workers on hazardous jobs, and compensation for work-related deaths or injuries. The AFL firmly rejected the lure of politics. Until Gompers died in 1924, the AFL never endorsed a political candidate.

Through the turbulent 1890s, the AFL grew. By 1904, the organization claimed 1.7 million members. For many, its appeal was its realistic view. It accepted American capitalism and intended to work within the system. It was not part of a coalition against the "new" America of the corporations. Gompers was simply trying to build an organization to match the power of the corporations. America had changed, and Gompers and the American Federation of Labor were asking for a "slice of the pie."

Other labor leaders and organizations did continue to fight for a different vision of America. For example, while he sat in federal prison after the Pullman strike, Eugene V. Debs read the writings of Karl Marx, a German social theorist and radical leader. When Debs got out of prison, he was a socialist.

Socialists believed in replacing capitalism (the private ownership of the means of production and distribution) with socialism (public ownership). Most socialists of the era were influenced by Karl Marx, who said that all history was a struggle between social classes. According to Marx, under capitalism workers would become increasingly poor and desperate. Finally they would revolt and establish socialism.

In 1901 Debs founded the American **Socialist party**. Unlike many Marxists, Debs and his followers believed that socialism could be established gradually and peacefully through the ballot, rather than by revolution.

SECTION 1 REVIEW

Identify: National Labor Union, blacklist, Molly Maguires, Great Railroad Strike of 1877, Knights of Labor, Terence V. Powderly, Haymarket riot, anarchists, John Peter Altgeld, Homestead strike, Pullman strike, injunction, Eugene V. Debs, American Federation of Labor, Samuel Gompers, Socialist party

Main Ideas

1. Why did many workers feel a need for national unions by the 1870s?
2. What methods did many employers use to prevent the growth of unions?
3. How did the Molly Maguires and the Great Railroad Strike of 1877 affect the cause of labor unions?
4. Who could join the Knights of Labor? What were their goals and achievements?
5. What were the causes and results of the Haymarket riot?
6. What were the causes of the Homestead and Pullman strikes? How did the state or federal government intervene in these strikes?
7. How did the goals and methods of the American Federation of Labor differ from those of the Knights of Labor? What were the goals and methods of the Socialist party?

2. WOMEN FIGHT FOR EQUALITY

I n the 1880s, many young American women joined the suffrage movement. Many had hoped to go to college and to train for a professional career, but faced discrimination at every turn. Their families were shocked by their "unfeminine" ambitions. Colleges often rejected these women simply because of their sex. The professions turned their backs on them because they were women. In the Gilded Age, feminist (women's rights) organizations struggled to win equality in education, in the marketplace, and in the voting booth for American women.

The Industrial Revolution
Affects Women

As you'll recall, in 1850 most states considered married women as dependents who did not have property rights of their own. Gradually, however, various states passed laws that improved women's legal status. By 1900 most American women could control their earnings and other property. But they could not vote and were still a long way from legal and social equality.

Industrialization and the growth of the cities had changed the world in which most women lived. Yet older ideas about femininity had not changed. For example, American leaders in politics, law, and religion still spoke of women as the domestic sex, and insisted that women confine their activities to domestic concerns. By 1880, however, at least 2.5 million women worked outside the home. Ten years later, the number had climbed to 4.5 million. By 1900, one in every five women over the age of ten was employed. Yet, most jobs were closed to women, discrimination in pay was practiced openly, and women usually earned about half the pay that men received for the same or similar work.

If all of the women entering the workplace had been poor or from immigrant families, their problems might have been ignored by middle-class Americans. But many of the working women were members of the middle class. These women rejected the view that the only role for women was within the family circle, and they sought careers and professions for themselves.

The Cult of True Womanhood

As you will see, such women met with great opposition. Members of their own sex accused them of being unnatural and unfeminine. Strong opposition also came from husbands and fathers. The competition and corruption of business life in the Gilded Age led many men to yearn for a haven, or refuge, from the daily struggle for survival. They turned to the home, and to the women in it, to provide comfort, gentleness, and escape from the tensions of the day. Through most of the 19th century, this sentimental image of a wife as a "ministering angel" was very strong. It had replaced the older image of the Republican Mother, who had important civic and educational duties, though few legal rights. Popular magazines, novels, and songs all promoted the idea that the two sexes lived in very different "spheres," and that women were morally superior angels within the home, but totally inappropriate outside of it.

This view of women as ministering angels who did not stray from their well-defined "women's sphere" is known as the "**cult of true womanhood.**" Among the women who rejected these ideas were pioneers in the fields of medicine, law, education, and politics. Many of these professional women would join the women's suffrage movement in order to win legal and political rights.

The Revolution in Education

One of the reasons for the new reform spirit among women was the improvement in education after the Civil War. Before the war the typical young woman could not hope to enter a college or university. She might attend a normal school (teacher training institution), but liberal arts colleges were closed to her. In 1837, **Mary Lyon** founded Mount Holyoke in Massachusetts. Though it was not the first women's college in the United States, its rigorous program served as a model for other women's colleges. In the next decades, other such colleges appeared. By the Gilded Age, Vassar, Smith, Radcliffe, Wellesley, and Bryn Mawr offered women the opportunity to educate themselves as well as any male student. In the Midwest, state universities also opened their doors to women. By 1890, 2,500 women were graduating from colleges and universities each year. By 1900, one in every four diplomas went to American women.

These figures do not tell the whole story, however. A college education was still a hard-won victory for young women, who continued to face opposition from family and friends. The story of M. Carey Thomas, who later became president of Bryn Mawr, is not unusual. Thomas set off to get a doctoral degree in 1879. But her family did not applaud her achievement. They disapproved of

her successes so strongly that they never again spoke her name in public. To the Thomas family, their brilliant daughter was rebelling against her proper destiny. Her ambition was a disgrace.

What could a young woman do with her diploma? In the Gilded Age, getting an education turned out to be only the first of several obstacles toward a career. Imagine, for instance, the difficulties faced by **Myra Bradwell** in the 1870s. Bradwell graduated from law school but was not permitted to practice law in her home state. Illinois, like many states, would not admit women to the bar. She took her case to the Illinois Supreme Court, which ruled against her, saying:

> That God designed the sexes to occupy different spheres of action, and that it belonged to men to make, apply and execute the laws, was regarded as an almost axiomatic [self-evident] truth. . . . This step, if taken by us, would mean that in the opinion of this tribunal, every civil office in this State may be filled by women—that it is in harmony with the spirit of our Constitution and laws that women should be made governors, judges and sheriffs. This we are not yet prepared to hold.

In 1873, Bradwell then took her case to the U.S. Supreme Court. Here, too, the justices ruled that this discrimination against women was totally legal.

Many of us might have given up at this point. But Myra Bradwell did not. Her continuing pressure on the state government helped force Illinois to change its law. Soon other states followed suit. By the turn of the century, about 1,000 women were practicing law in the United States.

The Fight for the Vote

The sight of women arguing before a jury, treating patients, or studying in a college library caused many traditional-minded Americans to shake their heads. But it was the suffrage issue that inflamed the passions of Americans in the Gilded Age. Opponents often portrayed suffrage as a plot to destroy the family, end marriage, and turn women into men. Some opponents truly wanted to protect women from the corrupt world of politics. Others, however, feared the power of the women's vote. Liquor interests, for example, feared that reform-minded women would vote for temperance laws. Whatever their reasons, these

Spinning cotton in Alabama, around 1900.
Chemistry class, Tuskegee Institute, Alabama, 1902.

fierce enemies of women's political rights were many, and they were powerful. And they alone had the key weapon in this struggle: They had the vote, and the women did not.

As you saw in Chapter 13, the women's rights movement began in the 1840s. In those years it called for broad reforms in the law, politics, and in the relationships between men and women. But the leaders of the women's movement were also strongly committed abolitionists. They set aside their own cause and worked for the emancipation of the slaves. After the Civil War, these feminists expected support from male reformers for the women's cause. They hoped, for example, that when black men received the right to vote, women of both races would also be granted suffrage.

The leaders of the women's movement were to be gravely disappointed. When the 14th Amendment was ratified in 1868, it guaranteed equal rights to black *men* only. This was a serious blow to the women's rights movement, for it was the first time the word "male" appeared in the U.S. Constitution. Women activists campaigned against the 14th Amendment and insisted that the proposed 15th Amendment include black and white women. But their demands were ignored.

Some women feared that the defeats on the 14th and 15th Amendments had killed the women's movement. In fact, these sharp blows seemed to breathe new life into feminism. New organizations and new leaders appeared to fight for women's rights. Unfortunately, as within most reform movements, these activists often disagreed about goals and tactics. Sometimes their quarrels with each other distracted them from the main goals of the movement. And, they always faced the serious problem of the widespread belief in separate rights and responsibilities for the sexes.

The two most important rival organizations in the Gilded Age were the **National Woman Suffrage Association (NWSA)** and the **American Woman Suffrage Association (AWSA)**. The NWSA was formed in 1869 by the Seneca Falls leader, **Elizabeth Cady Stanton,** and her friend **Susan B. Anthony**. The NWSA, like the Knights of Labor, was concerned with many reform issues. Its leaders called for equal education and better job opportunities as well as political rights. To achieve their ends, Stanton and Anthony led a national campaign for an amendment to the Constitution.

In 1869, **Lucy Stone**, along with her husband **Henry Blackwell** and other activists, created the American Woman Suffrage Association. More like the AFL, the AWSA preferred to focus sharply on one goal: political rights. Stone and Blackwell believed that involvement in too many reform issues made women activists look radical. This, they argued, hurt their chances of winning the vote. The AWSA also differed sharply with the Stanton-Anthony group on tactics. They favored a state-by-state approach, hoping that victories in the states would lead naturally to a change in federal law. It was not until 1890 that these two organizations joined forces.

Objections to the Vote

The most common argument against women voting was that politics was in the men's "sphere." But many opponents of women's suffrage had motives other than the view of women as "ministering angels." Three important groups feared that they would lose power if women won the vote. One group was composed of southern political leaders who still remembered the pre–Civil War alliance between abolition and women's rights. These politicians had slowly succeeded in taking away the rights blacks had won during Reconstruction. They feared that black and white women voters might stir up demands for a new Reconstruction. To keep the question of black voting from surfacing again, these men tried to squelch the women's issue. Ironically, in the Confederacy women had enjoyed more extensive rights and responsibilities than their northern counterparts.

The liquor industry also opposed women's suffrage, and spent millions of dollars in campaigns to defeat it. The liquor industry feared an alliance between the women's movement and the temperance movement, for women were the driving force behind the anti-liquor crusade. Leaders of the liquor industry knew that **Frances Willard**, head of the Women's Christian Temperance Union, was also an important spokeswoman for suffrage. Would temperance laws be passed if women won the vote? Liquor interests did not want to find out.

Finally, many of the new industrialists opposed women's suffrage. Millions of women were now in the work force and were actively participating in unions and national organizations like the

Knights of Labor. If these women could vote, there might be laws to regulate the working conditions in many factories.

The opposition of these three powerful groups spelled defeat for women's attempts to gain the vote throughout the late 19th and early 20th centuries. At first, women hoped to get around these groups by taking their cause to the courts. They created "test cases" that would reach the Supreme Court itself. There, they hoped, the Court would rule that the 14th and 15th Amendments applied to women as well as black men. The most famous such test case began in 1872, when Susan B. Anthony and 16 other women registered to vote in the presidential election. For her efforts, Anthony was tried by a lower court and convicted of breaking constitutional law.

The Anthony case never reached the Supreme Court. Before her appeal was made, the High Court sent down a ruling that crushed suffragist hopes. In 1874, in *Minor* v. *Happensatt*, the Supreme Court ruled that citizenship did not give one the right to vote. Women were certainly citizens, said the Court, but they should not expect to be voters, too.

Reluctantly, the women's movement gave up its struggle to win political rights on the national level. Activists now turned to Lucy Stone's strategy of winning the right to vote state by state. They had already won a small victory in 1870, when the Territory of Wyoming allowed women to cast their ballots in the congressional election. Washington and Utah territories also granted women political rights. But even these successes were misleading. When Washington became a state in 1889, its constitution barred women from voting.

Despite defeats and discouragements, women worked with great energy on their state-by-state strategy. Between 1870 and 1910, feminists ran 480 petition campaigns in 33 states, hoping to get the suffrage issue on the ballot. The women believed that a popular referendum, asking the male voters of the states to decide the issue, could lead to success. Seventeen states did hold referenda between 1874 and 1896, but most defeated the appeal for women's suffrage. By the turn of the century, only the states of Wyoming (1890), Colorado (1893), Utah (1896), and Idaho (1896) had given women the right to vote. These four victories were not enough to turn the tide of popular opposition.

The Women's Rights Movement Temporarily Fades

By 1890 the women's movement was more united than it had been since the end of the Civil War. The NWSA and AWSA had merged, and spoke with one voice as the **National American Woman Suffrage Association (NAWSA)**. Stanton took her turn at leading the organization, and so did Susan B. Anthony. But these women, giants though they were, were in their 70s and growing tired. Most of the pioneers in women's rights—some active ever since the 1840s—had died by 1900.

The loss of leadership and inspiration was a blow to the movement. Support for the NAWSA declined. Many young women felt that the suffrage movement had cut itself off too sharply from the era's larger struggles for social reform. These young women turned away from the issue of political rights and threw their energies and talents into the trade union movement or the settlement house movement (see Section 3). They took up the cause of the poor and the working classes, and temporarily gave up the cause of women's rights. But the fight for suffrage was not over, and it would revive in the new century.

SECTION 2 REVIEW

Identify: cult of true womanhood, Mary Lyon, Myra Bradwell, National Woman Suffrage Association, American Woman Suffrage Association, Elizabeth Cady Stanton, Susan B. Anthony, Lucy Stone, Henry Blackwell, Frances Willard, *Minor* v. *Happensatt*, National American Woman Suffrage Association

Main Ideas

1. Why did many women object to the 19th-century popular image of the "true woman"?
2. Why did the suffrage issue arouse so much opposition in the late 19th century?
3. Why did many feminists oppose the 14th and 15th Amendments? How did they try to win the vote by means of test cases?
4. Explain why *Minor* v. *Happensatt* led many feminists to Lucy Stone's strategy of winning the vote state by state.
5. What successes did the suffrage movement gain by 1900? Why did support for the NAWSA decline around 1900?

3. THE PROBLEMS OF THE CITIES

In 1800, the United States had only six "big cities." In 1800 a city was considered large if it had more than 8,000 people. By 1890, the definition of "bigness" had changed drastically. By that time, there were 14 American cities with more than 200,000 people. (See map, page 478.)

Still, the definition of size kept changing. By 1900, there were six American cities with more than 500,000 people. Three—Chicago, Philadelphia, and New York—had well over a million people living within their borders. Chicago had 1.7 million; Philadelphia had 1.3 million; and New York had a mind-boggling 3.4 million!

This growth of cities, or **urbanization**, did not take place at an even pace across the United States. If you looked at a map of the country, say in 1890, you would see dots across the United States representing cities. Most of those dots would be densely packed in the North Atlantic and Midwestern states. Few dots would be located in the South or West. The vast majority of city-dwellers lived in Illinois, Ohio, Pennsylvania, New York, and Massachusetts, for these tended to be the most industrialized states. Cities and factories grew together.

During the 19th century, the population of the country increased over 12 times. But, in the same period of time, the population in cities increased over 87 times. If you took that 1890 map of cities and changed it to a population distribution map like the one on page 478, which shows how many people lived in one area in 1890, you would see the same clustering of dots in the North Atlantic and Midwestern states.

America was becoming an urban nation. As the chart on the facing page shows, by 1900 two-fifths of all Americans lived in urban areas. People were leaving the countryside and moving to the cities, where they hoped to find jobs and opportunities that rural life did not offer. Most of the "new immigrants" also came from rural areas in southern and eastern Europe and Asia. The late 19th century saw millions of people, native-born and foreign-born, change from country "folk" to city "slickers."

It is hard to imagine such vast change in so short a time. And this rapid pace of urban growth brought new problems to American life, special problems tied to a new urban age. The cities grew so fast and filled up so quickly that the services city dwellers needed could not keep up with the demand. City dwellers needed efficient transportation to get to and from work, a water supply for drinking and washing, garbage disposal and sewage systems to take away wastes, decent housing, and protection from fire and crime. In the late 19th century, the cities' problems centered around these basic needs.

The Rise of "Streetcar Cities"

The growth of the city presented special problems for urban transportation. In the early 19th century, most urban areas had been "**walking cities**." This meant that the city was small enough to permit people to walk wherever they had to go. But, with the expansion of the city—and with

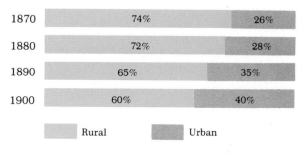

U.S. POPULATION, 1870–1900

Year	Total Population (millions)
1870	40
1880	50
1890	63
1900	76

RURAL AND URBAN POPULATION, 1870–1900

	Rural	Urban
1870	74%	26%
1880	72%	28%
1890	65%	35%
1900	60%	40%

For information on U.S. population growth and urbanization in other eras, see the Atlas and Reference Section in the back of your book for charts showing total population and rural/urban population for the years 1790–1980.

Italian district in New York City, around 1900

many middle-class people moving to suburbs—walking was no longer a realistic way to get about. To solve the new problem, the cities first tried horse-drawn streetcars. But these crowded vehicles were slow and noisy, and horses could only pull a limited passenger load. The streetcars caused pollution, too. Today we complain of smog in our cities, but horse droppings polluted the 19th-century urban environment with smells, flies, and disease.

By the late 19th century, cities had progressed to electric streetcars. The first electric streetcar system was set up in Richmond, Virginia, in 1887. By 1895, more than 800 cities had electric railway lines, and the cities expanded outward along the railway lines. Thus began the era of the "**streetcar cities.**"

The streetcars ran on tracks and were attached to electric wires strung above the street or, sometimes, to moving cables below the street. The electric cars were much larger and faster, and could go greater distances than the old horse-drawn vehicles. But they also led to fatal accidents in the crowded streets and contributed to terrible traffic jams.

New York and Chicago experimented with elevated railways set up on platforms above the streets. At first these trains were powered by steam engines that left billowing clouds of smoke and dangerous sparks in their wake. Soon, people were arguing that the only efficient transportation system would be an underground one. In 1897, Boston opened the first subway, and seven years later New York City had one too.

Clean Water and Sewage Disposal

Most cities lacked the facilities to supply water to millions of people. The streets of New York, Philadelphia, and other cities smelled of the raw sewage that stood in open gutters and exposed cesspools. Nearby rivers became undrinkable sewage canals. Urban drinking water tasted terrible, for it was filled with an assortment of chemicals to kill the mounting germs and mask the pollutants.

477

Toward the end of the century, cities did begin to set up procedures for water inspection and purification, and sewage disposal systems were constructed underneath the streets. But water and waste were constant problems in the late 19th century and remained serious threats to public health.

New States in the Union, 1860–1900

Kansas (1861)	North Dakota (1889)
West Virginia (1863)	South Dakota (1889)
Nevada (1864)	Washington (1889)
Nebraska (1867)	Idaho (1890)
Colorado (1876)	Wyoming (1890)
Montana (1889)	Utah (1896)

Crowded Housing and Fire Prevention

Perhaps the worst problem facing the city's residents was housing. The steady stream of new city dwellers put a strain on available housing facilities. Houses were often packed closely together, with new buildings rising in the alleys and backyards of the old. Housing dramatized the contrast between wealth and poverty in the city. You might take a stroll amidst the stately mansions and elegant shops of Fifth Avenue in New York City. But, hopping on a downtown streetcar, you would soon reach the desolate "Five Points" area of the city, with its packed and crumbling build-

ings and uncollected garbage. The crime rate in the cities soared in the late 19th century. Poverty and crime often went together, and the homicide rate tripled in the 1880s.

Millions of poor immigrants came to America to find work and a better way of life. By 1890, four out of every five New Yorkers had been born abroad or had foreign-born parents. A third of both Chicago's and Philadelphia's population was foreign born. As you learned in Chapter 18, many of these newcomers ended up the victims of the 19th-century boom-and-bust economy and were often out of work. With little money, they could usually find only crowded housing, often at high rents.

One example of the housing built for the poor in the Gilded Age was the **dumbbell tenement**. It was designed in New York City in 1879 by James E. Ware. Ware entered the dumbbell design in a contest. The judges were looking for a building to meet the *minimum* requirements of a new tenement house law, and Ware's design won. Its floorplan, shaped like a dumbbell to aid ventilation, managed to squash anywhere from 24 to 32 4-room apartments into a lot area measuring 25 x 100 feet. In other words, through the dumbbell design, a landlord could collect many rents from a small piece of property and still meet the limited requirements of the law.

As an immigrant child, you would not like Mr. Ware's prize-winning design. The hallways of

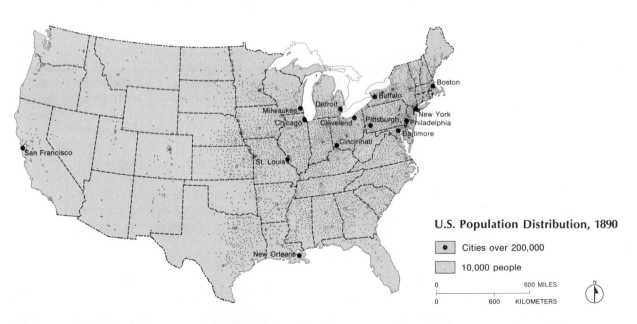

U.S. Population Distribution, 1890

● Cities over 200,000

▦ 10,000 people

478

LIFE IN AMERICA

THE WORK OF THOMAS EDISON

Electric streetcars were only one of the marvels of the last half of the 19th century. Electric elevators defied the laws of gravity, a tinfoil disc could capture the human voice, and electric lights pushed back the night. Only a wizard could catch sound or ban the darkness and that wizard was Thomas Alva Edison. Technologically speaking, he was probably the man of the century, with 1,093 patents to his name.

Born in 1847, he showed no special signs of outstanding intelligence as a child. He spent only two months of his life in school, but read anything he could get his hands on. At the age of 12 an accident left him almost completely deaf.

While working for a railroad, he invented a "quadruplex," which allowed four messages to be transmitted on the telegraph instead of only one. Then came a device for measuring small variations of heat, another for gauging the force of sound waves, and the stock ticker.

In 1877 Edison invented a carbon transmitter for Mr. Bell's equally remarkable telephone. Not long after that he hit upon the idea of the phonograph. The machine worked on the first try. Even Edison was surprised. "I was never

Thomas Edison with an early phonograph, 1888

so taken aback in my life—I was always afraid of things that worked the first time," he said.

The Menlo Park Laboratory

In 1875 Edison moved his family to Menlo Park, New Jersey, where he began to build another imaginative creation—the research laboratory. Keeping the laboratory supplied with rare elements and scientific instruments left him constantly short of cash, but that did not slow his search for his best-remembered invention, the light bulb.

Others had been experimenting with an incandescent bulb, and

Edison began work in 1878. Rather early he struck on the idea of a glowing filament encased in a vacuum tube. Finding a filament that would glow steadily without burning up quickly would consume him for the next 16 months.

Contrary to common belief, he did not work alone. He had assembled at Menlo Park a dozen or so researchers. One of them was Francis P. Upton. Upton's methodical and scientific nature was the perfect balance to Edison's experimentation.

The Search for a Filament

As the search for the perfect filament progressed, the two men tried hundreds of materials, from hemp to lime. In November 1879, Charles Batchelor, another researcher, cut two thin horseshoe shapes from a piece of cardboard, boiled them in sugar and alcohol, and then carbonized them. When this filament was placed inside a vacuum (creating a perfect vacuum had also been a problem) and a current passed through it, it glowed for 16 hours.

By New Year's Eve 1879, Batchelor, Upton, and Edison had put bulbs and wires in the railroad station, the lab, and half a dozen houses. That midnight more than a new decade began: A little town in New Jersey glowed, and the night was changed forever.

---

your building are dark, the apartments cramped. Many rooms have no direct access to light or air. You share a small sleeping space with your family, and probably some boarders, too. You also share a dirty, foul-smelling bathroom with other tenants in the building. The apartments are "sweatshops," where you and your family work, making artificial flowers, or parts of garments, or cigars.

Jacob Riis, the noted New York journalist, esti-

mated that there were 37,000 dumbbell tenements in New York City in 1890. They housed over half the city's population.

Health problems in the 19th-century city were serious. The poor living conditions of tenement housing brought a rising level of disease and death. Tuberculosis ran through the city slums, taking the lives of adults and children. By 1900, three out of every five babies born in the Chicago slums died before the age of one.

Family making artificial flowers, 1908

of these charitable groups were wealthy Protestants who tended to blame the poor for their own plight. They viewed poverty as the result of some moral defect in the poor. Their organizations opened missions in slum areas to help the "deserving" poor.

Although many of these charitable organizations helped people, some of the missionaries tried hard to change the customs and even the religions of the poor, and worked to convert Catholic and Jewish poor and their children to Protestantism. The response of the poor was often hostile. They turned to the urban political machines for help instead of to the missions. After all, the machine would perform services without demanding anything but their votes.

The Settlement House Movement

In the late 1880s a new approach to urban reform appeared. This was the **settlement house movement**. The settlement house was a community center within the city slums. Its workers performed needed services for the neighborhood and tried to create a sense of community. Settlement-house workers also worked hard to teach immigrants to deal with the mysterious ways of American life.

The settlement workers tended to be young and middle-class. They lived in the settlement house and took an active part in the daily life of the neighborhood. Unlike the earlier charity groups, these workers hoped to learn from their experiences with the poor. They were dissatisfied with their narrow lives as the children of a comfortable middle class. The settlement workers believed that engaging in "real life" would help them grow intellectually and morally.

Many of these young settlement workers were women, fresh from college. The settlement house offered these graduates a rare opportunity for active and important service to society. Their work gave them a feeling of self-fulfillment.

The settlement house movement spread rapidly through America's cities. The most famous settlement houses were Chicago's Hull House, set up by **Jane Addams** in 1889; Boston's South End House, founded by **Robert A. Woods** in 1892; and New York's Henry Street Settlement House, founded by **Lillian Wald** in 1893.

These settlement houses focused on the practical problems facing poor city residents. They held

Tenants spared by disease faced the constant threat of fire. Old wooden buildings stood packed together, needing only a spark to set off a disaster like the **Chicago Fire** of 1871, which destroyed most of the city. The homes of rich and poor alike could vanish in a great blaze. After the Chicago Fire, cities developed building codes to require more fireproof construction, and professional fire departments replaced the volunteer brigades.

Social Reform in the City

As you saw in the last chapter, the doctrine of laissez-faire worked against federal legislation to combat urban problems. Local governments did act, however. They passed fire and sanitary inspection laws, and even some laws regulating working conditions. For example, an 1882 New York law forbade the manufacture of cigars in apartment "sweatshops." But these laws were often weak and poorly enforced. Landlords and business owners easily sidestepped them, or had them repealed. Belief in the doctrine of laissez-faire led courts to narrowly interpret the powers of the cities and the states. Thus the courts limited the local governments' powers to interfere with the rights of landlords and business owners.

Individuals and private groups worked to help the urban poor throughout the 19th century. Many

An Excerpt from Jane Addams' Autobiography

Our very first Christmas at Hull-House, when we as yet knew nothing of child labor, a number of little girls refused the candy which was offered them as part of the Christmas good cheer, saying simply that they "worked in a candy factory and could not bear the sight of it." We discovered that for six weeks they had worked from seven in the morning until nine at night, and they were exhausted as well as satiated [had too much]. The sharp consciousness of stern economic conditions was thus thrust upon us in the midst of the season of good will.

During the same winter three boys from a Hull-House club were injured at one machine in a neighboring factory for lack of a guard which would have cost but a few dollars. When the injury of one of these boys resulted in his death, we felt quite sure that the owners of the factory would share our horror and remorse, and that they would do everything possible to prevent the recurrence of such a tragedy. To our surprise they did nothing whatever, and I made my first acquaintance then with those pathetic documents signed by the parents of working children, that they will make no claim for damages resulting from "carelessness."

The visits we made in the neighborhood constantly discovered women sewing upon sweatshop work, and often they were assisted by incredibly small children. I remember a little girl of four who pulled out basting threads hour after hour, sitting on a stool at the feet of her Bohemian mother, a little bunch of human misery. But even for that there was no legal redress, for the only child labor law in Illinois, with any provision for enforcement, had been secured by the coal miners' unions, and was confined to children employed in mines.

From Jane Addams, *Twenty Years at Hull House*, 1910.

classes in everything from arts and crafts to cooking. They organized social clubs for children and adults, set up day nurseries to help working mothers, and kept well-stocked libraries open to community residents. They also worked for government funding of playgrounds and parks.

Unlike the Mugwump reformers you read about in the last chapter, the settlement workers actively sought local and federal social legislation. They demanded laws to end child labor and to improve housing and education. They often worked with trade unions for legislation to regulate working conditions in factories and to abolish "sweatshops."

Critics of the settlement house workers say they tried to "Americanize" poor people and make them reject their ethnic cultures. Sometimes slum residents felt this and continued to turn to the political machine for help. On the whole, however, the settlement movement was greatly admired and popularly supported. It grew steadily as the century came to a close.

The Age of Reform Continues

The labor movement, the women's movement, and the settlement house movement were only three of the many organized efforts to reform the injustices of the Gilded Age. The issues that concerned these reformers—the rights of workers, the rights of women, and the problems of impoverished city dwellers—are issues that still concern Americans today. In the next chapter, you will see how the spirit of reform spread through the countryside and into the farmhouse. Finally, you will see how the reform spirit reached into the business world and the White House itself. The Gilded Age may have begun in scandal and corruption, but, as you will see, it ended with Americans working together to improve their country.

SECTION 3 REVIEW

Identify: urbanization, walking cities, streetcar cities, dumbbell tenement, Chicago Fire, settlement house movement, Jane Addams, Robert A. Woods, Lillian Wald

Main Ideas
1. How did the American population distribution change during the 19th century? Where did the new city dwellers come from?
2. What problems did the rapid pace of urbanization cause? Give examples.
3. What laws were passed to help solve urban problems? Why were city and state governments often ineffective?
4. What steps did the settlement house workers take to aid the urban poor?

CHAPTER 20 REVIEW

Key Terms
Explain the meaning of each of the following terms:

National Labor Union
blacklist
Molly Maguires
Great Railroad Strike of 1877
Knights of Labor
Haymarket riot
anarchists
Homestead strike
Pullman strike
injunction
American Federation of Labor
Socialist party
cult of true womanhood
National Woman Suffrage Association
American Woman Suffrage Association
Minor v. *Happensatt*
National American
 Woman Suffrage Association
urbanization
walking cities
streetcar cities
dumbbell tenement
Chicago Fire
settlement house movement

Reviewing the Main Ideas
Section 1
1. Why did many workers favor national labor organizations by the 1870s?
2. Why did the Molly Maguires and the Great Railroad Strike of 1877 frighten many Americans?
3. What tactics did employers and government officials use against unions in the late 19th-century? Give examples.
4. How did the goals and methods of the American Federation of Labor differ from those of the Knights of Labor? What was the aim of the Socialist party?

Section 2
1. Describe views about men's and women's spheres common throughout most of the 19th century. Why did many women join the movement to win equal rights and opportunities after the Civil War?
2. Why did feminists oppose the 14th and 15th Amendments? How did they try to win rights through test cases?
3. What groups opposed women's suffrage and why?
4. Describe the goals and strategies of the two major women's rights organizations. Why did they merge into one organization?
5. What successes did feminists achieve by 1900?

Section 3
1. What were five major problems that came with rapid urbanization in the late 19th century?
2. What laws were passed to help solve urban problems? How did the doctrine of laissez faire affect the ability of state and local governments to improve conditions in the cities?
3. What did settlement houses accomplish?

Special History Skills:
Working with Population Distribution Maps
Where do most people in the United States live today? Where did most live in 1890? Population distribution maps can give you this information. Look at the map on page 478 and Map 8 in the Atlas Section. Refer to these maps to answer the following questions:
1. Population distribution maps are sometimes called "dot maps." What does each small red dot on these two maps represent?
2. Refer to the map on page 478. Which part of the United States—the east or the west—had the most people in 1890?
3. A metropolitan area is a region that includes a large city and its suburbs. Refer to Map 8 in the Atlas Section. What symbol represents metropolitan areas with more than 3 million people? How many of these large metropolitan areas are there in the United States today?
4. By doing some simple arithmetic, you can roughly compare the number of people living in the largest cities in 1890 with the largest metropolitan areas today. For each map, multiply the number of cities or largest metropolitan

areas by the number of people living in them. Compare the results.

Other Skill Activities

1. A letter to the White House
You are living in Chicago at the time the Pullman strike is beginning. You might be a union member, a railroad executive, a Cleveland supporter, a storekeeper, or a settlement house worker. There is debate about whether President Cleveland should send in federal troops. Write him a letter saying what you think. Also give him your opinion about Governor Altgeld's statements.

2. Gaining political power
Imagine that you are an adult member of a group (for example, red-haired people). You are not allowed to vote because the average voter thinks that voting is in the non-redheads' sphere. What might you do if you wanted to win the vote for yourself and other redheads? First list as many ideas as you can. Then arrange them in order from the most likely to be effective to the least likely to be effective. Be prepared to defend your ideas.

3. A reformer's life
Write a short biography of one of the labor union leaders, women's rights leaders, or settlement workers mentioned in this chapter. Use more than one source.

4. In the news
Clip (if it is your own newspaper) or reproduce a newspaper article about unions, women's rights, or urban problems today. Underline the main ideas and write a short summary paragraph which includes your opinion.

Thinking Critically

1. In what ways did labor union organizers, women's rights leaders, and urban reform groups try to change state or local government's laissez-faire attitude? How successful were they in getting government on their side?
2. Have unions been a benefit or a hindrance to American workers? Explain your answer in the form of a two-minute speech.
3. "President Grover Cleveland believed in laissez faire for employers but not for employees." Defend or dispute this statement, and explain your reasoning.

Further Reading
Robert H. Walker. *Everyday Life in the Age of Enterprise, 1865–1900*. G. P. Putnam's Sons, 1967. Discusses the impact of technology and the growth of cities on daily life.

William and Jacqueline Katz. *Making Our Way*. Dial, 1975. Fourteen first-person accounts of daily life among the poor around 1900.

TEST YOURSELF

WRITE YOUR ANSWERS ON A SEPARATE SHEET OF PAPER.

Matching
Select the letter of the answer that best matches each item below.

1. met the minimum New York housing standards
2. founded to end capitalism in the United States
3. Chicago settlement house founded by Jane Addams
4. tried to organize both skilled and unskilled workers
5. ended by Pennsylvania state troops
6. its members were skilled workers; its goals were purely economic
7. a government weapon against unions
8. community centers in city slums
9. ruled that female citizens could not vote even though they were citizens
10. violent secret labor organization

a. settlement houses
b. NAWSA
c. Molly Maguires
d. *Minor* v. *Happensatt*
e. Hull House
f. Homestead strike
g. injunction
h. blacklist
i. Knights of Labor
j. dumbbell tenement
k. American Federation of Labor
l. Socialist party

Classifying
Identify the following people with an L for labor leaders, a W for women's rights leaders, or an S for settlement house leaders.

1. Elizabeth Cady Stanton
2. Susan B. Anthony
3. Samuel Gompers
4. Jane Addams
5. Terence V. Powderly
6. Mary Lyon
7. Lucy Stone
8. Eugene V. Debs
9. Myra Bradwell
10. Lillian Wald

Chapter 21

1870–1900

THE FARMERS' REVOLT

I n the Gilded Age, American cities were rocked by protest and swept up in reform. Urban Americans—rich and poor, native born and immigrant, female and male— were caught up in the problems of a changing society. But, you may be wondering, what did all this mean to the millions of Americans living in the countryside? Did the era of the railroad, industrialization, and the rise of the corporation affect the lives of farm families? Or did the farmers stand safely outside the cyclone of change and protest, free of the problems that haunted the city dwellers?

The farmers were not isolated from the growing pains of the nation in the late 19th century. In this chapter, you will see what new problems confronted rural Americans. You will learn the histories of the organizations farmers created to improve their daily lives. Finally, you will see how farmers wound up at the center of the era's most important political storm. This battle over "silver and gold" climaxed in one of the most bitter presidential elections in American history. The last great reform effort of the century, the Farmers' Revolt, began in the nation's quiet farmhouses.

Sections in This Chapter
1. The Changing Life of the American Farm Family
2. The Farmers Help Themselves
3. The Birth of the Populist Party
4. The Battle of Silver and Gold

Opposite: Tenant farmers' kitchen, around 1900

1. THE CHANGING LIFE OF THE AMERICAN FARM FAMILY

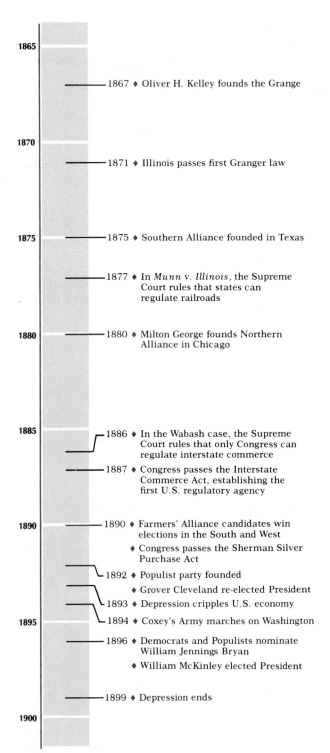

1865

1867 ♦ Oliver H. Kelley founds the Grange

1870

1871 ♦ Illinois passes first Granger law

1875

1875 ♦ Southern Alliance founded in Texas

1877 ♦ In *Munn* v. *Illinois*, the Supreme Court rules that states can regulate railroads

1880

1880 ♦ Milton George founds Northern Alliance in Chicago

1885

1886 ♦ In the Wabash case, the Supreme Court rules that only Congress can regulate interstate commerce

1887 ♦ Congress passes the Interstate Commerce Act, establishing the first U.S. regulatory agency

1890

1890 ♦ Farmers' Alliance candidates win elections in the South and West

♦ Congress passes the Sherman Silver Purchase Act

1892 ♦ Populist party founded

♦ Grover Cleveland re-elected President

1893 ♦ Depression cripples U.S. economy

1894 ♦ Coxey's Army marches on Washington

1895

1896 ♦ Democrats and Populists nominate William Jennings Bryan

♦ William McKinley elected President

1899 ♦ Depression ends

1900

griculture was changing in the Gilded Age. More land was being farmed, and harvests were greater than ever before. The railroads were responsible for the new acreage, for they carried settlers to America's plains and prairies. Railroads also brought older farming areas into contact with the growing markets of the cities. In fact, between 1860 and 1890, the number of American farms had risen from 2 million to over 4.5 million.

Improved farm machinery, better tools, and better scientific farming methods increased the farm family's productivity. The nation's wheat harvest rose from about 173 million bushels in 1860 to 449 million in 1890. In the same period, corn production grew from more than 800 million bushels to 1.6 billion bushels. Cotton, the South's staple crop, rose from less than 4 million bales in 1860 to 8.6 million by 1890.

This agricultural growth was impressive, but it did not mean that America was always going to be a nation of farmers. The number of farmers may have increased by 50% between the Civil War and the turn of the century, but the number of non-agricultural workers increased by 300%! As the chart on page 477 shows, the majority of Americans still lived in the countryside in the Gilded Age, but the cities were rapidly catching up.

The Life of the Farm Family

What was life like for the 41 million Americans who lived and worked on the land? Today, we often have a peaceful and romantic image of their lives. Actually, agricultural work was usually hard, lonely, and grueling. If you were a young man or woman growing up on a midwestern farm in the 1870s, you would begin work before the sun had risen and finish your tasks well after the sun had set. You would do your work by hand, whether it was helping around the house, taking care of the livestock, or planting or harvesting. Sometimes you might have a horse or a team of oxen to help pull wagons, or—if your family was a little more prosperous—a new reaper or thresher. Most of the time, though, you would have to rely on

your hands and your own strength to do the work. You would rarely see anyone outside your family, and even their company would be limited to mealtimes or after the day's work was done.

Sundays and holidays were welcome exceptions. You might go to the local church for services and see your neighbors. The other exception was school. You would walk long distances to the schoolhouse, and during planting or harvest time, you would not go at all. Winters could be terribly cold and lonely. Your family was imprisoned by snow and winds at home, and had few ties with the outside world.

Farm life was not all bad, of course. It had its positive side. Unlike the industrial worker, for example, you were your own boss. You worked closely with your family, and you shared a sense of independence. You produced much of what you needed, or traded with neighbors for necessities. The work might be hard, the weather difficult, but you had a feeling of satisfaction about working the land and feeding the country.

Falling Prices Plague the Farmers

Daily life on the farm did not change as dramatically as life did in the city during the Gilded Age. Yet new problems did arise that threatened the farmers' very existence. First, because of increased production, the price of farm products declined steadily throughout the period. (See graph, page 500.) In the late 1860s and early 1870s, you could sell your wheat for over $1.00 a bushel. But, by the mid-1890s, that same bushel would only bring you 60¢. If you grew corn, you watched it fall from 43¢ in the 1870s to 30¢ in the 1890s. If you lived in the South, the cotton crop brought your family less and less for your efforts. Cotton prices sank from 30¢ a pound in the 1860s to 15¢ in the 1870s, and then to 6¢ in the 1890s.

These falling prices do not tell the whole story, for they do not take into account the farmer's rising expenses. Farmers had to pay transportation costs to get their produce to market and warehouse costs to store their crops. For example, in 1889 Kansas corn was selling on the open market for 30¢ a bushel. But 20¢ of that went to shipping and storage costs, so the farmer made only 10¢. Thus, in 1889, Kansas farmers found it cheaper to burn corn to heat their homes and cook their food than to sell it. Cotton growers in Georgia faced a similar situation. After costs, they received 5¢ a pound. Yet it cost them 7¢ to grow that pound of cotton!

As you can see, farmers were growing more crops but were making less money. With their shrinking incomes, they had to pay for farm equipment, household goods, and clothes. The high tariff made these necessities expensive. Farmers everywhere had to borrow cash by mortgaging their property. A **mortgage** is a claim to property given in return for a loan. If farm prices sank again, or if a harvest was bad, they had to borrow more money. Many went bankrupt and gave up their property when the banks foreclosed the mortgages (took over the property to pay off the loan).

Many families gave up all hopes of saving for the future—or of ever being free of debt. The independent, self-sufficient farm family was disappearing. In its place came debt-ridden, dependent laborers. By 1890, almost a third of all American farms were mortgaged. In the states of Kansas, Nebraska, North and South Dakota, and Minnesota there were more mortgages than there were families.

The Rise of Widespread Farm Tenancy
If mortgages threatened the independence of American farmers, another system, called **farm tenancy**, turned farmers into landless workers. Tenant farmers might be either renters or sharecroppers. The renter paid a fixed amount of money or crops as rent for the land, while the sharecropper paid the landowner a given proportion, often half, of the crop at harvest time. In return, the sharecropper got the use of the land

and, usually, seeds and equipment. Whichever system the tenants used, they were almost certain to spend their lives working land that they would never own, paying interest on debts that would burden them until the day they died.

Tenants took as much as they could from the land and had no money nor inclination to use crop rotation and fertilizer to keep the soil productive. As the tenant system grew at the turn of the century, soil fertility decreased until much of the land became barren clay fit only for weeds. When the tenants could no longer make a living from their plots of ground, they would move on in search of less damaged places to farm.

Despite the harm it did, the tenancy system grew quickly during the Gilded Age. As you learned in Chapter 17, it had started after the Civil War with newly freed slaves and poor white farmers. By 1880 one-third of all Cotton Belt farmers were tenants. Within 40 years the proportion grew to two-thirds. The system spread quickly to the North as well, especially to the midwestern farm states. By 1900, one-third of all farmers in the United States were working other peoples' land.

The Crop-Lien System
Both tenants and independent farmers also fell victim to yet another harmful device, the **crop-lien system**. The farmers, faced with falling crop prices and rising seed and equipment costs, would turn to a local merchant, banker, or large landowner for a loan to be paid back when the crop came in. The merchant, often the same person as the owner of the sharecropper's land, charged as much as 50% more for goods than other stores did. Once the farmers owed the merchant money, though, they were forced to buy everything from that store and pay whatever prices were asked. When the farmers failed to pay the debt with the harvest, the debt would be added to next year's

Year	NUMBER OF FARMS Total number of farms	COTTON PRODUCTION Total bales	CORN PRODUCTION Total bushels	WHEAT PRODUCTION Total bushels
1860	2,044,000	3,841,000	838,793,000*	173,105,000†
1870	2,660,000	4,352,000	1,124,775,000	254,429,000
1880	4,009,000	6,606,000	1,706,673,000	502,257,000
1890	4,565,000	8,653,000	1,650,446,000	449,042,000
1900	5,737,000	10,124,000	2,661,978,000	599,315,000

* Figures for corn harvested for grain only, 1859
† Figures for 1859

loan. In this way, farmers found themselves deeper and deeper in debt, with almost no hope of ever freeing themselves from the lenders' power to run their lives. By 1900, two-thirds of all southern farmers were in that situation.

Increased Competition in the World Market

Why was the farmers' condition growing worse as the century ended? As you learned earlier, one reason was the very improvements in farming that had occurred. This agricultural revolution was not just an American development. New techniques and new tools had increased production in many parts of the globe. American farmers were producing surpluses, but so were Canadians, Australians, Russians, and Argentinians. The only steady market for surplus crops was western Europe, where cities demanded more than local farmers could produce. But, of course, the competition for the western European market grew fiercer every year.

The farmers were trapped by the **laws of supply and demand**: as the quantity of farm products rose, the prices buyers were willing to pay fell. As world production rose, Americans found it more difficult to sell their crops abroad. When a large quantity of crops stayed in the domestic market, prices at home fell. Thus a plentiful harvest was a disaster if foreign buyers could not be found.

Six Other Problems Facing Farmers

The average farmers found the mysteries of the world market puzzling. But they had little trouble understanding the problems that they saw closer to home. Some of these problems were tied directly to the expansion of the railroads and the developments in American business that you read about in Chapter 18.

Distributors First, farmers saw distributors taking a large share of income from the sale of produce. These distributors bought crops from the farmer and, in turn, sold the crops to wholesale merchants or to retail stores. You might ask, why did the farmers sell to the distributors? The answer, once again, was lack of cash. The farmers needed money desperately to pay the debts that came due at harvest time. They often had to sell crops to the distributors to get some money, no matter how low the price was. The distributors, who had no pressing debts, could take ad-

vantage of the farmers' need for cash. They could then make a sizable profit by storing the crops until prices went up.

Railroads The railroads were a second source of trouble. As you know, railroad companies competed heavily with one another for passengers and freight in the East. Here they often cut their rates to attract customers. But they made up for any financial loss from rate-cutting by charging southern and western farmers two or three times what they charged in the East. They also charged southern and western farmers high rates for short-distance shipments of goods.

Farmers claimed that freight rates were so expensive that they had to use one bushel of corn to pay the freight on another bushel. Again, you might ask, why did farmers use the railroads? The answer is they had little choice. Without the railroads, the crops could not get to market.

Banks Third, farmers got little help from banks. In fact, in the Gilded Age, banks were hostile to the farmers' needs. Most banks had their headquarters in the major cities of the East. The bankers had little knowledge of, or concern

LIFE IN AMERICA

TORNADO! AN AMERICAN PHENOMENON

From the far north they heard a low wail on the wind, and Uncle Henry and Dorothy could see where the long grass bowed in waves before the coming storm. There now came a sharp whistling in the air from the south. . . .

Suddenly Uncle Henry stood up.

"There's a cyclone coming, Em," he called to his wife; "I'll go look after the stock." . . .

Aunt Em dropped her work and came to the door. One glance told her of the danger close at hand.

"Quick, Dorothy!" she screamed; "run for the cellar!"

Everyone knows what happened next to Dorothy, perhaps the most famous little girl to come out of Kansas. L. Frank Baum used a tornado to spirit Dorothy to the land of Oz in his children's story, *The Wizard of Oz*, first published in 1900. He wanted to write a modern American fairy tale, and by using a tornado, he gave his story an unforgettably American quality. For though tornadoes occur in all parts of the world, no area rivals the American Great Plains for these sudden, intense, and destructive storms. Every year hundreds touch down, most often in Kansas, Iowa, Texas, Oklahoma, Arkansas, Missouri, Mississippi, and Alabama.

The Incredible Power of Tornadoes

Reports of tornado destruction by reputable meteorologists read like tall tales—five 70-ton railroad cars lifted off the track, one found in a ditch 80 feet away; a board driven through a solid iron sheet 5/8 inches thick. People caught in the tornado's path also feel its savage power. Victims suffer ruptures from pressure changes and death from flying debris or from actually being sucked up into the vortex, only to be spewed out encrusted with mud, sticks, and splinters.

Yet, at times, tornadoes can be incredibly gentle—live turkeys stripped of their feathers; a crate of eggs moved a quarter-mile without a cracked shell. Still, destruction remains the tornado's calling card. They have killed an average of 230 people every year since 1916.

Safety Measures

Civil Defense recommends going down to the basement in a home or public building, away from windows, and under a sturdy table, to protect yourself from falling debris. If you are in a car or mobile home, you should get out and seek the lowest ground, such as a roadside ditch. Lay down flat to avoid being hit by debris. These measures take only a few minutes and that's usually all the time you'll get.

During a "tornado watch," potential tornado-producing thunderstorms are tracked by radar. But a "tornado warning" is posted only after one has been actually sighted. Then it is time to head for the basement or a ditch! Dorothy's twister took her to Oz, but then she was also the luckiest little girl in Kansas.

How Tornadoes Are Formed

In spring and early summer, warm moist air from the Gulf of Mexico spreads north across the Great Plains. When this low-lying warm air meets a mass of cold, dry air, the warm air is pushed upward. When the warm air meets an upper stream of cold air, it is blocked and may begin to rotate very fast—thus forming a tornado.

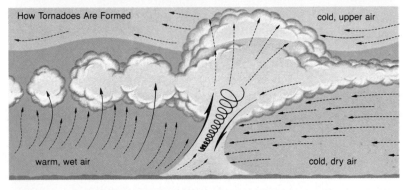

How Tornadoes Are Formed — cold, upper air — warm, wet air — cold, dry air

about, farmers' seasonal problems. They considered farming a risky business, and charged farmers much higher interest rates on loans than they charged manufacturers. The bankers pointed out that a bank could take over a factory and its products when bankruptcy occurred, but it could not take a crop which had failed.

Taxes The tax system was a fourth problem. Farmers paid more taxes than businesses did, in part because their assets (items of value, like crops and livestock) were clearly visible to the tax collector. A corporation could hide its assets, but a farmer's were out in the open for all to see. In addition, a business could pass on the tax burden to consumers in the form of higher prices, but the farmer could not.

Deflation The deflationary money policy of the government was a fifth problem for the farmer. **Deflation** means that there is a contracting, or shrinking, supply of money in circulation. When less money is available, a dollar is "worth" more. Bankers and other creditors usually prefer a stable currency or deflation because the money owed them keeps its value or increases in value. Debtors, on the other hand, usually prefer **inflation**, an increase in the money supply which makes the dollar "worth" less. With inflation, prices go up and debts are easier to pay off.

In the Gilded Age, the government's monetary policies caused farm prices to drop. The farmers were caught in a bind: they had to produce ever larger crops in order to make the same amount of money to pay off their debts. Like Alice in the world of the Looking Glass, a farmer had to run faster and faster—just to stay in the same spot! To combat deflation, farmers demanded that the government put more money in circulation. This, they argued, would create inflation to "cheapen" the dollar. Inflation would raise prices and make debts easier to pay off, they believed. However, inflation would also raise the level of their debts in following years.

Nature Sixth, even nature worked against the farmer. During the 1880s and 1890s, a series of natural disasters struck the land. There were terrible droughts in the West, floods in the Mississippi Valley, and freezing blizzards on the plains. Crops were destroyed, land eroded or was washed away, and livestock died. Whole agricultural communities disappeared.

A Period of Decline and Despair

As you can see, much had changed for the farm family since the Civil War. Chores may have been the same in 1880 as in 1850, but the attitude of the farmers was very different. Gone was the farmers' pride in an independent existence. Debts, poor crops, low prices, and tenancy had destroyed that pride. A popular rural song reveals the bitterness that had crept into the farmers' hearts:

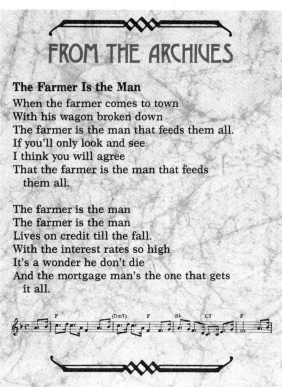

FROM THE ARCHIVES

The Farmer Is the Man
When the farmer comes to town
With his wagon broken down
The farmer is the man that feeds them all.
If you'll only look and see
I think you will agree
That the farmer is the man that feeds
  them all.

The farmer is the man
The farmer is the man
Lives on credit till the fall.
With the interest rates so high
It's a wonder he don't die
And the mortgage man's the one that gets
  it all.

SECTION 1 REVIEW

Identify: mortgage, farm tenancy, crop-lien system, laws of supply and demand, deflation, inflation

Main Ideas
1. Why did crop prices fall between 1860 and 1890?
2. Why did fewer and fewer farmers work their own lands in the late 19th century?
3. What problems did sharecropping and the crop-lien system create?
4. List six domestic problems that plagued farmers. Why did they think that they were not receiving a fair share of the profits?
5. Why did farmers want inflation?

2. THE FARMERS HELP THEMSELVES

In 1867 a Department of Agriculture clerk named **Oliver H. Kelley** became distressed over the plight of southern farmers. The result of his concern was a new organization, the National Grange of the Patrons of Husbandry. The name was impressive, but to farmers across the country it became simply **the Grange**. Kelley hoped that the Grange would soften the isolation of southern farm families and help make up for their lack of social and cultural opportunities. Each local chapter built its own Grange Hall, and that Hall became the hub of social life in the rural community. Dances, parties, and weddings took place here. Speakers, touring in the cotton or corn "belts," drew farmers to the Hall for lectures on literature, science, or agricultural topics. By 1872, 14 states had Granges, and by 1875 almost 1 million people had joined the Grange, mostly in the South and Midwest.

The Grange was more than a social club, however. It urged cooperation among farmers in their efforts to combat "eastern monopolies" like the railroads, distributors, and banks. The Grange sponsored many local efforts to build cooperative enterprises that were owned and run by farmers. These cooperatives sold farm products directly to markets and bought the materials and equipment farmers needed. Grange members experimented with cooperative mills and storage facilities as well. Some set up banks, and others tried to manufacture sewing machines and other products to be sold at low prices. Unfortunately, these enterprises often failed. Farmers lacked the business experience and the capital needed to succeed, while banks and other businesses did their best to eliminate this new competition.

The Grange's greatest impact was in the political realm, for members of the Grange entered political races throughout the Midwest and South. By the early 1870s, Granger-sponsored politicians controlled several state legislatures. The Grange used this power to pass state laws regulating railroads and storage rates. The first of these **"Granger laws"** was passed in Illinois in 1871. Here, a commission was set up to regulate the maximum rates that railroads could charge for hauling and storing freight. Other states soon followed the Illinois lead.

At first, these Granger laws seemed to win the blessing of the Supreme Court. In 1877, in the case of *Munn* v. *Illinois*, the High Court ruled that states did have the right to regulate businesses affecting the general public. For a time, railroads had no legal choice but to obey the Granger laws, although many lines simply ignored the laws or campaigned for their repeal.

In 1886, the Supreme Court changed its position on the Granger laws. In the case of *Wabash, St. Louis & Pacific Railroad Company* v. *Illinois*, known as the *Wabash* case, the Court declared that only the U.S. Congress could regulate interstate commerce. Since most railroad activity was interstate, the power of the Granger laws to keep railroad freight rates down vanished. A series of other Court decisions soon left the states with almost no power to regulate the railroads.

The defeat of the Granger laws did not silence demands for railroad rate reform. Popular pressure against the railroad policies actually increased. In 1887, Congress responded with the **Interstate Commerce Act.** This law required interstate railroads to charge "reasonable and just" rates. It prohibited pooling (secret rate agreements between lines) and forbade railroads to grant special rate privileges to preferred customers. The Interstate Commerce Act also required railroads to post their rates. Rates could be changed only after public notice of at least ten days. Most importantly for farmers, the law insisted that shipping charges be the same in the South and West as they were back East.

The 1887 law also created an Interstate Commerce Commission (ICC), made up of five members appointed by the President and approved by the Senate. The ICC had the authority to investigate railroad activities, to call witnesses, and to examine railroad company records. The companies were required to file annual reports with the Commission, explaining their operations.

Despite all these provisions, the ICC had little power. If railroads disobeyed its directives, the Commission could only appeal to the federal courts. In the laissez-faire atmosphere of the day, the courts nearly always reversed the ICC decisions. By 1898, the railroads had returned to their old, unfair practices. The ICC did little but collect and print railroad statistics.

The ICC did not succeed against the railroads. But the Interstate Commerce Act did set an important precedent. The ICC was, after all, the first federal regulatory agency. It marked a break away from the philosophy of laissez-faire government, even if—for the moment—it was blocked by that very same philosophy.

The Farmers' Alliance

By the late 1870s, the Grange had disappeared. But agricultural problems had not. New difficulties in the 1880s triggered a more powerful farmers' organization, the Farmers' Alliance. This Alliance was really two regional organizations, a large one in the South and a more modest one in the West.

In 1875 the Farmers' Alliance and Industrial Union of the South, or **Southern Alliance**, was founded in Texas. The organization grew slowly during the late 1870s and early 1880s. Then a strong, dynamic leader took over the Alliance. **C. W. Macune** was a lawyer and a doctor. But most of all, he was a successful organizer. Farmers joined his Southern Alliance by the hundreds of thousands, and the membership may have reached as many as 3 million by 1890. The Colored Farmers' National Alliance and Cooperative Union, or **Colored Alliance**, joined the Southern Alliance, adding more than 1 million black rural farmers to the membership rolls.

The Southern Alliance reached out to every type of farmer, from tenants to small landowners, through hundreds of weekly newspapers. These papers were read by millions, passed from hand to hand and home to home. The Southern Alliance made much stronger efforts to form cooperatives than had the Grange. Hundreds of Southern Alliance stores, warehouses, manufacturing firms, mills, and tanneries dotted the countryside. Once again, these projects met opposition from railroads, distributors, and wealthy planters. Sooner or later, most of the cooperatives failed.

In 1880, the National Farmers' Alliance of the Northwest, or **Northern Alliance**, was formed in Chicago. Its membership centered in the wheat-growing states of Kansas, Nebraska, Minnesota, and North and South Dakota. Its president was Milton George, the editor of a Chicago-based farm magazine. George was a dedicated man, but he was a conservative and less inspired leader than Macune. The Northern Alliance attracted about 1 million members at its height. It became a political force in some states, but it never won the mass support of wheat farmers.

The personalities of the two leaders were not the only differences between the Northern and Southern Alliance. There were four others: First, the Southern Alliance was a secret organization. This secrecy protected tenant farmers from their landlords, but the Northern Alliance disapproved of this policy. Second, the Southern Alliance was centrally controlled; the Northern was a loose-knit organization. Third, the two organizations differed on the question of membership and race. The Southern Alliance insisted on cooperating, but separate, organizations for blacks and whites, while the Northern Alliance supported an integrated membership. Finally, the two groups were divided by the heritage of the Civil War. The Southern Alliance was largely Democratic; the Northern Alliance was mainly Republican.

Despite all these differences, the Southern Alliance called for unity and merger. The Northern hesitated, for it was the smaller of the two, and feared that it would lose its identity and power. However, by 1889 Kansas and the Dakotas had thrown their lot in with the Southern Alliance. That same year, the Southern Alliance gained the endorsement of the Knights of Labor. The Alliances merged in 1889, becoming the National Farmers' Alliance and Industrial Union, or **Farmers' Alliance.** Within a year, the Farmers' Alliance would be a powerful force in American politics.

SECTION 2 REVIEW

Identify: Oliver H. Kelley, Grange, Granger laws, Interstate Commerce Act, Southern Alliance, C. W. Macune, Colored Alliance, Northern Alliance, Farmers' Alliance

Main Ideas

1. What function did the Grange serve for farmers, especially in the South?
2. How did the Supreme Court's decisions affect the Granger laws?
3. Describe the powers of the Interstate Commerce Commission. How were the railroads able to avoid the ICC regulations?
4. List the differences between the Southern Alliance and the Northern Alliance.

493

3. THE BIRTH OF THE POPULIST PARTY

Like the Grange, the Farmers' Alliance soon entered the world of politics and elections. In 1890, candidates from the Alliance ran for state and local office throughout the South and the West. The odds against Alliance victories in the South were overwhelming. Here, the Democratic party totally dominated politics, and the wealthy planters and landowners totally dominated the Democratic party. These wealthy leaders were nicknamed the **"Bourbon Democrats,"** for, like the French royal family in the 18th century, they ignored all calls for reform. The Alliance set its goals high: it wished to win control of the Democratic party from the Bourbon leaders.

When the votes were counted in the 1890 local elections, both Alliancemen and Bourbons were surprised. The new governors of Georgia, Tennessee, South Carolina, and Texas were all Alliance candidates, and Alliance members controlled eight state legislatures. Furthermore, 44 representatives and three senators sympathetic to Alliance principles were on their way to the nation's capital. In the West, the Alliance also triumphed, winning control of the Kansas and Nebraska legislatures and near-majorities in Minnesota and South Dakota. Unlike their southern counterparts, the western Alliancemen had won by forming local third parties instead of trying to win control of either established party.

A New Political Party Is Born

The political victories of 1890 encouraged farmers to think about expanding their new local parties into a new national party responsive to their needs. For a time, the Southern Alliancemen hesitated, for they now had high hopes of capturing the Democratic party. Finally, in February 1892, about 800 people gathered in St. Louis, Missouri. The majority were Alliance members, including about 100 blacks. But in the meeting hall there were also representatives of labor organizations and other reform groups.

Out of this meeting the People's or **Populist party** was born. In July, the new party held a convention in Omaha, Nebraska, and nominated its first presidential candidate, a former Union general, **James B. Weaver**. As his running mate, the Populists chose a former Confederate general, James G. Field. This balance of northern and southern candidates symbolized the desire to bury the sectional conflict that had long divided the country.

The Populist platform reflected the needs of the farmers. But it also addressed the concerns of many other reform groups. It called for government ownership of the "monopolies" that controlled transportation and communication. It demanded a graduated income tax. It called for an increase in the money supply by means of the "free and unlimited coinage of silver."

The platform also proposed a unique **"subtreasury plan"** that would eliminate distributors and solve the banking problems of many farmers. It would create a network of warehouses to hold the farmers' nonperishable crops off the market while prices were low. The government would provide loans on the basis of each farmer's "deposit" of crops in the warehouses. When prices rose again, the farmer could sell his or her crops and repay the loan.

The Populist platform also promised general reforms that would make the federal government more responsive to the needs of its citizens. The most important reforms were: the election of senators by popular vote, the adoption of the secret ballot, a single term for the President and Vice-President, and the procedures of **initiative and referendum**. Initiative would allow citizens to introduce bills in Congress or state legislatures by petition. Referendum would allow voters to reverse any action by Congress or state legislatures. Finally, the Populist platform contained demands to improve the lives of urban workers, like the 8-hour day and an end to the use of private police, like the Pinkertons, in labor conflicts.

Opposition to the Populist party arose at once, especially in the East. Here the Populist was pictured as a wild-eyed extremist, a hick with a sprig of barley in one corner of his mouth and dangerous ideas pouring out of the other. Much of the Populist language *was* laced with images of eastern conspiracies and threats of violence against farmers and workers. Nevertheless, the problems the farmers faced were serious, and many of their solutions were sound ones. As you know, reforms like the graduated income tax, the regulation of business practices, and the direct election of senators are all part of our system today. But in the era of laissez faire, the Populists' demands seemed very radical.

The 1892 Presidential Campaign

In the 1892 election the Republican President, Benjamin Harrison, faced former President Grover Cleveland. While their campaigns followed the usual pattern of the Gilded Age—that is, attacks on personalities—the tone and style of the Populist party campaign was different. Candidate Weaver traveled widely, speaking on the issues and about the party platform. In the West, large outdoor gatherings of farmers met to hear Populist candidates and to discuss the issues. These voters experienced a sense of unity, for their common enemy, the "eastern monopolies," were far away. That feeling of solidarity made the campaign exciting.

The southern campaign was less exhilarating. Here Populist leaders worked hard to break the barrier of social hostility. They urged blacks and whites to vote together against their "common enemy," the wealthy landowner. In the South, then, the common enemy was not far away, but next door. The Bourbon landowners destroyed the farmers' unity by dividing the races. They used terror to keep blacks from voting and called upon white voters to maintain white supremacy by supporting the Democrats. The Bourbon strategy of divide-and-conquer won, and the Populists' hard-fought attempt to pull white and black farmers together failed miserably.

On election day, Harrison lost the White House to his old enemy Cleveland. Weaver, however, received over 1 million popular votes and 22 electoral votes. The Populist party did extremely well in the West, even if it failed in the South. (See map below.) Both major parties were shocked by the Populists' strong showing. Much to their surprise, the Populist party had grown into an organized political force, challenging the basis of the Republican and Democratic parties. The possibility of a three-party system was clearly emerging. The Depression of 1893 would add even more fuel to the fires of the new party.

The Depression of 1893

In 1893, the United States was crippled by the worst depression thus far in its history. Farm prices plummeted, factories shut their doors, and railroad after railroad went bankrupt. By the end of the year, nearly 500 banks had closed and more than 15,000 businesses had disappeared. In 1894 unemployment reached an astonishing 3 million. This meant that about 20% of America's nonfarm workers had lost their jobs. In America today, an unemployed person can turn to unemployment insurance, and rely on other social services like welfare, food stamps, and social security. For us, it is hard to imagine the horrors of the 1890s depression. People went without clothes, people lost their homes, and people starved.

As the depression deepened, Americans cried out for relief and aid. But the government held to its laissez-faire policy. When Congress refused to pass a bill creating federal jobs for the unemployed, an "army" of desperate workers decided to march on Washington. **"Coxey's Army,"** led by Ohio businessman and Populist Jacob S. Coxey, reached the nation's capital on April 30, 1894. The government showed little sympathy for these tired and worried men. Coxey was immediately arrested for trespassing, and the 400 marchers were beaten and dispersed by the police. The threat of violence did not prevent at least 17 other "industrial armies" from marching toward Washington, but with little, if any, effect.

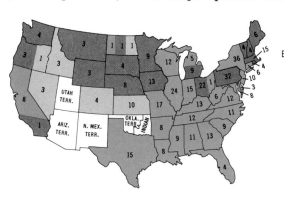

The Election of 1892

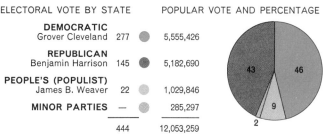

ELECTORAL VOTE BY STATE		POPULAR VOTE AND PERCENTAGE
DEMOCRATIC Grover Cleveland	277	5,555,426
REPUBLICAN Benjamin Harrison	145	5,182,690
PEOPLE'S (POPULIST) James B. Weaver	22	1,029,846
MINOR PARTIES	—	285,297
	444	12,053,259

National tensions grew worse as the depression continued. Industrialists cut wages in order to continue making profits. Workers, frightened and angry, responded with strikes. Public sympathy for the strikers was widespread, but President Cleveland strongly disapproved. He saw worker protests as rebellious and felt that labor "subversion" had to be stamped out. As you saw in the Pullman strike, Cleveland sent federal troops to many troublespots.

The depression was complicated by a financial crisis. When panic hit in 1893, Americans began redeeming their U.S. treasury notes, or paper money, for gold coins. By 1894 the treasury's gold supply was dwindling. This drain on the gold reserves had actually begun before Cleveland took office, but it grew to crisis proportions while he was President. By 1895 the country's gold reserves were only $41 million.

Cleveland was very disturbed about this gold crisis, for he believed it lay at the heart of the nation's problems. In a rash moment, he turned to private citizens for aid. A group of financial tycoons, led by J. P. Morgan, offered to bail out the government—for a price. These bankers agreed to lend the United States government $62 million in gold—at a very high interest rate. The gold reserve increased with this loan. Yet the depression continued. The only real effect the Morgan loan had was to destroy Clevelend's popularity. One thing was certain in those uncertain times: the upcoming presidential election would be a bitter one.

SECTION 3 REVIEW

 Identify: Bourbon Democrats, Populist party, James B. Weaver, subtreasury plan, initiative and referendum, Coxey's Army

Main Ideas

1. List some of the planks in the Populist party platform. Which reform proposals were aimed at making the federal government more responsive? Which directly related to the farmers' needs?
2. Describe the differences between the 1892 campaign in the West and in the South.
3. Why was President Cleveland so unpopular during the depression?

---

4. THE BATTLE OF SILVER AND GOLD

The long depression was hurting millions of Americans. People everywhere asked the same question: why had the depression happened? A powerful disagreement arose over its causes, and this disagreement flowed over into the political arena. It created one of the most bitter presidential elections in American history. The issues were often difficult to follow, as you will soon see.

The Gold Bugs and the Silverites

President Cleveland blamed the depression on the dwindling gold reserve, and he blamed the loss of gold on the **Sherman Silver Purchase Act of 1890.** The history of that act goes like this. To end the inflation after the Civil War, in 1873 the government passed a law removing the silver dollar from circulation. This left gold as the sole standard for U.S. currency. Because gold was scarce, the **gold standard** limited the amount of money possible, and this led to deflation.

In 1877, however, pressure from people in favor of "cheap money" and from silver mine operators helped push through the Bland-Allison Act. This bill instructed the Treasury Department to buy and mint into coins between 2 and 4 million dollars worth of silver each month. The additional silver coins would have meant a victory for those desiring inflation, but the government deposited most of the silver in the Treasury.

By 1890 the power of silver interests—including members of the Farmers' Alliance and silver mine operators—had increased. Six new western states—North and South Dakota, Montana, Washington, Idaho, and Wyoming—contributed their votes to help pass the Sherman Silver Purchase Act in 1890. This new bill authorized the purchase of 4.5 million ounces of silver each month, paid for in paper money that could itself be redeemed for gold or silver.

The farmers hoped that this large purchase of silver would increase the supply of money, raise the price of farm products, and relieve their debts. The motives of the silver mine operators were simpler. They hoped the act would raise silver prices.

Both hopes were dashed. The silver was purchased, but the government still chose not to mint it into coins. Thus the supply of money remained the same, as did the price of silver.

Cleveland and other "gold bugs" argued that the Sherman Silver Purchase Act had contributed to the shrinking gold reserve, for people tended to redeem their paper money for gold coins. He called for the repeal of the Sherman Silver Purchase Act and a return to the gold standard. This, he insisted, would end the depression.

"Cheap money" men disagreed. Instead, they blamed the depression on the establishment of the gold standard in 1873. They called for the free and unlimited coinage of silver dollars at a ratio of 16 ounces of silver to 1 ounce of gold. Clearly, the only thing "gold bugs" and "cheap money" men agreed on was that gold and silver ruled the economy.

Cleveland's call for the repeal of the Sherman Silver Purchase Act split the Democratic party but won the full support of the Republican party. Congress battled over Cleveland's proposal. In the end, Cleveland mustered enough votes to see the Sherman Silver Purchase Act repealed in 1895. Despite the heated tempers and the victory for gold, the depression only deepened. By 1896 the country was torn between the "sound money" gold-standard advocates and the "cheap money" supporters of silver. If nothing else, the depression had ended the Gilded Age political tradition of avoiding issues.

The 1896 Campaign

In 1896, the Republican party convention chose **William McKinley** as its presidential nominee. McKinley was well known and respected, and had fought gallantly for the North in the Civil War. He served in Congress from 1876 to 1892 and was governor of Ohio for two terms. He was recognized as an honest politician in the midst of Gilded Age corruption. McKinley ran on a platform that called for the gold standard and backed a series of pro-business policies.

The Democratic party had a more difficult time choosing its presidential candidate. Their convention hall bristled with boos, hisses, and applause as eastern gold advocates fought bitterly with southern and western silverites. The noisy debates meant little, for the silverites had a comfortable majority. They rejected Grover Cleveland's renomination and set to work writing a pro-silver platform. The first plank was the demand for free and unlimited coinage of gold and silver, or **bimetallism**. But the platform contained many other planks that reflected the reform views of the American farmers. It denounced the protective tariff and condemned banks and trusts. It criticized the Supreme Court's laissez-faire decisions and called for an end to labor injunctions that broke strikes. Like the Populist party, the Democrats called for a graduated income tax.

The problem of finding a suitable Democratic presidential candidate remained. The dilemma was solved when 36-year-old **William Jennings Bryan** walked up to the podium to address the convention. In a booming voice, the former Nebraska congressman caught the audience's attention and held them spellbound. He ended his remarkable reform speech with the words: "You shall not press down upon the brow of labor this crown of thorns, you shall not crucify mankind upon a cross of gold." The delegates were overwhelmed, and Bryan was chosen as their standard-bearer. Arthur Sewall, a Maine banker and businessman who opposed the gold standard, was the Democratic vice-presidential nominee.

The Populist Dilemma

Bryan's nomination put the Populist party in a difficult position. When the Populists met at their convention, they were split between those wishing to support Bryan and those opposed. Western Populists were eager to join with the Democrats in supporting Bryan as the Populist presidential candidate. But southerners, who were less devoted to the silver issue and more concerned with the party's other reform efforts, wanted a separate Populist candidate and campaign in order to keep their identity as a third party.

The deadlock was broken when Democratic party spokesmen promised that their party would replace Arthur Sewall with the Georgia Populist Tom Watson as the vice-presidential nominee. Acting on good faith, the Populist party nominated Bryan as their presidential candidate. The Democrats were less honorable. Despite their promise, Sewall remained on their ticket.

"With Bryan We Bust"

The Republicans were optimistic about victory. First of all, Bryan was inexperienced and practically unknown, while McKinley was a respected national figure. Secondly, the depression could not be blamed on their party, for the Democrats had been in power in 1894. Thirdly, almost every newspaper in the country—even those that were traditionally Democratic—came out for McKinley. Bryan was portrayed in the press as an anarchist and a dangerous lunatic. The *New York Times* declared him insane. Newspaper editorials warned that silver would bring about the end of the United States. As a popular Republican chant went, "In God We Trust, With Bryan We Bust." Finally, pressures put on urban workers helped the Republican candidate. Many factory owners threatened their employees that they would lose their jobs if Bryan were elected.

The odds were against him, yet Bryan turned out to be a powerful candidate. Like General Weaver, Bryan personally campaigned around the country. In 14 weeks he traveled 18,000 miles, visited 29 states, and made over 600 speeches to 5 million people. Never had so many

"Big Humbugs" attack the farmer in this 1896 cartoon against the Democrats.

people "met" a presidential candidate who addressed them about issues. Bryan was a big, impressive-looking man with a voice that carried clearly to every listener. Huge crowds met him at each stop, and went home persuaded by his arguments. Many well-known reformers and labor leaders campaigned for the young candidate. "Silver!" was the battle cry of the campaign, but Bryan's popularity showed the voters' concern for social reform as well.

McKinley's campaign style contrasted sharply with Bryan's. His bid for the presidency was managed by the wealthy Cleveland businessman, **Marcus Alonzo Hanna**. Hanna ran a brilliant campaign, pitting the Republican party's strengths against Bryan's strengths. For example, he knew that Bryan's reform demands troubled many businessmen. Hanna exploited that concern, raising a huge campaign fund from these conservatives. In our era of television commercials and campaigns costing millions, Hanna's $3.5 million campaign sounds modest. At the time, however, it was spectacular, especially when compared to Bryan's $300,000 budget. Hanna sent thousands of speakers into weak Republican areas and covered the country with 250 million pieces of literature.

Hanna also created a unique personal style for McKinley. McKinley pursued a **"front-porch campaign,"** never leaving his Canton, Ohio, home. Visitors and delegations came to him, in carefully planned appearances. As McKinley addressed his visitors, one arm draped around his proud mother, the other supporting his ailing wife, sympathetic reporters jotted down his every word and printed it without criticism.

Bryan lost the election to McKinley by more than 600,000 votes. McKinley carried the East and Midwest; Bryan won the South and most of the West. (See map.) Almost 14 million Americans had made their choice. Bryan's great failure was his inability to win the eastern labor vote. In the end, the country had split between the rural South and West and the urban, "moneyed" East. Sectionalism had not died in America.

The Aftermath of the Election of 1896
Three years after McKinley won the presidential election, the long depression ended. Neither McKinley's policies nor the return to the gold standard had much to do with the economic

upturn. In fact, fate and nature stood the arguments of gold bugs and silverites on their heads. In the late 1890s new gold deposits were discovered in Australia, Alaska, and South Africa. This plentiful gold supply, along with the invention of new processes to extract gold from ore, sent a flow of gold into the United States. The result was more money in circulation—and inflation. Business was stimulated, industry expanded, and the economy recovered. The situation of American farmers improved, and here too nature played a role. The European wheat crop failed in 1897, and American farm exports mushroomed.

The immediate result of the election of 1896 was political, not economic. The Populist party collapsed, in part because its support for a Democratic candidate in 1896 destroyed its image as an independent party. More importantly, the "silver and gold battle" had overshadowed the farmers' many other reform issues. As the radical journalist Henry Demarest Lloyd put it:

Free silver is the cow-bird of the reform movement. It waited until the nest had been built by the sacrifices and labour of others, and then it laid its eggs in it, pushing out the others which lie smashed on the ground.

The election of 1896 marked the beginning of a crisis in popular political participation in the United States. Never again would such a high proportion of voters participate in a presidential election. With Bryan's defeat and the end of the Farmers' Revolt, many of the country's poor and desperate citizens abandoned the political process. One era of reform had ended; another would soon rise. But, as you will see in Chapter 23, this new reform movement would not arise in the farmhouses or modest homes of America's working people.

SECTION 4 REVIEW

Identify: Sherman Silver Purchase Act of 1890, gold standard, gold bugs, "cheap money" men, William McKinley, bimetallism, William Jennings Bryan, Marcus Alonzo Hanna, front-porch campaign

Main Ideas

1. What did Grover Cleveland believe to be the cause of the depression? What did the "cheap money" advocates believe?
2. Describe the differences between the Democratic and Republican parties in the campaign of 1896. Contrast their platforms and the candidates' campaign styles.
3. Why did the depression end in the late 1890s?
4. How did the 1896 election affect the Populist party and voter attitudes?

The Election of 1896

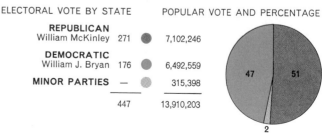

ELECTORAL VOTE BY STATE		POPULAR VOTE AND PERCENTAGE	
REPUBLICAN William McKinley	271	7,102,246	51
DEMOCRATIC William J. Bryan	176	6,492,559	47
MINOR PARTIES	—	315,398	2
	447	13,910,203	

CHAPTER 21 REVIEW

Key Terms
Explain the meaning of each of the following terms:

mortgage
farm tenancy
crop-lien system
laws of supply and demand
deflation
inflation
the Grange
Granger laws
Interstate Commerce Act
Southern Alliance
Colored Alliance
Northern Alliance

Farmers' Alliance
Bourbon Democrats
Populist party
subtreasury plan
initiative and referendum
Coxey's Army
Sherman Silver Purchase Act of 1890
gold standard
gold bugs
"cheap money" men
bimetallism
front-porch campaign

Reviewing the Main Ideas

Section 1
1. Why did farm productivity rise between 1860 and 1890? Why did crop prices fall during those years?
2. How did farm tenancy and the crop-lien system develop? What problems did these systems cause?
3. Why did farmers complain that distributors, railroads, banks, and other businesses were getting a better deal than they were?
4. Why did farmers want inflation?

Section 2
1. How did the Grange try to solve the farmers' problems and improve life on the farm?
2. How successful was the Grange in getting government to deal with farm issues?
3. Describe the activities of the Southern and Northern Alliances.

Section 3
1. What reforms did the Populist party propose in 1892?
2. Describe the campaign of 1892 in the West and South.

3. Describe economic conditions during the Depression of 1893.
4. Why was President Cleveland very unpopular during his second term?

Section 4
1. What did "cheap money" men hope the Sherman Silver Purchase Act would do? What did "gold bugs" think?
2. Describe the major candidates, parties, and platforms of the 1896 presidential campaign.
3. How did the election of 1896 affect the Populist party and voter attitudes?

Special History Skills:
Interpreting an Economic Graph
You learned in Chapter 21 that American farmers suffered from "deflation" in the late 1800s. More recently "inflation" has been a major economic problem. Using this chapter and the glossary, write a definition in your own words for these two important economic terms. Next, look at the graph below and answer the questions that follow.

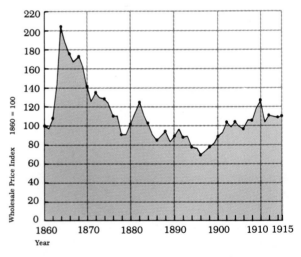

Price Level for Farm Products, 1860–1915

1. Judging from the title, what information will you gain from this graph?
2. What time period on the graph indicates deflation?
3. The early 1860s and the late 1890s show inflation. Give some reasons for inflation during these periods.

Other Skill Activities

1. Time line

Draw a time line for the period 1870–1900. On it place 12 important events—3 from each chapter—that you read about in Chapters 18 through 21. Be ready to defend your choices.

2. Graphing agricultural growth

Use the tables showing wheat, corn, and cotton production between 1860–1900 on page 488 to make a series of bar graphs.

3. A letter from the farm

In a letter to your cousin in the city, describe life on your family farm in 1890.

4. Current farm problems

Find an article in a magazine or newspaper that discusses current farm problems. Underline the main ideas and write a paragraph summarizing the main points.

Thinking Critically

1. Why might low farm prices continue to be a problem today, even though we suffer from inflation? In your answer, consider some of the causes of farm problems in the Gilded Age.

2. The Interstate Commerce Commission was the federal government's first attempt at regulation. Today many people are critical of federal regulation. Some want a return to laissez-faire government. What is your opinion? Use examples from the chapter and from current events.

3. How well would a front-porch presidential campaign work today? Explain your answer.

4. Many planks in the Populist platform of 1892 are now part of our government system. Which ones are they?

Further Reading

Alvin Schwartz. *When I Grew Up Long Ago.* J. B. Lippincott Co., 1978. Older people talk about recollections of family life and important events at the turn of the century. Many details of rural life.

Paul W. Glad. *McKinley, Bryan, and the People.* J. B. Lippincott Co., 1964. An in-depth study of the election of 1896 for the good reader. Discusses issues, personalities, and forces in American politics.

TEST YOURSELF

WRITE YOUR ANSWERS ON A SEPARATE SHEET OF PAPER.

True or False

Mark T if the statement is true, F if it is false. Change the italicized words in all false statements so they are true.

1. *William Jennings Bryan* believed a sound gold standard for currency would end the depression of 1893.

2. *William McKinley* became the presidential candidate of two parties in the 1896 campaign.

3. In the Gilded Age many farmers believed that the *railroads, distributors, and banks* were working against them.

4. Those who supported a gold standard only for American currency were called *"cheap money" men.*

5. The number of mortgaged farms in the United States *increased* sharply during the Gilded Age.

Labeling

Mark each statement P if it applies to the Populist party, D if it applies to the Democratic party, and R if it applies to the Republican party.

1. William Jennings Bryan was the 1896 presidential candidate.

2. It carried the South and most of the West in 1896.

3. William McKinley was the 1896 presidential candidate.

4. Its 1896 platform included reforms for farmers and laborers.

5. It grew out of the Farmers' Alliance.

6. It carried the eastern United States in the 1896 election.

7. Its 1896 candidate conducted a front-porch campaign.

8. It made a strong third-party showing in 1892.

9. It dumped Cleveland for his handling of the 1893 depression.

10. It supported bimetallism in 1896.

UNIT 6 TEST

WRITE YOUR ANSWERS ON A SEPARATE SHEET OF PAPER.

Matching (20 points)
Match each item with a definition from the list below.
1. Pendleton Act
2. limited liability
3. stock
4. Haymarket riot
5. Little Bighorn
6. Homestead strike
7. Pullman strike
8. laissez faire
9. Tweed Ring
10. Whiskey Ring

a. political group controlling New York City in the 1860s and 1870s
b. bombing that led to the trial of eight anarchists
c. conspiracy between politicians and distillers
d. belief that government should not interfere with business and other economic activity
e. a method by which the same group of directors controls several companies
f. battle between Plains Indians and the U.S. Army
g. broke union organization of the steel industry
h. certificate of partial ownership in a corporation
i. ended after federal troops sent and a federal injunction issued
j. another name for the Bourbon Democrats
k. concept that an investor's loss cannot exceed the original investment
l. basis for the civil service system

Vocabulary (20 points)
In each group, find the word or phrase that is least closely related to the other three.
1. **a.** rate wars **b.** standardization of time
   c. feeder lines **d.** merit system
2. **a.** civil service **b.** patronage system
   c. anarchists **d.** classified jobs
3. **a.** inflation **b.** new immigrants
   c. contract labor **d.** mass production

4. **a.** suffrage **b.** black list
   c. strike **d.** injunction
5. **a.** mortgage **b.** dumbbell tenement
   c. urbanization **d.** settlement house
6. **a.** sharecropper **b.** crop-lien system
   c. farm tenancy **d.** merit system
7. **a.** gold bugs **b.** bimetallism
   c. monopoly **d.** inflation
8. **a.** subsidies **b.** Bessemer converter
   c. coal **d.** open-hearth process
9. **a.** canyon **b.** cowboy
   c. mesa **d.** Colorado
10. **a.** bosses **b.** machines
    c. pools **d.** patronage

Time Line (20 points)
Match the letters on the time line with the events they stand for.
1. Coxey's Army marches on Washington, D.C.
2. Great Railroad Strike
3. Populist party founded
4. Transcontinental railroad completed
5. Dawes Act divides Indian tribal lands

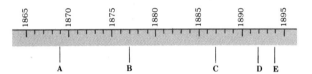

Essay Questions (40 points)
1. List three major changes that took place in American life between 1870 and 1890 and discuss the importance of each. In what ways did these changes bring about a better life for most Americans? Which of these changes made life poorer or less satisfying, in your opinion?
2. Why do you think that graft and corruption became so widespread after the Civil War? Describe some attempts at political reform at the local and national levels and weigh the success or failure of these efforts.

Unit Seven

Becoming a
World Power

Chapters in This Unit

Chapter 22

AMERICAN EXPANSION AND IMPERIALISM

Americans living in the last decade of the 19th century found themselves taking part in a great debate over foreign policy. Brought to a head by the American victory in the Spanish-American War of 1898, the debate centered around several issues. Should the United States expand overseas? Should it acquire island outposts to aid commerce and promote defense? Should it go further and build a great colonial empire as Britain and France had done? Or was the idea of building an American empire in conflict with the cherished principles of the Declaration of Independence?

Those who believed in overseas expansion began to speak of a "new Manifest Destiny." America, they said, now had a new and greater responsibility. It must take the benefits of its civilization to backward peoples in distant lands. Those who supported expansion asked what would happen if Americans were to turn their backs on opportunities to expand? What would become of Hawaii, the Philippines, and key Caribbean islands such as Cuba and Puerto Rico? Might they not fall into the hands of one of the great imperial powers of Europe? These lands would then be lost to American commerce and perhaps become a threat to American security.

From 1890 to 1914, the compelling issues of expansion and imperialism were passionately debated across the land. The way these issues were resolved did not please everyone. But for better or worse, the solutions reached would affect the lives of all Americans from that day to this.

Sections in This Chapter
1. A Great Debate over Expansion Beyond the Seas
2. The Architects of American Expansionism
3. The War with Spain and the Path of Empire
4. Consolidating the New American Empire
5. Building and Protecting the Panama Canal

Alaskan elkskin pillow made during the Klondike Gold Rush, 1896

1. A GREAT DEBATE OVER EXPANSION BEYOND THE SEAS

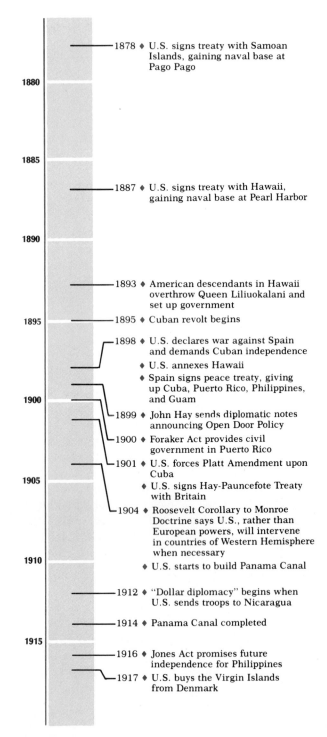

1878 ◆ U.S. signs treaty with Samoan Islands, gaining naval base at Pago Pago

1880

1885

1887 ◆ U.S. signs treaty with Hawaii, gaining naval base at Pearl Harbor

1890

1893 ◆ American descendants in Hawaii overthrow Queen Liliuokalani and set up government

1895 ◆ Cuban revolt begins

1898 ◆ U.S. declares war against Spain and demands Cuban independence

◆ U.S. annexes Hawaii

◆ Spain signs peace treaty, giving up Cuba, Puerto Rico, Philippines, and Guam

1900

1899 ◆ John Hay sends diplomatic notes announcing Open Door Policy

1900 ◆ Foraker Act provides civil government in Puerto Rico

1901 ◆ U.S. forces Platt Amendment upon Cuba

1905

◆ U.S. signs Hay-Pauncefote Treaty with Britain

1904 ◆ Roosevelt Corollary to Monroe Doctrine says U.S., rather than European powers, will intervene in countries of Western Hemisphere when necessary

1910

◆ U.S. starts to build Panama Canal

1912 ◆ "Dollar diplomacy" begins when U.S. sends troops to Nicaragua

1914 ◆ Panama Canal completed

1915

1916 ◆ Jones Act promises future independence for Philippines

1917 ◆ U.S. buys the Virgin Islands from Denmark

Those who lived during the years from 1890 to 1914 lived in a new age—the age of imperialism. **Imperialism** is the policy of extending the rule of one country over other countries or colonies, usually in order to control raw materials, markets, or military bases. Throughout the 19th century, American foreign relations had been governed by two great principles laid down in the early years of the Republic. One of these principles was first stated in Washington's Farewell Address in 1796.

Washington had called for Americans

to steer clear of permanent alliances, with any portion of the foreign world. . . . Taking care always to keep ourselves, by suitable establishments, on a respectably defensive posture, we may safely trust to temporary alliances for extraordinary emergencies.

Washington and the other early Presidents tried to stay neutral in the wars between England and France that erupted after the French Revolution. In Jefferson's words, the United States followed a **policy of noninvolvement**, or avoiding "entangling alliances" in European intrigues and wars. This was not a policy of "isolation," or lack of dealings with European countries. Rather, the United States tried to steer an independent course and follow its own interests.

The Monroe Doctrine Opposes Interference
The **Monroe Doctrine** added an important new element to the policy of noninvolvement. In 1823, President James Monroe reaffirmed that the United States would not interfere in the affairs of Europe. But Monroe added the important new principle that the United States would oppose further European colonization or political interference in the Western Hemisphere.

For about 100 years, the United States consistently followed these principles. We made no binding alliances with other nations, and on occasion we reminded the powers of Europe that we expected them to honor the Monroe Doctrine. In the 1860s, when France intervened militarily in Mexico, and in 1895, when Britain seemed ready to go into Venezuela to settle a boundary dispute, the United States invoked the Monroe Doctrine. In both cases, the United States was ready to use force if necessary. The Monroe Doctrine grew in importance as a result of both these incidents.

In the case of the French intervention in Mexico, in 1860 the French emperor, Napoleon III, sent a French army to Mexico. At that time the United States was occupied with the Civil War. In 1864, Napoleon III placed a puppet ruler, the Archduke Maximilian of Austria, on the throne of Mexico. Maximilian was unpopular with his new subjects, and when the French army withdrew in the winter of 1866–1867, he was deposed and shot. An important factor in the French decision to withdraw was the presence on the United States–Mexican border of 50,000 American troops. The Civil War over, the United States warned Napoleon III to withdraw from Mexico, backing up the warning by sending troops to the border.

In the case of the Venezuelan boundary dispute, the United States, in a strongly worded diplomatic note, objected to the refusal of the British to submit the disagreement to arbitration (the settling of a dispute by a third party). The British ignored the United States objection until 1899. Then, with mounting difficulties with Germany in South Africa, the British agreed to arbitrate the Venezuelan boundary dispute.

U.S. Expansion Before 1890

From its earliest days as a nation, the United States believed in and practiced territorial expansion. By winning independence from Britain, the 13 original states acquired most of the lands

"Johnson's Polar Bear Garden," one newspaper sneered when Seward bought Alaska in 1867.

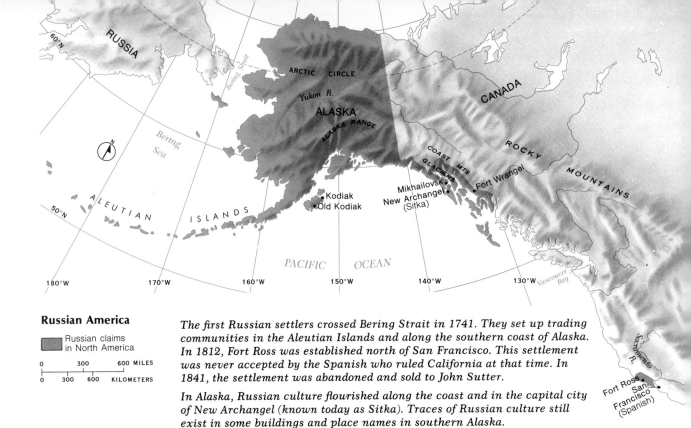

Russian America

Russian claims in North America

| 0 | 300 | 600 MILES |
| 0 | 300 | 600 KILOMETERS |

The first Russian settlers crossed Bering Strait in 1741. They set up trading communities in the Aleutian Islands and along the southern coast of Alaska. In 1812, Fort Ross was established north of San Francisco. This settlement was never accepted by the Spanish who ruled California at that time. In 1841, the settlement was abandoned and sold to John Sutter.

In Alaska, Russian culture flourished along the coast and in the capital city of New Archangel (known today as Sitka). Traces of Russian culture still exist in some buildings and place names in southern Alaska.

between the Appalachian Mountains and the Mississippi River. In 1803, Thomas Jefferson purchased the Louisiana Territory from France, expanding the nation in a majestic sweep westward to the Rockies. This was followed in 1819 by a treaty with Spain that added Florida to the nation. In the 1840s the United States annexed Texas and fought an expansionist war with Mexico, gaining the territories of New Mexico and California. In the same decade, an agreement with Britain gave us a large part of the Oregon Country. The expansionism of this period, called Manifest Destiny, seemed likely to continue.

Had it not been for the slavery issue, the nation might have given in to the call for further expansion—at the expense of Cuba, the rest of Mexico, or perhaps Canada. But with the firing on Fort Sumter, the nation's attention turned inward. Fighting the war consumed all the energies of the North and exhausted the South. Afterwards, the enormous tasks of rebuilding the South, winning the West, and developing American industries left little energy for expansion. Except for the purchase of Alaska from Russia in 1867, expansionism was dead.

Even in the case of Alaska, there was little enthusiasm. The suggestion that the United States might acquire Alaska seems to have originated with the Russians. Although Russia was aware that there was some gold in Alaska, the territory seemed otherwise of little value. Furthermore, Alaska was too far from European Russia to be defended in the event of a war. It happened also that during the 1860s, the United States and Russia were on very friendly terms. Aware of the U.S. interest in "Manifest Destiny," and aware of the danger of losing Alaska some day in any case, the Czar was willing to sell. The United States agreed to buy, but with a notable lack of enthusiasm. Andrew Johnson's Secretary of State, William H. Seward, who made the purchase, was ridiculed in some circles for spending $7 million for an "icebox," or "Seward's Folly."

When President Grant tried to annex the Dominican Republic in 1875, at the invitation of the Dominican government, he was stopped by the Senate. There was little support for adding lands that did not adjoin the continental United States.

Trade Arouses Interest in Faraway Places

At the same time that hardy pioneers were pushing the nation's frontiers westward, other Americans were finding profitable markets in distant lands. New England merchants and sea captains took the lead. Living in a land with a long seacoast and excellent harbors and with marketable products aplenty from fields, factories, and forests, enterprising Yankees were quick to find customers in faraway places.

New England sea captains, following Magellan's route around South America, reached China as early as the 1780s. Their ships carried cargoes of fur, raw cotton, and lead, which they traded for tea, silks, cotton goods, and chinaware. The highly profitable trade grew in volume as more and more Chinese ports were opened to trade. Next on the scene were American missionaries, who began going out to China as early as 1807. By mid-century, American missionaries were as familiar a sight in China as Yankee traders.

By this time, American sailors had also found their way to Japan. In 1853, **Commodore Matthew C. Perry**, after some difficulties, persuaded the local rulers to open the country to foreign contacts for the first time. A few years later Japan opened a number of her ports to American commerce. A small but lucrative trade with Japan quickly developed.

On their way to China and Japan, American ships began to stop at the Hawaiian Islands, "the Crossroads of the Pacific," for food and supplies. Located 2,000 miles southwest of San Francisco, these islands are much closer to North America than to any other landmass. (See map below.)

The Hawaiian Islands were completely unknown to the outside world until 1778, two years after the Declaration of Independence. Discovered in 1778 by the English explorer **Captain James Cook**, the Sandwich Islands, as they were named by Cook, quickly became a favorite port of call for the ships of many nations. The first American vessels visited the islands in 1789. Within a

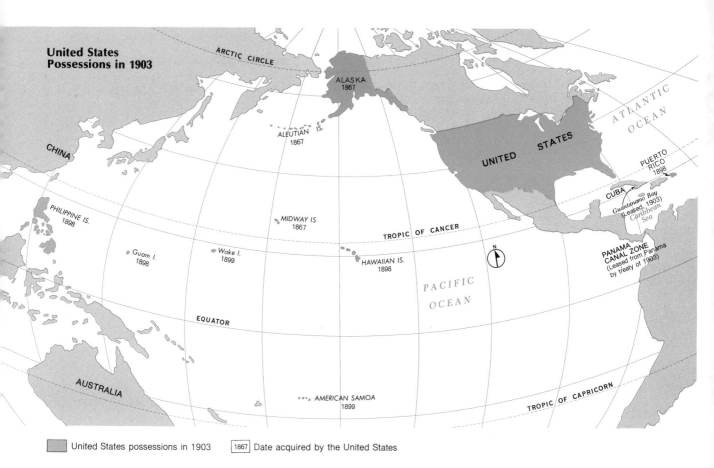

United States Possessions in 1903

ARCTIC CIRCLE

ALASKA 1867

ALEUTIAN IS. 1867

CHINA

UNITED STATES

ATLANTIC OCEAN

PUERTO RICO 1898

CUBA

Guantánamo Bay (Leased, 1903)
Caribbean Sea

PHILIPPINE IS. 1898

MIDWAY IS 1867

TROPIC OF CANCER

PANAMA CANAL ZONE (Leased from Panama by treaty of 1903)

Guam I. 1898

Wake I. 1899

HAWAIIAN IS. 1898

N

PACIFIC OCEAN

EQUATOR

AUSTRALIA

AMERICAN SAMOA 1899

TROPIC OF CAPRICORN

☐ United States possessions in 1903   1867 Date acquired by the United States

few years, there were many such visits and a developing trade.

Traders and Missionaries in Hawaii

In 1820, 200 years after the *Mayflower* arrived in New England, a shipload of New England missionaries reached Hawaii. Their success in spreading Christianity among the islanders had an important influence on later Hawaiian history. By the 1850s, the United States enjoyed a special position in Hawaii and a move was underway to annex the islands. It came to nothing at the time, mainly because Hawaii insisted on admission to the Union as a state.

By the 1890s, descendants of American missionary families dominated the native Hawaiian ruler. Many of the missionaries' descendants were now wealthy planters, engaged in raising sugar cane. An arrangement had been worked out in 1875 allowing Hawaiian sugar to enter the American market duty free. In return, in 1887 the United States had obtained the right to establish a naval base at Pearl Harbor on Oahu.

But in 1891, a new ruler, **Queen Liliuokalani** [lē-lē´ü ō kä lä´nē], came to the Hawaiian throne. Her attempt to end American control and lead a "Hawaii for the Hawaiians" movement failed. In 1893, John L. Stevens, the U.S. minister to Hawaii, ordered U.S. marines to land in Hawaii. With the help of the marines, the local Americans overthrew the Queen. They hastily organized a government and asked the United States to annex the islands. President Cleveland disapproved of

their actions and rejected the treaty. But he was unable to restore the deposed Queen. Thus in 1894 Cleveland formally recognized the new government of Hawaii, although it was not until 1898 that Hawaii was annexed.

During the late 1800s, the United States also established itself in the Samoan Islands in the South Pacific, located some 3,000 miles southwest of Hawaii. (See map, page 509.) In 1878, American naval officers reached an agreement with a Samoan chief. The agreement gave the United States use of the harbor at Pago Pago as a naval station. Since Germany and Britain were also interested in the islands, a three-power protectorate* of the islands was established. When Britain later withdrew, the United States shared control of the islands with Germany.

New States in the Union, 1900 to Present

Oklahoma (1907)
Arizona (1912)
New Mexico (1912)
Alaska (1959)
Hawaii (1959)

SECTION 1 REVIEW

Identify: imperialism, policy of noninvolvement, Monroe Doctrine, Matthew C. Perry, James Cook, Queen Liliuokalani

Main Ideas

1. List three questions asked during the great debate over foreign policy in the 1890s.
2. What two principles guided American foreign policy from the 1790s to the 1890s?
3. Name two instances in which the Monroe Doctrine was invoked during the 19th century. What happened?
4. Why did American expansion stop during and immediately after the Civil War? What was the response to Seward's purchase of Alaska and to Grant's attempt to annex the Dominican Republic?
5. How did the United States establish itself in the Hawaiian Islands? In the Samoan Islands?

160° 158° 156° 154°

Kauai

22°

Niihau

Oahu

Mòlokai

Lanai Maui

PACIFIC Kahoolawe

OCEAN 20°

MAUNA KEA

Hawaii
(Owhyhee)

Hawaiian Islands

0   75   150 MILES

0   75   150 KILOMETERS

N

Queen Liliuokalani

*protectorate [prə tek´tər it] a weak country under the protection and partial control of a strong country.

2. THE ARCHITECTS OF AMERICAN EXPANSIONISM

Individual Americans played key roles in getting the new age of imperialism underway. Perhaps foremost among the leaders was **Theodore Roosevelt**, who was assistant secretary of the navy between 1897 and 1898. Roosevelt had a lot of help from an enthusiastic group of senators. Among them were **Henry Cabot Lodge** of Massachusetts and **Albert Beveridge** of Indiana. Another man who influenced this group greatly and who was a powerful influence all by himself was a naval officer by the name of **Alfred Thayer Mahan** [mə han′].

Progress and the Survival of the Fittest

All of these men were firm believers in a number of powerful ideas that were popular in both Europe and America in the second half of the 19th century. One of these ideas was the belief in "progress," that is, the view that the human race was quickly making giant strides toward a higher form of civilization.

A second fashionable idea was that of the "survival of the fittest." According to this view, the nations with the more advanced technology were superior because, in the struggle to survive in a competitive world, they were likely to come out on top. As you recall from Chapter 19, this view of human society, called **Social Darwinism**, was popular among many Americans in the Gilded Age. They believed that the rise of the United States to greatness was a perfect illustration of Darwin's theories regarding survival of the fittest.

The ideas of Alfred Thayer Mahan also had a major impact on the thinking of many expansionists. In his book, *The Influence of Sea Power upon History* (1890), Mahan argued that a strong navy was the secret of world power. He drew most of his examples from British history, showing how command of the seas had given the small island kingdom of Great Britain control over a vast world empire "on which the sun never set." Influenced by Mahan, both Lodge and Roosevelt worked feverishly for a new modern navy. They were highly successful: by the turn of the century the United States Navy was strong enough to be a force in the world.

Belief in "the White Man's Burden"

A surge of optimism and idealism, mixed with a missionary zeal, was added to the ideas of Social Darwinism. Many people came to believe that a nation such as the United States, blessed with vast resources, wealth, and power, had an obligation to assist less fortunate and "backward" nations. This belief was also common in England at the time. A British poet, Rudyard Kipling, summed up the feeling by advising his audience to "take up the **white man's burden**." Kipling's phrase became world famous. It meant that England and America had an obligation to go into distant lands, taking their superior technology to "backward" people, civilizing and christianizing them. Kipling and his many supporters never questioned the superiority of western civilization over that of the peoples of Asia and Africa.

There was a strong element of racism in this kind of thinking. Believers in the new imperial-

FROM THE ARCHIVES

Albert J. Beveridge Argues for Imperialism

Here is an excerpt from Beveridge's famous speech, entitled "The March of the Flag," delivered at Indianapolis, Indiana, on September 16, 1898. He was elected to the Senate in 1899.

The ocean does not separate us from lands of our duty and desire—the oceans join us. . . . Steam joins us; electricity joins us—the very elements are in league with our destiny. Cuba not contiguous [next to the U.S.]! Porto Rico not contiguous! Hawaii and the Philippines not contiguous! Our navy will make them contiguous. . . .

   [Today] we are raising more than we can consume. Today we are making more than we can use. . . . Therefore we must find new markets for our produce, new occupation for our capital, new work for our labor. . . .

   Think of the thousands of Americans who will pour into Hawaii and Porto Rico when the republic's laws cover those islands with justice and safety! . . . Think of the hundreds of thousands of Americans who will build a soap-and-water, common-school civilization of energy and industry in Cuba, when a government of law replaces the double reign of anarchy and tyranny!

ism never asked whether the people of "backward" countries wanted western technology. They assumed that anyone without such technology would not only want it, but would also be grateful to the nation that provided it. Although it would be many years before the "beneficial" effects of modern imperialism were seriously questioned in England and America, there were voices of protest at the time. William Jennings Bryan, three times the Democratic candidate for President, questioned the wisdom of America's march along the path of empire. But Bryan's voice was that of a minority. By 1898, the opponents of imperialism were beginning to lose out in the great national debate over expansion.

By then, Americans such as Albert Beveridge were arguing that colonies were essential to trade. The United States, Beveridge and other expansionists said, was producing more than its citizens could consume. People in faraway lands would be ideal customers for the surpluses of its farms and factories. Its merchant ships, and the navy that protected them, needed coaling stations and supply bases along the routes of trade. The industrialized nations of Europe—Britain, Germany, and France—were rapidly staking out overseas bases to supply and protect their navies and merchant ships. We must, said the expansionists, do the same in this competitive world where the "survival of the fittest" was the governing principle. Although American businessmen and bankers usually opposed policies that might lead to war, for fear trade would be disrupted, they eagerly supported peaceful expansion overseas. More and more of them were persuaded by men like Beveridge of the need for an empire.

SECTION 2 REVIEW

Identify: Theodore Roosevelt, Henry Cabot Lodge, Albert Beveridge, Alfred Thayer Mahan, Social Darwinism, "white man's burden"

Main Ideas

1. Explain how ideas such as the belief in "progress," "survival of the fittest," and the "white man's burden" were used to justify America's expansionism.
2. How did the ideas of Mahan and Beveridge influence American foreign policy?

3. THE WAR WITH SPAIN AND THE PATH OF EMPIRE

A slim white battleship rides at anchor in a peaceful harbor. The Stars and Stripes fly from the masthead. Launches move regularly from ship to shore, carrying white-uniformed United States naval officers. Ashore the Americans enjoy a round of receptions, dinners, balls, and bullfights. The United States battleship *Maine* is paying a courtesy visit to Havana, Cuba. The year is 1898.

Suddenly the stillness of the February night is shattered by a powerful explosion. The battleship *Maine* sinks to a watery grave, carrying with her 260 American sailors. No one knows for certain what caused the explosion. But there are dark suspicions of treachery. Cuba belongs to Spain, and United States relations with Spain have not been good. Two months after the disaster in Havana Bay, with cries of "**Remember the *Maine***" ringing in the air, the United States goes to war with Spain.

Cuba: The Last of the Spanish Empire

The sinking of the *Maine* was one of the immediate causes that touched off the war with Spain. The real causes of the conflict ran deeper. The central cause of the Spanish-American War was America's growing concern over conditions on the island of Cuba. Along with Puerto Rico, Cuba was all that remained of Spain's once great empire in the Americas. Spanish misgovernment had left the island in turmoil, producing an insurrection every few years. The sufferings of the Cubans, just 90 miles from Florida, attracted widespread attention and sympathy in the United States.

Many Americans thought Cuba should be part of the United States. You may recall that southern expansionists of the 1850s had included Cuba in their Manifest Destiny plans. But northern opposition to the expansion of slave territory stood in the way of annexation. After the Civil War, various insurrectionist elements in Cuba tried to enlist United States aid in a move for Cuban independence. With great difficulty, the United States managed to remain neutral during a period of turmoil on the island that lasted from 1869 to 1878.

Then, in 1895, another revolt swept the island. By this time the ideas of men such as Mahan, Lodge, and Beveridge were popular with many Americans. Fully recovered from the Civil War, the nation was strong economically and politically. The U.S. army, relegated to reservation duty after the Indian Wars ended, was far from battle-ready. But the trim new navy was prepared for action. The nation was united in a belief that conditions on the strife-torn island of Cuba should not be permitted to continue.

Spain Tries to Crush Cuban Revolt of 1895

The 1895 revolt was partly the result of a change in United States tariff policy. The McKinley Tariff Act of 1890 admitted Cuban sugar to the United States duty free. This proved to be a bonanza to the island's economy, bringing unusual prosperity to the sugar industry. However, a new tariff in 1894 restored a sizable duty on Cuban sugar. Even in good times, Cuban workers were treated little better than slaves. Now, with sugar prices falling and the industry in trouble generally, conditions in Cuba became wretched. The resulting discontent erupted in another Cuban insurrection against Spanish rule. As before, the embattled Cubans sought and received aid from sympathizers in the United States.

Unable to crush the Cuban revolt by ordinary police methods, the Spanish government resorted to harsher measures. The kind of guerrilla warfare waged by the insurgents could be countered only by rounding up the civilian population of trouble zones and forcing them into fortified towns. This "reconcentration policy" brought strong protests from the United States government, particularly after serious epidemics of disease swept through some of the concentration camps. American newspapers added fuel to the flames by printing greatly exaggerated news stories of Spanish atrocities. Fed on a steady diet of such stories, the American people began clamoring for a war to free Cuba from Spanish misrule.

Two Events Lead to War

With the clamor for war rising, President McKinley doubled United States diplomatic efforts to persuade Spain to grant self-rule to Cuba. After considerable stalling, Spain finally agreed to end the reconcentration policy and to grant an armistice to the rebels. Spain did not agree to self-rule for Cuba, but it was willing to discuss the question. But by then it was too late. Two unexpected events intervened and made war all but certain.

The first of these was the **De Lôme letter**. Enrique Dupuy de Lôme was the Spanish minister to the United States. He wrote a private letter to a friend in Cuba in which he criticized President McKinley as "weak and a bidder for the admiration of the crowd, besides being a would-be politician who tries to leave a door open behind himself while keeping on good terms with the jingoes* of his party." The letter fell into American hands and found its way into the newspapers. There was a loud outcry. Americans reading their morning paper thought that their country and their President had been insulted.

Rage over the De Lôme letter was at a fever pitch when a violent explosion destroyed the United States battleship *Maine* in Havana harbor. It was widely believed at the time that Spain was responsible.

President McKinley continued to work for peace. He had vivid memories of the bloodshed and slaughter he had seen as a young soldier in the Union army during the American Civil War. He wanted peace, but he was not strong enough to withstand the demands for war. Spain was now ready to give in to all his demands. But time had run out. Congress and the public were screaming for war. "McKinley has no more backbone than a chocolate eclair!" Theodore Roosevelt is reported to have shouted.

His career at stake, McKinley reluctantly gave in to public opinion and sent a war message to Congress in April 1898. To show that the United States had no designs on Cuba, Congress adopted a resolution introduced by Senator Henry M. Teller of Colorado. The resolution, known as the **Teller Amendment**, stated that the United States claimed no sovereignty over Cuba. Once the island was free, the United States would leave.

Battle in the Philippines

The first action in the Spanish-American War occurred not in Cuba but half a world away in the Philippine Islands. (See map, page 509.) Spain had ruled the Philippines since the days of Magellan.

*__jingo__ term used to describe a supporter of an aggressive foreign policy.

Like the people of Cuba, the people of the Philippines were in rebellion against this rule. Although few Americans had ever heard of the Philippine Islands, Assistant Secretary of the Navy Theodore Roosevelt had long had his eyes on them as a possible American base for navy and merchant ships. When war with Spain over Cuba seemed about to erupt, Roosevelt acted. He cabled the United States naval commander in the Pacific, **George Dewey**, instructing him to sail to Hong Kong and be ready for news that war had been declared. Dewey was ordered to proceed at once to Manila, capital of the Philippines, and destroy the Spanish fleet stationed there.

Dewey carried out his assignment with ease. Before any American troops reached Cuba, Dewey had sent the Spanish squadron to the bottom of Manila Bay. The Spanish commander and his men fought gallantly, but their aging ships were no match for the new American navy. When news of the great naval victory reached home, Dewey became an instant hero.

America Prepares for the War

Attention now shifted to the island of Cuba. Preparations for the campaign to free Cuba began shortly after war was declared. An immediate invasion was out of the question, since the United States army at the time numbered only 30,000. But a call for volunteers brought over a million men into the army. Many weeks were needed to train and supply those who rallied to the call. Among the volunteers was Theodore Roosevelt, who resigned as Assistant Secretary of the Navy to accept a commission in a volunteer cavalry regiment later known as the "Rough Riders."

News of Dewey's easy win at Manila led President McKinley to believe that an invasion of Cuba could begin almost at once. He was certainly overly optimistic. In Tampa, Florida, mobilization camps were hurriedly set up to train the volunteers. All was chaos and confusion. Food and supplies arrived at one location while the men for whom they were intended arrived at another. Although war was declared in April 1898, it was not until June that the first transports left for Cuba.

The Spanish-American War: A Summer Long

The objective of the American invasion force was the port city of Santiago, where the Spanish Atlantic fleet was anchored. (See Atlas Map 2.) Theodore Roosevelt saw his first action in the successful effort to capture the hills protecting the city. The newspapers, eager for exciting material for their readers, followed the colorful Roosevelt. For his actions at the Battle of San Juan Hill they were ready to declare him a hero, although the key position in the engagement was captured by an infantry regiment.

The Spanish fleet, anchored in Santiago Harbor, now attempted to escape. The American fleet, including the battleship *Oregon*, which had made a 12,000-mile trip from Puget Sound, Washington, around South America, moved in for the kill. The resulting battle was a repeat of Dewey's smashing victory over Spain's Pacific squadron at Manila. The American ships sank the entire Spanish fleet as it tried to leave the harbor.

With the protecting fleet destroyed and the surrounding hills in American hands, Santiago surrendered. Cuba seemed free at last. A week later American forces took over Puerto Rico and before the summer was over the Spanish land forces in the Philippines surrendered. In the course of a single summer—from May to October 1898—the "splendid little war," as the American Secretary of State John Hay called the Spanish-American War, was over. The United States had obtained freedom for Cuba, and much more. In the peace treaty, Spain, in addition to giving up all claim to Cuba, ceded Puerto Rico, the Philippines, and the island of Guam to the United States. (See map, page 509.) For the Philippines, we agreed to pay Spain the sum of $20 million. During the fateful summer of 1898 the United States became a colonial power and assumed what soon proved to be vast new problems and responsibilities.

SECTION 3 REVIEW

Identify: "Remember the *Maine*," De Lôme letter, Teller Amendment, George Dewey

Main Ideas

1. What events led to the Spanish-American War? Discuss both the immediate causes and the long-term reasons for the war.
2. In what geographical areas was the Spanish-American War fought?
3. What were the terms of the peace treaty?

LIFE IN AMERICA

LEISURE TIME AT THE TURN OF THE CENTURY

Amusement park at Coney Island, New York, around 1903

While journalists were competing for the attention of the American people with gruesome stories from Cuba, William Randolph Hearst's *New York Journal* used another feature to boost circulation: baseball scores were printed in red ink on the paper's front page. Hearst sensed that baseball was becoming the national pastime. By the turn of the century, in fact, interest in leisure-time activities was at an all-time high.

More Leisure Time

While the poor had neither the time nor the money for games, many middle-class Americans had time on their hands and some extra money to spend. Per-capita income had risen from $779 to $1,164 between 1870 and 1900. The work day had been shortened to ten hours, with Saturday afternoons and Sundays off for many workers. Interest in books, plays, and music increased, and so did attendance at state fairs and circuses. But the most distinctive leisure-time impulse of the Gilded Age was the new interest in sports.

While the typical middle-class family often spent its Sunday afternoons playing checkers, staring into 3-D stereopticon viewers, or swinging on the porch swing, more strenuous activities such as tennis, golf, ice skating, boating, bicycling, and swimming were also popular.

Croquet and Bicycling

By far the two biggest sports crazes that the 1890s family enjoyed were croquet [krō kā′] and bicycling. Croquet was the first popular outdoor game designed for both sexes to play together. The wickets and pegs, brightly striped mallets and wooden balls cropped up in thousands of backyards.

During the 1890s, more than 10 million Americans took to bicycling after the invention of the "safety" bicycle in 1885. It featured two equal-sized wheels, much smaller and safer than the earlier version, which had featured a huge front wheel. By 1896 bike manufacturing was a $60 million business.

The Birth of Modern Spectator Sports

Modern spectator sports, such as basketball, boxing, and football, were also growing in popularity in the Gilded Age. But the budding sports fan let nothing rival his or her love for baseball. In 1886 *Harper's Weekly* announced: "The fascination of the game has seized upon the American people, irrespective of age, sex, or other condition."

No one knows for certain how baseball started, but organized play goes back to the 1840s. In later years new rules and equipment, including umpires, gloves, masks, shin guards, and chest protectors for catchers, made the game much like it is today.

In 1869 the Cincinnati Red Stockings became the first professional baseball team. The National League was founded in 1876, with teams in Boston, Hartford, New York, Philadelphia, Cincinnati, Louisville, Chicago, and St. Louis. By 1901 the American League was organized, and in 1903 the first World Series was played, the American League's Boston team defeating the National League's Pittsburgh team.

The popularity of baseball was unrivaled by any other spectator sport of the era. By 1890, 60,000 fans a day were going to the ball park. The New York Giants set an attendance record of 400,000 for the 1894 season. Americans had truly found their "national pastime." Sports in America were here to stay.

4. CONSOLIDATING THE NEW AMERICAN EMPIRE

The decision to annex the Philippine Islands was reached after a spirited debate in the United States Congress. Opinions expressed in Congress were probably a fairly accurate barometer of the shifting nature of public opinion. Although some American leaders such as Roosevelt and Lodge supported the idea of an American empire from the beginning, they were clearly a minority at the time the nation went to war against Spain. The spirit of the Teller Amendment—rejecting in advance any idea of territorial acquisition in Cuba—was much closer to the views of the majority.

But as the war progressed, all of this began to change. Once the flag had been raised over Cuba, Puerto Rico, and the Philippines, an increasing number of Americans believed that it would be wrong, if not actually unpatriotic, to haul it down. Gradually, the United States moved forward along the path of empire. Increasingly the American people came to believe that, unlike European imperialism, the American variety was unselfish and undertaken mainly for the purpose of uplifting "backward" peoples. It is highly doubtful that Americans would have accepted their new role as a colonial power if they had not convinced themselves that they had a responsibility to fulfill. But events in Cuba and the Philippine Islands soon brought into question the role of the United States as a liberator of oppressed peoples.

Cuba: Independence with Strings Attached

The idealism that helped propel the United States into the war against Spain was nowhere better illustrated than in the Teller Amendment. Overwhelmingly supported in Congress as an amendment to the war declaration of 1898, the resolution stated emphatically that the United States had no intention of exercising control over Cuba. The United States was concerned only in obtaining independence for the Cuban people.

This well-intentioned pledge soon brought the McKinley administration face-to-face with a serious problem. Once Spain was defeated, no effective government existed in Cuba. The United States army was in control and would remain so until a Cuban government could be formed. To have withdrawn immediately would probably have meant abandoning the Cuban people to a horrible fate—death for millions from starvation, disease, and crime. So the army stayed on and set about feeding the starving, caring for the ill, providing for basic sanitation needs, and keeping law and order. In effect, the army took over all the functions of a regular government. After two years of army rule, conditions in Cuba improved significantly. Under army supervision, the Cuban voters elected delegates to a convention which proceeded to draw up a constitution for an independent Cuba.

Cubans who expected the United States to live up to the Teller Amendment were in for a disappointment. The United States army authorities informed the Cuban Constitutional Convention that it must adopt a set of regulations defining Cuba's relationship with the United States. Those conditions became known as the **Platt Amendment** because they were first stated in an amendment to an army appropriations bill. The conditions severely limited Cuba's freedom of action.

Three of the most important conditions of the Platt Amendment were: (1) Cuba was not to enter into any agreements with foreign powers that would endanger its independence; (2) the Cuban government was to give the United States the right to intervene in Cuban affairs if necessary to maintain an efficient, independent government; (3) the Cuban government was required to lease harbor facilities to the United States for naval and coaling stations.

Much against their will, the Cubans accepted these conditions as part of their new constitution. Later they were required to sign a treaty with the United States that contained the same conditions. In this way, the United States gained control of an important naval base at Guantánamo Bay in Cuba. The United States still holds this base. The other provisions of the Platt Amendment continued in force until 1934. On several occasions between 1901 and 1934 the United States intervened in Cuban affairs under the terms of the agreement.

Puerto Rico: A Different Type of Control

In the case of Puerto Rico, the United States was not hampered by any pledge like that given to the

Cubans in the Teller Amendment. The United States took possession of Puerto Rico in 1898 with no thought of bringing independence to its people. Puerto Rico was to be a colony held by the United States as the spoils of war. After a year-and-a-half of army rule in Puerto Rico, in 1900 Congress passed the **Foraker Act**, which gave the island a system of civil government. The act made the people of the island citizens of Puerto Rico but not citizens of the United States. The people were permitted to elect a legislature, but administrative authority was vested in a governor and a council appointed by the President of the United States.

Puerto Ricans were unhappy with the type of colonial government provided by the Foraker Act. In 1917 Congress passed the **Jones Act**, making the people of the island citizens of the United States. Except for the governor, who was to be appointed by the United States, the government of the island was to be elected by the people. In 1952, Puerto Rico became a self-governing commonwealth with a new constitution. Since 1952, the island's relations with the United States have been close, but on a strictly voluntary basis. Some Puerto Ricans see their island as a potential 51st state of the Union. Others would like to continue as a commonwealth with close United States ties. There appears to be little support for complete independence.

The Insular Cases: Does the Constitution Follow the Flag?

The Foraker Act, which set up a civil government for Puerto Rico, raised a thorny constitutional issue. Among its many provisions was one which levied a duty on Puerto Rican goods coming into the United States. But if Puerto Rico was a part of the United States, were these import duties constitutional? The United States Constitution prohibits tariffs on goods shipped within the United States. The question raised was this: Does the Constitution follow the flag? When the United States acquires a foreign island (Puerto Rico), are its people guaranteed the constitutional rights of Americans?

This issue came before the United States Supreme Court in 1901 in cases called the **Insular Cases**. ("Insular" means "having to do with an island.") The Court ruled, in effect, that Puerto Rico and the other United States possessions were not fully part of the United States and that the tariff duties levied by the Foraker Act were legal. Thus the Supreme Court decided that the Constitution does not follow the flag. The people of the new American possessions were not automatically entitled to the same guarantees of the Constitution as were United States citizens. But, as we have seen, Congress gradually extended many of these rights to the people of Puerto Rico.

The Filipino Revolt and U.S. Expansionism

Long before most Americans had ever heard of the Philippine Islands, the Filipino people were waging a war of independence against Spain. Dewey's victory over the Spanish fleet at Manila did not give the United States control of the Philippines. The leader of the Philippine independence movement, **Emilio Aguinaldo**, was not about to exchange Spanish rule for American. When the United States decided to keep the islands, Aguinaldo and his followers took to the jungles. They became guerrillas once more, this time against United States rule.

The United States now found itself in a bitter struggle to impose its rule on a people fighting for their freedom. By the end of 1898, the insurgents held every important position in the islands except Manila. It was to take three years, the lives of 4,000 American soldiers and of at least 20,000 guerrillas, and more than $170 million to crush the independence movement. In crushing the revolt, United States troops resorted to the same kind of brutal warfare that the Spanish had used in Cuba. Finally Aguinaldo was captured, swore allegiance to the United States, and agreed to help pacify the country. Despite this unpromising beginning, American rule of the Philippines was gradually accepted.

Matters improved somewhat when **William Howard Taft** became governor of the islands in 1901. Taft proved adept at building local support. He brought about much needed reform in land ownership and quickly substituted civil for military government. Under Taft's leadership, public schools, hospitals, modern sanitation, and economic prosperity were introduced into the islands. But many Filipinos remained resentful and continued to work for independence. They saw the Americans as foreign conquerors who were destroying the culture of a people.

In 1902 Congress set up a system of government for the Philippines that allowed an important measure of self-rule. Under the act, the islands became an unorganized territory of the United States. Their people were to be citizens of the Philippine Islands, not citizens of the United States. The Philippine Islands were to have a legislative body, one house of which was to be popularly elected. But laws made by the Philippine legislature could be vetoed by the United States Congress.

When the first Philippine legislature met in 1907, over half of its members voted for independence from the United States. The Jones Act, passed by the United States Congress in 1916, made both houses of the Philippine legislature elective and promised independence some time in the future. This was delayed because many in the United States claimed that the Filipinos were not ready for independence. In 1934, an act of the United States Congress promised independence in ten years. Because of World War II and a Japanese invasion of the islands, however, independence was again delayed. Finally, in 1946, when the Japanese had been expelled from the islands and peace had returned, the Philippine Islands received their independence.

The Open Door in China

Among those who argued in favor of retaining the Philippines were American businessmen who were becoming increasingly concerned over American markets in East Asia, especially in China. The business community had not favored going to war with Spain, fearing war would disrupt the nation's economic life and endanger prosperity. But once the war was over, business interests tended to favor the annexation of Puerto Rico, Guam, and the Philippines. The annexation of the Hawaiian Islands in 1898 was eagerly supported, and in 1900 Hawaii became a U.S. territory. But the Philippines were of special concern to big business because of their nearness to the mainland of China.

China was a weak giant, unable to rule its vast lands and unable to beat back attempts of European powers to gain control over large parts of its territory. By the turn of the century, Britain, Germany, France, Russia, and Japan had carved out large trading areas in China. They called these areas "spheres of influence" and enjoyed special rights in them. Because the United States claimed no special privileges or spheres of influence in China, American merchants feared they would be frozen out of the areas where China had granted special privileges to other powers. But American presence in the Philippine Islands, 600 miles from the Chinese mainland, could greatly strengthen the United States position.

The American Secretary of State, **John Hay,** had a plan which he hoped would guarantee continued American access to China's market. He called it the **"Open Door Policy,"** meaning that the privilege of trading with China should remain open to all nations. Britain had originally followed this policy, but gave it up when other nations began to carve up China.

By the time Hay announced his Open Door Policy in 1899, the British had abandoned it as hopeless and had staked out a sphere of influence of their own. Thus Hay's Open Door Policy was declared after the door had been "closed." Consequently it had little effect. Hay knew this, but he wanted to make a clear statement of American rights in China. To do this, he sent diplomatic notes to all the great powers asking them to agree to keep open the ports of China to all nations and to guarantee equal trading rights and equal access to railroad and harbor facilities. The replies he received were discouraging. Nonetheless, Hay announced that the Open Door Policy was in effect. The United States continued to support the idea of the Open Door Policy, but in reality it meant very little.

The Defense of the Pacific Empire

The acquisition of the Philippine Islands strengthened the United States trading position in relation to China, but it also involved the nation more deeply in East Asian affairs. When, in 1900, a revolt against foreigners broke out in China, the United States took part in an armed intervention by the great powers. After the Boxer Rebellion, as the revolt was called, was crushed, the United States took a firm stand against those who wanted to punish China by dividing up more of its territory. China was required to pay an indemnity (payment for damages) to the powers instead of ceding them more territory. After compensating United States citizens for losses suffered during the rebellion, the United States government returned the remainder of its share of the indemnity to China. To show its appreciation for the return of the funds, the Chinese government used the money to send Chinese students to the United States. This educational program gave another boost to developing good will between China and America.

The United States kept a close watch on East Asian developments. Of particular concern was the growing rivalry between Russia and a modernized Japan. If one of these powers should become dominant (as Japan did in 1905–1906 by defeating Russia), it could pose a threat to United States control of the Philippines. How then was the United States to protect islands some 8,000 miles west of California?

American ownership of the Philippines placed an added strain on the nation's defense capabilities. In order to defend the Philippines and the growing American stake in China, it was necessary to revolutionize the nation's military strategy. Throughout our history, geographic isolation from Europe had been to our great benefit. We needed no large standing army or powerful fleet to defend our interests. All of this changed drastically at the turn of the century when the United States acquired a Pacific empire.

SECTION 4 REVIEW

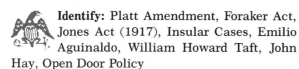

Identify: Platt Amendment, Foraker Act, Jones Act (1917), Insular Cases, Emilio Aguinaldo, William Howard Taft, John Hay, Open Door Policy

Main Ideas

1. How did America become an imperialist power? How did Americans consider their imperialism different from that of the European countries?
2. How did the Platt Amendment give the United States almost complete control of Cuba?
3. How did the United States gain control of Puerto Rico and the Philippines? Were their citizens given the same rights as Americans?
4. Why did friendly relations with China become important at the turn of the century? What actions did the United States take to maintain them?
5. How did the new possessions of the United States force a change in its defense needs?

5. BUILDING AND PROTECTING THE PANAMA CANAL

From the day Balboa sighted the mighty Pacific from a mountaintop in Panama, people dreamed of a waterway that would connect the Atlantic and Pacific oceans. But there was no natural passage through the Isthmus* of Panama. Ships had to sail around the tip of South America—a long and dangerous journey. For 400 years the mountainous terrain of Central America discouraged any idea of construction of an interoceanic canal. With the coming of the steam shovel, however, all of this changed.

During the mid-19th century, enterprising merchants and ship captains tried to interest their governments in digging an artificial waterway somewhere across the isthmus. They were encouraged by the success of the French company that dug the Suez Canal in Egypt in the 1860s. Finally, in the 1880s, a French company began work on a Panama Canal. But the task proved to be too great. The company went broke trying to cut through the rugged mountains and fever-infested swamps of Panama. The project was abandoned.

The Spanish-American War and the Panama Canal

Little more was heard of an interoceanic canal until the Spanish-American War. Overnight, interest grew. The event that triggered this interest was the dramatic rush of the new battleship *Oregon* from its base at Puget Sound around South America to the waters off Cuba. The 12,000-mile voyage took 68 days. The country held its breath for fear the mighty ship would be lost in the storm-tossed Straits of Magellan. The newspapers pointed out that a canal through Panama, controlled by the United States, could have solved the problem. The *Oregon* could then have reached Cuba in 20 days, completely avoiding the perils of the South Atlantic.

The war with Spain convinced American leaders that a canal must be built. The only questions

---

*isthmus [is′məs] a narrow strip of land with water on both sides, connecting two larger bodies of land.

U.S. Activities in the Caribbean, 1898–1917

U.S. protectorates

U.S. military expeditions

U.S. possessions are labeled in red

0 — 500 MILES

0 — 500 KILOMETERS

were where to build it and how to overcome the many obstacles that stood in the way.

The First Obstacle Removed

The first obstacle that had to be removed was an agreement with Britain known as the Clayton-Bulwer Treaty. By the terms of this treaty, signed in 1850, Britain and the United States had each agreed not to build a canal across the isthmus without the consent and participation of the other party. By the end of the century, however, the power relationship between the United States and Britain had changed. The United States had grown in strength and power and had become the dominant force in the Western Hemisphere. Meanwhile, Britain was feeling stiff competition elsewhere in the world from Germany and France. While British interests in the Caribbean were as great as ever, Britain could no longer support a large navy in the New World.

British leaders began to think of the United States more as a partner than as a threat. There was increasing talk of Anglo-American solidarity, based on common language and culture. Thus it proved fairly easy for the American Secretary of State, John Hay, to negotiate a new canal agreement with the British. By the terms of the new treaty, the **Hay-Pauncefote Treaty of 1901**, Britain agreed not to oppose a canal built and controlled solely by the United States. The only condition was that the canal would be open to the ships of all nations and would remain neutral in wartime.

With British opposition removed, other obstacles could now be faced. Where exactly should the canal be built? And how could the U.S. obtain the needed right-of-way through foreign territory?

The Route Is Determined

There were two favored routes for the projected canal. One lay through Panama, which was, at the time, a province of Colombia. (See map, facing page.) The other, a longer route, lay through the independent country of Nicaragua. A treaty would have to be negotiated with either Colombia or Nicaragua, allowing the United States to purchase the necessary right-of-way.

There were important arguments for and against each route. Some favored the route through Panama because it was shorter and because Colombia seemed willing to sell a right-of-way for a lower price. In addition, part of the work was already completed. The French company that had surveyed the route and completed part of the construction work was willing to sell its interests to the United States. But critics of the Panamanian route pointed to the rugged terrain and fever-ridden swamps through which the canal must pass. The United States would have to overcome the obstacles that had caused the French effort to fail.

Those who favored Nicaragua argued that the greater distance through that country was offset by the fact that Lake Nicaragua, which was navigable, formed part of the canal route. This would mean less excavation. The Nicaraguan route had other advantages as well. The land through which the canal would pass was less rugged and more healthful.

Ill Will Is Built

For many months Congress studied and debated the pros and cons of the two routes. In the end the Panamanian route was chosen for a number of reasons. For one thing, the French company that wanted to sell its rights to the United States hired a special agent, **Philippe Bunau-Varilla**, to promote the Panamanian route. A clever, resourceful man, Bunau-Varilla worked feverishly behind the scenes to smooth the way. When the Colombian government asked for more money than the United States was willing to pay, Bunau-Varilla was equal to the challenge. Knowing that the Panamanians were unhappy with Colombian rule, he set about organizing an independence movement in Panama. The people of Panama were afraid that if Colombia continued to hold out for more money, the United States would turn to Nicaragua. For this reason, they fell in with Bunau-Varilla's scheme for independence. An independent Panama could negotiate its own canal treaty with the United States.

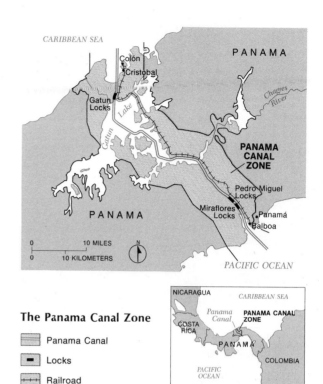

The Panama Canal Zone

▭ Panama Canal

▬ Locks

╫╫╫ Railroad

With the aid of a United States warship, which prevented Colombian troops from landing to crush the revolt, Bunau-Varilla's efforts succeeded. The Panamanians declared their independence, and the United States extended immediate diplomatic recognition to the new nation. Bunau-Varilla, now acting as foreign minister for an independent Panama, quickly negotiated a canal treaty with the United States. The United States purchased the assets of the French company and in 1904 began construction of the canal.

Colombia was furious with the high-handed actions of the United States government. Relations with Colombia were further strained when Theodore Roosevelt, who had become President in 1901, at first boasted that he had "taken Panama" and then later denied that he had in any way supported the revolution. Later United States efforts to wipe out the resulting ill will by a payment to Colombia of $25 million for the loss of Panama were taken as an admission of guilt. The belief that the United States was a big bully which pushed around smaller nations became widespread throughout Latin America.

President Roosevelt running a steam shovel at Culebra Cut, Panama Canal, 1906

Even before the Panama Canal was completed, protecting the waterway became a primary concern of United States foreign policy. The treaty with Panama gave the United States complete control over a strip of Panamanian territory ten miles wide. The United States paid Panama $10 million and an annual rent of $250,000 for the right-of-way. The United States fortified the Canal Zone itself and then began to consider ways of protecting the approaches to the Canal from the Caribbean. An important step in this direction had already been taken when the United States declared what amounted to a protectorate over Cuba. With a United States naval base at Guantánamo Bay in Cuba, one of the major sea approaches to the Panama Canal was protected.

The Roosevelt Corollary to the Monroe Doctrine

Soon other steps were taken to strengthen the Canal's defenses. President Theodore Roosevelt was afraid that one of the great European powers might try to establish itself in the Americas and become a threat to the Panama Canal. Germany was particularly feared. Several smaller Latin American countries had borrowed large sums of money from German, French, and British bankers. If the loans were not repaid, there was a danger that one of the European countries might use its navy in an effort to collect the money. This is exactly what happened in 1902 when Britain and Germany declared a blockade of Venezuela to force that country to pay its debts. Roosevelt feared that a naval blockade by a European power might lead to military intervention of the kind undertaken by France in Mexico during the American Civil War. This would be a violation of the Monroe Doctrine and a threat to the Panama Canal.

Although the Venezuelan crisis was solved by mediation (settlement with the help of an outside party), Roosevelt worried about the future. When, in 1904, a similar situation arose in the Dominican Republic, he acted. In his annual message to Congress in 1904, he told the European powers that if intervention in an American country became necessary because of "chronic wrong doing," it would be the United States that intervened. In other words, the United States would act as policeman of the Western Hemisphere.

The new U.S. policy of intervening to forestall

The Building and Defense of the Canal

The actual building of the canal proved more difficult than feared. The biggest problem was the unhealthy climate which promoted yellow fever and other tropical diseases. Eventually the efforts of Dr. Walter Reed and Major William Gorgas helped overcome these diseases. Their previous work in Cuba had identified a certain mosquito as the carrier of yellow fever. A vigorous campaign by United States doctors and engineers rid the swamps and jungles of the disease-carrying insects. Panama became a relatively healthy place and the work of construction got underway in 1904. The chief engineer, Colonel W. Goethals, succeeded despite numerous landslides, yellow fever, and the steaming climate. The canal took ten years to build and cost nearly $400 million. Completed in 1914, just as World War I was beginning, the canal was considered one of the greatest engineering feats of all time.

European intervention became known as the **Roosevelt Corollary** (extension) of the Monroe Doctrine. On several occasions the United States intervened financially or militarily in the Dominican Republic (in 1905 and 1916), in Haiti (in 1915), and in Nicaragua (in 1911) when these countries failed to make debt payments to European creditors. In this way, Roosevelt and his successors prevented European intervention in countries located in the Caribbean area, next door to the Canal. These countries resented United States interference in their affairs and complained that "the Colossus of the North" was trying to make the Caribbean a United States lake.

Taft and "Dollar Diplomacy"

Under President Taft, who succeeded Roosevelt in 1909, the United States continued to intervene in the Caribbean. Shortly after Taft took office, a revolution broke out in Nicaragua, bringing a new president, Adolfo Díaz, to power. Friendly to the United States, Díaz enlisted United States financial support. With the participation of United States bankers, Taft arranged to refinance the Nicaraguan national debt. As part of the agreement, United States bankers took charge of Nicaraguan custom duties and other Nicaraguan assets. When a revolt broke out against Díaz in 1911, he requested United States intervention. The following year Taft sent 2,000 United States marines to put down the revolt. The marines stayed on for many years, making Nicaragua in effect an American protectorate.

The forceful intervention of the United States in the financial affairs of Latin American countries in order to protect United States strategic interests was an extension of the Roosevelt Corollary which critics called "dollar diplomacy." "Dollar diplomacy" was the use of diplomatic efforts to encourage and protect American investments in foreign countries, particularly in Latin America. Sometimes United States banks, with or without urging from the State Department, made loans to Latin American countries. If and when those governments defaulted on the loans or failed to make interest payments, the United States intervened with troops to protect the bankers. Like the Roosevelt Corollary, "dollar diplomacy" created an increasing amount of ill will for the United States throughout Latin America.

Wilson Continues the Policy of Intervention in the Caribbean

Although Woodrow Wilson, Taft's successor in the White House, had criticized his predecessor's interventionist policy in the Caribbean, he found himself continuing it. In 1915, Wilson sent the marines into the Republic of Haiti. As a result of United States intervention, Haiti was required in 1916 to sign a treaty giving the United States control of the country's finances and police force. The same treaty provided for United States intervention in the future to maintain law and order. The United States marines stayed on in the riot-torn island for 18 years. By making Haiti a United States protectorate, Wilson and his successors continued Taft's policy of dollar diplomacy. Behind it all was the continuing desire of the United States for political stability in the Caribbean area adjacent to the Panama Canal.

To complete the protective shield for the Panama Canal, the United States purchased the Virgin Islands in 1917. This strategic island group, located to the east of Puerto Rico, belonged to Denmark. The Danes agreed to sell the islands to the United States for $25 million. The Caribbean defenses for the Panama Canal now extended in a giant arc from the Florida Keys through Cuba, Puerto Rico, and on to the Virgin Islands. (See map, page 520.) In addition, both Haiti and the Dominican Republic were subject to a large measure of United States influence as a result of the Roosevelt Corollary and "dollar diplomacy."

SECTION 5 REVIEW

 Identify: Hay-Pauncefote Treaty of 1901, Philippe Bunau-Varilla, Roosevelt Corollary, "dollar diplomacy"

Main Ideas

1. What prompted U.S. interest in a Panama Canal?
2. What obstacles to the building of the canal had to be overcome?
3. How did the United States acquire the land for the canal? What were the terms of the treaty?
4. What measures were taken to protect the canal?
5. How did the Roosevelt Corollary and "dollar diplomacy" create poor relations between the United States and Latin America?

CHAPTER 22 REVIEW

Key Terms
Explain the meaning of each of the following terms:

imperialism
policy of noninvolvement
Monroe Doctrine
Social Darwinism
"white man's burden"
"Remember the *Maine*"
De Lôme letter
Teller Amendment

Platt Amendment
Foraker Act
Jones Act (1917)
Insular Cases
Open Door Policy
Hay-Pauncefote Treaty of 1901
Roosevelt Corollary
"dollar diplomacy"

Reviewing the Main Ideas

Section 1
1. On what two principles was American foreign policy based before the 1890s?
2. How did the Civil War affect America's attitude toward expansion?
3. What changes did some Americans want to make in American foreign policy by the 1890s? Why?
4. Why did the United States become interested in Hawaii and the Samoan Islands?

Section 2
1. How were ideas such as the belief in "progress," "survival of the fittest," and the "white man's burden" used to justify American imperialism?
2. How did Alfred Thayer Mahan and Albert Beveridge influence Americans' views on foreign policy?

Section 3
1. Trace the events and concerns that led to the Spanish-American War.
2. In what geographical areas was the war fought?
3. What territories came under American control as a result of the war?

Section 4
1. Americans considered that their imperialism was different from European imperialism. How and why did they think so?

2. How did the United States gain control of Cuba, Puerto Rico, and the Philippines? What rights were their citizens given?
3. What changes in American military defense came about as a result of expansionism?

Section 5
1. Why did America want a canal through the Isthmus of Panama? What obstacles were overcome in order to build it?
2. What measures were taken to protect the canal?
3. How did these measures create ill will in Latin America toward the United States?

Special History Skills:
Working with Special Purpose Maps
In the early 1900s, the United States took a great interest in countries located in Central America and the Caribbean. The map on page 520 shows these countries and helps explain U.S. activities in the region. Refer to the map to answer the following questions.
1. What time period does the map cover?
2. Which places shown on the map were British possessions at that time?
3. Which places shown on the map were U.S. possessions?
4. Which countries were U.S. protectorates?
5. What area was leased by treaty in 1903?
6. Notice how close the Caribbean region is to the United States. What is the distance between the northern coast of Cuba and the southern tip of the United States?
7. Look at the location of the larger Caribbean islands in relation to the Panama Canal. Why was the U.S. interested in these islands?
8. Note that most, but not all, countries in Central America have coastlines on both the Caribbean Sea and the Pacific Ocean. Which country borders only the Pacific Ocean? Which country borders only the Caribbean Sea? What would be the advantage of bordering both?

Other Skills Activities
1. Mapping an empire
Draw a world map and label American Samoa, the Hawaiian Islands, Cuba, Puerto Rico, Guam, the Panama Canal, and the Virgin Islands. Color red those areas taken in war. Color blue those areas controlled by treaty or political

and economic influence. Color green those areas the United States purchased.

2. Engineering the canal

Find out more about the construction of the Panama Canal. Why was it considered an engineering feat? Give a report on the canal to the class. Include illustrations in your report. If you wish, you can build a model of the canal.

3. Expansionism crossword puzzle

Make a crossword puzzle using the names of people, places, and terms from this chapter.

4. Aguinaldo's speech

Suppose that you are Emilio Aguinaldo and your guerrillas have finally been defeated by the U.S. army after years of fighting. Give a two-minute speech to your fighters, telling them what you think they should do now.

Thinking Critically

1. In what ways was the "splendid little war" a turning point in American history?
2. Defend or reject any one of these concepts: "progress," "survival of the fittest," "white man's burden." Use examples from the text and current events to support your argument.
3. Explain the phrase, "The Constitution does not follow the flag." Use examples from the chapter to help your explanation.

Further Reading

Robert Conroy. *The Battle of Manila Bay*. Macmillan, 1968. Background and action of the war in the Philippines.

Irving Werstein. *1898: The Spanish-American War*. Cooper Square Publishers, 1966. Discusses role of journalists, military hardware, Cuban and Filipino freedom fighters.

TEST YOURSELF

WRITE YOUR ANSWERS ON A SEPARATE SHEET OF PAPER.

Matching

Write the letter of the item that best matches each description below.

1. author who advocated a strong navy
2. expansionist policy based on racism
3. sank the Spanish fleet in Manila Bay
4. denied that the United States would keep Cuba after the Spanish-American War
5. designed to help trade with China
6. decided that constitutional rights do not apply to citizens of territories won from Spain
7. made the United States the policeman of the Western Hemisphere
8. extending a nation's rule beyond its borders
9. animal studies applied to human society
10. helped U.S. gain land for Panama Canal

a. imperialism
b. progress
c. Social Darwinism
d. George Dewey
e. "white man's burden"
f. Teller Amendment
g. Insular Cases
h. Platt Amendment
i. Open Door Policy
j. Alfred Thayer Mahan
k. Philippe Bunau-Varilla
l. Roosevelt Corollary

Locating

Write the letter that best locates on the map the areas described below.

1. This area was purchased from Denmark to help the United States protect the Panama Canal.
2. The *Maine* explosion in this island's harbor was an immediate cause of war with Spain.
3. A long war with rebels followed U.S. takeover.
4. American settlers took over the government.
5. This country surrendered colonial lands to the United States.

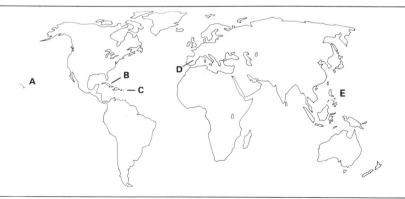

Chapter 23

1900–1916

THE PROGRESSIVE ERA

Where did you spend your vacation last summer? Perhaps you camped out in a beautiful national park. What kind of food do you like to eat? Perhaps you like a delicious sausage or a good, juicy steak. What about the money in your pocket? Perhaps you are carrying a few dollar bills. Did your parents vote in a recent election? Perhaps they selected a new mayor or U.S. senator, or picked a candidate in a primary. Check today's newspaper, and you may find an article exposing political corruption or a threat to public safety.

All these varied aspects of your life were changed and improved in the early 20th century. The national park you visited, the wholesome and tasty food you eat, the way your government is run, the type of money you have, and even the kind of reporting you might read in your newspaper—all these reflect the changes of the progressive era.

In this chapter, you will learn about a second great age of reform in America: the progressive era. You will see how reformers worked to transform local government and to end corruption and mismanagement. You will learn how progressives finally convinced national, state, and local government to regulate certain business practices and to protect consumer rights, public health, and natural resources. And you will see how the progressive movement made government itself more responsive to the needs and wishes of American citizens.

Sections in This Chapter
1. A New Movement for Reform Begins
2. Progressivism Reaches the White House: Roosevelt's Square Deal
3. The Taft Administration
4. Wilson's First Administration
5. Racism and Nativism

Opposite: For many years Americans discussed politics in general stores like this one, in use in West Virginia between 1861 and 1932.

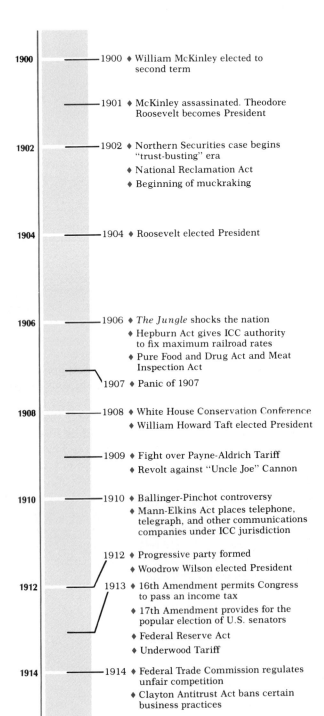

1900	1900 ◆ William McKinley elected to second term
	1901 ◆ McKinley assassinated. Theodore Roosevelt becomes President
1902	1902 ◆ Northern Securities case begins "trust-busting" era
	◆ National Reclamation Act
	◆ Beginning of muckraking
1904	1904 ◆ Roosevelt elected President
1906	1906 ◆ *The Jungle* shocks the nation
	◆ Hepburn Act gives ICC authority to fix maximum railroad rates
	◆ Pure Food and Drug Act and Meat Inspection Act
	1907 ◆ Panic of 1907
1908	1908 ◆ White House Conservation Conference
	◆ William Howard Taft elected President
	1909 ◆ Fight over Payne-Aldrich Tariff
	◆ Revolt against "Uncle Joe" Cannon
1910	1910 ◆ Ballinger-Pinchot controversy
	◆ Mann-Elkins Act places telephone, telegraph, and other communications companies under ICC jurisdiction
	1912 ◆ Progressive party formed
	◆ Woodrow Wilson elected President
1912	1913 ◆ 16th Amendment permits Congress to pass an income tax
	◆ 17th Amendment provides for the popular election of U.S. senators
	◆ Federal Reserve Act
	◆ Underwood Tariff
1914	1914 ◆ Federal Trade Commission regulates unfair competition
	◆ Clayton Antitrust Act bans certain business practices

1. A NEW MOVEMENT FOR REFORM BEGINS

As the new century began, Americans could look back on the last 30 years of their history with a sense of pride and achievement. The wealth, size, and power of the country had grown. Yet, prosperity carried with it its own problems. Precious natural resources were being squandered, young children labored in factories and mines, and giant corporations remained unregulated. Life in America's cities had grown worse, as slums bred crime and disease.

In the 1890s, a new group of reformers gathered to improve American conditions. Their movement, called **progressivism,** drew upon the heritage of Populism and the labor movement. But the progressives were middle-class men and women, living in the nation's towns and cities, rather than farmers or workers. Despite the enormous problems they faced, progressives were remarkably optimistic about the tasks ahead.

Progressivism was like a large umbrella under which many different reformers could huddle. Some who called themselves progressives worked against poverty; others focused on the regulation of corporations; and others devoted their energies to ending corruption and inefficiency in city government. Settlement-house and charity workers, writers and journalists, scientists, professors, housewives, and businessmen all carried the banner of progressivism.

Although progressives often disagreed on specific issues, there were some basic beliefs that unified the movement. First, progressives placed their faith in progress, technology, and science. They believed that society could be studied scientifically and that impartial experts could help politicians make good laws and regulations. Secondly, progressives rejected the laissez-faire attitudes of the Gilded Age. They called for an active government and pressed for legislation that would improve American life.

The Muckrakers

In our time, crusading reporters and newspaper exposés of corruption and illegality are common.

Writers of the progressive era were the ones who pioneered this investigative journalism. These men and women were called **muckrakers.** President Theodore Roosevelt coined this name in 1906 when he complained that certain journalists kept their eyes on the muck at their feet instead of raising their heads to the glories of the heavens above. Roosevelt intended his remark as an insult to these writers, but they bore the nickname proudly.

The progressives and the muckrakers were helped in their efforts to interest Americans in reform by the rise of inexpensive popular magazines like *McClure's, Cosmopolitan,* and *Collier's. McClure's* led the way to reform journalism with its 1902 fall issue. Here the reader found Part One of an exposé of Rockefeller's Standard Oil Trust by Ida M. Tarbell plus a report by Lincoln Steffens on the ties between business and corrupt urban political machines. The conclu-

sions to both exposé articles came in the next issue of *McClure's.* That issue sold out entirely. Clearly, muckraking was profitable! Soon other leading magazines hired well-known authors to keep their eyes on the muddy ground of American life.

Muckraking articles became muckraking books. The publishing industry put out hundreds of volumes, exposing everything from secret political deals in smoke-filled rooms to the cutthroat practices of business tycoons. Americans avidly read Lincoln Steffens' *Shame of the Cities,* Gustavus Myers' *History of the Great American Fortunes,* and David Graham Phillips' *The Treason of the Senate.*

Even novels took a muckraking turn, helping to dramatize reform issues. The most famous and shocking of these was Upton Sinclair's *The Jungle,* which, as you will see, was directly responsible for the passage of two federal reform laws.

Antimonopoly cartoon by George Luks, 1899, entitled "The Menace of the Hour"

The Efforts to Clean Up City Governments

Most progressives pointed to political corruption and to poorly run government as one of the major problems of the day. To combat this problem, in the 1890s and early 1900s progressives ran reform candidates in many cities and towns. To the surprise of the local political bosses, these reformers were often elected. Hazen S. Pingree of Detroit, elected in 1889, was the first of the reform mayors. Pingree was soon followed by others, including Edwin U. Curtis of Boston, George C. Cole of Chicago, Tom L. Johnson of Cleveland, and Seth Low of New York. All ousted notorious political bosses when they took office.

The most colorful and popular of the reform mayors was **Samuel "Golden Rule" Jones,** of Toledo, Ohio. As soon as Jones took office in 1897, he began sweeping reforms in that midwestern city. He pushed for lower electric, gas, and telephone rates and for lower fares on the streetcar system. He established a minimum wage for city employees and opened new parks for Toledo residents. Toledo soon boasted an improved criminal court system, free concerts, free public baths, and a limited form of welfare for the unfortunate. Not every reform mayor accomplished as much as "Golden Rule" Jones, but many did try.

The election of a progressive mayor did not, of course, automatically mean an end to political bosses and machines. A progressive could lose an election as easily as he could win one, and the bosses could return to power. What was needed, decided some progressives, was more than a change in personnel: The entire structure of city government had to be changed! To achieve this end, the progressives invented two new reforms of city government: the commission system and the city-manager plan.

The **commission system** was a radical departure from the tradition of elected officials. It separated politics entirely from the running of city government. Instead, a group of administrators were elected who had no party affiliations. They were chosen because they had special training or expertise in a particular area of municipal government. Each was placed in charge of a specific city function, and thus any improper behavior or any inefficient management could be pinpointed.

Galveston, Texas, was the first city to test the commission form of government. In 1900, this Gulf Coast town was hit by a terrible hurricane and a massive tidal wave that killed one-sixth of the population and destroyed one-third of all property. In this tense crisis, the town decided to try the commission system. Five people were given special powers to run the city and to repair the damage done to it by nature. The Galveston commissioners did such a fine job that the idea spread to other cities. Within two years, more than 200 communities had adopted the commission system. The system turned out to work well in middle-sized cities, but poorly in the more complex, giant American cities.

The **city-manager plan** was the progressives' second cure for badly run governments. Under this system, a board of commissioners was elected to make laws and set policy. These commissioners appointed a manager who was an expert in municipal government. He ran the city government without the pressures of political parties.

Staunton, Virginia, was the first town to try the new system in 1908. But in 1913, the city-manager plan became nationally known. That year, Dayton, Ohio, was devastated by a flood. Again, a natural disaster led citizens to experiment. Dayton successfully adopted a city-manager plan, and other cities followed suit. Like the commission system, the city-manager plan worked best in middle-sized American cities.

The Efforts to Clean Up State Governments

Progressives knew that city governments were part of a larger state system. If machines and bosses ran the state government, what hope was there for lasting reform on the local level? Mustering their energies, the reformers tackled corruption in the state capitals.

The most famous reform governor was Wisconsin's **Robert M. La Follette.** "Battling Bob," who had gained a reputation as a reformer in Congress, took over state office in 1901. The small, energetic governor rolled up his shirt sleeves and revamped Wisconsin's government. The voters supported him despite strong opposition from rich and powerful interests in the state.

First, he established a direct primary system for nominating political candidates. Then, laws against corruption were passed. For example, campaign spending was limited, and candidates were required to list campaign contributors. In addition, tax reforms forced the state railroads and utilities to pay a greater share of tax dollars.

La Follette was also sensitive to conservation issues. As governor, he saw to it that forests and water-power sites were made public trusts and were conserved. Finally, under Governor La Follette, Wisconsin workers won legal protection on the job. Like a true progressive, La Follette believed in employing experts. He often turned to social scientists at the University of Wisconsin for advice. He also established a legislative reference library to aid in creating new laws.

Wisconsin was soon known as the "laboratory of democracy," and the "Wisconsin Idea" spread across the country. Requests for information and ideas flooded into the state capital. By 1910, 15 states had legislative reference libraries. During the progressive era, state reform swept the nation, and state machine politicians were defeated, at least temporarily, in Iowa, Arkansas, Oregon, Minnesota, Kansas, Mississippi, New York, California, Missouri, Nebraska, New Jersey, and Colorado.

Ousting corrupt politicians was important. But making government more responsive to the demands of its citizens was the true achievement of this second age of reform. Almost all of the states followed Wisconsin's lead and instituted direct popular primary elections. In 1902, Oregon instituted the initiative and referendum, reforms the Populists had called for in the previous decade. Soon many other states would pass reform laws to make government more democratic.

SECTION 1 REVIEW

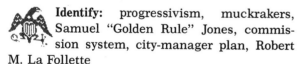 **Identify:** progressivism, muckrakers, Samuel "Golden Rule" Jones, commission system, city-manager plan, Robert M. La Follette

Main Ideas

1. What made the progressive reform movement different from earlier reform movements of the Gilded Age? List some of the ideas that progressives shared.
2. How did the muckrakers help bring society's problems to the public's attention?
3. How did progressives try to clean up city government?
4. Why was Wisconsin called the "laboratory of democracy"? Describe some of the reforms that La Follette instituted.

2. PROGRESSIVISM REACHES THE WHITE HOUSE: ROOSEVELT'S SQUARE DEAL

On September 6, 1901, President William McKinley visited the Pan-American Exposition in Buffalo, New York. Here, he met his death at the hands of an anarchist named Leon Czolgosz [chôl′ gôsh]. Shot, and mortally wounded, McKinley lingered until September 14. While the nation mourned, a new President solemnly took the oath of office. His name was Theodore Roosevelt.

When the short, stocky, mustachioed Roosevelt took the reins of government, a new era in national politics began. Progressivism had come to the White House.

Roosevelt was a remarkable man, loved by millions but hated by many. His personality dominated the era. Born into a wealthy New York family, Teddy Roosevelt had every advantage a young man could desire. He went to Harvard University, where a generation of gentlemen were educated to avoid the messy world of politics. But Roosevelt seemed to have politics in his blood. Straight out of school, he threw himself into New York politics, serving first as a state assemblyman and then as a member of the United States Civil Service Commission. Next, he took on the tough job of president of New York City's Board of Police Commissioners. In 1897, Roosevelt became Assistant Secretary of the Navy. In 1898, he returned to New York, this time as governor.

One term of this fiercely independent governor was enough for the state's Republican machine. When McKinley needed a running mate for his second term, New York's bosses arranged to have Teddy Roosevelt "kicked upstairs."

Now, in 1901, fate had made Roosevelt President. Would the conservative Republicans be sorry they had placed him a heartbeat away from the presidency? Many thought not. Roosevelt was, after all, a loyal Republican with a lot of political experience. He was basically a conservative, fond of saying that reformers had an "influence for bad hardly surpassed by that of the professional criminal class." Yet, there was another side to the new President that worried and upset many members of the Grand Old Party.

That other side was partly the result of a sickly childhood. As a boy, Teddy suffered from asthma and poor eyesight. He did not accept these weaknesses. Instead, he worked single-mindedly to strengthen his body. He took up exercising and boxing. He never stopped pushing himself.

As an adult, Roosevelt retained his fierce pride in overcoming all obstacles. Watching Roosevelt's delight in facing danger and difficulty, Mark Twain called the President "the Tom Sawyer of the political world . . . always hunting for a chance to show off." Roosevelt did seem to relish testing himself, shaking 6,000 hands on one occasion or hunting down cattle rustlers in the Dakota Territory on another. He worshiped action, aggression, and honor.

This love of what he called "the strenuous life" became obvious in 1898. That year, the war with Spain began. As you saw in the last chapter, Roosevelt immediately resigned his post as Assistant Secretary of the Navy and helped organize a voluntary cavalry regiment called the Rough Riders. Later he would gleefully recall his greatest moment of action when, he said, he had killed a Spaniard "like a Jack rabbit." It was this Roosevelt—whose wild exploits had gained him great popularity—that put even Republicans who agreed with his political views on edge.

As you will see, Roosevelt *did* change the presidency. He reversed the trend of the Gilded Age

with its weak Presidents and powerful Congresses. He became an active and strong chief executive, utilizing the powers of his office and his own personal popularity to get around congressional opposition. In this, he was the forerunner of our modern Presidents.

The Trust-Buster

Roosevelt was able to get his way by avoiding confrontations with Congress. A good way to understand his tactics is to look at how he handled a campaign to regulate trusts and monopolies. Instead of trying to get new, more effective antitrust laws from Congress, Roosevelt chose to revive an old law: the Sherman Antitrust Act of 1890.

In 1902, Roosevelt ordered the Department of Justice to sue the Northern Securities Company (NSC) under the provisions of the Sherman Act. The NSC was a "holding company," composed of the Great Northern, the Northern Pacific, and the Chicago, Burlington & Quincy railroads. It had been created to end the battle raging among the three railroads for control of transportation in the West. The public was worried about the giant NSC, and so Roosevelt's antitrust suit was very popular. Roosevelt won his fight against the holding company in 1904, when the Supreme Court ordered it dissolved. The Court decision breathed new life into the Sherman Antitrust Act. The President could continue his **"trust busting"** without fear of court interference and without Congress' help.

Roosevelt's next targets included the meatpacking and fertilizer trusts and the American Tobacco Company. Altogether, 44 antitrust suits were begun by Roosevelt, though not all were successful. With each one the President's popularity increased—and so did the power he exercised.

How did Roosevelt pick which trusts to bust? He did not select on the basis of size or power. In fact, the President did not believe that he should wipe out all trusts. Holding companies, trusts, and other such business devices were here to stay, Roosevelt felt. It made more sense to regulate them and to keep them honest than to attempt to restore the competition of a bygone age. There were "good" trusts, Roosevelt concluded, and there were "bad" trusts. "Good" trusts turned out to be those corporations that cooperated with Roosevelt.

Theodore Roosevelt (1858–1919)

IN OFFICE: 1901–1909

Republican from New York. Roosevelt tried to use the power of his office to solve national problems. Thus he helped conserve natural resources, regulated some business practices, aided settlement of the 1902 coal strike, and supported the Pure Food and Drug Act (1906). He believed in an expansionist foreign policy and was responsible for American control of the Panama Canal.

Cooperation meant, first, an informal meeting with the President. For example, in 1905 Roosevelt met with U.S. Steel Corporation president Elbert H. Gary. Together they worked out an informal understanding, or "gentlemen's agreement." They agreed that the new Bureau of Corporations, which had been established in 1903, would investigate U.S. Steel. If any business practices that restrained trade were uncovered, Roosevelt would permit Gary to correct the problems without court action or publicity. Similar agreements were made with International Harvester and John D. Rockefeller's Standard Oil Trust.

The Coal Strike and the Square Deal
Like his "trust busting" activities, Roosevelt's role in the 1902 coal strike increased the power of the presidency. In June of 1902 the United Mine Workers went out on strike. They demanded a 20% increase in wages, an 8-hour work day, recognition of their union, and better working conditions. But the mine owners refused to negotiate with the workers, and closed down the mines instead, hoping to drive the hard-pressed miners back to work by poverty. The miners and their families held out, however. The strike stretched out through the summer and into the fall. Coal prices shot up, and many Americans began to fear a cold winter without coal to warm their homes. Although popular support grew for the miners, who had remained peaceful, the mine owners would not relent.

In early October 1902, President Roosevelt called representatives of both sides to the White House. When the miners and mine owners showed up, even the blustery President was shocked by the mine owners' behavior. They refused to speak to the representatives of the United Mine Workers and demanded that Roosevelt send in federal troops to end the strike.

Roosevelt was enraged by the owners' attitude of defiance. He announced that unless an agreement was reached immediately, he *would* send in federal troops—to take the mines away from the owners! When the owners recovered from the shock of this threat, they agreed to negotiate with the strikers.

The President appointed an independent commission to help settle the strike. In March 1903, the commission granted the miners a 10% wage increase and a 9-hour workday. The mine owners were not required to recognize the union, however, and they were permitted to increase coal prices by 10%. Thus, both sides were granted something they demanded.

This kind of settlement represented what Roosevelt would later call a **"Square Deal."** In a "Square Deal," Roosevelt said, each side received what it deserved: fair treatment and consideration. Many miners felt disappointed at the outcome of their strike, but Roosevelt's action did mark a turning point in labor history. For unlike his predecessors, Hayes and Cleveland, Roosevelt had played a role as mediator, not strikebreaker, in a labor dispute. Later, the term "Square Deal" became identified in the public's mind with Roosevelt's first term as President.

A President in His Own Right
By 1904, Theodore Roosevelt was a powerful President, and a very popular one. When he stood for election in 1904, Roosevelt received 2.5 million more votes than the Democratic contender, Alton B. Parker. Roosevelt was now President in his own right. He was ready to do battle with Congress for reform legislation.

Roosevelt's opening jab at Congress was over railroad regulation. He demanded that the Interstate Commerce Commission be strengthened. The conservative Congress resisted, but by 1906, congressmen had come up with a compromise called the **Hepburn Act**. It gave the ICC authority to fix "just and reasonable" maximum railroad rates. It also empowered the Commission to investigate and regulate express and sleeping car companies, oil pipelines, ferries, terminals, and bridges if they did business across state lines. Finally, the Hepburn Act limited the right of railroads to issue free passes. The free passes were often given to politicians as a type of bribe to vote for laws supported by the railroads or against laws to regulate them. Roosevelt could take pride in this first victory against Congress. Railroad activity was at last under government regulation.

In the same year as the Hepburn Act, Upton Sinclair published his blistering novel, *The Jungle*. Its shocking description of the working conditions in Chicago's stockyards and meat-packing plants stunned the nation. Although Sinclair had hoped to raise an outcry over industry's working conditions, Americans were even more shaken by the book's revelations about the filthy, diseased

FROM THE ARCHIVES

Scenes from *The Jungle*

One Sunday evening, Jurgis sat puffing his pipe by the kitchen stove, and talking with an old fellow whom Jonas had introduced, and who worked in the canning-rooms at Durham's; and so Jurgis learned a few things about the great and only Durham canned goods, which had become a national institution. They were regular alchemists at Durham's; they advertised a mushroom-catsup, and the men who made it did not know what a mushroom looked like. They advertised "potted chicken." . . . Perhaps they had a secret process for making chickens chemically—who knows? said Jurgis's friend; the things that went into the mixture were tripe, and the fat of pork, and beef suet, and hearts of beef, and finally the waste ends of veal, when they had any. They put these up in several grades, and sold them at several prices; but the contents of the cans all came out of the same hopper. . . . Anybody who could invent a new imitation had been sure of a fortune from old Durham. . . .

There was another interesting set of statistics that a person might have gathered in Packingtown—those of the various afflictions of the workers. . . .

There were the men in the pickle-rooms, for instance, where old Antanas had gotten his death; scarce a one of these that had not some spot of horror on his person. Let a man so much as scrape his finger pushing a truck in the pickle-rooms, and he might have a sore that would put him out of the world; all the joints in his fingers might be eaten by the acid, one by one. Of the butchers and floorsmen, the beef-boners and trimmers, and all those who used knives, you could scarcely find a person who had the use of his thumb; time and time again the base of it had been slashed, till it was a mere lump of flesh against which the man pressed the knife to hold it. . . .

Worst of any, however, were the fertilizer-men, and those who served in the cooking-rooms. These people could not be shown to the visitor,—for the odor of a fertilizer-man would scare any ordinary visitor at a hundred yards, and as for the other men, who worked in the tank-rooms full of steam, and in some of which there were open vats near the level of the floor, their peculiar trouble was that they fell into the vats; and when they were fished out, there was never enough of them left to be worth exhibiting,—sometimes they would be overlooked for days, till all but the bones of them had gone out to the world as Durham's Pure Leaf Lard!

meat products they were being sold. As a contemporary rhyme put it:

> Mary had a little lamb,
>   And when she saw it sicken,
> She shipped it off to Packingtown,
>   And now it's labeled chicken.

Sinclair later observed, "I aimed at the public's heart and by accident I hit it in the stomach."

From the White House, Roosevelt quickly responded to public opinion. He appointed a commission to investigate the meat-packing industry. The commission's report confirmed the worst of Sinclair's claims, and in June 1906, Congress passed the **Pure Food and Drug Act**, which banned the manufacture, sale, or shipment of adulterated (impure) or mislabeled food and drugs in interstate commerce. At the same time, Congress also passed the **Meat Inspection Act** to enforce existing sanitary codes in the meat-packing industry. The law also required federal inspection of all companies selling meat in interstate commerce.

Roosevelt continued to push for further government regulation of American industry and for other reforms, such as income and inheritance taxes and minimum wage laws. But his early successes were not repeated. By 1907 a stalemate had developed between the President and the conservative Congress. No new reforms were passed, except in the realm of conservation.

Conservation

Today, we are all too aware of our fragile environment. Industrial waste, car exhausts, and chemical pollutants all threaten our health. It may be hard for you to imagine a time when pollution and conservation were not on the minds of the American people. Under the administration of Benjamin Harrison, the government began to set aside forest land as permanent reserves and parks. This policy was continued by Grover Cleveland. But, until Theodore Roosevelt brought the waste of America's national resources and the promise of conservation to national attention, there was no real government commitment to protect what then seemed to be an endless supply of resources and an inexhaustible wilderness. For years the government had been distributing lands, mineral deposits, and water-power sites with little concern for how they were used or what condition they were left in.

In June 1902, Roosevelt persuaded Congress to pass the **National Reclamation Act**, which set aside almost all the money from the sale of public lands in 16 western and southwestern states to pay for the construction of dams. These dams would provide water to irrigate and restore barren lands. The profits made from the sale of this water to farmers was to be used for other conservation projects. By 1906, 28 irrigation projects were under construction.

In May 1908, the President held the national White House Conservation Conference. From this conference came a **National Conservation Commission** to work with newly organized state commissions on natural resources. Headed by Gifford Pinchot, the Commission began a major study of mineral, soil, water, and forest resources throughout the United States.

Roosevelt helped create five national parks and over 50 wildlife sanctuaries. He also withdrew 148 million acres of forestland from public sale. By these acts, Roosevelt helped insure our generation's enjoyment of America's wilderness.

SECTION 2 REVIEW

Identify: trust busting, Square Deal, Hepburn Act, *The Jungle*, Pure Food and Drug Act, Meat Inspection Act, National Reclamation Act, National Conservation Commission

Main Ideas

1. Why is Theodore Roosevelt described as the forerunner of modern American Presidents?
2. What was Roosevelt's attitude toward trusts? Describe how he treated "good" and "bad" trusts.
3. Explain the circumstances of the 1902 coal strike and how Roosevelt worked out a "Square Deal." How was his role in a labor dispute unlike those of his predecessors?
4. List the reform legislation of Roosevelt's second term. What prevented further reform after 1907?
5. Describe government policy toward conservation before Roosevelt. Name several ways that Roosevelt pioneered in conservation.

U.S. National Parks Today

In addition to the 38 national parks shown above, there is also one national park in the U.S. territory of the Virgin Islands. There are more than 200 other national park lands, including historic sites, monuments, memorials, and recreation areas.

THE GEOGRAPHIC SETTING

THE PACIFIC COAST

Nowhere in the United States is the use and conservation of natural resources more an issue than in the Pacific Coast Region. Yosemite National Park, created by Congress in 1890, was only the first of many national parks and forests set aside there for protection and pleasure. During the era, groups like John Muir's Sierra Club pressured Congress to stop the destruction of natural wonders. Others began to plan the use of resources, especially water, to serve the growing population and economy of the region.

The Pacific Coast Region, which includes the states of Alaska, Washington, Oregon, and California, is a region of contrasts and contradictions. There are active volcanoes and violent earthquakes; arctic wastes and burning deserts; bountiful orchards, lush rainforests, and sunny beaches: these are the bold contrasts of the Pacific Coast Region.

Mountain Chains and Valleys

Linking all the states of the Pacific Coast is one of the world's greatest mountain systems. This chain of high mountains includes the Alaska Range and the Coast Mountains of Alaska and western Canada, the Cascades in Washington and Oregon, and the Sierra Nevada in California. Find these ranges on the maps opposite.

To the west of these tall mountains are several lower coastal ranges. Located between the high mountains and the coastal ranges are four important valleys—the Puget Trough in Washington, the Willamette Valley in Oregon, and the Central and Imperial valleys in California. These four valleys are the major fruit and vegetable growing regions of the United States. Find them on the map.

East of the Cascades and Sierras are the semiarid regions of eastern Washington and Oregon and the Mojave [mō hä′vē] Desert of southern California. North and east of the Mojave lies Death Valley, the lowest spot in North America.

Rivers of the Far West

Only a few rivers interrupt the north-south march of mountains and valleys. The Columbia of Washington and Oregon is second in water flow only to the Mississippi-Missouri River system. The Sacramento and San Joaquin rivers bring meltwater from the Sierras to the fertile Central Valley and empty into the Bay of San Francisco. The Colorado contributes water for southern California cities and irrigation. In Alaska, the mighty Yukon flows 2,000 miles to the Bering Sea.

Mountains, Winds Affect Climate

Much of the Pacific Coast, from southern Alaska to northern California, is blessed with a mild marine climate. The two most important climatic factors are the winds off the ocean and the high mountain ranges. Moist ocean air drops abundant rain west of the mountains. But beyond the mountain barrier, rainfall is scarce.

The coastal areas of southern California also enjoy a mild climate. However, the ocean breezes come off a cold water upwelling near the coast, causing them to hold less moisture. Thus Los Angeles and San Diego average less than 15 inches of rain a year while Portland, Oregon, gets almost 40 inches.

Along Alaska's southeastern coast as much as 150 inches falls annually. But the northern coast is a desert because the cold winds off the Arctic Ocean bring this region little moisture. Alaska's interior basin, bounded on the north by the Brooks Range and on the south by the Alaska Range, experiences the widest range of temperatures: −70°F in winter, 90°F in the summer. Most Alaskans live in the milder south-central region near Anchorage.

Throughout the Pacific Coast Region differences in rainfall and elevation are reflected in the natural vegetation. Rainfall is heavy in the dense forests of the Coast Range, the Cascades, and the Sierras, where the giant redwoods are found. In southern California are found grasses and scrublands along the coast and desert plants in the dry interior. Low, swampy, treeless plains called tundra cover the northern coast of Alaska.

Sleeping Giants in the Earth

No discussion of the physical features of the Pacific Coast would be complete without noting the forces that shaped them. Note on the map the volcanic peaks and the San Andreas fault. According to the theory of plate tectonics, the earth's surface is divided into great moving plates. The Pacific Coast is a kind of battleground between these plates, and the San Andreas fault system forms a boundary between two of them. The fault separates southwestern California from the rest of North America.

Hundreds of minor earthquakes are recorded each year as southwest California slips to the northwest. Major earthquakes, like those in San Francisco in 1906 and San Fernando in 1971, are judged inevitable to relieve pressure of the grinding plates. Alaska, too, is subject to devastating earthquakes, like the one that rocked Anchorage in 1964.

Volcanic eruptions are also caused by the movement of these plates. Mount St. Helens in Washington is a recent example.

Population Booms

Beginning with "Oregon Fever," in the 1840s, Americans have migrated to the Pacific Coast in a series of waves.

The humid climate and fertility of Oregon's Willamette Valley first attracted farmers who brought their familiar crops and place names—Salem, Portland, Albany, Springfield. Later the California Gold Rush brought half a million new residents in the 1850s.

The Central Valley was slow to be farmed because of climate differences from the East and complicated Mexican land grants. But after the 1870s, irrigation of the Central Valley changed this. Today one-third of the nation's fruits and vegetables are grown in the Central Valley, making California the leading agricultural state. The Imperial Valley is a desert, but with irrigation its 300-day growing season yields six harvests a year.

The dense forests of Washington and its uncertain border with Canada delayed settlement, but the railroad opened eastern markets for lumber and grain. By 1889 Washington was a state, and Seattle was larger than Portland.

A gold rush in Alaska in the late 1800s brought its first population surge. In recent years, the discovery of oil on the North Slope of the Brooks Range near Prudhoe Bay and the construction of the 800-mile Alaska pipeline (see map) have brought a new wave of residents to Alaska.

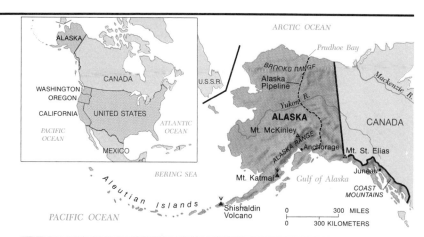

The Pacific Coast

- Volcanoes with volcanic activity after 1900
- Other volcanoes
- Mountain peaks

3. THE TAFT ADMINISTRATION

On the evening of his election victory in 1904, Roosevelt had shocked friends by announcing that "under no circumstances will I be a candidate for or accept another nomination." In 1908, the popular President regretted this rash statement, but his sense of honor prevented him from going back on his word. However, as the leader of the Republican party, Roosevelt was assured that the man of his choice would carry the party banner in 1908. Roosevelt picked as his successor his Secretary of War, William Howard Taft.

Both Taft and the three-time Democratic nominee, William Jennings Bryan, ran as progressives. But Roosevelt's popularity made all the difference. His friend Taft received 321 electoral votes to Bryan's 162, and carried the election by a margin of well over a million votes. The Republicans also continued to control the Senate and the House. Soon after Taft's inauguration, a smiling but obviously depressed Roosevelt went off to test his nerve against the big game of Africa.

Like Roosevelt, William Howard Taft could boast a long and distinguished career before entering the White House. He had graduated from Yale, served as a judge in Ohio, as U.S. Solicitor-General under President Harrison, and as a federal Circuit Court judge. In 1900, Taft led the Philippine Commission for President McKinley and then served as Philippine civil governor until Roosevelt made him Secretary of War in 1904.

Taft was no carbon copy of Roosevelt. In fact, the "Crown Prince"—as Taft was called—was the opposite of the "rough rider" in almost every regard. Even the physical differences were striking. Roosevelt was stocky, muscular, energetic; Taft had slow movements and sedentary ways, for the new President weighed 300 pounds.

The differences in character were equally obvious. Roosevelt loved the world of politics; Taft hated it. He longed to be Chief Justice of the U.S. Supreme Court rather than an elected official. Roosevelt was aggressive and combative. Taft liked to avoid conflict. Taft had a cautious temperament and a lawyer's respect for proper procedure. He did not like Roosevelt's broad use of executive power, and he was incapable of wheeling and dealing his way around the Congress.

Taft and Progressive Reform

No matter what their differences, Taft was a staunch supporter of Roosevelt's "Square Deal." He worked hard to continue the reform programs and policies that Roosevelt had begun. Under Taft, the U.S. Attorney General started 90 antitrust suits against giant corporations. This was twice the number of the Roosevelt years. Taft did his part to strengthen the regulatory agencies. In 1910, Congress passed the **Mann-Elkins Act**, which gave the Interstate Commerce Commission power to regulate telephone, telegraph, cable, and wireless companies. During the Taft years, a Department of Labor was created and an 8-hour day granted to all federal workers. A Children's Bureau was established to investigate continuing child-labor abuses.

Taft's reform record should have earned him a reputation as a progressive, but it did not. In 1909, a series of misunderstandings and disagreements began to drive a wedge between the President and the progressives in Congress. By 1910, Teddy Roosevelt had publicly denounced his hapless successor. What had gone wrong?

The Payne-Aldrich Tariff Controversy

The first problem arose in 1909 around the old issue of tariff reform. The progressives favored a tariff reduction, and Taft agreed. In fact, the new President called a special session of Congress on this very issue. Out of this session came the

William Howard Taft (1857–1930)

IN OFFICE: 1909–1913

Republican from Ohio. William Howard Taft's administration was active in the prosecution of trusts which violated the Sherman Antitrust Act. His support of the Payne-Aldrich Tariff (1909) lost him the support of progressives. His foreign policy, often called dollar diplomacy, was aimed at controlling the affairs of Caribbean nations through the pressure of financial investment and the sending of troops.

Payne-Aldrich Tariff, a genuine disappointment to the progressives. Payne-Aldrich lowered some rates, but kept most very high. Taft shared the disappointment of his congressional friends, yet he felt it best to avoid antagonizing Congress and sign the bill into law. Republican progressives were furious. Anger turned into outrage when Taft defensively called the new tariff "the best bill that the Republican party ever passed." Taft surely regretted this comment, but the damage was done.

The Ballinger-Pinchot Controversy

A conservation fiasco followed close on the heels of the tariff dispute. The problem arose from a clash of philosophies between two conservation officials. Taft's Secretary of the Interior, Richard A. Ballinger, was a nature lover and devoted to the preservation of America's natural wonders. But Ballinger did not support federal action to regulate or prevent the use of natural resources. He was greatly disturbed by Roosevelt's free-wheeling use of executive power in this kind of regulation. He charged that the former President had overstepped his powers by removing lands from public sale. Ballinger then returned several potential water-power sites in Montana and Wyoming to public sale.

Ballinger's opponent was Gifford Pinchot, head of the U.S. Forest Service under both Roosevelt and Taft. Pinchot applauded Roosevelt's use of executive power in the name of conservation, and appealed to Taft to stop Ballinger's sale of the water sites.

Taft did return the water sites to their protected status. But this victory did not satisfy Pinchot, who believed that Ballinger was an enemy of conservation with secret ties to private lumber interests. When Ballinger allowed some Alaskan lands to be sold, Pinchot called for his dismissal. Taft investigated the matter with his usual thoroughness and precision. He decided that Ballinger had done nothing illegal. Pinchot protested vigorously. The harassed Taft turned on Pinchot and fired him. Once again, congressional progressives were infuriated.

It was Taft's poor handling of personnel that damaged him in the **Ballinger-Pinchot controversy.** The President was not a foe of conservation at all. In fact, his administration had an excellent record in that area. Nevertheless, Taft now appeared to the progressives as an enemy, not an ally, on this reform issue. By 1911, public pressure forced Ballinger to resign. His successor immediately restored the Alaskan lands. This long and bitter controversy hurt the Republican party badly, and in the 1910 elections, the Democrats won control of the House for the first time in 16 years.

The Cannon Controversy

Trouble continued to plague Taft, as a third battle erupted in 1909. That setting was the floor of the House of Representatives. The issue was Representative Joseph Cannon's power over House affairs. Once again, Taft was caught in the middle.

Speaker of the House, **Joseph G. "Uncle Joe" Cannon** of Illinois, had been a congressman for 55 years. As Speaker, he had the power to appoint all the committees of the House and select their heads. Cannon personally headed the Committee on Rules which decided the order of business. In this role, he often prevented progressive legislation from reaching the floor for discussion. As Speaker, he had the power to decide who could speak during House debates and who could not. Cannon usually refused to recognize progressives during important debates. Thus "Uncle Joe" sabotaged many pieces of reform legislation.

The progressives first tried to remove Cannon from power in 1909. When both Cannon and the reformers called on Taft for aid, the President thought it best to remain neutral. Taft actually disliked Cannon and his power. Yet his neutrality contributed to the progressives' defeat.

In 1910, a new campaign against Cannon was mounted. George W. Norris of Nebraska rose on the House floor and announced: "We want the House to be representative of the people and each individual member to have his ideas presented and passed on." To carry out this goal, Norris proposed two amendments to the rules of the House. First, the members of the Committee on Rules should be elected by the whole House rather than appointed by the Speaker. Secondly, the Speaker should be excluded from membership on that committee.

The debate over these amendments was intense and split the Republicans into conservative and progressive camps. Finally, 40 progressive Republicans voted with the Democratic members, and the amendments passed. Cannon's power was struck a serious blow. A year later, the progressives ended Cannon's power to appoint the heads of the other committees. Thus, an important democratic reform had been instituted in the House. The progressive victory was far from complete, however. Cannon was still Speaker, and most committees were still headed by conservatives. Furthermore, Republicans paid a high price in this struggle, since their party was now divided into two fighting factions.

The Bull Moose Comes Home

While Taft watched his world fall apart, Theodore Roosevelt was traveling abroad. The former President was unaware of the controversies and the division in his party. But in 1910, Teddy returned from the African bush, dragging 3,000 trophies behind him. At home, Roosevelt found Taft allied with the conservatives, and the conservatives and progressives at each other's throats.

Roosevelt was not one to stay silent long. In August of 1910, at Osawatomie, Kansas, he entered the fray. In his Osawatomie speech, Roosevelt proposed a broad program of social reform which he labeled the **"New Nationalism."** Most Americans recognized in this New Nationalism an indirect attack on Taft's administration.

Roosevelt was now eager to challenge Taft for the Republican presidential nomination. Yet, he held back until 1911. That year, Taft infuriated Roosevelt by ordering an antitrust suit against U.S. Steel. As you recall, U.S. Steel was one of the corporations that had worked out a "gentlemen's agreement" with Roosevelt. That agreement was made in 1907, after a panic on Wall Street. Roosevelt had permitted U.S. Steel to take over a competitor, for he felt the move would help relieve the economic situation.

The Taft suit against U.S. Steel made Roosevelt look as if he had been fooled by the corporation or had openly aided the growth of a steel monopoly. Roosevelt was not a man to sit calmly when called a fool or a knave. In 1912, he declared himself a candidate for the Republican presidential nomination. A group of Republican progressives had set up the National Progressive Republican League to work to defeat Taft. They now dropped their candidate, Robert La Follette, and turned to Roosevelt.

In June, the Republican National Convention met in New York with battle lines drawn between Roosevelt and Taft. The progressives fought the conservatives over whose delegates would be seated. The conservatives won, for they controlled the credentials committee. When most of the seats went to Taft's delegates, Roosevelt's supporters stamped out of the hall shouting, "Naked thief!" The remaining delegates nominated Taft on the first ballot. Roosevelt had lost his bid for control of his party—but this defeat would not silence him.

Theodore Roosevelt finds President Taft rendered helpless by congressional antics.

SECTION 3 REVIEW

 Identify: Mann-Elkins Act, Payne-Aldrich Tariff, Ballinger-Pinchot controversy, Joseph G. Cannon, New Nationalism

Main Ideas

1. Describe the differences between Roosevelt and his successor, Taft.
2. List the progressive reforms carried out under the Taft administration. Do you feel that Taft was fairly viewed as antiprogressive?
3. Describe three issues that set progressive Republicans against Taft. What issue split the Republican party into two warring factions?
4. What was Roosevelt's reaction to his successor's action as President? Why was Roosevelt angered by Taft's suit against U.S. Steel?

4. WILSON'S FIRST ADMINISTRATION

In August 1912, Roosevelt's Republican supporters gathered in Chicago to form a third party: the **Progressive party,** which was nicknamed the "Bull Moose" party. The term came from Theodore Roosevelt's guarantee that he was "as fit as a bull moose."

The Bull Moosers were a determined and angry group. They sang "Onward Christian Soldiers" to show their readiness to do battle with Taft's party. Their platform was the "New Nationalism." This included a grab bag of reforms, like tariff reduction; greater regulation of monopolies; the direct election of U.S. senators; popular presidential nominating primaries; the initiative, referendum, and recall; women's suffrage; an end to child labor; and the minimum wage. Roosevelt proclaimed to the convention: "We stand at Armageddon, and we battle for the Lord!"

The New Nationalism Versus the New Freedom

Meanwhile, the Democratic convention met in Baltimore. After 46 ballots and much political maneuvering, the progressive governor of New Jersey, **Woodrow Wilson**, was chosen as the presidential candidate.

The Democratic platform, like the Progressive party platform, called for a wide range of progressive reforms. In one major regard, however, the two progressive platforms differed. Against Theodore Roosevelt's doctrine of the New Nationalism, Woodrow Wilson's party offered something called the **"New Freedom."** Both the New Nationalism and the New Freedom called for government control of monopolies. The major issue was how this control should be achieved.

As you saw in Section 2, Roosevelt was not against "bigness," as long as the government had the power to regulate the trusts. But Wilson said that trusts in general were bad because they destroyed America's old economy in which small businesses competed on an equal footing.

Although Taft was the Republican nominee, the real contest was between Roosevelt and Wilson. In the end, Democrats swept the election because the Republican party had split in two.

The Professor President

Imagine the wonder Thomas Woodrow Wilson must have felt as he took the presidential oath of office in 1913. Here he was, the first President from the South in 64 years. Even more surprising was the fact that two short years before Wilson had been president of a university. He entered the White House with very little political experience!

Wilson was born in Staunton, Virginia, five years before the outbreak of the Civil War. As the son of a Presbyterian minister, Woodrow Wilson was raised in an atmosphere of stern morality and commitment to public service. These values would color his perception of presidential responsibility later on. Wilson became a scholar of political science, teaching at Princeton University. The tall, angular, and intense young man with the spectacles was a conservative but popular lecturer. In private he seemed uncomfortable and cold.

Wilson spent two decades at Princeton University, where his reforms as president brought him national attention. Then, New Jersey's Democratic political boss approached him to run for governor of New Jersey. The New Jersey Democratic machine needed a respectable candidate that would not give Boss Jim Smith any trouble. "The professor" seemed perfect for the job.

Wilson won the election, and then shocked Boss Smith by attacking the very machine that had put him in power. New Jersey was considered one of the most corrupt states in the country, and in the two years he served as governor, Wilson worked hard for clean government. The conservative professor turned out to be a progressive governor.

An Activist President

Wilson took national office determined to be an active, progressive President. Unlike Roosevelt, Wilson was in a good position to do so for he had the support of a Congress controlled by Democrats and progressives.

Wilson quickly worked to get a series of reform bills through Congress. Many of these bills, calling for strong government regulation of business activity, soon made the differences between the New Nationalism and the New Freedom unimportant. In April 1913, he called Congress into special session to deal with the old problem of tariff reform. Wilson believed that high tariff rates helped create monopolies by cutting down the competition of European goods. Thus he wanted rates lowered. Breaking with tradition, Wilson appeared in person to present his proposals to Congress. Today, we are accustomed to seeing the President address the Congress, but Wilson was the first to take such an action since John Adams.

Industry generally opposed Wilson, but the public supported his tariff policy. Congress bowed to the popular will and passed the **Underwood Tariff** in October 1913. This law lowered rates on about 1,000 items, including cotton, woolen goods, steel, coal, and wood. It was the first real reduction in rates since the Civil War, and it permitted competition in industries that had been virtual monopolies for many years. Because revenues would be lost with lowered tariff rates, the Underwood Act provided for a graduated income tax. Such a tax had been authorized by the 16th Amendment in 1913.

Wilson next tackled banks and financial reform. A House committee had found that a small group of powerful investment banks controlled much of the U.S. money supply. Wilson sponsored the **Federal Reserve Act,** which established 12 Federal Reserve Districts, each with a Federal Reserve Bank. These banks would be "banker's banks": all national banks were required, and state banks invited, to belong to the system. Each would keep its cash reserves in the federal

banks. The federal government, too, would place its money in these Reserve Banks and issue paper money for public use. The Federal Reserve System could control the nation's money supply, putting more money in circulation or withdrawing it, depending on the needs of the economy.

Wilson's reform program continued. In 1914, he won passage of a law which established the **Federal Trade Commission**. The FTC, like Roosevelt's Bureau of Corporations, which it replaced, was created to prevent unfair methods of business competition in interstate commerce.

In 1914, Congress also passed the **Clayton Antitrust Act** to strengthen the old Sherman Antitrust Act of 1890. The Clayton Act outlawed certain business practices. They were: (1) lessening competition by setting different prices for different customers, (2) "tying contracts," which prohibited a customer from buying or handling the products of the seller's competitor, (3) interlocking directorates* in companies with capital over $1 million, and (4) stock purchases which lessened competition.

The Clayton Act also protected farmers' organizations and unions. This was a major change, for up to that time they had been considered conspiracies in restraint of trade. In fact, unions had been prosecuted under the old Sherman Act. For example, in 1912 the Danbury, Connecticut, Hatmakers Union had been sued in court for its boycott of hostile employers. The court had fined the union $250,000 in damages. To pay the fine, workers lost their savings and homes.

The labor movement hailed the Clayton Act. The AFL was now delighted that it had supported the "professor" for President. In the coming years, however, the courts weakened the Clayton Act and once again permitted the prosecution of unions under antitrust laws.

The Limits of the New Freedom

At the end of 1914, Wilson looked back at the work he had done and was satisfied. Then, to the surprise of progressives, he announced that his goals had been accomplished, and he would not seek any further reform laws.

Part of Wilson's decision was based on a deep

Woodrow Wilson (1856–1924)

IN OFFICE: 1913–1921

Democrat from New Jersey. Wilson's achievements in domestic affairs include the passage of the Underwood Tariff (1913), the creation of the Federal Reserve System (1913), and the Clayton Antitrust Act (1914). At the end of World War I, Wilson helped to create the League of Nations, but was unable to bring the U.S. into the League.

*interlocking directorates members of a company's board of directors sitting on the board of a competing company.

LIFE IN AMERICA

CHILD LABOR IN AMERICA

Certainly there was nothing new about children working. They had labored in fields and homes alongside their parents since the beginning of time. In fact, until the end of the Middle Ages, the idea of "childhood" as a distinct phase of life was unknown. Instead, the child of 5 or 7 was considered a small adult who lived, learned, and worked with mature adults.

The Concept of Childhood Develops

Several factors combined to create the idea of childhood. First, religious reformers of the 16th and 17th centuries insisted that youngsters needed moral training and protection. Then the coming of the industrial revolution increased the number of middle-class families who had the wealth and desire to shelter their children from the mainstream of life. Finally, the complexity of modern society made education essential. But while children of the wealthy went to school and played, the offspring of the poor went to work in the mines, mills, and factories of England and the Continent. For the first time, children did not work with their parents or learn a trade as apprentices. This was the beginning of child labor.

Child Labor in America

Child labor came to America as early as the first colony. Indentured pauper children arrived in Virginia in 1619. Puritans and Quakers believed idleness a sin and work a virtue, especially in light of early America's chronic labor shortage. In 1790, Samuel Slater, the "father of American manufacturing," used only 7- to 12-year-olds in his first factory. By 1820 almost half the textile workers in New England were children.

In the 1830s and 1840s American reformers became concerned

about the presence of children in factories. A few state laws were passed concerning schooling and limited hours for children. But without enforcement provisions, these laws were generally ignored.

Industrial Growth Affects Children

The huge industrial growth after the Civil War and the influx of immigrants put more children to work. Children rolled cigars and sewed garments in crowded New York tenement sweatshops. Ten-year-old boys worked 14-hour shifts in the Pennsylvania coal mines as "breakers," picking out slate with bleeding fingers, or they worked through the night in sweltering New Jersey glass factories. Worse off, perhaps, were the boys and girls so young that they had to climb up on the machines they tended in the hot, dust-laden cotton mills of the South. Wages were low, and chronic fatigue, injuries, tuberculosis, and ignorance were the "fringe benefits."

By 1880 over 1 million children aged 10 to 15 were employed, or 1 out of every 6 children in that age group. The number reached 2 million by the turn of the century.

Progressives Try to Regulate Child Labor

Many progressives worked to end this growing use of child labor. Muckraking journalists wrote magazine exposés to arouse the guilt and indignation of middle-class Americans, whose offspring were enjoying childhoods. Others worked for laws to regulate conditions, hours, and a minimum age for young workers.

In 1904 the National Child Labor Committee was formed to coordinate these efforts. But, progress in child-labor reform was slow. In 1912, President Taft agreed to set up a U.S. Children's Bureau to collect statistics and recommend programs. Wilson supported the passage of two laws in his second term, but they were both struck down by a conservative Supreme Court. It was not until 1938 that federal legislation finally became effective, after a change in views by the Supreme Court.

conservative streak in a man who had come late to politics and progressivism. He privately opposed many of the reforms he was hailed for or was expected to support. For example, the President did not like the provisions of the Clayton Act exempting unions and farm organizations from antitrust prosecution. He did not favor child-labor legislation. He absolutely refused to support a constitutional amendment for women's suffrage.

Another reason for Wilson's decision to lay aside reform was the change taking place in the U.S. economy. War had broken out in Europe and disrupted American trade. Business activity was slowing down; unemployment was on the rise. Business leaders blamed this slowdown on the tariff law and other New Freedom reforms.

Early in 1916, however, Wilson suddenly reversed his conservative direction, possibly to assure his re-election later that year. By this time, the Progressive party had all but collapsed. If its supporters reunited with the Republican party, Wilson, who had won only 42% of the popular vote in 1912, would be in trouble.

The President quickly shepherded through Congress a series of measures that practically made the 1912 Progressive party platform a reality. Wilson allied himself with the cause of women's suffrage, fought successfully for a child-labor law (later overturned by the courts) and a workers' compensation law, and signed a bill requiring railroads to give their employees an 8-hour day. The Democrats, he boasted in 1916, had come close to carrying out the Progressive platform as well as their own.

SECTION 4 REVIEW

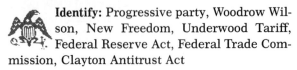 **Identify:** Progressive party, Woodrow Wilson, New Freedom, Underwood Tariff, Federal Reserve Act, Federal Trade Commission, Clayton Antitrust Act

Main Ideas
1. Compare the platforms of the Progressive and Democratic parties in 1912. How did each party view large corporations?
2. List four major reform bills passed under President Wilson's sponsorship in 1913 and 1914.
3. Why did Wilson stop pushing for reforms at the end of 1914? What was his attitude toward many of the programs that were passed?

5. RACISM AND NATIVISM

Like reformers in many eras, the progressives were victims of the prejudices of the world they hoped to reform. Thus, despite their concern for social justice and economic improvement, progressive reformers often remained blind to the plight of black people and other racial minorities in America. Ninety percent of the nation's black population still lived in the South. After the 1892 Populist attempt at black-white unity failed, a segregationist backlash spread across the South. The right of black men to vote was resented and opposed, and racial violence mounted.

From 1885 to 1900, 2,500 blacks were lynched, and in the first 14 years of the 20th century, over 1,100 more were murdered by white mobs. Southern blacks were also faced with discrimination in working and living conditions. In 1910, only 8,000 black children were attending high school in the entire South, and one-third of the nation's black population was illiterate. Yet, progressives did little to remedy these problems.

The national progressive movement, led by Theodore Roosevelt and Woodrow Wilson, had a shameful record on racial equality. Roosevelt himself harbored racist beliefs, which he revealed during his cowboy days in Dakota Territory. "I don't go so far as to think that the only good Indians are the dead Indians," Roosevelt said,

but I believe nine out of every ten are, and I shouldn't like to inquire too closely into the case of the tenth. The most vicious cowboy has more moral principle than the average Indian.

As President, Roosevelt overreacted to an incident in Brownsville, Texas, in 1906. Black troops stationed there were accused of terrorizing the town and, without investigating the matter, Roosevelt ordered the entire black battalion dishonorably discharged. This order was not overturned until 1972.

Woodrow Wilson's administration was openly hostile to black people. Wilson was an outspoken white supremacist who believed that black people were inferior. During his campaign for the presidency, Wilson promised to press for civil rights. But once in office he forgot his promises. Instead, Wilson ordered that white and black workers in federal government jobs be segregated from one another. This was the first time such segregation had existed since Reconstruction! When black federal employees in southern cities protested the order, Wilson had the protesters fired. In November 1914, a black delegation asked the President to reverse his policies. Wilson was rude and hostile and refused their demands.

Realizing that President Roosevelt would not help them, black leaders struck out on their own. In 1905, **W. E. B. Du Bois** [dü boiz′] and others met at Niagara Falls, New York. From this meeting came a list of demands, including civil rights, equal job opportunities, and an end to segregation. This call stirred into action some progressives like the settlement-house worker Jane Addams, the educator John Dewey, and magazine publisher Oswald Garrison Villard (the grandson of the abolitionist, William Lloyd Garrison). These progressives joined with Du Bois in 1910 to create the **National Association for the Advancement of Colored People (NAACP)**. As you will see, the NAACP would lead the struggle for black equality in the 20th century.

Prejudice Toward Immigrants

Many of the progressive reforms seemed to deny, rather than promote, equality among Americans. A nativist (anti-immigrant) impulse often lay beneath these reforms. For example, the commission system and the city-manager plan tended to end the influence of immigrants in city government. Many progressives believed that immigrants could not understand American institutions and thus should not have influence through their votes. The immigrants, these progressives argued, stood in the way of progress when they supported politicians rather than "impartial experts" in government. Yet, in destroying the political machines that ran these cities, the progressives also cut immigrants off from their one source of support. These new Americans relied on political bosses for jobs, housing, and other help in exchange for their votes.

Nativism and racism were also expressed by progressives in some scientific reform movements. One movement, called **eugenics**, sought to "improve" the American people by careful breeding, as if Americans were a breed of cattle or chickens. The eugenicists called for the govern-

Civil rights pioneer W. E. B. Du Bois at NAACP headquarters in New York City

ment to pass laws to improve American life by wiping out ethnic traits they thought were inferior. Immigrants, they said, were undermining American life. They were carriers of "feeble-mindedness" and "criminality." Some eugenicists called for laws restricting immigration, but others wanted more vicious legislation like the sterilizing of mentally ill and poor people. Many progressives rejected this movement. But, it was not until the rise of Nazism in Europe in the 1930s—with its similar racial outlook and policies—that the eugenics movement was finally discredited.

SECTION 5 REVIEW

 Identify: W. E. B. Du Bois, National Association for the Advancement of Colored People (NAACP), eugenics

Main Ideas
1. Describe the status of black Americans during the progressive era.
2. What were the attitudes and policies of Theodore Roosevelt and Woodrow Wilson toward blacks? How did black leaders respond?
3. Describe how some progressive reforms showed an underlying racism and nativism.

CHAPTER 23 REVIEW

Key Terms
Explain the meaning of each of the following terms:

progressivism
muckrakers
commission system
city-manager plan
trust busting
Square Deal
Hepburn Act
The Jungle
Pure Food and
    Drug Act
Meat Inspection Act
National Reclam-
    ation Act
National Conservation
    Commission
Mann-Elkins Act

Payne-Aldrich Tariff
Ballinger-Pinchot
    controversy
New Nationalism
Progressive party
New Freedom
Underwood Tariff
Federal Reserve Act
Federal Trade Com-
    mission
Clayton Antitrust Act
National Association
    for the Advance-
    ment of Colored
    People
eugenics

Reviewing the Main Ideas

Section 1
1. Describe the goals and ideas of the progressives and muckrakers.
2. What means were used to improve city governments?
3. How did Wisconsin lead the way in reform on the state level?

Section 2
1. Briefly describe Roosevelt's activities dealing with trusts, the coal strike, and conservation.
2. Why is Roosevelt described as the "forerunner of our modern Presidents"?
3. What reform legislation was passed during the Roosevelt administration?

Section 3
1. What reforms were passed during the Taft administration?
2. Briefly describe the three issues that led President Taft to lose favor with progressives.
3. What led to the split in the Republican party in the Taft administration?

Section 4
1. Name the candidates, parties, and major issues in the 1912 presidential campaign.
2. What major reforms were passed during the first Wilson administration?

Section 5
1. Were progressive reforms designed to help blacks and immigrants? Explain.
2. What was the black response to the racism of some progressives?

Special History Skills:
Identifying Primary and Secondary Sources
All historical information falls into two basic categories—primary sources or secondary sources. Primary sources are first-hand, direct descriptions of people, places, and events. They are written or recorded when and where the people lived or the event happened. Secondary sources are based on the study of one or more primary sources. They are written after the people lived or the event occurred.

Keep in mind that neither a primary source nor a secondary source is necessarily *accurate*. Both kinds of sources may be filled with errors. To gain a true picture of the past, a historian needs to analyze many primary and secondary sources, consider their accuracy, and then make a judgment about the nature of and relative importance of events that occurred in the past.

1. Identify each of the following as a primary or a secondary source:
    a speech by William Howard Taft
    Upton Sinclair's *The Jungle*
    a packinghouse owner's defense of the meat-packing industry
    a copy of the Sherman Antitrust Act
    a biography of Theodore Roosevelt
    a textbook
    a history of the NAACP
    an eyewitness account of McKinley's assassination
    minutes from the 1908 White House Conservation Conference
    an encyclopedia article on the ICC
2. Both primary and secondary sources are important research tools. List one possible advantage and one possible disadvantage of using each kind of source when studying an event, place, or person.

Other Skill Activities

1. **Be a muckraker**

   Write a muckraking article about a current problem in your community. Be sure to find out the facts before you write your opinion.

2. **Your city government**

   Find out what type of government your city (or the one closest to you) has. First, call or interview someone at city hall. Also use secondary sources.

3. **In the news**

   Federal agencies created by progressives are still an important part of government. Find and describe an action taken within the last year by one of the following: Interstate Commerce Commission, Federal Trade Commission, Federal Reserve, Pure Food and Drug Administration. Label each source you use "primary" or "secondary."

Thinking Critically

1. Many progressives believed that popular control of government would mean better government. Do you agree or disagree? Explain.
2. How did the progressives differ from the Populists? Compare the two movements on the basis of (**a**) background of the reformers, (**b**) goals, (**c**) accomplishments.
3. Are nativism and racism still prevalent in the United States? Define each in your answer.
4. In what ways did the progressive era improve American life? In what ways did it fail to do so?
5. Roosevelt believed that the President could do anything that the Constitution did not specifically prohibit. Was Ballinger right in believing that Roosevelt had overstepped his power? Give reasons for your answer.
6. Roosevelt is remembered as having been one of the best Presidents. Taft, on the other hand, is remembered as having been weak and ineffectual. How much of Roosevelt's reputation may be based on his public image rather than on his accomplishments as President? Explain.

Further Reading

Alice Fleming. *Ida Tarbell*. Thomas Y. Crowell Co., 1971. Biography of an early and successful muckraking journalist.

Ernest R. May. *The Progressive Era*. Time-Life Books, 1974. Discusses politics, social ills, leisure, and important people. Many photos.

TEST YOURSELF

WRITE YOUR ANSWERS ON A SEPARATE SHEET OF PAPER.

Matching

Write the letter of the item that best matches each description below.

1. led to regulation of the meat-packing industry
2. agency to prevent unfair business practices
3. movement advocating racial "improvement"
4. crusading journalists
5. reorganized the nation's banking system
6. gave the ICC the power to regulate telephone, telegraph, cable, and wireless companies
7. an appointed expert runs a city government
8. progressive governor of Wisconsin
9. provided for dam construction and irrigation
10. founder of the NAACP

a. muckrakers
b. W. E. B. Du Bois
c. city-manager plan
d. Robert M. La Follette
e. eugenics
f. National Reclamation Act
g. Mann-Elkins Act
h. Federal Trade Commission
i. Clayton Antitrust Act
j. *The Jungle*
k. Federal Reserve Act

Classifying

Mark each item R if it applies to Roosevelt, T if it applies to Taft, and W if it applies to Wilson. Some may apply to more than one President.

1. both conservative and progressive
2. became Bull Moose party candidate
3. unfairly discharged from the army a black battalion in Brownsville, Texas
4. lost the support of progressive Republicans during his single term of office
5. helped to end a long coal strike by acting as mediator
6. announced the end of reform in 1914 but continued it in 1916
7. created the National Conservation Commission
8. reformed the nation's banking and monetary system
9. created the Department of Labor
10. worked to regulate trusts

I WANT YOU
FOR U.S. ARMY
NEAREST RECRUITING STATION

Chapter 24

1914–1918

AMERICA GOES TO WAR

I t is late June 1914. Americans are enjoying a particularly pleasant summer. The weather has been glorious—perfect for boating, swimming, and camping. No one anywhere —least of all in America—is aware that the world they know is teetering on the brink of disaster.

On June 29th Americans read on the front pages of their newspapers of an assassination in the Balkans. A bullet has claimed the life of the heir to the throne of Austria-Hungary. Regrettable, of course, but of no particular concern to Americans—so it seems.

By the first week of August, the major European powers—Russia, Germany, France, Austria-Hungary, and Britain—are at war. From the Ural Mountains to the English Channel, armies are on the march. The bloodiest, costliest, and most destructive war in all history has begun.

Shocked and stunned by the news from Europe, Americans take satisfaction in the knowledge that the European war is none of their concern. After all, the United States has no quarrel with any of the warring powers. Its foreign policy concerns are with places nearer home—with Mexico, Canada, and Caribbean nations.

In the course of the next few months and years, the American people learn some sobering truths. Geographic isolation can now provide Americans only limited protection. The modern world has become a "global village." No man, no woman, and above all, no nation, is an island. World War I and its aftermath will soon force Americans to participate actively in European affairs.

Sections in This Chapter
1. The United States and World Affairs
2. Europe Explodes into World War I
3. Flying the Flag of Neutrality
4. America Goes to War
5. The Battle over the League of Nations

Opposite: Relics of World War I. The dramatic poster is still used to recruit American soldiers.

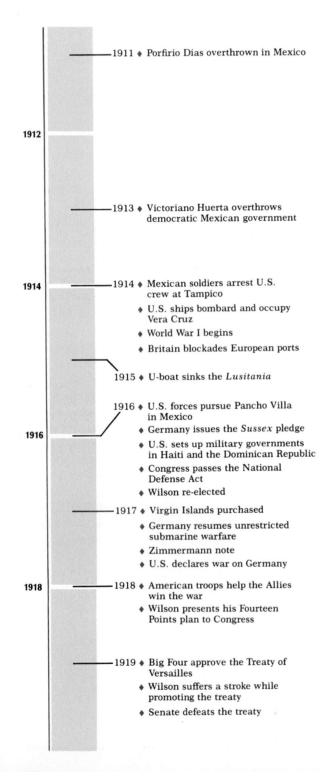

1911 ◆ Porfirio Díaz overthrown in Mexico

1912

1913 ◆ Victoriano Huerta overthrows democratic Mexican government

1914 ◆ Mexican soldiers arrest U.S. crew at Tampico
◆ U.S. ships bombard and occupy Vera Cruz
◆ World War I begins
◆ Britain blockades European ports

1915 ◆ U-boat sinks the *Lusitania*

1916 ◆ U.S. forces pursue Pancho Villa in Mexico
◆ Germany issues the *Sussex* pledge
◆ U.S. sets up military governments in Haiti and the Dominican Republic
◆ Congress passes the National Defense Act
◆ Wilson re-elected

1917 ◆ Virgin Islands purchased
◆ Germany resumes unrestricted submarine warfare
◆ Zimmermann note
◆ U.S. declares war on Germany

1918 ◆ American troops help the Allies win the war
◆ Wilson presents his Fourteen Points plan to Congress

1919 ◆ Big Four approve the Treaty of Versailles
◆ Wilson suffers a stroke while promoting the treaty
◆ Senate defeats the treaty

1. THE UNITED STATES AND WORLD AFFAIRS

As you saw in Chapter 23, when Woodrow Wilson was elected President, most of his experience and interest were in domestic policy. His overall program, the New Freedom, was mainly concerned with solving problems within the United States. Soon, however, more and more of the President's attention was drawn to foreign affairs.

Wilson's High Principles Guide Him in Foreign Affairs

Despite President Wilson's long study of American institutions as a college professor, he was not well prepared to deal with international relations. Nevertheless, when these problems presented themselves, he characteristically tried to deal with them quickly and in the manner he felt was right. As you know from Chapter 23, Wilson was a deeply religious person. He was the son of a Presbyterian minister, and his upbringing had instilled in him a strong sense of morality, or belief about what is right and wrong. It was this belief which guided the new President in his conduct of foreign affairs.

Wilson did not believe in following Teddy Roosevelt's imperialist policies. He felt that intervening in the affairs of other nations, in most cases, was wrong. He was also strongly opposed to war. The man he appointed Secretary of State, **William Jennings Bryan**, felt the same way. Together, Wilson thought, they could make a high sense of morality the key to United States dealings with the world. As we shall see, however, Wilson did not always act solely on these principles.

An Idealistic Beginning

One of the first problems the new President had to grapple with involved China. During the Taft administration, several American bankers had taken the government's advice to combine with bankers from other countries to finance a loan to China for a new railroad. Wilson believed that government support for such a transaction interfered with China's internal affairs. If the loan were made with government backing, he argued, the banks would expect "forcible interference" by the U.S. military to collect any missed repayments. Within two weeks of taking office, Wilson withdrew the government's support for the bankers' activities. Without government backing, the bankers were afraid to take the risks of the loan and withdrew from the project. It seemed an early victory for Wilson's goal of returning morality to foreign affairs.

Bryan's Cooling-Off Treaties

Almost as soon as he took office, Secretary of State Bryan, with Wilson's strong backing, began work on several conciliation treaties. Bryan, who hated war, believed that these treaties would help avoid armed conflict among the nations of the world. The countries signing these documents agreed to submit any disputes between them to an international investigating commission, though they did not have to abide by the commission's findings. They also pledged not to declare war until a "cooling-off" period of one year had passed. Both Bryan and Wilson felt that after a year had elapsed, most nations would have worked out their difficulties in a peaceful way.

Bryan eventually negotiated 30 of these **cooling-off treaties** before World War I broke out in Europe. Unfortunately, some European powers had declined to sign the treaties and others ignored them.

Trouble with Mexico

Another test of Wilson's ability to put his principles into practice came when Mexico entered a period of political unrest. Since 1877, Mexicans had been held in the iron grip of a ruthless dictator, Porfirio Díaz. During the decades that Díaz was in power, he permitted many foreign nations the right to develop Mexico's rich resources. Although this policy did help modernize Mexico's economy, the Mexican people gained little from it.

One of the largest investors in Mexican mines, oil wells, and factories was the United States. Almost 1.5 billion dollars had been plowed into Mexico by American businessmen, who owned 80% of Mexico's mines, 60% of the oil, 70% of the rubber plantations, and most of the railroads.

Because of this immense investment, and because some 50,000 American citizens lived below the Rio Grande, Americans were deeply concerned about what took place in Mexico.

In 1911 Díaz was ousted in a revolution. His successor, Francisco Madero, was liberal and a democrat who had been educated in the United States. Unfortunately for both Mexico and the United States, Madero's time in office was short. In 1913, he was murdered by one of his subordinates, Victoriano Huerta, who declared himself Mexico's ruler.

Wilson immediately faced the problem of whether or not he should recognize the blood-splattered Huerta regime as the rightful government of Mexico. Many other nations, including Britain, had quickly acknowledged the Huerta government, and American businessmen pressured Wilson to do the same. Furthermore, ever since Washington's administration, it had always been United States policy to recognize governments in power, even if they came into office through revolution.

The President decided to apply his view of morality to foreign affairs: breaking with tradition, he decided to refuse to recognize Huerta's government. Wilson believed that without United States recognition, Huerta's government would not last. At the same time Wilson initiated an embargo to keep weapons and ammunition from entering Mexico, where they would fall into the hands of the Huerta government.

Huerta scornfully rejected Wilson's proposal that he step down and allow the Mexican people to freely elect their President. Not only did Huerta continue in power, but several Americans were killed in the revolutionary disorders that erupted in attempts to remove him from office. Millions of dollars in American investments were lost.

Wilson's embargo and refusal to recognize the Huerta government soon revealed the dangers of his "watchful waiting" policy. Huerta refused to back down. Because of Wilson's public stand, the United States was now in a difficult position: either it had to back its words with the very military intervention Wilson so hated, or it had to back down and lose respect in the eyes of other nations—and the American voters. Wilson tried to hasten the dictator's downfall by allowing American weapons to get through the embargo to reach rebel leader Venustiano Carranza. He also stationed U.S. Navy ships off the Mexican coast to block European arms shipments to Huerta.

These efforts only strengthened Huerta's support. Wilson's problem grew worse. By this time, United States intervention would have turned both sides in the Mexican struggle against the American "busybodies." Then, in April 1914, the crisis came to a head. Mexican soldiers arrested a group of American sailors who had come ashore illegally at the port city of Tampico. (See map, page 520.) The Mexican commander released the men at once, with apologies. The American admiral in command of the naval squadron, however, demanded a 21-gun salute to the Stars and Stripes. This Huerta refused to do.

Wilson deeply believed the Mexican people should have the right to a free and democratic government. Angered at Huerta's dictatorial methods and at the failure of his own Mexican policy, the President decided to take action. He asked Congress for authority to intervene in Mexico with armed force. But even before Congress could approve (which it did, two days later), the President sent the American navy into action. Ordered to prevent an arms delivery by a German merchant vessel, American ships bombarded and seized the seaport of Vera Cruz. Nineteen Americans and 126 Mexicans were killed. Mexicans united behind Huerta, and the two nations teetered on the brink of war.

It was at this critical point that Argentina, Brazil, and Chile—the "ABC Powers"—came forward with an offer to mediate the crisis. Wilson, thankful for an opportunity to avoid an actual war, quickly accepted.

The mediation conference was held in Niagara Falls, New York. Although the attempt at mediation failed in the end, Huerta's regime was in difficulty and soon collapsed. The dictator's chief rival, Venustiano Carranza, became Mexico's new ruler.

But Wilson's troubles with Mexico were far from over. One of Carranza's generals, **Pancho Villa**, soon broke from his leader and led a revolt against him. In 1916 Villa, to show his contempt for and hatred of the United States, raided the town of Columbus, New Mexico, killing 17 Americans. Wilson ordered a 6,000-man army expedition, under the command of the stern and disciplined General John "Black Jack" Pershing, across the border with instructions to capture

Villa. But Villa and his men escaped Pershing, and Wilson, faced with the likelihood of war with Germany, called the expedition home.

The expedition outraged the Mexican people, including Carranza, and provoked hostility from much of Central and South America. The episode fueled Mexican suspicion of American intentions for years to come.

In this first major test of his moral policies, Wilson had been unable to resist interfering with Mexico's internal problems. His dislike of traditional "immoral" diplomacy had led him into errors that resulted in the very kind of intervention he despised. On the other hand, Wilson did manage to resist strong pressure at home to invade and even annex Mexico, and he had tried, however clumsily, to act in what he saw as Mexico's best interest.

Caribbean Involvement

Wilson's attention was also drawn to other Latin American countries during his first administration. As with his predecessors Roosevelt and Taft, Wilson's goal was to protect American interests in the Panama Canal. The President ordered marines into the small nation of Haiti when revolution flamed across that country in 1914. A treaty was negotiated in 1916 which permitted the United States to oversee Haitian financial transactions. Supervision of the country's police force was also a part of the agreement, which in effect made the island country an American protectorate. The period of American military rule lasted until 1934.

Similar events occurred in the Dominican Republic in 1916. When the Dominicans stated that they would no longer permit the United States to supervise the collection of their customs duties as provided in an earlier agreement, Wilson again sent in the marines. His action continued the United States protectorate established by President Roosevelt in 1905, and American rule lasted until 1934.

In 1917 the United States acquired more territory in the Caribbean by the purchase of the Virgin Islands from Denmark for $25 million. These tiny specks of land had their main value in protecting the approaches to the Panama Canal and providing locations where the United States could establish naval bases for the Atlantic fleet.

As you have read, President Wilson launched his administration on a note of morality and idealism. He soon discovered that because of forces he could not control, his ideas of morality and idealism had to give way to practical action. Thus, though he believed it morally undesirable to send marines into the Caribbean, he saw no way to avoid it. On the other hand, he thought it was morally right to fight a dictator in Mexico, though many Americans and Mexicans disagreed with his idea of morality in this matter.

Trouble Brews Across the Atlantic

While the President dealt with problems in this hemisphere, dangerous events were taking place elsewhere overseas. As you recall from Chapter 22, since the country's earliest days under President Washington, America had followed a policy of noninvolvement in European affairs. The Atlantic Ocean kept us from being drawn into Europe's quarrels. Most Americans agreed with this policy of "isolationism," as it was later called. They felt we should deal with problems here at home or in the Western Hemisphere and stay out of European affairs as much as possible.

This view of America's role was still prevalent when Wilson took office. Soon, however, the President and the American people were to be swept into European affairs far more deeply than anyone could have imagined.

SECTION 1 REVIEW

 Identify: William Jennings Bryan, cooling-off treaties, Pancho Villa, isolationism

Main Ideas

1. What beliefs guided President Wilson in his conduct of foreign affairs?
2. Why did President Wilson intervene in Mexican affairs, though he said that he was opposed to interference in the affairs of other countries?
3. What actions did the Wilson administration take in Haiti, the Dominican Republic, and the Virgin Islands? Did these actions fit his views on American intervention?

2. EUROPE EXPLODES INTO WORLD WAR I

It has been said that Europe in 1914 was a powder keg and that the nations of the Balkan Peninsula were the fuse. In 1914, the independent Balkan nations included Albania, Bulgaria, Greece, Montenegro, Romania, Serbia, and part of the Ottoman Empire. (See upper map, page 566.) The northwestern part of the peninsula was ruled by Austria-Hungary. Here lived the South Slavs, a variety of related peoples including Bosnians, Serbs, Croats, and Slovenes. For many years the Slavs who lived in Bosnia, Herzegovina, and other small provinces had been under the control of first the Ottoman Empire and then Austria-Hungary.

Unfortunately for the world, the Balkan fuse was lit on Sunday, June 28. That was the day the **Archduke Franz Ferdinand**, heir to the throne of Austria-Hungary, and his wife, Sophie, were visiting the city of Sarajevo. Sarajevo was the capital of the province of Bosnia, which had been annexed by Austria-Hungary in 1908. As the Archduke and his wife rode in an open car through the streets of the city, they were assassinated by a 19-year-old Bosnian student named Gavrilo Princip.

Princip was a member of a terrorist group called the Black Hand, whose goal was to free all the South Slavic peoples who lived under Austrian rule. The Black Hand group supported the idea of **nationalism**. Nationalism is the belief that one's own country and the independent government of that country are more important than anything else in international relations. Princip and his fellow conspirators wanted all Slavs in the Balkan area to have a nation of their own.

Anatomy of an Explosion

The Great Powers of Europe—Britain, France, Germany, Austria-Hungary, and Russia—had been at peace since 1870. But during those years European diplomats had built an extensive system of alliances. Through these alliances they guaranteed assistance to each other in the case of war. By 1907 two major sets of alliances had developed. On one side, allied in the **Triple En-**

tente, was Britain, France, and Russia. Opposing the Triple Entente was the **Triple Alliance** of Germany, Austria-Hungary, and Italy. After November 5, 1914, the Ottoman Empire also sided with the Triple Alliance.

During the years in which the Great Powers were lining up against each other, often secretly, many international tensions and rivalries were developing. The same nationalism which made the South Slavs want a nation of their own caused the people in each of the European countries to have an intense pride in their own countries. Along with this, the citizens of these nations were proud of their governments' actions, whether those actions were right or wrong.

Imperialism and Nationalism Lead to an Arms Race

During this same time most of the major powers were pursuing a policy of imperialism through which they controlled far-off colonies in Asia, the

Franz Ferdinand and Sophie were assassinated moments after this photograph was taken.

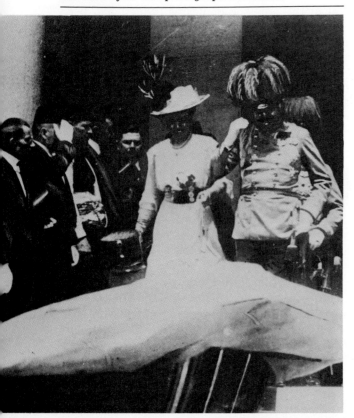

Pacific, and Africa. Britain, France, and Russia had been colonial powers for centuries, but countries such as Germany, Austria-Hungary, and Italy were "new to the game." In their race for "a place in the sun" all these countries frequently came into conflict with each other. Meanwhile, in the Balkans, smaller nations, such as Serbia and Romania, were constantly at each other's throats, again moved by the forces of nationalism.

The twin forces of nationalism and imperialism produced a great arms race among the European powers. To instill patriotism among its citizens and to ensure that it could defend itself and carry out its colonial policies, each European country became involved. Huge sums were spent to build up armies and to strengthen navies with larger and more powerful warships. As the powers competed with each other to improve their military capabilities, each of the two alliance systems looked at each other with growing suspicion. It was in this atmosphere of mistrust, fear, and almost continual crisis that the tragic event in Sarajevo occurred. And it was because of these conditions that the "powder keg" blew up.

War Breaks Out

When Princip and his friends were caught, it became known that Serbians were responsible for Archduke Franz Ferdinand's death. The Archduke's uncle, the 83-year-old Franz Josef, emperor of Austria-Hungary, believed he had to punish Serbia to discourage further rebellion. He won a promise from Germany to support any actions he took against Serbia, then issued a set of demands that infringed on Serbia's independence. These demands included an order to cease all anti-Austrian activities, to allow Austro-Hungarian officials to suppress such activities, and to dismiss all Serbian officials who engaged in anti-Austrian propaganda.

The Austrians knew that Serbia would refuse to meet all the demands in the ultimatum. They knew, too, that their challenge would very likely lead to war. The emperor and his advisers felt, however, that any conflict would only be between Austria and Serbia. In this judgment the Austrians proved to be tragically wrong. Serbia refused to give in, and Austria-Hungary declared war on Serbia on July 28—just one month after the Archduke's murder. Serbia turned to Russia for help, and the Czar mobilized the Russian army.

Germany, alarmed at the Czar's action, declared war on Russia four days later, on August 1. To eliminate the threat on its western border, Germany also declared war on France, and attacked it through the tiny country of Belgium. (See map, page 557.) Germany hoped to defeat France quickly so that it could turn its full attention to Russia without fear of being attacked from the west. As we shall see, this plan failed. When Germany attacked France, Britain—France's partner in the Triple Entente—was pulled into the conflict. Now most of Europe was ablaze.

Because of the great system of alliances, each nation that entered the fight had forced its treaty partners to go to war. Thus, the nations of Europe fell into the war like chained prisoners pulling each other, one by one, over a cliff. Only Italy did not follow through on its treaty obligations. In return for a promise of certain territories at the war's end, it deserted the Triple Alliance and joined the Triple Entente in 1915.

Thirty-three nations, including the United States, eventually entered the "Great War" or "World War," as it was called at the time. (See chart, page 560.) At least 15 million persons were killed during the four-year conflict, and millions more died from starvation and epidemics in the immediate postwar years. Four empires were toppled, and the maps of Europe, the Middle East, and Africa would have to be redrawn.

SECTION 2 REVIEW

 Identify: Franz Ferdinand, nationalism, Triple Entente, Triple Alliance

Main Ideas
1. Why was Franz Ferdinand assassinated?
2. Why did the leaders of Austria-Hungary present such a stiff ultimatum to Serbia if they believed it would cause war?
3. What was the impact of imperialism and nationalism on European affairs before the outbreak of World War I?
4. How did the assassination of the Archduke lead to all-out war in Europe?

3. FLYING THE FLAG OF NEUTRALITY

When war broke out in Europe, quickly engulfing one nation after another, most Americans believed there was no reason for the United States to become involved. Thousands of miles of ocean separated us from the warring states, and none were our enemies. Why get involved? A feeling of isolationism dominated American attitudes in August of 1914.

The President Hopes for Non-Involvement
On August 4, 1914, President Wilson issued a **Neutrality Proclamation** which stated that the United States was officially committed to neither side, and was to be considered a neutral nation by all those at war. Later, on August 19, just one week after the last of the Great Powers had entered the war, Wilson asked United States citizens to be "neutral in fact as well as in name . . . impartial in thought as well as in action."

Wilson, backed by Secretary of State Bryan, truly hoped America could remain above the conflict. Neutrality, however, was not the President's only goal. He also hoped that somehow, someway, he could stop the fighting by speaking the "counsels of peace and accommodation" to the belligerent nations.

Unfortunately, Wilson's desires were dashed in both instances. At the outset of the war, each of the alliance systems fought frantically to obtain as much as possible as quickly as possible. In these circumstances the European nations were not ready to listen to the "counsels of peace and accommodation" from Wilson or anyone else. Nor would Americans long remain neutral "in thought as well as in action."

The War Divides Americans
Of the total American population of 100 million, about 32 million, or one-third, had at least one foreign-born parent. Most of these persons were of European descent and naturally had strong feelings about one or another of the nations at war. Millions of German-Americans and other relatively recent arrivals from central and southern Europe favored the Triple Alliance countries, or

"**Central Powers**." Many Irish Americans, most of whom opposed the English who ruled their homeland, also backed the Central Powers.

But the overwhelming majority of United States citizens supported the Triple Entente countries, or "**Allies**." Many cultural and historic ties linked the United States and Britain. The two nations spoke a common language, and almost 50 million Americans had British ancestors. Most Americans also had a warm spot in their hearts for France, which gave us the Marquis de Lafayette and supplied indispensable aid during the American Revolution. A verse of the time summed up this feeling admirably:

> Forget us God, if we forget
> The sacred sword of Lafayette.

Many Americans were *against* Germany more than they were *for* the Allies. They were repelled by the warlike attitude of Kaiser Wilhelm, Germany's ruler, and the German emphasis on militarism. When Germany invaded the tiny country of Belgium and then called a previously signed agreement not to do so a "scrap of paper," American support for Germany dropped to a new low. But no matter which side Americans favored, most of them wanted the United States to stay out of the war, and they wanted the war to end quickly.

The War Becomes Deadlocked

In Europe, meanwhile, both the Allies and the Central Powers also hoped for an early end to the war. However, they did not want to stop fighting until each had gained the best possible position for its forces. Thus the war continued.

Since 1905, the German army's General Staff had developed a plan to launch a quick strike against France in the event war broke out. According to this "Schlieffen plan," German forces would first knock France out of the war, then concentrate on Russia on the Eastern Front. To avoid the heavily fortified Franco-German border, Germany attacked France through Belgium on August 4. The German master plan called for crossing the Belgium countryside in only six days. Then, once the Franco-Belgian border was reached, the German armies would thrust deep into France, pivot left, and destroy all French resistance. (See map, facing page.)

This carefully thought-out master plan failed. The Belgian army, with much hard fighting,

managed to delay the German advance for 18 days—three times as long as called for in the German plan. In the 18 days it took the German forces to crush Belgium, the British and French were able to deploy* troops to northern France. Fighting furiously, the Allied troops retreated before the superior German army until they reached the Marne River. (See inset map.) There, in the **First Battle of the Marne** (September 5–12) the Allies finally stopped the German advance. Both armies settled into defensive positions in 475 miles of trenches dug into the French soil. From the North Sea to the border of Switzerland stretched the battleline—and the trenches.

In other parts of Europe, particularly in the east where Germany and Austria-Hungary battled Russia, fierce fighting also took place. But for the most part the combatants were deadlocked.

Britain Blockades Europe

Under these circumstances new tactics soon began to appear. England, long mistress of the seas, blockaded the ports of Europe, including those of neutral countries. Supplies to the Central Powers were not allowed to go through. All ships approaching the blockaded area, including those of the United States, were stopped and searched. In some instances the vessels were taken into a British harbor where they were subjected to thorough and time-consuming searches. Those carrying **contraband** (war-related materials) had their cargoes confiscated. The British were the sole judges of what was contraband.

The policy of blockading neutral ports, along with other British actions such as opening U.S. mail found on vessels being searched, infringed on America's right to freedom of the seas. A century earlier the United States had gone to war with Britain to defend its neutral rights. Now, in this war, President Wilson protested vigorously, but Britain again refused to budge. Friction between Britain and the United States mounted.

Germany Attacks with U-Boats

On the other hand, American problems also soon developed with Germany. To break the blockade, which was keeping food from German civilians as well as from soldiers at the front, the German navy turned to a terrifying new weapon—the submarine, or **U-boat**. (The term comes from the

*__deploy__ spread out troops from a column into a long battle line.

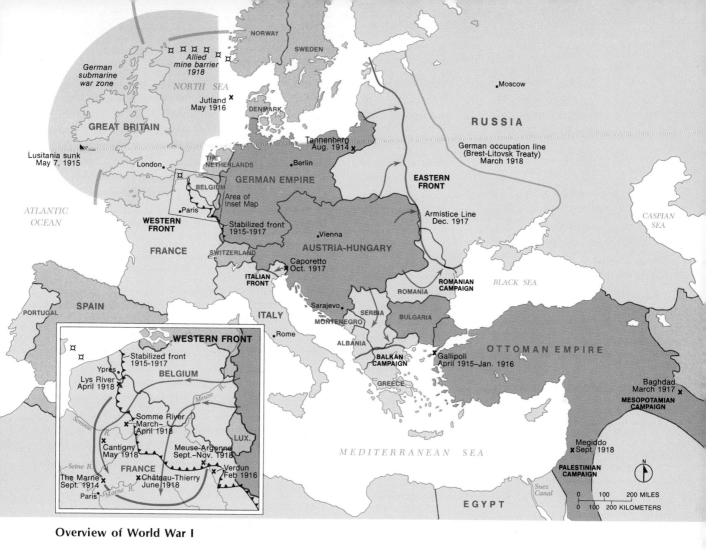

Overview of World War I

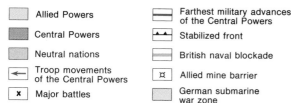

- Allied Powers
- Central Powers
- Neutral nations
- ← Troop movements of the Central Powers
- x Major battles
- ⌐ Farthest military advances of the Central Powers
- ▲▲ Stabilized front
- ▬▬ British naval blockade
- ⌷ Allied mine barrier
- German submarine war zone

World War I was fought on many fronts. After Germany's initial plunge across Belgium into France, a two-year stalemate developed along the Western Front. The worst of many deadlocked battles during that time was Verdun, which cost nearly a million lives and resulted in no change of position for either side.

German word *unterseeboot*, meaning "undersea boat.") With these silent and murderous marauders, Germany intended to destroy English and French merchant ships bringing war supplies to the Allies. Even neutral vessels would not be safe, said the Germans, because "mistakes" most likely would occur.

Wilson sharply protested Germany's violation of neutral rights. Germany, he stated, would be held "strictly accountable" for any destruction of American ships or the death of any American citizens. Five months later, on May 7, 1915, the inevitable mistake occurred. A German torpedo

sliced through the water off the coast of Ireland, striking the British liner **Lusitania**. The huge ship went to the bottom in 18 minutes, with the loss of 1,200 lives, including 128 American men, women, and children.

Many Americans, especially those along the East Coast, clamored for war. Wilson, more level-headed, resisted. Stating that in some instances nations should be "too proud to fight," he sent a severe note of protest to Germany. Secretary of State Bryan, totally opposed to war, believed Americans should not be permitted on ships sailing in the war zone. When an even stronger second note of protest was sent, Bryan refused to sign it and resigned. He was replaced by the handsome and distinguished-looking Robert Lansing, who was pro-British.

Nearly a year later, in March 1916, the French passenger ship *Sussex* was torpedoed and sunk by a German U-boat. Several Americans were injured, and it seemed as if the United States would break diplomatic relations or possibly even go to war. But still Wilson waited. In an ultimatum to Germany, the President demanded that the German navy cease its submarine warfare, or the United States would break diplomatic relations. Wilson's protest was so strong that in May 1916 Germany issued the so-called *Sussex* **pledge**. In this pledge the German government announced that no more merchant ships would be sunk "without warning and without saving human lives." Temporarily, at least, the submarine problem appeared to be solved.

The United States Builds Up Its Strength

Despite the German promise, public opinion in the United States now favored the Allies. Many Americans felt that the United States should prepare to enter the war. British propaganda about "the Hun," along with Germany's submarine tactics, had turned the tide. Across the land Americans called for preparedness.

Wilson also believed the nation should be better prepared for war. The previous year, in July 1915, he had asked the Secretaries of War and the Navy to tell him what was necessary to bring the nation's armed forces up to strength. In June of 1916 Congress passed the National Defense Act which increased the size of the army. In August the Naval Appropriations Bill was passed by Congress. This bill authorized the building of many new ships for the navy. By November, when the presidential elections were held, the country had started down the long road to preparedness.

The Election of 1916

With the submarine threat somewhat lessened and preparedness underway, Americans turned their attention to the presidential election of 1916. Convinced they had a winner, the Democratic party enthusiastically renominated Woodrow Wilson. Pointing to the President's diplomatic achievements in dealing with Britain and Germany, the Democrats used the phrase "He kept us out of war" as their campaign slogan.

The Republicans named the distinguished Supreme Court justice Charles Evans Hughes as their candidate. The Progressives nominated their 1912 candidate, Teddy Roosevelt. When Roosevelt refused the nomination, most of the Progressives threw their support to Wilson. The election turned out to be one of the closest in the country's history. Wilson was returned to the White House by a popular margin of 600,000 votes, but in the electoral college, the President mustered only 277 votes to Hughes' 254.

The U-Boats Strike Again

Peace efforts took on a hollow ring when on January 31, 1917, the Germans announced that unrestricted submarine warfare would be resumed at once. The German government knew that this decision would draw the United States into the war. They believed, however, that Britain could be knocked out of the fighting before United States troops could begin fighting in Europe.

Wilson severed diplomatic relations with Germany on February 3. He also authorized the arming of American merchant ships for protection against U-boat attacks.

FROM THE ARCHIVES

Wilson's War Message to Congress

The present German submarine warfare against commerce is a warfare against mankind. It is a war against all nations. . . .

We have no quarrel with the German people. We have no feeling towards them but one of sympathy and friendship. It was not upon their impulse that their government acted in entering this war. . . .

The world must be made safe for democracy. Its peace must be planted upon the tested foundations of political liberty. We have no selfish ends to serve. We desire no conquest, no dominion. We seek no indemnities for ourselves, no material compensation for the sacrifices we shall freely make. We are but one of the champions of the rights of mankind. We shall be satisfied when those rights have been made as secure as the faith and the freedom of nations can make them.

Address given before Joint Session of Congress, April 2, 1917.

In early March 1917, the President released to the Associated Press news service a captured coded message from German foreign minister Arthur Zimmermann to the German minister to Mexico. The **Zimmermann note** promised to give Texas, New Mexico, and Arizona to Mexico if the Mexicans entered the war against the United States. When the American people read Zimmermann's message, a sense of outrage swept across the country. War fever heightened, and it became evident to almost everyone that neutrality was no longer possible. When several American merchant ships were sunk later in March, most citizens sensed that American participation in the war was inevitable.

On April 2, 1917, Wilson went before Congress to ask for a declaration of war against Germany. In an eloquent and moving address, the President explained why the United States must enter the war. The war had been forced upon America, he said. Although Britain had also violated America's rights, Germany had been far more ruthless. "Property can be paid for," said Wilson, "lives of peaceful and innocent people cannot." The "world must be made safe for democracy" the President stated, and this could be done only if the "military masters" of Germany were defeated. Four days later Congress voted overwhelmingly to declare war against Germany. The flames of war had at last reached across the Atlantic and engulfed the United States.

SECTION 3 REVIEW

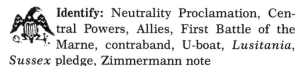

Identify: Neutrality Proclamation, Central Powers, Allies, First Battle of the Marne, contraband, U-boat, *Lusitania*, *Sussex* pledge, Zimmermann note

Main Ideas

1. List two factors which kept Americans from being really neutral during the years 1914–1917.
2. What were the two new tactics employed by the European powers during the war?
3. How did the Zimmermann note affect U.S. neutrality?
4. Why did many Americans feel that Germany's tactics were worse than Britain's during the period of neutrality?

4. AMERICA GOES TO WAR

For the first time since 1898 Americans prepared for war with a European power. One of the President's first jobs was to raise an army. Despite Wilson's earlier efforts at preparedness, the United States still needed much more military manpower.

To overcome the troop shortage Congress passed the Selective Service Act in May of 1917. Through this legislation all men between the ages of 21 and 30 were registered by their local draft boards. After registration the men were classified by physical condition and other factors in order of availability for the draft. In August 1918 the Act was modified to register men between 18 and 45. By the time the fighting was over, 24 million men had been registered. Over 4 million were drafted, and 2 million were sent to France.

The Desperate Plight of the Allies

The American decision to enter the war came not a moment too soon. Exhausted from almost four years of fighting, the Allies were nearly bled white. The Central Powers seemed on the verge of a stunning victory. Fighting alongside Austrian forces, the Germans struck Italy a staggering blow at Caporetto in October 1917. (See map, page 557.) In Russia, the Communists had seized power in a revolution in November and in effect removed that country from the war. Though a German-Russian peace treaty was not signed until March, huge numbers of seasoned German veterans were shifted to the Western Front in the fall. At sea, U-boats were making quick work of the Allies' merchant ships.

The American Navy Goes into Action

In the face of these circumstances, immediate American assistance was indispensable. The American navy, which was much better prepared for war than the army, was put into use almost at once. Under **Admiral W. S. Sims**, American vessels swept the icy waters of the North Sea, searching for the deadly U-boats. Sims also directed his forces to assist the Royal Navy in laying a mine barrier across the North Sea. The barrier was highly effective in bottling up the powerful

COMBATANTS IN WORLD WAR I

The Allies		The Central Powers
Australia	Japan	Austria-Hungary
Belgium	Liberia	Bulgaria
Brazil	Montenegro	Germany
Britain	New Zealand	Ottoman Empire
Canada	Nicaragua	
China	Panama	
Costa Rica	Portugal	
Cuba	Romania	
France	Russia	
Greece	San Marino	
Guatemala	Serbia	
Haiti	Siam	
Honduras	South Africa	
India	United States	
Italy		
Maximum total mobilized strength: 42 million troops		Maximum total mobilized strength: 23 million troops

German navy. The U.S. navy also brought to the Allies the technique of the convoy, in which several ships traveled together under the protection of destroyers. Soon, thanks to these efforts, losses in Allied shipping began to drop.

New Agencies Help Mobilize America

The war affected every aspect of American life. Mobilized along with the military services were the nation's industrial workers, farmers, business leaders, and everyday citizens. The responsibility for overseeing America's economic mobilization was given to the Council of National Defense, a body made up of cabinet members and officials from business, industry, railroads, and labor unions. The Council soon created several other bodies to carry out the country's mobilization.

Charged with the responsibility of increasing the nation's industrial output was the **War Industries Board**, headed by the wealthy American businessman **Bernard Baruch**. The WIB soon became the most powerful agency in America. The Board regulated every area of the American economy. It set quotas, controlled the use of raw materials, developed new industries, fixed prices, and standardized many products. The Board was so effective that it increased the nation's industrial production by some 20%.

The National War Labor Board, with former President Taft and Frank Walsh as co-chairmen, helped ensure that labor problems were mini-

mized during the war by serving as an arbitration body. With the cooperation of American workers, the country's industrial output was assured. Throughout the war, labor unions supported the war effort, and there were few strikes.

American agriculture was marshaled into war service through the **Food Administration**. Headed by the young and talented **Herbert Hoover**, this agency encouraged farm production by guaranteeing a set price for specified crops. Hoover encouraged Americans to plant "Victory Gardens." He also instituted "Meatless Mondays" and "Wheatless Wednesdays" to provide food for the Allies as well as for American fighting men.

Efforts to conserve coal, gasoline, oil, kerosene, and other fuel products were carried out by the Fuel Administration, headed by Harry Garfield, a college president and son of the assassinated James A. Garfield. Daylight-savings time was put into effect to help save coal.

The Emergency Fleet Corporation was created to provide ships for the transportation of men and materials overseas. During the war the total tonnage of the American merchant marine grew to ten times its prewar size.

Bond Drives Go over the Top

All of these special efforts called for vast sums of money. How could the necessary funds be raised? It was the decision of Congress to finance the war by increasing taxes and by selling bonds to the American people. The bonds were sold in four huge Liberty Loan Drives and a Victory Loan Drive. Children were encouraged to buy savings stamps. By the time the fighting had stopped, a staggering total of more than 21 billion dollars had been raised.

Increased Opportunities for Women

One of the results of mass mobilization of the nation's industry was increased opportunity for American women. Just as they had done in the Civil War, women stepped forward to fill the vacancies created when millions of men entered the armed forces. Many women were able to take jobs which were unavailable to them before. Their work in the defense plants and in war industries which manufactured equipment and other items necessary to the military had a large impact on the success of the war effort.

For the first time in American history women

donned official uniforms of the nation's armed services. Almost 11,000 wore Navy blue as "yeomanettes." About 300 joined the Marine Corps, where they were called "Marinettes." The servicewomen in World War I were the predecessors of the much larger number of women who volunteered for service in World War II.

Women were leaders in wartime organizations such as the Women's Camouflage Corps and in the Liberty Bond drives. Many other women joined the Red Cross and the U.S. Army Corps of Nurses, where they often served in the military hospitals in France. The war thus opened up many doors that had been closed to women, although almost all of the gains made by women during the war were lost when the fighting stopped.

Many Blacks Move North During the War

When America's industries began to expand to meet war needs, hundreds of thousands of southern black men and women saw an opportunity to improve their lives and moved north. Here they took advantage of the new demands for labor created by the war. Many found the good jobs and better pay they had hoped for. On the other hand, discrimination and prejudice did not end, and in some cases they even intensified. Blacks and unskilled whites, often competing for the same jobs, came into frequent conflict. Racial tensions and in some instances lynchings and other violence resulted.

Blacks in the military also encountered discrimination, though it was far less than in the civilian world. Nearly 400,000 blacks served in uniform during World War I, although they were blocked from service in the Marine Corps. Almost 200,000 blacks served overseas, many with distinction. Two black infantry divisions served in France, the 92nd and 93rd. Blacks made a considerable stride forward when over 600 were commissioned as officers in the military. In the navy, a small group of black women served in the Navy Department headquarters as yeomanettes.

Blacks made some economic gains during the war, but the real impact of the war was on the distribution of the black population. In fact, the large-scale migration of blacks to the major cities of the north brought about one of the greatest social changes in our country's history. Until World War I, about 90% of all black Americans lived in the southern states, and three out of four lived in rural areas. The hundreds of thousands of blacks who moved north during World War I were not the first blacks to do so, but they did set in motion a stream of population that would continue into the 1960s. By 1960 half of all black Americans would live outside the southern states, and three out of four would reside in urban areas.

Molding Public Opinion

To ensure continued support of the war effort, Wilson created the **Committee on Public Information**, headed by a young newspaperman, George Creel. Soon Creel was hard at work with an extensive campaign to sell the war to the American people. Many artists, writers, and speakers were pressed into service to publicize the American cause and whip up hatred for the "Huns." Women's groups, social clubs, the media, and even the pulpits of the nation's churches became platforms for what Creel called "the world's greatest adventure in advertising."

Unfortunately the fervor whipped up by Creel had its ugly side. Patriotism became an excuse for persecuting people with German names. The teaching of the German language was stopped in many schools, and the music of German composers such as Bach, Beethoven, and Wagner was banned. Less serious effects of Creel's work resulted in people calling sauerkraut "liberty cabbage" and dachshunds "liberty pups." Even German food became less accepted during the war.

New Laws Enforce Loyalty

Though the vast majority of Americans supported the war, a small group of socialists and pacifists stood in opposition to the fighting. Some progressives such as the Wisconsin senator, Robert La Follette, also opposed the war because they were afraid the war effort would cause a decline in progressive reform in the United States.

Creel's public relations efforts soon unleashed a tide of hysteria against these opponents of the war. Congress reacted by passing the 1917 **Espionage Act** and the 1918 **Sedition Act** which were aimed at controlling dissent and disloyalty. Newspapers and magazines were censored, and in some cases even freedom of speech was repressed. A movie producer, for example, was sentenced to jail for making a film about the American Revolution because it could have

aroused hatred against the British. About 1,500 people, including Socialist party leader Eugene V. Debs, were convicted of violating these laws.

The Espionage and Sedition Acts seemed to violate Americans' constitutional rights, but the Supreme Court upheld their constitutionality. The Court said that in some instances, such as war, absolute freedom could legally be restricted. Just as no one has the right to shout "fire" in a crowded theater, said Justice Oliver Wendell Holmes, Jr., disloyalty cannot be allowed during wartime or the nation might not survive to ensure its citizens' freedoms.

Americans Help Win the War in Europe

In June of 1917 the first troops from the American Expeditionary Force (A.E.F.) arrived in France under the command of **General John "Black Jack" Pershing**, the army officer who had earlier led American troops into Mexico. In a little over a year more than 2 million American "doughboys"* were serving in France.

The Americans were desperately needed. Hoping to win the war before the American troops arrived, the Germans launched a major offensive on March 21, 1918, against the Allies in the valley of the Somme River. (See inset map, page 557.) Because of Russia's withdrawal from the war, Germany had great numbers of troops released from service on the Eastern Front. They struck savagely again on April 9, at the Lys River.

Then, on May 31, American soldiers for the first time were placed in the thick of the action at Château-Thierry. Here, fighting furiously, they shoved the Germans eastward across the Marne. In September, 1.2 million doughboys fought with

*doughboys U.S. infantrymen in World War I. The nickname originated in the 1800s and was used by cavalrymen to describe infantrymen, who wore white belts which they cleaned with a pipe clay "dough."

Far left: British soldiers in the trenches. Center: American troops on the way to the front in the Meuse-Argonne offensive. Above: A French couple welcomes two Americans.

distinction in the Meuse-Argonne offensive, the last major campaign of the war and the largest in the history of warfare up to that time.

Realizing all was lost, Kaiser Wilhelm fled from Germany to the Netherlands on November 9, 1918. Two days later, on the 11th hour of the 11th day of the 11th month, the armistice was signed. Stillness fell across the battered French countryside as the fighting stopped. World War I had ended, but it had been the most terrible bloodbath in history. Some 112,000 Americans had died, 49,000 in combat. Most of the rest lost their lives in the deadly influenza epidemic of 1918, which swept across the world, killing tens of millions. Altogether, at least 10 million troops and 5 million civilians had been killed in the war, while starvation and disease had claimed—or would soon claim—the lives of countless millions more. A whole generation of Europeans had been consumed in the carnage.

SECTION 4 REVIEW

 Identify: W. S. Sims, War Industries Board, Bernard Baruch, Food Administration, Herbert Hoover, Committee on Public Information, Espionage and Sedition Acts, John "Black Jack" Pershing

Main Ideas
1. Why was the American entry into the war so important for the Allies? What was the role of the American navy in aiding the Allies?
2. Describe four boards or commissions created to deal with the war.
3. How did opportunities for women and blacks temporarily increase during the war?
4. Describe the work of the Committee on Public Information. How did it affect civil liberties?
5. How did the American army help the Allies win the war? Refer to the map on page 557 to locate specific battles.

5. THE BATTLE OVER THE LEAGUE OF NATIONS

Even before the war had ended, politicians and diplomats had formed very definite ideas about the kind of peace that should follow. On January 22, 1918, President Wilson outlined his concept of the peace settlement to the American Congress.

The Fourteen Points
The outcome of the war, he said, must be "a peace without victory" if war were not to flare again in Europe or elsewhere. To obtain such a peace, Wilson outlined his hopes in what he termed the "**Fourteen Points**." The adoption of these ideas as the basis for a peace treaty would ensure a just and lasting settlement, said Wilson.

The Fourteen Points called, in Points One through Five, for the end of secret treaties, for the freedom of the seas, for the reduction of tariffs and armaments, and for a fair adjustment of all claims to colonies. (See chart, facing page.) Points Six through Thirteen outlined a plan to give European national groups their own nations, where possible, by redrawing the map of prewar Europe; the removal of German troops from France and Belgium; and the transfer of Alsace-Lorraine back to France (see lower map, page 566).

It was the Fourteenth Point, however, that was most dear to Wilson's heart. In it he called for "a general association of nations" which would afford "mutual guarantees of political independence and territorial integrity to great and small states alike." This was the President's cherished plan for a **League of Nations**. Wilson was determined to make the League part of the peace settlement.

Wilson Goes to France
The peace conference was scheduled for January 1919. On December 4, 1918, Wilson sailed for France. Little did he know that he was sailing into one of the most troublesome times of his political career. For the first time an American President was going to Europe. For the first time as well, he was going to act as the negotiator for America at a peace conference with leaders from the Great Powers of Europe. It was a departure from American tradition, but Wilson felt that only his presence could ensure a just peace.

When the President arrived in France, he was greeted by mammoth crowds that paid homage to the great "peacemaker from America." In Britain and Italy he received similar attention. Unfortunately, before the final peace was made, much of this reservoir of goodwill toward Wilson had been depleted.

The Peace Conference
The peace conference began at the Palace of Versailles on January 18, 1919. Though many nations were represented, the major decisions were made by the leaders of the Allied nations. Called the "Big Four" they included Wilson; Georges Clemenceau of France, who was called "the Tiger"; David Lloyd George of Britain; and Vittorio Orlando of Italy. In small sessions with these practical politicians of the Old World, the idealistic Wilson soon ran into difficulty.

The President quickly learned that the European leaders were more interested in pursuing their own national interests than in making a "peace without victory." Lloyd George, the master politician from Britain, had just won re-election by promising to squeeze Germany for large **reparations** payments, that is, payments of money to countries damaged in the war. Clemenceau, "the Tiger," was 29 years old when Germany defeated France in 1871. Now after seeing his country invaded anew in 1914, he was determined to ensure that the Germans could never make war again. Orlando's Italy had been promised territorial gains at the start of the war, and Orlando intended to see that these promises were kept. How in these circumstances did Wilson hope to win adoption of his Fourteen Points?

Wilson's Diplomacy
The President soon realized that he must compromise. But what was most important and was not to be given away? To Wilson there was but one answer—the League of Nations. Thus he gave ground on many of the Fourteen Points while standing fast on Point Fourteen. He reluctantly agreed that Germany should have to pay massive reparations. He also agreed that Britain could reconsider the point about freedom of the seas.

Wilson was also forced to compromise on the

important question of the territory which formerly made up the Ottoman Empire (Turkey), which had also been defeated by the Allies. Turkey retained eastern Thrace and Armenia, while Syria was given to France. Mesopotamia and Palestine went to Britain. Italy received the Dodecanese Islands. As you will see later, these decisions at the end of the war were to have long-range effects on Middle East affairs.

The President held firm on his idea that colonies taken from Germany should not go to the Allies. Instead the Allies were to administer them as mandates (protectorates) of the League. Wilson also held his ground against some of Italy's territorial demands while agreeing to others. But upon his beloved idea of the League of Nations, however, Wilson would make no compromise. He insisted to the other members of the Big Four that the covenant, or charter, of the League be made a part of the peace treaty with Germany. Threatening to make a separate peace with Germany, the President scored a major victory when the Allied leaders agreed to this demand.

Opposition to the League Grows at Home

While Wilson was in Paris, a growing opposition to his plans was mounting in Congress. The President had made a major misstep when he failed to make his peace delegation bipartisan—composed of both Democrats and Republicans. All those who traveled to Paris were Democrats save Henry White, a retired Republican diplomat who had no influence with his party. Many Republicans felt left out by the President's actions, and when he returned to the United States in July he faced a serious situation.

Chief critic of the President and his plans was his long-time political enemy, **Senator Henry Cabot Lodge** of Massachusetts. Lodge felt that the United States should not join the League of Nations without certain reservations, or changes, in the covenant. His main concern, among others, was that the League seemed to commit American troops to war without congressional approval. Unless this was changed, said Lodge, he and his followers, called "reservationists" would not support the Treaty of Versailles.

Another group, led by **Senators William E. Borah** and **Hiram W. Johnson**, also opposed the treaty. This group was termed the "irreconcilables" because they felt that the United States should not join the League under any circumstances. Strong isolationists, they did not want the United States to remain involved in European affairs. A third group in the Senate supported the treaty. These were mostly Democrats who, as loyal followers of the party, backed the President and his plans.

Lodge and the other treaty opponents had by early fall marshaled their strength. The tide of public opinion seemed to be running against Wilson, the treaty, and the League. It appeared that if something were not done, the chance for the United States to work for peace through the League would forever vanish. Under these circumstances Wilson decided to use his personal prestige as President to fight for the Treaty of Versailles. He would go directly to the people. He would, through speeches and personal appeal, overcome the opposition that had been created by League opponents.

The President's Last Trip

In early September 1919 Wilson began an ambitious speaking tour. A special train carried him west across the autumn countryside, deep into America's heartland. Weak and frail in health,

---

WILSON'S FOURTEEN POINTS

1. An end to all secret diplomacy
2. Freedom of the seas in peace and war
3. The reduction of trade barriers among nations
4. The general reduction of armaments
5. The adjustment of colonial claims in the interest of the inhabitants as well as of the colonial power
6. The evacuation of Russian territory and a welcome for its government to the society of nations
7. The restoration of Belgium
8. The evacuation of all French territory, including Alsace-Lorraine (which Germany took from France in 1871)
9. The readjustment of Italian boundaries along clearly recognizable lines of nationality
10. Independence for various national groups in Austria-Hungary
11. The restoration of the Balkan nations and free access to the sea for Serbia
12. Protection for minorities in Turkey and the free passage of the ships of all nations through the Dardanelles
13. Independence for Poland, including access to the sea
14. An association of nations to protect "mutual guarantees of political independence and territorial integrity to great and small states alike."

Europe in 1914

Europe after World War I

Boundaries in 1914

Boundaries after World War I

New nations

the President had spent most of his energy in the long months of negotiations at Paris. Now, as he undertook a journey of 9,500 miles with 37 speeches, his health began to fail rapidly. As he traveled farther west, the President's appeal seemed to be working. Huge crowds thronged to hear him speak. But on September 25th he collapsed after a moving speech at Pueblo, Colorado. Too sick to continue, the stricken President was hastily brought back to Washington. There, on October 2, his wife found him on the bathroom floor in the White House, half paralyzed by a stroke.

The League Is Defeated

For many months the President was so ill that he could carry on almost none of his duties. While Wilson was in his sickroom, his enemies continued to oppose the treaty. Wilson, however, refused to compromise. Rising partially from his sickbed, he whispered "Let Lodge compromise!"

Lodge proposed his own amended version of the treaty. It accepted United States membership in the League of Nations, but made reservations about the extent of American responsibility for defending other League members. Lodge's amendments also gave Congress the power to veto any actions the President might take to fulfill commitments to the League.

Wilson remained firm. "Better a thousand times to go down fighting than to dip your colors to dishonorable compromise," he told his wife. Using his position as head of the Democratic party, Wilson ordered Senate Democrats to vote against the amended treaty. When the Senate vote came up on November 19, 1919, both the amended and the original versions of the treaty were defeated. But the battle had not quite ended.

Debate continued, but frantic efforts by treaty supporters still failed to move either Lodge or Wilson toward compromise. A large majority of senators, as well as most of the American people, favored ratifying the treaty, including League membership, but most wanted some kind of amendments. The treaty came up for a second vote in March of 1920, and was again voted down. Wilson, the great wartime leader, had failed in peace. The United States would not be in the League.

Who was to blame for the situation? Why did the treaty fail? Without question much of the responsibility must be shouldered by Lodge and the

LIFE IN AMERICA

EDITH WILSON'S STEWARDSHIP

On October 2, 1919, Woodrow Wilson suffered a stroke which partially paralyzed his left side and left him close to death. It was then that Edith Wilson began her stewardship. She was not, as some have said, our first woman President, but she did closely control who saw the President, how long the visit lasted, and, to some degree, what was said.

What the Constitution Said
Had the President died, the Constitution was clear: Vice-President Thomas Marshall would have become President. Wilson, however, remained lucid, although he was very ill for some time and remained partially paralyzed until his death in 1924.

Secretary of State Robert Lansing decided to force the issue. He called a cabinet meeting and read the Constitution:

In case of the removal of the President from office, or of his death, resignation, or inability to discharge the powers and duties of the said office, the same shall devolve on the Vice-President.

But who was to declare that the President was unable to carry on? The Constitution had no answer. Mrs. Wilson then made a crucial decision of national importance. She and the President's doctor reasoned that Wilson's resignation would ensure defeat of the League of Nations and that this knowledge would kill him.

So there it stood. An unelected person controlled access to President Wilson for the rest of his term and even guided his hand to sign legislation for six weeks.

The 25th Amendment
In 1965, after President Kennedy's assassination, the Constitution was amended to provide for such situations. If the President will not or cannot declare himself or herself unable to carry on, the Vice-President and a majority of the cabinet can vote to do so; the Vice-President will then become Acting President.

Republican senators who worked against Wilson's peace plan. But Wilson, who refused to compromise, even in the face of impending failure, must also bear the burden of failure. And finally, much of the American public was responsible for the nation's decision to remain out of the League in the decades that followed. The desire of United States citizens to remain uninvolved with Europe was too much to overcome once the President fell ill.

Had America joined the League of Nations the course of European history might have been different. But with the United States out of the new international body, events took place which, as you will see in Chapter 30, led to a second and much more terrible world war.

SECTION 5 REVIEW

 Identify: Fourteen Points, League of Nations, reparations, Henry Cabot Lodge, William E. Borah, Hiram W. Johnson

Main Ideas
1. What was Wilson's main goal at the Versailles peace conference? What were the main goals of the Big Four leaders?
2. List several points on which Wilson was willing to compromise. On what point did he refuse to compromise?
3. What was Henry Cabot Lodge's main objection to the League of Nations?
4. Why was the Treaty of Versailles defeated in the Senate?

CHAPTER 24 REVIEW

Key Terms
Explain the meaning of each of the following terms:

cooling-off treaties
isolationism
nationalism
Triple Entente
Triple Alliance
Neutrality
   Proclamation
Central Powers
Allies
First Battle of the
   Marne
contraband
U-boat

Lusitania
Sussex pledge
Zimmermann note
War Industries Board
Food Administration
Committee on Public
   Information
Espionage and Sedition
   Acts
Fourteen Points
League of Nations
reparations

Reviewing the Main Ideas
Section 1
1. What was President Wilson's guiding principle in his conduct of foreign affairs?
2. Why did President Wilson intervene in Mexico, Haiti, and the Dominican Republic when he said he was opposed to interference in the affairs of other countries? Why did the United States buy the Virgin Islands?

Section 2
1. How did the assassination of Franz Ferdinand lead to the start of World War I?
2. How did imperialism, nationalism, and the alliance system make World War I more likely?

Section 3
1. Name two factors which kept Americans from being really neutral during the years 1914–1917.
2. What were the two new naval tactics employed by the European powers during the war?
3. Why did the United States enter the war on the side of the Allies and not the Central Powers?

Section 4
1. Why was American entry into the war so important to the Allies in 1917?

2. List three ways the country organized itself to deal with wartime needs.

Section 5
1. How did the goals of Wilson, Clemenceau, Lloyd George, and Orlando differ at Versailles?
2. What factors led to the Senate's defeat of the Treaty of Versailles?

Special History Skills:
Working with Military Maps
World War I lasted four years, from 1914 to 1918. The map on page 557 shows alliances and major battles of this war. Refer to the map to answer the following questions.
1. Which battle marks the farthest advance of the Central Powers on the Western Front in 1914? Did the Central Powers reach Paris?
2. The Stabilized Front stretched from the North Sea to Switzerland—this front was one long line of trenches. Find this line on the map. How many years did the Stabilized Front remain unchanged? What major battles were fought along this front in 1918?
3. Which nation was surrounded by the German submarine zone?
4. How did the Allies try to cut off German access to the North Sea?
5. Did the Central Powers advance into Russia? When was the Armistice Line established on the Eastern Front?
6. What campaigns took place in Southern Europe and the Middle East?

Other Skill Activities
1. **Political cartoons**
   It is often said that the start of World War I was the result of a "domino effect." With this as your title, make a political cartoon which shows the beginning of the war. Be sure to label the dominoes.
2. **Extra! Extra!**
   After doing some research on the sinking of the *Lusitania*, construct the front page of your local paper as you think it would have looked that day.
3. **Face to face**
   President Wilson and Henry Cabot Lodge never debated the League of Nations face to face.

With a classmate, stage that debate now with one person playing Lodge and the other Wilson. Use research, acting ability, and props.

Thinking Critically

1. Do you think Secretary of State Bryan's "cooling-off" treaties were a workable idea? Why or why not?
2. Imperialism, nationalism, and the alliance system were all given as contributing causes of World War I. Which of these was probably most responsible for the outbreak of that war?
3. Do you think that President Wilson and George Creel should have used public opinion the way they did? Explain.
4. What are the dangers of laws like the Espionage Act and the Sedition Act? What are the arguments in their favor?
5. Was the American public ultimately responsible for the defeat of the Treaty of Versailles in the Senate? Explain your answer.
6. What is your opinion of Senator Lodge's reason for opposing the treaty? Should Wilson have tried harder to see Lodge's point of view?

Further Reading

Gene Smith. *When the Cheering Stopped.* William Morrow, 1964. The story of the period between Wilson's stroke and the end of his term. Who ran the country?

Steven Jantzen. *Hooray for Peace, Hurrah for War.* Alfred A. Knopf, 1972. Much use of original sources such as songs, letters, and diaries to explain World War I.

Erich Maria Remarque. *All Quiet on the Western Front.* Little, Brown, 1929. A classic German novel which tells the horrors of war as seen by young men in the trenches.

TEST YOURSELF

WRITE YOUR ANSWERS ON A SEPARATE SHEET OF PAPER.

Chronology of Events

Arrange the following events in the order in which they occurred.
1. The United States enters the war.
2. Germany invades Belgium.
3. The *Lusitania* is sunk.
4. The Archduke Franz Ferdinand is murdered.
5. Germany resumes its policy of unrestricted submarine warfare.

True or False

Read each statement below. Mark T if the statement is true, F if it is false. Rewrite the italicized words in all false statements so that they are true.

1. Wilson wanted his foreign policy to stress *morality and fairness.*
2. Wilson ordered General Pershing to invade *Mexico.*
3. Austria-Hungary's ultimatum to *Serbia* led the Great Powers of Europe into war.
4. Austria-Hungary belonged to the *Triple Entente.*
5. Germany's plans for an alliance with *Mexico* were outlined in the Zimmermann note.
6. German *battleships* were called U-boats.
7. America's entry into World War I was important because the *Allies were exhausted.*
8. The *Committee on Public Information* helped stir up American public opinion against anything German.
9. Senator Henry Cabot Lodge was a leading *supporter* of the League of Nations.
10. Wilson insisted on *making changes* in the Treaty of Versailles when it came before the Senate.

Matching

Match the man with his country.
1. William Jennings Bryan
2. Georges Clemenceau
3. George Creel
4. Porfirio Díaz
5. Franz Ferdinand
6. David Lloyd George
7. Henry Cabot Lodge
8. Vittorio Orlando
9. Kaiser Wilhelm
10. Woodrow Wilson

a. Austria-Hungary   g. Mexico
b. Belgium   h. Russia
c. Britain   i. Serbia
d. France   j. Spain
e. Germany   k. United States
f. Italy

VISITING THE PAST

The Brooklyn Bridge

New York had not seen such a celebration since the opening of the Erie Canal. New York City and Brooklyn were covered with flags. The President, Governor, and city mayors were in attendance. Bands played as navy vessels sailed down the river. That evening, a solid hour of fireworks lit up the city.

It was May 24, 1883. Fourteen long years after construction had begun, the Brooklyn Bridge was open. An opening-day sign announced: "Babylon had her hanging gardens, Egypt her Pyramids, Athens her Acropolis, Rome her Atheneum; so Brooklyn has her bridge." This was not just a bridge, it was the "eighth wonder of the world."

Since 1800 there had been talk of connecting the island of Manhattan to Brooklyn, which lay across the East River. But could anyone in the world build such a gigantic bridge?

In fact, there were two people who could: the father and son engineering team of the Roeblings. John Roebling's plan was to build the largest and strongest suspension bridge in the world. Its towers would be taller than most buildings, and the four massive cables suspended from them would hold the bridge high above the passing ships. John Roebling died in 1869. Though his son, Washington, took over the project, the father's vision created the bridge.

Washington was seriously injured while working on the bridge, just as his father had been. But with the help of his wife and assistants, he guided the bridge to its completion.

Today, in the space age, the Brooklyn Bridge is still an awe-inspiring sight. Though designed to be a functional transportation link, it was also designed to be beautiful. Its two great stone towers, with their gothic arches, have become landmarks of New York City.

When it was built, the bridge was physical proof of the nation's growing industrial strength and technological genius. Today the Brooklyn Bridge is a continual and beautiful reminder of the miracles that can be accomplished with ingenuity, technology, and commitment.

Chicago's "El"

A squeal announces its arrival. You step on the train and then you are traveling above ground, elevated over the street, looking at the rich architecture of the Windy City. You look into offices and up at skyscrapers. The steel ribbing of the elevated tracks takes you on a 5-by-7 block rectangular loop through the commercial center of Chicago. The loop shape of the tracks has given the area its name, the Loop. The "El" (short for elevated) is an important Chicago structure and symbol.

Completed in 1897, the elevated train system was a critical factor in the growth of Chicago. Skyscrapers could be built only when it was possible to get those who would work and shop in them to and from the city easily. The "El" did not just shape the commercial portion of the city—it made possible its growth.

As with many early urban mass-transit systems, the elevated was privately financed. Four different transit companies used the tracks. The trains were initially powered by steam, but they were among the first in the country converted to electricity. By 1947 the Chicago Transit Authority was running the complete elevated system.

Today the "El" still serves Chicago. Though threatened by a subway replacement, the "El" survives. Not only does it work, but it has become more than just a way to get to and from work—it has become a landmark. The "El" was built at a time when even practical structures were treated as architecture. Its metalwork reveals a classical flavor in its decorative details. The "El's" riveted steel structure rivals that of the Eiffel tower. The "El" is more than functional, it is beautiful. It has character.

The "El" is a landmark for several reasons. First, it is a monument to engineering. Almost a century old, it still serves its original purpose. Second, its influence on the size and shape of Chicago is unrivaled by any other single structure. Finally, it is also a landmark symbol that makes the city distinctive. St. Louis has its arch, Brooklyn its bridge, and Chicago its "El."

The Indianapolis Speedway

Engines roar. The crowd cheers. Thirty-three of the finest racing cars in the world speed around the track. Over 300,000 spectators watch from the stands and raceway grounds. It is May in Indiana, and that means the Indianapolis 500.

Located a few miles northwest of Indianapolis, the Indianapolis Motor Speedway is the oldest continually operated automobile race course in the world. On its track the likes of A. J. Foyt, Jr., Al Unser, and Johnny Rutherford have raced to victory. Since the grueling contest began in 1911, over 60 Indy 500s have been held. But the Speedway is more than a racetrack. It is listed on the National Register of Historic Places.

The Speedway's history is the story of the growth of a sporting event and the evolution of the automobile. The Speedway was opened on August 19, 1909, by four Indianapolis businessmen. In 1911 it was decided to focus energy on one big annual event: a 500-mile race. From a winner's purse of $25,000 the prize has grown to over $1.5 million. That first race saw speeds climb to 75 miles an hour. Today they more than double that. The Speedway's importance, however, is more than that of a popular sporting site.

The original intent of the Speedway founders was to create a "giant outdoor laboratory." There new developments in the automobile industry could be evaluated. The Speedway became a major test course where innovative items that we now take for granted were developed. Front-wheel drive, low-pressure tires, hydraulic shock absorbers, front-wheel suspension, high-compression engines, and the rear-view mirror saw early action at the Speedway. Experimental fuels and lubricants were also put to the test in this laboratory for automobile science.

The key role the Speedway played as a proving ground for innovations decreased as auto makers built their own test courses. Still, today the development of spark plugs, piston rings, safety devices, and auto design are furthered through information gained at the Speedway.

In the Speedway's Hall of Fame Museum you can see many of the cars that won races as well as a display of antique cars, historic photos, and trophies.

America's historical sites include more than battlefields and restored homes. Places like the Indianapolis Motor Speedway have also made important contributions to our history.

UNIT 7 TEST

WRITE YOUR ANSWERS ON A SEPARATE SHEET OF PAPER.

Matching (20 points)

Match each "ism" discussed in Unit 7 with a definition from the list below.

1. progressivism   4. imperialism
2. isolationism   5. Social Darwinism
3. nationalism

a. concept that the superior individual, group, or nation is most likely to survive in a competitive world
b. reform movement among farmers in the late 19th century
c. policy of extending the rule of one country over others in order to control raw materials, markets, or military bases
d. belief that one's own country and its independence are more important than anything else in international relations
e. policy of noninvolvement in European affairs or in problems outside the Western Hemisphere
f. reform movement that tried to improve government, working conditions, and business practices through laws and commissions

Multiple Choice (20 points)

Write the letter of the answer that best completes each statement. There may be more than one correct answer.

1. United States involvement in the financial affairs of Latin American countries
   a. was called "dollar diplomacy."
   b. spread good will toward the United States throughout Latin America.
   c. was influenced by the Roosevelt Corollary to the Monroe Doctrine.
   d. was motivated by a desire for political stability in the area near the Panama Canal.
2. The progressive movement
   a. was never effective at the national level.
   b. generally favored high protective tariffs.
   c. controlled the House of Representatives through its speaker, Joseph G. Cannon.

d. invented both the commission system and the city-manager plan.
3. Democrats under Woodrow Wilson passed most of the Progressive party's reforms including
   a. tariff reductions.
   b. child-labor laws.
   c. the exemption of unions and farm organizations from antitrust action.
   d. government regulation of certain business practices.
4. The Espionage and Sedition Acts sought to
   a. curb dissent and disloyalty.
   b. silence pacifists and other war opponents.
   c. uphold freedom of speech and other basic freedoms guaranteed in the Bill of Rights.
   d. further the socialist movement.

Time Line (20 points)

Match the letters on the time line with the events they stand for.

1. United States fights Spain
2. William Howard Taft elected President
3. Americans in Hawaii overthrow Queen Liliuokalani
4. Pure Food and Drug Act
5. President McKinley assassinated
6. United States declares war on Germany
7. 16th Amendment permits an income tax
8. Progressive party formed
9. Senate rejects the Treaty of Versailles
10. Open Door policy in China proposed

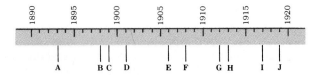

Essay Questions (40 points)

1. What factors contributed to the progressive movement and what were its goals? Give two examples of effective progressive programs.
2. America fought two wars beyond its borders between 1870 and 1918. Describe the reasons why we fought each war and what we had accomplished when each was over. Also discuss whether or not American involvement should have been avoided.

572

Unit Eight

Prosperity and Depression

Chapter 25

1919–1928

THE POLITICS OF PROSPERITY

B y 1920, the American people had been through a period of reform and change in the progressive era. They had also been through a world war—one that was supposed to "end all wars" and "make the world safe for democracy." Yet the world war brought not harmony, but squabbling, vengefulness, and revolution. The American people were tired of causes. They wanted to forget their cares; they wanted to celebrate and enjoy the nation's wealth. They were tired of missions and tired of thinking about others; they wanted to think only about themselves.

But the celebration mood of the 1920s did not begin immediately. It could not, because the end of World War I brought with it tens of thousands of demobilized troops who came home to find no jobs waiting for them. It brought labor unrest, since wages had not kept up with inflation. It brought a continued demand for social reform on the part of groups such as the Socialist party, as well as terrorist bombs from extremists. In turn, these things brought reaction—the Ku Klux Klan, racist immigration laws, the "red scare," the Palmer raids, and race riots.

The 1920s became known as the "Roaring Twenties" or "Jazz Age." It was a decade of tremendous prosperity and new lifestyles: the radio, automobiles, wild parties, movies, advertising, magazines, new clothing styles, and new hair styles. The "Roaring Twenties," however, were ushered in by a rejection of reform and a turn toward intolerance. The progressive spirit that began the 20th century was renounced. The decade of celebration of self began.

Sections in This Chapter
1. An End to Reform
2. The Republican Ascendancy
3. Prohibition
4. Two Groups That Prosperity Forgot

Opposite: A typical American home, around 1925. The newspaper and keepsakes on the table reflect the family's Italian origins.

1. AN END TO REFORM

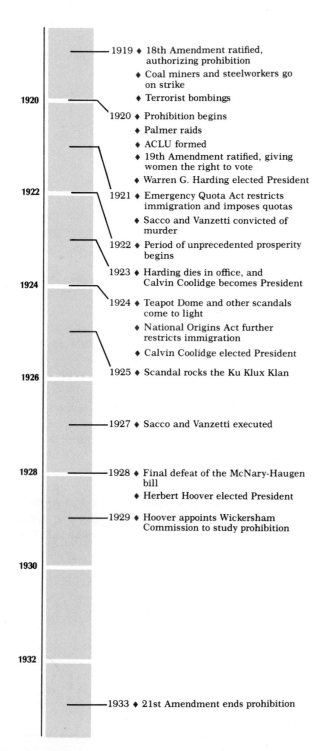

1919 ◆ 18th Amendment ratified, authorizing prohibition
◆ Coal miners and steelworkers go on strike
◆ Terrorist bombings

1920 ◆ Prohibition begins
◆ Palmer raids
◆ ACLU formed
◆ 19th Amendment ratified, giving women the right to vote
◆ Warren G. Harding elected President

1921 ◆ Emergency Quota Act restricts immigration and imposes quotas
◆ Sacco and Vanzetti convicted of murder

1922 ◆ Period of unprecedented prosperity begins

1923 ◆ Harding dies in office, and Calvin Coolidge becomes President

1924 ◆ Teapot Dome and other scandals come to light
◆ National Origins Act further restricts immigration
◆ Calvin Coolidge elected President

1925 ◆ Scandal rocks the Ku Klux Klan

1927 ◆ Sacco and Vanzetti executed

1928 ◆ Final defeat of the McNary-Haugen bill
◆ Herbert Hoover elected President

1929 ◆ Hoover appoints Wickersham Commission to study prohibition

1933 ◆ 21st Amendment ends prohibition

The war was over! The troops were returning at last, to trade "doughboy" uniforms for "civvies," or civilian clothes. But the shift from a wartime economy to a peacetime one was not as simple as a change of clothing. With peace, life in America changed suddenly. War contracts with industries were canceled, and machinery ground to a halt in factories across the nation. Some factories closed entirely, while others operated at half capacity. This left many workers without jobs. As the government's wartime agencies closed, office workers likewise lost their incomes. Unemployment was not the only problem. Prices for consumer goods were on the rise. Peace was welcomed, yet it came hand-in-hand with a postwar recession.*

Inflation Leads to Labor Unrest

Even those factory workers who kept their jobs found peacetime a difficult experience. During the war, they had received higher wages than they ever had before. The **National War Labor Board**, created in 1918, had helped regulate wages and settle industrial disputes. Once peace returned, however, the NWLB ended its regulations and the struggle between employers and workers began again.

Thus, in 1919, there was a new wave of strikes. In that year alone there were more than 3,000 strikes involving over 4 million workers. And 1920 saw almost as much unrest. By 1919 the cost of living had increased by 77% above the 1914 level. In 1920, it climbed to 105% of the 1914 level. And, as inflation climbed so did union membership. In 1916 the American Federation of Labor (AFL), the largest union organization in the country, had 2 million members; in 1920 it had more than 4 million. Organized or unorganized, workers in 1919–1920 demanded higher wages, and if they could not get them, they were ready to strike.

*recession   period of temporary business reduction, shorter and less extreme than a depression.

The Coal Miners Strike, and President Wilson Intervenes

During the war, coal miners, as a sign of patriotism, had agreed not to strike. This meant a sacrifice of income and an inability to keep up with inflation. Coal miners expected some relief when peace returned, but their paychecks remained the same despite the Armistice.

On November 1, 1919, some 394,000 members of the United Mine Workers struck the soft-coal industry. Their new president was **John L. Lewis,** whose bushy brows and craggy face would become familiar to all Americans. The miners, who had not had a raise in pay since 1917, demanded better wages and a shorter work week. The government was not sympathetic. Within a week of the strike, Attorney General **A. Mitchell Palmer** had an injunction issued against the UMW leadership, ordering it to stop the strike. John L. Lewis agreed to have the miners return to work, but to his surprise, the miners refused. The strike continued for a month, then President Wilson stepped in. Wilson took the demands of the UMW to a board of arbitration. The board granted the strikers a 27% wage increase but did not shorten the long work day or do anything about the unsafe working conditions in the mines. Lewis and other UMW leaders accepted the proposal and the miners returned to work.

Steel: The Seven-Day Week Continues

The second major strike of 1919 came in the steel industry. Unlike the coal strike, the steel strike ended in violence and defeat. In the steel industry, men worked 12 hours a day, 7 days a week. These workers had turned to the AFL in the hope that a union could reduce their hours in the mills. But the United States Steel Corporation refused to recognize the union. In the fall of 1919, 343,000 steel workers went out on strike, most of them in Chicago, Illinois, and nearby Gary, Indiana. The employers brought in strikebreakers, many of them unemployed blacks, to man the machinery. Violence erupted between the striking workers and the strikebreakers. The town of Gary, in the heart of steel country, was placed under martial law, and federal troops kept an uneasy peace there.

The United States Steel Corporation, which had long resisted any unionization efforts, claimed that the strike was a communist plot to overthrow the government. The American public, sick of war, violence, and plots, forgot the real goals of the strikers: higher wages and shorter hours. Public opinion went against the steel men. Bitter and disheartened, the strikers returned to work in January 1920.

The Red Scare

Why were Americans so sensitive to the threat of communists and revolution? The answer lay in recent events in faraway Russia. In March 1917, the Czar, with his centuries-old tradition of absolute power, was overthrown. In November 1917, the Bolsheviks, or Communists, had grabbed power. Inspired by the theories of the German writer Karl Marx, the Bolsheviks declared a "people's government," henceforth to be known as the Union of Soviet Socialist Republics. They outlawed private property and launched a propaganda war against private enterprise in all industrial countries. This communist revolution gave new hope to Marxist radicals in other nations. Soon the call for revolution spread through war-torn, starving Europe. It even reached America.

In 1919, radical members of the Socialist party left that organization to form a Communist party. As it was, they formed two Communist parties, the Communist party and the Communist Labor party. These two groups were no sooner born than they faced the arrest of their leaders and the deportation of hundreds of members. The call for radical change of any kind was greeted as a threat to the nation. Thus, the **"red scare"*** began.

It was not only the communists who were arrested during the "red scare." Members of many other groups that advocated radical change, among them the Socialist party, were arrested as well. During the prewar years, the Socialist party had grown in the United States. Socialism was the theory that the people, or public, should own and operate the means of production and distribution in society. Like the communists, socialists were opposed to private property, but the Socialist party, unlike the communists, supported democratic methods to win its goals.

In the prewar years, a number of Socialists were elected to public office. In 1912, **Eugene V. Debs** ran for the presidency on the Socialist party

---

***red**   a communist or other Marxist radical, so called because of the party's red flag, which symbolizes Marxist revolution.

ticket and won 900,000 votes, about 6% of the popular vote. The Socialists lost favor, however, when the war began. Debs and his followers opposed American involvement in a war waged by kings against kings. In 1920, Debs again ran for President and, despite the "red scare," again received 900,000 votes, or about 5%.

During the war, Wilson's government grew impatient with criticisms, and the President moved to silence them. As you recall from Chapter 24, during the war Congress enacted two laws to end public opposition. The Espionage Act of 1917 and the Sedition Act of 1918 punished people who actively opposed the war, with sentences of up to 20 years in prison. The Socialist party refused to give up what it believed was the right of free speech, and two socialist leaders—Eugene V. Debs and Victor L. Berger—were tried and imprisoned under the Sedition Act for speaking out against U.S. participation in World War I. The government also raided party offices and banned socialist publications.

Terrorist Bombs

The socialists were attacked primarily because they spoke out against the war and thus seemed unpatriotic. Communists were attacked because they advocated violence. A series of anonymous violent acts in 1919 and 1920 did little to soothe American minds. For example, on April 28, 1919, a package delivered to Senator Thomas W. Hardwick of Georgia exploded, injuring an employee who had unwrapped it. When federal authorities investigated, they discovered 18 other bomb packages in the New York post office. Each was addressed to a noted American, such as John D. Rockefeller and Supreme Court Justice Oliver Wendell Homes, Jr. On June 2, 1919, a series of bombs exploded in eight different cities, including one which destroyed the front of the home of Attorney General A. Mitchell Palmer. The bomb-thrower, who was killed, is believed to have been a foreign anarchist.

Other bombing incidents took place later, including an explosion on Wall Street on September 16, 1920. During the crowded noontime rush, this explosion killed 38 people and injured hundreds. The culprits were never found.

The U.S Attorney General, A. Mitchell Palmer, was ready and willing to launch a campaign against the "red menace." His Justice Depart-

Crowds gather after a terrorist bomb explodes on Wall Street, killing 38 people.

ment took command in the move against radicals of all sorts. Palmer, a progressive before the war, was now a firm conservative. He believed that the demand for reform could pave the way for revolution. His own brush with violence helped shape this view.

Palmer argued that radicalism was a disease brought to America from Europe. To rid the nation of foreign ideas, Palmer said, we must get rid of the foreign agitators. In August 1919 Attorney General Palmer set up a General Intelligence Division in the Justice Department. **J. Edgar Hoover,** who would later run the Federal Bureau of Investigation, was picked to head this agency. Hoover was told to collect information about subversive or politically dangerous activities.

Soon information gathering turned to action. In November 1919 Hoover's agents raided the offices of a small organization called the Union of Russian Workers. Although 650 persons were arrested, most were American citizens; only 43 were aliens, eligible for deportation. The Union of Russian Workers was an unlikely threat to the American government, yet Palmer was praised for his actions. This public applause led Palmer to dream of winning the Democratic presidential nomination in 1920. He could not resist using the "red scare" to get his name on the front page of every newspaper in the nation.

The Palmer Raids

In January 1920, Palmer authorized a sweep of raids on suspected radicals. Federal agents, local police, and private citizens, none of them with warrants, raided homes, offices, and meeting halls in 33 cities. Altogether, 6,000 persons were arrested in the **Palmer raids.** Many of these persons were American citizens. Many were men and women with no connection to radical groups. All were roughly treated and stuffed into crowded jail cells, and some were beaten and had false confessions forced out of them. Their civil liberties were violated in the name of American freedom and "safety."

Had Palmer nipped a revolution in the bud? Had be brought foreign agitators to justice? The facts did not support Palmer. Few of those arrested were aliens. And, while they found many revolutionary pamphlets, Palmer's men found only three guns.

The absence of any real revolutionary threat did not ease American minds. In fact, harsher precautions followed. Almost one-third of the states passed laws designed to punish radicals. These laws applied to people who *advocated* violence as well as to the few who actually committed violent acts. Again, the peaceful advocates of social change suffered, too. For example, Victor L. Berger, who was a legally elected Socialist representative from Wisconsin, was barred from taking his seat in the House of Representatives. In New York, the state legislature expelled five elected Socialist assemblymen.

Reaction to the Palmer Raids

Opposition to Palmer, the raids, and the whole "red scare" movement soon developed. First, there were Americans who felt that the "red scare" was a greater threat to American liberty than the communists were. In 1920, a group of these citizens formed the **American Civil Liberties Union (ACLU).** The ACLU challenged the constitutionality of all government laws that it felt violated the Bill of Rights. Second, many Americans grew suspicious of Attorney General Palmer's motives. Was there a real threat to American security, or was Palmer engaging in political showmanship?

Palmer's downfall came when he announced that a massive communist demonstration would take place in New York City on May 1, 1920. Thousands of police and federal agents gathered to defend the city. When nothing happened, Americans withdrew their support of Palmer and his tactics.

The Sacco-Vanzetti Case

Just as Attorney General Palmer was losing his public support, attention became focused on two laborers whose conviction turned into a worldwide *cause célèbre*—the **Sacco-Vanzetti case.** Nicola Sacco and Bartolomeo Vanzetti were Italian immigrants. Both were anarchists; they believed that government was an unnecessary evil that should be abolished.

In April 1920, five armed men in a car robbed a shoe company in South Braintree, Massachusetts. The paymaster and a guard were shot and killed. In May, the police arrested Sacco and Vanzetti. They were linked with the robbery car, carried pistols, and made false statements upon their arrest. However, neither had a criminal record, and none of the stolen money showed up in their possession. In 1921, they were both found guilty of murder.

The truth in the case has never been determined. (A 1961 ballistics test indicated that the gun found on Sacco was used to murder the guard.) Defenders of Sacco and Vanzetti charged that the evidence was flimsy and that they were really convicted for their political views, not for robbery and murder. Despite appeals, the verdict of the lower court was upheld, and in 1927 Sacco and Vanzetti were executed. Mass demonstrations to prevent their execution were held by Sacco-Vanzetti defense committees in the United States, Europe, and Latin America. After their deaths, they were viewed by many people as symbols of the poor, the foreign-born, and the politically radical. Their persecution, said their defenders, was an attempt to silence opposition to conservative politics and to discourage independent thinking.

Immigration Is Restricted

Just as unionism and communism were linked in the public mind in 1919, so were "Americanism" and national origin. Most industrial workers were immigrants or the children of immigrants, and many were in the forefront of the union movement. And many radicals were also immigrants. This increased the call by some Americans for immigration restrictions.

Anti-immigrant feelings may have been an inevitable product of the war. As you'll recall from Chapter 24, to arouse patriotism, the President had established agencies such as the Committee on Public Information. This committee churned out reels of film and millions of pamphlets. Most had a strong anti-German message. When peace came, it was hard for Americans to abandon the anti-German and other anti-foreign feelings created or fueled by the Committee. A general suspicion of foreigners and a fear of foreign ideas lingered and even increased. Perhaps even more important, however, was the knowledge that millions of Europeans were planning to immigrate to America to find refuge from starvation and revolution.

Thus, America abandoned its role as a haven for the oppressed people of Europe, just as more people than ever wanted to come to our shores. In May 1921, the Emergency Quota Act was passed. The law limited immigration to quotas based on the ethnic population of the United States in 1910. For example, Irish immigration after 1921 was limited to 3% of the number of Irish Americans in 1910. In 1924, the **National Origins Act** reduced each quota to 2% and changed the "base year" to 1890. As you know, most immigrants to America before the 1890s were from the British Isles and northwestern Europe. Thus the 1924 law admitted 140,000 immigrants from these countries each year, but let in only 21,000 per year from southern and eastern Europe. Special laws excluded Japanese, Chinese, and other Asian immigrants. The idea of an American "melting pot" no longer seemed a good one to postwar America. However, the 1924 law did not restrict immigration from Mexico, Canada, and other countries of the Western Hemisphere.

The Rebirth of the Ku Klux Klan

In the atmosphere of fear and intolerance following World War I, the **Ku Klux Klan**, revived in 1915, gained membership rapidly. By 1924, the Klan had about 5 million members. The Klan, born in the troubled days of Reconstruction, once again raised the banner of racism and preached white supremacy.

The new Klan may have seemed just like the old one, with the same secret rituals, the white-hooded robes, the burning crosses. But this new Klan was centered mainly in the towns and cities of the Midwest, Southwest, and Far West. The new Klan was especially strong in Indiana, Ohio, and Illinois. It attracted Americans who wished to preserve a Protestant, Anglo-Saxon America. Although it continued the old Klan's anti-black violence, the new Klan's targets were mainly Roman Catholics and Jews, foreigners, and people it considered immoral, such as bootleggers (sellers of illegal liquor). Attempting to restore a "pure America," the new Klan spread its program through terror and violence, often beating, mutilating, and sometimes murdering its victims.

As the Klan grew in the 1920s, its political power grew, too. At one point, five U.S. senators and four governors were members. The KKK was strong enough to prevent the major parties from publicly opposing it. By 1925, the Klan was confident enough to march in the nation's capital. On August 8, 1925, some 50,000 hooded Klansmen marched down Pennsylvania Avenue. The hooded parade took three-and-a-half hours.

The prejudice and violence of the Klan did not destroy it. Instead, the hypocrisy and greed of its leaders caused its downfall. Men vied for control of the organization. Millions of dollars in membership dues were pocketed by the leadership. Finally, in 1925, at the height of its popularity, a scandal rocked the Klan. A prominent Klan leader was convicted for assaulting and killing a young woman. Many Klan members turned away from their organization in disgust. The moral world they believed they were protecting was not respected by their own leaders. By 1930, its membership had declined to about 9,000.

Women Win the Vote

Although the spirit of reform was declining in America after the First World War, reform did triumph in one area. In 1920, the **19th Amendment** to the Constitution was passed, giving women the right to vote in national elections.

Under the leadership of **Carrie Chapman Catt,** the National American Women's Suffrage Association (NAWSA) had fought long and hard for full citizenship for women. **Alice Paul's** Congressional

Nighttime rally for women's suffrage, 1915

Union had joined Catt's organization in the slow process of winning the vote in state after state. But by 1916, the movement for the vote was grinding to a halt. The cooperation so necessary for the women to succeed was faltering, and there were too many battling factions or groups within the women's movement. Catt realized that something dramatic and effective must be done or much time would be lost. She therefore proposed her **"Winning Plan"** for suffrage.

At the 1916 NAWSA convention, the officers of over 36 state suffrage associations signed a secret agreement. They agreed to follow Catt's leadership, to set aside old disagreements, and to concentrate on a national rather than a state-by-state strategy for winning the vote. State leaders vowed to follow Catt's directions in a carefully coordinated campaign. Each state suffrage association was given a specific role to play in Catt's "Winning Plan."

The "Winning Plan" did indeed work. By January 10, 1918, support for the national amendment on suffrage had mushroomed. On that cold winter day in January, thousands of suffragists gathered outside the House of Representatives and waited

FROM THE ARCHIVES

The Campaign to Win the Vote

In her book on the women's suffrage movement, Carrie Chapman Catt described the tremendous effort that it took to secure passage of the 19th Amendment:

To get the word "male" in effect out of the Constitution cost the women of the country fifty-two years of pauseless campaign. . . . During that time they were forced to conduct fifty-six campaigns of referenda to male voters; 480 campaigns to get Legislatures to submit suffrage amendments to voters; 47 campaigns to get State constitutional conventions to write woman suffrage into state constitutions; 277 campaigns to get State party conventions to include woman suffrage planks; 30 campaigns to get presidential party conventions to adopt woman suffrage planks in party platforms, and 19 campaigns with 19 successive Congresses.

From Carrie Chapman Catt and Nettie Rogers Shuler, *Woman Suffrage and Politics* (New York, 1923), p. 107.

to hear its vote on women's suffrage. Three short years before, the House had voted down the measure. But now, by a vote of 274 to 136, the House approved the following historic amendment: "The right of citizens of the United States to vote shall not be denied or abridged by the United States or by any State on account of sex." It took two more years for the state legislatures to approve the House vote by a two-thirds majority. On August 26, 1920, the 19th Amendment became part of the Constitution.

The right to vote did not, of course, end the struggle for equality for women in America. Women were still discriminated against in many areas of their lives, from the paycheck they received in the workplace to their rights under law in marriage. Many women saw the need for the passage of an Equal Rights Amendment to end all discrimination based on sex. Thus, in 1923, Alice Paul's National Women's Party began a new political campaign to complete the process toward equality for women.

SECTION 1 REVIEW

Identify: National War Labor Board, John L. Lewis, A. Mitchell Palmer, red scare, Eugene V. Debs, J. Edgar Hoover, Palmer raids, American Civil Liberties Union, Sacco-Vanzetti case, National Origins Act, Ku Klux Klan, 19th Amendment, Carrie Chapman Catt, Alice Paul, Winning Plan

Main Ideas

1. What were the reasons for the strike wave of 1919? What happened in the coal miners' and steel strikes?
2. What caused the "red scare"? How did it affect the Socialist party?
3. What were the Palmer raids? Why did opposition to them develop?
4. Why did some people feel that the Sacco-Vanzetti case was a miscarriage of justice?
5. Why did the United States limit immigration in the early 1920s? Why were the quotas set up as they were?
6. What caused the rebirth of the Ku Klux Klan? Why did it decline after 1925?
7. Describe the strategy that led to the passage of the women's suffrage amendment.

2. THE REPUBLICAN ASCENDANCY

In 1920, the Republicans, out of office since the prewar days of William Howard Taft, were determined to regain the White House. Their candidate was **Warren G. Harding**, an Ohio newspaper publisher who had served in the state legislature and later in the U.S. Senate. Harding was a handsome, well-liked, friendly man. He was not, however, a particularly quick or bright man. Nor was he driven by ambition. In truth, he had no desire to be President. His party, on the other hand, saw him as the ideal candidate. After eight years of the activist Woodrow Wilson, the nation seemed to want a slow, easy-going man such as Harding.

Harding's Election Signals the End of Reform

Harding's great appeal to the public proved to be just what wise heads among the Republicans suspected: his lack of ambition and his mild, pleasant character. Even though he made a host of embarrassing mistakes in his campaign speeches, and even though it was clear he had no ideas beyond a return to "normalcy," Warren G. Harding captured the nation's heart. On election day, he overwhelmed the Democratic candidate, Ohio Governor James M. Cox, winning 16 million votes to Cox's 9 million.

With Harding's election, a new mood settled over Washington. The old fighting reform spirit of the "New Freedom" and the "New Nationalism" faded. Regulation of business and intervention in the economy faded, too. The laissez-faire principles of the Gilded Age were restored. Harding himself did little to influence this return to laissez faire. Instead, he let his high-level appointees set policy for his government.

For example, the multi-millionaire financier and industrialist **Andrew W. Mellon** worked as Secretary of the Treasury to dismantle the progressive-era restraints on business. Mellon lowered taxes for the wealthy and used his influence to cut back the budgets of many reform programs. Mellon also supported the 1922 Fordney-McCumber Tariff, which again raised import duties. Many business leaders applauded the new tariff, for it reduced foreign competition. Progressives, however, saw the tariff as a symbol of their defeat and mourned the end of reform.

The end to reform was further ensured by Harding's Supreme Court appointments. Four well-known conservatives took their place on the High Court bench. Among them was former President William Howard Taft, who became Chief Justice. The Harding Court often ruled against reform bills in the 1920s and 1930s.

President Harding Dies in Office

Harding's popularity might have guaranteed him many years in the White House. Tragedy struck, however, in 1923, when the jovial President returned to San Francisco from a trip to Alaska. The President was in poor health; his doctor diagnosed the problem as ptomaine poisoning caused by a meal of Japanese crab. Harding had confidence in the doctor, whom he had appointed United States Surgeon General. But the physician was wrong. Far from having ptomaine poisoning, the President had suffered a heart attack. On August 2, Harding died.

The American people were shocked and deeply saddened. Three million citizens watched the President's coffin as it was transported from San Francisco to Washington, D.C. Soon, however, this public outpouring of grief would turn to an outpouring of anger. The Harding scandals were about to be made public.

The Ohio Gang

What caused a grieving nation to turn on the deceased Harding? The President's willingness to let others run his government proved his undoing. It became clear that most of Harding's appointees had been his old friends and political cronies. The only qualifications for office these men could boast was that they were good poker companions for the easy-going President. This **"Ohio Gang,"** as they were called, used the President's friendship badly. They were corrupt men who deceived Harding and brought shame to his memory.

Soon after Harding's death, the "Ohio Gang" scandals became public. In 1924, it was discovered that **Harry M. Daugherty** [dô′ėr tē], the Attorney General, had *sold* pardons to criminals and had received payoffs from people who had violated prohibition laws. (See Section 3 of this chapter.) Daugherty, guilty of other crimes as well, was forced to resign. He was then prosecuted for fraud. In court, the wily Daugherty refused to testify. He hinted that if he talked Harding himself might be implicated in the corruption. A troubled jury could not agree on a verdict, and Daugherty, head of the Ohio Gang, went free.

The Teapot Dome Scandal

More scandals followed rapidly. In 1924, several senators grew suspicious of the luxurious life led by the Secretary of the Interior, **Albert B. Fall.** Their investigation unearthed the **"Teapot Dome scandal."** Fall, it appears, had convinced the Secretary of the Navy to transfer the administration of certain oil-rich properties in Teapot Dome, Wyoming, and Elk Hills, California, to the Interior Department. These lands were specifically reserved for the needs of the navy, yet Fall secretly leased them to private interests.

The reserves at Elk Hills, California, were secretly leased to Edward L. Doheny of the Pan-American Petroleum Company. The reserves at Teapot Dome, Wyoming, were secretly leased to Harry F. Sinclair of the Mammoth Oil Company. For these secret and illegal actions, Fall received $200,000 in government bonds and $85,000 in cash from Sinclair. Doheny's $100,000 payoff was delivered to Fall in a "little black bag." All three conspirators were tried for defrauding the government, and all were acquitted (judged not guilty).

Warren G. Harding   (1865–1923)

IN OFFICE: 1921–1923

Republican from Ohio. The major achievement of the Harding administration was the limitation of naval armaments agreed upon at the international conference held in Washington, D.C., in 1922–1923. A short time after Harding's death, the exposure of corruption involving some of his appointments damaged the reputation of his administration.

Fall was later convicted of bribery, fined $100,000, and sentenced to a year in prison. Neither Sinclair nor Doheny were convicted for paying the bribes, although Sinclair did serve a short prison sentence and paid a small fine for attempting to tamper with the jury.

Harding's Error: Bad Judgment

The scandals continued. The Alien Property Custodian, Thomas W. Miller, was found to be stealing money. The head of the Veterans Bureau, Charles R. Forbes, had siphoned off millions of dollars earmarked for the construction of hospitals.

Most Americans realized that Harding had taken no active part in the corruption and cynicism of his "Ohio Gang." His only fault was bad judgment. He had appointed men to important and responsible offices because he liked them and felt they deserved a reward for their loyalty to him. Before his death, even Harding had begun to realize his mistaken judgment. He had grown to hate his position as President. When he died he was a defeated and broken-hearted man. "This is a [terrible] job," he exclaimed before his death. "I have no trouble with my enemies. . . . But my . . . friends. . . . They're the ones who keep me walking the floors nights!"

Vice-President Coolidge Takes Over

Harding's death put Vice-President **Calvin Coolidge** in the political spotlight. Coolidge took the oath of office at his father's house near Plymouth,

Vermont. The modest family setting, framed by the light of kerosene lamps, contrasted sharply with the Washington scenes of the Ohio Gang scandals. The new President clearly understood that his first task was to restore the tarnished reputation of the Republican party.

Coolidge began his government house-cleaning by asking for the resignation of the infamous Daugherty. By the time of the Republican nominating convention for the 1924 election, the honest and conservative Coolidge had rid Washington of the Harding era scoundrels. His party rewarded him with the presidential nomination. "Keep Cool with Coolidge" was the catchy slogan of the Coolidge campaign.

The Democrats and Progressives Choose Their Candidates

Things were far from cool at the Democratic party convention. It was a sweltering New York City summer, and inside the convention hall the temperature of rural and urban delegates continued to rise. After 103 ballots, delegates still could not agree on a suitable candidate!

At last, both sides conceded defeat and approved a compromise candidate, John W. Davis. Davis was a conservative lawyer with J. P. Morgan's company. The Davis nomination meant that both major parties were running conservative candidates.

Faced with a choice between Coolidge and Davis, the Progressives decided to run a third-party candidate. Many farmers, socialists, and organized workers joined the Progressive camp. The aging but still determinedly reform-minded Bob La Follette was the Progressive party's choice for President. La Follette did receive 5 million votes, but the Progressives failed to attract the majority of Americans, who were content with the new conservative stand of the federal government. Business was booming, the country seemed richer than ever, and the American people saw no reason to unseat the Republican President. Coolidge won the election by a landslide.

Coolidge Speaks Out for America's Business

Calvin Coolidge was an excellent spokesman for the new mood of his nation. He could boast a long career in Massachusetts politics. He gained a national reputation in 1919 when, as governor, he took a strong stand against striking Boston police-

Calvin Coolidge (1872–1933)

IN OFFICE: 1923–1929

Republican from Massachusetts. During President Coolidge's administration, the United States enjoyed a period of unprecedented prosperity. Coolidge favored conservative business interests. He supported lower tax rates and at the same time reduced the national debt. In 1928, the United States signed the Kellogg-Briand Pact which renounced war as a national policy.

men, sending federal troops into the city, and winning widespread public admiration.

Coolidge's style matched his conservative politics. "Silent Cal" was small, frail, solemn, and shy. He suffered from repeated stomach aches and insisted on taking long naps every day, even in the demanding office of President. The President should not be a leader, Coolidge argued, and he slept more than any other chief executive in the 20th century. "Four-fifths of all our troubles in this life would disappear," he once declared, "if we would only sit down and keep still." Silent Cal's determined inactivity was welcomed by an American people wearied of Woodrow Wilson's activity. The thrifty Coolidge was also a welcome relief from the high-spending Ohio Gang.

Coolidge's policies were much like Harding's. The new President was a great admirer of the businessmen of America. "The man who builds a factory," Coolidge said, "builds a temple." He favored giving private enterprise great freedom from government control or regulation. In fact, he used his influence to transform regulatory agencies into agencies supporting private business policies. Both the Interstate Commerce Commission and the Federal Reserve Board thus became allies of private enterprise rather than its watchdogs. Coolidge's philosophy was summed up in his favorite saying: "The business of America is business."

A Campaign of Intolerance

Calvin Coolidge chose not to run for re-election in 1928. The Republicans therefore nominated Secretary of Commerce **Herbert Hoover**, who campaigned on a platform promising continued prosperity.

The Democratic party nominated the Governor of New York, **Alfred E. Smith.** Smith was hardly a typical national candidate. Raised in the Lower Eastside slums of New York City, he was a Roman Catholic and a politician who had risen without the big-city political machine. Although Smith was personally a reformer, his party did not give him a progressive platform. Like the Republicans, the Democrats drew up a conservative platform. In fact, as far as policies went, it was not easy to tell the two parties apart. The one big issue in the campaign was "Al" Smith himself.

The magazine *The New Republic* described the 1928 campaign well:

For the first time, a representative of the unpedigreed, foreign-born, city-bred, many-tongued recent arrivals on the American scene has knocked on the door and aspired seriously to the presiding seat in the national Council Chamber.

Smith represented the immigrant, the political machine, Catholicism, and all the elements of city life that many rural Americans thought were destroying America. Unfortunately, Smith's religion and his city orientation became *the* issue, bringing the intolerance of the era into the campaign. What was left of the Ku Klux Klan came out in force against Smith. Droves of Democrats crossed over to the Republican party, calling themselves "Hoovercrats." If Smith became President, ran the hysterical cry, the Pope would run America.

The differences in style between Hoover and Smith were clearly evident to millions of Americans, for their campaign was the first to be broadcast on the radio. Smith's casual, eastside voice contrasted sharply with Hoover's clipped and statesmanlike speech.

As expected, Hoover scored an overwhelming victory, carrying 444 electoral votes to Smith's 87. The Republicans even won the southern vote from the Democrats, their first such success since Reconstruction. To a great extent, the Republicans won because Americans were happy with the prosperity and wealth of the period. Yet Hoover's victory also revealed many Americans' fear of anything or anyone different.

SECTION 2 REVIEW

Identify: Warren G. Harding, Andrew W. Mellon, Ohio Gang, Harry M. Daugherty, Albert B. Fall, Teapot Dome scandal, Calvin Coolidge, Herbert Hoover, Alfred E. Smith

Main Ideas

1. What did Americans especially like about Warren G. Harding? How did Harding's election signal the end of the reform era?
2. How did the Ohio Gang betray the public trust? Give four examples.
3. What were Calvin Coolidge's views on the role of the President and the federal government?
4. Give two reasons why Herbert Hoover won an overwhelming victory in the 1928 election. In what way did the election reveal intolerance?

3. PROHIBITION

The fierce emotions that rose to the surface in the 1928 Hoover-Smith campaign were also apparent in the great debate over alcohol in the 1920s. No other issue drew the lines so sharply between rural America and the cities, between immigrant cultures and the older, Protestant society. As you know, the battle against liquor was an old one, dating back to 1826 and the founding of the American Temperance Society. By the 20th century, many reformers saw the saloon as a meeting place for machine politicians and immigrant voters. They hoped that if they could get rid of alcohol, it would be easier to get rid of corrupt politics.

The **Anti-Saloon League**, formed in 1895, had long worked for a national prohibition amendment. When World War I came, many who were against drinking and against immigrants used the argument that brewers were German, Germans were the enemy, and therefore alcohol was an evil. Arguments such as these helped the **18th Amendment** pass Congress in 1917. The amendment was ratified in January 1919 and became law in January of 1920. Specifically, the 18th Amendment forbade the manufacture, sale, or transportation of alcoholic beverages.

The **Volstead Act** became the law which was used to enforce the 18th Amendment. It defined any liquor containing 1/2 of 1% of alcohol as intoxicating and therefore illegal. The power to enforce the Volstead Act and treat as criminals anybody who manufactured, sold, or drank alcohol was given to the Bureau of Internal Revenue. The nation was launched on a crusade against drink, a "noble experiment" to impose morality on people, whether they wanted it or not.

The "noble experiment," as Herbert Hoover called prohibition, lasted over ten years, until 1933, when it was abandoned. During this dry decade, alcohol consumption declined, and, with it, the number of deaths due to alcoholism. Arrests for drunkenness also decreased. But many people considered the total ban on drinking— including beer and wine—to be a violation of their personal liberties.

Almost as soon as the Volstead Act became law, many Americans became lawbreakers. The once-legal corner saloons were replaced by underground **"speakeasies,"** secret clubs the local police usually knew about but ignored. In many "wet" areas, such as the cities, local officials did nothing to prevent drinking. Because federal enforcement agencies were grossly understaffed, they could take only limited action against offenders.

Smuggling of alcohol became a big business, and illegal stills and breweries manufacturing "bootleg," or unlawful, liquor sprang up everywhere. Even in the White House, prohibition was ignored. When President Harding met with his poker cronies in the "little green house on K Street," he served liquor confiscated by federal authorities. This liquor was delivered to the President by a Wells Fargo armored truck!

Organized Crime Benefits

Very quickly organized crime moved in to profit from the "wet" rebellion to prohibition. Gangsters seized control of the illegal liquor business, and the violence in American cities escalated. The manufacture, sale, and transport of bootleg liquor became a big business, one controlled by gangsters. Trucks carrying bootleg liquor were highjacked by rival gangs, and competitors were murdered in broad daylight.

Chicago, a shipping, trucking, and rail center, had a large number of notorious gangs. The Bureau of Internal Revenue estimated that **Al Capone**, leader of one of the crime syndicates, took in $105 million in 1927, most of it made by control of liquor, gambling, and prostitution. The crime syndicates such as Capone's gang terrorized the citizens. In Chicago on St. Valentine's Day 1929, "Scarface" Al Capone had seven members of a rival gang assassinated by men masquerading as police. Capone was never prosecuted for this massacre. More people were killed on the streets of Chicago in a year, it was said, than in all of Great Britain.

The violence of the crime syndicates against each other was interrupted when they fought federal law enforcement agencies. Prohibition officials seized millions of dollars worth of property in raids against bootleggers. Between 1920 and 1928, 135 people were killed by law enforcement officers seeking to enforce prohibition. In addition, 55 officials were killed.

The End of Prohibition

By the end of the 1920s, it was clear to almost everyone that the "noble experiment" had failed. Polls taken in 1926 showed that only 19% of Americans favored the 18th Amendment. Prohibition failed because most people did not believe in it or support it. It no longer seemed to be an effective way to cure alcoholism or corruption.

In 1929 President Herbert Hoover appointed a special commission, headed by former Attorney General George W. Wickersham, to investigate the effectiveness of the prohibition law. In 1931, after two years of study, the **Wickersham Commission** presented an inconclusive—and contradictory—report. Prohibition was a failure, the Commission admitted, because the public was indifferent or actually hostile to it, but the ban on alcohol should continue. The political power of the "dry" forces prevented the Wickersham Commission from recommending an end to prohibition. A New York newspaper mocked the government:

> Prohibition is an awful flop.
>   We like it.
> It can't stop what it's meant to stop.
>   We like it.
> It's left a trail of graft and slime,
> It's filled our land with vice and crime,
> It don't prohibit worth a dime,
>   Nevertheless we're for it.

The pressure for repeal of the 18th Amendment grew stronger as the 1930s began. In 1932, President Hoover threw his support to the "wets." Finally, on December 5, 1933, the **21st Amendment** was ratified, repealing the 18th Amendment.

SECTION 3 REVIEW

Identify: Anti-Saloon League, 18th Amendment, Volstead Act, speakeasies, Al Capone, Wickersham Commission, 21st Amendment

Main Ideas

1. Why was the 18th Amendment passed?
2. How did the government attempt to enforce prohibition?
3. List some of the positive and negative results of prohibition.
4. When and why was the 18th Amendment repealed?

4. TWO GROUPS THAT PROSPERITY FORGOT

I t would be wrong to imagine that all Americans prospered in the 1920s. Many Americans in all parts of the nation suffered from poverty, including Indians and immigrants. Two of the largest groups to find the decade a trying and disappointing time were American farmers and American blacks.

Farm Prices Drop; Costs Rise

During the war, American farm produce was in great demand. American wheat sold for $2.50 a bushel. Our European allies needed to import food from us, for their farms were often battlefields. American farmers responded to this wartime demand by expanding their production. When peace came and farming was restored in France, Britain, and other European countries, American farmers, especially in the Midwest, were left with an unwanted surplus. Farm prices plummeted. Wheat sold for less than a dollar a bushel. A serious agricultural depression set in.

Just as prices began to drop, costs began to rise for American farmers. To remain competitive, farmers had to purchase new power-driven equipment such as tractors and trucks. Yet this machinery only added to the dilemma. Not only did it call for a large investment—which most farmers could ill afford—but with power equipment came larger crops, and larger crops drove prices down further. New farming techniques and the use of chemical fertilizers added to this strange cycle of greater production and lower profits.

In the 1920s, midwestern and southern farmers organized a congressional farm bloc to press for government aid to agriculture. From 1924 to 1928, the farm bloc fought for passage of the **McNary-Haugen bill**. This bill proposed to raise the domestic prices of wheat, cotton, and corn by setting up a federal farm board that would buy a given amount of the farmers' annual crops. The government would then sell these crops on the world market. The farmers would pay the government for any losses that it suffered by selling the crops at the lower world price.

The McNary-Haugen bill was vetoed twice by President Coolidge. He felt that such price fixing would encourage overproduction on farms and would force consumers to pay higher prices for farm goods.

During the 1920s farm families suffered an economic setback from which they never recovered. A half-million farm families lost their farms in this decade because they could not make ends meet. During the Great Depression of the 1930s *millions* of farms were lost. When agriculture recovered from the blow in the 1940s, it had a new look: fewer but larger farms, owned by agricultural companies, not by individuals.

Blacks Move North Toward Opportunity

As you learned in the last chapter, during the war hundreds of thousands of black people migrated from southern farms to northern cities. Here many found work, for America's war industries were desperately shorthanded. Black Americans were soon working in the meatpacking industry of Chicago, in the steel mills of Pittsburgh, and in the auto plants of Detroit. But if the migration northward brought opportunities, it also brought disappointments and problems. Blacks were often given the hardest and the lowest-paying jobs. Racial tensions mounted, for many whites felt their jobs were threatened by the growing numbers of black workers. By 1918, a series of race riots had erupted in northern cities.

Like other Americans, blacks looked forward to peacetime and hoped to share in the prosperity it would bring. After all, 367,000 black men had served in the armed forces during the war, more than half of them in Europe. In Europe these soldiers had experienced more freedom and less discrimination, particularly among the French, than they had ever enjoyed at home. If they had helped fight to make the world safe for democracy, black veterans believed, surely they could hope for more opportunities at home.

Race Riots Sweep the Nation

Black optimism was dashed by the short postwar economic recession, which produced fierce competition for the few jobs available. The continuing shortage of housing in the North also increased the anger and frustration of whites and blacks. In 1919, a new wave of race riots swept 26 towns and cities across the country.

The worst of these riots occurred in Chicago. It began when a black youth, playing in the waters of Lake Michigan, floated ashore on a white beach. The boy was stoned by an angry white crowd, knocked unconscious, and drowned. Black Chicagoans were both shocked and angry. Soon Chicago's streets were filled with blacks and whites taunting and fighting each other. After five days of mob violence, 6,000 federal troops were called in to restore order. When calm returned, the casualties were counted: 38 people died in the riots, and 537 were injured. About 1,000 blacks were left homeless, their houses destroyed by white mobs.

Harlem Becomes a Cultural Center

By 1930, almost 2.5 million blacks had settled north of the Mason-Dixon line. In parts of northern cities that had once been white neighborhoods, the black sections, or ghettos, that we know today were born. For example, New York's **Harlem** was a white residential neighborhood in the early 20th century. But by 1920, 73,000 blacks lived in the area. Only ten years later the black population there reached 165,000. As the number of blacks in Harlem increased, a housing shortage occurred. Soon enterprising landlords had converted private homes into many small apartments. Rents soared despite the cramped living quarters. Life in Harlem was difficult, yet here a vibrant culture was born and flourished.

A New Militancy

With the disappointment and hardship of life in the city ghetto came a new black militancy. This spirit was strengthened by the Jamaican immigrant, **Marcus Garvey,** who organized the Universal Negro Improvement Association in Harlem in 1914. Garvey believed that blacks would never be treated as equals by a white majority, so he called for a "back to Africa" movement. Garvey preached black nationalism and black pride—and thousands listened and agreed.

Garvey organized black-run businesses, such as restaurants, grocery stores, a printing plant, and a company that manufactured black dolls for the children of the ghetto. In 1921, with over 4 million people in many cities paying dues to his organization, Garvey set up the Black Star Line Steamship Company. The company was to provide transportation for the return to Africa. However, the dream quickly fell apart. In 1923 the steamship company went bankrupt, and Garvey

LIFE IN AMERICA

JAZZ: THE MUSIC THAT NAMED THE AGE

Louis Armstrong and George Gershwin

As blacks moved out of the South and into the great industrial cities of the North, they developed a new style of music—jazz. This new kind of music gave its name to the 1920s, or Jazz Age.

In jazz, the melody is subordinate to the rhythm. In the 1920s, many considered jazz scandalous because of the strong, syncopated beat, which was not found in the mainstream popular music of the day. Jazz is also characterized by improvisation, the sliding from tone to tone, and the imitation of vocal effects by the instrument.

New Orleans Jazz and Swing

In Chicago, black jazz groups were led by famous musicians such as "King" Oliver and "Jelly Roll" Morton. But none were as famous as Louis Armstrong, called "Satchmo." Armstrong was a very young man in the 1920s, but he had already formed his own jazz band. He was an outstanding trumpet player and vocalist and, in fact, helped give the vocal a place in jazz. The bands of Oliver, Morton, and Armstrong played what was called New Orleans jazz.

In New York City and Kansas City, another kind of jazz was played, called "swing." Swing bands were much larger than the New Orleans bands. Edward Kennedy Ellington, better known as Duke Ellington, was the most famous of the New York jazz musicians.

The Influence of Jazz

One important white musician of the Jazz Age was George Gershwin, the American-born son of Russian immigrant parents. Gershwin wrote musical shows as well as works such as *Rhapsody in Blue* (1923) and *An American in Paris* (1928), which are played by symphony orchestras. His music combines two major musical traditions—that of European orchestras and American-born jazz.

Jazz was the changing music of American blacks, developed from work songs, spirituals, and blues. It revolutionized the sound of music in America, and, indeed the world. Go to some of the most remote places on earth, and you'll hear jazz.

---

was tried and convicted for defrauding his followers. He went to prison and was later deported.

Garvey's movement collapsed, but other leaders arose in the black communities of both the urban north and the rural south. The National Association for the Advancement of Colored People (NAACP), founded in 1910, continued to work for civil rights. The name of W. E. B. Du Bois, the professor who had helped found the NAACP and who served as its director of publicity and research, became familiar to white and black Americans alike. As you will see in later chapters, the struggle for civil rights and racial equality would prove a long and difficult one.

SECTION 4 REVIEW

 Identify: McNary-Haugen bill, Harlem, Marcus Garvey

Main Ideas

1. How were American farmers left out of the prosperity of the 1920s? What did farmers try to do about their worsening conditions?
2. Why did American blacks expect greater freedom and equality in the postwar period? Give some examples of how their expectations were met or not met.
3. What trends affected many American blacks in the 1920s?

CHAPTER 25 REVIEW

Key Terms
Explain the meaning of each of the following terms:

National War Labor Board
red scare
Palmer raids
American Civil Liberties Union
Sacco-Vanzetti case
National Origins Act
Ku Klux Klan
19th Amendment
Winning Plan
Ohio Gang
Teapot Dome scandal
Anti-Saloon League
18th Amendment
Volstead Act
speakeasies
Wickersham Commission
21st Amendment
McNary-Haugen bill
Harlem

Reviewing the Main Ideas
Section 1
1. Why were there so many strikes in 1919 and 1920?
2. Explain the red scare and discuss three concrete cases as well as the general results.
3. What happened to immigration laws in the 1920s? Why?
4. How did women win the right to vote?

Section 2
1. Why was Harding able to win the presidency easily? What happened to him? Why did public opinion toward Harding change?
2. Explain the issues in the 1928 presidential campaign.

Section 3
1. What was the "noble experiment," and why was it supported and opposed?
2. Why and how did organized crime grow during the 1920s?
3. Why did the "noble experiment" fail?

Section 4
1. What happened to many American farmers in the 1920s? What steps did they take to try to improve conditions?
2. Why did race riots break out in the postwar period? What trends affected many black Americans during the 1920s?

Special History Skills:
Analyzing a Historian's Interpretation
Historians look back upon an era and try to relate it to previous periods and trends. The following passage is by William E. Leuchtenburg from his 1958 book *The Perils of Prosperity, 1914–1932.* Read the passage and then answer the questions that follow:

The 1920s represent not the high tide of laissez faire but of Hamiltonianism, of a hierarchical concept of society with a deliberate pursuit by the government of policies most favorable to large business interests. . . .

If, as Republican orators promised, this alliance succeeded in maintaining prosperity, the wisdom of single interest politics would be proven. If it failed, a sharp reaction against single interest politics would be inevitable.

1. What do you think Leuchtenburg meant when he wrote that the 1920s were dominated by "Hamiltonianism" rather than "laissez faire"?
2. Do you think that his view was probably affected by his knowledge that there was a depression in the 1930s? If your answer is yes, give reasons for your answer.
3. Compare Leuchtenburg's view of the period 1920–1928 to the one given in this chapter.

Other Skill Activities
1. **Write a letter**
   Write a letter to your cousin in Italy, describing his or her chances for emigrating to the United States in 1924.
2. **On strike**
   Make four picket signs which could have been used by miners or steel workers in 1919–1920 to advertise their point of view.
3. **Investigative reporter**
   Research the Teapot Dome scandal. Then write a series of newspaper articles which show how the scandal developed.
4. **Hold a debate**
   Have two students debate the idea of prohibition, one for, one against.

5. Write a song

Write a song about the situation of a Nebraska farm family during the 1920s.

Thinking Critically

1. Were the Palmer raids justified by the red menace? Why or why not?
2. Explain Coolidge's statement that "The business of America is business." Do you think this is true? Why or why not?
3. Should the federal government have the right to outlaw drinking, smoking, and other personal habits if they contribute to poor health? Why or why not?
4. Should the federal government help family farmers keep their farms? Give arguments both for and against this idea.

Further Reading

Frederick Lewis Allen. *Only Yesterday: An Informal History of the 1920s.* Harper & Row, 1931. Classic reading on the 1920s.

John Kobler. *Capone: The Life and Times of Al Capone.* G. P. Putnam & Sons, 1971. A biography of the public and private life of this notorious gangster.

TEST YOURSELF

WRITE YOUR ANSWERS ON A SEPARATE SHEET OF PAPER.

Matching

Write the letter of the name that best matches each description below.

1. a popular President whose administration was later marred by scandal
2. a popular President who believed that a President should be generally inactive
3. a leader who encouraged black pride and a return to Africa
4. an attorney general who authorized the arrest of suspected radicals
5. a two-time presidential candidate on the Socialist party ticket

a. Eugene V. Debs
b. Marcus Garvey
c. A. Mitchell Palmer
d. Carrie Chapman Catt
e. John L. Lewis
f. Warren G. Harding
g. Calvin Coolidge

Multiple Choice

Write the letter of the phrase which best completes each statement.

1. The following workers staged major strikes in 1919 and 1920:
   a. teamsters and steelworkers.
   b. steelworkers and miners.
   c. auto workers and miners.
2. The Palmer raids were conducted against
   a. Americans and foreigners suspected to be radicals.
   b. only known communists.
   c. only socialists eligible for deportation.
3. The red scare was caused by
   a. fear of a Bolshevik revolution.
   b. terrorist bombings.
   c. both of the above.
4. Harding's friends were called
   a. the Kitchen Cabinet.
   b. the Ohio Gang.
   c. Socialists.
5. Albert B. Fall sold oil rights in return for a bribe in the
   a. Pentagon scandal.
   b. Teapot Dome scandal.
   c. Crédit Mobilier scandal.
6. One reason that Herbert Hoover beat Alfred E. Smith was that
   a. Hoover was a war hero.
   b. Smith was a Catholic.
   c. Hoover called for an end to prohibition.
7. The National Origins Act
   a. set up the same quotas for all countries.
   b. favored southern Europeans, eastern Europeans, Asians, and Africans.
   c. discriminated against southern Europeans, eastern Europeans, Asians, and Africans.
8. The McNary-Haugen bill
   a. tried to raise domestic farm prices.
   b. ended prohibition.
   c. was an anti-union law.
9. Al Capone built his criminal empire by means of
   a. Bolshevik activities.
   b. illegal liquor.
   c. the Ku Klux Klan.
10. Prohibition
    a. encouraged the growth of organized crime.
    b. led to race riots.
    c. was abolished during the administration of Calvin Coolidge.

Chapter 26

1920–1929

LIFE IN THE JAZZ AGE

Today the average American spends part of each day reading a newspaper or magazine, watching baseball, basketball, or football on television, traveling to school or work by bus or car, listening to music on the radio or record player, or going to a movie. Americans across the country can read the same news, read the same magazines, watch the same sporting events or films, ride in similar cars or buses, or use the same appliances. These experiences are so familiar, so routine, that most Americans take them for granted.

Yet all these everyday experiences became part of American life only as recently as the 1920s, the period of history known as the Jazz Age or the Roaring Twenties. Just as the railroad in the Gilded Age pulled Americans together into a national market, the technology of the Jazz Age—the automobile, radio, and film—united Americans culturally and psychologically.

In many ways, the Jazz Age was a logical outgrowth of the political conservatism of the period. America's artists and intellectuals, instead of being concerned with the welfare of society, were concerned almost exclusively with the individual, with the idea of self-expression (although it was not called that during the Jazz Age). The search for pleasure replaced the search for progress.

Americans had found new ways of enjoying the new inventions and the period of prosperity: life in the Jazz Age was radically different from life in any previous decade.

Sections in This Chapter

1. The Miracles of Technology
2. The New Consumer Society
3. The Revolution in Manners and Morals
4. "The Lost Generation" and the Criticism of America

Opposite: On display at the National Air and Space Museum is the single-engine airplane that Charles A. Lindbergh flew in 1927 on the first solo nonstop flight across the Atlantic.

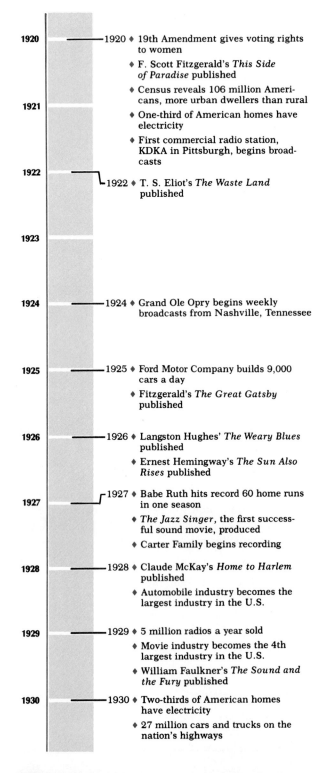

1920 — 1920 ♦ 19th Amendment gives voting rights to women

♦ F. Scott Fitzgerald's *This Side of Paradise* published

♦ Census reveals 106 million Americans, more urban dwellers than rural

1921 ♦ One-third of American homes have electricity

♦ First commercial radio station, KDKA in Pittsburgh, begins broadcasts

1922 — 1922 ♦ T. S. Eliot's *The Waste Land* published

1923

1924 — 1924 ♦ Grand Ole Opry begins weekly broadcasts from Nashville, Tennessee

1925 — 1925 ♦ Ford Motor Company builds 9,000 cars a day

♦ Fitzgerald's *The Great Gatsby* published

1926 — 1926 ♦ Langston Hughes' *The Weary Blues* published

♦ Ernest Hemingway's *The Sun Also Rises* published

1927 — 1927 ♦ Babe Ruth hits record 60 home runs in one season

♦ *The Jazz Singer,* the first successful sound movie, produced

♦ Carter Family begins recording

1928 — 1928 ♦ Claude McKay's *Home to Harlem* published

♦ Automobile industry becomes the largest industry in the U.S.

1929 — 1929 ♦ 5 million radios a year sold

♦ Movie industry becomes the 4th largest industry in the U.S.

♦ William Faulkner's *The Sound and the Fury* published

1930 — 1930 ♦ Two-thirds of American homes have electricity

♦ 27 million cars and trucks on the nation's highways

1. THE MIRACLES OF TECHNOLOGY

Two new energy sources—oil and electricity—fueled the production and prosperity of the 1920s. They remain the major fuels of our country today. In 1859, near Titusville, Pennsylvania, a retired railroad conductor named Edwin L. Drake drilled the first U.S. oil well. By the 1880s kerosene (used in lamps and stoves) and lubricants were the nation's fourth largest exports. Oil refineries became a common part of the landscape around Cleveland, Pittsburgh, Baltimore, and New York.

New technology made oil even more valuable in the early 20th century. The invention and mass production of the automobile created a demand for gasoline to run the nation's cars and trucks.

Ever since Benjamin Franklin's kite experiment in the mid-1700s, electricity was known as a potential source of energy. It was not until 1880, however, that electricity was effectively harnessed for manufacturing and lighting. In 1882, the famous inventor of the light bulb and phonograph, **Thomas Alva Edison**, built the first central electric power plant. This New York City plant supplied electrical power for lighting to only 85 customers, for the "direct current" (DC) supplied by the Edison Illuminating Company could be transmitted only short distances. Nevertheless, Edison's concept was a breakthrough.

In the 1890s, **George Westinghouse** improved on Edison's idea by inventing an "alternating current" (AC) which, at a higher voltage, could be sent greater distances. With AC, electricity became available to run gadgets and machinery larger than the light bulb. Soon the tiny electric industry was growing, supplying electricity for railway systems and factories. But, as in the case of oil, the true impact of electricity was not felt until the early 20th century, when it became the common source of lighting in American homes and of power in American industry.

By the end of the 1920s, the United States was producing more electricity for homes and industry than was the rest of the world combined. And, as in other industries, a few massive companies took over control of electrical generation in the 1920s. By 1930, ten huge corporations controlled 75% of America's electrical power.

The Father of Scientific Management

By the 1920s, electrically powered machines were typical of American industry. Industrial production almost doubled while the size of the work force remained about the same.

At the same time that electrically powered machinery increased production, more efficient methods of mass production became the hallmark of American industry. The champion of mass production, engineer **Frederick W. Taylor**, became the father of "scientific management," as he called it, before the 1920s began. For Taylor and his followers, speed and efficiency were the keys to mass-production success.

To determine the best speed, Taylor did "time and motion" studies of every step in a worker's routine. Under the principles of scientific management, unnecessary steps were eliminated, some steps were combined, and workers were able to produce more consistently and more rapidly. Unfortunately, as the industrial worker sped up to keep pace with machinery, individual judgment and decision making became things of the past. Products were produced more efficiently, but at the cost of human satisfaction. Work became more and more boring and exhausting.

The greatest symbol of efficiency and speed in production was the moving **assembly line**. A product, such as an automobile, was moved along on a conveyor belt; as it passed, each worker added a part. Work speed was determined by the movement of the line. Far more could be produced by the assembly-line method, and at lower costs.

Henry Ford, the "Flivver King"

It was **Henry Ford** with his assembly-line production of the automobile who best symbolized the new methods of mass production in the 1920s. Ford was a self-taught Michigan mechanic who loved to build cars. For a time he worked for the Edison Illuminating Company in Detroit as its chief engineer. In 1903 Ford organized his own company, the Ford Motor Company. Although many people think of Ford as the inventor of the car, he was not. Ford's fame came from his mass-production techniques, which made cars affordable to the average American.

In 1908, Ford designed the **Model T Ford**, a strong but very stark automobile. Compared to the comfortable and sleek cars of today, the Model T probably seems unattractive. But the public wanted a cheap, durable automobile, and in one year Ford sold an astonishing 11,000 Model T's. The Model T was called a "flivver," which was slang for a cheap, small automobile.

In 1911, Ford opened his Highland Park, Michigan, plant. There, by introducing the assembly line, he further cut costs, raised efficiency, and increased the number of cars produced. By 1925, Ford was putting out 9,000 cars a day—or approximately one car every five seconds! You can imagine the speed and intensity automobile workers had to maintain every moment on the assembly line. But the American public was happy: the price of a Ford automobile fell below $300, and Henry Ford became known as the "flivver king."

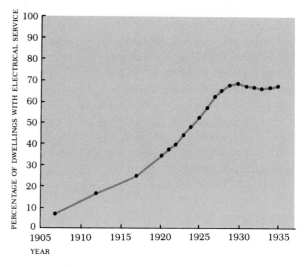

HOUSEHOLDS WITH ELECTRICITY, 1907–1935

SECTION 1 REVIEW

Identify: Thomas Alva Edison, George Westinghouse, Frederick W. Taylor, assembly line, Henry Ford, Model T Ford

Main Ideas

1. What new energy sources changed American life by the 1920s?
2. How did the theories of Frederick W. Taylor change production techniques in American factories? How did this change affect workers?
3. What factors combined to make the price of a car fall below $300 in the 1920s? How did the public react to this?

2. THE NEW CONSUMER SOCIETY

The automobile was the single most important influence on Americans' style of life in the 1920s. It changed the way Americans traveled, and it transformed the way America looked. By 1930, there were almost 27 million cars and trucks traveling along the nation's roadways, approximately one vehicle for every five Americans. Annual car sales in the 1920s rose to 5 million, and by 1928 the automobile industry was the largest industry in the United States.

The Economic Impact of Cars

The automobile had a powerful impact on the American economy. The business boom of the 1920s was due largely to the automobile industry, for in its own growth it spawned new and allied industries. Automobile manufacturers needed great quantities of steel, rubber, glass, paint, lead, nickel, and petroleum. By 1929, the automobile industry was using 15% of the nation's steel production, 75% of its plate glass production, and 80% of its rubber production. The oil industry adjusted to the new car culture, switching from kerosene production to gasoline production. By the end of the 1920s, almost 4 million Americans were employed in some industry related to the construction, maintenance, or powering of the automobile.

The Automobile Changes the Appearance of America

It was in the way Americans lived that the automobile made its greatest impact. The car revolutionized the way Americans spent their leisure time, the places they could visit, and the new distances they could live from their work places. Suburbs, outside the center of cities, could be reached easily with the automobile. Businesses moved outside of cities to less expensive or more convenient locations, for their employees were now able to reach work by car.

The appearance of the American countryside changed. It became filled with gasoline stations and billboards. In cities, streets were widened, parking spaces were created, and traffic was sent in new one-way directions. But it was the construction of roads and highways that most changed the nation's appearance. Can you imagine a United States without the endless and complicated roadways that exist today?

In the 1920s, America's car culture promoted the first burst of road construction. By the end of the decade, the construction of roadways was the largest item in the federal budget, with more people working on them than on any other project. If you had fallen asleep in 1919 and awakened in 1930, it is unlikely that you would recognize your country!

Advertising Creates More Consumers

Ford was not the only name in automobiles. General Motors, Chrysler, and Dodge competed with one another and with Henry Ford. Each wooed the consumers, hoping to win their loyalty. At the same time a host of mass-produced new products were also competing for customers. Americans had the opportunity to buy radios; electrical appliances such as vacuum cleaners, washing machines, refrigerators, irons, and fans; and inexpensive items such as wristwatches, cigarette lighters, and cameras. In an era of prosperity, Americans proved eager to buy. Their eagerness prompted the appearance of even more new items on the market. Over 90,000 patents for new or improved gadgets were applied for each year of the Jazz Age.

But would Americans continue to buy? Many Americans had been brought up to believe in thrift and saving. Manufacturers had to get Americans to overcome these attitudes toward money. They had to persuade Americans to spend, to live for today, to buy products whether they needed them or not. To help develop a new attitude toward money and living on the part of Americans, business turned to advertising.

Today, we are used to the endless chain of commercials on television and radio. We can all recite jingles and other advertising messages; advertising has become a part of everyday life. This kind of advertising began in the 1920s. In order to sell more cars, car manufacturers changed the models of their cars yearly. Soap and deodorant manufacturers warned of the terrible effects of not using their products. The psychology of packaging products was carefully studied and buyers' reactions analyzed. Advertisers worked to create new wants in consumers by making them unhappy with what they had. As one General Motors executive put it, advertising was there to make people "healthily dissatisfied with what they have." Manufacturers spent more and more on advertising, broadcasting their messages over the radio and plastering them across the pages of the nation's press.

The new emphasis on buying *now*, rather than saving for tomorrow, was helped along by the availability of easy credit. Automobiles, refrigerators, sewing machines, and radios, as well as other items, were sold on the **installment plan**, permitting people with modest incomes to buy items once out of their reach. As one popular song put it, Americans could now buy anything with "a dollar down and a dollar a week."

The Promotion of Sports Heroes

With better incomes, easy credit, and new forms of transportation, many Americans had more time for leisure. New industries and pastimes developed to fill that time. Several new forms of entertainment became quite popular, reaching Americans everywhere and creating a national popular culture.

Spectator sports were typical of the new national popular culture. Thousands of Americans filled stadiums to see their favorite baseball and football players, while millions of others listened to the games over their radios. Sports figures be-

LIFE IN AMERICA

AMERICANS AND CARS: A LOVE STORY

Lack of funds has never stood in the way of owning a car in America. By 1926, 75% of all cars produced were bought on the installment plan.

Even roads built for horses and wagons did not deter the national passion for cars. The 1916 Federal Aid Road Act put the federal government in the road construction business. By 1919 the states had hit upon the idea of gasoline taxes for roads and repairs. In 1956 the U.S. government began to pay for 90% of the cost of the interstate highway system.

"Automobile Cities"
Before autos, people usually lived within walking distance of their jobs or depended upon public transit. Recall the "walking cities" and "streetcar cities" described in Chapter 20. After Americans fell in love with the automobile, their cities gradually changed. The depression of the 1930s and then World War II delayed suburban develop-

ment until the 1950s. Then, in the early 1950s, millions left the city to find their own patch of green lawn and quiet.

With these suburbs came a new way of life. In these new "automobile cities" everything was spread out. Although merchants naturally followed the migration, shopping malls were seldom within walking distance from one's house. Acres were devoted to parking lots, drive-in theaters, drive-in restaurants, and drive-in banks.

Life without wheels seems hard to imagine. Many places would be totally unreachable. In addition, millions owe their jobs to the automobile industry and its related industries. This huge investment in jobs, roads, and lifestyles seems to assure that the automobile is here to stay, even though its form may change. In an effort to make the machine fit human needs, technology is helping to decrease its pollution and to increase its fuel efficiency.

Plans for Mickey Mouse. Note basic ear design.

came national heroes, often helped along by skillful public relations that emphasized their good qualities and hid their less admirable ones. The nation adored athletes such as George H. **"Babe" Ruth**, an outstanding player who brought power hitting back to baseball, making it an exciting spectator sport. In 1927, Ruth hit a record-breaking 60 home runs in one season. He also drew record crowds to Yankee Stadium each summer. And in 1921, when Jack Dempsey knocked out Georges Carpentier to become heavyweight champion of the world, he was cheered by a crowd which had paid more than $1 million to watch the bout. The Jazz Age saw the beginnings of the sports extravaganzas we see today.

The Growth of Standardized News
The way in which people learned about world events, politics, or sports followed a similar pattern by the 1920s. By the 1920s many American newspapers had become part of large national newspaper chains that had bought out the local, independent owners. Thus Americans began to read standardized news, written by national press associations such as the Associated Press, United Press, and International News Service. They also read the same syndicated columnists, editorials,

comic strips, and, of course, advertisements. More people were tempted to read the paper each day because of a new style of paper called a **tabloid**. This smaller, easier-to-hold paper was first developed in New York City by *The Daily News*. Banner headlines, photos, and stories of violence and sex, typical of many tabloids, drew readers. At the same time, mass circulation magazines multiplied.

Hollywood Entertains Millions
The major entertainment industry of the 1920s soon became the motion-picture industry. By the Jazz Age, huge, lavishly decorated movie palaces were showing films to over 100 million Americans a week. The movie industry was the fourth largest industry in the country, and Hollywood was its center. Movie actors such as Rudolph Valentino, Mary Pickford, Douglas Fairbanks, and Charlie Chaplin became popular idols. Their fame was encouraged by clever public relations and by coverage in the tabloids and magazines.

In 1927, Warner Brothers presented *The Jazz Singer*, the first successful "talkie," or sound motion picture. With the rise of the talkie, audiences grew even larger. Although most films were tales of adventure or glitter and wealth, appealing to people's fantasies, there were many serious films of the times. For example, Lewis Milestone's *All Quiet on the Western Front* portrayed the terror and pointlessness of warfare. Most Hollywood films, though, provided light entertainment.

HOUSEHOLDS WITH RADIO SETS 1922–1935

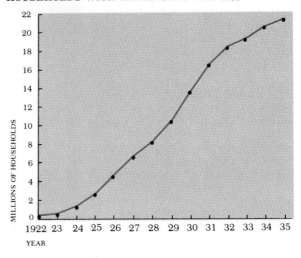

Moviemakers such as Max Fleischer and Walt Disney invented a new form, the animated cartoon. Hollywood, entertaining the nation with silver-screen heroes and heroines, with cartoons, and with larger-than-life action, earned its reputation as the "dreammaker."

The Radio Enters American Homes

Hollywood reached millions weekly, yet the radio reached millions daily. No other invention or industry changed the daily lives of Americans as much as the radio did. The first commercial broadcast occurred on November 2, 1920, over station **KDKA** in Pittsburgh, Pennsylvania. By 1927 there were nearly 700 radio stations across the country. In 1924, the National Broadcasting Company began the first nationwide broadcasting of radio programs, transmitting shows, news, and sports coast-to-coast. By the end of the decade, 5 million radios were sold annually. In our era of television, it is hard to imagine the impact of radio. Yet it was the radio that brought news, music, serialized drama, comedy, and sports into Americans' homes.

The movies, radio, and newspapers meant that Americans were no longer restricted to local or regional sources of information. Major broadcasting centers, located in major cities, spread urban culture to all areas of the country. Just as Americans of the Gilded Age were tied together economically by the railroad, Jazz Age Americans were united culturally by the new media.

SECTION 2 REVIEW

 Identify: installment plan, Babe Ruth, tabloid, *The Jazz Singer*, KDKA

Main Ideas

1. Explain how the automobile transformed American life in the 1920s. How did it affect the nation's economy, the way Americans lived and traveled, and the way the nation looked?
2. Why did the 1920s become the era of advertising? What old habits did advertisers want to change?
3. Describe three of the most popular entertainment industries of the 1920s.
4. Explain how standardized communications helped create a common popular culture throughout America.

3. THE REVOLUTION IN MANNERS AND MORALS

With the postwar rejection of progressivism, many young Americans of the 1920s turned to a life of self-indulgence. As the writer F. Scott Fitzgerald put it, they had "grown up to find all Gods dead, all wars fought, all faiths in man shaken." Having no faith in the desirability, necessity, or even possibility of changing things, many young people decided to live for the "here and now."

The key to the new style was freedom and spontaneity. Many young people seemed to act as if all the traditional rules of behavior had to be ignored. To the shock and outrage of their elders, young people danced to the rhythms of jazz music, drank bootleg liquor out of hip-pocket flasks, and raced their new cars at breakneck speeds.

The symbol of the period was the **flapper**. The flapper was a young woman who rejected traditional views of femininity and women's domestic nature. She smoked in public, drank liquor, and peppered her language with swear words. A new style of clothing became fashionable. Hemlines rose. Waistlines dropped. Tight corsets were abandoned, and long hair, for centuries worn elaborately piled high on the head, was cut off, severe and short. This "bobbed" hair was the rage, as was the use of make-up, which defied the old view that only "cheap" women used cosmetics.

Freud and Psychoanalysis

Part of the Jazz Age urge for self-expression was tied to a radical new method of treating human unhappiness: psychoanalysis. The ideas of the Viennese doctor, **Sigmund Freud**, became popular in the United States in the 1920s. At the turn of the century, Freud had concluded that abnormal behavior was often the result of unconscious or suppressed fears or desires. Through his work in psychoanalysis (the examining of a person's mind to discover the unconscious desires, fears, or anxieties which produce mental or emotional disorder), he theorized that people often became emotionally disturbed when human "drives" were

kept hidden or repressed. Without reading Freud's complex theory, many people came to the simple conclusion that *any* social controls on emotions and behavior were bad for them. Human problems could be solved, said the Jazz Age sages, if everyone were free and uninhibited.

The "Flask and Flapper" Generation

The flapper and her friends probably do not seem very shocking to you now. In fact, they probably seem tame. But in the 1920s many older or conservative people were scandalized and disturbed by the "flask and flapper" generation. Their new lifestyle seemed to represent the collapse of America's moral standards. Parental authority had been undermined, it was said, and the result was a younger generation gone wild.

All the head-wagging and concern was not foolish. Traffic fatalities due to drunken drivers ended the happy-go-lucky life of many young people. And the pursuit of thrills could be dangerous for innocent bystanders. The most notorious case

of thrill-seeking took place in Chicago in 1924. There, two young men named Nathan Leopold and Richard Loeb killed a boy simply to "experience" murder.

Women in the Jazz Age

The flapper was the most obvious example of a changing identity for women. But not every woman bobbed her hair, drank, and flirted openly. In fact, these changes in personal appearance and behavior may not have been the important ones to millions of married women. For them, it was the new technology of the era and the multiplication of consumer goods and labor-saving devices that revolutionized their lives. Canned food, commercial laundries, ready-made clothes, appliances such as the electric washing machine and vacuum cleaner—all these shortened the workday for homemakers. Leisure time became a reality for many American women for the first time.

Equally important in the lives of women was the trend toward smaller families. For the first time in American history the national birth rate was falling. And in 1920, more women entered the paid work force outside the home than ever before. By the end of the decade, almost 11 million women were working outside the home in the United States. Most worked as men did, out of necessity. But there were many who rejected the traditional role of "wife and mother" and embarked on their own careers. The symbol of importance for these women was the vote, guaranteed in 1920 by the 19th Amendment.

Flappers, professional women, political equality—did all these new options and gains mean that the woman's equality movement had achieved its goals? The answer was no. In the work place, women faced both obvious and hidden discrimination. Women's work still tended to be in service to men—as secretaries, clerical workers, and salespeople—or as domestics. Even when women worked at the same jobs as men, their pay scale was still far below that of men. Thus in many vital areas of life a double standard remained strong.

The Country Versus the City

The **1920 census** indicated that the population of the United States had grown to 106 million people. But the startling news was that for the first time more people were living in towns and cities than in the countryside. About 54 million Americans lived in urban areas, while only 52 million were country dwellers. These numbers were a bit misleading, of course, since only one person in four lived in a city of over 100,000. Nevertheless, the shift was significant. You have already seen one effect of this balance between urban and rural population in the deep division within the Democratic party of this era: 103 ballots were required to choose a presidential candidate in 1924!

Although the urban population of the United States continued to grow throughout the 1920s, rural culture remained strong. Many rural groups rejected the new "urban" culture being spread by radio, syndicated newspapers, and movies. Rural-based churches led the fight to preserve the older traditions and ways of thinking from this invasion of new manners, morals, and ideas. Prohibition was one such reaction against urban life.

Some rural cultures, however, used the radio and record player to entertain themselves and others. In the process, they spread their own culture and influenced mainstream America as well. Singing groups such as the **Carter Family** became famous to Americans of the time. Coming from the mountains of Virginia, the Carters started recording together in 1927 and were, for probably 15 years, one of the country's most famous singing groups. Their music, which is today the "country" part of "country and western music," stemmed from the folk songs and ballads of English, Scottish, and Irish settlers of the southeastern, mountainous United States. The Carters, like many other country musicians of the period, performed on the Grand Ole Opry, which has broadcast weekly from Nashville, Tennessee, every Saturday night since 1924.

SECTION 3 REVIEW

 Identify: flapper, Sigmund Freud, 1920 census, Carter Family

Main Ideas

1. Describe the behavior and beliefs that characterized young people in the Jazz Age.
2. In what ways were the lives of American women transformed during the Jazz Age? In what ways did they remain the same?
3. Why did rural and urban America come into sharp conflict in the 1920s?

4. "THE LOST GENERATION" AND THE CRITICISM OF AMERICA

Not all young people greeted the politics and the lifestyle changes of the 1920s with a carefree attitude. There were artists and intellectuals among this new generation who viewed the America of the Jazz Age with anger and scorn. They looked at the lost causes of reform, the war, the postwar repression, and the complacency of prosperity and turned away in anger.

These young people were a "**lost generation,**" alienated from a society whose values they rejected. They were critics of that society, but, unlike the progressives of an earlier age, the critics of the "lost generation" were pessimists, not reformers. They felt that all ideals, all causes, were pointless. As H. L. Mencken, editor of the *American Mercury*, cynically put it: "If I am convinced of anything, it is that Doing Good is in bad taste."

This group of young Americans took refuge in art. Out of their rejection of society came a second great flowering of American creativity. (The first, as you'll recall, was during the period 1820–1850.) Some of these artists and thinkers retreated to places such as New York City's Greenwich Village. Others fled to Europe, particularly to Paris and Rome. Yet all carried America with them in their hearts and minds. Their art had only one motif: America. They were constantly critical, yet, like the artists of the 1820s–1840s, they were obsessed with American themes.

Writers of the Lost Generation

Two young novelists became the major chroniclers, or historians, of the "lost generation." They became symbols of that generation as well. One was Minnesota-born **F. Scott Fitzgerald.** Handsome, gifted "Scotty" Fitzgerald rose to sudden fame in 1920 with his first book, *This Side of Paradise*. The novel described the life of his generation, a life of frenzied activity and gaiety hiding fear and bewilderment, testifying to the pointlessness of living the "here and now." Fitzgerald, who lived the lavish, carefree life he wrote about, went on to write books such as *The Great Gatsby* (1925) and *Tender Is the Night* (1934), portraying in each the wealth and glitter of the era and its underlying tragedy and disillusionment.

The second major writer of the "lost generation," **Ernest Hemingway**, began his career as a newspaper reporter when he was only 17 years old. When World War I began, he served as an ambulance driver in France and Italy. In Italy, he was badly wounded just before his 19th birthday. He was also greatly disillusioned by what he saw on the battlefield.

When peace came, Hemingway did not return to America. Like others of the "lost generation," he settled into exile in Europe. He soon attracted attention because of his terse writing style and because his heroes were all men who lived lonely, dangerous lives but faced their circumstances with courage. In *The Sun Also Rises* (1926), a novel, Hemingway told the story of the Parisian café world of the American refugees, who lived lives of aimlessness and quiet desperation.

Other writers stayed in America and wrote of the confining, narrow, often hypocritical world of small-town life. Sinclair Lewis, who attacked the behavior of American businessmen and religious fundamentalists in books such as *Babbit* (1922) and *Elmer Gantry* (1927), became one of the most successful novelists of the period.

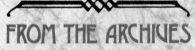

FROM THE ARCHIVES

A Poet of the Lost Generation

In her 1922 poem "First Fig," Edna St. Vincent Millay described the self-destructive spirit of the Jazz Age generation and the philosophy of living for the "here and now":

My candle burns at both ends;
It will not last the night;
But ah, my foes, and oh, my friends—
It gives a lovely light!

The South produced a group of novelists who presented an unromantic and complicated portrait of the life of their region. The greatest one was **William Faulkner**, whose finest works began with *The Sound and the Fury* (1929), just as the Jazz Age was ending. In his novels, Faulkner created a complex world of a fictional Mississippi community, Yoknapatawpha County.

American poetry and drama also blossomed in this era of disillusionment. **T. S. Eliot** was born in St. Louis in 1888 but moved to England in 1914, becoming a British subject. In his collection of poems called *The Waste Land* (1922), he showed how people feel alone and alienated in modern life. In "The Hollow Men" (1925), Eliot wrote of the "stuffed men" of his age:

Shape without form, shade without colour,
Paralysed force, gesture without motion;

The poem ends with the chilling lines:

This is the way the world ends
This is the way the world ends
This is the way the world ends
Not with a bang but a whimper.

Other poets—including Edna St. Vincent Millay, e. e. cummings, Ezra Pound, Edgar Lee Masters, Amy Lowell, Carl Sandburg, Robert Frost, Stephen Vincent Benét, and Edward Arlington Robinson—experimented with new forms of expression as they dissected society in the Jazz Age.

Painters and Photographers

Artists, too, were breaking new ground in the Jazz Age. Talented Americans such as **Georgia O'Keeffe** and Edward Hopper were expanding the subject matter and techniques of art. O'Keeffe painted the natural environment using powerful simplicity of form and dramatic color. Hopper painted starkly lighted scenes of lonely roads, vacant rooms, and women seated alone lost in thought, surrounded by empty chairs.

During the 1920s, American photography rose to an art form through the work of photographers such as Edward Steichen. Steichen had helped develop aerial photography in World War I, then gone on to produce pictures that had an astounding clarity and detail.

The Harlem Renaissance

With the migration of blacks northward, black artists and writers of the 1920s began to express their own unique view of American life. New York City's Harlem district, which had become the largest black urban area in the world, also became a cultural capital, housing theatrical companies, libraries, poets and writers, painters and musicians. This outburst of artistic talent was called the **Harlem Renaissance**. The excite-

Black Hollyhocks and Blue Larkspur, *by Georgia O'Keeffe, 1929. She painted flowers large so people would notice them, and they did.*

ment of the place and time was captured by poet **Langston Hughes**, who described his arrival in Harlem:

I can never put on paper the thrill of the underground ride to Harlem. I went up the steps and out into the bright September sunlight. Harlem! I stood there, dropped my bags, took a deep breath and felt happy again.

The black artists, writers, and poets of the Harlem Renaissance were often harsh critics of American race relations. They used their artistic skills to dramatize the injustices of segregation and lynching, and the poverty of black families. But writers such as James Weldon Johnson, Claude McKay, Jessie Redmond Fauset, Countee Cullen, and Langston Hughes also expressed the pride of black Americans in their own history and culture. Together, the men and women of the Harlem Renaissance gave other Americans a better understanding of the daily lives of American blacks. Today we can still turn to Jean Toomer's *Cane* (1923) or to Claude McKay's *Home to Har-*

lem (1928) to recapture the everyday life of the 1920s' black community.

By the end of the 1920s, the spirit of the Harlem Renaissance had spread to other American cities, such as Detroit, Chicago, Houston, and Los Angeles. The influence of the Harlem Renaissance can also be seen in the works of important later writers like Richard Wright, James Baldwin, and Toni Morrison.

SECTION 4 REVIEW

Identify: lost generation, F. Scott Fitzgerald, Ernest Hemingway, William Faulkner, T. S. Eliot, Georgia O'Keeffe, Harlem Renaissance, Langston Hughes

Main Ideas

1. What aspects of American society did the lost generation scorn? How did they express their disillusionment?
2. Who were some of the major figures in the Harlem Renaissance?

CHAPTER 26 REVIEW

Key Terms
Explain the meaning of each of the following terms:

assembly line	KDKA
Model T Ford	flapper
installment plan	1920 census
tabloid	lost generation
The Jazz Singer	Harlem Renaissance

Reviewing the Main Ideas

Section 1
1. What developments in energy changed American life in the 1920s?
2. What developments in production methods changed life in the 1920s? How?

Section 2
1. How did the automobile change America and Americans?
2. What techniques did advertisers use to sell new products? What changes took place in Americans' buying habits?
3. Describe four entertainment or leisure-time industries that helped create a common American culture. How did they do this?

Section 3
1. Describe the "revolution in manners and morals" in the Jazz Age.
2. How did the lives of American women change in the 1920s?
3. What were some causes and effects of the clash between rural and urban Americans?

Section 4
1. What was the lost generation's attitude toward America?
2. Who were some of the writers and artists of the 1920s?

Special History Skills:
Using the *Readers' Guide to Periodical Literature*
You know that the card catalog will tell you what books and pamphlets a library has on a topic. But do you have to look through every magazine to find an article that will help you research a topic? Thanks to the *Readers' Guide to Periodical Literature*, you don't.

The *Readers' Guide* is published every month in paperback and every year in hardcover volumes. Each issue includes magazine articles listed according to subject and author, and fiction by title and author. The *Readers' Guide* includes more than 150 magazines, which are listed in the front, along with a "translation" of the special abbreviations used in the entries.

Here is an example:
Pressure-packed ad game. M. N. Carter. il Money 9:72–4 D '80
This entry means that an article entitled "Pressure-packed Ad Game," written by M. N. Carter, can be found, with illustrations, in the December 1980 issue of *Money*, Volume 9, pages 72–74.

Try translating the following entry. (+ means the article is continued on additional pages.)
Great series of the '70s. B. Ryan. il Sports Illus 53: 55–6+ O 6 '80
Now copy down one magazine article listed in the *Readers' Guide* for each of the following topics: (1) baseball, (2) radio, (3) advertising, (4) motion pictures, (5) collecting automobiles.

Other Skill Activities
1. **Write a commercial**
   Write a 30-second radio commercial which creates a need for a product that people do not really need.
2. **Paint a mural**
   Use the library to study pictures of the Fords and other cars of the 1920s. Also study the dress styles of men and women. Paint a mural showing the influence of the automobile on American life in the 1920s, incorporating the "look" of the 1920s.
3. **The Scopes Trial**
   Research the famous "monkey trial" of 1925. What were the issues? What roles did William Jennings Bryan, Clarence Darrow, the ACLU, and the communications media play? Did this trial reflect a rural-urban conflict?
4. **Make a crossword puzzle**
   Make a crossword puzzle using the names of inventors, critics, artists, and other personalities of the 1920s.

5. Assemble an essay

Choose a topic to write on, such as the automobile or technology. Write an essay on the topic using "assembly-line" techniques. One student should write the first sentence and pass the paper on to the second student, and so on.

6. Write a radio script

Write a 5- to 10-minute radio drama or comedy, using special sound effects. Present the production to the class.

Thinking Critically

1. The automobile's popularity changed America in the 1920s. How would America change if car use were eliminated in the 1980s?
2. Advertising became an important part of the American economy in the 1920s, and still is today. What are the advantages and disadvantages of advertising to the consumer?
3. Compare the ideas and attitudes of young people in the Jazz Age with those of young people today. What are similarities and differences?
4. Discuss the pros and cons of having a "national" culture. Do we lose anything when local styles and customs begin to disappear?

Further Reading

Editors of Time-Life Books. *This Fabulous Century*, Volume III, 1920–1930. Time-Life Books, 1969. The era is captured in photographs, quotations, and excerpts from literature.

Ken W. Purdy. *Motorcars of the Golden Past*. Galahad Books, 1966. Beautiful color photos and discussion of restored vintage autos from Harrah's collection in Reno, Nevada.

TEST YOURSELF

WRITE YOUR ANSWERS ON A SEPARATE SHEET OF PAPER.

True or False

Mark T if the statement is true, F if it is false. Rewrite the italicized words in all false statements so that they are true.

1. Henry Ford used the *assembly line* to mass produce cheap durable cars.
2. The 19th Amendment gave women *full equality under the Constitution.*
3. The *Harlem Renaissance* was a flowering of black culture.

4. The lost generation was a group of young people *attempting to reform a "lost" America.*
5. The *Model T Ford* made car ownership possible for millions of Americans.
6. The first U.S. oil well was drilled in *Texas.*
7. The 1920 census reported that *more* people lived in the country than in cities and towns.
8. *Road building* was the largest item in the federal budget by the end of the 1920s.
9. Advertising and easy credit terms *increased* consumer buying in the 1920s.
10. Movies, newspapers, and radio helped *preserve* regional differences in America.

Multiple Choice

Write the letter of the phrase that best completes each statement. There may be *more than one* correct answer.

1. Prosperity in the 1920s was partly the result of
   a. the development of the assembly line.
   b. the invention of the alternating current.
   c. the availability of oil for fuel.
   d. increased consumer buying aided by easy credit.
2. Women in the 1920s
   a. entered the paid work force in record numbers.
   b. were all flappers.
   c. benefited from new labor-saving devices.
   d. often faced on-the-job discrimination.
3. The national popular culture of the 1920s
   a. stressed the virtues of saving money.
   b. was spread by radio, newspapers, and films.
   c. included sports heroes.
   d. was influenced by advertising.

Matching

Write the letter of the name that best matches each description below.

a. Frederick W. Taylor
b. T. S. Eliot
c. Langston Hughes
d. George Westinghouse
e. Georgia O'Keeffe
f. Ernest Hemingway

1. poet of the Harlem Renaissance
2. inventor of the alternating current
3. painter of the 1920s
4. author of the "lost generation"
5. poet of the "lost generation"

Chapter 27

1929–1932

HARD TIMES BEGIN

The year is 1929, the month, September. It is the height of the Jazz Age. A rising tide of prosperity is flowing across America. The new President, Herbert Hoover, has promised Americans a "chicken in every pot and two cars in every garage."

In the concrete canyon of Wall Street thousands of stockbrokers, bankers, and investment counselors are hard at work, buying and selling stocks. Here profits are to be made. And what profits! Look at the stock of RCA. In March it sold for $94.50 a share. Now, just six months later, it is selling for $505 per share. And Wright Aeronautics—from $69 to $289 per share! In Chicago, two workers at an "El" station discuss market prices. In New York, a barber has retired, wealthy from his investments.

Few Americans see anything ahead but fair skies and continued prosperity. Joseph P. Kennedy, a man of immense wealth whose son is destined to be President, hears market predictions from a shoeshine boy. Realizing how dangerously far speculation has gone, he sells his stock.

In the Midwest farm earnings are down; in the cities housing construction has slumped sharply. But these are small clouds on the horizon. Most Americans see no cause for concern.

Within the course of a few short weeks, the nation will plunge headlong into the worst economic disaster in its history. Unemployment, hunger, bank closings, and bankruptcies will continue for more than ten years. What caused this collapse and how did it affect Americans? You will learn the answers in this chapter.

Sections in This Chapter
1. The Meaning of the Stock-Market Crash
2. President Hoover Tries to Restore the Economy
3. The Collapse of Faith in American Business Leaders
4. Franklin D. Roosevelt and the Election of 1932

Opposite: Apple-selling became a symbol of hardship during the Great Depression.

607

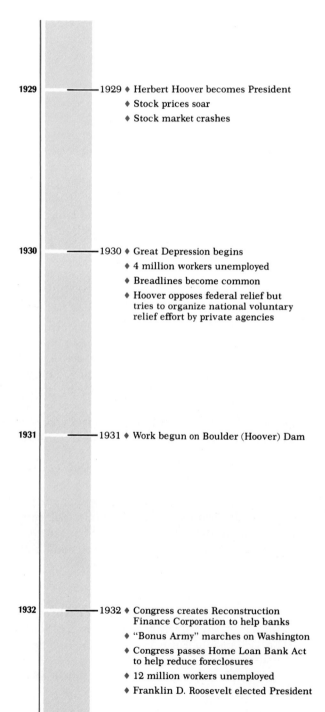

1929	1929 ♦ Herbert Hoover becomes President
	♦ Stock prices soar
	♦ Stock market crashes
1930	1930 ♦ Great Depression begins
	♦ 4 million workers unemployed
	♦ Breadlines become common
	♦ Hoover opposes federal relief but tries to organize national voluntary relief effort by private agencies
1931	1931 ♦ Work begun on Boulder (Hoover) Dam
1932	1932 ♦ Congress creates Reconstruction Finance Corporation to help banks
	♦ "Bonus Army" marches on Washington
	♦ Congress passes Home Loan Bank Act to help reduce foreclosures
	♦ 12 million workers unemployed
	♦ Franklin D. Roosevelt elected President

1. THE MEANING OF THE STOCK-MARKET CRASH

President Hoover, a former mining engineer and a self-made millionaire, had won fame as the administrator of Belgian relief during World War I. He earned further respect as Secretary of Commerce during the Harding and Coolidge administrations. With a reputation as a successful businessman, a good administrator, and a dedicated government official, Hoover seemed the ideal President for the times.

On October 24, 1929, just a little more than seven months after Hoover became President, came the stock-market crash and the beginning of an economic nightmare in America. The events of October 1929 caught almost everyone by surprise, but the forces that led to the Great Crash had been at work for years.

After the United States recovered from the postwar recession in 1922, the American economy began to boom. By the late 1920s Americans from New York to California were infected with a bad case of "prosperity fever." Except for many unskilled workers and small farmers, most Americans thought that the future never looked better. Workers' wages were increasing while the profits of corporations grew rapidly. In these circumstances, Americans began to spend more and more money. As you recall from Chapter 26, automobiles and consumer goods, such as washing machines, vacuum cleaners, and kitchen stoves were sold almost more quickly than they could be made.

Stock-Market Speculation Hits America

Cars and consumer goods were not the only things Americans were buying. With extra money on hand and with credit easy to obtain, many persons began to buy stocks—shares of ownership in companies—in the fast-rising stock market. Almost anyone could buy stock. All that was needed was a down payment. Buying stock with only a down payment was called **"buying on margin."** When a person bought on margin, only a portion —or margin—of a stock's value was paid to a stockbroker (a person who buys and sells stocks for others). The broker then borrowed the rest of the money. If the stock went up in value and was sold, the broker would keep part of the money to pay for the loan and the broker's fee, and give the rest to the stockholder as profit. If, however, the stock declined in value, the broker would demand more money from the stockholders—money which many small investors might not have. Today buying on margin is regulated, and many of the dangers of 1929 have been reduced.

The Great Crash

The system of buying stocks on margin in the hope of making vast fortunes caused thousands of persons to risk their hard-earned savings in the stock market. By late summer of 1929, transactions on the market were taking place at a dizzying rate. Then, in early September, prices began a slide downward: the market seemed unstable. Still, few people believed that anything was seriously amiss. As the days passed, however, uncertainty began to grow, and on October 24—**Black Thursday**—catastrophe struck the market. A colossal wave of selling swept over Wall Street. As fear and panic spread, millions of shares of stock were traded. By the end of the day, over 13 million shares had been traded. On normal days, less than 5 million shares of stock changed hands.

After this first disastrous decline, an even worse crash came some five days later, on October 29. On that day, known now as "Terrifying Tuesday," stockholders offered more than 16 million shares for sale, many at any price. Everybody wanted to sell, but nobody wanted to buy. The result was that by the close of the day, hundreds of thousands of shareholders and thousands of stockbrokers, bankers, and business owners had lost everything. Over $15 billion in paper value had disappeared in less than 30 days. Even so, few Americans realized that the stock-market crash signaled the beginning of the greatest economic crisis in the country's history—the Great Depression.

The Causes of the Great Depression

Though events on Black Thursday and Terrifying Tuesday began the Great Depression, they were not the cause. Even today economists are not sure what brought the catastrophe about. However, it is generally agreed that the following factors contributed to the depression:

Agricultural problems Many farmers purchased more land and new equipment to meet the demands for farm goods during World War I. When the war ended, demand dropped and farm income declined, making it difficult for farmers to pay their debts. As you recall from Chapter 25, many farmers had been in a deep depression since 1920. This, in turn, meant that one part of the population could not afford to buy the goods being produced. More goods were being produced than the population could eventually consume.

High tariffs and war debts Another contributing factor was the **Fordney-McCumber Tariff**, passed by Congress in 1922. This tariff, the highest in U.S. history, prevented foreign countries from repaying war debts because they could not sell to the American market. Furthermore, foreign nations raised tariff rates in retaliation against the

Crowds jam Wall Street as the stock market crashes, October 29, 1929.

Common scenes of the depression: apple sellers, bread-lines, and desperate attempts to find work

United States, thus reducing trade still further (and worsening the farmer's plight). Insistence by Harding and Coolidge that the European powers pay their large war debts to the United States also contributed to a decline in international trade.

Concentration of wealth The prosperity in the United States was not as widespread as it seemed. About 5% of the population received about 30% of all income. This 5% invested their wealth in stocks or placed it in savings accounts. Too small a portion of the national income went to workers and farmers, who would have purchased consumer goods and thus kept money in circulation.

Overproduction and credit buying The productive capacity of the United States increased rapidly during and after World War I. Because workers' wages were rising more slowly than were production and the price of goods, and because overseas trade was declining, American plants and factories were producing more than could be consumed. This development did not seem serious until the late 1920s because millions of Americans were buying on "time payment," or credit

plans. Installment buying thus concealed the fact that there was an actual decline in purchasing power.

A frail system of banks Many banks, especially in rural areas and in small towns, were weak and badly managed. These banks were prone to fail (close) because they had unwisely used depositors' money. When one bank failed, many people grew uneasy and withdrew their money from other banks, thus causing more failures.

The domino effect When one segment of the economy was affected by the depression, it soon affected others. Let us take as an example a man who loses his job because the company he works for fails. Without income from his job, this man must reduce some of his expenditures. He cancels his plans to buy a new vacuum cleaner, a refrigerator, or an automobile. Because of his decision, sales of these items will decrease.

In 1930, when similar decisions were made by thousands of people in the same circumstances, manufacturing slowed, and factory workers were laid off. These workers then lost their purchasing power, further slowing down the economy. Such a chain of events is called a "domino effect." With this happening to millions and millions of persons, it is easy to see how the depression spread like a prairie fire from one part of the economy to another.

The Depression Deepens

Throughout the winter of 1929–1930 the depression spread with frightening speed. By the end of 1930, over 4 million Americans were without jobs. Breadlines became common in large cities. At the beginning of 1931, there were 82 breadlines in New York City alone, serving 85,000 meals every day. Across the nation, the gloom deepened as hundreds of banks failed and hundreds of thousands of citizens lost their savings.

FROM THE ARCHIVES

Despair and Want During the Depression

The following clipping from The New York Times, *September 7, 1932, shows the misery that many unemployed and homeless Americans suffered during the Great Depression.*

DANBURY, CONN., Sept. 6.—Found starving under a rude canvas shelter in a patch of woods on Flatboard Ridge, where they had lived for five days on wild berries and apples, a woman and her 16-year-old daughter were fed and clothed today by the police and placed in the city almshouse.

The woman is Mrs. John Moll, 33, and her daughter Helen, of White Plains, N.Y., who have been going from city to city looking for work since July, 1931, when Mrs. Moll's husband left her.

When the police found them, they were huddled beneath a strip of canvas stretched from a boulder to the ground. Rain was dripping from the improvised shelter, which had no sides.

LIFE IN AMERICA

HISTORY OF THE CREDIT CARD

Credit is an ancient arrangement, but credit cards are relatively new. In just a few short years, they have become a multi-billion dollar industry. In 1887 Edward Bellamy, a lawyer and journalist, wrote *Looking Backward, 2000–1887,* in which he conceived of a credit card. His idea was of a card issued by the government with a value equal to one's contribution to society. Each time a purchase was made, a portion of the card would be punched out. No money would be needed.

The First Credit Cards

The first credit cards, as we know them, were used in 1900 by hotels and issued to their most prominent customers. By 1914 department stores, which long had been extending credit to wealthy customers, starting using credit cards in order to urge monthly payments on accounts.

The real growth of credit cards,

A radio store of the 1920s

however, depended on the development of computers. Once the cost of all the paperwork involved in credit extension could be minimized, the industry took off. In 1958 the Chase Manhattan Bank and the Bank of America revolutionized the industry by introducing one credit card accepted almost everywhere. Now one need not carry dozens of cards—a single piece of plastic could be used to charge everything from fun to funerals. That handy piece of plastic has been a mixed blessing ever since.

Everywhere suffering and hardship seemed to grow. Some Americans tried to earn a living by peddling apples on street corners while others sold newspapers or shined shoes. President Hoover, once highly respected for his humanity in helping the refugees of World War I, became one of the most despised men in America. Though the depression was not his fault, he received the blame. His name became a symbol of the depression. Homeless persons sleeping under newspapers were said to be wearing "Hoover blankets." Jack rabbits, caught by hungry people with nothing else to eat, were called "Hoover hogs." Near the edges of cities, clusters of rough, makeshift shacks made of packing crates, boxes, and scrap lumber sprang up almost overnight. Called **"Hoovervilles,"** they served as residences for thousands of unemployed and homeless citizens. Clearly something had to be done. But what?

SECTION 1 REVIEW

 Identify: buying on margin, Black Thursday, Fordney-McCumber Tariff, Hoovervilles

Main Ideas

1. Why did so many Americans join the stock buying craze of the 1920s? How did buying on margin weaken the market?
2. Why did American farmers have economic problems before the rest of the nation?
3. What international factors helped bring on the Great Depression?
4. How did overproduction hurt the economy?
5. How did installment buying conceal the declining purchasing power of American workers?
6. Why did banks often fail? What was the result?
7. Describe how the depression spread through the economy.

2. PRESIDENT HOOVER TRIES TO RESTORE THE ECONOMY

As you have seen, President Hoover was well known as a humanitarian. Between 1914 and 1917 he had administered a mammoth program of aid to help Belgian refugees. Later, he was in charge of a similar program in Russia, until the new Communist government there forced him to leave. In 1927 he ran a relief program to assist people in the flood-stricken state of Mississippi. Yet for many months, as President during the Great Depression, Hoover did almost nothing for the unemployed, the homeless, or the hungry. Why?

Hoover's Personal Philosophy

Born in a small Iowa town, Hoover was orphaned at the age of eight. He was raised by relatives and worked his way through Stanford University. Then Hoover became a mining engineer. Through hard work, intelligence, and wise investments, the future President became a self-made millionaire by the age of 40.

Hoover's personal philosophy held that **"rugged individualism"** was the foundation of the American way of life. It was his belief that Americans were self-reliant, and that direct relief for the needy should come from private charities or local communities. President Hoover believed that if the federal government distributed aid, it would erode the character of those who received it.

Thus, the President did not direct the government to provide relief. Instead, he tried to reassure Americans. In several speeches he stated that prosperity was "just around the corner" and that business was fundamentally sound. Still, the depression deepened.

The President Releases Federal Funds

It soon became evident that the President's methods were doing little to deal with the problems facing the nation. By 1932 over 12 million people were unemployed, 9,000 banks had failed, and 32,000 businesses had closed their doors. Hoover realized that something else must be done.

One of the President's first steps was to release federal money for use in public works programs. Through these programs the federal government gave jobs to the unemployed by hiring them to build roads and dams and to work on land reclamation projects. The largest such project was **Boulder Dam** on the Colorado River between Arizona and Nevada. In 1947 the dam was renamed Hoover Dam in honor of the President.

The President also created the **Reconstruction Finance Corporation (RFC)** in 1932. This agency loaned money to banks, to city and state governments, and to certain large businesses. It was the President's hope that if the federal government supported key elements of the economy, businesses could remain open and banks would not be forced to foreclose mortgages on homes and farms. Local and state governments were to use RFC funds to provide local relief programs. Eventually the RFC pumped more than $2 billion into the American economy.

The President departed from his previous outlook even more when he recommended to Congress that it pass the **Home Loan Bank Act**. This legislation established 12 new regional banks which received money from the RFC. This money was then made available to other lenders, such as savings and loan associations, insurance companies, and savings banks to reduce foreclosures of mortgages they held.

Despite the President's efforts, the downward spiral of the economy continued. Unemployment worsened, businesses continued to close, and prices slid downward. Still, many historians now believe that the economic situation of the country would have worsened even more had President Hoover not taken the actions he did. As we will see in Chapter 28, these Hoover projects paved the way for many of the programs of Franklin D. Roosevelt's New Deal.

The Bonus Army Confronts Hoover

Meanwhile, as Hoover started to put his new programs into effect, he faced yet another problem almost at the White House door. Camped on the swampy banks of the Anacostia River and in empty government buildings in downtown Washington were thousands of unemployed veterans. In 1924, Congress had approved a bonus bill for veterans of World War I. The bill provided for a life insurance policy for each veteran. The policies could be redeemed for their full value in 1944.

When the depression came, thousands of former soldiers were soon among the unemployed.

By 1932 many of these veterans were demanding that their bonuses be paid immediately, rather than in 1944 as scheduled. To emphasize their demands, in May of 1932 a small group of former soldiers traveled in freight trains and borrowed trucks across America to Washington. In a matter of weeks, hundreds and then thousands of other hungry and jobless veterans joined them. Newspapers soon nicknamed this group of ragged and unhappy men the Bonus Expeditionary Force or BEF. It was popularly called the **Bonus Army**.

Although as many as 25,000 men and their families crowded into the nation's capital, there were few acts of violence, theft, or disorder. The men organized into units and elected leaders to speak for them. President Hoover and other government officials were, however, alarmed by the Bonus Army. The President refused to meet with the leaders. Instead he locked the gates to the White House lawn and ordered a heavy police patrol of the area.

MacArthur Charges the Bonus Army

By the last part of July, the President decided that the bonus marchers must go. On July 28, he directed **General Douglas MacArthur** to clear Washington of the marchers. Soldiers, using bayonets and tear gas and accompanied by tanks, charged the defenseless veterans. The camps were burned, and two veterans were killed.

Many Americans criticized President Hoover for the way he dealt with the bonus marchers. Some historians now believe that the President's intention was to clear the buildings near the Capitol, not to burn the camps. General MacArthur, some think, disobeyed Hoover's orders and drove the veterans away. The incident helped cause the President's defeat in the 1932 election.

SECTION 2 REVIEW

Identify: rugged individualism, Boulder (Hoover) Dam, Reconstruction Finance Corporation, Home Loan Bank Act, Bonus Army, Douglas MacArthur

Main Ideas
1. Why did President Hoover try to avoid giving federal aid to the victims of the depression?
2. Once Hoover acted, what did he do?
3. Why did veterans march on the Capitol? Why did Hoover disband their camps?

3. THE COLLAPSE OF FAITH IN AMERICAN BUSINESS LEADERS

As you saw in Chapter 26, the decade of the 1920s was one in which the nation's businesses and industries were growing as never before. New technology and new methods of marketing goods helped American business prosper. Along with the great expansion in business came an increased respect for those who were leaders in finance, business, and industry. Men such as Henry Ford, Andrew Mellon, Samuel Insull, William C. Durant, J. P. Morgan, and many others were considered heroes by most Americans. Bruce Barton, an advertising executive, wrote a book in which he went so far as to depict Jesus and his Disciples as businessmen who had "sold" Christianity to the world.

It was felt by many in high political office that big business was the most important part of the American way of life. "The business of America is business," said President Calvin Coolidge. President Hoover had won wide respect for his success as a businessman and for his businesslike approach to government.

The Depression Changes Attitudes Toward Business

Soon, however, the attitude of Americans toward big business and business leaders began to change. The stock-market crash and the depression that followed caused a loss of faith in the country's business leaders. In the years and months just before the depression began in 1929, many business leaders encouraged Americans to invest in stocks. When the market crashed and these citizens lost their savings, they began to doubt the judgment of business leaders.

Americans also believed that business leaders had encouraged them to buy on credit. As workers became unemployed, many were unable to meet payments on refrigerators, stoves, and cars. When this happened and the items were repossessed, business leaders were blamed.

Later, well-known industrialists and bankers tried to convince the public that the economy was sound even though they knew otherwise. Finally, when businesses went bankrupt and when banks began to fail, trust and confidence in business leaders reached an all-time low.

Communists and Socialists Seek Support

As the depression continued to worsen, some critics began to attack not only business leaders but the entire system of capitalism. Soon after the 1917 revolution in Russia, **Communist parties** were established in several other nations, including the United States. Because the depression signaled serious problems for capitalism, the Communists in the United States were able to become more active. They believed that the time was at hand for a Communist revolution to overthrow America's system of capitalism and privately owned business.

Under the leadership of William Z. Foster and Earl Browder, the Communist party ran several candidates for office during the years of the Great Depression. To attract support the party stressed that there was little unemployment in the Soviet Union. The American Communists did not mention, however, the other side of life in the Soviet Union—the planned elimination of millions of kulaks (well-to-do peasants), the outlawing of religion, the lack of choice in the kinds of jobs a person could hold, the strict regulation, and the absence of even the most basic freedoms.

A few Americans, however, did sympathize with communism because they felt it would end the nation's economic problems. Some even joined the Communist party or otherwise supported it. But the great majority of American citizens did not rally to communism or Communists. In 1936, only about 41,000 citizens were members of the party. Communist candidates did poorly and never won a major office.

The Socialist party, led by Norman Thomas after Eugene V. Debs' death in 1926, was also small. It numbered only 21,000 members at its height in 1934. Like the Communists, the Socialists believed that the time was right for capitalism to be replaced with another economic system. As you recall from Chapter 20, the Socialists thought that the government should own factories, farms, and other means of production. Like the Communists, the Socialists gained a few supporters because of the depression. Unlike the Communists, however, the Socialists did not propose violent means to obtain their goals.

In 1932 and 1934 the **Farmer-Labor party,** a Minnesota political party with some socialist ideas, grew in strength. The party was made up of those who had lost faith in American business

Herbert C. Hoover (1874–1964)

IN OFFICE: 1929–1933

Republican from California. Because he was afraid that federal intervention would destroy individualism, Hoover hesitated to extend the role of the federal government in combatting the depression of 1929. However, in 1931, he requested that Congress establish the Reconstruction Finance Corporation to help industry recover. His efforts were not enough to restore prosperity.

and capitalism. A governor and several state and federal legislators were elected on the Farmer-Labor ticket. The party merged with the Democrats after the start of the New Deal.

Most Americans were interested in neither communism nor socialism but in ending the unemployment, starvation, and suffering of the depression. To do this, they turned not to economic systems or to forms of government foreign to American traditions but to the constitutional processes which had been a part of U.S. history since the nation's earliest days. In the election of 1932, U.S. citizens voted for new leaders whom they believed would try to solve America's problems. The election of 1932 confirmed once more the Americans' support for private enterprise as well as the respect Americans have for the law, the Constitution, and peaceful change through the ballot box.

SECTION 3 REVIEW

Identify: Communist party, Farmer-Labor party

Main Ideas

1. Why did many Americans during the 1920s consider business leaders as heroes?
2. List three reasons why Americans changed their attitude toward big business around 1930.
3. How did the depression cause the growth of various radical political parties?

4. FRANKLIN D. ROOSEVELT AND THE ELECTION OF 1932

By the spring of 1932, the depression had strengthened its hold on the nation. Nearly everyone seemed to be affected. In the winter of 1932–1933, a New York husband and wife moved into a cave in that city's Central Park. They lived there a year. In back alleys behind Chicago restaurants, people fought for scraps of garbage. Over 2 million men, women, and children were wandering the countryside, riding in boxcars or hitchhiking across the nation, looking for jobs. Everywhere fear held millions of Americans tightly in its grip.

During the late spring of 1932, the Democratic and Republican parties prepared to hold their national nominating conventions. The Republican leaders realized that if they nominated anyone other than Hoover it would appear that he and the Republicans were at fault for the depression. Consequently, at their convention in Chicago, they once again nominated Hoover as their candidate for the presidency.

The Democrats sensed that for the first time since Wilson's election in 1916 they had a real chance to place a member of their party in the White House. There was an attempt at the Democratic convention to again nominate the 1928 candidate, Al Smith. The effort failed, however, and to face Hoover the party nominated the dynamic and energetic governor of New York, **Franklin Delano Roosevelt**.

Franklin Delano Roosevelt's Background

FDR, as the nation's press soon began to call him, came from a wealthy and distinguished old New York family. A distant cousin of President Theodore Roosevelt, Franklin grew up on his family's estate at Hyde Park on the Hudson River. He graduated from Harvard College and then earned a law degree from Columbia University.

Roosevelt was best known in 1932 as governor of New York, but by then he had been in politics for more than 20 years. Able to win the confidence of voters with his jaunty manner, ready smile, and quick wit, Roosevelt had served two terms in the New York state legislature. He later became Assistant Secretary of the Navy during the administration of Woodrow Wilson. In 1920 Roosevelt ran on the Democratic ticket for Vice-President, but he and his running mate, James Cox, were defeated by Harding and Coolidge.

In 1921, while vacationing at Campobello Island off the coast of Canada, Franklin D. Roosevelt was stricken with the crippling disease of polio. It seemed as if a brilliant career were over. But with cheerfulness, determination, and hard work, Roosevelt fought his way to recovery. Though forced to use leg braces to walk, he was able to return to an active life in politics. In 1928 he won election as governor of New York, and as governor, he began many new programs designed to help fight the depression.

The Election of 1932

The 1932 presidential campaign got underway in July of that year. The main issue, of course, was the Great Depression. But other questions, such as prohibition, played a minor part in the campaign. President Hoover blamed the depression on international problems. He argued that his relief programs would solve the nation's problems. He also said that things would have been worse if he had not taken the action that he did.

Roosevelt blamed Hoover and the Republicans for the depression. The Democratic platform promised to regulate stock exchanges, to begin unemployment assistance, and to start a social security program.* While Hoover still believed that "rugged individualism" was the best solution to America's problems, Roosevelt argued that it was the duty of the federal government to help individual citizens when necessary.

Roosevelt's sunny and commanding personality radiated confidence. He campaigned extensively, speaking all across America, and did not let his physical handicap slow his efforts. Candidate Roosevelt promised a "new deal" for Americans and programs to help "the forgotten man" who was poor, unemployed, and disheartened. Hoover, on the other hand, seemed to feel the weight of the depression personally. He was serious and

---

*social security program   government system of old-age, disability, and other benefits financed by employers, employees, and taxpayers.

gloomy, and his speeches and public appearances reflected his mood. He declared that it would be a calamity for the United States if Roosevelt were elected. The President believed that the relief programs proposed by Roosevelt would harm the character and strength of the American people. To Hoover, the Roosevelt program seemed dangerously close to radicalism.

On election day Americans went to the polls to decide who would govern for the coming four years. When the ballots were counted, Roosevelt had defeated President Hoover by an overwhelming majority. FDR received nearly 23 million votes while Hoover's total was about 16 million. In the electoral college, Roosevelt polled 472 votes to Hoover's 59.

The Significance of Roosevelt's Victory

When Franklin D. Roosevelt entered the White House on March 4, 1933, the United States faced its worse crisis since the Civil War. During the campaign, and later while Roosevelt was President, many wealthy and conservative Americans were concerned about Democratic promises and programs. Some called Roosevelt a "traitor to his class" and were afraid he was planning a socialist way of life. Others felt he was on the road to becoming a dictator. Some, like President Hoover, believed that Roosevelt's election signaled the ruin of the country. What did the election of Franklin Delano Roosevelt actually mean? Was he as radical as some of his opponents feared?

There is no question that Roosevelt's election heralded a dramatic change in the role of the federal government. Under Roosevelt's programs, collectively called the **"New Deal,"** the federal government began to play a larger part in the lives of most American citizens. As we shall see in Chapter 28, a host of government agencies came into being to help combat the mammoth economic problems gripping the country. Some of these agencies regulated major aspects of the American economy. But Roosevelt was not a radical. The actions he took were like those taken by Lincoln and Wilson during wartime. They were taken in a time of crisis, not with the desire to diminish American liberty but to preserve it. Had Roosevelt not offered vigorous new programs to ease the problems of the depression, it is possible that a far more radical leader would have emerged to grasp the reins of the nation.

Franklin Delano Roosevelt suffered a crippling bout of polio in 1921.

SECTION 4 REVIEW

 Identify: Franklin Delano Roosevelt, New Deal

Main Ideas

1. What was Franklin D. Roosevelt's political and personal background?
2. What kind of campaigns did the two presidential candidates of 1932 wage?
3. What was the significance of Roosevelt's victory? Why did many Americans fear it?

617

CHAPTER 27 REVIEW

Key Terms

Explain the meaning of each of the following terms:

> buying on margin
> Black Thursday
> Fordney-McCumber Tariff
> Hoovervilles
> rugged individualism
> Boulder (Hoover) Dam
> Reconstruction Finance Corporation
> Home Loan Bank Act
> Bonus Army
> Communist party
> Farmer-Labor party
> New Deal

Reviewing the Main Ideas

Section 1

1. Describe how each of the following contributed to the onset of the Great Depression: (a) buying on margin, (b) farm problems, (c) high tariffs, (d) war debts, (e) overproduction, (f) credit buying, and (g) bank failures.
2. Why did the depression spread throughout the economy?

Section 2

1. What steps did Hoover take to try to end the depression and relieve suffering?
2. Why did some veterans march on the nation's capital? Why did the Hoover administration attack the marchers' settlements?

Section 3

1. Why did the attitude of many Americans toward big business and business leaders change after the stock-market crash?
2. How did the Great Depression cause some people to question the capitalist system?

Section 4

1. In the campaign of 1932, how did Hoover and Roosevelt differ in their approaches to the problem of the Great Depression?
2. Why did many people fear FDR's election?

Special History Skills:

Oral History

History often becomes more interesting when we talk to the people who lived it. Interviewing people about their experiences during a particular period is the gathering of oral history. People 60 years old or more have many memories about the Great Depression. Look around your community, apartment building, church, or family and find several older citizens who are willing to help you with this assignment.

Ask them how old they were and where they lived during the Great Depression. In what ways were economic conditions then the same as or different from today's? What did these people do for fun? What was school like? Then ask at least one other question of your own and make a report to the class of your interview.

Other Skill Activities

1. **Domino effect**
   Briefly explain the "domino effect" of unemployment. Does it seem to you that it might also work in reverse? Use as an example a person employed in the auto industry.

2. **Protest marches**
   Research other protest marches on Washington, D.C. Recall Coxey's Army and other "armies" in the depression of the 1890s (see Chapter 21). In 1963 there was a major civil-rights march, and during the 1960s and 1970s there were several large anti-war and anti-draft marches. How were various demonstrators treated in the capital?

3. **Debate**
   With the help of some friends stage a debate between Herbert Hoover and Franklin D. Roosevelt. The topic is, "Resolved: the federal government should not give direct aid to citizens during a severe depression."

4. **Library research**
   How did the Great Depression affect people in Britain, Germany, France, and other European countries? Why did many of them blame the United States for causing the depression?

5. **Depression songs**
   Write one or more songs about the Depression.

6. **You solve it**
   Finding the best way to end the Great Depression was a major goal of Republicans

and Democrats both before and after the 1932 election. What was the best way to accomplish this goal? Make up your own plan, drawing from the ideas in this chapter and adding some of your own.

Thinking Critically

1. Do you agree with President Hoover's view that state and local government and private charities, not the federal government, should aid the needy? Explain.
2. How might Hoover's background have led him to his belief in rugged individualism?
3. Why do independent parties often grow in times of national crisis? At what other times in our nation's history have such parties grown?
4. How do you think the rest of the world fared during the Great Depression? Which countries were probably hit the hardest? Which the least? Why?

Further Reading

Studs Terkel. *Hard Times*. Pantheon Books, 1970. Terkel, a Chicago journalist, records the oral history of the depression with numerous interviews of people in all conditions and walks of life. Excellent reading in whole or in part.

William E. Leuchtenburg. *The Perils of Prosperity, 1914–1932*. University of Chicago Press, 1958. A highly readable book for advanced students, this covers the period from the outbreak of World War I to the election of 1932.

TEST YOURSELF

WRITE YOUR ANSWERS ON A SEPARATE SHEET OF PAPER.

Matching

Write the letter of the item that best matches each description below.

1. the day the stock market first crashed
2. veterans who marched on the Capitol in 1932
3. work-relief program initiated by President Hoover
4. hurt foreign trade
5. the way unemployment affected the rest of the economy
6. buying stocks on credit
7. buying appliances on credit
8. shantytowns built during the Depression
9. wanted to end capitalism through revolution
10. wanted to end capitalism by means of the ballot

a. buying on margin
b. Hoovervilles
c. Bonus Army
d. Communist party
e. Fordney-McCumber Tariff
f. Boulder Dam
g. Terrifying Tuesday
h. domino effect
i. Socialist party
j. installment buying
k. Black Thursday

True or False

Mark T if the statement is true, F if it is false. Rewrite all false statements so that they are true.

1. In the 1920s, a high tariff contributed to good times for farmers.
2. In the 1920s, overproduction caused a surplus of some goods.
3. Buying on margin helped cause the stock-market crash.
4. In 1932 the Reconstruction Finance Corporation lent money to state and local governments and some businesses to help improve the economy.
5. The Bonus Army marched on Washington, D.C., demanding payment of back pay.
6. After the stock-market crash many Americans blamed business leaders for the hard times.
7. As the depression deepened, people often drew their money out of well-managed banks, causing these banks to fail.
8. Hoover thought that it was the responsibility of local government and private charities to help the people.
9. FDR believed that rugged individualism was the best solution to America's problems.
10. FDR's program for change was called the Square Deal.

Chapter 28

THE FIRST NEW DEAL

1933–1935

The buildings of the city of Washington stand stark and desolate against an overcast sky. The bare trees and brown grass give evidence of a winter not quite past. Bitter gusts of wind cut through the vast crowd gathered along the broad expanse of Pennsylvania Avenue. It is March 4, 1933, Inauguration Day in America, and the weather in the capital—somber and bleak—seems to reflect the mood of the nation's people.

As the crowd watches, an open black limousine rolls slowly down the street. In the rear seat are two top-hatted figures: President Herbert Hoover, looking glum and serious, and Franklin D. Roosevelt, smiling and waving to the crowd.

At the Capitol building the President-elect, walking stiffly because of the heavy braces on his crippled legs, makes his way slowly up a sloping ramp to the speaker's platform and takes the oath of office. Turning to face the forest of microphones in front of him, Roosevelt looks across the sea of people gathered to hear his inaugural address. Unseen by the President are millions of other citizens, seated near radios in homes all across America.

"I am certain," begins the President, "that my fellow Americans expect that . . . I will address them with a candor and a decision which the present situation of our Nation impels." During the campaign, Roosevelt had promised the country a "new deal." With his inaugural remarks, that new deal begins.

Sections in This Chapter
1. Background to the New Deal
2. Fear and Fireside Chats
3. The NIRA
4. An Alphabet of Agencies
5. Critics from the Left and Right Attack the New Deal

Opposite: This post office in Chicago is one of thousands of public buildings, schools, bridges, parks, and other facilities constructed by relief workers during the New Deal.

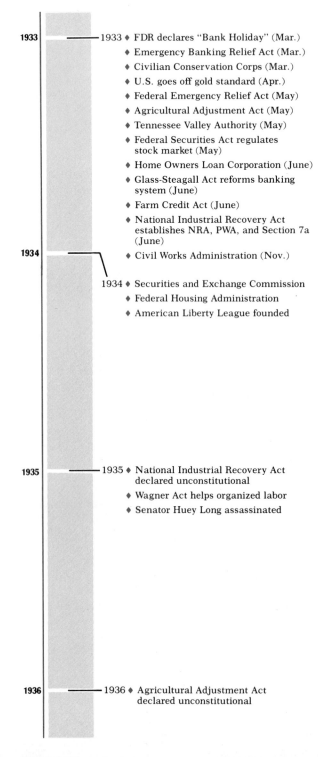

1933 — 1933 ♦ FDR declares "Bank Holiday" (Mar.)
♦ Emergency Banking Relief Act (Mar.)
♦ Civilian Conservation Corps (Mar.)
♦ U.S. goes off gold standard (Apr.)
♦ Federal Emergency Relief Act (May)
♦ Agricultural Adjustment Act (May)
♦ Tennessee Valley Authority (May)
♦ Federal Securities Act regulates stock market (May)
♦ Home Owners Loan Corporation (June)
♦ Glass-Steagall Act reforms banking system (June)
♦ Farm Credit Act (June)
♦ National Industrial Recovery Act establishes NRA, PWA, and Section 7a (June)

1934 — ♦ Civil Works Administration (Nov.)

1934 ♦ Securities and Exchange Commission
♦ Federal Housing Administration
♦ American Liberty League founded

1935 — 1935 ♦ National Industrial Recovery Act declared unconstitutional
♦ Wagner Act helps organized labor
♦ Senator Huey Long assassinated

1936 — 1936 ♦ Agricultural Adjustment Act declared unconstitutional

The inauguration of Franklin D. Roosevelt as the nation's 32nd President began a special era in American history. Before his death 12 years later, Roosevelt, like Jefferson and Jackson, had given his name to an age. During those years, he had presided over some of the most far-reaching changes our country has ever seen. And, by the time he died in 1945, he had become one of the most loved and one of the most hated Presidents ever elected by the American people.

Roosevelt Begins Without an Exact Plan

The new President promised action against the depression, and he soon lived up to his word. In the first **"Hundred Days"** of his administration (from March 9 to June 16), Roosevelt and the Congress produced an amazing amount of legislation. Roosevelt became President without an exact plan for attacking the depression. He did know, however, that action was required. "Take a method and try it," the President once told his staff members. "If it fails, try another. But above all, try something!"

Franklin D. Roosevelt seemed to be especially suited to lead the nation in a time of crisis. His own struggle and suffering during his battle with polio had made him personally familiar with fear and misfortune. During his illness he learned to face problems cheerfully and with determination, rather than with despair. FDR brought these qualities to the White House with him.

Some of his ideas and programs came from a small group of intellectuals called the **"brain trust."** Some were lawyers or social workers. Others were college professors, such as Rexford Tugwell, a young economist from Columbia University. Tugwell became Under Secretary of Agriculture. Raymond Moley, another college professor, became Assistant Secretary of State.

The President's wife, Eleanor, was one of his most important advisers, and she served as a spokeswoman for the administration throughout his long term of office. Other members of the President's staff included political advisers he had known for many years, such as Louis Howe and Samuel Rosenman. Still others were persons who were asked to join the New Deal because of their special backgrounds or experience. Frances Perkins, who was Roosevelt's Industrial Commissioner when he was governor of New York, became America's first female cabinet member as Secretary of Labor. Harry Hopkins, a shabbily dressed New York social worker, held many important jobs, in both domestic and foreign affairs, during the Roosevelt years. Harold Ickes, a gruff Republican from Illinois, became the New Deal's Secretary of the Interior.

Origins and Goals of the New Deal

The concepts of the New Deal struck many Americans as novel and revolutionary. Some felt that the President's thoughts were heavily influenced by ideas from foreign lands. But Roosevelt's actions for ending the depression generally had their roots in American history. New Deal ideas for the regulation of business, for example, dated from the days of Teddy Roosevelt. Steps taken by the American government during World War I guided the new administration in setting up an elaborate web of federal agencies to fight the depression. Reform measures in banking and finance drew much from programs started by President Wilson. Still other ideas came from the progressives and Populists of years before.

President Roosevelt and his advisers believed that to deal effectively with the depression, the New Deal should have three basic goals—relief, recovery, and reform. The most immediate need during the first days of the New Deal, believed President Roosevelt, was relief for the victims of the depression.

Immediate recovery, and later, long-range recovery, was also a major part of FDR's program. The "Bank Holiday," the Emergency Banking Relief Act, the National Recovery Administration, and other measures that you will study in this chapter were all recovery efforts created during the first "Hundred Days" of the New Deal.

The President's longer range plans also included reform measures to ensure that another disastrous depression would not take place. Among the reform efforts of the New Deal were the creation of the Securities and Exchange Commission and the Social Security Act.

As you will learn, many of the President's efforts overlapped. Many times the efforts conflict-ed with one another. And the President's assistants often argued with each other about which project should receive priority and which should not. Overall, however, the New Deal moved forward with more speed and more effect than anything Americans had ever seen before.

SECTION 1 REVIEW

 Identify: Hundred Days, brain trust

Main Ideas
1. What factors in Roosevelt's personal life seemed to make him particularly suited to lead the nation during a time of crisis?
2. What was the historical background for many of the New Deal programs?
3. What were the three main goals of the New Deal?

FROM THE ARCHIVES

Franklin D. Roosevelt's First Inaugural Address

This is preeminently the time to speak the truth, the whole truth, frankly and boldly. Nor need we shrink from honestly facing conditions in our country today. This great Nation will endure as it has endured, will revive and will prosper. So, first of all, let me assert my firm belief that the only thing we have to fear it fear itself—nameless, unreasoning, unjustified terror which paralyzes needed efforts to convert retreat into advance. . . .

I am prepared under my constitutional duty to recommend the measures that a stricken nation in the midst of a stricken world may require. These measures, or such other measures as the Congress may build out of its experience and wisdom, I shall seek, within my constitutional authority, to bring to speedy adoption.

But in the event that the Congress shall fail to take one of these two courses, and in the event that the national emergency is still critical, I shall not evade the clear course of duty that will then confront me. I shall ask the Congress for the one remaining instrument to meet the crisis—broad Executive power to wage a war against the emergency, as great as the power that would be given to me if we were in fact invaded by a foreign foe.

2. FEAR AND FIRESIDE CHATS

When Franklin D. Roosevelt became President, Americans everywhere were fearful of the future. Unemployed workers were frightened that they would be unable to feed their families or that they would never be able to find a job. Home owners feared that their mortgages would be foreclosed and that they would lose their homes. Bankers were afraid that their banks would fail. Business owners and industrialists were concerned lest their enterprises go bankrupt. Farmers trembled at the thought that their already pitifully small incomes might shrink still more. Roosevelt knew that if he were to be successful in his attempt to conquer the depression, he must help restore confidence in the future.

The Banking Crisis

The most critical problem confronting the nation at the moment Roosevelt took office was the banking crisis. Between the election in November and Roosevelt's inauguration in March, millions of citizens rushed to banks to withdraw their money from savings and checking accounts. Because some banks had failed and others were failing, depositors withdrew their money and took it home, where they kept it in mattresses, coffee cans, and shoe boxes.

Franklin Delano Roosevelt (1882–1945)

IN OFFICE: 1933–1945

Democrat from New York. Roosevelt's programs to combat the depression shifted more power from the states to the federal government. During his third term, the United States became involved in World War II (1939–1945). His decisions at various conferences during the war helped to determine national policies in the postwar world. He died soon after his election to an unprecedented fourth term.

By the time Hoover left office on March 4, almost every bank in the country had either failed or had closed to keep from failing. Business had ground to a standstill, and anxiety lay like a heavy blanket across the nation.

On March 6, just two days after his inauguration, the new President took action. By means of a presidential proclamation, Roosevelt suspended the operation of all banks in what he called a **"Bank Holiday."** At the same time he halted the trading of gold. Three days later, the President called a special session of Congress and obtained overwhelming approval for the Emergency Banking Act. This act not only confirmed the President's actions but established new regulations that allowed sound banks to reopen their doors. The Reconstruction Finance Corporation was instructed to make loans to banks which needed additional funds to reopen. Newly issued currency was also used to help other banks open.

To renew the faith of Americans in banks, the President gave the first of his famous **"fireside chats."** Speaking simply and calmly, as though he were talking informally with a small group of friends sitting around the fireside, Roosevelt assured Americans that the government was correcting the banking problem. The President also explained that because of his action money would be safer in a bank than at home. Roosevelt's message was so effective that confidence in the banks was restored almost at once. By the end of March, most of the nation's banks were crowded with people who trusted them again. More than 5,000 banks were reopened within a few days. Those banks found to be completely unsound, however, were closed for good.

Three months later Congress passed the **Glass-Steagall Act,** which brought badly needed reform to the banking business. The act prohibited commercial banks from selling stock or financing corporations. An even more important provision of the act created the Federal Bank Deposit Insurance Corporation. The FDIC, as it was soon called, insured individual bank deposits of up to $2,500 (later increased). The new measure further increased public confidence in the country's banking system and effectively ended bank failures in the United States.

New Regulations of Securities and Stocks

Uncontrolled trading in the stock market was one

of the causes of the crash of 1929. To help prevent a recurrence of such a disaster, Congress passed the Federal Securities Act of 1933. This new law required any company which had stock for sale to fully inform investors of all financial information about the company. The Securities Act also gave the Federal Trade Commission the authority to oversee any new issue of stocks.

Later, in 1934, Congress created the **Securities and Exchange Commission,** or SEC, to administer the Securities Act. The President appointed his friend Joseph P. Kennedy, a wealthy business-man, to head the SEC. The Commission regulated buying on margin and other practices and tried to prevent unfair manipulation of stock exchanges throughout the United States.

Roosevelt's action protected many investors, but it also had the effect of turning some businessmen and businesswomen against him. Those who did not like the Securities Act or the Securities and Exchange Commission believed the President's actions were unnecessary government interference in the business world.

Roosevelt Repudiates the Gold Standard

Most of the President's financial advisers believed that rising prices would stimulate business and that the dollar had to be inflated if prices were to rise. Many senators and representatives agreed, but differed on what action to take. Some believed that billions of dollars of new currency should be printed and placed into circulation. A few invoked the ghost of William Jennings Bryan and demanded the purchase of silver by the government (see Chapter 21).

The President decided on a third plan. Following the lead of Britain, Roosevelt took America off the **gold standard** in April of 1933. When a country's currency is on the gold standard it means that the paper currency is redeemable for gold. Once America was taken off the gold standard, it meant that each paper dollar was no longer backed by gold and could not be redeemed in gold. In 1934, the dollar's value was set at 59¢ in gold, a little more than one half its previous worth. Through this measure, the dollar was inflated dramatically.

Roosevelt's action was condemned by many persons who believed that the gold standard was essential to the financial stability of the United States. Among those critical of Roosevelt's action were the financier Bernard Baruch and the President's fellow Democrat, Al Smith. Smith called the newly devalued currency "baloney dollars." Others, such as J. P. Morgan, believed that Roosevelt had done the proper thing. As with so many of the new President's actions, public opinion was deeply divided over the repudiation of the gold standard.

Roosevelt Orders an End to Gold Hoarding

President Roosevelt also ordered an end to the hoarding of gold. The Secretary of the Treasury was empowered to call in all gold certificates and gold coins in circulation. Citizens charged with hoarding gold were subject to a $10,000 fine and ten years in jail. These measures, along with a later decision to authorize the Reconstruction Finance Corporation to buy and sell gold in the world market, helped to some extent to "pump up" the drastically deflated economy and to stabilize the monetary situation.

How effective was Roosevelt's manipulation of the currency? This is a difficult question to answer. America's economy improved during the years following the President's actions. How much of this was due to abandoning the gold standard and devaluing the dollar no one really knows. Perhaps the economy's improvement was due to other actions the New Dealers were taking at the same time. The President's efforts did prove, however, that gold did not have to serve as the monetary yardstick in America. Thus the fears that had haunted the nation since the days of Bryan and the silverites in the 1890s were laid to rest.

SECTION 2 REVIEW

Identify: Bank Holiday, fireside chats, Glass-Steagall Act, Securities and Exchange Commission, gold standard

Main Ideas

1. What steps did the President take to end the banking crisis? What were the results?
2. Explain two ways in which the New Deal tried to reform the stock market.
3. Why did Roosevelt and many of his advisers want to inflate the country's currency? How did they do this? What were the results?

3. THE NIRA

Another immediate task confronting Roosevelt and the New Dealers was how to start the nation's industries on the road to recovery. The President and his advisers knew that most of the dollars paid to workers were quickly spent on food and clothing, while any extra money generally was used to buy a house, automobile, or other purchases. Such expenditures would soon put millions of dollars into circulation.

The New Dealers knew also that materials such as lumber, steel, cement, paint, and masonry products were used in the construction of homes and businesses. All of these items had to be manufactured or processed by other workers, who put yet more money into the economy. Thus, industrial recovery, because it would put money into circulation and create jobs, seemed to be the best medicine for improving the economy.

The NIRA and the NRA

The main step the President took to initiate industrial recovery was to sign into law the **National Industrial Recovery Act.** The NIRA went into effect in June of 1933. Inspired by President Wilson's wartime administration, it was designed to join the federal government with business and labor in a single team to fight the depression. Roosevelt hoped that through this joint effort, wages would increase, the jobless would be re-employed, and production would be balanced with consumption to avoid surpluses that kept prices down.

The heart of the NIRA was a series of **"codes of fair competition"** which limited production, established minimum wages, and reduced the hours of labor so that employment could be spread over more workers. Many of these codes had been drawn up by business associations after World War I, but under the NIRA they became enforceable by law. The old antitrust laws such as the Sherman Antitrust Act and the Clayton Antitrust Act were temporarily set aside as industries were urged to cooperate with each other.

To write, coordinate, and implement the codes in this sweeping program, Roosevelt established the **National Recovery Administration**, or NRA. The President appointed General Hugh Johnson, a red-faced and aggressive ex-cavalry officer, to lead the new agency. Johnson had worked closely with Bernard Baruch during World War I. Though Johnson was experienced and dedicated, his rough manner and colorful personality were to cause Roosevelt problems later.

At first the NRA appeared to be a splendid success. Ten of the nation's major industries signed the codes of fair competition.* To identify those who participated, General Johnson created the emblem of the Blue Eagle, based on an Indian thunderbird symbol. Businesses cooperating with the NRA were permitted to display the Blue Eagle with the words "We Do Our Part" printed beneath it. A giant parade in support of the NRA was held in New York City. Nearly 250,000 persons participated and a Navy dirigible flew overhead, towing a banner which read "We Do Our Part." Housewives were urged to buy only products that displayed the Blue Eagle. Shop owners displayed the symbol on their windows. The NRA appeared to be off to a vigorous start.

The NIRA was designed not only to aid industry but to assist labor as well. Some of the most important measures of the act were those found in **Section 7a**, which guaranteed certain rights to labor. This section stated that all employers who were operating under an NRA code must grant workers the right to organize and bargain collectively. Section 7a also said that employers could not exert pressure upon workers to keep them from joining the union of their choice. Other parts of Section 7a prohibited child labor and established a minimum wage for workers.

Because it protected the rights of employees to unionize, the NIRA had the effect of promoting membership in the nation's labor unions. In the six months between May and October of 1933, 1.5 million workers joined the American Federation of Labor. After this first surge, the growth of union membership began to level off.

The NIRA Runs into Problems

Despite its initial success, the NIRA soon experienced problems. One grew out of confusion over the codes. Did small industries, such as button makers, for example, need a code of their own, or should they be included under the garment man-

---

*Those industries signing codes were textiles, woolens, electrical, oil, garments, automobiles, cotton, coal, lumber, and shipbuilding.

ufacturers' code? Another problem came when owners of small businesses claimed that they were treated unfairly because their codes had been written by big businesses. They also charged that the minimum-wage sections of the codes drove their costs up disproportionately because they used more manual labor than the larger businesses did.

Other troubles came when "chiselers" or cheaters disregarded the codes. Having agreed to reduce hours and control wages according to the codes, they ignored the agreement. When this happened, no new jobs were created. Though Johnson often threatened to crack down on code violators, many escaped prosecution.

Furthermore, businesses had to raise the prices of their products to meet the increased labor costs created by the NIRA requirements. This in turn had the effect of raising many prices beyond the consumers' reach.

Perhaps the biggest criticism of the NIRA, however, came from business owners who believed the act was too pro-labor. Section 7a helped bring unionization into industries which had never been unionized before. Other provisions, such as those which established the maximum length of the work week and a minimum wage, seemed to many employers to be infringements on their rights. Questions about which union was to serve as bargaining agent in a particular plant were often raised. In addition, some employers established company unions, which were dominated by management.

In an attempt to solve some of these many problems, Congress created the **National Labor Board**, or NLB. This body conducted elections in

LIFE IN AMERICA

GOING TO THE MOVIES

Like the circus of the late 19th century, movies were more than just entertainment; they were a great experience, transporting people out of their ordinary lives into great adventures and fantasies. Before television, movies were the way to relax and become informed. More than 80 million Americans a week went to the movies in the 1930s.

The first movies were little more than still photos mounted on a revolving paddle wheel. In 1889 George Eastman invented celluloid film and Thomas Edison developed a camera for use in nickelodeon peep shows which showed travel and adventure films. Directors soon began experimenting with different camera angles and special effects. The hit of 1902 was a space thriller entitled *A Trip to the Moon.* D. W. Griffith made the first full-length motion picture, *Birth of a Nation,* in 1915. Sound arrived in 1927. "Talkies" meant that ac-

tors could use a more subtle acting style. For some actors this meant they were out of a job.

When World War I shut down European studios, the United States became the movie capital of the world. Big studios were financed by stock issues and moved their operations from New York City to the sunshine and cheap land of California. Hollywood was on its way to stardom!

King Kong, 1933

plants and factories to decide which union would serve as the bargaining agent for the employees. The Board also engaged in arbitration of disputes between labor and management. However, the NLB had little authority, and employers often ignored its rulings. The NIRA continued to have problems as labor troubles swept the country.

The Supreme Court Rules Against the NIRA

Criticisms of the NIRA continued to mount. In the summer of 1934, General Johnson resigned. And in May 1935, a lawsuit, *Schecter Poultry Corp.* v. *United States*, came before the United States Supreme Court. The Court determined that the NIRA and the NRA were unconstitutional. The ruling stated that the codes of fair competition were illegal because Congress did not have the power to place such authority into the hands of the President and the NRA officials. Thus one of the first and most ambitious of the New Deal's recovery measures came to an end.

The Wagner Act

Though the NIRA was wrecked, parts of it survived in the Wagner-Connery Act, or National Labor Relations Act, passed in July 1935. Usually known as the **Wagner Act**, this law saved many of the provisions of Section 7a of the NIRA. One of the main sections of the act was the one which created the **National Labor Relations Board**, or NLRB, which still exists today. This is a permanent body which helps to prevent unfair labor practices, such as coercion of employees, dismissal of an employee simply for belonging to a union, and the establishment of company unions dominated by management. As you'll see in Chapter 29, the Wagner Act soon became known as organized labor's "Magna Carta."

SECTION 3 REVIEW

Identify: National Industrial Recovery Act (NIRA), codes of fair competition, National Recovery Administration (NRA), Section 7a, National Labor Board, Wagner Act, National Labor Relations Board

Main Ideas
1. What was the main goal of the NIRA? Why were many business owners against it?
2. What happened to the NIRA?

4. AN ALPHABET OF AGENCIES

When Roosevelt took office in 1933, about 13 million Americans, or 25% of the labor force, were jobless. Many of these citizens had exhausted their personal savings and had sold their property and possessions to keep from starving. Though Roosevelt opposed the dole, or outright giving of money to the needy, he believed that it was necessary to head off the possibility of starvation which faced many citizens.

The FERA and the CWA

In May 1933, just two months after Roosevelt became President, Congress established the **Federal Emergency Relief Administration.** Its purpose was to funnel federal money to state and municipal governments. These governments then made direct payments to persons in need.

The FERA was headed by the President's close associate, **Harry Hopkins.** The new agency had a beginning budget of $500 million, which it soon made available to state and local governments. In his first two hours at a desk set up in the hall of a government building because his regular office was unfinished, Hopkins spent over $5 million of relief money. Food, clothing, and outright payments of money were made during the spring and summer to millions of jobless Americans.

As the summer faded into the fall, Hopkins and Roosevelt realized that even the considerable efforts of the FERA were not going to be enough to meet the needs of millions of citizens during the cold weather months ahead. Therefore, in November 1933, Congress established the **Civil Works Administration.** Roosevelt's friend Hopkins also headed the CWA, which employed persons directly on the federal payroll. During its short life, the CWA employed 4 million people and spent $933 million on nearly 200,000 projects.

Unemployed men and women raked leaves in parks, repaired roads, and improved schools. Critics of the CWA charged that it "made work" and that its jobs were meaningless and unimportant. In fact, however, the CWA did much excellent work during its few months of existence. Before the agency was phased out in April 1934, its workers had repaired or improved nearly 500,000 miles of roads, 100 airports, and 40,000 schools. Most important, the CWA kept millions of citizens from facing the winter of 1933–1934 without money for food, fuel, or clothing.

The Public Works Administration (PWA)

Roosevelt struck still another blow at the depression when, as part of the NIRA, Congress established the **Public Works Administration**, soon known as the PWA, in June of 1933. The PWA was a **"pump-priming"** effort by the New Deal. Before running water was common, hand pumps often had to be "primed," or started, by pouring a small amount of water down the pump shaft so that the pump washer would seal and bring water from the well. In the same way, Roosevelt hoped that a small amount of government spending would create additional private spending.

The pump-priming idea was intended to work something like this: The PWA would contract with a construction company to build a large bridge. From this project not only would construction workers get jobs, but so would cement workers, workers who helped make the bridge's steel beams, truck drivers who delivered materials, and so on. Because all these workers would be employed and earning money, they would begin to buy items, and the economy would improve.

The PWA was headed by **Harold Ickes**, Roosevelt's Secretary of the Interior. The Public Works Administration eventually pumped almost $12 billion into the economy. It worked on some 35,000 projects, including bridges, municipal water and sewer systems, schools, parks, auditoriums, and public swimming pools. The PWA even built two new aircraft carriers, the *Enterprise* and the *Yorktown*.

The Civilian Conservation Corps (CCC)

One of the most successful of the New Deal relief agencies was the **Civilian Conservation Corps**. Created in March of 1933, the CCC employed young men between the ages of 18 and 25 to help replant forests, restore historic battlefields, stock streams and lakes with fish, build parks, and fight forest fires. Each member lived in a camp and earned $30 a month, a portion of which he was required to send home to his family.

By 1940, more than 2 million men had served in the CCC. The work of the agency could be seen long after the Depression years in restored historic sites, well-groomed parks, and freshly forested mountains. Many trails, roads, and buildings in use in our state and national recreational areas today were created by the men of the CCC.

The Farm Credit Administration (FCA)

In 1933 two out of every five farms in America were mortgaged. Hundreds of family farms were being reclaimed monthly by banks, insurance companies, and other mortgage holders. Under these circumstances farmers grew desperate. In Iowa a judge who was presiding over foreclosure proceedings was dragged from his courtroom to a rural crossroads where he was beaten by a band of angry farmers masked in blue bandanas. Other desperate farmers disrupted eviction sales and attacked public officials who attempted to foreclose mortgages on their farms.

To help farmers threatened with foreclosures and eviction, Roosevelt proposed the **Farm Credit Administration**. Passed by Congress in June 1933, the FCA financed outstanding mortgages at a 4% interest rate (later reduced to 3%). Payment schedules were also extended, in some cases up to 50 years. Farmers whose lands were already lost to foreclosure could borrow money from the FCA to repurchase their homesteads. Thousands of farmers had their homes and farms saved by the Farm Credit Administration.

The Agricultural Adjustment Administration (AAA)

Another major problem facing farmers was the low farm income prevailing since the early 1920s. In 1933 farmers made up about one-fourth of America's population. Roosevelt and his advisers knew that if farmers had more income, they would spend it on manufactured goods such as machinery, clothing, and farm supplies. This in turn would create jobs in industries and businesses. As the workers in plants and factories were re-employed, they would also purchase items, thus creating still more jobs. But how could the income of farmers be increased? How could this particular economic chain reaction be started?

The New Dealers based their answer to this problem on the laws of supply and demand. When an item or product is in short supply, the price generally goes up. When it is plentiful, the price generally drops. Roosevelt and his agricultural experts knew that if there were fewer farm prod-

629

ucts on the market, prices would rise. This was the purpose of another New Deal agency, the **Agricultural Adjustment Administration.**

Through the AAA, farmers across the country were asked to remove from cultivation one-fourth to one-half of their tillable land. Farmers who did so were paid a "benefit subsidy" for each acre removed from production. The money for these subsidies came from a special tax placed on the processors of farm products, such as vegetable canners, meat packers, and flour millers.

Soon millions of acres were removed from cultivation. About 6 million baby pigs were also killed to keep them off the market and thus prevent a pork surplus. Despite the great outcry against this destruction, farm income began to rise.

By 1936 prices of farm products had increased markedly, and farmers' incomes had risen to more than 50% above what they had been in 1932. Still, there were a number of problems with American agriculture, and the AAA came under sharp criticism.

One of the biggest problems was that tenant farmers and sharecroppers, who were often those most in need, were left out of the AAA benefits subsidy payments because the payments went to the owner of the property. Second, many urban citizens complained about higher food prices. In addition, large, one-crop farmers, such as cotton planters, often received more benefits than smaller, multi-crop farmers.

The AAA continued to assist farmers despite mounting criticism, until it was declared unconstitutional in 1936. In a 6–3 decision in the case of the *United States* v. *Butler*, the Supreme Court ruled that the government had no right to levy a processors' tax which took "money from one group" of citizens for the "benefit of another." The ruling temporarily stopped the New Deal efforts to aid agriculture under the AAA.

Help for Home Owners

In 1933, millions of Americans who lived in cities and towns were in danger of losing their homes to banks and other mortgage holders. To ease this situation, Roosevelt proposed to Congress the **Home Owners Loan Corporation**, or HOLC. Congress approved the new measure in June 1933.

The HOLC provided a loan fund of $2 billion. Home owners who could not meet their house payments could borrow from the HOLC. Interest

rates were low, and repayment could be extended for up to 15 years. When an HOLC office opened in Akron, Ohio, a double line three blocks long waited to get in. The HOLC eventually helped to re-finance one in every five mortgaged homes in America, enabling more than 1 million families to keep their homes.

Another New Deal agency to help home owners was the **Federal Housing Administration,** created in 1934. Through FHA loans, many families were able to modernize existing homes or to build new ones, and thus to stimulate the building industry.

The Tennessee Valley Authority (TVA)

In January 1933, Roosevelt and **Senator George Norris** of Nebraska visited the Muscle Shoals Dam on the Tennessee River where it flows through northern Georgia. The dam had been started during World War I to help in flood control on the river and to make nitrates for the ammunition needed during the war. When the war ended, the project was left uncompleted.

As Norris and Roosevelt viewed the river, they could visualize a vast network of dams which would control floods, produce electricity, and manufacture fertilizer for the farmers of the Tennessee Valley. The two men believed such a project would vastly improve the well-being of the poverty-stricken people who lived in the valley. Senator Norris had earlier proposed a similar idea to Congress, but the project had been vetoed by both Coolidge and Hoover. Shortly after his election, Roosevelt proposed legislation to put the program into effect. On May 18, 1933, Congress created the **Tennessee Valley Authority**. The TVA was authorized to buy or build dams, generate electrical power, help establish flood control, and manufacture and sell fertilizer.

The TVA was perhaps the most successful and enduring of all the programs created by the New Deal. The independent public corporation which carried out the project built 20 dams and took control of five others in a seven-state area. The region under its control included some 40,000 square miles. (See map, facing page.)

By 1940 over 400,000 residents of the area were using electricity, many for the first time. Now electric lights, vacuum cleaners, electric fences, milking machines, and many other modern and

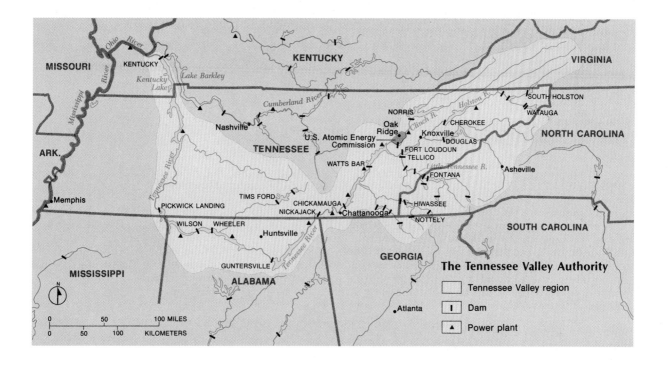

The Tennessee Valley Authority

- Tennessee Valley region
- I Dam
- ▲ Power plant

labor-saving devices could be used by the area's farmers. The dams of the TVA controlled the floods which had previously made much of the region useless for farming. Millions of acres of cut-off forests were replanted. The Tennessee River became a major waterway for barge shipping, connecting the interior of the South with the Great Lakes, Ohio River, and Mississippi-Missouri river systems. Thousands of workers were employed to build dams, power plants, and fertilizer factories. TVA-produced power was used as a "yardstick" to compare the costs which private utilities companies were charging for electricity.

The TVA was criticized by private power companies, who believed the yardstick concept was unfair because part of the cost of the TVA was paid by the government. Other critics argued that the TVA was socialistic interference with private enterprise.

The New Dealers defended the TVA by arguing that the yardstick did work, that costs of electricity went down all over the nation after the TVA began to operate. They also argued that the socialistic aspects of the project were more than offset by the private enterprises that grew up in the region because of the TVA. However, public utility companies and others continued to oppose

the TVA and kept other similar projects, such as a proposal for an "MVA" in the Missouri River Valley, from getting off the ground.

SECTION 4 REVIEW

Identify: Federal Emergency Relief Administration, Harry Hopkins, Civil Works Administration, Public Works Administration, pump priming, Harold Ickes, Civilian Conservation Corps, Farm Credit Administration, Agricultural Adjustment Administration, Home Owners Loan Corporation, Federal Housing Administration, George Norris, Tennessee Valley Authority

Main Ideas
1. What did the FERA and the CWA accomplish?
2. How did the PWA seek to "prime the pump" of the economy?
3. What did the CCC accomplish?
4. What programs did the New Deal provide for farmers? Why did the Supreme Court declare the AAA unconstitutional?
5. How did the New Deal help home owners?
6. What did the TVA accomplish? What were the criticisms of the TVA?

631

THE GEOGRAPHIC SETTING

Effect of dust storms in Oklahoma, 1936

DROUGHT AND DUST BOWL

American farmers in the 1930s suffered severe drought as well as economic depression. From 1932 to 1936 the entire United States received lower than average rainfall. Lakes and rivers dried up, plants withered, animals died. This was hard on all farmers, but on the High Plains from the Dakotas to Texas worse happened. The withered crops were blown away by the wind. Nothing now anchored the land in place. As you can see on the map below, the westerly winds picked up the precious topsoil, which had taken centuries to accumulate, and blew it eastward. In 1934 a huge storm dropped mil-

lions of pounds of dust on Chicago in one day. Winds carrying the topsoil turned the New England snow red and dusted ships at sea with a layer of silt.

During 1935–1937 dramatic "black blizzards" or "rollers" came across the plains with a boiling turbulence. Blowing dirt buffeted houses, cars, cattle, and humans with 60-mile-per-hour force, covering barren fields with dunes and interiors of houses with half-inch layers of grit.

The map shows the Dust Bowl area where drought conditions caused the most damage. It centered in the panhandles of Texas and Oklahoma and parts of Kansas, Colorado, and New Mexico.

The lighter brown area shows other parts of the High Plains also affected by severe wind erosion.

As you recall from the Geographic Setting in Chapter 14, the Great Plains had experienced drought many times in the past, and winds were ever present. Why then did the Dust Bowl occur? And what were the short- and long-term effects of this disaster?

Breaking the Land

The sodbusters of the 1880s came to the Great Plains in the wake of the cattlemen. New dry-farming methods and a few years of ample rainfall produced bumper crops and many new farms. Drought years might ruin some farmers, but enough of the native short grasses remained to hold down the soil.

World War I in Europe resulted in a huge market and high prices for American wheat, causing an agricultural boom on the High Plains. Farmers plowed up more and more sod in order to respond to the appeal. The newly developed farm machinery made this agricultural bonanza possible, and farmers spent their profits on an expanding array of tractors, plows, and threshers. Between 1920 and 1930 5 million acres of natural vegetation were plowed up on the southern Plains. Production jumped 300%, producing a severe glut and sharply falling prices.

When drought struck with particular intensity in the 1930s, Plains farmers were ill-prepared. Unplanted fields and scorched croplands had no protection against the wind. Machinery had encouraged overtilling. Too many people plant-

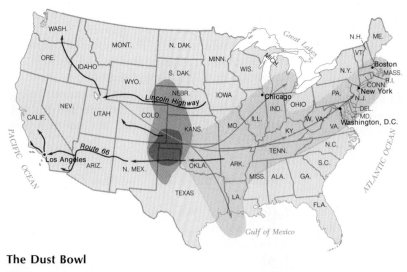

The Dust Bowl

- The heart of the Dust Bowl
- Other areas severely affected by wind erosion
- Major routes of migration
- Prevailing winds
- Distribution of dust

0   500 MILES
0   500 KILOMETERS

ing too much wheat on too many acres had upset the balance of nature. Now there was nothing to keep the dust down.

Okies and Exodusters

The dust and drought meant hard times for all Plains farmers, but the hardest hit were those tenant and small farmers who barely earned a living even in the best of years. The increased mechanization of farming in the 1920s had begun to force these people off the land. The Dust Bowl sent increased numbers packing.

Since a large portion of these people came from Oklahoma, they were called "Okies." Soon all farm workers leaving the Plains for other agricultural areas were called "Okies," or "dustbowlers," or "exodusters." Many families headed west to California, where they hoped to find work in the fields and orchards. Those who owned cars packed their families and possessions and set off down Route 66. Others walked or hitched rides. More than 1 million migrant farm workers reached California, where their economic plight rarely improved. In addition, nearly half a million migrants from the northern Plains traveled the old Lincoln Highway to the Pacific Northwest. Find these routes on the map.

Changes in Agriculture

The growing mechanization of agriculture had caused the exodus of people from the Plains as much as the drought and depression. This trend was encouraged by AAA relief measures which gave farm owners money to spend on additional machinery. Recovery measures also included the replanting of native grasses, contour plowing, and the planting of trees as windbreaks by the CCC. But it was the return of ample rainfall in 1941 that assured the end of the Dust Bowl.

Today agriculture on the Great Plains is even more highly mechanized. The cost of machinery, fuel, and fertilizers has made the small

family farm uneconomical, and "agribusiness" has taken over the landscape. Farmers combat soil erosion through a variety of planting techniques. Windbreaks around fields and farmsteads cut wind velocity and cool the air. Irrigation is used to circumvent the inconsistencies of rainfall. The former Dust Bowl region now grows a variety of crops watered by huge sprinkler systems that paint bright green circles across the brown land. Rivers on the Plains have never been reliable sources of water, so underground water is the source for most irrigation in the region.

Future Dust Bowls?

Droughts are inevitable on the Great Plains. Thought to coincide with sunspot activity, a severe drought can be expected every 20 years with milder ones every 3 to 4 years. Scientists think that weather on the Great Plains has actually been unusually stable for the past 40 years, but could become more variable in the future. What are the chances that another Dust Bowl will occur?

Some experts think that the chances are quite good if more steps are not taken to prevent soil erosion. In recent years water levels have dropped in the Ogallala Aquifer, a giant underground reservoir below the Great Plains. The rate of recharge—of water seepage back into the aquifer—is extremely slow and does not keep up with current usage rates. Irrigation may become too expensive for all but the largest agribusiness farms. Perhaps dry farming methods and careful soil management practices will be needed to prevent another disaster.

Two families on their way to California, 1936

5. CRITICS FROM THE LEFT AND RIGHT ATTACK THE NEW DEAL

Despite the great strides taken by President Roosevelt and the New Deal against the depression, not all Americans were satisfied. As in almost every political situation, there were those who criticized the government for going too far in its actions while others believed it had not gone far enough. During the first year the President was in office there was little criticism of the new administration. Most of the nation was caught up in the whirlwind of the "Hundred Days" and the host of new agencies, programs, and projects that followed. But by 1934 and 1935, a few political leaders were dissatisfied enough to begin attacking the New Deal. These critics were from both the left and right sides of the political spectrum.

Conservatives Criticize the President

Conservative opposition to the Roosevelt administration came mostly from big businessmen and the Republican party, but a few discontented

Anti–New Deal cartoon: Uncle Sam is shown as Gulliver, tied down by alphabet agencies.

Democrats joined the chorus of criticism as well. In August of 1934, the **American Liberty League** was founded as a powerful conservative voice. Many American industrialists, including members of the Du Pont family and the automobile executive William Knudsen, were members. A few prominent members of the President's own party, such as Al Smith, the 1928 Democratic candidate for the presidency, and John Davis, the conservative Democrat who had run against Coolidge in 1924, also added their names to the list of Liberty Leaguers. The Liberty League said it had two objectives: to teach respect for the rights of persons and property, and to teach the government to encourage private enterprise.

Most of those who opposed the President from the right believed that the New Deal was far too expensive (it had created a debt of $34 billion by 1936) for the good which had been accomplished. These conservative citizens also believed that the New Deal programs interfered with business. The provisions of Section 7a of the NIRA and later the Wagner Act, both of which were pro-union, created fierce opposition among businessmen and businesswomen. Other conservatives were alarmed by the growing power of the presidency and the federal government.

The Supreme Court, which was dominated by a majority of conservative justices appointed by earlier Presidents, reflected this opposition to some of the New Deal measures. When it declared the NIRA and the AAA unconstitutional, the Court was voicing conservative resistance to the direction the Roosevelt administration was taking.

Radicals Also Criticize Roosevelt

Just as the conservatives objected to many New Deal measures, so, too, did radicals. Many of the radicals offered promises to those citizens who had not benefited from the New Deal, including the elderly and some of the remaining unemployed.

In California, **Dr. Francis E. Townsend,** a physician who had lost all his savings in the depression, proposed the Townsend Plan, a plan by which the government would pay $200 each month to every American over 60. The money, said Townsend, would come from a nationwide 2% sales tax. Townsend's only provision was that each recipient had to spend the money within a month in order to keep it in circulation. Although economists calculated that the doctor's plan would tumble the nation into bankruptcy, Townsend attracted some 5 million followers. By 1935 elderly citizens had organized 2,000 Townsend Clubs in California and elsewhere.

Another voice from the left was that of **Father Charles Coughlin** [kog′lən], the Roman Catholic "Radio Priest" from Royal Oak, Michigan. Though Coughlin at first supported Roosevelt and the New Deal, he later violently attacked the President on his weekly radio broadcasts. As many people listened to Coughlin's broadcasts as listened to the President's fireside chats.

Like Roosevelt, Coughlin was a masterful radio personality. Using his immense popularity, he called for government ownership of banks, natural resources, and public utilities. Coughlin's programs attracted an audience of millions, especially among working-class citizens in the northeastern part of the nation. Later, during the 1936 presidential campaign, Coughlin worked against the President's re-election.

Perhaps the most colorful of all the radicals to emerge during the Great Depression was **Senator Huey P. Long** of Louisiana, nicknamed the "Kingfish." A skillful politician with a strong backing in his own state, where he had helped build schools, roads, and bridges, as well as state hospitals, Long attracted nationwide attention by 1935. Sporting purple shirts, pink ties, suspenders, and a straw hat, he built an immense following in the South and along the West Coast.

Long began a national organization which had as its slogan "Share Our Wealth." The "Share Our Wealth" program promised to make "Every Man a King" by giving every family a guaranteed annual income, a home, and a college education for the children. With such claims, the "Kingfish" soon attracted millions of dispossessed to his banner.

By early 1935 Long's organization had grown so large that some of Roosevelt's advisers believed the Louisiana senator could siphon off enough Democratic votes in the election of 1936 to cause a Republican victory. However, before he could challenge the President, Long was assassinated in the Louisiana capitol by a political enemy.

As we shall see in the next chapter, Roosevelt met this "thunder from the left" by shifting the New Deal itself further to the political left in his attempts to pull the nation out of the depression.

GLOSSARY OF POLITICAL TERMS

Here is a list of commonly used political terms. Keep in mind that they are all emotional labels that express personal opinions, not clear-cut categories. The terms "left," "center," and "right" come from the French National Assembly of the 18th century and refer to the practice of seating radicals on the left, moderates in the center, and conservatives on the right of the presiding officer.

left, left-wing person or group who wants major social, political, or economic changes at a fast rate. Usually wants to take power from the rich and redistribute it to the general populace.

right, right-wing person or group who does not want major changes or who wants them to come at a very slow rate. Usually wants to keep the existing distribution of power.

center the position of a person or group who supports moderate change. People in the center usually side with the left on some questions and the right on other questions.

moderate person or group who is in the center.

liberal person or group who wants changes in the existing social, political, or economic system. Usually in the center or on the left, prefers federal over state and local action, and supports government regulation of the economy.

progressive a liberal.

conservative person or group who defends the existing social, political, or economic system. Usually in the center or on the right, prefers state and local over federal action, and opposes government regulation of the economy.

radical person or group who favors extreme changes. Generally refers to persons or groups on the extreme left, but the term "radical right" is used to describe those on the extreme right.

reactionary person or party who wants political or social changes that represent a return to an earlier period.

extremist synonym for a radical of the extreme left or extreme right.

SECTION 5 REVIEW

Identify: American Liberty League, Francis E. Townsend, Charles Coughlin, Huey P. Long

Main Ideas

1. Why did many conservatives oppose the New Deal?
2. What were the programs called for by Dr. Townsend, Father Coughlin, and Senator Long?

CHAPTER 28 REVIEW

Key Terms
Explain the meaning of each of the following terms:

Hundred Days
brain trust
Bank Holiday
fireside chats
Glass-Steagall Act
Securities and Exchange Commission
gold standard
National Industrial Recovery Act
codes of fair competition
National Recovery Administration
Section 7a
National Labor Board
Wagner Act
National Labor Relations Board
Federal Emergency Relief Administration
Civil Works Administration
Public Works Administration
pump priming
Civilian Conservation Corps
Farm Credit Administration
Agricultural Adjustment Administration
Home Owners Loan Corporation
Federal Housing Administration
Tennessee Valley Authority
American Liberty League

Reviewing the Main Ideas

Section 1
1. What was the inspiration for the New Deal?
2. What were the general goals of the New Deal?

Section 2
1. What steps did Roosevelt take to end the banking crisis that faced the nation?
2. How did he try to reform the stock market?
3. How did Roosevelt try to end deflation?

Section 3
1. What were the goals of the NIRA and the NRA? Why did many business owners oppose them?
2. How did the New Deal help organized labor?

Section 4
1. What did the FERA and CWA accomplish?
2. What is "pump priming," and how did the PWA try to use this principle?
3. What problems were faced by farmers, and how did the New Deal try to help?
4. What did the TVA accomplish, and why was it criticized?

Section 5
1. Why did many conservatives object to the New Deal?
2. Describe three radical plans to end the depression.

Special History Skills:
Applying Economics to History
"Pump priming" by the PWA and other New Deal agencies was based on an economic effect called the "multiplier effect": each dollar added to the economy creates more dollars as it travels through the economy. For instance, suppose the Smith family receives $100. The Smiths will spend that money on rent, groceries, clothes, etc. The people who receive this money will also spend it. Not all the money each family receives will be spent, however. Some will be saved.

Let's say that, on the average, Americans spend $75 out of every $100 (or 75%) and save the rest of it. The percentage of dollars spent is called the "marginal propensity to consume," or MPC.

Now imagine that, in our example above, the Smith family receives $100 in "Round 1" and spends it in "Round 2." The people who receive that money spent it in "Round 3" and so on. The table shows how, if the MPC is 75%, all the "rounds" add up to create $400 out of the Smiths' original $100.

Round	Amount Spent If MPC Is 75%
1	100.00
2	75.00
3	56.25
4	42.18
5	31.64
6	23.73
7	17.79
8	13.35
9	10.00
10	7.50
All remaining rounds	22.56
Total	$400.00

In this example, $100 has created $400. Thus, the "multiplier" is 4. If the MPC changes, the multiplier will change. Economists use the following formula to show how the MPC affects the multiplier:

$$\text{multiplier} = \frac{1}{1 - \text{MPC}}$$

In the example above, the multiplier $= \frac{1}{1 - .75}$ or 4. You now have enough information to answer the following questions:

1. What would be the multiplier if the MPC were 90%?
2. How much money would be added to the economy if a worker earned $100 and the MPC were 90%?

Other Skill Activities

1. Get a job

Research the alphabet agencies and decide which one you would most like to work for during the Depression and why. Give a five-minute report on the reasons for your decision.

2. Economics collage

Make a collage of pictures, headlines, charts, and graphs which illustrate present-day economic problems and attempts to solve them.

3. Fireside chat

Write a five-minute script for one of FDR's fireside chats, then give it to the class as if you were on radio.

Thinking Critically

1. Were the alphabet agencies merely make-work projects, or did they fulfill legitimate needs? Explain.
2. What laws or public works or ideas from the New Deal affect our lives today? Explain.

Further Reading

Robert Penn Warren. *All the King's Men.* Random House, 1960. Written in 1946, this novel has a plot which closely follows Huey P. Long's life.

John Steinbeck. *The Grapes of Wrath.* Penguin Press, 1976. A classic novel of an Oklahoma family's struggles during the Depression.

William Loren Katz. *An Album of the Great Depression.* Franklin Watts, Inc., 1978. Simply written, with many photos, this book focuses on the years between the crash and World War II.

TEST YOURSELF

WRITE YOUR ANSWERS ON A SEPARATE SHEET OF PAPER.

True or False

Mark T if the statement is true, F if it is false. Rewrite the italicized words in all false statements so that they are true.

1. New Deal reforms had *no precedents* in American history.
2. The goals of the New Deal were *relief, recovery, and reform.*
3. The Bank Holiday was meant to end *panic withdrawals by depositors.*
4. The goal of the SEC was to *restore the Dust Bowl lands.*
5. The main step taken to initiate industrial recovery was the *NIRA.*
6. The NRA was declared unconstitutional because it *limited competition.*
7. The FERA funneled relief money to *state and local governments.*
8. The CWA directly employed people in *public works projects.*
9. The American Liberty League felt the New Deal was spending too much money and *hurting private enterprise.*
10. *Francis E. Townsend* wanted to make "every man a king."

Matching

Select the letter of the item that best matches each description below.

1. built dams and produced electricity
2. controlled stock speculation
3. joined government and business in fighting the depression
4. conducted elections to establish union representation
5. funneled money to state and local governments for payment to needy people
6. directly employed needy people
7. employed young men to replant forests and build parks
8. helped finance farm mortgages
9. paid farmers not to produce a surplus
10. helped home owners meet mortgage payments

a. HOLC	**e.** NLB	**i.** CCC
b. FCA	**f.** NIRA	**j.** TVA
c. AAA	**g.** SEC	**k.** MVA
d. FERA	**h.** CWA	

Chapter 29   1935–1940

THE SECOND NEW DEAL

As the year 1934 turned into 1935, the Great Depression stubbornly persisted in America. Although the New Deal had taken important steps toward restoring the nation's economy, prosperity had not returned. In 1932, 24% of the labor force were unemployed; in 1934, 22% were still unemployed. The millions of unemployed workers, elderly people, farm laborers, and sharecroppers were still suffering acutely from the continuing years of depression. Understandably, these Americans wanted an end to their suffering. Soon some of them began listening more closely to the provocative voices of Senator Huey Long, Dr. Francis Townsend, and the "radio priest," Father Coughlin.

Roosevelt faced the challenge of the continuing depression by beginning to turn the New Deal in a more liberal direction. In his State of the Union speech of 1935, he admitted that the New Deal had not accomplished all that he had hoped. The President spoke of the importance of giving economic security to the aged and of assisting the needy. He wanted the New Deal to help reform some of America's institutions and traditions. The depression, he believed, showed that such social reform was needed.

In this chapter you will study the goals and effects of further New Deal reform laws. You will also study the strengthening of American labor unions, Roosevelt's "court-packing" fight, and the impact of the New Deal on the nation's minorities. And you will learn how the New Deal still affects Americans today.

Sections in This Chapter
1. The Increasing Emphasis on Social Reform
2. The Growth of Labor Unions
3. FDR and the Supreme Court
4. Minorities and the New Deal
5. The Legacy of the New Deal

Opposite: This charming pavilion at the 1939 New York World's Fair represented optimism in the nation's economic recovery.

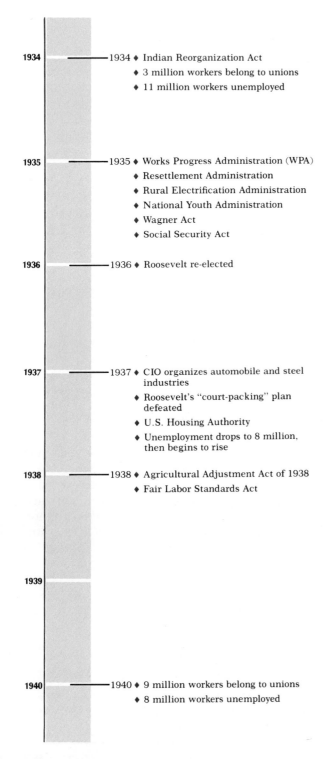

1934 — 1934 ♦ Indian Reorganization Act
        ♦ 3 million workers belong to unions
        ♦ 11 million workers unemployed

1935 — 1935 ♦ Works Progress Administration (WPA)
        ♦ Resettlement Administration
        ♦ Rural Electrification Administration
        ♦ National Youth Administration
        ♦ Wagner Act
        ♦ Social Security Act

1936 — 1936 ♦ Roosevelt re-elected

1937 — 1937 ♦ CIO organizes automobile and steel
             industries
        ♦ Roosevelt's "court-packing" plan
          defeated
        ♦ U.S. Housing Authority
        ♦ Unemployment drops to 8 million,
          then begins to rise

1938 — 1938 ♦ Agricultural Adjustment Act of 1938
        ♦ Fair Labor Standards Act

1939

1940 — 1940 ♦ 9 million workers belong to unions
        ♦ 8 million workers unemployed

1. THE INCREASING EMPHASIS ON SOCIAL REFORM

One of the most important new steps Roosevelt took was to provide some monetary security for citizens who could not provide it for themselves. Throughout much of American history, the responsibility for the care of the elderly and the handicapped had been assumed by the families of those affected. For those whose families could not provide for them or for those who had no families, the only roads to survival were working until they died, or going to private, state, or county poorhouses. But during the Great Depression, city and county resources were so strained that local poorhouses could no longer provide even minimal care for the needy. A few states passed laws to try to deal with this serious problem, but the nation lacked a unified plan to help those needing assistance.

The Social Security Act

To remedy this serious situation, Congress passed the **Social Security Act** in 1935. This law was designed to provide a system of old-age insurance which required most American workers and their employers to participate. The Social Security Act provided for monthly pensions for those over age 65, beginning in 1942. The pensions were funded by taxes on the wages of the workers and by a 1% tax on the payrolls of the employers. After 1937, employers had to pay a 3% tax.

The act also funneled money to the states for the care of dependent children and the handicapped. Another part of the Social Security package provided joint state-national funding for the care of those already over 65.

Although Roosevelt considered the Social Security Act the "supreme achievement" of the New Deal, the program had its flaws. Many of the benefits, ranging from $10 to $85 a month in 1942, were inadequate even in those days, when prices were much lower than they are today. The act also omitted coverage of many groups of workers such as farm employees, civilian sailors, and domestic employees, who, because their jobs seldom provided benefits of any sort, were often most in need of aid. Still, the creation of the Social

Security system was a milestone in the history of the United States. It reflected the growing opinion that the federal government had a responsibility to help the elderly as well as those put out of work by the unpredictable nature of the economy. In the 1980s, the Social Security program would come under a different kind of criticism, as you'll see in Section 5 of this chapter.

The WPA and Other Work Relief Efforts

Roosevelt struck another blow at the Great Depression when he signed a law passed by Congress to establish the **Works Progress Administration,** or WPA. Harry Hopkins was made administrator of the WPA, which began its work with an appropriation of $5 billion. Hopkins' goal was the employment of 5 million of America's unemployed, mostly in public works projects. This goal was never achieved, but more than 2 million people were employed by the WPA in any given month. The WPA built about 13,000 playgrounds, 6,000 schools, and 2,500 hospitals. In addition, 78,000 bridges were built, 800 airports were improved, and more than half a million miles of roads were constructed or repaired.

As a result of the influence of **Eleanor Roosevelt,** the WPA also provided jobs for thousands of artists, actors, and other unemployed white-collar workers. The Federal Writers' Project, for instance, put writers to work writing state and city guides, handbooks about America's rivers, and many other types of historical and informative publications. The Federal Art Projects employed out-of-work artists, many of whom painted murals on the walls of post offices and other public buildings. Under the WPA, nearly 10,000 works of art were produced, most of them depicting scenes of our American heritage. Actors and directors found work with the Federal Theatre Project, which staged plays across the country, many times in locations where live performances had never been seen before. Approximately 4,000 musical performances a month were given under this project.

During its existence, the WPA spent more than $11 billion on 250,000 public projects. Though

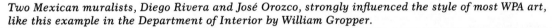

Two Mexican muralists, Diego Rivera and José Orozco, strongly influenced the style of most WPA art, like this example in the Department of Interior by William Gropper.

there was wasted money and effort, the WPA provided a fresh chance for many who would otherwise have continued in the ranks of the jobless.

The Second Agricultural Adjustment Act

As you saw in Chapter 28, in 1933 the Supreme Court declared the Agricultural Adjustment Act of 1933 unconstitutional. The drought year of 1934 had been a low point in farm production. By 1937, however, farm production had greatly increased and this, in turn, could have led to lower farm prices and a return to the severe unemployment levels of 1932–1934. Congress sought to prevent such an occurrence by passing the second **Agricultural Adjustment Act** in 1938.

The second AAA attempted to raise farm income in two ways: (1) by restricting production, and (2) by paying subsidies to farmers. The goal of the law was to restore farm prosperity and purchasing power to what it had been during the favorable period from 1909 to 1914. This earlier period became the yardstick for comparison and was called the **"parity base."** How well farmers were doing in any future year was determined by asking whether the prices they received for their crops were above or below "parity." If market prices were below parity, it was believed, the farmer probably spent more than he or she made. When prices were above parity, the farmer's income was probably more than his or her expenses.

The second AAA also encouraged soil conservation by paying farmers benefits for each acre removed from crop production and planted with soil-conserving crops such as clover and alfalfa.

To answer the immediate problem of surplus crops, the new AAA made provisions for the storage of surplus crops, to be used in years when harvests were low. Farmers were loaned money for the stored crops, and the loan was to be repaid when the crops were sold. This feature of the act was very much like the subtreasury plan that the Populists had proposed 40 years earlier.

Other Agencies of the Second New Deal

Other new agencies were created to supplement the WPA in the continuing struggle against the Great Depression. The **Rural Electrification Administration**, or REA, was established to lend money at low interest rates for the building of power lines in areas never before served by electricity. Millions of farmers had electrical power for the first time for their homes, barns, and other buildings, as well as for electrical farm equipment. Before REA, only 10% of American farms had electricity, but afterwards, 90% did so.

The **National Youth Administration**, or NYA, was designed to help both high-school and college students find part-time jobs so that they could continue their educations. Some 600,000 college students and more than 500,000 high-school students found work with the NYA. In addition, the NYA assisted over 2.5 million young people who were not in school.

The **Resettlement Administration**, headed by one of Roosevelt's early brain trust advisers, Rexford Tugwell, was established to place farmers on more productive land. It also created three new "greenbelt" towns near Washington, D.C.; Cincinnati, Ohio; and Milwaukee, Wisconsin. These were model small towns, located in rural areas near places of employment in the cities.

The Resettlement Administration was largely unsuccessful, due to a limited budget and other

LIFE IN AMERICA

ELEANOR ROOSEVELT'S INFLUENCE ON THE NEW DEAL

Eleanor Roosevelt was probably the nation's most controversial wife of a President. Throughout her life, she was an active reformer and supporter of unpopular causes. Millions loved her: in the 1950s, American women consistently voted her the woman they most admired. To those who disliked FDR, however, she was a symbol of everything wrong with the New Deal.

Her uncle was President Theodore Roosevelt, and FDR was her fourth cousin. In the 1920s, Eleanor Roosevelt became an active political campaigner for FDR. During his presidency, she was one of his closest advisers, a key figure in establishing policies for the CWA, the WPA, the NYA, and other agencies. She fought to win jobs and equal pay for women, and she actively lobbied for civil rights laws at a time when support for racial equality was extremely controversial.

Constantly traveling on fact-finding trips, she acted as FDR's "eyes and ears," visiting communities, relief projects, schools, and citizens' groups. One famous *New*

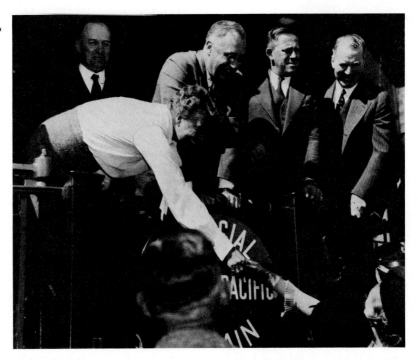

Yorker cartoon depicted a coal miner saying to his co-worker: "For gosh sakes, here comes Mrs. Roosevelt!" Later she did go down in a coal mine. She also reached the public through twice-weekly radio broadcasts, press conferences, a daily newspaper column, and a monthly magazine column. To millions she represented the innovative energy and humanitarian spirit of the New Deal.

---

difficulties. Later it was replaced by the Farm Security Administration, or FSA. This agency loaned money to farmers to rehabilitate run-down farmsteads and to some farm tenants to purchase farms of their own.

Although the New Dealers focused a great deal of their attention on farm problems, they also tried to solve some of the problems of the urban poor. Under the **United States Housing Authority,** created by Congress in 1937, a sum of $500 million was earmarked for low-cost housing loans to local governments. The money was used to build housing units and to clear the slums festering in almost every large American city. By the end of 1940, nearly 350 USHA projects had been completed.

SECTION 1 REVIEW

Identify: Social Security Act, Works Progress Administration (WPA), Eleanor Roosevelt, Agricultural Adjustment Act of 1938, parity base, Rural Electrification Administration, National Youth Administration, Resettlement Administration, United States Housing Authority

Main Ideas

1. What were the provisions of the Social Security Act?
2. Describe the role played by the WPA during the depression.
3. How did the "Second New Deal" try to help farmers? The urban poor?

2. THE GROWTH OF LABOR UNIONS

As you learned in the last chapter, Roosevelt's efforts to enable labor unions to organize through Section 7a of the NIRA were blocked when the Supreme Court declared the act unconstitutional. Consequently, in 1935 he signed into law the Wagner Act, which created the National Labor Relations Board (NLRB). The NLRB was authorized to hold elections in factories to determine whether or not workers wanted to unionize, and if so, which union would represent them.

The Wagner Act served as a green light for the growth of American labor unions. It also helped protect this growing labor movement. The American Federation of Labor, headed by William Green, was the beneficiary of much of this growth. The AFL, however, was founded in the late 19th century and was made up largely of **craft unions**, while most of the new growth in union membership was in **industrial unions**.

A craft union is an organization representing one craft or skill, such as carpentry or plumbing. An industrial union, on the other hand, is made up of all the workers in one industry, such as all the workers in mining or automobile manufacturing, regardless of the job (craft) each worker has.

John L. Lewis and the CIO

In 1935, the **Committee for Industrial Organization (CIO)**, headed by the colorful and aggressive **John L. Lewis,** president of the United Mine Workers, was formed within the American Federation of Labor. Because the AFL leadership opposed the organizing of workers along industrial lines, the CIO members were suspended in 1936 and, in 1937, expelled. This did not stop them from conducting union organizing drives in two huge industries: automobile and steel.

The strength of an industrial union that organized every worker in a shop regardless of job or skill was quickly demonstrated when the United Automobile Workers, formed in 1935, organized a **sitdown strike** against General Motors in the Fisher Body Plant in Flint, Michigan. The event that sparked the strike was GM's refusal to engage in collective bargaining or recognize the union. In a sitdown strike, the workers refuse to leave their places of employment, thus keeping the employer from bringing in non-union workers to replace them. The UAW and General Motors came to terms in February of 1937 with General Motors meeting the demand for union recognition as well as most of the union's other demands. Soon thereafter, the UAW organized the workers at Chrysler.

As head of the CIO, Lewis was also busy in the smoke-blackened cities of Pennsylvania, where he and the head of the United Steel Workers Union, Phillip Murray, organized workers at the U.S. Steel Corporation. When the strength of the union became apparent, the company, which had long resisted recognizing the union, decided to negotiate a contract, thus avoiding a strike. In South Chicago and Gary, Indiana, however, Republic Steel refused to recognize the union. In May 1937, police attacked demonstrating strikers with guns, tear gas, and clubs. Ten strikers were killed, and many were injured.

The success of industrial unions in the auto and steel industries began a chain reaction in other industries throughout the nation. The United Rubber Workers won an important victory after an eight-week strike against the Firestone Tire and Rubber Company. The United Electrical and Radio Workers Union was recognized by Philco, General Electric, and other giant electrical appliance manufacturers.

In 1938, the CIO, still headed by Lewis, changed its name to the Congress of Industrial Organizations, thus keeping the same initials— the CIO. Despite the split in labor's ranks, the union movement was stronger by 1939 than it had ever been in United States history. Almost 9 million workers belonged to either the AFL or the CIO. The split between the AFL and the CIO lasted until 1955, when the two organizations merged to form the new AFL–CIO.

The Fair Labor Standards Act

An additional boost for workers came in 1938 with the passage of the **Fair Labor Standards Act,** also known as the "wages and hours law." This law provided for a 40¢-per-hour minimum wage and a 40-hour maximum work week in businesses engaged in interstate commerce. The law allowed a three- to eight-year time period for the new regulations to take effect. The act also contained a child labor provision, forbidding labor by children under 16 years old.

The Election of 1936

In 1936 the Democrats nominated President Roosevelt for a second term. In his acceptance speech, Roosevelt prophetically told his audience:

There is a mysterious cycle in human events. To some generations much is given. Of other generations much is expected. This generation of Americans has a rendezvous with destiny.

The Republicans chose as their candidate the friendly and competent governor of Kansas, Alfred M. Landon. The supporters of Townsend, Coughlin, and those who had followed Huey Long before his death united under the banner of the Union party. North Dakota Congressman William Lemke was chosen as the Union party candidate.

While Republicans spoke out against Roosevelt and the New Deal, the Republican platform included many of the New Deal programs and ideas. The Republicans said, however, that they could carry out the programs more effectively than the Democrats were doing under Roosevelt. The Democratic platform stressed continuation of the New Deal. Lemke and his followers in the Union party put forth a platform which tried to appeal to the demands of most of the radicals, such as Townsend and Coughlin.

President Roosevelt's chief political adviser, "Big Jim" Farley, predicted that the President would win a massive victory on election day, with only the states of Maine and Vermont voting Republican. When Americans went to the polls on November 3, they proved Farley correct. In the election of 1936, Roosevelt won every state except Maine and Vermont, collecting 523 electoral votes to Landon's 8 votes. Lemke polled 900,000 votes and the various socialists and communists received fewer than 300,000 votes combined.

SECTION 2 REVIEW

Identify: craft unions, industrial unions, Committee for Industrial Organization (CIO), John L. Lewis, sitdown strike, Fair Labor Standards Act

Main Ideas

1. How did the Wagner Act influence the growth of the organized labor movement?
2. Why did the CIO form? What happened to it?
3. Describe the candidates, issues, and outcome of the election of 1936.

3. FDR AND THE SUPREME COURT

President Roosevelt felt that his overwhelming victory in the 1936 election was a signal from the American people to continue the New Deal. But how could he continue it when the Supreme Court kept declaring unconstitutional key programs such as the NIRA and the AAA? FDR believed that before his programs could go forward, he would have to have a friendly Court.

The Composition of the Court

Of the nine men on the Supreme Court, seven had been appointed by Republican Presidents. Since Roosevelt's election in 1932, none of the justices had left the bench. Thus the President did not have the opportunity to appoint justices who supported his programs. Several of the justices were past 70, and one, who had been on the Court since Taft's administration, was 75. Some people felt that the age of the justices meant that their interpretations of the law were out of date. Others felt, however, that the age of the justices indicated that experience would help them interpret the law in the best way.

The Court was composed of four conservatives, three liberals, and two justices who sometimes voted with the conservatives and at other times sided with the liberals. It was Roosevelt's hope to increase the number of liberal judges on the Supreme Court.

Roosevelt's Proposal and the Outcry

The Constitution does not specify the number of Supreme Court justices or their age of retirement. According to Article III of the Constitution, Congress has the power to make rules regarding the Court. In the past, the Court has had as few as five justices and as many as ten.

Roosevelt consulted only with his Attorney General as he drew up a plan to reform the Court. The President's proposal contained plans to reform the lower courts of the federal judiciary, adding more justices so as to speed up the trying of cases, but the main thrust of the scheme was to alter the composition of the Supreme Court. The Judiciary Reorganization bill that Roosevelt submitted to

Congress in February of 1937 asked that the President be authorized to appoint one new justice to the Supreme Court for every sitting justice who had reached age 70 and failed to retire. The proposal limited the Court's size to 15 members. Roosevelt justified his plan by stating that the Court needed "a constant infusion of new blood" to "face modern complexities."

Almost as soon as the President's plan was made public, a tidal wave of alarm washed through both houses of Congress and across the country. Conservative Republicans accused the President of **"court packing"** and of tinkering with the independence of one of America's most sacred institutions. Many prominent members of Roosevelt's own party added their voices to the chorus of criticism. Throughout the spring and summer of 1937, the fight over the President's plan continued. Finally, in July, the bill was defeated.

The President stated that he "lost the battle but won the war" in the Court fight because the Court, even before the bill's defeat, began to reverse itself. In several decisions the justices upheld administration-sponsored bills. But Roosevelt's attempt to "pack the court" had cost him severely. Not only did he suffer a major defeat, but he divided the Democratic party as well. He also lost some support from those who had given him unquestioning backing earlier, making it harder to win laws in Congress. Few major reform laws were passed in his second term.

The composition of the Court soon changed with the resignation of several of the older justices. Roosevelt was then able to appoint justices to the Court who shared many of his views about the programs of the New Deal. As a result, the Court's decisions were less conservative than at any time since World War I.

SECTION 3 REVIEW

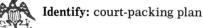

Identify: court-packing plan

Main Ideas

1. What was Roosevelt's plan to change the Supreme Court, and why did he propose it?
2. Why did the plan meet so much opposition?
3. What did Roosevelt mean when he said that he "lost the battle but won the war" over the Court?
4. What were some of the results of Roosevelt's attempt to "pack the court"?

4. MINORITIES AND THE NEW DEAL

Among those hardest hit during the depression years were black Americans, and the early New Deal programs failed to aid them. For example, NRA codes did not apply to most of the jobs that black Americans held. Most of the FERA relief money did not get to blacks because the funds were usually administered locally. In areas where prejudice against blacks was greatest, local relief officials often ignored black needs.

But some New Deal programs did help blacks, and most of these new opportunities grew out of Eleanor Roosevelt's constant efforts to secure fair treatment for black Americans. As a result of her efforts, the National Youth Administration, for example, helped thousands of blacks with educational assistance. Likewise, the Civilian Conservation Corps employed some 200,000 black workers, and many rural black families received help from New Deal farm agencies.

Another step was taken when FDR began to appoint blacks to positions in the New Deal. Among these leaders was **Mary McLeod Bethune,** a college president who became Director of the Division of Negro Affairs in the National Youth Administration. Other prominent blacks in the New Deal included Robert L. Vann, a lawyer who was named as Special Assistant to the United States Attorney General; E. K. Jones, who served in the Commerce Department; William Hastie, who was appointed by the President to a federal judgeship in the Virgin Islands; and Robert C. Weaver, who was an adviser to the Department of the Interior. Many other blacks, including economists, engineers, lawyers, and architects, found within the New Deal agencies jobs which had never before been open to them.

During the 1930s, the South was very badly hit. Not only was it poorer than the North to begin with, but it was made poorer by the depression and the great drought of 1932–1936. As a result, many southern blacks moved to the northern cities of New York, Detroit, and Chicago, as well as to Los Angeles. The Great Depression saw the largest-yet migration of American blacks out of the South. The war years of 1941–1945 would see an even greater movement.

The efforts by the Democratic administration to aid blacks caused black Americans to turn from the party of Lincoln, the Republicans. In 1932 most of the black vote went to Hoover. In 1936, however, blacks voted overwhelmingly for Roosevelt and the Democrats. Black Americans have generally been an important source of Democratic strength ever since the New Deal.

Indians and the Great Depression

America's 250 to 300 Indian tribes were having serious economic problems before the Great Depression struck the rest of the country. In 1924, all Indians born in the United States were granted U.S. citizenship. Other policies toward them had not changed, however, and they continued to suffer from attempts to destroy their cultures. Furthermore, unemployment was widespread on the Indian reservations, and many Indian families lived on the edge of starvation.

As you learned in Chapter 18, the Dawes Act of 1887 tried to make the Indians just like white Americans by dissolving the tribes and pressuring Indians to become independent farmers on individual plots of land. Such a concept directly violated Indian traditions. In addition, much of the land that the Indians were supposed to farm was dry and infertile. Furthermore, the Bureau of Indian Affairs, which administered the Indians, did not serve their interests. By 1934, almost 90 million acres of land held by Indians in 1887 had been taken back or sold to white settlers.

Thus the Dawes Act had failed on all accounts. It trampled on Indian traditions and customs. It ignored the fact that most of the nation's 330,000 Indians did not want the white Americans' ways forced on them. And it did not help the Indians to survive in the economy of the United States. Under these circumstances, the majority of Indians lived in sickness, illiteracy, and poverty, with little hope for the future.

To help overcome these conditions, in 1934 Congress passed the Wheeler-Howard Act, usually known as the **Indian Reorganization Act.** This act stopped land allotments to individuals and provided for tribal ownership of Indian lands. The act also established schools, authorized the tribes to re-create their own governments if they so desired, and provided for loans for Indian business efforts. The law also stopped the practice of destroying tribal identity by forcing unwanted ways on the Indians. The Indian Reorganization Act did not solve all of the problems of the nation's Indians, but it did end many of the worst abuses of the past.

President Roosevelt appointed **John Collier** as Commissioner of Indian Affairs in 1933. Collier's work, along with the Indian Reorganization Act, made the New Deal years a better time than previous decades had been for American Indians. Land holdings which had melted away during the years since the Dawes Act began to increase under the New Deal. Between 1933 and 1938, for example, about 2.5 million acres were added or restored to Indian holdings.

Mexican Americans and the New Deal

Thousands of the nation's Mexican American citizens were placed in desperate circumstances by the depression. Many of these men and women were employed as migrant workers, traveling from place to place around the country to harvest crops. Most lived in substandard housing, and because of the transient nature of their work, most owned little property. Many Mexican American children did not have the opportunity for even the most elementary education, and migrant incomes were extremely low.

The New Deal failed to help this group of Americans. Most of the programs did not touch the migrants, though some efforts were made through the Resettlement Administration. The terrible conditions these Americans faced continued until long after the Great Depression had ended for most of the rest of the nation.

SECTION 4 REVIEW

 Identify: Mary McLeod Bethune, Indian Reorganization Act, John Collier

Main Ideas
1. What problems did black Americans face during the depression? What role did Eleanor Roosevelt play in securing fairer treatment for blacks under the New Deal?
2. What political change took place among American blacks in the New Deal period?
3. How did the New Deal help Indians?
4. What problems facing Mexican Americans did the New Deal fail to address?

5. THE LEGACY OF THE NEW DEAL

By 1940, although more than 8 million Americans remained unemployed (see graph, facing page), the United States had regained some of its economic strength, and Americans their optimistic attitude. During the years between 1933 and 1940, Franklin Roosevelt's New Deal brought great changes to America. Almost every citizen, it seemed, was affected one way or another by the programs, agencies, and laws that came from the President's efforts to restore prosperity.

Two Sides of the New Deal
Though the New Deal was never able to fully restore economic prosperity, steps toward that goal were made. A comparison of America in 1932 and in 1939 demonstrates this improvement. In agriculture, farm prices were up; in industry, profits were higher; among workers, unemployment, though still extensive, was down. Per capita income (after taxes) had risen by $246 above the 1932 level, though it still did not equal the 1929 level.

These, of course, were the gains. On the other side of the ledger were some important liabilities for which the New Deal was responsible. The Roosevelt years saw an immense increase in the federal debt. In 1930 the public debt was $16 billion; in 1940 it was $42 billion. The New Deal created a large government bureaucracy to administer the new programs and agencies. There was a great deal of waste and duplication, and some New Deal programs limited the freedom of private enterprise.

The Expansion of Government
Probably the most significant aspect of the New Deal that still affects Americans today was the rapid expansion of government functions and responsibilities. During the New Deal, government agencies entered into almost every area of the country's economic life. Nearly all this government activity was designed to help the millions of depression victims, such as unemployed workers and disaster-stricken farmers.

By 1939 government spending at the local, state, and national levels made up 15% of the Gross National Product.* In 1929 government expenditures accounted for only 3% of the GNP. This widespread government spending continues today. In 1982, for example, government spending accounted for about 20% of the GNP.

Social Security for Those in Need
Another legacy of the New Deal is America's Social Security system. The original Social Security Act of 1935, which provided for old age pensions, unemployment insurance, and aid to dependent children, has been expanded over the years until it offers many more programs for the needy.

Social Security is today considered by millions of citizens as their chief means of support after retirement. However, the income provided by Social Security benefits has not been able to protect retired citizens against mounting inflation. In addition, so many citizens are now collecting Social Security that the entire system is in financial jeopardy. In order for current workers to support those retired, the government is taking a larger and larger portion out of already heavily taxed paychecks. And since today's Social Security taxes pay for today's retired citizens, who will pay for the retirement of the current working generations? The Social Security system is thus in great trouble, threatening the old-age security of both current and future retirees.

Wages and Working Conditions
Labor unions were active in America for many years before the Roosevelt administration took office in 1933. It was during the New Deal, however, that organized labor made its greatest gains. First under Section 7a of the NIRA and then through the Wagner Act, labor unions took important steps that resulted in higher wages and better conditions for many working men and women. The passage of the 1938 "wages and hours" law and the reform of child labor were also noteworthy steps in American labor history.

There were some negative effects of the organized labor movement, however. Many workers, such as those in agriculture and in other non-union jobs, did not benefit from the efforts of organized labor. And while workers in labor unions earned higher wages, these increased costs

*Gross National Product (GNP) value of all goods and services produced in a nation during a certain period of time.

to management were passed along in the form of higher prices to all consumers—including those who were not in unions and whose wages had not increased.

Conservation of Natural Resources

As a result of the efforts of the Civilian Conservation Corps and the work of the TVA, much of the nation's natural beauty and many of its precious resources were saved during the New Deal. The CCC planted millions of trees, thereby renewing the forest cover of thousands of timber-stripped acres. Hundreds of parks were built or renewed by the same agency. Many historical sites were also preserved or restored by the CCC.

The TVA not only sent millions of kilowatts of electricity humming over wires to remote areas, but also added to the productivity of the entire seven-state region it served. The TVA's flood control and land reclamation projects brought lasting improvements to the area. However, many conservatives continued to oppose the TVA. They questioned the wisdom and fairness of government ownership of the project in a country dedicated to the principles of free enterprise and business competition.

Financial and Banking Reform

Unrestrained stock-market speculation and badly managed banks combined to deal a fatal blow to the savings of millions of Americans between 1929 and 1932. During the Roosevelt administration some of the earliest measures were designed to avoid these same problems in the future. The Federal Deposit Insurance Corporation, or FDIC, which was created during the early New Deal days, still insures the money of those who have placed their funds in FDIC member banks. The initial insurance protection of $5,000 of savings by the FDIC now extends to deposits of $100,000.

The Securities and Exchange Commission, created in 1934, continues to oversee transactions on the stock exchanges of the country. The SEC protects investors against illegality in stock and bond issues. It monitors financial institutions that deal with members of the stock exchange. And the SEC has supervisory authority over investment trusts and regulates the use of credit in margin transactions.

The New Deal's Place in History

The years of the New Deal were one of the most influential peacetime periods in American history. The activity and power of the national government, as well as the public debt, was greatly increased during the New Deal years. During those same years perhaps more persons were helped and aided in a humanitarian way than in any other time in America's past.

Although the New Deal did not succeed in ending the Great Depression, millions of citizens who lived through the period remember New Deal programs as helping them and giving them hope for the future. Perhaps this hope was the most important legacy of the New Deal.

SECTION 5 REVIEW

 Identify: Gross National Product

Main Ideas
1. List specific ways in which the New Deal made progress over the years against the Great Depression.
2. What were some negative effects of the New Deal?
3. Which New Deal agencies had a long-term effect on conservation in America?
4. List two agencies in the fields of banking and finance which have their origins in the New Deal.

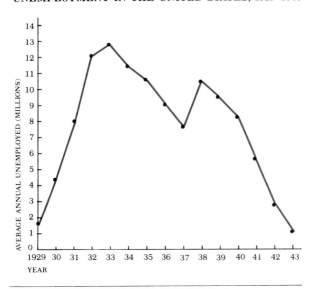

UNEMPLOYMENT IN THE UNITED STATES, 1929–1943

CHAPTER 29 REVIEW

Key Terms
Explain the meaning of each of the following terms:

Social Security Act
Works Progress Administration
Agricultural Adjustment Act of 1938
parity base
Rural Electrification Administration
National Youth Administration
Resettlement Administration
United States Housing Authority
craft unions
industrial unions
Committee for Industrial Organization
sitdown strike
Fair Labor Standards Act
court-packing plan
Indian Reorganization Act
Gross National Product

Reviewing the Main Ideas
Section 1
1. What were some provisions of the Social Security Act of 1935?
2. What was the role of the WPA?
3. How did the Second New Deal help farmers? The urban poor?

Section 2
1. How did the Wagner Act influence the growth of the labor union movement?
2. Describe the basic split between the AFL and the CIO.
3. How did the efforts of the unions to organize the auto and steel industries affect the union movement in other industries?
4. Describe briefly the candidates, issues and results of the election of 1936.

Section 3
1. Why did Roosevelt propose to alter the Supreme Court? How did he propose to do it?
2. What were some of the results of Roosevelt's attempt to "pack the court"?

Section 4
1. Why did the New Deal win blacks away from the Republican party?
2. How did the New Deal help Indians?
3. What problems did Mexican Americans face during the depression?

Section 5
1. How did the New Deal make progress against the Great Depression? How did it fail?
2. What New Deal programs or approaches survive in government today?

Special History Skills:
Political Labels
The terms "radical," "liberal," "moderate," "conservative," and "reactionary" often confuse people. Useful as generalizations, these political labels tend to confuse because a person may be a "conservative" regarding one issue and a "liberal" regarding another. Rarely, if ever, can you expect a political label to describe a person's views on all things. With this in mind, an analogy may be useful. Try thinking of these political labels in relation to an automobile's automatic transmission.

The Neutral (N) position could represent the "moderate" center in which the car could be pushed either forward or backward. Moderates will sometimes favor and sometimes oppose changes.

In the "conservative" Park (P) position, the unmoving car will be held in place, representing the conservatives' desire to preserve the existing society.

"Reactionaries," in their desire to return to an earlier time and undo recent changes could be represented by the Reverse (R) position which will move the car backwards.

Low (L), in which the car moves slowly forward could correspond with the "liberals," who favor gradual changes in society.

Those favoring more rapid change, the "radicals," could then be compared to the Drive (D) position which will move the car forward at high speed.

Obviously, people using these political labels are expressing their personal opinions. What is conservative to one person is radical to another. The five political terms, though commonly used, are merely shortcuts and labels, not precise categories. This is why they are so confusing.

Write a brief essay explaining which of these five political terms describes the New Deal. Give specific reasons why you think so.

Other Skill Activities

1. **WPA art**

   Assemble a picture presentation for your class, showing artistic projects completed for the WPA. Are there any examples of these works in your town?

2. **Eleanor Roosevelt**

   Research the life of Eleanor Roosevelt and give a report to the class.

3. **New Deal crossword puzzle**

   Make a crossword puzzle out of the names and terms that appear in this chapter.

4. **Union growth**

   Choose a large labor union that has been in existence since at least 1927. Research the membership figures. Graph the figures in five-year intervals. Was there an increase or decrease in union membership during the New Deal?

5. **Everyday life**

   For one week make a list of the government agencies started during the New Deal which directly or indirectly affect your life and the lives of members of your family. (For instance, upon entering a bank you may see a sign in the window which says that deposits are insured by the FDIC.)

Thinking Critically

1. Today millions of America's older citizens depend on Social Security payments for their well-being. Do you think this is good or bad? What alternative possibilities exist?

2. Do you believe that the federal government should be permitted to regulate minimum wages and maximum hours, or should an employer be free to decide whatever he/she wants in regard to these things? Discuss.

3. The Roosevelt administration tried to solve the problems of the day. However, one legacy of the New Deal era is the greatly expanded role of the federal government, accompanied by a huge national debt. Discuss the pros and cons of the New Deal era in terms of its impact on succeeding generations.

Further Reading

Ann Banks. *First-Person America*. Alfred A. Knopf, 1980. Oral histories based on Federal Writers' Project interviews during the 1930s.

Harvard Sitkoff. *A New Deal for Blacks*. Oxford University Press, 1978. The importance of the black vote to the Democratic party and Eleanor Roosevelt's contribution to civil rights are considered here.

Francis V. O'Connor. *The New Deal Art Projects*. Smithsonian Institution Press, 1972. Many pictures show the contribution WPA made to our culture through its support of artists.

TEST YOURSELF

WRITE YOUR ANSWERS ON A SEPARATE SHEET OF PAPER.

Matching

Write the letter of the item that best matches each description below. Some letters can be used more than once.

1. provided monthly pensions financed by a payroll tax and employers' tax
2. helped high-school and college students find part-time jobs so they could continue their educations
3. employed artists, writers, and actors
4. loaned farmers money to store surplus crops
5. restricted agricultural production and paid subsidies to farmers
6. encouraged soil conservation by paying farmers to plant soil-conserving crops
7. provided monthly funds for handicapped people and dependent children
8. loaned money for the building of power lines in rural areas
9. constructed three greenbelt towns to serve as model communities
10. built schools, hospitals, airports, roads, and other public works

a. REA	d. Social Security
b. AAA	e. Resettlement Administration
c. NYA	f. WPA

Listing

List three problems the New Deal left America and three improvements the New Deal made in the lives of average Americans.

VISITING THE PAST

Miami Beach, Florida

Mention Miami Beach, Florida, and what comes to mind? Sun, sand, retirement? Would you believe historic preservation? Yes. Miami Beach is the home of one of the nation's largest historic districts.

Miami Beach hardly seems old enough to be considered historic. Only in the 1920s did it become a vacation spot for the nation's upper middle class. During the 1930s and 1940s it grew, and during this period its architecture evolved from a Spanish style to an exciting modern style called Art Deco.

Art Deco was fashionable in the 1920s and 1930s in New York and Paris. Yet it was a perfect style for the fantasy feeling of a resort. The style was energetic and glamorous. In Miami Beach architects incorporated the exotic aspects of the area into the details of their buildings. Dolphins, waves, shells, ships, flamingos, and mermaids appeared in the decorative elements of the new buildings.

In its day, Art Deco was the elegant style of the great oceanliners, of Hollywood movies, and of the big city skyscrapers. It incorporated molded chrome and etched glass. It was sleek and chic. Art Deco brought a sense of playfulness to whatever it touched. In Miami Beach it touched almost everything, including, of course, most hotels and apartment buildings.

Today there is a new appreciation of the Art Deco style. For years it had been ignored, unappreciated, and rejected. In the mid-1970s, however, it experienced a revival. After years of looking at stark, glassy boxes, people were willing to be amused by fanciful architectural details.

Certain residents of Miami Beach realized that they had an architectural treasure around them. South Miami Beach still had hundreds of buildings from its Art Deco days. More than that, a 1930s character remained. So distinct was the area's sense of place and time, and so rich was its collection of buildings, that in 1979 it was listed on the National Register as a historic district.

Several years ago very few people would have believed that a 1930s neighborhood could be considered historic. Fewer still would have fought for its preservation. Today attempts to demolish Art Deco buildings are met with demonstrations and court orders.

Individuals and organizations in Miami Beach are at work to give these Art Deco treasures a new lease on life. The magic of Art Deco has captured the imagination of a new generation.

Hoover Dam

Its rushing waters ran untamed from the Rocky Mountains to the Pacific Ocean. Spring floods and late summer droughts put much of the Southwest at its mercy. The Colorado River, one of the largest rivers in the nation, was its own master.

After disastrous flooding in the early 1900s, however, people felt that something had to be done. A comprehensive water-control system was needed. The major element of the system would be the world's biggest dam, located on the border between Arizona and Nevada. Behind its massive walls, this dam would create the largest reservoir in the world. Together the dam and the reservoir would tame the Colorado.

This ambitious project was unique because of its size and its approach. Not only would flooding be controlled, but water for drink-

landscape that has resulted from it are an important chapter in the story of 20th-century America. The home of a President or the site of an important battle are clearly places of historic importance, but what about a site that represents the role of the automobile in American life? Can a gas station be a national landmark?

In Winston-Salem, North Carolina, at the northwest corner of Sprague Street and Peachtree Street, sits a small national landmark. Dating from the early years of the 1930s, this gas station is a rare survivor. Built to sell Shell motor oil products, the station reflects an advertising technique popular in the 1920s and 1930s.

The shape of the building is related to the brand name of the gas it was built to sell—this station was built in the shape of a giant seashell! In those days other roadside businesses took the same direct approach. A giant milk bottle might loom over a road, with milk for sale inside. You could buy a hamburger at a giant hamburger.

These odd structures are a part of our recent history. Today there is a growing appreciation for these fanciful roadside creations from the early days of the automobile culture. Efforts are being made to keep them as part of our landscape. They are fun to pass on the road.

Such sites from the recent past also help us understand our own time. In future years they will help others understand life in the distant days of the 20th century. When you think of the impact the car has had on our lives and country, you can understand that, like the Erie Canal, or like an old railroad station, an old-fashioned gas station represents an important chapter in our history.

ing, irrigation, and industry would be secured. Electricity would be generated by the river. Recreational areas and fish and wildlife preserves would be created.

After much study, engineers selected a huge canyon as the best site for the dam. The location was isolated. Everything from power lines to railroad tracks had to be moved in. A complete town, with roads, parks, and houses had to be built for the workers. This monumental project provided much needed work for Americans from all across the nation.

To construct the dam, the mighty river had to be moved. Four huge tunnels were blasted through the canyon walls to direct the river around the construction site. The site was then excavated to solid rock and the concrete dam built.

Despite the difficult conditions, the project moved ahead rapidly. The dam was finished in five years,

two years ahead of schedule. President Roosevelt dedicated it in 1935. The American Southwest continues to benefit from this multi-purpose project.

Today, you can tour Hoover Dam. It stands as tall as a 60-story building. One look at this impressive structure and you will understand why the American Society of Civil Engineers named it one of the seven modern civil-engineering wonders in America.

A Gas Station in Winston-Salem, North Carolina

Imagine America in the days before the car. Not only did people live in a radically different way, but the country looked very different. There were no interstate highways, no drive-in restaurants, no regional shopping malls, no parking garages, and no automobile junkyards.

The automobile culture and the

UNIT 8 TEST

WRITE YOUR ANSWERS ON A SEPARATE SHEET OF PAPER.

Fill in the Blanks (30 points)

Choose the correct answer from the pair that follows each statement.

1. In the January 1920 _____, 4,000 radicals were arrested throughout the United States. (Palmer raids—general strike)
2. _____ was the first President for whom the majority of American women were able to vote. (Warren Harding—Calvin Coolidge)
3. Frederick W. Taylor's studies of efficiency in manufacturing are called _____. (the consumer society—scientific management)
4. The flowering of black culture during the 1920s is called the _____. (black ghetto—Harlem Renaissance)
5. Buying stock with only a down payment was called _____. (time payment—buying on margin)
6. President Hoover feared that government welfare programs would destroy Americans' _____. (rugged individualism—psychoanalysis)
7. FDR called his program for economic recovery the _____. (fireside chats—New Deal)
8. Flood control and electrification were the purposes of the _____. (SEC—TVA)
9. Business leaders criticized the New Deal because measures such as the NIRA and the Wagner Act favored the _____. (gold standard—labor unions)
10. One significant drawback of the New Deal was the increase in _____. (the public debt—unemployment)

Multiple Choice (30 points)

Write the letter of the answer that best completes each statement. There may be more than one correct answer.

1. All of the following contributed to the Great Depression *except*
   a. low tariffs.
   b. a frail system of banks.
   c. overproduction and credit buying.
2. Some important differences between Hoover's approach to depression problems and that of FDR include
   a. Hoover's refusal to involve the federal government in any public works projects or programs aiding the nation's financial institutions.
   b. FDR's aristocratic background, which prevented him from really understanding the problems of unemployed citizens.
   c. Hoover's reluctance to give direct government aid to the needy.
3. The Great Depression affected American farmers
   a. severely, in part due to the extensive drought of 1932–1936.
   b. very little, because banks had long been accustomed to extending credit to farmers.
   c. only slightly, because farm families could grow their own food.
4. The Supreme Court's decisions attacking New Deal legislation reflected the Court's
   a. conservative view of the role of government.
   b. hostility toward big business.
   c. belief that New Deal programs did not go far enough.
5. FDR's second term differed from the first in that
   a. his "court-packing" plan undermined his political influence.
   b. unemployment dropped to 1929 levels.
   c. FDR was unable to get much major legislation through Congress.

Essay Questions (40 points)

1. Describe three problems created by the Great Depression. Compare the solutions to these problems put into effect by Hoover and by Roosevelt.
2. Describe several social reforms enacted by the New Deal that are still in effect and explain their purposes.

Unit Nine

War and Cold War

A watch found in the ruins of Hiroshima records the instant that the Nuclear Age began.

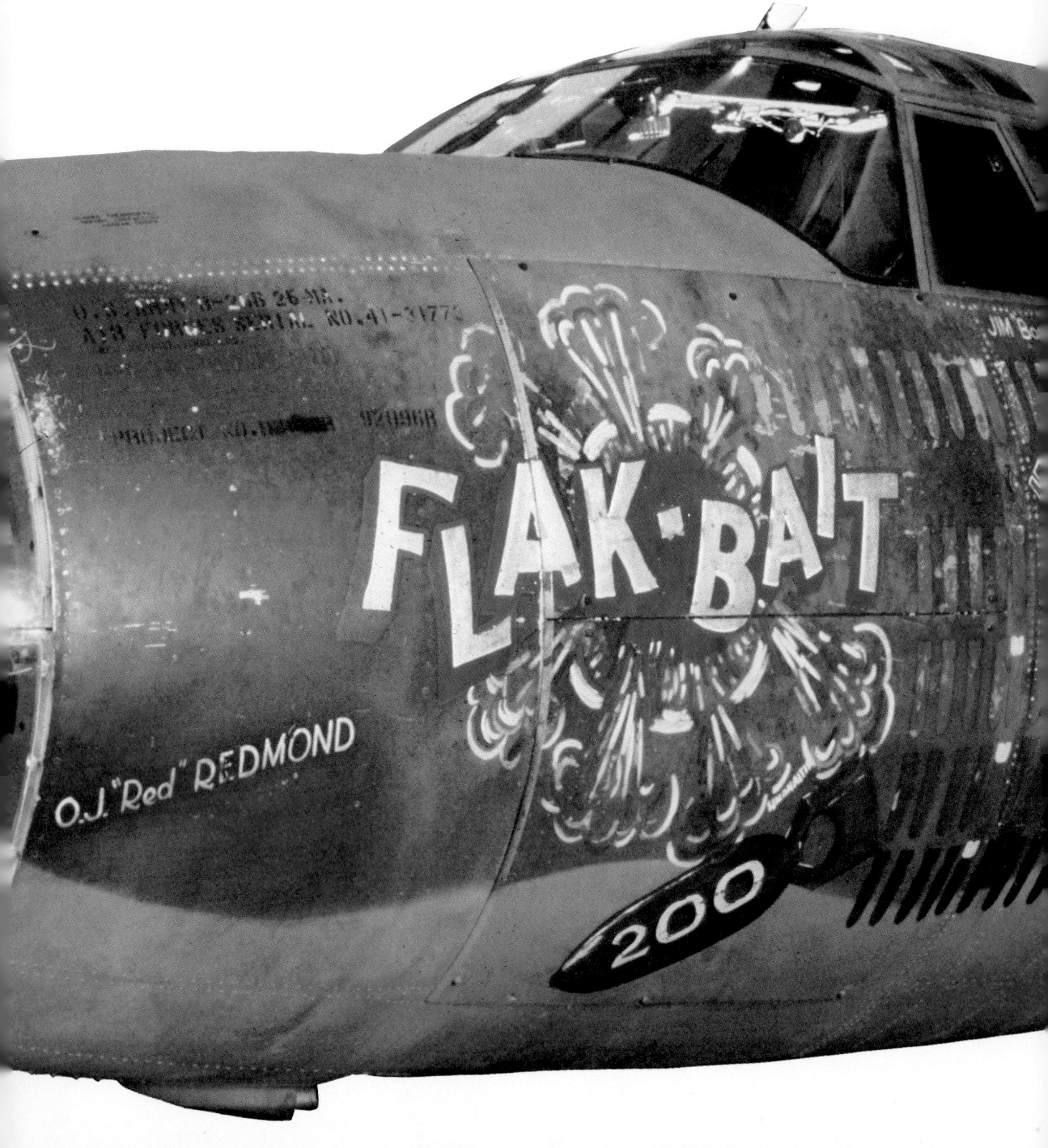
FLAK-BAIT
O.J. "Red" REDMOND
200

Chapter 30

1939–1945

WORLD WAR II

I t is before sunrise on September 1, 1939. Across the countryside of western Poland, in ancient farmhouses and tiny hamlets, a strange and frightening noise fills the air. It drones through the darkness, rushing eastward like a tidal wave. It is the sound of hundreds of German bombers winging their way to attack Poland's largest cities. As the bombs fall earthward, blasting their Polish targets, Poles realize that the wild threats of the German dictator, Adolf Hitler, have become reality. Poland is under attack!

With the first light of dawn, five German armies, made up of some 60 divisions and 1.3 million troops, roll across the Polish border. Many of the divisions are armored units—fast-moving groups of tanks, armored cars, and self-propelled artillery pieces. These are followed by infantry divisions riding in trucks and armored carriers. The German *blitzkrieg* (lightning war) strikes with terrifying speed, sweeping aside the brave but poorly equipped and badly outnumbered Polish army.

Within a week, German tanks surround Warsaw, Poland's capital. Within another week, the Polish government flees the country. By October 5, after a month of fighting, the last Polish army unit surrenders. Hitler's army has begun its drive for world domination with a great victory.

In this chapter, you will learn how the most destructive war in the world's history began. And you will learn how the United States, still reacting to World War I, moved from isolationism to involvement in this new conflict.

Sections in This Chapter
1. The European Situation
2. Isolationism at High Tide
3. America's Entry into War
4. The War in Europe
5. The Home Front
6. The War in the Pacific

Opposite: B-26 bomber "Flak Bait"

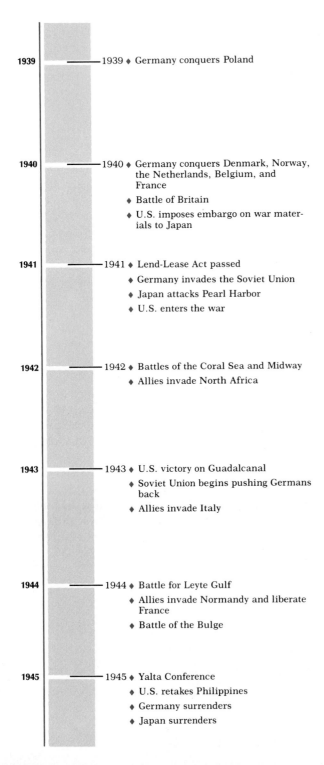

1939 — 1939 ♦ Germany conquers Poland

1940 — 1940 ♦ Germany conquers Denmark, Norway, the Netherlands, Belgium, and France
♦ Battle of Britain
♦ U.S. imposes embargo on war materials to Japan

1941 — 1941 ♦ Lend-Lease Act passed
♦ Germany invades the Soviet Union
♦ Japan attacks Pearl Harbor
♦ U.S. enters the war

1942 — 1942 ♦ Battles of the Coral Sea and Midway
♦ Allies invade North Africa

1943 — 1943 ♦ U.S. victory on Guadalcanal
♦ Soviet Union begins pushing Germans back
♦ Allies invade Italy

1944 — 1944 ♦ Battle for Leyte Gulf
♦ Allies invade Normandy and liberate France
♦ Battle of the Bulge

1945 — 1945 ♦ Yalta Conference
♦ U.S. retakes Philippines
♦ Germany surrenders
♦ Japan surrenders

1. THE EUROPEAN SITUATION

Throughout the 1930s, while President Roosevelt and most other Americans were preoccupied with the problems of the Great Depression, dangerous events were developing across the Atlantic. Separated from the Old World by thousands of miles of ocean, the United States gave scant attention to the rise of military dictators in Europe.

Bent on aggression and conquest, the dictators grew more powerful year by year. As they raised large armies and navies and geared their industries for war production, these rulers became increasingly reckless and belligerent. In time they plunged not only their own nations but the entire world into the most destructive war in history.

The Rise of Fascist Dictators

During the years following World War I, the long shadow of **fascism** fell across Europe. Fascism was the view that individuals existed only to serve the military goals of the state. Under fascist dictators, individual rights and freedoms were ruthlessly crushed. First in Italy and then in Germany and Spain, dictators came to power. Economic conditions were partly to blame. The Great Depression had struck Europe with devastating force. Foreign trade declined, unemployment soared, and many nations stood one step away from economic collapse. Millions were jobless, hungry, and fearful of the future.

Under these circumstances, conditions were ripe for the rise of dictators. Riding on the crest of a wave of popular discontent, **Benito Mussolini** in Italy, **Adolf Hitler** in Germany, and Francisco Franco in Spain were able to seize control of their nations' governments. Forthwith, the light of democracy gave way to the darkness of terrorism, fear, repression, and the intimidation of the police state.

Italy and Mussolini

After World War I, Benito Mussolini organized a powerful political party—the Fascists. Made up at first of former soldiers, the Fascists—nicknamed "black shirts" because of their black uniforms—

bullied their way with threats and violence to a place of prominence in the Italian government. By 1922, Mussolini was powerful enough to be named Prime Minister of Italy. Two years later, in 1924, he seized total control of the government.

Mussolini's dream was to restore Italy to the strength and glory of the ancient Roman empire. To do this, he began to enlarge the Italian army and navy and to turn his country's industry to the manufacture of war materials. Many Italian citizens, unemployed or otherwise affected by the Great Depression, applauded Mussolini's actions.

In October of 1935, Mussolini, who was called "Il Duce" (the leader), sent the Italian army into Ethiopia, in eastern Africa. Using modern weapons against the almost defenseless Ethiopians, Italy defeated Ethiopia. Less than a year later, Italy signed a pact with Hitler's Germany, another totalitarian government. The two nations were called the **"Axis Powers"** because Mussolini said that the line between Berlin and Rome would be the axis on which the world would turn.

Germany and Hitler

At the Berlin end of that axis, Germany, too, struggled with the effects of worldwide depression. More importantly, many Germans blamed the Treaty of Versailles for their poverty and sense of humiliation. The treaty blamed Germany for World War I and forced its government to make huge war reparations payments to the Allies, causing economic chaos. The democratic German government, known as the Weimar Republic, could do little to relieve the situation. Hundreds of thousands of Germans looked hopelessly for work, and bitterly sought someone to blame for their troubles.

When enough people in a society become ready to hand over their responsibility to a strong leader, such a leader is likely to emerge. In Germany, an Austrian housepainter told the citizens that their troubles were the work of Jews, foreigners, and the democracies. Adolf Hitler promised to destroy these enemies and lead the nation to world domination.

In March 1933, Adolf Hitler was elected Chancellor of Germany. A persuasive orator with immense popular appeal, Hitler seemed to millions of German citizens to have the answers to their country's problems. In less than a year, Hitler's National Socialist party, or **Nazi party**, seized total control of the German government. Political opponents were either executed or jailed as Hitler began to act on the plans outlined in his book, *Mein Kampf* (My Struggle), written years before while in prison.

Hitler preached that the Germans were a "master race" destined to rule Europe and dominate the world. People of inferior races, like Slavs and Jews, said Hitler, must be enslaved or killed to make way for German ambitions.

Despite the efforts of many Germans to resist the growth of Nazism, Hitler's attitudes spread in Germany with alarming speed. Soon Nazis were beating Jews in the streets without interference from police or government. Houses and businesses owned by Jews, foreigners, and political enemies were burned and looted. A nation once seen as one of the most civilized in Europe had fallen under the control of brutal savages.

Hitler soon began secretly to rearm Germany, defying a ban in the Treaty of Versailles. In 1936, just three years after he gained power, Hitler sent German troops marching into the Rhineland (see map, next page). As the Nazi soldiers goose-stepped across the Rhine River, the world saw for the first time the highly trained and well equipped military machine Hitler had created illegally.

Adolf Hitler in a Nazi parade, 1938

Axis-Soviet Takeovers, 1936-1939

That machine had a major test in Spain shortly after the German-Italian alliance was formed. A civil war pitted the democratic government against a fascist officer named Francisco Franco. Germany and Italy sent modern weapons and well-trained troops to help Franco, who won control of the government after bloody fighting. German weapons and tactics had proven their power to change the fate of nations.

In 1938, Hitler sent his army into his smaller neighbor, Austria, and annexed that nation to Germany. When there was no real opposition to his actions from the democratic nations of England and France, Hitler believed he had a free hand. He soon threatened to move again. The Sudetenland [sü dāt′n land′], located in the western part of Czechoslovakia, had a large German population. Hitler claimed that these Germans

were being mistreated by the Czech government and desired to be a part of Germany. Czechoslovakia, with one of the best armies in Europe, refused to yield to Hitler's demands. War seemed inevitable.

Appeasement at Munich

The Czechoslovakian crisis was at its peak when, in September 1938, Hitler and Mussolini agreed to meet in Munich, Germany, with British Prime Minister Neville Chamberlain and French Premier Edouard Daladier. Hitler promised to make no more territorial demands in Europe if he were permitted to take the Sudetenland from Czechoslovakia. "We want no Czechs," he declared. Neither France nor Britain believed the Sudetenland was worth another war. Therefore, Chamberlain and Daladier decided to appease Hitler by agreeing to his demands in the hope that he would not ask for more concessions.

On September 30, 1938, the **Munich Pact** was signed. The western leaders met Hitler's demand for the Sudetenland in return for his promise to seek no more territorial concessions. The Czechs, without the support of England and France, were forced to give up the Sudetenland. Although Chamberlain told the British people that he believed the Munich Pact meant "peace in our time," many doubted that Hitler would live up to his end of the bargain.

The doubters were right to be skeptical. Barely six months later, in March of 1939, Hitler seized the rest of Czechoslovakia. The following month, Mussolini advanced on the tiny nation of Albania. When Hitler began to threaten Poland as his next victim, Britain and France realized that appeasement had failed. In a last desperate effort to stop the German leader, the British and French promised to aid the Poles if Poland were attacked.

At this point, Hitler surprised the world by negotiating a nonaggression treaty with the Soviet Union. The two nations pledged not to attack each other. A secret section of the treaty also permitted the Soviets to occupy the Baltic states (Lithuania, Latvia, and Estonia), Bessarabia, and a portion of eastern Poland (see map opposite). Hitler, with nothing to fear now from Russia, ordered the German army across the Polish border on September 1. Two days later, Britain and France, honoring their treaty with Poland, declared war on Germany. World War II had begun.

SECTION 1 REVIEW

 Identify: fascism, Benito Mussolini, Adolf Hitler, Axis Powers, Nazi party, Munich Pact

Main Ideas
1. What factors contributed to the rise of dictatorships in Europe after World War I?
2. What were the goals of Mussolini and Hitler?
3. Trace, country by country, the course of Germany's aggression which resulted in the outbreak of World War II.
4. Why did the leaders of Britain and France sign the Munich Pact with the Axis Powers?
5. How did the nonaggression treaty with the Soviet Union help Hitler's plans?

2. ISOLATIONISM AT HIGH TIDE

As events in Europe during the 1930s moved toward a deadly climax, the United States chose to remain uninvolved. Americans were more concerned with the Great Depression than with the activities of European dictators. Few wanted to see the United States drawn once more into the "slaughter pens of Europe."

The Spirit of Isolationism

As you learned in Chapter 24, the spirit of **isolationism** had deep roots in our nation's past. Throughout American history, leaders such as George Washington, Abraham Lincoln, William Jennings Bryan, and Robert La Follette had all preached the merits of staying out of Europe's quarrels. Now with war clouds gathering again, this feeling increased.

Another cause for the growing spirit of isolationism was the disillusionment Americans felt about the First World War. A popular book published in 1934, *The Merchants of Death* by Helmuth Engelbrecht, contributed to the disenchantment. The book convinced large numbers of citizens that the United States had been drawn into World War I by bankers, ammunitions manufacturers, and other war profiteers who made vast sums of money from the death and destruction of the war. The findings of a 1934 Senate committee headed by Gerald Nye of North Dakota seemed to confirm the "merchants of death" theory, thus turning America in an even more isolationist direction.

Neutrality Legislation

American determination to avoid war was reflected in the neutrality laws passed by Congress in 1935, 1936, and 1937. These laws were designed to keep the United States from having to confront once again the neutrality problems faced by the Wilson administration during World War I. The **Neutrality Acts** contained the following provisions: (1) The transportation of weapons and other specified items of war to belligerents (warring nations) was banned. (2) Other materials which could also be used for war, such as copper, oil, and steel, were to be sold only on a "cash and carry" basis. In other words, the warring parties were extended no credit and had to carry the materials in their own ships. (3) No warring nations could borrow money from the United States. (4) American citizens were prohibited from traveling on ships belonging to belligerent nations.

Congress and the American people hoped that by reducing trade with belligerents the United States would remain at peace. President Roosevelt believed that cooperation with Britain and France would be a better protection against war, but he did little to insist on his ideas. By 1937, however, Roosevelt's attitude had changed.

In his so-called "Quarantine Speech," delivered in October 1937, Roosevelt compared aggression to a disease that must be quarantined if peace were to be preserved. "When an epidemic of physical disease starts to spread," the President said,

the community approves and joins in a quarantine of the patients in order to protect the health of the community against the spread of the disease.

Isolationists across the country were alarmed by this seemingly new outlook. After a storm of criticism from newspapers and magazines, Roosevelt said nothing more on the subject.

The *Panay* Incident and the Ludlow Amendment

In the meantime, the flames of military expansionism were licking across Asia. An aggressive and warlike Japan was attempting to spread its influence throughout the Pacific. In December 1937, Japanese and United States interests collided in the *Panay* **incident**. The incident grew out of a war then in progress between China and Japan. Several Japanese pilots bombed an American gunboat, the *Panay*, on the Yangtze River in China. Two American sailors were killed and 30 others were wounded. In the United States there was no reaction over the *Panay* such as had swept the country 39 years earlier, when the *Maine* was sunk. Instead, Americans were worried that the episode would cause a war. The Japanese, who claimed that the bombing was accidental, officially apologized and paid an indemnity (compensation) to the United States. It is the opinion of most historians that the Japanese government was testing American will power in the Pacific with the *Panay* incident.

Shortly after the *Panay* affair, the tide of American isolationism flowed even more strongly. Representative Louis Ludlow of Indiana proposed that the Constitution be amended to forbid Congress to declare war without a popular referendum, unless the country were actually invaded. President Roosevelt vigorously opposed the Ludlow resolution, which was only narrowly defeated. American willingness to accept the *Panay* incident and the near success of the Ludlow Amendment encouraged Japanese aggression.

The U.S. Embargoes Trade of War Materials to Japan

As time passed, Japan grew increasingly belligerent, and its armies continued to thrust deep into China. There, two Chinese military men, the Nationalist Chiang Kai-shek and the Communist Mao Tse-tung, temporarily put aside their differences to cooperate in the fight against the Japanese. In 1938 the Japanese declared the Open Door Policy (see page 518) null and void. There was now a **"New Order"** in East Asia, said Japan, under which the Japanese would control China and the rest of eastern Asia.

The United States openly denounced the "New Order" and began to take economic actions against Japan. In September 1940, an embargo was ordered against shipping certain war materials to Japan. By early 1941, the list of embargoed items included gasoline, steel, oil, copper, iron ore, and brass. As this economic noose was tightened, Japan became more willing to negotiate about affairs in the Pacific. These negotiations, unsatisfactory to both nations, continued as late as December 1941, although the Japanese government was secretly preparing for war.

SECTION 2 REVIEW

Identify: isolationism, Neutrality Acts, *Panay* incident, "New Order"

Main Ideas

1. Why was isolationism so strong in the United States in the years between World War I and II?
2. What did the *Panay* incident and the Ludlow Amendment indicate about American sentiment toward war in the late 1930s?
3. How did the United States try to force Japan to abandon its goals of conquest?

3. AMERICA'S ENTRY INTO WAR

As Hitler's armies pushed deep into Poland, no one could doubt any longer that Germany had built a truly formidable military machine. Although Britain and France had promised aid to the Poles, there was little they could do to help. In just over a month, the black, white, and red swastika fluttered over all of Poland. In the meantime, Britain rushed more than 300,000 troops across the Channel to northern France while the French began to strengthen a series of fortifications—the Maginot Line—along their eastern frontier.

In the United States, President Roosevelt asked Congress to reconsider the Neutrality Acts it had passed earlier. The arms embargo kept needed war materials from Britain and France. If the embargo were lifted, these nations had the sea power to protect shipments across the Atlantic. Germany, with a small navy, would be unable to protect ships carrying war goods to Europe. Thus repeal of the neutrality laws would be of no help to Germany, but would greatly aid Britain and France. In November 1939, after six weeks of heated debate, Congress amended the law to permit the sale of war supplies if the country carried the goods in its own ships. Across the Atlantic, meanwhile, the guns fell silent. Hitler was regrouping his forces.

War in Western Europe

For almost seven months after Poland's defeat, an uneasy calm settled over Europe. People in France and elsewhere began to refer to the "sitzkrieg" or "sitting war." Others called this time of quiet the **"phony war."** But on April 9, 1940, the European tranquillity was shattered as Hitler unleashed his armies once more.

Between April and June of 1940, the Nazis attacked, conquered, and occupied Denmark, Norway, Belgium, Luxembourg, and the Netherlands. As the German army pounded across Belgium, Britain was forced to withdraw its troops from France during the **Battle of Dunkirk.** There, under heavy attack, over 330,000 troops were miraculously evacuated by a flotilla of ferries, fishing boats, yachts, and many other vessels which were pressed into emergency service. **Winston Churchill**, who had replaced Chamberlain as Prime Minister, rallied British spirits with his stirring words before the House of Commons:

We shall prove ourselves again able to defend our island home, to ride out the storm of war, and to outlive the menace of tyranny, if necessary for years, if necessary alone. . . . [We] shall defend our Island, whatever the cost may be. We shall fight on the beaches, we shall fight on the landing grounds, we shall fight in the fields and in the streets, we shall fight in the hills; we shall never surrender; and even if, which I do not for a moment believe, this Island or a large part of it were subjugated and starving, then our Empire beyond the seas, armed and guarded by the British Fleet, would carry on the struggle, until, in God's good time, the New World, with all its power and might, steps forth to the rescue and liberation of the Old.

After the British army escaped, Hitler turned on France, whose weak defenses rapidly crumbled. On June 14 Paris fell, and by June 17 France was defeated. In an act of revenge, Hitler forced the French to sign an armistice on the exact spot in the Compiègne Forest where, 22 years before, Germany was compelled to accept defeat.

The peace terms allowed Hitler to occupy the northern half of France. The southern half, the **Vichy regime**, which was ruled by the German puppet Marshal Pétain, cooperated with the Nazis. The French watched helplessly as their own government recruited workers for German weapons factories, and French police shipped French Jews to torture and death in German concentration camps.

With the fall of France, Germany seemed unstoppable. Nearly all of western Europe lay under the Nazi heel. Britain, separated from the continent by the protective waters of the English Channel, now stood alone.

American Aid to Britain

Most Americans opposed Hitler and Nazism, yet the majority still did not believe the United States should enter the war. The American public was divided into groups: interventionists, who wanted to aid Britain short of actual war, and isolationists, who opposed any involvement. To make their views known, the interventionists formed a group called "The Committee to Defend America by Aiding the Allies" which pressed for U.S. aid to Britain. The isolationists also formed an organization, called the "America First Committee," to air their views.

The British, in the meantime, were engaged in a life or death struggle known as the **Battle of Britain**. In an attempt to destroy British defenses before his invading armies lunged across the channel from France, Hitler began an intensive air assault in August 1940. The skies above England were darkened with fighters and bombers as the Royal Air Force battled furiously around the clock. Winston Churchill urged the British people to stand firm against the almost overwhelming odds of the Nazi onslaught. "Hitler," said Churchill,

knows he will have to break us in this island or lose the war. If we can stand up to him all Europe may be free and the life of the world may move forward into broad, sunlit uplands. But if we fail, then the whole world,

including the United States . . . will sink into the abyss of a new Dark Age.

By October it was clear that Germany had not gained air superiority over the RAF. Britain had withstood Hitler's assault.

By the time of the Battle of Britain, President Roosevelt was firmly committed to Britain's cause. In September 1940 he announced the transfer of 50 "over-age" destroyers to Britain in return for British naval bases in Newfoundland, Bermuda, and the Caribbean. This action sparked intense outrage among isolationists, who believed that Roosevelt was acting like a dictator.

The Election of 1940

While Europe was ablaze with war, the political processes continued as usual in the United States. Although it was in violation of the "No Third Term" tradition begun by President Washington in 1796, the Democrats in 1940 again nominated President Roosevelt. At the Republican convention, Wendell Willkie, a lawyer from Indiana and president of a large utilities company, won the nomination.

During the campaign, the Republicans attacked Roosevelt with the slogan "No Third Term" while criticizing Democratic overspending during the New Deal. Willkie's views on foreign policy—in which he called for increased military strength and promised to keep America out of the war unless attacked—were almost identical to those of Roosevelt. When Americans went to the polls in November, they once again elected Roosevelt to the presidency, although by a much smaller majority than in 1932 or 1936.

The U.S. Enters the War Unofficially

While Americans continued to hope for peace, stories of Nazi brutality turned more and more of them into interventionists. In January 1941, a poll showed a massive shift in public opinion: 70% of those polled favored aid to Britain, even if that meant risking war. In March Congress passed the **Lend-Lease Act** which permitted the President to "sell, transfer, exchange, lease, lend, or otherwise dispose of," any defense article for "any country whose defense the President deems vital to the defense of the United States."

With the lend-lease plan, the United States gave up the last pretenses of remaining neutral. To

FROM THE ARCHIVES

The Four Freedoms

In his State of the Union speech given on January 6, 1941, President Roosevelt recommended the Lend-Lease Act to Congress and described America's ideals:

In the future days, which we seek to make secure, we look forward to a world founded upon four essential human freedoms.

The first is freedom of speech and expression—everywhere in the world.

The second is freedom of every person to worship God in his own way—everywhere in the world.

The third is freedom from want—which, translated into world terms, means economic understandings which will secure to every nation a healthy peacetime life for its inhabitants—everywhere in the world.

The fourth is freedom from fear—which, translated into world terms, means a world wide reduction of armaments to such a point and in such a thorough fashion that no nation will be in a position to commit an act of physical aggression against any neighbor—anywhere in the world.

That is no vision of a distant millennium. It is a definite basis for a kind of world attainable in our own time and generation. That kind of world is the very antithesis of the so-called new order of tyranny which the dictators seek to create with the crash of a bomb.

protect arms shipments to Britain, Roosevelt extended a "neutrality zone," almost to Iceland (see map, page 675). Within that zone, American naval patrols escorted shipments and radioed to British ships the location of German U-boats. In July, the United States occupied Iceland. In September, when the American destroyer *Greer* was attacked by a Nazi U-boat, the President authorized American naval forces to attack all German submarines on sight. Then, in November, Congress repealed the portion of the 1939 Neutrality Act which restricted American ships from sailing into the European combat zone. President Roosevelt armed the ships and stationed Navy gun crews aboard. The United States was for all practical purposes at war.

Japan Attacks Pearl Harbor

As you learned earlier, American relations with Japan had deteriorated rapidly after 1940. By 1941, trade between Japan and the U.S. was almost at a standstill. The Japanese, however, desperately needed the oil and scrap-iron shipments which had previously come from America. In a last attempt to achieve their goals, Japan sent a peace delegation to Washington late in 1941.

The Japanese diplomats demanded that the United States release the Japanese assets which had been frozen earlier, that the trade restrictions against Japan be removed, and that the United States stop sending aid to China, which was receiving American lend-lease assistance. In return, **General Hideki Tojo,** the Japanese Prime Minister, promised to withdraw Japan's forces from Indochina.

Secretary of State Cordell Hull refused General Tojo's offer. Because the American military had broken Japan's secret code, Hull knew Japan would make no more serious offers. President Roosevelt and the Secretary of State believed from what had been picked up in code that the Japanese would go to war. They did not know, however, where the attack would be made.

Even as Tojo's diplomats were preparing to meet once more with Hull, Japanese leaders launched a strike force of carriers, destroyers, cruisers, and other ships toward Hawaii. At 7:55 A.M. Honolulu time, December 7, 1941, waves of Japanese aircraft streaked low over the unsuspecting naval base at **Pearl Harbor.** As the enemy

The West Virginia *aflame in Pearl Harbor, December 7, 1941*

bombs struck in giant explosions, the nucleus of America's Pacific fleet was destroyed. The next day, President Roosevelt asked Congress for a declaration of war against Japan. The declaration was quickly passed by the House and Senate, with only one opposing vote. America was at war.

SECTION 3 REVIEW

 Identify: phony war, Battle of Dunkirk, Winston Churchill, Vichy regime, Battle of Britain, Lend-Lease Act, Hideki Tojo, Pearl Harbor

Main Ideas
1. Why did President Roosevelt ask Congress to reconsider the Neutrality Acts?
2. Contrast the two main viewpoints Americans held concerning aid to Britain in 1940.
3. How did the United States, though not officially at war, aid Britain after March 1941?
4. What did the Japanese delegation try to negotiate with the United States? Why did it fail?

4. THE WAR IN EUROPE

Just three days after the U.S. declared war on Japan, Hitler and Mussolini, following the terms of a treaty with Japan signed in 1940, declared war on the United States. For Americans, this new war was far more complex than World War I. World War II was truly a global struggle, and the United States was forced to carry on the fight not just in Europe but in Asia, Africa, and across the vast reaches of the Pacific. Under these circumstances, the biggest question facing Roosevelt was where to begin the war effort.

Roosevelt's Military Strategy

After consulting with his military advisers, it was Roosevelt's decision as commander-in-chief to place the bulk of United States military force against the Axis Powers in Europe. Churchill and Roosevelt agreed that Hitler and Mussolini must be defeated first because of their greater military strength. The war against Japan took a lower priority, although much hard and bloody fighting took place in the Pacific throughout the war.

The Allied strategy was made easier by a great blunder on Hitler's part. During the summer before the United States officially entered the war, Hitler decided to invade the Soviet Union, breaking the nonaggression agreement he had made two years earlier. Many military experts feared that the Soviets would fall within a few months, but the Red Army resisted at a terrible cost in lives. The Germans pushed slowly forward until they were at the gates of Moscow. Aided by lend-lease supplies and the terrible Russian winter, the Soviets kept the massive German army pinned down. The Allies thus gained time to plan a second front to threaten the German forces.

Operation Torch in North Africa

England, meanwhile, was the scene of feverish Allied activity. Thousands of troops were assembled in 1942 to open that second front. After careful planning and with the advice of such military leaders as **General George C. Marshall,** the American chief-of-staff, Roosevelt and Churchill decided to strike first in North Africa. Command of the offensive, code-named **Operation Torch,** was

given to a then-obscure American general, **Dwight D. Eisenhower.**

The British had been fighting German forces in Africa since 1940. By the time Operation Torch was launched, the elite German Afrika Korps, commanded by Field Marshall Erwin Rommel, had been stopped by the forces of the British general Bernard Montgomery. On November 8, 1942, over 100,000 U.S. and British troops landed on the shores of North Africa. The German forces were attacked by Eisenhower's troops from the west and the British Eighth Army under Montgomery from the east. After much hard fighting, including one stunning American defeat at the

Kasserine Pass in Tunisia, the German and Italian forces were defeated by the end of May 1943. The Allies had won their first major victory of the war.

The "Soft Underbelly of Europe"

Once the Axis forces were swept from North Africa, the Allies' attention could be focused on Europe itself. General Marshall and other American planners wanted a cross-channel invasion from England to France. Churchill, on the other hand, wanted to strike a blow at what he called the "soft underbelly of Europe"—Italy. In the end this became the Allied plan, but at the same time preparations for an Allied assault across the English Channel were also begun.

In July and August of 1943, Allied troops launched an offensive against Sicily. By September, the Italian island was in Allied hands. On September 9, Allied forces landed on the mainland of southern Italy, but they found the "soft underbelly" of Europe to be cold, mountainous, and well defended. By June 1944, the Allies had advanced only as far as Rome. Although the Italian campaign went more slowly than hoped, it did keep hundreds of thousands of German soldiers tied down when the Allies invaded western Europe through France in the spring of 1944.

June 6, 1944: Allied troops land at Normandy, France, in a massive invasion of occupied Europe.

Attack on a German aircraft factory at Bremen

Assault on Fortress Europe

For almost two years—since 1942—the Allied Powers prepared for the invasion of France. Millions of troops and shiploads of supplies flooded into Britain as plans went forward. All of Britain became a giant military camp, used to house troops and equipment. By the spring of 1944, almost 3 million troops, along with 6 million tons of supplies and thousands of tanks, trucks, and jeeps, had been assembled in preparation for **Operation Overlord**—code name for the cross-channel invasion of France. In Supreme Headquarters, Allied Expeditionary Forces (SHAEF) General Eisenhower, overall commander of the invasion, and Field Marshal Montgomery made final plans, taking into account the tides and weather.

At daybreak on June 6, 1944, German defenders on the Normandy coast of France saw thousands of ships emerge from the early morning mist on the Channel. Three divisions of American troops, two divisions of British soldiers, and one Canadian division landed on the French beaches. This first assault—which included 176,000 troops, 12,000 planes, 600 warships, 1,500 tanks, and 4,000 landing craft—was the largest amphibious (sea to land) operation in all history. The German shore defense troops, commanded by Field Marshal Rommel, fought furiously. On Utah and Omaha beaches the Americans gained a foothold, while on Gold, Juno, and Sword beaches British and Canadian troops inched their way ashore. American and British paratroopers, dropped behind enemy lines the night before, fought to link up with the beachheads. By nightfall, after hours of bloody fighting, the beaches were taken.

In August the Allied armies began to break out of the Normandy area, a difficult terrain because its thousands of small farms were separated by high hedgerows. During the late summer and fall, the Allied armies, often led by the flamboyant American tank general, George S. Patton, raced across Europe toward Germany. Paris was liberated on August 25, just after another Allied invasion—this time in southern France—was launched on August 15. By September, Allied forces had reached Germany's last line of defense—the Rhine River. There General Eisenhower decided to consolidate his armies before making a final lunge deep into Germany.

The Defeat of Hitler's Germany

In the meantime the Nazis were suffering devastating defeats at the hands of Soviet troops. As British, French, and American forces hammered at Hitler from the west, the Soviet armies rolled across Poland from the east. In the west, in December, Hitler mounted one last, desperate counteroffensive through the heavily wooded Ardennes forest near Bastogne, Belgium. Although the German thrust caught American troops off guard and for a time threatened the Belgian port of Antwerp, it was halted and then turned back by American forces in the famous **Battle of the Bulge**. The Allies then advanced on Berlin.

Allied troops advancing through Poland, Austria, and Germany got the first sight of the Nazi atrocities that would shock the world. In places whose names would come to stand for all that is most repulsive in human history—Dachau, Treblinka, Bergen-Belsen, Auschwitz—the Nazi savagery had found its final expression. Allied soldiers freed thousands of half-dead, mutilated prisoners from each of the Nazi **death camps** they found. Here Jews rounded up in Poland, Italy, France, Holland, Greece, and other countries under German control had been murdered, tortured, and subjected to the criminal "experiments" of German doctors and scientists.

By the end of the war, Nazis had murdered more than 12 million civilians. Six million were European Jews (including 2 million children), but other targets of Nazi mass killings included elderly, handicapped, and mentally ill people, Poles, Russians, Gypsies, homosexuals, and "traitors" who had dared speak out against the sick dreams of the "master race."

By the spring of 1945, Germany was shattered. Its cities were in ruins, its army destroyed or captured, and its civilian population dispirited. American and Soviet troops met at Torgau on the Elbe River in central Germany on April 25. On April 30, inside his bunker deep under the ruins of the Chancellory in Berlin, Adolf Hitler committed suicide. On May 7, Admiral Karl Doenitz, who had succeeded Hitler, surrendered Germany unconditionally. The war in Europe was over.

The Politics of War

Behind the Allied military forces were their leaders—Roosevelt, Churchill, and the Soviet dictator, **Joseph Stalin**—who were pursuing the poli-

German soldiers seizing Jewish families in Warsaw

tics of war. So long as Hitler stood as a common enemy, the Big Three presented a united front and pursued a common objective—the defeat of Nazi Germany. However, the postwar goals of Roosevelt and Churchill differed dramatically from those of Stalin.

Three major Big Three conferences hammered out strategy. The first of these, the Teheran [te/ə ran/] Conference was held in the capital of Iran in November and December of 1943. The Americans and British agreed to invade France in June of 1944, with the invasion of southern France to follow. The Soviets, in turn, agreed to launch a concentrated offensive from the east at the same time. Stalin, in a successful attempt to gain Soviet control of southeastern Europe, obtained an agreement that there was to be no American or British invasion through the Balkans—thus leaving that area open to Russian influence at the end of the war.

The second Big Three meeting occurred in February of 1945 at **Yalta**, an old seaport town on the Crimean Peninsula. President Roosevelt, at this meeting, had barely two months to live, and was an ill, frail, and tired man. The three leaders decided that after the war Germany would be divided into four zones of occupation—one each for the French, English, Americans, and Russians. Stalin promised free elections in the countries overrun by the Red Army in its drive through eastern Europe—a pledge that he violated almost immediately. The Soviet Union also promised to enter the war against Japan once Hitler was defeated—an agreement that the Americans soon realized was unnecessary and probably unwise. The meeting at Yalta has been the subject of much historical controversy. Many historians now believe that an ill and tired Roosevelt made arrangements which were overbalanced in favor of the Soviet Union, and which in the long run contributed to the Cold War—the decades-long period of East-West tensions that followed.

The last meeting of the three Allied leaders was held at Potsdam, Germany, in July of 1945. **Harry S. Truman**, who became President when Roosevelt died in April 1945, represented the United States. Churchill, England's representative, was turned out of office during the meeting and was replaced by Clement Attlee. Stalin represented Russia. Little was decided, and the first cracks of disagreement appeared. At one point the American delegation threatened to leave because Stalin demanded huge German war reparations. The meeting marked the end of cooperation between the western democracies and the Soviet Union.

SECTION 4 REVIEW

Identify: George C. Marshall, Operation Torch, Dwight D. Eisenhower, Operation Overlord, Battle of the Bulge, death camps, Joseph Stalin, Yalta Conference, Harry S. Truman

Main Ideas

1. Where did Roosevelt decide to begin America's war effort, and why?
2. What major campaigns were American forces in Europe involved in between 1942 and 1945?
3. What were the three major conferences held by the Big Three during World War II? What was the significance of each?

5. THE HOME FRONT

The attack on Pearl Harbor found the United States unprepared for war, but the nation quickly converted to a wartime economy. As in the First World War, government bureaus and boards quickly sprouted to oversee and guide the nation's industrial output. Many capable executives from civilian business and industry rushed to Washington to assist with war planning and programing.

The collection of agencies and commissions directing the war effort was controlled by the **Office of War Mobilization (OWM)**, headed by the distinguished **James F. Byrnes,** a former senator and Supreme Court justice. Under the OWM was the War Production Board, headed by Donald Nelson, a Sears, Roebuck executive. The WPB assumed almost complete control of industrial production. Like the War Industries Board of World War I, the WPB fixed production priorities, awarded contracts, and set production quotas. That the Board accomplished its mission was evident in the tremendous number of tanks, guns, planes, uniforms, farm products, and other items produced by the nation's mines, farms, and factories in a short period of time.

To control the inflation which grew from sudden full employment and rapidly increased spend-

Two of the millions of women who worked in wartime defense plants

ing, the President created the **Office of Price Administration (OPA)**. This agency tried to keep prices at a reasonable level by imposing controls on wages and prices. Thus a ceiling was placed on the amount any person or firm could charge for goods or services. The OPA also rationed many everyday items in order to conserve supplies, prevent hoarding, and keep the prices down. Among the products which American families had to use ration coupons to obtain were gasoline, meat, canned foods, sugar, and tires.

Mobilizing Workers and Troops

As in World War I, it was essential that labor and management keep their differences to a minimum. To accomplish this difficult task, President Roosevelt appointed a War Labor Board. The Board dealt with wartime labor disputes (of which, fortunately, there were few), monitored workers' pay scales, and in general enforced the provisions of the 1935 Wagner Act.

Other important wartime agencies included the Office of Defense Transportation and the War Shipping Administration, both of which supervised America's railroads, truck lines, express agencies, and merchant marine. The Office of War Information kept America and the Allies informed about the war effort through broadcasts, news articles, posters, and speeches. Finally, the War Manpower Commission operated the Selective Service System and recruited workers for war industries. More than 15 million men and

---

LIFE IN AMERICA

JAPANESE AMERICANS AND THE WAR

At the outbreak of the war, thousands of Japanese Americans resided in the states located along America's West Coast. In a wave of concern that approached hysteria, many Americans in these states unjustifiably regarded Japanese Americans as a threat to national security.

The Relocation Camps

Officials on the West Coast asked the U.S. government to move all Japanese Americans to other parts of the country. President Roosevelt then authorized the immediate movement of some 112,000 persons of Japanese ancestry to relocation camps, where they were kept throughout most of the war. So sudden was this development, many Japanese Americans had to sell their homes and other property at sacrifice prices, causing financial ruin to thousands of families.

Although the loyalty of most was soon established, they were not allowed to return to their homes. Instead they were given the choice of moving to the interior of the country or joining the armed forces. About 36,000 took one of these options.

A Continuing Controversy

The controversy over the legality and justice of the relocation of the Japanese Americans continues even today. Some Americans view it as one of the greatest violations of civil liberties in American history. Others maintain that a wartime emergency places hardships on all Americans. According to this view, the relocation of the Japanese Americans, while probably not necessary, appeared so at the time and was therefore justified.

Japanese Americans awaiting relocation, 1942

671

250,000 women served in the armed forces during World War II. As the draft swept up male workers, and as industry expanded rapidly, millions of women joined the wartime civilian work force, providing a key labor force for the war industries.

The Election of 1944

In 1944 the Democrats nominated Franklin D. Roosevelt for a fourth term, arguing that it would be unwise to change leaders while the war continued. Harry S. Truman, a senator from Missouri, replaced Henry Wallace as FDR's running mate. The Republicans nominated the energetic governor of New York, **Thomas E. Dewey**, who had a reputation for fighting organized crime. Winning with only 53% of the popular vote, the smallest margin of his four terms, President Roosevelt was again returned to the White House.

Plans for the Postwar World

While the Allies were beginning to crush the Axis Powers, diplomats were meeting to plan for peace. During the summer of 1944, representatives from the United States, Britain, China, and the Soviet Union met at **Dumbarton Oaks**, a lovely estate in Washington, D.C., to discuss plans for the United Nations. The delegates wrestled with many prickly problems, including the Soviet demand for 16 representatives, one for each so-called republic within the Soviet Union. They also discussed membership in the Security Council, and the question of the veto. Many issues remained unsettled, but at least a beginning was made for an organization that would help keep peace in what was to become a very troubled postwar world.

SECTION 5 REVIEW

Identify: Office of War Mobilization, James F. Byrnes, Office of Price Administration, Thomas E. Dewey, Dumbarton Oaks

Main Ideas

1. How did the United States quickly change from a peacetime economy to a wartime economy?
2. Why were wages and prices controlled during the war?

6. THE WAR IN THE PACIFIC

In the hours and days following the attack on Pearl Harbor, Japan's military steamroller rapidly overran other American positions in the Pacific. The United States base in the Philippines was hit just ten hours after the raid on Pearl Harbor. On December 9, Japan attacked Wake Island, which finally surrendered after a bloody fight on December 23. Guam was attacked on December 10 and surrendered on December 12. When Japanese troops landed on Luzon, the main island of the Philippines, they met a stiff wall of resistance from American troops commanded by **General Douglas MacArthur**. Between December 1941 and May 1942, some 15,000 American soldiers put up a heroic fight as they slowly retreated down the Bataan Peninsula and fortified themselves on the island of Corregidor in Manila Bay. After a three-month siege, food and ammunition ran out, and the Americans had to surrender. General MacArthur was able to escape to Australia, where he assumed overall command of Allied forces in the Pacific.

In the meantime, Japan had also swept up British, French, and Dutch possessions with stunning speed. At Singapore, on the Malay Peninsula, England suffered the worst Far East defeat in its history when 70,000 troops surrendered. The Dutch East Indies, along with the French Solomon Islands, also fell to the dazzling Japanese attack.

The Battle of the Coral Sea

By May of 1942, the white and red flag of the rising sun fluttered in an arc across the Pacific from northern New Guinea in the south to the western Aleutians in the north. (See map, page 674.) The Japanese military command, however, had still another objective—Port Moresby in southern New Guinea. Japanese possession of this city would ensure a strong outer defensive perimeter for the home islands. It would also serve as a staging area for attacks on Australia. On May 7, 1942, a Japanese task force moved to occupy Port Moresby. On the way, it was intercepted by an American fleet which included the two carriers, the *Yorktown* and the *Lexington*, in the Coral Sea.

In the **Battle of the Coral Sea** that followed, a historic event occurred. For the first time two surface fleets did battle without exchanging a shot. The entire engagement was fought by aircraft from the carriers. Technically the Japanese won the battle because their losses were lower, but strategically the Allies won: Port Moresby remained in Allied hands.

The Battle of Midway

A month later Japanese and American naval forces again clashed in a battle which was a turning point in the war in the Pacific. In an effort to engage and destroy the American Pacific fleet, a huge Japanese force, commanded by Admiral Isorobu Yamamoto, steamed toward the American-held island of Midway. Yamamoto did not know that American intelligence had cracked his secret code. From Pearl Harbor Admiral Chester Nimitz prepared for the attack by ordering an American carrier force to reinforce the fleet, sailing near Midway.

As was the case at the Battle of the Coral Sea, the **Battle of Midway** was fought entirely by aircraft. In a spectacular victory, the U.S. fleet sank three Japanese carriers on the first day's fighting and one on the second day of battle. The Americans lost one carrier, the *Yorktown,* and 151 airplanes, but Japanese naval strength in the Pacific was blunted. The strategic outlook had shifted in favor of the United States.

Victory at Guadalcanal

The Japanese threat to Australia was lessened by the results of the Battle of the Coral Sea, but it was not eliminated. Japanese troops occupied **Guadalcanal** in the Solomon Islands where they built an air base from which they could threaten Australia. (Refer to the map, page 674.) General MacArthur knew that if he were to protect Australia, he must eliminate Japan's force on Guadalcanal. MacArthur also wanted the island as a stepping stone to the Philippines.

Just after dawn on August 7, 1942, landing craft from an Allied naval force landed 20,000 marines on the island's beaches. The initial landings were made with little Japanese resistance because of the heavy pre-invasion shelling. Later waves, however, met stiff resistance from the enemy, and the fighting for Guadalcanal soon bogged down into a deadly stalemate. After six months of fighting, in February 1943, U.S. forces finally pushed the Japanese off the island. For the first time, American ground troops had defeated Japanese soldiers in the Pacific.

General MacArthur's Strategy

To close the ring on Japan, General MacArthur decided upon a policy of island-hopping. Under this plan, marine and army units were to seize one by one the islands of the western and central Pacific which were held by Japanese troops. On the islands closest to Japan, air fields were to be constructed and used for launching bombing runs on the major Japanese cities. Finally, Japan itself would be invaded by Allied forces.

With the new naval superiority gained at the Battle of Midway, the United States was able to advance steadily toward Japan. The first objectives were the Gilbert, Marshall, and Mariana island chains. (See map, page 674.) In these chains, the islands of Tarawa, Kwajalein, and Eniwetok [tä rä′wä, kwä′jə län′, en′ä wē′tok] were seized by United States forces. Some of these, such as Tarawa, cost many lives, but the enemy was slowly pushed across the Pacific.

The Invasion of the Philippines

When General MacArthur was forced to leave the Philippines in 1942, he had promised, "I shall return!" Two years later, on October 20, 1944, he was able to make good on his promise. On that day American troops began the invasion of the Philippine Islands. The smaller island of Leyte [lā′tē] was taken first. Then, in a last desperate attempt to stop the Americans, Japan threw its navy into the battle. During the ensuing **Battle for Leyte Gulf** (October 23–26, 1944), Japanese seapower was shattered. General MacArthur's troops then invaded the main island of Luzon. After five months of hard fighting the last Japanese troops were swept from the Philippines.

Victory Over Japan

In early 1945 the United States struck at two islands that were almost in Japan's backyard—Iwo Jima and Okinawa. These two islands had been held by Japan for centuries, and they were among the most strongly defended in the entire Pacific. Bloody battles were fought for both of them. Five thousand marines were killed on Iwo Jima, and 11,000 more died on Okinawa.

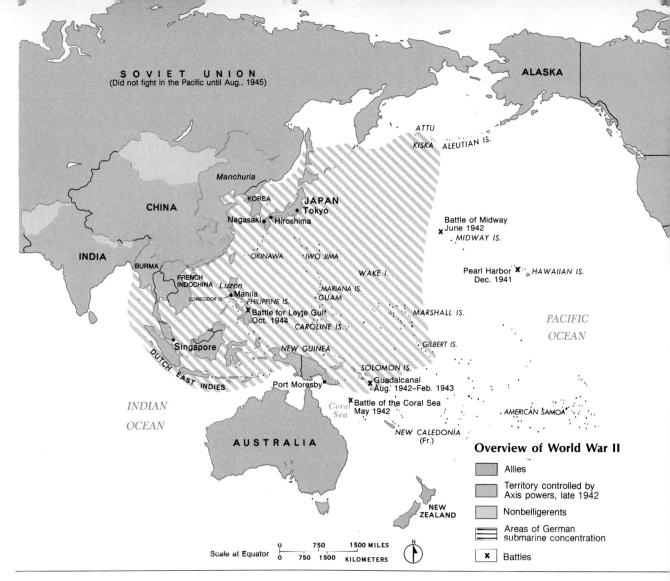

SOVIET UNION
(Did not fight in the Pacific until Aug., 1945)

ALASKA

ATTU

KISKA ALEUTIAN IS.

Manchuria

CHINA

KOREA

JAPAN
• Tokyo
Nagasaki • • Hiroshima

Battle of Midway
June 1942
x • MIDWAY IS.

INDIA

BURMA

OKINAWA

IWO JIMA

WAKE I.

Pearl Harbor x • HAWAIIAN IS.
Dec. 1941

FRENCH
INDOCHINA Luzon
CORREGIDOR IS. • Manila
• PHILIPPINE IS.
x Battle for Leyte Gulf
Oct. 1944

MARIANA IS.
• GUAM

MARSHALL IS.

PACIFIC
OCEAN

CAROLINE IS.

• Singapore

DUTCH EAST INDIES

NEW GUINEA

GILBERT IS.

SOLOMON IS.

x Guadalcanal
Aug. 1942–Feb. 1943

Port Moresby •

Coral
Sea

x Battle of the Coral Sea
May 1942

• AMERICAN SAMOA

INDIAN

OCEAN

AUSTRALIA

NEW CALEDONIA
(Fr.)

Overview of World War II

Allies

Territory controlled by
Axis powers, late 1942

Nonbelligerents

NEW
ZEALAND

Areas of German
submarine concentration

x Battles

Scale at Equator 0   750   1500 MILES
0   750 1500   KILOMETERS

N

In the meantime a group of scientists working on a secret program had unleashed a powerful new force. On December 2, 1942, scientists led by Enrico Fermi had set off the world's first controlled nuclear chain reaction at the University of Chicago. The Army then took charge and set up an atomic bomb research center at Los Alamos, New Mexico. Physicist J. Robert Oppenheimer headed the operation, code-named the **Manhattan Project**. Three years and 2 billion dollars later, on July 16, 1945, the first atomic bomb in history was detonated at Alamagordo, New Mexico. Oppenheimer later recalled how words from a Hindu scripture had flashed through his mind: "I am become Death, the shatterer of worlds."

President Truman learned of the success of the test bomb while at the Potsdam Conference. He issued an ultimatum to Japan to surrender or face "prompt and utter destruction." There was no response from Japan. Truman, after learning from his military advisers that an invasion of Japan would probably cost 1 million American lives, ordered the bomb to be dropped.

On August 6, 1945, an American B-29 bomber droned through the empty sky high above **Hiroshima** [hir/ə shē/mə], an important Japanese military center. When directly over the city, the bomber, called the *Enola Gay*, dropped an atomic bomb. In the unsuspecting city far below, a blinding flash of light was followed by an enormous ball of fire. Within a fraction of a second, the entire center section of Hiroshima disappeared into a giant mushroom cloud. Nearly 100,000 men, women, and children were killed outright. Thousands of others died later from burns, wounds, and radiation sickness. Still Japan refused to surrender. On August 9, a second atom bomb devastated the city of Nagasaki, killing

① 1940: Germany conquers Denmark, Norway, Belgium, Luxembourg, the Netherlands, France. Vichy regime set up in France.

② June 1941: Germany invades the Soviet Union

③ 1942: Operation Torch— Allied invasion of North Africa

④ 1944: Operation Overlord— Allied invasion of Europe at Normandy

another 36,000. The next day, Japanese leaders asked for peace talks, and on August 15, a cease-fire went into effect. The war was over.

SECTION 6 REVIEW

Identify: Douglas MacArthur, Battle of the Coral Sea, Battle of Midway, Guadalcanal, Battle for Leyte Gulf, Manhattan Project, Hiroshima

Main Ideas

1. What was the significance of the Battle of the Coral Sea? What was unique about this battle?
2. Why were the Battle of Midway and the victory at Guadalcanal important?
3. What was General MacArthur's strategy for the war against Japan?
4. Why did the United States drop atomic bombs on Hiroshima and Nagasaki?

CHAPTER 30 REVIEW

Key Terms
Explain the meaning of each of the following terms:

fascism
Axis Powers
Nazi party
Munich Pact
isolationism
Neutrality Acts
Panay incident
"New Order"
phony war
Battle of Dunkirk
Vichy regime
Battle of Britain
Lend-Lease Act
Pearl Harbor
Operation Torch

Operation Overlord
Battle of the Bulge
death camps
Yalta Conference
Office of War Mobilization
Office of Price
  Administration
Dumbarton Oaks
Battle of the Coral Sea
Battle of Midway
Guadalcanal
Battle for Leyte Gulf
Manhattan Project
Hiroshima

Reviewing the Main Ideas
Section 1
1. List in chronological order the factors that led to the outbreak of World War II.
2. How did Britain, France, and the Soviet Union deal with the Axis before the invasion of Poland?

Section 2
1. Why was isolationist feeling so strong among Americans in the 1930s?
2. How did the United States try to persuade Japan to stop its program of conquest?

Section 3
1. How did the United States aid Britain in the period before it officially entered the war?
2. What events led to American involvement in World War II?

Section 4
1. List the major campaigns Americans fought in Europe between 1942 and 1945.
2. Describe the significance of the Big Three conferences in Teheran, Yalta, and Potsdam.

Section 5
1. What measures did the United States take to change to a wartime economy?
2. Why were wages and prices controlled during the war?

Section 6
1. What was the Allied strategy for Japan's defeat?
2. Describe the significance of at least three important battles in the Pacific.
3. Why did President Truman order atomic bombs to be dropped on Japan? What was the result?

Special History Skills:
Using an Index
If you want to know what a book is about, the easiest place to look is the Table of Contents. But if you want to find specific information, look in the index. An index is a detailed alphabetical guide to the book's contents. By using a book's index properly, you can save yourself hours of fruitless hunting for information. Instead of taking out a stack of library books and reading them all, you can pick out those that have the best information on the topic you are studying.

Use the index in the back of this book to find the page(s) on which each of the following appears:
1. U.S. battle casualties in World War II
2. origins of isolationism
3. women in the U.S. armed forces
4. the League of Nations
5. the causes of World War I and II

Most libraries have many books on World War II. The best way to find out which has the specific information you need is to use the index of each book you look at.

Other Skill Activities
1. Making Hypotheses
List the ways in which each of the following could have changed World War II:
a. What if the Japanese had not attacked the United States at Pearl Harbor?
b. What if Germany had not declared war on the United States after Pearl Harbor?
c. What if Germany had not invaded the Soviet Union?
d. What if the United States had not cracked the Japanese code before the Battle of Midway?

e. What if the United States had not dropped the atomic bomb?

f. What if Roosevelt had been strong and healthy at the Yalta Conference?

g. Think of some of your own "what ifs."

2. **Using Indexes**

Choose a topic that relates to this chapter—a battle, a wartime leader, the war effort at home, the development of the atomic bomb, etc. Then look for information on your topic in the indexes of books on World War II in your library. Write the titles of two books which have information on your topic and summarize what you learned in a paragraph.

Thinking Critically

1. How were the seeds of World War II sown by the peace terms following World War I?

2. Should the United States have tried harder to avoid war with Japan? Discuss.

3. Why do you think the U.S. government relocated Japanese Americans but not German or Italian Americans? Should the government be allowed to take such wartime measures?

4. What justification was given for the use of the atomic bomb against Japan? Do you feel its use was justified? Explain your answer.

Further Reading

Dwight D. Eisenhower. *Crusade in Europe*. Doubleday, 1948. A fascinating account of the war in Europe by one of America's greatest military heroes. For advanced students.

Richard Lidz. *Many Kinds of Courage*. G. P. Putnam's Sons, 1980. A collection of first-hand accounts of war experienced by "the little guy."

Anne Frank. *The Diary of a Young Girl*. Doubleday, 1967. The compelling diary of a Jewish Dutch girl who lived with her family in a secret apartment in Amsterdam for three years in an attempt to escape from the Nazi terror.

Charles Mercer. *Miracle at Midway*. G. P. Putnam's Sons, 1977. Discusses the Pearl Harbor attack, the Battle of the Coral Sea, and cracking the Japanese code.

John Hersey. *Hiroshima*. Alfred A. Knopf, 1946. Based on interviews with survivors of the bombing of Hiroshima, this book provides a glimpse of the effects of nuclear warfare.

TEST YOURSELF

WRITE YOUR ANSWERS ON A SEPARATE SHEET OF PAPER.

Matching

Write the letter of the item that best matches each description below.

1. resulted in the first atomic bomb
2. final German offensive
3. first American victory over Japanese ground forces
4. leader of Britain
5. appeasement agreement signed by Britain and France
6. leader of the Soviet Union
7. commander of Operations Torch and Overlord
8. Allied invasion of France
9. fought entirely by aircraft
10. many Americans held this belief in the 1930s

a. fascism **g.** Dwight D. Eisenhower

b. Munich Pact **h.** Winston Churchill

c. isolationism **i.** Manhattan Project

d. Guadalcanal **j.** Operation Overlord

e. Joseph Stalin **k.** Battle of the Bulge

f. Adolf Hitler **l.** Battle of the Coral Sea

Chronology

List the following events in the order in which they occurred.

1. Battle of Britain
2. Atomic bomb dropped on Hiroshima
3. U.S. declares war on the Axis
4. *Blitzkrieg* invasion of Poland
5. Attack on Pearl Harbor

Locations

Match the letters on the map with the campaigns and battles listed below.

1. Battle of the Coral Sea 4. Battle for Leyte Gulf
2. Operation Overlord 5. Operation Torch
3. Battle of the Bulge 6. Guadalcanal

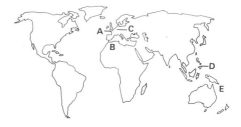

Chapter 31

1945–1952

THE TRUMAN YEARS

V-J Day. After six years of slaughter in which an estimated 55 million people died, the guns fell silent. World War II was over.

In New York City, 2 million ecstatic Americans hugged and danced with strangers in Times Square as news of the armistice flashed above them in lights. The scene repeated itself all across the country to Los Angeles, where thousands of drivers blew their horns and flashed their lights to mark the great day. Americans looked forward to an "American Century" of worldwide peace and prosperity inspired by American ideals of freedom and democracy.

For a time, for many people, that vision appeared to come true. The wartime "miracles" in technology and industrial production now created an endless river of consumer goods, and the easy credit to buy them with. The U.S. government promised to keep the world at peace by the wise but firm use of its military and economic power. At home, the economic pie grew large enough to provide more for nearly everyone, so there seemed no reason to expect domestic conflict. And yet, the dream had its dark spots.

In this chapter, you will discover the problems that arose in postwar America along with the progress. You will also see how two former allies, the United States and the Soviet Union, became locked in a seemingly endless struggle that threatened to engulf the world in yet another orgy of mass destruction.

Sections in This Chapter
1. Mr. Ordinary, Harry Truman, Becomes President
2. Coming Home to a Dream of Greatness
3. The Election of 1948
4. The Cold War Heats Up
5. The Korean War

Opposite: A 1940s TV set glows like the dawn of a new age. In 1948, only 172,000 families had TV sets. By 1950, 5 million did. Soon, almost every American home would have one.

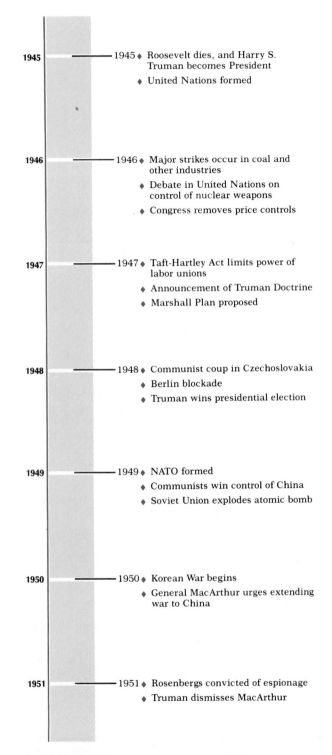

1945	1945 ♦ Roosevelt dies, and Harry S. Truman becomes President
	♦ United Nations formed
1946	1946 ♦ Major strikes occur in coal and other industries
	♦ Debate in United Nations on control of nuclear weapons
	♦ Congress removes price controls
1947	1947 ♦ Taft-Hartley Act limits power of labor unions
	♦ Announcement of Truman Doctrine
	♦ Marshall Plan proposed
1948	1948 ♦ Communist coup in Czechoslovakia
	♦ Berlin blockade
	♦ Truman wins presidential election
1949	1949 ♦ NATO formed
	♦ Communists win control of China
	♦ Soviet Union explodes atomic bomb
1950	1950 ♦ Korean War begins
	♦ General MacArthur urges extending war to China
1951	1951 ♦ Rosenbergs convicted of espionage
	♦ Truman dismisses MacArthur

1. MR. ORDINARY, HARRY TRUMAN, BECOMES PRESIDENT

On April 12, 1945, the giant of 20th-century American politics, Franklin D. Roosevelt, died suddenly from a cerebral hemorrhage. The person who stepped into his shoes was **Harry S. Truman**, "the average man's average man."

Truman was a Missouri farm boy and lifelong Democrat who had served in World War I and then returned home to fail as the owner of a men's clothing store. He went into politics where, as a loyal but honest member of the Democratic machine, he rose to become a county judge and later a United States senator. After an undistinguished career as a supporter of the New Deal, Truman emerged as the compromise choice for vice-presidential candidate in 1944.

Truman was stunned by Roosevelt's death. He had never expected to be a senator, let alone President, and he felt unprepared for the task ahead. As Vice-President, he had little to do but ask about FDR's health. He was kept in the dark about the complex questions of foreign policy that he was soon to face. The day after he took the presidential oath he told reporters:

Boys, if you ever pray, pray for me now. I don't know whether you fellows ever had a load of hay fall on you, but when they told me yesterday what had happened, I felt like the moon, the stars, and all the planets had fallen on me.

The man who had the sky drop on him was not yet aware that the United States was developing a revolutionary new weapon, the atomic bomb.

Truman's strength was his plain talking, no nonsense, take-the-bull-by-the-horns style. A plaque in his office read, "The buck stops here." He was fond of saying, "If you can't stand the heat, get out of the kitchen." But his abrupt style was also his weakness. He could be like a bull in a china shop. He could make quick decisions about complex issues without carefully studying the details. And he was sometimes so forceful in presenting his views that he did not leave an opponent room to compromise.

Truman's diplomatic skills were tested from his very first day in office. The Yalta agreements, which were the key to the postwar relationship between America, Britain, and the Soviet Union, were coming unraveled because of a dispute over Poland. Under the Yalta agreements Stalin was supposed to allow free elections in Poland. In return, the United States and Britain were to recognize Russia's right to dominate its western borders militarily. Having suffered 20 million war dead at German hands, the Russians understandably feared future German aggression. But the Soviets also wanted to expand Russia's imperial domain.

The Yalta accords began to break down even before Roosevelt died. Stalin realized that free elections in Poland would result in an anti-Russian government. Britain, which had gone to war against Germany to defend Poland, and the United States, which had gone to war in the name of democracy and freedom, were faced with the Russian military domination of Poland and Eastern Europe. **W. Averell Harriman,** the American ambassador to Moscow, called the Russian expansion westward "a new barbarian invasion." Faced with Russian territorial ambitions, many Americans, including President Truman, began to equate Russian communism with Nazism.

Harriman advised Truman to get tough with the Russians. Truman took the advice, perhaps too enthusiastically. When Soviet Foreign Minister Molotov visited Washington in April 1945, President Truman, in his own words, gave him a "straight one-two to the jaw." Truman told Molotov to honor the Yalta agreement or else! Molotov left furious.

Soviet-American Differences and the UN

President Roosevelt had placed many of his hopes for postwar peace on the idea of collective security (maintenance of peace by group action) through a world organization. The United Nations (UN) was his brain child. Roosevelt, who greatly admired Woodrow Wilson, planned to make the new organization an improvement over the unsuccessful League of Nations.

The United Nations was established in 1945. It was composed of two bodies, the **Security Council** and the **General Assembly.** The big powers, including of course the United States and the Soviet Union, were to be permanent members of the Security Council. It was to be the police authority of the world. The less powerful General Assem-

bly, in which all nations were to be represented, was to be the "town meeting of the world."

Right from the start the Americans and Russians fought over the United Nations. The Russians saw that America's allies controlled a majority of the votes in the Security Council. Their answer was to use their veto in the Security Council to block American initiatives. For their part, the Americans were upset by the Russian insistence on receiving General Assembly seats for such internal subdivisions of the Soviet Union as Mongolia, Byelorussia, and the Ukraine.

The limitations of the United Nations became clear in 1946 during the debate on the control of the atomic bomb. The United States saw the bomb as the equalizer to Russia's superior military manpower. In order to maintain this nuclear edge and head off the dangerous proliferation of atomic weapons, the United States proposed that all atomic production be placed under the supervision of an international agency. This agency, as part of the UN, would inspect every country to ensure the peaceful use of atomic power.

Speaking for the United States, Bernard Baruch warned of the dangers of atomic weaponry. He told the United Nations, "We are here to make a choice between the quick and the dead. . . . If we fail we have damned every man to be the slave of fear." The Russians, however, were against the proposal, seeing it as a threat to their sovereignty and independence. The Soviet am-

Harry S. Truman (1884–1972)

IN OFFICE: 1945–1953

Democrat from Missouri. Soon after President Truman took office, he authorized the first use of an atomic bomb (on Hiroshima, Japan, August 1945) in order to shorten the war. His administration was largely concerned with the politics of the Cold War. The threat of Communist aggression led to the Truman Doctrine, the Marshall Plan, the Point Four foreign aid program, and the founding of NATO. The Korean War began during his second term.

bassador proposed that all nations destroy their atomic bombs and that the UN prohibit their further manufacture. To the United States this would have meant giving up its advantage without having any way of knowing whether Russia was secretly building bombs. It became clear that the United Nations would not be able to stop the atomic weapons race.

UN Successes

Despite the failure of the United States and the Soviet Union to cooperate, the UN scored a few important successes between 1945 and 1950. It helped preserve, at least temporarily, the peace between the newly created nations of India and Pakistan. It also played an important role in creating the new nation of Israel.

Israel was the original homeland of the Jewish people. It had been rebuilt, beginning in the late 19th century, primarily by Jews fleeing from oppression in Europe. After World War II, it served as the haven for the survivors of the Nazi holocaust who had been denied entry into the allied nations, including the United States. The United Nations officially recognized Israel in its 1947 partition plan. The plan recognized the existence of two nations in what had been, since World War I, the British mandate of Palestine. There was to be a very small Jewish state along the coast and a larger Arab state to the east.

The Arabs, however, refused to recognize the right of Israel to exist. In May 1948 they attacked the new nation minutes after it was created. Israel held off the attackers and extended its boundaries along the cease-fire lines. Meanwhile, the Arab Palestinian state called for in the UN partition plan was swallowed up by Jordan.

Tensions Increase Between the United States and the Soviet Union

The wartime alliance between Russia and the United States was never more than a military necessity. Even before the defeat of the Axis Powers, the old tensions between the most powerful capitalist nation and its communist challenger began to reappear. The Russians had deepseated fears of encirclement by capitalist nations. They pointed to the Allied intervention in Russia during World War I and the failure of the United States to recognize the Communist government until 1933. For their part many Americans had not forgotten the Nazi-Stalin pact of 1939. They feared the Russians' determination to destroy private enterprise and to conquer neighboring countries. And they were repelled by the authoritarianism of Russian life and government.

A host of specific problems also divided the two nations. The Russians were angry because the U.S. abruptly ended economic aid to their wartorn country when Germany was defeated. The Americans were upset because Soviet troops occupied northern Iran. Americans were also alarmed by reports of mass killings, deportations, and slave-labor camps in Eastern Europe. The most serious problem dividing the U.S. and the Soviet Union concerned the future of Germany. The Americans were at first inclined to dismantle the Nazi industrial and military machine and make Germany into a "potato patch," a nation

The Iron Curtain

In March 1946, Winston Churchill visited the United States. In a famous speech delivered at Fulton, Missouri, he warned Americans of the new dangers to peace and freedom that threatened the world.

From Stettin in the Baltic to Trieste in the Adriatic, an iron curtain has descended across the Continent. . . . In front of the iron curtain which lies across Europe are other causes for anxiety. . . . Communist fifth columns [traitors and spies] are established and work in complete unity and absolute obedience to the directions they receive from the Communist center. . . . [The] Communist parties or fifth columns constitute a growing challenge and peril to Christian civilization. . . .

I do not believe that Soviet Russia desires war. What they desire is the fruits of war and the indefinite expansion of their power and doctrines. But what we have to consider here today, while time remains, is the permanent prevention of war and the establishment of conditions of freedom and democracy as rapidly as possible in all countries. . . .

From what I have seen of our Russian friends and allies during the war, I am convinced that there is nothing they admire so much as strength, and there is nothing for which they have less respect than for military weakness.

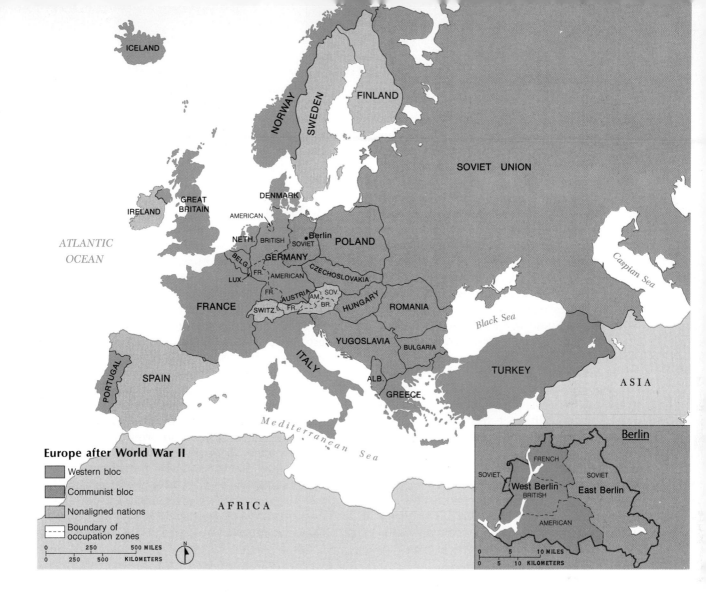

Europe after World War II

Western bloc

Communist bloc

Nonaligned nations

Boundary of occupation zones

Berlin

without industry or an army. These thoughts were soon forgotten when the United States saw what the Russians were doing in Eastern Europe.

During the period of the Nazi-Stalin pact, the Russians had annexed Lithuania, Latvia, and Estonia. At the war's end they added chunks of Poland and Romania while establishing their rule over those countries. In the early postwar years, they also took over control of Hungary, Czechoslovakia, and the eastern part of Germany.

As a counter to the creation of this zone of Soviet satellite countries, in 1946 the Americans and their western allies consolidated their hold on the western part of Germany despite strong Russian objections. They began to revive the German economy, hoping that western Germany would serve as a barrier against future Soviet expansion.

SECTION 1 REVIEW

Identify: Harry S. Truman, W. Averell Harriman, Security Council, General Assembly

Main Ideas

1. What was Harry Truman's greatest strength and greatest weakness?
2. What aspects of the Yalta agreement caused the rift between the United States and the Soviet Union?
3. Why did the UN fail to prevent a nuclear arms race?
4. List the reasons for the tensions between the Soviet Union and the United States in the postwar period.
5. Why did the United States begin to help revive the economy of western Germany?

2. COMING HOME TO A DREAM OF GREATNESS

For Americans generally, World War II restored the confidence shaken by the depression. The United States emerged from the conflict clearly the strongest nation on earth. Americans expected that strength to show itself at home as well as abroad. As one writer put it: "To have been an American then—the world must have seemed at one's feet."

To the American GIs in Europe and Asia, the chief desire was to get home as quickly as possible. But the government, with one eye on Soviet troop strength and the other on the dangers of massive unemployment, wanted to demobilize slowly.

The government's plan for gradual demobilization brought angry reactions at once. Yielding to public pressure, the government brought the GIs quickly home. Within a year, the armed forces were cut from 12.5 million to 2 million.

Readjusting the Economy

With the end of the war, depression-era fears of unemployment returned to haunt the nation. Economists predicted that the nation would be unable to reabsorb returning veterans. Some experts believed that unemployment would reach between 8 and 20 million people.

Thousands of women did lose their jobs to the returning GIs. For example, in 1943 women made up 25% of all automotive workers. By 1950, they were only 10%. These women did not give up their jobs willingly. But company policies and social pressures forced them to make room for the veterans.

Although many women were thrown out of work, jobs for men in the postwar years were generally available. The credit for preventing a crisis in unemployment for men belongs in part to effective government planning.

Even before the war ended, the government began planning for the postwar economy. During the war, half of all the nation's economic activities involved war orders. When peace came, Washington moved quickly to reduce the government's role to prewar levels. Surplus government property was sold to private enterprise, and taxes were reduced to pump money into the economy.

In contrast to the period following World War I, reconversion after World War II was a great success. The economy returned to peacetime production more smoothly and efficiently than anyone had expected. By the end of 1945, more than 90% of the wartime industries were back to civilian production. This rapid revival of civilian production plus GI unemployment benefits meant that the breadlines of the depression never returned.

Inflation, not unemployment, became the biggest postwar problem. During the war years, military production and strict rationing had limited the purchases people could make. With few consumer goods available, Americans saved some $140 billion. When the war ended, those dollars were waiting to buy goods that had not yet been produced. As a result, the prices of the limited goods available went sky high.

President Truman tried to halt the rapid rise in prices by at first maintaining and then only gradually lifting wartime wage and price controls. But the public responded in much the same way that they responded to plans to bring the GIs home slowly. After 15 years of war and depression, people had money in their pockets, and they wanted to spend it. For a time the nation had the worst of both worlds—government controls and a flourishing black market (the sale of goods at unlawful prices).

On the issue of controls, President Truman found himself opposed by the nation's businesses and by Republicans in Congress. Manufacturers were anxious to return to what they regarded as the good old days of "supply and demand." Republican politicians denounced controls as political tyranny over the economic system.

After a series of bitter fights in Congress, Truman lifted controls in November 1946. Prices jumped 25% in one month while earnings declined 12%. A headline in the New York *Daily News* on beef prices read:

PRICES SOAR, BUYERS SORE
STEERS JUMPED OVER THE MOON

The enormous growth of the economy, however, came to Truman's rescue. With more and more goods available, prices began to level off by 1950. Critics of the New Deal saw in this a vindication of their point of view. They argued that business, not government, had solved the problem of inflation. To them the end of wage and price controls signaled the end of the New Deal.

The Fair Deal

President Truman ignored his conservative critics and laid plans to extend the New Deal. He called his proposals the **Fair Deal**. Truman's Fair Deal plans called for an expansion of the Social Security system, an increase in the minimum wage from 40¢ to 65¢ an hour, and a full employment bill. He also called for an end to racial discrimination in housing, for a stronger Fair Employment Practices Commission, for new public housing and slum clearance programs, for federal aid to education, for national health insurance, and for government support of scientific research.

In 1949 Congress raised the minimum wage and passed the Public Housing Act. In 1950 it extended Social Security coverage to 10 million more Americans. But Congress refused to pass most of Truman's other proposals.

Business Versus Labor

After the war, business and labor resumed the fierce fighting of the depression years. As we have seen, the depression of the 1930s greatly weakened the public's view of American business. But the great success of industry in arming the Allies revived public support of the business community. Their confidence renewed, members of the National Association of Manufacturers and other business owners began to take the offensive against organized labor and its allies.

But organized labor, too, had gained in strength. It emerged from World War II far stronger than it had from World War I. But it had some new problems. During the war, workers had not gone on strike because of patriotism and high wages. At the war's end prices rose sharply, and

LIFE IN AMERICA

THE GI BILL

To help the returning veterans adjust to civilian life the government passed the Servicemen's Readjustment Act, popularly called the GI Bill of Rights. (GI—or "government issue"—was the slang term for American soldiers.) The GI Bill helped veterans buy homes and farms and start businesses. For those who could not find work, the GI Bill provided special unemployment benefits.

The greatest impact of the GI Bill, however, was on education. The veterans of World War II, many of whom remembered the breadlines of the depression years, came home with great expectations for the future. The GI Bill allowed the veterans to live up to their new faith in themselves and in their country. It offered monthly income payments to all veterans who enrolled in a college or voca-

tional school. As a result, millions of men and women who could never have afforded to go to college had a chance to better themselves. Some 8 million "vets" eventually took advantage of the educational benefits of the GI Bill. It was the largest and probably the most successful higher education program in American history.

Emergency housing for veterans in Los Angeles

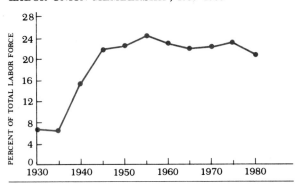

LABOR UNION MEMBERSHIP, 1930–1980

wages declined. Wages fell because of the end of overtime pay for war production, the end of well-paid defense work, and the growing surplus of labor as veterans flooded the labor market.

Once more workers began to "hit the bricks"— to go out on strike. By January of 1946, more than 2 million workers were on strike in the auto, oil refining, electrical, and steel industries.

The conflict between business and labor centered on how to divide growing profits. Between 1939 and 1945, productivity in American industry had doubled, but wages had not kept pace. Many companies grew prosperous on wartime contracts and then saw profits soar even higher after the war. Union leaders pointed to these enormous profits and argued that wages could be greatly raised without increasing prices. Management rejected these suggestions in an atmosphere of bitterness, arguing that such a path would lead to tyranny and socialism.

The coal-mining industry provided a dramatic illustration of the need for better labor conditions. In 1946 alone, dangerous conditions in the mines claimed the lives of nearly 1,000 miners. John L. Lewis, the flamboyant head of the United Mine Workers, led 400,000 miners out on strike. In addition to wage increases, Lewis called for improvements in mine safety and demanded that mine owners contribute to a special miner's health and retirement fund. The owners rejected these proposals.

The mine workers' strike threatened to cripple the entire economy. President Truman accused Lewis of ignoring the greater good of the nation. Truman then seized the coal mines. This was the first act of a long drama which saw the government greatly reduce the power of labor unions.

The Taft-Hartley Act

The efforts of labor unions to win their goals led to growing resentment on the part of business. Even many unorganized workers objected to union demands. In 1947, anti-union sentiment led to the passage of the **Taft-Hartley Act** over President Truman's veto. The principal author of the measure was **Senator Robert A. Taft** of Ohio. Taft, the highly respected leader of the conservative forces in the Republican party, wanted to limit the power of unions, which he claimed had been made too great by New Deal labor laws.

The Taft-Hartley Act outlawed a number of labor practices such as the "closed shop," which prevented employers from hiring nonunion members. ("Union shops," which required workers to join a union after they were hired, were still permitted.) The Taft-Hartley Act also required unions to accept a 60-day "cooling-off period" before striking, and it empowered the President to issue an injunction to prevent strikes that hurt the national safety. In addition, the law forbade unions to contribute to political campaigns, made unions file financial statements, and required all union leaders to take an oath that they were not Communists.

Labor denounced the act as a "slave-labor law" designed to keep workers docile. The passage of the law over Truman's veto was only one sign of the growing conservative mood in the country and of increased opposition to the President.

SECTION 2 REVIEW

 Identify: Fair Deal, Taft-Hartley Act, Robert A. Taft

Main Ideas
1. Why did the U.S. government want gradual demobilization after World War II? Why did a rapid demobilization occur?
2. Why did President Truman want to continue wage and price controls? Why did business oppose him?
3. Why did Truman's Fair Deal proposals yield few results?
4. Why did many workers go out on strike in 1945 and 1946?
5. What was Senator Taft's objective in seeking passage of the Taft-Hartley Act? Why did unions oppose the act?

3. THE ELECTION OF 1948

As the nation approached the presidential election of 1948, "Truman-can't-win" talk filled the air. Despite the popularity of Truman's militantly anti-Russian foreign policy, the tide seemed to be moving with the Republicans. The Republicans thought the country was finally turning away from the active government spawned by the New Deal and back to business-oriented politics. They had captured Congress in 1946. And in the past, when the party out of power won control of Congress during an off-year election, it had always gone on to win the next presidential election.

As their candidate in 1948, the Republicans nominated **Governor Thomas E. Dewey** of New York. Dewey, who had also been the Republican nominee in 1944, was confident about his chances. He expected to capitalize on the feeling that the Democrats had been in office for 16 years and "it was time to throw the rascals out."

Before Truman could face Dewey he had to fight off numerous challenges from within his own party. A number of middle-of-the-road Democrats approached General Dwight D. Eisenhower and asked him if he would be their standard bearer. "Ike" declined. On his political left, Truman faced Henry Wallace, who had left the Democratic party over what he felt was Truman's unnecessary belligerence toward the Soviet Union. Wallace's followers considered him the true heir to FDR. To his right, Truman faced the States' Rights Democrats, which the press called **Dixiecrats**, led by Senator Strom Thurmond of South Carolina. The Dixiecrats wanted to protect southern white interests and to limit the political and economic power of blacks.

After the Populist movement of the 1890s, southern politics had been dominated by a small number of Democratic voters, voting in white-only primaries. The war years began to change this. Black and poor white voters were gradually allowed to enter the political process. At the same time, southern influence in the national Democratic party declined when the rule was changed that had, in effect, given the South veto power over the presidential nominee. This rule had required the party nominee for President to win the support of two-thirds of the delegates to the national nominating convention.

Civil Rights Becomes a Political Issue

Many white southerners were upset by President Truman's proposal to establish a stronger Fair Employment Practices Commission (FEPC). The FEPC, an agency designed to end discrimination in federal hiring, was the forerunner of more extensive government efforts to abolish discrimination that would come in the 1960s.

The proposed Commission was an effort on behalf of blacks that went far beyond anything attempted under the New Deal. In 1941, Roosevelt had created an FEPC to ban discrimination in hiring by companies holding government contracts. He did so after **A. Philip Randolph,** head of the Brotherhood of Sleeping Car Porters, threatened a massive march of blacks on Washington. As a result of the agency's work, blacks received fairer treatment in hiring during the war. But Roosevelt depended on white southern support for many of his programs and had always moved very cautiously in the area of civil rights.

Although Congress did not strengthen the FEPC, Truman used his executive powers to attack discrimination. In 1948, for example, he issued an executive order that ended segregation in the armed forces.

The greatest changes in race relations in the postwar period came not from presidential actions but because of a dramatic shift in black attitudes and living patterns. Blacks, particularly veterans, pointed to the obvious contradiction of the United States fighting a war against Hitler's racism while maintaining racial discrimination at home. Similarly, the Cold War rivalry between America and Russia made racism an international embarrassment for the United States. Black leaders such as A. Philip Randolph took advantage of the situation to press for racial equality.

Millions of black workers who had moved north during the war into high-paying defense jobs supported Randolph's militancy. They made it clear that they were unwilling to return to the racist climate of the prewar years. At the same time black veterans who had experienced a measure of equality in the wider world were reluctant to return to their old jobs. The headline in one Memphis newspaper read, "Cotton pickers, where are you?" The black "vets," like the white "vets," not only expected better jobs upon their return, but they often engaged actively in politics. The white response was sometimes violence against black voters.

Truman's "Miraculous" Victory

With many traditional Democratic votes lost to him because of the Fair Deal and his stand on civil rights, Truman seemed to have little chance of winning in 1948. One split would have been bad enough; a Democratic party split three ways seemed easy for the Republicans to beat.

But Truman was stronger than he appeared. As a campaigner, his opponent was "as dull as a dishrag." Riding around the country on his "Victory Special" train, Dewey was overconfident. And what was worse, he let his overconfidence show. Many people found him cold, smug, and overly slick. Truman, on the other hand, was an exciting campaigner. He crisscrossed the country by rail on a whistle-stop campaign, giving as many as a dozen speeches a day in his folksy, no-holds-barred style.

It was a nasty campaign. The Republicans accused Truman of being soft on communism. Truman accused the Republicans of being tools of big business. Truman's master stroke was to call the Republican Congress back into session midway through the campaign to enact measures which he said would relieve the average American of the burden of inflation. When Congress refused to go along with his proposals, Truman scored crucial points with the public. He then turned to crowds, like the farmers he spoke to in Iowa, and shouted that "Congress had stuck a pitchfork in the farmer's back."

Even Truman's weakness turned out to be a source of strength. The Republicans accused him of being soft on communism. But they were unable to make the charge stick because Wallace supporters were, at the same time, accusing him of being an imperialist warmonger who was trying to start a war with Russia. Liberals who compared Truman unfavorably with FDR still preferred him to the Dixiecrats. In fact, the Dixiecrat attack on Truman's civil rights record forced liberals to swallow their pride and support his campaign.

The day after the election, the headline in the Chicago *Tribune* read "Dewey Defeats Truman." But the *Tribune* was wrong. To the surprise of almost everyone, Truman had won an upset victory. He had gained almost 50% of the popular vote, while Dewey received 45%.

Elections are more than personal popularity contests. Looked at closely, they can be seen as X rays that reveal the inner anatomy of the country. When we analyze the 1948 election, we can see that Truman's victory was a testimony to the number of groups that had come to look to the federal government for assistance. The farmers, for instance, who were supposed to be mainly Republican, voted heavily for Truman. They had come to depend on New Deal price supports and were unwilling to risk a Republican administration. Blue-collar Americans feared that a Dewey presidency might bring more in the way of Taft-Hartley legislation. And black Americans, voting in increasing numbers, abandoned the party of Lincoln for the party of civil rights legislation.

SECTION 3 REVIEW

 Identify: Thomas E. Dewey, Dixiecrats, A. Philip Randolph

Main Ideas
1. What opposition did President Truman face in the campaign of 1948?
2. How did the position of American blacks change during and after World War II? What part did civil rights play in the 1948 campaign?
3. List two reasons why Harry Truman won the 1948 election.

4. THE COLD WAR HEATS UP

In the late 1940s Russian expansion abroad and "communist subversion" at home became the preoccupation of both official Washington and millions of Americans. The peace that had seemed so secure just a few short years earlier now seemed increasingly fragile. A "Cold War" began—a continuing rivalry between the two nations that threatened to turn into World War III.

The Truman Doctrine

In 1947 one of the major trouble spots was the eastern Mediterranean. Soviet leaders demanded that Turkey give up control of the strategic waterway leading from the Black Sea to the Mediterranean. At the same time, in Greece, Moscow-backed rebels tried to overthrow a conservative regime supported by Britain, the traditional guardian of western interests in the Mediterranean.

The situation in Greece and Turkey, combined with the earlier Russian attempt to take over northern Iran and the establishment of Russian puppet regimes in Romania and Bulgaria, led the United States to fear the worst. Undersecretary of State **Dean Acheson** came before a private meeting of congressional leaders to say that "like apples in a barrel infected by one rotten one, the corruption of Greece [by Communist rebels] would infect Iran and all to the east." In an early version of what would later be called the "domino theory," Acheson warned that the infection could spread to Egypt, Turkey, and then Europe itself.

Acheson's dark vision of the future was based on a new view of Soviet intentions developed by Secretary of Defense **James Forrestal** and U.S. ambassador in Moscow **George Kennan**. These men argued that the revolutionary heritage of communism and Stalin's need for an external enemy led Russia toward endless expansion. Kennan compared Russia's actions to those of a toy car. When wound up, it would run over everything in its path until it struck a more powerful object. This view was bolstered by the growing belief that all totalitarian governments were alike. If Stalin's Russia were like Hitler's Germany, the chief problem of American foreign policy was to avoid another "Munich."

Thus it was that in early 1947 when an ailing Britain announced that it could no longer afford to support the anti-Communist regime in Greece, President Truman boldly stepped in to fill the breech. His words to the nation were, "We must not go through the Thirties again." To prevent this he proposed in March 1947 what became known as the **Truman Doctrine.** By the terms of this doctrine, the United States promised not only to aid Greece, but to support free peoples anywhere in the world who were "resisting attempted subjugation by armed minorities or by outside pressures." In effect, Truman pledged to fight communism the world over. Truman's policy also became known as the **policy of "containment"** after a magazine article by George Kennan used the term in July 1947.

The Marshall Plan

The military tone of the Truman Doctrine angered some of the President's liberal supporters. They were much happier with the second prong of his counter to the Russians, the **Marshall Plan.** This plan, launched in June 1947, was designed to aid America's European allies who were still suffering from the destruction of World War II.

European railroads, factories, power plants, banking houses, and farms had been devastated by the war. The people of these nations were anxious to buy American goods and machinery to rebuild but lacked the dollars to do so. In the two years since the fighting ended, Europe lurched from crisis to crisis. Churchill later remarked that Europe at the time was "a rubble heap, a charnel house, a breeding ground of pestilence and hate." To add to the woe, the continent suffered the worst snowstorms in a half century.

Secretary of State George Marshall responded to Europe's plight with an imaginative plan to aid Europe and at the same time provide a market for American goods. Avoiding the narrow anti-Communist focus of the Truman Doctrine, the plan called for funneling massive funds to rebuild Europe. According to Marshall the plan, which was originally to include Russia, was directed "not against any country or doctrine but against hunger, poverty, desperation, and chaos." The American government asked only that the European governments cooperate fully and take the initiative in devising long-term programs.

The nations of Western Europe responded enthusiastically and plunged at once into the planning effort. The Russians attended the early discussions but withdrew when they realized that they would have to be open about their economic condition. They also feared that the Marshall Plan would relieve discontent in Western Europe and thus hinder the spread of communism.

The Marshall Plan turned out to be a great success. During the four years of the Marshall Plan from 1948 to 1951, the United States loaned or gave $12 billion to the countries taking part in the plan. As a result, by 1951 Western Europe was economically healthy. The Marshall Plan also provided a large market for American goods, and it held back the spread of Soviet influence in Western Europe.

Czechoslovakia, Yugoslavia, and Berlin

While Congress was still debating the Marshall Plan in February 1948, the nation was hit with the first of several shocks that would be felt that year. The Soviets staged a military coup in democratic Czechoslovakia. Congress responded by passing the Marshall Plan despite the criticism of some Republicans that it amounted to a global New Deal. Next, when Yugoslavia asserted its independence from the Soviets, Stalin expelled it from the world Communist movement. He then set about purging the non-Communist leaders holding office in other Eastern European countries. The most dramatic Soviet challenge to the Marshall Plan came in June 1948 when Stalin set up a blockade of the western-occupied section of Berlin. Here was a direct challenge that could not be ignored.

The **Berlin blockade** caught Truman by surprise. After the war, Germany had been divided into four zones. (See inset map, page 683.) Berlin, which had been Hitler's capital, was located in the Russian zone. But at the end of the war the armies of the western powers occupied the western half of the city. They assumed that their stay in Berlin would last only until Germany was de-Nazified and reunited. But when the Cold War erupted, West Berlin became a western island, 100 miles inside Soviet-occupied East Germany.

The Berlin blockade presented President Truman with three choices. He could simply withdraw from a militarily indefensible position in West Berlin. He could threaten the Russians with military force. Or, on a lesser scale, he could send an armed convoy through the Soviet zone.

Any one of the steps would risk war. Truman rejected the first as appeasement. The second he believed too dangerous. So he chose an imaginative air-age version of the third. The U.S. Air Force began a giant airlift of food and provisions for the 2 million people of West Berlin. Every three minutes, 24 hours a day, American and British planes flew food, clothing, fuel, and even machinery into Berlin.

The Berlin airlift was a great display of western resourcefulness. But most important, without being overly warlike, it demonstrated to the Europeans that America could be counted on in a crisis. The Russians, taken aback by Allied determination, lifted the blockade in May 1949.

The Birth of NATO

In the wake of the Berlin blockade, Truman moved quickly to provide Europe with the kind of military guarantees needed to counteract the fears of Russian aggression. "Tired of babying the Russians," Truman called for a dramatic break with American diplomatic and military traditions. He called for a sweeping military alliance between the United States and Western Europe.

Secretary of State Dean Acheson became the architect of the North Atlantic Treaty Organization, or **NATO**, signed in 1949 by 12 nations.* Elegant and mustachioed, Acheson was both loved and hated. His enemies, particularly old-line isolationists, saw him as a snob and an imitation Englishman. His supporters described him as a brilliant tactician and the man responsible for securing the safety of Western Europe.

SECTION 4 REVIEW

Identify: Cold War, Dean Acheson, James Forrestal, George Kennan, Truman Doctrine, policy of containment, Marshall Plan, Berlin blockade, NATO

Main Ideas

1. What were the goals of the Marshall Plan? How did Russia react to it?
2. What were two effects of the Berlin blockade crisis?

*The original members were Belgium, Britain, Canada, Denmark, France, Iceland, Italy, Luxembourg, the Netherlands, Norway, Portugal, and the United States. Greece and Turkey joined in 1952, West Germany in 1955.

5. THE KOREAN WAR

The creation of NATO was the high-water mark of the Truman administration. Shortly thereafter, Truman's domestic and foreign policies were hampered by growing fears about Communist subversion at home and Communist gains abroad.

China Becomes Communist

The promise of the Truman Doctrine to support anti-Communist governments around the world was soon put to the test in China. **Chiang Kai-shek,** the Nationalist Chinese leader, had been at war off and on since 1947 with the Chinese Communists led by **Mao Tse-tung.** Chiang's cause had strong support from many Americans who saw the destiny of the United States as lying more in Asia than in Europe.

President Truman made several attempts to aid Chiang, but despite American military and economic support, Chiang's corrupt regime was unable to withstand the rising power of the Communists. Truman refused to become more deeply involved. Defeated on the mainland, Chiang fled to the island of Formosa in 1949, where he established the government known today as Taiwan.

The Communist victory in China stunned many Americans. Liberals who believed that "history was on our side" and that the Communist regime could not win popular support were dismayed. But an even more intense reaction came from conservatives who demanded to know, "Who lost China?" Conservatives pointed to the Truman Doctrine and asked why the administration stood by while "China went down the drain."

The Search for Traitors

With China in the Communist camp, the balance of power seemed to have shifted against the United States. Many believed that the shift could only have resulted from internal subversion (traitors).

The U.S. emerged from World War II so powerful relative to the war-ravaged nations that many Americans believed their country was capable of controlling the destiny of the entire world. When things did not go their way, they thought that the problem must be traitors in their midst.

Fears of internal subversion grew rapidly when, shortly after the Communists' victory in China, the Russians announced that they had exploded an atomic bomb. The Soviet achievement took place long before American scientists had believed it could. Because it had demobilized quickly after the war, the United States relied on its atomic monopoly to counter Russia's superiority in manpower. Without that monopoly Americans began to feel terribly vulnerable. In 1950 the FBI, searching for possible leaks of atomic secrets, arrested two U.S. citizens, Julius and Ethel Rosenberg, and charged them with passing classified atomic information to the Russians.

The **Rosenberg case** helped create an atmosphere of fear in the nation. The trial of the Rosenbergs in 1951 and their controversial execution in 1953 focused public attention on the threat of subversion. U.S. Attorney General J. Howard McGrath warned that Communists "are everywhere—in factories, offices, butcher shops, on street corners, in private business—and each carries in himself the germs of death for society."

The Korean War Begins

When the Japanese surrendered in 1945, Korea was divided, temporarily it was thought, between the Russian armies in the North and the Americans in the South. Four years later the Russians and Americans withdrew, leaving a bitterly divided country. The North, heavily armed and far more industrially developed, was ruled by the Communist boss Kim Il-Sung. The less-developed South was controlled by strongman Syngman Rhee, whose army was useful primarily to eliminate domestic opponents. Kim, aggressive and ambitious, saw a chance to conquer the South when Dean Acheson publicly stated that Korea was outside the American defense perimeter.

For reasons of their own, the Russians encouraged Kim. Although Russia and China were both Communist countries, there was a deep animosity between Stalin and Mao. The Russians knew that a unified Korea under Russian control would be a blow to Chinese prestige and a potential enemy on China's flank. It would also pose a threat to Japan.

When the North Koreans attacked the South on June 25, 1950, Truman was determined to halt aggression in its tracks. He appealed at once to the United Nations, and because the Russians happened to be boycotting the UN at the time, he received its support. The resulting war in Korea was fought under a UN command with several member nations contributing troops and supplies. In fact, however, the support for South Korea was overwhelmingly an American affair.

The American involvement was not officially a "war." Truman called it a "police action" because only Congress has the right to declare war, and he never asked for congressional approval. Truman justified his actions on the grounds that in the atomic age the President must be able to make quick decisions without waiting for Congress to move through its lengthy debates.

MacArthur's Brilliant Strategy

Despite all the tensions of the Cold War, the United States was unprepared for combat. Army troop strength was less than half what it had been at the start of World War II. Thus the Americans were of little immediate aid to the South Koreans, who were overrun and pushed back into the area around Pusan in southeastern Korea. (See map, below left.)

The situation was desperate, but the American Far Eastern Commander Douglas MacArthur responded with a brilliant stroke. Rather than fight his way out of the corner in which he was trapped, MacArthur executed an end run. In mid-September he staged an amphibious attack at Inchon to the north, well behind North Korean lines. The bold gamble paid off brilliantly, and within two weeks the North Korean army was driven back north of the 38th parallel which divided the two Koreas.

China Enters the War

Flushed with success, MacArthur and Truman aimed next at driving the Communists out of all of Korea. This new American objective alarmed the Chinese. They openly warned that if American troops approached the Yalu River separating North Korea from China, they would respond with force. Despite this warning, MacArthur as-

American paratroopers practice jumping at Taegu, Korea, in 1951.

The Korean War

- Area occupied by Communist forces
- Area occupied by UN forces
- Communist forces
- UN forces

0 — 200 MILES
0 — 200 KILOMETERS

North Korean Invasion
JUNE–SEPT. 1950

CHINA
Yalu R.
NORTH KOREA
Sea of Japan
Pyongyang
38th Parallel
Seoul
Pusan Perimeter
SOUTH KOREA
Yellow Sea
Pusan
JAPAN

UN Offensive
SEPT.–NOV. 1950

CHINA
Yalu R.
NORTH KOREA
Sea of Japan
Pyongyang
Inchon
Seoul
38th Parallel
SOUTH KOREA
Yellow Sea
JAPAN

Communist Chinese Offensive
NOV. 1950–JAN. 1951

CHINA
Yalu R.
NORTH KOREA
Sea of Japan
Pyongyang
Seoul
38th Parallel
SOUTH KOREA
Yellow Sea
JAPAN

UN Counteroffensive and Truce
JAN. 1951–JULY 1953

CHINA
Yalu R.
NORTH KOREA
Sea of Japan
Pyongyang
Panmunjom
Seoul
Armistice Line
38th Parallel
SOUTH KOREA
Yellow Sea
JAPAN

sured Truman that the Chinese would not intervene. The President then authorized MacArthur to push northward. The confident general promised to "have the boys home by Christmas."

The war appeared all but over when disaster struck. Some 200,000 Chinese troops crossed the Yalu, inflicting huge casualties on the Americans. In the retreat that followed, the South Korean capital of Seoul, liberated at Inchon, was again lost to the Communists. It was only after further heavy fighting that the Americans were able to reestablish their lines near the 38th parallel. The war dragged on for three more indecisive years. The fighting seesawed back and forth, inflicting heavy casualties without changing the military stalemate.

The Truman-MacArthur Controversy

General MacArthur wanted to commit massive American forces to win a decisive victory. If necessary, he favored using the A-bomb against China. "There is no substitute for victory," he declared. Truman, however, insisted on a limited war for limited objectives. He feared that a broader war in Asia could not be won. And he was even more worried by the prospect of the conflict over Korea turning into an atomic World War III.

Truman's policies were bitterly attacked by many conservative politicians. They idolized MacArthur and wanted to "unleash" Chiang Kai-shek and use the Korean conflict to defeat communism in China. When MacArthur sided publicly with this viewpoint and insisted that he be allowed to pursue the war by bombing China if necessary, Truman relieved him of his command. Backed by most of the other generals, Truman insisted that a commander, even one as popular as MacArthur, could not be allowed to override civilian authority.

MacArthur's dismissal in April 1951 set off a great debate in Congress over the conduct of the war. Truman's critics denounced him as an imbecile and an appeaser. Truman's insistence on civilian authority received wide support, but his policy of limited war came under heavy attack. The concept of limited war ran counter to the national spirit. Many Americans assumed that if there was reason enough to go to war there was reason enough to fight on to victory, using any means necessary.

Unhappiness over the policy of limited war

Americans held huge sympathy parades for General MacArthur after his dismissal.

destroyed Truman's administration. His Fair Deal programs were buried by the resulting furor. Disagreements over Korea paved the way for the election of a former general, Dwight D. Eisenhower, as President and touched off a new hunt for Communist subversives in government.

SECTION 5 REVIEW

 Identify: Chiang Kai-shek, Mao Tse-tung, Rosenberg case

Main Ideas

1. What was Truman's policy toward China, and why was it criticized?
2. How did the Soviet A-bomb and the Rosenberg case affect American attitudes?
3. How did the Korean conflict start? Why was it called a "police action" instead of a "war"?
4. How did the Truman-MacArthur controversy arise? What was the outcome?

693

CHAPTER 31 REVIEW

Key Terms
Explain the meaning of each of the following terms:

    Security Council
    General Assembly
    Fair Deal
    Taft-Hartley Act
    Dixiecrats
    Cold War
    Truman Doctrine
    policy of containment
    Marshall Plan
    Berlin blockade
    NATO
    Rosenberg case

Reviewing the Main Ideas

Section 1
1. What issues divided the United States and the Soviet Union at the end of the war?
2. Why did the UN fail to prevent a nuclear arms race?
3. What steps did the United States take in 1946 to counter Soviet influence in Eastern Europe?

Section 2
1. What was Truman's Fair Deal program, and what happened to it?
2. What was the dispute between President Truman and business owners over continuation of wage and price controls? How was the issue resolved?
3. What were the main provisions of the Taft-Hartley Act? Why did labor unions oppose it?

Section 3
1. What opposition did President Truman face in the campaign of 1948? What part did the civil rights issue play in the campaign?
2. What factors led to Truman's surprise victory in 1948? Why did most people expect him to lose?

Section 4
1. What led to the formation in 1947 of the policy known as the Truman Doctrine?
2. Describe the goals and results of the Marshall Plan.
3. Why was NATO created, and what were its objectives?

Section 5
1. Why was Truman's policy toward China criticized in 1949 and after?
2. How did the Soviet A-bomb and the Rosenberg case affect American attitudes?
3. Why did Truman declare the Korean conflict a "police action" and not a war?
4. How did General MacArthur and President Truman differ on Korean War objectives?

Special History Skills:
Using a Specialized Vocabulary
Many words have a specialized meaning when used in reference to a particular time in history. Write a definition for each of the following words and use it in a sentence dealing with the Cold War. Use your textbook and a dictionary as your sources.

    proliferation
    iron curtain
    Soviet sphere
    fifth column
    satellite
    imperialist warmonger
    puppet regime

Other Skill Activities
1. **Speechwriter**
   Imagine you are a speechwriter for President Truman in 1948. Write a speech for one of his whistle-stop tours. Before you write the speech, consider who his audience will be.
2. **Research**
   Research the Berlin airlift. What sorts of goods were airlifted? How many planes were involved? How were the goods collected and distributed?
3. **Make a political map**
   Draw a map of the world that shows Communist countries in 1950. Use a key to indicate which ones were controlled by Russia and

which ones had independent Communist governments.

4. Biography

J. Robert Oppenheimer, a developer of the atomic bomb, had reservations about its use. What were they, and what happened to Oppenheimer when he voiced these reservations?

Thinking Critically

1. Why do you think the United States joined the United Nations even though it did not join the League of Nations?
2. If you were President Truman, how would you have reacted to the Berlin blockade? Why?
3. Should the United States have done more to prevent the Communist victory in China? If so, what?
4. Why did the United States move from a position of supporting total victory in World War II to supporting a limited war in Korea?

Further Reading

Nancy Garden. *Berlin City Split in Two*. G. P. Putnam, 1971. Reasons for the division of Berlin, the airlift, and the Berlin Wall are covered in this easy-to-read book.

A. B. Lane. *I Saw Poland Betrayed*. Bobbs-Merrill, 1948. An account of the Soviet takeover of Poland.

Robert and Michael Meeropol. *We Are Your Sons*. Houghton Mifflin Co., 1975. Julius and Ethel Rosenberg's children tell the story of their parents' lives and why they believe their parents to have been innocent.

TEST YOURSELF

WRITE YOUR ANSWERS ON A SEPARATE SHEET OF PAPER.

Matching

Write the letter of the description that best matches each person below.

1. W. Averell Harriman
2. Harry S. Truman
3. A. Philip Randolph
4. Thomas E. Dewey
5. Douglas MacArthur
6. Chiang Kai-shek
7. Mao Tse-tung
8. Syngman Rhee
9. Ethel Rosenberg
10. George Marshall

a. South Korean dictator during the Korean conflict
b. leader of Nationalist China
c. leader of Communist China
d. secretary of state who proposed a program of economic aid for Europe
e. union leader who pushed for racial equality
f. conservative senator who proposed that the United States "unleash" the forces of Chiang Kai-shek
g. convicted and executed for disclosing atomic secrets
h. U.S. general who took command from General MacArthur in Korea
i. ordered the Berlin airlift
j. U.S. ambassador who advised Truman to "get tough" with the Russians
k. Republican candidate for President in 1948
l. U.S. general who wanted to invade China

True or False

Mark T if the statement is true and F if it is false. Change the italicized words in all false statements so that they are true.

1. The Truman Doctrine was developed to *counteract* Communist intervention in Greece.
2. The *Fair Deal* gave Western Europe loans and economic aid.
3. The GI Bill provided veterans with *money for education*.
4. Business leaders opposed Truman because he *favored* the Taft-Hartley bill.
5. Veterans returned to an era of *depression*.
6. Goods were airlifted to *Munich* when the Soviets blockaded that city.
7. General MacArthur wanted to invade *China* in order to end the Korean conflict.
8. NATO is a military association of *Communist* countries.
9. The Rosenbergs were executed for passing *atomic information* to the Soviets.
10. In 1950 Yugoslavia and China *were close allies* of the Soviet Union.

Chapter 32

1952–1960

THE EISENHOWER ERA

I t is 6:20 A.M., May 1, 1960. On an isolated airstrip in Pakistan, a strange black airplane, with no markings on its long, slender wings, moves swiftly down a runway and gracefully lifts into the sky. The aircraft is an American U-2—the "black lady of espionage"— and it is starting out on a mission that will take it deep into the territory of the Soviet Union.

Four hours later, 68,000 feet above the Soviet city of Sverdlovsk, the U-2 jerks suddenly forward, as if struck violently from the rear. An orange flash fills the cockpit and the plane lurches wildly out of control. A Soviet surface-to-air missile has hit the American plane. A few seconds later the pilot, 30-year-old Francis Gary Powers, hurls himself out of the plane. The U-2 crashes onto Soviet soil, and a few minutes later Powers is a prisoner of the Soviet government. A new international crisis has begun.

The U-2 incident, as this event was soon called, was one of several international crises that occurred during the Eisenhower era. In this chapter you will learn of America's growing prosperity at home and of the deepening chill of the Cold War abroad. You will see how the irresponsible tactics of an American senator brought a second "red scare" to the United States. You will also study how a major Supreme Court decision and a bus boycott started the nation on the road to ending segregation in education and in other public facilities. And, finally, you will see how millions of Americans achieved unimagined affluence.

Sections in This Chapter
1. The Rise and Fall of Senator Joseph McCarthy
2. Dwight D. Eisenhower—The General Becomes President
3. American Foreign Policy and the Cold War
4. Eisenhower at Home
5. Eisenhower's Second Term
6. The Impact of the Fifties on America

Opposite: Mid-century jukebox. Early rock and roll was played on gaudy machines like this one.

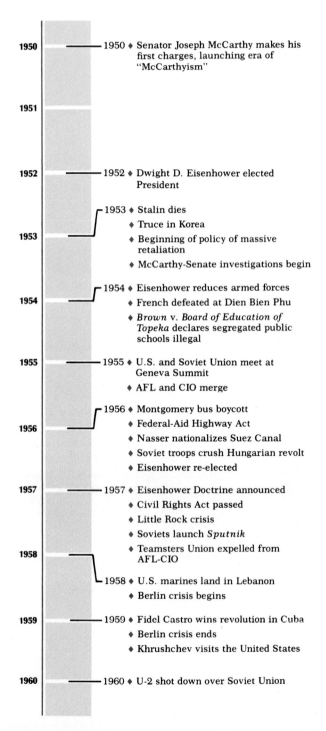

1950 ♦ Senator Joseph McCarthy makes his first charges, launching era of "McCarthyism"

1952 ♦ Dwight D. Eisenhower elected President

1953 ♦ Stalin dies
♦ Truce in Korea
♦ Beginning of policy of massive retaliation
♦ McCarthy-Senate investigations begin

1954 ♦ Eisenhower reduces armed forces
♦ French defeated at Dien Bien Phu
♦ *Brown v. Board of Education of Topeka* declares segregated public schools illegal

1955 ♦ U.S. and Soviet Union meet at Geneva Summit
♦ AFL and CIO merge

1956 ♦ Montgomery bus boycott
♦ Federal-Aid Highway Act
♦ Nasser nationalizes Suez Canal
♦ Soviet troops crush Hungarian revolt
♦ Eisenhower re-elected

1957 ♦ Eisenhower Doctrine announced
♦ Civil Rights Act passed
♦ Little Rock crisis
♦ Soviets launch *Sputnik*
♦ Teamsters Union expelled from AFL-CIO

1958 ♦ U.S. marines land in Lebanon
♦ Berlin crisis begins

1959 ♦ Fidel Castro wins revolution in Cuba
♦ Berlin crisis ends
♦ Khrushchev visits the United States

1960 ♦ U-2 shot down over Soviet Union

1. THE RISE AND FALL OF SENATOR JOSEPH McCARTHY

The tremors set off by the Chinese Revolution and the explosion of the first Soviet A-bomb became full-scale earthquakes with the political arrival of **Senator Joseph R. McCarthy.** McCarthy, a Republican from Wisconsin, seemed to be able to make sense of all these calamities. There was, he said, evidence of a gigantic Communist conspiracy in the very heart of the American government.

McCarthy, a genius at creating publicity, dominated American political life from early 1950 through 1954. Even the election of Dwight D. Eisenhower took place under the shadow of what became known as **"McCarthyism."**

McCarthy's Charges

Senator McCarthy first came to the nation's attention in February 1950 as the result of a sensational speech he gave in Wheeling, West Virginia. The exact words of his talk remain in dispute. What is clear, however, is that during his rambling remarks he waved a piece of paper and shouted something like the following:

I have here in my hands a list of 205—a list of names that were made known to the Secretary of State [Dean Acheson] as being members of the Communist party and who nevertheless are still working and shaping State Department policy.

The newspaper reporters present immediately recognized McCarthy's accusations as the makings of a big story. They followed him from his talk to the airport and asked for a copy of his list. McCarthy refused to show one. The next night he gave a speech in Reno, Nevada, and there he mentioned a list of 57 Communists. A week later in Salt Lake City, the number was 81. The press trumpeted these charges without checking on their truthfulness. This enormous attention given by the press to McCarthy's charges paved the way for his prominence. Although a Senate investigating committee soon concluded that these charges were false and malicious, McCarthy kept on making them.

McCarthy's Target: New Dealers

McCarthy was not the first person to make charges about Communist subversion in government. But his personal style and his ability to express the fear and anger many Americans felt may have come at a time when Americans wanted to hear such charges. There were some actual spies in Washington, but McCarthy showed little interest in them. They were not his true target. The people he was really after were the New Dealers and other liberal Democrats.

McCarthy appealed to Americans by posing as an avenging private eye out to right the wrongs that the "New Deal Establishment" had supposedly covered up. A Marine Corps veteran, he billed himself as "Tailgunner Joe," the fighting hero from World War II. Actually, as a Marine intelligence officer, he had held a desk job interviewing pilots returning from bombing missions. To show the public how different he was from "stuffed shirt" politicians, McCarthy had himself photographed coming out of the shower with a towel wrapped around his waist in the manner of the famous prizefighter, Rocky Marciano. McCarthy liked to think of himself as the representative of the common people, taking on what he called the "Commiecrats" and "perverts" of Washington. He once commented acidly: "I don't think we need to fear too much about the Communists dropping a bomb on Washington. They would kill too many of their friends that way."

McCarthy's supporters were welded together by a strong dislike of one or another of Roosevelt's policies during the New Deal and his wartime dealings with the Soviet Union, especially at Yalta. Many Republican party officials saw McCarthy as a godsend for the GOP. The Wisconsin senator had put the Democrats on the defensive. For the first time since the Great Depression, Republicans had a chance to seize the political initiative.

A Second Red Scare

Many Republicans, however, were troubled by the way McCarthy abused his power. Because of McCarthy's accusations, thousands of officials were driven from their jobs. Others were blacklisted (cut off from employment possibilities). Many people were afraid to voice their political feelings. Some local schools tried to remove *Robin Hood* from their libraries because its theme of robbing the rich and giving to the poor was "red." Even the Cincinnati Reds changed their name to "Redlegs."

A new red scare called McCarthyism swept the nation. McCarthyism was the use of unsubstantiated accusations of treason, support of communism, or "un-American" thinking. When people are caught up in such a mood of fear and intolerance they often take accusation for proof. Thus mere *accusations* were enough to ruin the government careers of many innocent people. In such a national mood, there is little defense against slander.

There were some officials in both parties who were troubled by the senator's tactics, but many went along. Even the respected and normally principled Robert Taft urged McCarthy on. Said Taft: "If one case doesn't work, try another." Taft hoped that McCarthy's influence would set the stage for a Republican, preferably Taft himself, to

The Army-McCarthy Senate hearings, 1953

win the presidential election in 1952. Republican support of McCarthy's accusations was strong while Truman was in the White House. After a Republican President was elected, however, the party began to consider McCarthy an embarrassment.

None of McCarthy's charges were proven, but his reckless accusations did a great deal of damage. Careers of a number of government officials, college professors, and entertainment figures were ruined or severely harmed because of the fear generated by McCarthy. People distrusted their neighbors and friends. The only protection, it seemed, was conformity and silence.

McCarthy's Downfall

In 1954, Senator McCarthy, seeking even more attention and power, accused the United States Army of being a hotbed of communism. The charge was the beginning of the senator's downfall. When in 1953 the Senate began to hold public hearings to examine McCarthy's charges, the proceedings were televised and open to the public. Here McCarthy's abrasiveness and groundless accusations offended the sense of fairness of most Americans. No one could seriously believe the charge that the United States Army fostered communism. In addition, McCarthy's bullying rudeness worked against him.

In December of 1954, McCarthy was censured by his colleagues in the Senate for "conduct unbecoming a member." To "censure" is to publicly criticize or rebuke. The Senate's censure of McCarthy swept away much of his support, and he quickly faded from the public view. Two years later McCarthy died as a man with little influence and no respect, ignored by the public which had once feared and perhaps even admired him.

SECTION 1 REVIEW

Identify: Joseph McCarthy, McCarthyism

Main Ideas

1. What were Senator McCarthy's charges? How did the press bring them to the attention of the public?
2. Why did Senator McCarthy appeal to so many Americans?
3. How did McCarthyism hurt many Americans?
4. What finally brought a halt to McCarthy?

2. DWIGHT D. EISENHOWER— THE GENERAL BECOMES PRESIDENT

As the election of 1952 approached, the Democrats were in deep trouble. President Truman could muster an approval rating of just 26% in the public-opinion polls. His administration was saddled with scandals, an unpopular war in Korea, and accusations of being soft on communism. At home, however, the economy was growing, employment was up, and Americans were prospering. In the midst of these somewhat confusing times, the nation's two political parties prepared for the election of 1952.

The Election of 1952

President Truman, even though he was eligible for re-election, decided not to run again. After a long series of ballots at the Democratic convention in Chicago, **Adlai E. Stevenson,** the witty and urbane governor of Illinois, won the nomination.

The main contenders for the Republican nomination were Senator Robert A. Taft of Ohio, the son of a former President, and General **Dwight D. Eisenhower,** the World War II hero. Taft entered the convention with more support than Eisenhower, but after a bitter fight Ike won the nomination. A young senator from California, **Richard M. Nixon,** won the vice-presidential nomination.

Eisenhower's choice of Nixon as his running mate threatened to sink the ticket when the New York *Post* published a story about a secret "Nixon fund" which had been set up by some of the vice-presidential candidate's supporters. The story claimed that a millionaire's club in California had illegally provided Nixon with an $18,000 secret fund. Eisenhower considered dropping Nixon from the ticket, but, in a dramatic television speech, the vice-presidential candidate described his financial troubles and explained how one of the gifts he had received was a small cocker spaniel named Checkers. The little dog, said Nixon, was the only gift he had kept personally. The Checkers speech, as it was known, saved the day for Nixon. His frank discussion of his financial status and the emotionalism of the speech won the sympathy of many Americans.

During the campaign, Ike's twinkling eyes and famous grin made him an attractive candidate. Although many Americans thought that Stevenson was witty, polished, and brilliant, he was unable to counter Eisenhower's enormous appeal. When the former general promised to go personally to Korea and end the war, his election was assured. When Americans went to the polls in November, Eisenhower won 442 electoral votes to Stevenson's 89. In the congressional elections a narrow Republican majority won control of Congress.

The Eisenhower White House

President Eisenhower brought a military crispness to the White House, where he built a thoroughly Republican administration. Almost all cabinet positions went to business executives. The cabinet also began to play a much larger role than it had before. Sherman Adams, the former governor of New Hampshire, became Eisenhower's Chief of Staff. It was Adams' job to decide who could see the President and what information should be made available to him. Although this system maintained order, it had the effect of insulating the President from much of the activity of his subordinates.

Peace in Korea

Eisenhower was elected partly on his promise to travel to the war-battered peninsula of Korea and end the fighting there. His Secretary of State, **John Foster Dulles,** wanted to end the war by defeating the Chinese, who were siding with North Korea. Other presidential advisers also believed the United States should wage total war to win in Korea. The President, however, felt that an all-out war would wreck the nation's economy. Eisenhower did not believe Korea was worth such a risk. Thus, he decided that a negotiated peace settlement would best serve the interests of the United States.

When the President entered office in January 1953, two years of back-and-forth fighting had left the two sides essentially where they were when the North Korean invasion began the war. Both North Korea and the United States appeared interested in a truce. Peace efforts, however, were snagged over the issue of prisoners of war. The Chinese and North Koreans insisted that all their troops held captive be returned. The South Kore-

ans and the United States refused this demand because many enemy prisoners were unwilling to return to their native lands. The truce negotiations seemed hopelessly deadlocked when Stalin's sudden death in early 1953 brought a less rigid leadership into control in the Soviet Union, and Eisenhower's threat to use nuclear weapons cleared the way for a settlement.

Although the war had cost more than 54,000 American lives, and perhaps as many as 2 million Chinese and Korean casualties, little was achieved by either side. The peace settlement divided the peninsula along the armistice line, which was surrounded by a demilitarized zone. (See map, page 692.) Thus, South Korea gained about 1,500 square miles of territory. An uneasy peace has been maintained at this line since the armistice agreements were signed in July of 1953.

Dwight D. Eisenhower (1890–1969)

IN OFFICE: 1953–1961

Republican from New York. Eisenhower was the first Republican President in 20 years and the first professional soldier to serve in that office since Ulysses S. Grant. During his administration, the Korean War was ended (1953), the McCarthy hearings (1953–1954) attracted national attention, and the Supreme Court declared school segregation unconstitutional (1954).

SECTION 2 REVIEW

Identify: Adlai E. Stevenson, Dwight D. Eisenhower, Richard M. Nixon, John Foster Dulles

Main Ideas

1. Who were the main candidates in the 1952 presidential election? What was the outcome?
2. How did Richard M. Nixon clear his name during the "Nixon fund" accusations?
3. How did Eisenhower's election affect the Korean War? What was the outcome of the war?

3. AMERICAN FOREIGN POLICY AND THE COLD WAR

When Dwight Eisenhower became President, he and his Secretary of State, John Foster Dulles, hoped to create a new American foreign policy. This foreign policy would reflect Republican principles, ideals, and needs. The President had confidence in Dulles and left it to him to put the new policy into effect. The ideas formulated by Dulles left a deep imprint on the entire decade of the Fifties.

Dulles Calls for a Roll-back of Communism

Dulles wanted to make a clean break with Truman and Acheson's policy of containment—that is, of confining communism to its present boundaries. To Dulles, containment was a "treadmill which at best might keep us in the same place until we drop exhausted." Dulles wanted to "roll back" communism to its pre–World War II borders. This roll-back, he said, would liberate the people of Eastern Europe from "communist despotism and Godless terrorism." The Secretary of State's promise to free the people of Eastern Europe left no room for compromise. Dulles believed the struggle between America and the Soviet Union was a confrontation between good and evil. He compared Stalin to Hitler and viewed the Soviet Union as a threat to all free and peaceful nations.

Eisenhower personally held a somewhat less rigorous view. As President, he had to balance a desire for a tougher foreign policy with his hope to cut government spending. Thus, with one hand he extended peace offerings while with the other he reshaped the American armed forces into the so-called "New Look." The "New Look" reduced expensive ground troops and placed greater emphasis on atomic weapons, which were to be launched by the Air Force.

Massive Retaliation and Brinkmanship

The new administration's idea of relying on nuclear weapons in case of war was known as the policy of "massive retaliation." Under this policy, the United States said it would respond to any Soviet aggression with the threat of massive nuclear war. These threats were a part of the policy of "brinkmanship," which meant going to the brink of war without going over the edge. Dulles believed he could convince the Soviet Union that the United States had the will to use atomic weapons as a counter to the immense Soviet army. Thus, believed Dulles, the Soviet Union would back down, and no weapons at all would have to be used. In the days when America had a nuclear monopoly, the doctrine of "massive retaliation" was plausible. But with the Soviet Union developing its own nuclear arsenal, the policy became highly dangerous.

Although the policy of massive retaliation continued to be part of American foreign policy, both Eisenhower and Dulles soon realized that it could not be the nation's only option. The Soviet Union had exploded its first atomic weapon in 1949. By the early 1950s both sides in the Cold War knew that a total nuclear war would destroy civilization. Under these circumstances the United States and the Soviet Union faced each other in an uneasy peace. Meanwhile, both nations engaged in a nuclear arms race in which more and larger weapons were developed and stockpiled.

Trouble in Indochina

In the early 1950s France was bogged down in a losing fight to hold its colony, French Indochina, which included the present-day countries of Cambodia, Laos, and Vietnam. During World War II, a coalition of Communist and nationalist organizations formed a group popularly called the Viet Minh. The Viet Minh fought against both the Japanese and the French—they wanted an independent Vietnam. From 1946 to 1954, the Viet Minh fought the French. In 1954, the Viet Minh, commanded by the Communist Ho Chi Minh, surrounded a large French garrison in the fortress of **Dien Bien Phu** [dyen′ byen′ fü′]. (See map, page 711.) The French called for American intervention in order to prevent a French defeat. Secretary of State Dulles believed that Dien Bien Phu should not be allowed to fall. He urged President Eisenhower to order massive air strikes to save the fortress from defeat.

Eisenhower believed that America had vital concerns in Vietnam. In 1953, in fact, he had announced that the American government was giving $60 million to the French to help them win the war in Vietnam. He also felt that if Vietnam were lost to U.S. influence, several other nations in Southeast Asia might fall to communism, like dominoes in a row. Despite his concern, however, the President declined to send American air power into the fight at Dien Bien Phu. A man with vast military experience, Eisenhower believed that it would not be prudent to risk another land war in Asia.

Eisenhower's decision was a critical one. When the United States allowed the French to be defeated, long-range changes began in Southeast Asia. Vietnam was divided in half. Ho Chi Minh, a Communist, ruled in the North. The South was ruled by a series of corrupt strongmen backed by the United States. The stage was set for America's tragic involvement in Vietnam a decade later.

A Short Thaw in the Cold War

With war averted in Indochina, there was an apparent thaw in the Cold War. Eisenhower extended the olive branch to the Soviet Union, and the Soviet Premier, Nikolai Bulganin, reached out and grasped it. The two men met in a summit conference in Geneva, Switzerland, in 1955. Eisenhower opened the conference with a heartfelt appeal for a "new spirit of cooperation."

"It is not always necessary," Eisenhower declared, "that people should think alike and believe alike before they can work together." Eisenhower then startled Bulganin by suggesting that each nation give the other "complete blueprints" of its military establishments and permit the other to fly over its territory to take aerial photographs. Such an inspection could allow each country to be sure that it was not being threatened by the other. Although little came of this proposal, the conference did generate some feelings of good will known as "the spirit of Geneva." This new spirit seemed to grow when, in 1956, **Nikita Khrushchev,** head of the Communist party in the Soviet Union (and later Premier), openly denounced the bloody purges of the late Joseph Stalin.

The Hungarian Revolt

Unfortunately, the hopes for a new spirit of cooperation were dashed a few months later. In 1956, a revolution in Hungary brought a new chill to the Cold War. In Hungary people rebelled, demanding that Soviet troops leave the country. For a few splendid days, the Hungarians appeared to have won their demand. Then, on November 4, 1956, Soviet tanks and 200,000 troops streamed across the Hungarian border. Young Hungarian Freedom Fighters fought Russian troops and tanks with little more than rocks and Molotov cocktails (homemade gasoline bombs). Budapest, the Hungarian capital, became a slaughterhouse, and thousands of Hungarians fled their native land. Although Dulles had once spoken of "rolling back" communism, the United States chose not to aid the embattled Hungarians. Dulles and Eisenhower believed that there was too much risk of a nuclear holocaust for America to assist the Freedom Fighters.

NATO tactical missiles in West Germany, 1958

703

Crisis in the Middle East

Meanwhile, clouds appeared on the horizon in the Middle East. In Egypt in 1952 a radical nationalist regime headed by **Colonel Gamal Abdel Nasser** came to power. Nasser stirred the peasant masses of the Arab world with visions of a return to the glories of ancient Egypt, free from foreign control and domination. Already the most popular leader in the Arab world, Nasser outlined his aims. First he planned to seize control of the Suez Canal, which was on Egyptian territory but owned by the British and French. Then he planned to make war on Israel, the Jewish state created at the end of World War II.

When the British removed their troops from the Suez Canal area in 1954, Nasser took control of the canal. In 1956, he nationalized (made Egypt the owner of) it in order to collect funds for the Aswan Dam project. The United States had promised Egypt money for the dam, but then withdrew its offer, precipitating the nationalization of the Suez Canal. Tension shrouded the Middle East like a fog.

In October 1956, when Israel saw that the Soviet Union was concentrating on the situation in Hungary, Israeli troops struck swiftly at Egypt's army on the Sinai Peninsula. Shortly afterwards, France and Britain dropped paratroopers on the Suez Canal in order to regain control of the strategic waterway from Egypt. Their objective was to keep open the main route for oil supplies from the Middle East to Western Europe.

Britain, France, and Israel were publicly condemned for their actions by most of the rest of the world, including the United States and the Soviet Union. Privately, however, Eisenhower was prepared to use force against the Soviets if they decided to attack British or French forces in the Sinai. When a financial crisis at home caused the British to accept a cease-fire, France and Israel had to follow suit. The Middle East crisis quickly cooled down.

The Middle East crisis, which pitted the NATO allies of Britain, France, and the United States against each other, caused serious problems for the West. Nasser, now friendly with the Soviet Union, kept control of the Suez Canal. France, disillusioned with its allies, began plans for building its own nuclear force and for withdrawing from NATO. The Soviet Union, which appeared to be the backer of a victorious Egypt, gained influence in the Middle East.

The Eisenhower Doctrine

To repair America's damaged prestige in the Middle East and to keep the Soviets from gaining a foothold there, Eisenhower and his advisers took a bold step. In January 1957 the President asked Congress for the authority to help militarily any nation in the Middle East that was threatened by an "aggressor controlled by international communism."

The **Eisenhower Doctrine,** as this policy was known, was employed in 1958 when army officers believed to be inspired by Nasser and the Soviet Union assassinated the king and crown prince of Iraq and proclaimed a republic. Next, chaos broke out in Lebanon, and the Lebanese President, Camille Chamoun, fearing a leftist coup, asked for American help. Although reluctant to interfere, in July 1958 Eisenhower sent 15,000 United States marines into Lebanon. Order was soon restored, and the marines were withdrawn. Although there was no immediate Communist threat to Lebanon, Eisenhower demonstrated that the United States could react quickly. As a result, tensions in the region receded.

SECTION 3 REVIEW

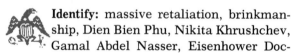

Identify: massive retaliation, brinkmanship, Dien Bien Phu, Nikita Khrushchev, Gamal Abdel Nasser, Eisenhower Doctrine

Main Ideas

1. How did Secretary of State Dulles hope to change America's policy toward communism?
2. During the Eisenhower administration, why did the United States place less emphasis on ground troops and more emphasis on nuclear weapons? What was the effect of this policy?
3. What did President Eisenhower believe were America's vital interests in Indochina? What was the political situation in Vietnam after the fall of Dien Bien Phu?
4. How did the Hungarian Revolt intensify the Cold War? What was the U.S. response to the revolt?
5. How did the Suez Canal crisis of 1956 lead to problems within NATO?

4. EISENHOWER AT HOME

Although Eisenhower's foreign policy was understood by most Americans, the President found it difficult to define his approach to domestic problems. At various times Ike described his administration as representing "dynamic conservatism," "progressive moderation," and "moderate progressivism." When all labels were placed aside, however, the President was an economic conservative. He wanted to undo what he described as the "creeping socialism" of the New Deal. But President Eisenhower was also a practical man. Long years as a military leader and as president of Columbia University had taught him the value of compromise. Thus, when he met strong opposition to his plans to uproot the New Deal, he drew back.

The President's Public Power Policy

The President and his advisers hoped to balance the budget and to return as much of the economy as possible to private interests. Eisenhower was particularly anxious to dismantle the Tennessee Valley Authority, the giant public power company created by President Roosevelt during the New Deal. Although he wanted to sell the TVA, Eisenhower realized this would be impractical. "I suppose we can't go that far," Ike said to an aide.

Eisenhower's plan to substitute private power for the TVA failed. In a move to bring the private utility interests back into the Tennessee Valley area, in 1954 the government awarded a new contract for a major power plant to a private firm known as the Dixon-Yates group. In 1955, however, a congressional investigation uncovered improprieties in the way the contract was awarded, and a scandal erupted. An embarrassed administration had to sue to block the same contract it had negotiated, and the TVA continued as a government enterprise.

Offshore Oil Is Returned to the States

The President was more successful in his effort to take the government out of the offshore oil business. President Truman had argued that the rich deposits of oil just off the coast of the country were public property. Truman felt that these valuable resources should be held by the federal government in trust for the entire nation. During his administration he vetoed two bills passed by Congress to return these deposits to the states.

Eisenhower disagreed. With the cooperation of the Republican Congress in 1953, these valuable deposits were turned over to the states of Texas, California, and Louisiana. In the years since Eisenhower's decision, these offshore oil reserves have become more valuable than ever.

Eisenhower's Policies Toward Federal Spending

The President was also successful initially in reducing government spending and the federal payroll. In the first year of his administration he eliminated 200,000 federal jobs. He also reduced federal spending by 10%. Eisenhower was forced to reverse himself, however, when a recession swept the nation in 1953 and 1954. Ike's first response was to issue statements saying that the problems would pass and that there was no need for government action. To many Americans this sounded too much like a return to the discredited policies of Herbert Hoover. Protests from private citizens, economics professors, and business people flooded into the White House.

This wave of public opinion caused Eisenhower to reconsider his policies. He decided to use government spending and an adjustment in the nation's interest rates to stimulate the economy, even though these were policies he had disliked about the New Deal. The President's turnabout

The Interstate Highway System

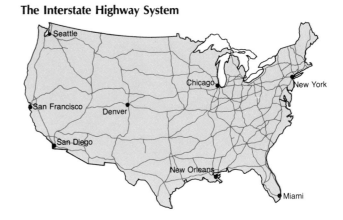

helped to establish ever more firmly the opinion that government should intervene in the economy in times of economic difficulty.

On balance, Eisenhower slowed the growth of the federal government, but he did not halt it. The President himself supported some very costly programs, such as the **Federal-Aid Highway Act** (1956). This was the largest public-works project in the nation's history. It provided for more than $32 billion over 13 years to create a 41,000-mile system of interstate highways. Eisenhower supported it by saying that it would link the nation in the 20th century the way the railroads had tied America together in the 19th century. At the end of Eisenhower's first term, the federal government was still playing a large role in the nation's economy.

The 1954 Supreme Court Decision on School Segregation

It was also in Eisenhower's first administration that important developments in civil rights occurred. In 1954 the United States Supreme Court made a landmark decision in ***Brown v. Board of Education of Topeka.*** In this historic decision, the Court ruled that separate schools for black and white students were unconstitutional.

The *Brown* decision reversed the 1896 precedent-setting decision of *Plessy* v. *Ferguson*. The *Plessy* v. *Ferguson* decision stated that separate railroad cars and other public facilities for blacks and whites were not a violation of the 14th Amendment so long as these facilities were equal. As you have seen, this provided the basis for the "Jim Crow" era in the South.

In the *Brown* decision, by contrast, the Court—led by Eisenhower's newly appointed **Chief Justice Earl Warren**—ruled unanimously that segregation in public education was a denial of the equal protection of the laws. Warren argued that separating schoolchildren

solely because of their race generates a feeling of inferiority as to their status in the community that may affect their hearts and minds in a way unlikely ever to be undone.

Reactions to the Decision

The *Brown* decision was the first major victory in the long and difficult fight of black citizens for equality in American life. The decision was hailed by many. In some of the border states

FROM THE ARCHIVES

Brown v. Board of Education of Topeka

Here are excerpts from the famous Supreme Court decision which declared that segregated public schools were a denial of the equal protection clause of the 14th Amendment.

In these days, it is doubtful that any child may reasonably be expected to succeed in life if he is denied the opportunity of an education. Such an opportunity, where the state has undertaken to provide it, is a right which must be made available to all on equal terms.

We come then to the question presented: Does segregation of children in public schools solely on the basis of race, even though the physical facilities and other "tangible" factors may be equal, deprive the children of the minority group of equal educational opportunities? We believe that it does. . . .

We conclude that in the field of public education the doctrine of "separate but equal" has no place. Separate educational facilities are inherently unequal. Therefore, we hold that the plaintiffs and others similarly situated for whom the actions have been brought are, by reason of the segregation complained of, deprived of the equal protection of the laws guaranteed by the 14th Amendment.

progress was quickly made in carrying out the intent of the law. In much of the South, however, there was strong opposition. The Supreme Court recognized the deep-seated hostility to the decision and did not call for immediate enforcement. Instead, it recommended that the states proceed with "all deliberate speed." As one justice said, "Not even a court can in a day change a deplorable situation into the ideal."

President Truman had been an activist President who was a strong supporter of civil rights. Eisenhower, by contrast, was far less willing to use the government as an instrument of social reform. Ike even regretted his choice of Earl Warren as Chief Justice of the Supreme Court. There had been nothing in Warren's record to indicate his strong stance on civil rights. His decision in *Brown* took the President by surprise. Eisenhower refused to take the lead in urging Americans to obey the new law. By his silence, he encouraged opponents of the ruling to believe that their resistance could be successful.

Many white southerners resisted the integration of the schools. One hundred and one of the South's senators and representatives signed a "Southern Manifesto" which denounced *Brown* as "a clear abuse of judicial power . . . which is destroying the amicable relations between the white and Negro races." Of the South's senators, only Lyndon B. Johnson of Texas and Albert Gore and Estes Kefauver of Tennessee refused to sign.

Southern blacks were soon faced with a far more immediate enemy in the form of **White Citizens' Councils** and increased violence. The White Citizens' Councils, which originated in 1954 in direct response to the Supreme Court decision, stood for continued segregation of the races. They used economic pressure such as mortgage foreclosures, job dismissals, and withdrawal of credit, as well as legal maneuvers to block integration. For a time, they were largely successful. One year after the *Brown* decision, in eight southern states not a single black child was attending school with whites.

Crisis in Little Rock

Eisenhower tried to remain above the conflicts resulting from the Court's decision. In September 1957, however, a serious challenge to federal authority forced him to act. The governor of Arkansas, **Orval Faubus,** ordered Arkansas National Guard units to surround Central High School in **Little Rock** in order to prevent nine black students from attending. Eisenhower met with Faubus to discuss the situation, but the Governor refused to change his mind. A court order finally forced him to remove the National Guard and to bring in the state police to ensure the safety of the black students who were finally enrolled at Central.

The nine black students were then brought into the school through a back door. When an angry white mob discovered that the blacks were actually in the building, it rushed the school. The crowd was turned back by the police, but the mob turned on several black reporters, some of whom were beaten to the ground.

The outcry over this situation, along with the claim by the Arkansas state police that they could not maintain order, finally forced Eisenhower to act decisively. He ordered 1,000 troops of the 101st Airborne Division to Central High School to keep order. In addition, he put the Arkansas National Guard under federal command. The nine black students were escorted to and from classes by the soldiers. As it became clear to those in the white mobs around the school that order would be maintained, the crowds withered away, and this confrontation between the federal government and a state thus ended.

The same month that saw the events in Little Rock also saw the passage of the first civil rights legislation since the end of Reconstruction. Eisenhower sent Congress a bill which empowered federal judges to oversee voting registration to ensure that blacks and other Americans could register to vote without harassment. The bill seemed sure to fail because previous attempts had been killed by Senate filibuster. But **Lyndon B. Johnson** of Texas, the Democratic leader of the Senate, arranged a compromise which led to the passage of the Voting Rights Act of 1957. Even with this law and the passage of additional supporting ones, however, it was still difficult for blacks to exercise their voting rights in the South. Under these circumstances, blacks began to work more diligently for their rights.

The Montgomery Bus Boycott

The **Montgomery bus boycott** was the first major example of blacks directly challenging racial segregation. As in other southern cities, the standard

Rosa Parks started a major civil rights boycott.

Martin Luther King, Jr., greets supporters.

leaders in this critical struggle.

King believed that the principles of Christian love could be a tool of social progress through nonviolent direct action. He called for actions that would protest segregation and, by setting an example of nonviolence, persuade opponents of equality of the error of their ways. He told his followers:

If we are arrested every day, if we are exploited every day, if we are trampled over every day, don't ever let anyone pull you so low as to hate them. We must use the weapon of love. We must have compassion and understanding for those who hate us.

King led the boycott to victory. Blacks refused to ride the buses. Some formed carpools while others walked. The boycott began to have its effect as the bus company slid toward bankruptcy, losing 65% of its income because of the boycott. One year after Rosa Parks was arrested, King's followers won a nonviolent victory. Segregation was declared illegal on Montgomery's buses. Shortly thereafter King formed the **Southern Christian Leadership Conference,** which became one of the most important organizations in the fight for civil rights. The success of the boycott in Montgomery also gained national media attention for the civil rights struggle.

practice in Montgomery, the capital of Alabama, was for blacks to sit only in the back of city transit buses. Blacks were also expected to give up their seats if whites were standing. On December 1, 1955, a black seamstress named **Rosa Parks,** tired from a hard day's work, took a seat just behind the white section. When the driver later ordered her to move to make room for a boarding white passenger, she refused. She left her seat only when she was arrested by the police.

Rosa Parks' defiance sparked a boycott of the city's buses by Montgomery's 50,000 blacks. The boycott took effect quickly because of organizing efforts by the National Association for the Advancement of Colored People (NAACP) and the Brotherhood of Sleeping Car Porters. During the course of the boycott, a new black leader emerged in the person of the **Reverend Dr. Martin Luther King, Jr.** Just 27 years old, Dr. King was already a magnetic figure. As the boycott continued, he came to the fore as one of the most important

SECTION 4 REVIEW

Identify: Federal-Aid Highway Act, *Brown* v. *Board of Education of Topeka,* Earl Warren, White Citizens' Councils, Orval Faubus, Little Rock crisis, Lyndon B. Johnson, Montgomery bus boycott, Rosa Parks, Martin Luther King, Jr., Southern Christian Leadership Conference

Main Ideas

1. What economic actions did President Eisenhower take during his first term?
2. What was the significance of the Supreme Court's ruling in the case of *Brown* v. *Board of Education of Topeka?* How did the President and the country react?
3. Why did President Eisenhower send federal troops to Little Rock, Arkansas?
4. Describe the philosophy of nonviolent protest of Dr. Martin Luther King, Jr., and the tactics he used during the Montgomery bus boycott.

5. EISENHOWER'S SECOND TERM

In 1956, the nation once again prepared for a presidential election. The Republicans again nominated Eisenhower to run, and the Democrats once again chose Adlai Stevenson. Although Stevenson campaigned hard, he faced an uphill battle against the enormously popular President. Eisenhower's record of peace abroad and prosperity at home combined with his genial personality and friendly manner to carry the day.

The President, however, won a purely personal victory. Many people voted for Eisenhower for President but selected Democrats for senators and representatives. The Democrats regained the control of Congress which they had lost in 1952. For the first time since 1848, a President was elected without carrying at least one house of Congress as well.

Health Problems and Scandal

President Eisenhower had had a heart attack in 1955, and although he recovered, he suffered a mild stroke in 1956 shortly after winning re-election. As the President recuperated, he turned more and more of the everyday affairs of government over to his advisers. John Foster Dulles, Eisenhower's dependable Secretary of State, represented the President in determining the nation's foreign policy. In domestic affairs, **Sherman Adams,** Ike's chief of staff, became even more important.

Americans began to wonder if the President would live through the rest of his term. During President Eisenhower's convalescence, his critics charged that he spent more time on the golf course than in his office. As the President recovered, many Americans, including newspaper reporters covering the capital, began to believe that Adams, and not Eisenhower, was running the government.

In 1958 a scandal struck the Eisenhower administration, deeply involving Adams. A House investigating committee revealed that Adams had used his influential position to aid a friend's private business interests. Adams, the committee reported, had interceded with certain federal agencies on behalf of Bernard Goldfine, a New England textile manufacturer. In return, Goldfine had given Adams an expensive vicuna* coat. The Democrats clamored for Adams' resignation. President Eisenhower, however, was reluctant to let his chief adviser go. After increased pressure from both Republican and Democratic leaders, Eisenhower accepted Adams' resignation.

Corruption in the Labor Unions

Political corruption was not the only problem to attract national attention during Ike's second administration. Organized labor suffered from corruption as well. A Senate investigating committee learned that the **Teamsters Union,** one of the nation's most powerful labor organizations, had used questionable tactics to acquire a string of gambling houses and taverns. In addition, some $320,000 in Teamster funds could not be accounted for. The Senate committee summoned the Teamsters' president, Dave Beck, who had a reputation for dealing with underworld figures, to appear for testimony. Later, when Beck was sent to prison, he still managed to retain influence over the union through his handpicked successor, vice-president Jimmy Hoffa. Hoffa, who was also alleged to have underworld connections, mysteriously disappeared many years later, in 1975.

Organized labor had made a major step forward two years earlier, in 1955, when the AFL and the CIO put aside their differences and reunited into one organization. The combined organization, with a membership of 17 million, was headed by George Meany, a former New York plumber.

The Teamster revelations stunned much of the rest of organized labor. In 1957 the AFL-CIO expelled the Teamsters on the basis of the Senate investigating committee hearings. Public opinion toward labor unions sank drastically. Despite these difficulties, however, labor was able to organize its supporters politically when Eisenhower's economic policies helped to bring on a severe recession in late 1957. The economic slowdown brought on the highest peacetime unemployment since the Great Depression.

The Democrats Win Large Majorities

Although the Republicans had won a majority in both houses of Congress in 1952, the 1956 elec-

*A vicuna is a South American animal that looks like and is related to the llama. Its fine wool is very expensive.

tions had returned congressional control to the Democrats. In the mid-term elections of 1958, the Democrats again won a majority in the House and Senate. In the Senate the Democrats held a two-to-one lead, while in the House they enjoyed the largest majority since the election of 1936. The election made it clear that the economy was the people's main concern.

The huge Democratic majorities in Congress pitted against a Republican President produced a political stalemate. Eisenhower was unable to impose his will on the Congress. On the other hand, the Democrats, split between liberals and conservatives, were unable to present a united front against the Republican administration.

The deadlock in Washington left an enormous amount of power in the hands of two extraordinary congressional leaders, both from Texas. Sam Rayburn, the Speaker of the House, and Lyndon B. Johnson, the Majority Leader of the Senate, tried to set a moderately liberal course for the government in the face of Eisenhower's fears of "creeping socialism" and the liberals' complaints about Democratic timidity. Few significant laws were passed, however, and the Eisenhower administration rolled slowly to a standstill.

Sputnik Shocks America

In October 1957, a Soviet rocket zoomed into outer space, carrying a small satellite known as *Sputnik* (companion). A shock wave of surprise and embarrassment rolled across the United States. Most Americans had believed that the United States would launch the first space shot. When the Soviets beat them to it, Eisenhower's space program was discredited in the eyes of many citizens. The problem was made worse when the *Vanguard* rocket, designed to carry America's first satellite into orbit, crashed on launch. Although the United States was able to launch its first satellite in January of 1958, the nation feared it might not catch up to the Soviets.

While American industry was concentrating on automobiles and color television sets, the Soviet Union was devoting itself to rocketry with a single-minded dedication. Secret U.S. government reports showed that it might be possible for the Soviets to use their superior rocketry to launch a successful surprise attack on the United States. Eisenhower responded by calling for greater aid to education to improve the quality of America's military technology. Thus, in 1958 Congress passed the National Defense Education Act, which provided loans for college students and teachers who took additional courses in science and mathematics.

Critics of President Eisenhower began to speak of a "missile gap" which threatened America's security. As you will see, this became one of the main issues in the presidential election of 1960.

Communism in Cuba

Meanwhile, another storm cloud appeared on the horizon in Cuba, just 90 miles from America's shores. Fulgencio Batista, Cuba's dictator, was overthrown on January 1, 1959, after a long struggle by guerrillas led by **Fidel Castro.** Although Batista had been friendly to the United States, many Americans initially supported Castro's revolution. Soon after he came to power, Castro confiscated U.S.-owned oil refineries and seized American business firms which he felt were exploiting Cubans and making Cuba poor. Castro developed friendly relations with the Soviet Union and soon declared that the Cuban revolution must turn to communism. The U.S., in turn, cut the import of Cuban sugar and placed an embargo on the export of products to Cuba.

Troubles in Berlin

In 1958 and 1959 Nikita Khrushchev, the Soviet Premier, referred to Berlin as "a bone in my throat," implying that the problem of a divided Berlin had to be resolved. The prosperity of West Berlin, occupied by the United States, France, and Britain, when compared to the rubble-strewn drabness of the eastern half of the city, occupied by the Soviets, was an embarrassment to Khrushchev and the Soviet Union. On November 27, 1958, the Soviet leader gave the Western Powers six months to withdraw from the divided city. At the end of the six months, said Khrushchev, the East Germans would take control of all of Berlin. Eisenhower refused to give in to Khrushchev's demands, and when the deadline passed, the Soviet leader backed down.

Khrushchev Visits America

In 1959 President Eisenhower invited Khrushchev to visit the United States. In a visit in September which was a mixture of diplomacy, showmanship, and low comedy, Khrushchev met

American showgirls, petted a prize pig in Iowa, and created a minor crisis when he was not allowed to visit Disneyland (because of security problems).

The trip ended with Khrushchev and Eisenhower in a meeting at Camp David, the presidential retreat in Maryland. There, agreements were worked out for a summit meeting in Paris. The apparent good will generated by the meeting was known as the **"spirit of Camp David."**

The U-2 Incident

Plans for the Paris summit conference were dashed on May 5, 1960, when an American U-2 spy plane, piloted by Francis Gary Powers, was shot down deep inside Soviet territory. Powers was captured and put in a Soviet prison pending a spy trial. The Soviet Union leaders refused to meet with Eisenhower when the President finally assumed personal responsibility for the spy flights. Because of the **U-2 incident,** the conference scheduled for Paris was canceled, and the Soviets withdrew a previously offered invitation to President Eisenhower to visit the Soviet Union.

Thus, President Eisenhower left office in 1961 with a mixed legacy. America had in general been peaceful and very prosperous. But the na-

tion's prestige had been dealt some severe blows. Although Eisenhower retired as an enormously popular figure, he was unable to transfer this popularity to the Republican nominee, Vice-President Richard M. Nixon. As you shall see, Nixon faced a tough fight for the presidency with the Democratic nominee, the dynamic John Fitzgerald Kennedy.

SECTION 5 REVIEW

Identify: Sherman Adams, Teamsters Union, *Sputnik*, Fidel Castro, spirit of Camp David, U-2 incident

Main Ideas

1. What two officials carried on much of President Eisenhower's work during the first part of his second administration? Why?
2. Why were Americans so shocked when the Soviet Union placed a satellite in orbit? How did the government react?
3. What was the attitude of many Americans toward Fidel Castro when he first came to power in Cuba? Why did this attitude change?
4. How did the U-2 spy plane incident affect Cold War tensions?

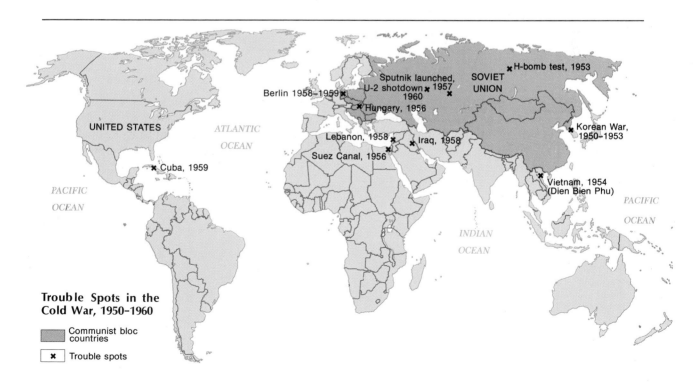

Trouble Spots in the Cold War, 1950–1960

- Communist bloc countries
- **✗** Trouble spots

6. THE IMPACT OF THE FIFTIES ON AMERICA

By the middle of the Eisenhower years the United States was enjoying an extraordinary economic boom which changed the face of the nation. By the end of Ike's second term, most of the nation's white population lived free of material want. With Europe and Japan still recovering from the war, the United States, with only 6% of the world's population, produced half of the world's manufactured goods.

Real Income Increases

The enormous burst of productivity in America after World War II increased **real income** (income adjusted for inflation) by a third between 1947 and 1956. At the same time, the number of families owning homes grew by some 50%. Disposable income more than tripled. This boom greatly increased the size of the American middle class.

Previously, the country's social structure had been shaped like a pyramid. The pyramid had a very broad base of poor people at the bottom with very few wealthy people at the top. In the Eisenhower years, however, the growing number of people in the middle class made the social structure look like a diamond, bulging at the center. The proportion of families and individuals with annual incomes of $10,000 or more steadily increased throughout the decade. At the same time, the number of families or individuals whose income was $3,000 or less declined. These changes helped to make America the richest nation on earth. Yet, as you shall see, these developments also had negative effects on American society.

The Growth of the Suburbs

The new prosperity produced new ways of living. In the prosperous 1920s, the average industrial worker labored 10 hours a day, 6 days a week, and worked year round without a vacation. During the 1950s, that same worker was working approximately 8 hours per day, 5 days a week, and had 2 weeks' paid vacation.

Many of these well-paid workers used their earnings to buy a home. One out of every four houses standing in 1960 had been built after 1950. These new homes were likely to be equipped with indoor plumbing and refrigerators.

In 1925 less than 1% of American homes had an electrical refrigerator; most people relied on daily deliveries from the ice man. But by 1960, 98% of all American homes had electrical refrigerators.

These new homes were usually built outside the city limits in what came to be called the suburbs. Homes in the suburbs often had spacious lawns, large garages, and wide streets. **"Suburbia,"** as the suburbs were sometimes called, seemed to beckon to many Americans, offering them the "American dream" of a happy life.

Records and Televisions

Americans used much of their new wealth and leisure time on recreational activities. Record sales, which had previously been counted in the thousands, were, in the mid-1950s, now tabulated in the millions. The records of the great jazz artists were popular, but they were overshadowed by a new music called rock and roll, which started to become popular in 1954. The new music quickly became a craze among teenagers, who went wild over rock and roll stars such as Chuck Berry and Elvis Presley.

The new leisure in America was brought about by the new technology of World War II applied to consumer use after the war. The old, brittle 78 rpm records were replaced by smaller, flexible 45 rpm records which were far cheaper to produce and sell. But the biggest change came with the advent of television.

In 1945 television was a rarity. By 1953, however, two out of every three American homes had a television set. Older forms of entertainment, such as vaudeville and live theater, could play at most to a few thousand people at a time. Even motion pictures could accommodate only limited audiences in any one place at a time. Television, however, reached into millions of homes, and a farmer in Maine and a lawyer in New Orleans could watch the same program at the same time.

Although television tied the country together by giving people something in common, it also had undesirable effects. For example, it undermined live entertainment and local cultures, resulting in the loss of local differences and a growing homogenization of our culture.

Problems of the New Affluence

America's new affluence also produced some unexpected problems. For example, earlier generations of young people often had to work to help support their families. The children of the newly well-to-do of the Fifties were freed from the need to work. Often they lacked any sense of what to do with themselves. Lacking direction, they sometimes identified with screen heroes such as James Dean, who played a confused teenager in the hit motion picture *Rebel Without a Cause* (1955). Or, like the characters in the popular novel and film, *The Blackboard Jungle* (1955), they sometimes drifted into acts of senseless violence and hostility. Teenagers increasingly became part of a distinct subculture. Catered to by record companies and film makers and pampered by their parents, they were cut off from adult society. The teenage rebels of the Fifties were the forerunners of the "youth culture" of the Sixties.

Another example of an unexpected by-product of the new affluence was the enormous growth of giant corporations and the decline of small, independently owned businesses. This development meant that more people than ever before were working for someone else, usually a large corpo-

ration. As a result, white-collar workers in these giant companies sometimes complained about being swallowed up by the large organizations which employed them. They felt they had no power, no ability to influence the decisions of the corporation.

But the dominant mood of the 1950s was probably best summed up by the symbol of those years, President Eisenhower, when he told the country, "Everybody ought to be happy every day. Play hard, have fun doing it, and despise wickedness."

SECTION 6 REVIEW

 Identify: real income, suburbia

Main Ideas

1. In what ways did the economic boom of the 1950s change the way Americans lived?
2. How did the size of the middle class change during the Eisenhower era?
3. What were some effects of the new technology and affluence of the 1950s?

LIFE IN AMERICA

THE BABY BOOM

At the end of the war, many Americans resumed interrupted careers, got married, and started families. So many babies were born in the postwar period of 1946 to 1964 that it has come to be called a boom— the baby boom. The 76 million "boomers" (as babies born during this period have been called) have traveled through American society with some difficulty.

When they were born, there were too many of them in the maternity wards. When they entered grade school, they sat two to a desk and shared textbooks. They competed fiercely for limited college and job openings, experienced a housing shortage in the 1980s, and will pose a serious problem for the Social Security system when they reach retirement age.

"Diaper derby," New Jersey, 1946

A Child-Centered Society

The sheer number of the "boomers" gives them enormous power. As children, they were the first generation to grow up with TV, and advertisers have aimed many products at them. When they were teens the record industry prospered from their purchases. As young adults they were called the Pepsi Generation. "Never trust anyone over 30" they were told. Now, as some of them reach middle age, they are told, "You're not getting older, you're getting better."

The Future

The hopes and aspirations of the baby boom generation are important because the baby boomers are the generation now taking charge, and they will be at the center of power well into the next century.

CHAPTER 32 REVIEW

Key Terms
Explain the meaning of each of the following terms:

McCarthyism
massive retaliation
brinkmanship
Dien Bien Phu
Eisenhower Doctrine
Federal-Aid Highway
    Act
Brown v. *Board of*
    Education of Topeka
White Citizens'
    Councils
Little Rock crisis

Montgomery bus
    boycott
Southern Christian
    Leadership
    Conference
Teamsters Union
Sputnik
spirit of Camp David
U-2 incident
real income
suburbia

Reviewing Main Ideas

Section 1
1. What were Senator McCarthy's charges?
2. Why did McCarthy become so popular?
3. What effect did McCarthyism have on the nation?

Section 2
1. Describe briefly the election of 1952.
2. What changes did Eisenhower make in the presidency?
3. How did Eisenhower end the Korean War? What were the results of the peace agreements?

Section 3
1. What was the goal of Secretary of State Dulles' foreign policy?
2. How did the Eisenhower administration reshape the American armed forces? What was the danger in this "New Look"?
3. What was Eisenhower's policy in Vietnam between 1954 and 1956?
4. How did the Hungarian Revolt intensify the Cold War?
5. What was the effect of the Suez Canal crisis of 1956 on NATO?

Section 4
1. In what ways did President Eisenhower try to reduce the size and power of the federal government? How successful was he?
2. What was the significance of the Supreme Court's decision of *Brown* v. *Board of Education of Topeka*? How did the President and the country react?
3. Why did Eisenhower send troops to Little Rock, Arkansas?
4. Describe the views of Martin Luther King, Jr., on methods to win an end to segregation. What was the goal of the Montgomery bus boycott?

Section 5
1. What were Americans' reactions to *Sputnik*? Why?
2. How did Fidel Castro's victory in Cuba and the U-2 spy plane incident affect Cold War tensions?

Section 6
1. What were the effects of economic prosperity and technological change on the way Americans lived in the 1950s?
2. What culture changes took place in the 1950s?

Special History Skills:
Recognizing Anachronisms
An anachronism [ə nak′rə niz′əm] is the placing of a person, object, custom, or event in an incorrect time period. Popular media, especially television programs and advertisements, are often guilty of anachronisms, showing hairstyles, clothes, cars, customs, slang words, inventions, and events in the wrong years. Pay careful attention to the details in old photographs and illustrations as well as learning facts from the text of your textbook, and you will soon be able to spot many anachronisms. Test your skill by doing the following:
1. Describe the anachronisms in each of the following situations:
(a) A 1952 newspaper headline reads, "President Nixon's Pet Dog Wins Voter Sympathy."
(b) A movie shows flappers driving a Model T across the country on an interstate highway.
(c) A World War I GI celebrates the end of the war with a Soviet paratrooper.
(d) During the Korean War an American soldier plays an Elvis Presley song on a cassette tape recorder.
(e) News of Lincoln's 1860 vote lead reaches Cali-

fornia before the polls close.

(f) Andrew Jackson receives a telegram announcing the end of the War of 1812 but fights the Battle of New Orleans anyway.

2. Make up your own list of four anachronisms.

Other Skill Activities

1. King and Gandhi

In developing his philosophy of nonviolent protest, Martin Luther King, Jr., was greatly influenced by Mohandas K. Gandhi [gän′dē], a political leader from India. Research Gandhi's life and ideas. How do they relate to those of King?

2. Desegregation

The process of desegregation that began in 1954 continues today. Write summaries of the main ideas of three newspaper or magazine articles that discuss desegregation.

3. Suburbia

If you live in a suburb or near one, find out when and how it was founded and how it has grown. What ties it to the city? Use your town hall, public library, and historical society as resources. Give a report to the class, using maps, charts, and pictures.

Thinking Critically

1. Discuss two policies and/or decisions of the Eisenhower era that still affect our country today.

2. How effective do you think the policies of massive retaliation and brinkmanship were? Did they ever get in the way of effective reaction to the Soviets in the 1950s? Could they work today? Why or why not?

3. Do you agree or disagree with the statement by Chief Justice Earl Warren on the psychological effects of segregation? Explain your answer.

4. The "Eisenhower Doctrine" should really be called the "Dulles Doctrine." Explain.

Further Reading

Janet Stevenson. *The School Segregation Cases.* Franklin Watts, 1973. Details several cases, including *Brown* v. *Board of Education of Topeka,* that made legal history.

Betty Schechter. *The Peaceable Revolution.* Houghton Mifflin, 1963. Traces the development of nonviolent resistance from Thoreau to Gandhi and to the American civil rights movement.

TEST YOURSELF

WRITE YOUR ANSWERS ON A SEPARATE SHEET OF PAPER.

Matching

Write the letter of the name that best matches each description below.

1. led nonviolent movement against segregation
2. fought a successful revolution in Cuba
3. leader who took control of the Suez Canal
4. precipitated the Montgomery bus boycott
5. charged that Communists ran U.S. government

a. Fidel Castro
b. Rosa Parks
c. Joseph McCarthy
d. Gamal Abdel Nasser
e. Martin Luther King, Jr.

Multiple Choice

Write the letter of the phrase that best completes each statement. There may be more than one correct answer.

1. In his "Checkers speech," Richard M. Nixon
   a. explained his "checker theory" of foreign policy.
   b. resigned from public office.
   c. used a pet dog to win voter sympathy.
   d. saved his vice-presidential candidacy.

2. The policy of massive retaliation
   a. was supported by the Eisenhower administration.
   b. meant using nuclear weapons instead of ground forces.
   c. was a way of making promised cuts in the federal budget.
   d. became more dangerous as more nuclear weapons were stockpiled.

3. Senator Joseph McCarthy
   a. seemed more interested in discrediting New Deal liberals than in finding Communists.
   b. used solid evidence to make his charges.
   c. made accusations resulting in a wave of political fear and blacklisting.
   d. was honored by the Senate after retirement.

Recognizing Trends

Mark I those things which were increasing in the 1950s. Mark D those things that were decreasing.

1. middle class
2. rock and roll music
3. independent businesses
4. live entertainment
5. home ownership

VISITING THE PAST

Pearl Harbor, Hawaii

They flew through Kolekole Pass, a break in the hills overlooking the harbor. The roar of their engines broke the quiet of that Sunday morning. Soon the exploding bombs woke the sleeping island. It was 7:55 A.M. It was December 7, 1941, at Pearl Harbor, Hawaii.

That morning over 200 Japanese planes and 8 mini-subs attacked the United States Naval Base at Pearl Harbor. When the planes left, 2,400 Americans lay dead, and 1,200 lay wounded. Eight battle-ships and 10 other vessels were either resting on the harbor floor or seriously damaged.

News of the surprise attack on Pearl Harbor shocked the nation. Americans gathered around their radios, anxiously awaiting details. President Franklin D. Roosevelt described December 7th as "a date which will live in infamy." The next day, the U.S. declared war on Japan.

Many Americans have personal memories of that day. Today, a visit to Pearl Harbor keeps alive the infamy of that day for those who lived through it and for new generations.

The focal point of a visit to Pearl Harbor today is one of the vessels sunk in the attack: the U.S.S. *Arizona*. On that December Sunday morning, an armor-penetrating bomb turned the U.S.S. *Arizona* into an underwater tomb for 1,102 of its crew. The mural in the new National Park Service visitor's center depicts the ship in its full glory. The site awaiting the visitor offers a sharp contrast to this mural.

A boat takes you from the visitor's center to the U.S.S. *Arizona* Memorial. This strikingly modern memorial spans the stern of the sunken ship. Most of the vessels lost during that attack were raised. Attempts to remove the *Arizona* failed, and it remains where it sank.

Several parts of the ship break through the water of the harbor. From the memorial, one looks down into the water to see the barnacle-covered hull of that mighty ship. This site makes the attack on Pearl Harbor seem more than just another story out of our history. It brings that event to life.

The sunken vessel itself is more powerful than any monument that could be built to commemorate it. It is more than a monument to a particular battle and a painful event. It is a constant reminder of both the need for military preparedness and the horror of war.

Oak Ridge, Tennessee

It seems more like a suspense movie than history. The terrible world war is suddenly and dramatically ended by a secret super-powerful weapon. Too unbelievable to be true? No, it is the story of the end of World War II. The secret weapon was the atomic bomb.

In 1939, Albert Einstein informed President Roosevelt of the possibility of an atomic weapon with terrific strength. It was feared that Germany might develop such a weapon first. It was crucial that America be the first to have the bomb. This was the goal of the Manhattan Project.

The Project brought together the best minds and all the resources needed to develop this bomb. Those working on the project needed a large secret research facility and a nuclear reactor. These needs were met with the creation of Oak Ridge, Tennessee (see map, page 631), and the building of a graphite reactor.

The site in eastern Tennessee was selected for the hidden city because sheltered wooded valleys with limestone ridges gave the site

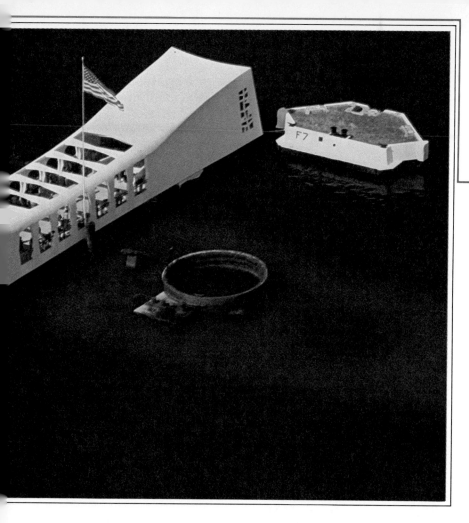

U.S.S. Arizona *Memorial, Pearl Harbor, Hawaii*

security. The Tennessee Valley Authority could meet the Project's large power needs. The climate allowed work year round.

Speed and secrecy were essential. In record time, facilities were built and a town for 13,000 families was constructed. Oak Ridge soon swelled to 100,000. Shortages were common in the secret city. Some companies would not ship supplies to a city that did not exist. Supply orders were always kept low so that no observer could guess the city's real size.

The graphite reactor at the Oak Ridge National Laboratory, 10 miles outside of the city, was essential to the work of the Project. It was both a pilot plant and a producer of quantities of purified plutonium.

On August 6, 1945, the *Enola Gay* dropped an atomic bomb on Hiroshima, Japan. The work at Oak Ridge had helped make this possible.

After the war, Oak Ridge continued its leadership role in nuclear research. Its facilities were turned to peaceful ends. In 1963, after 20 years of use, the reactor was shut down. It is now a National Historic Landmark and open to the public.

Today the visitor to the world's oldest nuclear reactor sees where history was made. Oak Ridge is now home of the American Museum of Science and Energy. There the story of energy is told through movies and demonstrations of how various tools and appliances work.

Oak Ridge and its nuclear reactor are monuments to the development of our nuclear knowledge. They are also tangible proof of what is possible when a country commits itself and its resources to achieving a goal, no matter how unreachable that goal appears to be.

Disneyland, California

This Main Street seems typical of many that might have been found at the turn of the century. However, if you follow it past the City Hall you will find that it is an unusual Main Street. Its residents include such celebrities as Mickey Mouse, Donald Duck, and Goofy. The street leads to such fanciful places as Sleeping Beauty's Castle and the Swiss Family Treehouse. This is no ordinary street. This is Main Street, U.S.A., at Disneyland.

For over 25 years Disneyland has attracted visitors from all over the world. Since it opened on July 17, 1955, over 187 million guests, ranging from people like you and your neighbors to kings and presidents have visited this magic kingdom.

The amusement park is located in Anaheim, California, on more than 75 acres of a strange and exotic landscape that includes jungles, lakes, mountains, and a monorail. Many of the fantasy attractions are made realistic by means of voices, music, and lifelike mechanical figures.

Disneyland was the dream of Walt Disney, the famous cartoonist. His goal was to create a place that the whole family could enjoy. This meant more than creating exciting things to see and do. It meant creating a wholesome atmosphere that could be enjoyed by people of all types.

It reinforces traditional values, and its attractions highlight places and episodes in our country's history. It is a mixture of fact, fantasy, and fun. Disneyland itself keeps improving and developing its magic and mystery.

It is a product of, and a tribute to, America's prosperity. The almost daily parades and fireworks at Disneyland celebrate America as much as they celebrate this magical kingdom.

UNIT 9 TEST

WRITE YOUR ANSWERS ON A SEPARATE SHEET OF PAPER.

Fill in the Blanks (10 points)
Choose the correct answer from the pair that follows each statement.

1. Americans who wanted to take an active role in helping Britain fight German aggression were called _____. (isolationists—interventionists)
2. The _____ Project was a secret program to build the atomic bomb. (U-2—Manhattan)
3. The first atomic bomb was dropped on _____. (Hiroshima—Nagasaki)
4. In 1948, southerners who bolted the Democratic party over the civil rights issue formed the _____ party. (Dixiecrat—America First)
5. _____ was a military defense pact binding the United States and European countries. (Truman Doctrine—NATO)
6. _____ was executed for passing American atomic secrets to the Soviets. (Ethel Rosenberg—Francis Gary Powers)
7. The policy of _____ meant using nuclear weapons instead of ground forces. (containment—massive retaliation)
8. In 1957 President Eisenhower sent troops to maintain order during the school integration crisis in _____. (Little Rock, Arkansas—Montgomery, Alabama)
9. _____ played a leading role in the bus segregation boycott. (A. Philip Randolph—Rosa Parks)
10. The small, unmanned satellite that pointed up a temporary Soviet superiority in space exploration was called _____. (Khrushchev—Sputnik)

True or False (40 points)
Read each statement below. Mark T if the statement is true, F if it is false. Rewrite the italicized words in all false statements to make them true.

1. The Munich Pact gave Germany a free hand to invade *Poland.*
2. After the Japanese sank an American gunboat in China in 1937, the United States *started* preparing for war with Japan.
3. Roosevelt and Willkie had *greatly different* views on foreign policy.
4. The *Battle of Dunkirk* was the largest amphibious operation in all history.
5. Russia's differences with the United States began *when World War II ended.*
6. Truman's Fair Deal legislation was *successful* in extending the New Deal programs of FDR.
7. MacArthur was relieved of command in Korea because he insisted that he be allowed *to bomb the Soviet Union.*
8. The popularity of Joseph McCarthy's crusade against Communists in government *rose dramatically* after the election of a Republican President in 1952.

Time Line (10 points)
Match the letters on the time line with the events they stand for.

1. Truman Doctrine
2. Korean War begins
3. Germany conquers Poland
4. Truman dismisses MacArthur
5. Dwight D. Eisenhower elected President
6. Berlin blockade
7. Japan attacks Pearl Harbor
8. Little Rock crisis
9. Germany and Japan defeated
10. NATO formed

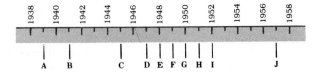

Essay Questions (40 points)

1. Describe the civil rights movement between 1939 and 1960. Identify several of the leaders and compare their ideas.
2. What was the most important element in American foreign policy between 1940 and 1960, in your opinion? What effect did nuclear weapons have on this policy?

Unit Ten

Modern America

Chapter 33

THE NEW FRONTIER AND THE GREAT SOCIETY

I t is wintertime, 1961. America's new President, John F. Kennedy, has been in office almost a year. Americans are fascinated with their new leader. In newspapers and magazines, on radio and television, even in barbershops and supermarkets, President Kennedy and his family seem always to be mentioned.

The President, the youngest person ever elected to the country's highest office, has brought a fresh sense of purpose and a new style to Washington. His young wife, Jacqueline, and their two small children make the White House come alive with activity. And, as the First Family settles in, a new glamor colors governmental affairs. Famous musicians perform at presidential concerts; artists and poets are invited to receptions for the Congress. Reporters refer to the new administration as "Camelot" after the fairy-tale reign of King Arthur in England long ago.

The President promises bold new leadership for America. He declares that the nation will always assist its friends and oppose the enemies of freedom. A vigorous spirit of enthusiasm and pride sweeps the country. Then, in the middle of his term in office, the President is cut down by an assassin's bullet.

Soon America's mood is different. The nation becomes entangled in a long war in Vietnam. There are more assassinations, and they shock Americans. Race riots flare in the large cities. The hopes and promises of just a few years before seem to vanish. In this chapter, you will examine the pride and the shame, the conflicting senses of purpose and confusion that characterized America during the years from 1960 to 1968.

Sections in This Chapter
1. The New Frontier at Home
2. The New Frontier and the Cold War
3. Lyndon B. Johnson Takes the Helm
4. The Black Revolt
5. President Johnson and the Vietnam War

Embroidered jeans from the 1960s

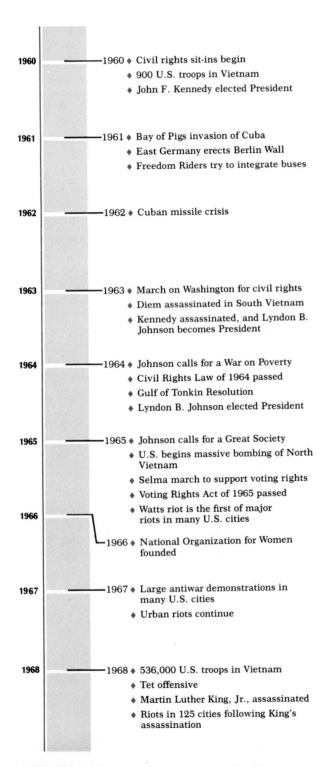

1960	1960 ♦ Civil rights sit-ins begin
	♦ 900 U.S. troops in Vietnam
	♦ John F. Kennedy elected President
1961	1961 ♦ Bay of Pigs invasion of Cuba
	♦ East Germany erects Berlin Wall
	♦ Freedom Riders try to integrate buses
1962	1962 ♦ Cuban missile crisis
1963	1963 ♦ March on Washington for civil rights
	♦ Diem assassinated in South Vietnam
	♦ Kennedy assassinated, and Lyndon B. Johnson becomes President
1964	1964 ♦ Johnson calls for a War on Poverty
	♦ Civil Rights Law of 1964 passed
	♦ Gulf of Tonkin Resolution
	♦ Lyndon B. Johnson elected President
1965	1965 ♦ Johnson calls for a Great Society
	♦ U.S. begins massive bombing of North Vietnam
	♦ Selma march to support voting rights
	♦ Voting Rights Act of 1965 passed
1966	♦ Watts riot is the first of major riots in many U.S. cities
	1966 ♦ National Organization for Women founded
1967	1967 ♦ Large antiwar demonstrations in many U.S. cities
	♦ Urban riots continue
1968	1968 ♦ 536,000 U.S. troops in Vietnam
	♦ Tet offensive
	♦ Martin Luther King, Jr., assassinated
	♦ Riots in 125 cities following King's assassination

For the campaign of 1960, the Republicans chose Vice-President **Richard M. Nixon** for their candidate and UN ambassador Henry Cabot Lodge of Massachusetts as his running mate. At the Democratic convention, Massachusetts Senator **John F. Kennedy** won the nomination on the first ballot. With an eye to winning southern support in the general election, Kennedy then picked as his running mate his only important opponent, Senate majority leader Lyndon B. Johnson of Texas.

During the campaign, Kennedy criticized the Eisenhower administration for letting America fall behind the Soviet Union in military might. In particular, Kennedy charged that there was a **"missile gap"** developing between the United States and the Soviet Union which left America vulnerable to surprise attack.

Although it was later determined that Kennedy's accusations were groundless, they were effective in putting Nixon on the defensive. John F. Kennedy won the election by a narrow margin.

A Call for Action

The 43-year-old Kennedy was the youngest person ever elected President, and he made a striking appearance on his inauguration day, January 20, 1961. Standing before the nation without hat or topcoat, JFK stirred Americans with his call for action:

Let every nation know, whether it wishes us well or ill, that we shall pay any price, bear any burden, meet any hardship, support any friend, oppose any foe to assure the survival and the success of liberty. This much we pledge—and more. . . .

In the long history of the world, only a few generations have been granted the role of defending freedom in its hour of maximum danger. I do not shrink from this responsibility—I welcome it. . . .

And so, my fellow Americans: ask not what your country can do for you—ask what you can do for your country.

Eisenhower had viewed the President as a trustee of the nation's interests. Kennedy saw the holder of the office as a shaper and creator of a national purpose. He called his program the "**New**

Frontier," relating it to the "New Deal." The new President assembled one of the youngest cabinets on record. Its members included Robert McNamara, the head of the Ford Motor Company, as Secretary of Defense; Dean Rusk, the president of the Rockefeller Foundation, as Secretary of State; and Kennedy's brother Robert as Attorney General. Several advisers had been faculty members at Harvard University, Kennedy's alma mater.

Problems with Congress

Hoping that his first months in office would rival FDR's Hundred Days, Kennedy quickly presented Congress with an ambitious and energetic program. It included Medicare (medical insurance) for the elderly, federal aid to education, a program to combat unemployment, and a new department for urban affairs. But Congress, dominated by Republicans and conservative southern Democrats, was uninterested in some of Kennedy's proposals and hostile to others.

JFK soon discovered that his power over the nation's domestic life was rather limited. Unlike FDR, who was carried into office by a landslide, Kennedy had barely won election. Thus he could not claim any national mandate for his programs. Then, too, Kennedy's popularity with the press sometimes worked to his disadvantage. Magazines found the charming young President and his fashionable wife, Jacqueline, fascinating and glamorous. But in the Senate, where Kennedy had served without distinction, this kind of attention was resented. However, the most serious limitation on the President's power was the coalition of Republicans and conservative Democrats who blocked many of Kennedy's proposals.

Kennedy failed to win congressional votes for his major proposals such as Medicare and federal aid to education. He did, however, score some limited victories. Social Security benefits were increased, some public works money was pumped into depressed areas, and a Federal Water Pollution Control Act was approved.

A Troublesome Economy

The new President's most serious domestic problem was a sluggish economy. When JFK entered the White House, the nation was faced with both a recession and creeping inflation. Seven percent of the work force was unemployed as the nation suffered its fourth recession since World War II.

Kennedy tried to stimulate the sluggish economy by legislation which made grants and loans available for public projects in parts of the country where unemployment was high. He also hoped the economy would be spurred by increasing the minimum wage from $1.00 to $1.25 per hour. In addition, the President encouraged trade through the lowering of tariffs between the United States and the European Common Market. He believed the increased trade would expand the economy. Kennedy used increased military and highway spending as another means of lifting the economy out of the recession.

Kennedy Threatens the Steel Industry

In an attempt to curb the inflation which was hurting the country's economy, JFK established economic guideposts which were to be used in making wage and price increases. Using these guidelines, American steelworkers negotiated a new contract containing a small wage increase.

The President and his advisers did not think that the higher wages would lead to higher steel prices. However, the steel companies, led by Roger Blough, the president of U.S. Steel, raised their prices by $6 per ton. Kennedy called the price increases "a wholly unjustified and irresponsible defiance of our public interest" and mobilized the power of the government to force the steel companies to back down. He threatened

John F. Kennedy (1917–1963)

IN OFFICE: 1961–1963

Democrat from Massachusetts. Kennedy won the presidency in the closest election since 1884. He was the first Catholic and the youngest man ever elected to that office. During his administration, the U.S. supported an unsuccessful invasion of Cuba (1961), the first American was launched into space (1961), the Cuban missile crisis occurred (1962), and a nuclear test ban treaty was signed (1963).

a Defense Department boycott of steel companies that raised prices, and he promised tax investigations by the Treasury Department. Blough and the other steel company leaders soon capitulated by canceling their price increases.

The Struggle for Civil Rights Steps Up

Kennedy faced another serious problem during his administration—the struggle of black Americans for their civil rights. Despite his announced concern for the rights of black Americans, JFK moved slowly at first on civil rights. The President was careful in his approach because he needed the support of white southern congressio-

nal leaders to achieve his top priority of revitalizing the economy.

To avoid a congressional fight which he was sure to lose, Kennedy instructed his brother **Robert Kennedy,** the Attorney General, to enforce civil rights laws already in effect. For example, during the Eisenhower administration only 49 school districts began desegregation. By contrast, 183 did so in the three years of the Kennedy presidency. Robert Kennedy also pursued a vigorous campaign for black voting rights.

Encouraged by the success of the Montgomery bus boycott, more and more blacks, along with white supporters, turned to nonviolent direct ac-

LIFE IN AMERICA

THE ROLE OF TELEVISION IN PRESIDENTIAL ELECTIONS

The 1960 campaign was the first election in which television played a central role. The two candidates, the Republican Vice-President, Richard M. Nixon, and the Democratic Senator John Kennedy, were products of "media politics," a term that was later used to describe campaigns that relied on television. Both were extremely young for presidential candidates— Nixon was 47 and Kennedy 43. Both had used the techniques of modern public relations to leapfrog over their older and more established party rivals.

The Television Debates

When Americans went to the polls in November, it became clear that the election may have been decided by the nation's first televised presidential debates. These debates were held in September and October and consisted of four hour-long programs in which the two candidates answered questions from news reporters. In order to allow the debates to be held, Congress suspended the "equal time" provision of the Communications Act of 1934, thereby permitting the television networks to refuse equal time

Would George Washington win election today?

to four other candidates from minor parties.

Nixon, who had used television to great advantage with his famous 1952 "Checkers speech," thought that the debates could clinch the election for him. Kennedy, however, wanted to use the debates to become better known. He displayed a poise and maturity on television that undercut fears about his youth and inexperience.

Charisma Wins

Although there was little in the way of policy differences between the two candidates, Kennedy's charisma—his personal magnetism and attractiveness—persuaded many voters to support him. Since 1960, the "public image" of presidential candidates as seen on television has either enhanced or detracted from the candidates' appeal with millions of voters.

tion to end segregation and discrimination. Beginning in February 1960, civil rights activists staged "sit-ins" at segregated lunch counters in the South, refusing to move until the blacks among them were served. In 1961, "Freedom Riders" rode on interstate buses into the South in an effort to integrate previously all-white buses and bus terminals.

James Meredith, Birmingham, and the March on Washington

A crisis in Kennedy's civil rights program took place in October of 1962. **James Meredith,** a 29-year-old black Air Force veteran, tried to enroll at the University of Mississippi, a school which had never admitted blacks. Although Meredith was authorized by a court order to enroll, the University refused to admit him. The Justice Department then directed the U.S. Circuit Court to order his admission.

The governor of Mississippi, Ross Barnett, personally blocked the doorway to prevent Meredith from registering for classes. President Kennedy responded by sending 200 U.S. marshals to escort Meredith onto the campus. Their presence touched off a bloody riot in which 2 persons were killed and many wounded. Meredith continued to attend classes with marshals at his side, but one barrier to racial equality was removed.

The following spring the entire nation was shaken by a new confrontation in Birmingham, Alabama. Millions of Americans saw on their TV screens a shocking spectacle. Hundreds of men, women, and children, black and white, who were demonstrating for civil rights in Birmingham, were assaulted by police, who used dogs, electric cattle prods, and fire hoses to break up the nonviolent demonstration. This event won many more whites over to the civil rights cause.

President Kennedy, sensing the explosiveness of the situation, responded with a powerful address on national television. Speaking with great feeling, he described what the lack of jobs and housing meant for blacks. He concluded by asking Congress for laws guaranteeing equal access to all public accommodations and outlawing discrimination in voting and employment. Conservatives in Congress, however, blocked the passage of these measures.

Several months later, in August of 1963, Martin Luther King, Jr., led a quarter of a million demon-

FROM THE ARCHIVES

"I Have a Dream"

Here is an excerpt from Martin Luther King, Jr.'s speech on the steps of the Lincoln Memorial, August 28, 1963.

I say to you today, my friends, that in spite of the difficulties and frustrations of the moment I still have a dream. It is a dream deeply rooted in the American dream.

I have a dream that one day this nation will rise up and live out the true meaning of its creed: "We hold these truths to be self-evident; that all men are created equal."

I have a dream that one day on the red hills of Georgia the sons of former slaves and the sons of former slaveowners will be able to sit down together at the table of brotherhood. . . .

I have a dream that my four little children will one day live in a nation where they will not be judged by the color of their skin but by the content of their character.

I have a dream today.

strators in a march on Washington. On the steps of the Lincoln Memorial, King delivered a stirring speech in which he called for jobs and for an end to segregation and racial intolerance. King's address signaled the start of an even greater wave of black civil rights activity which swept across America throughout the 1960s.

SECTION 1 REVIEW

Identify: Richard M. Nixon, John F. Kennedy, missile gap, New Frontier, Robert Kennedy, sit-ins, James Meredith

Main Ideas

1. How did Eisenhower and Kennedy differ in their views on the presidency?
2. Why did JFK have problems getting his programs passed? How did he hope to stimulate the economy?
3. What steps did JFK take regarding civil rights legislation?
4. What types of direct action did the struggle for civil rights take? What was the reaction?

725

2. THE NEW FRONTIER AND THE COLD WAR

Kennedy's concept of an active presidency was also found in his foreign policy. He inspired Americans with his plans for a Peace Corps to help people in poverty-stricken areas of the world. However, many of his plans were military in nature, and he greatly expanded the nation's nuclear arsenal.

JFK's chief criticism of Eisenhower's foreign policy was that it had been too inflexible. Kennedy believed that "massive retaliation" meant that in a crisis the nation was faced with the unhappy choice between humiliating retreat or nuclear incineration. Kennedy wanted other alternatives. To gain these alternatives, the President turned to the doctrine of **"flexible response."**

In keeping with the doctrine of flexible response, conventional forces capable of fighting in limited or "brushfire" wars were built up. This was a strategy particularly suited to the third world,* where Kennedy saw the greatest challenges to America.

The Bay of Pigs Invasion

When JFK came into office, he learned that President Eisenhower was preparing a Central Intelligence Agency (CIA)–supported invasion of Cuba. The goal of the invasion, which was to be launched from Central America, was to trigger an anti-Communist uprising in Cuba. Kennedy sought and obtained assurances from the CIA and the military that the invasion would succeed and decided to go ahead with the plan.

The invasion force consisted of about 1,500 Cuban exiles. The invaders landed on April 17, 1961, in a swampy and isolated region of Cuba called the *Bahia de Cochinas,* or **Bay of Pigs.** The expected internal uprising did not occur. The plan to knock out Cuba's small air force with attacks on Cuban airfields failed. The invasion was a disaster. When Kennedy did not commit the U.S. Air Force in support of the invaders, their chances evaporated. Within three days the invaders were captured by Castro's forces.

*Refers to the world of neutral nations, mainly new nations in Africa and Asia, which take neither side in the Cold War between Communist and Western nations.

When the failure of the invasion became public, President Kennedy quickly acknowledged his full responsibility. Although the public generally reacted to Kennedy's confession of failure with increased support, many historians now believe that the Bay of Pigs disaster made him appear vulnerable in the eyes of the Soviets. This may have encouraged Soviet leaders to challenge America later in Europe, and to bring about a crisis over Berlin, Kennedy's next test in foreign affairs.

Crisis over Berlin

Berlin remained a divided city after the Soviets lifted the blockade you read about in Chapter 31. As you know, that city lay entirely within East Germany. Thousands of East Germans were fleeing dictatorship, using West Berlin as their doorway to freedom. This caused East Germany and the Soviet Union great embarrassment. The Berlin crisis of 1961 began when Khrushchev threatened to sign a separate peace treaty with East Germany. If such a treaty were signed, East Germany could seal off West Berlin and starve it into capitulation as it had tried to do earlier during the blockade of 1948–1949.

In the midst of this increasing tension, Khrushchev informed American diplomats in Moscow that he would like to meet with the new President. In June of 1961, JFK traveled to Vienna, Austria, for a summit meeting with the Soviet leader. The meeting did not go well, and the chill of the Cold War continued.

To show America's determination not to abandon Berlin, Kennedy called up the Army Reserve and increased the nation's military expenditures. In August the East Germans built the **Berlin Wall**—a grim, gray barrier cutting through the heart of the city. No longer could East Germans escape to freedom through West Berlin. Although the wall stood as a confession of Communist failure, the crisis was defused.

The Cuban Missile Crisis

Only a year after the Berlin crisis, America again seemed on the brink of war with the Soviet Union. In October 1962, American U-2 reconnaissance planes discovered evidence through high-altitude photographs that Soviet-built missiles were being installed in Cuba. Premier Khrushchev may have hoped to regain lost prestige by placing nuclear weapons there. The missiles installed in Cuba could strike cities in the United States as far away as Washington and St. Louis. Americans were not accustomed to living with any military threat just 90 miles from their border.

President Kennedy thus faced a momentous decision—should he move against this threat from the Soviet Union and risk war? Or should he avoid the possibility of war at the price of permitting hostile weapons in America's backyard? Some of Kennedy's advisers called for an invasion of Cuba, but JFK decided that would be too dangerous. Instead, he surrounded the island with a naval blockade to halt approaching Soviet ships.

For six terrifying days the world trembled on the brink of war. Nearly unbearable tension gripped the entire world as Soviet ships steamed toward Cuba while a huge American invasion force gathered in Florida. Then, to the great relief of everyone involved, the Soviet ships turned around. "We were eyeball to eyeball," said Secretary of State Dean Rusk, "and I think the other fellow just blinked." The crisis finally ended when the Soviets agreed to dismantle the missiles already in place in Cuba. In return, the United States agreed not to invade the island.

Twice in two years, Kennedy had successfully called Khrushchev's bluff. But the President had won a hollow victory. Khrushchev came under great pressure from Kremlin "hawks" and the hard-line Chinese Communists. Within a year the Soviet leader was replaced by men who had as their chief priority an increase in Soviet military might. These leaders were determined that the Soviet Union would never again give in to the Americans. As a result, they began the largest peacetime military buildup in history.

Trouble in Vietnam

As you learned in the preceding chapter, in 1954 a Communist government took control of the northern part of Vietnam when the French were defeated at Dien Bien Phu. To keep the rest of the nation from becoming Communist, President Eisenhower sent military advisers to South Vietnam. President Kennedy increased the number of American servicemen in South Vietnam from about 900 in 1961 to 17,000 by 1963. These troops were sent to aid the South Vietnamese leader **Ngo Dinh Diem.**

Kennedy was aware of the problems in Vietnam. Diem was a Catholic in a nation of Buddhists. Diem's government lacked the support of the mass of the people, and he had called off the 1956 elections on reunification of the North and South that had been called for in the Geneva Agreements (1954). In response, local Communist insurgents formed guerrilla bands called the **Viet Cong.** The Viet Cong guerrilla movement, supplied and aided by the Communist North, was strong and well organized.

Despite these facts, the President decided that it was important symbolically for the United States to oppose communism in Southeast Asia. In addition, JFK's advisers told him that the United States could win a war there.

Vietnam turned out to be an extremely difficult place in which to fight. It was a long, narrow country that stretched along the sea to southern China. (See map, page 734.) Along the coast ran a narrow plain covered with thick jungles. Farther inland were mountains. At the southern tip was the rich rice-growing area of the Mekong Delta. In the north were the mountainous, forested "highlands." In both areas American advisers found themselves facing an enemy who seemed to melt away with the daylight hours or with the approach of a strong opposing force.

It soon became apparent that victory was not possible with Diem in power. The South Vietnamese leader was then deposed in a coup approved by the United States government. The coup went further than the Kennedy administration wished when Diem and some of his family were executed. A new government better able to fight the war was installed at Kennedy's direction. The United States was now committed to fighting a war against communism in Southeast Asia. President Kennedy, however, did not live to carry out his new policies in regard to the war.

Death in Dallas

President Kennedy's term in office came to a sudden and tragic end in the third year of his administration. On November 22, 1963, he visited Dallas, Texas, to help mend a split in the Texas Democratic party. Just before noon, the President was shot as he traveled in a motorcade en route to a speaking engagement. The Secret Service rushed the dying President to Parkland Hospital, where a team of doctors tried to save his life. The wounds, however, were fatal. Two hours later, on board Air Force One, which was returning the young President's body to Washington, Vice-President Lyndon B. Johnson was sworn in as President of the United States.

Within a few hours of JFK's death, Dallas police seized a suspect in the assassination—Lee Harvey Oswald. A neurotic, confused young man who had once asked for political asylum in the Soviet Union, Oswald was in turn killed two days later. As he was being taken to the Dallas County jail, he was shot at point-blank range by Jack Ruby, a Dallas nightclub owner, in full sight of millions of television viewers.

America was stunned by the terrible events in Dallas. Had Oswald acted alone? If not, who else was responsible? Had Ruby killed Oswald to keep him from talking?

To answer these and other questions, President Johnson appointed the **Warren Commission,** a body of distinguished citizens headed by Chief Justice Earl Warren, to investigate the assassination. At the end of nine months of investigation, the Commission issued a report stating that there had been no conspiracy. Oswald and then Ruby, the report said, had acted alone.

In the years since the Warren Report was issued, new investigations have been conducted. One of these was a lengthy study made in 1979 by a congressional committee. Using new techniques for analyzing sound, the committee concluded that more than one rifle was used in the assassination. If there was a second rifle, who fired it? The committee also suggested that Ruby may have acted for others when he killed Oswald. If so, who were they? Today, these questions about the death of President Kennedy remain unanswered.

SECTION 2 REVIEW

Identify: flexible response, Bay of Pigs invasion, Berlin Wall, Ngo Dinh Diem, Viet Cong, Warren Commission

Main Ideas

1. Give two reasons why the Bay of Pigs invasion failed.
2. Why was the Berlin Wall built? How did it ease tensions in the Cold War?
3. What were the short-term and long-term results of the Cuban missile crisis?
4. List three problems the United States faced in aiding the South Vietnamese.

3. LYNDON B. JOHNSON TAKES THE HELM

Lyndon Baines Johnson was a figure who seemed larger than life. A tall man from Texas, a state with a reputation for producing outsized characters, Johnson had the legislative skills of a master politician. He was only ten years older than Kennedy, but he came from a different generation and a different political world. Johnson was a product of depression-era poverty, and his political views were shaped by his hero, Franklin D. Roosevelt.

Johnson was a self-made man who had worked his way to the top of the political heap. Elected majority leader of the Senate in 1954, he soon became one of the most powerful and effective majority leaders that the Senate had ever known. Johnson was a genius at using his extraordinarily persuasive skills to engineer a consensus among diverse interests. In the Senate he created agreement through what was known as the "Johnson treatment." The Senator would find a colleague in a hallway, a cloakroom, or at a party. He would charm, plead, promise, and threaten, his expressive face reflecting his approach. Usually Johnson would get what he wanted.

Civil Rights and the War on Poverty

As President, Johnson used his endless energy and skill to push through the sort of legislative program that John Kennedy, the Senate outsider, had not been able to push through when he was President. Within months of taking office, LBJ, as he was soon known, guided through Congress the most sweeping civil rights act since the days of Reconstruction. The **Civil Rights Act of 1964** barred discrimination in public places, gave the Attorney General the authority to bring suits to desegregate schools or other public facilities, and banned discrimination in employment on the basis of race, color, sex, nationality, or religion.

Johnson also secured laws to conserve wilderness areas, improve mass transit systems, and provide aid to education. He planned to finance these measures through a massive tax cut designed to increase economic growth and federal revenues.

Johnson hoped to outdo even his idol FDR in his efforts to help the disadvantaged. In his 1964 State of the Union message, he called for a **"War on Poverty"** to combat unemployment and illiteracy. Under Johnson's leadership Congress passed a vast array of measures to help poor people. Among the new programs were a Neighborhood Youth Corps and a Job Corps that provided counseling, training, and work for young people. Operation Head Start helped disadvantaged preschoolers.

The Campaign and Election of 1964

Lyndon Johnson was the uncontested nominee of the Democrats in 1964. The Republicans, however, had a fight on their hands. The two chief rivals were Nelson Rockefeller, the multi-millionaire governor of New York, and **Senator Barry Goldwater,** a square-jawed former fighter pilot and businessman from Arizona. Rockefeller represented the old-line "Eastern establishment" wing of the party. Rockefeller Republicans accepted most of the ideas of the New Deal. They were also internationalist in their approach to foreign policy. Their candidates had dominated the Republican party for over 20 years.

The Goldwater Republicans described Rockefeller Republicanism as "me-tooism," a reference to the tendency of the liberal Republicans to go along with many Democratic ideas. The Goldwater Republicans were very conservative. Generally from the western United States, they believed that the U.S. was becoming a welfare state that was rapidly destroying the traditional American values of individual initiative, thrift, and self-support. They opposed big government, big business, and particularly big labor, and they were concerned that America was moving down the road to socialism.

When Goldwater defeated Rockefeller for the Republican nomination, the conservatives won control of the Republican party. Goldwater refused to try to attract more middle-of-the-road voters. He campaigned as a strict conservative who was opposed to civil rights legislation, the Social Security system, the TVA, and deficit spending* by the federal government.

During the campaign, Johnson skillfully tagged

*__deficit spending__ The practice by a government of spending more than it collects in taxes. The extra money is raised by the sale of government bonds.

Goldwater as an extremist who could not be trusted with the nation's security. The Republican candidate played into Johnson's hands when he suggested that the United States use low-yield nuclear weapons in Vietnam. Johnson used these and other statements to portray Goldwater as a trigger-happy cowboy who would lead the United States and the world into a nuclear war.

When Americans cast their ballots in November, LBJ was elected by a landslide, winning 486 electoral votes to Goldwater's 52. Once he was elected, LBJ set out to end poverty in America. His job was seemingly made easier by the fact that the conservative coalition of Republicans and southern Democrats which had opposed so many of Kennedy's programs had been shattered by the 1964 election.

A Wave of Reform Legislation

In his 1965 State of the Union address to the nation, Johnson called for programs to achieve the **"Great Society,"** in which hunger, disease, discrimination, pollution, and other social problems would be banished from the land. One of his top priorities was medical care for the elderly.

For nearly 30 years there had been many proposals to extend Social Security to include medical care for the aged. Each time the proposals were blocked by lobbying from the American Medical Association. In July 1965, however, Medicare

Lyndon B. Johnson   (1908–1973)

IN OFFICE: 1963–1969

Democrat from Texas. Johnson assumed office when Kennedy was assassinated, then won election on his own. At first he was a very popular President, and he used his influence in Congress to secure the passage of many social programs, including the Economic Opportunity Act (1964), the Civil Rights Act (1964), the Voting Rights Act (1965), and Medicare (1965). His escalation of the Vietnam War without raising taxes caused inflation to soar. He lost much support as the war continued, and this led to his decision not to run for re-election.

Selma march for voting rights, 1965

was passed by Congress. Financed through the Social Security system, Medicare helped provide medical aid for persons 65 years old and older.

The War on Poverty moved into high gear after Johnson's election. Congress approved over $1 billion to rehabilitate the poverty-stricken Appalachian region. Most of the money went to build roads, airports, parks, and other public facilities. To administer similar programs to rebuild the nation's decaying cities, Johnson asked for and Congress created a new cabinet department—the Department of Housing and Urban Development. LBJ named as its secretary Robert C. Weaver, who became the nation's first black cabinet officer.

The President also supported the first major additions to the nation's parks and recreation areas since the days of the New Deal. "Our common goal," he said, "is an America of open spaces, fresh water, of green country—a place where wildlife and natural beauty cannot be despoiled." Congress also passed a series of air and water pollution bills.

The President and Congress were also influenced by Ralph Nader's 1965 book, *Unsafe at Any Speed.* **Ralph Nader** was a lawyer who drew a whirlwind of public attention by demonstrating that many American cars were safety hazards because of faulty design and construction. Nader also criticized many other products on the market and sparked the first interest in a wave of "consumerism" which would soon wash from coast to coast. The Johnson administration responded by passing new laws to protect consumers.

The most hotly contested set of Johnson's reforms centered around civil rights for blacks. The Johnson administration soon found itself involved in this continuing issue. In March of 1965 the nation was again shocked by the sight on national television of civil rights demonstrators being beaten. State troopers near Selma, Alabama, attacked a group of peaceful demonstrators who were marching to protest the lack of voting rights. Public sympathy for the civil rights struggle increased.

Congress reflected the public mood by passing the **Voting Rights Act of 1965.** The new law banned the literacy tests which had been used for decades to prevent blacks from voting. It also empowered the U.S. Attorney General to send examiners into any area where there was a charge of voting discrimination. The Johnson administration believed that blacks would best be able to advance their interests through the ballot box. Their faith in the ballot box, however, was shaken by the racial hostilities which seemed to grow more violent and dangerous even as Congress acted to calm them.

The Civil Rights Struggle and the Women's Rights Movement

The Civil Rights Act of 1964 also outlawed discrimination in employment on the basis of sex. Although not enforced at the time, this provision was to be of importance in the following decade when the women's movement gained momentum. The law could be used against employers who discriminated against women in their hiring practices. This possibility was seen at the time by some supporters of women's rights.

In her influential book *The Feminine Mystique* (1963), **Betty Friedan** had argued that women were treated as second-class citizens with fewer opportunities than men. In 1966, spurred by the passage of the Civil Rights Act, Friedan and 31 other people founded the **National Organization for Women (NOW)**. Among the organization's goals was that of obtaining legal and social equality for women. The women's movement, inspired by the gains made by blacks in the 1960s, would win its greatest victories in the 1970s.

SECTION 3 REVIEW

Identify: Civil Rights Act of 1964, War on Poverty, Barry Goldwater, Great Society, Ralph Nader, Voting Rights Act of 1965, Betty Friedan, National Organization for Women

Main Ideas

1. Why was Johnson more successful in getting legislation through Congress than Kennedy? How did the election of 1964 increase Johnson's ability to get his programs passed?
2. What were the issues in the campaign of 1964?
3. What did President Johnson hope to see accomplished through his Great Society programs?
4. What were the goals of the civil rights laws passed in 1964 and 1965?
5. How did the Civil Rights Act of 1964 affect the women's movement?

4. THE BLACK REVOLT

During LBJ's administration the legal basis for segregation was at last toppled. The Civil Rights Act of 1964 and the Voting Rights Act of 1965 legally ended the Jim Crow status of blacks. Although many whites bitterly opposed black rights, their voices were no longer politically respectable. A new national consensus had emerged concerning the need for integration. American blacks could no longer legally be denied their right to vote or to use public facilities. Racial discrimination in housing and employment was barred by law.

The social and economic condition of many blacks across America was also improving. The massive migration from the rural poverty of the South into the large cities of the North brought some improvement in medical care, though not always in living standards. The number of blacks attending college grew sharply between 1940 and 1965. Black income steadily increased, and blacks were increasingly moving into skilled and professional jobs. But unemployment among blacks remained a serious problem. From 1949 to 1964 the unemployment rate of blacks was twice that of whites. The vast majority of blacks remained at the bottom of the economic ladder.

Riots in the Ghettos

The civil rights movement seemed to be moving toward success, but the apparent progress was deceptive. While some blacks had improved their lot, others remained mired in poverty. In 1964, riots broke out in black slum areas of New York City, Philadelphia, and other cities. Within five days after LBJ signed the 1965 Voting Rights Act, one of the worst riots in the nation's history broke out in Watts, the black area of Los Angeles. The riots were a protest against entrenched unemployment and low living standards.

During the **Watts riot** black mobs burned and looted the white-owned businesses in the ghetto and shot at the police and National Guardsmen who came to quell the violence. Thirty-four people were killed, hundreds more were wounded, over 4,000 citizens were arrested, and some $200 million worth of property was destroyed.

Those who had supported the civil rights movement were thrown off balance by the Watts riot and the other disorders that followed in slum areas in Chicago, Philadelphia, Newark, Cleveland, and Detroit. In Detroit in 1967, the rioting lasted for weeks. More than 40 people were killed, and 5,000 left homeless by the wave of violence.

The Black Power Movement

In the mid-1960s, some blacks had begun to question the goals of the civil rights movement. They argued that the goals and methods of the nonviolent protest movement led by Martin Luther King, Jr., would not solve the problems of the urban slums. Instead, more and more blacks began to call for **"Black Power."**

The Black Power movement was largely inspired by the ideas of **Malcolm X,** one of the leaders of a religious movement called the Black Muslims. Malcolm X called for separatism, not integration. He and other Black Muslims believed that blacks should own their own factories and businesses so that whites could no longer have economic control over blacks. Malcolm X also rejected King's view that blacks should engage only in nonviolent protest. Instead, he said, blacks should defend themselves when attacked.

Malcolm X's views spread to other groups, including some which had been in the forefront of the civil rights movement. The phrase "Black Power" came to represent a general attitude that blacks should control their own neighborhoods, businesses, and schools. Some supporters of Black Power hoped to forge a powerful nation within a nation rather than work for the integration of blacks into white society. Others viewed the phrase as a call to re-examine their African origins and to study black achievements. Some Black Power advocates used revolutionary slogans and called for a black uprising if their demands were not met.

Opposition to the Black Power Movement

Many black leaders criticized the call for Black Power. Martin Luther King, Jr., who was still the most influential black leader in the country, warned that violence and separatism were self-defeating, both in moral and practical terms. **Bayard Rustin,** the main organizer of the 1963 march on Washington, cautioned that Black Power would isolate the civil rights movement.

Blacks, Rustin insisted, had to enter into political coalitions with other groups if they were to gain their goals. Rustin feared most of all that Black Power would burn itself out in spectacular gestures which would produce no concrete changes but would enrage the white population. Groups such as the NAACP continued to work for peaceful change with integration and equality as their goals.

Tragically, the most effective voice against violence, Martin Luther King, Jr., was assassinated by a white sniper, James Earl Ray, early in April 1968. In response to King's slaying, violence erupted in 125 cities across the nation. In the nation's capital giant plumes of smoke towered skyward when rioters burned ghetto areas.

The Legacy of the Black Struggle

King's death left the civil rights movement in a weakened position. The tactics it had developed to combat legal discrimination in the South had proved ineffective in dealing with the economic problems of life in northern cities. At the same time the Black Power movement also slowly burned itself out.

Although racial problems did not end, and the problems of poverty and slums were not solved, the decade of protest did win some major victories. Segregation was ended, and many black citizens gained access to jobs that had formerly been denied them. More and more blacks moved into middle-class jobs, as white-collar workers, technicians, journalists, teachers, lawyers, and doctors. The political gains were substantial. Thousands of blacks won public office in the South and elsewhere, and black voters wielded increased political power throughout the nation.

SECTION 4 REVIEW

Identify: Watts riot, Black Power, Malcolm X, Bayard Rustin

Main Ideas
1. What was the cause of the Watts riot and other riots that took place in black slums of the cities during the 1960s?
2. What were various meanings of the term "Black Power"? Why did many civil rights leaders oppose the call for Black Power?
3. Describe some major victories that blacks won during the years of protest.

5. PRESIDENT JOHNSON AND THE VIETNAM WAR

The same qualities that made Lyndon Johnson an effective leader at home led him into a disaster abroad. LBJ was a man of extraordinary political skills. He used his electoral mandate to dominate the nation's government as few Presidents had dominated it before. As a result, few of LBJ's early decisions were questioned by Congress or the American people. Even as the President began to lead the United States further into the expanding war in Vietnam, he retained the support of most citizens.

The Gulf of Tonkin Resolution
In the summer of 1964 LBJ told Congress that U.S. warships had been attacked by North Vietnamese torpedo boats in the Gulf of Tonkin, located off the shore of North Vietnam. What the President did not tell Congress (or the American public) was that the American ships had been engaged in intelligence operations in support of South Vietnamese attacks on the coast of North Vietnam.

Unaware of all the facts, Congress accepted the President's version of the events. On August 7, 1964, Congress approved the **Gulf of Tonkin Resolution** with only two dissenting voices in the entire House and Senate. The resolution was a statement by Congress supporting the power of the President to "take all necessary measures to repel any armed attack against the forces of the United States and to prevent further aggression." In effect, Congress had surrendered its war-making powers to the President, giving him a blank check for his policies in Southeast Asia.

Johnson's Plans for Vietnam
Not all of LBJ's plans for Vietnam involved military actions. He hoped to make South Vietnam a model of non-Communist development. He proposed to do this through a plan similar to Roosevelt's New Deal of the 1930s. Just as the TVA had remade the Tennessee Valley in America, LBJ hoped that a similar development project on the Mekong River would help remake South Vietnam. This plan would be supplemented by a host of other projects designed to transform and modernize all of South Vietnam.

As the President soon discovered, however, neither the Communists in North Vietnam nor the peasants in the South were much interested in his vision. The fact that in South Vietnam power was wielded by army officers, none of whom had widespread popular support, was a major problem. South Vietnam's leaders seemed incapable of fighting the Communists, remaking their country, or gaining the support of the people.

By 1965, the Viet Cong and their North Vietnamese allies were clearly defeating the American-equipped and American-advised South Vietnamese army. LBJ responded by sending more and more American troops and advisers to Vietnam. Little by little, the United States was drawn into a land war in Asia. By 1966, there were 190,000 U.S. troops in Vietnam. The escalation of the war was destroying the President's vision for a new and better Southeast Asia. And, little by little, the war was destroying Vietnam itself.

The United States Escalates the War
The President and his advisers continued to increase the level of the fighting in the Vietnam War. They believed that the North Vietnamese would be defeated only if sufficient pressure were applied to their home territory. To carry the war to the North Vietnamese, "Operation Rolling Thunder," the massive bombing of North Vietnam, began in March 1965. The country was carpeted with bombs. Vast areas of the countryside were turned into crater-pitted moonscapes.

In the South, the American and South Vietnamese armies increased their efforts to root out the North Vietnamese and Viet Cong guerrillas, who blended so easily and quickly into the local population. American troops employed "search and destroy" missions which often devastated villages suspected of being Communist sanctuaries. In an attempt to restrict Viet Cong mobility, "free-fire" zones were designated, where massive firepower destroyed every living thing, sometimes including friendly civilians.

Many Americans Question the War
At home, meanwhile, the administration was faced with growing criticism of the war. Many Americans were shocked by the monstrous

Saigon residents return to their destroyed homes after the Tet offensive, 1968.

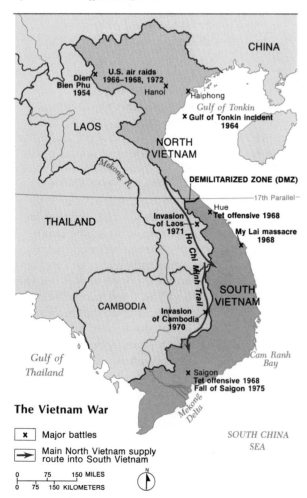

The Vietnam War

x	Major battles
→	Main North Vietnam supply route into South Vietnam

0   75   150 MILES
0 75 150 KILOMETERS

human cost of a war in which 150,000 civilians were killed each year and in which 5 million people had been forced into refugee camps. Religious leaders questioned the morality of the war, while college professors and other intellectuals doubted the wisdom of American efforts to try to help the Vietnamese. Business leaders became concerned with the cost of the war, as the expense of the fighting spiraled from $8 billion in 1966 to $25 billion in 1968. The cost of the war fueled inflation and began to drive the price of consumer goods upward. The war was hurting the very people at home that the Great Society was designed to help.

The President responded to his critics by reminding them of the Munich Conference, at which Britain and France tried to appease Hitler. Johnson and Secretary of State Dean Rusk believed that if we did not defeat the Communists in South Vietnam, there could be an even more serious confrontation later on. Johnson also did not want to be the President who was responsible for losing Vietnam. "I am not going to be the President," said LBJ, "who saw Southeast Asia go the way China went."

The Tet Offensive Increases Opposition to the War

The administration's problems were compounded by the **Tet offensive** of January 1968. During Tet, the Vietnamese New Year season, the Viet Cong and North Vietnamese launched an offensive which overran most of the major South Vietnamese cities. They laid siege to the United States embassy in Saigon and captured villages throughout the countryside thought to be loyal to the South Vietnamese government. Although the Tet offensive cost the Viet Cong and the North Vietnamese so many casualties that armies were bled white, it severely shocked the American military. It also helped turn the tide of American public opinion at home decisively against the war in Vietnam.

Newspapers raised the question of a "credibility gap." How was it possible, they asked, for the North Vietnamese to launch such an offensive if the administration had been telling the truth about American progress in the war? College students, faced with the prospect of being drafted to fight in what seemed to be a meaningless war, asked awkward questions. Why were we supporting a government in Vietnam that did not even have the backing of its own citizens? Even some military men, such as the Marine Corps Medal of Honor winner General David Shoup, opposed the war. Perhaps most disturbing to Americans was the comment by returning troops that we were fighting an unseen enemy in a land where the majority of the common people did not care who won, but only wanted an end to the carnage.

The President Changes His Views

In June 1967, Robert McNamara, who had been Secretary of Defense since the Kennedy administration, began to doubt the wisdom of American policy in Vietnam. In the fall he resigned and was replaced by Clark Clifford. Clifford began to examine carefully the military reports coming out of Vietnam. Although he was at first a "hawk," or supporter of the war, Clifford soon changed his mind. He too advised LBJ that it was a mistake to continue the fighting. Other advisers began to have the same opinion. The President decided to reconsider his war policies.

While LBJ was reassessing his policy toward Vietnam, the 1968 presidential campaign began. In the New Hampshire primary, the Democratic party and most supporters of the war were stunned when an antiwar senator, Eugene McCarthy, accumulated more than 40% of the vote. Four days later, Senator Robert Kennedy, who also was now opposed to the fighting, entered the presidential race.

Two weeks later, on March 31, President Johnson appeared on national television with an announcement that the American government was taking immediate steps to de-escalate the war. All bombing attacks on North Vietnam were to be halted. LBJ also asked the North Vietnamese leader, Ho Chi Minh, to come to the conference table to discuss a negotiated settlement.

Then the President made another announcement, unexpected by most of the nation. "I shall not seek, and I will not accept the nomination of my party for another term as your President."

The war in Vietnam had damaged both a large part of Vietnam and the Great Society. Johnson's splendid plans, which had begun with such high hopes, ended in disaster. Inflation, racial strife, and the bitter conflict over the war divided the American people. Abroad, the United States appeared to some nations as an imperialistic country. Even some of our allies criticized us for fighting the wrong war at the wrong time in the wrong place.

Americans began to question their country and its role in world affairs. It was the beginning of a period of doubt and uncertainty among Americans which would plague the nation for many years into the future.

Peace march in San Francisco, 1972

SECTION 5 REVIEW

 Identify: Gulf of Tonkin Resolution, Tet offensive

Main Ideas

1. How did the Gulf of Tonkin Resolution enable the President to escalate the war?
2. What factors made it difficult for the U.S. to aid the South Vietnamese government?
3. Describe how the war caused great hardship for the Vietnamese.
4. List reasons why many Americans began to oppose the war. Why did Johnson continue to try to win it?
5. Why did Johnson decide to de-escalate the war? What were the effects of the war on American society?

CHAPTER 33 REVIEW

Key Terms
Explain the meaning of each of the following terms:

missile gap
New Frontier
sit-ins
flexible response
Bay of Pigs invasion
Berlin Wall
Viet Cong
Warren Commission
Civil Rights Act
    of 1964
War on Poverty

Great Society
Voting Rights Act of
    1965
National Organization
    for Women
Watts riot
Black Power
Gulf of Tonkin
    Resolution
Tet offensive

Reviewing the Main Ideas
Section 1
1. How did Eisenhower and Kennedy differ in their views on the presidency?
2. Why did Kennedy have trouble getting his programs passed? What steps did he take to improve the economy?
3. What civil rights actions and laws date from the Kennedy years?

Section 2
1. Why did the Bay of Pigs invasion fail?
2. What happened in Berlin during Kennedy's presidency?
3. What were the most important results of the Cuban missile crisis?
4. What problems did the United States face in aiding the South Vietnamese during the Kennedy administration?

Section 3
1. Why was Johnson more successful than Kennedy in getting legislation through Congress?
2. What were the goals of the Great Society?
3. What civil rights laws were passed during the Johnson administration?
4. What effect did the Civil Rights Act of 1964 have upon the women's movement?

Section 4
1. What was the cause of the Watts riot and other riots that took place in black poverty-stricken sections of cities in the 1960s?
2. What were the various meanings of the term "Black Power"?
3. What political and economic gains did black Americans make during the 1960s?

Section 5
1. How did the Gulf of Tonkin Resolution help President Johnson escalate the war in Vietnam?
2. Why was it difficult for the United States to help the South Vietnamese government win the war?
3. How did the war affect the Vietnamese land and people?
4. Why did many Americans begin to oppose the war effort? Why did President Johnson continue the American involvement?
5. How did the war affect American society?

Special History Skills:
Summarizing Viewpoints
The 1960s saw Americans deeply divided over the best solution to racial problems. Some favored the status quo, some favored gradual change, others favored nonviolent direct action, while still others supported calls for Black Power. First, write a paragraph explaining the economic and social conditions blacks faced between 1960 and 1968. Then write a paragraph that summarizes views supporting nonviolent direct action that were commonly held during the period. Next, write a paragraph that summarizes commonly held views supporting Black Power. For paragraphs 2 and 3, include a discussion of the spokesmen and women for the various points of view. To do so, you will need to do library research. Finally, write a paragraph that expresses your own point of view.

Other Skill Activities
1. Biography
Write a short biography of Martin Luther King, Jr. Be sure to use at least three sources.
2. Letters to the editor
The country was deeply divided over the Viet-

nam War. Write two letters to the editor which might have appeared in a newspaper after Lyndon Johnson decided not to run for re-election. One letter should give reasons for supporting the war, and the other should give reasons for pulling American troops out of Vietnam.

3. **Art that shows the 1960s**

   Draw a series of pictures or make a collage that reflects the change in the mood of the nation between 1960 and 1968. Over your art work make a time line which shows the events that changed the nation's mood.

4. **Songs of protest**

   Using the library or a record collection, find a song of antiwar protest and one of black protest from the 1960s. Play them for the class. Discuss what the songs reflect.

Thinking Critically

1. Defend or reject the following statement: "Television has helped clarify election issues for Americans."
2. Do you think Kennedy used unfair tactics to force the steel companies to follow his price guidelines? Why or why not?
3. Was Kennedy's position on the Cuban missiles an act of brinkmanship? Why or why not?
4. There was never a formal declaration of war in either Korea or Vietnam. Is this a violation of the Constitution? Discuss. Is a declaration of war less likely to be passed than it was earlier? Why or why not?
5. After the Tet offensive, the United States might have been able to win the war if it had mounted a major offensive against the Viet Cong and North Vietnamese. Do you think that it should have tried to do so? Explain.
6. What attitudes and actions of the 1960s still affect our lives today? How?

Further Reading

Tom Wicker. *JFK and LBJ*. Penguin, 1969. An excellent comparison of the two men and their administrations. Contains a facsimile of the Gulf of Tonkin Resolution.

John Hope Franklin. *From Slavery to Freedom*. Knopf, 1974. A history of black Americans for advanced students.

Don McKee. *Martin Luther King, Jr*. Putnam, 1969. A simply written biography.

Guenter Lewy. *America in Vietnam*. Oxford University Press, 1978. The war is traced from the defeat of the French through the American escalation and the bombing of North Vietnam. For advanced students.

TEST YOURSELF

WRITE YOUR ANSWERS ON A SEPARATE SHEET OF PAPER.

Chronology

List the following events in their chronological order.

1. Bay of Pigs invasion
2. Civil Rights Act of 1964
3. beginning of sit-ins
4. march on Washington for civil rights
5. JFK election
6. LBJ election
7. Watts riot
8. Tet offensive

Fill in the Blanks

1. JFK accused Eisenhower of allowing a _____ to develop between the United States and the Soviet Union.
2. In 1960 _____ was used for the first time in presidential debates.
3. JFK chose to strictly enforce existing _____ legislation rather than ask Congress for new laws.
4. JFK called his administration and its proposals _____.
5. The U.S.–backed invasion of _____ was called the Bay of Pigs invasion.
6. Kennedy gave increased support to the unpopular Diem regime in _____.
7. President Johnson called his administration and its proposals the _____.
8. Martin Luther King, Jr., supported _____ tactics to win an end to segregation.
9. The North Vietnamese attack which changed President Johnson's policies toward the Vietnam War was called the _____.
10. In the 1960s, the term _____ was used to describe the belief that blacks should control their own neighborhoods, businesses, and schools.

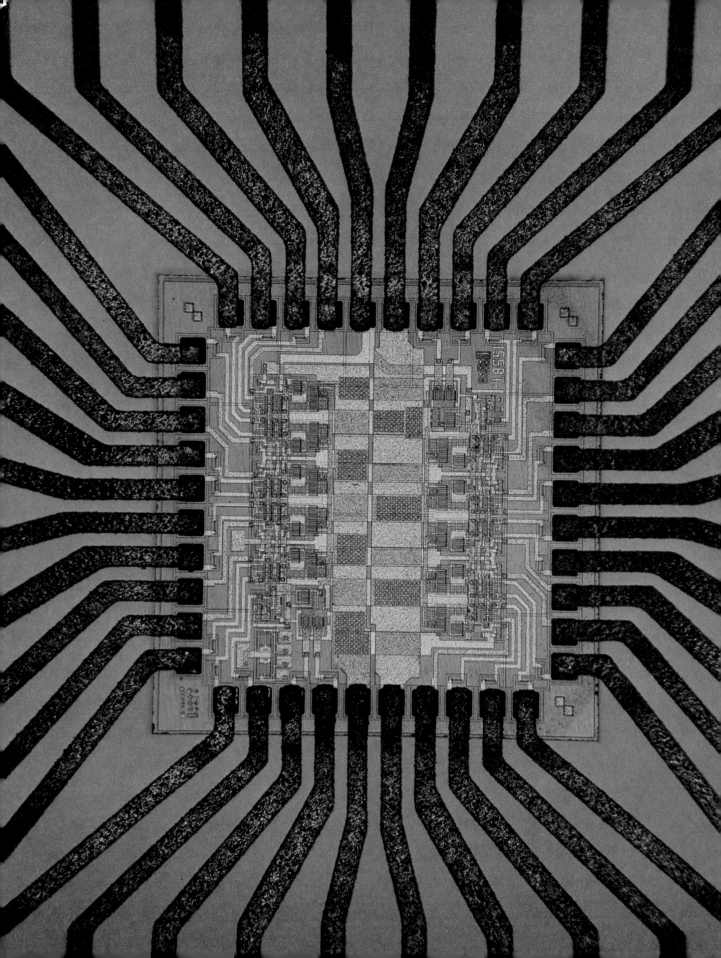

Chapter 34

THE NIXON–FORD YEARS

1968–1976

I t is February 21, 1972. On the windswept runway of an airport near Peking, the capital city of China, a giant American airplane rolls slowly to a halt. Inside the plane, called the *Spirit of '76*, is Richard M. Nixon, President of the United States. At the foot of the ramp to the plane's door stands China's Premier, Chou En-lai, wrapped in a heavy overcoat against the chill of the Chinese winter. President Nixon, in one of the most historic gestures in modern American history, descends the ramp and clasps the hand of the Chinese leader in a show of friendship and peace. Nixon is the first American official to publicly visit China in more than 25 years.

During the next week the President and his staff meet with several high-ranking Chinese leaders, including Chairman Mao Tse-tung. At receptions and banquets held in the gaily decorated Great Hall of the People in Peking, toasts are made to the new relationship between the two nations. Although no final decisions are reached about the problems that confront them, everyone agrees that a historic step has been taken.

In this chapter you will learn how President Nixon, the man responsible for America's new relationship with China, was first elected to the presidency in 1968. You will study his domestic and foreign policy decisions, including his successful effort to end America's involvement in Vietnam. And you will see how, after winning a second term, Nixon resigned from office because of the Watergate scandal.

Sections in This Chapter
1. The Election of 1968
2. Nixon's First Administration
3. President Nixon Confronts Problems at Home
4. The Imperial Presidency
5. A Scandal Called Watergate

Computer technology zoomed in the mid-1970s with the development of microelectronic circuits on tiny silicon chips like the one opposite, ¼-inch square and greatly magnified.

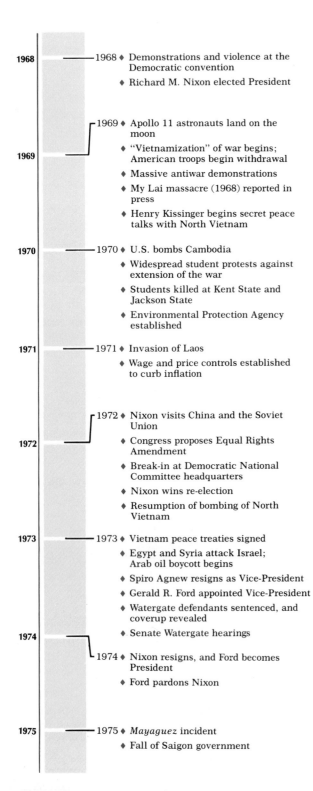

1968 ♦ Demonstrations and violence at the Democratic convention
     ♦ Richard M. Nixon elected President

1969 ♦ Apollo 11 astronauts land on the moon
     ♦ "Vietnamization" of war begins; American troops begin withdrawal
     ♦ Massive antiwar demonstrations
     ♦ My Lai massacre (1968) reported in press
     ♦ Henry Kissinger begins secret peace talks with North Vietnam

1970 ♦ U.S. bombs Cambodia
     ♦ Widespread student protests against extension of the war
     ♦ Students killed at Kent State and Jackson State
     ♦ Environmental Protection Agency established

1971 ♦ Invasion of Laos
     ♦ Wage and price controls established to curb inflation

1972 ♦ Nixon visits China and the Soviet Union
     ♦ Congress proposes Equal Rights Amendment
     ♦ Break-in at Democratic National Committee headquarters
     ♦ Nixon wins re-election
     ♦ Resumption of bombing of North Vietnam

1973 ♦ Vietnam peace treaties signed
     ♦ Egypt and Syria attack Israel; Arab oil boycott begins
     ♦ Spiro Agnew resigns as Vice-President
     ♦ Gerald R. Ford appointed Vice-President
     ♦ Watergate defendants sentenced, and coverup revealed
     ♦ Senate Watergate hearings

1974 ♦ Nixon resigns, and Ford becomes President
     ♦ Ford pardons Nixon

1975 ♦ *Mayaguez* incident
     ♦ Fall of Saigon government

1. THE ELECTION OF 1968

The 1968 political campaign was one of the most disturbing in American history. It took place against a backdrop of riots and assassinations at home and a continuing war abroad. The antiwar candidate, Senator Eugene McCarthy of Minnesota, who had made a surprisingly strong showing in the New Hampshire primary, was in turn challenged by Senator Robert F. Kennedy, the brother of the late President John F. Kennedy.

McCarthy's support was based almost entirely on college students and a few middle-class white professionals. Kennedy's support included blacks, Mexican Americans, and a sizable number of white blue-collar workers who had supported his brother.

McCarthy and Kennedy battled each other in a series of grueling primaries until Kennedy won overwhelmingly in the decisive California primary of June 5, 1968. That night, exactly two months after Martin Luther King's murder, Robert F. Kennedy was assassinated by a Palestinian fanatic who wanted to punish Kennedy for his support of the state of Israel.

Hubert H. Humphrey, Johnson's Vice-President, became the main Democratic candidate. Although Humphrey entered no primaries, Democratic officials all across the country supported him. Since most of the delegates to the nominating convention were picked by these officials, Humphrey was all but assured the nomination.

Violence in Chicago
Many Democrats were deeply disillusioned by the Johnson-Humphrey administration's continuation of the war. Deprived by an assassin's bullet of one of their heroes and embittered by the certainty of a Humphrey victory, they went to the convention in an angry mood. They were joined by antiwar protestors who wanted an antiwar candidate, and by radicals who had gone to the convention to disrupt it.

At the convention, McCarthy supporters fought a losing battle to change the party's war policy. Outside, thousands of people demonstrated. They ranged from middle-class reformers and antiwar protestors to "Yippies" who wanted to "start a revolution for the heck of it" and radicals who supported the Viet Cong. The hostility between the delegates inside the hall was matched outside by the hostility between the mainly middle-aged blue-collar policemen and the generally young protestors.

On the night Humphrey was nominated, millions of Americans watching the convention on TV saw the police attack demonstrators, onlookers, newspaper reporters, and television crews. As the demonstrators ran they shouted, "The whole world is watching!" Sadly, it was. The violence in Chicago tarnished the image of the Democrats, widened the hostilities between young Americans of military age and those who were much older, and made much of the world think that American society was destroying itself.

The Republicans Nominate Nixon

The violence in Chicago set the stage for a Republican revival and the nomination of Richard M. Nixon. Just four years earlier the Republicans had been trounced so badly in the Johnson-Goldwater campaign that some people believed that the party was dead. Richard Nixon's political career had also been given up for dead. After his defeat for the presidency in 1960 and for the California governorship in 1962, Nixon had announced his retirement from politics. The events in Chicago, however, gave both the Republicans and Nixon a new lease on political life.

The 1968 Campaign

Nixon entered the campaign as the voice of unity. After experiencing five consecutive summers of ghetto rioting, antiwar campus disorders, and a sharp upsurge in crime, many American voters wanted peace. Nixon promised to restore calm. He announced that he had a plan for stopping the war in Vietnam, but stated that he could not reveal the details. Nixon consulted television and public relations experts and put together a campaign that ran smoothly.

Humphrey, however, was not so lucky. The deep divisions in the Democratic party dogged him wherever he went. If Humphrey had followed his own sentiments and denounced the war, he would have cut himself off from President Johnson and the Democratic officials who won the nomination for him. But because he did not denounce the war, the McCarthy Democrats

threatened to withhold their support on election day. This dilemma created many embarrassing situations for Humphrey and the Democratic party.

The wild card in the race was **Governor George Wallace** of Alabama, the candidate of the newly formed **American Independent party**. Wallace and the American Independent party symbolized the resentment many white Americans felt toward both blacks and what they regarded as privileged college student protestors. The governor was a force to be reckoned with in the North as well as in the South. Six weeks before election day, Wallace was only slightly behind Humphrey in the popularity polls. Nixon was well in the lead.

In the last month of the campaign Humphrey staged a comeback while Nixon began to slip in the polls. Humphrey, who was tied to LBJ's war policies, gained some support when Johnson ended all bombing in North Vietnam. Nixon, in order to retain some of the conservative support which was drifting to Wallace, began to adopt some of the Governor's themes. He spoke increasingly of bringing "law and order" once again to America, and of controlling the hippies* and protestors who threatened to disrupt society.

In the end Nixon's judgment proved correct, and the law and order issue carried him to victory over Humphrey. Nixon narrowly won the popular vote, but gathered 301 electoral votes to Humphrey's 191 and Wallace's 46. Democrats, however, continued to control both houses of Congress.

SECTION 1 REVIEW

Identify: Hubert H. Humphrey, George Wallace, American Independent party

Main Ideas

1. What unusual events occurred at the 1968 Democratic convention? What were the goals of the demonstrators?
2. Why did Hubert Humphrey refuse to denounce the war? How did this refusal affect his campaign?
3. What issues were the key to Richard M. Nixon's victory in 1968?

---

*hippies commonly used term in the 1960s and 1970s to describe people who rejected conventional standards of dress and behavior. Many of them lived in groups and acted with complete freedom in their private lives.

2. NIXON'S FIRST ADMINISTRATION

Nixon had been elected by a narrow margin of popular votes, and the Democrats controlled both Houses of Congress. Thus the President knew that he would be unable to pass any major pieces of social legislation. Blocked from affecting domestic policy in a dramatic way, the President turned to foreign policy to make his mark. Nixon told a friend that

the country could run itself domestically without a President. All you need is a competent cabinet to run the country . . . you need a President for foreign policy.

At his inaugural, President Richard M. Nixon told the audience that

In these difficult years, America has suffered from a fever of words. . . . We cannot learn from one another until we stop shouting at one another—until we speak quietly enough so that our words can be heard as well as our voices.

Despite his call for openness, however, President Nixon remained suspicious and mistrustful. He soon cut himself off from all but his most trusted political aides and advisers. His closest aides were people with limited experience in the bartering and compromise of legislative politics. They were people from business and advertising backgrounds whose main qualification for office seemed to be their loyalty to the President. Nixon kept even the senior members of his own party at arm's length. He relied entirely on his enormous White House staff, directed by former advertising man H. R. Haldeman, lawyer John Erlichman, and Attorney General John Mitchell.

A New Approach to Foreign Policy

President Nixon was a great admirer of the majestic and haughty General Charles de Gaulle, the President of France from 1959 to 1969. Nixon believed that de Gaulle's great success in foreign policy was due to his ability to rise above party squabbles and petty politics in order to serve the national interest. Nixon hoped to do the same thing in America. He thus adopted some of the techniques of the French leader.

Nixon's chief aide in creating a bold new foreign policy was **Henry Kissinger,** who in 1969 was appointed Assistant to the President for National Security Affairs. Kissinger was a German Jew whose family had fled to America to escape Nazi persecution. A witty intellectual and a Harvard University political science professor, Kissinger became known for trying to apply the European doctrine of *realpolitik* (practical politics) to American foreign policy.

Traditionally, American foreign policy was based on either the outward-looking idealism of an internationalist such as Woodrow Wilson or on the inward-looking idealism of an isolationist such as Herbert Hoover. Kissinger proposed a dramatic change. He took as his model the 19th-century German leader, Otto Von Bismarck. There was no room for idealism in Bismarck's policy. For Bismarck there were no permanent friends or enemies, but only permanent German interests. On the basis of those interests, Bismarck attempted to maintain a **"balance of power"** between the nations of Europe so that no one nation or group of nations could ever be powerful enough to threaten Germany.

Kissinger's version of balance-of-power diplomacy was based on the fact that there were five "economic superpowers" in the world—the United States, the Soviet Union, China, Japan, and the European Common Market countries. Of the five, there were two—the United States and the Soviet Union—that balanced each other militarily.

Thus the real contest was to see which grouping of powers would determine the world's economic future. According to Kissinger, economic power was the key to other kinds of power. Kissinger also believed that the deepest conflict was not between America and the Soviet Union, but between the Soviet Union and China. He hoped to use the Chinese-Soviet conflict to reorganize the world order and to find an honorable way out of the Vietnam War for the United States.

"Vietnamization" and the Invasion of Cambodia

Before Nixon and Kissinger could put their plans into effect, they were faced with the thorny problem of what to do about the war in Vietnam. Kissinger recognized that the ever increasing opposition to the war meant that the United States could never commit enough forces to win. He therefore decided to look for a way out.

Since a simple withdrawal of American troops would make the United States appear weak and untrustworthy, Kissinger and Nixon decided on a different plan—a plan they called **"Vietnamization."** Vietnamization meant that the United States would continue to support the anti-Communist government of South Vietnam by supplying it with more money and material, but not with more troops. Instead, the U.S. would train and equip South Vietnamese soldiers to be the front-line troops. Henceforth, the actual fighting in Asia was to be done by Asians.

Opposition to the war continued despite Nixon's announcement of Vietnamization. In October of 1969 a wave of enormous demonstrations in which millions of Americans participated rocked the nation. In November 1969 many Americans were shocked by the reports of a bloody massacre that had occurred in March 1968. American troops killed more than 450 Vietnamese civilians, including babies and small children, in the village of **My Lai.**

In late April 1970, the President decided that despite U.S. assistance, the South Vietnamese government would fall if the North Vietnamese were able to continue to launch attacks on South Vietnam from Cambodia. (See map, page 734.) Without consulting Congress, the President sent

American forces into Cambodia to clear out the North Vietnamese. He argued that the attack would bring the North Vietnamese more quickly to the bargaining table. He also said that only by punishing the North Vietnamese could he bring them to negotiate on terms the United States could accept.

Massive and sometimes violent demonstrations broke out all across America in opposition to the Cambodian invasion. At two colleges, events took a particularly ugly turn. On May 4, 1970, Ohio National Guardsmen fired into a crowd of students at Kent State University. Four students were killed, and several were wounded. At Jackson State College in Mississippi, the state highway patrol shot and killed two students on May 14. Although the antiwar protests flared to their highest level, Nixon insisted that Vietnamization and the American invasion of Cambodia were necessary to protect the nation.

Nixon was able to continue the war for several reasons. One, there was a growing "backlash" (reaction) developing among working-class people towards the "privileged" students who were leading the peace movement. All along, of course, many Americans had supported the war and saw no reason to stop supporting it. Two, some elements of the antiwar movement had hurt their cause by turning to violence and demonstrating a hatred for America. Three, there was no move by Congress to stop the war. Under these circumstances, the President was able to proceed with Vietnamization. Supplies continued to flow to Vietnam, but the American troop level there began to decrease. In December 1968 there had been 536,000 troops in Vietnam. By the end of 1970, there were 335,000.

In early 1971 President Nixon and his advisers decided to test how well the Vietnamization program was working. They also hoped to cut the Ho Chi Minh Trail—a network of roads and trails running through Laos that was used by the Communists to bring supplies and reinforcements into South Vietnam. (See map, page 734.) No American ground forces were used in the invasion of Laos, which began in late January and ended on March 24. South Vietnamese Army units were ferried into combat by American helicopters, however, and supplies were also delivered by United States planes. When the Laos invasion ended, the President claimed it proved that South

Richard M. Nixon (1913–   )

IN OFFICE: 1969–1974

Republican from California. During Nixon's first term Americans landed on the moon, the Environmental Protection Agency was established, and détente with the Soviet Union and China was achieved. During his second term, American participation in the Vietnam War was ended. When the Watergate scandal broke, Nixon was implicated in helping to cover up the crime. Rather than face probable impeachment proceedings, he resigned, the first President to do so.

President and Mrs. Nixon in Peking, 1972

the secret talks, and in early 1972 North Vietnam launched one of its largest attacks of the war. Thousands of North Vietnamese troops invaded South Vietnam. The United States responded with heavy air strikes near Hanoi, North Vietnam's capital, and at Haiphong, a major seaport. These were the first U.S. bombings of North Vietnam since 1968. As the North Vietnamese began to capture provinces in South Vietnam, American troops continued to leave Vietnam. By mid-August 1972, all American ground combat units were withdrawn from South Vietnam, and by the end of the year there were only 24,000 American troops left in South Vietnam.

On October 12, Kissinger and Le Duc Tho reached a cease-fire agreement. But the arrangement was opposed by South Vietnam's President Thieu. Negotiations finally began again in November, but the North Vietnamese attempted to win additional concessions from the United States. In December 1972, the U.S. resumed bombing North Vietnam in order to force it to conclude negotiations.

New Approaches to the Soviet Union and China

Once President Nixon had his critics on the defensive on the peace issue, he was ready to make the diplomatic moves for which he would be long remembered. Nixon knew that American power was vastly overcommitted in the world. He knew, too, that the United States could no longer police the entire globe. But rather than simply reduce the American role in the world, the President and Henry Kissinger decided to take advantage of the divisions between the other major powers to maintain American supremacy. First and foremost in their plans was a desire to take advantage of the deep hostility between the two great Communist powers, the Soviet Union and China.

Nixon hoped to use America's technological know-how and agricultural surpluses, both of which were badly needed by the Soviet Union and China, to bend those nations' policies in a new direction. By holding out the bait of increased trade, the President hoped to gain access to the vast Chinese and Soviet markets for American business. He also hoped to gain Soviet and Chinese help in bringing North Vietnam to the bargaining table.

Vietnam could survive on its own. Critics, however, charged that while some South Vietnamese troops had done well, others had not.

Early in 1972, President Nixon revealed that between 1969 and 1972, Kissinger had held 12 secret meetings in Paris with Le Duc Tho, the North Vietnamese representative. The purpose of the secret meetings, which were held at the same time as the open peace talks, was to work out an agreement with North Vietnam directly to end the war. In late 1971, however, Hanoi broke off

In July 1971, Nixon, a person who had made his political reputation as a hard-line anti-Communist, stunned the world. He told a vast television audience that he had accepted an invitation to visit China. Conservative Republicans were shocked. They could not believe that this was the same Richard Nixon who had blamed China for the Korean War or who had fought so hard to keep China out of the United Nations. In February 1972, President Nixon visited Peking. A new era in American diplomatic relations was underway.

The new relationship between China and the United States upset the Soviet Union, which had long been engaged in a war of words with China. On occasion the two powers had clashed militarily along their mutual border. Anticipating Soviet concern, President Nixon's next trip, in May 1972, was to the Soviet capital of Moscow. There, in a televised address to the Soviet and American people, Nixon expressed the need for friendship and arms reduction as a part of a **détente** (relaxation of tensions) between the United States and the Soviet Union. With Nixon's two trips, "détente" became a word on everyone's lips.

President Nixon had accomplished an extraordinary diplomatic feat. He had gained a degree of Communist cooperation at a time when the United States was at war with Communist North Vietnam. At the same time, he had made it clear to the world that national interest had become more important than ideology in American foreign policy.

SECTION 2 REVIEW

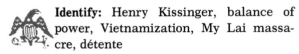

Identify: Henry Kissinger, balance of power, Vietnamization, My Lai massacre, détente

Main Ideas

1. Why did President Nixon concentrate on foreign policy during his first administration?
2. What was Henry Kissinger's approach to foreign policy? How did it differ from traditional American foreign policy?
3. Describe the policy of Vietnamization and the reasons for the invasion of Cambodia and Laos. What was the result?
4. Why did President Nixon establish new relationships with China and the Soviet Union?

3. PRESIDENT NIXON CONFRONTS PROBLEMS AT HOME

Even though Republicans were a minority in Congress, President Nixon brought about the passage of several new laws. In 1969 he signed a bill that changed the military draft and placed America's Selective Service on a lottery basis. Later, a law was passed to prohibit radio and TV advertising of cigarettes. In 1970 the President signed a bill creating the National Railroad Corporation. This agency, known as Amtrak, was to rebuild and operate America's passenger railroads. In 1970 he also established the **Environmental Protection Agency**, which was to fight for conservation of natural resources and against pollution.

Other laws were signed by the President to establish and enforce standards of safety for consumer products, to increase the pay of military personnel, and to increase Social Security benefits. In 1971, the 26th Amendment was ratified, lowering the voting age from 21 to 18.

Nixon's first administration also saw a triumph in the American space program. On July 20, 1969, the *Apollo 11* space shot landed two men—Neil Armstrong and Edwin Aldrin—on the moon's surface while a third astronaut, Michael Collins, orbited the moon in a command ship. Other Apollo missions followed. Vehicles were landed and driven about on the moon's surface. Samples of lunar soil were returned to Earth for study. America had fulfilled the goal set by President Kennedy in 1961 of reaching the moon with a manned landing before the end of the decade. When the Apollo program was ended in 1972, it had been an enormous success.

Another major Nixon domestic program was revenue sharing. This was a plan to take tax money collected by the federal government and return it to the states. Although liberals feared that such revenue sharing spelled the end of federal programs for the needy, and conservatives hoped that the federal government would shrink in size, neither expectation came to pass.

During Nixon's first administration, in 1972, Congress proposed an Equal Rights Amendment which attempted to end discrimination against

women. The amendment stated: "Equality of rights under the law shall not be denied or abridged by the United States or by any state on account of sex." Although supported by many women's groups and labor unions, the Equal Rights Amendment fell three states short of the 38 needed to win ratification.

Changes in the Supreme Court

Nixon had long believed that the Court was dominated by liberals who had failed to uphold the Constitution. When four vacancies appeared on the Court during the President's first term, he used the opportunity to change the direction of the Supreme Court.

The President's first move was to replace Chief Justice Earl Warren, who was retiring, with **Warren Burger**, a conservative from Minnesota. But Nixon ran into trouble with his next two nominees, Clement Haynesworth of South Carolina and Harold Carswell of Florida. The Senate challenged the legal qualifications and civil rights records of both men. As a result, neither man was approved. Later the President succeeded in appointing Harry Blackmun, a respected Minnesota lawyer, to the Court. Because of Nixon's appointments, the Court took a conservative swing.

Problems with the Economy

President Nixon's most difficult domestic problem was how to deal with the economy. Because of the war in Vietnam, Nixon inherited a high rate of inflation from the Johnson administration. President Johnson had been unwilling to finance an unpopular war by increasing taxes. Instead, he had resorted to **deficit spending**—in effect, printing more money to pay for military expenditures. As the amount of money in circulation grew faster than the rate at which new goods were produced, prices began to rise. As a result of rising prices, American products were unable to compete effectively with foreign products. This in turn caused the United States to lose business overseas, and an unfavorable balance of trade threatened to develop.

President Nixon at first decided against any drastic action. He announced that he would fight inflation by the traditional Republican means of reducing government spending, improving government efficiency, and regulating more closely the nation's money supply.

By 1971, however, the President realized his economic policy was throwing America into a recession. In order to overcome the unemployment and falling production which were affecting the nation, Nixon and his economic advisers changed their economic plan. The President decided to expand the nation's money supply through a larger federal budget and deficit spending—much as had been done by the Democratic party during the Johnson administration. The new budget submitted to Congress in January 1971 called for a deficit of $11.6 billion in 1972. Many conservative Republicans were shocked by the President's turnaround.

In August of 1971 President Nixon shocked some of his supporters even more when he announced that he was imposing **wage and price controls** on the nation's economy for 90 days. This policy meant that the wages of American workers would be frozen at their present level for three months. Businesses and industries were also required to freeze prices, fees, professional charges, and rents at their August 1971 level. Through this program the President hoped to slow the spiraling rate of inflation which continued to drive prices upward. The first phase of the new anti-inflation plan also called for a reduction by 5% of the persons employed by the federal government. The

President then announced that Phase II of his plan would go into effect in November. Nixon stated that under Phase II the government would permit wage and price increases if they corresponded with increases in productivity. Nixon also established the Cost of Living Council to oversee the fight against inflation.

Phase II of the President's plan began on November 13, 1971. Under this part of the plan, a 5% cost of living wage increase was approved by the Cost of Living Council. Price hikes of 2.5% were also authorized. For a time Nixon's new program seemed to be working. Price increases declined by almost 2% while unemployment dropped by 1% from pre-freeze levels. Under these circumstances Nixon was able to curb inflation until the next presidential election.

During his second administration, however, the President's program did not work as well as he and his advisers hoped. When controls were removed, prices shot up even more. The use of controls had also increased the government's bureaucracy needed to enforce the freeze program. In addition, both labor and business were unhappy with the wage and price freeze because it interfered with economic freedom.

The Election of 1972

As the nation prepared for the 1972 presidential elections, President Nixon confronted a Democratic opposition that was deeply divided. The wounds left by the 1968 Democratic convention had barely healed when the pro- and anti-Humphrey forces again began attacking each other.

The Democratic reformers felt that they had been cheated out of the 1968 nomination by the Humphrey regulars. The reform element was led by **George McGovern**, a senator from South Dakota and a foe of the war in Vietnam. Under his leadership in 1970, the party delegate and convention rules had been rewritten. The new rules enabled all enrolled party members to help select delegates to the convention. In addition, minorities, women, and young people were given proportional representation within committees and as delegates. These new rules took away the power of party officials and enabled McGovern to secure the nomination in 1972.

McGovern ran an inept campaign, however, and was unable to capitalize on the country's growing criticism of the war. Nixon, in contrast, used his presidential powers to command the media's attention. He painted himself as a candidate who would bring peace with honor in Vietnam, thus implying that McGovern, who favored immediate and unconditional withdrawal, represented dishonor.

Nixon also gained support when the hero of the "hawks," Alabama Governor George Wallace, was forced to withdraw from the race after being wounded by a would-be assassin's bullet. To hold on to the support of the hawks and to force the North Vietnamese to the bargaining table, Nixon ordered the military to bomb and strafe the harbors of North Vietnam. A week before the election, Henry Kissinger announced that he and the North Vietnamese would soon agree on a cease-fire. The announcement was premature, but it had the desired effect by causing some of the antiwar vote to slip away from McGovern.

McGovern tried (without success) to make an issue of a break-in at the Democratic National Committee in the Watergate office complex. Try as he might, however, McGovern could not get the press or the public to take seriously charges of Republican wrongdoing.

Under these circumstances, Nixon won in a crushing landslide that almost equaled Franklin Delano Roosevelt's great victory of 1936. Nixon captured 47 million popular votes (60%) to McGovern's 29 million (37%). In the electoral college, Nixon received 520 votes to McGovern's 17. The Democrats, however, retained sizable majorities in both houses of Congress.

SECTION 3 REVIEW

Identify: Environmental Protection Agency, *Apollo 11*, Warren Burger, deficit spending, wage and price controls, George McGovern

Main Ideas
1. What new laws did Congress pass or consider during Nixon's first term?
2. What successes in the space program occurred during the first Nixon administration?
3. How did Nixon influence the Supreme Court?
4. What steps did President Nixon take to deal with inflation? What success did he achieve?
5. Name two factors which led to President Nixon's landslide victory in 1972.

4. THE IMPERIAL PRESIDENCY

Once President Nixon won re-election for a second term, he made clear his intention to exert his power to the fullest extent possible. In a stunning move, the President asked for the resignation of all his cabinet members. Although he did not intend to replace these officials, he wanted to show that they served completely at his pleasure. The President also wanted it understood that he demanded strict personal loyalty from his subordinates.

Nixon demonstrated his idea of a strong presidency in a number of other ways as well. He upgraded the power of his own staff—those persons appointed by him without the need for Senate approval. The President also created what has sometimes been referred to as a "Super Cabinet" by giving four cabinet members and three other close advisers posts as "White House Counselors." President Nixon moved to dismantle agencies and departments left over from Democratic administrations, but soon found himself at odds with the Democratic Congress.

President Nixon seemed to be moving more and more toward the extremely powerful chief executive described by the historian Arthur Schlesinger, Jr., in his book entitled *The Imperial Presidency* (1973). Schlesinger believed that American Presidents were becoming too powerful for the good of the country. Little did Schlesinger—or even Nixon himself—know where this drive toward power would end.

Nixon's Relations with Congress

President Nixon began his second term with a hard line against Congress. He created a minor constitutional crisis when he refused to spend funds Congress had appropriated for the War on Poverty. In addition, when Congress refused to grant Nixon a $250 billion budget for fiscal year 1973, Nixon impounded (seized) money for his own programs and departments. In 1974 federal courts ruled that these actions were illegal. Congress then drew up procedures to prevent future Presidents from impounding funds.

The President seemed far more outspokenly conservative in his second term than he had during his first administration. This brought him into conflict with liberal and Democratic opponents on Capitol Hill. Without requesting the lawmakers' approval, Nixon began to dismantle the Office of Economic Opportunity, which Congress had created under President Johnson. After Nixon left office, President Ford continued the former President's plan, and the OEO was ended in 1975. In 1973, during Nixon's second term, the Selective Service Act expired and, for the first time since 1948, the U.S. Army was an all-volunteer army.

America Withdraws from Vietnam

President Nixon found it far more difficult to deal with North Vietnam than he did with Congress. After round-the-clock bombing raids—the heaviest in the entire war—on Hanoi and Haiphong in December 1972, negotiations were resumed. In January of 1973, peace treaties were finally signed between the United States, North Vietnam, South Vietnam, and the Provisional Revolutionary Government of the Viet Cong. The terms that the U.S. agreed to were a death warrant for the South Vietnamese government, which could not exist without American support. These terms included: (1) a cease-fire in Vietnam, (2) a pledge that the people of South Vietnam could determine their political future, (3) the release of all American prisoners, and (4) the withdrawal of all U.S. forces from South Vietnam within 60 days.

The North Vietnamese were permitted to keep about 150,000 troops in South Vietnam. It was also understood that despite pledges of continued U.S. military and economic aid, it would be only a matter of time before the South Vietnamese, unaided by American troops, would be crushed by the North. Clearly, South Vietnam had been abandoned by the United States. Within two years, the North again went to war and easily conquered the South Vietnamese government. It was difficult to explain why the United States had fought so long and hard for a settlement which could have been obtained far earlier and with far less bloodshed all around.

The Aftermath of the Vietnam War

When Saigon fell to the Communists in 1975, most Americans tried not to notice. They preferred to forget our most unpopular war. Vietnam had cost 58,000 American lives, 110 billion dollars, and an untold number of physical and mental wounds. Within America the war had set generation against generation. Some veterans of the conflict came back addicted to dangerous drugs and unable to cope with the problems of readjusting to civilian life.

American foreign policy was affected by the war for years to come. Because of the American tragedy in Vietnam, the American people and their leaders were hesitant to exert their power in other parts of the world. As a result, there was a withdrawal of American influence in many parts of the world.

Crisis in the Middle East—the 1973 Arab-Israeli War

In October 1973, less than a year after the United States came to terms with the North Vietnamese, a new foreign crisis broke out—this time in the Middle East. The Arab states in the area, unwilling to accept the existence of Israel, made another attempt to destroy their neighbor. Heavily equipped by the Soviets, Egypt and Syria unleashed a crushing surprise attack on Yom Kippur [yōm′ kē pür′], the most sacred holiday in the Jewish calendar.

After suffering severe initial setbacks, the Israelis beat back the Arab armies. When Israel turned the tide and began to take the offensive, the Soviet Union threatened to intervene with troops on behalf of the Arab nations. At that point the United States placed its armed forces on a worldwide alert. America then sent several huge shipments of supplies to the beleaguered Israelis. The Soviet Union then agreed that a UN force should try to keep peace in the area.

The Arab states retaliated against the United States for its support of Israel by instigating an oil boycott. Although at that time the United States received only a small percentage of its oil from the Arab states, the cutoff was enough to create gas shortages all across the nation. For the first time in history Americans found themselves face to face with a national energy crisis. The boycott made clear what careful observers had known for a long time—the United States had become far too dependent on the Middle East for its energy supplies. Arab and non-Arab oil producers alike took advantage of the energy crisis to raise the price of oil fourfold.

Energy Conservation Measures

Faced with a growing shortage of oil, the United States took a number of steps to conserve dwindling supplies. For a short time daylight savings time was instituted year round, to cut down on the need for lighting at night. The national speed limit on highways was lowered to 55 miles per hour. Americans were asked to set their thermostats at lower temperatures. These efforts helped to some extent, but the energy shortage still persisted.

The Nixon administration was not able to focus its full attention on the energy problem. The President and his chief aides were increasingly occupied by what had become known as the "Watergate affair,"—or simply **Watergate**—named after a seemingly minor break-in at the Democratic National Committee headquarters in the Watergate office and apartment building in Washington.

A Mysterious Break-in

Two years earlier, in the early morning hours of June 17, 1972, Frank Wills, a security guard in the Watergate office complex in Washington, had noticed something odd. While making his routine rounds, he came across a taped latch on a door leading from the building's parking garage to one of its corridors. Wills removed the tape and thought no more of it until he found it retaped on his next round. Realizing that something strange was taking place, Wills called the Washington police to the scene. The police searched the upper floors of the building. When they reached the sixth floor, they found five men inside the office of the Democratic National Committee. The men carried electronic bugging devices and tools for picking locks.

During the arrest that followed, an address book discovered on one of the men contained the name of **G. Gordon Liddy**, a White House staff member and counsel to the Committee to Re-Elect the President. Reporters routinely covering the story eventually came to realize that the break-in was more than an ordinary burglary. In 1973, well over six months after it happened, Watergate became front-page news, driving all other news to the back pages. Watergate became the greatest political scandal in the history of the United States.

LIFE IN AMERICA

AMERICANS AND WORLD TRADE

The Arab oil embargo of 1973 brought to everyone's attention an important economic and geographic fact of modern life—the United States and other nations depend on each other for many essential products. Many Americans consider this dependence dangerous. But world trade also brings a wide variety of goods to American consumers and provides employment for many workers.

No other nation in the world buys and sells as much abroad as the United States. In fact, one out of every six American workers has a job linked to world trade. Farmers have an even bigger stake in this commerce. One out of every three acres under cultivation produces crops for export, and these exports account for 25% of the total income earned by American farmers. Over half the wheat and soybeans grown in America is sold to other countries.

Our Chief Trading Partners

The tables show the countries that are today our best customers and our main suppliers. Note that Canada, Japan, and Mexico top both lists. Canada alone provides 20% of all our imports and buys 20% of all our exports.

Economists use the term "comparative advantage" to refer to one of the benefits of world trade. It is cheaper to grow coffee in Brazil, for example, than to try to grow it in the United States. Therefore, the money we save by buying coffee from Brazil can be used to purchase other goods. A similar argument can be made for purchasing cars from Japan and textiles from Taiwan, although U.S. firms may be put out of business.

Current Trends

Multinational corporations have developed since World War II to take advantage of unrestricted world trade. These huge companies make their headquarters in one country, make their goods in other countries, and sell their products to the world. Names like Coca-Cola and General Motors (both U.S. firms), Sony (Japanese), and Nestlé (Swiss) are familiar to consumers throughout the world.

Another trend is the formation of cartels, or monopolies, by nations that produce certain important raw materials. OPEC is the most powerful example of an international cartel that tries to control prices.

In the 1970s the availability of inexpensive well-made foreign goods and the huge increase in petroleum prices created an unfavorable balance of trade, or trade deficit. In other words, the United States imports more than it exports. In 1980 this gap exceeded $20 billion.

Some industries that have been hard hit by foreign competition, like the automobile, textile, and steel industries, have called for a return to protectionism. This would increase the cost of imported goods in this country and tend to decrease sales. Others feel that a return to protectionism would be a mistake. Rather, they argue, America should strive to increase exports, especially to OPEC countries. By decreasing government regulations and increasing efficiency, they believe, American exports can outdistance imports once again. Those who support free trade believe that more world trade, not less, is the answer to America's economic problems.

Our Ten Best Customers	
Canada	$35
Japan	21
Mexico	15
Britain	13
West Germany	11
Netherlands	9
France	8
Saudi Arabia	6
Italy	6
Venezuela	5

U.S. sales in billions, 1980

Our Ten Main Suppliers	
Canada	$41
Japan	31
Mexico	13
Saudi Arabia	13
West Germany	12
Nigeria	11
Britain	10
Taiwan	7
Venezuela	5
France	5

U.S. purchases in billions, 1980

SECTION 4 REVIEW

 Identify: Watergate, G. Gordon Liddy

Main Ideas

1. Give two examples of Nixon's move to an "imperial presidency" during his second term.
2. What were the terms of the peace treaty that ended the Vietnam War? What happened to the South Vietnamese government after American troops were withdrawn?
3. How did the aftermath of the Vietnam War affect America?
4. Why did the United States suffer an energy crisis in 1974? What steps did Americans take to conserve energy?
5. How were the Watergate burglars connected to the White House?

5. A SCANDAL CALLED WATERGATE

In March of 1973, the eyes of the nation were focused on the courtroom of "hanging judge" **John J. Sirica**. Sirica's court had passed sentence on the seven defendants convicted of breaking into the Democratic National Committee headquarters in Washington's Watergate complex. Sirica refused to believe that the incident had been a simple burglary. He put pressure on the defendants to tell the court who was really behind the break-in.

Under the threat of a long sentence, one of the defendants broke. James McCord, a former CIA employee, revealed that some of the defendants had been paid "hush money" to plead guilty and to guarantee their silence. He also told Judge Sirica that some who had testified during the trial had perjured themselves (lied under oath) and that many other persons involved with the Watergate episode had not been named.

During his testimony, James McCord told the court that the Committee to Re-Elect the President (CRP) was behind the Watergate burglary. The director of CRP had been **John Mitchell**, Nixon's hard-line law-and-order Attorney General who had resigned his chairmanship of CRP in June of 1972. When Mitchell, in the middle of the investigation, attempted to shift the blame to some of his aides, they began to reveal what had taken place during the scandal. One of these aides, White House counsel John Dean, accused President Nixon's two closest advisers, H. R. Haldeman and John Ehrlichman, of deep involvement in the events leading to Watergate. Within a short time several officials within the Nixon administration were making accusations against other administration officials.

The FBI, the CIA, the IRS, and the "Plumbers"

Soon it was revealed that the Federal Bureau of Investigation, the Central Intelligence Agency, and the Internal Revenue Service had all been improperly used by the White House to harass the President's political opponents. Acting FBI Director L. Patrick Gray, a retired naval officer, was forced to withdraw as nominee for Director when it was revealed that he had burned files relating to Watergate.

On the day Gray withdrew his nomination in April 1973, startling new disclosures were made about the original Watergate break-in. It was disclosed that the burglars were part of a White House group called the **"Plumbers"** which had been created to stop leaks of confidential or secret information from the administration. The "Plumbers" had carried out a number of break-ins, buggings, and other illegal activities for the Nixon White House.

The President Reacts to the Scandal

As wave after wave of scandal shocked the public —the Attorney General had authorized a burglary! the Acting Head of the FBI had burned files needed by the Court!—President Nixon declined to comment. Finally, however, he was forced to announce that he would begin investigations. Then, on the night of April 30, 1973, he went before the American people on national television. The President described the whole Watergate episode as a sordid and unfortunate affair but shed no light on his own role. He announced that Haldeman, Ehrlichman, and Attorney General Kleindienst were all resigning. Few people, however, were satisfied with the President's report. Nixon recognized that the speech had failed to silence or slow his critics. A month later he issued another statement in which he said that the White House had tried to "cover up" the crime, but that he himself knew nothing of the Watergate burglary or the cover-up that followed.

The Watergate Hearings

In May 1973, a Senate hearing on the Watergate burglary and related crimes began. The **Watergate hearings** were televised nationally. The Senate committee, led by the widely respected **Senator Sam Ervin** of North Carolina, attracted widespread national attention. The hearing uncovered more and more wrongdoing. CRP, the Senators found out, had used various "dirty tricks" to try to disrupt Democratic primaries in several states. These efforts had included relatively harmless activities, such as releasing mice during press conferences or setting off stink bombs at rallies, as well as criminal activities, such as sending false and malicious campaign literature through the mail and stealing documents and data from political headquarters. The Senate hearings revealed that Jeb Stuart Magruder, who had been deputy director of CRP, had committed perjury before the grand jury. Magruder also said that Attorney General John Mitchell had helped plan the Watergate burglary. Then John Dean, counsel to the President, said in June 1973 that the President had known about Watergate and the cover-up for eight months.

Vice-President Agnew Resigns

Day after day the headlines revealed new cases of criminal actions, cover-up, and corruption on the part of the White House. In the midst of these revelations, it was disclosed that the nation's Vice-President, **Spiro Agnew,** was involved in a scandal of his own. Investigators determined that when Agnew was Governor of Maryland, he had accepted payments of kickback money for contracts awarded to companies doing state business. Although Agnew proclaimed his innocence at first, the evidence against the Vice-President was soon overwhelming. In October 1973, Agnew pleaded no contest on a charge of income tax evasion and resigned from office. The remaining charges against him were dropped, and President Nixon appointed **Gerald R. Ford**, a Republican congressman from Michigan, to take Agnew's place as Vice-President.

Senator Sam Ervin at the Watergate hearings

The Presidential Tapes

Despite all the revelations, one question remained—"How much did the President know?" Was he the chief conspirator, or the victim of overzealous aides? During the Senate investigation it was revealed that the White House staff had taped, for future reference, all the conversations that had taken place in the Oval Office.

Nixon refused to turn the tapes over to the Ervin committee on the grounds of executive privilege. Executive privilege is the right of the executive branch to deny, under certain conditions, the Congress access to White House documents and papers and for White House staff members to decline to give legal testimony. Nixon claimed executive privilege for the tapes on the grounds that they contained nothing of value to the investigation and that national security would be damaged if they were revealed publicly or to the Congress.

The deadlock, which continued for nearly a year, threatened a constitutional crisis. It was broken when the U.S. Court of Appeals ordered the tapes handed over to the Ervin committee. The Court's decision spelled President Nixon's doom. The critical tapes, turned over to the Senate in 1974, contained a conversation between Nixon and Haldeman less than a week after the break-in. That conversation made it clear that the President had known about the Watergate break-in from the start.

The President Resigns

Although President Nixon continued to "stonewall" (behave in an uncooperative manner) against Watergate, the tapes convinced even his die-hard supporters that the President had acted improperly, if not criminally. Several prominent Republicans urged the President to resign as a patriotic gesture. Nixon continued to hold firm, but when a group of respected Republican congressional leaders informed him that he was certain to face impeachment if he failed to resign, the President decided to step down. On August 8, 1974, President Nixon announced that he was going to resign from office. On August 9 he resigned, and Vice-President Gerald Ford took the reins of government.

The growing power of the "imperial presidency" had claimed Richard Nixon as its victim. In the end, Nixon's deep suspicions, mistrust, and obsession with combating his "enemies" was his undoing. In order to be elected for a second term he had resorted to burglary and lies. In order to hide the crime, he engaged in cover-ups and further crimes and lies.

Yet during his administration President Nixon had made some giant advances. The end of the bloodshed in Vietnam, his handling of the Middle East crisis, and his resumption of relations with China were all great accomplishments. The Watergate scandal, however, took away much of the luster from Nixon's accomplishments in foreign policy and tainted his reputation and his presidency.

A New President Takes Office

Gerald R. Ford was the first President in American history to assume the leadership of the nation without having been elected to either the presidency or the vice-presidency. An affable and easygoing man, well liked by his congressional colleagues, Ford was at first a popular chief executive. He pledged an honest, respectable, and open administration, free from the problems of the past.

A conservative Republican in Congress, Ford carried conservative views with him to the presidency. During his administration of some two and one-half years, the new President vetoed 49 bills sent to him by a Democratic Congress. Many of his vetoes were against liberal legislation which would have required expenditures of federal funds.

A month after he became President, Ford damaged his popularity when he unconditionally pardoned Richard Nixon of any and all crimes he may have committed while in office. Impeachment proceedings had begun, and many Americans who believed that the former President should be tried and, if necessary, punished, deeply resented Ford's actions. The President added to his problems when, in an effort to heal the wounds of Vietnam, he granted amnesty to those who had fled the country to avoid American military service during the war.

Problems with the economy continued under President Ford's administration. Inflation continued to be the main difficulty. In an attempt to control rising prices the President launched what he termed the WIN—Whip Inflation Now—Program. The campaign, which asked businesses

Gerald R. Ford (1913–   )

IN OFFICE: 1974–1977

Republican from Michigan. Appointed Vice-President by Nixon, Ford became President when Nixon resigned, the first U.S. President to reach office without being elected to it. During his term the nation faced continuing inflation and a business recession. Ford supported tax cuts, limited social spending, high defense spending, and heavy taxes on imported oil, but was unable to effectively curb inflation.

and labor to hold down wages and prices voluntarily, was largely unsuccessful.

The President regained a measure of popularity when he acted strongly in a foreign crisis. When the Communist government of Cambodia captured the American merchant freighter *Mayaguez* in May 1975, the President sent American marines to free it. Although casualties were heavy, the ship was freed and its crew members were released. The *Mayaguez* incident established Gerald Ford as a decisive leader, and as 1975 drew to a close it was clear that the President would have a good chance to become his party's candidate in 1976.

SECTION 5 REVIEW

Identify: John J. Sirica, John Mitchell, Plumbers, Watergate hearings, Sam Ervin, Spiro Agnew, Gerald R. Ford

Main Ideas

1. What happened in the courtroom of Judge John J. Sirica when the Watergate defendants were sentenced? What did the defendants reveal?
2. How was the FBI involved in Watergate?
3. What did the Watergate hearings reveal?
4. Why were the presidential tapes requested by the Senate? Why did President Nixon resign?
5. What actions did President Ford take that damaged his popularity? How did the *Mayaguez* incident increase his popularity?

CHAPTER 34 REVIEW

Key Terms
Explain the meaning of each of the following terms:

American Independent party
balance of power
Vietnamization
My Lai massacre
détente
Environmental Protection Agency
Apollo 11
deficit spending
wage and price controls
Watergate
Plumbers
Watergate hearings

Reviewing the Main Ideas
Section 1
1. What events made the 1968 Democratic convention a particularly bitter affair?
2. Why was Democratic candidate Hubert H. Humphrey unable to make a strong showing? What issues helped Richard M. Nixon win the election?

Section 2
1. How did Henry Kissinger's views on foreign policy differ from those of advisers in previous administrations?
2. What was the goal and result of the policy of Vietnamization? How did the invasion of Cambodia affect antiwar opinion?
3. Why did President Nixon establish new relationships with China and the Soviet Union?

Section 3
1. List some laws passed during the first Nixon administration. How did President Nixon influence the Supreme Court?
2. What measures did Nixon pursue to try to control inflation? What results did he achieve?
3. What factors enabled Nixon to win such an overwhelming victory in the election of 1972?

Section 4
1. How did Nixon demonstrate his view of a strong presidency during his second term?
2. Describe the peace settlement that ended U.S. participation in the Vietnam War. How did the settlement affect the South Vietnamese government?
3. What caused the energy crisis of 1974, and how did Americans try to deal with it?

Section 5
1. How was Judge John J. Sirica instrumental in bringing to light facts about the Watergate break-in?
2. What did the Watergate hearings reveal about the 1972 campaign?
3. Explain how the discovery of presidential tapes led to the resignation of President Nixon.
4. What actions did President Ford take that decreased his popularity? What action increased his popularity?

Special History Skills:
Sources for Newspaper Stories
Newspapers and investigative reporters played a major role in uncovering the Watergate story. Since papers can be sued for printing untruths, editors usually insist that reporters have at least two sources to confirm what is printed. For instance, to confirm that the Watergate burglars had been paid "hush money," reporters contacted Judge John Sirica and James McCord and checked bank records.

If you were an investigative reporter, what sources would you use to write a story about the following cases?
1. There are suspicions that the mayor has been paid money to give Smith Construction Company a contract to build a new road for the city.
2. City council members are suspected of using confidential information to buy cheap property and then resell it at a high profit to a commercial development firm.
3. It appears as if an elected official is cheating on his expense account.

Other Skill Activities
1. You decide
In 1972 Richard M. Nixon won a huge election victory, but by 1974 he resigned rather than face the growing risk of impeachment. At what

point, if any, would the Watergate evidence have probably convinced you that the President had done wrong? Why? Write your answer in a well thought-out paragraph.

2. **Analyzing policy**

Henry Kissinger's views on foreign policy are discussed in Section 2 of this chapter. Reread that section and then give a report explaining how the policy of Vietnamization was a direct result of Kissinger's views.

3. **How would you vote?**

The election of 1968 troubled many Americans. The Vietnam War had become unpopular, yet most Americans did not support the antiwar demonstrations at the Democratic convention. How would you have voted in 1968? Give your answer in the form of a two-minute speech designed to get others to vote with you.

4. **Nixon crossword puzzle**

Make a crossword puzzle from the names and events prominent in the Nixon years, 1969–1974.

5. **Vietnam after the American withdrawal**

Research Vietnamese events from 1973 to the present. Give a five-minute report to the class on the state of the country.

6. **Headline collage**

Use library microfilms to study newspaper headlines from 1968 to 1973. Copy the headlines and make a collage from them.

Thinking Critically

1. Was the end of the Vietnam War an "honorable" peace for the United States? Discuss.
2. Why would wage and price controls be difficult to implement in our economy?
3. What do you think is the effect of assassinations and assassination attempts on our political system? On the morale of citizens?
4. Do you think that "executive privilege" should put a President above the law? Explain.

Further Reading

Carl Bernstein and Bob Woodward. *All the President's Men.* Simon and Schuster, 1974. The book was written by the reporters most responsible for uncovering the Watergate scandal. Well written in dramatic reporting-type style. For advanced students.

William C. Westmoreland. *A Soldier Reports.* Doubleday, 1976.

TEST YOURSELF

Matching

Write the letter or letters of the descriptions that best match each name below.

1. George Wallace
2. Eugene McCarthy
3. Hubert Humphrey
4. Robert Kennedy
5. Richard Nixon
6. Henry Kissinger
7. H. R. Haldeman
8. John Erlichman
9. George McGovern
10. Gerald Ford

a. two scandals made this congressman President
b. sought the Democratic nomination in 1968
c. presidential adviser
d. Democratic candidate in 1972
e. Republican candidate in 1968
f. independent candidate in 1968 and 1972

True or False

Mark T if the statement is true, F if it is false. Rewrite the italicized words in all false statements so that they are true.

1. In February of 1972 Richard Nixon stunned the world by visiting *Taiwan.*
2. The protestors outside the 1968 Democratic convention *wanted* Hubert Humphrey to be the party's candidate for President.
3. In 1968, George Wallace was the candidate of the *American Independent party.*
4. In 1972 Congress proposed the *Equal Rights Amendment*, but it did not win ratification.
5. President Johnson resorted to *deficit spending* to finance the war in Vietnam.
6. There was *little opposition* to the U.S. invasion of Cambodia.
7. Richard Nixon won the 1972 election by a *close margin.*
8. In 1975, the *Saigon* government fell to the North Vietnamese and the Viet Cong.
9. George McGovern complained about the Watergate break-in in 1972, and the nation was *shocked* at that time.
10. Richard Nixon was succeeded in office by his Vice-President, *Spiro Agnew.*

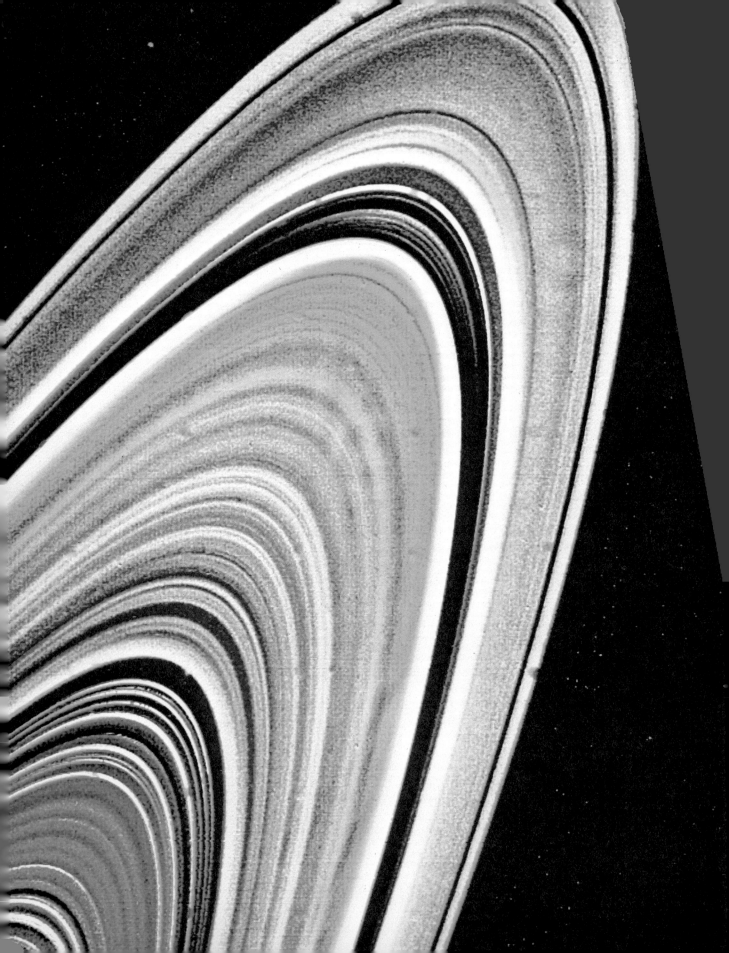

AMERICA ENTERS A THIRD CENTURY

1976 to the Present

When the American people celebrated their nation's bicentennial in 1976, they remained deeply disturbed by the events of the Watergate scandal and the Vietnam War. Americans questioned themselves and their country, perhaps more than at any other time in United States history. Many citizens wondered if the country could put its recent troubles behind and go on to a better future. They wondered if politicians and the government could be trusted. They had questions about the effects of a rapidly developing technology and worsening economic problems.

Both of America's major political parties suffered from deep divisions as the election of 1976 drew near. Many Americans seemed to be anti-government in their outlook, and a number of prominent public officials had differing views on the major issues confronting the nation.

A policy of détente with the Soviet Union, the opening of a new relationship with China, and the end of the war in Vietnam were the most striking developments of the Nixon-Ford years. Although international tensions lessened, the next two Presidents would also face many serious problems in foreign policy.

In this chapter you will examine how one crisis after another seemed to face the United States in the late 1970s and early 1980s. You will see how America and Americans reacted to these problems. And you will study how in 1980 American voters took a turn toward conservatism and elected a new leader in the hope of once again bringing strength and respect to the United States.

Sections in This Chapter
1. Jimmy Carter Becomes President
2. America's Minority Groups in the 1970s
3. President Carter Faces Challenges Abroad
4. Crises in Iran and Afghanistan
5. Ronald Reagan Becomes President

Opposite: The robot eyes of U.S. spacecraft Voyager 2 *swoop over Saturn's rings, 1 billion miles from home.*

JIMMY CARTER BECOMES
PRESIDENT

1975	1975 ♦ Congress passes the Indian Self-Determination Act
1976	
1977	1977 ♦ Jimmy Carter becomes President ♦ Carter initiates human rights policy ♦ U.S. signs treaty ending its control of the Panama Canal
1978	1978 ♦ Carter convinces Sadat and Begin to sign Camp David accords
1979	1979 ♦ Carter and Brezhnev sign SALT II agreement; Senate fails to approve it ♦ Shah of Iran deposed ♦ Iranian militants seize U.S. embassy and take hostages
1980	1980 ♦ Congress creates the Synthetic Fuels Corporation ♦ Soviet Union invades Afghanistan
1981	1981 ♦ Ronald Reagan becomes President ♦ Iran releases U.S. hostages ♦ Martial law declared in Poland ♦ Crisis deepens in El Salvador
1982	1982 ♦ Reagan announces "New Federalism" ♦ Recession deepens

1. JIMMY CARTER BECOMES PRESIDENT

In the Republican party in 1976 the anti-administration mood was best expressed by **Ronald Reagan,** the former governor of California. A movie star turned politician, Reagan decided to challenge President Ford for the Republican nomination. Ford, a genial man, was well liked, but he had no personal political following. Reagan, by contrast, was the hero of millions of conservative Republicans. The same Republicans who had once supported Barry Goldwater now viewed Reagan as their new champion. For the most part these were people who believed that big government was unnecessary and undesirable. They believed that the size of government could be reduced by ending government regulation of business and cutting back in social services. In effect, these citizens wanted to repeal much of the legislation of the New Deal and of the other liberal administrations of recent decades.

Reagan's enthusiastic and well-organized supporters attacked Ford as soft on both big government and communism. They were especially critical of Henry Kissinger's policy of détente. Many conservatives believed that the policy of détente was not in the best interests of the United States.

The Republican primaries showed that the battle between Ford and Reagan was extremely close. The President finally won renomination on the floor of the Republican Convention by the narrow margin of 57 votes. When Gerald Ford gained the nomination, he was forced to accept a Republican platform drafted by the Reaganites. Ford, however, made the best of a platform that sometimes criticized the policies he had supported as President.

The Democrats Nominate a Newcomer

Because Ford seemed to many a sure loser, and because of the Watergate scandal, the Democrats were confident that they could win the presidency easily. Among the many candidates was a political newcomer—James Earl Carter, better known as **Jimmy Carter.** A peanut farmer and former governor of Georgia, Carter was virtually unknown in national politics. Polls showed that at the beginning of his long campaign, Carter was known by only 2% of the voters.

Carter overcame this handicap by an ambitious speaking schedule that took him into many parts of the country. Accompanied by his able wife, Rosalyn, he caught the imagination of the voters with a simple, direct approach. He entered primary after primary and to the surprise of party leaders began to win. By the time the Democrats met in New York City for the nominating convention, Carter had won 18 of the 31 states' primary contests. Nominated on the first ballot, he chose Walter Mondale of Minnesota as his running mate.

The former governor's homespun style appealed to voters angered by the "imperial presidency." Carter presented himself as a common, down-home fellow who knew what it was like to be an ordinary citizen. He made a point of carrying his own luggage on the campaign trail. He stayed in the homes of his supporters to show his belief in the common man. Reporters soon began to notice that Carter's campaign style and driving ambition were making him a formidable candidate.

A deeply religious man, Carter was warmly embraced by the growing number of "born-again" Christians who appreciated the way he publicly identified himself with Christian values. Carter emphasized his morality to stress the difference between his outlook and that of former President Nixon.

Both candidates tended to be somewhat conservative. Both also emphasized that there were no quick solutions to the nation's complex problems. Ford criticized Carter for his lack of experience in national government, but Carter turned Ford's comments to advantage by portraying himself as an outsider uncorrupted by Washington. In the November election the American people elected Carter by a narrow margin. He received 50% of the popular vote to Ford's 48% and won 297 electoral votes to Ford's 240.

Troubles with Congress

Carter had campaigned for the presidency as an outsider who would whip the flabby federal government into shape. Once he arrived in Washington, however, he found that he knew very little about how the federal government really worked. Carter's staff was of little help, because the President surrounded himself with White House aides who had been his campaign associates. They were almost all fellow Georgians with little standing in the Democratic party or experience in the national government.

Carter and his aides discovered that the same Washington politicians they had campaigned against were the men and women they had to go to for help if any of their legislation was to be passed. Nor could Carter turn to his party for support. Although Carter was a Democrat and the Democrats controlled both houses of Congress, the President had few ties to the national Democratic leadership.

The Energy Crisis

A major problem for the new administration was the energy crisis. As late as 1950, the U.S. had exported oil. Due to the enormous consumption of gasoline and other petroleum products, however, most of America's readily available oil was gone by the late 1960s. By the end of the 1970s much of the oil used in America was imported from countries in Latin America and the Middle East. Several of these oil-producing nations banded together to control oil prices through an organization called **OPEC**—the Organization of Petroleum Exporting Countries. During President Carter's administration the OPEC oil cartel* succeeded in dramatically raising prices.

*__cartel__ an association for establishing a monopoly by price fixing or other means.

James E. Carter (1924–   )

IN OFFICE: 1977–1981

Democrat from Georgia. Carter established the Department of Health and Human Services, a cabinet-level Department of Education, and the Department of Energy. He kept the U.S. out of the 1980 Summer Olympics in Moscow and began a grain embargo of the Soviet Union to protest its invasion of Afghanistan. He gained a treaty ending U.S. control of the Panama Canal and was instrumental in working out a peace treaty between Egypt and Israel. The Iranian hostage issue caused his popularity to fluctuate. The hostages were freed on the day he left office.

Because of OPEC's efforts, the foreign oil on which American industry depended was not only expensive, it was also undependable. The supply might be shut off without warning. In addition many of the nations that supplied oil, particularly those in the Middle East, were unstable. Furthermore, many Americans argued that the oil crisis was an invention of the oil companies. These citizens pointed to the immense profits made by oil giants such as Mobil and Exxon and suggested that the crisis had been created to fill the treasuries of these companies.

Various solutions to the energy crisis were proposed. Radicals suggested that the government break up the giant oil corporations. Liberals emphasized conservation and alternative sources of renewable energy like solar and water power. And conservatives called for an end to federal price regulation of the domestic oil and gas industry. Deregulation, they argued, would greatly expand United States oil production, thus reducing American dependence on Arab oil. Finally, the coal and nuclear power industries claimed they could solve the problem if they were freed of what they termed "excessive" environmental regulations.

President Carter wanted "a moral equivalent of war" to make America energy independent again. He called on people to save fuel by insulating their homes and by giving up their gas-guzzling cars. He proposed an energy "windfall profits tax" to divert oil company profits into research to develop other forms of energy and to provide fuel subsidies for the poor.

President Carter warned Congress that failure to act on his proposals would be very costly to the nation. He pointed out that expensive oil was both a major source of inflation and the basis for enormous trade deficits. His proposals, however, were debated back and forth in congressional committees with no results. The President, his prestige on the line, was infuriated as Congress battled over different compromises month after month without passing a bill which provided for an energy program for the nation.

Congress finally approved part of President Carter's energy package in 1980. This program—the synthetic fuels bill—created the Synthetic Fuels Corporation to increase development of alternate fuels. By the end of the Carter administration, the energy crisis had eased off. Americans

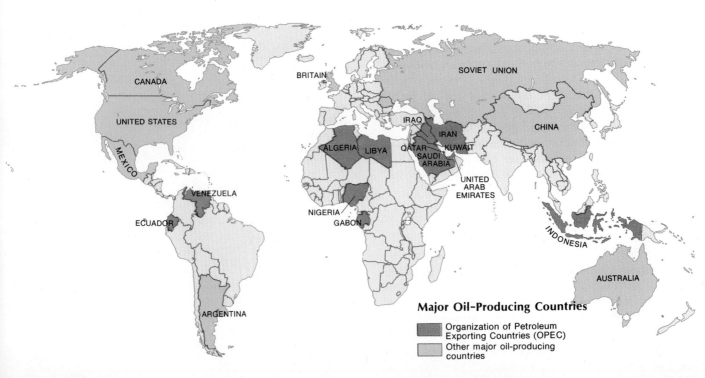

Major Oil-Producing Countries

Organization of Petroleum Exporting Countries (OPEC)

Other major oil-producing countries

LIFE IN AMERICA

THE GROWTH OF THE SUNBELT

A conflict over tax monies between the sunbelt (the warm weather states of the South and Southwest) and the snowbelt (the old industrial states of the Northeast and Midwest) grew sharper during the past 30 years as many Americans moved to warmer climates.

Attractions of the Sunbelt

Mild winters, more jobs, lack of unions, cheaper labor and energy, and limited state government interference attracted many people and businesses from the snowbelt.

Between 1970 and 1975, the snowbelt lost over 1 million people, while the sunbelt gained more than 2 million. Almost half of this growth came in just three booming states—California, Texas, and Florida. As a result, in 1976—for the first time in American history—more people lived in the sunbelt than in the northern states. See Map 9 in the Atlas Section for a look at this trend. Note that for the first time, the center of population was located west of the Mississippi River and south of Louisville, Kentucky. This means that as many Americans lived west and south of this point as lived north and east —the political center of the nation was shifting sunward, too.

Effects of the Shift

The movement worried some citizens of the snowbelt. The fast-growing states, they argued, bene-fited more from government spending for defense and highway construction. Other people feared that the poor and minority residents were stranded in the poverty of the snowbelt's decaying cities.

The trend toward the sunbelt is expected to continue for the rest of this century, but at a slower rate. Thus the different interests of snowbelt and sunbelt will trigger many future political debates.

---

were building and buying smaller cars. They were driving fewer miles by using such energy-saving techniques as car and van pooling. In addition, differences of opinion and policy among the oil-producing nations made OPEC less effective.

"Stagflation" Hits America

America was also faced with what economists call "Stagflation"—stagnation (business slowdown) plus inflation. Never before had the nation been faced with both high unemployment and rapidly rising prices. Carter's dilemma was that steps taken to curb inflation were likely to increase unemployment and vice versa.

Since the Truman administration, Democratic Presidents faced with high unemployment usually increased taxes to fund programs to aid the unemployed. Carter was unable to take such action because such programs helped fuel inflation. In addition, taxes were already at record levels, and taxpayers were angry. Since Truman, Democratic Presidents faced with inflation had resorted to wage and price controls. But because such controls proved ineffective during the Nixon years, Carter hesitated. He also did not want to go back on his campaign pledge to reduce the power of government.

Caught between these difficulties, Carter tried to find a solution. He implemented a system of voluntary wage and price controls which depended for its effectiveness on the good will of companies and labor unions. He created some public works projects designed to aid the unemployed. But both actions were half-measures which left his critics and his supporters unsatisfied. And neither measure had much impact on the nation's economic problems.

SECTION 1 REVIEW

 Identify: Ronald Reagan, Jimmy Carter, OPEC, "stagflation"

Main Ideas

1. What were the issues in the campaign of 1976? What led to Carter's victory?
2. What problems did Carter face as a Washington outsider?
3. How did the President try to deal with the energy crisis? What action did Congress take to deal with the problem? What happened to the energy crisis?
4. How did President Carter try to deal with stagflation? What success did he achieve?

2. AMERICA'S MINORITY GROUPS IN THE 1970s

I n the 1970s, minority-group Americans and women made some significant advances in American society. Most striking of these advances was the gaining of employment in fields formerly closed to them. After the tumultuous decade of the 1960s, the 1970s brought a relative calm and a participation in the opportunities now open to many of these Americans.

The Gains for Black Americans

In the 1960s, as you recall, black Americans struggled for their civil rights. During those years black slum areas in many American cities exploded in violence. By 1969, however, most such social unrest had ended. In the late 1960s and throughout the 1970s, black middle- and upper-class Americans achieved unparalleled success as they took advantage of the new opportunities that the civil rights movement had opened up to them. For many black families segregation and discrimination no longer barred the way to the enjoyment of middle-class affluence.

Yet, for many, life remained the same. As unemployment rose throughout the 1970s, black Americans were hardest hit. In the late 1970s and early 1980s, the unemployment rate for black men and women was more than double that for whites. The unemployment rate of black teenagers was a continuing problem, reaching about 40% in the early 1980s. In the cities, a growing population of poor black people seemed increasingly cut off from job opportunities.

The increasing number of unemployed blacks in urban slums gave rise to an increase in the crime rate, which, however, leveled off in the mid-1970s. In most cases, the victims of black criminals were other blacks, but the fear of violent crime caused a reaction on the part of the white population. White reaction, called the "white backlash," also appeared in attitudes toward school integration and employment. Programs for busing children to achieve school integration supported by the Carter administration met with stiff opposition.

As the rate of unemployment climbed and as jobs became harder to get, many white Americans refused to support affirmative action programs* for blacks and other minorities, charging that such programs were unfair and caused reverse discrimination. In the early 1980s, unemployment and all its repercussions was one of the main problems all Americans wanted to see solved.

Hispanic Americans

In the 1960s and 1970s, the programs designed to aid black Americans were also extended to the nation's fastest growing minority population, Hispanic Americans. These citizens and immigrants of Latin American descent were concentrated mainly in the Southwest, the Northeast, and Florida. Hispanic Americans had a high birth rate, and their numbers were also enlarged by a huge migration, both legal and illegal, from Mexico and the Caribbean. In 1980 about 19 million Americans were Hispanic Americans. About 7.2 million of all Hispanic Americans were of Mexican origin. The second largest group was comprised of some 1.8 million Puerto Ricans. Other Hispanic Americans included Mexican Americans whose ancestors became Americans when the United States took over their lands after the Mexican War. In addition, 3.1 million Hispanic Americans were of Cuban, Central American, and South American ancestry.

Separated from other Americans by language, customs, and to some extent by skin color, most Hispanic Americans traditionally were employed as low paid *braceros* (field hands) in agriculture or as subminimum-wage service workers in the nation's cities. Inspired by the successes of the black civil rights movement, Hispanic Americans increasingly organized to better their conditions in the 1960s and 1970s.

One such attempt to improve conditions was led by **Cesar Chavez,** who organized the United Farm Workers Union. One of the tactics Chavez used was the boycott. He urged all Americans to boycott nonunion lettuce and nonunion grapes. In this manner the United Farm Workers hoped to put pressure on the agricultural corporations to accept the union. After an eight-month strike in

---

*affirmative action programs programs that set goals and timetables for the hiring of minority groups and women. To meet these goals, some employers were charged with preferential hiring, choosing black and female applicants over equally qualified or even more qualified white male applicants.

Cesar Chavez in a United Farm Workers strike

1979, members of the United Farm Workers Union won a marked increase in wages.

In New Mexico, some Hispanic Americans organized to fight for legal return of the lands that were taken from Mexican families when the U.S. took over New Mexico. These efforts, conducted through the courts, met with little success.

Another area in which Hispanic Americans sought reform was in education. In the 1960s and 1970s, many schools introduced bilingual programs to help non-English-speaking Hispanic Americans learn the skills necessary to enter the job market on an equal footing with English-speaking citizens. By the late 1970s and early 1980s, many of these bilingual programs were being cut in schools for economic reasons.

Once mainly an agricultural area, the Southwest is rapidly becoming highly industrialized, and Hispanic Americans are entering the industrial labor force. Today most Hispanic Americans live in cities, not on farms. Immigrants from Mexico have tended to become citizens at a much lower rate than have other immigrants. Perhaps many of them continue to think of Mexico as "home," the place they would like to retire to. Many simply do not want to give up their Mexican citizenship. During the 1970s, however, two Hispanic Americans became governors of southwestern states: Jerry Apodaca in New Mexico and Raul Castro in Arizona. Cuban Americans have increasing political power in Miami, Florida, and Puerto Ricans in New York City.

American Indians

Today there are approximately 170 distinct groups of American Indians, and their total population is about 1.4 million. As you recall, the Indian Reorganization Act of 1934 encouraged Indians to develop their own local government on the reservations and to preserve their tribal cultures, lands, and resources. During the 1950s, however, the Eisenhower administration began a new government policy toward Indians. Called "termination" and adopted in 1953, this policy tried to eliminate the special protection granted to Indian reservation lands. The policy was adopted so that Indians would not be "wards of the state." But in practical terms the termination policy meant that the reservations of several tribes, such as the Menominees in Wisconsin and the Klamath in Oregon, both of which contained valuable timber, were taken away from them.

Almost all Indians opposed the termination policy, as did most other Americans who understood what it meant. In 1961, when President Kennedy came to office, the government dropped the termination policy. Later, some of the tribes sued in federal court to regain their reservation land and had it returned to them.

Like other Americans, Indians have moved in increasing numbers to urban areas. By 1980 approximately 200,000 Indians lived in cities. When, in the 1970s, Indians began to win lawsuits based on treaties signed in the 18th and 19th centuries, differences arose between the reservation Indians and the urban Indians. Generally, the reservation Indians tended to vote to spend the money on developing the reservation, while the urban Indians tended to vote for per capita payments to be distributed to the individual members of the tribe.

In 1975, Congress passed the **Indian Self-Determination and Educational Assistance Act**. The purpose of this act was to free Indians from government control without, at the same time, taking away the reservation lands. The act sought to provide maximum Indian participation in the governing and educating of Indians and to provide for the full participation of Indian tribes in all available government programs. Like the

Indian Reorganization Act of 1934, the Indian Self-Determination Act of 1975 tried to encourage Indian self-government. But many tribes opposed the law because they lost various health and other services formerly supplied by the federal government.

The Women's Movement

Unlike blacks, Hispanic Americans, and Indians, women in America, as in the world, are a majority, not a minority. Women comprise more than 50% of the population; yet many women in the 1960s and 1970s felt that they had much in common with minority groups.

As inflation increased throughout the 1960s and 1970s, women entered the job market in ever increasing numbers. By 1980, 43% of the labor force was female. (In contrast, 30% was female in 1955.) Some of these employed women had participated in the social movements of the 1960s, especially the civil rights and antiwar movements. As they struggled for social reform, many women came to believe that they needed to fight against discrimination and prevalent views about women's place in society. As a result, many activists worked for passage of federal, state, and local antidiscrimination laws and for better opportunities for women in education, in sports, and in family life.

The various groups that comprised the **women's movement** of the 1960s and 1970s strongly attacked the view that women had a special, more passive, role to play in society. Instead, these feminists argued, individual women should be free to follow their own interests and have the same job opportunities as men. Men should share the housework and child rearing, rather than assuming that these jobs were particularly "feminine." In short, the workload at home and outside the home should be more evenly distributed.

During the 1970s, some women were able to take advantage of affirmative action programs to gain jobs in industries and professions formerly closed to them. But most women remained in jobs that paid less than men typically received. Thus, in 1980, women as a group still earned only about two-thirds of what men earned.

In raising the question of women's roles in society, the women's movement managed to shake up some of the traditional views toward "men's" work and "women's" work. In certain industries, for example, paternity leave was granted to fathers so that they could spend time at home with their newborn children. More women moved into jobs that were traditionally thought of as "men's" work—the legal profession, for example. In general, men and women both felt freer to pursue the careers that interested them, and to share the work of raising children and running the home.

Newly sworn-in Supreme Court Justice Sandra O'Connor meets photographers, 1981

SECTION 2 REVIEW

Identify: Cesar Chavez, Indian Self-Determination and Educational Assistance Act, women's movement

Main Ideas

1. How did the civil rights movement benefit many black Americans? What major problems continued?
2. How were many Hispanic Americans influenced by the civil rights movement?
3. What changes took place in federal policy toward Indians between 1950 and 1980? Why did American Indians oppose the termination policy? Why did many oppose the Self-Determination Act?
4. What were the goals of many groups that participated in the women's movement? What trends took place in women's employment in recent years?

3. PRESIDENT CARTER FACES CHALLENGES ABROAD

President Carter hoped to create a new, post-Vietnam foreign policy for the United States. Like Woodrow Wilson, Jimmy Carter was a deeply religious man. And, like Wilson, he wanted to place moral principles in the forefront of the nation's foreign policy. While campaigning for President, Carter criticized the amoral character of Henry Kissinger's policy of *realpolitik* (practical politics). Without specifically criticizing America's involvement in Vietnam, Carter implied that the tragedy in Southeast Asia had come about because Americans had abandoned their traditional moral concerns. Carter's "new morality" in foreign policy emphasized human rights.

The Human Rights Policy
In 1977, President Carter proclaimed that, whenever possible, American foreign policy would be guided by a concern for **human rights** that would help end acts of political repression such as imprisonment without trial, torture, and murder. Carter and two of his foreign policy team, Cyrus Vance, the Secretary of State, and Andrew Young, the Ambassador to the United Nations, insisted that this policy was both morally right and politically effective. To show even allies that he meant business, the President cut off military aid to countries such as Brazil and Argentina, considered friendly to the United States, when the State Department accused them of violent repression of their own people.

The President's new policy allowed the United States to regain from the Soviet Union the moral upper hand lost over Vietnam. The human rights policy also helped to reaffirm America's position in the world as a place of freedom, justice, hope, and human dignity. However, the policy did create some new problems. European allies complained that Carter's emphasis on human rights introduced a self-righteous tone into American policy. Other critics pointed out that the emphasis on human rights undercut another prime goal of the new administration—better relations with the Soviet Union. The Soviets could understand

Kissinger's dealings, but they were upset and concerned by Carter's idealistic concepts. Few lasting positive effects resulted from the President's efforts.

Relations with the Soviet Union
The President wanted to change the way the United States dealt with the Soviet Union. Carter condemned America's "inordinate fear" of communism. "The great challenge we Americans confront," he wrote,

is to demonstrate to the Soviet Union that our good will is as great as our strength, until, despite all obstacles, our two nations can achieve new attitudes and new trust.

Carter's critics called this idea "mirror imaging." Carter, they said, acted as if the Soviet Union was fundamentally no different than the United States, a notion that the critics believed to be mistaken.

In order to enter into a new relationship with the Soviet Union, Carter scuttled a number of weapons programs that he feared would add to the arms race. He canceled a new bomber, the B-1, and shelved a new missile system, the MX. He also canceled the neutron bomb, a nuclear weapon that destroyed people but not property. Liberals generally supported Carter's actions in this regard while conservatives were critical.

The SALT II Treaty
The keystone of Carter's new policy toward the Soviet Union was to be the ratification of the Strategic Arms Limitation Treaty, or **SALT II**. The SALT II treaty put a lid on the arms race by limiting the number, type, and deployment of ICBMs (intercontinental ballistic missiles), the most powerful weapons in either nation's arsenal. The idea behind the treaty was that if a strategic balance could be maintained by agreement, neither nation would have to fear a nuclear strike which would leave it helpless. Underpinning the balance idea was the concept of MAD, or mutually assured destruction. MAD meant, in effect, that as long as the balance was maintained, neither nation would be powerful enough to destroy the other without being destroyed in return.

In June of 1979, President Carter and Soviet Premier Leonid Brezhnev met in Vienna to sign the SALT II agreement. But, as you know, before

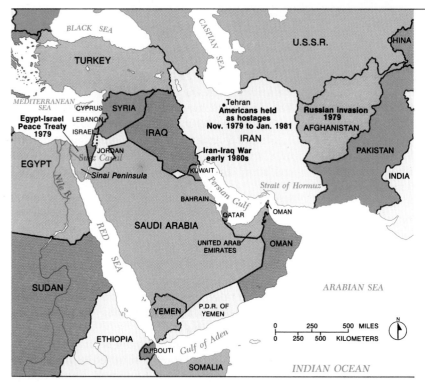

The Middle East

Note the central location and huge size of Saudi Arabia relative to the other Middle Eastern countries. It is about the size of the U.S. east of the Mississippi but is mostly desert with a population of only 8 million. Also notice how the Strait of Hormuz holds the key to oil shipments from the Middle East to the rest of the world.

a treaty is binding on the United States, the Senate must approve it. When SALT II reached the Senate, a long and bitter debate ensued. Supporters of the treaty met stiff opposition from senators who argued that the treaty was written in such a way as to favor the Soviet Union. Other opponents of SALT II pointed to the Soviet penetration of Africa either with Soviet "advisers" or through Cuban and East European surrogates (substitutes).

The Soviet military presence was felt in Ethiopia, where a bloody revolution killed over a million people. In Angola, pro-Western forces were locked in rebellion against a government supplied with Soviet and Cuban arms. And South Yemen, located on the oil-rich Arabian Peninsula, had become virtually a Soviet satellite. President Carter's supporters argued that the involvement of the Soviet Union in these countries would prove to be self-defeating. The Soviets, they said, were on the same path that led America to disaster in Vietnam. They predicted that the Soviet Union would get bogged down and be weakened by involvement in civil and revolutionary wars. Supporters of SALT II also emphasized the im-

pact of China on the global balance of power. One-third of the Soviet army, they pointed out, was tied up along the Sino-Soviet border. Neither side in the debate was able to convince the other, however, and the SALT II treaty was trapped in the Senate until new developments in Iran and Afghanistan killed it.

Although the President's failure to receive congressional approval of SALT II was a major defeat for his administration, his policies bore fruit elsewhere. After a bitter fight, he succeeded in getting the Senate to pass a new treaty with Panama in 1977. The treaty secured the safety of the Canal while ending American domination over the Canal Zone. In Africa, patient British and American diplomacy paved the way for an end to white racist rule in Rhodesia. A bloody civil war came to an end, and the new nation of Zimbabwe was born.

The Middle East Settlement

President Carter's greatest foreign policy success came in the Middle East. The Arab countries and the terrorist Palestine Liberation Organization (**PLO**) were pledged to destroy Israel. But Egypt, the most powerful of the Arab nations, began to take a new position on Israel.

First, Egyptian President **Anwar Sadat** removed all Soviet advisers from his country and established closer relations with the United States. Sadat also decided that solving Egypt's extremely severe economic problems was more important than destroying Israel. The next development came when Muammar el-Qaddafi, the leader of Egypt's oil-rich neighbor, Libya, made several attempts at overthrowing Sadat. When the Israeli secret service, the Mossad, saved Sadat from assassination by one of Qaddafi's gunmen, the stage was set for a historic development. Egypt became the first Arab nation to recognize the right of Israel to exist.

Egypt was bitterly criticized by other Arab states for breaking ranks. Cut off from the rest of the Arab world and exposed to military and economic pressure from Libya and Saudi Arabia, Egypt needed to conclude a treaty with Israel that would bring glory to Sadat by returning to Arab hands the land that Israel had captured in the 1967 Six-Days' War.

Negotiations between Sadat and Israeli Prime Minister **Menachem Begin** began in November 1977 but by August of 1978 they had broken down. At this moment President Carter stepped in. He invited both Sadat and Begin to the Camp David presidential retreat in the mountains of western Maryland. There, in 13 grueling days of negotiations, Carter was able to convince the two leaders to sign on September 12, 1978, an agreement called the **Camp David accords,** which paved the way for peace in the Middle East. Carter was widely hailed for his success at Camp David. It was the President's finest moment.

SECTION 3 REVIEW

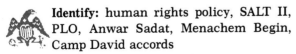

Identify: human rights policy, SALT II, PLO, Anwar Sadat, Menachem Begin, Camp David accords

Main Ideas

1. What was the goal of President Carter's human rights policy? How was it successful? Why was it criticized?
2. What was the purpose of the SALT II treaty?
3. What is considered to be President Carter's finest achievement in office?

4. CRISES IN IRAN AND AFGHANISTAN

Iran, the ancient land of Persia, was for many years one of America's closest allies. In the 19th century, Iran had been exploited by both Russian and British imperialism. After World War II, Iran turned to the United States as a protector and ally against its old enemies. Over time the United States turned out to be as interested in oil as in friendship.

In 1941, the United States had placed on the throne Muhammud Reza Shah Pahlevi after his father, suspected of collaborating with Nazi Germany, was deposed by British and Soviet troops. In 1953, a Communist-backed political party seized control of the government and attempted to assert control over Iran's oil resources. The **Shah of Iran** was deposed. A few months later, the United States secretly helped overthrow the Communist-dominated government and reinstated the Shah as ruler of Iran.

In the years that followed, the Shah attempted to use his country's oil riches to modernize his nation. He brought education and western ideas to Iran, but such things were opposed by many Iranians. Deeply attached to their Islamic beliefs, many Iranians viewed the Shah's reforms as the work of the devil.

The Shah Encounters Opposition

The Shah's western ideas as well as the wealth and corruption of the royal family cut him off from his potential allies in Iran, the new middle class created by his economic and social reforms. During the Nixon administration, the United States encouraged the Shah in his grand efforts to make Iran a world power. The Shah purchased vast amounts of modern military and industrial equipment and boasted that he would make Iran's influence felt everywhere in the world.

But beneath the facade of modernity and power, the foundations of the Shah's kingdom were crumbling. The fighter jets he bought meant little to the peasants, who thought that the Shah's decision to educate women and to allow them to wear western dress was little short of blasphemous. Islamic religious fundamentalists criticized the Shah's introduction of western morals while radicals criticized the inequality of wealth brought about by the Shah's actions. Business owners and middle-class citizens made fun of the Shah's pretensions. The Shah soon found himself isolated from his own people.

As the discontent in Iran grew, the Shah relied on his secret police to harass and imprison his opponents. In 1978 Iran teetered on the brink of revolution. Although the Shah could have tried to reach a compromise with the more moderate of his critics or use the military to crack down on the opposition, he did neither. In early 1979 he was forced to flee his native land.

The revolution in Iran was carried out by a group of forces. But the Moslem clergy, led by **Ayatollah Ruhollah Khomeini,** quickly became the dominant element. The Ayatollah (holy man) announced a cut-off of oil production. He publicly blamed the United States for the decline of Iranian religious virtue. Khomeini wanted to return Iran to a pre-modern state where Islam was the law and the nation was ruled by its clergy.

The American Embassy Is Seized

In the summer of 1979 President Carter permitted the Shah to enter the United States for medical treatment. The Iranian leader's arrival sparked violent demonstrations in Iran against the United States. Then, in a move calculated to humiliate America, on November 4, 1979, militant supporters of the Ayatollah seized the United States embassy in Tehran, the capital city of Iran.

When the militants seized the embassy, they violated international law. Even in times of war, embassies are traditionally protected from such harassment. The 52 diplomats and other Americans taken prisoner at the embassy were publicly humiliated by the militants. Their plight stirred an extraordinary reaction in the United States.

The seizure of the embassy caused a wave of anti-Iranian feeling in the United States. Although Carter was under enormous public pressure to free the hostages, there was little he could do. The Iranians threatened to kill the hostages if the President used military force. When he tried to negotiate for their release, the Iranians were uncooperative. The Khomeini government seemed, in fact, uninterested in freeing the American prisoners. Because the hostages had become the symbol of the revolution against the Shah, they were essential to the new regime. In these difficult circumstances Carter finally decided to

try to rescue the captives. In April 1980 he launched a special force on a rescue raid which not only failed to free the hostages but also took the lives of eight servicemen when a helicopter and transport plane collided.

A few years earlier the fall of Saigon had come and gone quietly. But all the resentment, anger, and frustration that had built up during the defeat in Vietnam expressed itself during the 14-month long Iranian hostage crisis.

Each night Americans from Maine to Hawaii watched their television sets to hear news of the hostages. As the nation's anger grew, people tried to understand what had happened to the United States. Conservatives believed that ever since America's failure in Vietnam, our leaders had suffered a loss of nerve. They argued that America was being humiliated because the nation had become weak and indecisive. Many liberals, previously hostile to an increase in American military power, began to rethink their position.

The Soviet Invasion of Afghanistan

In December 1979, in the midst of the hostage crisis, the Soviet Union invaded Afghanistan, a nation of 16 million people which lay to the east of Iran. Although Afghanistan had been in the Soviet sphere since 1978, the invasion produced opposition in the West. The little that was left of détente with the Soviet Union quickly disappeared, and the conservative political trend was further increased.

President Carter joined the conservatives in calling for increased American military strength. In addition, he called for a grain embargo against the Soviet Union. While many supported such an action as patriotic, farmers were against it because it hurt them economically.

SECTION 4 REVIEW

 Identify: Shah of Iran, Ayatollah Ruhollah Khomeini

Main Ideas

1. How did the Shah of Iran come to power? Why was he overthrown?
2. What prompted the Iranian militants to take over the U.S. embassy? What was President Carter's response?
3. How did the invasion of Afghanistan affect government policy toward the Soviet Union?

768

5. RONALD REAGAN BECOMES PRESIDENT

By 1980, President Carter had become extremely unpopular. Although the majority of Americans still thought highly of his personal character, they questioned his abilities as a leader. At his lowest point in popularity, only 29% of the public gave Carter their support. This was a lower percentage than Richard Nixon had received at the height of the Watergate scandal.

The Election of 1980

An incumbent President has a certain advantage, however. Carter could distribute government funds and jobs in a way that discouraged support for his opposition. Carter also used the Iranian hostage crisis to his advantage. He refused to debate his chief rival, Senator Edward Kennedy of Massachusetts, on the grounds that he was too busy in the White House trying to free the captives. He appealed to voters to support him as a way of showing the Iranians that Americans were behind his efforts. President Carter won most of the Democratic primaries and thus received the nomination. Vice-President Walter Mondale was again chosen as his running mate.

The Republican party chose Ronald Reagan as its candidate and George Bush as his running mate. Reagan promised to reduce the size of the federal government, strengthen the military, and dramatically reduce taxes. In 1964 these proposals were supported by only a small number of citizens. Barry Goldwater, the Republican candidate for President that year, was badly defeated.

However, much had changed by 1980. The voters were discontented with Carter's administration, and conservative sentiment had been building since 1968. Millions of Americans did not vote on election day. Only 51% of the voters went to the polls. But Reagan won a resounding victory, defeating Carter in 44 of the 50 states. The Republicans also gained control of the Senate for the first time in more than 25 years. In so doing they defeated some of the most prominent liberals in the Senate. A coalition of Republicans and increasingly conservative Democrats formed the majority in the House of Representatives.

The Reagan Presidency

At the outset the new President seemed to be blessed with good luck. On inauguration day in January 1981, the Iranians announced the long-awaited release of the American hostages. The captives were freed after the Iranian revolution was beset by internal conflicts and a war with neighboring Iraq. The Iranians decided that it was better to accept the deal which the outgoing Carter administration offered than to renegotiate with a new, hard-line Reagan administration. Early in 1981 Reagan also ended the Soviet grain embargo, which American farmers had opposed.

Reagan's easy affability and pleasant personality contributed to his early popularity. As one aide put it, "He has no dark side like Richard Nixon. What you see is what you get." Reagan's critics agreed but felt that many of the new President's ideas were simplistic and shallow. Reagan had campaigned on a promise to raise military spending and to reduce taxes sharply. Many economists suggested that while such a program might make for a good campaign promise, it was likely to lead to hyper-inflation.

When Reagan became President, the United States, along with many other industrial nations, was plagued with serious economic problems. High unemployment and inflation were felt nationwide, causing hardship unknown since the Great Depression. Taxes were high, and American industry was suffering from foreign competition. The steel, automotive, and electronics in-

Ronald W. Reagan (1911–   )

IN OFFICE: 1981–

Republican from California. Reagan won election on the promises that the federal government would govern less and that he would turn around the sagging economy. He supported an economic program of tax cuts with a wide reduction in federal social spending and an increase in defense spending. During his administration, inflation slowed but unemployment increased.

dustries were losing out to Japanese and other foreign competitors. One major auto maker was saved from bankruptcy only by massive government loans. Layoffs in major industries such as automobiles and steel were causing a ripple effect throughout the economy.

To add to these problems, interest rates (the cost of borrowing money) had risen to the point where those who needed to borrow money to buy homes or cars or to expand businesses could not afford to do so. In addition, the new President had bi-partisan support in his determination to match the military strength of the Soviet Union, which many observers believed had grown alarmingly, leaving the United States in the number two position.

Supply-Side Economics and Reaganomics
In his campaign, Ronald Reagan had promised to cut taxes, reduce spending, cut inflation, rebuild the nation's armed forces, and balance the federal budget. Influenced by the views of economist Arthur Laffer, the President and other Republican leaders thought they could solve the nation's economic problems by reversing some of the policies of the federal government that had been followed by every President, Democrat and Republican, since World War II. They held that the federal government had grown too large. They also believed the government interfered too much in the individual lives of citizens and in the business life of the nation.

These leaders felt that social programs such as Social Security, welfare, food stamps, Medicare, and a whole host of others had caused taxes to rise to the point where there was too little money left to invest in business and industry. If these social programs could be cut, they believed, taxes could be lowered, and individuals would have more money to invest. These investments would, in turn, stimulate the economy. American industry could then modernize and expand and become more competitive. Employment would increase and inflation would be brought under control. With a return of prosperity, tax revenues would increase to the point where the federal budget could be balanced.

This view of how to solve the nation's economic problems came to be called "**supply-side economics,**" meaning that emphasis should be placed on how to increase the nation's supply of goods rather than on how the government, through high taxes, should redistribute the nation's wealth. Although something needed to be done to solve the country's economic problems, there were many who questioned the soundness of supply-side economics. The economic policies of the new administration, based largely on the supply-side theory, were called "Reaganomics."

The New Federalism
A guiding belief of the Reagan administration was that too much power had come to be concentrated in the federal government. According to this view, many of the programs run from Washington would be better run at the state or local level. These governmental units were closer to the people, understood their needs better, and could operate more efficiently. Thus the Reagan administration called for turning welfare, food stamps, and certain other social programs back to the states. This aspect of Reaganomics was called the "**New Federalism.**"

Critics of the New Federalism feared that turning programs such as welfare over to the states would result in inadequate and unequal services for needy Americans. Some states had far greater resources than others to take care of the needs of their citizens. The New Federalism was hotly debated in and out of Congress.

During his first two years in office, President Reagan won some notable victories. His tax cuts —an important part of the supply-side program— were enacted, and large reductions were made in federal spending. The inflation rate slowed but business did not revive. By 1982, with the economy still sluggish and with 9.5% of the work force unemployed, Reaganomics faced its toughest battles in Congress. The administration's budget proposals were under attack because of large cuts in social programs and huge anticipated federal deficits caused by increased defense spending.

Reagan and Foreign Affairs
During the 1980 campaign, Reagan had criticized the Carter administration for what he called a weak American response to the threat of international communism as advanced by the Soviet Union. Thus the Reagan administration budgets contained huge increases for the Defense Department. The B-1 bomber and the MX missile program were revived. The navy received large sums

for new ships. The neutron bomb and chemical warfare programs were given the green light. Huge outlays for defense were one of the chief reasons for the projected budget deficits that caused alarm even on the part of the President's staunchest supporters. Attempts to bring down the deficits without cutting military spending led to deeper cuts in domestic programs. Critics also feared that a renewed arms race would lead the world to an even greater threat of mass destruction.

After Ronald Reagan took office, the internal situation in Poland deteriorated rapidly. Faced with the threat of a Soviet invasion, the Polish government cracked down on Solidarity, the labor union that had won many liberal concessions. The union, led by a former electrician, Lech Walesa, had opposed much of the control that the Polish Communist party exerted over Poland's workers. When the Polish government moved against Solidarity, declared martial law, interned (confined) Walesa, and muzzled the press, radio, and TV, the Reagan administration responded by imposing economic sanctions.

The inability of the United States to influence developments in Poland pointed up a hard fact of international relations in the nuclear age. Even if American military strength had been as great as President Reagan wanted to make it, there was little the United States could do in an area next to the Soviet Union without risking nuclear war and global destruction.

The situation in the Caribbean region, an area as close geographically to the United States as Poland was to the Soviet Union, was reversed. Here the United States could follow a policy that did not depend for its success on the threat of a nuclear strike. El Salvador, the smallest of the Central American nations, was in the midst of a civil war. The right-wing government was attempting to overcome a leftist insurrection. The rebels were receiving support from Cuba, Nicaragua, and indirectly from the Soviet Union. Determined to prevent further Communist gains in the Western Hemisphere, the Reagan administration began to supply greater military aid to El Salvador, including a small number of military advisers. Critics in the United States said that this policy was leading to another Vietnam and that the right-wing government of El Salvador did not merit American support.

FROM THE ARCHIVES

The New Federalism

A wide range of federal activities can be more appropriately . . . carried out by the states. . . .

- We should leave to private initiative all the functions that individuals can perform privately.
- We should use the level of government closest to the community involved for all the public functions it can handle. This principle includes encouraging intergovernmental arrangements among the state and local communities.
- Federal government action should be reserved for those needed functions that only the national government can undertake.

From *Economic Report of the President,* transmitted to the Congress, February 10, 1982.

Americans Remain Optimistic

Among the qualities that Ronald Reagan brought to the presidency was an optimistic spirit that was singularly American. The times were admittedly rough, the nation faced a number of serious problems that defied easy solutions—economic difficulties, competition from foreign manufacturers, dwindling natural resources, foreign threats, and the ever present danger of nuclear destruction. But most Americans remained optimistic about the nation's future. They were convinced that their free institutions, their great natural wealth, and the genius of the American people would enable the United States to continue to be—as it always has been—THE LAND OF PROMISE.

SECTION 5 REVIEW

 Identify: supply-side economics, New Federalism

Main Ideas

1. How did the Reagan administration attempt to use supply-side economics to solve the nation's economic problems?
2. What was the goal of Reagan's "New Federalism," and why was there opposition to it?
3. How did Reagan attempt to increase America's military strength? What were criticisms of this policy?

CHAPTER 35 REVIEW

Key Terms
Explain the meaning of each of the following terms:

OPEC
"stagflation"
Indian Self-Determination and Educational Assistance Act
women's movement
human rights policy
SALT II
PLO
Camp David accords
supply-side economics
New Federalism

Reviewing the Main Ideas
Section 1
1. What were the issues in the 1976 presidential campaign? Why did Jimmy Carter win?
2. How did Carter's background make it difficult for him to get his programs passed in Congress? Give an example.
3. Describe two major economic problems faced by the Carter administration. Why was President Carter unable to resolve them?

Section 2
1. In what ways was the civil rights movement of the 1960s a success? What major problem facing blacks continued to be unsolved?
2. How were many Hispanic Americans influenced by the civil rights movement?
3. What changes took place in Indian policy between 1950 and 1980?
4. What were the goals of the activists in the women's movement? What results were achieved by the early 1980s?

Section 3
1. On what concept did President Carter base his foreign policy? How was this received by allies and enemies?
2. What were some foreign policy accomplishments of the Carter administration? What were some failures?

Section 4
1. What events led to the seizing of the U.S. embassy and hostages in Iran?
2. How did Americans react to the hostage crisis?
3. What was President Carter's response to the problems in Iran and Afghanistan?

Section 5
1. What factors led to Ronald Reagan's victory in the 1980 election?
2. What economic problems did President Reagan face? How did he attempt to solve them?
3. What was the goal of the New Federalism, and why was this policy criticized?

Special History Skills
Recognizing Bias
When reading about recent history or current events, one of the most important skills you need is the ability to recognize bias. A biased statement is one based on emotion or prejudice instead of on a rational consideration of facts.

Let's see how good you are at recognizing bias. Read the following statements. On a separate sheet of paper mark R any statement that you feel is a reasonable conclusion based on facts. (Note that you do not necessarily have to agree with the conclusion to label it "reasonable.") Mark B any statement that you feel is biased. Be sure to keep in mind that it may be "biased" even though you agree with it. Mark X any statement that you feel cannot be labeled R or B. Then compare your answers with those of your classmates.
1. Movie actors do not make good Presidents.
2. President Carter's human rights policy was ineffective.
3. Unemployment is worse than inflation.
4. Iranians are all crazy.
5. Neither Carter nor Ford had much to offer the American public in 1976.
6. During the 1970s, a population shift to the South and West occurred, affecting the political power of these areas.
7. More women than ever before were employed outside the home in the 1970s.
8. In 1980, a majority of white middle-class suburbanites voted for Ronald Reagan.
9. Jimmy Carter was a better President than Richard Nixon or Ronald Reagan.
10. Today millions of Americans suffer from unemployment.

Other Skill Activities

1. The hostage crisis

Read three articles in news magazines, one from 1979, one from 1980, and one from 1981, on the hostage crisis. Summarize each article. Then describe similarities and differences you notice in the articles. For instance, what was the attitude toward the militants? How optimistic about release were the articles?

2. Human rights debate

Prepare a two-minute speech supporting or rejecting the following statement: "The United States should give aid to repressive governments as long as they are anti-Communist."

3. Presidential popularity

What is the current popularity of the President? Find out how presidential popularity polls are taken, what the figures mean, and how they are used. Give a report to the class on your findings.

4. Writing recent history

Write another section of this chapter, bringing it up to date. Before you begin, write a brief outline of the important events you would include. Compare your new section with those of your classmates. How are they the same? How are they different? Discuss reasons for the differences.

5. Current history crossword puzzle

Make a crossword puzzle using people and events from this chapter and from current newspapers.

Thinking Critically

1. Is presidential "image" important? Should a chief executive be concerned with portraying himself or herself as a certain kind of person with certain values and personality traits? Why or why not? If so, what would be the ideal presidential image?

2. Why weren't traditional solutions to economic problems able to work in the Carter administration? Do you think they will ever be able to work again? Why or why not?

3. What have been the most important political and social trends in the past five years?

4. Predict the future for our country.

Further Reading

Jimmy Carter. *Why Not the Best?* Broadman Press, 1975. Jimmy Carter's life and ideas in his own words.

Time, Newsweek, U.S. News and World Report, The New York Times, and other current periodicals will help you keep up with current events and issues.

TEST YOURSELF

WRITE YOUR ANSWERS ON A SEPARATE SHEET OF PAPER.

Matching

Write the letter of the item that best matches each description below.

1. a solution to the energy crisis
2. Egyptian leader at Camp David
3. influential theorist of supply-side economics
4. organizer of the United Farm Workers Union
5. oil cartel
6. winner of the 1976 presidential election
7. Israeli leader at Camp David
8. inflation and unemployment at the same time
9. religious leader of Iran
10. deposed leader of Iran

a. Arthur Laffer	**g.** Anwar Sadat
b. Jimmy Carter	**h.** Shah of Iran
c. Cesar Chavez	**i.** deregulation
d. Gerald Ford	**j.** stagflation
e. Menachem Begin	**k.** PLO
f. Ayatollah Khomeini	**l.** OPEC

Cause and Effect

Read each pair of statements. Mark C the statement that causes the other statement in the pair. Mark E the statement that is the effect. Mark O any pair of statements that do not have a cause-and-effect relationship.

1. The deposed Shah of Iran comes to the U.S. for medical treatment.
   The U.S. embassy in Iran is seized.

2. Ronald Reagan is elected President.
   Conservative sentiment grows among voters.

3. OPEC sharply raises prices.
   President Carter proposes conservation and a windfall profits tax.

4. Jimmy Carter runs for President as a Washington outsider.
   Ronald Reagan is supported by conservative Republicans.

5. SALT II is rejected by the Senate.
   Poland is put under martial law.

The Astrodome: Houston, Texas

It has been called the "eighth wonder of the world." Whether this title survives the test of time or not, there is no question that the Astrodome is as much a symbol of modern America as it is a symbol of its hometown—Houston, Texas.

When the Astrodome opened on April 19, 1965, it made sports history: the first major-league indoor baseball game was played there. Since then, the dome has earned a long series of firsts. This is no surprise, for it was the first of its type—a totally enclosed, all-weather, multi-purpose sports stadium.

Under its 642-foot clear-span dome, Americans have witnessed events that represent all aspects of our culture. Elvis Presley and Frank Sinatra have performed on its stage; Muhammad Ali has boxed in its ring; Hubert Humphrey held a political rally in its arena; Billy Graham held a religious crusade there. Even the circus has brought its three rings to the stadium.

Regularly, Americans follow the sports of baseball, football, and basketball in the Astrodome. This monument to American sports has set the standard for spectator-sport stadiums in the United States. Totally enclosed and fully equipped with soft opera-type chairs, the Astrodome has elevated the sports arena from the days of hardback wooden bleachers in the hot sun to a temperature-controlled environment in comfortable chairs. The sun may be baking spectators elsewhere, or the rain may be canceling other contests, but when an event is held at the Astrodome, the weather is always 72°F and dry.

The Astrodome sits in a 260-acre complex six miles from downtown Houston. It was built at a cost of $38 million. Seating for events ranges from 66,000 for a boxing match to 45,000 for a baseball game. The Astrodome is tall enough to contain an 18-story building.

The Astrodome is worth a visit, whether you want to see a particular sporting contest or just tour the facility. Daily tours take visitors on a two-mile exploration of the stadium. Just as the Roman Colosseum tells us much about the life and times of the society that built it, so too, the Astrodome reflects on our times.

Renaissance Center: Detroit, Michigan

It rises up from the waterfront, a gleaming symbol of faith in the future of this midwestern industrial city. Its central city location, its vast size, and its immense cost underscore its commitment to downtown Detroit. The Renaissance Center is both unique and one of a group. For Detroit, it is a dramatic new civic symbol. Seen from a national perspective, it is an example of the dramatic hotel development complex appearing in our urban areas.

The Center features a breathtaking interior space, almost a fantasy land. This distinctive environment was created by John Portman, an architect who has created several such special places. The Center's interior features an eight-story atrium with a half-acre pond, hanging gardens, suspended trees, five levels of aerial walkways, sculpture, and acres of skylights. Glass elevators soar to the 73-story hotel at the heart of the complex.

The space shuttle Columbia *lifts off at Cape Canaveral.*

The Center is a self-contained, self-sustained environment.

In addition to the hotel, the complex consists of major office facilities. At the base of its hotel and office towers is a 14-acre podium that houses a vast commercial area. Here over 100 shops and restaurants provide a wide range of goods and services. Such variety gives Renaissance Center a cosmopolitan flavor. The architecture and activities of the Center make it a tourist attraction. It was designed to attract people to the city, and it is doing just that.

The leading figure behind the creation of the complex is a man whose family name is almost synonymous with Detroit—Henry Ford II. A partnership of 51 companies was organized to invest in this $350 million, privately financed development. The project was formally dedicated in 1977.

As its name suggests, the Renaissance Center was intended to generate downtown Detroit's rebirth. It was to breathe new life into this troubled city's economy and to foster a new civic pride in this depressed area.

Only time will tell if this ambitious project succeeds in revitalizing the center of Detroit. It is, however, already obvious that Renaissance Center has begun to transform the image of Detroit. Renaissance Center, with its bold architecture and its exotic environment, has launched the nation's "Motor City" into the space age.

Cape Canaveral, Florida, and the Kennedy Space Center

October 4, 1957. Space history was made. The first satellite was successfully launched. America was shocked, for the satellite was called Sputnik and its maker was the Soviet Union.

America's pride was hurt and, more importantly, some thought our security was threatened. The Cold War was on and now the Soviets were taking the lead in space. President Kennedy announced in May of 1961 that the United States would take up the challenge. America would demonstrate its leadership in space by placing a man on the moon by the end of the decade.

In the next years, America and the world would focus attention on a place in Florida where history would be made, over and over again. The place was Cape Canaveral.

By the time the country put two men on the moon in July of 1969, Americans had become space fans, and astronauts were national heroes. Millions of Americans eagerly followed the details of the various space missions.

Today you can visit Cape Canaveral and the Kennedy Space Center and see where space history is made. Flight training equipment, launch pads, Mission Control, space suits, space capsules, and space shuttle facilities are all on display for you to explore. You can see where the first U.S. manned space flight lifted off. In the Hall of History you can follow the whole story of space exploration from its beginnings to the projects that are now being planned.

America's journey into space is more than a historically significant event for America. It is a new chapter in the history of the human race. Our explorations in space are a part of history that you can see in the making.

775

UNIT 10 TEST

WRITE YOUR ANSWERS ON A SEPARATE SHEET OF PAPER.

Multiple Choice (30 points)

Write the letter of the answer that best completes each statement. There may be more than one correct answer.

1. President Kennedy sought to
   a. rival the "Hundred Days" with social programs such as Medicare and federal aid to education.
   b. enforce existing civil rights laws.
   c. pull the country out of an economic slump.
2. During the Cuban missile crisis President Kennedy
   a. called for an immediate invasion of Cuba.
   b. threatened to sink Soviet ships that approached Cuba.
   c. humiliated the Soviets, possibly precipitating their massive arms buildup.
3. Among Lyndon B. Johnson's chief characteristics as President was his
   a. effectiveness in working with Congress.
   b. belief in laissez-faire government.
   c. opposition to civil rights.
4. President Nixon's policies in Southeast and East Asia included
   a. invasions of Cambodia and Laos in an effort to cut off Viet Cong supply routes.
   b. increased hostility to Communist China.
   c. a program of Vietnamization that permitted the eventual withdrawal of American troops.
5. A major problem of the Carter administration was the
   a. Watergate scandal.
   b. Iranian hostage crisis.
   c. energy crisis.

True or False (30 points)

Read each statement below. Mark T if the statement is true, F if it is false. Rewrite the italicized words in all false statements to make them true.

1. In August 1963 *James Meredith* led a massive civil rights demonstration in Washington, D.C.

2. In 1963, the Kennedy administration backed a coup to depose the *North Vietnamese leader* Ngo Dinh Diem.
3. The call for "Black Power" in the late 1960s *did little* to develop pride among American blacks.
4. In the *Bay of Pigs Resolution,* Congress in effect surrendered its war-making powers to the President.
5. Henry Kissinger applied the European doctrine of *pacification* to American foreign policy in an effort to maintain a balance of power among major nations.
6. President Nixon continued President Johnson's policies of *wage and price controls,* which means increasing the amount of money in circulation in order to meet the government's needs.
7. White House staff members were involved in *break-ins, buggings, and other illegal activities,* known collectively as the Watergate scandal.
8. A major achievement of the American space program in the late 1960s and early 1970s was *the landing of American astronauts on the moon.*
9. The goal of President Carter's *energy policy* was to help end acts of political repression in the world and to regain America's position as a moral leader.
10. *Stagflation* was the term coined to describe President Reagan's economic theory that lower taxes would stimulate private enterprise and thus help the economy.

Essay Questions (40 points)

1. Trace the American commitment to Vietnam from 1960 to 1975. How and why did it change? How does the Vietnam experience continue to affect American foreign policy?
2. Rank in order of greatness Presidents Kennedy, Johnson, Nixon, Ford, Carter, and Reagan. Give a brief explanation of the accomplishments of each and your reasons for ranking them as you did.

ATLAS AND REFERENCE SECTION

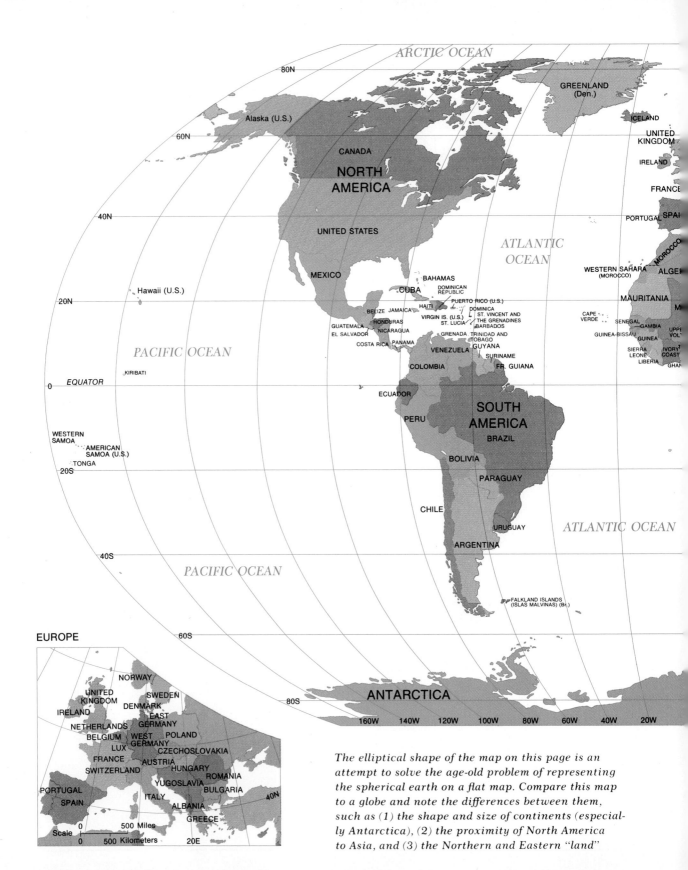

ARCTIC OCEAN

80N

GREENLAND
(Den.)

Alaska (U.S.)

ICELAND

60N

UNITED
KINGDOM

CANADA

IRELAND

NORTH
AMERICA

FRANCE

40N

PORTUGAL

SPAI

ATLANTIC
OCEAN

UNITED STATES

MOROCCO

WESTERN SAHARA
(MOROCCO)

ALGE

MEXICO

BAHAMAS

MAURITANIA

M

20N

Hawaii (U.S.)

DOMINICAN
REPUBLIC

CUBA

PUERTO RICO (U.S.)

HAITI

CAPE
VERDE

BELIZE

JAMAICA

DOMINICA

SENEGAL

GAMBIA

UPPI
VOL

GUATEMALA

HONDURAS

ST. VINCENT AND
THE GRENADINES

VIRGIN IS. (U.S.)

ST. LUCIA

GUINEA-BISSAU

GUINEA

EL SALVADOR

NICARAGUA

BARBADOS

SIERRA
LEONE

IVORY
COAST

GHAN

COSTA RICA

PANAMA

GRENADA

TRINIDAD AND
TOBAGO

LIBERIA

PACIFIC OCEAN

KIRIBATI

VENEZUELA

GUYANA

SURINAME

COLOMBIA

FR. GUIANA

0

EQUATOR

ECUADOR

SOUTH
AMERICA

WESTERN
SAMOA

PERU

BRAZIL

AMERICAN
SAMOA (U.S.)

TONGA

BOLIVIA

20S

PARAGUAY

CHILE

URUGUAY

ATLANTIC OCEAN

ARGENTINA

40S

PACIFIC OCEAN

FALKLAND ISLANDS
(ISLAS MALVINAS) (Br.)

EUROPE

60S

ANTARCTICA

80S

160W   140W   120W   100W   80W   60W   40W   20W

NORWAY

UNITED
KINGDOM

SWEDEN

DENMARK

IRELAND

EAST
GERMANY

NETHERLANDS

POLAND

BELGIUM

WEST
GERMANY

LUX

CZECHOSLOVAKIA

FRANCE

AUSTRIA

SWITZERLAND

HUNGARY

40N

ROMANIA

YUGOSLAVIA

BULGARIA

PORTUGAL

ITALY

SPAIN

ALBANIA

GREECE

Scale

0   500 Miles

0   500 Kilometers

20E

*The elliptical shape of the map on this page is an
attempt to solve the age-old problem of representing
the spherical earth on a flat map. Compare this map
to a globe and note the differences between them,
such as (1) the shape and size of continents (especially Antarctica), (2) the proximity of North America
to Asia, and (3) the Northern and Eastern "land"*

778

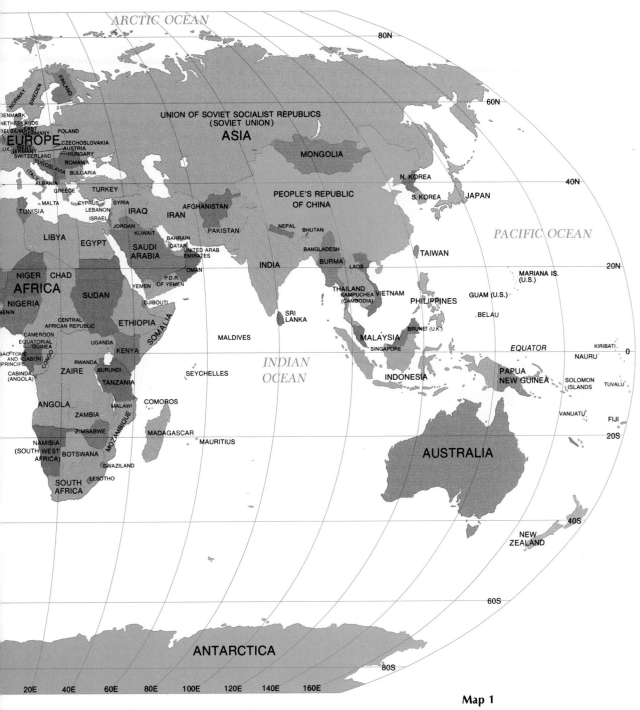

ARCTIC OCEAN

80N

NORWAY
SWEDEN
FINLAND

DENMARK
NETHERLANDS
BELGIUM
EUROPE
EAST GERMANY
LUX
WEST GERMANY
SWITZERLAND
ITALY
ALBANIA
GREECE
MALTA
TUNISIA
POLAND
CZECHOSLOVAKIA
AUSTRIA
HUNGARY
ROMANIA
YUGOSLAVIA
BULGARIA
TURKEY
CYPRUS
LEBANON
ISRAEL
SYRIA
JORDAN
KUWAIT

UNION OF SOVIET SOCIALIST REPUBLICS
(SOVIET UNION)
ASIA

60N

MONGOLIA

N. KOREA

40N

S. KOREA   JAPAN

PEOPLE'S REPUBLIC
OF CHINA

PACIFIC OCEAN

AFGHANISTAN

IRAN

IRAQ

PAKISTAN

LIBYA   EGYPT

SAUDI
ARABIA

BAHRAIN
QATAR
UNITED ARAB
EMIRATES

NEPAL   BHUTAN

BANGLADESH

BURMA

TAIWAN

20N

MARIANA IS.
(U.S.)

NIGER   CHAD

AFRICA

SUDAN

P.D.R.
OF YEMEN
YEMEN

OMAN

INDIA

LAOS

THAILAND
KAMPUCHEA VIETNAM
(CAMBODIA)

PHILIPPINES

GUAM (U.S.)

NIGERIA

DJIBOUTI

BELAU

BENIN

CENTRAL
AFRICAN REPUBLIC

ETHIOPIA

SRI
LANKA

MALDIVES

MALAYSIA

BRUNEI (U.K.)

CAMEROON
EQUATORIAL
GUINEA

UGANDA

SOMALIA

SINGAPORE

EQUATOR

KIRIBATI

0

SAO TOME
AND
PRINCIPE
GABON

KENYA

NAURU

CABINDA
(ANGOLA)

ZAIRE

RWANDA
BURUNDI

SEYCHELLES

INDIAN
OCEAN

INDONESIA

PAPUA
NEW GUINEA

SOLOMON
ISLANDS

TUVALU

CONGO

TANZANIA

ANGOLA

MALAWI

ZAMBIA

COMOROS

VANUATU

FIJI

ZIMBABWE

MOZAMBIQUE

MADAGASCAR

MAURITIUS

20S

NAMIBIA
(SOUTH WEST
AFRICA)

BOTSWANA

SWAZILAND

AUSTRALIA

SOUTH
AFRICA

LESOTHO

40S

NEW
ZEALAND

60S

ANTARCTICA

80S

20E   40E   60E   80E   100E   120E   140E   160E

*hemispheres. The map shows boundaries and names
of all independent countries and some dependencies.
Because boundaries and names often change, use the
most recent map available. This map uses a latitude
and longitude grid to show directions. The latitude
lines run east and west. The longitude lines meet at
the Poles and run north and south.*

Map 1

World: Political Boundaries

Scale at Equator

0	500	1000	1500 Miles
0	500	1000 1500	Kilometers

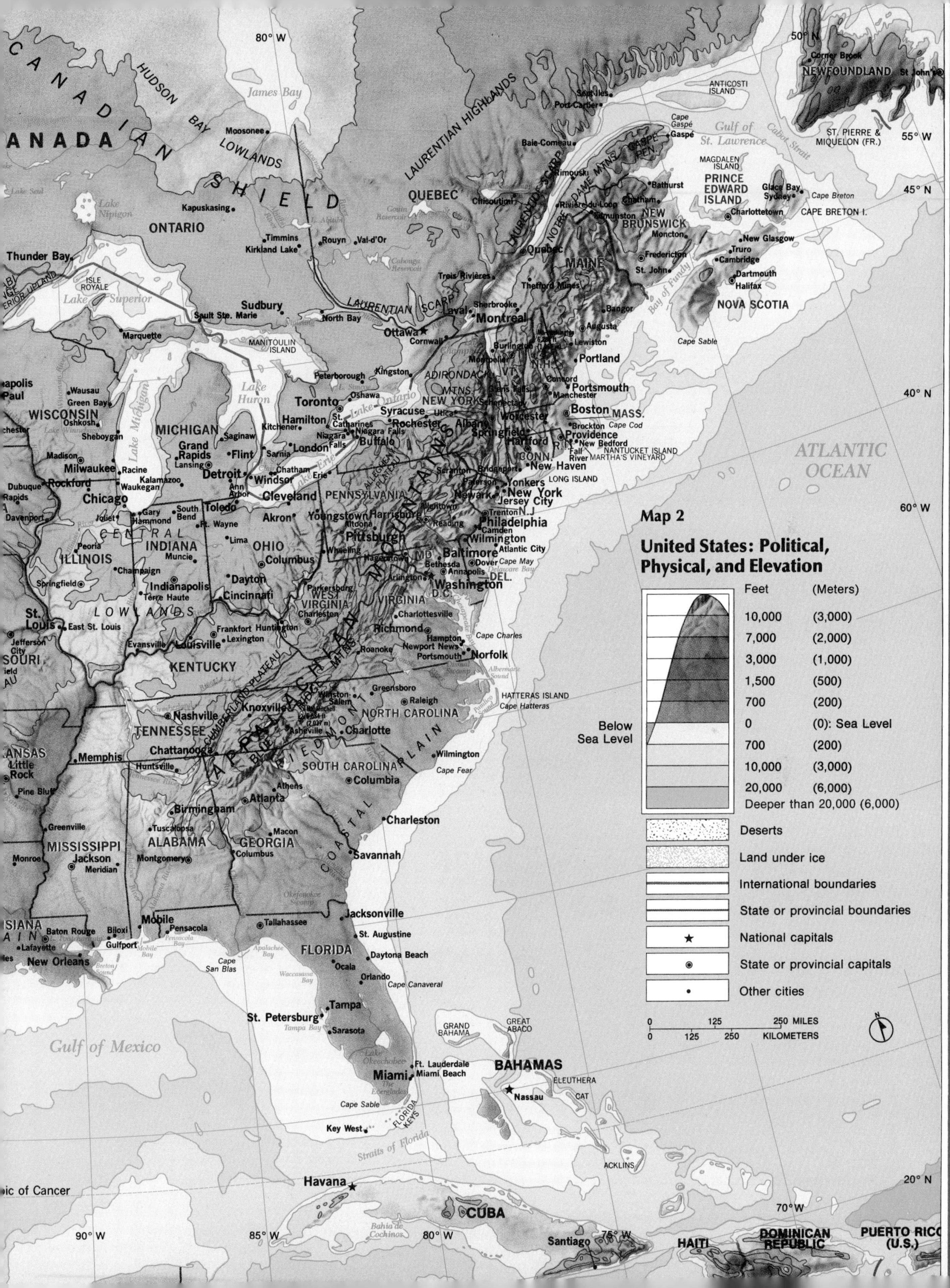

CANADIAN SHIELD
CANADA
HUDSON BAY LOWLANDS
James Bay
LAURENTIAN HIGHLANDS
LAURENTIAN SCARP
NOTRE DAME MTNS.
GASPÉ PEN.
QUEBEC
ONTARIO
Moosonee
Kapuskasing
Timmins
Kirkland Lake
Rouyn
Val-d'Or
Thunder Bay
ISLE ROYALE
Lake Superior
Lake Nipigon
Sudbury
Sault Ste. Marie
North Bay
Marquette
MANITOULIN ISLAND
Ottawa
Cornwall
Laval
Montreal
Sherbrooke
Trois Rivières
Quebec
Chicoutimi
Baie-Comeau
Sept-Îles
Port-Cartier
Rimouski
Rivière-du-Loup
Edmunston
Thetford Mines
ANTICOSTI ISLAND
Cape Gaspé
Gaspé
Gulf of St. Lawrence
Cabot Strait
MAGDALEN ISLAND
PRINCE EDWARD ISLAND
Charlottetown
Glace Bay
Sydney
Cape Breton
CAPE BRETON I.
NEWFOUNDLAND
Corner Brook
St John's
ST. PIERRE & MIQUELON (FR.)
NEW BRUNSWICK
Bathurst
Chatham
Moncton
Fredericton
St. John
New Glasgow
Truro
Cambridge
Dartmouth
Halifax
NOVA SCOTIA
Bay of Fundy
Cape Sable
MAINE
Bangor
Augusta
Lewiston
Portland
Burlington
Montpelier
VT.
N.H.
Concord
Portsmouth
Manchester
ADIRONDACK MTNS
Kingston
Peterborough
Oshawa
Toronto
Hamilton
Kitchener
St. Catharines
Niagara Falls
Lake Ontario
Lake Huron
Lake Michigan
Lake Erie
NEW YORK
Syracuse
Rochester
Utica
Schenectady
Albany
Buffalo
Worcester
Springfield
Boston
MASS.
Brockton
Cape Cod
Providence
New Bedford
Fall River
R.I.
CONN.
Hartford
NANTUCKET ISLAND
MARTHA'S VINEYARD
New Haven
Bridgeport
LONG ISLAND
Yonkers
Paterson
Newark
New York
Jersey City
Scranton
Trenton
N.J.
Allentown
Reading
Harrisburg
Philadelphia
Camden
Wilmington
Atlantic City
Cape May
Delaware Bay
Dover
DEL.
Baltimore
MD
Bethesda
Annapolis
Arlington
Washington D.C.
PENNSYLVANIA
ALLEGHENY PLATEAU
Erie
Youngstown
Altoona
Pittsburgh
Wheeling
Hagerstown
APPALACHIAN MOUNTAINS
WEST VIRGINIA
Parkersburg
Charleston
VIRGINIA
Charlottesville
Richmond
Roanoke
Hampton
Newport News
Portsmouth
Norfolk
Cape Charles
Chesapeake Bay
Albemarle Sound
Pamlico Sound
HATTERAS ISLAND
Cape Hatteras
NORTH CAROLINA
Greensboro
Winston-Salem
Raleigh
Charlotte
Asheville
Mt. Mitchell
BLUE RIDGE MTNS.
PIEDMONT
COASTAL PLAIN
Wilmington
Cape Fear
SOUTH CAROLINA
Columbia
Charleston
Athens
Atlanta
GEORGIA
Macon
Columbus
Savannah
Okefenokee Swamp
Jacksonville
St. Augustine
Tallahassee
FLORIDA
Daytona Beach
Ocala
Orlando
Cape Canaveral
Tampa
St. Petersburg
Tampa Bay
Sarasota
Lake Okeechobee
Ft. Lauderdale
Miami
Miami Beach
The Everglades
Cape Sable
FLORIDA KEYS
Key West
Straits of Florida
Gulf of Mexico
Apalachee Bay
Cape San Blas
Pensacola
Pensacola Bay
Mobile
Mobile Bay
Biloxi
Gulfport
Breton Sound
New Orleans
Baton Rouge
Lafayette
MISSISSIPPI
Jackson
Meridian
Greenville
Monroe
ALABAMA
Tuscaloosa
Birmingham
Montgomery
Huntsville
Chattanooga
TENNESSEE
Nashville
Knoxville
Memphis
CUMBERLAND PLATEAU
KENTUCKY
Louisville
Frankfort
Lexington
Huntington
Evansville
Little Rock
Pine Bluff
St. Louis
East St. Louis
Jefferson City
CENTRAL LOWLANDS
ILLINOIS
Springfield
Peoria
Champaign
Chicago
Joliet
Gary
Hammond
INDIANA
South Bend
Ft. Wayne
Muncie
Indianapolis
Terre Haute
OHIO
Toledo
Lima
Dayton
Columbus
Cincinnati
Cleveland
Akron
MICHIGAN
Saginaw
Flint
Grand Rapids
Lansing
Kalamazoo
Ann Arbor
Detroit
Windsor
Sarnia
London
Chatham
WISCONSIN
Wausau
Green Bay
Oshkosh
Sheboygan
Madison
Milwaukee
Racine
Waukegan
Rockford
Dubuque
Davenport
ATLANTIC OCEAN
GRAND BAHAMA
GREAT ABACO
BAHAMAS
Nassau
ELEUTHERA
CAT
ACKLINS
CUBA
Havana
Bahía de Cochinos
Santiago
HAITI
DOMINICAN REPUBLIC
PUERTO RICO (U.S.)
Tropic of Cancer
80° W
50° N
55° W
45° N
40° N
60° W
20° N
70° W
90° W
85° W
75° W
Feet (Meters)
10,000 (3,000)
7,000 (2,000)
3,000 (1,000)
1,500 (500)
700 (200)
0 (0): Sea Level
Below Sea Level
700 (200)
10,000 (3,000)
20,000 (6,000)
Deeper than 20,000 (6,000)
Deserts
Land under ice
International boundaries
State or provincial boundaries
National capitals
State or provincial capitals
Other cities
0 125 250 MILES
0 125 250 KILOMETERS
N

Map 2

United States: Political, Physical, and Elevation

NORTH POLE

GREENLAND SEA

ARCTIC OCEAN

GREENLAND

ARCTIC CIRCLE

ICELAND

BERING SEA

Bering Strait

Aleutian Islands

BROOKS RANGE

Yukon R.

Beaufort Sea

Viscount Melville Sound

Baffin Bay

ATLANTIC OCEAN

Gulf of Alaska

ALASKA RANGE

Mt. McKinley

KLONDIKE REGION

Mackenzie River

Great Bear Lake

Victoria Island

Baffin Island

Davis Strait

Mt. Logan

CANADIAN

Hudson Strait

Queen Charlotte Islands

Great Slave Lake

Reindeer Lake

UNGAVA PENINSULA

Hudson Bay

SHIELD

LABRADOR

Lake Athabaska

James Bay

Vancouver Island

COAST MOUNTAINS

North Saskatchewan

Nelson R.

LAURENTIAN

Gulf of St. Lawrence

Newfoundland

Columbia River

ROCKY MOUNTAINS

South

Red R.

Lake Winnipeg

Lake of the Woods

HIGHLANDS

St. Lawrence R.

PACIFIC

Cascade

Snake R.

GREAT

Missouri R.

L. Superior

SUPERIOR UPLANDS

Michigan

Huron

Niagra Falls

L. Champlain

Cape Cod

OCEAN

SIERRA NEVADA

Great Salt Lake

BLACK HILLS

L. Ontario

Hudson R.

GREEN MTS.

Mt. Whitney

COASTAL RANGE

GREAT BASIN

DEATH VALLEY

GRAND CANYON

CENTRAL

LOWLAND

L. Erie

APPALACHIAN

Chesapeake Bay

BERMUDA

MOJAVE DESERT

Colorado

COLORADO PLATEAU

PLAINS

OZARK PLATEAU

Arkansas R.

Mississippi

Ohio R.

LOWLAND

PIEDMONT

Cape Hatteras

INTERIOR

ATLANTIC COASTAL PLAIN

TROPIC OF CANCER

BAJA CALIFORNIA

Gulf of California

Rio Grande

SIERRA MADRE ORIENTAL

Gulf of Mexico

THE BAHAMAS

WEST INDIES

ATLANTIC OCEAN

Cape San Lucas

SIERRA MADRE OCCIDENTAL

MEXICAN PLATEAU

CUBA

GREATER ANTILLES

HISPANIOLA

PUERTO RICO

JAMAICA

ISTHMUS OF TEHUANTEPEC

YUCATAN PENINSULA

CARIBBEAN SEA

L. Nicaragua

ISTHMUS OF PANAMA

Gulf of Panama

Isla del Cocos

Kauai

Niihau

Oahu

Molokai

Maui

Lanai

Kahoolawe

HAWAIIAN IS.

Hawaii

PACIFIC OCEAN

Map 3
North America: Physical Features

782

Scale at 40°

0   350   700 Miles

0   350   700 Kilometers

Map 4
Territorial Growth of the United States

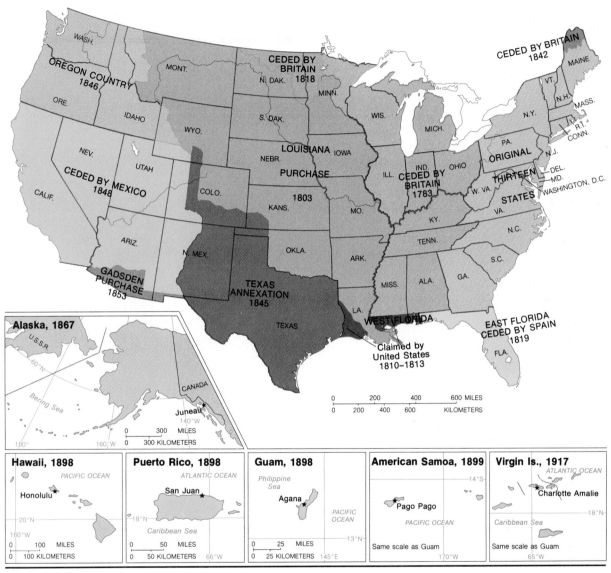

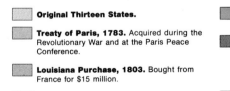

Original Thirteen States.

Treaty of Paris, 1783. Acquired during the Revolutionary War and at the Paris Peace Conference.

Louisiana Purchase, 1803. Bought from France for $15 million.

West Florida, 1810–1813. Claimed by the U.S. and Spain. To secure its claim, the U.S. sent troops to occupy the area.

Northern Boundary, 1818. A treaty with Britain set the northern boundary of the U.S. at the 49th parallel. The U.S. and Britain shared control of the Oregon Country.

East Florida, 1819. Spain ceded East and West Florida to the U.S. by treaty and gave up its claim to the Oregon Country. The U.S. gave up its claim to Texas.

Maine Boundary, 1842. A treaty with Britain divided the disputed land.

Texas Annexation, 1845. In 1836, the Republic of Texas declared its independence from Mexico. Texas then petitioned the U.S. for annexation. The U.S. annexed this area in 1845.

Oregon Country, 1846. Claimed by Spain, Russia, the U.S., and Britain. Spain gave up its claim in 1819; Russia, in 1824. By treaty, the U.S. and Britain split the disputed area along the 49th parallel.

Mexican Cession, 1848. Ceded by Mexico after the Mexican War. Under the Treaty of Guadalupe Hidalgo, the U.S. agreed to pay $15 million for the territory.

Gadsden Purchase, 1853. Bought from Mexico for $10 million.

Alaska was purchased from Russia in 1867 for $7 million. It became a territory in 1912 and a state in 1959. In **Hawaii,** Americans led a revolt against the queen in 1893. They petitioned the U.S. for annexation. The U.S. annexed Hawaii in 1898. It became a territory in 1900 and a state in 1959. **Puerto Rico** and **Guam** were ceded by Spain under the treaty ending the Spanish-American War in 1898. Puerto Rico is a commonwealth; Guam is a territory. **American Samoa** became an American territory under a treaty with Britain and Germany in 1899. It had been an American protectorate since 1878. The territory of the **Virgin Islands** was purchased from Denmark in 1917 for $25 million.

783

U.S. POPULATION, BY SEX, RACE, RESIDENCE, AND MEDIAN AGE, 1790–1980

(Nearest million. Total resident population, excluding Armed Forces abroad.)

| Census date | Total population | Sex | | Race | | | Residence | | | Median age |
		Male	Female	White	Black	Other	Urban	% Urban	Rural	
1790	4	NA	NA	3	1	NA	.20	5%	4	NA
1800	5	NA	NA	4	1	NA	.32	6%	5	NA
1810	7	NA	NA	6	1	NA	.53	7%	7	NA
1820	10	5	5	8	2	NA	.69	7%	9	17
1830	13	7	6	11	2	NA	1	9%	12	17
1840	17	9	8	14	3	NA	2	11%	15	18
1850	23	12	11	20	4	NA	4	15%	20	19
1860	31	16	15	27	4	.08	6	20%	25	19
1870	40	19	19	34	5	.09	10	26%	29	20
1880	50	26	25	43	7	.17	14	28%	36	21
1890	63	32	31	55	7	.36	22	35%	41	22
1900	76	39	37	67	9	.35	30	40%	46	23
1910	92	47	45	82	10	.41	42	46%	50	24
1920	106	54	52	95	10	.43	54	51%	52	25
1930	123	62	61	110	12	.60	69	56%	54	26
1940	132	66	66	118	13	.59	74	57%	57	29
1950	151	75	76	135	15	1	97	64%	54	30
1960	179	88	91	159	19	2	125	70%	54	30
1970	203	99	104	178	23	3	149	73%	54	28
1980	227	110	116	188	26	17	167	74%	60	30

NA Not available

U.S. TOTAL POPULATION, 1790–1980

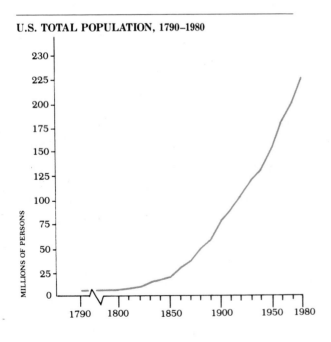

U.S. URBAN & RURAL POPULATION, 1790–1980

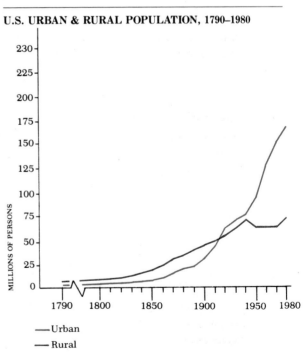

— Urban
— Rural

IMMIGRATION TO THE UNITED STATES

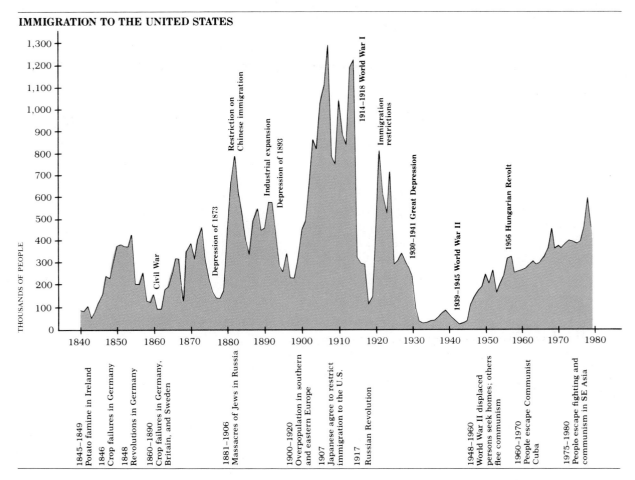

THOUSANDS OF PEOPLE
0
100
200
300
400
500
600
700
800
900
1,000
1,100
1,200
1,300
1840
1850
1860
1870
1880
1890
1900
1910
1920
1930
1940
1950
1960
1970
1980
Civil War
Depression of 1873
Restriction on Chinese immigration
Industrial expansion
Depression of 1893
1914–1918 World War I
Immigration restrictions
1930–1941 Great Depression
1939–1945 World War II
1956 Hungarian Revolt
1845–1849 Potato famine in Ireland
1846 Crop failures in Germany
1848 Revolutions in Germany
1860–1890 Crop failures in Germany, Britain, and Sweden
1881–1906 Massacres of Jews in Russia
1900–1920 Overpopulation in southern and eastern Europe
1907 Japanese agree to restrict immigration to the U.S.
1917 Russian Revolution
1948–1960 World War II displaced persons seek homes; others flee communism
1960–1970 People escape Communist Cuba
1975–1980 People escape fighting and communism in SE Asia

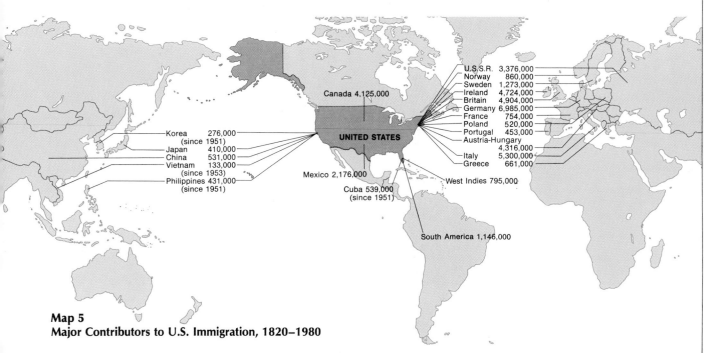

U.S.S.R. 3,376,000
Norway 860,000
Sweden 1,273,000
Ireland 4,724,000
Britain 4,904,000
Germany 6,985,000
France 754,000
Poland 520,000
Portugal 453,000
Austria-Hungary 4,316,000
Italy 5,300,000
Greece 661,000
Canada 4,125,000
UNITED STATES
Korea 276,000 (since 1951)
Japan 410,000
China 531,000
Vietnam 133,000 (since 1953)
Philippines 431,000 (since 1951)
Mexico 2,176,000
Cuba 539,000 (since 1951)
West Indies 795,000
South America 1,146,000

Map 5
Major Contributors to U.S. Immigration, 1820–1980

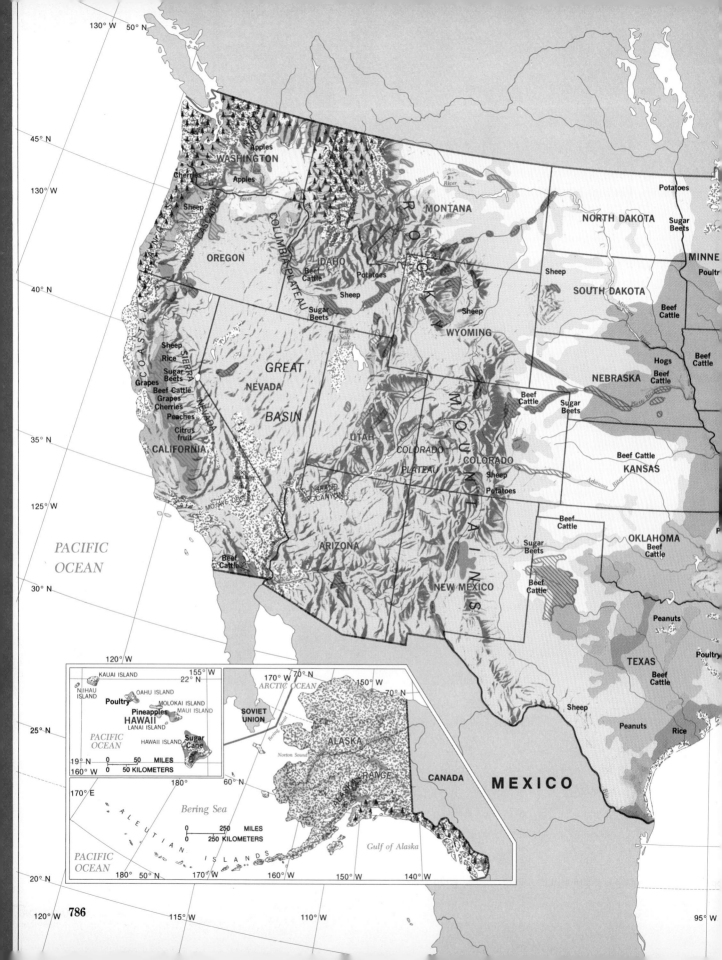

50° N

130° W

45° N

130° W

40° N

35° N

125° W

PACIFIC
OCEAN

30° N

120° W 786

115° W

WASHINGTON

Apples

Cherries

Apples

Snake River

Sheep

OREGON

COLUMBIA PLATEAU

IDAHO
Beef
Cattle

Potatoes

Sheep

Sugar
Beets

Great
Salt
Lake

GREAT

NEVADA

BASIN

Sheep
Rice
Sugar
Beets
Grapes
Beef Cattle
Grapes
Cherries
Peaches

Citrus
fruit
CALIFORNIA

DEATH VALLEY

MOJAVE DESERT

Beef
Cattle

GRAND
CANYON

ARIZONA

UTAH

COLORADO
PLATEAU

Missouri   River

MONTANA

ROCKY

WYOMING

Sheep

COLORADO

COLORADO

Sheep

Potatoes

NEW MEXICO

M
O
U
N
T
A
I
N
S

Beef
Cattle

Sugar
Beets

Beef
Cattle

Sugar
Beets

Beef
Cattle

Potatoes

NORTH DAKOTA

Sugar
Beets

MINNE

SOUTH DAKOTA

Poultry

Beef
Cattle

NEBRASKA

Hogs
Beef
Cattle

Platte River

Beef
Cattle

Sugar
Beets

Missouri River

Beef Cattle

KANSAS

OKLAHOMA
Beef
Cattle

Peanuts

Arkansas River

Poultry

TEXAS

Beef
Cattle

Sheep

Peanuts

Rice

MEXICO

CANADA

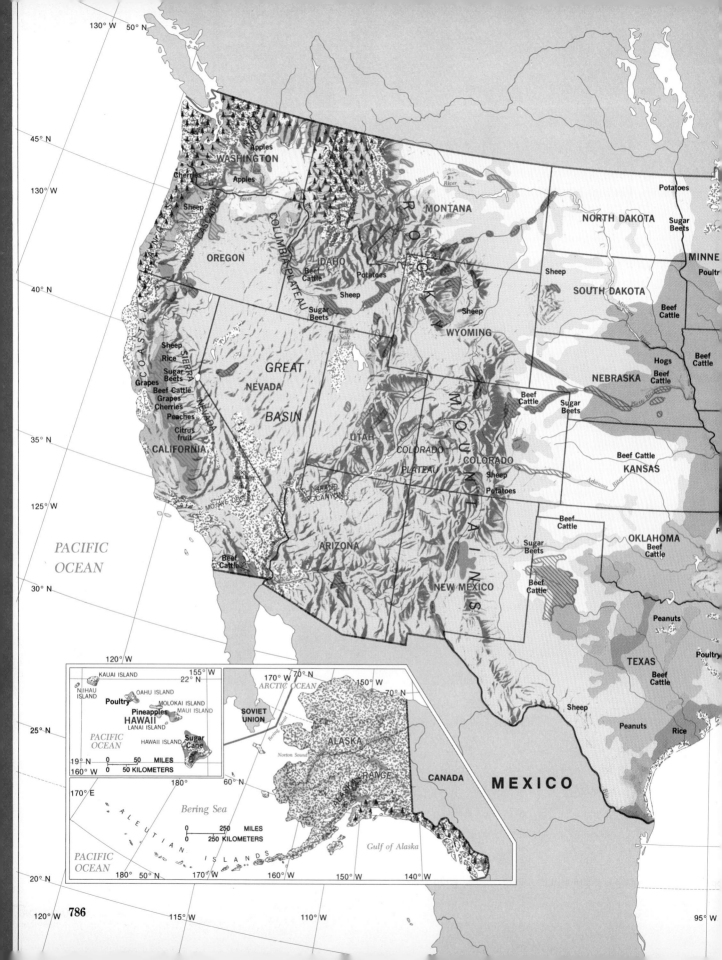

120° W

KAUAI ISLAND

NIIHAU
ISLAND

OAHU ISLAND

Poultry
Pineapples
HAWAII
LANAI ISLAND

MOLOKAI ISLAND
MAUI ISLAND

155° W
22° N

PACIFIC
OCEAN

HAWAII ISLAND
Sugar
Cane

19° N
160° W

0   50   MILES

0   50 KILOMETERS

170° E

170° W 70° N

ARCTIC OCEAN

SOVIET
UNION

Norton Sound

Bering Strait

150° W

70° N

ALASKA

ALASKA RANGE

60° N

Gulf of Alaska

170° E

Bering Sea

PACIFIC
OCEAN

A L E U T I A N   I S L A N D S

0   250   MILES

0   250 KILOMETERS

180°

50° N

170° W

160° W

150° W

140° W

20° N

180°

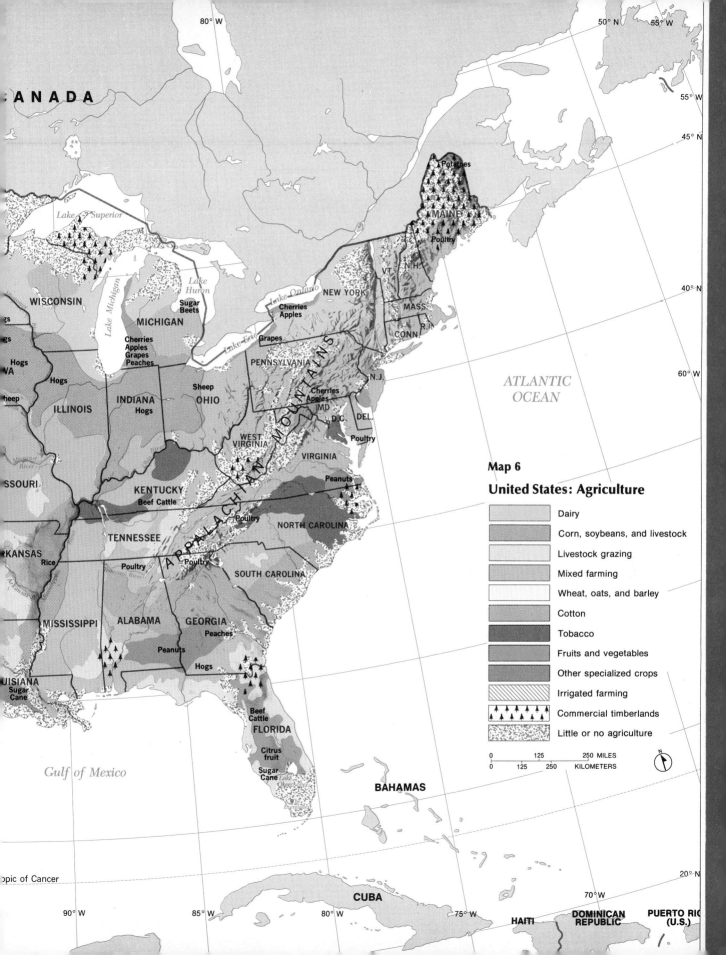

Map 6

United States: Agriculture

	Dairy
	Corn, soybeans, and livestock
	Livestock grazing
	Mixed farming
	Wheat, oats, and barley
	Cotton
	Tobacco
	Fruits and vegetables
	Other specialized crops
	Irrigated farming
	Commercial timberlands
	Little or no agriculture

0   125   250 MILES
0   125   250 KILOMETERS

CANADA

Lake Superior

Lake Michigan

Lake Huron

Lake Ontario

Lake Erie

WISCONSIN

MICHIGAN

Sugar Beets

Cherries
Apples
Grapes
Peaches

Cherries
Apples

Grapes

NEW YORK

PENNSYLVANIA

N.J.

MASS.

CONN.

R.I.

VT.   N.H.

MAINE

Potatoes

Poultry

ATLANTIC OCEAN

Hogs

Hogs

ILLINOIS

INDIANA

Hogs

Sheep

OHIO

WEST VIRGINIA

VIRGINIA

Cherries
Apples

MD.

D.C.   DEL.

Poultry

Peanuts

Missouri River

SSOURI

KENTUCKY

Beef Cattle

Poultry

NORTH CAROLINA

APPALACHIAN MOUNTAINS

TENNESSEE

Poultry

Poultry

SOUTH CAROLINA

RKANSAS

Rice

Arkansas River

MISSISSIPPI

ALABAMA

Peanuts

GEORGIA

Peaches

Hogs

UISIANA

Sugar Cane

Peanuts

Beef Cattle

FLORIDA

Citrus fruit

Sugar Cane

Lake Okeechobee

The Everglades

Gulf of Mexico

BAHAMAS

Tropic of Cancer

CUBA

HAITI

DOMINICAN REPUBLIC

PUERTO RIC (U.S.)

80° W
90° W
85° W
80° W
75° W
70° W
50° N
55° W
45° N
40° N
55° W
60° W
20° N

N

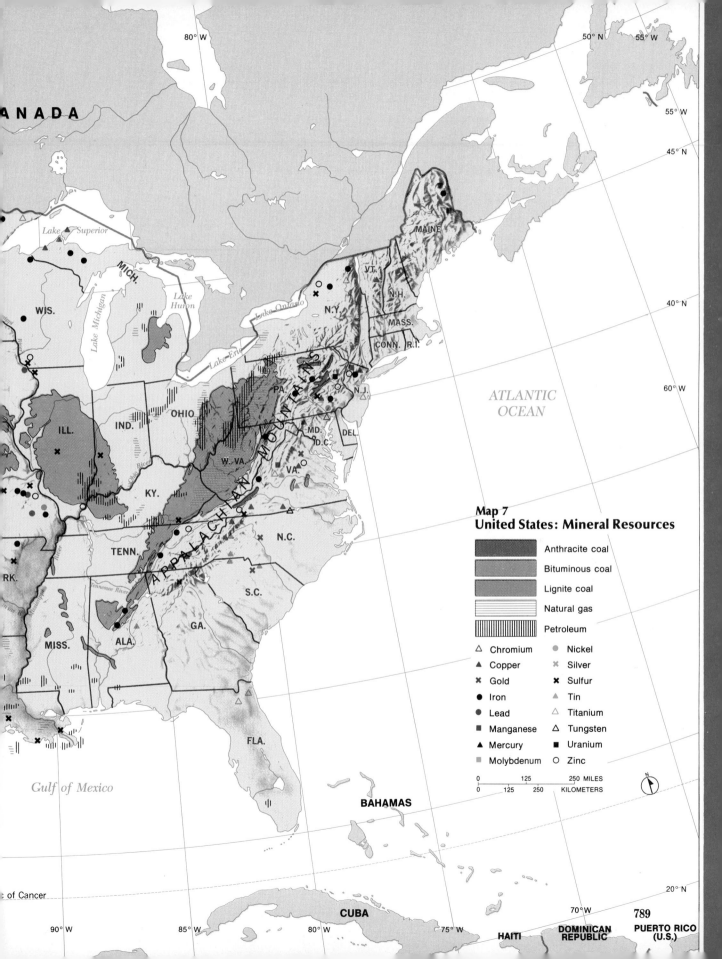

Map 7
United States: Mineral Resources

	Anthracite coal
	Bituminous coal
	Lignite coal
	Natural gas
	Petroleum

△ Chromium	● Nickel
▲ Copper	✖ Silver
✳ Gold	✕ Sulfur
● Iron	▲ Tin
● Lead	△ Titanium
■ Manganese	△ Tungsten
▲ Mercury	■ Uranium
Molybdenum	○ Zinc

0   125   250 MILES
0   125   250 KILOMETERS

789

LARGEST AMERICAN CITIES, 1690–1980

*By modern standards, colonial cities could hardly be called cities. In the
19th century, northern cities grew faster than southern cities. The most
rapid gains were made by new cities in the interior of the country, such
as St. Louis and Chicago. In the late 20th century, the cities of the
North have stopped growing, while the cities of the Southwest and West
have made tremendous gains.*

1690		1760		1775		1840			
Boston	7,000	Philadelphia	19,000	Philadelphia	40,000	New York	313,000	Cincinnati	46,000
Philadelphia	4,000	Boston	16,000	New York	25,000	Baltimore	102,000	Albany	34,000
New York	4,000	New York	14,000	Boston	16,000	New Orleans	102,000	Charleston	29,000
Newport, R.I.	3,000	Charleston	8,000	Charleston	12,000	Philadelphia	94,000	Washington, D.C.	23,000
Charleston	1,000	Newport	7,000	Newport	11,000	Boston	93,000	Providence	23,000

1870		1900		1940		1980	
New York	1,478,000	New York	3,437,000	New York	7,455,000	New York	7,071,000
Philadelphia	674,000	Chicago	1,699,000	Chicago	3,397,000	Chicago	3,572,000
St. Louis	311,000	Philadelphia	1,294,000	Philadelphia	1,931,000	Los Angeles	2,967,000
Chicago	299,000	St. Louis	575,000	Detroit	1,623,000	Philadelphia	1,688,000
Baltimore	267,000	Boston	561,000	Los Angeles	1,504,000	Houston	1,554,000
Boston	251,000	Baltimore	509,000	Cleveland	878,000	Detroit	1,203,000
Cincinnati	216,000	Pittsburgh	452,000	Baltimore	859,000	Dallas	904,000
New Orleans	191,000	Cleveland	382,000	St. Louis	816,000	San Diego	876,000
San Francisco	149,000	Buffalo	352,000	Boston	771,000	Phoenix	790,000
Pittsburgh	139,000	San Francisco	343,000	Pittsburgh	672,000	Baltimore	787,000

Map 8
U.S. Largest Metropolitan Areas

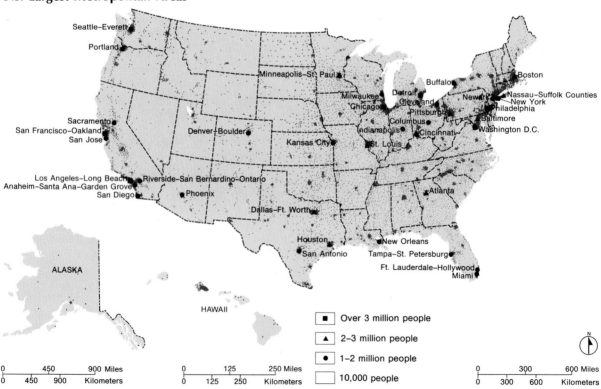

Map 9
Population Centers in the United States, 1790–1980

The settlement of the United States was the largest movement of people in history. In 1790 the population was concentrated along the East Coast. Note on the map how the center of population has gradually shifted westward and southward. Compare this map to the population distribution map on page 790. Most of the western half of the country is still thinly settled, except along the Pacific Coast.

FACTS ABOUT THE NORTHEASTERN STATES

State	Population per Square Mile	Percent Urban	Largest City
Connecticut	639	79	Bridgeport
Maine	36	48	Portland
Massachusetts	733	84	Boston
New Hampshire	102	52	Manchester
New Jersey	979	89	Newark
New York	367	85	New York City
Pennsylvania	264	69	Philadelphia
Rhode Island	903	87	Providence
Vermont	55	34	Burlington

Map 10

· = 10,000 people

State	Origin of State Name	State Nickname	State Capital	Area in Square Miles	Year Admitted to Union	Order of Entry	Population	Number of Representatives in Congress*
Connecticut	Algonquin, "beside the long river"	Nutmeg State	Hartford	5,009	1788	5	3,108,000	6
Maine	after former French province of Mayne	Pine Tree State	Augusta	33,215	1820	23	1,125,000	2
Massachusetts	Algonquin, "large mountain place"	Bay State	Boston	8,257	1788	6	5,737,000	11 (−1)
New Hampshire	after English county of Hampshire	Granite State	Concord	9,304	1788	9	921,000	2
New Jersey	after island of Jersey in English Channel	Garden State	Trenton	7,836	1787	3	7,364,000	15 (−1)
New York	honors English Duke of York	Empire State	Albany	49,576	1788	11	17,557,000	34 (−5)
Pennsylvania	honors Admiral William Penn, father of founder of colony	Keystone State	Harrisburg	45,333	1787	2	11,867,000	23 (−2)
Rhode Island	after Greek island of Rhodes	Ocean State	Providence	1,214	1790	13	947,000	2
Vermont	French, "green mountain"	Green Mountain State	Montpelier	9,609	1791	14	511,000	1

*Figure in parentheses shows number of representatives gained or lost after 1980 census.

FACTS ABOUT THE SOUTHERN STATES
(including District of Columbia)

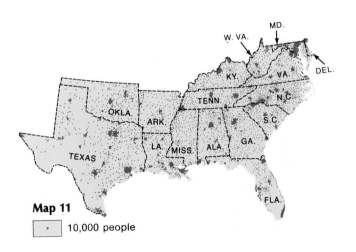

Map 11

▢ · ▢ 10,000 people

State	Population per Square Mile	Percent Urban	Largest City
Alabama	77	60	Birmingham
Arkansas	44	52	Little Rock
Delaware	300	71	Wilmington
District of Columbia	10,453	100	Washington
Florida	177	84	Jacksonville
Georgia	94	62	Atlanta
Kentucky	92	51	Louisville
Louisiana	94	69	New Orleans
Maryland	426	80	Baltimore
Mississippi	53	47	Jackson
North Carolina	120	48	Charlotte
Oklahoma	44	67	Oklahoma City
South Carolina	103	54	Columbia
Tennessee	111	60	Memphis
Texas	54	80	Houston
Virginia	134	66	Norfolk
West Virginia	81	36	Charleston

State	Origin of State Name	State Nickname	State Capital	Area in Square Miles	Year Admitted to Union	Order of Entry	Population	Number of Representatives in Congress
Alabama	tribe of the Creek confederacy	Yellowhammer State	Montgomery	51,609	1819	22	3,890,000	7
Arkansas	French version of "Kansas," a Sioux word meaning south wind people	Land of Opportunity	Little Rock	53,104	1836	25	2,286,000	4
Delaware	honors Lord De La Warr, early governor of Virginia	Diamond State	Dover	2,057	1787	1	595,000	1
District of Columbia	honors Columbus	—	—	69	—	—	638,000	—
Florida	Spanish, "feast of flowers"	Sunshine State	Tallahassee	58,560	1845	27	9,740,000	19 (+4)
Georgia	honors King George II	Peach State	Atlanta	58,876	1788	4	5,464,000	10
Kentucky	Iroquois, "meadowland"	Bluegrass State	Frankfort	40,395	1792	15	3,661,000	7
Louisiana	honors Louis XIV of France	Pelican State	Baton Rouge	48,523	1812	18	4,204,000	8
Maryland	honors Queen Henrietta Marie	Free State	Annapolis	10,577	1788	7	4,216,000	8
Mississippi	Chippewa, "great river"	Magnolia State	Jackson	47,716	1817	20	2,521,000	5
North Carolina	honors King Charles I	Tar Heel State	Raleigh	52,712	1789	12	5,874,000	11
Oklahoma	Choctaw, "red people"	Sooner State	Oklahoma City	69,919	1907	46	3,025,000	6
South Carolina	honors King Charles I	Palmetto State	Columbia	31,055	1788	8	3,119,000	6
Tennessee	name of Cherokee villages on the Little Tennessee River	Volunteer State	Nashville	42,244	1796	16	4,591,000	9 (+1)
Texas	Caddo, "friendly tribe"	Lone Star State	Austin	267,339	1845	28	14,228,000	27 (+3)
Virginia	honors "Virgin Queen" Elizabeth I	The Old Dominion	Richmond	40,815	1788	10	5,346,000	10
West Virginia	honors "Virgin Queen" Elizabeth I	Mountain State	Charleston	24,181	1863	35	1,950,000	4

FACTS ABOUT THE NORTH CENTRAL STATES

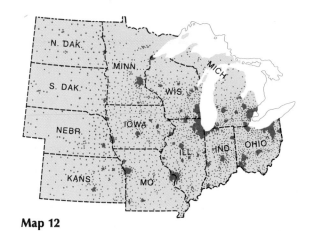

Map 12

☐ 10,000 people

State	Population per Square Mile	Percent Urban	Largest City
Illinois	205	83	Chicago
Indiana	152	64	Indianapolis
Iowa	52	59	Des Moines
Kansas	29	67	Wichita
Michigan	163	71	Detroit
Minnesota	51	67	Minneapolis
Missouri	71	68	St. Louis
Nebraska	21	63	Omaha
North Dakota	9	49	Fargo
Ohio	264	73	Cleveland
South Dakota	9	46	Sioux Falls
Wisconsin	86	64	Milwaukee

State	Origin of State Name	State Nickname	State Capital	Area in Square Miles	Year Admitted to Union	Order of Entry	Population	Number of Representatives in Congress
Illinois	Algonquin, "men" or "warriors"	Prairie State	Springfield	56,400	1818	21	11,418,000	22 (−2)
Indiana	land of the Indians	Hoosier State	Indianapolis	36,291	1816	19	5,490,000	10
Iowa	Sioux, "beautiful land"	Hawkeye State	Des Moines	56,290	1846	29	2,913,000	6
Kansas	Sioux, "south wind people"	Sunflower State	Topeka	82,264	1861	34	2,363,000	5
Michigan	Chippewa, "great water"	Wolverine State	Lansing	58,216	1837	26	9,258,000	18 (−1)
Minnesota	Sioux, "sky-tinted water"	North Star State	St. Paul	84,068	1858	32	4,077,000	8
Missouri	tribe named after Missouri River, or "muddy water"	Show Me State	Jefferson City	69,686	1821	24	4,917,000	9 (−1)
Nebraska	Omaha name for Platte River, "broad river"	Cornhusker State	Lincoln	77,227	1867	37	1,570,000	3
North Dakota	Sioux, "friend" or "ally"	Sioux State	Bismarck	70,665	1889	39	653,000	1
Ohio	Iroquois, "beautiful river"	Buckeye State	Columbus	41,222	1803	17	10,797,000	21 (−2)
South Dakota	Sioux, "friend" or "ally"	Sunshine State	Pierre	77,047	1889	40	690,000	1 (−1)
Wisconsin	Chippewa, "grassy place"	Badger State	Madison	56,154	1848	30	4,705,000	9

FACTS ABOUT THE WESTERN STATES

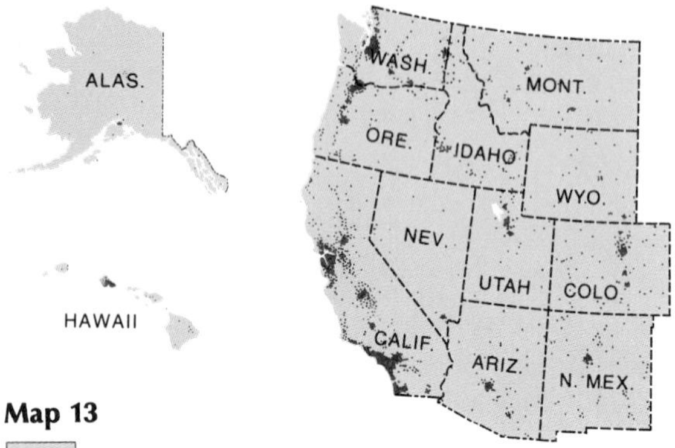

Map 13

☐ · 10,000 people

State	Population per Square Mile	Percent Urban	Largest City
Alaska	1	65	Anchorage
Arizona	24	84	Phoenix
California	151	91	Los Angeles
Colorado	28	81	Denver
Hawaii	150	87	Honolulu
Idaho	11	54	Boise
Montana	5	53	Billings
Nevada	7	85	Las Vegas
New Mexico	11	72	Albuquerque
Oregon	27	68	Portland
Utah	18	84	Salt Lake City
Washington	62	38	Seattle
Wyoming	5	63	Casper

State	Origin of State Name	State Nickname	State Capital	Area in Square Miles	Year Admitted to Union	Order of Entry	Population	Number of Representatives in Congress
Alaska	Russian version of Aleut word meaning "great land"	The Last Frontier	Juneau	589,757	1959	49	400,000	7
Arizona	Spanish version of Pima word meaning "little spring place"	Grand Canyon State	Phoenix	113,909	1912	48	2,718,000	5 (+1)
California	mythical island paradise in Spanish literature	Golden State	Sacramento	158,693	1850	31	23,669,000	45 (+2)
Colorado	Spanish, "red"	Centennial State	Denver	104,247	1876	38	2,889,000	6 (+1)
Hawaii	Polynesian word for "homeland"	Aloha State	Honolulu	6,450	1959	50	965,000	2
Idaho	Shoshone, "salmon tribe" or "light on the mountains"	Gem State	Boise	83,557	1890	43	944,000	2
Montana	Spanish, "mountainous"	Treasure State	Helena	147,138	1889	41	787,000	2
Nevada	Spanish, "snow-clad"	Silver State	Carson City	110,540	1864	36	799,000	2 (+1)
New Mexico	Aztec war god, "Mexitil"	Land of Enchantment	Santa Fe	121,666	1912	47	1,300,000	3 (+1)
Oregon	Indian, "beautiful water"	Beaver State	Salem	96,981	1859	33	2,633,000	5 (+1)
Utah	Navajo, "higher up," referring to the Utes	Beehive State	Salt Lake City	84,916	1896	45	1,461,000	3 (+1)
Washington	honors George Washington	Evergreen State	Olympia	68,192	1889	42	4,130,000	8 (+1)
Wyoming	Algonquin, "large prairie"; honors Wyoming Valley, Pennsylvania	Equality State	Cheyenne	97,914	1890	44	471,000	1

PRESIDENTS OF THE UNITED STATES

President	Party	State[2]	Term of Office
George Washington (1732–1799)	None	Virginia	1789–1797
John Adams (1735–1826)	Fed.	Massachusetts	1797–1801
Thomas Jefferson (1743–1826)	Rep.[1]	Virginia	1801–1809
James Madison (1751–1836)	Rep.[1]	Virginia	1809–1817
James Monroe (1758–1831)	Rep.[1]	Virginia	1817–1825
John Quincy Adams (1767–1848)	Rep.[1]	Massachusetts	1825–1829
Andrew Jackson (1767–1845)	Dem.	Tennessee (S.C.)	1829–1837
Martin Van Buren (1782–1862)	Dem.	New York	1837–1841
William Henry Harrison (1773–1841)	Whig	Ohio (Va.)	1841
John Tyler (1790–1862)	Whig	Virginia	1841–1845
James K. Polk (1795–1849)	Dem.	Tennessee (N.C.)	1845–1849
Zachary Taylor (1784–1850)	Whig	Louisiana (Va.)	1849–1850
Millard Fillmore (1800–1874)	Whig	New York	1850–1853
Franklin Pierce (1804–1869)	Dem.	New Hampshire	1853–1857
James Buchanan (1791–1868)	Dem.	Pennsylvania	1857–1861
Abraham Lincoln (1809–1865)	Rep.	Illinois (Ky.)	1861–1865
Andrew Johnson (1808–1875)	Rep.	Tennessee (N.C.)	1865–1869
Ulysses S. Grant (1822–1885)	Rep.	Illinois (Ohio)	1869–1877
Rutherford B. Hayes (1822–1893)	Rep.	Ohio	1877–1881
James A. Garfield (1831–1881)	Rep.	Ohio	1881
Chester A. Arthur (1829–1886)	Rep.	New York (Vt.)	1881–1885
Grover Cleveland (1837–1908)	Dem.	New York (N.J.)	1885–1889
Benjamin Harrison (1883–1901)	Rep.	Indiana (Ohio)	1889–1893
Grover Cleveland (1837–1908)	Dem.	New York (N.J.)	1893–1897
William McKinley (1843–1901)	Rep.	Ohio	1897–1901
Theodore Roosevelt (1858–1919)	Rep.	New York	1901–1909
William Howard Taft (1857–1930)	Rep.	Ohio	1909–1913
Woodrow Wilson (1856–1924)	Dem.	New Jersey (Va.)	1913–1921
Warren G. Harding (1865–1923)	Rep.	Ohio	1921–1923
Calvin Coolidge (1872–1933)	Rep.	Massachusetts (Vt.)	1923–1929
Herbert C. Hoover (1874–1964)	Rep.	California (Iowa)	1929–1933
Franklin Delano Roosevelt (1882–1945)	Dem.	New York	1933–1945
Harry S. Truman (1884–1972)	Dem.	Missouri	1945–1953
Dwight D. Eisenhower (1890–1969)	Rep.	New York (Tex.) Pennsylvania	1953–1961
John F. Kennedy (1917–1963)	Dem.	Massachusetts	1961–1963
Lyndon B. Johnson (1908–1973)	Dem.	Texas	1963–1969
Richard M. Nixon (1913–	Rep.	New York (Calif.)	1969–1974
Gerald R. Ford (1913–	Rep.	Michigan (Neb.)	1974–1977
James E. Carter (1924–	Dem.	Georgia	1977–1981
Ronald W. Reagan (1911–	Rep.	California (Ill.)	1981–

[1]Also called the Democratic-Republican party because in the 1820s it became the Democratic party.
[2]State of residence at time of election. If state of birth is different, it is shown in parentheses.

Glossary

hat, āge, fär; let, ēqual, tėrm;
it, īce; hot, ōpen, ôrder;
oil, out; cup, pùt, rüle;
ch, child; ng, long; sh, she;
th, thin; ᴛʜ, then; zh, measure;

ə represents *a* in about, *e* in taken,
i in pencil, *o* in lemon, *u* in circus.

Page numbers show where each term is
first discussed.

abolitionist   person in the 1830s to 1860s who favored the compulsory ending of slavery in the United States. (p. 316)

absolute monarch   a king or queen who controls all the powers of government. (p. 34)

affirmative action programs   programs that set goals and timetables for the hiring of minority groups and women. (p. 762)

affluence [af′lü əns]   great abundance of material goods; wealth. (p. 697)

amnesty   a general pardon for past offenses against a government. (p. 161)

anarchist [an′ər kist]   person who opposes all forms of government. (p. 469)

annul   destroy the force of; make void; nullify; cancel. (pp. 184, 204)

apportion   divide and give out in fair shares, distribute according to some rule. (p. 193)

apprenticeship   in colonial America, a practice in which a worker, usually a young boy or girl about ten years old, was contracted or bound to work for a master or mistress in exchange for room, board, clothing, and an opportunity to learn a special craft. (p. 99)

armada [är mä′də]   a large fleet of warships. (p. 32)

artillery   large caliber, crew-served mounted firearms, such as cannons. (p. 161)

artisan [ar′tə zən]   skilled worker in an industry or craft, such as carpenter, seamstress, or weaver. (p. 59)

assembly line   row of workers and machines along which work is passed until the final product is made. (p. 595)

balance of power   distribution of strength among independent nations so that no one nation or group of nations becomes strong enough to dominate or conquer the others. (p. 742)

bicameral   having two legislative houses. (p. 120)

bill of attainder   a law passed by a legislature to convict a person of a crime. (p. 206)

Bill of Rights   statement of the fundamental rights of the people of a state or nation; the first ten amendments to the U.S. Constitution. (pp. 183, 207)

bimetallism   the use of both gold and silver as the basis of the money system of a nation. (p. 497)

blacklist   a list of workers who are considered union organizers or troublemakers. (p. 467)

brinkmanship   a policy of going to the brink of nuclear war without going over the edge. (p. 702)

cabinet   group of advisers chosen by the head of a government to aid in administration. (p. 245)

capital   in financial matters, the amount of money or property that a company or a person uses in carrying on a business; resources. (p. 296)

carpetbaggers   northerners who went to the South during the ʀᴇᴄᴏɴsᴛʀᴜᴄᴛɪᴏɴ ᴘᴇʀɪᴏᴅ, so called because some came carrying a type of luggage popular at the time made of carpeting material. (p. 416)

cartel [kär tel′]   an association for establishing a monopoly by price fixing or other means. (p. 759)

caste [kast]   a legally established and inherited position within a society. (p. 104)

caucus [kô kəs]   a private meeting at which a political party selects candidates or decides how it is going to vote. (p. 291)

chattel [chat′l]   property that is not real estate. (p. 102)

Chisholm Trail   a cattle trail which stretched from San Antonio, Texas, to Abilene, Kansas. (p. 430)

civil liberties   the freedom of a person to enjoy the rights guaranteed by the laws or constitution of a state or country without any undue restraint by the government. (p. 206)

civil service   the branch of the government service responsible for the routine maintenance and running of the government. (p. 454)

clipper ship   a large sailing ship built and rigged for speed. (pp. 346, 363)

Communist   member of a revolutionary party who seeks to overthrow private enterprise, or capitalism, and place the ownership, production, and distribution of goods in the hands of the government. (p. 577)

concurrent powers   powers held in common by the state and federal governments. (p. 204)

Confederacy   a group of 11 southern states that seceded from the Union in 1860–1861. (p. 340)

conquistadors [kon kē′stə dôrz]   Spanish conquerors in North and South America during the 1500s. (p. 21)

contraband [kon′trə band]   goods imported or exported contrary to law; smuggled goods. (p. 556)

contract labor   foreign laborers who were brought to the United States under a prearranged work contract with an employer. (p. 445)

corporate colonies   self-governing colonies. (p. 121)

corporation   a group of people who obtain a charter that gives them as a group certain legal rights. In the eyes of the law, the corporation acts as a single person, apart from the people who own it. As a legal entity, it can make its own contracts, buy and sell property, and take legal action in court. (p. 440)

coureurs de bois [kü rər′də bwa′]   runners of the woods, a name given to the colonial French fur traders. (p. 41)

court-packing   appointing members to the Supreme Court who would support certain programs. (p. 646)

craft union   an organization representing one craft or skill, such as carpentry or plumbing. (p. 644)

culture [kul′chər]   all the things that describe how a group of people live, their language, literature, art, religion, the way they organize their lives, how they govern themselves, and how they make a living. (p. 13)

dame school   in the 1700s, a combination day-care and elementary school. (p. 115)

deficit spending   the practice by a government of spending more than it collects in taxes. (p. 729)

deflation [di flā′shən]   reduction of the amount of available money in circulation so that the value of money increases and prices go down. (p. 491)

deism [dē′iz′əm]   a form of Christianity popular among intellectuals in the late 1700s. God was viewed as a "Heavenly Clockmaker." (p. 112)

Democratic party   one of the two main political parties in the United States; in the 1800s, a political party that upheld the doctrine of states' rights and represented the agricultural interests. (p. 293)

depression   in economics, an especially long or severe decline in general business activity. (p. 186)

détente [dā tänt′]   relaxation of tensions between nations. (p. 745)

division of labor   distribution of separate small parts of a process among many workers, as on an ᴀssᴇᴍʙʟʏ ʟɪɴᴇ, in order to facilitate ᴍᴀss ᴘʀᴏᴅᴜᴄᴛɪᴏɴ. (p. 443)

dollar diplomacy   the use of both diplomacy and dollars to protect American interests in foreign countries, particularly in Latin America. (p. 523)

dragoon [drə gün′]   heavily armed, mounted soldier who fought both on foot and on horseback. (p. 340)

due process of law   legal proceedings carried out in accordance with established rules and principles. (p. 70)

electoral college   group of people who elect the U.S. President and Vice-President. (p. 194)

encomienda [en kō myen′da]   large tract of land, which included the Indians who lived on it, that was given by the Spanish ruler to important colonists. (p. 34)

Enlightenment   a philosophical movement in Europe in the 1700s that emphasized rational thought and scientific discovery. (p. 138)

established church church that is a national institution recognized and supported by the government. The Church of England is an established church. (p. 112)

excise tax a tax on the manufacture, sale, or use of certain articles made, sold, or used within a country. (p. 249)

ex post facto **laws** laws that impose punishment for acts that were not crimes at the time they were committed but were declared illegal later. (p. 206)

factions in politics, competing alliances within a party. In the 1790s, political parties were called factions. (pp. 253, 451)

fascism [fash′iz′əm] the principles or methods of a government favoring rule by a dictator, with strong control of industry and labor by the central government, great restrictions upon the freedom of individuals, and extreme nationalism and militarism. (p. 658)

federal having to do with the central, or national, government of the United States. (p. 204)

federalism system of government in which power is shared by a central government and by local governments. (p. 204)

financier [fin′ən sir′] person who is active in matters involving large sums of money. (p. 296)

Forty-Niners the gold seekers who rushed to California in 1849 after gold was discovered there. (p. 346)

freedom of the seas the right of a neutral country to trade with any other country during wartime. (pp. 268, 556)

frigate from the 1600s to the 1800s, a fast, square-rigged, three-masted sailing warship of medium size; in the modern U.S. Navy, large warships equipped with guided missiles. (p. 68)

gag rule in 1836, a rule passed by the Senate to forbid discussion of the issue of abolition in the Congress. (p. 303)

galleon a heavy, square-rigged sailing ship with three or four decks, used especially in the 1400s and 1500s. (p. 32)

ghettos [get′ōz] sections of European towns and cities where Jews were once required to live. The word now means the section of a city where racial or other minority groups are concentrated because they find it difficult to find housing elsewhere. (p. 588)

gold bugs advocates of the gold standard. (p. 497)

gold standard use of gold as the standard of value for the money of a country. The nation's unit of money value is declared by the government to be equal to and exchangeable for a certain amount of gold. (pp. 496, 625)

greenbacks U.S. paper money, having the back printed in green. Greenbacks were originally issued in 1862 without any gold or silver reserve behind them. (p. 398)

Gross National Product (GNP) value of all goods and services produced in a nation during a certain period of time. (p. 648)

habitant [à bē tän′] a tenant in New France who held one of the smaller parcels of land which was part of the estate of the SEIGNEUR. (p. 42)

Hessian [hesh′ən] a German soldier hired by the British to fight against the Americans in the Revolutionary War. (p. 166)

hippies commonly used term in the 1960s and 1970s to describe people who rejected conventional standards of dress and behavior. (p. 741)

holding company a means of business consolidation in which the holding company owns stocks or bonds of other companies and often controls them. (p. 442)

Hoovervilles makeshift shacks made of packing crates, boxes, and scrap lumber that served as residences for thousands of unemployed and homeless citizens in the 1930s. (p. 612)

impeach accuse a public official of wrong conduct during office before a competent tribunal. (pp. 208, 414)

imperialism policy of extending the rule of one country over other countries or colonies, usually for the purpose of controlling raw materials, markets, or military bases. (p. 506)

impressment seizing of property for public use or of men to serve in the armed forces. (p. 250)

inalienable rights basic rights that cannot be taken away. (p. 120)

indentured servant a person who signed an agreement to work for three to seven years in return for passage to America. (pp. 48, 99)

industrial union an organization made up of all the workers in one industry, such as all the workers in mining or automobile manufacturing, regardless of the particular job each worker holds. (p. 644)

inflation [in flā′shən] a general rise in prices resulting from an increase in the amount of money or credit. (pp. 296, 491)

initiative and referendum initiative is a procedure which allows citizens to introduce bills in Congress or state legislatures by petition. Referendum is a process which allows voters to reverse any action by Congress or state legislatures. (p. 494)

injunction [in jungk′shən] a formal order from a court of law ordering a person or group to do something or to stop doing something. (pp. 470, 577)

installment plan a plan permitting people to buy an item for a small down payment, with the balance to be paid in weekly or monthly payments. (p. 597)

interlocking directorate a method of business consolidation in which the same group of directors takes control of several companies. The companies remain legally separate but can operate as one large business. (p. 442)

investor person who invests money. (p. 296)

isolationism principle or policy of avoiding involvement in European affairs, especially in the years between World War I and World War II. (pp. 553, 661)

isthmus [is′məs] a narrow strip of land with water on both sides, connecting two larger bodies of land. (p. 519)

judicial review power of the Supreme Court to declare acts of Congress or actions of the President unconstitutional. (p. 208)

judiciary system of courts of law of a country. (p. 184)

joint-stock company a business organization formed to finance new settlements in America in which many individuals could invest small amounts of money and thereby share their resources as well as the financial risks. (p. 44)

laissez faire [les′ā fer′] the belief that government should not interfere with business activity. From a French phrase, meaning "to let one do." (p. 460)

latitude lines imaginary lines which circle the globe running parallel to the Equator. Also called parallels. (p. 9)

laws of supply and demand the "law of supply" is an economic pattern wherein suppliers usually want to produce more of an item as the price increases and less as the price declines. The "law of demand" means that as the price of a good or service increases, the quantity people will buy usually declines, and vice versa. (pp. 489, 629–630)

limited liability a term which means the owners of a corporation cannot be held legally liable for the debts of the business. If the company fails, the stockholders lose only the money they have invested in shares of stock. (p. 440)

longitude lines imaginary lines on the globe which run between the North Pole and the South Pole. Also called meridians. (p. 10)

machine [mə shēn′] in politics, an organized group that controls the activities of a political party. (p. 451)

Manifest Destiny in the 1840s, the belief that the United States was destined to bring progress and democracy to the Western Hemisphere by territorial expansion. (p. 331)

man-of-war, *pl.* **men-of-war** term used mainly in former times to describe a warship; combatant warship of a recognized navy. (p. 32)

manumit release from slavery. (p. 213)

massive retaliation the idea of relying on nuclear weapons in case of war. (p. 702)

mass production the making of goods in large quantities, especially by machinery. (p. 443)

McCarthyism the use of unsubstantiated accusations of treason and support of communism. (p. 698)

mercantilism the economic system of Europe in the 1500s and 1600s in which a nation tried to maintain a favorable balance of trade by exporting as much as possible and importing as little as possible, so that gold would be brought into the country rather than drained out. (p. 84)

mercenary soldier serving for pay in a foreign army. (p. 166)

middle passage the slave trade between Africa and the Americas. (p. 102)

midnight judges in 1800, Federalist judges of the circuit and lower courts whose commissions were signed by President John Adams the day and evening of his last day in office, so that the Federalists might secure the judicial branch for their party. (p. 258)

militia citizen soldiers. (p. 122)

monopoly the exclusive control of a commodity or service. (p. 441)

mortgage [môr′gij] a legal right or claim to a piece of property given in return for a loan. (p. 488)

muckrakers writers in the era of PROGRESSIVISM who exposed social and political evils. (p. 529)

nationalism devotion to one's nation; the doctrine that national interests and security are more important than international considerations; the desire for national independence. (p. 553)

nativism prejudice against immigrants. (p. 445)

NATO the North Atlantic Treaty Organization formed in 1949 as a military alliance between the United States and 11 countries of Western Europe. (p. 690)

Nazi party, Nazism the National Socialist party of Adolf Hitler, German dictator. Its doctrines and practices included suppression of civil liberties, militarism, racism, anti-Semitism, and quest for world conquest by the German "master race." (p. 659)

noninvolvement, policy of traditional U.S. policy of avoiding alliances with European nations. (p. 506)

nullify make not binding; render void; cancel. (pp. 257, 295)

OPEC (Organization of Petroleum Exporting Countries) an organization of countries exporting petroleum who banded together to control oil prices. (p. 759)

Oregon Trail a route used by settlers beginning in the 1840s that began at Independence, Missouri, and continued 2,000 miles across the Great Plains and the Rocky Mountains to Fort Vancouver in Oregon, headquarters of the Hudson's Bay Company. (p. 334)

outflank go or extend beyond the far right or far left side of an opposing army. (p. 391)

panic a widespread fear of the collapse of the financial system that leads to hasty, ill-advised attempts to avoid loss by turning property into cash, withdrawing money from banks, etc. (pp. 280, 297)

parity base a favorable period for an agricultural commodity which can be used as the yardstick for comparison in future years. (p. 642)

Patriot an American colonist who supported the movement for independence. (p. 153)

patronage the granting of government jobs in return for support. (pp. 122, 294, 454)

patroon [pə trün′] the owner of a large tract of land in the Hudson Valley. (p. 43)

Pennsylvania Dutch German settlers in colonial Pennsylvania and their descendants. Also, their dialect of German with English intermixed. (p. 88)

Piedmont [pēd′mont] foothills that extend between the Appalachian Mountains and the Atlantic Coastal Plain. They begin near the coast of New York and run southwest to Alabama. (p. 95)

Pilgrims members of a small community of religious exiles from England who had been living in Holland. They were offered the opportunity to emigrate to Virginia by the London Company. In 1620, they sailed for America on the *Mayflower,* landing instead at Plymouth where they founded the first permanent colony in New England. (p. 61)

pocket veto method of vetoing a bill presented within 10 days of the end of a session of Congress. If the President does not sign the bill before Congress adjourns, it does not become a law. (p. 409)

pool a form of merger in the 1870s and 1880s in which corporations in the same industries united together and operated as one large business. They divided up the market, agreed on rates and charges, and shared their profits. (p. 440)

popular sovereignty a doctrine which meant letting the voters who lived in a territory decide whether or not to allow slavery there. (pp. 348, 366)

power of the purse control of taxation. (p. 183)

presidio [pri sid′ē ō] a military post or fortified area of a settlement in Spanish America. (p. 39)

primogeniture [prī′mə jen′ə chùr] the right of inheritance or succession by the first-born, especially the inheritance of a family estate by the eldest son. (p. 92)

privateer privately owned warship. (p. 251)

progressivism a reform movement of the early 20th century that worked to improve various aspects of American life such as city and state governments, conservation, working conditions, and regulation of certain business practices. (p. 528)

proprietary colony the property of an individual or group of individuals who had been granted American lands by the Crown of England. (p. 121)

protective tariff tax on imported goods to protect local industries. (p. 187)

protectionist supporter of a high protective tariff. (p. 460)

protectorate [prə tek′tər it] a weak country under the protection and partial control of a strong country. (p. 510)

public facilities facilities which include both private and public services, such as railroads, restaurants, schools, parks, theaters, that are open to the general public. (p. 212)

pueblo [pweb′lō] an Indian village consisting of houses built of stone and adobe, often several stories high; also a member of any of a group of Indian tribes of the American Southwest living in these villages. (p. 15)

pump priming pouring a small amount of water down the pump shaft so that the pump washer will seal and bring water from the well. President Roosevelt applied this idea to the economy in 1933, when he hoped that a small amount of government spending would create additional spending in other areas. (p. 629)

Puritans members of a Protestant group in the Church of England during the 1500s and 1600s who wanted simpler forms of worship and stricter morals. (p. 59)

Quakers [kwā′kərs] members of a small Protestant sect that were persecuted in the mid-1600s because of their opposition to the Anglican Church. (p. 69)

quorum number of members of an assembly required on hand to carry on legal business. (p. 197)

ratification adoption or formal approval. (p. 196)

real income income adjusted for inflation. (p. 412)

recession a period of temporary business reduction, shorter and less extreme than a depression. (p. 576)

Reconstruction period the years following the Civil War between 1865 and 1877. (p. 405)

red a COMMUNIST or other Marxist radical, so called because of their red flag, which symbolizes Marxist revolution. (p. 577)

Renaissance [ren′ə säns′] period of time when a great revival of art and learning took place in Europe. (p. 4)

reparations payments made by a defeated country for the devastation of territory during war. (p. 564)

Republican party in 1792, persons who followed the Jefferson-Madison group, known as the Jeffersonians, or Democratic-Republican party; in 1854, a new party which opposed the expansion of slavery, made of northern Whigs, antislavery Democrats, and Free-Soilers. (pp. 253, 367)

reservations areas of land set aside by the U.S. government for Indian tribes. (p. 436)

royal colony a colony ruled directly by the Crown according to the laws of England. (p. 121)

rugged individualism strong, hardy self-reliance. (p. 613)

salutary neglect English policy of letting the 13 colonies develop without close regulation. (p. 141)

scalawags white southerners who cooperated with the new governments of the RECONSTRUCTION PERIOD. (p. 416)

Scots-Irish the largest immigrant group to America in the early 18th century. They were Scottish Presbyterians who had colonized northern Ireland in the 1500s, and were persecuted by the English government. (p. 88)

sea dog another name for dogfish, which are several species of small shark. English sailors who plundered Spanish ships were called "sea dogs." (p. 29)

segregate separate the races. (pp. 103, 418)

seigneur [sā nyėr′] a large landowner or noble who received land in New France from the French ruler. (p. 42)

separation of powers dividing of powers within one government. (p. 208)

sharecropping system a system in which a farm family made a contract with a landlord, agreeing to pay for the use of the land with a share of the crop. The landlord provided the tools and seed, a mule, and a house or shack for the TENANT FARMER to live in. (p. 419)

shifting cultivation a system also called slash-and-burn agriculture in which farmers clear a field by slashing tree trunks, allowing the trees to die. The trunks are burned and the wood ash is used to fertilize the soil. In a few years, the soil loses its fertility and the farmers move to another area to repeat the same process. (p. 20)

sit-down strike a strike in which the workers refuse to leave their places of employment, thus keeping the employer from bringing in non-union workers to replace them. (p. 644)

sit-ins protest demonstrations in the 1960s in which blacks and whites sat down at segregated lunch counters and refused to move until the blacks were served. (p. 725)

slander spread false statements in order to harm a person's reputation. (p. 207)

slave codes laws which regulated all aspects of the institution of slavery. (pp. 102, 411)

social contract in the 1700s, a new theory of government in England, in which the contract required the ruler to protect the property and the lives of the people. In return, the citizens were obliged to be loyal, to pay taxes, and to obey laws. (p. 119)

Social Darwinism a philosophy which held that success came to the deserving in society. (pp. 458, 511)

Socialist supporter of an economic and social system based on public ownership of land, factories, and other means of production. (p. 471)

social security program government system of old-age, disability, and other benefits financed by employees, employers, and taxpayers. (p. 616)

sovereignty [sov′rən tē] independence; complete control of a state over its own affairs. (p. 193)

speakeasy secret place where alcoholic liquors were sold contrary to law. (p. 586)

specie [spē′shē] money in the form of coins; metal money. (p. 296)

speculation buying and selling when there is a large risk, with the hope of making a profit from future price changes. (p. 94)

squatter a person who settles on another's land without legal right. (p. 67)

stagflation stagnation, or business slowdown, plus inflation. (p. 761)

stock certificates of partial ownership in a corporation. (p. 440)

subsidies grant or contribution of money, especially one made by a government. (p. 428)

subsistence economy economy of small-scale farmers, hunters, or gatherers who consume all that they produce. (p. 82)

suburbia suburbs, or residential sections near the boundary of a city or town. (p. 712)

suffrage the right to vote; also called the franchise. (p. 214)

sumptuary laws laws which regulated the consumption by workers of various luxuries, such as silk, lace, or gold buttons. In colonial America, it was feared the rich and their servants would soon dress alike. (p. 99)

syncopate [sing′kə pāt] begin a note on an unaccented beat and hold it into an accented one; play in a "swing" style. (p. 589)

tabloid a newspaper, usually smaller and easier to hold than the ordinary size newspaper page, that has many pictures, short articles, and large, often sensational, headlines. (p. 578)

tariff tax on imported goods. (p. 187)

temperance movement against the use of alcoholic beverages; being moderate in the use of alcoholic drinks. (p. 303)

tenant farmer a farmer who raises crops and lives on land belonging to another person, paying as rent a share of the crops. (p. 58)

Tory an American who favored continued British rule of the 13 colonies; a Loyalist. (p. 293)

trunk lines major routes of a railroad. (p. 429)

trust a common type of business consolidation in the 1880s and early 1890s. A trust could operate as one giant company, control the production and price of some commodity, and reduce or eliminate competition. (p. 441)

Underground Railroad term used to describe the escape routes used by the blacks from the slave states to Canada. (p. 365)

unicameral having one legislative house. (p. 120)

urbanization the growth of cities. (p. 475)

utopian societies groups formed during the 1840s and 1850s, from New England to Texas that tried to establish perfect societies. (p. 309)

veto the right or power to prevent an action proposed by a lawmaking body. (p. 120)

viceroy [vīs′roi] governor of a country or province who rules as the monarch's representative. (p. 34)

vigilante [vij′ə lan′tē] member of a self-appointed and unauthorized group of citizens organized to punish law-breakers or unpopular citizens. (p. 190)

virtual representation the English view that the House of Commons was pledged to represent fairly *all* Englishmen and women, regardless of where they lived or if they had the right to vote. (p. 142)

walking cities cities that were small enough to permit people to walk wherever they had to go. (p. 476)

wampum beads made from shells, often used by the colonists for money in the 1600s. (p. 94)

Whig party in 1834, an American political party, formed in opposition to the Democratic party, led by the wealthiest city people. (p. 300)

writ of *habeas corpus* a court order requiring that a prisoner be brought before a court for the purpose of determining whether the accused is being held legally. (p. 206)

yeoman farmers farmers who owned their own small farms, as opposed to tenant farmers whose farms were owned by others. (p. 63)

Index

Presbyterians, 88, 111, 114, 333, 541
Prescott [pres'kət], Samuel (1751–1777?), 150, *map* 151
President(s), election of, 194–195, 254, 291; impeachment of, 208, 414; legislative role of, 211; powers of, 208–210, 228–230, 533, 538–539; succession, 240; term of, 193, 664; title of, 244; war powers, 206, 414, 418, 733. *See also* Elections, national
Presidios [pri sid'ē ōs], 37, 39, 338
Presley, Elvis (1935–1977), 712, 774, 779
Presque Isle [pre skil], Pennsylvania, 272
Press, 208, 319, 370–371, 747; freedom of, 183, 206–207. *See also* Magazines; Newspapers; Radio; Television
Preston, Thomas (1824–1891), 144–145
Primary elections, 531, 541
Princeton [prins'tən], N.J., Washington at, 166–167, *map* 166
Princeton University, 114, 360, 541
Prisons, 302, 314–315, 320
Privateers, 151, 251, 276–277
Proclamation Line of 1763, 137, *map* 140
Proclamation of Neutrality, 251
Progress, faith in, 313, 511, 528. *See also* Technology
Progressive party, 541
Progressivism [prə gres'ə viz'əm], and Cannon controversy, 539–540; and child labor, 543; and corruption, 527–531; and minorities, 544; and tariffs, 538, 583
Prohibition, 238, 586–587, 616; crime, 586–587; gangs, 586; Harding and, 586; payoffs, 583; repealed, **239**, 587; at state level, 315
Promontory [prom'ən tôr'ē] Point, Utah, 428
Property and society, 117, 214, 577; among Indians, 15, 123, 188, 439
Proprietary [prə pri'ə ter'ē] colonies, 120–121
Prosperity, 608, 610, 712, 717; problems of, 528; and religious attitudes, 112
Protectorate [prə tek'tər it], *def.* 510
Protestant(s), in England, 29, 111; and social issues, 480, 586. *See also* Catholics and Protestants; denominations
Protests, 142, 277, 545, 557–558, 730. *See also* Demonstrations; Public opinion; subjects
Prudhoe [prəd'hō] Bay, 537
Prussia, 135, 282
Public health, 460, 477–479
Public Housing Act of 1949, 685
Public opinion, 208, 259, 533–534, 539, 577, 625, 705–706; and wars, 251, 513, 516, 556–558, 561, 664. *See also* Compromise of 1850; Congress, pay raises; Demonstrations; Protests
Public Works Administration, 629
Public works programs, 613, 628–629, 641, 723
Pueblo [pweb'lō], Colo., 566
Pueblo Bonito [pweb'lō bə nē'tō], N.M., 38
Pueblo Indians, 36, 38
Pueblos, 15, 38, *illus.* 38
Puerto Rico [pwer'tō rē'kō], 33, 282, 512, 514, 516–517, 523, 762–763
Pulaski, Count Casimir (1748?–1779), 169
Pullman, George (1831–1897), 431
Pullman strike, 470
Pure Food and Drug Act, 534
Puritans, 70, 73, 110, 112, 114, 119, 123, 292, 314, 543

Qaddafi [gut dä'fē], Muammar el- (1941–), 767
Quadruple Alliance, 282
Quaker(s), and abolition, 103, 214, 320–321; and child labor, 543; in colonial America, 70–72, 88; and education, 115; Indian policy, 123; meeting house, *illus.* 112; pacifism of, 70; persecuted, 111; and religious tolerance, 111
"Quarantine Speech," 662
Quartering Acts, 141–142, 147
Quasi-war with France, 254–255
Quebec, Can., 28, *map* 30, 40, 135, 147, 163
Quebec Act, 146–147, *map* 146
Queen Anne's War, 125
Quinault [kwi nôlt'] Indians, 16
Quincy Market, 219
Quotas, immigration, 580; wartime, 560, 660

Racism, 445, 511–512, 545, 580–582, 687. *See also* Lynchings; Riots
Rackham [rak'əm], "Calico Jack," 277

Radcliffe [rad'klif] College, 473
Radical Republicans, and A. Johnson, 410–415; and Lincoln, 388, 401, 407, 409; and Reconstruction, 415–418
Radicals, 578–580
Radio, *illus.* 612, 624, 635, 745; impact of, 599
Railroad(s), 372, *illus.* 426, 427–433, *illus.* 429, 460, 479, 530, 550, 671; and agriculture, 337, 362, 489, 492; bankruptcies, 495; and circus, 432–433, *illus.* 432; companies, 431; construction, 361, *illus.* 426, 427–433, *illus.* 429, 445; impact of, 326–327, 360; and Indians, 436–438passim; and industry, 431–432, 439, 440; and labor, 445, 467–469; land grants to, 428–429, 460; during Reconstruction, 408, 416; rise of, 361–363
Raleigh [rô'lē], Sir Walter (1552?–1618), 31
Rall [räl], Johann Gottlieb (1720?–1776), 166
Ranching, 33, 336–337, 435, 438
Randolph, Asa Philip (1889–1979), 687
Randolph, Edmund (1753–1813), 192, 196, 246
Rationing, 671, 684
Ray, James Earl (1928–), 732
Rayburn [rā'bərn], Sam (1882–1961), 710
REA. *See* Rural Electrification Administration
Read, Mary (?–1720), 95, 277
Readmission of states, 410, 413, 416, *map* 420, *table* 421
Reagan, Ronald (1911–), 758, 769–770
Realpolitik [rā äl'pō li tēk'], 742, 765
Reconstruction, election fraud in, 419; end of, 420–421; under A. Johnson, 410–414; legislatures, 416–417, *illus.* 417; under Lincoln, 406–407, 409–410; military, 414–421; Radical, 415–418; reversed, 474; and women's rights, 417
Reconstruction Finance Corporation, 613, 624–625
Red Cross, 561
Redemptioners, 100
Red scare, 577–579, 699
Redwoods, 536
Reed, Walter (1851–1902), 522
Referendum [ref'ə ren'dəm], 475, 494, 531, 541
Reform movement, 302–303, 313–319, 458–461, 480, 492, 527–531, 585; decline of, 576–583; and L. Johnson, 729–731; labor, 466–471; Populist, 494–499passim. *See also* Abolition; Populist party; Progressivism; Religion; Women's rights
Refugees, Civil War, 408, 411; Indian, 19, 299; Loyalist, *illus.* 177; Vietnam, 734; World War I, 608, 613
Regulation of business and industry, 541, 623–625, 758. *See also* Antitrust; Monopolies; Trade and Commerce; Trusts
Regulator movement, 124, 164
Religion, and abolition, 317; in colonial America, 110–114; and education, 114, 314; freedom of, 71, 73, 77, 111, 147, 234; and government, 112, 121; and pacifism, 70, 734; persecutions, 70, 88, 111; and presidential elections, 585; and reform, 308–311, 314, 543; revival of, 113–114, 303, 308–309, 311, 317. *See also* Catholics and Protestants; Jews; Roman Catholics; Toleration; denominations
Relocation camps, 671
Renaissance [ren'ə säns'], European, 4–5; Harlem, 602–603
Representative government, colonial, 70, 75, 119–121, 124; and Constitution, 193, 198
Republican Motherhood, 320, 472
Republican party, 388, 455, 686; ascendancy of, 582–585; birth of, 366–373; and blacks, 420, 646; and business, 688; and farming, 493; Independent, 451, 458; and A. Johnson, 411; on League of Nations, 566–567; and J. McCarthy, 699–700; and New Deal, 634, 646; and Populism, 495; Radical, 388, 401, 407, 409–418; and reform, 458, 460; scandals in, 452; silver platform, 497. *See also* Elections, national; names, subjects
Republican party (Jeffersonian), 253–257, 277–279, 292
Resettlement Administration, 642–643
Reservations, 436, *map* 437, 439, 647, 763
Reserved powers, 205
Revenue sharing, 745
Revere, Paul, 99, *illus.* 145, 150, *map* 151
Revolutionary War, *map* 162, 166, *illus.* 167, *illus.* 174; army, 166, 168–170; black Americans in, 145, 152; campaigns, *map* 166, *map* 173, in Canada, 162; casualties, 168–170, *chart*

396; causes of, 135–137, 140–147; espionage, 170, 173; finances and debts, 170, 176, 187; France in, 168–169, 171, 175, 176, *map* 172; guerrilla warfare, 174; Hessians in, 166; and independence, 168, 182; Indians in, 167, 176; in the Middle Colonies, 164–169, *map* 168, *map* 172; morale, 166, 168–169; naval forces, 163–165, *illus.* 165, 171, *map* 172, 175; in New England, 160–163; in New Jersey, 166–167; peace treaty, 176–177; perceived goal of, 198; in the South, 171–174, *illus.* 174; women in, 169–170
Revolution(s), in Europe, 363; French, 250; Russian, 559, 577
Rhee [rē], Syngman, 691
Rhineland, 87, 659, *map* 660
Rhode Island, 99, 111, 145, 187, 303; colonial government, 120–121; and ratification of Constitution, 199; and slavery, 213–214
Rice, 74, *map* 88, 93–94, 129, 356, *map* 358
Richmond, Va., 98, 139, 317, 477; Civil War, 382–384, *map* 386, 391, 394–395; Confederate capital, 380; Reconstruction, 408
"Rights of Englishmen," 119, 207
Riis [rēs], Jacob (1849–1914), 479
Rio Grande, 36, 341–342, *map* 343
Riots, 90, 116, 319; anti-immigrant, 309; draft, 397; race, 397, 420, 588, 731–732, 740
Rivera [ri ver'ə], Diego (1886–1957), 641
Roads, 278, 283–285, 408, 416, 596; New Deal, 629, 641. *See also* Highways
Roanoke [rō'ə nōk] Island, *map* 30, 31
Roberts, Bartholomew (1682?–1722), 276
Robinson, Edward Arlington (1869–1935), 602
Rochambeau [rō shäm bō'], comte Jean-Baptiste (1725–1807), *map* 172
Rochester, N.Y., 318, 322
Rockefeller, John Davison (1839–1937), 128, 441, 529, 578
Rockefeller, Nelson Aldrich (1908–1979), 729
Rocky Mountains, 267, 334, 336, 434
Roebling [rōb'ling], John (1806–1869), 570
Roebling, Washington (1837–1926), 570
Rolfe, John (1585–1622), 47, 92
Roman Catholic(s), in Canada, 147; Church and diplomacy, 21, 29; in colonial America, 71–72, 111; missionaries and monks, 37, 39, 338; protection of Indians, 34; sentiment against, 309, 458, 585, 727; in Texas, 338–339. *See also* Catholics and Protestants
Romania, 553–554, 689
Rommel [rom'əl], Erwin (1891–1944), 666, 668
Roosevelt, Eleanor (1884–1962), 622, 641, 643
Roosevelt, Franklin Delano (1882–1945), *illus.* 617, 621, 665, 680, 681; brain trust, 622; elections, 616–617, 645, 672; "fireside chats," Four Freedoms, 667; Hundred Days, 622–623; and Japanese relocation, 671; and neutrality, 662–663; *quoted* 623, 667, 716; and Supreme Court, 645–646; and Wilson, 681; and World War II, 666, 669–670; at Yalta, 670. *See also* New Deal
Roosevelt, Theodore (1858–1919), *illus.* 540; and African game-hunting, 538, 540; Bull Moose, 541; career, 511, 513, 514; and Congress, 533; and conservation, 534–535; and expansionism, 511, 516; foreign policy of, 522–523; and New Deal, 623; and Panama Canal, 521; presidency, 521–523, 531–535, 538; and the press, 529; *quoted* 513, 531, 541; on racial equality, 544–545; and reform, 531; Rough Riders, 514, 532; in Spanish-American War, 513–514; and strikes, 533; and W. Taft, 538–540
Roosevelt Corollary, 522–523
Rosenberg, Julius (1918–1953) and Ethel Greenglass (1915–1953), 691
Rosecrans [rō'zən krans], William, 394
Rosenman, Samuel I. (1896–1973), 622
Rough Riders, 514, 532
Rousseau, Jean-Baptiste (1712–1778), 112
Royal African Company, 101
Royal Air Force, 664
Royal Navy, 147, 152
Ruef, Abraham (1864–1936), 453
Rule of '56, 268
Rules Committee, 539
Rum, 84, 314; Romanism, and rebellion, 458
Rural America, blacks in, 646; communications in, 431; culture of, 600–601; politics of, 585; population of, 601
Rural Electrification Administration, 642
Rush, Benjamin (1745–1813), *quoted* 203
Rush-Bagot Agreement, 281

Acknowledgments

Quoted Material

19 *The Letter of Columbus on the Discovery of America* with introduction by Wilberforce Eames. (New York 1892). **100** Gottfried Mittelberger. *Journey to Pennsylvania in the Year 1750 and Return to Germany in the Year 1754;* tr. from the German by Carl Theo. Eban. Philadelphia: John Joseph McVey, n.d. **102** Helen T. Catterall, ed., *Judicial Cases Concerning American Slavery and the Negro* (5 vols., Washington, Carnegie Institution of Washington, 1926–1936), I, 77. **116** From Philip Fithian's letter to the Reverend Enoch Green, December 1, 1773, *Journal and Letters of Philip Vickers Fithian*, edited by Hunter D. Farish. Reprinted by permission of The Colonial Williamsburg Foundation. **175** "The World Turned Upside Down" by J. F. Lehmeier. **323** Carrie Chapman Catt and Nettie Rogers Shuler, *Woman Suffrage and Politics* (New York, 1923), p. 107. **346** From "An Account of a Trip Across the Plains in 1855" by Lydia Milner Waters, *Quarterly of the Society of California Pioneers*, Vol. VI, No. 2, June 1929. Reprinted by permission. **409** Mary Boykin Chesnut, *A Diary from Dixie*. New York: D. Appleton and Company, 1905. **481** Jane Addams, *Twenty Years at Hull House*. New York: The Macmillan Company, 1910. **490** L. Frank Baum, *The Wizard of Oz*. New York: The Macmillan Company, 1962, p. 3. **491** "The Farmer Is the Man" by Tex Fletcher, Leonard Whitcup and Richard S. Kuhn. Used by permission of Broadway Music Corporation. **602** "First Fig" by Edna St. Vincent Millay from *Collected Poems*, Harper & Row. Copyright 1922, 1950 by Edna St. Vincent Millay. Reprinted by permission of Norma Millay Ellis. **602** From "Hollow Men" in *Collected Poems 1909–1962* by T. S. Eliot. Reprinted by permission of Harcourt Brace Jovanovich and Faber and Faber Ltd. **611** Copyright © 1932 by the New York Times Company. Reprinted by permission. **642** "Brother, Can You Spare a Dime?" by E. Y. Harburg. Copyright 1932 (Renewed) by Warner Bros. Music, Inc. Reprinted by permission of Warner Bros. Music, Inc. and Chappell Music. All rights reserved. **650** Adaptation of "Political Spectrum Analogy" by David Russell from *Social Education*, October 1980. Adapted with permission of the National Council for the Social Studies and the author. **725** Abridged from *I Have a Dream* by Martin Luther King, Jr. Copyright © 1963 by Martin Luther King, Jr. Reprinted by permission of Joan Daves.

Illustrations

The abbreviations indicate the position of the illustrations on the page: *t* is top, *b* is bottom, *c* is center, *l* is left, *r* is right.

Cover Courtesy West Point Museum Collection, U.S. Military Academy. Photograph by Robert W. Caudy. **Back Cover:** Mastai Collection. **v** Noval after Nicholas Garrison: *View of Bethlehem, Pennsylvania, 1757*. Prints Division. The New York Public Library. Astor, Lenox and Tilden Foundations. **vi** Courtesy of The New-York Historical Society. **viii** State Historical Society of Wisconsin. **x** T. Lesley/Black Star. **xii** A. E. Nordenskiold, Facsimile—*Atlas to the Early History of Cartography*. Stockholm, 1889, The Newberry Library. **xiii** The National Maritime Museum, London. **xiv** Joseph F. Viesti. **xv** Anonymous collector.

1 Courtesy Victoria and Albert Museum. **2** Erich Lessing/Magnum. **5** The Granger Collection, New York. **8** University Museum of National Antiquities, Oslo, Norway. **9** Joel Gordon 1980. **10** (t) Historical Pictures Service, Inc., Chicago. (b) The Granger Collection, New York. **13** Courtesy National Museums of Canada. **15** Courtesy of Field Museum of Natural History, Chicago. **16** Courtesy of Museum of the American Indian, Heye Foundation. **17** Courtesy of National Collection of Fine Art, Smithsonian Institution. **18** Courtesy National Gallery of Canada, Ottawa. **19** Edwin Tunis, *Indians*. **20** Historical Pictures Service, Inc., Chicago. **26** Robert Frerck, Odyssey Productions. **29** The Granger Collection, New York. **36, 37, 38** Robert Frerck, Odyssey Productions. **40–41** Courtesy of the Newberry Library, Chicago. **41** (r) Thomas Gilcrease Institute of American History and Art. **42** New York Public Library, Rare Book Division, Astor, Lenox and Tilden Foundation. **43** New York Public Library, Stokes Collection, Astor, Lenox and Tilden Foundation. **45** New York Public Library, Rare Book Division, Astor, Lenox and Tilden Foundation. **46** (inset) Courtesy of the Newberry Library, Chicago. **46–47** Sidney C. King. **48** John R. Freeman and Company. **49** The Granger Collection, New York. **52–53** Robert Frerck, Odyssey Productions. **55** Philadelphia Museum of Art. **56** John Lewis Stage. **60** Culver Pictures. **62–63** Cal Sacks. **65** (t) Reproduced by permission of The World Publishing Company and Curtis Brown, Ltd. from *Colonial Living* by Edwin Tunis. Copyright © 1957 by Edwin Tunis. **71** Abby Aldrich Rockefeller Folk Art Museum. **75** New York Public Library, Prints Division, I.N. Phelps Stokes Collection of American Historical Prints. **77** Bonoeil. Letter to the Earl of Southhampton, 1622. **80** John Lewis Stage. **83** Colonial Williamsburg Foundation. **86** City Art Museum of St. Louis, Missouri. **90** (t,b) The New-York Historical Society. **91** Chandler Wedding Tapestry, Courtesy American Antiquarian Society. **92** New York Public Library. Map Room. **93** Metropolitan Museum of Art. Gift of Edgar William and Bernice Garbisch, 1963. **94** Il Gazettieri Americano, Livorno, 1763. Vol. 1. **96** Chuck Rydlewski. **98** The New-York Historical Society. **103** (l) The Granger Collection, New York. (r) New York Public Library, Schomburg Center for Research in Black Culture. Astor, Lenox and Tilden Foundation. **104** Courtesy of The Essex Institute, Salem, Mass. **105** Abby Aldrich Rockefeller Folk Art Center. **108** John Lewis Stage. **111** Courtesy The Newport Historical Society. **112** Courtesy Museum of Fine Arts, Boston. **113** The Historical Society of York County, York, Pa. **115** Historical Pictures Service, Chicago. **117** Colonial Williamsburg Foundation. **118** The Historical Society of York County, York, Pa. **121** (t) Historical Pictures Service, Chicago (b) John Lewis Stage. **125** The Franklin Institute, Philadelphia. **128–129** Freelance Photographers Guild. **131** *Presentation Sword and Scabbard*. Thomas and Andrew E. Warner. Museum of Fine Arts, Boston. **132** Courtesy The Rhode Island Historical Society. **136** Colonial Williamsburg Foundation. **139** University of Virginia Library. **141** Library of Congress. **142** Metropolitan Museum of Art, Bequest of Charles Allen Munn, 1924. **145** American Antiquarian Society. **158** John Lewis Stage. **163** Anne S.K. Brown Military Collection, Brown University Library. **165** Courtesy Office of the Architects of the Capitol. U.S. Capitol Historical Society. **167** Metropolitan Museum of Art, Gift of John Stewart Kennedy, 1897. **168** Bettmann Archive. **171** Courtesy United States Naval Academy Museum. **173** Bettmann Archive. **174** Cliche Musees Nationaux, Paris. **177** Public Archives of Canada. **180** John Lewis Stage. **184** New York Public Library, Rare Book Division. **188** (all) United States Department of Agriculture. **190** New York Public Library. **195** Courtesy Office of the Architects of the Capitol. U.S. Capitol Historical Society. **198** Brown Brothers. **199** The New-York Historical Society. **202** Office of Charles and Ray Eames/National Archive. **205** The New-York Historical Society. **211** Wide World. **212** The New York Times. **213** New York Public Library, Astor, Lenox and Tilden Foundation. **218–219** Peter Gridley/FPG. **220** Angel Weathervane (MASS-ME-19) National Gallery of Art, Washington. Index of American Design. **242** Joseph F. Viesti. **245** The New-York Historical Society. **249** The Granger Collection, New York. **251** New York State Historical Association, Cooperstown, NY. **255** U.S. Bureau of Engraving and Printing. **262** Whitney Museum of American Art. **265** U.S. Bureau of Engraving and Printing. **267** American Museum of Natural History. **269** The New-York Historical Society. **270** U.S. Bureau of Engraving and Printing. **273** The New-York Historical Society. **278** U.S. Bureau of Engraving and Printing. **279** Metropolitan Museum of Art. **283** H. Armstrong Roberts. **284** Maryland Historical Society. **288** Collection of the Chester County Historical Society, West Chester, Pa. **291** Historical Society of Pennsylvania. **293, 295** U.S. Bureau of Engraving and Printing. **296** The New-York Historical Society. **298–299** Philbrook Art Center, Tulsa, Oklahoma. **300** U.S. Bureau of Engraving and Printing. **301** (t) Ladies Hermitage Association, Hermitage, Tenn. (b) Courtesy of Smithsonian Institution. **302** Yale University Art Gallery. Mabel Brady Garvan Collection. **306** Henry Groskisky. **309** New York Public Library, Astor, Lenox and Tilden Foundation. **312** Metropolitan Museum of Art, Bequest of Maria DeWitt Jesup, 1915. **315, 318, 320** New York Public Library, Astor, Lenox and Tilden Foundation. **321** (all) The Sophia Smith Collection (Women's History Archive) Smith College, Northampton, Mass. **322** Historical Pictures Service, Chicago. **326–327** Wm. Franklin McMahon. **328** Mastai Collection. **330** Joel Monture-Knecht. **333** Collection of Everett D. Graff, Winnetka, IL. **335** U.S. Bureau of Engraving and Printing. **336** Grant Heilman. **340** Gary Foreman. **347** Wells Fargo Bank, History Room, San Francisco. **348** (t) Courtesy Texas Memorial Museum, Austin (b) Society of California Pioneers Library. **349, 350** U.S. Bureau of Engraving and Printing. **354** Dewitt Jones Productions. **357** Museum of the City of New York, Harry T. Peters Collection. **362** Harper's New Monthly Magazine, March 1854. **363** Marine Historical Association. **365, 369** U.S. Bureau of Engraving and Printing. **370** (both) Library of Congress. **376** Fred J. Maroon. **379** U.S. Bureau of Engraving and Printing. **383** Chicago Historical Society. **385** Library of Congress. **387** National Archives. Library of Congress. Lee. **389** (t) Library of Congress. (b) The Sophia Smith Collection, Smith College. **390** Chicago Historical Society. **394–395, 398, 398–399, 399, 400** Library of Congress. **404** Mastai Collection. **408** Library of Congress. **411** U.S. Bureau of Engraving and Printing. **412** Harper's Weekly, June 23, 1866. **415** (t) Harper's Weekly. (b) U.S. Bureau of Engraving and Printing. **417** Confederate Museum, Richmond, VA. **419** The Lightfoot Collection. **425** J. Doyle DeWitt Collection, University of Hartford From The National Museum of American History by Shirley Abbott. (c) 1981 Smithsonian Institution. All rights reserved. Published 1981 by Harry N. Abrams, Inc., New York. **429** The Oakland Museum. **432, 433** Circus World Museum, Baraboo, Wisconsin. **434** Scott Foresman. **438** University of Nebraska Press. **444** George Eastman House Collection, Lewis W. Hine. **448** From The National Museum of American History by Shirley Abbott. (c) 1981 Smithsonian Institution. All rights reserved. Published 1981 by Harry N. Abrams, Inc., New York. **452** Thomas Nast. Harper's Weekly, September 23, 1871. **455–456** U.S. Bureau of Engraving and Printing. **457** Culver Pictures. **459** (tl) (b) Library of Congress. (tr) University of Hartford, J. Doyle DeWitt Collection. **460** U.S. Bureau of Engraving and Printing. **461** (t) Culver Pictures. (b) U.S. Bureau of Engraving and Printing. **462** Thomas Nast. Harper's Weekly, August 19, 1871. **464** Fred J. Maroon. **467** George Eastman House. **468** From Stefan Lorant's *Pittsburgh, The Story of an American City*, Doubleday. **470** Culver Pictures. **472** Courtesy of the Smithsonian Institution. **473** Courtesy Tuskegee Institute. **476–477** Library of Congress. **479** U.S. Department of Interior, National Park Service, Edison National Historic Site. **480** Lewis W. Hine, George Eastman House. **484** From The National Museum of American History by Shirley Abbott. © 1981 Smithsonian Institution. All rights reserved. Published 1981 by Harry N. Abrams, Inc., New York. **487** National Archives. **489** Kansas State Historical Society. **490** NOAA. **498** From Stefan Lorant's *Glorious Burden*. **499** U.S. Bureau of Engraving and Printing. **503** Mastai Collection. **504** Mastai Collection. **507** Edgar William and Bernice Chrysler Garbisch Collection. **510** Brown Brothers. **515** Museum of the City of New York. **522** Library of Congress. **526** From The National Museum of American History by Shirley Abbott. © 1981 Smithsonian Institution. All rights reserved. Published 1981 by Harry N. Abrams, Inc., New York. **529** The New York Public Library, General Research and Humanities Division. Astor, Lenox and Tilden Foundation. **532** U.S. Bureau of Engraving and Printing. **536** Robert Frerck, Odyssey Productions. **538** U.S. Bureau of Engraving and Printing. **540** The New York Public Library, General Research and Humanities Division, Astor, Lenox and Tilden Foundation. **543** Brown Brothers. **545** N.A.A.C.P. **548** Fred J. Maroon. **554** UPI. **562** (1) Imperial War Museum, London. **562–563** © U.S. Signal Corp, National Archives. **563** (r) National Archives. **567** Bettmann Archive. **570–571** Walter Olden. **573** Scott Foresman. **574** From The National Museum of American History by Shirley Abbott. © 1981 Smithsonian Institution. All rights reserved. Published 1981 by Harry N. Abrams, Inc., New York. **578** Culver Pictures. **581** Sophia Smith Collection, Smith College. **583–584** U.S. Bureau of Engraving and Printing. **589** (l,r) Culver Pictures. **592** The National Air and Space Museum by C.D.B. Bryan, published by Harry N. Abrams, Inc. **597** Brown Brothers. **598** © Walt Disney Productions. **600** Schomburg Center for Research in Black Culture. The New York Public Library. Astor, Lenox and Tilden Foundation. **603** Georgia O'Keeffe, "Black Hollyhocks and Blue Larkspur." Photo by Malcolm Varon, NYC. **606** Scott Foresman. **609** UPI. **610** (l) Wide World. **610–611** Library of Congress. **611** Detroit News. **612** Brown Brothers. **617** Wide World. **620** Jay Wolke. **624** U.S. Bureau of Engraving and Printing. **627** Museum of Modern Art, Film Stills Archive. **632, 633** Library of Congress. **634** Copyright © 1935 (renewed 1963) by Conde Nast Publications, Inc. **638** Frank Sobeck Collection. **641** Department of the Interior, Washington DC. **643** UPI. **652–653** David J. Kaminsky. **655** Lohn Launois/Black Star. **656** The National Air and Space Museum by C.D.B. Bryan, published by Harry N. Abrams, Inc. **659** Hugo Jaeger, LIFE Magazine, © Time, Inc. **665** Wide World. **666–667** U.S. Coast Guard. **668** U.S. Air Force. **669** H. Roger Viollet. **670** Library of Congress. **671** Photo by Dorothea Lange. War Relocation Authority in the National Archives. **675** Hydrogen bomb test, 1954. U.S. Navy. **678** Fred J. Maroon. **681** U.S. Bureau of Engraving and Printing. **685** Wide World. **688** UPI. **692** U.S. Army photo. **693** McArthur parade and inset. **696** Kaz Tsuruta. **699** Hank Walker, Life Magazine, © Time, Inc. **701** U.S. Bureau of Engraving and Printing. **703** Cornell Capa/Magnum. **707** UPI. **708** Leonard Freed/Magnum. **713** Cornell Capa/LIFE Magazine 1958. Time Inc. **716–717** Werner Stoy/Camera Hawaii. **720** Baron Wolman from *American Denim*. **723** U.S. Bureau of Engraving and Printing. **724** © Rube Goldberg. King Features Syndicate 1975. **729** U.S. Bureau of Engraving and Printing. **730** James Karales/ © 1965 LOOK Magazine/Library of Congress. **734** Philip Jones Griffith/Magnum. **735** Stephen Shames/Magnum. **738** Fritz Goro. **743** U.S. Bureau of Engraving and Printing. **744** UPI. **752** Wide World. **753** U.S. Bureau of Engraving and Printing. **756** NASA. **759** U.S. Bureau of Engraving and Printing. **761** Cameraman International. **763** George Ballis/Black Star. **764** Owen Franken/Sygma. **769** The White House. **774–775** NASA.